# BARRON'S
# Guide to
# Medical
# & Dental
# Schools

# BARRON'S
# Guide to
# Medical
# & Dental
# Schools

12th Edition

**Saul Wischnitzer, Ph.D. with Edith Wischnitzer**

**About the Author:**
Dr. Saul Wischnitzer is a nationally recognized authority on career guidance for the health professions. He has extensive experience as a college advisor. Dr. Wischnitzer's unique program has helped hundreds of applicants gain admission to U.S. medical and dental schools.

*All inquiries should be addressed to:*
Barron's Educational Series, Inc.
250 Wireless Boulevard
Hauppauge, NY 11788
**www.barronseduc.com**

ISBN-13: 978-0-7641-4122-5
ISBN-10: 0-7641-4122-8
ISSN: 1935-7559

PRINTED IN THE UNITED STATES OF AMERICA
9 8 7 6 5 4 3 2 1

3 2903 30056 9529

# CONTENTS

v

# LIST OF TABLES

# LIST OF SAMPLE DOCUMENTS

# ACKNOWLEDGMENTS

Acknowledgment is made to the following organizations for allowing us to reprint copyrighted or previously published material in this book.

The American Association of Colleges of Osteopathic Medicine for permitting us to reprint the current AACOMAS application form.

The American Dental Association Survey Center for allowing us to use data in Tables 20.1 and 20.2 from its Annual Supplemental Reports on Dental Education 2003–04, as well as for the sample DAT material used in Chapter 21.

Hugo R. Seibel and others for permission to reprint a Model MCAT exam from their book *Barron's MCAT*, 12th Edition. © Copyright 2008 by Barron's Educational Series, Inc.

The efforts and cooperation of Mr. David Rodman, Editor, and Ms. Lena Perfetto, Project Assistant, for this book at Barron's, is very much appreciated.

Finally, the very valuable advice of my brother-in-law, Dr. Judah N. Lefkovits, is greatfully acknowledged.

# DEDICATION

This quarter-of-a-century anniversary edition of this book is dedicated to our children, Judah and Rachel, whose help, cooperation, and encouragement made its publication possible. We are especially grateful to our son Judah who applied his computer skills in preparing the format for the data capsules for all the professional schools. His contribution has significantly enhanced both the appearance and value of the book.

# PREFACE

This book has served as a guidance manual for preprofessional students for more than a quarter century. In 1974 *Barron's Guide to Medical, Dental, and Allied Health Science Careers* was published. Its favorable reception resulted in the publication of updated versions in 1975 and 1977. Subsequently, a marked rapid increase of interest in health science careers generated a need for an expanded new edition; however, this would have resulted in a book too cumbersome for convenient use. Thus, in 1982 two separate volumes were published: one, *Barron's Guide to Medical and Dental Schools,* dealing with medical and dental careers, and the other, *Futures in Health,* describing allied health science careers. The present tenth edition is actually the thirteenth, if one includes the three editions of the previous title.

In this book, as in the previous editions, medical and dental careers are discussed together. This is because they have in common the following: (1) There is no need to make even a tentative choice between these two careers while in high school; (2) due to their similar educational requirements, a definitive career decision can be deferred until the junior year of college; (3) applying to both medical and dental schools for some students may be desirable; (4) at a number of institutions medical and dental students take basic science courses together; (5) often teaching hospitals also have dental clinics that serve as a center for postgraduate dental training; (6) medical and dental practices overlap in the surgical specialties relating to the mouth and neck; (7) the interrelationship of the two sciences is reflected by the fact that some dental schools award a Doctor of Dental Medicine (DMD) degree, while others award the traditional Doctor of Dental Surgery (DDS).

In this new edition the facts and statistics have been optimally updated. The following major changes and additions have been introduced: (1) All medical and dental school profiles have been reviewed, updated, and where required, expanded; (2) the comprehensive data for all relevant tables have been made current; (3) the sequencing of chapters has been significantly altered, because of the addition of new chapters to be more consistent with the educational process associated with becoming a practicing physician; (4) additions have been made to the historical overview of medical education; (5) important advice was added on how to stay healthy during the demanding educational phase of a medical student's life; (6) advice is given to high school students on getting exposure to the field of medicine, so that they can judge the demands of the profession they may be getting into; (7) a section providing advice or how to satisfactorily adjust to living with college roommates is now included; (8) a discussion of various types of interview formats, which is of special value to applicants in the last phase of the admission process, has been added; (9) a listing of medical schools stressing research in their curriculum is now available to prospective applicants; (10) a special chapter is devoted to nontraditional older students, which provides comprehensive guidance concerning the issues of importance relative to such individuals successfully becoming medical students, has been incorporated in this new edition; (11) Postbaccalaureate Medical Programs has been updated and incorporated into a new chapter; (12) additional information about the MCAT has been added; (13) since the publication of the last edition, seven allopathic medical schools, five osteopathic schools, and one new dental school are described in the appropriate sections; (14) a discussion of interview formats has also been added, and relative to this subject, a section dealing with relaxation techniques is now included, which may be useful prior to interviews; (15) additional useful information for minority applicants is presented; (16) useful definitions relative to educational financial considerations is included; (17) a list of legitimate questions you may wish to ask at an interview are given; (18) a discussion of selection factors for admission to medical school is presented; (19) additionally, a premed financial aid primer is included; (20) a discussion on taking the DAT is now available; (21) in a variety of places, concise summaries entitled **Bottom Line**, have been added, to consolidate the reader's grasp of an important subject under discussion; and (22) plans for the next revision of the MCAT are outlined. And finally, a new appendix (I) was added showing the distribution of osteopathic medical schools on a nationwide map.

Some of the book's new material stems from the author's experience as a private, professional consultant for premedical and predental students. This has resulted in exposure to a large pool of individuals with a variety of pre- and postcollegiate backgrounds from many different schools. Consequently, a broader dimension to this work has been added.

Finally, some information has been added because prospective physicians should become aware of the rapidly changing climate in medicine. Medical practice has been revolutionized by dramatic improvements in the diagnosis and treatment of diseases, which has transformed medicine during the second half of the twentieth century. Parallel major changes in medical education have also taken place during this period. As a result, students will be better prepared for practice in the twenty-first century. This will have a significant positive impact on their future professional life.

## To the Reader

One of the most important decisions facing you is choosing a life-long career. Consequently, this requires very careful and thorough consideration. The competitive nature of our contemporary society has created marked pressure for early career selection. However, this should be determined only after honestly evaluating your interests, abilities, and goals. Since you are considering medicine or dentistry, you will need sound advice as well as the most current information about schools, admission policies, and educational programs. All of these elements are necessary in order to make the appropriate decisions about how to successfully overcome the numerous obstacles that lie ahead.

This book will provide you with both essential facts and proper guidance on planning a career in medicine or dentistry; you will find answers to critical questions you will face in the future. Proper advice and up-to-date information are important because of strong competition for admission that exists today, as well as the continually changing nature of professional education.

Ultimate success depends on your own abilities; however, the guidance offered in this book will facilitate your decision making during high school and college. As a result, your chances for admission to a professional school should be enhanced by the information and advice provided herein.

This comprehensive guidance manual is aimed at assisting a broad spectrum of motivated individuals seeking to become physicians and dentists. For well past the middle of the twentieth century, the overwhelming number of applicants were upper- and middle-class white males, who had completed their junior year of college. In recent decades this situation has dramatically changed; therefore, this book will be of very significant help not only to traditional male applicants, but also to women, minority group members, and older career changers. Moreover, it provides vital assistance to borderline candidates, unsuccessful applicants, and premedical dropouts. It can also serve to fill the gap for students who do not have access to a health career advisor or where they seek a second opinion. For those who never seriously considered a career in medicine or dentistry, this guide may provide a vision of a possible new, attractive future.

It is common knowledge that getting into medical or dental school is competitive. This is especially true about medicine where more than half the applicants are rejected. You should therefore recognize at the very outset that regardless of your credentials, there is no guaranteed admission; a student with an outstanding average and MCAT scores may be rejected. This might be the result of failing to apply to enough schools or the appropriate ones. Rejection might be due to a disqualifying personal statement or because of negative interviews. There are a host of issues that have a bearing on the end result of the admission process. This manual is specifically designed to ensure that you not stumble along the way; making the right choices at the proper time, can make all the difference!

This detailed handbook is designed to provide you with decisive advice that you will need at many critical junctions. It starts with vital issues that are relevant in high school and extends all the way through college and medical school as well as postgraduate medical training and even beyond.

The following is a list of a dozen major decisions and critical issues that you will have to face:

1. Choosing a suitable high school program of studies.
2. Selecting appropriate colleges to apply to.
3. Securing admission into college.
4. Choosing a college major.
5. Planning how to succeed in college.
6. Preparing for the Medical College Admission Test or Dental Aptitude Test.
7. Designing a strategy for getting into medical or dental school.
8. Selecting appropriate medical or dental schools to apply to.
9. Preparing a winning personal statement.
10. Training how best to sell yourself at an interview.
11. Responding appropriately to acceptance or rejection decisions from professional schools.
12. Preparing for what to anticipate in medical school.

In summary, this comprehensive manual will do more than assist you in your quest to gain admission to a professional school. It also serves, especially for those seeking careers in medicine, as a guide into and through postgraduate training or both residency and fellowship levels. In addition, it provides an insight into the various options available when you are considering the practice of medicine. No matter what educational stage you are at, this book will be valuable for many years; therefore, it should be kept accessible in your personal library.

The author welcomes comments from readers. I can be contacted by mail via the publisher's address on the copyright page or by e-mail at *ewischnitzer@yahoo.com*.

Saul Wischnitzer, PhD
Queens, New York
March 2009

# ABBREVIATIONS

| | |
|---|---|
| AACOMAS | American Association of Colleges of Osteopathic Medicine Application Service |
| AADS | American Association of Dental Schools |
| AADSAS | American Association of Dental Schools Application Service |
| AAMC | Association of American Medical Colleges |
| ABMS | American Board of Medical Specialties |
| AMA | American Medical Association |
| AMCAS | American Medical College Application Service |
| AMSA | American Medical Student Association |
| AOA | American Osteopathic Association |
| CACMS | Committee on Accreditation of Canadian Medical Schools |
| CDA | Commission on Dental Accreditation |
| COA | Commission on Osteopathic Accreditation |
| COTRANS | Coordinated Transfer Application System |
| CSA | Clinical Skills Assessment Examination |
| DAT | Dental Admission Test |
| FLEX | Federation Licensing Examinations |
| GPA | grade point average |
| HMO | Health Maintenance Organization |
| IMG | International Medical Graduate |
| IPA | Independent Practitioners' Association |
| LCME | Liaison Committee on Medical Education |
| MCAT | Medical College Admission Test |
| Med-MAR | Medical Minority Applicant Registry |
| MSKP | Medical Sciences Knowledge Profile |
| MSTP | Medical Scientist Training Program |
| NBME | National Board of Medical Examiners |
| NIH | National Institute of Health |
| NIRMP | National Intern and Resident Matching Program |
| OMSAS | Ontario Medical School Application Service |
| PPA | Private Practitioners' Association |
| TMDSAS | Texas Medical Doctor School Application Service |
| USMLE | United States Medical Licensing Examination |
| WWAMI | Washington, Wyoming, Alaska, Montana, Idaho |
| WHO | World Health Organization |
| WICHE | Western Interstate Commission for Higher Education |

# PART ONE

# MEDICINE

# Medicine as a Career

On being a physician
Why study medicine?
The reality of a physician's career
The challenge ahead
Self-evaluation
Historical overview
The need for physicians
Physician supply: current debate
Desirable attributes for a medical career
Facing the future

## ON BEING A PHYSICIAN

Physicians are acknowledged practitioners of the art of medicine. They are expected to be people of high ethical standards since they are entrusted with the intimate details of life and death. They are expected to have the capacity and enthusiasm for difficult work extended over long hours, and they must be able to perform efficiently under a chronic load of heavy responsibility.

Physicians are expected to be able to reason quickly and accurately and to have life-long desires to continually add to their accumulated body of medical knowledge by learning about new developments in their profession. They are expected to be able to communicate with their patients in order to teach them hygienic measures and to adequately explain the nature and significance of a disease. They are also expected to be willing to serve the community in a capacity beyond that of their professional training. Physicians are people who have ordinary physical and emotional needs, yet who have a great purpose in life. Their practice can be the source of enrichment of their own life as well as the lives of others.

When setting your sights toward a medical career, your goal should be to become a *good* physician. Ideally, this means becoming a doctor who will (1) blend book knowledge with common sense; (2) provide compassion with candor; (3) strive to maintain perspective by focusing on the whole patient rather than solely on the disease; (4) allow time to listen to those seeking help; (5) perceive the real meaning of the patient's words; (6) communicate with patients in a way they can easily understand; (7) think independently; (8) rely on your own mind and clinical judgment; (9) utilize tests and consultants to verify hypotheses; (10) be aware of limitations of lab procedures; (11) be cognizant of your own fallibility; and (12) not be afraid to admit when you don't know something.

## WHY STUDY MEDICINE?

The medical profession offers much to a young person. It provides an avenue for attaining satisfaction of many of the most fundamental human desires. Medicine can satisfy your intellectual curiosity; it permits you to successfully apply the enormous body of information that has been accumulated in recent decades to reduce pain and suffering and extend the average life span. At the same time, it presents the challenge of the many unsolved problems that await solution through laboratory or hospital work.

Medicine can satisfy your desire for human service by enabling you to bring help and comfort to others. Medicine can satisfy your desire to work in a profession that has prestige. While prestige is no longer granted automatically, it does come with the faithful discharge of responsibilities and obligations. Medicine can also satisfy your desire for a substantial income. This income, which is superior to that of most other professions, is earned by the long and difficult hours demanded of the physician. Medicine is a profession that can, to a significant extent, satisfy your desire for independent and individual achievement in a society that is becoming increasingly overstructured.

An MD degree and the completion of all three components of the United States Medical Licensing Examination (USMLE) enables you to practice medicine anywhere in the United States. With this degree, you can care for people at all stages: you can bring them into the world, treat their childhood and young adult illnesses, help them deal with their middle-age crises, and assist them in coping with the increasingly frequent and troublesome illnesses of advancing years.

If teaching appeals to you, you can enjoy guiding the next generation of physicians. Educating medical students, residents, and postdoctoral fellows will enhance your own creative abilities and stimulate your own thought processes.

If you have a flair for writing, there is a vast potential to use literary expression in writing lucid scientific papers, analytic essays, or even nonscientific works. Just remember the background of Arthur Conan Doyle, W. Somerset Maugham, or Lewis Thomas, to mention a few prominent physician-writers.

Should laboratory work be more to your liking, with suitable postdoctoral training (or an MD-PhD degree), you may want to become involved in valuable research that can lead to finding cures for diseases and possible disease prevention. Much work is being done today in the field of genetic engineering, which impacts greatly on congenital disorders and various metabolic abnormalities.

Medicine therefore represents the broadest spectrum of opportunities for an individual to render service to others while at the same time attaining his or her own goals in life in a satisfying manner. Medicine provides the widest range of career options in a variety of roles, such as small-town doctor, family practitioner, specialist, superspecialist, clinical investigator, academician, public health officer, administrator, and varying combinations of these positions. Making the choice, rather than having the choice, is the issue medical students and residents face at some point in their training.

## Bottom Line

The profession of medicine offers physicians many specific advantages. These include

- respect from patients whose lives they seek to help.
- an opportunity to gain much personal satisfaction by using one's knowledge, talents, and skills to enhance the well-being of others.
- the option of being able to select from the wide variety of possible career pathways that medical specialties and subspecialties offer.
- an opportunity to set up a practice in a wide variety of possible geographic locations and select the type of practice one prefers.
- being assured of receiving, in due course, a steady income that can provide a comfortable life.

## THE REALITY OF A PHYSICIAN'S CAREER

On average, the professional career of a physician can extend close to 40 years, assuming he or she starts to practice at 27 and retires at 65. Obviously, quite a number of physicians will work beyond the traditional retirement date. The pattern of an average physician can be portrayed in a linear fashion as follows:

| College (4 years) | Medical School (4 years) | Residency (3-6 years) | Practice (about 38 years) | 65 | Post-practice (5 plus years) |

It is imperative for every premedical student to have a genuinely realistic view of a medical career, in order to avoid disillusionment at a later date. However, it is challenging to obtain such a perspective. Bear in mind, that the response of individual physicians largely depends on the nature of the specialty and on their own professional success (or the lack thereof). Each field has its own demands in terms of working hours per week (range: 45–65), the frequency of night calls (from none to heavy), and stress due to the nature of one's responsibilities (from none to very intense).

The best picture of what might lie ahead, can come from, in addition to reading, autobiographical accounts written by physicians (see Bibliography, page 730), personal visits to hospitals (both wards and emergency rooms), as well as speaking to physicians, (both satisfied and dissatisfied), from a wide range of specialties.

When practicing physicians reach the last phase of their professional career, many options are available; thus, they can slow down the pace of their activities, yet retain a professional link to medicine. Some older physicians found a second career in some medical-associated activity following retirement. This can include administrative work for insurance companies, local government, etc. Thus, medicine can offer a life of financial security and respect as well as a deep sense of accomplishment that continues until retirement and even beyond.

## THE CHALLENGE AHEAD

As noted, medicine can be a most attractive and fulfilling profession, but before one seriously embarks upon the journey to become a physician, it is most essential to fully recognize the potential obstacles that lie ahead and that need be overcome. These can be briefly summarized as follows:

- a lengthy and vigorous period of premedical education as an undergraduate.
- an intensely competitive medical school admission process to secure a place.
- a lengthy and most challenging program of medical education and training.
- a need to pass standardized national exams as a medical student to graduate.
- a formidable challenge to select an appropriate residency training area appointment at a suitable medical teaching facility.
- a multiyear arduous period of graduate clinical responsibility as a resident.
- a possible need to secure a fellowship for advanced subspecialty training.
- a need to pass specialty examinations to qualify for "board" certification.
- a need to secure recertification at later intervals in one's career.
- a need to overcome obstacles associated with establishing a practice.

In addition to the aforementioned hurdles, the fact is that physicians face potentially long working hours, stressful situations, and a need to cope with governmental or managed care bureaucratic obstacles. It is therefore not surprising that reliable surveys suggest that a significant number of doctors have serious doubts about recommending their profession to others, including members of their own family.

In light of the rewards and obstacles of medicine as a career, you are well advised to give outmost serious consideration to the true nature of your motives and the strength of your convictions to achieve your goal. After all the above facts are considered, you will need to answer the following two fundamental questions, to the best of your ability, namely:

1. Do I have genuinely valid motives that serve to compel me to choose medicine as a career?

2. Do I have the necessary perseverance to retain my career commitment in the face of numerous potential impediments that extend over many years of schooling and training?

If you elicit affirmative responses to these basic, critical questions, you will feel much more confident to proceed ahead. This guidance and self-assessment manual (see Appendix A, page 657) is designed to facilitate your coming up with the correct answer to these questions so that you achieve the goal that is in your best interest.

## SELF-EVALUATION

The road to becoming a practicing physician is a long and difficult one. It requires from the candidate a very substantial expenditure of time, effort, and money. To achieve your goal necessitates self-awareness of the extent of your motivation, abilities, and determination to succeed. To achieve one's full potential, self-evaluation can prove to be a useful and desirable approach to introspection. This can be facilitated somewhat for asking yourself the following questions:

- Do you find information on how the body functions especially interesting?

- Is gaining knowledge meaningful to you beyond rewards of good grades?

- Is your desire for knowledge such that you seek information beyond that taught?

- Are you impressed by the ability of physicians to enhance the quality of human life?

- Are you excited to read about the many current advances in medicine and surgery?

- Do you find the demanding lifestyle of a practicing physician acceptable?

- Do you feel a sense of satisfaction and gratification from helping others?

Determine how many of these questions are answered in the affirmative. If the overwhelming majority is affirmative, then I have some supporting evidence favoring your desire to become a physician.

It is now desirable to explore your interests in greater depth. You should look into your past life experiences and evaluate whether or not you have the determination or "staying power" for the long haul that preparation for a career in medicine requires. Do you sincerely feel that your motivation is intense enough to face the multitude of challenges that lie ahead? If you are certain or at least reasonably confident that you do, then proceed—give it a try. This can best be done by starting to take the prerequisite biology and chemistry courses in order to test your innate abilities and strength of your conviction.

For those uncertain about the correct direction for their career, if the above assessment is inconclusive, both school and private career counselors employ formal interest inventory tests whose results shed useful light on one's employment potential. The results from those tests are an objective indicator. They can serve to reinforce one's current subjective views or serve to dissuade one away from them. The results of such tests, however, should not be taken as a definitive judgment, independent of your own personal viewpoint. In addition, such tests may bring to light hidden areas of interest that can serve to expand a person's career horizon.

## Gearing Up

Once you have firmly decided to choose medicine as a career, you should recognize that on the long road to achieving your goal obstacles may come your way and there may even be setbacks. There are, however, a number of enabling guidelines that can assist you in overcoming adversity. These are

- No matter how challenging the situation, don't panic—a solution does exist.
- Motivate yourself emotionally in order to face difficult issues that you can foresee.
- Tackle a cluster of problems systematically, in order of importance.
- Break up a large problem into a group of smaller issues.
- Accept the reality that your chosen career is a long and demanding one.
- Learn from your mistakes rather than dwell upon them.
- Let your successes strongly motivate you to think positively about challenges.
- Remember that there is help available when you need it, so seek and use it.

The aforementioned guidelines can facilitate getting through the difficult times that are not uncommon and thus facilitating your successfully attaining your career goal.

## Bottom Line

Although there are a minority of physicians who will not recommend the medical profession to others, and some who are genuinely unhappy with their lot, the conclusion from these observations in reality is

- Medicine is not a profession for everyone, no matter how bright or talented they are.
- The bulk of physicians enjoy their work and are fully satisfied with their career choice.
- Thoughtful consideration through self-assessment, meaningful exposure, and competent guidance from an advisor and/or recognized occupational test can assist you in making the appropriate career choice.
- If you can anticipate any specific problems, such as poor interview skills, a low grade in a critical required science course, etc., seek advice, and consider reasonable steps to overcome handicaps before they become a liability.
- If faced with a complex problem, try, if possible, to dismantle it into smaller components that may allow you to better manage the situation.
- Generate within yourself the self-confidence that assures you that you are on the right path. However, be prepared to make course corrections when it is both reasonable and essential to do so.
- Try to always be of good cheer, even in the face of formidable obstacles. This can be achieved by trying to find a brighter side to things to help you overcome many issues and ultimately attain your goal.
- There are about 20,000 freshmen slots open in allopathic and osteopathic medical institutions that need to be filled annually. You need to be accepted by only one, when all is said and done. If you feel you really deserve a spot, and have only a fair chance of getting it, seek to get it with all you've got!

## HISTORICAL OVERVIEW

In seeking to become a physician, you are planning to join a fraternity of professional men and women who have a profound influence, both physically and emotionally, on the lives of many millions of people. The roots of medicine penetrate deeply into the history of humankind. Cave paintings reveal the existence of "healers" as far back as the Ice Age. The medical practitioners of ancient China developed acupuncture and a small-pox vaccination method. Western medicine is indebted to the "scientific" approach developed in ancient Greece and Rome by men such as Hippocrates and Galen. These advances were preserved through the Dark Ages by the Arab world. In medieval Europe medical science stagnated until the rebirth of learning and experimentation in the Renaissance.

In the United States during the colonial era, medicine was largely a hit-or-miss affair. The pushing of the frontiers westward developed a pioneer type of doctor. A step forward was achieved in the last half of the eighteenth century when medical schools in the United States began conferring the MD degree and it was no longer necessary to journey abroad to obtain one. In 1910 the Flexner report, Medical Education in the United States and Canada, brought about a revolution in medical education and placed it on a sound basis by establishing standardized requirements of medical education. Flexner's basic recommendations included the following:

1. Medical education should be conducted in the context of a university. This would help ensure that students would gain a scientifically oriented foundation for the practice of medicine.

2. Schools should be changed from a "diploma mill" or trade school status to that of providing a professional school education.

3. The upgraded medical schools should be provided with a full-time faculty, because practicing physicians lacked time to devote themselves adequately to teaching.

Flexner's report resulted in a drastic reduction in the number of then-existing medical schools.

The impact of the Flexner report extended far beyond improving the quality of medical education. Ultimately it was responsible for the preeminence in biomedical research and the development of specialty medicine in this country.

Well before the turn of this century, Americans made major contributions to medical science, especially in the battle against infectious diseases. In the last half of the twentieth century, American medicine has become a world leader. Thus, to become a physician means entering a fellowship with a healing tradition that extends back to the beginnings of civilization.

Major highlights in American medical education are summarized below:

1765—University of Pennsylvania opens the nation's first medical school.

1848—Elizabeth Blackwell is the first American woman to receive a medical degree.

1870—An estimated 15,000 Americans travel to Germany and Austria over the course of the next four decades for modern medical education.

1871—Harvard transforms its curriculum by introducing the basic science courses along with hands-on lab experience.

1890—AAMC is founded and a three-year curriculum is mandated for all U.S. medical schools.

1893—Johns Hopkins University Medical School opens and is the first to require a baccalaureate degree for admission and four years of study for a medical degree.

1910—The Flexner report recommends closing half of American medical schools.

1912—AMA conducts its first survey of hospitals for the training of interns.

1922—AMA establishes guidelines for approved hospital residencies and fellowships.

1952—Case Western University introduces an organ system-based curriculum.

1956—Federal Health Facilities Research Act enhances research efforts in medical schools.

1958—University of Toronto Medical School introduces its experimental fourth-year program in comprehensive medicine, incorporating relevant psychological and sociological aspects.

1968—McMaster University of Canada introduces problem-based learning.

1992—About 18% of U.S. physicians and 42% of medical students are women.

—Number of students applying to medical schools reaches an all-time high.

1993–1996—A record number of medical school applicants during these years.

## THE NEED FOR PHYSICIANS

Until about 1980, the increasing need for additional manpower in the health professions, and particularly medical manpower, was shown in governmental studies of both urban and rural areas. Thus medical educators strongly urged that efforts be made to increase the number of physicians and other health science personnel. As a result, increased financial support, especially from the federal government, resulted in expanding first-year enrollment by both enlarging existing medical school class size and by establishing new colleges of medicine. Thus, for example, the number of first-year students increased from about 8,000 in 1960–1961 to more than 11,000 in 1970–1971 and then to about 16,500 first-year places in the early 1980s. All of the six two-year basic science schools were converted to four-year MD-granting institutions. Also, in the 1980s nine new schools became operational, thereby ultimately providing about 750 to 1,000 additional places.

The increase in the number of medical schools and their class size has resulted in a significant narrowing of the gap between physician supply and demand. The number of active physicians increased roughly 12% from 285,000 to 318,000 in the 1965 to 1970 period as against a population growth of only 5%. A similar rate of increase also occurred between 1970 and 1980 as well as in the following decade. The total number of active physicians is approximately 750,000 in the year 2000. This results in a physician-to-population ratio of about 300 per 100,000 in 2000, which is much higher than the 1988 ratio of 223 per 100,000. As a matter of fact, since 1960 the number of physicians has grown four times faster than the population. Thus, on a numerical basis, the gap between physician supply and demand apparently will be closed. A major study of future physician manpower needs, known as the GEMENAC report, which projected an oversupply of physicians, has given rise (not surprisingly) to anxiety among some premedical and medical students, as well as to residents, regarding the need for their services in the twenty-first century.

There are a number of factors to consider when evaluating the conclusion of this report. First, as with all projections based on statistical analysis, they need not be self-fulfilling. Second, a major and unknown impact on the validity of the report's conclusions is the very significant (and long overdue) increase in the enrollment of women in medical schools; women now constitute more than 35% of the student population and their number may rise to 45% or more. An unknown, but perhaps significant, number of these women may initially opt for a specialty of their primary interest but later, to meet personal and/or family needs, gravitate to fields that demand less time. This may leave a void in the supply of physicians specializing in internal medicine, surgery, and other time-intensive fields. Third, the number of American graduates of foreign medical schools may diminish, in view of the drastic change in the "atmosphere" with regard to this option. Fourth, with the size of the applicant pool subject to cyclical fluctuation, there could at some point possibly be a sharp decline (as took place in the mid-1980s). There would then be a tendency for some schools to reduce the size of their entering class, and thus the total number of medical school graduates may, under these conditions, diminish. All the while the population will undoubtedly continue to grow, increasing the demand for medical services (already being fueled by public health education programs).

The aforementioned considerations may have contributed to the significant downward revision in the size of the projected physician surplus that was made by the Department of Health and Human Services over that originally contained in the 1980 GEMENAC report. The overall question of whether there will be a physician surplus, and how big the surplus will be, cannot be resolved with any degree of certainty. The situation is more complex than simply the ratio of the number of physicians to the total population. There is an important issue of an unequal distribution of physicians with rural and inner city areas remaining underserved even when the overall number of physicians has significantly increased. In addition, there is an increasing pressure to deemphasize specialization and strongly encourage the expansion of the number of primary care or family practice physicians. In view of these considerations, the increased number of physicians will definitely have its impact. *It will require that prospective practitioners be more flexible in the choice of a specialty and in the location of their practice, and above all be very dedicated to their chosen profession.*

## PHYSICIAN SUPPLY: CURRENT DEBATE

A new major debate is developing over the issue of physician surplus. It was fueled by a report by a commission of health care policy experts funded by the Pew Foundation. The commission recommended that 20% of the nation's medical schools be closed by the year 2005. It warned of a surplus of 100,000 to 150,000 physicians in the next century, and urged closing some schools as the best way to solve the problem, although it did not identify which schools should be shut down.

The conclusion by the Pew commission that there will be a surplus of physicians is consistent with the earlier findings of other organizations and the GEMENAC report discussed above. Not surprisingly, there has been a cool reaction by those in academic medicine to the recommendation that schools be closed. They advocate two other courses of possible action, namely downsizing schools and limiting access to graduate training by foreign graduates. Currently, U.S. schools graduate about 17,000 physicians a year, but there are 24,000 first-year graduate positions available. The 7,000 extra spaces are filled by foreign medical graduates. The commission did recommend that graduate medical training be capped at 110% of U.S. medical graduates. Some educators believe that solving the foreign graduate problem by itself will resolve the issue and downsizing will be unnecessary. This is because they feel that once this number is down, the marketplace will in a natural way readjust the specialist-to-generalist ratio and uneven geographic distribution of physicians, thus eliminating surplus physicians.

One major element strongly impacts upon the issue of physician surplus, namely managed care. Since the number of specialists will be reduced under managed care, more physicians will enter primary care, altering our health care system's infrastructure more rapidly than expected.

More recently a total contradictory view on physician supply has emerged, suggesting that there may be a physician shortage by the beginning of the next decade. The rationale behind this suggestion is that (1) the current population of physicians is aging; (2) the workload for residents is diminishing, generating a need for more of them; (3) there is a markedly increased number of female physicians with a prospective decrease in lifetime work; and (4) the professional activity work schedule of physicians is dminishing, but the need for medical services is increasing. While these considerations are resonable, a physician shortage may nevertheless fail to materialize. This would be comparable to the surplus that did not take place toward the end of the twentieth century as originally predicted.

The current serious difficulty in assessing the future need for physicians is clearly evident by the highly conflicting reports published in recent times. On one hand, the Council on Graduate Medical Education (CGME) called for more medical schools to help stem what it believes is a looming physician shortage. This is a reversal of its prior policy. The CGME has called for a 15% increase in the number of medical school graduates. The impetus for this decision was a report by the Center for Health Workforce Studies at the State University of New York at Albany. The council predicted an 85,000 physician shortfall by 2020 at current rates.

On the other hand, the General Accounting Office (GAO) has come to a completely opposite conclusion. In the study of the nation's physicians' work force, the GAO found that physician numbers grew at twice the rate of the general population in the decade between 1991 and 2001. Comparing data from the AMA and the AOA against the U.S. Census Bureau figures, the GAO determined that all of the nation's statewide and rural areas and all but 17 metropolitan areas gained physicians per 100,000 people. Moreover, of those 17 cities, only two saw a decline in the total number of physicians, while the large remainder gained physicians, albeit below the general rate of increase. In addition, it was found that the ratio of generalist to specialist remained about one-third to two-thirds during this ten-year interlude. Also, the disparity in the distribution of physicians between urban and rural areas, while narrowed, still exists.

It is clear that the present decade is an era of change and uncertainty; it will take time till this situation becomes clarified. The current debate reinforces the conclusion noted above that prospective physicians must be strongly committed, need to show flexibility and openmindedness, and above all stay informed.

## Bottom Line

In recent years the picture regarding physician supply has become somewhat clearer. The following is an updated summary.

- Conflicting opinions still exist about whether there will be a physician shortage or surplus, but current projections favor the former. The reality is that the medical education system seeks to increase the number of graduates in anticipation of a possible physician shortage.

- Even those favoring an increased number of physicians are unsure of how many and what kind will be needed in the future.

- There has been a call by the AAMC for a 15% increase in medical school enrollment by 2015. The response to this call has resulted in a record number of acceptees (c. 17,000) in 12/2005, representing a meaningful increase over previous years.

- Osteopathic medical schools have contributed significantly to the higher pool of new enrollees. Allopathic schools tend to increase their class size by 5–15 slots annually. About half of all allopathic schools have thus made plans for increases in class size.

- Some medical educators are advocating even greater increases in student enrollments, ranging up to 40% or more. They believe there is an adequate pool of qualified applicants to fill such an enlarged student body.

- The underlying rationale behind the argument that a physician shortage is looming stems from research data derived from analyzing population and economic projections.

- The concept has been advanced that while few medical innovations result in a need for fewer physicians, some advances may serve to stimulate the creation of new subspecialties. At the very least, they create the necessity for more patient service time, as an indirect consequence of which there is a greater need for physicians.

- Possibly contributing to a physician shortage may be the tendency for some younger physicians to seek to better balance family life and work; thus they are devoting fewer hours to their practices. Simultaneously, on the other hand, many older physicians are diminishing their service availability as they approach retirement; consequently, a heavier load is shifting to those in real full-time practice.

## DESIRABLE ATTRIBUTES FOR A MEDICAL CAREER _____

The changing environment for medical practice that is gradually taking place, which is discussed later in this chapter, will fully impact on those who will practice in the twenty-first century. Thus, while ten specific desirable attributes are noted below, one major personal quality should be emphasized at this point, namely, the need for a strong commitment to medicine. Having such a commitment will serve to overcome the inevitable obstacles, which include a less attractive environment in which to practice, high tuition costs, a long education and training period, and lower income expectations. An intense commitment will permit one to meet the inevitable challenges and overcome any setbacks that may be encountered. It will also serve to avoid incurring the disappointment that withdrawal from a career goal for nonacademic reasons would generate.

There are ten basic qualities that are desirable for prospective physicians to have.

1. *Intelligence.* Medical studies and practice require an ability to learn, retain, and integrate a vast amount of scientific data through study, experimentation, and experience.

2. *Scientific interest.* Medicine, while an applied science, rests upon an understanding of the fundamental biological and chemical activities that we define as life. An understanding of its dynamic processes requires a solid grounding in chemical, physical, and biological principles. What is especially desirable is a mastery of the scientific mode of inquiry and the attainment of good manipulative skills.

3. *Favorable personality.* A successful practice involves an ability to establish and maintain a good rapport with people at all levels. Thus, you must realize that you will have to treat people coming from different walks of life and associate with colleagues who have different backgrounds. It is very desirable to have warmth and empathy and, thus, be able to reflect a positive response to the needs, suffering, and fears of others in a manner that can provide both reassurance and respect. Another desirable personality characteristic is broadmindedness. This is reflected by a wide breadth of interests, the desire for a wide range of experiences, the habit of forming value judgments independently, the ability to establish close friendships, an open-mindedness to nonconforming ideas, and the capacity of putting issues in their proper perspective.

4. *Physical and emotional strength.* Those who plan a career in medicine must possess the capability of enduring the rigorous physical and emotional demands of many years of study and training. You must be able to maintain the self-discipline required during such a prolonged preparatory period. Medical school and specialty training require a disposition capable of expending an enormous amount of energy. This innate characteristic is reflected in the records of those achieving a high degree of academic success while being simultaneously involved in a variety of extracurricular activities. This suggests that as busy practitioners such individuals will also be able to participate in a variety of nonprofessional activities.

5. *Ability to tolerate uncertainty and frustration.* The practice of medicine is based on the fact that every patient is unique, that frequently one must intervene therapeutically before all the facts are available, and that even after securing all relevant data it may be necessary to select from several courses of action that are quite different and possibly contradictory. Thus you must have a personality that enables you to function in an atmosphere of ambiguity where clear-cut and pre-

cisely defined treatment modalities are lacking. Moreover, since the response to even the most appropriate therapeutic regime may prove disappointing, you also must be able to withstand the frustrations of clinical failure in spite of excellent medical treatment.

6. *Well-organized work habits*. It is crucial to professional success that prospective medical students maximize their expenditure of time and effort. This will ensure that opportunities will not be lost and information will not go to waste.

7. *Capacity for self-education*. Willingness to learn a great deal about a topic without the prospect of gaining external reward for doing so is essential. The reason is that much of what will be learned in medical school will either be forgotten and/or become obsolete. Inherent in self-education is the necessity to hone one's critical faculties. This will permit clear thinking and independent formulation of judgments. Self-education also includes an ability to assimilate and sustain by continual learning a large knowledge base, as well as the ability to define and solve problems by interpreting data, reasoning critically, and applying learned information.

8. *Social awareness*. A gradual change is taking place in health care delivery, in which the focus is not exclusively on the individual patient out of the context of the many psychological and social factors that affect health and produce illness. It is thus incumbent to have an awareness of the current climate relative to the sociomedical issues involved in providing health care to the varying population groups.

9. *Achievement*. Evidence of some special achievement, in any one of a variety of fields, is an asset for a prospective medical school applicant. Thus an applicant may have climbed a well-known mountain, organized a band, or learned how to captain a small fishing boat. Achievements that demonstrate initiative, leadership potential, and/or the ability to establish satisfactory interpersonal relationships are indicative of the potential for achievement in the challenging field of medicine.

10. *Creativity*. The ability to marshall one's intellectual resources to meet challenges is an especially valuable asset. This capability for creativity may be reflected in self-confidence and by an ability to detect and define problems, to think originally, to question established scientific dogmas, and to demonstrate intellectual courage.

The four years of high school and first three years of college provide the opportunity to determine to what extent you possess these basic attributes. The grades you receive, especially in your science courses, will provide a basis for judging your intellectual ability. Your response to various science courses, as well as other contacts with experimentation and scientific inquiry in class or possibly in summer work, will enable you to evaluate your natural response to this area of studies. Your ability to get along with your fellow students and friends should provide a basis for judging your personality. Finally, how you stand up to the demands of your school work and personal problems will provide some basis for evaluating your inner tenacity and determination.

Objective self-analysis at the end of high school and at the end of each college year will help to ensure that your choice of a medical career is realistic and will provide a stimulus for greater performance. Such analysis may, on the other hand, call for reconsideration and a possible change in your career goal. If this is the case, the change should be made promptly after consultation with your guidance counselor and parents, in order to avoid loss of time and almost certain disappointment at a later date.

The aim of the self-evaluation should not be to determine if you are outstanding in all the basic attributes necessary for a successful medical career; rather you should ascertain if you are above average in the sum total, at least average in each, and do not have very serious deficiencies in any. What is to be sought is a determination of how close one actually comes to a hypothetical standard, realizing that there is a broad spectrum of acceptability determined by a balancing of all factors.

# FACING THE FUTURE

The first step to becoming a physician is to decide that at all times you will be realistic and honest with yourself. Before you reach the stage of applying to a medical school, you should periodically reevaluate your abilities and the sincerity of your conviction to become a physician. You should determine if you possess the intelligence, scientific aptitude, personality, and inner strength—that are essential for success as a physician.

Each prospective medical school applicant must in time face the reality that he or she will be but one out of more than 45,000 applicants competing for a place in freshman medical school classes. The competition is very intense and more than 50% of the applicants fail to attain their goal (at least on the first try). You should also be aware that since each applicant applies to about ten medical schools, there are more than 300,000 applications to be processed. This means screening 500 to 7,500 applicants to fill 50 to 250 places. The initial screening process rejects some individuals outright and ranks others for further action, determining if they merit a prompt interview or should be put on hold for an interview at a later date. It is, therefore, important to realize at the outset that in addition to your intellectual achievements and potential, the mechanics of the admission process itself is critical. Knowing which schools and how many schools to apply to, presenting your qualifications, writing your essay, and handling yourself well at interviews are all vital elements in achieving your goal. The admission process is the culmination of your efforts to become a physician. It involves marketing your personal assets to the maximum extent possible. It is therefore important for you to get to know your strengths and weaknesses in order to make sure that you accentuate the strengths and minimize or, if possible, even eliminate the weaknesses. The image that you indirectly project by means of the transcripts, recommendations, and MCAT scores submitted in your behalf, and that you directly project in your interview, will determine the success of your attempt to secure a place in a medical school. Once you have been accepted for admission, it is almost a certainty (because of the negligible failure rate) that in due course you will be awarded your medical degree.

## Future Challenges

After completing their studies and training, the challenge of the practitioners of the twenty-first century will be (1) to maintain the traditional commitment to service as the central theme of their work in spite of increasing regulation; (2) to remain committed to life-long learning as medical knowledge has an increasingly shorter half-life of validity; (3) to seek to resolve the social and ethical problems that arise as technological capabilities increase within a humanistic framework. For further discussion of these challenges, see Chapter 18, Physicians and Medicine in the Twenty-first Century.

# 2 Preparing for College

## HIGH SCHOOL: AN OVERVIEW

High school is a period of social adjustment and a time when the student becomes increasingly aware of what adult responsibilities are. Thus, while high school is a transitional era, it is a critical one in that it is usually the time when your career goals become tentatively formulated. Career ambitions may change as you become exposed to new areas of knowledge and as old ones are explored more deeply, but it is advantageous to have some general educational goals rather than to drift aimlessly.

A *final* decision to choose medicine as a career need not be made in high school and probably should be deferred until the end of the sophomore year of college. Two questions, however, need to be answered in high school: Do you intend to go to college? Do you have a genuine interest in science? It is essential to plan an educational program of high school studies that will make it feasible to gain admission to a suitable college as well as to test the validity of your preliminary career decision.

Especially gifted high school students should be aware that there are integrated BA-MD or BS-MD programs offered by about 35 schools (see page 152). These combine undergraduate and medical education into a continuum that in some cases facilitates the completion of one's studies in less time than required by the traditional programs.

## PROGRAM OF HIGH SCHOOL STUDIES

Having decided to attend college and possibly become a premedical student, you should select your high school program to include courses that meet at least the minimum requirements for admission to a liberal arts college. The program should therefore include:

English: 4 years

Laboratory science: 2 years

Modern foreign or classical language: 2 years

Mathematics: 2½ years

Social studies: 2 years

You should enlarge upon these requirements as much as is feasible by taking electives to obtain a well-rounded academic background. Concentrate in a science with the aim of making your other college courses less demanding, and thereby enhance your chances of securing higher grades in all your courses. This approach can help strengthen your science course average, which is one of the factors in the medical school selection process.

Mastering good study habits and computer literacy are essential elements that should be achieved in high school, since they will have a significant impact on your success in college. Set up regular hours for study, learn how to read quickly and effectively, and learn how to take lecture notes and develop test-taking skills. Good achievement in your academic studies, especially in science, should be a major challenge of your high school education.

During high school you should participate in a variety of extracurricular activities, including athletics and science clubs, especially premedical groups such as the Future Physician Club or Medical Explorer Post of the Boy Scouts of America. While in high school you should acquire a good ability to communicate—both orally and in writing. Seek help if there is a serious problem in these areas. Your summers should be spent profitably and should involve activities that bring you into active contact with people. Working in a hospital or laboratory may also provide some useful experience, but such activities are probably best deferred until the college years.

Take the appropriate college entrance examination required by the colleges you plan to apply to—either SAT I or the ACT (American College Testing program). If your scores are in the upper percentiles, you should feel encouraged about your potential success.

## STAY HEALTHY

The road to becoming a practicing physician passes through four-educational stages, starting from high school, then college, next medical school, and finally postgraduate training. During these stages the demands placed on the individual become increasingly intense and adequate time to achieve all goals seems to be diminishing as one moves up the ladder. To compensate for these pressures, students, especially in medical school, have made lifestyle changes that can be deleterious to one's health. It is thus important to recognize potential pitfalls *early on* so that they cannot harm your well-being and become habit forming. Negative reactions to the demands of a challenging educational program can include:

*Staying up all night.* There is a strong tendency, especially when the pressures to cram for exams are strong, to sacrifice sleep in response to the need for more study time. It may start off by staying up one hour longer, with the conviction that this will solve the problem. This eventually may lead to staying up several hours more and in time all night. Should this pattern become established, its potential harmful consequences on health are obvious.

*Fast food.* School leaves little time to prepare your own meals. Consequently, students become dependent upon their school cafeterias and fast food restaurants, which unfortunately usually fail to provide the healthiest choices. The food selection is further narrowed by eating out, because, aside from the time issue, food at these sources tends to be rather expensive. With little time and a limited budget, the dollar menu at a fast food establishment doesn't seem like such a bad option to students under pressure. Given these issues, pizza and snack bars have substantial appeal, especially for those with severe time or financial containments.

*No sweat.* The time pressure impact has other lifestyle casualties than sleeping and eating habits. Among these is exercise, what should be a vital component of everyone's routine, especially students who tend to be sedentary. Failure to exercise adequately can further contribute to undermining one's basic health status.

*No life.* There is a fourth potential area that can suffer when pressure of school work excludes other interests. This situation can and should be remedied by some positive distraction to ameliorate a critical gap in a student's life. This may be achieved by involvement in entertainment, sports, and hobbies during free time.

*Seek guidance.* Look for a mentor who can help you to achieve your vision. Get him/her to share his/her wisdom with you. The mentor can then guide you through your own journey, which is a long road, and show you how to avoid potential pitfalls.

*Maintain a support system.* Seek to maintain your ties with your family and friends. Their support can help get you through the tough periods by their encouragement and advice.

*Stick to a routine.* Establish a schedule and adhere to it as much as possible. By doing so one can use time more efficiently. However, rigidity on scheduling activities should be avoided.

## Bottom Line

- Your goal should be to learn how to establish a *proper balance* between responsibilities, so that under all circumstances one's health is not jeopardized in order for you to be able to face the challenge of advancing your career while under pressure.

- It is important that *early on,* even during the premedical phase of life, you make a genuine effort to avoid distorting your lifestyle in order to meet vital educational commitments.

- Focus on maintaining your health by eating properly on a regular basis. Avoid shortcuts to satisfy your need for food.

- Don't undervalue sleep, but try to maintain an adequate amount of it (about seven hours per night). This is recommended especially for the night before an examination, so that you can perform optimally the next day when faced with the challenge.

- Make a meaningful effort to set aside some time daily for exercise. This may even be as little as a 10-minute walk around the block during lunch hour and using stairs even when an elevator is available.

- See if you can retain elements of your life prior to the start of school, such as social contacts and an interesting hobby. This will help you remain a person, not only a student.

- Take your own advice. This means that since you are aware of the critical factors involved in maintaining health, seek to apply your knowledge to yourself in a consistent manner.

## EVALUATING A COLLEGE

It is essential to get as detailed an assessment as possible of any prospective institution you are seriously considering attending. To do this is a comprehensive matter. It is important to obtain data from reliable sources (such as upper-level students) and record your information for comparative purposes on a chart such as the one shown in Form 2.1. A separate copy of this form should be prepared for each college.

## Bottom Line

- Since you will have to spend four years attending college, you should seek an institution (a) where you will feel comfortable, (b) that you can afford, and (c) whose program can help you succeed in your future career.

- Prioritize the factors you identified by an asterisk and then compare evaluations from several schools to facilitate finalizing your decision.

## Form 2.1. EVALUATION OF PROSPECTIVE UNDERGRADUATE SCHOOL

School Name and Address: _____

| Factor | Superior | Acceptable | Deficient |
|---|---|---|---|

**Location**
Section of country
City/Suburban
Community

**Program of Studies**
Range of majors offered
Premed requirements available
Science course available
Laboratory facilities
Average class size

**Curriculum**
Quality
Extent of basic requirements
Combined degrees available
Career counseling services
Examination frequency
Problem-solving learning
Computer-based instruction
Group-seminar teaching
Premedical counseling services

**Faculty**
Accessibility
Faculty-student relations

**Facilities**
Classroom lecture halls
Laboratories
Computer support
Library
Parking
Bookstore
Cafeteria
Recreation Center
Learning Center

**Other Facilities/Services**
Housing on Campus
Health care facilities
Social facilities

**Finances**
Tuition
Other costs
Scholarship support

**Student satisfaction**
Lower level
Upper level

**Summary:**
**Subjective impression:**
**The college is acceptable _____ Possibly acceptable _____ , Not acceptable _____**
Place an asterisk next to the factors listed above that are most important to you.

- Colleges vary as to the level of high school performance and SAT scores applicants need in order to be seriously considered for acceptance.

- Colleges vary in their reaction to initial academic weakness and subsequent improvement in one's performance as time goes on. Some favor consistent performers, while others will acknowledge the determination of students who come from behind.

- During an interview, if granted, seek to determine the school's admissions policy in regard to issues that concern you.

## SELECTING A COLLEGE

There is a wide choice of colleges open to the high school graduate whose ultimate goal is medical school. Students should make their choice from one of the liberal arts colleges or universities accredited by one of the six regional accrediting agencies. This helps ensure that the school has met at least the minimum educational standards for institutions of higher learning. You should determine your personal preference either for a small school, with its opportunities for more personalized instruction and closer interaction with faculty and fellow students, or for a larger university, with its wider curricular and extracurricular opportunities. Factors such as cost should also be carefully considered. Take into account also the size of the library, the student-faculty ratio, the local environment, and the academic pressures. In addition, evaluate each college keeping in mind the following points:

1. Does the college offer the premedical courses that are prerequisites for admission to medical school? Examine the school's catalog to determine this.

2. Does the college have dynamic and modern science departments and adequate laboratory facilities?

3. Does the list of faculty members in the catalog indicate a competent staff? (Note, for example, the number of faculty with doctorate degrees.)

4. When you visit the school, do students speak well of the science and mathematics departments?

5. Does the school have good library facilities? A visit to the library will give you an insight into its quality.

6. Does the college have a high academic reputation? Examination of the freshman class profile, which should be available from high school counselors, will shed light on this point.

7. Does the college consistently send a significant portion of its premedical graduates to medical school? This information is very helpful in assessing the school's reputation and the quality of its premedical students. Discuss this question with the college's seniors, its premedical advisor, and its science professors.

8. Does the college have a premedical advisory program? A knowledgeable and dedicated premedical advisor will help ensure academic guidance, current information, and assistance at the time the student is planning to apply to medical and/or dental school.

A comparative evaluation of these and other issues involves reading the schools' catalogs and visiting each of the campuses under consideration. A visit offers the opportunity of meeting students, admissions and guidance personnel, and professors, and of discussing the aspects of the schools with those who are most familiar with them.

It is very important to give careful consideration to the college you select, for it will undoubtedly have a major impact upon your career. The undergraduate school at which you matriculate can affect your performance. In addition, it is one of the factors in the selection of medical students. Because of this, it is very desirable to secure a quality education at a well-established or prestigious college or university. A private school may give you an edge. To secure admission to a college that will improve your career potential requires competitive grades, attractive SAT I or ACT scores, impressive recommendations, and personal achievement(s).

## Bottom Line

Guidelines for selecting a college, can be summarized as follows:

- If you have not chosen a major, then check to make sure you have an adequate choice of offerings along with good-quality courses.
- If you have chosen a major, determine if you will be offered adequate choices in your area of concentration and how good the quality of teaching is.
- If you elect to attend a community college, be certain that your upper-level courses are taken at a four-year college to provide evidence of your ability to handle the demands of medical school.
- Determine if the atmosphere of the prospective school is conducive to enhancing your chances for a pleasant, lengthy educational experience.
- College rating guidelines have inherent technical problems that may make them a questionable source of information relative to selecting a college. Nevertheless, it may be worthwhile ascertaining the rating of possible schools from an acceptable reference source.

# GETTING INTO COLLEGE

Two groups of individuals are associated with filling freshman college classes. One group consists of the schools' admissions personnel who are given the difficult responsibility of selecting students for their schools' incoming class who are bright, self-confident high achievers and energetic learners. The other group consists of the large applicant pool of high school seniors who seek admission into colleges of their choice. Each group has a perspective of its own. This section will focus on the issues that will influence your achieving the educational goal you seek and how you can best facilitate your chances for getting accepted by one or more appropriate schools.

## Admission Considerations

It is important to recognize that your acceptance will depend not only on your credentials and applications, but also on how intense the competition is for admission to the particular institutions. Some have a one out of two acceptance ratio, while others have only one out of five or more.

There are several important areas relative to your application for admission to college. These are: academic profile, essay (personal statement), extracurricular activities, and the interview. Each of these areas will be discussed separately. It should be clearly realized that some issues that impact upon admission potential are outside of your control. These include the number of applicants, your high school's reputation, and the section of the country you come from.

## Academic Profile

This consists of a number of components that in composite provide a picture of your educational accomplishments and thus may indicate possible future academic potential. These three items are: courses completed and their grades, standardized test scores, and class rank. Colleges seek students who are capable of successfully meeting the challenge that their curriculum presents, as well as other significant factors. It should be noted that the first item of interest is the content and quality of the student's record. Subsequently, each school follows its own procedure for screening applicants.

## Your Transcript

This document provides a list of courses taken in the past, or presently, and the grades assigned to those you have completed. The two elements, courses and grades, provide a picture of your effort and achievement and need to be carefully interpreted in order to draw the appropriate conclusion about your future potential. This information is a key ingredient in the college admission assessment process. However, the nature of your transcript is not taken at face value.

While a predominance of As on your record is obviously very desirable, it is clear that what is especially impressive are those grades in challenging courses that have been completed. Taking such courses and achieving superior grades in them is the best recipe for making a favorable impression on admissions personnel. Your choice of courses is therefore a significant factor in setting the "tone" of your transcript. Most schools offer such honors work as Advanced Placement (AP) classes. Where this is the case, admissions committees would expect you to enroll in several of these, preferably balanced between the sciences and nonsciences. Admissions personnel, based on their school site visits and experience with prior applicants, have a reasonably good perspective of a school's course offerings; thus they are likely aware of the essay and difficult courses that appear on your transcript.

In viewing your transcript the admission personnel's search for trends is a standard approach. Special attention is frequently given to your most recent level of performance, namely your junior and lower senior year grades. Also, the consistent direction of the level of your work is a significant factor. Consistent superior work over the years, or a marked upward trend from a mediocre start, can prove helpful in advancing your case toward the acceptance goal.

## Standardized Tests

High schools vary in size, character, and the quality of their education. The use of standardized tests "levels the playing field," because it provides for uniformity in judging performance. It therefore makes it possible for candidates who come from different high schools to be compared in an objective manner. Consequently, a more reliable comparative assessment can be made between candidates for admission.

There is a consensus among admissions officers that the combination of both transcript and standardized test scores is a better predictor of performance than the use of the transcript by itself. Because of this enhanced predictive value, most colleges mandate taking either the SAT or ACT as a prerequisite for applying for admission. Some require specific achievement tests.

### Scholastic Aptitude Test (SAT)

This standardized exam measures verbal and mathematical reasoning abilities that are relevant to college performance. The verbal section will emphasize critical reading, while the math section will require students to produce some of their own results (with the aid of a calculator). There is also a standard written English test that reflects your familiarity with its usage.

A copy of your scores is sent to you and each college specified on your application. The scale for the verbal and math tests is 200–800 and the written component has a 20–80 scale. In addition, the College Board provides you with several percentile rankings. These will indicate how your scores compare with: (1) all other high school students; (2) other college-bound students; and (3) students in your state who attend high school.

### American College Testing Program Assessment (ACT)

This test is required for admission to many schools in some parts of the country. It consists of English, mathematics, reading, and science reasoning components.

Scoring on this exam involves separate subtest scores in the 1–56 range and a composite score, representing the average of the four subtests. Scores are also provided for specific content areas within English, math, and reading.

### Achievement Tests

These are also sponsored by the College Board and they measure knowledge in specific subjects. They are curriculum-based and intended to assess outcomes of courses that you have recently completed. Therefore, if you are aware of the achievement tests you will need to take, it is best to do so as soon as possible after you have completed those subjects. By this means you can maximize your performance, since your knowledge base in the subject will be optimal.

### Role of the Test Scores

The impact of your scores on your admission chances varies widely and is dependent on the particular school's admissions policy. Larger institutions place considerable weight on the results of standardized tests. In general, the scores are commonly considered in the context of the student's transcript. While the test scores may be indicators of academic ability, their validation is determined by whether the scores are consistent with one's grade point average in high school. A wide discrepancy between the two will raise concerns (see Table 2.1 below).

**Table 2.1**
**RELATIONSHIP OF STANDARDIZED TEST SCORES**
**AND HIGH SCHOOL AVERAGE**

| Test Scores | H.S. Average | Impact |
|---|---|---|
| High | High | Confirmatory |
| Low | High | Requires evaluation |
| Average | Average | Confirmatory |
| High | Low | Requires evaluation |
| Low | Low | Confirmatory |

Another factor that needs to be kept in mind is that the more your score is close to the college's median, the less significant role it will have. If there is a meaningful deviation from the median, however, this will catch the attention of the admissions officers. Depending on the direction and how extreme the deviation is, its impact upon your admission chances will be positive or negative.

If you are not satisfied with your performance and you feel that you can do *significantly* better, then (and only then) is it advisable to retake the test. To do so and not find a significant change will mean that you have merely confirmed the accuracy of your initial performance. If you decide to repeat the test, you should be aware that some schools have a policy of averaging the two scores, while others elect to count only the highest score. To retake a standardized exam more than twice is not advisable. Where your performance was negatively impacted by a major problem (such as being ill) you should call attention to such mitigating circumstances in your personal statement.

Experienced admissions officers have gained subjective perceptions of the caliber of schools that send abundant numbers of applicants for entrance to their colleges. These schools need no introduction to admissions personnel. If you are attending a small, less well-known institution, admissions personnel may need to be enlightened about the nature of your school and its program. You can try to do this briefly in your essay. If your transcript of courses does not clearly identify its character, see if you can get a guidance counselor to elaborate on it and on how demanding its program is, when he or she communicates with the college on your behalf. Finally, it should be noted that some schools have prepared their own profile to familiarize admissions officers with their program. If this is the case, make sure it is sent off with your transcript.

## Class Rank

Your transcript will not only contain a list of courses, but may frequently also indicate your class rank. The value of this figure depends on whether it is "weighted or unweighted." In the latter case, class rank is formulated without taking the difficulty of course load into consideration. In such cases, class rank is less valuable to admissions officers, unless there are several students from your school applying and each is taking courses that are equally challenging. A weighted rank provides a more meaningful appraisal, since more difficult courses are given greater weight than others. Schools that cite weighted rank usually use ranking guidelines adopted by the professional organization of school principals, registrars, and admissions officers. Where the school has its own ranking system, it will describe it in its profile.

There are schools that use modified ranking systems. They do not provide a specific rank; rather, students are placed into levels based on parameters, such as, for example, deciles, or divided into 10 groups of equal size. Thus, a student in the second decile falls in between the 10th and 20th percentile. Similarly, a quintile (five-part) or quartile (four-part) system can be used to define rank.

Some academically highly competitive or small high schools elect not to rank their students. In such cases, admissions officers will seek to compare grades with other members of the class from the same school.

Finally, it needs to be emphasized that rank *per se* is but one item on the transcript. It does not define the quality of your high school academic accomplishments; it is merely an indicator and not a decisive one at that. It fails, for example, to identify the direction of your progress, namely, if it was consistent or erratic; if it is progressing or faltering. These are important issues, where a prolonged effort and strong determination to succeed are vital, as is the case when choosing medicine as a career.

# THE ESSAY: YOUR PERSONAL STATEMENT

As part of the application procedure you will be expected to write an essay. At the outset it is desirable to recognize the significant role the essay can play in the admission process.

## Importance of the Essay

It is obvious that in the screening of applicants, priority is given to your high school record and aptitude test scores. Nevertheless, it needs to be emphasized that your essay can have a pivotal influence on the admissions process. This is especially important in borderline situations, such as when an applicant is on the threshold of being accepted, wait-listed, or rejected. There is a consensus that the essay in general has a critical role that may not always be appreciated by students because they may rely for success too heavily on their academic achievement. While grades and test scores can open up the admission gates, the essay may serve to tilt the balance in your favor. It is even possible, in some situations, that by submitting a very memorable essay, you can "write your way" into a college.

## Nature of the Essay

The essay you write may need to respond to a specific topic proposed by the school to which you are applying, or you may have the option of writing on a topic of your own choice.

Where a school requests a response to a specific question, it naturally will vary from one institution to another. Moreover, the same school can change the topic periodically. Therefore, reading an essay written for a prior year may not always prove directly helpful.

When presented with one or a choice of essay topics, these may be conventional or they may be "offbeat." In the former category are requests to write on (1) why you wish to attend college; (2) more specifically, why you are applying to this college; (3) how you define success; (4) a story about yourself; (5) who you are; (6) what life issues are of importance to you. Most conventional questions asked can serve as vehicles to bringing your personal attributes to the reader's attention.

## Preparing Your Essay

At the outset, when you are preparing to write your essay, the following considerations need to be taken into account:

- The success of your essay depends on the manner in which you present yourself.
- What you want to say and how effectively you convey your message is what counts.
- Do not try to respond to what you think the admission committee wants to hear.
- Write about yourself in a forthright manner, but without baring your soul.
- Write about a subject that is important to you, and do so in a convincing manner.
- Write an essay that reflects your uniqueness as a prospective college student.
- Keep your essay focused on the message you wish to convey.
- Present your accomplishments, but don't overdo it to the point of bragging.
- Don't feel you must respond to an offbeat question with an offbeat essay.
- Feel free to insert appropriate humor, so as to add spice to your essay.
- Respond to an ordinary question by using a distinctive approach.

With these guidelines in mind, we will consider two important issues: selecting a topic and how to approach it.

## The Essay Topic

It may prove easier to respond to a specific question posed by the school than to prepare an essay on a topic of your own choosing. When this is the case, the options are unlimited and this is why choosing a topic presents such a challenge. However, you shouldn't view this feature as a burden, but rather as a chance to "sell" yourself. It offers an opportunity to present yourself in a nonacademic context. Namely, you can, in an appropriate fashion, bring to light information about your skills, philosophy, talents, experiences, character, background, personal interests, and life goals. In other words, you have a valuable opportunity to generate a meaningful image of yourself as a unique individual. This can significantly add to the desirability of the school wanting to have you as a member of their next incoming class.

Most conventional topics discussed in essays relate to school activities, trips, and vacations. This is because they reflect the norm of a high school student's lifestyle. The key is to fit your personal message into the context of the specific topic you select.

Essay topics of a conventional nature that you may wish to write about are

- What career objectives do you have, and how will attending college help you achieve them?
- In what way will college help you fulfill your specific life goals and aspirations?
- What contribution can you make to the college you wish to enter?
- What would you write in your recommendation for admission?

In addition, you may find a topic to write about by thinking of answers to the following:

• What do you excel at?

• What do you consider to be the most impressive accomplishment so far in your life?

• What achievement has given you the most satisfaction?

• What are your strongest personal commitments?

• If you came into great wealth, how would you spend your life?

To decide on the topic for your essay, you may need to set aside time for undisturbed reflection. Moreover, this warm-up time should be used not only to identify the subject, but to clarify its focus so that you can say all you want in the limited space allotted (approximately 300 words).

If your efforts at initiating writing are not productive and the results of the drafts are mediocre, then you should try to approach the problem by placing the title of your topic on a page and then writing about 15 relevant questions beneath it. Leave enough space between questions for responses. The challenge is to come up with questions, and the answers can serve to generate a viable topic and draft the message you seek to send.

If the above formula to find an essay topic still doesn't produce a satisfactory response, another approach is to spend an hour or two a day for five days drafting an essay outline on five different topics, possibly using different styles. Allow the essays to "hibernate" for a weekend, then on the following Monday read them all through and select the one that most appeals to you and is most suitable for use in your application.

## Preparation

By the time you have to prepare your application for admission to college you will have already written numerous essays. In developing these you used your own modes of preparation. This may simply involve expressing your thoughts on a sheet of paper and handing it in, or you may have written a rough draft, set it aside, and then come back and reorganized and/or edited it. You may also have given a subject some prior thought and then prepared an outline to guide your writing. Finally, you may have used a combination of approaches to fit each particular need. In any case, you used the approach you felt most comfortable with and one that you believed to be most appropriate for the project at hand.

For your college application essay, you also have several approach options at your disposal. While the reader of your essay at the admissions office is obligated to thoughtfully review it, your challenge is to take hold of and maintain the reader's interest as he or she proceeds.

Since you wish to fit a personal image into the context of your essay, it may prove desirable to prepare an inventory of your attributes. These can be ranked in order of your estimate of their importance. Such a list may consist, for example, of the following qualities:

| | |
|---|---|
| idealistic | dedicated |
| broad minded | motivated |
| competitive | reliable |
| good listener | determined |
| energetic | tolerant |
| ambitious | empathetic |
| conscientious | realistic |

Find a way to demonstrate your individuality by exemplifying some of your attributes in your essay. You should try to do so in a creative manner, even when you have to respond to some specific question. Thus, you need not confine yourself exclusively to a topic in its narrowest perspective. There usually is a degree of liberty afforded with any topic so as to get your personal message across.

Once you have a rough draft of your essay on paper or in your mind, you have set the basis for the next step.

## Organization of the Essay

There is a simple, basic, three-step pattern that is recommended in regard to organization of your essay. It involves an *introduction,* where you present the general theme of your essay; the *body,* where you convey in-depth your message; and a *conclusion,* which summarizes the points you wish to emphasize.

### Introduction

The introduction should convey to the reader the subject of your essay in an appealing way. Your goal is to grab the reader's attention as early as possible. The most appealing essays are those that are initiated with a phrase, sentence, or idea that intensely attracts the reader's interest. The most incisive your remarks, the sharper will be the "hook" that grabs hold of the reader. Naturally, your initial remarks should be suited to the topic and the tone of your essay. The introduction should also indicate to the reader the direction in which you are heading.

Among the lead-off approaches you may consider using are to:

• ask one or two questions that will be responded to in the course of the essay.

• present a relevant real or fictional incident that will leave an impact.

• state an ordinary idea in a provocative manner or vice versa.

• use a meaningful quotation that will serve to set the tone for your essay.

• debunk some common assumption and then show why.

### The Body

Once you have determined what you wish your reader's reaction to be, such as whether to inform, inspire, or entertain, your thoughts need to be presented in a logical order. To do this, rank your ideas in order of their importance. You can build up your ideas toward the major one, which should come at the end, rather than present it at the very outset. Start off with the second major point you wish to convey. The least significant point can be placed in the middle. Thus, in a typical essay, the body will consist of three sections. These do not have to be of equal length; each may contain one or more paragraphs with each segment aiming to convey its distinct message. Your aim should also be to link the three sections together as well as to keep your message in sight as the reader is moved forward.

### The Conclusion

When finishing your essay you need to leave your reader with something substantive. This may be in the form of an impressive remark, memorable phrase, or poignant quotation. A stylish ending can remain in the reader's mind and may serve to tilt the balance of one's reaction to the essay in your favor.

## Following the Draft

Having labored to prepare your draft essay, you now need to look at it objectively and determine if it conveys your thoughts in the most meaningful and impressive manner. To arrive at a decision, set your draft aside entirely for a short interlude. Then see if it meets the goal of selling your potential as a future college student. The criteria you should use to determine the suitability of your essay should be:

1. *Purpose.* Does your essay meet the challenge of making a solid case for your admission?
2. *Clarity.* Does the essay succeed in getting its main idea across lucidly?
3. *Focus.* Does the essay keep the main message in sight for the reviewer to take note of?
4. *Organization.* Does each of the parts of the essay meet its goal?
5. *Accuracy.* Is the information contained in the essay accurate and clear?

If any of these goals are not met, then rewrite the text where necessary to meet deficiencies that you came across. Test your satisfaction with the revised version by

- reading your essay out loud. Your reaction to hearing it will clue you in to how good it really is.

- having another person read the essay aloud. Note their facial reaction to see if they are satisfied as they proceed.

- setting the revised draft aside again for an interlude and then coming back for another reading.

In rereading your essay evaluate your choice of words. You should avoid: (1) using complex or elegant words merely to impress the reader; (2) using words in unnecessary excessive numbers that do not serve to clarify your thoughts; (3) repetition, since making your point once should be enough.

## The Final Check

After carefully evaluating your essay for the varied parameters that were previously defined, and critically checking your word usage, you should give your essay one final review. This should be done after a brief interlude following the last revision and editing the text. Once completed you should prepare a neat copy using a computer and laser printer. Naturally, where a hand-written copy is required, print it rather than use script, if your penmanship is poor. The goal is to make your essay look good and clearly readable. This should be done by double-spacing, making use of high-quality $8\frac{1}{2} \times 11$-inch paper, and leaving a one-inch margin all around. Make sure to stay within the word guidelines set by the school. If necessary, find a way to reduce the text to meet the limit set.

The next phase involves proofreading your near-finished product. You may wish to show it to one or more responsible and qualified individuals to read it carefully and offer their *frank* comments.

If you still feel insecure about the state of your essay, you can set it aside while it is being reviewed by outsiders and await their comments and reaction. In making your final review, focus your attention on spelling and punctuation. If you are distracted by the meaning of the text, then try and read the sentences not only forward but also backward. This will facilitate being able to concentrate on the spelling. Particular attention should be paid to words that are similar (such as *there* and *their*). When uncertain, check a dictionary for spelling, even after spell-checking on your computer.

After receiving comments from others about your draft essay, if rewording one or two sentences or even changing several words or clarifying an idea are called for—suggestions that you agree with—by all means make them. However, if you are urged to drastically alter your essay with numerous radical alterations, try and resist making such changes that will, *drastically*, alter *your* essay into someone else's. To "polish" your essay to this point may prove self-defeating because it may raise questions in the reader's mind that the essay is too good, and whether it is really yours. By this means its value can be diluted and you may not fully benefit from your efforts at change, and possibly even be hurt.

# EXTRACURRICULAR ACTIVITIES

As part of your college application you will be asked to describe what extracurricular activities you have been participating in. Since the space allotment for this information may be substantial, you should not panic if your response does not fill all or even most of the available space.

You need to realize that the number of listed activities will not be counted up by the committee, so padding your profile of extracurricular activities can be self-defeating. The issue that is important is not only the nature of your outside activities, but the extent of your commitment to them. In other words, the admissions committee wants to know the importance you place on the individual activities you are or were involved in during your free time. Your list provides an indication of your interests and talents. Since such activities vary widely among applicants, it indicates your potential contribution toward class diversity. What to include on your list of extracurricular activities is a key issue. By considering those activities that are time consuming, require creative thinking, and demand responsibility you should hopefully find a significant number to formulate an impressive preliminary list.

To initiate your list, note down any activity meeting the above three criteria you have been involved in, along with any relevant details. This includes not only those at school, at home, and also within your community, but you should include work experience on your list, indicating the length of time you were employed each week. This will indicate the amount of time you were unable to devote to classwork or other activities.

In the event of involvement in some community activity, whether of a political or service character, it should be identified and explained. If you gained a commendation for any activity, such as becoming an Eagle Scout, or have been presented an award, this should be noted next to the activity or under a separate heading. It is best not to include hobbies unless they are substantive.

Care needs to be taken in finalizing your list of extracurricular activities. Consider what impression you wish to relate by the way in which you present them. You may wish to emphasize a balance between sports and leadership roles in the clubs you were active in. Carefully select the activity listed first, since it reflects the one you consider most important. This should be reinforced by demonstrating the substantial time and effort you have expended in this area.

In composing the final list, be selective and informative. It need not be an activity you participated in each year. The list as a whole should generate an impression that contributes to the image you wish to create. It should also fit into the image you believe is being provided by any recommendations submitted in your behalf.

Review the application as a whole when you have come to this end point; it is desirable to carefully look at the overall image of yourself that your application generates. Ask yourself if this is the image that you really wish to give the admissions committee. Be sure that your unique talents and interests are reflected and your potential contribution as a member of the incoming class can be clearly visualized.

# THE INTERVIEW

An interview is an absolute requirement to get into medical school or obtain a residency appointment; however, most colleges that you may apply to will *not* require you to have an on-campus interview. Many may not even offer one, but if they do, it will likely be optional. This indicates that an interview is of secondary importance. Moreover, only a small part of the applicant pool will be interviewed. While an interview does provide an opportunity to establish your identity as an individual, it should not be construed as a way to get the committee to overlook significant defects in your record. Nevertheless, if you (1) are very anxious to gain admission to a specific school; (2) can afford the expense; and (3) are a presentable and articulate individual, you should try to set up an appointment. You can then take this opportunity to do your very best to personally "sell" yourself. Obviously, you need to have good reason to believe that you have a realistic chance of getting in to the college before asking for an interview.

Plan to set up appointments for interviews early (as in the first part of the summer). Determine the best time for you to interrupt your routine schedule to attend an interview. When scheduling, arrange that you can arrive at your interview in a good physical state and not be suffering from travel fatigue. When you arrive for your interview, be dressed in a presentable manner, so that the initial impression you give is a favorable one.

It is essential that you adequately prepare for any interview you decide to schedule. Your initial source of information should be the college's catalog. Therefore, issues that are of special interest to you but are not discussed in the catalog, such as choice of major or class size, can be raised at the interview.

You will probably be allotted only about a half-hour for the interview so it is important to prepare your personal message that presents your personality and potential, and fit it in somewhere in the course of the interview. You might use a well-placed question to move the interview in a direction that is in your favor and allows you to come across most effectively.

Remember that the basic goal of the interview is for the admissions personnel to get to know you better and exchange thoughts about getting an education at their college. Your responses should be in this context. If you can establish a favorable rapport with your interviewer right away, things will most likely move along more smoothly. Two elements to attain this goal are to be as relaxed as possible and respond to questions in a thoughtful and accurate manner—if a question is asked that you don't know the answer to, you should say so rather than try and obfuscate when responding.

To help your interview skills, you should

- maintain eye contact throughout the session.

- avoid brisk, one-word, or one-sentence, answers.

- get involved and demonstrate interest, thereby generating a dialogue.

- ask about school strengths, but don't ask for comparisons.

- don't try to explain deficiencies in your record (unless specifically asked).

- have a transcript and test score reports with you, but do not present them unless requested to do so.

# RECOMMENDATIONS

Recommendations in support of your application are usually expected by colleges. It is *your* obligation to arrange for them to be sent to the schools to which you are applying. The usual sources for recommendations are current or former teachers. The expectation is to receive an evaluation of your academic skills in the teacher's subject and an assessment of your level of maturity as well as other personal assets. The college will commonly ask the applicant to arrange that specific recommendation forms be given to the individuals to be completed.

You need to take care when selecting teachers to give recommendation forms to be completed on your behalf. You should realize that the comments provided should enhance the impression generated by your transcript and related data. This can be the case if the individuals writing on your behalf hold you in high regard. There are situations that provide teachers at a large school with an opportunity to get to know their students better, such as when you are a member of a small class where individual student interaction with the instructor is high, if more than one course has been or is being taken with the teacher, or if the teacher also serves as a coach in some area and knows you also in this context. All of the aforementioned assume that you have performed well in courses whose instructors are writing your recommendation.

As to the teachers' subject, what is expected is a recommendation from one (or two) from the traditional courses in the social or physical sciences. Where you have special interests that you wish to pursue at a college, a solid letter from a teacher in the same field may well serve to strengthen your admission chances. Other considerations in choosing a subject are how recently the course was completed. The more recent, the more valuable will be the teacher's opinion of you. Finally, a recommendation from an instructor of an advanced course will surely be more impressive and indicate effectively your intellectual assets in that field.

A potentially good source for a recommendation is a guidance counselor who knows you well. This means that he or she has had contact with you over an extended length of time. Such individuals should be able to write in depth about your abilities and your academic progress and personnel growth over the years.

## SUMMER ENRICHMENT PROGRAMS

Even at this early stage in your career, it is beneficial to gain exposure to the activities associated with a medical environment or with social service. This may involve contact with patients as well as working with individuals in need of personal help. Possible opportunities for such experiences may be secured at hospitals, nursing homes, assisted living facilities, and clinics. Working with impaired children privately or at a facility or tutoring disadvantaged youngsters are valuable experiences.

## GET EXPOSURE TO MEDICINE

Deciding on marriage and choosing a career have much in common. They both involve long-term commitments, a great deal of effort, time, and considerable expenditure of money. Usually one dates the person one wishes to marry, to get to know that person. Similarly, in choosing medicine as a possible future profession, it is clearly advantageous to become familiar with the basic characteristics of practicing medicine, even at this relatively early stage in your education.

While a significant amount of exposure to medicine is expected from a college premedical student, one should seek to gain insight into what the profession is all about, as well as eliminate some myths that one may have. Approaches that are commonly used to secure some exposure are

- "Shadow" a physician both during office hours and hospital rounds. Observe the level of patient care provided, to the extent the sponsoring physician feels comfortable with having you present.

- Obtain training as an EMT to gain clinical exposure during the educational phase. Some volunteer ambulance services make use of EMT volunteers, which can provide additional opportunities for exposure during emergency care situations.

Clinical exposure can serve to further stimulate your interest in medicine and encourage you to proceed and eventually to become a college premedical student. Should your experience change your mind and your course away from a possible medical career, it will, in a sense, also be beneficial, because it will minimize your expenditure of effort and time in the wrong direction. Your altered course will give you a chance to choose an educational program that may prove more beneficial to your future. Thus it is essential to be open-minded at this stage and review your options with a knowledgeable guidance counselor and others whose judgment you can rely on.

# CHECKLIST OF PRECOLLEGE ACTIVITIES _____

Indicate with a check or an x, when the task has been completed.

_____ Selected a high school that offers a strong academic program (especially in the sciences), has a solid track record of its graduates being admitted to quality undergraduate schools, and has a strong career guidance program.

_____ Demonstrated an interest in the sciences and received good grades (B+ or better), in these courses.

_____ Completed four years of English so as to develop good written communication skills.

_____ Completed a speech course that enhances one's abilities to communicate orally.

_____ Completed at least three years of a foreign language (preferably Spanish).

_____ Completed at least one year of biology.

_____ Completed four years of humanities (including a psychology course).

_____ Engaged in voluntary community service in a meaningful manner.

_____ Considered applying to an accelerated or combined program.

_____ Joined a premed club at school and actively participated in its functions.

_____ Spent time observing the activities of a physician who has a successful practice.

_____ Properly prepared for and took the SAT (or ACT) exam.

_____ Received the necessary applications from appropriate undergraduate schools.

_____ Visited schools (even if not invited for an interview), to see if it meets the necessary level, both scholastically and socially.

# 3 Preparing for Medical School

Program of college studies
Succeeding in college
Extracurricular and summer activities
The premedical advisor and/or committee
Humanistic aspects of premedical education
Checklist of college activities

## PROGRAM OF COLLEGE STUDIES

You should realize at the outset of your college career that every medical school admissions committee will initially screen your application by viewing your grades as a whole. This is expressed by your grade point average (GPA), which simply represents the total of your average for each academic year divided by the number of years you have attended college (usually three at the time you apply, plus any summer school work completed). Then your science course average, your achievement in your major and in the more challenging premedical requirements (such as organic chemistry and physics), and honors work or independent study are all scrutinized. This means that it is imperative that you apply all your talents (and remedy any deficiencies) at the time you begin college studies. It is risky to wait until you are faced with serious academic problems to decide to buckle down to the demands of your courses. It is difficult, although certainly not impossible, to rectify the results of one unimpressive semester, let alone an entire year. Thus, for example, a B or 3.0 for your first freshman semester will give you a maximum B+ or 3.5 average for the year only if your second semester is straight A or 4.0. Similarly, a 3.0 for the entire freshman year would demand a perfect sophomore year to bring you up to a B+ level. In addition, a mediocre semester or a mediocre year can seriously undermine your self-confidence and raise doubts about the wisdom of your career decision. This type of situation is undoubtedly one of the underlying factors in the significantly high incidents of changes in majors among freshman premeds.

### Your Major

Historically, premedicine has changed to keep pace with advancements in medical education. In colonial America, premedical education as such was nonexistent. However, as medical education became more sophisticated, so by necessity did premedical education come into existence. During this century there have been varying trends in premedical programming. The older school of thought was that a specialized preprofessional program was mandatory. As a result, a formal "premedical major" with a prescribed program of study was established. A strong movement away from this approach began in the mid-1950s. Students were encouraged to select any major that was of interest, but if it was in one of the sciences (as was frequently the case) they were also urged to obtain broad exposure to the humanities and social sciences as well. Currently the pressure, due to diminished time allotted to the basic sciences in medical school, has given impetus to encouraging students to complete more science courses in college, so that the pendulum has swung somewhat in the direction of a science major. While completing a science major, students automatically take the required premedical courses.

The specific choice of which science to major in is yours alone. You should, before making a decision, evaluate your school's science departments in terms of their requirements, quality of teaching, and grading attitudes. To do so, you should read the school catalog and talk to faculty members and senior-level students. The choice should be the one in which you will be academically most successful and in which you stand a good chance of developing a good relationship with members of the department staff. A correct decision as to your major will help ensure that your GPA, science cumulative average, and the quality of your recommendations—three critical medical school selection factors—will be strong.

Most premedical students major in biology (zoology) or chemistry, but some major in biochemistry, physics, or even computer science, all of which have a relevance to medicine. However, choosing to major in a science unrelated to the art of healing, such as geology or engineering, will certainly not impede an applicant from gaining admission.

It should be strongly emphasized that being a nonscience major is not a liability so far as medical school admission is concerned, but may even be an asset. Humanities majors, although representing the smaller segment of the applicant pool, have as good an admissions track record as science majors. Thus, should your current interest lie in the classics, foreign languages, history, or philosophy, and your career goal is medicine, you should pursue a humanities major and seek to develop an attractive set of credentials supported by solid achievement in the premedical science prerequisites. This approach is especially valid now that medical educators are stressing the importance of developing and retaining the humanistic attributes as medical and postgraduate students. Thus what is critical is not your major, but the nature of your achievement and development as a college student.

These remarks should alleviate the concerns of those who fear that being a liberal arts major would impede their chances for admission into medical school. Another factor influencing prospective medical students against becoming liberal arts majors is the concern that they would then be less competitive in facing the demands of a science-oriented curriculum. A comparative study of science and nonscience majors from three medical schools has shown, however, that this is not the case. This conclusion was based on performance on both parts of the National Board Examination (now USMLE) and on clinical-year grade point averages. There is no reason not to assume that the same is applicable to medical students as a whole. This finding should further encourage college freshmen to feel free in their choice of a major.

In support of the conclusion mentioned above, it is useful to consider the relevant statistics with regard to the choice of a major by recent acceptees to medical school. It was reported that they fell into groups.

| | |
|---|---|
| Biological sciences | 47% |
| Physical sciences | 19% |
| Nonsciences | 13% |
| Other health professions | 2% |
| Mixed disciplines | 8% |
| Other | 11% |

These findings demonstrate that while the overwhleming majority of acceptees (70%) were science majors, a significant number (at least 17%) were not. These facts demonstrate that the acceptee is no longer almost exclusively made up of science majors, as it was for many decades. Thus, prospective applicants can, under appropriate circumstances, seriously consider majoring in one of the nonsciences if their interests and talents encourage them to do so.

## Bottom Line

The following considerations should be taken into account when choosing a major:

- Past experience indicates that you have talent in and interest in the area.
- You have good reason to believe that you would enjoy the subject matter.

- You could be able to utilize the knowledge obtained in the major, if you were to drop out as premed or not get into medical school.

- You should be able to meet all basic premedical requirements at the same time as fulfilling those of your major.

- As a nonscience major, you will need to demonstrate your strong ability in the basic premedical science courses.

- If you do not major in science, it is preferable to select an area that is "people"-oriented.

- It is appropriate to take a biochemistry course, regardless of your major, since it can prove to be a significant help in lightening your first year of medical school.

- In whatever area you focus your efforts, develop good problem-solving and critical-thinking skills; they will be vital assets in medical school.

- Organic chemistry courses, while in themselves are of little future benefit, are essential areas of study for the MCAT, which is critical for admission.

- Be flexible when choosing your major by preparing options that may be used if the situation calls for it.

- To protect your future interests, you should also have an alternative career choice. This will allow you to remain calm in the face of any unforeseen adversity, which is a key to success.

## Premedical Requirements

Regardless of your choice of a major, you should arrange to include the basic premedical science courses plus lab requirements, namely, two years of chemistry and one each of biology and physics, in your first three years of college study. The purpose of premedical science course requirements is twofold: (1) to determine the compatibility between the student and science, since medicine academically is the science of the human body, and (2) to provide the premedical student with a background on which to launch future studies in the basic medical sciences.

The required premedical science courses you take should not be those designed for the nonscience major. If possible, stagger your laboratory courses so that you don't take too many at one time. These courses require additional time both in the laboratory and outside of the classroom. However, none of these courses should be deferred to the senior year. They are all needed in preparation for the MCAT. One or more of these courses may be in progress when taking the spring MCAT.

The science course requirements are purposely limited in order to allow broad latitude for the planning of individualized programs. Table 3.1 lists the courses required by medical schools.

You need to recognize that you should strive for *at least* a 3.5 (B+) science commutative average; this will keep you competitive during the admission process. To maximize your chances of obtaining superior grades, you should avoid registering for courses catering to specialty students (such as inorganic or organic chemistry for chemical engineers). Similarly, avoid courses whose instructors are known to be outrageously demanding or have a reputation for rarely giving out As. If really necessary, take a course in summer school or even at a community college, but do not do so for the majority of your science course reqirements and certainly not for all of them. This will generate a "red flag" when your record is reviewed, and require an explanation. Moreover, it would mandate your getting especially attractive science subtest scores on your MCAT to confirm your abilities in the sciences.

It should be noted that some advanced science courses, as well as some nonscience courses, while not officially required for admission by some schools, may nevertheless be listed in their catalogs as "recommended" or "desirable."

In summary, while the premedical core studies in the sciences will usually absorb the greatest portion of one's time and energy, one must place these in the proper perspective of the entire program of undergraduate education. For just as the patient should be viewed as a whole rather than as merely a collection of organ systems, so too should the person be educated as a whole in order to face both the academic as well as the nonacademic challenges that lie ahead. In essence this means that the student should attempt to secure a meaningful balance between the physical and biological sciences, and the humanities and social sciences. In this way, not only will the college experience be more pleasurable, but also one's sense of purpose and ethical values will be developed, and a more humanistic physician can evolve in a mechanistically oriented society.

**Table 3.1**
**SUMMARY OF REQUIRED COURSES**
+ required by more than 100 schools
− required by fewer than 20 schools

| Course | |
|---|---|
| **Chemistry** | |
| Inorganic (or General) Chemistry | + |
| Organic Chemistry | + |
| Qualitative Analysis | − |
| Quantitative Analysis | − |
| Physical Chemistry/Quantitative Analysis | − |
| *Biochemistry | |
| Other | − |
| **Biology** | |
| General Biology (or Zoology) | + |
| Embryology | − |
| Genetics | − |
| Comparative Anatomy | − |
| Cell Biology | − |
| Molecular Biology | − |
| Other | − |
| **Physics** | |
| General Physics | + |
| Other | − |
| **Mathematics** | |
| College Mathematics | − |
| College Algebra | − |
| Analytical Geometry | − |
| Trigonometry | − |
| Calculus | − |
| Other | − |
| **Humanities** | |
| English | + |
| Language | − |
| Other | − |
| **Social and Behavioral Sciences** | |
| Sociology | − |
| Psychology | − |
| Behavioral Science | − |
| Social Science | − |
| Other | − |

*For some schools biochemistry is required or may be used as a substitute for one semester of organic chemistry.

# Special Educational Opportunities

Most liberal arts colleges offer special educational opportunities that can enhance the character of your program of study. These programs not only improve the quality of your college educational experience but also increase the strength of your medical school application and thereby improve your admission chances. You should not arbitrarily utilize any of these programs but should incorporate them into your program only if you are sure that they will definitely help you attain your career goal. The six special programs discussed below are advanced placement credit, honors courses, independent study, graduate-level courses, pass/fail courses, and summer school courses.

## Advanced Placement Credit

When a student has acquired advanced placement credit for excelling in a science on the high school level, one or more required premedical courses will be waived. As a result, there will be a gap in grade information in this area. It is frequently desirable in such cases to substitute a suitable number of elective courses for the waived courses. You should select substitute elective courses carefully, determining that your high school background is adequate, and discussing the course requirements with the instructor. You should also consider auditing the basic science course from which you have been excused in advance of taking the elective; this would not only provide a useful background but would also enable you to develop a set of lecture notes that could prove helpful for review when you are studying for the MCAT. For example, if your general biology requirement has been waived, you should review the principles of biology by yourself or audit a course if possible. This preparation is essential, even if you do not major in biology. In this case, your elective course grades will serve to indicate to the admissions committee your academic potential in this important area. If you do major in biology, a good grounding in its principles will serve you well for a variety of electives you choose during the course of your studies.

## Honors Courses

There is no question that completing an honors section of a course can strengthen your admission potential. This, however, is true only if you get an A in such a course. Receiving a B grade may serve to depress your GPA (and, where applicable, your science average) even though in reality a B in an honors section may be equivalent to an A in a standard section. In some cases, however, grades for honors courses may be weighted, in order to provide an equivalency factor. Thus, before enrolling in an honors section, you should determine, by talking to the instructor and students involved in the course, just how much additional work it requires and how the grade is evaluated. If you have the time and are confident of your ability to master the requirements, then enrolling in an honors section is reasonable. In any case, the honors credit should be noted in your application documents. The course can be educationally rewarding and provide a good source for securing an impressive letter of recommendation.

## Independent Study

Another approach that can add significantly to the attractiveness of your credentials is satisfactory completion of an independent study program. Such an undertaking can demonstrate that you are willing and able to accept the responsibility of a special educational challenge. Your motives must, however, be sincere so that you will apply yourself maximally in order to ensure that your research is impressive and is completed on schedule. As a result of such an activity you will undoubtedly develop a special favorable relationship with your mentor, who will then be able to strongly support your candidacy for admission to medical school at the appropriate time.

Independent study should be undertaken only if you are sure that it will not have a negative impact on your educational responsibilities as a whole. You need to be especially careful in selecting a project that can be realistically completed by the date you set. It is best if you can complete any independent study project before you apply to medical school so that recommendations resulting from this work can be submitted when they can be most effective. A good time to carry out such a project may be the summer after you complete your junior-year studies. By then you should have completed all your premedical science course requirements and satisfactorily taken your MCAT. Your only remaining commitment will be preparing your application(s) to medical school. There is no objection, if time is available, to undertake independent study during the regular academic year.

### Graduate Courses

Occasionally, the option of taking a graduate-level course is available to undergraduates. You should not assume, unless specifically told, that you will be graded differently from the graduate students taking the course with you. Thus the note of caution regarding the impact of the grade applicable here. Graduate courses can be demanding, and successful completion of such a challenge can demonstrate impressively your ability to respond effectively to the academic challenge of medical school. If you do successfully complete graduate courses, make sure to bring it to the attention of the medical school by noting it on your essay or in your interview.

### Pass/fail Courses

These are courses that your school permits you to take for credit without getting a grade. It is not advisable to take any courses in biology or chemistry on this basis since the implication would be that your level of performance was not satisfactory. Thus while the absence of a grade would preclude any negative impact on your GPA and science average, your image could suffer. On the other hand, taking a medically unrelated science (such as geology) or a nonscience course of special interest on a pass/fail basis is quite legitimate. It shows evidence of your desire to secure a broad education, which certainly is desirable.

### Summer Courses

There is no inherent objection to the completion of courses during the summer. Moreover, it may prove useful or even desirable to do so in order to get some required nonscience courses out of the way and thereby lighten your course load during the regular academic year. Thus some students take one or two nonscience courses at the end of their sophomore year so they can lighten their course load during their junior year when they have to take organic chemistry or physics and also study for the MCAT.

It may even prove advantageous to take one or more science electives during the summer, if they are not offered at your school during the regular academic year, or if you cannot fit them into your schedule. In addition, summer electives can help improve your science average. Thus if your BCPM (biology, chemistry, physics, and math) average comes close to a critical level, taking summer courses can bring these figures up. It is worthwhile to consider attending summer school to do so. Again, it is important to realize that it can take an A or two A's to do this, and that special care needs to be taken before utilizing this double-edged option.

## SUCCEEDING IN COLLEGE

Four factors are involved in doing well in college: academic ability, determination, good study skills, and proper time management. There are, however, a good number of pitfalls that should and can be avoided to enhance your chances for success. The following are ten tips that may prove helpful:

#### TIP 1    Prepare for lectures

Being acquainted with the general subject material in advance of a lecture will permit you to understand it better as well as to integrate the new information with the knowledge you already have.

#### TIP 2    Guard your time

The social demands of college life can be very time consuming. You need to determine your obligations and priorities. Study time needs will inherently vary. Thus, you should not feel pressured by classmates to give up needed study time for social activities.

### TIP 3 Avoid test cramming

The proven method of successful studying involves repetition. Thus, earlier review of material covered and keeping up with class assignments will serve to reduce the need for cramming prior to examinations.

### TIP 4 Seek assistance

Failure to comprehend a topic should not be a source of embarrassment. Instead, you should be motivated to secure help from teachers, upperclass students, or other classmates.

### TIP 5 Utilize free time

Free time between classes can be an occasion for extra study. This time can be useful because you may not be as tired then as in the evening hours. Also, use the free time for class preparation or review purposes.

### TIP 6 Listening is an art

When sitting in on a lecture, avoid being distracted by a classmate or even by the instructor's mannerisms. Rather, focus your attention on the content of the talk.

### TIP 7 Proper note taking

Students vary in their ability to take accurate lecture notes, which can be sketchy or disorganized. It is well worth the effort to review and, if necessary, rewrite lecture notes so that they will be legible, complete, and accurate.

### TIP 8 Review

Daily brief review and regular periodic review of the material being studied will serve to enhance your knowledge of the subject matter and reduce the time needed for study for examinations.

### TIP 9 Proper reading

If you read an assigned chapter in its entirety for the first time, you may be overwhelmed by its detail. To get the most out of your reading, skim the subject titles and subheadings, opening and concluding sentences, in order to get a knowledge of the main ideas and to be better prepared to absorb the details.

### TIP 10 Underlining with purpose

If reading material is first "screened," as noted above, and then read, you are in a better position to judge what to underline. You will then be able to underscore with discrimination and to highlight passages that will prove more meaningful when you review them at a later date.

The following discussion covers (1) organizing oneself, (2) writing term papers, and (3) taking examinations.

## Organizing for College Life

It is important to be aware of the fact that during high school, competition may not necessarily be very intense, because not all students are considering college or postgraduate careers. Under these circumstances, students may not be motivated to acquire good study habits in order to succeed. This is especially true if they find that, with a modest amount of work, they can attain adequate grades to be admitted to a college, even the one of their choice. Upon entering college, where competition is usually much more intense, knowing how to study is obligatory if the student is to have a good enough academic record to get into a professional school.

College life is very time consuming; it preempts the largest block of one's daily activities. It has built-in time commitments, such as: (1) the need to attend lecture and recitation classes, as well as laboratory sessions; (2) library research and term paper writing; and (3) study in preparation for periodic midterm and final examinations. In addition to these educational time demands, there are those of a personal nature, such as eating, relaxation, social life, and participation in extracurricular activities. Leading a balanced college life that meets both your personal and educational needs is the most desirable formula for achieving academic success. It also ensures enjoying your stay in college, which is a unique time in one's life.

The key to adequately meeting both your school and personal obligations is the proper allocation of your time. This can be done either in a disorganized or in an orderly manner (without the need for extreme regimentation). Thus, if you establish a seven-day grid (Table 3.2, page 40), with a time plan schedule from 8:00 A.M. to 10:00 P.M., you can readily see: (1) if you have allotted the needed time to meet all your responsibilities, and (2) how much spare time you have available and where it is in order to meet unforeseen demands and unexpected challenges.

Having formulated your semester's course of study, you should initially fill in the time where you have scheduled lectures, recitations, and laboratory sessions. Next, you should factor into your schedule that one hour of class time on average requires two hours of study time. Thus, a typical 16-hour semester course load requires 32 hours of study time, resulting in a basic total weekly educational time commitment of 48 hours (exclusive of special test study time). Place any other regular commitments into the time grid, such as travel to and from school, attendance at religious services, social obligations, etc. With these items placed in their proper time frame, your actual available free time becomes readily evident and can then be allotted to meet your personal needs.

You should recognize that allocation of study time also needs to be flexible, since: (1) the same course may demand a varying amount of study time at different intervals during the course of a semester, depending on such variables as complexity of topics and frequency of examinations; and (2) different courses vary significantly in their overall study time requirements, depending on their inherent difficulty, quality of the instruction, and ability of the student. With this in mind, you should be prepared to make appropriate adjustments in your initial study time schedule to accommodate changing circumstances. It is obviously also essential that you prioritize your study time so that you place appropriate emphasis not only on time allotment, but also in the sequence in which you study your subjects in the context of their importance and difficulty. Successfully completing the highest priority assignments should be satisfying enough to motivate you to proceed with other, perhaps less appealing, projects. It is vital for your health and the success of your study efforts that you allot adequate time for meals, recreation, relaxation, and sleep.

Failure to provide time for any of these four vital areas can diminish the efficiency of your study efforts. A consistent fulfillment of your study plans will allow you more freedom to enjoy your rest periods without feeling any sense of guilt for having taken time off.

It is also important that you put to good use the time breaks between classes for relaxation, makeup reading, or review of material, prior to a lecture or lab. This will allow you to get the most out of these learning opportunities.

Time-demanding projects, such as term papers or laboratory reports, should be placed into your study time schedule as soon as it is practical. You can then work on them in a timely fashion, rather than hastily completing them in order to meet a competing assignment.

Genuine study involves intense concentration that can usually be done more efficiently in short time intervals. Thus, you should try to utilize study time blocks of 30 to 60 minutes to avoid mental fatigue. Also, try to avoid studying closely related subjects in sequence, so as to minimize the confusion between them.

Another major benefit that comes from having and adhering to a study schedule is that it reduces the possibility of your work piling up. Such a situation can produce stress that may impede your academic progress. It is obvious that studying under pressure is not as effective as studying under favorable conditions.

**Table 3.2**
**TIME PLAN**

|  |  | Monday | Tuesday | Wednesday | Thursday | Friday | Saturday |
|---|---|---|---|---|---|---|---|
| A.M. | 8:00 |  |  |  |  |  |  |
|  | 9:00 |  |  |  |  |  |  |
|  | 10:00 |  |  |  |  |  |  |
|  | 11:00 |  |  |  |  |  |  |
|  | 12:00 |  |  |  |  |  |  |
| P.M. | 1:00 |  |  |  |  |  |  |
|  | 2:00 |  |  |  |  |  |  |
|  | 3:00 |  |  |  |  |  |  |
|  | 4:00 |  |  |  |  |  |  |
|  | 5:00 |  |  |  |  |  |  |
|  | 6:00 |  |  |  |  |  |  |
|  | 7:00 |  |  |  |  |  |  |
|  | 8:00 |  |  |  |  |  |  |
|  | 9:00 |  |  |  |  |  |  |
|  | 10:00 |  |  |  |  |  |  |

With an appropriate study plan—one that has periodically been reviewed and adjusted—potential problems with exams can be avoided. You will find that, under these circumstances, you will not need to cram for tests, but, rather, you will be able to review intensively. Moreover, you will likely retain the basic information longer and be able to build upon it, as you absorb more advanced material.

Mastering the art of time management will surely pay substantial dividends during your professional education and training. It may prove to be one of the keys to your future success. Medical students and residents face the challenge of mastering knowledge and technical skills in order to attain diagnostic and treatment proficiency. To achieve such formidable goals, it is essential that health professionals-in-training maintain good physical and mental health, which is constrained by intense time demands.

It is assumed that since healing practitioners are devoted to improving the lifestyle of their patients, they surely will be alert to their own well-being. Unfortunately, this is frequently not the case. Their concerns focus so intensely on career responsibilities and their daily obligations as to frequently result in neglecting their own health status.

A recent published report claimed that medical students felt an incessant need to study while giving little thought to properly managing their time. To achieve study goals and to compress them into a restricted time frame often leads to formulating strategies that are not beneficial to one's well-being. This may include staying up all night, living on fast food and snacks, getting minimal exercise, and having no social life. To avoid such deleterious practices in the future, mastering the art of time management early on can prove to be a most valuable asset.

## Physical Setting

After establishing an appropriate study schedule, it is essential to secure a suitable and conducive atmosphere, where your study plan can be carried out. The first place to consider is your home or dorm room. This location is a good choice if you are its sole occupant and can enjoy the privacy and solitude that is necessary for successful study. However, the presence of siblings in the home or roommates in the dorm may make this location impractical, unless you can control entry or gain the cooperation of the occupant(s).

## Learning in the Classroom

### Benefiting from Lectures

Lectures provide an excellent way of securing ideas, facts, and viewpoints. To get the most out of lectures, it is important to improve your listening skills. To accomplish this, the following should be taken into consideration:

#### TIP 1    Your lecture seat

Your position in the classroom can influence your level of concentration. If you find your attention wandering, try to move to a place that is preferably near the front and, if possible, near the center. Try to avoid sitting in a crowded area.

#### TIP 2    Preparation

Orient yourself before the lecture as quickly as possible. This may take the form of a brief review of the previous lecture and/or highlights of a reading assignment.

#### TIP 3    Note taking

Take notes with discrimination. You need to use judgment as to the extent of note taking that a course requires. Speaking to students who took the course with the same instructor, and did well, will give you some general guidelines as to the extent of note taking that is desirable.

When presented with new information, fresh ideas, complex or condensed information during the course of a lecture, detailed note taking is mandatory. Similarly, concepts or facts that may be inconsistent with those known or held by you should be recorded because this type of information tends to be easily disregarded or dismissed because of the inherent conflict between what you hear and what you believe to be true.

#### TIP 4    Identifying main ideas

The central themes of a lecture should be determined. Their significance should be enhanced by "fleshing them out" with illustrations, diagrams, or supporting numerical data. Major ideas become genuinely meaningful when one associates some details with them.

#### TIP 5    Accuracy

Lecture notes are a condensation of the teacher's presentation. If you use the note-taking approach, as is commonly done, rather than taping the lecture, an accurate representation of the information is needed. This should be done with the aim of using as condensed a written record as possible, while concentrating on making sure that you secure all of the principles and facts. To achieve this goal, you may find it helpful to develop a personalized shorthand system. This requires consistently using abbreviations and symbols and not being concerned with the presence of incomplete sentence flow.

#### TIP 6    Reworking notes

At the first available opportunity, your rough notes should be rewritten so that their meaning is clear and the notes can be used at a future date for review and to prepare for exams. In rewriting your notes, you should rework them by filling in gaps and adding any relevant details that you recall. The process of reworking your notes can be valuable because it helps you better understand and absorb the material and it enhances your note-taking skills—an essential part of the learning process.

### TIP 7   Rethinking concepts

After the lecture, discuss the principles presented with your classmates to be sure that you understood them properly. Only when your notes are intelligible should you raise any counter-arguments to the issues discussed.

## *Recitation Classes*

Many courses consist of two (or three) lectures per week and one recitation or discussion hour. This arrangement is especially desirable where lecture classes are large and the only opportunity available to discuss the course material is during a recitation hour. The following is suggested in order to get the most from the recitation interval:

### TIP 1   Complete assignments

The need to finish assignments and be prepared is especially important in recitation classes. Being knowledgeable about the issues, both in terms of general principles and specific facts, facilitates participation in recitation classes. Thus, reading the assigned material is essential to feeling comfortable in and getting the most out of these classes.

### TIP 2   Supplemental reading

The lecturer may provide a list of or refer to supplemental reading material. Becoming familiar with at least some of this material can enhance your ability to participate in discussions. Therefore, you should have notes available that contain highlights from any of the supplementary material you have read so that you can use that material appropriately and efficiently. You may wish to bring copies of relevant articles with you to class.

### TIP 3   Prepare questions

During the lecture sessions, especially where large groups are involved, questions may arise that invariably remain unanswered. These should be noted and the list of questions should be brought to the recitation session, where they can be raised as topics for discussion. Getting a clear definition of terms is especially desirable. In addition, you may also wish to identify any discrepancies or apparent contradictions between the lecture and reading material that deserves resolution. Questions that arise in the course of reading should also be noted.

### TIP 4   Clarify lectures

Rewriting your lecture notes may bring to your attention areas where further clarification is desirable. The recitation hour provides an opportunity to eliminate any confusion.

### TIP 5   Test preparation exercise

Listen to the questions being asked and note your answers in order to compare them with those of your instructor. This will provide you with an estimate of your level of knowledge and you can see where there are gaps in your pool of information.

## Writing Term Papers

Term papers are traditional college assignments. In general, they are usually not favored by students because they challenge the individual much more than study assignments. However, the preparation of term papers provides a useful vehicle to learn how to properly and clearly express yourself. This is a vital communication skill that is invaluable in the world you will work in.

Our educational system in large measure is a structured one, requiring that you simply recall information that has been presented. Preparing term papers requires independent thought, since it necessitates your evaluating and synthesizing information from multiple sources. As a result, you can formulate conclusions that you support with facts, thereby reflecting your ability to reason along logical lines.

Writing an attractive and effective term paper requires proper topic selection (assuming you have a choice), ability to obtain appropriate information (research skills), talent at organization, and clearly expressing your thoughts.

Instructors usually provide submission deadlines for the term paper. Once you know the deadline, you should set up a work schedule so that you can meet it. This should consist of the following interim deadlines:

topic selection date

rough draft date

semifinal draft date

final draft date

Obviously, you will need adequate and appropriate spacing between these four stages. By getting right to work, you can proceed in a systematic manner. You will also find yourself under less pressure. Concentrate on the quality of your work rather than only progressing toward its completion. If you delay working on your term paper, you will eventually need a crash program to catch up. This could impair the quality of your end product as well as your other educational obligations, which may then have to be neglected to meet this commitment. The above schedule should allow about one week between each of the drafts so that you can have a fresh look at the material before you move on to the next stage. These time intervals should be included in your overall work schedule.

### Selecting a Topic

Your instructor will usually provide you with general guidelines on dealing with the term paper, including the general topic. The choice of a specific topic may well be left to you. The idea is to find a topic that will be of strong interest. This is especially important because it will serve to motivate you to face up to the challenging task in a forceful and positive manner.

If the instructor does not assign a specific topic nor offer a list of topics from which to choose, your initial approach should be to look at your text and determine relevant issues that fall into the general topic category. The bibliography dealing with the topic may provide some clues that are worth pursuing. Some additional research involving encyclopedias and/or current periodicals may shed light on possible appropriate topics that deserve consideration.

In selecting a topic, it is critical that you avoid choosing one that is too broad and thus cannot be readily covered, or, on the other hand, selecting a topic that is too narrow for you to find adequate source material to meet the needs of the topic. Even after making a topic decision, you need to be prepared to be flexible in determining its ultimate scope. As you proceed with organizing and writing your first draft, you may decide to enlarge or shorten the original desired coverage. Your initial clue as to the possible need to make any adjustment will come from the review of the library index and periodical index, which will provide insight as to the amount of information that is available. You must bear in mind the approximate length of the term paper as prescribed by the course instructor. Excessive length or brevity relative to the guidelines set should be avoided.

Before you invest extensive effort, but after you have formulated your term paper topic, you should check its appropriateness with your instructor. If you have selected more than one topic, present them all to your instructor, but indicate your preference. If you have difficulty choosing a topic, but have ideas that merit further discussion, arrange to do so with your instructor. Your discussions should be prearranged, by appointment, so that you can receive the time and attention you need. Avoid a spur-of-the moment inquiry. Also avoid any arranged meeting that you attend without any ideas to discuss. Offering some ideas of your own will demonstrate that you have given serious consideration to selecting a topic. This may lead to an exchange of ideas with your instructor that can produce possible subjects for further consideration. If you have no ideas to offer, you will convey a negative impression that is obviously not in your best interest.

### Researching a Term Paper

Prepare an outline to serve as an organizational guide. This guide will enhance the presentation of your thoughts in a clear, organized, and concise manner.

There are two types of outlines that are used—topic and sentence outlines. Topic outlines are used in short essays and consist of a few words or phrases that highlight the major topics or subtopics that the essay will cover. Sentence outlines are used in longer writing projects and consist of one-sentence summaries for each of the topics or subtopics. This is used in term papers and will force you to determine exactly what you want to say. Such a sentence outline can serve to help determine the overall validity of the organizational scheme you have formulated for the project.

A suitable starting point for your research is an encyclopedia. Consult both general and specialized types. Try to have the reference librarian help you in your search for source material.

One of the keys to successful research is taking adequate notes. A useful way to do this is to record information on 5 × 7 cards, writing on one side only so that the cards can later be spread out. You should fully identify your reference source for sorting. For books, you should indicate title, author(s), publisher, year of publication, page where information is found, and total number of pages. For articles, you need to identify the name of the periodical, title of article, author(s), volume, issue number, date, and inclusive page numbers.

Material in books that contain important information or tables and/or charts should be photocopied, using the library's (coin operated) copy machine.

In cases where you copy text verbatim, you must use quotation marks, or you should paraphrase the text, using your own words to summarize the author's views. If you do not do this you will be guilty of plagiarism—a serious academic offense.

If your topic involves an issue that has more than one view, seek material that presents the alternative viewpoints, using the various reference sources noted earlier. You may need to broaden your reference heading if you are unable to adequately secure information under the headings you are currently using. If the standard sources are inadequate, you may want to make use of *The New York Times Index* and/or *Readers' Guide to Periodical Literature* (starting with the most recent edition). You probably will need to look through back issues as well as microfilm in your search for source material. You also may have to utilize the resources of other libraries to acquire all of the material you need. These include public, central municipal, and college libraries. Universities frequently have specialized departmental libraries that can prove to be invaluable in your research.

To facilitate your effort, avoid repeating the information you have already recorded. Merely note the additional source for inclusion in your bibliography. Any work done by the instructor should obviously be noted in the body of the text, if appropriate, and certainly in the bibliography. (The reason for this should be obvious.) Avoid working on a project with someone else, even if you have the instructor's approval, because collaboration has inherent difficulties and an especially superior product is usually expected.

When you find that you have obtained the information you seek and sources provide only confirmatory data, you can begin preparing the rough draft of your term paper. Using a computer is strongly recommended.

### The Rough Draft

Before starting your rough draft, review your outline and amend it as necessary. Then arrange your research index cards according to your outline. Number your cards in sequence.

Make a special effort to draft the initial paragraph so that it contains the premise of your paper and so that it comes across in a forceful manner. Next, you should clarify how you intend to achieve the goal of establishing the proposed premise.

Having defined your goals, you can now proceed to outline your research data, using the information from your cards to present your ideas. When presenting an author's ideas or providing support from one of your sources for a statement you are making, note with a superscript the card number containing the reference source. At this writing phase, place your emphasis on quality of the ideas, rather than on the flow of the language. At the next stage you can concentrate on improving the paper by elaborating on the details of your presentation. This rough draft should be clear and concise and should accurately present the information you secured in the course of your research. If it is appropriate to use a chart or table to support your argument, note the place in the text where it belongs.

After presenting the facts and viewpoints based on your research and evaluating them, you need to arrive at a concluding paragraph that can be supported by what you have established.

At the conclusion of this phase of the project, it is essential to pause for several days, so that you will have an opportunity to gain a fresh overview of what you have written in your rough draft. After the appropriate interlude, reread the draft to see if it is properly organized and if there is continuity between the paragraphs. If not, amend it by relocating paragraphs or merely adding appropriate connecting phrases. While making any of these necessary changes, make notes about any other alterations you wish to incorporate in the text and proceed to work on the next stage of the term paper.

### Semifinal Draft

Examine each paragraph carefully to see that the opening sentence serves to introduce the theme of the paragraph. The balance of the paragraph should provide the supporting detail. Evaluate the paragraph for clarity and elaborate where necessary to be sure that you have fully expressed your thoughts. However, try to avoid excessively lengthy paragraphs.

The effort that you put into preparing the semifinal draft will determine how much work will be needed for the final draft. You should use a word processor or computer to prepare your paper. This makes correcting much easier and should obviously facilitate carrying out any alterations due to grammatical errors.

At this point, you should once again set your paper aside for a few days before you tackle the final draft. During this interlude, it would serve you well if you were able to arrange for an outsider to review your draft, especially a person who is qualified to check for spelling, grammar, and punctuation, as well as for clarity and continuity. With potentially useful comments in hand, you are now in a position to review your semifinal draft and get the paper ready for submission.

### Final Draft

Your term paper will need a title page. If a format has not been assigned by the instructor, prepare a title page on your own. It should contain the title of your paper, the course name, number, and section, the name of the instructor, and your own name. The title you select should be informative and attention-grabbing.

Your final draft should incorporate the comments that you feel are appropriate from an outside reader. In rereading it, try to avoid radical alterations that may introduce new difficulties in continuity and exposition. This stage is designed to put the final touches on your paper, rather than make major revisions of it.

The final copy should have a two-inch border along the left margin (for comments) and should be double-spaced (except for lengthy quotations, which can be single-spaced).

All text pages should be numbered, preferably using the format page 1 of 10, page 2 of 10, etc. Place your name at the top of each page to ensure that it will not be lost. If a table of contents is needed, prepare one.

References should be numbered sequentially in Arabic and placed as close to the relevant material as possible. They should be identified, preferably on separate pages at the end of the paper. Your instructor may provide references and a style manual or sheet showing how these should be presented. If none is provided, your librarian can show you a source for this information.

Find a suitable presentation binder for your term paper, one that will make a positive impression without being flashy or costly. Make sure the pages are in the proper order before you insert them in your binder.

# Taking Examinations

An integral part of our educational system is taking examinations. While it is acknowledged that they are imperfect measures of an individual's knowledge or ability, they are an accepted means of determining academic progress and thus help to establish a basis for advancement.

In addition to being a grading tool, exams can have a positive value in that they can encourage or motivate the student to achieve. Doing well on exams can improve one's self-esteem.

Students sometimes tend to fear exams, being concerned that they will not perform well. This can become a self-fulfilling prophecy, because it can lead to anxiety and this, in turn, can interfere with one's performance on the exam. Intense pre-examination anxiety must be avoided (realizing, of course, that some degree of nervousness is reasonable).

Knowing that you have done everything necessary to prepare for an exam should provide you with a sense of self-confidence that is strong enough to achieve a potentially good performance. Relaxing just before an exam is therefore very desirable.

## Reducing Anxiety

A major prerequisite for reducing anxiety is to get a good night's sleep just prior to the exam. This should be obtained, if at all possible, without the use of any sleep-inducing aids so as to avoid any chance of a hangover that could interfere with your performance the next day.

A more active approach that may prove helpful is to employ one of the common tension-reducing methods. A common exercise is to sit down (in a comfortable chair, when possible), close your eyes, and take deep breaths. Hold each breath for about five seconds before exhaling. You should find your tension diminishing as you proceed with counting your breaths (approximately 20). Practicing this exercise will improve the results.

When possible, avoid mingling with other anxious students just prior to the exam, since this can have a negative effect on your state of mind. Waiting just outside the door of the exam room for the instructor to arrive is not recommended, nor is trying to get information from others at the last minute. You should, however, avoid being too far from the exam room at the appointed time, since being there on time is essential to remaining calm. If the exam room was or is one of your classrooms, try to sit in your usual seat, if possible. Remember that once the exam starts, and you focus attention on it, your nervousness should be gone.

## General Exam Advice

Here are some important tips:

### TIP 1    Readiness
Be prepared with several pens, pencils, and erasers; wear a watch, if possible.

### TIP 2    Record data early
If you are afraid you will forget some vital memorized information, put it down in an appropriate place in your exam booklet for possible future reference (if your test proctor permits it).

### TIP 3    Read instructions
Before beginning the exam, read all the instructions carefully. Underline key words (such as compare, differentiate, causes, reasons, etc.) in the instructions. The same advice applies to any essay questions. Note whether you are given a choice of parts of the exam or questions within a part and if there are any extra credit questions.

### TIP 4    Record clues
If, while reading the essay question, highlights of answers come to mind, put them down so they can be referred to at a later time.

### TIP 5    Balance your time
If you know how the exam is weighted pointwise, allot your time in answering the questions in a proportional manner.

# Nature of Exams

Your exam can have three formats: objective, subjective, or a combination of both types of questions. Objective questions appear in the form of true-false, multiple-choice, matching, or completion. Science and mathematics exams are usually presented using an objective format. This is also true in other areas, where a large class size is involved, since it facilitates rapid grading. Objective exams are thought by some to entail less bias. Subjective examinations, on the other hand, consist of essay questions, with reasoning, analysis, and opinion rendering. This is the preferred type for humanities and social science courses. Subjective exams are viewed favorably because they are thought to measure the depth of knowledge and understanding.

# Taking Objective Exams

Objective exams are recognition tests; you should not read into the question any elements that are not self-evident. The most straightforward, rather than obscure, meaning should be considered. Your answer should be based on the lectures and reading assignments for the course.

Questions have equal value, so avoid spending too much time on any one in particular. Answering all the questions that you know at the outset will provide you with time to consider and act on those you do not know. This includes guessing.

Accept questions at face value; do not add, change, or delete words to make the meaning more acceptable to you.

On multiple-choice completion questions, try to answer the question in your own words first, then find the answer that most closely approximates it. This is likely to be the correct one. In alloting time, expect multiple-choice questions to take twice as long per question as true-false questions. Also, when entering answers on an IBM card, one solid black stroke is enough; multiple strokes are superfluous and avoiding them will save some time.

## True-false Questions

1. Beware of mandatory words: "never," "always," "must." They presuppose that, if any exceptions exist, the answer must be false. If guessing an answer to a question that has a mandatory word, then the answer chosen should also be false.

2. Similarly, you have to beware when such mandatory words as "generally," "normally," and "seldom" are used, since they clearly imply exceptions to the question and these would make the statement false. When guessing in this context, it is best to choose true.

## Multiple-choice Questions

If you are uncertain about any of these questions and you have to guess, use the following guidelines:

1. If two answers contain similar sounding words, pick one of these.

2. If two answers are almost identical, choose one of these.

3. If among the choices an answer is unusually short or long, select one of these.

4. Eliminate extreme answers from consideration and choose from among the others.

5. If you are unable to make any choice, select the third answer. It has the highest probability of being correct.

## Taking Subjective Exams

Subjective exams, in addition to recall, require organization and, frequently, conclusions. The following suggestions can prove helpful:

1. Read all the questions carefully and then select the easiest question to answer first.

2. After selecting the question, do not begin writing your response immediately. Rather, organize your answer in a logical order by noting down headings and subheadings, and then proceed.

3. The essay should be structured so that you initially present your position, follow it up with relevant data or arguments, and then draw the appropriate conclusions (offering other options when desirable).

4. Allot an appropriate amount of time for each question. When the time is up, wrap up your conclusions and move on.

5. At the outset, merely identify the question without repeating it. This will save time.

6. Try to have a strong lead sentence in each paragraph, with the following sentences supporting or flowing from this opening one.

7. When possible, use the technical vocabulary of the course.

8. Try to make your sentences short and as uncomplicated as possible. The sentences should not be mere definition statements, but should be supported by facts or arguments when possible. These should, preferably, be arranged in order.

9. If providing a definition, try to give it a broad meaning and use the instructor's wording when possible.

10. If you have answered in what you consider a satisfactory manner, do not seek to "flesh it out" with irrelevant information.

11. If you do not know an answer to an essay question and have left it to the end and still have no recall, write on a closely related issue in the hope that you will get partial credit.

12. Leave some space after each essay question in the case you recall some additional information later and time permits you to come back.

13. Neatness is very desirable; if it is difficult to read your writing, the instructor may be negatively biased. Write your essay in ink to enhance neatness.

14. Write your essay on one side of the page, leaving the other side for use, if necessary, later.

## Upon Exam Completion

When you finish the exam, you will have a natural impulse to want to leave the room. You should make use of any remaining time to review your answers. Answers to objective questions should be altered if you feel that they were misinterpreted or answered wrong. Do not do so merely on impulse.

Review of your answers may also bring to your attention any questions that have inadvertently gone unanswered or may have been answered in the wrong place (a not uncommon situation that can prove disastrous). In a situation where you were forced to guess, rereading a question may bring the correct answer to mind. For essays, rereading can bring to light a point or issue that was overlooked, probably because we think faster than we write. Computations should be rechecked, especially the position of decimal points.

After leaving the classroom, make notes pertaining to the questions asked so that you have an idea of the type of exams the instructor gives, a useful reference for future exam preparation.

# Memorization Techniques

Over the past several decades medical educators have been carefully scrutinizing the curriculum in order to update it and keep it relevant to the demands of a modern medical practice. One of the unstated goals is to reduce the extent of memorization needed and concentrate on the reasoning processes involved in problem solving. While some progress has been made, there is and will always remain a mass of essential information that has to be memorized, in college, medical school, and postgraduate training, in order to successfully complete these programs.

Below are some memorization techniques that may prove beneficial during your education. They can be divided into three categories:

## A. Organize

### TIP 1    Remove distractions
If you are not distracted by some outside elements, such as conversation, radio, or television, you obviously will be able to concentrate more effectively on the task at hand.

### TIP 2    Get a good night's sleep
After a good night's sleep, one is usually mentally more alert in the morning than later in the day. Take advantage of this fact and try to grasp the major concepts early in the day, before you start to memorize the details.

### TIP 3    Relax
When you are relaxed, new data can be absorbed more readily and you will likely retain it with a greater degree of accuracy. Being tense will prove mentally distracting and counterproductive.

### TIP 4    Stand while studying
Some people find it helpful to try memorizing while standing up. You should determine if this works for you.

### TIP 5    Create associations
Store information that you already know in some way that you can recall. When you want to add new data, it is desirable to link the "new" with similar data that you already know.

### TIP 6    Generate images
Draw sketches and/or diagrams and use them to link together facts and illustrate relationships.

### TIP 7    Scan over the material
Before beginning a reading assignment, skim over it in order to recognize the main ideas the writer seeks to convey.

### TIP 8    Recite and repeat
When you recite material out loud, you double the effect by first reading the item and then hearing it, thereby involving two different senses. The effect will be further reinforced by repeating the information.

### TIP 9    Write it
When an important fact comes spontaneously to mind, promptly write it down. Even if you do not refer to it later, the act of recording it will serve to place it in your mind's memory bank.

## B. Think

### TIP 10    Overstudy
Study somewhat more than you feel is necessary to ensure a feeling of self-confidence. This will also reinforce your prior memorization efforts.

**TIP 11   Spread out learning**

Make use of the valuable intervals between required assignments and commit information to memory that you expect to need later.

**TIP 12   Look for connections**

Interesting things are remembered more readily; if you have a subject that is not especially appealing, try to find something that is more interesting to relate it to. By establishing a connection, you will elevate your interest in the subject and be more likely to remember it.

**TIP 13   Be selective**

In committing material to memory, choose what is necessary or essential. Do not fill your mind with trivia or data that does not need to be memorized and can be easily retrieved.

**TIP 14   Combine memory techniques**

To secure maximal effect, memory techniques should be combined, with one technique reinforcing another.

### C. Recall

**TIP 15   Unblocking**

You can possibly unlock your memory by stimulating the recall of related information; therefore, if you cannot recall an answer, try jotting down answers to related questions. This may cause the sought-after answer to come to mind.

**TIP 16   Determine your memory style**

Determine from experience what techniques work best for you. Also, ascertain what memory vehicle leaves the most lasting impression: reading, hearing, or seeing. Try wherever possible to use the one approach that works best for you.

**TIP 17   Use your information**

Repeated use will help you retain data. This is best exemplified by one's recall of telephone, social security, or bank account numbers.

**TIP 18   Be positive**

Develop the conviction that you do not really forget but that you simply misplace information and all you need to do is to find where in your memory file you stored that needed information.

## Living with College Roommates

Quite frequently students relocate in order to attend college and thus find it necessary to dorm. Getting along with one's roommate(s) is an essential part of college life. It can significantly impact one's social as well as educational activities. On occasion, roommates form lifelong friendships. Frequently the friendships generated are very enjoyable although transitory, but on occasion, difficulties arise between roommates that can lead to considerable unpleasantness if not handled appropriately.

In an effort to ensure pleasant dorm life, here is some advice on how to establish a harmonious relationship with one's roommates, in other words, guidance on how to keep the peace when sharing close living quarters with other students. This information may be relevant to you both as a college and medical student and, if unmarried, possibly as a resident.

It should be recognized that rooming together sets up a far different relationship than that generated by residing separately but in close proximity to a good friend. Moreover, roommates in college may come from entirely different backgrounds. In addition, many college students had their own room at home, which provided significantly more freedom and privileges, all of which compounds the problem of living in a dorm. In spite of these challenges, there is evidence that suggests that potential problems can be overcome and students can learn to tolerate and even enjoy the dorm experience. The following guidelines can prove helpful and help make dorm life a success.

### TIP 1    Be forthright

Students enrolling at a college and seeking to use dormitory facilities are sent by their school questionnaires that need to be completed. These may inquire whether the applicant smokes, stays up late at night, and keeps his/her room neat. Providing inaccurate responses to such questions can result in your being placed in a room with someone who is not compatible with you in these or other areas, consequently, a built-in potential for a serious source of friction. Make sure that you are straightforward in answering such questions but also be sure that you answer them yourself and do not pass them on to your parents or others to complete. Through an open approach, your chances of getting more compatible and congenial roommates is increased.

### TIP 2    Be realistic

It should be recognized at the outset that you should not set your goal at having your roommate become your best friend. While it may happen, it may not be so, and having a good roommate should be the reasonable goal to aim for.

It is possible that were one to room with a close friend, the relationship might become impaired. As a result, many colleges discourage students from requesting that their high school friend become their roommate, although they may offer them that option. In addition, getting to know someone new may prove to be a meaningful experience.

### TIP 3    Be communicative

You should recognize that you don't have to like your roommate in order to get along. However, you should be able to communicate effectively with the person in order to express your needs, and your roommate should be able to do the same. By means of an open exchange of views, issues can be resolved before they become problems. This approach allows for compatibility and mutual respect. It may take a special effort to get difficult relationships to work, but it is worth it, both in the short and long run, for in life, one needs to know how to get along with both congenial and difficult people.

### TIP 4    Be open

It is not in anyone's interest to gloss over troublesome issues by being excessively nice. Don't let the issue fester, but approach potential underlying concerns in a courteous, thoughtful manner. Having them lie dormant will not solve problems nor make them disappear. When necessary, discuss troubling issues with a dorm counselor for a more objective perspective.

There is good reason to believe that in retrospect you will look upon your dorm experience as one of the decisive interludes in your life. It can provide an opportunity for relative independent living, meeting new people, and facing some of life's challenges head on. In fact, the experience can help prepare one for the vicissitudes of life that lie ahead for a prospective professional.

## Succeeding as a Premedical Student

In the preceding section detailed advice is outlined on various important aspects affecting your potential success as a college student in general. This section focuses on ways to enhance your career prospects, specifically as a college premedical student.

It is essential that throughout your college career, you evaluate your progress at regular intervals, certainly at the end of each semester. While doing this, it is important that you keep abreast of the admissions criteria and standards at medical schools that traditionally accept students from your school. To secure this information, you may have to tap several sources; tips on potential sources for useful information are outlined below:

### TIP 1    Make connections

Establish early contact with other premed students, especially those on academic levels above you. This may most easily be done at premed club meetings. Discuss with others their plans and application experiences, where appropriate. Remember, however, that such students, while able to relate personal insights, may not have authoritative opinions. If what they say doesn't sound correct, seek clarification from your premed advisor.

### TIP 2 Get information

Seek to obtain additional data (beyond that provided in Table 6.1), regarding current admissions criteria relative to grade point average, science cumulative average, and MCAT scores. This information will allow you to put your own performance in perspective as you progress through college. If such a self-evaluation raises concerns on your part, discuss them with your advisor as early as possible so as to not be negatively impacted psychologically and filled with self-doubt.

### TIP 3 Obtain publications

Determine if your premed society or advisory office has prepared a student handbook or has a file with current admissions information, charts, and tables. This will add to your knowledge base.

### TIP 4 Attend meetings

Many premedical groups organize "career nights," where speakers, frequently alumni, discuss different career options in the health professions. This may be supplemented by field trips that may involve visits to local medical schools. Additional information can be obtained by attending meetings where medical school representatives report on their admissions policies and procedures.

### TIP 5 Seek advice

Arrange to meet with your advisor periodically so that he or she can assess your progress and get to know you. Your meetings can be both formal and informal, as an individual and as part of a group. It is important, especially at a large school, that you lose anonymity and become known to your advisor, who, in due course, will be writing recommendations on your behalf.

Another set of factors associated with your success as a premed student involves academic components (such as GPA and science cum). The following additional tips are relevant to this important area:

### TIP 1 Plan well

Work out for yourself a basic four-year curriculum that fulfills the college's general prerequisites as well as those in your major (and minor) and premed course for graduation requirements. Discuss your plan with students who may have followed a similar program as well as with your advisor, to see if it is realistic.

### TIP 2 Schedule appropriately

Once your overall college program is in place, structure your semesters' schedules so that there is a suitable balance of time blocks allotted to lectures, laboratory sessions, study, and relaxation intervals, as well as extracurricular activities.

### TIP 3 Select carefully

In choosing the course section, bear in mind that more demanding courses such as chemistry or physics might best be taken earlier in the day, when you are more alert and receptive. In addition, ask other students about the different faculty members offering the same course, to determine their teaching characteristics. Are they devoted to educating their students? Do they mark their exams excessively hard? Are their exams aimed at eliciting what you really know? Are they reasonable to deal with? Avoid being influenced by students who may be biased because they feel that they were unfairly treated by a professor, unless there is a consistent pattern to this teacher's actions. In other words, you are seeking to obtain information to ensure that your chances for succeeding in your coursework are good.

**TIP 4  Improve your average**

To meet the credit requirement for graduation, you usually have to take electives. These should be carefully selected in terms of your general interest, rounding out your educational background, how the course fits in your schedule, time demands of the course, and the projected grade for the course. By selecting wisely, you can help boost your grade point average, since the computer does not distinguish between elective and required courses in automatically computing your GPA.

**TIP 5  Elect a summer session**

As the term proceeds you may find your schedule to be too demanding and that it is jeopardizing your overall performance. You should then consider dropping a course to lighten your load, perhaps making up the course during the following summer. Consult an appropriate school advisor before doing so.

# EXTRACURRICULAR AND SUMMER ACTIVITIES

Your nonacademic activities usually will not be decisive elements in your admission to medical school but they can be helpful. You would be well advised to participate in your college premedical society, as well as other organizations that may be related to medicine less directly. Participation in community, political, or sports activities helps in presenting the image of a well-rounded and adjusted individual to admissions officers.

If possible, plan your summer activities so that they can be useful for your career goals. Such activities include hospital work, research, or other activities involving interpersonal contacts. For example, at the end of the freshman year, try to find activities that involve working with people, such as youth camp work or community projects. During the summer following the sophomore year, try to gain some hospital experience. Though summer positions in hospitals are not readily available, try for employment as an orderly, operating or emergency room assistant, or nurse's aide. Also consider a position as a clinical laboratory assistant or a position in a mental hospital or nursing home.

The summer between the junior and senior year could also be spent in hospital work. Students with an interest in research might try obtaining a position at a medical school or in a government laboratory. In addition, a summer spent participating in a research project can provide an understanding of the scientific method in action. It will afford experiences in designing experiments and in collecting and evaluating data.

When working on a summer project, make a definite effort to ensure that your supervisor becomes acquainted with both you and your work. It may prove useful later when you begin securing letters of recommendation to be sent to the medical schools.

As a prospective professional, you should take a job in a hospital, not just to be able to list this activity on your application, but to be able to look at yourself and your reactions to the sick patient, to understand that medical practice is not all heroics and glory, but many hours of hard work. You should try to familiarize yourself with the roles of the various members of the health care team so that you recognize that each has a crucial function in the entire process. In this way you can see if it is the physician's role that is most compatible with your life goals.

Your competitors for a place in a medical school freshman class will present evidence of participation in one or more of three areas: clinical experience, volunteer service, and/or research. Each of these activities will be discussed separately.

## Clinical Experience

The overwhelming majority of applicants seek, to some degree, to demonstrate exposure to clinical aspects of medicine. This may result from professional medical activities (such as being a PA, EMT, nurse, etc.) or from involvement in volunteer work. The nature of your experience and duration are the two important factors relative to this issue. Your contact with physicians, patients, and ancillary staff, and the type of environment you were in can suggest the impact it will have on your thoughts on your career choice and possible future plans.

If a clinical opportunity comes your way, inquire if it offers the possibility of obtaining the experiences you seek, such as working with patients, observing physicians during rounds and at clinical conferences, being exposed to emergency room activities, etc. The latter has the potential of offering invaluable exposure into the world of medicine from a variety of perspectives and, when possible, should be included as part of one's clinical experiences.

It is critical that you convince admissions committees of your solid potential for a medical career. Obtaining clinical exposure to the nature of medical work, its demands, stresses, and emotional rewards can prove to be a meaningful educational experience.

## Volunteer Service

Becoming actively involved in volunteer work in a medical or nonmedical service area at some time in your college career can also help to improve your prospects of gaining admission to medical school. It is vital to your future success and happiness that you convincingly demonstrate to yourself that of all possible professions, medicine is the service-oriented career that appeals to you most. Choosing and finding a suitable volunteer position can prove challenging. Some are available at local hospitals but if you have difficulty securing one, ask your premedical advisor for suggestions based on prior student activities.

To determine what you would prefer to do, most, ask yourself:

1. Based on my interests and talents, what services am I especially suited for?
2. How much real free time do I currently have available on a regular basis?
3. In what kind of professional or social setting would I feel most comfortable?
4. What do I wish to gain out of my volunteer experience that can be of future help?

While you may possibly find an individual physician's practice or group practice in which to secure volunteer experience, most premeds obtain exposure at an institutional setting. These include medical centers, hospitals, hospices, nursing homes, assisted living facilities, community clinics, or with volunteer ambulance services. The preferred site, from among the aforementioned, depends in large measure on your responses to the above-mentioned four considerations.

## Research

Research, whether the laboratory or nonlab type, such as data collection and evaluation, reference library activity, etc., should be focused on (a) broadening your scientific interests, (b) expanding your analytical skills, and (c) developing improved powers of observation and/or analysis. Naturally, premedical students who can clearly visualize a career in academic medicine will find a research stint to be especially advisable. In any case, securing a research position is difficult, given a premeds student's very limited background, but with some effort and luck you may find one, so it is worth pursuing this goal.

## Other Activities

When reviewing your application, admissions people frequently seek to gain an insight into your personality by noting what you do during your free time. They are anxious to see if you have any general activities that you pursue regularly. Such outlets can serve as a means of diminishing stress and providing relaxation. This is critical for those considering entering a profession that, by its very nature, may at times be particularly stressful. Thus, being active in sports, hiking, or bicycle riding, or being an avid reader, is viewed in a positive light.

## Bottom Line

Active participation in extracurricular activities in college is expected, and you need to realize that:

- Opportunities for free time as a premedical student naturally are very limited. Such activities offer a meaningful way of releasing the stress of school demands and the tension from the competitive atmosphere that is generated.

- Summer activities, such as doing research, taking a responsible job, pursuing volunteer hospital work, are viewed by medical school admissions committees in a favorable light.

- The nature of the extracurricular activities you select can serve to enhance your personal growth, demonstrate altruism, and indicate a people-oriented personality.

- The choice of activity, while possibly having a potential positive impact on your admission potential, should also serve to give you personal satisfaction.

- It is preferable to select an activity that can extend over to a relatively longer period, such as working with underprivileged youth, disabled individuals, educationally challenging students, etc., rather than being engaged in many short stints of volunteer work.

- If you need to use your free time to secure needed funds, do not use that fact as an excuse to avoid extracurricular activities. Rather, focus any available time you may have on more limited activities, such as a charitable fund-raising campaign, organizing campus society programs, etc.

## Summer Enrichment Programs

The importance of spending time in a medical environment has already been emphasized. This can help you to more firmly determine the extent of your interest in medicine. It can also enhance the extracurricular activities segment of your resume, thereby furthering your chances for admission to medical school.

The section below consists of two parts, medical and nonmedical school-sponsored programs.

### Medical School-sponsored Programs

A list of medical schools that have been offering summer enrichment programs is presented below. These offerings vary from year to year and may be sponsored by different departments within an institution, moreover, openings frequently are restricted to underrepresented students. To follow up and determine if opportunities are available, contact the Dean of Students at the school, using information provided for each school in Chapter 8 (allopathic medical schools) and Chapter 16 (osteopathic medical schools). Checking Web sites may also prove useful.

**Alabama**
University of Alabama
University of South Alabama

**Arizona**
University of Arizona

**California**
Loyola University
Stanford University
University of California—Davis
University of California—Irvine

University of California—Los Angeles
University of California—San Diego
University of California—San Francisco
University of Southern California

**Colorado**
University of Colorado

**Connecticut**
University of Connecticut
Yale University

**District of Columbia**
Georgetown University

**Florida**
Florida State University
University of Florida
University of Miami
University of South Florida

**Georgia**
Emory University
Medical College of Georgia

**Hawaii**
University of Hawaii at Manoa

**Illinois**
Finch/Chicago University
Loyola University of Chicago
Northwestern University
Rush University
Southeastern Illinois University
University of Chicago, Pritzker

**Indiana**
Indiana University

**Iowa**
University of Iowa

**Kansas**
University of Kansas

**Kentucky**
University of Louisville

**Louisiana**
Louisiana State University—Shreveport

**Maryland**
Johns Hopkins University
University of Maryland

**Massachusetts**
Boston University
Harvard University
University of Massachusetts

**Michigan**
University of Michigan

**Minnesota**
University of Minnesota—Duluth
University of Minnesota

**Mississippi**
University of Mississippi

**Missouri**
St. Louis University
University of Missouri—Columbia
University of Missouri—Kansas City
Washington University

**Nebraska**
Creighton University
University of Nebraska

**Nevada**
University of Nevada

**New Hampshire**
Dartmouth University

**New Jersey**
UMDNJ—New Jersey
UMDNJ—Robert Wood Johnson
UMDNJ—School of Osteopathic Medical School

**New Mexico**
University of New Mexico

**New York**
Albany Medical College
Albert Einstein
Columbia University
Cornell
Mt. Sinai
New York College of Osteopathic Medicine
SUNY—Buffalo
SUNY—Downstate
University of Rochester

**North Carolina**
Duke University
East Carolina University
University of North Carolina
Wake Forest University

**Ohio**
Case Western University
Medical College of Ohio
Ohio State University
University of Cincinnati
Wright State University

**Oregon**
Oregon Health Science Center

**Pennsylvania**
University of Pittsburgh
Lake Erie College (osteopathy)
Temple University

**Rhode Island**
Brown University

**South Carolina**
Medical University of South Carolina

**Tennessee**
East Tennessee State University
University of Tennessee
Vanderbilt University

**Texas**
Baylor College
University of Texas-Houston
Texas A&M University
Texas Tech University
University of North Texas (osteopathy)
University of Texas—Galveston
University of Texas—Health Science Center at San Antonio
University of Texas—Southwestern

**Utah**
University of Utah

**Vermont**
University of Vermont

**Virginia**
Eastern Virginia University
Medical College of Virginia
University of Virginia

**Washington**
University of Washington

**West Virginia**
West Virginia

**Wisconsin**
Medical School of Wisconsin

Your inquiry should be addressed to the Dean of Students.

### *Nonmedical School-sponsored Programs*
The following is a list of nonmedical school institutions that at various times have offered summer enrichment programs. If you are interested in securing an appointment, use the list below to obtain information.

**California**
American Heart Association
Research Department
1710 Gilbreth Road
Burlingame, CA 94010

San Diego State University
Collegiate Union for Health-Related Education (CUHRE)
Aztec Center
San Diego, CA 92182

San Jose State University
HCOP Summer Enrichment Program
1 Washington Square
San Jose, CA 95192

University of California
Personnel Department
Lawrence Livermore Laboratory
P O Box 808-N
Livermore, CA 94550

**Illinois**
Michael Reese Medical Center
Summer Student Research Fellowship Program
Office of Research Administration
29th Street and Ellis Avenue
Chicago, IL 60616

**Maine**
The Jackson Laboratory
Research Training Office
Bar Harbor, ME 04609

**Massachusetts**
Tufts University
Biomedical Sciences Summer Enrichment Program for Sackler School of Graduate
    and Undergraduate Minority Students
136 Harrison Avenue
Boston, MA 02111

University of Massachusetts Medical Center
Summer Enrichment Program
Office of Outreach Programs
55 Lake Avenue North
Worcester, MA 01655

**Michigan**
University of Michigan
School of Public Health
Summer Enrichment Program in Health Administration
Ann Arbor, MI 48109

**Minnesota**
University of Minnesota
Summer Biology Program
515 Delaware Street, SE
1-125 Moos Tower
Minneapolis, MN 55455

**New York**
Brookhaven National Laboratory
Science Education Center
Building 438, P O Box 5000
Upton, NY 11973

Roswell Park Cancer Institute
Research Participation Program in Molecular Biology
Elm and Carlton Streets
Buffalo, NY 14263

**Oklahoma**
University of Oklahoma Health Sciences Center
Headlands Indian Health Careers
Summer Programs
BSEB, Room 200, P O Box 26901
Oklahoma City, OK 73126

**Pennsylvania**
Western Psychiatric Institute and Clinic
Mellon Research Summer Program in Psychiatry for Undergraduates
3811 O'Hara Street
Pittsburgh, PA 15213

**Tennessee**
Fisk University
Premedical Summer Institute
1000 17th Avenue North
Nashville, TN 37208

**Wisconsin**
Marquette University
School of Dentistry/Physical Therapy
Summer Science Enrichment Program
P O Box 1881
Milwaukee, WI 53201

# THE PREMEDICAL ADVISOR AND/OR COMMITTEE

The premedical advisor can help you in planning the sequence of courses needed to meet the requirements at most medical schools. He or she will also offer suggestions as to which schools to apply to, when to take the MCAT, and how to interpret the scores. The advisor is usually assisted by a committee of faculty members who evaluate your academic performance and potential as well as your overall fitness to study medicine. The premedical committee maintains a file of your records and evaluations by individual members.

Most schools reognize their obligation to appoint an individual who will serve as a preprofessional health sciences advisor. The administration may select someone who is a faculty member, usually from one of the sciences, a person from the school's career guidance center, or an individual from a dean's office who is actively involved with student advising.

The advisor will generally have set office hours and require that appointments be made in advance so as to ensure that adequate time will be allotted to meet the students' needs.

Students at any class level—and even graduates—should feel free to seek guidance from their school's premedical advisor. Naturally, the nature of the advice may vary depending on the stage of the student's career and a variety of other factors. The possible issues at different stages are reflected in Appendix G, Table 1. The general responsibilities that advisors may assume in part or entirely, depending on the school, can be grouped into five categories.

1. *Academic advising.* This may involve guiding individuals in selecting a major, or, if necessary, changing it, helping to select and schedule courses, and ensuring proper sequencing of courses.

2. *Support services.* This may cover a broad spectrum of activities—being merely a good listener or sounding board for troubled or overworked students. Advisors may also help students who are caught in some bureaucratic maze with the administration, or assist those who are finding the premed curriculum too challenging and therefore desperately need guidance. A sympathetic and knowledgeable advisor can be an invaluable asset in all such cases.

3. *Resource center.* Many questions may arise that require checking, such as specific school requirements, deadlines, and so on. These may require access to reference sources or specific medical school catalogs, both of which may be part of the advisor's library. In addition, advisors may have information files dealing with preparing for the MCAT, medical school interviews, sample essays, and a list of summer job opportunities, all of which are useful for prospective applicants. Some schools that have Web sites will provide space for their premedical advisor to post information that may be tapped into by high school students and can serve as a useful recruitment device.

4. *Extracurricular programming.* The advisor can enhance the quality of the school's overall premedical program by facilitating the group activities of prehealth students. Advisors are in a position to help with planning extracurricular activities by helping secure appropriate speakers to discuss topics of relevance to prehealth students. Speakers may include representatives from medical schools and other schools that train health professionals, and alumni who can share their professional experiences and/or discuss their work. Frequently, the advisors may ask seniors to relate their interview experiences. In this case, a mock interview session may be conducted and the advisor can then voice some constructive criticism.

5. *Facilitating admission.* An important function of premedical advisors is to actively assist in the admissions process, which goes beyond providing the documentary information sought by the medical schools. The extent of their individualized help will vary. Clearly they should be able to assess your chances for success, help determine how many and which schools you should apply to, and answer any specific questions. They may offer to read and/or even edit your application essay and give you personalized advice about how to improve your interview performance. The advisor may also serve as a useful source of support during this stressful time, while you are awaiting responses from the schools to which you applied.

Finally, it should be noted that prehealth advisors have a national organization, the National Association of Advisors for the Health Professions, P.O. Box 1518, Champaign, Illinois 61824. The organization issues a variety of publications and has a current list of advisors. Its Web site is *www.naahp.org*.

It is the obligation of the advisor or committee to provide the medical schools with supporting information in your behalf (see pages 71 and 72). Some medical schools will utilize their own recommendation forms that they send out to be completed. Most rely on the college's forms and even accept them in lieu of their own. Undergraduate schools vary in the format they use to provide their evaluation. Many use a letter of recommendation drafted by the advisor or a member of the committee who knows the student. It may include written comments about the applicant submitted by faculty members, and it will reveal the committee's consensus of the student's abilities and potential and may rate the applicant in comparison to others applying during the year from the same school. Some schools provide a letter of recommendation and a separate sheet of faculty comments. Others may provide a letter and a quantitative rating sheet (see page 73) and possibly also a comment sheet.

Attributes listed on rating sheets, and the ratings used, vary from school to school. However, in general they refer to the applicant's personal as well as academic attributes and attempt to portray them in a quantitative and objective manner.

In view of the generally high caliber of applicants to medical school, recommendations (and interviews) have assumed major importance in the application process. Thus, students should make themselves and their abilities well known to faculty members. Their knowledge of you should be as thorough as possible so that they can rate you not only quantitatively but also qualitatively. Recommendations by science professors, whether they know you from coursework or as an individual, are of special value. Of particular usefulness are evaluations from honors work or independent study supervisors who can comment on such qualities as initiative, determination, and reliability.

To facilitate preparation of letters of recommendation in your behalf, some college premedical committees require that prospective applicants complete a standard form that may be several pages long (see pages 67 to 70). This mechanism provides the committee with data relative to your personal life, family background, outside jobs, extracurricular activities (both school or non-school related), and special interests. They may also request that you submit a tentative list of the schools you wish to apply to as well as an essay relevant to your application to medical school. By this means, not only is a database available to the committee to formulate your letter of recommendation, but you will also be able to secure advice on where to apply and how many schools to apply to (see also pages 117–119). In addition, your premedical committee essay can serve as a prototype for your AMCAS essay. If your school does not use such a form, you may, nevertheless, wish to use the sample format shown to provide information to your premedical advisor and/or committee. In addition, you may wish to solicit your advisor's (or an English composition instructor's) reaction to your essay as to content, style, and effectiveness in "marketing" your candidacy for admission.

Finally, a word of caution about advisors. It is essential that you are courteous and respectful at all times in your dealings with members of your college faculty and especially with your preprofessional advisor. Your advisor will be responsible for transmitting the qualitative impression of the faculty to the medical schools. Thus, your advisor's good will is most desirable and can be developed, not by ingratiating yourself, but by establishing a genuine relationship.

On the other hand, it is not necessary to accept your advisor's recommendations as the only truth if you have valid reasons to question it. As with physicians, there are both good and mediocre advisors. Moreover, there are no licensing or certification processes for accrediting advisors as there are for MDs or DDSs. The institution usually selects a member of its science faculty who may be interested in doing advisory work and assigns the responsibility to this individual, in turn relieving that person of some teaching responsibilities. The quality of the advice you will receive will depend upon the advisor's innate ability, experience, conscientiousness, other academic responsibilities, and number of other advisees. Thus, the extent of personal attention students receive varies greatly. All too frequently, student counseling is provided on a "clinic"-type basis. Students frequently turn to upperclass-level premeds (especially seniors) for advice; their advice can be misleading since their experience is limited, even if they have been successful in getting into medical school. In the event that you have reservations about some important issue, you can seek to validate your advisor's recommendations by discreetly discussing them with another faculty member on a confidential basis, by asking a friend at another school to pose the same question or problem there, or by contacting a medical school admission office or a private counseling service.

Some undergraduate schools, especially those with large premedical populations, may utilize the services of peer advisors and/or mentors.

*Peer advisors.* Where such a program exists, premedical advisors select high-performing upperclass students to serve in such a capacity. They may be qualified to respond to many common questions based on their own recent experience. You should not, however, use them as a replacement for your premedical advisor. It is especially important to consult with your advisor relative to the selection of prospective medical schools, essay and interview preparation, and other key elements in the premedical experience.

*Mentors.* Many schools appoint official student mentors. Should you decide to make use of a mentor, you need to select one with care, in order to obtain the most benefit from him or her. In making your choice, ask successful upperclass students for their recommendations in terms of the mentor's availability, knowledge, judgment, and compatibility.

## Bottom Line

Where a premedical advisor is conscientious, he or she can be of help to the student body in a wide variety of ways, such as:

- offering incoming freshmen with health science career interests an in-depth orientation to the school's advisory and guidance programs. They have multiple functions.

- providing information as to course and other requirements for admission to U.S. medical schools.

- counsel students on a one-on-one basis about the advisability of pursuing a medical career as well as an appropriate major (and minor), and the appropriate program of courses and best sequence for taking them.

- assisting students having academic difficulties with advice and information as to the best services for help.

- conducting group seminars on appropriate preparation for the MCAT examination, the AMCAS application, and medical school interviews.

- counseling students individually as to which schools to apply to, what choice to make if they receive multiple acceptances, or the best option if, unfortunately, they fail to get into a medical school.

- helping organize a premedical club or honor society (such as Alpha Epsilon Delta) to provide student-directed programs during the academic year, featuring both appropriate speakers and relevant events.

- providing information on summer and year-long volunteer and research opportunities.

- distributing AMCAS medical school applications and other materials as well as maintaining a library of reference sources including current relevant AAMC literature, medical school catalogs, and listings of important Web sites.

- meeting with the premedical committee to facilitate preparation of letters of recommendation and also arrange that they be sent out in a timely fashion.

- providing students with moral and psychological support during the stressful application time until all responses from medical school are in.

# HUMANISTIC ASPECTS OF PREMEDICAL EDUCATION

Aside from the intellectual and technical challenges that medical education presents, there are a variety of other considerations that must be faced by professional school students. Among these are the realizations that:

1. There is a great diversity in the patients that one sees. One is not surrounded by a homogeneous population, but by all types of people—rich and poor, young and old, educated and illiterate.

2. There are emotional as well as physical factors to be dealt with in patient care, including crises in the lives of patients.

3. The issues of pain and suffering, of dying and death are aspects of life that are distant from the young, healthy student who must learn to cope with them in a sympathetic, although somewhat detached, manner.

4. There are ethical issues to consider that cannot be defined scientifically, such as who shall be born, who shall live, who shall die.

Medical school does not adequately prepare one for the aforementioned problems and thus it is the premedical experiences and training that tend to mold one's values on these subjective issues. Only by an in-depth exposure to the human condition through literature, religion, and philosophy can the student develop the capacity to face the nonacademic aspects of the medical professions.

The inexperienced medical student is usually unable to assess the issues that defy scientific definition—the issues of human diversity, suffering, life and death. These questions are peripheral to mastering the mass of scientific information and technical skills during the preclinical years. It is during the premedical years that the opportunity exists to acquire the exposure that molds values relative to nonquantifiable moral issues. If these ethical guidelines can be acquired by formal and/or informal education in the course of one's college years as a premedical student, then a solid foundation will have been laid for the medical training that will follow, and ultimately a well-rounded physician will emerge to practice in the twenty-first century.

# CHECKLIST OF COLLEGE ACTIVITIES

Indicate with a check or x when the task is completed.

### First Year

\_\_\_\_\_ Become acquainted with your school's general course requirements for graduation.

\_\_\_\_\_ Familiarize yourself with the basic course requirements for admission to medical school.

\_\_\_\_\_ Determine if there are any specific school premedical requirements for graduation.

\_\_\_\_\_ Learn about your school's program of extracurricular activities and career guidance department services.

\_\_\_\_\_ Work out a program outline for meeting the general and specific premedical course requirements over the balance of your college career.

\_\_\_\_\_ Consider what major challenges you anticipate facing in the year ahead and how best to deal with them.

\_\_\_\_\_ Evaluate your study and test-taking skills and make improvements where necessary.

\_\_\_\_\_ Become personally acquainted with your premedical advisor and discuss possible majors and any other concerns you may have.

\_\_\_\_\_ Try to meet upper-level premedical students who can discuss with you what "pitfalls" to avoid in various aspects of your education.

\_\_\_\_\_ Set your sights on and make a concerted effort to become a high academic achiever (B+ or better).

\_\_\_\_\_ Initiate participation in extracurricular activities of interest and value to a premed student.

_____ Join the school's premed society and seek to be an active participant in its activities.

_____ Establish and maintain a healthy lifestyle to protect your physical and mental health.

_____ Use any free time available for accreditation as well as volunteer activities in a relevant area of interest.

_____ Formulate summer plans that may include hospital work, social service work, or possibly participating in a research program.

_____ Seek to secure exposure to medical school and residency activities by, if possible, linking up for a short time with an upper-class medical student or resident.

_____ Toward the end of the academic year, review your performance and draft a tentative program of studies for the balance of your college stay and evaluate it with your premedical advisor.

_____ Evaluate your year's performance and determine if and where improvements can be made.

## Second Year

_____ Initiate your studies in your selected major as part of your program of studies.

_____ Continue your academic efforts to achieve an impressive GPA (B+ or better).

_____ Thus far, explore, through general medical reading, a variety of areas of medicine.

_____ Continue volunteer work relevant to medicine in an area of interest.

_____ Become familiar with the basic organization and contents of the MCAT examination.

_____ Evaluate your performance at the end of the year and then make a reality check about your prospects for gaining admission to a medical school.

_____ Determine your future educational and career plans in light of your achievements of medicine.

_____ Establish your junior and senior year programs in consultation with your premedical advisor.

## Third Year

_____ Establish a feasible systematic program of studies for the MCAT and apply to take it in April (or August, if necessary). Incorporate your preparation into your schedule of summer activities.

_____ Continue your efforts to attain an attractive GPA and science course average.

_____ Get a good night's sleep before the scheduled day to take the MCAT so as to perform optimally.

_____ Get information about medical schools of special interest to you from their catalog and/or Web site.

_____ Meet with your premedical advisor and discuss your application strategy and review and basically finalize your list of prospective medical schools to apply to.

_____ Get a copy of the AMCAS or AACOMAS application (around March) and review it carefully before completing it.

_____ Continue medical reading to become familiar with the general current information.

_____ Make an outline of the structure of your personal statement (essay) and then prepare a preliminary draft.

_____ Review your overall three-year performance and, if necessary, adjust the number and list of schools you will be applying to in light of your admission potential.

_____ Arrange for faculty letters of recommendation to be submitted on your behalf to your Premedical Office.

_____ Prepare for an interview by your school's Premedical Committee, if called for. This is aimed at facilitating preparation of a composite recommendation to go with your application to medical school.

_____ Formulate plans to obtain research or volunteer work in medically related activities during the summer.

_____ If necessary, study for the August MCAT during the summer intersession.

_____ Finalize your personal statement or (essay) early in the summer in consultation with your advisor and a person who writes well.

_____ Complete your AMCAS/AACOMAS application and send it off in a timely fashion (June–July).

_____ Review a student copy of your college transcript for accuracy before arranging for it to be sent out.

_____ Make preliminary preparations for medical school interviews that you will face.

**Fourth Year**

_____ Check to confirm that your AMCAS/AACOMAS application has been received.

_____ Carefully and thoroughly complete and promptly return all your secondary applications.

_____ When invited, schedule interviews on a convenient date.

_____ Prepare intensively for each of your medical school interviews and try to benefit from each.

_____ Following each interview, evaluate both your performance and the suitability of the school for possible enrollment.

_____ In consultation with your advisor, make a definitive medical school selection in the event you receive multiple acceptances.

_____ Advise your chosen school of your acceptance promptly and withdraw from all others (so that places can be filled by other applicants).

_____ Consider how best to respond, in the event an acceptance is not received.

_____ Discuss your options and formulate an action plan in consultation with your advisor.

_____ Appropriately acknowledge the assistance of your premedical advisor and faculty members who supported your application.

_____ Make plans to spend the summer profitably depending on the outcome of your application process. In any case, plan how best to prepare for your postgraduate activities.

### *Request Form for a Letter of Recommendation*

_____ UNIVERSITY

Prehealth Professions Committee

Re:  Request for Preparation of a Letter of Recommendation

Please prepare supporting material on the applicant's behalf for (check one or more):

medical _____, dental _____, osteopathy _____, podiatry _____,

optometry _____, other (specify) _____

Application for class entering: _____  Today's date _____

Name:_____  Date of birth: ____/____/____
    (last)         (first)        (middle)

Local address: _____
         (number and street)        (city)     (state)    (zip)

Permanent address: _____
         (number and street)        (city)     (state)    (zip)

Telephone number: _____
        (area code)      (number)

Citizenship: U.S. _____  Other: (specify) _____

Father's occupation: _____  Mother's occupation: _____

Credits transferred (if any): _____, Completed: _____, In progress: _____

The data below should refer only to the applicant's performance at _____ University.

Current Grade Point Average: _____  Science cum (including math): _____

Major: _____  Major average: _____  Minor: _____  Minor average: _____

Has the applicant's education to date been continuous other than for vacations?

Yes: _____  No: _____

If the answer to the previous question is in the negative, indicate what the applicant has done while out of attendance or since graduation.

_____

_____

_____

Has the applicant ever been placed on probation (academic or disciplinary)?

Yes: _____  No: _____

If the answer to the previous question is yes, clarify the circumstances involved.

_____

_____

_____

Employment history: Complete as fully as possible.

| | Position | Place of employment | Dates of employment | Hours worked/week |
|---|---|---|---|---|
| Summer prior to beginning college | | | | |
| Freshman year | | | | |
| Summer between freshman and sophomore years | | | | |
| Sophomore year | | | | |
| Summer between sophomore and junior years | | | | |
| Junior year | | | | |
| Summer between junior and senior years | | | | |
| Senior year | | | | |

Furnish, in detail, the following information:

Extracurricular (school-related) activities (clubs, projects, positions in student government, student organizations, college or university committees, etc.)

_____

_____

_____

_____

Non-school-related activities (social, fraternal, religious, community, political, etc.)

_____

_____

_____

Hobbies: _____
_____
_____

Special interests (not previously covered):_____
_____
_____

Provide a TENTATIVE list of those schools to which the applicant plans to apply:

| | | |
|---|---|---|
| _____ | _____ | _____ |
| _____ | _____ | _____ |
| _____ | _____ | _____ |
| _____ | _____ | _____ |
| _____ | _____ | _____ |
| _____ | _____ | _____ |

Is the applicant interested in a professional degree (DDS, MD, OD, DO, DPM, DVM) only? (Check one.) Yes: _____ No: _____

Is the applicant interested in a combined MD/PhD degree? Yes: _____ No: _____

TYPE an essay (limited to two pages), in which the applicant considers the following topics, as they personally relate:

1. How did your interest in the sciences begin and how did it develop?

2. What circumstances and considerations have motivated you to consider undertaking a career in the health sciences?

3. From where does your knowledge of the health sciences and of health care delivery stem (is it based on family exposure, work, reading, talking with practitioners, volunteer work, etc.)?

4. Why do you seek to enter the health professions? What do you hope to contribute? What do you feel you have to offer? What do you hope to derive from working in this area?

5. What are your plans in the event that you are not accepted (aside from reapplication)?

**Type the essay, double-spaced, on this page.** If you need more space, you may use additional pages.

AMCAS or AADSAS applications should be single-spaced. The suggestion for double spacing here is to permit emendation by your advisor.

*Letter of Recommendation in Support of a Superior Candidate*

_____ University
Premedical Advisory Committee

August 15, 2005

Chairperson
Admissions Committee

Re: Steven B. _____

Dear Doctor:

In the course of several extended interviews with Steven B. _____, I have gotten to know him academically and personally. I found that he is an attractive individual from both perspectives and therefore I am writing this recommendation.

Steve has been a solid achiever his entire life. After a superior (94) performance at Stuyvesant High School, one of New York City's top three, he enrolled at _____ College. He selected this school because of its modest size and the quality liberal arts education it offers. After adjusting to college life during his first semester, his record over the past three years has gone from about B+ to above A−. His science performance has been consistently superior in both the required premedical courses and in all his electives. He has a special aptitude for mathematics and has even tutored in this area.

What I found especially interesting in Steven's background is that he is one of the rare breed of premeds who is a genuine liberal arts student, having majored in East Asian studies. One of his professors cultivated his interest in this area, which blends well with his innate interest in people. This quality is also reflected by his involvement in a hospice program, which prospective medical students rarely get exposed to. Steve's perspective of medicine is well rounded, from having become an EMT, and also because he worked in the emergency and operating rooms at several local hospitals.

Steve is very affable, outgoing, open, and has a ready sense of humor. It is easy to establish a good rapport with him, which his future patients will surely come to appreciate. He has impressed me with his perceptive analysis of people and tolerant attitude toward them. Steve is a hard worker whose unusual physical strength permits him to be employed in his free time for very extended periods (a quality that should serve him well during his residency). He is also self-disciplined, having to resist a predisposition to becoming overweight. Being on the rugby team at _____, and now its captain, has been an asset in this regard. Steven is a young man of high integrity, with a genuine service orientation and a keen sense of observation.

In summary, Steven B. _____ stands out not merely on a quantitative paper profile, but rather as a total person. His warm personality, open-mindedness, and motivation make him attractive even among a large pool of qualified applicants.

Sincerely,


Chief Premedical Advisor

### Letter of Recommendation to Enhance a Candidate's Status

_____ University

July 31, 2009
Chairperson
Admissions Committee                                    Re: Daniel H. _____

Dear Doctor:

I am writing on behalf of Daniel H. _____, whom I have gotten to know very well during the course of his extended visits to my office.

I am especially stimulated to write on behalf of Daniel in the light of what I foresee as the special qualities that I think physicians planning to practice in the next decade should have. It is my feeling that there is a need for prospective physicians to feel that their sense of satisfaction will be the major fulfillment factor in their future medical practice. Daniel _____, to my mind, is an individual with such an outlook.

Daniel was born and raised on Long Island, where he attended private elementary and high schools. His parents both have a higher education. He enrolled at _____ University for his undergraduate studies because he desired the advantages that a smaller institution affords. _____ University premedical curriculum is rather unusual in that organic chemistry precedes inorganic chemistry. Daniel was academically unprepared for this regimen; nevertheless, by intensively applying himself he received a satisfactory grade in this course. This situation, however, impacted negatively on his freshman GPA (approximately 3.0). Subsequently, his performance steadily improved to the point where his GPA for junior year was 3.85. Clearly, his ability to face up to challenges and his determination to achieve his goal are most evident from his overall performance during the past three years. His science GPA (excluding freshman year) is superior and is reflected and confirmed in his strong showing on both of the science subtests of the spring, 2008 MCAT. His low quantitative score is probably an aberration. I believe it is to be of no significance in terms of a reflection on his ability. Nevertheless, he is retaking the exam because of his determination to rectify this situation.

What is especially striking about Daniel is that he comes from a family that has passed on a very successful business (wholesale fruit and vegetables) through several generations. His father, not surprisingly, would be quite amenable to his becoming active in the business upon graduating college and eventually attaining financial success. However, Daniel is seeking a service-oriented career.

Daniel has impressed me with the genuineness of his motivation and the sincerity of his conviction. He clearly realizes that the component of personal satisfaction is one of the most important aspects of a career in medicine. His considerable exposure to medicine has not only reinforced his interest in this field, but has provided him with evidence that such service can provide a unique means of personal gratification.

In summary, Daniel possesses solid academic and personal credentials and, in my mind, has the innate attributes that a prospective physician should possess. I strongly recommend him to your next freshman class.

Sincerely,


Chair, Premedical Advisory Committee

_____UNIVERSITY
_____
_____

**CONFIDENTIAL REPORT ON CANDIDATE FOR ADMISSION TO PROFESSIONAL SCHOOL**

Date _____

The following evaluation is submitted for your guidance by the Health Sciences Advisory Office of _____ (the college of arts and sciences for men of _____ University). This evaluation is based on a careful study of written evaluations by, and consultation with, those members of the faculty who have had personal knowledge of the candidate and his work in both lecture and laboratory courses.

NAME OF CANDIDATE _____ I.D. No._____
This student has completed _____ years of college. His cumulative average to date is _____ (A = 4).
Candidate for School of ( ) Medicine     ( ) Dentistry     ( ) Podiatry     ( ) Optometry     ( ) Other _____

| | OUTSTANDING | VERY GOOD | GOOD | AVERAGE | POOR |
|---|---|---|---|---|---|
| **PERSONAL ATTRIBUTES** | | | | | |
| 1. Appearance and Social Manner | | | | | |
| 2. Maturity and Emotional Stability | | | | | |
| 3. Communication Skills | | | | | |
| 4. Interpersonal Relations | | | | | |
| 5. Cooperation and Reliability | | | | | |
| 6. Self-Confidence | | | | | |

| | OUTSTANDING | VERY GOOD | GOOD | AVERAGE | POOR |
|---|---|---|---|---|---|
| **ACADEMIC ATTRIBUTES** | | | | | |
| 7. Industry and Perseverance | | | | | |
| 8. Originality and Resourcefulness | | | | | |
| 9. Laboratory Skills | | | | | |
| 10. Native Intelligence and Judgment | | | | | |
| 11. Scientific Aptitude | | | | | |

Summary evaluation of the applicant's
fitness for professional study and practice.*

*Determined by averaging the student's ratings of items 7 through 11 together with his cumulative academic average, according to a mathematical formula under which 4.0 is the highest possible rating. Students whose combined index falls between:

   3.7 and 4.0 are rated "outstanding"
   3.4 and 3.6 are rated "very good"
   2.9 and 3.3 are rated "good"
   2.3 and 2.8 are rated "average"
   2.0 and 2.2 are rated "poor"

_____
_Health Sciences Advisor_

REMARKS_____
_____

NOTE: The above student has waived his right to inspect and review this recommendation under the Family Education Rights and Privacy Act of 1974. Therefore please keep this document confidential.

# The Postbaccalaureate Premedical Student

**Introduction**
**Action plan**
**Preparing for the challenge**
**Postbaccalaureate programs**

## INTRODUCTION

While the vast majority of medical school applicants are college seniors, a small, yet increasingly significant, number consists of those with a postbaccalaureate premedical education. This group is made up of individuals who: (1) seek to change their present career, (2) have been uncommitted as to a career choice and now have decided on medicine as a profession, or (3) sought but failed to secure admission to medical school and are now trying to improve their chances upon reapplying.

A prerequisite for applying to all medical schools is to satisfactorily complete the required premedical courses, namely two years of chemistry and one year each of biology and of physics. Schools may have additional course requirements such as English, mathematics, or biochemistry. Even in the case of the few schools that do not formally require the basic sciences, these courses are needed in order for the student to do well on the MCAT. Students can elect to meet the requirements by enrolling in a structured postbaccalaureate program (see page 76), which usually requires a significant time commitment. On the other hand, for those with time constraints, a less structured approach is advisable. Before enrolling in a postbaccalaureate program, which is usually costly, it is important to determine its educational quality and the school's placement record. Premedical advisors at your local college may be able to provide guidance on this subject, or you can check with a medical school admissions office.

## ACTION PLAN

As an older, nontraditional premed, it is absolutely essential to have a well-thought-out action plan in place prior to the time you initiate your journey toward admission into medical school. This action plan should focus on the following six components:

1. Evaluate as objectively as possible your motivation for applying to determine if it is genuine and consider your intellectual abilities; are they adequate for the many difficult challenges ahead?

2. Determine the time frame that establishes the feasibility of your making it through medical school and completing clinical training at a reasonable stage in your life.

3. Begin to establish the essential groundwork that will provide you with the required premed academics and clinical awareness about the field of medicine.

4. Formulate a strategy for adequately preparing for the MCAT exam.

5. Set your sights on attaining the highest possible grade and test scores to enhance your chances to be admitted to medical school.

6. Formulate a fall-back position to possible options, in the event you don't succeed in attaining your goal initially and in the long run.

# PREPARING FOR THE CHALLENGE

Many postbaccalaureate students find themselves returning to college studies after a hiatus of varying lengths of time, which can prove especially challenging. Since they must attain good results, they are under considerable pressure to succeed. Under these unique circumstances, special advice for such college returnees is needed. The following tips should prove beneficial:

### TIP 1  Focus on time management

Your most essential commodity is time. Once you begin your studies again, you will find that little of your previous free time is available to you. Thus, as with finances, budgeting your time to accomplish the multiple tasks at hand will allow you to accomplish the best results.

### TIP 2  Secure family support

Hold periodic family meetings to seek cooperation and support. This is an especially useful opportunity if you need a more amenable study atmosphere and added space. You might invite your family to visit the school campus, making them feel that they are an important component of your ambitious undertaking.

### TIP 3  Get to know your instructors

It can be very beneficial if your instructors get to know you personally, rather than just as a name on the class roster. The instructor should become familiar with your goals, concerns, and constraints, as well as your background. A sympathetic instructor can provide special consideration when it comes to assignments and deadlines.

### TIP 4  Establish suitable transportation

It may prove very beneficial for you to join a car pool and also to participate in study groups. You can possibly gain valuable information from fellow classmates on the nature of some instructors, their expectations, and the type of examinations they give. If you aren't driving, you may find that you will have some additional free study time.

### TIP 5  Pace yourself

Going back to school after a hiatus, especially a long one, requires some personal psychological adjustment. Should you find yourself overwhelmed by undertaking too demanding a program, slow down—but don't quit. This approach will have a two-fold benefit, namely, easing the stress while at the same time keeping you on schedule toward graduation. You may well still find time for vacation breaks so essential to maintaining your overall well-being.

### TIP 6  Secure financial support

By tapping appropriate resources you may well find a wide variety of financial aid available. Your college Financial Aid Office is a prime source of information and help.

### TIP 7  Seek guidance

It is important that you get to know your Prehealth Advisor. Determine if the person seems qualified and if you can establish a good rapport. A guidance counselor may have the knowledge and skills that can provide you with help and vital assistance, especially when you will be applying to medical school. Get to know this individual early on, since he/she usually will have to write a letter supporting your application. The better you are known and, hopefully, liked, the greater the chances for a more positive and more supportive letter.

**TIP 8   College can be enjoyable**

While recognizing that you have returned to college with the important goal of getting into medical school, recognize that you should not deny yourself the pleasant life experiences that attending college can afford. Given the limited time available to you, seek to enjoy the company of fellow collegians at lunch, club meetings, and organizational events. As an older student, you may be looked up to for leadership, which you should provide whenever possible. In the end, you may come to look upon this college experience as a particularly meaningful and hopefully memorable phase of your life.

## POSTBACCALAUREATE PREMEDICAL PROGRAMS

The following schools offer structured postbaccalaureate educational programs that provide a wide range of academic and nonacademic support. Programs extend for one or two years. Some are geared toward non-science majors, while others assist in preparation for the MCAT.

### Alabama
*Postbaccalaureate Program*
Spring Hill College
Department of Biology
4000 Dauphin Street
Mobile, AL 36608
(251) 380-3082

### Arizona
*Postbaccalaureate Program*
Arizona State University
Main Graduate College
P O Box 871003
Tempe, AZ 85287
(602) 965-3521

*Biomedical Sciences Program*
Midwestern University
Biomedical Sciences Program
19555 N. 59th Avenue
Glendale, AZ 85308
(623) 572-3291

### California
*Reapplication Program*
UCLA School of Medicine
Office of Academic Enrichment and Outreach
13-154 Center of Health Sciences
Los Angeles, CA 90095
(310) 825-3575

*Postbaccalaureate Premedical Program*
University of Southern California
College Academic Services
Las 120
Los Angeles, CA 90089
(213) 740-2534

*Postbaccalaureate Program-Reapplicant*
University of California—Irvine
Office of Admissions and Outreach
College of Medicine (125 Medical Surge I)
P O Box 4089
Irvine, CA 92697
(949) 824-5388

*Postbaccalaureate Program*
University of California—San Diego
Student Outreach Services
School of Medicine
9500 Gillman Drive
La Jolla, CA 92093
(858) 534-4170

*Postbaccalaureate Premedical Program*
Mills College
Office of Graduate Studies, Room 226
5000 MacArthur Boulevard
Oakland, CA 94613
(510) 4430-2317

*Health Professions Postbaccalaureate Advancement Program*
California State University—Fullerton
Health Profession Office, Room 24203
800 North State College Boulevard
Fullerton, CA 92384
(714) 278-3980

*Postbaccalaureate Reapplicant Program*
University of California—Davis
Office of Medical Education
School of Medicine
1 Shields Avenue
Davis, CA 95616
(530) 752-8119

*Postbaccalaureate Program*
California State University—Dominguez Hills
1000 East Victoria Street
Carson, CA 90747
(310) 243-3388

*Postbaccalaureate Premedical Certificate Program*
Scripps College
W. M. Keck Science Center
925 North Mills Avenue
Claremont, CA 91711
(909) 621-8764

*Postbaccalaureate Program*
California State University—Hayward
Hayward, CA 94542
(510) 885-2741

*Postbaccalaureate Program*
Loyola Marymount University
1 LMU Drive
Los Angeles, CA 90045
(310) 338-5954

*Postbaccalaureate Reapplicant Program*
University of California—San Francisco
School of Medicine
1855 Folsom Street
Box 0409
San Francisco, CA 94143
(415) 476-5348

*Biological Sciences*
San Jose State University
San Jose, CA 95192
(408) 924-4900

**Connecticut**
*Postbaccalaureate Program*
University of Connecticut
School of Medicine
263 Farmington Avenue
Farmington, CT 06030
(203) 679-2152

**District of Columbia**
*Postbaccalaureate Program*
American University
Department of Chemistry
4400 Massachusetts Avenue NW
Washington, DC 20016
(202) 885-1770

*Georgetown Experimental Medical Studies Program*
Georgetown University School of Medicine
Office of Programs for Minority Student Development
School of Medicine
3900 Reservoir Road NW
Washington, DC 20007
(202) 687-1406

*Postbaccalaureate Premed Certificate Program*
Trinity College
Office of the Dean of Faculty
125 Michigan Avenue NE
Washington, DC 20017
(202) 939-5000

**Florida**
*Postbaccalaureate Program*
Barry University
School of Natural and Health Sciences
11300 NE Second Avenue
Miami Shores, FL 33161
(305) 899-3541

*Postbaccalaureate Bride Program*
Florida State University
College of Medicine
Tallahassee, FL 32306
(904) 644-7678

*Postbaccalaureate Program*
Nova Southeastern University
Medical Sciences Admissions
3200 S University Drive
Ft. Lauderdale, FL 33328
(954) 262-1101

*Postbaccalaureate Program*
Dean of Graduate School
University of Florida
Box 115515
Gainesville, FL 32611
(352) 392-1365

*Postbaccalaureate Premedical Program*
University of North Florida
4567 St. Johns Bluff Road South
Jacksonville, FL 32224
(904) 620-2608

*Postbaccalaureate Program*
University of Miami—Coral Gables
College of Arts and Sciences
P O Box 248004
Coral Gables, FL 33124
(305) 284-5176

**Georgia**
*Postbaccalaureate Premedical Program for Women*
Agnes Scott College
Office of Graduate Studies
141 E. College Avenue
Decatur, GA 30030
(404) 471-6361

*Postbaccalaureate Program*
Armstrong Atlantic State University
Savannah, GA 31419
(912) 927-5279

**Hawaii**
*IMI Ho' Ola Postbaccalaureate Program*
University of Hawaii
1960 East–West Road, Biomedicine C-203
Honolulu, HI 96822
(808) 956-3466

## Illinois
*Postbaccalaureate Program*
Finch University Health Science/Chicago Medical School
Applied Physiology Program
3333 Green Bay Road
North Chicago, IL 60064
(847) 578-3209

*Chicago Area Health and Medical Careers Program*
Illinois Institute of Technology
3200 S. Wabash Avenue
Chicago, IL 60616
(312) 567-3890

*Postbaccalaureate Program*
Rosary College
Dominican University
7900 W. Division Street
River Forest, IL 60305
(708) 524-6800

*Postbaccalaureate Program*
Midwestern University
Biomedical Sciences
555 31st Street
Downers Grove, IL 60515
(630) 515-6392

*Postbaccalaureate Program*
Roosevelt University
Department of Biology
430 S. Michigan
Chicago, IL 60605
(312) 341-3676

*Medical—Dental Education Preparation Program*
Southern Illinois University
Admission Coordinator
MEDPREP, Wheeler Hall
School of Medicine
Carbondale, IL 62901
(618) 452-1554

*Postbaccalaureate Premedical Preparation Program*
Mundelein College of Loyola University
6525 North Sheridan Road
Chicago, IL 60626
(773) 508-6054

## Indiana
*Postbaccalaureate Program*
Indiana University School of Medicine
Department of Cellular and Integrative Physiology
635 Barnhill Drive, MS 446
Indianapolis, IN 46202
(317) 274-7772

*Postbaccalaureate Program*
Indiana University—Purdue University at Indiana
Biology Department
723 W. Michigan Street
Indianapolis, IN 46202
(317) 274-0589

**Iowa**
*Postbaccalaureate Program*
Iowa State University
102 Carrie Chapman Catt Hall
Ames, IA 50011
(515) 294-4831

**Louisiana**
*Postbaccalaureate Program*
Tulane University
Prehealth Advisory Office
106 Hebert Hall
New Orleans, LA 70118
(504) 865-5370

**Maryland**
*Postbaccalaureate Premedical Program*
The Johns Hopkins University
Wyman Park Buildings, Room G-1
3400 N. Charles Street
Baltimore, MD 21218
(410) 516-7748

*NIH Postbaccalaureate Training Program*
National Institutes of Health
2 Center Drive, MSC 0240
Bethesda, MD 20892
(301) 402-1917

*Postbaccalaureate Program*
University of Maryland
College of Life Sciences
Mitchell Bldg. 1st Floor
College Park, MD 20742
(301) 314-3572

*Postbaccalaureate Premedical Program*
Goucher College
1201 Dulaney Valley Road
Baltimore, MD 21204
(800) 414-3437

*Postbaccalaureate Premedical-Predental Program*
Towson State University
Department of Biological Sciences
8000 York Road
Towson, MD 21252
(410) 830-3042

**Massachusetts**

*Postbaccalaureate Program*
American International College
1000 State Street
Springfield, MA 01109
(413) 747-6379

*Medical Science Degree Program*
Boston University School of Medicine
Division of Graduate Medical Science
715 Albany Street
Boston, MA 02118
(617) 638-5120

*Postbaccalaureate Certificate Program*
Brandeis University
Office of Undergraduate Academic Affairs
Kutz 108/MS001
Waltham, MA 02454

*Postbaccalaureate Program*
University of Massachusetts—Amherst
Premedical Office, N. 330 Mohill
Amherst, MA 01003
(413) 545-3674

*Postbaccalaureate Program*
University of Massachusetts—Boston
McCormack Hall, 3rd Floor
Boston, MA 02125
(617) 287-5519

*Postbaccalaureate Studies Program*
Mount Holyoke College
6 Stafford Hall
50 College Street
South Hadley, MA 01075
(413) 538-2077

*Postbaccalaureate Program*
Wellesley College
Office of Continuing Education
106 Central Street
Wellesley, MA 02181
(617) 283-2660

*Postbaccalaureate Program*
Worcester State College
Premedical Advisory Committee
486 Chandler Street
Worcester, MA 01602
(508) 793-8000

*Health Careers Program*
Harvard University Extension School
Health Career Program
51 Brattle Street
Cambridge, MA 02138
(617) 495-2926

*Postbaccalaureate Prehealth Program*
Tufts University
Office of Professional and Continuing Studies
419 Boston Avenue
Medford, MA 02155
(617) 627-2321

*Postbaccalaureate Certificate Program*
Assumption College
Division of Natural Sciences
500 Salisbury Street, P O Box 15005
Worchester, MA 01615
(508) 767-7545

## Michigan
*Advanced Baccalaureate Learning Experience Program*
Michigan State University
A 254 Life Sciences Building
College of Human Medicine
East Lansing, MI 44824
(517) 355-2401

*Postbaccalaureate Premedical Program*
University of Michigan Medical School
Office of Student and Minority Affairs
1301 Catherine Road
5109C Medical Science I Bldg.
Ann Arbor, MI 48109
(313) 764-8185

*Postbaccalaureate Program*
Wayne State University
540 East Canfield Avenue, Rm. 1320
Detroit, MI 48201
(313) 577-1598

## Missouri
*Postbaccalaureate Program*
Rockhurst University
College of Arts and Sciences
1100 Rockhurst Road
Kansas City, MO 64110
(816) 501-3590

*Graduate Experience in Medical Educational Program*
Saint Louis University School of Medicine
1402 S. Grand Boulevard
St. Louis, MO 63104
(314) 268-5398

*Postbaccalaureate Premedical Program*
Avila University
11901 Wornhall Road
Kansas City, MO 64145
(816) 501-3655

**Nebraska**
*Postbaccalaureate Program*
Creighton University School of Medicine
Medical Administration
2500 California Plaza
Omaha, NE 68178
(402) 280-2799

**New Hampshire**
*Postbaccalaureate Program*
Dartmouth Medical School
Center of Evaluative Clinical Sciences
Hinman Box 7252
Hanover, NH 03755
(603) 650-1782

**New Jersey**
*Postbaccalaureate Program*
Ramapo College of New Jersey
School of Theoretical and Applied Science
Mahway, NJ 07430
(201) 684-7727

*Postbaccalaureate Certificate Program*
Richard Stockton College of New Jersey
Health Professions
JIM Leeds Road
Pomana, NJ 08240
(609) 652-4462

*Postbaccalaureate Program for Prehealth Profession Studies*
Rutgers University
University College, Office of the Dean
35 College Avenue
New Brunswick, NJ 08903
(732) 932-7683

*Postbaccalaureate Program*
University of Medicine and Dentistry of New Jersey
Graduate School of Biomedical Sciences
30 Bergen St.
Newark, NJ 07107
(973) 972-4631

**New Mexico**
*Cultural and Ethnic Programs*
New Mexico Health Sciences Center
Basic Medical Sciences Bldg., Room 106
915 Camino de Salud, NE
Albuquerque, NM 87131
(505) 272-2728

**New York**

*Postbaccalaureate Program*
City College of New York/CUNY
Convent Avenue at 138th Street
New York, NY 10031
(212) 650-6622

*Postbaccalaureate Program*
Hofstra University
Office of Continuing Education
Hempstead, NY 11549
(516) 463-5016

*Postbaccalaureate Program*
Long Island University
Division of Science
University Plaza
Brooklyn, NY 11201
(718) 488-1209

*Postbaccalaureate Program*
Manhattanville College
Prehealth Advisory Committee
2900 Purchase Street
Purchase, NY 10577
(914) 694-2200

*Postbaccalaureate Program*
New York College of Osteopathic Medicine
P O Box 8000
Old Westbury, NY 11568
(516) 686-3800

*Postbaccalaureate Program*
New York Medical College
Graduate School
Basic Medical Science
Basic Sciences Building, Rm. A-41
Valhalla, NY 10595
(914) 594-4110

*Postbaccalaureate Program*
SUNY—Albany
School of Public Health
One University Place
Rensselaer, NY 12144
(518) 402-0333

*Postbaccalaureate Program*
SUNY—Buffalo
408 Research Studies Center
Buffalo, NY 14263
(716) 845-2239

*Postbaccalaureate Program*
SUNY—Stony Brook
Faculty Committee of Health Professions
Melville Library E. 2360
Stony Brook, NY 11794
(516) 632-7082

*Postbaccalaureate Program*
Syracuse University
Department of Bioengineering and Neuroscience
Institute of Sensory Research
621 Skytop Road
Syracuse, NY 13244
(315) 443-4164

*Postbaccalaureate Program*
Union College
Graduate Education
Lamont House Graduation Center
Schenectady, NY 12308
(518) 388-6239

*Postbaccalaureate Premedical Program*
Columbia University
Office of Preprofessional Programs
2970 Broadway
New York, NY 10027
(212) 854-2772

*Postbaccalaureate Program*
New York University, College of Arts and Sciences
Prehealth Advising Office, Main Bldg. Room 9L
100 Washington Square East
New York, NY 10003
(212) 998-8160

*Postbaccalaureate Program*
SUNY—Buffalo
Coordinator, Post-Bac Program
School of Medicine and Biomedical Sciences
3435 Main Street, 40 CFS Building
Buffalo, NY 14214
(716) 829-2802

**North Carolina**
*Postbaccalaureate Program*
Fayetteville State University
Department of Natural Science
1200 Murchison Road
Fayetteville, NC 28301
(910) 672-1691

*Premedical and Predental Postbaccalaureate Program*
University of North Carolina, Greensboro
Department of Biology
P O Box 26170
Greensboro, NC 27402
(336) 256-0071

*Postbaccalaureate Development Program*
Wake Forest University, School of Medicine
Office of Minority Affairs
Medical Center Boulevard
Winston-Salem, NC 27157
(336) 716-4271

## Ohio

*Postbaccalaureate Program*
Cleveland State University
Department of Health Sciences
2121 Euclid Avenue
Cleveland, OH 44115
(216) 687-3567

*Postbaccalaureate Program*
University of Cincinnati College of Medicine
Pathways Office
231 Albert Sabin Way
Cincinnati, OH 45267
(513) 558-7212

*Postbaccalaureate Program*
Ohio State University College of Medicine
MEDPATH Office
1072 Graves Hall
370 W. 9th Avenue
Columbus, OH 43210
(614) 292-3161

*Postbaccalaureate Program*
Ohio University, College of Osteopathic Medicine
Director, Center for Excellence
030 Grosvenor Hall
Athens, OH 45701
(740) 593-0898

## Oregon

*Postbaccalaureate Program*
Portland State University
College of Liberal Arts and Science
P O Box 751
Portland, OR 97207
(503) 725-3514

*Postbaccalaureate Program*
University of Oregon
Academic Advisor
364 Oregon Hall
Eugene, OR 97403
(541) 346-3211

### Pennsylvania
*Postbaccalaureate Certificate Program*
Beaver College
Office of Enrollment Management
Glenside, PA 19038
(215) 572-2836

*Medical Science Preparatory Program*
Drexel University College of Medicine
245 N. 15th Street
Philadelphia, PA 19102
(215) 762-4692

*Postbaccalaureate Program*
Bryn Mawr College
101 N. Merion Avenue
Bryn Mawr, PA 19010
(215) 526-7350
(610) 526-7350

*Postbaccalaureate Program*
Lake Erie College of Osteopathic Medicine
1858 W. Grandview Boulevard
Erie, PA 16509
(814) 866-8436

*Postbaccalaureate Program*
LaSalle University
Prehealth Professions
1900 W. Olney Avenue
Philadelphia, PA 19141
(215) 951-1248

*Postbaccalaureate Certificate Program*
The Pennsylvania State University
213 Whitmore Laboratory
University Park, PA 16802
(814) 865-7620

*Biomedical Science Program*
Philadelphia College of Osteopathic Medicine
4170 City Avenue
Philadelphia, PA 19131
(800) 999-6998

*Postbaccalaureate Program*
Temple University
Prehealth Advice Center
Curtis Hall 113
1301 Montgomery Avenue
Philadelphia, PA 19122
(215) 204-8669

*Posbaccalaureate Program*
West Chester University
Premedical Program
117 Schmucker Science Center South
West Chester, PA 19383
(610) 436-2978

*Postbaccalaureate Premedical Linkage and Nonlinkage Programs*
Duquesne University
Postbac Premedical Programs
B101-Bayer Learning Center
Pittsburgh, PA 15282
(412) 396-6335

*Postbaccalaureate Program*
Immaculate College
Department of Biology
1145 King Road
Immaculate, PA 19345
(215) 647-4400

*Postbaccalaureate Premedical Programs*
Pennsylvania State University
213 Whitmore Laboratory
University Park, PA 16802
(800) 778-8632

*Postbaccalaureate Prehealth Program*
University of Pennsylvania
Assistant Dean, Prehealth Program
3440 Market Street, Room 100
Philadelphia, PA 19104
(215) 898-7326

*Postbaccalaureate Program*
University of the Sciences in Philadelphia
600 South 43rd Street
Philadelphia, PA 19104
(215) 596-8508

**Rhode Island**
*Postbaccalaureate Program*
Brown University
Brown Learning Community
Box 1959
Providence, RI 02906
(401) 863-3452

*Postbaccalaureate Program*
University of Rhode Island
Advisory Committee
Health Professions
A-129, Biological Science Center
100 Fleggs Road
Kingston, RI 02861
(401) 874-2670

**Tennessee**
*Postbaccalaureate Program*
Carson–Newman College
CNC Box 71992
Russell Avenue
Jefferson City, TN 27760
(865) 471-3257

*Postbaccalaureate Program*
Christian Brothers University
Biology Department
650 East Parkway South
Memphis, TN 38104
(901) 321-3447

*Postbaccalaureate Program*
East Tennessee State University
Fast Track Program
P O Box 70592
Johnson City, TN 37614
(423) 439-6903

*Postbaccalaureate Program*
Fisk University
UNF Premed Summer Institute
1000 17th Avenue N
Nashville, TN 37208
(615) 329-8796

**Texas**
*Postbaccalaureate Program*
Lamar University
Department of Biology
Beaumont, TX 77710
(409) 880-7970

*Postbaccalaureate Program*
Texas Christian University
Sid Richardson Bldg.
Forth Worth, TX 76129
(817) 257-6337

*Postbaccalaureate Program*
University of Houston
The University Studies Division
Student Service Center
Houston, TX 77204
(713) 743-8982

*Postbaccalaureate Program*
University of Texas—Arlington
Life Science Building
P O Box 19047
Arlington, TX 76019
(817) 273-2310

*Postbaccalaureate Program*
University of Texas Medical Branch
Director, Medical Student Recruitment
Ashbel Smith G120
Galveston, TX 77555
(409) 772-5256

## Vermont
*Postbaccalaureate Premedical Program*
University of Vermont
Continuing Education
322 S. Prospect Street
Burlington, VT 05405
(800) 639-3210

*Postbaccalaureate Premedical and Allied Health Sciences Program*
Bennington College
Chief Health Science Advisor
Bennington, VT 05201
(802) 440-4320

## Virginia
*Postbaccalaureate Program*
Eastern Virginia Medical School
Biomedical Science Program
Fairfax Hall
721 Fairfax Avenue
Norfolk, VA 23507
(757) 446-8480

*Postbaccalaureate Program*
Old Dominion University
OCNPS 133
Norfolk, VA 23529
(757) 683-5200

*Postbaccalaureate Program*
Virginia Commonwealth University
School of Graduate Studies
P O Box 843051
Richmond, VA 23298
(804) 828-6916

*Medical Academic Advancement Program*
University of Virginia School of Medicine
Office of Student Academic Support
Health Sciences Center, Box 446
Charlottesville, VA 22909
(804) 924-2189

**Washington**
*Postbaccalaureate Program*
Premed/Predent Department of Biology
Seattle, WA 98122
(206) 296-5486

**West Virginia**
*Postbaccalaureate Program*
Glenville State College
Division of Science and Math
200 High Street
Glenville, WV 26351
(304) 462-4126

**Wisconsin**
*Postbaccalaureate Program*
University of Wisconsin—Madison
Graduate Education
1656 Linden Drive
Madison, WI 53706
(608) 263-1008

*Postbaccalaureate Program*
University of Wisconsin—Milwaukee
Certificate of Premed Studies
Holton Hall 130
Milwaukee, WI 53201
(414) 229-3922

# 5 Opportunities for Nontraditional (Older) Applicants

Introduction
Nature of the challenge
Admission planning
Choice of preparatory program
The MCAT
The post-application interlude
Postbaccalaureate programs

## INTRODUCTION

Almost all students applying to medical school are college seniors and, if accepted, are around 22 years of age when starting medical school. Those who are significantly older, in their upper 20s and beyond, are usually already in the workplace in a wide variety of careers. They are classified as nontraditional applicants when they become premedical students. Such individuals, whose age can range up to about 50, face a special challenge when seeking admission to medical school. This chapter is devoted to discussing their unique situation, insofar as gaining entrance to a first-year class is concerned. From this special group each year, a relatively small, but nevertheless, significant number have succeeded in getting in and achieving their goal, in spite of the obvious obstacles their situation presents. This chapter is designed to help those having the courage to consider this route and significantly improve their chances toward self-fulfillment.

## NATURE OF THE CHALLENGE

### Being a Nontraditional Applicant

It is understandable that your status as an older applicant certainly puts you at a disadvantage, when compared to the typical applicants. However, you are not unique, since one out of every 50 first-year medical students is 36 or older. Moreover, nearly 10% of medical students is 30 or older.

Why the delay in applying by nontraditional students? Some of the common reasons offered are

*Combining careers.* Ambitious individuals wish to add a new component to their existing professional activities. These include artists, lawyers, engineers, computer specialists, and so on. They can use their existing talents and knowledge in medicine. How realistic is one's concept to combine careers is the critical element that has to be established by applicants to the satisfaction of an admission committee.

*Late bloomers.* There are talented individuals who delay applying to medical school due to a lack of drive, out of sheer inertia, or an underlying insecurity of successfully attaining a long-cherished goal of becoming a physician. Now prior obstacles have disappeared and their goal of attaining admission dominates their lives. One's sincerity of purpose needs to be convincingly made to enhance one's chances of success.

*Post-child rearing.* Many older women applicants feel that now that they have put their child-rearing responsibilities essentially behind them, their time is available to focus their attention on undertaking a demanding and perhaps long hoped-for career in medicine, as they seek a new and different level of satisfaction. Demonstrating that it is a medical career that they want rather than just an occupation is what such an applicant must do.

*Career change.* This impulse is not infrequent for individuals in midlife. It is especially common among engineers, architects, and lawyers and may result from no longer gaining the personal satisfaction that they envisioned early in life. Justifying that they will find genuine fulfillment in medicine is the challenge such applicants face when seeking admission to medical school.

*Postcareer individuals.* These are not typical career changers, but individuals who are eligible to retire after 20 years of some career service and are prepared to move from one career to another. Such individuals need to convincingly demonstrate that they are not merely looking for a new career, but that medicine is a most appropriate choice for reasons that need to be convincingly established by the applicant.

## Testing One's Sincerity

Nontraditional individuals who have firmly decided to become applicants presumably will respond in the *affirmative* when they ask themselves the following questions:

- Do I feel young and courageous enough to change my career at this point in life?
- Am I capable and ready to absorb a vast amount of new scientific information?
- Can I (and my family) satisfactorily maintain an adequate lifestyle for the four years that I am a medical student?
- Do I have the basic academic ability and intense motivation to attain my goal over the entire course of a lengthy educational and training time?
- Have I given adequate thought to my proposed career plans and their wide-ranging ramifications?
- Can I fully justify my desire for a career change to everyone who will be seriously affected by my decision?
- Can I adequately and satisfactorily justify why I plan a career change at this point in my life?
- Do I have the support of my family in undertaking this radical course of action?

If you are unable to respond positively to these questions, you should carefully rethink your decision to determine its reality.

## Special Considerations

When responding to the above questions you should bear in mind that there are a number of issues that are especially relevant to older applicants considering applying to medical school. Some of these are

- Having been away from an academic environment, your study skills may well be below your optimal level. Taking premedical prerequisite courses and preparing for the MCAT will provide an opportunity to refresh these skills and retrain yourself. Doing well in these courses should provide a degree of reassurance that you can handle the demands of the medical curriculum.
- Your career experiences will have given you an opportunity to develop time-management skills that should serve you well as a medical student.
- You need to recognize that going to medical school is a demanding full-time job. It requires your committing yourself fully and withdrawing largely from many of your previous activities that have brought you satisfaction and enjoyment.
- Attending medical school will undoubtedly add significantly to any existing college debt and/or create new debt if the original was paid off by your career income.

- Medical school responsibilities will radically alter your lifestyle both socially and economically. These facts need to be taken into serious consideration.

- Gaining admission to a medical school may well force you (and your family) to relocate to an entirely new community. Should you desire an M.D. degree, be exceptionally intense; you may even visualize the need to go to an overseas school to achieve your goal, with all the hardships this will entail.

- You need to digest the fact that your training may involve such demanding experiences as staying up all night to study for exams and possibly working a 36-hour shift. This requires both stamina and willpower. You are the best judge of whether these attributes are present in your personal makeup.

- It is vital that you have genuine family support and an awareness of the impact of your decision on the standard of their personal lives. This may require your spouse to help provide financial assistance in support of the family. Also, care for elderly parents may be a consideration, in light of the minimal seven-year commitment that physician training entails. One needs to take into account the possibility of compounding serious personal issues with the rigorous demands of medical school.

- It should be recognized that if and when you become a resident, you likely would have to submit to the orders (and whims) of younger supervisory attendants and residents. This may not be so comfortable, but this situation should be tolerable.

- Occasionally, some medical schools will accept attractive candidates (for instance, those with high GPA and MCAT scores) with 90 or more college credits. Should you be in such a position, you might consider this route in order to possibly save a year of college studies.

Any existing or potential issues that the above points raise should be resolved before a commitment to proceed is made.

## ADMISSION PLANNING

At the outset, you should read Chapter 6, *Applying to Medical School*. While admission requirements for nontraditional applicants are nominally identical to those for traditional ones, there are subtle, but significant, differences. Although the major objective criteria of grade point average and MCAT scores apply to both groups of applicants, the subjective negative aspect of age is present as an unspoken potential barrier that needs somehow to be overcome in order to gain admission. A special effort should be made, therefore, to impress the admissions personnel with a well-prepared application (especially the essay) and impressive interview performance. Advice on these and other highly relevant subjects follow.

## CHOICE OF PREPARATORY PROGRAM

The initial and critical fist step if you decide to proceed is to determine at which institution you will look to complete your premedical academic studies. Your two choices are: (a) matriculating at an undergraduate college/university, or (b) enrolling in a postbaccalaureate premedical program. Your decision depends on whether you already hold a bachelor's degree or not.

*Standard prerequisites*. Essentially almost every medical school expects applicants to have a baccalaureate degree at the time of matriculation, regardless of one's major, as long as the following prerequisites are included in your program of studies:

- One year each of inorganic and organic chemistry along with corresponding laboratory sessions

- One year of college biology plus associated laboratory

- One year of college physics plus associated laboratory

*Supplementary prerequisites.* There are three of these, namely:

- One year of English Composition (most schools)
- One year of college mathematics or calculus (some schools)
- Humanities electives (several schools)

It is *essential* to consult the individual medical school catalog, to be certain that you will meet the school's specific admission requirements.

## Selection of Major

For nontraditional students who have completed their undergraduate degree, this is not an issue; however, those without an undergraduate degree need to select a college major. The choice could be either a science, such as biology, or a nonscience area in one of the humanities, or a social science. When selecting a specific major, one should take into consideration the following elements:

1. It should have intellectual appeal so that you will have a strong incentive to perform well.
2. Select a major whose subject matter you think you will very likely perform well in (B+ or better).
3. The major will not be excessively demanding, but will allow adequate time to study for the required science prerequisites and MCAT exam, and for volunteer work.
4. The major has potential for use toward an alternate career in the event you don't succeed in getting accepted into medical school (or to help you in your present career).

**Note:** It may be difficult to find one major that meets all of the above criteria, so you should select the one that comes closest to doing so.

*Supplementary courses.* For some, such as reapplicants, you may need to take additional college courses other than your major. These may be taken for a variety of reasons, such as: to help meet specific medical school requirements, assist in preparation for the MCAT, elevate your GPA, or for educational refresher purposes.

## Recommendations

Recommendations provide an essential information source for supporting your application for admission. This can come in the form of a composite Premedical Committee letter of recommendation or individual faculty letters written on your behalf. In the latter case, the letters should, when possible, come from two science and one nonscience instructor. It is essential that, for this purpose, you select individuals who know you well, so it is important that you: (a) arrange for the appropriate instructors to become familiar with you, both as a person and a student, as a result of your having relatively extensive contact with them, and (b) utilize faculty who are experienced in writing such letters from past years on behalf of premeds and thus are aware of what issues to emphasize. By selecting the appropriate faculty, you will be appointing strong advocates in support of your cause. Given your status as a nontraditional student, you need as strong a group of "lawyers" on your team as you can find.

## Volunteer Service

Having some meaningful exposure to clinical medicine is expected, in order to ensure that you are aware of the general nature of the field you want to enter. This type of experience is vital in order to demonstrate your seriousness of purpose. To achieve this goal, there is nothing better than firsthand exposure to the practice of medicine. For those who work in a relevant health care field (for example, as a physician's assistant) this requirement obviously is not so essential, but letters from physicians familiar with your work will prove helpful. However, for all others, it is best to secure appropriate exposure to clinical medicine, especially via an appointment at a hospital emergency service. This opportunity should be obtained through the hospital's volunteer office. Try to offer the hospital as much time as possible, without jeopardizing your academic work. You should be entitled to a confirming letter, establishing that you were an active volunteer and indicating the duration of your service (assuming that the length of time was meaningful and your work was satisfactory).

## Application Basics

An applicant seeking admission is comparable to a general planning for a major battle. You need to have a timetable and the knowledge of resources available for the execution of the offensive.

*Timetable.* When scheduling your activities you need to be aware of the following considerations:

- Applying to medical school and securing a definitive response is a lengthy process that can take well over a year—a great deal of patience is mandated.

- Medical schools for the most part, use a rolling admissions policy, which by its very nature tends to benefit those who apply early.

As to the specific time frame, the following guidelines can prove useful:

- Take the MCAT when you feel fully prepared, especially in August of the year before you apply or in April of the year you apply, but repeat it in August if necessary.

- In rolling admissions, you should prepare your AMCAS or AACOMAS applications for submission as close to the date as possible, then it will be accepted (which is usually around June 1st).

- Arrange for transcripts of your relevant academic records (undergraduate plus postbacclaureate program) to be sent out promptly. Then check to make sure that this has taken place.

*Resources.* These are your AMCAS and/or AACOMAS applications (see below), MCAT scores, recommendations, and application essay. The stronger these are, the more effective will be your application for admission.

## Your Applications

Two applications have to be filed during a successful applicant's route to medical school. These applications are

*Preliminary application.* This is the primary document that initiates the application process, submitted through the American Medical College Application Service (AMCAS) or the American Association of Colleges Osteopathic Medicine Application Service (AACOMAS). These organizations are *not* involved in the decision-making aspects of the application process. Rather, they merely serve to disseminate your application to the schools you designate.

*Supplementary applications.* These are secondary forms, sent to applicants directly by individual medical schools. Receiving one means that your application has been carefully screened and merits serious further consideration by the admissions committee of the school that sent it to you. Upon its receipt, complete it promptly and carefully and then return it, so that you can then be considered and it can be determined if you merit an interview.

# THE MCAT

The MCAT is a national exam for all premeds. It is the "gold standard" that medical schools use to rate applicants. It is one of the most important tests you will need to take and one of the two most important decisive elements in the admission process along with your GPA.

The MCAT differs from other standardized tests you may have taken because it requires an intense and sustained effort to properly prepare for it. You should be prepared to study 20 to 40 hours a week consistently, for a full three months, in order to be competitive and feel confident. Your study time should be extended if there has been a long gap since you completed your science prerequisites; consequently, more recall effort needs to be expended to refresh your memory.

## Commercial Test Prep Courses

It is essential that you take several practice tests to build up your endurance and hopefully your confidence, as well as to allow you to become familiar with the nature of the proceedings on test day. Make the most out of any free time you may have in the months preceding the test, so that you will be maximally prepared for it. If you feel very insecure, consider taking one of the commercial MCAT preparation courses offered. These courses serve to teach you test-taking skills and/or to give you the impetus to study if you need such stimulation. Nevertheless, bear in mind that it is still imperative, even if you take a prep course, to continue your self-study. You will have no choice but to invest additional study time in preparing, when using a supplementary preparatory program, in addition to all your other obligations. In addition, commercial courses are expensive and, to benefit fully, you must attend them regularly; there is no supporting evidence that they *significantly* improve final test scores.

## Study Timetable

A *sample* study timetable for anyone who has been away for many years from the premedical curriculum and is planning to take the MCAT, as well as those who need a schedule guide, is suggested as follows:

- August—review general biology
- September through January—if possible, take a review science course in cell biology and genetics
- January—review organic chemistry I
- February through June—if possible, audit organic chemistry II; otherwise, review on your own
- December through April—study a different science *each* week using a continuous cycle. The sequence should be general biology, general chemistry, organic chemistry, and then general physics. Also make sure to practice verbal passages biweekly.

Having an appropriate study plan and following it consistently may prove the key to successful performance on the MCAT.

## Test Taking: Special Tips

- To facilitate admission, bring your MCAT admission card, a photo identification document, several sharpened number two pencils, a reliable eraser, two ballpoint pens containing black ink (for the essay), and a watch (without built-in accessories such as a camera, calculator, timer, etc.). Also take along some high-caloric snacks to eat when break is called.

- Do not plan on taking notes, a calculator, a computer, or a timer into the examination room. The same applies to colored pencils, highlighters, scrap paper, or a clip board.

- Make every effort to get a good night's sleep before the examination day. Make use of a facility that can ensure this goal.

- You can reduce anxiety and stress by avoiding studying the morning of the exam and, if possible, the evening before.

- It is recommended that your breakfast on the morning of the exam be, when possible, high in protein and low in carbohydrates so that you maximize your energy resources.

- Dress comfortably. To avoid feeling cold due to intense air conditioning, bring a sweatshirt or a sweater. Also wear comfortable shoes.

- If you wish, you may visit the exam room a day or so before the test. Your seat assignment, however, will be determined by the proctor.

- Since all answers must be recorded on the answer sheet in order to be scored and counted, allow sufficient time to transfer them from the test booklet.

- During breaks, make use of the rest room, stretch, or just close your eyes and meditate. Avoid discussing the exam with another examinee, since it can be stress generating.

- When the test is over, plan to go out with someone (but not a test-taking friend) and reward yourself by spending a pleasant evening and putting the test behind you.

## Interview

Receiving an interview invitation, especially for a nontraditional applicant, is a major leap forward. It means that the medical school is genuinely interested in your candidacy and wants to get to know you personally. It therefore is important for you to prepare intensively for the interview, since you never know how many such opportunities will come up. To do so, you should read pages 125–137, especially the section dealing with the interview process. What applies to the general applicant certainly applies to you, but being a nontraditional student, you can anticipate an especially intense interview experience, focusing on such basic questions as:

- How did you arrive at your decision to apply to medical school?

- What consideration motivated you to become a physician at this point in your life?

- What have you done to test the validity of your decision to apply to medical school?

- Why do you wish to enroll in this particular medical school?

- Assuming you get admitted, what area of medicine do you wish to enter?

- Where do you see yourself, personally and professionally, in about 10 years from now?

- What do you believe are some of the positive and negative aspects of being a physician?

## Responding to Challenging Questions

You may be faced with tough questions that need to be prepared for; samples of these are listed below and possible answers are also given.

- Are there any issues in your past that might affect your acceptance?

  *Answer:* If you decide to reveal sensitive, negative information, be very brief. Also do not make any excuses, but demonstrate, in concrete terms, that the previously existing serious problems were completely overcome (and perhaps indicate how).

- Why should you be accepted this time around (if you are a reapplicant)?

  *Answer:* Demonstrate your progress and positive changes in your application status that enhance your position since you applied last. Simply saying you are a better candidate for admission is not enough; you have to prove this with facts (for example, improved MCAT scores).

- Do you consider yourself too old to go to medical school and why not?

  *Answer:* I never let age be the deciding factor in making presumably major decisions in my life. I sincerely believe that I have the ability, energy, and motivation to achieve my goal. I (and my family) are prepared to make the necessary adjustments and believe I can meet all my personal obligations while I am a medical student.

- Does your family support your decision and if so how did you get them to do so?

  *Answer:* I made my case to my family that I am a highly responsible spouse and parent and have a solid track record of meeting all my obligations. I pointed out that I merit their trust and support. I indicated that it is feasible to meet our basic needs as a family, and I assured them that over time, when they see things working out for the best, everyone will benefit from my decision to become a physician.

## THE POSTAPPLICATION INTERLUDE

The process of gaining admission into medical school is lengthy, costly, and emotionally challenging. Particularly difficult are time gaps, where one is just waiting for results to arrive relative to some major activity.

There are four such interludes:

1. Awaiting one's MCAT scores
2. Awaiting supplementary applications
3. Awaiting interview invitations
4. Awaiting the final medical school decision

These are stressful periods in every applicant's life. However, they should be recognized for what they are, namely, an integral and essential part of the lengthy admission process. The fourth waiting phase is the most difficult, because there is little that you can do (other than sending updated transcripts of any positive changes in your academic record). Otherwise, it means marching to the mailbox daily until all the results are in.

At the decision time, the results may fall into three categories:

1. You may be offered a place in an incoming class.
2. You may be placed on a waiting list.
3. You may be rejected.

If you are put on a waiting list or are rejected, do not despair; the "game" is far from over. Many schools have considerable turnover as time goes on, during the late spring and summer. It is the waiting list from which they draw prospective students to fill vacancies. The number of vacancies is unpredictable and varies from school to school and year to year—this serves to provide hope and encouragement to those on waiting lists.

Even if the class is filled by mid-August, and things look definitely bleak, since you have not yet been accepted, there is always a chance, even if it's remote, that you may be chosen from a short alternate list. Those on this list are ranked and offered positions in the freshman class if a last-minute opening should occur due to withdrawal of accepted candidates. They do occur!

**Note:** Since being notified by a medical school of having been accepted is unpredictable, it is *absolutely* critical that the school have your e-mail address and cell phone number on file, so that, if you have to be away from home for any reason for any length of time, you can be contacted. It is essential that you also have a reliable person check your phone and answering machine and regular mail; be certain to give that person your contact number.

The bottom line is to stay in touch with the medical school admissions office by contacting them periodically to express your continued interest. Try to leave a positive impression with the admissions staff that you have a genuine interest in their school (but avoid becoming a pest). The school catalog may tip you off as to their interest in maintaining contact with applicants. Finally, a well-written brief on your own behalf, laying out your case, as a lawyer does on behalf of a client, may not be out of order. Should one of those who recommended you or your Premedical Adviser feel strongly that you deserve to be accepted, you may consider asking if they would think it appropriate for them to directly contact the Director of Admissions on your behalf.

For nontraditional students, in particular, receiving rejection letters, which can be recognized by their thin, trim number 10 envelope, can well be anticipated. Nevertheless, their receipt does have its negative impact emotionally so you should strengthen yourself psychologically by feeling that you have done and still are doing your best. Remember, the ultimate decision is not in your hands.

Since there are no guarantees for anyone of acceptance and the challenge is significantly greater for nontraditional applicants, you can use your free waiting time to review what has transpired up to this point and consider what you would do better if you have to reapply, such as study harder for the MCAT or prepare more for the interviews. Remember, you can only be expected to do what is humanly possible. Good Luck!

## POSTBACCALAUREATE PROGRAMS

See pages 74 to 92 for further information.

# 6 Applying to Medical School

General considerations
Selection factors
The application process
Recommendations
The interview
The selection process
Selection factors
Acceptance
Ranking of medical schools
Rejection
Special educational programs
Canadian medical schools
The admission process: timetable

## GENERAL CONSIDERATIONS

There are two basic factors that determine admission to medical school *independent* of the personal qualifications of each candidate. These factors are the total number of first-year places available and the total number of applicants for admission. Presently, fewer than half of those that apply are accepted to American medical schools; about half of those that are rejected are considered qualified to attend medical school.

Starting in 1930, in the decade between the Great Depression and World War II, the number of medical schools remained substantially unchanged and the number of first-year students actually decreased slightly. In the next two decades (1940–60), nine new schools were established and, as a result, first-year enrollment increased by about 50%. In the 15-year period 1960–75, 27 new schools came into being, bringing with them nearly another 65% increase in enrollment. Over the next decade (1976–86), only seven new schools became operational. Since the mid-1980s only a few new schools have been established. All of this points to the end of the era of medical school expansion, at least for the foreseeable future, even if a few new schools open in the coming years.

During the long period of expansion (1940–86), the total number of freshman places changed as a result of the opening of new institutions or the enlarging of class size at existing schools. The data indicates that two-thirds of the increase in enrollment was due to the latter and one-third to the former. This is understandable because new schools usually start with small enrollments and then expand.

### Bottom Line

A prospective applicant to medical school should have not only a general understanding of the profession, but should also demonstrate an interest in and an awareness of medical and social issues. Other relevant considerations are

- One's level of maturity, degree of poise, and humanitarism
- Realization that medical schools are looking for candidates with superior personal attributes in such areas as integrity, responsibility, leadership, initiative, curiosity, common sense, perseverance, breadth of interests, and communication skills

- A broad background in the biological sciences and humanities, knowledge of and exposure to the needs of people and society, and an awareness of the current health care delivery system

While few individuals excel in all areas, one should seek to improve one's personal image in areas that one feels they are deficient. A frank discussion with close friends or one's mentor can pinpoint areas of weakness that should be worked on to enhance one's image. The strong qualities that one does possess should be emphasized in the essay and interviews.

## Prospects for the Future

As noted, the era of major medical school expansion has ended. The long-term goal of the 15,000 first-year enrollments, set by medical educators to meet national health care needs, has not only been met but even surpassed. For many years, approximately 16,000 freshman medical students have enrolled each year. All indications are that the available number of freshman places has peaked, since no new schools are likely to open and significant expansion of first-year class size will not take place.

During the mid-1980s there was a continuous and marked decline in the number of medical school applicants, which reached an all-time low in 1988, with a 1.6:1 applicant/acceptee ratio. Since then, the decline has not only bottomed out, but the applicant pool consistently increased until 1996. By 1993 the number of applicants surpassed the previous peak year of 1974, and reached new heights over each of the next three years.

After seven straight years of increases, a decline in the applicant pool began in 1997 and continued to 2002. The past three years have shown a modest recovery and an upswing in applicants may possibly be in the making (see graph). Of special interest to prospective applicants should be the (rounded-off) applicant figures for the past nine years. These can be extrapolated from the graph of applicants.

**Medical School Applicants (A) and Matriculates (M)**
**1950–2006**

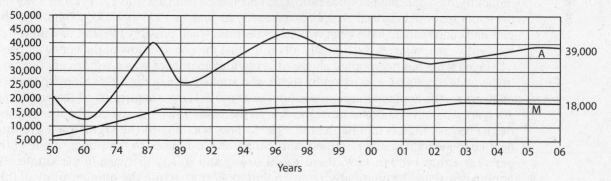

Also encouraging is the fact that, in 2005, 17,000 freshmen enrolled in medical schools. This is the highest number in several decades. New medical schools are anticipated to open in Florida and Texas, which should further increase allopathic medical school enrollment.

Some educators linked the increase in the applicant pool during most of the 1990s to the prolonged economic recession in the early 1980s, when many professions no longer provided assured job opportunities. Medicine has retained its appeal as a means of providing a secure economic future; therefore, students with a variety of majors were applying to medical school. Moreover, the surge in applicants has also been fueled by women, who now make up more than 40% of all medical students, and by Asian Americans, although representation in medical school by other groups such as African-Americans and Hispanic Americans has not been growing.

In the light of the exceptional circumstances associated with the change in size of the applicant pool, it is very difficult to predict at this time what the admission prospects will be during the next decade. Clearly, a variety of conditions over the next few years will impact strongly on the issue.

There has been about a 25% decline in the applicant pool over the five years 1997–2001. As a result, by 2001 the applicant pool declined to about 35,000 or close to 12,000 below the peak year of 1996, bringing it down to the 1994 level. From the events of recent years it would appear that in 1997 we may have entered the third major decline in the applicant pool of this past half century, the others being 1959–61 and 1984–88. It is not possible to predict where and when the decline will bottom out. What is clear is that as a result of the decline over the past few years, the applicant/acceptee ratio has finally gone down well below the long-standing 3:1 ratio (the general meaning of this ratio change is discussed on page 105).

One can only speculate as to the reasons for the current decline in the applicant pool. Perhaps prospective medical students are becoming concerned about the economic and social forces that are transforming the nature of the practice of medicine. They may also be reacting to the growing chorus of discontent with their profession, reflected by some physicians, due to the negative impact of managed care and a litigious society. The existing climate has not been enhanced by reports of a prospective oversupply of physicians, which some believe may exceed 100,000. Finally, the prospects of potentially incurring a heavy debt burden during the course of one's medical education undoubtedly adds significantly to the concerns of prospective students as they contemplate a medical career.

## First-Year Applicants

During the decade from 1950 to 1960, the number of applicants significantly decreased, from 22,000 to 14,000 per year, and there was a corresponding decrease in the applicant/acceptee ratio, from 3.1:1 to 1.7:1. From the early 1960s to its peak in 1974 there was a continual increase in the number of applicants, from 14,000 to 43,000 per year. Since then the number of applicants has markedly declined, to under 28,000 in 1988; consequently, the applicant/acceptee ratio again decreased from 2.8:1 to 1.7:1. From 1989 on, the applicant pool has risen sharply and steadily to peak in 1996 at 47,000. Thus, over the past half century there have been two major declines—and possibly the start of a third—as well as two major increases, dramatically reflecting the ebb and flow of the applicant pool.

From what has been noted above, it is obvious that there was a significant increase in the odds of gaining admission by those who applied during the 1975–88 period, when on average, the applicant/acceptee ratio was about 2:1, over applicants of the preceding 10 years when the ratio was closer to 3:1. In the years 1987–92, the competition turned out to be less than it had been since 1975. This was due to the significant gradual decline in the total number of applicants, which was estimated to have been about 1,000 per year. From 1989 to 1996 there was a strong and steady increase in the number of applicants, rising dramatically from 26,900 to 47,000, while the number of available places has remained about the same (approximately 16,000). As noted, since 1997 the applicant pool has declined for six successive years, lowering the applicant/acceptee ratio proportionately. The impact of this reversal is considered below.

While the current near 2:1 ratio still presents a formidable challenge, it need not be taken as reflecting any particular individual's chance for admission. Rather, it should be taken as a general reflection of the level of competition. The reason for this is that the applicant pool no longer consists almost entirely of white males as it did for well over the first half of this century. The pool now contains a very sizable female segment and a smaller minority segment, which together make up more than 50% of the freshman class each year. This situation makes it more difficult to define the exact odds for any particular individual to gain admission solely on the basis of the applicant/acceptee ratio. The problem of mathematically defining the intensity of competition is compounded by the fact that about one-fourth of the total applicant pool may be repeaters, whose chances for admission usually are significantly less than are those of new applicants. Thus, in trying to assess your own overall chances, many factors come into play. These include sex, race, residency, age, and financial status in addition to intellectual achievement and potential.

## Impact of Applicant Pool Size

Over the eight-year span (1988–96), the most dramatic fluctuation in the size of the applicant pool in a half century took place, from a very depressed number (about 27,000), to a remarkable record high (about 47,000). Such an enormous change in so short a time is unlikely to recur in the foreseeable future. It does, however, serve to impressively demonstrate how the size of the applicant pool significantly influences one's chances of getting into medical school as well as a variety of factors associated with the admissions process. Even under more normal circumstances, there are cyclical phases in the size of the pool of applicants and the impact of an above or below average number of applicants (about 35,000) will also be felt, although to a lesser degree, in a variety of ways. Therefore, consideration of the multifaceted influence of the impact of the applicant pool size is very important.

During interludes when the applicant pool is very large (such as the mid-1970s and mid-1990s), competition to secure a place is naturally extremely high. Under these circumstances, the following also takes place:

1. The chances for applicants with average credentials to gain admission is markedly diminished.

2. For the more attractive applicant the number of multiple acceptances received will likely be reduced.

3. The number of schools to which an applicant should apply will probably increase; consequently, the overall cost to applicants of the entire admissions process (such as application fees and interview expenses) will be higher.

4. The response from medical schools may be slower due to the large volume of applications that need to be processed when the pool is large.

5. Less attractive financial aid packages may be offered to applicants.

6. Competition will also be intense in the selection of women and minority group applicants who make up a sizable segment of most freshman classes.

7. Marked deficiencies in an applicant's record will carry more weight than usual, to the applicant's disadvantage; therefore, chances of the applicant securing an interview, which would allow the opportunity to explain a possible weakness in that applicant's record, are unfortunately diminished.

8. Tuition will more likely remain high when the applicant pool is large.

During a period when the applicant pool is low (as in 1984–87), the reverse of the above considerations come into play, to a degree dependent on the extent of the depression in the number of applicants.

In light of these considerations, it is important for all applicants to be alert to the status of the current size and direction of movement of the applicant pool for the few years prior to the time they plan to apply. They could then anticipate the general impact that the existing applicant pool situation will have upon them.

## Early Admission

Most applicants to medical school plan to have their baccalaureate degree before beginning medical study. For a typical entering class, less than 5% of the first-year students lacked their bachelor's degree.

There is considerable variation in policy regarding the admission of students after only three years of college study. The percentage of early admissions varies between none and 25%. In any case, only the exceptional student should consider applying for early admission, since only such an applicant will have a good chance of being accepted and the best chance of successfully completing his/her study. Applying early and not being accepted, however, does not prejudice your chances for admission the following year.

If you are interested in the early admission program, compare the colleges that offer such programs, using the information included in Table 8.1.

# SELECTION FACTORS

The admissions process is theoretically geared to recognize applicants who measure up to a hypothetical image of the person who, in the consensus of the medical school's admissions committee, will prove to be a successful medical student and in time a qualified and dedicated practitioner. Those who are accepted may not have all the qualities that a committee seeks. There may even be some areas of weakness in a candidate's profile. The weaknesses, however, can be offset by strengths in other areas so that on balance the applicant's overall picture is one that meets the standards that each school sets. In other words, one need not be the ideal candidate in order to achieve success.

It should also be realized, as was implied earlier, that some applicants may, at first glance, possess an impressive array of qualifications but nevertheless do not succeed in gaining admission. These candidates unfortunately proved unable to effectively project to the committee, either indirectly through their application or directly at their interviews, all the strengths they possess. Having solid credentials and being able to market yourself as a prospective good physician make up the winning combination that will open the door to a place in a freshman medical school class.

Some selection factors, such as GPA or MCAT scores, can readily be put into quantitative terms, while others, such as personality or motivation, cannot. Nevertheless, both types of factors are important and have a strong bearing on the outcome of the admissions process. Specifically, they determine if you qualify to be placed at some point into the applicant interview pool and at a later time into the applicant acceptance pool.

## Academic Achievement

Academic achievement is measured in terms of your grade point average, science course performance, and college(s) attended.

### Grade Point Average (GPA)

The application that each medical school receives on behalf of an individual applicant will contain a facsimile of the candidate's college transcript and, where applicable, any postgraduate record. It will show the courses taken and grades received during the regular academic year as well as during any summer. (Those high school courses and grades for which advanced placement credit were given are also listed.) Courses that the applicant is taking or is planning to take are also frequently requested. This self-designed record is checked for accuracy against official transcripts sent by your school and will form the basis of your GPA.

Recently, with the competition for places in entering classes intense because of the large number of applicants, the GPA for the *average* matriculant was 3.5. This can be interpreted to mean that a significant number of the approximately 16,000 students accepted—which represents only 35% of the applicant pool—had an average below 3.5. On the other hand, the entire pool average was 3.3. This indicates that some applicants with 3.5 or higher failed to gain admission, thus emphasizing that a high GPA by itself does not guarantee acceptance into medical school. The corollary is also true, namely, that having an average below 3.3 also does not mean you will not be accepted. As a matter of fact, 5% of those accepted had averages of 3.0 or less. All this suggests that your chances will be markedly diminished if your average goes below 3.3. The lower the GPA, the greater the need to compensate for this weakness by high MCAT scores and recommendations. Also, achieving improved grades in the later years of college, especially in the sciences, will contribute to a more favorable reception of your application. All this emphasizes the fact that you should not view the GPA as an entity in itself; rather, it has to be taken along with all other considerations, and a low GPA by itself should not discourage you from applying. Therefore, the quantitative factors will remain a very vital, and for most applicants, a critical element of the selection process. You should strive to attain as high a level of achievement as possible. This is essential because passing the initial admissions screening is usually dependent on your academic achievement.

While the GPA is one of the major factors examined as part of the initial screening process, it is usually viewed in the context of the applicant's overall educational data. The reasons are that the GPA is subject to grade inflation, is relative to the college attended and the course of studies pursued, and only represents an overall level of performance rather than the direction of the performance.

Medical school admissions officers know that grade inflation—namely, artificially high grades that do not accurately reflect the level of academic achievement—is a common phenomenon of undergraduate education. Thus, while they do not minimize the value of a high GPA, they do not necessarily take it at face value. Admissions officers seek to establish how authentic the GPA is by checking to see at which college the grades were earned. Therefore, an applicant with a good GPA attending a college with low admission selection standards will not be much better off than another applicant with somewhat lower grades who is enrolled at a more selective school. Also, the GPA is viewed in the context of the applicant's course of study. An applicant who met the premedical course requirements by completing bona fide courses designed for science majors will obviously be favored over one whose courses were intended for nonscience majors. Similarly, an applicant who is successfully completing a science major will tend to be more credible than one who is not doing so.

The breakdown of an applicant's GPA frequently provides a more significant insight into an applicant's achievement than does the numerical value of the GPA. Thus, a consistent level of performance would tend to imply that this is the applicant's optimal achievement level. On the other hand, an erratic performance pattern, either upward or downward, may well reflect a person's response to the academic challenge being faced. An upward pattern suggests an ability to adjust to college, overcome an initial disappointing performance level, and then proceed to attain a high level of achievement even when the educational demands are increasing. A downward pattern would tend to indicate the reverse—namely, the inability to maintain a sustained high level of achievement in the face of increased educational pressures. In other words, when the values of GPAs are the same, a GPA with a consistently good achievement level and an upward pattern will have a greater impact on the screening and selection process than a similar GPA with a downward achievement trend.

### Science Course Grades

The science course grades on your record are another factor considered in the admissions process. This is reasonable since medicine is the application of scientific principles that are intensively studied during the first two years of professional school. While a straight A science average is certainly not mandatory for admission to medical school, a solid level of consistently good performance (3.5 or better) will serve to demonstrate the potential to cope with the intellectual demands of the basic medical sciences.

Your science grades and the effort it took to achieve them will also help you evaluate your own abilities and the wisdom of your career choice. Incidentally, it is not essential to enjoy all your premedical science courses, but a genuine interest in science is essential.

It should be emphasized that just as the GPA's impact is relative to the college attended, so too is the science coursework judged. Similarly, the grade pattern for work completed over a three-year period can be of special value. Consistently good grades and an upward trend clearly present a positive image of your science potential.

### College Attended

It has already been noted that the college attended affects the evaluation of an applicant's GPA and science coursework by the admissions committee. It also has an overall impact on admission chances in general, for three reasons. First, attendance at a university that has an affiliated medical school offers a degree of priority for acceptance into the university's own medical college, because medical schools traditionally accept a significant number of freshman from their own college. Second, it appears, at least statistically speaking, that an applicant from a private undergraduate institution has a greater chance of acceptance at a private medical school. Third, coming from a college that has established a good medical school admission track record is a decided advantage. There is an initial favorable bias because of the positive image that such an institution's name generates.

## Intellectual Potential

Your academic performance, usually after a three-year period of undergraduate studies, provides a reasonable measure of your intellectual potential. Its usefulness, however, is tempered by the status of the school you attend, by the possibility of grade inflation, and possibly by the impact of pass/fail grades. For these reasons there are two additional factors considered in obtaining a comprehensive and reliable determination of the future performance of a medical student: MCAT scores and recommendations.

### MCAT Scores

The Medical College Admission Test (MCAT) is a lengthy, standardized, multiple-choice examination that is given twice each year. It is designed to determine your skills in problem solving in the natural and biological sciences, your verbal reasoning ability, and your written expository aptitude. The MCAT is an indicator of your academic potential. The test is designed in such a manner that the value of memorization is deemphasized, while analysis and synthetic intellectual capabilities are tested. This clearly implies that one of the major goals in college should be to develop "thinking" skills in exactly these areas. This can best be done over an extended period of time rather than by cramming for a few weeks or even months, and/or depending on commercial MCAT preparation programs.

The MCAT score is particularly important because it provides a quantitative measurement that easily lends itself, together with your GPA (and science average), to a screening formula. Because of the large volume of applications, such formulas are used by *some* medical schools as a rapid preliminary evaluation technique. The formula baseline figure, which can be adjusted during the admission season, can determine if your application deserves more careful examination. This may involve reviewing your recommendations, essay, and extracurricular activities to determine the possibility of an invitation for an interview. The MCAT score by itself will also be used to assess the validity of your academic record. This is especially true when the problem of grade inflation exists and when the academic caliber of a school is unknown or uncertain.

The MCAT is therefore an admission obstacle that must be overcome by all premedical students because almost all schools require this examination (for exceptions, see for example, the University of Rochester or Johns Hopkins profile, Chapter 8). This examination should not be looked upon as a major admission barrier, but rather, from a positive perspective, as a potential asset that can enhance your admission potential. Therefore, if you have a high GPA, good MCAT scores will confirm your status as an attractive applicant and thus speed processing your application toward the interview stage. On the other hand, if you are a borderline or weak applicant, impressive MCAT scores can significantly strengthen the chance of having your application reviewed more thoroughly. It is at this point that your letters of recommendation will have a special influence in determining your true intellectual potential.

### Letters of Recommendation

Letters of recommendation supplement the quantitative data provided by transcripts and MCAT scores. They add a positive or negative tone to the overall impression that your college work and aptitude test have established. All medical schools expect recommendations, preferably from your Health Professions Advisory Committee or from several natural science and other faculty members at your school.

## Personal Attributes

Aside from your academic achievements and intellectual potential, a number of personal attributes can have an impact of varying degree on your admission chances. These attributes can be placed into categories, which will be discussed below.

### Extracurricular and Summer Activities
See discussion in Chapter 3, page 53.

### Exposure to Medicine
This factor was, in part, discussed in Chapter 3 in "Extracurricular and Summer Activities." It should be noted that in addition to unstructured observation and service opportunities as a hospital volunteer, some institutions offer formal premedical observation programs on a group basis. In the course of such a program, premedical students, like medical interns, rotate through various departments and may even be given lectures by attending physicians on the staff. Some programs provide a small stipend. These types of programs can provide an invaluable opportunity for prospective medical students, by permitting them a direct personal view of the actual world of medicine and the realities of medical training. To learn about such exceptionally meaningful opportunities, make inquiries at the volunteer office of local hospitals; also ask your premedical advisor or senior premedical students who may have already participated in such a program.

### Special Achievements
Medical schools usually look for applicants who, for one reason or another, stand out among the large pool of qualified individuals seeking admission. Therefore, gaining acceptance into honor societies or receiving awards for scholastic achievement or service will strengthen your admission potential. Demonstrated leadership capacity will also enhance your appeal. Achievements such as serving as a student senator at your college, gaining election to an important student office, organizing a band, forming a volunteer group of students to visit the sick at your school infirmary or the elderly and handicapped in the neighborhood, or tutoring underprivileged youngsters would all be a strong plus on your credentials. These kinds of accomplishments demonstrate that you have initiative, concern for others, an ability to interact constructively as part of a team effort (a requirement for modern patient care), and the determination to succeed. All these qualities are desirable in applicants seeking to enter such professions as medicine.

## Individual Status

Your individual status can have a significant bearing on your chances for admission. Five factors are involved: citizenship, state of residence, age, sex, and minority status. Each of these factors is discussed separately, below.

### Citizenship
U.S. medical schools have more qualified applicants than places available to train them. Moreover, the tuition paid by medical students covers only part of the actual training costs, with the balance made up by the school, state, and federal funding. Consequently, medical schools naturally have as their primary obligation the training of U.S. citizens and thus only rarely accept noncitizens into their freshman classes. Applicants not holding citizenship status, including Canadians, are clearly at a great disadvantage when applying for admission to U.S. schools. This handicap can be somewhat diminished if the applicant can secure a green card and establish permanent residency status, as well as initiate the first formal steps toward citizenship.

### State of Residence

The state where you reside is another major factor in determining your chances for success. Many state schools have significantly lower tuition levels for their residents and exclude nonresidents from admission as well. They have this policy because they are funded by state taxes and thus believe that their primary obligation is to train professionals who not only live in the state but who are likely to set up practice there. The state of your residence should be carefully considered when the time comes to make up the list of schools to which you plan to apply.

If your state has only a few medical schools, you need not consider this an insurmountable obstacle because there are quite a few private schools that do not discriminate against out-of-state residents, although they may demonstrate geographical preferences to applicants from a general section of the country.

To be classified as a legal or bona fide resident of a state, you usually must maintain domicile in that state for at least 12 months preceding the date of first enrollment in an institution of higher education in that state. Student status at an institution of higher education (for example, as an undergraduate) does not constitute eligibility for residence status with regard to graduate-level work in the same state. You must maintain residence in a non-student capacity for the prescribed time in order to gain residence status. The student's eligibility to establish residence is also determined by his or her status as an adult or a minor. (A minor is any person who has not reached the age of 21, 18 in some states.) For minors, the legal residence is that of his or her parents, surviving parent, or legal guardian. As a result of Supreme Court rulings, the right of state schools to charge higher fees for out-of-state students has been upheld, but it may now be easier for such nonresident students who are 18 or older to establish legal residence and thus take advantage of the lower rate.

Two groups of states generally offer prospective applicants a statistically better chance of admission: those with many freshman places and relatively few in-state applicants (such as Illinois and Texas) and those with no in-state medical school but with special admission arrangements with other state schools (such as Maine and Wyoming).

### Age

Medical schools prefer applicants who are in the 20–25 age group. Exceptions are made for select individuals, but the upper acceptance limit is usually about 35. The most favored applicants of the older group are those whose postcollege careers have been associated with medicine: research assistants, physician assistants, graduate students in one of the biomedical sciences, or holders of advanced degrees in one of these areas. Less attractive are applicants who would like to give up established careers as dentists, podiatrists, engineers, lawyers, accountants, or physicists, and who now seek to become physicians because of personal disillusionment with present activities. The latter group, seeking a career change instead of personal advancement, represent a higher risk than the former, because of concern that the pattern of giving up one's existing career might be repeated at a later time when this same individual is in medical school, training, or practice.

In the light of the aforementioned, an applicant whose age is above 25 (and preferably under 35) should present solid credentials in science course requirements, acceptable MCAT scores, good evidence of familiarity with the demands and responsibilities of a medical career, and above all, very convincing reasons for giving up a current career and seeking one as a physician (see Appendix A, page 657).

That there exists a significant pool of postbaccalaureate students who become premeds is evident from the fact that there are many schools (see list in Chapter 4) that offer special programs designed so these students can meet the premedical science course requirements. In addition, the University of Miami may offer advanced placement for those having a science PhD. Thus, it is possible that highly motivated and well-qualified career changers can succeed in spite of inherent difficulties, if they can establish a strong case for themselves and present it effectively.

### Sex

The applicant's sex can influence the admission process. All medical schools accept both males and females as applicants and most encourage strongly motivated and well-qualified women to seek admission. Women currently make up at least 40% of the national freshman class admitted. Some schools are more liberal in admitting women than others (see Table 10.1). A detailed discussion of women in medicine is found in Chapter 10.

### Minority Status

If you can claim minority status—namely, if you are African-American, Native American/Alaskan native, Mexican American, Puerto Rican, Asian or Pacific Islander, or other Hispanic—you will be given special consideration, because most schools actively seek to enroll minority group members in their freshman classes. As a result, minority students currently make up about 10% of the national freshman class. A more detailed discussion of minority opportunities can be found in Chapter 11.

## Disability

Reliable surveys indicate that there are over 100 medical students with disabilities and upwards of 1,000 physicians-in-training with physical or learning disabilities. In 1970 Temple University Medical School in Philadelphia accepted a blind student who is currently a practicing child psychiatrist. The goal of disabled students is to gain admission on their own merit, and to secure reasonable accommodations from the school in order to be able to attend it. However, what constitutes "reasonable" accommodations and whether severely impaired students can be adequately trained has been a subject of considerable debate. The Americans with Disabilities Act (ADA) has greatly enhanced educational opportunities for disabled students; however, the law's loophole of allowing tests to measure skills provides a legal basis for a medical school to reject disabled applicants, claiming that they are lacking critical faculties and abilities that are fundamentally essential to practice medicine. Therefore, deficiencies in sensory skills could prevent them from observing patients or taking a history, deficiencies in motor skills could prohibit performing diagnostic procedures, and problems in communication skills may inhibit contact with patients or fellow physicians. Such limitations may serve as a basis to disqualify a disabled individual from gaining admission to any medical school. Not everyone shares this view, and a small, active group of disabled physicians is seeking to educate the medical community about the compensatory technology available for the handicapped medical student or physician.

Disabled students who feel that they have been rejected because of their disability can sue on grounds of discrimination as this is a violation of the ADA legislation. A blind Ohio premed student did so and won (but only after years of court battles). More recently, profoundly deaf and quadriplegic premedical students were admitted to medical school.

The current effort toward encouraging production of more primary care physicians, a physically demanding practice area, is not favorable to potential disabled applicants. Nevertheless, no generalization can be made regarding the chances of disabled premeds to gain admission. All individuals seeking a medical career have to judge for themselves their chances for gaining admission, satisfactorily completing their studies and training, and establishing a successful practice. Indeed, while there are major obstacles in the path of the disabled, they do not need to be insurmountable in the face of solid ability and intense determination.

## Personal Characteristics

These include a wide variety of factors, such as personality, maturity, appearance, and ability to communicate, many of which become evident at the interview. They can have a decisive impact on your admission chances at that time.

In summary, there are more than ten factors that, to varying degrees, play a role in the admission process. An honest assessment of yourself in terms of each of these factors will give you an insight into your own chances for admission.

## Bottom Line

Serious consideration should be given to the following suggestions to enhance your admission potential.

- *Nonacademic qualities*. Undoubtedly your GPA and MCAT scores are the critical and decisive factors in determining the outcome of your application process. There are, however, other qualitative issues that are of special concern to admissions committees. These include evidence that you have sensitivity for the needs of others, an appreciation of the complexity of patient care, as well as a sense of responsibility to face challenges in a mature manner and resolve them properly. It is your task to demonstrate that you have such qualities during the course of your interviews and in your personal statement.

- *Being a nonscience major*. In this situation, attractive science course grades and MCAT scores are especially essential in order to demonstrate your innate abilities in the sciences. If your academic record does not effectively demonstrate this, advanced science courses (such as cellular and/or molecular biology, genetics, biochemistry, etc.), and doing well in them, is essential to becoming a competitive candidate for admission.

- *Older applicants*. These individuals complete postbaccalaureate programs that are now widespread. (See Chapter 5.) They usually are judged on the same basis as traditional applicants, so they need suitably impressive academic credentials in order to be accepted. Older applicants need to convincingly demonstrate what specifically motivates them to change careers in order to enter the medical profession. A well-written personal statement is the key to achieving this goal.

- *Application enhancements*. The potential of your application will increase when you demonstrate that you have acquired some organizational and communication skills during the course of an activity not related to your college work. In addition, some service activity in a health field is important so as to develop an awareness of some of the issues associated with being a professional in this area.

- *Selling yourself*. The decisive element that frequently determines one's fate is the interview. Demonstrating that you are a mature, motivated, and committed individual is essential. You should aim to leave a clear impression that your career goal is realistic in terms of your intellect, personality, and character. Your argument relative to these three elements needs to be supported. This is usually evident from your academic record, as suggested by your transcript, what your faculty thinks of you, as reflected by recommendations, and by your personal statement as well as interview performance.

- *Maximize your efforts*. Work diligently and effectively to achieve the highest level of academic performance that you possibly can. At a *minimum*, your GPA should be 3.3–3.4 and your total MCAT scores should be 29–30. These numbers should still keep you in the running, but you should aim for more than borderline status.

- *Emphasize your strengths*. Both in your personal statement and during your interviews emphasize the fact (if true) that you have been able to manage a tough undergraduate curriculum and still have time for extracurricular activities. Prepare yourself adequately to respond to a wide range of questions at the interview to demonstrate that you have strong communication skills.

- *Don't procrastinate*. Submit your application in a timely fashion, namely, after thorough review of the completed form; send it off in early or mid-summer (June–July).

In summary, remember, that the admission process is a highly subjective one, as demonstrated by the fact that the same individual may gain several acceptances as well as several rejections. As with a social date, not every person will appeal to you, nor will you appeal to every person. Take the outcome in stride. Your job is to do your best and then hope for a favorable outcome.

# THE APPLICATION PROCESS

## Gearing up

Having come to the conclusion that medicine is an appropriate career for you, it is vital to become mentally charged up to face the potential changes in your lifestyle that may be necessary on the long road toward admission into medical school. It therefore, is necessary for you to:

- decide to remain calm, regardless of *any* problems that may arise. In other words, never panic, no matter what obstacles you come up against. By maintaining your composure, you will more easily be able to resolve the issues that may arise and find solutions to the problems that lie in your way.

- prepare yourself mentally by recognizing that you are facing a lengthy, stressful period in which you will, by necessity, be competing against other able applicants for a place in a freshman medical school class.

- carefully review all the potential issues that you can anticipate and plan how you might possibly respond to them in a constructive manner, in order to overcome any difficulties.

## How to Apply

### Traditional Application

There are currently two means of applying—directly to the school and indirectly through the American Medical College Application Service (AMCAS).

### Non-AMCAS Schools

The direct approach involves submitting a separate application to any school that is *not* a member of AMCAS. The application for each of these schools should be returned with a check covering the fee, which varies in amount from school to school. Table 8.1 in Chapter 8 gives the application fee for each of the non-AMCAS schools. The non-AMCAS schools requiring separate applications are

Baylor

Brown

*Texas A&M

*Texas—Galveston

*Texas—Houston

*Texas—San Antonio

*Texas—Southwest

*Texas Tech.

University of Missouri–Kansas

University of North Dakota

As is indicated by an asterisk (*), six non-AMCAS schools receive their applications through the University of Texas Medical System and Dental Application Center. For further information check the Web site *www.system.edu/tmdsas*.

Naturally, all Canadian medical schools do not participate in AMCAS. However, the three schools located in Ontario Province belong to the Ontario Medical School Application Service (OMSAS).

### AMCAS Schools

Most premedical students quite properly apply to a considerable number of medical schools. Originally it was necessary to apply to each institution individually, a time-consuming, costly, and cumbersome process. To expedite matters, the Section for Student Services of the American Association of Medical Colleges (AAMC) developed a booklet containing a lengthy standardized application form. Upon its completion, it had to be sent, along with relevant fees, to The American Medical Colleges Application Services (AMCAS), 2501 M Street, NW, Lobby 26, Washington, DC 20037, Phone: (202) 828-0600, mcas@aamc.org. The application, along with supporting transcript(s) and MCAT scores, was then duplicated and transmitted to all schools designated by the applicant. The cost to apply was determined by the number of applications submitted to AMCAS-linked schools. Currently, 115 out of 125 U.S. medical schools are affiliated with AMCAS.

The paper application system, while convenient, worked very efficiently for a long period of time. In the late 1990s AMCAS introduced an alternative electronic medical school application process. Starting in 2001, however, AMCAS mandated exclusive use of a Web-based application, hoping to be more efficient than the traditional format. Unfortunately, this new approach was plagued by serious difficulties. There were very lengthy delays in executing applications. This was especially frustrating for all concerned, since the Web-based application was designed to make the process smoother and quicker. Apparently AMCAS servers were unable to adequately cope with the high volume of incoming applications. Later, to relieve the congestion, computer servers were reconfigured.

The extraordinarily slow electronic application procedure induced an additional level of stress to an already tension-filled admission process. This situation forced some schools to revise their admission timetable, while others provided their own paper applications. As a result, a more reliable system will soon be available for applicants.

While completing your AMCAS application, consider the following suggestions:

1. Answer all questions carefully, accurately, and fully.

2. Use available space for comments judiciously.

3. Outline your motivation for applying to medical school (see page 3 and Appendix C, page 668).

4. Where clarification is required, such as a transfer to another school or a poor grade due to an illness, explain the circumstances appropriately.

5. Arrange to send your transcript(s) to AMCAS.

6. Request that letters of recommendation be directly mailed to all schools that receive your AMCAS application.

7. Make sure that letters of recommendation to AMCAS are identified by your personal AMCAS ID.

8. Use the AMCAS Transcript Request Form for submission of transcripts.

9. When applying to non-AMCAS schools (see Appendix B, page 660), submit individual school applications directly to their admissions offices.

10. For non-AMCAS schools, make sure that your transcript(s) and recommendations are sent to the admissions offices.

11. If browser-related problems occur while preparing your electronic AMCAS application, try to change from Internet Explorer to Netscape or vice versa.

12. You cannot simultaneously apply through AMCAS for both standard (MD) and combined medical/graduate (MD/PhD) degree programs at the same medical school; however, you can do so to different institutions.

13. After applying, if you wish to designate additional medical schools to receive your AMCAS application, it is necessary to resubmit your application.

14. Make sure to enter all official transcript grades in the application.

15. Determine if there is a grading system conversion applicable to your situation.

16. Enter an estimated end date for postsecondary experiences you are involved in at the time the application is being completed.

17. Repeated postsecondary experiences should be entered only once.

18. Check drop-down menu before making the choice of "other" to identify your race.

19. Make sure that your e-mail notifications are not blocked by filters used by some e-mail providers. Do this by turning the filter off or having a junk mail file.

20. It is essential that you keep a printed copy of your application for future reference in order to insure against loss due to an unforeseen computer crash.

## When to Apply

The earliest date when medical schools begin accepting applications varies; the exact dates for each school are indicated in Table 8.1. As a rule, your application should be submitted in July or August of the year preceding your planned enrollment. Naturally, the earlier your application is received, the earlier you will receive consideration. Thus, in the case of superior students, it may ensure an early acceptance that would reduce anxiety and make it unnecessary to apply to additional schools. Moreover, prolonged delay in applying means that you will be competing for a smaller number of openings since part of the class may be filled by the time your application is received. Deadlines for receipt of applications at each college are also listed in Table 8.1.

## Bottom Line

- AMCAS is a centralized application processing service for the first-year entering classes at participating U.S. medical schools.

- Most U.S. medical schools use AMCAS as the primary application.

- Applicants to the few U.S. medical schools that do not use AMCAS (see page 113), as well as advanced standing and transfer applicants, should contact the Admissions Offices for application instructions.

- Other relevant application services are

  Texas Medical and Dental Schools Application Service (TMDSAS)

  Ontario Medical School Application Service (OMSAS)

  American Association of Colleges Osteopathic Medicine Application Service (AACOMAS)

## Early Decision Program (EDP)

From the students' point of view, applying to medical school is both an expensive and an emotionally trying experience. From the medical schools' point of view, selection is both a time-consuming and laborious process. To reduce the burden somewhat for both parties, the procedures of early decision have been introduced and adopted by some schools. Thus, if you are anxious to attend a particular school and you feel that you have a good chance of gaining admission, you should submit your application before the early decision deadline (usually August 1) to the selected school (but to none other at this time). Once your supporting data have been received, an interview will be scheduled if desirable and a prompt decision will be sent to you (usually about October 1). If this decision is in the affirmative you are obligated to accept the offer and refrain from seeking admission elsewhere. If you are rejected, you can then go ahead and apply to as many schools as you wish. Only if you have a sincere interest in attending a particular school and only if you have a good chance of being accepted should you use the early decision approach.

Medical schools participating in the early decision plan are indicated in Table 8.1. It should be realized that schools offering this option will fill only a part of their freshman class by this means. The remainder of the places, which will probably be the bulk of the class, will be filled by students applying under the standard procedure.

## How Many Schools to Apply to

There are over 125 U.S. medical schools. Most of these will undoubtedly *not* be suitable for you to apply to because a very large number of schools offer places almost exclusively to their own state residents. This makes you eligible for admission only to schools in your home state as well as privately owned institutions nationwide. Many individuals, for a variety of personal reasons, are not willing or able to relocate very far from their existing residence. In addition, private schools are very costly and thus may be out of range, especially for those not willing to run up a large debt. Prestigious medical schools are inundated with very highly qualified applicants, making it extremely challenging for an average, solid applicant to secure a place. All of these factors significantly reduce the number of medical schools potentially available to you.

Making matters more difficult in this regard is the fact that the list of prospective schools will shrink further if you eliminate minority-run schools and institutions designed to develop a specially focused physician, such as primary care or research-oriented one. Nevertheless, your choices of prospective schools, while reduced, will still be adequate in number.

When selecting from the preliminary list you formulate, your approach should be to:

1. Apply to your state schools but only if you would seriously consider attending if accepted, no matter what the location. Thus, for example, not every New York City resident will apply to SUNY—Buffalo when there are state schools nearby (Stony Brook and Downstate).

2. Apply to schools where, for some reason, you can be considered equivalent to an in-state resident on the basis of an existing cooperative program (such as WICHE).

3. Using Table 8.1, identify which schools on your tentative application list accept students with a GPA and MCAT scores in your general range and also are affordable.

These three steps will help narrow down your list to those schools to which you have the best chance of being admitted. Once this prospective list is prepared, you may wish to take into consideration the other factors discussed in the next section to, if necessary, further narrow down your choices to a desirable number.

The actual number of schools you should apply to is suggested in Table 6.1; this table should merely serve as a general guide. You can apply to more or fewer schools, depending how comfortable you think you are with the choices you make.

Regarding whether to apply or not, which is relevant to a borderline student, the basic rule of thumb should be whether you believe that you have even somewhat of a chance to get in. If you do, then don't even hesitate to apply, even if your chances are remote. If you don't make it, you will never say in later life that had you applied you might have gotten in. Should you not get in, you still have a good number of options, such as reapplying or applying to an allopathic school or seeking entrance to a foreign medical school or an osteopathic school (see Chapters 15 and 16), or obtaining a doctorate in one of many health-associated professions. (See page 120 for more detailed advice.)

**Table 6.1**
**RELATIONSHIP OF ACADEMIC RECORD TO SUGGESTED NUMBER OF APPLICATIONS**

| Academic Record | Number of Applications |
|---|---|
| A– to A+ | 5–10 |
| B+ to A– | 10–15 |
| B to B+ | 15–20 |
| C to B | 20–30 |

## Where to Apply

The decision as to which schools to apply to is in part determined by the total number of applications you plan to file. The estimated national average for the past 20 years has remained 9–10 per applicant. The actual number you should send out is best determined by your financial means and a realistic evaluation of your chances for gaining acceptance. One of the financial considerations that should be taken into account is the cost for out-of-town interviews.

Table 6.1 offers a generalization regarding the number of applications that should be submitted in accordance with your academic record. The exact number of applications within each range should be determined by financial considerations, test scores, and possibilities for favorable interviews. A large volume of applications may be less important than selectivity as to which schools you should apply to since, in many cases, applications to some schools for some students are a waste of time, money, and effort.

Consider the following criteria when determining which schools to apply to.

- *School's track record.* Where have students from your undergraduate college been accepted in recent years?

- *Finances.* Which schools can you afford to attend? Determine what your financial means are and exactly how much you can pay for tuition and living expenses without overextending yourself excessively by borrowing too heavily.

- *Location.* Which schools are located in areas that meet your personal needs? Do you prefer a large metropolitan area or a smaller town environment?

- *Out-of-state schools.* If you are planning to apply to an out-of-state school, does the institution accept a significant number of nonresident students? Consider the possibility of attending a suitable school located further from home, even though it may not be the choice of your fellow students. This may enhance your chances.

- *Curriculum.* Determine whether the school's curriculum is amenable to your style of intellectual endeavor. Carefully evaluate it to determine if you find it most appealing, challenging, and stimulating. Review the school's performance in Chapter 9.

- *Mission.* A key piece of information that you should seek, is to uncover the school's mission. Does it focus on producing primary care physicians, clinicians, or research-oriented doctors? The school's literature and Web site may clue you in as to the type of physician the school aims to produce. School profiles are also useful.

- *Class size.* Regarding class size, the faculty-to-student ratio for the preclinical years is important, as well as whether there are adequate clerkships available for training during the clinical years. To get answers regarding these two issues, contact current medical students or alumni. Ask your advisor for suitable individuals that must be contacted.

ASSOCIATION OF AMERICAN MEDICAL COLLEGES

Section for Student Services
2450 N Street, N.W., Suite 201
Washington, D.C. 20037-1131
Telephone (202) 828-0600

**AMCAS** ®

Your AMCAS Application has been forwarded to the schools listed below, with the biographic and academic information and MCAT scores which appear on this Transmittal Notification (TN). Please check all items carefully and notify AMCAS in writing immediately of any discrepancies. In all correspondence with AMCAS or medical schools, be sure to indicate your complete name, cycle/file number, Social Security Number and telephone number.

11/04/03     Cycle: 000-NEW

To:     Alice Smith
        70 Poss Street.
        Brooklyn, N.Y. 11211

Soc Sec #: 105-47-5167
Cycle/File #: 096-25130
Entering Class: 2008

Phone: 718-768-6325
Leg Res:
    KINGS        NY

Self Desc: WHITE
Minority/Consider/Ethnic:     NO
Financial:     YES

Citizenship: UNIDENTIFIED
Visa Type: PERMANENT RESIDENT
Birthplace: WARSAW
    POLAND
**Birthdate: 05/07/83**    Age: 21    Sex: FEMALE
Num of Dep: 02

Fee Waiver:     NO
Military Service:     NO
Previous Med School:     YES

Early Decision:     NO
Advisor Information Release:     YES

| Colleges Attended | Major | Program | Degree | Degree Dates | Attended |
|---|---|---|---|---|---|
| NY UNIVERSITY | BIOLOGY | UNDERGR | BS | 06/05 | 02–05 |

| | BCPM | | AO | | Total | | MCAT Scores |
|---|---|---|---|---|---|---|---|
| | GPA | HOURS | GPA | HOURS | GPA | HOURS | Test Date(s) Oct. |
| | | | | | | | **Series Number** |
| FR | 3.00 | 19.0 | 3.70 | 15.0 | 3.31 | 34.0 | Verbal Reasoning 9 |
| SO | 3.68 | 11.0 | 3.50 | 15.0 | 3.58 | 26.0 | Physical Sciences 9 |
| JR | 3.58 | 16.0 | 2.70 | 4.0 | 2.40 | 20.0 | Writing Sample N |
| SR | | | | | | | Biological Sciences 10 |
| PBU | | | | | | | |
| CUG | 3.38 | 46.0 | 3.48 | 34.0 | 3.42 | 80.0 | |
| GRD | | | | | | | |

Supplementary Hours: 13.0
Pass/Fail-Pass     0.0
Pass/Fail-Fail     0.0
Advanced Placement     0.0
CLEP     0.0

Number of MCAT(S) Taken: 0
MCAT Date: 9/07

| Your application was Transmitted to: | Date of Application | Yr(s) Prev Applied |
|---|---|---|

| Code | School | | |
|---|---|---|---|
| 115 | CORNELL | 100102 | |
| 120 | ALBERT EINSTEIN | 100102 | |
| 136 | SUNY-BROOKLYN | 100102 | |
| 151 | NEW YORK MED | 100102 | |
| 801 | MOUNT SINAI | 100102 | |
| 805 | SUNY-STONYBROOK | 100102 | |

- *Teaching.* Be sure to become familiar with the teaching methods used at the schools you are considering. There currently are a variety of approaches being used, aside from the traditional lecture-laboratory sequence. These include problem-based learning, integrated teaching, and computer-assisted teaching/learning. The school's Web site, as well as its profile, should be able to clarify this issue.

- *Evaluation.* It is also important for you to learn what student performance evaluation methods are used. There are generally five different types used in medical schools: multiple-choice exams, oral exams, structured patient exams, computer-based simulation exams, and personal observation. Different types are used, depending on the course. Check the school literature regarding this issue. In addition, the national standardized tests, required by almost all medical schools, are the USMLE and the objective structured clinical examination (OSCE). You may wish to learn to what extent they are required for promotion and graduation.

- *Grading.* Another consideration of interest is the nature of the grading system employed by prospective medical schools. There are two basic systems currently in use: a numeric/letter or pass/fail. Some institutions use a combination of both grading systems, with the least significant courses usually employing the pass/fail standard. The pass/fail approach is currently favored by most medical schools since it serves to diminish the level of stress at examination time. It also encourages the student to focus on learning rather than on just achieving good grades. To facilitate the residency evaluation process, most schools currently are using a three-tier grading system: honors/pass/fail, which probably approximates the letter grades A, B-, F. This approach facilitates better differentiation between students when recommendations for residency appointments need to be prepared.

- *Faculty.* To judge the overall quality of the school's faculty is quite difficult. For prospective women medical students, it may be of interest to note that on average, 25% of preclinical and 30% of clinical faculty currently are women. The percentages at a school you are interested in may have some implications as to your comfort level at the institution. This information, obviously, should be taken in the context of the number of women enrolled in the school, which likely is the major consideration relevant to this entire issue.

- *Reputation.* A school's reputation can, to some degree, influence one's chances for securing a residency. How important this factor is depends on how competitive the specialty is. The Dean of Students at a medical school, upon request, may be prepared to inform you as to the school's residency placement for the last graduating class. This data will allow you to determine how many residency appointments of the school's graduates were secured at prestigious training institutions.

- *Attrition.* A final factor that might be of possible interest is the attrition rate at the school. Nationwide, it has been calculated that less than 3% fail to graduate for academic or other reasons. If you wish, you may inquire from the Dean of Students office about the attrition rate at his or her school. But based on national statistics, you can assume that once you gain acceptance and enroll in medical school, the odds are very much in your favor that you will in due course be awarded an M.D. degree.

After reviewing the above criteria, determine which of them are most significant for you. Obtain and take note of the data regarding the issues of concern to you, then make a determination of each school's suitability. Prepare a prioritized list of schools, based on the recommendations in Table 6.1 and use this list when filling out your AMCAS application.

## Advice to Borderline Applicants

Your GPA and MCAT scores, as discussed earlier, are the key factors impacting on your chances for admission to medical school; therefore, these two parameters should provide guidelines for future action.

- If you have potential acceptance-level credentials, namely a GPA of at least 3.5 and 9s and 10s on your MCAT, then you should definitely apply. This obviously assumes that you have such attributes as motivation, competence in science, and a desire to serve others.

- If you are a borderline applicant, having a GPA of 3.3 and 9s or less on your MCAT, then your admission chances are uncertain or precarious. Under these circumstances: (1) elect to apply to an increased number of medical schools (see Table 6.1); or (2) consider postponing applying until your academic record improves.

- If your science cumulative average is weak (less than 3.3), taking some advanced science courses and doing well (B+ or better), will improve your position. Your choice of courses clearly should be in an area where you have already demonstrated academic strength.

- If your MCAT scores are weak (9s or less), retaking the exam *may* be advisable. This is valid only if you and your advisor believe that the scores will definitely improve. This can be done preferably in the fall of your senior year (which allows the preceding summer for test preparation), or if necessary, in the spring of your senior year; then apply soon after graduation.

A borderline candidate should determine the following:

1. Is your essay impressive enough? Does it maximize your admission potential? Find this out by getting an opinion from your premedical advisor and/or an English professor, then make any necessary improvements.

2. How strong is your school's track record in getting people into medical school? Where have your school's applicants been most successful? Don't hesitate to contact your premedical office, which should have this information and be willing to provide it. This will clue you in as to where it is most worthwhile applying.

3. How supportive do you think your recommendations will be? Have you selected the most suitable faculty to write on your behalf? Talk to those who know you well and think highly of you. Explain your borderline situation regarding admission and ask them for as strong supporting letters as possible.

4. How adequate are your financial resources? Could you afford to apply to more schools than originally planned and, if necessary, in more than one academic year? Talk to those who are assisting you financially to see if this is feasible.

5. How strong are your interview skills? How well do you perform on mock interviews? Ask your interviewers for their frank criticism. Strive to improve your interview potential to an optimal level.

In the event you decide to defer applying, your time can best be spent, besides taking courses, for research work at a medical school. Where possible, this should be at one to which you plan to apply and stand a chance of getting in. An impressive recommendation from a faculty member can help facilitate admission at any medical school. The downside of this approach is that you will have to invest two years beyond college, one to do your research and a second to apply and await the result.

In summary, a borderline applicant can best determine the desirable course of action by judging how far away he or she is from the threshold for admission, as defined above. If you are relatively close and the other factors are positive, such as essay, recommendations, and interview skills, it may well be advisable to apply. This is especially true if you can afford, if necessary, to try again. Try to obtain impressive grades in your lower senior year. These should be sent off in January to all medical schools to which you have applied. If, however, you are a substantial distance from the borderline acceptance level, deferring applying may be the wiser alternative. Taking additional courses and/or securing a research position should improve your chances for admission. In any case, before selecting from the various options available, discuss this issue thoroughly with your premedical advisor. In addition, it may be worthwhile to consult an authoritative individual at the admissions office at a local medical school. This matter merits careful consideration before you finalize your future path.

## The Essay (See also Appendix C)

The AMCAS application is four pages long and the questions asked are straightforward. Detailed instructions are included.

Page 2 of the application is entitled "For Personal Comments" and is completely blank. It enables you to communicate directly with the admissions personnel who screen the applications and with those who evaluate the candidates. Your essay can thus be considered your brief or appeal for a place in the next freshman class. It affords you the opportunity to express yourself and to present your attributes in the most appealing manner possible, so the reader will want to get to know you personally by means of an interview.

One approach to drafting your essay can be to itemize all the information you wish to convey: biographical highlights, motivational factors behind your career choice, significant life experiences, and information about yourself or your past performance that needs elaboration or clarification. Having identified the key elements, you can next proceed to preparing a preliminary draft. The lead and concluding paragraphs probably deserve special attention since they will more likely be read during an initial scan of your essay. Once the draft is prepared, put it aside for a few days and then reread it and revise it as much as you feel is required. You may want to repeat this once again before your rough draft is completed.

You should next seek one or more outside reviewers to read and frankly criticize your essay. This may come from an able senior premed student, an English professor at your school, a young physician, or your premedical advisor. Since the essay is yours, you have the final decision of how much to revise your draft essay. You should realize that the more people you ask, the more pressure for revision there will be. Thus, a reasonable cutoff point is desirable; that is, when you are satisfied that your essay presents an honest image of you in the best possible light. When you reach that point, have your essay typed neatly and accurately and make sure it stays within the allotted one page.

There is no "ideal" essay; the samples of conventional and unconventional essays shown on pages 122 and 123 are designed only to give you an insight into what other premeds have written. If your essay "sells" you as a potential attractive candidate, you have done your job. Appendix C contains sample essays that will be very helpful.

## RECOMMENDATIONS

Letters of recommendation can have a significant impact if they describe you in realistic, qualitative terms (and when they rank you with respect to others applying from your class). When the letter writers discuss not your quantitative achievements (midterm and final or course grades), but you as a person (in terms of your innate potential, motivation, personality, reliability), the communication will be effective. If your recommendation profile makes you stand out as a potential quality medical student and physician, your admission chances will be significantly enhanced and the possibility of your being invited for an interview will be strengthened. If, on the other hand, your letters of recommendation are bland or noncommittal, your chances of getting an interview will not be helped.

## *Sample Conventional Essay*

During my freshman and sophomore years at University A, I worked as a physical therapy assistant on a voluntary, part-time basis at Medical Center B in Hometown. In the course of this experience, the most important conversation I had relevant to my career goal was with a nurse. I had observed that she was exceptionally intelligent, knowledgeable, and competent and I asked her why she had elected to become a nurse rather than a doctor. "A physician has to make a lifetime commitment to medicine; his profession must be his first priority. I am not prepared to have my profession dominate my life." Her response did not surprise me, it only served to reinforce my commitment to a profession in which I had become actively involved.

For the summer of 20-, while I could have continued my work in physical therapy, I chose to seek a position which I felt would provide a new perspective from which to view medicine. Upon returning to Bigtown, I began working at the Department of Radiology of Medical Center C. My activities were concentrated in the Special Procedures Division where one of my duties involved assisting the nurses to prepare the patient and the room for the scheduled test. I observed the procedures which usually were angiograms, venograms, or percutaneous nephrostomies. I was usually provided with a detailed explanation in the course of the procedure which was informative and educational. At the conclusion of the procedure, I listened to the radiologist read the X-rays and learned about the patient's problems and the appropriate treatments mandated. The staff, after getting to know me, encouraged my spending time with many of the apprehensive patients to try to alleviate some of their anxieties and to be generally supportive. In addition, for one hour each day, I attended classes with the interns where I learned basic human anatomy, how to interpret some of the nuances of complicated X-rays and listened to a discussion of some of the interesting cases that occurred each week. My experiences at Medical Center C were so stimulating that I immediately applied for placement for the following summer and was accepted.

In June 20-, I began to work as a research assistant for Dr. Teicher, a surgeon at Medical Center C. The research concerns the reliability of the criteria for the diagnosis of appendicitis. The justification for the research is the problematic nature of diagnoses as evidenced by the significant negative laparotomy rate. The aim of this study is to assess the feasibility of increasing the diagnostic accuracy. A large part of my activities involves using the hospital computer to retrieve, study, and evaluate appropriate patient charts in order to enlarge the statistical sample. My activities have not only made me more appreciative of the importance of medical research, but also it has shown me how some physicians combine their practice with clinical research.

After reading the article "The Ordeal: Life As a Medical Resident" in *The New York Times Magazine*, my understanding of the strong commitment a physician must make was strengthened. Unlike the nurse in Hometown, I have been impressed by the many doctors who lead rich and rewarding home lives as well as being totally dedicated to their profession.

Besides a sense of dedication, I am aware that appropriate academic ability is needed to meet the demands of medical school and postgraduate training. I elected to attend University A because it is an excellent institution of high education and I wanted to be on my own so as to develop the self-confidence necessary to manage my life. My high academic performance and my science MCAT scores confirm my ability to handle the anticipated demands of the basic medical sciences. In the light of both my clinical exposure and educational preparation, I feel confident that I will be prepared for the demands of medical education, training, and practice. I look forward to beginning this exciting and challenging adventure.

*Note:* Names and places in this and the following essay have been changed.

## Sample Unconventional Essay

Raindrops pelted my body as I absently stared at the small concentric circles formed from the fusion of a raindrop and a puddle. I loosely gripped the 14-foot fiberglass pole with my perspiring hands, and thought: the pole vault—decathlon—third event—second day—the bar set at a logically impossible height, as Mr. Spock would say. Pressure. Whatever the outcome, I would not deny myself the challenge. So I strode down the slick runway, planted the pole, and launched myself up and over the bar—and subsequently into the giant sponge of a pit that sucked me into its depths. Of course, a requirement after a successful vault is back flip in the pit, which I immediately performed to the delight of the roaring crowd—all 23 of them. Thus ends another chapter in THE LIFE AND TIMES OF JOE WHITE.

Now let us turn to a later chapter, Joe White: The Road to Becoming a Physician.

My ambition to become a physician arose from my desire to help people. But not to help people like a waiter or a mechanic helps people. I want to help people who truly require my services. The first thing that anyone must do in order to help another is to care. I believe this to be the most important quality of a physician. And I believe that I possess this quality. I do, however, realize that it is not always easy to care about someone—especially if he does not seem to care about himself. My experiences with many different types of people will be valuable when caring for patients. However, my motives are not all so unselfish. I have always been fascinated with the structure and functions of the body. My high school and college educations have given me a broad background from which to build. By becoming a physician I will be able to further pursue my inquiry into the functioning of the body.

The road to becoming a physician may be full of potholes, detours, and do not enters. The way is not easy. But, I do not know the meaning of the word "quit" and do not intend to look it up.

Now that I have explained my motivation, let me explain my commitment. When I arrived at Chatham College, I obtained employment in the Health Center as an assistant laboratory technician/phlebotomist, where I have been working ever since. This job has provided me the important experience of interacting with patients. Then the director of the Health Center requested that I join his Student Health Advisory Committee, which functions to inform the student body of various health issues.

To obtain more knowledge about physicians and the practice of medicine, I served as a volunteer in a cardiology department. From this experience I learned much (relatively speaking) about cardiology and realized that the life of the physician was not all roses.

My academic life has not been limited to books. I worked with Dr. Jim Pike of Chatham College on epilepsy research. I enjoyed this very much and found it to be an interesting and informative experience.

There was much more to my life than scholastics. I spent many a night with the love of my life—hockey. My club team was able to successfully compete against Division II and III teams. I also spent a good deal of time playing the gentleman's game of rugby.

Through my various activities I have encountered many different types of people. This fall I will be exposed to an entirely new environment. I will be taking a break from my regular science courses in order to study in Paris, where I hope to expand my cultural and intellectual horizons.

I hope that these excerpts from the book of my life have given you a little insight into me as a person. The next chapter is still in the planning stages, but after it is written I will be sure to send you a copy of Joe White: The Physician.

It is *your* responsibility to see that recommendations in your behalf are sent to the medical schools. You can strengthen the quality of your recommendations by making sure that your health professions advisor gets to know you and has a favorable impression of you. In addition, you will be called upon to submit faculty evaluations to the health professions committee or to send out separate letters of recommendation. It is clearly advantageous to ensure that these individuals really know you. This can best be achieved by asking appropriate questions during recitation periods, at personal conferences, or better still, in the course of doing a research or independent study project. All this requires appropriate initiative on your part, which can pay rewarding dividends at the time you apply to medical school.

Letters from prestigious professors, as reflected by their academic rank, are obviously more impressive and effective than those from teaching assistants or faculty instructors. It is not advisable to ask for a recommendation unless you are fairly confident that the individual knows you well enough and is known to follow through on such requests. Otherwise you may end up with a perfunctory recommendation and such a letter may even be late in coming. Therefore, you should tactfully ask the people from whom you are requesting letters if they feel that they are in a position to write about you in a manner that will help your admission chances.

It is also appropriate to arrange to have letters of recommendation sent in your behalf (to your school committee or directly to the medical schools) by a hospital staff member where you have worked (in a volunteer or paid capacity), or other employers, or by faculty members who have known you well as the result of working for them on a special project; these letters can supplement your committee's recommendation. Letters from clergy, family physicians, relatives, friends, or alumni (unless the latter know you exceedingly well) are not only ineffective but may be self-defeating. Such letters leave the clear impression that you have weak credentials that need such unsolicited outside support to merit attention.

In order to arrange that a committee recommendation be sent out in your behalf, your advisory office may require that you complete forms comparable to an AMCAS application and be interviewed by your premedical advisor and/or advisory committee. These proceedings can serve as a "trial run" in preparation for the actual application process. It is therefore advantageous for you to prepare, early in your upper junior semester, a short statement incorporating autobiographical highlights, an outline of your personal attributes, relevant information about your exposure to medicine, and a brief discussion of your motives for selecting a medical career. This statement should be given to professors from whom you have requested recommendations at the time you request them, in order to facilitate their task; it can also be used in completing forms requested by your committee and later by AMCAS.

## Bottom Line

*Premedical Advisor: Office Recommendations:* Bear in mind the following, regarding recommendations:

- Have your premedical office set up a file for holding your incoming letters of recommendation.
- Aim to secure by the end of your junior year letters from at least three science and two social science faculty and, if possible, two from project supervisors.
- Request letters from individuals as soon as the course has been completed so that their impression of you is fresh.
- Periodically check with the premedical office to determine if the letters you requested have been received.
- Provide stamped self-addressed envelopes to nonfaculty members who are writing on your behalf so as to expedite matters.

- To allow letter writers the option of freely expressing themselves, you should sign a waiver relinquishing your right of review.

- It is essential that you secure a letter of recommendation from your premedical advisor or committee. An evaluation from such a source carries special weight, and failure to receive one implies a strong caution signal about you.

- Provide an opportunity for those who will write on your behalf to get to know you relative to your intellectual potential, personal attributes, and character.

- Provide potential letter writers with a brief résumé of your background and achievements so they will have source material to use when preparing their letters.

*Faculty recommendations.* Faculty are more than teachers: they also serve as subject advisors. Getting them to know you is valuable both in the short and long run.

- If you feel you are not keeping up with the class, seek advice early on from the course professor to determine where the problem(s) lies.

- Prepare for your meeting with your professor so that you can present your problems in a clear and concise manner.

- Make an appointment to see your professor in advance and arrive on time.

- Try to be specific in describing a particular problem and indicate how you are attempting to resolve it.

- Professors who get to know you and with whom you develop a positive relationship may be good sources to provide recommendations for you at a later date.

- Remember, however, that in most cases, your premedical advisor should be your primary source of information and guidance.

# THE INTERVIEW

At the outset, it should be realized that the interview is not just a brief exchange between yourself and one or more representatives of the school that has requested your appearance. The interview should not be looked upon as a one-sided affair, but rather as an opportunity for a dialogue that has advantages for both the school and you.

The school uses the interview to determine

1. if your personal attributes are as appealing as your academic record (this goes, of course, for a student who is already academically acceptable), and if your personal attributes will enable you to overcome any deficiency that may appear.

2. if your personal attributes will place you in the overall acceptable range (if you are considered academically borderline).

3. if you are considered to have some obvious academic or physical deficiency, whether you have the personal attributes to overcome the deficiency.

4. if your combination of qualities will most likely enable you to succeed as a medical student, therefore meriting your interviewer's recommendation for acceptance to the school's admission committee.

5. if you possess the qualities that will enable you to fit in with the individual school's mission (such as primary care).

6. if the interviewer can entice you to enroll by means of a "soft" or "hard" sell in the event you are an exceptionally attractive applicant.

The interview will permit you to

1. have an opportunity to sell yourself by projecting as favorable an image as possible, and thus overcoming any deficiencies in your record.

2. familiarize yourself with the campus and with its facilities, as well as with members of its student body.

3. obtain firsthand answers to questions about the school that may not yet have been answered.

## Significance of the Interview

It has been previously noted that there are five primary criteria for admission to medical school. These are your nonscience GPA, science cumulative average, MCAT scores, letters of recommendation, and the interview. More than a decade ago *Academic Medicine,* the journal that focuses on medical educational issues, carried out a survey of U.S. medical schools to determine which of these five criteria ranks highest in importance. The result was that the criterion selected was the interview. It was chosen because they felt that by means of an interview the medical school could determine better than in any other way the noncognitive skills of an applicant. The interview also provides the possibility of obtaining the essential segments of information noted above.

The receipt of the letter requesting that you come for an interview clearly indicates that the medical school is seriously interested in you. The large volume of applications has meant that admissions officers have to be highly selective in granting interviews. Admissions officers have at their disposal only a limited number of interviewers, who are usually faculty members and whose time is obviously very valuable. Thus, obtaining an invitation to come for an interview means either that they wish to confirm a tentative decision that you are acceptable or they think that you deserve a chance to prove that you merit admission in spite of some possible weakness. The interviewer will endeavor to appraise such personal qualifications as responsiveness, a warmth of personality, poise, ability to communicate ideas clearly and concisely, and soundness of motivation.

In the interviewer's written report, these criteria will usually be touched upon.

1. *Physical appearance:* Grooming, bearing, and self-confident manner.

2. *Personality:* Friendliness, ability to establish rapport and charm, sense of humor.

3. *Communication skills:* Ability to express ideas clearly, fluently, and intelligently.

4. *Motivation:* Soundness of career choice, conviction of interests.

5. *Maturity:* Ability to undertake responsibility that the career entails.

6. *Interests:* What educational, social, and cultural interests do you have?

7. *Level of concern:* Do you have a genuine interest in people, their problems, and helping them solve them—empathy?

8. *Emotional stability:* Composure while under pressure.

9. *Intellectual potential:* Have you truly demonstrated superior intellectual abilities?

10. Overall subjective reaction of the interviewer to the applicant.

Evaluate yourself in terms of items 1 to 9 as honestly as possible and work to improve your weaknesses. By subjecting yourself to mock interviews by your peers, you can determine where your weaknesses are, and how well you are doing to overcome them. Allow your mock interviewers to be honest and candid (even if it hurts your feelings).

## Interview Format

The interview format can vary widely, although some types obviously predominate.

*Standard interview.* The most common format is a one-on-one scenario, in which you proceed from one interviewer to another. In some cases, only one interviewer is involved, but most others use two interviewers. On average, an interview takes three-quarters of an hour. The format used generally consists of the interviewer gathering information about the applicant's background as a premedical student and the nature of the applicant's interest in a medical career and what direct exposure he/she has had to the medical field. Interviewers may also ask some personal questions. You may be asked about your family, personal interests, and any issues that need clarification. Time is usually allotted for the applicant to ask any questions he/she may have. Applicants who impress the interviewer may be encouraged, in a subtle manner, to join the student body if accepted.

Most schools use an open interview approach. They provide their interviewers with basic information about a prospective interviewee taken from their file. This avoids rehashing information that is already available and allows for a more productive line of questioning. Such schools are not concerned about prejudicing the interviewer either way when he/she is exposed at the outset to the candidate's academic record.

*Unstructured interview.* There is variability as to the extent of information given to the interviewer about the applicant's background. As noted, some schools provide the basic information, and the interviewer fills in the details. Others provide interviewers with only the applicant's name and then assume that a dialogue will follow that will add to the information.

*Panel interviews.* A *small* number of schools use this format to save the interviewer time. The panel consists of a group of interviewers who will question the applicant. Students generally do not favor this approach for obvious reasons.

*Multiple-interviewee panels.* Only a *few* schools use this format. After including a routine interview, several applicants are brought together into a common site with faculty members. The faculty questions the applicants at random intensively. This can be an intimidating experience, and thus fortunately it is rarely used.

*Stress interviews.* This type of interview is not as common as in the past. It was aimed at seeing how the applicant would respond to being treated in a somewhat hostile manner. An indirect means of doing this may occur if there is a brief period of silence during the interview. The applicant feels uncomfortable, uncertain, and possibly bewildered. This is not a time for the applicant to reveal his/her understandable nervousness or insecurity. Rather, it is clearly an occasion to demonstrate self-assurance. While it is possible that a period of silence may be used to test self-confidence, such an incident may also result from some innocuous reason; in any case, one should not feel that it is intentionally directed for a negative purpose. Some interviewers may even be oblivious to this sort of situation, for they may be lost in thought.

## Bottom Line

- Medical schools interview only those applicants who are being seriously considered for admission.

- Interviews serve to evaluate an applicant's personal characteristics firsthand, so as to better judge prospective candidates for admission.

- Characteristics commonly assessed are motivation, maturity, interpersonal and communication skills, a sense of empathy, social behavior, and innate judgment.

- For most schools the results of the interview are the most important factor in determining the final selections from the acceptable pool of candidates.

- Remember that it is not only your formal interview performance, but also conduct throughout your entire time at the school that will be observed and may have an impact on the outcome.

- Check your e-mail regularly in the immediate days before your interview date to be certain that for some unforeseen reason, your appointment has not changed.

- See if you can obtain a copy of your interview schedule (by e-mail or fax). This may allow you to prepare to use any free time to visit nearby sites such as hospitals and clinics in addition to affording you the opportunity of anticipating and planning for your activities.

- Allow extra time in your departure schedule so that if the interview process runs late or you wish to explore some issues further, you will be able to do so.

- Be upbeat and positive in your facial appearance, even if things might have, at some point, not gone well. This may suggest that you can stand up to adversity and are an amiable person to have as a member of the next student body.

- When meeting other applicants, don't feel that you are less qualified by virtue of what you may hear about them. All applicants have strengths and flaws; the critical issue is to get the interviewer to recognize your assets. You should therefore manage to bring these factors to his/her attention in an appropriate manner, during the course of the interview.

## Preparation for the Interview

There are a number of steps that you can take that will help to prepare you for your interview.

1. Read the catalog of the school and become familiar with any special facilities or programs it has to offer.

2. Discuss with fellow applicants from your college the nature of their experiences at interviews at various schools.

3. Dress neatly and be properly groomed.

4. Arrive for the interview early, so that you locate the interview site with time to spare for an adjustment to your surroundings.

5. If your interviewer is late, do not indicate annoyance for being kept waiting. (He or she probably was delayed by something important.)

6. Act naturally and avoid looking nervous.

7. Answer the questions raised without trying to anticipate what you think the interviewer may wish to hear.

8. Avoid controversial subjects and don't raise sensitive issues.

9. Be prepared to explain your specific interest in the school you are visiting.

10. If you inadvertently flub a question, don't let it upset you for the rest of your interview.

11. Be well rested, alert, and honest. Do not exaggerate your scholastic achievements or extracurricular activities.

12. If you worked on a research (or other) project, be prepared to discuss it fluently and concisely.

13. If you have had exposure to medicine by working at a hospital, be prepared to discuss it if asked, or work it into the conversation in an appropriate manner.

14. If you can, find out the departmental affiliation of your interviewer in advance from an admissions office secretary, or by checking his or her name in the school catalog. You may then be able to raise a topic of special mutual interest (if being interviewed by a surgeon, you may wish to mention that you observed an appendectomy).

15. Do not hesitate to ask questions about the school and its program—or about the interviewer's activities (such as how much time does he or she have for research).

16. Talk to a classmate who has had an interview at the school. Get his or her

impressions of the school and interview. Remember that it is unlikely that you will get the same interviewer—but it is possible.

17. If the school is of special interest to you, you may wish to contact an alumnus in attendance or a recent graduate.

18. Bear in mind that the school is trying to get a sense of you as a person—to see what motivates you—to understand why you want to enter the health sciences, and to become convinced that you are a worthy, potential colleague.

The following steps will be of additional help in preparing for the interview:

19. Prepare rehearsed answers to the typical questions that may be asked at an interview. You can tape record your responses and hear how you sound.

20. See if you can appropriately fit or slip your rehearsed answers in during the interview in a manner that is casual and doesn't sound canned. The latter can be accomplished by pausing for a moment before answering a question that you are prepared for, acting as if you are preparing your answers.

21. Try to sell your favorable assets by fitting them into the interview (hospital work, research experience, community activities, research articles published, etc.). Know your strengths thoroughly.

22. Try to establish a rapport with the interviewer from the very outset. Walk in with a greeting, a smile on your face, and a firm handshake. On leaving, express your appreciation for the time the interviewer gave you.

23. Try to avoid, where possible, "yes" or "no" answers. Rather, give the pros and cons of the issue and your views in a brief and concise manner. Show that you can be analytical while at the same time avoid being overly talkative.

24. If you don't understand the question, ask the interviewer to clarify it.

25. Look directly at your interviewer; act relaxed; avoid squirming in your seat.

26. If you don't know an answer, admit it rather than guess wildly. If pressed for a reply, qualify it as being an "on the spur of the moment" judgment, that is open to change on further reflection.

27. Don't open up discussions on your own, such as on politics or religion. If asked, don't be defensive. Interviewers seek a sense of confidence even on controversial issues.

28. Avoid disparaging your school or specific instructors or students. It will not help make you look better.

29. If you have a video camera and VCR, tape yourself during a practice interview and see how you look and sound. Note if your body language conveys a positive or negative impression. Try to improve your performance in a second taping at a later session.

30. If you have serious problems handling interviews (such as being very shy or having a speech defect), seek professional help by taking a course that teaches interview skills.

## Travel Advice

The following travel tips can prove valuable in expediting your interview visit:

• Try to arrive early on your interview day, if possible, even the day before.

• If you are not going directly to the interview, dress comfortably for your flight.

• Carry with you high-energy snacks and a bottle of water (if permitted on the flight).

• Plan your trip to allow for any unforeseen delay that may arise.

- Promptly contact your travel agent in the event your flight is cancelled.
- Have an official flight schedule with you so that you will know flight options.
- Pack all your clothes and accessories in one piece of carry-on luggage.
- Board your flight early to secure storage space for your carry-on items.
- Choose a seat near the front for more rapid exit upon the plane's arrival.
- If you plan to sleep during the flight, get an inside seat to ensure comfort.
- For those planning to sleep, ear plugs and eye shades can prove helpful.
- For those who are not planning to sleep, an outside seat will allow more rapid exit.

## Keys to Success

The following tips summarize the major factors that can decisively influence the outcome of your interview:

### TIP 1   Be knowledgeable

When invited for an interview, be well informed about the school. To do this, study its catalog, talk to fellow students who already had an interview there, and, if possible, alumni of the school. Also you should review your application and refresh your memory as to what you wrote so that you are able to respond to any specific questions raised by its contents.

### TIP 2   Be on time

Do everything possible to be on time. Preferably you should be ahead of time, since this will allow you to become used to your new surroundings. Take a cell phone with you so that, if necessary, you can call the admissions office if you are unavoidably delayed. If your interviewer is late, take no notice, since undoubtedly it wasn't intentional.

### TIP 3   Be properly dressed

Make sure to dress appropriately. A conservative suit is appropriate for a man, while jeans or a sweater are likely to be self-defeating. Similarly, for women, a skirt suit or demure dress is acceptable, while an appropriate pantsuit is a suitable option. Avoid too much jewelry and makeup.

### TIP 4   Be honest

Obviously you cannot know in advance the questions that you will face; you can prepare for them as discussed below. It is in your best interest that you avoid any suggestion of being devious. If you cannot answer a question, simply say "I don't know," rather than trying to obfuscate an issue. If you have a legitimate reason for having done poorly in a critical major course (such as an illness at the time of the final exam), it is not appropriate to bring it to the interviewer's attention. Remember that for physicians, interviewing is a component of their daily work, so it is naïve to feel that you can proceed in any but a straightforward manner.

### TIP 5   Be a salesperson

Having been given an opportunity to impress the medical school that you are the type of student it is looking for, make the most of it. Determine the message you wish to convey, namely, "You should accept me because . . . ." Find an appropriate way and time to weave it into the conversation. If you are unable to fit it in unobtrusively during the course of the interview, do it at the very end by saying, "May I make a final comment, . . . that as a potential medical student in your school I could be an asset by virtue of my . . . ."

### TIP 6   Be different

You need to call attention to yourself by your accomplishments so that you stand out in the interviewer's mind. Even if you have noted them in your essay, do not hesitate to make the interviewer aware of your achievements. This may have involved being a member of a band, a school newspaper editor, an artistic achievement, a special job experience, a bicycle race winner, completing a long wilderness hike, and so on. What is desirable is that you demonstrate that you can undertake a project and see it through to a satisfactory conclusion. Schools seek individuals of diverse backgrounds and interests. By emphasizing your uniqueness, in a sense you are presenting yourself as an outstanding person.

### TIP 7  Be prepared

Aside from being ready to discuss answers to the sample questions outlined elsewhere in this chapter, you should be ready to cover the following subjects very commonly raised by interviewers, namely, (a) the motives encouraging you to pursue a medical career, (b) the personal qualities you possess that will enhance the quality of your medical practice, (c) the specific reasons for choosing the medical school at which you are being interviewed, and (d) the qualities you feel are essential for a physician to possess.

### TIP 8  Be knowledgeable

Medical ethics is a very common topic raised at interviews. You should therefore be prepared to discuss such subjects as patient privacy, the rights of the handicapped, organ donation, care for the elderly or mentally handicapped, determination of death, and the physician's responsibility for societal health.

### TIP 9  Be relaxed

While recognizing that an interview intrinsically is a stressful situation, especially when your future is at stake, a concerted effort should be made to at least outwardly act in a relaxed manner. It is essential that your body language not convey an underlying tenseness, even if it exists. Avoid fidgeting or nervous gestures, smile or laugh when appropriate, avoid tightening or loosening your facial expression, maintain eye contact with the interviewer when speaking. (See also the discussion on relaxation techniques below.)

### TIP 10 Be impressive

You need to extrude a degree of self-confidence, even if you are aware of a marked weakness, which you should be able to convincingly explain. Remember the fact that you have been granted an interview because the school does not consider your weakness to be a fatal flaw. You should make the most of your opportunity to present yourself as a very viable candidate, but do so without evincing a sense of arrogance.

## Relaxation Techniques

One needs to recognize that most applicants, even the best of them, will experience some anxiety prior to an interview; do not consider it unnatural if you also do so. The issue is to avoid an excessive amount of insecurity. You can mitigate stress-related feelings and generate confidence by both mental and physical means. For the former, it is essential that you adopt a positive and determined spirit, realizing that you are being interviewed because the school is only interested in you for a spot in the next freshman class. This can reinforce your confidence by reminding you of all the achievements in your past life's experiences. Physical ways for reducing anxiety include

- Taking a stroll around the block before entering the interview site (assuming time is available).
- Breathing in deeply, holding back for a number of seconds, and then exhaling for as long as possible. Repeat this exercise several times, each time lengthening the time you hold your breath and the exhalation stage. This exercise can be carried out even while in a room waiting for the interviewer to appear.

• Realize that a degree of anxiety is to be expected under the circumstances, but also that, if limited, it can have a positive effect, energizing you and thus enhancing your interview performance.

## Typical Interview Questions

Be prepared to answer some typical questions that frequently come up, some of which follow.

1. Why did you attend _____ College/University?
2. What are your extracurricular activities?
3. Why do you want to become a physician?
4. What books and newspapers do you read?
5. What do you do during the summer?
6. How will you finance your education?
7. What other schools have you applied to?
8. What do you plan to specialize in?
9. Why did you get a poor grade in _____?
10. Do you have any questions?
11. Which medical school is your first choice?
12. What kind of social life do you have?
13. Describe your schedule at _____ .
14. What were your favorite courses taken?
15. Did you participate in any special science projects in high school or college?
16. Will your religious convictions interfere with your studies or practice?
17. How did you arrive at your decision to become a physician?
18. What area of medicine do you wish to enter?
19. Describe a typical day in your life.
20. Do you feel you should have gone to a different college?
21. What do you do in your spare time?
22. Tell me about yourself and your family.
23. What do you think are the most pressing social problems?
24. Describe your study habits.
25. What are your hobbies?
26. What experiences led you to your career choice?
27. What are your plans for marriage and a family?
28. Why isn't _____ your first choice?
29. What are the characteristics of a good physician (or dentist)?
30. Why do you think you are better suited for admission than your classmates?
31. What is the status of the medical doctor in modern society?
32. What has been your most significant accomplishment to date?
33. If you had great willpower, how would you change yourself?
34. What are the characteristics of a mature person?
35. What can be determined about an applicant at an interview?

36. What books have you read recently?

37. Describe your research at _____ .

38. What is your opinion on _____ (major current event issues)?

39. What newspaper do you read and which columnist do you like the best?

40. How do you cope with frustrating situations?

41. What will you do if you are not accepted?

42. How do you rank among the preprofessional students at your school?

43. Have you ever worked with people, and if so in what capacity?

44. Who has had the greatest influence on your life?

45. What made you apply to our school?

46. What are your weaknesses?

47. Describe your exposure to medicine at _____ .

48. If you are accepted to more than one school, how will you decide which to attend?

49. How do you see yourself ten years from now?

50. Why did your grades go down in your _____ semester?

51. Why do you want to work with people who are ill?

52. How will you finance your education and yourself while you are a medical student?

53. At what point in your life did you decide to become a physician?

54. How do you know you will be happy if you become a physician?

55. Will the level of income affect your choice of a specialty, and do you think physicians are overpaid?

56. How do you feel about treating HIV-positive or AIDS patients?

57. What do you think about legalizing medically sanctioned euthanasia?

58. What is an HMO? Would you want to be employed by one as a physician?

59. Will the question of the likelihood of malpractice suits affect your choice of a specialty?

60. What makes you think you will be prepared for medical school by the time you graduate from college?

## Atypical Interview Questions

1. What is your favorite piece of music?

2. Do you know enough about hockey to compare the _____ and the _____ teams?

3. What would you do to improve the quality of life in large cities?

4. Describe the difference between lactose and glucose.

5. What movies did you see recently?

6. If you were to have a year off, what would you do with it?

7. What is your favorite form of entertainment?

8. What is your opinion of socialized medicine?

9. What do you feel are physicians' obligations to their patients?

10. How would you respond to a patient who you learn is terminally ill?

11. How do your parents feel about your career goals?

12. What are the characteristics of aromatic compounds?

13. Why do you think that life was based on the carbon atom?

14. What do you think about and how did you prepare for the MCAT?

15. Can you explain why your MCAT scores went up (down) when you took the test a second time?

16. Would you be willing to serve in an area where there is a physician shortage?

17. What subspecialty are you considering?

18. What message would you like me to convey to the admissions committee in your behalf?

19. What were your most favorite and least favorite courses in college?

20. What demands do you think medicine will make upon you?

21. How will marriage and having a family fit in with your career plans?

22. Have you been interviewed or accepted at any other school?

23. What are your thoughts about the expected physician surplus?

24. What are your views on abortion, gay rights, capital punishment, and animal experimentation?

25. What are your thoughts about the use of animals for medical research?

26. What do you feel should be the physician's role as far as abortion is concerned?

27. What are your opinions about the issue of universal health care?

28. How do you feel about the level of compensation of interns and residents (house staff)?

29. Do you feel an obligation to treat the indigent or uninsured patients?

30. What three words describe you best?

31. What do you do for recreation?

32. What do you think of the idea of closing some medical schools to limit the output of physicians and thus avoid a physician surplus?

33. Do you have a physician role model? If so, who and why do you perceive that person as a role model?

34. If you were an interviewer, what one question would you always ask an applicant?

You can improve your performance by preparing for it (as indicated in the preceding sections) and by learning from the mistakes you may have made at the interviews you have had. Thus, after each interview, evaluate your performance along the following lines.

1. Did I come across effectively?

2. Where did I flounder and become excessively talkative?

3. Did I keep my cool after a blunder?

4. Was there some basic information I should have known, but didn't?

5. Were my prepared responses effective?

6. Did I sell myself, especially my assets, adequately and effectively?

7. Did I establish a good rapport and behave in a well-mannered way?

8. Did I seem to show the appropriate interest in the school at which I was being interviewed?

9. Was I able to slip in information that I wanted the interviewer to know about me?

10. What would I have done differently?

With honest answers, you can then go on and prepare more effectively for the next interview. The results should be better. The first interview is usually the toughest. Try to schedule it with a school that is not your first choice, if this is at all possible.

## Questions You May Wish to Ask the Interviewer

Frequently, time is available for the applicant to ask the interviewer questions. The questions you ask will leave an impression on the interviewer. If you are asked, "Do you have any questions?" be prepared to respond appropriately.

The following questions should serve to favorably benefit the impression you leave:

1. To what extent is problem-based learning incorporated in the curriculum?

2. How successful have students been in their courses at your school?

3. Do you anticipate any changes in the curriculum in the next academic year?

4. Could you tell me about the advisory system that is available to students?

5. How would you describe the nature of the population seen in clinical training?

6. Do medical students serve on any of the school's committees?

7. Do students obtain assistance from the support staff during their rotations?

8. What, on average, is the dropout rate among the student body and its cause?

9. To what kinds of training sites are students assigned for their clerkships?

10. To what extent do students gain clinical exposure during the basic science years?

## Questions to Ask Medical Students

You should always allow time to meet any unexpected needs that may arise during the course of an interview visit. Some of this free time should be used to talk to medical students who, in spite of their busy schedule, may be willing to provide you with relevant information from a prospective schoolmate. Try to find adequate sources to form a reliable judgment.

Among the relevant questions to ask are

1. How available is housing and is it accessible to the school by foot?

2. How accessible is parking to the school and to clinical training sites?

3. How adequate are the library and computer facilities?

4. Is there a note-taking service available and how does it operate?

5. What extracurricular facilities are available?

6. How good is the socialization among the students themselves?

7. What is the on-call schedule like during your clinical rotations?

8. To what extent do students have interaction with clinical faculty?

9. Based on your experience, what do you like best and least about this school?

10. Are you, on the whole, satisfied that you decided to attend this medical school?

## Questions Not to Ask or Things Not to Do

Since your goal is to leave the most favorable impression possible on interviewers, some questions should not be asked of them, even if they are not unreasonable, since they may leave the wrong impression. These are, for example

1. Don't ask how much vacation is provided. (The information is available in the catalog.)

2. Don't inquire about competitors seeking admission. (The focus should be on enhancing your own chances.)

3. Don't reflect a negative outlook if you feel that things did not go right at a certain point. (Your impression may be wrong.)

4. Don't express negativity about other schools you have been invited to for interviews. (Indicate that you are evaluating the pluses and minuses of all these institutions, and you will judge what best meets your specific needs when you have received acceptances.)

5. Respond honestly to questions. (If you raise a suspicion of an untrue event and seek to be misleading, your career may be in jeopardy; while you wish to "sell yourself" to the interviewer, don't go beyond the limits of the truth in doing so. The consequences may be too severe.)

6. Avoid personal habits that give a negative impression about yourself such as chewing gum, smoking, or biting your nails. Even accepting an offer of coffee can be distracting when you wish to concentrate exclusively on the interview process.

## Bottom Line

- The interview is a major element in admission processes and it frequently is decisive as to success or failure in getting into medical school.

- There is much that you can do to harm your chances for success; the essential keys are being prepared as well as knowing your strengths and weaknesses.

- Gently seek to steer the interview in a direction that is in your favor. This can be done by responding to questions, bringing up the points you wish to emphasize in a way that benefits you most. This process needs to be done tactfully and subtly so as not to offend the interviewer.

- Avoid giving an impression of arrogance, even if all your credentials are "top-notch." While it is beneficial to convey an air of self-assurance, don't let your ego carry you too far.

- Become knowledgeable about the field of medicine, your own career goals, the mission of the school you will visit, something about the faculty, and appropriate answers to typical interview questions.

- It is most essential that you listen very intentionally to your interviewer's questions, especially those having a "why" or "what" component.

- If the question is unclear, rephrase it in your own words so that you know that you are responding to what has been asked.

- Do not become annoyed by any insensitive remarks made by an interviewer—you will leave a better impression if you always stay "cool." Part of doing so is by *not* interrupting the interviewer during an exchange. Listen to the interviewer and then respond calmly.

- Avoid providing needless or pointless conversation that merely is time consuming. If the interviewer has nothing further to say, ask your questions.

- Finally, but most importantly, it is essential that you list your resources (positive attributes and accomplishments) and find the appropriate means of effectively expressing them during the course of the interview. This will facilitate the interviewer's task of defining you on favorable terms, such as your being personable, enthusiastic, self-confident, and possessing good communication and analytical skills. This is your job and it is in your best interest to facilitate your interviewer's task by leaving a favorable impression.

# THE SELECTION PROCESS

Every medical school has an Office of Admissions. This office processes the voluminous paperwork associated with the admissions process and usually carries out the initial screening as discussed below. When student files are complete they are referred to the school's admissions committee. Medical school admissions committees have a complicated and difficult task. Selecting future medical students requires assessing diverse information about each applicant in order to make decisions that affect the lives and careers of applicants, the attainment of their schools' educational goals, and those of society as a whole. This information about every applicant includes family, ethnic, and geographic background, activities that may reflect motivation and career aspirations, letters of recommendation, personal statements, academic records, interviews, and MCAT scores.

The selection task is further complicated by the fact that medical schools vary with respect to their educational goals. Some are dedicated to educating primary care physicians and/or physicians for specific sites or regions; many are committed to care for underserved populations. Some seek to educate academic physicians, while others educate missionaries. Various educational missions motivate schools to select students with different characteristics deemed by individual schools to be vital for their specific missions. These attributes may be academic background, geographic origin, ethnic background, career motivations, and value systems.

As an autonomous institution, each medical school has its own selection process and admissions criteria (see profiles, Chapter 9). There is considerable procedural variability among schools and one scheme cannot be applicable for all. Even the makeup of admissions committees is not fixed, although 15 seem to be the average number of members, with representatives coming from the schools' basic and clinical science departments, each serving for terms of one to three years. Some schools have appointed students (usually seniors) to their admissions committee as voting or nonvoting members.

The basic selection process takes three steps. At each step some of the variable approaches are noted.

## Preliminary Screening

The first step is designed to narrow down the large pool of applications that a school receives to those who merit further serious consideration.

### Screening Personnel
After your application and supplementary supporting data (in whole or in part) have been received, your folder will be screened either by two admissions officers independently or by a subcommittee of the school's admissions committee.

### Screening Criteria
This is subject to variation and may include:
- Total GPA and MCAT percentile (with average GPA levels usually varying between 3.2 and 3.7 and MCAT levels between the 60th and the 80th percentiles).
- Total GPA, science GPA, nonscience GPA, and total MCAT scores.
- Quantitative data as well as letters of recommendation.
- Total application packet including letters of recommendation and application essay.

### *Supplementary Application*

Certain schools have designed their own supplementary applications containing questions that they require you to answer (such as, How do you see yourself ten years from now? What will medicine be like in the next century?) or that are optional (List the medical schools that you have applied to). Receipt of a supplementary application to be completed suggests that the school is interested in you. However, not all schools have supplementary applications and not getting one should not be interpreted as a lack of interest in you. You may also merely receive a postcard asking if you have ever been convicted of a felony.

If you receive a supplementary application, it is essential that you respond promptly. Your application for admission cannot move forward without the information they want. Once your supplementary application is received, as well as your letters of recommendation, the basis is available for determining if you should be invited for an interview, placed on a waiting list, or rejected.

## Interview

After you have been screened, your application will be rated to determine your eligibility for an interview. You may be invited for an interview promptly if your rating is high, relative to the established numerical standard; you may be placed on an interview-eligible list making it quite likely that you will be invited in due course; you may be placed on hold for further review; or you may be put on an ineligible list. The last classification may result in your receiving a rejection, which may or may not require full committee confirmation.

## Determination

After your interview, a report drafted by the interviewer will be placed in your file, which subsequently will be presented to the entire committee. It will then be discussed and rated, and depending on the rank it receives, an acceptance, hold, or rejection letter will follow.

In general, there are three areas of consideration that influence admissions committees when formulating their definitive decision as to acceptance, hold, or rejection. These are:

1. *Success potential.* Committees are aware that medical school is a demanding program and they want all students to succeed. They need to feel confident that to the best of their ability, this will likely happen with every applicant they accept. They formulate an initial judgment on the basis of the applicant's GPA, science com, and MCAT scores.

2. *Motivation and character.* The committee is anxious to enroll individuals who have an intense desire to achieve their professional goal and have the drive to do so. They therefore seek people who have done well in college while being active in various extracurricular activities. This serves to demonstrate their intense energy level, which bodes well for those undertaking medical studies. Similarly, they are impressed by those who have undertaken a challenge, applied their skills, and followed the project to successful conclusion. This information should be obtainable from your application and essay. In addition, your character is an important factor in the assessment process. Entering such a sensitive profession as medicine requires individuals of emotional stability, high ethical standards, and sound personal values. Information in this regard can be obtained from your letters of recommendation and interview evaluation report.

3. *Personal suitability.* Given the very large volume of qualified applicants, with more than two applicants for each place, an unbiased, but subjective dimension associated with admission undoubtedly exists. Committee members come with

their own vision of suitability for acceptance based on an idealized model that each of them has. This hypothetical image includes considerations such as the school's mission, the need for a level of balance among the sexes, incoming class desire to give disadvantaged students opportunities, a bias toward the undergraduate school where the applicant may have studied, and originally an inner feeling of the suitability of the individual for admission. Therefore, comments by your interviewer(s), especially if they are admissions committee members, and a variety of fortuitous circumstances, including the stage in the admissions cycle when when your application comes up for review, can decisively influence your chances.

## SELECTION FACTORS

Members of admissions committees are appointed by the medical school administration. These individuals serve for limited and varied periods of time, according to their commitments to teaching, practice, and possibly research. Each member obviously comes with his/her own subjective opinions; however, the members are all guided by the school's established general selection criteria, which remain in effect regardless of the composition of the admissions committee.

Admission criteria to medical school can be grouped into two categories according to their level of importance. These groups are

*Primary factors.* These are the decisive criteria that strongly influence committee members (whose order of importance is subjective, relative to individual committee members).

- GPA from undergraduate and any graduate schools
- Medical College Admission Test scores (and the number of times taken)
- Evaluation of medical school interviewer comments and conclusions
- Letters of recommendation from premedical committees/advisers and individual faculty members
- The extent of your motivation and commitment to a career in medicine as reflected by your volunteer medical or social service commitments
- Your choice of a college major and evidence of negative academic discrepancies.

*Secondary factors.* These are issues of less significance in the admission evaluation process.

- The degree of your knowledge of current major health care issues
- The depth of science coursework and the quality of your performance
- Level of extracurricular participation in college activities
- Extent of your civic activities in your community
- Reputation of the school you attended in providing quality premeds
- Compatibility of the applicant with the typical students attending the school

### Bottom Line

Regarding admissions committees and their operating procedures, it is useful to be aware of the following:

- Admissions Committees and admissions procedures vary among medical schools.
- The typical Admissions Committee consists of the Dean of Admissions, representatives from the basic and clinical science faculties, and in most cases at least one or more (voting or nonvoting) medical student(s). A small number of committees

may also include alumni, a physician-in-training (or resident), and an Admissions Office staff member as nonvoting members.

- Admissions Committees set their own criteria for acceptance and prioritize their importance. These criteria frequently differ between state-supported and private institutions.

- Admissions criteria for minority or underrepresented applicants differ from those of other applicants and vary from one institution to another.

- After screening your AMCAS application, a determination is made regarding whether you should be sent the school's supplementary application. If affirmed, this, plus payment of a fee, will enable your application to be processed further. Not being sent a supplementary form terminates further consideration of your application and is equivalent to rejection.

- A special subcommittee initially screens all incoming applications, and supplementary forms, to determine which candidates are most suitable as prospective interviewees. These individuals are usually placed into one of four categories: interview, hold for possible later interview, reinterview, and decline to interview (i.e., reject).

- After the interview has taken place, the entire committee will examine each applicant's completed portfolio. These usually include a completed AMCAS application, the secondary form, MCAT scores, letters of recommendation, and the interviewer(s)' evaluation(s). The committee will then be ready to make a definitive decision.

- All eligible members will vote on each applicant during each review cycle. Those with the highest number of votes above a cut-off point will receive a letter of acceptance. All other applicants will either be put on a waiting list or rejected, depending on how they are ranked in committee voting.

- During subsequent cycles, the committee will review new applicant portfolios as well as those who are on the waiting list.

- The admissions process continues until the class is filled and an adequate pool of qualified waiting list applicants is available to replace any accepted applicants who withdraw their names before the start of class.

# ACCEPTANCE

Attaining an acceptance to medical school, especially the one of your choice, is your goal (see letter on page 141). In responding to an acceptance, bear in mind that the Executive Council of the AAMC has approved a set of guidelines regarding acceptance. Among the recommendations are:

1. that an applicant should not have less than two weeks in which to reply to an offer;

2. that medical schools should not notify applicants of acceptance before November 15 of each admission cycle;

3. that by April 1 any applicant holding more than one acceptance for more than two weeks (and having received all necessary financial aid information) should choose the school the applicant wishes to attend and withdraw from all others;

4. that after June 1 a medical school seeking to enroll an applicant already known to be accepted elsewhere should advise the school of its intentions;

5. that an offer of acceptance does not constitute a moral obligation to matriculate at that school.

THE
GEORGE
WASHINGTON
UNIVERSITY
MEDICAL CENTER

*Office of Admissions*
*(202) 676-3506*

*School of Medicine and Health Sciences / 2300 Eye Street, NW / Washington, DC 20037*

February 11, 2005

Mr. Robert Brown
1234 56th Street
Belle City, MD 20000

Dear Mr. Brown:

On behalf of the George Washington University School of Medicine and
Health Sciences and the Committee on Admissions, I am pleased to
invite you to become a member of the First-year Class entering the
Doctor of Medicine degree program starting in the fall of 2005.

You are to be congratulated on your fine record: your academic and personal qualities as assessed by a multiplicity of factors led the Committee
on Admissions to believe that you will have a fine future here at George
Washington and in the community of physicians.

Please read the enclosed Notice of Acceptance carefully and return the
signed copy not later than the date noted. The original is enclosed for
your records. I suggest that you keep it for future reference. I particularly call your attention to the need to plan your future program at the
earliest possible date. Until your record is fully up to date, we cannot
certify you for matriculation.

We look forward with pleasure to welcoming you next fall.

Sincerely,

Rachele I. Klein, M.D.
Associate Dean for Student
   Affairs and Admissions

RIK/pac
Encl.

## Choosing Among the Acceptances

Naturally, if you have received only one acceptance, your course of action is restricted. If you receive multiple acceptances, then carefully consider each school so that you select the school that best meets your needs.

It is not in the best interest of the students or medical schools for an acceptee to hold on to more than one place at a time. The basic criteria in determining where to attend will be just as well known to the applicant at the time of notification of acceptance as a month or two later. If it is easy to make a choice, then it should be made promptly and a polite letter of withdrawal should be sent to the appropriate school(s). If, however, it is difficult to choose between schools, a choice should nevertheless be made rapidly (using the criteria noted below) rather than agonizing over the decision for a prolonged period. By making a decision with all deliberate speed, you can then concentrate on other important matters. At the same time, this will enable the medical school(s) you have withdrawn from to offer the place made vacant to others, perhaps even a student from your own school. (This is also the time to withdraw from schools you have not yet heard from, that you would not attend if accepted.)

In making your selection, you should bear in mind that, while all medical colleges in the country are acceptable, there are significant variations among them. Evaluate each school, keeping in mind the following criteria:

1. *Financial considerations.* You should evaluate tuition and living costs coupled with your financial means and offers of financial assistance. Bear in mind that expenses among medical schools vary markedly especially for state and out-of-state residents. Over the past decades costs have risen dramatically and they can be anticipated to continue to increase in the future years.

2. *Location.* Consider the geographic location as well as the proximity of the school to where you wish to live. The accepted state residency is usually a major consideration insofar as location is concerned. Other factors are the place where you wish to live and practice, location of family and friends, and specific attraction for the locale.

3. *Faculty-student relationships.* What are the opportunities for informal and personal assistance and guidance in academic and general problems? What cooperation is there with the staff and administration? What is the role of the students in various policy-making organs of the school?

4. *Teaching program.* How recently has the curriculum been updated? How are the innovations working out in practice? Do the senior faculty members actively participate in teaching? Is the faculty as a whole interested in teaching or is their primary concern research and clinical services?

5. *Student performance.* Determine the current attrition rate and what percentage is due to academic failure. Of interest also is the number of students asked to repeat an academic year; compare the figure with the national average.

6. *Facilities.* Familiarize yourself with the character of the basic science teaching laboratories and what up-to-date equipment is available. How many hospital beds are available for teaching purposes? What kinds of hospitals are used (private, city, or state)?

7. *Student body.* What is the class size? What is their morale, attitude, and enthusiasm for the school? Determine the nature of student competition—is it stimulating or cut-throat?

8. *Reputation.* Speak with recent graduates about the school's standing. Find out what percentage of the school's graduates are placed as interns in prestigious teaching hospitals.

9. *Grading systems*. There are two types of grading systems in use at medical schools: pass/fail and numerical letter grades. Schools may use both of these systems. There has been differing emphasis in grading systems over the course of time. Currently the three-grade system—honors/pass/fail—is most popular. It is equal to the A, C, and F of the letter grade system. Grades are important when applying for residencies.

10. *Curriculum/teaching methods*. It is significant to determine what teaching approach is taken by the faculty. Students who are self-directed learners will prefer problem-based learning or independent-study teaching methods, but significant numbers prefer the more formal lecture-laboratory arrangement.

There is a wide variation among schools as new teaching approaches have been employed within their curriculum. The curricula for U.S. and Canadian medical schools are outlined in Chapter 9. In some descriptions the teaching method employed may be indicated. Another source of information is the school catalog. In addition, during your interviews you should try to secure from students firsthand information on this subject. You can then judge your compatibility with the new approaches (described below), or whether straightforward lecture-lab is your preference.

Alternative teaching approaches are

*Problem-based learning*. This approach requires students to work through and solve problems, which are usually clinical, using sources that are at their disposal. Students must integrate the best available sciences and clinical knowledge, comparable to the way in which practicing physicians think. When carried out under faculty supervision, students thereby learn to master clinical practice skills. To strengthen this process, many schools supplement their problem-based learning approach with formal lectures.

*Small group sessions*. This approach is also aimed at enhancing student communication, abilities, teamwork, and learning skills. Considerable faculty input is needed to be meaningful. This approach is most commonly used in clinical teaching, since it is suited to situations where small numbers of students (and residents) are involved in providing patient care.

*Integrated teaching*. This is an approach aimed at integrated knowledge about body systems from the perspective of various disciplines. It presents considerable pedagogical challenges, so only a small component of the curriculum has employed this approach.

*Computer-assisted instruction*. This approach has gained popularity for use in one or more of the basic science courses in most schools. Many are using computer-based simulations to teach and evaluate student diagnostic or therapeutic decision-making skills. Most schools employ computer-based programs as study aids.

## Evaluation Methods

There are four evaluation methods used at medical schools. These testing methods include multiple-choice exams, computer-based structured patient exams, computer-based exams, and direct observation. The most critical multiple-choice exams are the USMLE and the OSCE. Performance on the first two components, Step 1 and Step 2, of the USMLE can determine promotion to the third year of medical school or graduation, respectively, depending on school policy. The information is also provided in the individual school descriptions.

There is no authoritative list of distinguished U.S. hospitals; however, an unranked sampling of 20 institutions that many would agree fall into this category is listed in Table 6.3. Other prestigious hospitals can undoubtedly be added to this list. By examining postgraduate training appointment lists, usually found in the back of medical school catalogs, one can see if any graduates were placed in these hospitals. Although the absence of placement need not be taken as reflecting negatively on a medical school's status, since the hospital sample is a very small one (20 out of 2,500), the presence of placed graduates should be considered a positive sign as to the quality of its education.

# RANKING OF MEDICAL SCHOOLS

There is a natural tendency to seek admission to the "best" medical school possible. The problem is identifying which medical schools are the best. It is quite possible that in reality the best school is the one that has accepted you and is also most suitable to *your own* special needs, rather than one whose only attraction is its distinguished reputation. Nevertheless, a list ranking medical schools can be useful; it may provide information that can help you decide which schools to apply to and which school to select in case of multiple acceptances.

In considering any ranking list, the following factors should be taken into consideration.

1. The ranking of a school should be only one of a number of factors affecting your final choice.

2. Formulating a ranking list that cannot be challenged is almost impossible, because there are so many variables to consider (size, curriculum, faculty, basic and clinical facilities, student services, supporting resources).

3. Since the educational philosophy of schools varies (for example, some are research oriented while others seek to train primary care physicians), one cannot objectively compare relative values. A judgment can be made only as to how well each meets its defined mission.

4. A list that ranks the schools in numerical order can be misleading, because it would suggest that a school ranked number 21 is superior to 22 when in reality the difference is based solely on minute statistical differences between the two, within the data collected.

5. A school's place on a list cannot be used as a definitive measure of the school's status, but merely serves as an estimate of its perceived reputation.

6. Any list should be considered in the context of your own observations, your advisor's opinion, and alumni comments.

Because of the absence of any recognized ranking list, an awareness of some of the most prestigious U.S. medical schools may prove helpful to prospective applicants and acceptees. To this end an *unranked* list of some of the top U.S. medical schools is provided in Table 6.2. This list correlates well with the list of the most prestigious hospitals (see Table 6.3) and the mean MCAT admission scores (see Chapter 8). Obviously, on such a short list, there may be omissions.

## Bottom Line

It is desirable to use the following criteria when selecting which medical school to attend, assuming that you have multiple choices. Much of the information needed to make an assessment should come from information acquired during the course of your interviews. Check your notes carefully.

- *Get the facts.* Find out as much as you can about each institution from its literature, Web site, and present and former students.

- *School mission.* Medical schools have different orientations as to the type of physician they seek to graduate. Determine from the school's literature its specific mission and see if it is compatible with your ultimate goal.

- *Size and cost.* Evaluate your preference for a small or large student body. Determine to what extent total costs, namely, tuition-related school expenditures as well as living expenses, will strain your finances. Evaluate whether your debt potential after four years of school will be acceptable.

- *Reputation.* Schools are known to have different cultures, with some considered to be competitive, high powered, or laid back. Determine what atmosphere you favor and see if it is comparable to that of the institution in question.

- *Curriculum/teaching methods.* There are various curricula in use at medical schools. Determine how recent the school in question reviews and updates its own curriculum. Determine if a problem-based approach is used as part of the educational methodology, an approach that is currently favored by many institutions. Determine to what extent computer-assisted instruction is used at the school.

- *Early clinical exposure.* Traditionally, students get their clinical exposure only near the beginning of the third year of medical school; the modern trend has now been to introduce clinical exposure early on. Determine when and to what extent this is done at the schools you are considering.

- *Clinical facilities.* The essence of learning medicine takes place at a clinical facility. There are various types of settings. Your interview notes may indicate if you can obtain diversified exposure, such as at respected tertiary-care teaching hospitals, community hospitals, long-term care facilities, and ambulatory care settings. Such exposure provides strong preparation for a successful medical career.

- *Outside learning experience.* Determine if the medical school offers a realistic option of taking electives at nonaffiliated domestic or foreign institutions.

- *Evaluating performance.* Consider whether you are comfortable with the major evaluation system in use at the institutions, be it letter grade or honors/pass/fail.

- *Faculty relationships.* Evaluate what you have heard about the general level of interaction between students and faculty. It is important to get a sense of how supportive faculty are to student academic needs.

- *Residency placement.* The Dean of Students Office is the best source to obtain information in the school's ability to place its graduates in strong postgraduate training programs. Of importance also is the range of specialties in which graduates have gained appointments.

- *Research.* Consider how significant a role research is for medical students at the school. It is important to learn about research opportunities offered to students in the form of electives or summer positions.

- *Social attributes.* How far is the school from your family's residence? Are the amenities that the community in which the school is located attractive to you? What is the general school environment?

- *Attrition rate.* While nationally the attrition rate is extremely low—about 3%—only one-third of these who left did so for academic reasons, thus, this issue need not be a source of concern to you. Your acceptance should be taken as a vote of confidence.

- *School ranking.* While it is comforting to feel you will attend a school that is ranked high, even if true, that does not necessarily mean that it is the best one for you. Your assessment of the aforementioned criteria should determine your choice.

In summary, accumulate all of the facts relevant to the schools you are considering and determine which of these are especially important, to you. By this time you should be able to ascertain, with a considerable degree of confidence, at which institution you will thrive. It is there that your personal success probably lies.

**Table 6.2**
**SOME OF THE MOST PRESTIGIOUS U.S. MEDICAL SCHOOLS**

**California**
  Stanford University
  University of California—Los Angeles
  University of California—San Diego
  University of California—San Francisco
**Connecticut**
  Yale University
**Illinois**
  University of Chicago
**Louisiana**
  Tulane University
**Maryland**
  Johns Hopkins University
**Massachusetts**
  Harvard University
**Michigan**
  University of Michigan
**Minnesota**
  University of Minnesota—Minneapolis

**Missouri**
  Washington University
**New York**
  Albert Einstein
  Columbia University
  Cornell University
  New York University
  University of Rochester
**North Carolina**
  Duke University
**Pennsylvania**
  University of Pennsylvania
**Tennessee**
  Vanderbilt University
**Texas**
  Baylor College of Medicine
  University of Texas—Dallas

**Table 6.3**
**SOME OF THE MOST PRESTIGIOUS U.S. HOSPITALS**

**California**
  Medical Center at University of California
    (San Francisco)
  University of California at Los Angeles—
    Center for Health Sciences
  Stanford University Medical Center
**Connecticut**
  Yale-New Haven Hospital
**Florida**
  Jackson Memorial Hospital
**Illinois**
  Northwestern University Medical Center
**Maryland**
  Johns Hopkins Hospital
**Massachusetts**
  Massachusetts General
  Brigham and Women's Hospital
**Michigan**
  University of Michigan Medical Center

**Minnesota**
  Mayo Medical Center
**Missouri**
  Barnes Hospital
**New York**
  Mount Sinai Hospital
  New York Hospital–Cornell Medical Center
  The Presbyterian Hospital
**North Carolina**
  Duke Medical Center
**Pennsylvania**
  Hospital of the University of Pennsylvania
  University Health Center (Pittsburgh)
**Tennessee**
  Vanderbilt University Medical Center
**Texas**
  Baylor College of Medicine Hospital
  University of Texas Health Sciences Center
    (Dallas)

# REJECTION

## Meaning of Rejection

When you apply to medical school you obviously risk the possibility of rejection. While such a response is a major setback, it need not necessarily mean that the rejection terminates your career prospects. To a considerable degree, gaining admission lies outside of your powers to control, since it is *in part* governed by factors over which you have no control. Such factors include the total applicant pool and the ratio of men, women, and minority applicants. For a long time white males felt assured that they would stand the best chance of being accepted. With a larger applicant pool and a substantial female segment, the situation has changed considerably to a much more competitive one. The impact of an increasing number of minority applicants, especially those of Asian background, has made admission even more unpredictable. The uncertainty surrounding the admission process is further demonstrated by the fact that even superior applicants who apply to a number of schools will usually find that they are accepted by some and rejected by others.

The aforementioned considerations point to the fact that if you are rejected, this should not be automatically equated with being unqualified or unfit to become a physician. As noted in detail below, careful, thorough, and objective analysis of your specific situation is needed to judge possible reasons for your rejection and to determine the most appropriate response.

Further complicating the interpretation of the meaning of rejection is the fact that many such applicants may possess the qualities that make a good physician, such as compassion, listening skills, excellent judgment, a keen sense of observation, the ability to solve problems independently, and a desire to help others. The fact is that because of the large volume of applicants and the pressure to quantify the admissions process, great weight is placed on GPA, science cumulative average, and MCAT scores. Weakness in any of these areas seriously compromises one's admission potential, even when the less quantifiable elements are present. Some applicants are able to overcome grade and test score deficiencies, but many others are not, and in spite of their potential must make alternative career plans. Some applicants may clearly not merit admission. It is the rejected borderline cases that deserve special review and analysis to determine the appropriate course of action.

## Responding to Rejection

Each year many thousands of applicants to medical school are rejected for one reason or another. If you unfortunately find yourself in this category, very careful examination of your future plans is needed.

Try to determine the reasons for your rejection. Weigh the advantages and disadvantages of the various alternatives that present themselves and then select a course of action that is *realistic*. Almost all rejected applicants fall into one of the six categories listed below:

1. Those who plan to reapply to U.S. medical schools the following year.

2. Those who plan to apply to foreign medical schools.

3. Those who will apply to enter a different health profession.

4. Those who will apply for admission to a graduate school to enter a career in teaching and research or in the basic medical sciences.

5. Those who plan a career in science education on the high school level or lower.

6. Those who will seek a nonscience-oriented career.

Seriously consider the reasons why you might have been rejected. If your academic record has been consistently poor, your SAT I and MCAT scores were low, and there were no genuine extenuating circumstances for your unimpressive performance, then you should consider either another health profession or a nonscience career. If your academic record is good, but for obvious reasons—physical or mental health—you were considered unsuitable for a medical career, consider another health career, a career in science education, or a nonscience program.

If you were a borderline candidate and you have had a consistently fair academic record at a recognized college, satisfactory test scores, a pleasant personality, and good motivation, and were probably rejected because of a very competitive admissions situation, then you should consider attending graduate school and studying for a career in teaching or research. If your test scores were low because of some unusual circumstances, you should consider retaking the examination and reapplying.

If you think that your record, as a whole, is not exceptional but does reveal the possibility of considerable capability as reflected by occasional high performance in some key courses, high test scores, and so forth, you should seriously consider reapplying to schools the following year. You should also consider applying to foreign schools or beginning a nonscience career. The schools you select to apply to the second time should be those that offer the best possibility of accepting you.

If you believe that you were rejected because of possible late applications, delay in receiving or loss of supporting data, poor selection of schools to which you applied, too few applications submitted, poor performance at the interview, or some similar explainable factor, you should consider reapplying, and think about other options open to you. A percentage of students who reapply do succeed; therefore, you should feel encouraged to do so.

A study was made of the career choices of 98 unsuccessful applicants to an entering medical class. Of that group of 57 men and 41 women, it was discovered that 52% entered occupations outside the health care field. Forty-eight percent ultimately entered health-related occupations, of which 10 men and 2 women became physicians, 7 became dentists, and 1 became an optometrist. These data indicate that a medical career is still possible if one is rejected initially and that a career in one of the many health care professions is a realistic alternative.

A later study, consistent with the aforementioned findings, showed that unsuccessful applicants to medical school tended to reapply at least once and that 51% of those employed after being rejected initially were engaged in health-related occupations (with laboratory technology being the leading choice, especially for women). This study also noted that of the respondents who were still students, 29% of the men and 20% of the women were in health-related training. The largest group among men was in dental school and among women was in the study of microbiology or other medical sciences. Women were found to be less likely than men to enter doctoral-level health science study. Careers in the new mid-level health fields such as physician's assistant and nurse practitioner attracted a few rejected premedical students. This conclusion is strongly supported by an even more recent study of a larger sampling of unaccepted applicants to the medical school class. It was found that a majority had reapplied and that 27% had gained entrance to either a U.S. or a foreign medical school. Of those still unaccepted, about half were studying or working in health-related fields or occupations. Because the state of medical school admissions is currently somewhat more competitive than it has been in the past, reapplying to U.S. schools is clearly a less attractive option than it has been in a very long time.

In any event, you should carefully consider the risks involved with medical study overseas before applying to such schools. See Chapter 15, "Foreign Medical Study" for the problems involved with transferring credits, obtaining American licenses, and other difficulties of foreign study. If you should decide to undertake an alternative health profession or graduate study, you must determine if you have sufficient motivation to do so. Without sufficient motivation, the chances for success are slim.

## Coping with Rejection

A second major facet of relevance to the unsuccessful applicant is the psychological impact of falling into this category.

Occupational choice results from a combination of conscious and subconscious elements involving both rational and emotional factors. The manner in which these factors are synthesized and compromised, leading to the ultimate career choice, is unclear. Although the making of a vocational choice is, for many individuals, a long-term process spanning the college years, this is not the case for most premedical students. It has been shown that about half of these had made a definite career decision before entrance to college and that 60% never changed their vocational choice once it was made.

Thus, as a group, premedical students are likely not only to enter college with a pre-determined career goal, but also to insulate themselves from situations perceived as threats to their decision, as well as from faculty members who may challenge the wisdom of their career choice. Moreover, they surround themselves with peers who share their values and reinforce their beliefs.

Many premeds have, therefore, at an early (and perhaps premature) stage fixed their vocational goal irrevocably and insulated themselves from any possibility of change. Consequently, such individuals are potentially incapable of anticipatory coping with rejection to medical school. If this situation comes to pass, the potential exists for a crisis due to a thwarted career goal. Moreover, it is believed that, since our society equates self-worth with success, a career crisis becomes equivalent to an identity crisis, which can produce serious negative psychological manifestations. At the initial stage these may be evident as a sense of shame, inadequacy, and guilt-producing feelings of isolation. This phase may be followed by a second stage characterized by denial, resentment, and anger. This leads to placing the blame for failure to attain admission on others rather than oneself. A third stage may follow in which depressive behavior, instead of the rational self-appraisal that is called for, becomes apparent. Lethargy and fantasizing, as well as anxiety, dominate the individual's personality.

It is obvious, then, that students who fail to gain admission are confronted with a major crisis that easily lends itself to perception as having been brought about by others or by uncontrollable factors. Most individuals eventually work through the trauma of rejection successfully, begin a realistic appraisal, and successfully adjust to their new situation. Some, however, remain in one of the reactive stages noted above and may need help to cope with the stress produced by the circumstances in which they find themselves.

For those unable to handle the impact of admission failure, counseling by the premedical advisor may prove beneficial. The advisor, if necessary with the help of other relevant and qualified personnel, should initially seek to help the individual maintain his or her sense of self-worth and thus facilitate working through the crisis. The individual next should be made to realize that the failure should be perceived as another of life's problems that needs resolving and can be resolved successfully. Finally, the advisor should offer assistance in developing a strategy for meeting this problem.

There are a significant number of rejected applicants who, after careful consideration, have concluded that neither reapplying to or enrolling in a foreign medical school is a viable option. Many of these individuals, due to their background and interests, can find a rewarding career in one of the health sciences other than medicine, both allopathic and osteopathic. Listed below are the addresses of the professional organizations for the fields of dentistry (see also Chapter 19), podiatry, optometry, pharmacy, and veterinary medicine. These organizations can provide detailed literature about their respective professions.

American Association of Colleges of Podiatric Medicine
1350 Piccard Drive, Suite 322
Rockville, MD 20850

Association of Schools and Colleges of Optometry
6110 Executive Boulevard
Rockville, MD 20852

American Association of Colleges of Pharmacy
1426 Prince Street
Alexandria, VA 22314

Association of American Veterinary Medical Colleges
1101 Vermont Avenue NW, Suite 710
Washington, DC 20005

## Keys to Bouncing Back

Rejection of any sort has its negative impact on an individual's personality. This is especially true when it applies to medical school admission; a serious blow to one's self-esteem and psychological composure may occur because a dream appears to have been shattered. The nature of the response to this crisis may determine whether the individual will ultimately succeed, so a critical choice must be made between passive acceptance or taking appropriate action. Obviously, the latter approach is logical and hence preferable.

In summary, you should thoroughly reevaluate your candidacy and carefully consider the following options:

1. *Perform a reality check.* At the outset, reassess your chances for admission. You should determine, preferably in consultation with your premedical advisor, if there is anything reasonable you can do to *significantly* enhance your admission potential. Determine what deficiencies exist and whether they can be remedied. A frank evaluation of the likelihood to succeed if you reapply should indicate the best course of action. The problem may not be intrinsic but merely structural; in other words, there may be no serious academic deficiencies, only a weakness in the quality of your essay or recommendations or interview performance. There may be a need for more convincing evidence of your commitment to medicine. This may have been reflected by your essay or a lack of adequate exposure to the profession. If so, an appropriate course of action should be self-evident.

2. *Improve your admission potential.* Merely reapplying with the same credentials will probably not improve your chances. This assumes that you applied to an adequate number of schools (see Table 6.1) and chose the right ones (see Chapter 9), as well as having handled your interviews competently. If so, determine how you can *meaningfully* enhance your status. You may take advanced courses in your senior year to improve your GPA, or repeat the MCAT if you are convinced that you could have done better. If you won some significant school awards or completed a special impressive project, this should be clearly stated in your new application. Obviously, the second time around, you must provide the admissions committees with a valid reason to take a fresh look at your case. Additionally, try to identify schools that you may have overlooked and would be receptive to your case with an improved application.

3. *Trying again.* If you decide to reapply, you should do your utmost to maximally enhance your chances. Carefully review your list of schools and select those to which you realistically stand the best chance of getting in. Consider applying to osteopathic medical schools (see Chapter 16). Intrinsic defects can be remedied by taking advanced courses or by taking the MCAT or doing research at a medical school. Such steps can make a difference and may well "push you over the bar" (see discussion on Advice to Borderline Applicants, page 120).

4. *Finding success elsewhere.* Should you and your advisor conclude that your rejection is irreversible, this certainly is not the end of a meaningful future career. Your skills, intellect, and desire for service can be expressed through other health care careers. Explore such viable options as dentistry (see Chapter 19), podiatry, and physician assistant. These professions are comparable in many aspects to medicine, and provide satisfaction, status, and substantial remuneration. Therefore, they have proven to be suitable careers for many whose initial option could not be realized.

5. *Doing it the hard way.* Should you find none of the aforementioned options appealing, and you are absolutely determined to become a physician, there is another alternative. This is to enroll in a foreign medical school (see Chapter 15). During the period of 1950 to 1970, this option usually meant going to Europe, but over the past several decades, this has involved attending an offshore medical school in the Caribbean or Mexico. You need to be extremely cautious, if proceeding along this tract, since there are potential serious obstacles along the road. These include the lack of accreditation comparable to U.S. or Canadian medical schools, the need to secure acceptable clinical clerkship experience in America, and the need to pass appropriate qualifying exams in order to obtain a residency appointment. Graduating from a foreign medical school can be done if you are highly motivated, can financially afford it, and pick the right school. Speak to individuals who currently are students at any of these institutions, and to recent graduates of these for-profit medical schools. It is essential to get the lowdown before you decide.

# SPECIAL EDUCATIONAL PROGRAMS

The programs discussed below will be of special interest to those seeking admission to only one specific school, minority students, high school students anxious to complete the college-medical school sequence earlier, those interested in becoming physician-scientists, and those seeking a career in primary care.

1. **Early Decision Program (EDP)** — see page 115.
2. **Flexible Curriculum Programs**
3. **Integrated Degree Programs**
4. **Combined Programs**—see page 154.
5. **Interdisciplinary Programs**
6. **Primary Care Training Programs**

## Flexible Curriculum Programs

A few schools offer some minority students the possibility of completing the required courses at a slower pace (usually five years). Such students must meet regularly with faculty advisors to demonstrate their progress and they must pass the standard comprehensive examinations for promotion and graduation.

## Integrated Degree Programs: BA-MD or BS-MD

These programs permit selected students to participate in combined undergraduate college and medical school curricula thus enabling them to obtain the MD degree in six or eight years from the time they graduate from high school. In such cases, individual students can obtain their baccalaureate degrees while enrolled in medical school. You must realize that the advantage is balanced off by the fact that in these programs you are committed to attend one specific medical school that is linked to the undergraduate institution, and you are locked into a medical career at an early stage in life. Thus, students who find these two significant limitations acceptable, and who have excelled academically, are exceptionally mature, socially adjusted, and able to communicate well, should carefully investigate integrated programs in depth. Consultation with advisors in high school and college as well as with medical school admissions personnel is highly recommended, as is securing adequate exposure to medicine at a medical facility. Beginning the medical phase of these dual programs is obviously important in order to have a successful record as an undergraduate.

The following list includes schools presently offering such programs:

**Alabama**
University of South Alabama College of Medicine

**California**
University of California at Riverside with UCLA School of Medicine
University of Southern California with School of Medicine

**Connecticut**
University of Connecticut School of Medicine

**District of Columbia**
Howard University with George Washington University School of Medicine

**Florida**
University of Florida
University of Miami School of Medicine

**Illinois**
Illinois Institute of Technology with Chicago Medical School
Northwestern University
University of Illinois at Chicago

**Massachusetts**
Boston University

**Michigan**
Michigan State University College of Human Medicine
University of Michigan

**Missouri**
Drury College with St. Louis University College of Human Medicine.
Drury College with University of Missouri—Columbia School of Medicine
Rockhurst University with St. Louis College of Human Medicine
Southeast Missouri State University with University of Missouri—Columbia
Truman State University with University of Missouri—Columbia School of Medicine
University of Missouri—Columbia School of Medicine
University of Missouri—Kansas City School of Medicine

**New Jersey**
College of New Jersey with New Jersey Medical School
Drew University with New Jersey Medical School

Montclair State University with New Jersey Medical School
New Jersey Institute of Technology
New Jersey Medical School
Robert Wood Johnson Medical School
Rutgers University with Robert Wood Johnson Medical School

**New York**
Marist College with New York College of Osteopathic Medicine
New York University
Rensselaer Polytechnical Institute with Albany Medical College
Siena College and Albany Medical College
Sophie Davis School of Biomedical Education—CUNY with Mount Sinai School of
    Medicine
SUNY Downstate Medical Center, Brooklyn College
SUNY Genesco with New York College of Osteopathic Medicine
SUNY New Paltz with New York College of Osteopathic Medicine
SUNY at Stony Brook School of Medicine
SUNY Syracuse College of Medicine
SUNY Upstate Medical University, Binghamton University
Union College with Albany Medical College
University of Rochester School of Medical and Dentistry

**Ohio**
Case Western Reserve University
Miami University of Ohio with University of Cincinnati College of Medicine
Northeastern Ohio Universities College of Medicine
Ohio State University College of Medicine
University of Akron with Northwestern Ohio University College of Medicine
University of Cincinnati College of Medicine
Xavier University with University of Cincinnati College of Medicine
Youngstown State University with Northeastern Ohio University College of Medicine

**Pennsylvania**
Duquesne University with Temple University School of Medicine
Jefferson Medical College
Lehigh University with Drexel University College of Medicine
Penn State University with Jefferson Medical College
Rosemont College with Drexel University College of Medicine
Villanova University with Drexel University College of Medicine
Widener University with Temple University School of Medicine
Wilkes University with Drexel University College of Medicine

**Rhode Island**
Brown Medical School

**Tennessee**
East Tennessee State University
Fisk University with Meharry Medical College

**Texas**
Baylor University—Waco with Baylor College of Medicine
Rice University with Baylor College of Medicine
Texas A&M University College of Medicine
University of Houston with Baylor College of Medicine
University of North Texas Health Science Center
University of Texas—Panam with Baylor College of Medicine

**Virginia**
Eastern Virginia Medical School
Old Dominion University with Eastern Virginia Medical School
Virginia Commonwealth University

**Wisconsin**
University of Wisconsin Medical School

## Bottom Line

- Integrated programs are designed for outstanding high school students who have firmly concluded that medicine should be their career.

- Integrated programs are designed for those who aim to reduce the lengthy educational process as well as to be accepted early to medical school.

- Only a tiny fraction (well under 5%) of freshman medical students are enrolled in medical schools by means of integrated programs.

- Program enrollees are awarded Bachelor of Arts or Sciences and Medical Doctor degrees upon satisfactory completion of prescribed studies at the affiliated undergraduate medical school unit.

- Eligible applicants for these programs are senior high school through second-year college students.

- Premed required courses must be completed at the specific undergraduate school affiliates of the medical schools that offer integrated programs. Obviously, the same is true for one's medical studies.

- If the student demonstrates the program's required level of performance as an undergraduate, he or she basically automatically is eligible to continue studies at the affiliated medical school.

- Some, but not all, programs require students to take the MCAT prior to finalizing their acceptance into medical school.

- Each program has its requirements and these should be carefully evaluated before a commitment is made.

- Being in an integrated program early on may facilitate a student's adjustment to medical school as well as reduce the stress generated by the regular application program.

- Being enrolled in an integrated program, however, commits you, possibly prematurely, to a medical career.

- If you are not accepted into the medical school phase of the integrated program, you still have an option of applying to any number of these schools like any regular applicant.

## Combined Programs: MD-MS, MD-PhD

These programs permit combined study for an MS or PhD degree in basic medical science, along with study for the MD degree. Average time for these programs ranges from six to seven years. A special *Medical Scientist Training Program* (MSTP) sponsored by the National Institutes of Health offers annual stipends and full tuition coverage for students accepted into the program at the schools offering it, listed below.

Albert Einstein College of Medicine
Baylor College of Medicine
Case Western Reserve University
Chicago-Pritzker

Columbia University
Cornell University
Duke University
Emory University
Harvard Medical School
Johns Hopkins University
Mount Sinai School of Medicine
New York University
Northwestern University
Pennsylvania State University
Stanford University
SUNY at Stonybrook Health Sciences Center
Tufts University
University of Alabama
University of California—Los Angeles
University of California—San Diego
University of California—San Francisco
University of Colorado
University of Iowa
University of Michigan
University of Minnesota
University of Pennsylvania
University of Rochester
University of Texas, Dallas
University of Virginia
University of Washington
Vanderbilt University
Washington University
Yale University

Currently more than 30 medical schools receive funding and about 75 more launched MD-PhD programs on their own. All told, about 2,500 students are enrolled in such programs. The MSTP was inaugurated by the National Institute of Health (NIH) more than 30 years ago and it has supplied the nation with a significant number of its physician-scientists. Many program graduates have succeeded in securing senior administrative research appointments where they have gained access to investigative grants, laboratory staffs, and other benefits that have furthered their careers. Some have become Nobel laureates. In spite of the seven-to-ten-year length of MD-PhD programs, schools report that the program is as popular with prospective students as ever.

The changes taking place in the health care system have raised questions about the future of the program. This is because research funds are beginning to dry up due to the cutback in funding by the government and in reimbursement by the managed care system. With reduced income for academic medical centers, they have less funds to support in-house research. There has been criticism by some that combined MD-PhD programs are no longer necessary. They argue that these programs emphasize the basic rather than clinical disciplines and that the physician can perform research, as many do, without the PhD component.

The majority of graduates of combined programs ultimately end up with academic careers, being engaged in research, teaching, and perhaps some limited clinical duties. These individuals have met the goals of the original NIH concept. There still is very strong support for the MD-PhD program within the academic community as being a vital approach in generating physician-scientists.

In reaction to the existing climate, there appears to be a tendency to readjust the ratio of activities of MD-PhD candidates, with increased clinical responsibilities delegated to them. One program mandates a full month of medical work on the wards before even entering the lab. Others require a more equitable sharing of time between clinical and research work. The combined program candidates generally respond positively to this change, even when their research is far removed from patient care.

One of the negative side effects of increasing the clinical obligations of combined-degree candidates at the expense of research is that it will inevitably slow down lab work and thus lengthen the PhD phase of the program. This will further strengthen the voice of critics who claim that the program already takes up too much of the candidate's career development segment.

Besides usually interrupting the candidate's medical education with a three- to five-year research interlude, an additional three to five years of specialty (residency) training usually takes place after receiving the dual degrees. This brings the education-training phase to a minimum of 10 years and maybe more if a postdoctoral fellowship is elected (which can in extreme situations almost double the training time). Critics of the length of the program suggest that medical students interested in research have other options, such as taking a research elective during the school year, spending a summer or even taking off an entire year for research, or doing it on a postdoctorate (MD) level. While these options are feasible, they can't provide the solid background and training that is essential for physician-scientists.

A second major issue raised by the MD-PhD program is the disruption caused by the research phase right in the middle of medical studies. Students find themselves removed from their class (and classmates), where the social environment is support-ive, and they are transferred into the relative isolation of the laboratory. Having to transfer back and forth between two radically different academic cultures—medical student, graduate student, then medical student again—can be destabilizing. The med-ical training is in the context of a hierarchical system, while that of graduate research is basically egalitarian. In response, some schools are allowing candidates greater flexibility in planning their program. Thus, in some cases candidates may start their research immediately or after one year of medical school, or complete either one of the degrees first, or pursue a personalized schedule. Nevertheless, there are, by the program's very nature, built-in social disadvantages that are unavoidable in a com-bined-degree program.

Critics of the MSTP do not deny its attractiveness in providing candidates with full funding and making them potentially very marketable. They argue that MDs can and do learn how to do sophisticated research, although the start-up time may be longer. With the dual-degree program perhaps being subjected to fiscal pressure, future candidates can anticipate a lower threshold of support.

## Interdisciplinary Programs

This arrangement permits a combination medical degree program with a degree in another field such as engineering, statistics, law, physics, chemistry, administration, dentistry, or agriculture. Schools offering such programs are identified in the special features section of their profiles in Chapter 9.

The vast majority of dual degree programs are obviously linked with the biomedical sciences. There are a small number of prospective physician-scholars who set their goal to secure a doctorate in one of the humanities of social sciences. For such individuals, there are a very limited number of formal programs available. The biggest is probably the Illinois Medical Scholars program at the University of Illinois College of Medicine at Urbana-Champaign. It offers PhDs not only in the biomedical and physical sciences but also in subjects ranging from anthropology to philosophy. Similarly, the program in Medicine, Arts, and Social Sciences at the University of Chicago attracts medical stu-dents from around the country who pursue PhD's in a wide range of subjects. A third program of note is the Clinical Scholars program at the University of Michigan.

The most popular of the nonscience dual programs, relatively speaking, is the MD-JD program. There are presently at least six medical schools that offer opportunities for interested students who wish to secure a law degree along with an MD. These schools include Chicago-Pritzker, Duke, University of Pennsylvania, University of Illinois Urbana–Champaign, and Yale. Many graduates with this dual degree enter the field of medical malpractice or health policy work. Finally, it may be noted, a master's degree in Public Health is offered by Tufts University School of Medicine.

## Primary Care Training Programs

You may be interested in specializing in primary care after graduation from medical school; there are a number of schools whose aim is to train specialists in this area. Shown below are a list of medical schools from whose recent graduating classes more than 60% entered primary care residencies.

> Brown University
> Case Western Reserve University
> East Tennessee State University
> Meharry Medical College
> Mercer University
> Michigan State University
> Morehouse School of Medicine
> Robert Wood Johnson Medical School
> University of Arkansas
> University of Hawaii
> University of Illinois—Rockford
> University of Kansas
> University of Missouri—Kansas City
> University of Nebraska
> University of New Mexico
> University of South Alabama
> University of Washington
> Wright State University

It should be noted that a number of these schools have developed a special program in order to encourage students to enter primary care (family practice or internal medicine). It combines the last year of medical school with the first year of postgraduate training thus accelerating the entire education process.

## Medical Schools Stressing Research

While research is conducted at all medical schools, some emphasize its value more in their curriculum. Should you have a strong research interest, you may want to consider these schools when formulating a list of where you should apply.

> Brown University
> Case Western Reserve University
> Columbia Physicians and Surgeons
> Duke University
> Emory University
> Harvard University
> Indiana University
> Johns Hopkins University
> Michigan State University
> New York University
> Northwestern University
> Ohio State University
> Pennsylvania State University

Stanford University
Tulane University
University of Arizona
University of California-Davis
University of California-San Diego
University of Chicago, Pritzker
University of Florida
University of Kansas

## CANADIAN MEDICAL SCHOOLS

There are 16 Canadian medical schools. They are accredited jointly by the CACMS and LCME; therefore, these schools provide their students with assured high-quality medical education. They have admissions policies and procedures similar to U.S. medical schools. However, except for McGill University, Canadian schools admit very few U.S. applicants.

The basic premedical science courses plus English are usually one requirement for admission. Because the educational system in Canada differs from the United States, the prerequisite educational level requirement varies with different schools. In addition, two schools have a three-year program and three require fluency in French.

Additional information about Canadian schools can be secured from the Association of Canadian Medical Colleges, Suite 120, 151 Slater Street, Ottawa, Canada K1P 5N1. It should be noted that the five medical schools of Ontario province belong to a common application service and that applications to them should thus be directed to OMSAS, Ontario Universities' Application Center, P.O. Box 1328, 650 Woodlawn Road West, Guelph, Ontario, Canada N1H 7P4.

## THE ADMISSION PROCESS: TIMETABLE

Based on what you have read up to this point, you can see that the admission process in reality begins when you start to think you might want to become a physician. It is a complex and prolonged ordeal that all students must pass through. Doing it right is critical to success. Deadlines need to be met and careful thought and preparation is imperative. It is also a costly process. It is to your advantage to be as well informed as possible. Sources of information, aside from this book, are your advisor, upper-class students, admissions personnel, and alumni.

Tracking Table 1 (page 705) provides you with a checklist of your activities that extend from the time you enter college until you complete the process. You can mark off each step as it is completed and thus know what you have done and what tasks lie ahead.

# 7

# The Medical College Admission Test (MCAT)

Overview of the MCAT
MCAT update
Importance of the MCAT
Validity of the MCAT
Contents of the MCAT
Preparing for the MCAT
Reference data for model test
Model MCAT
Scoring of the MCAT
Future MCAT Plans

## OVERVIEW OF THE MCAT

Essentially all applicants to the U.S. and Canadian medical schools, as well as some applicants to foreign schools, are expected to take the MCAT. It is given on a Saturday in April and in August at test centers located throughout the country and at some overseas locations. The test is computer administered and scored by The MCAT Program, P.O. Box 4056, Iowa City, IA 52243, (319) 337-1357. Score reporting is the responsibility of the AAMC (MCAT Operations, Association of American Medical Colleges, Section for Student Services, 2450 N Street NW, Suite 201, Washington, DC 20037, (202) 828-0600). You can arrange to take the test by filing an application (frequently obtainable at your Premedical Advisory Office), along with the examination fee (currently $155) and a recent snapshot. Special test centers are open on Sundays for students whose religious convictions prevent them from taking the exam on Saturday. An additional fee (currently $10) is required for taking the exam on Sunday.

Scores are sent automatically in mid-June or mid-October both to you and to your advisor. Your scores will also be sent automatically to AMCAS schools. You can indicate on your test application six non-AMCAS schools you wish to receive your scores; if you are applying to more than six AMCAS schools, you must pay a fee for each additional school.

The MCAT can be retaken without special permission, but it is usually advisable to do so only if there is a significant discrepancy between your college grades and MCAT scores, if the test was taken before you completed your basic biology and chemistry courses, if you were quite ill or emotionally upset at the time the test was taken, or if you are encouraged by your Premedical Committee to do so. When the MCAT is taken twice, the AAMC recommends that the initial and retest scores on the verbal reasoning tests be averaged, and the retest scores for the physical and biological sciences tests be used, unless there is evidence that unusual circumstances might have affected scores on either exam.

As a general rule, you should take the MCAT at the session at which you feel you could perform best. The overwhelming majority of students take the test in the spring and this is justified for a number of reasons:

1. Scores become available earlier and therefore prompter action on your application can be taken by admissions committees.

2. Additional knowledge accumulated between the two test periods does not significantly affect test scores.

3. Most schools interpret the scores in light of the actual coursework completed at the time the exam was taken.

4. You still have the option of retaking the examination in the fall if you missed it in the spring or if you feel that the scores, for some reason, did not reflect your true capabilities.

5. A significant number of places may already be filled by the time the schools receive the scores from the fall exam (usually after Thanksgiving).

6. You can get a necessary hurdle out of the way and you can then concentrate better on your studies.

Students who have not had basic courses in chemistry and biology and who plan to take these courses during the summer and students whose academic record is B– or less and who will have additional time to study for the examination during the summer and therefore may perform better on the exam in the fall should give serious consideration to the later test administration. In any event, the exam should not be taken in the spring as if it were a trial run, with the intention of taking it definitively in the fall since medical schools are aware that the exam is taken twice and can secure both sets of scores.

Test scores are sent to the student usually four to six weeks after the test is taken. The student also receives a copy to be given to his or her advisor. The advisor receives a computer printout of the scores from those students electing to release them.

## MCAT UPDATE

In 2007 the fully electronic MCAT replaced the manual version. The test of all procedures, the delivery software, and computers, proved to be highly successful.

The new test should cut score reporting delays significantly and the testing day should be about half as long. Perhaps the most striking development is that the MCAT can now be taken on 22 different dates throughout the year, rather than only in April and August. Students will be able to take the test up to three times a year, although they will only be allowed to register for one date at a time.

## IMPORTANCE OF THE MCAT

The MCAT scores provide admissions committees with nationally standardized measures of both academic ability and achievement. This permits comparison of applicants even though they have widely different academic backgrounds and attend different colleges. The scores attained on the MCAT do not by themselves determine admission and are supplemental in interpreting the academic record, since they help to shed light on the academic abilities of the applicant. The extent of their importance varies among medical schools because committees place different degrees of stress on the scores. In general, the MCAT scores are significant in relation to the academic record of the individual. When the scores are high or low for a student with a good or a weak record, respectively, they simply confirm the academic record. When they are significantly different from the student's record, they raise questions that can be critical in determining admissions. Thus students with poor records and high scores may have greater potential than their records indicate. In such cases, more intensive evaluation may be warranted, and the applicants may be called for an interview that they otherwise may not have been granted. At the interview, the discrepancy between the academic record and the MCAT scores can be clarified, and the applicants will have the opportunity to "sell themselves," perhaps significantly improving their chances for admission.

On the other hand, when the academic record is high and the MCAT scores are low, the applicant's interview will not be perfunctory but will be aimed at clarifying the discrepancy. He or she will have to convince the interviewer of potential ability and overcome the uncertainty that has been created. One way of doing this is to retake the test and perform significantly better.

In summary, the implication of your MCAT score is as follows:

**Table 7.1**
**RELATIONSHIP OF MCAT SCORES TO ADMISSION**

| GPA | MCAT | Impact on Admission |
| --- | --- | --- |
| High (3.7) | High (12) | Confirmatory; enhances chances |
| High | Low | Diminishes chances |
| Average (3.5) | High | Supportive; improves chances |
| Average | Average (10) | Status unchanged |
| Average | Low (9) | Diminishes chances |
| Low (3.3) | High | Improves chances |
| Low | Low | Confirmatory, seriously diminished |

# VALIDITY OF THE MCAT

Since the introduction of the revised MCAT in 1991, there has been an important study by the AUMC of the extent to which MCAT scores impact on predicting success in medical schools. The relationship was examined in terms of three parameters: (1) medical school grades, (2) USMLE, Step scores, and (3) academic difficulty. The study of this issue involved two groups of students and extended from their entrance into medical school through residency. The individuals whose performance was followed came from 14 different medical schools.

## Bottom Line

The results of this long-term study were:

- Medical school grades are best predicted by a combination of MCAT scores and GPAs, with MCAT scores being the more valuable component.

- MCAT scores were better predictors of Step scores of all three Step examinations, especially Step 1.

- MCAT scores also served as predictors of academic difficulty.

From this study one can see why MCAT scores play such an important role in the admissions process and therefore why it is essential that an applicant maximize his/her effort to achieve the best results possible and thereby enhance his/her chances for admission to medical school.

# CONTENTS OF THE MCAT

Over the past several decades, there has been a gradual but nevertheless dramatic change in the medical profession in terms of knowledge amassed, technological advances, and delivery of health care. This has brought about the belief that premedical and medical education for practitioners in the twenty-first century needs revision. This realization has similarly motivated a review of the MCAT exam for relevancy, especially since its relevance in predicting clinical success has been seriously questioned.

A study over a period of several years, including field testing, resulted in a new MCAT format that was introduced in the fall of 1991. The new format is designed to assist medical school admissions committees to identify applicants who have a broad liberal arts education as well as a solid scientific background and adequate writing skills.

The MCAT now consists of four separate subtests:

| | |
|---|---|
| Verbal reasoning | 85 minutes |
| Physical sciences | 100 minutes |
| Writing sample | 60 minutes |
| Biological sciences | 100 minutes |

The tests are designed so that nearly everyone will have enough time to finish each section without undue pressure, since the emphasis will be on preparation rather than on speed of response.

## Timetable for the MCAT

TOTAL TIME: $5\frac{3}{4}$ hours, plus 1 hour for lunch, two 10-minute breaks

| 85 minutes | Verbal Reasoning | 65 questions |
|---|---|---|
| | Rest Period—10 minutes | |
| 100 minutes | Physical Sciences | 77 questions |
| | Lunch—60 minutes | |
| 60 minutes | Writing Sample | 2 questions |
| | Rest Period—10 minutes | |
| 100 minutes | Biological Sciences | 77 questions |

## Verbal Reasoning

This section consists of a 500- to 600-word selected text taken from the natural or social sciences or humanities. The source of the text will be identified. Following the text will be a set of questions presented in order from easiest to hardest. The goal of this subtest is to ascertain quantitatively the applicant's skills in several, but not necessarily all, of the following:

(a) comprehending the essence of the text,

(b) utilizing the information of the text,

(c) determining the validity of the information in the text, and

(d) integrating new data on the context of that which is in the text.

## Physical Sciences

This subtest seeks to measure an applicant's comprehension of basic concepts and problem-solving ability in physics and chemistry. (This may require an understanding and ability to use basic college-level mathematical concepts to solve some of the problems in the physical sciences.) Of the 77 questions making up this subtest, 62 are based on a text that discusses a problem or situation that may be presented in a prose, graphic, tabular, or illustrative format. About ten problem sets consisting of four to eight questions each are associated with each such unit. In addition, 15 questions unrelated to the text are presented. The questions are not predicated on an ability to memorize scientific facts. Rather, they require knowledge of constants and equations commonly used in basic physics and chemistry courses.

## Physics

This segment of the physical sciences subtest will judge your ability to utilize fundamental physics theories in solving problems (on a noncalculus basis). Topics that you should be familiar with include:

**Mechanics:** namely, concepts in equilibrium, momentum, force, motion, gravitation, translational motion, work, energy, fluids, and solids.

**Wave Motion:** namely, wave characteristics, periodic motion, and sound.

**Electricity and Magnetism:** namely, concepts in electrostatics, electromagnetism, and electric circuits.

**Light and Optics:** namely, concepts in visible light and geometric optics.

**Modern Physics:** namely, concepts in atomic and nuclear structure.

## Chemistry

This segment of the physical science subtest will judge your ability to apply fundamental theories of general chemistry to solving problems. (Organic chemistry is included as part of the biological sciences subtest.) Topics you should be familiar with include:

**Stoichiometry:** namely, metric units, molecular weight, Avogadro number, mole concept, oxidation number, chemical equation reactions.

**Electronic Structure:** namely, understanding the complexities and dynamics of chemical reactions, as well as the link between quantum theories and physical and chemical properties of elements and compounds.

**Bonding:** namely, ionic and covalent bond formation characteristics should be understood so as to appreciate chemical and physical properties of substances.

**Phases:** namely, understanding the concepts involved in the dynamic phases of elements (gas, liquid, and solid) as well as phase equilibria is necessary to respond to some of the questions.

**Solution Chemistry:** namely, familiarity with ions in solution, solubility, and precipitation reactions.

**Acids and Bases:** namely, the concepts associated with acid/base equilibria and acid/base titrations.

**Thermodynamics and Thermochemistry:** namely, concepts associated with the evolution and absorption of heat during a reaction should be understood.

**Rate of Chemical Reactions:** namely, an understanding of rate concepts and reaction equilibrium is necessary.

**Electrochemistry:** namely, an understanding of concepts in the analysis of galvanic, electronic, or concentration cells.

## Mathematics

Noncalculus prerequisite knowledge in mathematics that will permit solving some of the problems in the physical science subtests includes:

**Arithmetic Computation Skills:** namely, exponents, logarithms, quadratic equations, simultaneous equations, scientific notation, graphic presentation of data and functions.

**Trigonometry:** namely, functions (sine, cosine, tangent), the values of sines and cosines of $0°$, $90°$, and $180°$; inverse functions ($\sin^{-1}$, $\cos^{-1}$, $\tan^{-1}$); lengths relationships of sides of right triangles containing angles of $30°$, $45°$, and $60°$.

**Vectors:** namely, addition, subtraction, and right hand rule.

**Probability:** namely, capability to determine the mathematical probability of an event (on an elementary level).

**Statistics:** namely, capability to calculate the arithmetic average and range of a set of numerical data; comprehension of statistical association and correlation concepts; appreciating the value of standard deviation as a measure of variability (its calculation is not required).

**Experimental Error:** namely, relative magnitude as well as propagation of error, comprehension of reasonable estimates as well as the significant digits of a measurement.

## Writing Sample

Written communication skills are deemed important elements for a successful medical practitioner. They provide an essential vehicle for an effective relationship with both colleagues and patients. The measure of an applicant's capability in the area is determined on the MCAT by two 30-minutes essays. Each item is made up of a short, usually one-line, statement of a policy or an opinion on a topic that can come from a broad range of issues. The applicant is then presented with three tasks: (1) to provide an in-depth interpretation of the meaning of the statement, (2) to provide a detailed rebuttal of the point of view expressed in the statement, and (3) to demonstrate how one can resolve the statement and the opposing viewpoint that was offered.

The response to all three tasks should be provided in a detailed, thoughtful, and logically expressed essay.

## Biological Sciences

This subtest seeks to measure an applicant's comprehension of basic concepts of molecular biology, cell structure and function, genetics, and evolution as well as the organization of body systems. Topics in organic chemistry are also covered in the 77 questions of this subtest because it forms the bases of many biological (biochemical) reactions.

### Biology

The major topics covered are:

**Molecular Biology:** namely, understanding enzyme regulation of cell metabolism as well as DNA and protein synthesis is necessary.

**Microbiology:** namely, familiarity with the structure and life histories of the bacteriophage, animal versus "fungi," and prokaryotic cell is necessary.

**Eukaryotic Cell:** namely, knowledge of the principal components of the typical eukaryotic cell and their functions is required.

**Specialized Eukaryotic Cell:** namely, the unique features of cells and tissues of connective, muscular, nervous tissues, and skin should be understood.

**Body Systems:** namely, the organs that compose the major body systems (skeletal, muscular, circulatory, digestive, respiratory, excretory, nervous, reproductive, and endocrine) should be known.

**Genetics and Evolution:** both Mendelian and modern concepts of genetics should be understood as well as concepts of evolution such as natural selection, speciation, and basic structure of chordates.

### *Organic Chemistry*

This area requires a knowledge of organic compounds, including nomenclature, classification of functional groups, and reactions including reaction mechanisms. The major topics covered are:

**Biological Molecules:** namely, knowledge of the types of biologically active molecules (e.g., amino acids and proteins, carbohydrates, lipids, and phosphorus compounds) is required.

**Oxygen-Containing Compounds:** namely, knowledge of the principal reaction of the oxygen-containing compounds (e.g., alcohols, aldehydes, ketones, carboxylic acids, ethers, and phenols) is required.

**Amines:** namely, knowledge of the nitrogen-containing compounds is required.

**Hydrocarbons:** namely, knowledge of the alkanes, alkenes, and benzene derivatives is required.

**Molecular Structure:** namely, knowledge of the structure of organic compounds in terms of bonds; bond strengths, and stereochemistry of bonded molecules is necessary.

**Separation and Purification:** namely, familiarity with the methodology and the characteristics of different organic compounds as related to their separation and possible purification if needed. This requires knowledge of the processes of extraction, distillation, recrystallization, and chromatography.

**Spectroscopy:** namely, knowledge of nuclear magnetic resonance (NMR) and infrared (IR) spectroscopy is necessary.

A full description of the test is included in *The MCAT Student Manual,* obtainable from AAMC, 2450 N Street, NW, Washington, DC 20037.

# PREPARING FOR THE MCAT

It can be categorically stated that your performance on the MCAT will be better if you prepare for it in an organized manner. This means that a *structured study plan* should be developed before initiating your review process.

Developing a study plan involves (1) setting a realistic starting date to begin your study program (such as one and a half to three months prior to the test date, depending on your ability, time available for study, etc.); (2) requisitioning fixed blocks of time on a weekly basis to be used exclusively for study (with alternate time-blocks if you cannot keep to your schedule); (3) proportioning your study time relative to each of the subtests, in direct proportion to your strength or weakness in each area; (4) arranging your study schedule to allow for completion of preparation for taking the exam a few days *before* the test date. This will reduce the chance or need for cramming, which would be counterproductive. Moreover, a brief interlude available just prior to the test will afford you a chance to relax physically and mentally in preparation for the examination. You can then better meet the very demanding challenge for a $5\frac{3}{4}$-hour test.

## General Study Guidelines

The following nine suggestions should aid in your preparation for taking the MCAT.

1. Your first step should be to familiarize yourself with the major topics that must be mastered for each of the subtests (see pages 168–169). This will give an overview of areas that may require greater or lesser emphasis in your study schedule.

2. It is probably desirable to begin your study with the subject that you are most knowledgeable or comfortable with. Thus the learning process, which under the circumstances should be a productive one, will also serve to reinforce your self-confidence as you prepare for more challenging segments of the exam.

3. Consider utilizing a study plan that involves a preliminary review of the material, before initiating intensive study. If areas of weakness are identified during the initial review, seek to fill in the void without excessive delay. This will lessen your anxiety due to concern over your knowledge gap. Excessive worry over your deficiencies can seriously impede preparation for and attainment of your goal.

4. Determine the inherent sequence of the information you seek to master. Try to master it within the context of a logical "framework" rather than as isolated data.

5. You should try to determine your most successful study techniques (such as repeated reading of material outlining the subject, written summary of the text, or verbalizing the highlights of the information being studied).

6. Before you commit information to memory, be certain that you comprehend it fully. It is more difficult to unlearn erroneous material and replace it with a correct version than to learn it right in the first place.

7. The length of your individual study session should be reasonable and adjusted to the state of your physical and mental well-being. If fatigue sets in during your learning period, take a break or terminate it. Pushing yourself beyond your limit will be unproductive because of inefficiency, and consequently potentially frustrating.

8. The major determinant of success on the MCAT (like any other exam) is retention of the material learned. Meaningful information—that is, knowledge associated with principles or concepts—is retained longer than nonmeaningful information—this is, isolated facts. In both cases, however, repetition at spaced intervals after initial learning will enhance retention. Thus, frequent, short, intense review periods will definitely enhance your incorporating the material for an extended interval.

9. Getting a good night's (REM) sleep after an initial intense study session in the evening is important, because (dream) sleep has been shown to consolidate long-term memory, thus enhancing retention.

## Specific Study Guidelines

One can and should prepare for each of the four specific subtests. Preparation for these should be an integral part of your overall study plan.

## Science Subtest Preparation

As indicated in the preceding section, a preliminary review of the major topics in the physical and biological sciences will provide you with a general assessment of your strengths and weaknesses. This can be done using well-written college textbooks or reading the Science Review chapter in *MCAT—Medical College Admission Test* by Hugo R. Seibel et al. (Barron's Educational Series, Inc., 2008). Your goal should be to refresh your memory with the general concepts and principal facts in each of the three science areas you will be tested in.

It is best that you begin intensive study only after you have completed your preliminary survey.

The major topics to be covered are summarized in the chart on pages 168–169, which is consistent with the contents of the MCAT.

## Verbal Reasoning Subtest Preparation

It should be recognized that reasoning is a skill and requires practice. Some basic rules for proper reasoning are the following:

1. Strive to ascertain the meaning of the central theme of the passage under consideration.

2. Try to identify the premises upon which the passage is based, both explicit or implicit.

3. Evaluate critically the premises in terms of how strongly or poorly they support the conclusion.

4. Seek other relevant arguments to support the conclusion.

5. Be alert to being led astray in your thinking.

Newspaper or magazine articles, especially editorials, provide source material to test your verbal reasoning skills.

In responding to the paragraph under consideration, you can chose to read it first, then take note of the questions next. Conversely, you may wish to read the questions first, then read the relevant paragraph. In either case, underlining appropriate key words or phrases in the paragraph should prove helpful in your analysis of its contents.

## Writing Sample Subtest Preparation

This subtest will, for some applicants, represent the greatest challenge. Meeting this challenge will depend on how successfully you have mastered the art of essay writing. Given a statement, you will have to respond to three writing tasks pertaining to the statement.

First, you must determine the meaning of the statement and do so in an orderly, thorough, and coherent manner. Second, you will have to translate the meaning of the statement in the context of some example that illustrates an opposing attitude. The third task will be to reconcile the conflict between the statement or interpretation (task 1) and its opposite viewpoint (task 2). While you may respond to the three tasks in any order, all three tasks must be met in order to maximize your credit potential.

In responding to the challenge of the writing sample, the following guidelines should prove helpful.

1. Carefully read and analyze the statement presented before you initiate your response.

2. Determine specifically what you are really being asked to do.

3. Prepare a brief outline of how you wish to respond, using key words, ideas, facts, or examples.

4. Write legibly and in direct response to the task under consideration. Focus your responses as specifically as possible.

5. Present your ideas clearly and in an organized rather than haphazard fashion.

## MCAT STUDY TOPICS

### Biological Sciences

Microbiology
  Viral structure
  Prokaryotic cell
  Fungi

Molecular Biology
  Cell metabolism
  Enzyme structure
  Enzyme function
  Glycosis

The Cell
  Plasma membrane
    Ultrastructure
    Function
    Membrane transport

  Cytologic research methods
  Cytoplasmic organelles
    Mitochondria
    Golgi apparatus
    Endoplasmic reticulum
    Lysosomes and peroxisomes
    Annulate lamellae

Skeletal System
  Organization
  Bone characteristics
  Function
  Joints

Muscular Tissue
  Classification
  Terminology
  Gross and fine structure
  Function
  Control of activity

Circulatory System
  Components
  Structure
  Circulation path
  Blood
  Oxygen transport
  Lymph system
    Spleen

Cytoskeleton
  Microtubules
  Microfilaments
  Cilia

Mitosis
  Process
  Structures
  Movements and mechanisms
  Nucleus
    Nuclear envelope
    Nuclear structures

Human Body Organization
  Basic tissues
  Epithelial tissue
  Connective tissue
  Muscle tissue
  Nerve tissue

Respiratory System
  Function
  Gas exchange
  Thermoregulation
  Components
    Rib cage
    Diaphragm

Digestive System
  Organs
  Digestive glands
  Functional control
  Nutrition

Urinary System
  Organs
  Structure
  Function
  Hormonal control

Nervous System
  Components
  Central system
  Autonomic system

Immune System
  Bone marrow
  Thymus
  Function

Neuron
  Classification and groups
  Supportive cells

Special Sensory Organs
    Eyes
        Structure
        Sensory reception

    Ear
        Structure
        Mechanism of hearing

    Nose
        Structure
        Mechanism of olfaction

Endocrine System
    Major glands
    Function
    Mechanism of action

Reproductive System
    Organs

Reproductive System cont.
    Gametogenesis
    Meiotic cycle
    Menstruation
    Placenta
    Embryogenesis
        Early stages
        Germ layers
    Chordate body plan
    Vertebrate body plan

Genetics
    Mendelian concepts
    Sex-linked features
    Mutation

Evolution
    Natural selection
    Formation of species
    Origin of life

*Note:* While organic chemistry is covered in the biological sciences subtest, its topical outline here is given in its traditional position under chemistry.

---

## Physical Sciences

| *Inorganic Chemistry* | *Organic Chemistry* | Energy cont. |
|---|---|---|

**Inorganic Chemistry**

The Atom
Components of the atom
Energy levels
The Periodic Table
    Gases
    Liquids
    Solids
    Phase changes
    Chemical compounds
    Bonding
    Balanced chemical equations
    Solutions
    Acids and bases
    pH and buffers
    Electrochemistry
    Thermodynamics
    Rate of chemical reactions

**Biochemistry**

Enzymes
Amino acids
Proteins
Carbohydrates
Lipids
Nucleotids and nucleic acids

**Organic Chemistry**

Alkanes
Cycloalkanes
Alkenes
Alkynes
Aromatic compounds
Grignard reagent
Alcohols
Amines
Amides
Aldehydes
Ketones
Carboxylic acids
Esters
Ethers

**Physics**

Accelerated motion
Forces and motion
Projective motion
Friction
Work and power
Energy
    Momentum
    Uniform circular motion
    Fluids at rest

**Energy cont.**

    Gravity
    Temperature calculations
    Temperature measurements
    Heat
    Thermodynamics
    Electrostatics
    Electricity
    Electric circuits
    Electric energy
Machines
    Advantages of machines
    Harmonic motion
Waves
Sound waves
Light rays
Mirrors
Lenses
Atom composition
Radioactivity
Nuclear energy
Photons
Atomic energy units

# REFERENCE DATA FOR MODEL TEST

## Logarithms and Exponents

### *Logarithms*

The logarithm of any number is the exponent of the power to which 10 must be raised to produce the number. The logarithm $X$ of the number $N$ to the base 10 is the exponent of the power to which 10 must be raised to give $N$ (for example, $\log_{10} N = X$). Logarithms consist of two parts. First, there is the "characteristic," which is determined by the position of the first significant figure of the number in relation to the decimal point. If we count leftwards from the decimal point as positive and rightwards as negative, the characteristic is equal to the count ending at the right of the first significant figure. Thus, the characteristic of the logarithm of 2340 is 3, and of 0.00234 is –3. Second, there is the "mantissa." It is always positive, is found in logarithm tables, and depends only on the sequence of significant figures. Thus, the mantissa for the two numbers is the same, namely 0.3692. The logarithm of a number is the sum of the characteristic and the mantissa. Thus, log 2340 = 3.3692 while log 0.00234 = –3 + 0.3692 = –2.6308.

The logarithms of the whole integers 1 to 10 are given below.

| | | | |
|---|---|---|---|
| log 1.0 = 0.000 | log 4.0 = 0.602 | log 7.0 = 0.845 | log 10.0 = 1.000 |
| log 2.0 = 0.301 | log 5.0 = 0.699 | log 8.0 = 0.903 | |
| log 3.0 = 0.477 | log 6.0 = 0.778 | log 9.0 = 0.954 | |

### Useful Rules in Handling Logarithms

1. The logarithm of a product is equal to the sum of the logarithm of the factors:
$$\log ab = \log a + \log b$$
(Check this out by solving for log 6, using log 2 + log 3.)

2. The logarithm of a fraction is equal to the logarithm of the numerator minus the logarithm of the denominator:
$$\log \frac{a}{b} = \log a - \log b \qquad \text{Example: } \log \frac{10}{2} = \log 10 - \log 2 = \log 5$$
How about log 2.5? The answer from the log tables is 0.398.

3. The logarithm of the reciprocal of a number is the negative logarithm of the number:
$$\log \frac{1}{a} = \log 1 - \log a$$
Since log 1 = 0, then
$$\log \frac{1}{a} = - \log a$$
Equally,
$$\log \frac{1}{2} = - \log 2 = -0.301$$

4. The logarithm of a number raised to a power is the logarithm of the number multiplied by the power:
$$\log a^b = b \log a$$
$$\log 2^2 = 0.603$$

### *Exponents*

It is convenient to express large numbers as $10^x$, where $x$ represents the number of places that the decimal must be moved to place it after the first significant figure. This also represents 10 • 10 for $x$ times. For example, 1,000,000 may be expressed as $1 \times 10^6$; 3663 as $3.663 \times 10^3$; and so on. To multiply, the exponents are added, but coefficients are multiplied. To divide, the exponents are subtracted but coefficients are divided.

Multiplying: $(1 \times 10^x) \cdot (1 \times 10^y) = 1 \times 10^{x+y}$   $(4 \times 10^2) \cdot (2 \times 10^3) = 8 \times 10^5$

Dividing: $(1 \times 10^x) \div (1 \times 10^y) = 1 \times 10^{x-y}$   $(4 \times 10^2) \div (2 \times 10^3) = 2 \times 10^{-1}$

Numbers less than 1 are $10^{-x}$. For example, 0.000001 is $1 \times 10^{-6}$.

Multiplying: $(1 \times 10^{-x}) \cdot (1 \times 10^{-y}) = 1 \times 10^{-(x+y)}$   $(4 \times 10^{-2}) \cdot (2 \times 10^{-3}) = 8 \times 10^{-5}$

A large number multiplied by a small number: $(4 \times 10^{-2})(2 \times 10^3) = 8 \times 10^1$

(Logarithms and Exponents are reproduced through the courtesy of Dr. Richard B. Brandt, Dept. of Biochemistry, MCV, VCU, Richmond, Virginia, 23298).

# Table of Common Logarithms

| Numbers | 0 | 1 | 2 | 3 | 4 | 5 | 6 | 7 | 8 | 9 |
|---|---|---|---|---|---|---|---|---|---|---|
| 10 | 0000 | 0043 | 0086 | 0128 | 0170 | 0212 | 0253 | 0294 | 0334 | 0374 |
| 11 | 0414 | 0453 | 0492 | 0531 | 0569 | 0607 | 0645 | 0682 | 0719 | 0755 |
| 12 | 0792 | 0828 | 0864 | 0899 | 0934 | 0969 | 1004 | 1038 | 1072 | 1106 |
| 13 | 1139 | 1173 | 1206 | 1239 | 1271 | 1303 | 11335 | 1367 | 1399 | 1430 |
| 14 | 1461 | 1492 | 1523 | 1553 | 1584 | 1614 | 1644 | 1673 | 1703 | 1732 |
| | | | | | | | | | | |
| 15 | 1761 | 1790 | 1818 | 1847 | 1875 | 1903 | 1931 | 1959 | 1987 | 2014 |
| 16 | 2041 | 2068 | 2095 | 2122 | 2148 | 2175 | 2201 | 2227 | 2253 | 2279 |
| 17 | 2304 | 2330 | 2355 | 2380 | 2405 | 2430 | 2455 | 2480 | 2504 | 2529 |
| 18 | 2553 | 2577 | 2601 | 2625 | 2648 | 2672 | 2695 | 2718 | 2742 | 2765 |
| 19 | 2788 | 2810 | 2833 | 2856 | 2878 | 2900 | 2923 | 2945 | 2967 | 2989 |
| | | | | | | | | | | |
| 20 | 3010 | 3032 | 3054 | 3075 | 3096 | 3118 | 3139 | 3160 | 3181 | 3201 |
| 21 | 3222 | 3243 | 3263 | 3284 | 3304 | 3324 | 3345 | 3365 | 3385 | 3404 |
| 22 | 3424 | 3444 | 3464 | 3483 | 3502 | 3522 | 3541 | 3560 | 3579 | 3598 |
| 23 | 3617 | 3636 | 3655 | 3674 | 3692 | 3711 | 3729 | 3747 | 3766 | 3784 |
| 24 | 3802 | 3820 | 3838 | 3856 | 3874 | 3892 | 3909 | 3927 | 3945 | 3962 |
| | | | | | | | | | | |
| 25 | 3979 | 3997 | 4014 | 4031 | 4048 | 4064 | 4082 | 4099 | 4116 | 4133 |
| 26 | 4150 | 4166 | 4183 | 4200 | 4216 | 4232 | 4249 | 4265 | 4281 | 4298 |
| 27 | 4314 | 4330 | 4346 | 4362 | 4378 | 4393 | 4409 | 4425 | 4440 | 4456 |
| 28 | 4472 | 4487 | 4502 | 4518 | 4533 | 4548 | 4564 | 4579 | 4594 | 4609 |
| 29 | 4624 | 4639 | 4654 | 4669 | 4683 | 4698 | 4713 | 4728 | 4742 | 4757 |
| | | | | | | | | | | |
| 30 | 4771 | 4786 | 4800 | 4814 | 4829 | 4843 | 4857 | 4871 | 4886 | 4900 |
| 31 | 4914 | 4928 | 4942 | 4955 | 4969 | 4983 | 4997 | 5011 | 5024 | 5038 |
| 32 | 5051 | 5065 | 5079 | 5092 | 5105 | 5119 | 5132 | 5415 | 5159 | 5172 |
| 33 | 5185 | 5198 | 5211 | 5224 | 5237 | 5250 | 5260 | 5276 | 5289 | 5302 |
| 34 | 5315 | 5328 | 5340 | 5353 | 5366 | 5378 | 5391 | 5403 | 5416 | 5428 |
| | | | | | | | | | | |
| 35 | 5441 | 5453 | 5465 | 5478 | 5490 | 5502 | 5514 | 5527 | 5539 | 5551 |
| 36 | 5563 | 5575 | 5587 | 5599 | 5611 | 5623 | 5635 | 5647 | 5658 | 5670 |
| 37 | 5682 | 5694 | 5705 | 5717 | 5729 | 5740 | 5752 | 5763 | 5775 | 5786 |
| 38 | 5798 | 5809 | 5821 | 5832 | 5843 | 5855 | 5866 | 5877 | 5888 | 5899 |
| 39 | 5911 | 5922 | 5933 | 5944 | 5955 | 5966 | 5977 | 5988 | 5999 | 6010 |
| | | | | | | | | | | |
| 40 | 6021 | 6031 | 6042 | 6053 | 6064 | 6075 | 6085 | 6096 | 6107 | 6117 |
| 41 | 6128 | 6138 | 6149 | 6160 | 6170 | 6180 | 6191 | 6201 | 6212 | 6222 |
| 42 | 6232 | 6243 | 6253 | 6263 | 6274 | 6284 | 6294 | 6304 | 6314 | 6325 |
| 43 | 6335 | 6345 | 6355 | 6365 | 6375 | 6385 | 6395 | 6405 | 6415 | 6425 |
| 44 | 6435 | 6444 | 6454 | 6464 | 6474 | 6484 | 6493 | 6503 | 6513 | 6522 |
| | | | | | | | | | | |
| 45 | 6532 | 6542 | 6551 | 6561 | 6571 | 6580 | 6590 | 6599 | 6609 | 6618 |
| 46 | 6628 | 6637 | 6646 | 6656 | 6665 | 6675 | 6684 | 6693 | 6702 | 6712 |
| 47 | 6721 | 6730 | 6739 | 6749 | 6758 | 6767 | 6776 | 6785 | 6794 | 6803 |
| 48 | 6812 | 6821 | 6830 | 6839 | 6848 | 6857 | 6866 | 6875 | 6884 | 6893 |
| 49 | 6902 | 6911 | 6920 | 6928 | 6937 | 6946 | 6955 | 6964 | 6972 | 6981 |
| | | | | | | | | | | |
| 50 | 6990 | 6998 | 7007 | 7016 | 7024 | 7033 | 7042 | 7050 | 7059 | 7067 |
| 51 | 7076 | 7084 | 7093 | 7101 | 7110 | 7118 | 7126 | 7135 | 7143 | 7152 |
| 52 | 7106 | 7168 | 7177 | 7185 | 7193 | 7202 | 7210 | 7218 | 7226 | 7235 |
| 53 | 7243 | 7251 | 7259 | 7267 | 7275 | 7284 | 7292 | 7300 | 7308 | 7316 |
| 54 | 7324 | 7332 | 7340 | 7148 | 7356 | 7364 | 7372 | 7380 | 7388 | 7396 |

| Numbers | 0 | 1 | 2 | 3 | 4 | 5 | 6 | 7 | 8 | 9 |
|---|---|---|---|---|---|---|---|---|---|---|
| 55 | 7404 | 7412 | 7419 | 7427 | 7435 | 7443 | 7451 | 7459 | 7466 | 7474 |
| 56 | 7482 | 7490 | 7497 | 7505 | 7513 | 7520 | 7528 | 7536 | 7543 | 7551 |
| 57 | 7559 | 7566 | 7574 | 7582 | 7589 | 7597 | 7604 | 7612 | 7619 | 7627 |
| 58 | 7634 | 7642 | 7649 | 7657 | 7664 | 7672 | 7679 | 7686 | 7694 | 7701 |
| 59 | 7709 | 7716 | 7723 | 7731 | 7738 | 7745 | 7752 | 7760 | 7767 | 7774 |
| 60 | 7782 | 7789 | 7796 | 7803 | 7810 | 7818 | 7825 | 7832 | 7839 | 7846 |
| 61 | 7853 | 7860 | 7868 | 7875 | 7882 | 7889 | 7896 | 7903 | 7910 | 7917 |
| 62 | 7924 | 7931 | 7938 | 7945 | 7952 | 7959 | 7966 | 7937 | 7980 | 7987 |
| 63 | 7993 | 8000 | 8007 | 8014 | 8021 | 8028 | 8035 | 8041 | 8048 | 8055 |
| 64 | 8062 | 8069 | 8075 | 8082 | 8089 | 8096 | 8102 | 8109 | 8116 | 8122 |
| 65 | 8129 | 8136 | 8142 | 8149 | 8456 | 8162 | 8169 | 8176 | 8182 | 8189 |
| 66 | 8195 | 8202 | 8209 | 8215 | 8222 | 8228 | 8235 | 8241 | 5248 | 8254 |
| 67 | 8261 | 8267 | 8274 | 8280 | 8287 | 8293 | 8299 | 8306 | 8312 | 8319 |
| 68 | 8325 | 8331 | 8338 | 8344 | 8351 | 8357 | 8363 | 8370 | 8376 | 8382 |
| 69 | 8388 | 8395 | 8401 | 8407 | 8414 | 8420 | 8426 | 8432 | 8439 | 8445 |
| 70 | 8451 | 8457 | 8463 | 8470 | 8476 | 8482 | 8488 | 8494 | 8500 | 8506 |
| 71 | 8513 | 8519 | 8525 | 8531 | 8537 | 8543 | 8549 | 8555 | 8561 | 8567 |
| 72 | 8573 | 8579 | 8585 | 8591 | 8597 | 8603 | 8609 | 8615 | 8621 | 8627 |
| 73 | 8633 | 8639 | 8645 | 8651 | 8657 | 8663 | 8669 | 8675 | 8681 | 8686 |
| 74 | 8692 | 8698 | 8704 | 8710 | 8716 | 8722 | 8727 | 8733 | 8739 | 8745 |
| 75 | 8751 | 8756 | 8762 | 8768 | 8774 | 8779 | 8785 | 8791 | 8797 | 8802 |
| 76 | 8808 | 8814 | 8820 | 8825 | 8831 | 8837 | 8842 | 8848 | 8854 | 8859 |
| 77 | 8865 | 8871 | 8876 | 8882 | 8887 | 8893 | 8899 | 8904 | 8910 | 8915 |
| 78 | 8921 | 8927 | 8932 | 8938 | 8943 | 8949 | 8954 | 8960 | 8965 | 8971 |
| 79 | 8976 | 8982 | 8987 | 8993 | 8998 | 9004 | 9009 | 9015 | 9020 | 9025 |
| 80 | 9031 | 9036 | 9042 | 9047 | 9053 | 9058 | 9063 | 9069 | 9074 | 9079 |
| 81 | 9085 | 9090 | 9096 | 9101 | 9106 | 9112 | 9117 | 9122 | 9128 | 9133 |
| 82 | 9138 | 9143 | 9149 | 9154 | 9159 | 9165 | 9170 | 9175 | 9180 | 9186 |
| 83 | 9191 | 9196 | 9201 | 9206 | 9212 | 9217 | 9222 | 9227 | 9232 | 9238 |
| 84 | 9243 | 9248 | 9253 | 9258 | 9263 | 9269 | 9274 | 9279 | 9284 | 9289 |
| 85 | 9294 | 9299 | 9304 | 9309 | 9315 | 9320 | 9325 | 9330 | 9335 | 9340 |
| 86 | 9345 | 9350 | 9355 | 9360 | 9365 | 9370 | 9375 | 9380 | 9385 | 9390 |
| 87 | 9395 | 9400 | 9405 | 9410 | 9415 | 9420 | 9425 | 9430 | 9435 | 9440 |
| 88 | 9445 | 9450 | 9455 | 9460 | 9465 | 9469 | 9474 | 9479 | 9484 | 9489 |
| 89 | 9494 | 9499 | 9504 | 9509 | 9513 | 9518 | 9523 | 9528 | 9533 | 9538 |
| 90 | 9542 | 9547 | 9552 | 9557 | 9562 | 9566 | 9571 | 9576 | 9581 | 9586 |
| 91 | 9590 | 9595 | 9600 | 9605 | 9609 | 9614 | 9619 | 9624 | 9628 | 9633 |
| 92 | 9638 | 9643 | 9647 | 9652 | 9657 | 9661 | 9666 | 9671 | 9675 | 9680 |
| 93 | 9685 | 9689 | 9694 | 9699 | 9703 | 9708 | 9713 | 9717 | 9722 | 9727 |
| 94 | 9731 | 9736 | 9741 | 9745 | 9750 | 9754 | 9759 | 9763 | 9768 | 9773 |
| 95 | 9777 | 9782 | 9786 | 9791 | 9795 | 9800 | 9805 | 9809 | 9814 | 9818 |
| 96 | 9823 | 9727 | 9832 | 9836 | 9841 | 9845 | 9850 | 9854 | 9859 | 9863 |
| 97 | 9868 | 9872 | 9877 | 9881 | 9886 | 9890 | 9894 | 9899 | 9903 | 9908 |
| 98 | 9912 | 9917 | 9921 | 9926 | 9930 | 9934 | 9939 | 9943 | 9948 | 9952 |
| 99 | 9956 | 9961 | 9965 | 9969 | 9974 | 9978 | 9983 | 9987 | 9991 | 9996 |

# Periodic Table of the Elements

**KEY**

- Common oxidation states
- Atomic number
- Element symbol
- Element name
- Atomic mass (or mass number of longest-lived isotope)
- Electron configuration

$1$  $+1$  $-1$
**H**
Hydrogen
$1.00794$
$1s^1$

Note: Atomic masses are based on carbon-12 = 12.000...u

*s-block* · *p-block* · *d-block* (Transition Elements) · *f-block*

## Main Table

| Group | Z | Symbol | Name | Oxidation states | Atomic mass | Electron config. |
|---|---|---|---|---|---|---|
| 1 | 1 | H | Hydrogen | +1, −1 | 1.00794 | $1s^1$ |
| 18 | 2 | He | Helium | 0 | 4.00260 | $1s^2$ |
| 1 | 3 | Li | Lithium | +1 | 6.941 | $[He]2s^1$ |
| 2 | 4 | Be | Beryllium | +2 | 9.01218 | $[He]2s^2$ |
| 13 | 5 | B | Boron | +3 | 10.81 | $[He]2s^22p^1$ |
| 14 | 6 | C | Carbon | +2, +4, −4 | 12.011 | $[He]2s^22p^2$ |
| 15 | 7 | N | Nitrogen | −3, +1, +2, +3, +4, +5 | 14.0067 | $[He]2s^22p^3$ |
| 16 | 8 | O | Oxygen | −2 | 15.9994 | $[He]2s^22p^4$ |
| 17 | 9 | F | Fluorine | −1 | 18.998403 | $[He]2s^22p^5$ |
| 18 | 10 | Ne | Neon | 0 | 20.1797 | $[He]2s^22p^6$ |
| 1 | 11 | Na | Sodium | +1 | 22.98977 | $[Ne]3s^1$ |
| 2 | 12 | Mg | Magnesium | +2 | 24.305 | $[Ne]3s^2$ |
| 13 | 13 | Al | Aluminum | +3 | 26.98154 | $[Ne]3s^23p^1$ |
| 14 | 14 | Si | Silicon | −4, +2, +4 | 28.0855 | $[Ne]3s^23p^2$ |
| 15 | 15 | P | Phosphorus | −3, +3, +5 | 30.97376 | $[Ne]3s^23p^3$ |
| 16 | 16 | S | Sulfur | −2, +4, +6 | 32.066 | $[Ne]3s^23p^4$ |
| 17 | 17 | Cl | Chlorine | −1, +1, +3, +5, +7 | 35.453 | $[Ne]3s^23p^5$ |
| 18 | 18 | Ar | Argon | 0 | 39.948 | $[Ne]3s^23p^6$ |
| 1 | 19 | K | Potassium | +1 | 39.0983 | $[Ar]4s^1$ |
| 2 | 20 | Ca | Calcium | +2 | 40.078 | $[Ar]4s^2$ |
| 3 | 21 | Sc | Scandium | +3 | 44.9559 | $[Ar]3d^14s^2$ |
| 4 | 22 | Ti | Titanium | +2, +3, +4 | 47.88 | $[Ar]3d^24s^2$ |
| 5 | 23 | V | Vanadium | +2, +3, +4, +5 | 50.9415 | $[Ar]3d^34s^2$ |
| 6 | 24 | Cr | Chromium | +2, +3, +6 | 51.996 | $[Ar]3d^54s^1$ |
| 7 | 25 | Mn | Manganese | +2, +3, +4, +7 | 54.9380 | $[Ar]3d^54s^2$ |
| 8 | 26 | Fe | Iron | +2, +3 | 55.847 | $[Ar]3d^64s^2$ |
| 9 | 27 | Co | Cobalt | +2, +3 | 58.9332 | $[Ar]3d^74s^2$ |
| 10 | 28 | Ni | Nickel | +2, +3 | 58.69 | $[Ar]3d^84s^2$ |
| 11 | 29 | Cu | Copper | +1, +2 | 63.546 | $[Ar]3d^{10}4s^1$ |
| 12 | 30 | Zn | Zinc | +2 | 65.39 | $[Ar]3d^{10}4s^2$ |
| 13 | 31 | Ga | Gallium | +3 | 69.72 | $[Ar]3d^{10}4s^24p^1$ |
| 14 | 32 | Ge | Germanium | +2, +4 | 72.61 | $[Ar]3d^{10}4s^24p^2$ |
| 15 | 33 | As | Arsenic | −3, +3, +5 | 74.9216 | $[Ar]3d^{10}4s^24p^3$ |
| 16 | 34 | Se | Selenium | −2, +4, +6 | 78.96 | $[Ar]3d^{10}4s^24p^4$ |
| 17 | 35 | Br | Bromine | −1, +1, +5 | 79.904 | $[Ar]3d^{10}4s^24p^5$ |
| 18 | 36 | Kr | Krypton | 0 | 83.80 | $[Ar]3d^{10}4s^24p^6$ |
| 1 | 37 | Rb | Rubidium | +1 | 85.4678 | $[Kr]5s^1$ |
| 2 | 38 | Sr | Strontium | +2 | 87.62 | $[Kr]5s^2$ |
| 3 | 39 | Y | Yttrium | +3 | 88.9059 | $[Kr]4d^15s^2$ |
| 4 | 40 | Zr | Zirconium | +4 | 91.224 | $[Kr]4d^25s^2$ |
| 5 | 41 | Nb | Niobium | +3, +5 | 92.9064 | $[Kr]4d^45s^1$ |
| 6 | 42 | Mo | Molybdenum | +6 | 95.94 | $[Kr]4d^55s^1$ |
| 7 | 43 | Tc | Technetium | +4, +6, +7 | (98) | $[Kr]4d^55s^2$ |
| 8 | 44 | Ru | Ruthenium | +3, +4, +6, +8 | 101.07 | $[Kr]4d^75s^1$ |
| 9 | 45 | Rh | Rhodium | +3 | 102.9055 | $[Kr]4d^85s^1$ |
| 10 | 46 | Pd | Palladium | +2, +4 | 106.42 | $[Kr]4d^{10}$ |
| 11 | 47 | Ag | Silver | +1 | 107.8682 | $[Kr]4d^{10}5s^1$ |
| 12 | 48 | Cd | Cadmium | +2 | 112.41 | $[Kr]4d^{10}5s^2$ |
| 13 | 49 | In | Indium | +3 | 114.82 | $[Kr]4d^{10}5s^25p^1$ |
| 14 | 50 | Sn | Tin | +2, +4 | 118.710 | $[Kr]4d^{10}5s^25p^2$ |
| 15 | 51 | Sb | Antimony | −3, +3, +5 | 121.757 | $[Kr]4d^{10}5s^25p^3$ |
| 16 | 52 | Te | Tellurium | −2, +4, +6 | 127.60 | $[Kr]4d^{10}5s^25p^4$ |
| 17 | 53 | I | Iodine | −1, +1, +5, +7 | 126.9045 | $[Kr]4d^{10}5s^25p^5$ |
| 18 | 54 | Xe | Xenon | +4, +6 | 131.29 | $[Kr]4d^{10}5s^25p^6$ |
| 1 | 55 | Cs | Cesium | +1 | 132.9054 | $[Xe]6s^1$ |
| 2 | 56 | Ba | Barium | +2 | 137.33 | $[Xe]6s^2$ |
| 3 | 57 | La | Lanthanum | +3 | 138.9055 | $[Xe]5d^16s^2$ |
| 4 | 72 | Hf | Hafnium | +4 | 178.49 | $[Xe]4f^{14}5d^26s^2$ |
| 5 | 73 | Ta | Tantalum | +5 | 180.9479 | $[Xe]4f^{14}5d^36s^2$ |
| 6 | 74 | W | Tungsten | +6 | 183.85 | $[Xe]4f^{14}5d^46s^2$ |
| 7 | 75 | Re | Rhenium | +4, +6, +7 | 186.207 | $[Xe]4f^{14}5d^56s^2$ |
| 8 | 76 | Os | Osmium | +3, +4, +6, +8 | 190.2 | $[Xe]4f^{14}5d^66s^2$ |
| 9 | 77 | Ir | Iridium | +3, +4 | 192.22 | $[Xe]4f^{14}5d^76s^2$ |
| 10 | 78 | Pt | Platinum | +2, +4 | 195.08 | $[Xe]4f^{14}5d^96s^1$ |
| 11 | 79 | Au | Gold | +1, +3 | 196.9665 | $[Xe]4f^{14}5d^{10}6s^1$ |
| 12 | 80 | Hg | Mercury | +1, +2 | 200.59 | $[Xe]4f^{14}5d^{10}6s^2$ |
| 13 | 81 | Tl | Thallium | +1, +3 | 204.383 | $[Xe]4f^{14}5d^{10}6s^26p^1$ |
| 14 | 82 | Pb | Lead | +2, +4 | 207.2 | $[Xe]4f^{14}5d^{10}6s^26p^2$ |
| 15 | 83 | Bi | Bismuth | +3, +5 | 208.9804 | $[Xe]4f^{14}5d^{10}6s^26p^3$ |
| 16 | 84 | Po | Polonium | +2, +4 | (209) | $[Xe]4f^{14}5d^{10}6s^26p^4$ |
| 17 | 85 | At | Astatine | −1 | (210) | $[Xe]4f^{14}5d^{10}6s^26p^5$ |
| 18 | 86 | Rn | Radon | 0 | (222) | $[Xe]4f^{14}5d^{10}6s^26p^6$ |
| 1 | 87 | Fr | Francium | +1 | (223) | $[Rn]7s^1$ |
| 2 | 88 | Ra | Radium | +2 | 226.0254 | $[Rn]7s^2$ |
| 3 | 89 | Ac | Actinium | +3 | 227.0278 | $[Rn]6d^17s^2$ |
| 4 | 104 | Rf | Rutherfordium | | (261) | $[Rn]5f^{14}6d^27s^2$ |
| 5 | 105 | Db | Dubnium | | (262) | $[Rn]5f^{14}6d^37s^2$ |
| 6 | 106 | Sg | Seaborgium | | (263) | $[Rn]5f^{14}6d^47s^2$ |
| 7 | 107 | Bh | Bohrium | | (262) | $[Rn]5f^{14}6d^57s^2$ |
| 8 | 108 | Hs | Hassium | | (265) | $[Rn]5f^{14}6d^67s^2$ |
| 9 | 109 | Mt | Meitnerium | | (266) | $[Rn]5f^{14}6d^77s^2$ |
| 10 | 110 | Uun | Ununnilium | | (269) | $[Rn]5f^{14}6d^87s^2$ |
| 11 | 111 | Uuu | Unununium | | (272) | $[Rn]5f^{14}6d^97s^2$ |
| 12 | 112 | Uub | Ununbium | | (277) | $[Rn]5f^{14}6d^{10}7s^2$ |

## f-block

### Lanthanides

| Z | Symbol | Name | Oxidation states | Atomic mass | Electron config. |
|---|---|---|---|---|---|
| 58 | Ce | Cerium | +3, +4 | 140.12 | $[Xe]4f^15d^16s^2$ |
| 59 | Pr | Praseodymium | +3 | 140.9077 | $[Xe]4f^36s^2$ |
| 60 | Nd | Neodymium | +3 | 144.24 | $[Xe]4f^46s^2$ |
| 61 | Pm | Promethium | +3 | (145) | $[Xe]4f^56s^2$ |
| 62 | Sm | Samarium | +2, +3 | 150.36 | $[Xe]4f^66s^2$ |
| 63 | Eu | Europium | +2, +3 | 151.96 | $[Xe]4f^76s^2$ |
| 64 | Gd | Gadolinium | +3 | 157.25 | $[Xe]4f^75d^16s^2$ |
| 65 | Tb | Terbium | +3 | 158.9254 | $[Xe]4f^96s^2$ |
| 66 | Dy | Dysprosium | +3 | 162.50 | $[Xe]4f^{10}6s^2$ |
| 67 | Ho | Holmium | +3 | 164.9304 | $[Xe]4f^{11}6s^2$ |
| 68 | Er | Erbium | +3 | 167.26 | $[Xe]4f^{12}6s^2$ |
| 69 | Tm | Thulium | +3 | 168.9342 | $[Xe]4f^{13}6s^2$ |
| 70 | Yb | Ytterbium | +2, +3 | 173.04 | $[Xe]4f^{14}6s^2$ |
| 71 | Lu | Lutetium | +3 | 174.967 | $[Xe]4f^{14}5d^16s^2$ |

### Actinides

| Z | Symbol | Name | Oxidation states | Atomic mass | Electron config. |
|---|---|---|---|---|---|
| 90 | Th | Thorium | +4 | 232.0381 | $[Rn]6d^27s^2$ |
| 91 | Pa | Protactinium | +4, +5 | 231.0359 | $[Rn]5f^26d^17s^2$ |
| 92 | U | Uranium | +3, +4, +5, +6 | 238.0289 | $[Rn]5f^36d^17s^2$ |
| 93 | Np | Neptunium | +3, +4, +5, +6 | 237.048 | $[Rn]5f^46d^17s^2$ |
| 94 | Pu | Plutonium | +3, +4, +5, +6 | (244) | $[Rn]5f^67s^2$ |
| 95 | Am | Americium | +3, +4, +5, +6 | (243) | $[Rn]5f^77s^2$ |
| 96 | Cm | Curium | +3 | (247) | $[Rn]5f^76d^17s^2$ |
| 97 | Bk | Berkelium | +3, +4 | (247) | $[Rn]5f^97s^2$ |
| 98 | Cf | Californium | +3 | (251) | $[Rn]5f^{10}7s^2$ |
| 99 | Es | Einsteinium | | (252) | $[Rn]5f^{11}7s^2$ |
| 100 | Fm | Fermium | | (257) | $[Rn]5f^{12}7s^2$ |
| 101 | Md | Mendelevium | | (258) | $[Rn]5f^{13}7s^2$ |
| 102 | No | Nobelium | +2, +3 | (259) | $[Rn]5f^{14}7s^2$ |
| 103 | Lr | Lawrencium | +3 | (262) | $[Rn]5f^{14}6d^17s^2$ |

# List of Elements with Their Symbols

| Element | Symbol | Element | Symbol |
|---|---|---|---|
| Actinium | Ac | Mendelevium | Md |
| Aluminum | Al | Mercury | Hg |
| Americium | Am | Molybdenum | Mo |
| Antimony | Sb | Neodymium | Nd |
| Argon | Ar | Neon | Ne |
| Arsenic | As | Neptunium | Np |
| Astatine | At | Nickel | Ni |
| Barium | Ba | Niobium | Nb |
| Berkelium | Bk | Nitrogen | N |
| Beryllium | Be | Nobelium | No |
| Bismuth | Bi | Osmium | Os |
| Boron | B | Oxygen | O |
| Bromine | Br | Palladium | Pd |
| Cadmium | Cd | Phosphorus | P |
| Calcium | Ca | Platinum | Pt |
| Californium | Cf | Plutonium | Pu |
| Carbon | C | Polonium | Po |
| Cerium | Ce | Potassium | K |
| Cesium | Cs | Praseodynium | Pr |
| Chlorine | Cl | Promethium | Pm |
| Chromium | Cr | Protactinium | Pa |
| Cobalt | Co | Radium | Ra |
| Copper | Cu | Radon | Rn |
| Curium | Cm | Rhenium | Re |
| Dysprosium | Dy | Rhodium | Rh |
| Einsteinium | Es | Rubidium | Rb |
| Element 106 | | Ruthenium | Ru |
| Erbium | Er | Samarium | Sm |
| Europium | Eu | Scandium | Sc |
| Fermium | Fm | Selenium | Se |
| Flourine | F | Silicon | Si |
| Francium | Fr | Silver | Ag |
| Gadolinium | Gd | Sodium | Na |
| Gallium | Ga | Strontium | Sr |
| Germanium | Ge | Sulfur | S |
| Gold | Au | Tantalum | Ta |
| Hafnium | Hf | Technetium | Tc |
| Helium | He | Tellurium | Te |
| Holmium | Ho | Terbium | Tb |
| Hydrogen | H | Thallium | Tl |
| Indium | In | Thorium | Th |
| Iodine | I | Thulium | Tm |
| Iridium | Ir | Tin | Sn |
| Iron | Fe | Titanium | Ti |
| Krypton | Kr | Tungsten | W |
| Lanthanum | La | Uranium | U |
| Lawrencium | Lr | Vanadium | V |
| Lead | Pb | Xenon | Xe |
| Lithium | Li | Ytterbium | Yb |
| Lutetium | Lu | Yttrium | Y |
| Magnesium | Mg | Zinc | Zn |
| Manganese | Mn | Zirconium | Zr |

# Reference Tables for Chemistry

## PHYSICAL CONSTANTS AND CONVERSION FACTORS

| Name | Symbol | Value(s) | Units |
|---|---|---|---|
| Angstrom unit | Å | $1 \times 10^{-10}$ m | meter |
| Avogadro number | $N_A$ | $6.02 \times 10^{23}$ per mol | |
| Charge of electron | $e$ | $1.60 \times 10^{-19}$ C | coulomb |
| Electron-volt | eV | $1.60 \times 10^{-19}$ J | joule |
| Speed of light | $c$ | $3.00 \times 10^8$ m/s | meters/second |
| Planck's constant | $h$ | $6.63 \times 10^{-34}$ J·s | joule-second |
| | | $1.58 \times 10^{-37}$ kcal·s | kilocalorie-second |
| Universal gas constant | $R$ | 0.0821 L · atm/mol·K | liter-atmosphere/mole-kelvin |
| | | 1.98 cal/mol·K | calories/mole-kelvin |
| | | 8.31 J/mol·K | joules/mole-kelvin |
| Atomic mass unit | U | $1.66 \times 10^{-24}$ g | gram |
| Volume standard, liter | L | $1 \times 10^3$ cm$^3$ = 1 dm$^3$ | cubic centimeters, cubic decimeter |
| Standard pressure, atmosphere | atm | 101.3 kPa | kilopascals |
| | | 760 mmHg | millimeters of mercury |
| | | 760 torr | torr |
| Heat equivalent, kilocalorie | kcal | $4.19 \times 10^3$ J | joules |

### Physical Constants for H$_2$O

Molal freezing point depression ................ 1.86°C/m
Molal boiling point elevation .................... 0.52°C/m
Heat of fusion ....................................... 79.72 cal/g
Heat of vaporization ..............................539.4 cal/g

## STANDARD UNITS

| Symbol | Name | Quantity | Selected Prefixes | | |
|---|---|---|---|---|---|
| | | | Factor | Prefix | Symbol |
| m | meter | length | $10^{12}$ | tera | T |
| kg | kilogram | mass | $10^9$ | giga | G |
| Pa | pascal | pressure | $10^6$ | mega | M |
| K | kelvin | thermodynamic temperature | $10^3$ | kilo | k |
| mol | mole | amount of substance | $10^{-1}$ | deci | d |
| J | joule | energy, work, quantity of heat | $10^{-2}$ | centi | c |
| s | second | time | $10^{-3}$ | milli | m |
| C | coulomb | quantity of electricity | $10^{-6}$ | micro | μ |
| V | volt | electric potential, potential difference | $10^{-9}$ | nano | n |
| L | liter | volume | $10^{-12}$ | pico | p |

## RELATIVE STRENGTHS OF ACIDS IN AQUEOUS SOLUTION AT 1 atm AND 298 K

| Conjugate Pairs | $K_a$ |
|---|---|
| *ACID*        *BASE* | |
| $HI = H^+ + I^-$ | very large |
| $HBr = H^+ + Br^-$ | very large |
| $HCl = H^+ + Cl^-$ | very large |
| $HNO_3 = H^+ + NO_3^-$ | very large |
| $H_2SO_4 = H^+ + HSO_4^-$ | large |
| $H_2O + SO_2 = H^+ + HSO_3^-$ | $1.5 \times 10^{-2}$ |
| $HSO_4^- = H^+ + SO_4^{2-}$ | $1.2 \times 10^{-2}$ |
| $H_3PO_4 = H^+ + H_2PO_4^-$ | $7.5 \times 10^{-3}$ |
| $Fe(H_2O)_6^{3+} = H^+ + Fe(H_2O)_5(OH)^{2+}$ | $8.9 \times 10^{-4}$ |
| $HNO_2 = H^+ + NO_2^-$ | $4.6 \times 10^{-4}$ |
| $HF = H^+ + F^-$ | $3.5 \times 10^{-4}$ |
| $Cr(H_2O)_6^{3+} = H^+ + Cr(H_2O)_5(OH)^{2+}$ | $1.0 \times 10^{-4}$ |
| $CH_3COOH = H^+ + CH_3COO^-$ | $1.8 \times 10^{-5}$ |
| $Al(H_2O)_6^{3+} = H^+ + Al(H_2O)_5(OH)^{2+}$ | $1.1 \times 10^{-5}$ |
| $H_2O + CO_2 = H^+ + HCO_3^-$ | $4.3 \times 10^{-7}$ |
| $HSO_3^- = H^+ + SO_3^{2-}$ | $1.1 \times 10^{-7}$ |
| $H_2S = H^+ + HS^-$ | $9.5 \times 10^{-8}$ |
| $H_2PO_4^- = H^+ + HPO_4^{2-}$ | $6.2 \times 10^{-8}$ |
| $NH_4^+ = H^+ + NH_3$ | $5.7 \times 10^{-10}$ |
| $HCO_3^- = H^+ + CO_3^{2-}$ | $5.6 \times 10^{-11}$ |
| $HPO_4^{2-} = H^+ + PO_4^{3-}$ | $2.2 \times 10^{-13}$ |
| $HS^- = H^+ + S^{2-}$ | $1.3 \times 10^{-14}$ |
| $H_2O = H^+ + OH^-$ | $1.0 \times 10^{-14}$ |
| $OH^- = H^+ + O^{2-}$ | $< 10^{-36}$ |
| $NH_3 = H^+ + NH_2^-$ | very small |

Note: $H^+(aq) = H_3O^+$

Sample equation: $HI + H_2O = H_3O^+ + I^-$

## CONSTANTS FOR VARIOUS EQUILIBRIA AT 1 atm AND 298 K

| | |
|---|---|
| $H_2O(\ell) = H^+(aq) + OH^-(aq)$ | $K_w = 1.0 \times 10^{-14}$ |
| $H_2O(\ell) + H_2O(\ell) = H_3O^+(aq) + OH^-(aq)$ | $K_w = 1.0 \times 10^{-14}$ |
| $CH_3COO^-(aq) + H_2O(\ell) = CH_3COOH(aq) + OH^-(aq)$ | $K_b = 5.6 \times 10^{-10}$ |
| $Na^+F^-(aq) + H_2O(\ell) = Na^+(OH)^- + HF(aq)$ | $K_b = 1.5 \times 10^{-11}$ |
| $NH_3(aq) + H_2O(\ell) = NH_4^+(aq) + OH^-(aq)$ | $K_b = 1.8 \times 10^{-5}$ |
| $CO_3^{2-}(aq) + H_2O(\ell) = HCO_3^-(aq) + OH^-(aq)$ | $K_b = 1.8 \times 10^{-4}$ |
| $Ag(NH_3)_2^+(aq) = Ag^+(aq) + 2NH_3(aq)$ | $K_{eq} = 8.9 \times 10^{-8}$ |
| $N_2(g) + 3H_2(g) = 2NH_3(g)$ | $K_{eq} = 6.7 \times 10^5$ |
| $H_2(g) + I_2(g) = 2HI(g)$ | $K_{eq} = 3.5 \times 10^{-1}$ |

| Compound | $K_{sp}$ | Compound | $K_{sp}$ |
|---|---|---|---|
| AgBr | $5.0 \times 10^{-13}$ | $Li_2CO_3$ | $2.5 \times 10^{-2}$ |
| AgCl | $1.8 \times 10^{-10}$ | $PbCl_2$ | $1.6 \times 10^{-5}$ |
| $Ag_2CrO_4$ | $1.1 \times 10^{-12}$ | $PbCO_3$ | $7.4 \times 10^{-14}$ |
| AgI | $8.3 \times 10^{-17}$ | $PbCrO_4$ | $2.8 \times 10^{-13}$ |
| $BaSO_4$ | $1.1 \times 10^{-10}$ | $PbI_2$ | $7.1 \times 10^{-9}$ |
| $CaSO_4$ | $9.1 \times 10^{-6}$ | $ZnCO_3$ | $1.4 \times 10^{-11}$ |

**STANDARD ENERGIES OF FORMATION**
**OF COMPOUNDS AT 1 atm AND 298 K**

| Compound | Heat (Enthalpy) of Formation* $(\Delta H_f°)$ | | Free Energy of Formation $(\Delta G_f°)$ | |
|---|---|---|---|---|
| | kJ/mol | kcal/mol | kJ/mol | kcal/mol |
| Aluminum oxide $Al_2O_3(s)$ | −1676.5 | −400.5 | −1583.1 | −378.2 |
| Ammonia $NH_3(g)$ | −46.0 | −11.0 | −16.3 | −3.9 |
| Barium sulfate $BaSO_4(s)$ | −1473.9 | −352.1 | −1363.0 | −325.6 |
| Calcium hydroxide $Ca(OH)_2(s)$ | −986.6 | −235.7 | −899.2 | −214.8 |
| Carbon dioxide $CO_2(g)$ | −393.9 | −94.1 | −394.7 | −94.3 |
| Carbon monoxide $CO(g)$ | −110.5 | −26.4 | −137.3 | −32.8 |
| Copper(II) sulfate $CuSO_4(s)$ | −771.9 | −184.4 | −662.2 | −158.2 |
| Ethane $C_2H_6(g)$ | −84.6 | −20.2 | −33.1 | −7.9 |
| Ethene (ethylene) $C_2H_4(g)$ | 52.3 | 12.5 | 68.2 | 16.3 |
| Ethyne (acetylene) $C_2H_2(g)$ | 226.9 | 54.2 | 209.3 | 50.0 |
| Hydrogen fluoride $HF(g)$ | −271.3 | −64.8 | −273.3 | −65.3 |
| Hydrogen iodide $HI(g)$ | 26.4 | 6.3 | 1.7 | 0.4 |
| Iodine chloride $ICl(g)$ | 18.0 | 4.3 | −5.4 | −1.3 |
| Lead(II) oxide $PbO(s)$ | −215.6 | −51.5 | −188.4 | −45.0 |
| Methane $CH_4(g)$ | −74.9 | −17.9 | −50.7 | −12.1 |
| Magnesium oxide $MgO(s)$ | −601.9 | −143.8 | −569.7 | −136.1 |
| Nitrogen(II) oxide $NO(g)$ | 90.4 | 21.6 | 86.7 | 20.7 |
| Nitrogen(IV) oxide $NO_2(g)$ | 33.1 | 7.9 | 51.5 | 12.3 |
| Potassium chloride $KCl(s)$ | −437.0 | −104.4 | −409.4 | −97.8 |
| Sodium chloride $NaCl(s)$ | −411.5 | −98.3 | −384.3 | −91.8 |
| Sulfur dioxide $SO_2(g)$ | −296.8 | −70.9 | −300.1 | −71.7 |
| Water $H_2O(g)$ | −242.0 | −57.8 | −228.6 | −54.6 |
| Water $H_2O(\ell)$ | −285.9 | −68.3 | −237.3 | −56.7 |

*Minus sign indicates an exothermic reaction.
Sample equations:

$$2Al(s) + \frac{3}{2} O_2(g) \rightarrow Al_2O_3(s) + 400.5 \text{ kcal}$$

$$2Al(s) + \frac{3}{2} O_2(g) \rightarrow Al_2O_3(s) \quad \Delta H = -400.5 \text{ kcal/mol}$$

# MODEL MCAT

Some useful reference material can be found beginning on page 170.

The full-length model MCAT that follows will provide you with helpful practice. Be sure to take the model test under strict test conditions, timing each section as instructed. First, remove the answer sheets.

After you complete the test, check your answers with the explanations that begin on page 216.

# The MCAT
# Model Examination

From *Barron's MCAT*, 12th ed., by Hugo R. Seibel et al. (Barron's Educational Series, 2008).

## ANSWER FORM

*DIRECTIONS:*  After locating the number of the question to which you are responding, fill in the circle containing the letter of the answer you have selected. Use pencil (not a ballpoint pen) to completely blacken the circle.

**PHYSICAL SCIENCES**

1. Ⓐ Ⓑ Ⓒ Ⓓ
2. Ⓐ Ⓑ Ⓒ Ⓓ
3. Ⓐ Ⓑ Ⓒ Ⓓ
4. Ⓐ Ⓑ Ⓒ Ⓓ
5. Ⓐ Ⓑ Ⓒ Ⓓ
6. Ⓐ Ⓑ Ⓒ Ⓓ
7. Ⓐ Ⓑ Ⓒ Ⓓ
8. Ⓐ Ⓑ Ⓒ Ⓓ
9. Ⓐ Ⓑ Ⓒ Ⓓ
10. Ⓐ Ⓑ Ⓒ Ⓓ
11. Ⓐ Ⓑ Ⓒ Ⓓ
12. Ⓐ Ⓑ Ⓒ Ⓓ
13. Ⓐ Ⓑ Ⓒ Ⓓ
14. Ⓐ Ⓑ Ⓒ Ⓓ
15. Ⓐ Ⓑ Ⓒ Ⓓ
16. Ⓐ Ⓑ Ⓒ Ⓓ
17. Ⓐ Ⓑ Ⓒ Ⓓ
18. Ⓐ Ⓑ Ⓒ Ⓓ
19. Ⓐ Ⓑ Ⓒ Ⓓ
20. Ⓐ Ⓑ Ⓒ Ⓓ
21. Ⓐ Ⓑ Ⓒ Ⓓ
22. Ⓐ Ⓑ Ⓒ Ⓓ
23. Ⓐ Ⓑ Ⓒ Ⓓ
24. Ⓐ Ⓑ Ⓒ Ⓓ
25. Ⓐ Ⓑ Ⓒ Ⓓ
26. Ⓐ Ⓑ Ⓒ Ⓓ

27. Ⓐ Ⓑ Ⓒ Ⓓ
28. Ⓐ Ⓑ Ⓒ Ⓓ
29. Ⓐ Ⓑ Ⓒ Ⓓ
30. Ⓐ Ⓑ Ⓒ Ⓓ
31. Ⓐ Ⓑ Ⓒ Ⓓ
32. Ⓐ Ⓑ Ⓒ Ⓓ
33. Ⓐ Ⓑ Ⓒ Ⓓ
34. Ⓐ Ⓑ Ⓒ Ⓓ
35. Ⓐ Ⓑ Ⓒ Ⓓ
36. Ⓐ Ⓑ Ⓒ Ⓓ
37. Ⓐ Ⓑ Ⓒ Ⓓ
38. Ⓐ Ⓑ Ⓒ Ⓓ
39. Ⓐ Ⓑ Ⓒ Ⓓ
40. Ⓐ Ⓑ Ⓒ Ⓓ
41. Ⓐ Ⓑ Ⓒ Ⓓ
42. Ⓐ Ⓑ Ⓒ Ⓓ
43. Ⓐ Ⓑ Ⓒ Ⓓ
44. Ⓐ Ⓑ Ⓒ Ⓓ
45. Ⓐ Ⓑ Ⓒ Ⓓ
46. Ⓐ Ⓑ Ⓒ Ⓓ
47. Ⓐ Ⓑ Ⓒ Ⓓ
48. Ⓐ Ⓑ Ⓒ Ⓓ
49. Ⓐ Ⓑ Ⓒ Ⓓ
50. Ⓐ Ⓑ Ⓒ Ⓓ
51. Ⓐ Ⓑ Ⓒ Ⓓ
52. Ⓐ Ⓑ Ⓒ Ⓓ

**VERBAL REASONING**

53. Ⓐ Ⓑ Ⓒ Ⓓ
54. Ⓐ Ⓑ Ⓒ Ⓓ
55. Ⓐ Ⓑ Ⓒ Ⓓ
56. Ⓐ Ⓑ Ⓒ Ⓓ
57. Ⓐ Ⓑ Ⓒ Ⓓ
58. Ⓐ Ⓑ Ⓒ Ⓓ
59. Ⓐ Ⓑ Ⓒ Ⓓ
60. Ⓐ Ⓑ Ⓒ Ⓓ
61. Ⓐ Ⓑ Ⓒ Ⓓ
62. Ⓐ Ⓑ Ⓒ Ⓓ
63. Ⓐ Ⓑ Ⓒ Ⓓ
64. Ⓐ Ⓑ Ⓒ Ⓓ
65. Ⓐ Ⓑ Ⓒ Ⓓ
66. Ⓐ Ⓑ Ⓒ Ⓓ
67. Ⓐ Ⓑ Ⓒ Ⓓ
68. Ⓐ Ⓑ Ⓒ Ⓓ
69. Ⓐ Ⓑ Ⓒ Ⓓ
70. Ⓐ Ⓑ Ⓒ Ⓓ
71. Ⓐ Ⓑ Ⓒ Ⓓ
72. Ⓐ Ⓑ Ⓒ Ⓓ

73. Ⓐ Ⓑ Ⓒ Ⓓ
74. Ⓐ Ⓑ Ⓒ Ⓓ
75. Ⓐ Ⓑ Ⓒ Ⓓ
76. Ⓐ Ⓑ Ⓒ Ⓓ
77. Ⓐ Ⓑ Ⓒ Ⓓ
78. Ⓐ Ⓑ Ⓒ Ⓓ
79. Ⓐ Ⓑ Ⓒ Ⓓ
80. Ⓐ Ⓑ Ⓒ Ⓓ
81. Ⓐ Ⓑ Ⓒ Ⓓ
82. Ⓐ Ⓑ Ⓒ Ⓓ
83. Ⓐ Ⓑ Ⓒ Ⓓ
84. Ⓐ Ⓑ Ⓒ Ⓓ
85. Ⓐ Ⓑ Ⓒ Ⓓ
86. Ⓐ Ⓑ Ⓒ Ⓓ
87. Ⓐ Ⓑ Ⓒ Ⓓ
88. Ⓐ Ⓑ Ⓒ Ⓓ
89. Ⓐ Ⓑ Ⓒ Ⓓ
90. Ⓐ Ⓑ Ⓒ Ⓓ
91. Ⓐ Ⓑ Ⓒ Ⓓ
92. Ⓐ Ⓑ Ⓒ Ⓓ

**WRITING SAMPLE**

93. Use separate sheets
    of paper.
94. Use separate sheets of
    paper.

**BIOLOGICAL SCIENCES**

95. Ⓐ Ⓑ Ⓒ Ⓓ
96. Ⓐ Ⓑ Ⓒ Ⓓ
97. Ⓐ Ⓑ Ⓒ Ⓓ
98. Ⓐ Ⓑ Ⓒ Ⓓ
99. Ⓐ Ⓑ Ⓒ Ⓓ
100. Ⓐ Ⓑ Ⓒ Ⓓ
101. Ⓐ Ⓑ Ⓒ Ⓓ
102. Ⓐ Ⓑ Ⓒ Ⓓ
103. Ⓐ Ⓑ Ⓒ Ⓓ
104. Ⓐ Ⓑ Ⓒ Ⓓ
105. Ⓐ Ⓑ Ⓒ Ⓓ
106. Ⓐ Ⓑ Ⓒ Ⓓ

107. Ⓐ Ⓑ Ⓒ Ⓓ
108. Ⓐ Ⓑ Ⓒ Ⓓ
109. Ⓐ Ⓑ Ⓒ Ⓓ
110. Ⓐ Ⓑ Ⓒ Ⓓ
111. Ⓐ Ⓑ Ⓒ Ⓓ
112. Ⓐ Ⓑ Ⓒ Ⓓ
113. Ⓐ Ⓑ Ⓒ Ⓓ
114. Ⓐ Ⓑ Ⓒ Ⓓ
115. Ⓐ Ⓑ Ⓒ Ⓓ
116. Ⓐ Ⓑ Ⓒ Ⓓ
117. Ⓐ Ⓑ Ⓒ Ⓓ
118. Ⓐ Ⓑ Ⓒ Ⓓ
119. Ⓐ Ⓑ Ⓒ Ⓓ
120. Ⓐ Ⓑ Ⓒ Ⓓ

121. Ⓐ Ⓑ Ⓒ Ⓓ
122. Ⓐ Ⓑ Ⓒ Ⓓ
123. Ⓐ Ⓑ Ⓒ Ⓓ
124. Ⓐ Ⓑ Ⓒ Ⓓ
125. Ⓐ Ⓑ Ⓒ Ⓓ
126. Ⓐ Ⓑ Ⓒ Ⓓ
127. Ⓐ Ⓑ Ⓒ Ⓓ
128. Ⓐ Ⓑ Ⓒ Ⓓ
129. Ⓐ Ⓑ Ⓒ Ⓓ
130. Ⓐ Ⓑ Ⓒ Ⓓ
131. Ⓐ Ⓑ Ⓒ Ⓓ
132. Ⓐ Ⓑ Ⓒ Ⓓ
133. Ⓐ Ⓑ Ⓒ Ⓓ

134. Ⓐ Ⓑ Ⓒ Ⓓ
135. Ⓐ Ⓑ Ⓒ Ⓓ
136. Ⓐ Ⓑ Ⓒ Ⓓ
137. Ⓐ Ⓑ Ⓒ Ⓓ
138. Ⓐ Ⓑ Ⓒ Ⓓ
139. Ⓐ Ⓑ Ⓒ Ⓓ
140. Ⓐ Ⓑ Ⓒ Ⓓ
141. Ⓐ Ⓑ Ⓒ Ⓓ
142. Ⓐ Ⓑ Ⓒ Ⓓ
143. Ⓐ Ⓑ Ⓒ Ⓓ
144. Ⓐ Ⓑ Ⓒ Ⓓ
145. Ⓐ Ⓑ Ⓒ Ⓓ
146. Ⓐ Ⓑ Ⓒ Ⓓ

TEST BEGINS ON NEXT PAGE.

# The MCAT Model Examination

---

## PHYSICAL SCIENCES

52 QUESTIONS
70 MINUTES

*DIRECTIONS:* The following questions or incomplete statements are in groups. Preceding each series of questions or statements is a paragraph or a short explanatory statement, a formula or set of formulas, or a definition. Read the written material and then answer the questions or complete the statements. Select the ONE BEST ANSWER for each question and indicate your selection by marking the corresponding letter of your choice on the Answer Form. Eliminate those alternatives you know to be incorrect and then select an answer from among the remaining alternatives. A periodic table is provided (see p. 173). You may consult it whenever you wish to do so.

### Passage I (Questions 1–5)

An X-ray tube consists of two metal electrodes, a heated filament cathode, and an anode containing the metal target sealed under high vacuum in a glass envelope. The heated filament in the cathode emits electrons which are accelerated by a high DC voltage and collide with the positive anode target. Two different types of X-ray spectra may be seen. The continuous or "bremsstrahlung" spectrum that is always present is produced when the electron penetrates through the outer electron cloud and is abruptly accelerated by the large positive charge on the nucleus of a heavy atom. The production of X-rays increases with increasing atomic number but is typically no more than 1% efficient, the remaining energy appearing as heat in the target metal. The sharp line spectra that can be seen at higher voltages occur when the incident electrons eject an inner shell electron, such as an $n = 1$ shell electron. The spectral line is produced when an electron, say from $n = 2$, fills the vacancy in the $n = 1$ shell, emitting an x-ray photon whose energy corresponds to the energy difference between the $n = 2$ and $n = 1$ shells. The intensity of X-rays is proportional to the number of photons created. The photon energy $E = hf = hc/\lambda$ where h is Planck's constant and $c$ is the speed of light. Figure 1 is a sketch of intensity versus wavelength for a molybdenum target with an accelerating voltage of 35,000 V.

1. Figure 1 shows that the continuous X-ray spectrum has a minimum (cut-off) wavelength. No shorter wavelengths are emitted from the tube. This minimum wavelength corresponds to:

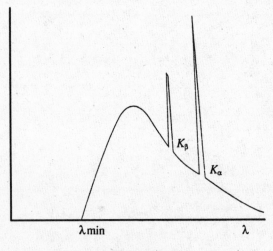

**Figure 1.**
X-ray intensity versus wavelength

  **A.** the smallest number of emitted photons.
  **B.** the highest energy photons emitted.
  **C.** the type of cathode used.
  **D.** the type of anode material used.

2. The sharp $K_\alpha$ peak in Figure 1 corresponds to an electron transition from state $n = 2$ to $n = 1$, whereas $K_\beta$ corresponds to a transition from state $n = 3$ to $n = 1$. The $K_\alpha$ peak is higher than the $K_\beta$ peak. Which peak corresponds to higher-energy X-ray photons? Which transition is more probable?

   A. $K_\alpha$ is higher energy; $K_\alpha$ is more probable.
   B. $K_\alpha$ is higher energy; $K_\beta$ is more probable.
   C. $K_\beta$ is higher energy; $K_\beta$ is more probable.
   D. $K_\beta$ is higher energy; $K_\alpha$ is more probable.

3. The current to the heated filament in the cathode is increased while the accelerating voltage is kept constant. This increased current increases the number of electrons striking the target increasing the overall intensity. What effect does this have on the minimum wavelength value?

   A. The minimum value will move to shorter wavelength values.
   B. It will move to longer wavelength values.
   C. There will no longer be a cutoff wavelength.
   D. The minimum wavelength will remain the same.

4. If the accelerating voltage, $V_o$, is increased while keeping the filament current constant, the overall intensity will also increase. What effect will this have on the wavelength position where the two peaks are observed?

   A. They will occur at the same wavelengths.
   B. The peaks occur at shorter wavelengths due to the higher energies available.
   C. They may disappear because all energies may exceed those of the $n = 3$ to $n = 1$ transition.
   D. The $K_\alpha$ occur at longer wavelengths but the $K_\beta$ occur at shorter wavelengths.

5. The energy of those x-ray photons that have the minimum wavelength ($\lambda_{min}$) is:

   A. 35,000 eV  C. 17,500 eV
   B. 0 eV  D. $5.6 \times 10^{-15}$ eV

## Passage II (Questions 6–10)

   A safety engineering firm is producing a film for high school driver education classes. The firm uses skilled test drivers driving both small cars and larger vans. The vans weigh three times as much as the cars and have larger tires with twice the tread width. In a demonstration that tests reaction times and skid-to-stop distances and shows them on the film, three guns that fire a yellow paint onto the road are mounted on the bumpers and fired electrically. When the driver hears the report of the first gun, he locks the brakes, and the touch of his foot on the brake pedal fires a second yellow pellet. The third pellet is fired when the car stops. The safety engineers also design several remote controlled cars and vans in order to film crash results.

6. Drivers of a car and a van brake hard and skid to a stop from 50 mph. The skid marks are measured to be the same length for both. Why are the stopping distances the same length?

   A. The mechanical work done by friction to stop both is the same.
   B. The frictional force between tires and road is three times greater for the heavier van so it slides the same distance as the car.
   C. The frictional force for the car and van are the same.
   D. The wider tires on the van require less friction force than the narrow tires on the car.

7. Two drivers in identical cars skid to a stop from speeds of 20 mph and 40 mph. How do the lengths of the skid marks compare?

   A. They are the same length.
   B. The 40 mph mark is twice as long.
   C. The 40 mph mark is four times as long.
   D. The 40 mph mark is eight times as long.

8. A remote-controlled car and van are crashed head-on at the same speed. Why does the car suffer more damage in the collision?

   A. The car and van had the same momentum.
   B. The forces during collision are equal and opposite, so the smaller and weaker car suffers more damage.
   C. The van exerts a larger force on the car.
   D. The mechanical work done in stopping the car is greater.

9. The van going at a speed of 15 mph collides head-on with a car going at a speed of 45 mph. Because the van weighs three times as much, their vector momenta are equal and opposite. However, examination shows that the car suffers more damage than the van. Why?

   A. The massive van exerts a larger force on the car.
   B. The lighter car exerts a smaller force on the van.
   C. The forces exerted during the collision are equal and opposite, so the weaker car suffers more damage.
   D. The mechanical work required to stop the van is smaller.

10. For the reaction time test, one driver is tested at 20 mph and 60 mph. It is noted that the distance between the first two paint marks is three times farther for the 60 mph test than the 20 mph test. How do his reaction times compare at 20 mph and 60 mph?

    A. His reaction time at 60 mph is three times faster.
    B. His reaction times remain the same.
    C. His reaction time at 20 mph is three times faster.
    D. His reaction time at 20 mph is one-third as long as at 60 mph.

## Passage III (Questions 11–16)

Calcium carbonate reacts with water and carbon dioxide to produce soluble calcium bicarbonate according to the reaction:

$$CaCO_3(s) + CO_2(g) + H_2O(l) \rightarrow Ca(HCO_3)_2(aq)$$

This reaction is responsible for the erosion of caves containing large deposits of calcium carbonate. Calcium carbonate reacts with hydrochloric acid to produce calcium chloride, according to the reaction:

$$CaCO_3(s) + 2HCl(aq) \rightarrow CaCl_2(aq) + CO_2(g) + H_2O(l)$$

Heating calcium carbonate at high temperatures produces calcium oxide, which is used to neutralize acidic soils, as follows:

$$CaCO_3(s) \rightarrow CaO(s) + CO_2(g)$$

11. A chemist places a sample of calcium carbonate into a sealed container under pure carbon dioxide gas. Will the sample react to form calcium bicarbonate?

    A. Yes, because carbon dioxide is present.
    B. Yes, because calcium carbonate is present.
    C. No, because water is absent.
    D. No, because hydrochloric acid is absent.

12. A sample of calcium oxide is placed into water. What is the approximate pH of the solution:

    A. 2         C. 7
    B. 6         D. 9

13. Which of the following is a strong electrolyte?

    A. $CO_2(g)$         C. $CaCl_2(aq)$
    B. $H_2O(l)$         D. $Ca(s)$

14. A lake contains runoff from a mountain that has large deposits of calcium carbonate and freezes at a point 1.6°C lower than other lakes at similar altitude. What is the most likely explanation for this?

    A. Dissolved calcium bicarbonate lowers the freezing point.
    B. Dissolved calcium carbonate lowers the freezing point.
    C. Dissolved calcium bicarbonate raises the freezing point.
    D. Dissolved calcium carbonate raises the freezing point.

15. What is the charge of the calcium ion in calcium chloride?

    A. −1         C. +1
    B. −2         D. +2

16. Decomposition of a sample of calcium carbonate produced 56.1 g CaO. How much carbon dioxide is produced at STP?

    A. 11.2 L         C. 33.4 L
    B. 22.4 L         D. 40.6 L

**Passage IV** (Questions 17–20)

A large cylindrical tank 5 meters in radius is filled to the top with water. A small amount of water is then added until it mounds up slightly above the edges of the tank (because of surface tension). The tank is 3 meters high. A stopcock 2 meters below the top edge can be opened to allow water to flow out horizontally. The tank sits in a catch basin to catch any water that flows over the top edge. If the stopcock is opened, the water will flow out in a smooth jet that lands on the floor beyond the edge of the catch basin. A closed top can be clamped onto the top of the tank and connected to an air pump so that the air pressure on the top surface of the water can be increased above one atmosphere. Wooden cubes that are 10 cm on an edge and have a mass density of 700 kg/m$^3$ are available.

The mass density of water is 1000 kg/m$^3$.
1 atmosphere pressure = $1.03 \times 10^5$ N/m$^2$.

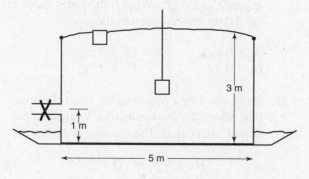

17. A single cube of wood is placed carefully on the mounded water surface, causing water to overflow into the catch basin. How much water overflows into the catch basin?

    A. A volume of water equal to 30% of the volume of the wood block.
    B. A mass of water equal to 70% of the mass of the wood block.
    C. A volume of water equal to the volume of the wood block.
    D. A volume of water the weight of which equals the weight of the block.

18. The block of wood is now submerged completely under the water surface by pushing down on it with a very thin rigid rod, and some more water overflows into the catch basin. How much *total* water is now in the catch basin?

    A. A mass of water equal to the mass of the block of wood.
    B. A weight of water equal to the weight of the block of wood.
    C. A volume of water equal to the volume of the wood block.
    D. A weight of water equal to 70% of the weight of the wood block.

19. The buoyant force the water exerts on the submerged block is:

    A. equal to the weight of the block.
    B. smaller than the weight of the block by 30%.
    C. equal to the weight of the water in the catch basin.
    D. equal to 70% of the weight of the block.

20. The blocks are removed and the water in the tank is adjusted until the water surface is level with the top edge of the tank. A smaller tank is only 2 m in radius but is filled to the same height with water as the large tank and also has a stopcock 2 m below its top edge. How do the speeds of water exiting through the two stopcocks compare?

    A. The water from the large tank is 67% faster.
    B. The water from the small tank is 33% slower.
    C. The water from the large tank is about 6 times faster because it has 6 times the volume of the small tank.
    D. The speeds are the same.

## Passage V (Questions 21–25)

A pendulum system consists of a bob of mass 2 kg on the end of a cord that is 80 cm long from the cord support to the center of the bob. The system behaves as a simple pendulum if one displaces the pendulum through a small angle (less than about 10°) from the vertical. The period is given by:

$$T = 2\pi\sqrt{L / g}$$

Other masses and cord lengths are available.

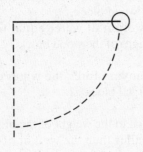

**21.** The bob is raised to the position where the cord is horizontal (90°) and then released. What is the speed of the bob as it passes through the lowest point of its swing?

**A.** 2.0 m/s     **C.** 5.1 m/s
**B.** 4.0 m/s     **D.** 5.9 m/s

**22.** The bob is now raised until the cord makes an angle of 4° with the vertical. What is the period of oscillation when the bob is released?

**A.** 1.8 s     **C.** 1.4 s
**B.** 2.8 s     **D.** 2.6 s

**23.** The bob is raised higher so that the cord makes the angle of 8° with the vertical. What is the period of oscillation now?

**A.** 3.6 s     **C.** 1.8 s
**B.** 3.2 s     **D.** 0.9 s

**24.** The bob is replaced with a bob of 3 kg. A new cord is of unknown length. When the period is timed, it is found to be 2.0 s for small angles. What is the length of the new pendulum?

**A.** 1.0 m     **C.** 1.8 m
**B.** 2.0 m     **D.** 2.4 m

**25.** NASA, upon renewing the moon landing program in preparation for sending men and women to Mars, sends the 2.0-second pendulum system to the moon. What happens to the measured period of the pendulum when used on the moon?

**A.** $T$ increases.
**B.** $T$ decreases.
**C.** $T$ hardly changes at all.
**D.** The pendulum will not work on the moon where there is no gravity.

## Questions 26–32 are independent of any passage and of each other.

**26.** Water flows without friction through a water-filled pipe of cross-sectional area 3.0 m² at a speed of 2.0 m/s. The pipe's cross-sectional area first constricts to 1.0 m² and then expands to 2.0 m². What is the water speed in the 2.0 m² cross section of the pipe?

**A.** 9.0 m/s     **C.** 3.0 m/s
**B.** 4.0 m/s     **D.** 1.0 m/s

**27.** Rutherford first observed nuclear transmutation when $^{14}$N was bombarded with alpha particles ($^4$He nuclei). The reaction is written as:

$$^4_2\text{He} + {}^{14}_7\text{N} \rightarrow {}^{17}_8\text{O} + ?$$

What is the missing particle ?

**A.** $^4_2$He (alpha particle)
**B.** $^1_1$H (proton)
**C.** $^1_0$n (neutron)
**D.** $^0_{-1}$e (electron)

**28.** Two charged particles, A and B, are a distance $r$ apart so that a certain force exists between them. The charge on A is tripled while the distance between the charges is also tripled. How does the force between the particles change?

**A.** It does not change.
**B.** It increases by a factor of 3.
**C.** It decreases by a factor of 9.
**D.** It decreases by a factor of 3.

**29.** A 3-ohm resistor and a 6-ohm resistor are connected in parallel and a 2-ohm resistor is connected in series with this combination as shown. If a current of 3 amperes is sent through the 2-ohm resistor, the currents through the 3- and 6-ohm resistors are, respectively:

A. 3 and 2 amperes
B. 1 and 2 amperes
C. 2 and 1 amperes
D. 0.5 and 2.5 amperes

**30.** A golf ball is dropped from the top of a very tall building. (Air friction is present.) Which graph below correctly shows the velocity of the ball as a function of time?

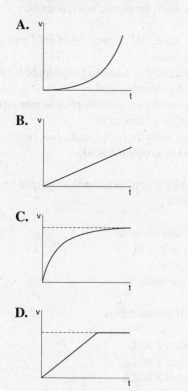

A. v

B. v

C. v

D. v

**31.** A box slides on a frictionless surface from rest at point A, which is 10 m above the ground, to point C at 5 m above the ground. What is the speed of the box at point C?

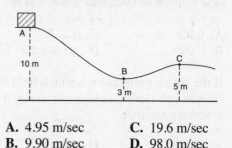

A. 4.95 m/sec      C. 19.6 m/sec
B. 9.90 m/sec      D. 98.0 m/sec

**32.** A lighted object produces an image on a screen. The screen is 30 cm from the lens. The lens is exactly midway between the object and the screen. What is the focal length of the lens?

A. +30 cm      C. +60 cm
B. +15 cm      D. −30 cm

## Passage VI (Questions 33–38)

The colorimeter is a device for measuring the amount of light that passes through a solution. When the color (wavelength) of light is selected properly, the colorimeter is a useful tool for determining the amount of a particular light-absorbing material in solution.

A colorimeter is equipped with a meter that responds in linear fashion to the amount of light reaching it. The meter is set to zero with no light and it is found that a cuvette containing pure water gives a reading of 81 for light of a particular wavelength. When the same cuvette with an aqueous solution is placed in the light path, a reading of 72 is obtained.

**33.** The transmittance of the solution is:

A. 0.811.      C. 0.889.
B. 81.1.        D. 0.722.

**34.** The absorbance of the solution is:

A. 0.189.      C. 0.278.
B. 0.111.      D. 0.051.

35. If the light is of a particular wavelength that is specifically absorbed by the solute (or one of its functional groups), dilution of the solution with an equal volume of water will produce a new solution whose absorbance will be:

    A. 0.026.      C. 0.282.
    B. 0.095.      D. greater than 0.5.

36. If the path length through which light travels in the above solution is halved, the absorbance will be:

    A. 0.013.      C. 0.041.
    B. 0.052.      D. 0.190.

37. If the solute concentration for the first reading in this question set is doubled, the reading for this higher concentration will be:

    A. 64.      C. 18.
    B. 51.      D. 5.

38. If the wavelength of the light in this previous question is doubled, the reading will:

    A. be doubled.
    B. be halved.
    C. show no change.
    D. change by an amount that cannot be predicted.

## Passage VII (Questions 39–45)

A 0.01 mole sample of HCl is diluted to 1000 mL with water and mixed in a beaker to produce solution A. To this is added 1000 mL of water. After mixing, the resulting solution is solution B. To this is added 0.02 moles sodium propionate. After mixing, the resulting solution is solution C. To this is added 0.01 mole sodium propionate and 0.01 mole propionic acid. After mixing, the resulting solution is solution D. To this is added 1000 mL more water. After mixing, the resulting solution is solution E. To another beaker is added 0.005 mole of pyruvic acid. Water is added to a total volume of 500 mL. After mixing, the resulting solution is solution F. To solution F is added 0.005 mole of sodium pyruvate. After mixing, the resulting solution is solution G. $K_a$ values are $1.3 \times 10^{-5}$ for propionic acid, $1.4 \times 10^{-4}$ for pyruvic acid, and $5.9 \times 10^{-10}$ for boric acid. $pK_a$ values are 4.89 for propionic acid, 3.85 for pyruvic acid, and 9.23 for boric acid. (For the purpose of this problem, assume no volume change occurs after the addition of small quantities of liquid or solid.)

39. The pH of solution A is:

    A. 2.0.      C. 4.0.
    B. 3.0.      D. 6.0.

40. The pH of solution B is:

    A. less than 2.
    B. between 2 and 3
    C. between 3 and 4.
    D. between 4 and 7.

41. The pH of solution C is equal to the $pK_a$ of the weak acid, propionic acid, because:

    A. there are equal quantities of HCl and propionic acid.
    B. the quantity of sodium propionate is twice that of propionic acid.
    C. the quantity of sodium propionate equals that of propionic acid.
    D. all the sodium propionate has been converted to propionic acid.

42. The strongest acid used in the sample preparations was:

    A. hydrochloric acid.
    B. propionic acid.
    C. boric acid.
    D. pyruvic acid.

43. The pH of solution E is:

    A. between 2 and 3.
    B. between 4 and 5.
    C. between 5 and 6.
    D. greater than 6.5.

44. Among pyruvic acid, propionic acid, and boric acid:

    A. pyruvic acid is most acidic because it has the lowest $pK_a$.
    B. propionic acid is most acidic because it has the lowest $pK_a$.
    C. boric acid is most acidic because it has the lowest $pK_a$.
    D. boric acid is most acidic because it has the highest $pK_a$.

**45.** The percent of ionization of pyruvic acid is:

**A.** 0.12.  **C.** 12.
**B.** 1.2.  **D.** greater than 20.

**Questions 46–52 are independent of any passage and of each other.**

**46.** Compound A is known to have a molecular weight of 20. The molecular weight of Compound B is not known. Upon observing that gaseous Compound B will diffuse half as fast as gaseous Compound A, we can calculate the molecular weight of Compound B as:

**A.** 10.  **C.** 40.
**B.** 20.  **D.** 80.

**47.** In the titration of a 0.100 N solution of NaOH, it is found that 20.0 ml of a 0.200 N solution of an unknown acid will neutralize 40.0 ml of the 0.100 N NaOH. This indicates that the unknown acid is:

**A.** monoprotic.
**B.** diprotic.
**C.** triprotic.
**D.** none of the above.

**48.** If it is known that the pH of a solution is 4.5, we can calculate that the pOH is:

**A.** 4.5.  **C.** 9.5.
**B.** 7.5.  **D.** 12.5.

**49.** The $pK_a$ of an acid HA is 4.2. The pH at which equal concentrations of $A^-$ and HA are present in solution is:

**A.** 2.4.  **C.** 7.0.
**B.** 4.2.  **D.** 9.8.

**50.** A buffer is made of a weak acid ($pK_a = 5.9$) and its salt. Such a buffer functions best to suppress changes of pH on addition of acid when the pH of the solution is:

**A.** 3.9.  **C.** 7.0.
**B.** 5.9.  **D.** 8.9.

**51.** One liter of a gas is held at a pressure of 1 atm. If there is no change in temperature, increasing the pressure to 2 atm will result in a volume change to:

**A.** 2.0 liters.  **C.** 0.50 liter.
**B.** 0.95 liter.  **D.** 0.20 liter.

**52.** In recovery of silver from photographic film, you have decided to dissolve the silver ion with dilute nitric acid. Addition of dilute HCl to precipitate AgCl seems to result in unacceptable losses. You might improve recovery by addition of _____ in the latter step.

**A.** $NaNO_3$  **C.** $Ag_2SO_4$
**B.** NaCl  **D.** sodium acetate

# VERBAL REASONING

40 QUESTIONS
60 MINUTES

*DIRECTIONS:*    The questions are based on the accompanying seven passages. Read each passage carefully, then answer the following questions. Consider only the material within the passage. For each question, select the ONE BEST ANSWER and indicate your selection by marking the corresponding letter on the Answer Form.

## Passage I (Questions 53–58)

Periodic demands for educational reform, in conjunction with the corresponding efforts of the nation's public school systems to improve their instructional programs, are not an unusual phenomenon in the annals of this country's history. The most recent reform movement, however, which is viewed by many as a demand on the part of legislatures and the public for more effective schools, might be classified as unique. During the last 20 years, monumental amounts of research and discussion have been generated regarding all facets of public education.

The outcry was created in part by declining economic conditions and by the publication of such exhaustive studies of school resources and their impact as the Coleman et al., (1966) report on the *Equality of Educational Opportunity* and others (Jensen, 1969; Jenks et al. 1970; Rist, 1970; Avech, 1974), which seemed to point out the failure of the American educational system. The results of their findings caused considerable dismay in the educational community and the population at large, since they suggested that schools make little, if any, difference in the lives of the children who attend them. The socio-economic status of the individual's family (Hodgson, 1975) as well as a measure of "pure luck" (ERIC Action Brief, 1981) were credited with influencing student achievement and other educational outcomes to a much greater degree than a pupil's school experiences.

After the initial reaction of shock, neither researchers nor practitioners were content to stand by and accept the pessimistic picture that had been painted for them as a final verdict. In response, literally hundreds of studies have been conducted in schools across the country that focus on every aspect of public education.

Researchers have gone into the field in great numbers to obtain a firsthand view of the educational process in action. One early example of a now classic study that made an attempt to overcome the existing attitude of fatalism was that conducted by Weber (1971) in four Washington, D.C., schools. The results indicated that by placing a consistent school-wide emphasis on the teaching of basic skills, school leaders could be influential in improving the reading achievement of disadvantaged inner-city youngsters.

Many other research efforts, both ethnographic and quantitative in nature, have produced positive results and have infused practitioners with a new hope and a renewed belief that what takes place in schools can indeed make a significant difference in both the academic lives and the personal development of the pupils that they serve.

Although the negative effects of the early findings have been lessened, they have not been wiped away. The call for further reform continues, as evidenced by the continuing wave of national, state, and public demands contained in such reports as *A Nation at Risk* (Goldberg & James, 1983) and *Making the Grade* (Graham, 1983). Consequently, the research effort has intensified and has resulted in the translation of many of its findings into positive plans of action.

53. The central thesis of the passage is:

   **A.** schools do not make a difference in the lives of the students who attend them.
   **B.** instructional programs must always be improved and updated so that educational critics will be satisfied.
   **C.** although the call for educational reform in the United States has been an ongoing process, the past 20-year period has been an extremely research-oriented time in the public education arena.
   **D.** middle class parents should consider providing academic instruction for their children in the home setting.

Adapted from E. E. Seibel, "Principal Change Facilitator Style: Its Relationship to School Climate and Student Achievement." Doctoral Dissertation, Virginia Commonwealth University, 1986.

**54.** According to this passage, what factors were partially responsible for triggering the educational reform movement that is discussed therein?

   **A.** The fact that the majority of citizens in the United States have attended the public schools themselves and therefore knew that instructional programs needed to be changed.
   **B.** The fact that many people wanted to teach their children at home and did not want to pay taxes to support the public school system.
   **C.** Anger over the implication that the amount of money a family has, as well as the amount of "luck" they encounter, can make a difference in a child's education.
   **D.** A decline in the national economy and the publication of exhaustive school resource studies.

**55.** The demand for educational reform and the resulting research that has been conducted over the past 20 years has been centered on:

   **A.** public schools.
   **B.** private schools.
   **C.** home education.
   **D.** correspondence courses.

**56.** The fourth paragraph states: "Researchers have gone into the field in great numbers to gain a firsthand view of the educational process in action." Which of the following statements would be reasonable assumptions to make as a result of that sentence?

   I. Many studies have been conducted in school settings.
   II. The people conducting the research are not simply basing their results on educational theories.
   III. There appears to be a great deal of interest in the educational process.

   **A.** I only      **C.** I and II only
   **B.** II only      **D.** I, II, and III

**57.** What groups might the word "practitioners," used in paragraph three, stand for?

   **A.** doctors, dentists, lawyers
   **B.** educators
   **C.** superintendents, principals, teachers
   **D.** both B and C

**58.** The author of this passage gives the impression that:

   **A.** there is little hope for the successful future of public education in the United States.
   **B.** although serious problems exist in the educational arena, progress is being made, partially, as a result of the hands-on involvement of researchers.
   **C.** the field of education is so large that effective change cannot occur.
   **D.** too many people are involved in doing educational research.

## Passage II (Questions 59–64)

The fairy tale of Cinderella is one of the most widely known folk stories in the world. In its various versions it captures the struggle for the young girl's passage into womanhood. It covers, in its scope, several of Karen Horney's ideas, as well as the trials, totems, and family patterns found in primitive cultures. The Cinderella story chronicles the transformation of the girl into the woman, the profane into the spiritual; ending in the heroine's resolution of her feminine powers.

The Cinderella story goes back as far as seventh-century China. It is classified among the most well-known folktales in the world, and there is a version in nearly every language. The plot is universal: Cinderella, a beautiful, kind, and loving girl, suffers within her family, and is aided by some form of magic through which she meets the man she is destined to marry. After the initial meetings with this man, she loses some article symbolic of the womb, and the man uses this article to find and betroth her.

---

Adapted from Heather Tuttle, "If the Shoe Fits," VCU, 1990.

Several of Karen Horney's theories from "The Distrust Between the Sexes" are evident in this folktale. One of the main ideas in Cinderella is the concept of the evil stepmother or foster mother. Even in instances where Cinderella's father is still living, the stepmother is allowed to abuse her. Her elder sisters are also given this privilege. This is because the mother and sisters are older and less attractive than the heroine. Cinderella's persecution is permitted because, as Horney says, ". . . it is only the sexually attractive woman of whom [man] is afraid and who . . . has to be kept in bondage." In the cultures from which the story derives, old women are not sexually threatening to men and so the stepmother is given the power (by the father) to make the heroine submissive. Horney continues: "Old women, on the other hand, are held in high esteem, even by cultures in which the young woman is dreaded and therefore suppressed." Not only is the stepmother granted more power over Cinderella due to her position, but she feels her power potentially jeopardized by the sway that Cinderella's beauty may have over men. The sisters also feel jeopardized by the heroine's sexual attractiveness, which leads to greater resentment and cruelty on their part.

Another of Horney's theories prevalent in the story is the duality of motherhood. There are two aspects of motherhood, the virgin mother who is self-sacrificing, nurturing, and selfless, and the mother goddess, warm, earthy, sensual, and fertile. Both aspects are visible in the heroine. Cinderella, as she is first seen, sleeps in the cold, empty hearth, reflective of the virgin's womb, empty until acted upon by some outside force. She is covered in ashes, dressed in rags; in general a picture of self-effacing humility. Despite the hardships put upon her by her family, she is kind to them and even tries her best to beautify her stepsisters for the ball. She is virtuous, in contrast to her stepsisters and stepmother. After marriage to the prince, in the end, the heroine does not seek any revenge on her persecutors. In some renditions, she actually invites her family to come live with her and her new husband. Further evidence of this virginal mother aspect is the part that the prince plays in her life at this point. Like the ultimate example of nurturing motherhood, Mother Mary, who waits for the male god to act upon her, Cinderella lies in wait for the prince to come and save her. He is the aid she needs to be freed of her harsh life.

The other aspect of motherhood is revealed in her when magic help arrives from the outside. She is bestowed with sensual, material things: beautiful clothes, ornaments, cosmetics; things to make her desirable to men. The heroine is also gifted with the famous shoes, reflective of the womb. This prince is usually attracted to her for her physical appearance. She is displaying her sensual, seductive, earthy side and the prince is a reward for her power to act on him with her seductive ability. This dichotomy provides some confusion to the heroine, her family, and her suitor. The journey to resolve the puzzle of her twofold womanhood is a main theme in this folklore.

The passage from a girl to a woman is only one of the several transitions that take place within our heroine. She also undergoes a spiritual transformation. In the beginning of every account, the heroine is dirty and ragged. In at least three versions, she is made to wear animal skins. These things are representative of the material, animalistic, profane world. As she is put through the trials for entering into adulthood, she is also put through trials to test her spirituality. In spite of hardships, she manages to remain pious, loving, and kind. These trials come to an end and she becomes clean and well dressed. She is described as radiant, angelic, and fairylike. The heroine is then presented to the prince. The image of the prince embracing the servant girl is heavily laden with religious meaning, especially during the period when this story became popular. This analogy was very often used by the convents of the Middle Ages to relate the relationship of the nuns to Jesus Christ. Cinderella's spiritual ascent is completed with her royal wedding.

The heroine's time of testing is not completely at an end until the two sides of her femininity merge. They have been in the process of merging since the time of her totem's arrival. Since the arrival of the totem, she has actively struggled with her two female aspects, the virginal/nurturing and the earthy/seductive. The heroine in each version of the tale is given a womb symbol: either a shoe or a ring. This symbol accompanies her when she meets the prince in her state of beauty and sensuality. She then loses this article with the prince, who uses it to find her. When he sees her again, she is once more virginal, modest; covered in dirt and ashes, yet she is missing this symbol of her womanhood. The prince is confused; this is not quite the girl he thought he came for. After he places the shoe on her foot (or the ring on her finger, as the case may be) he sees her as whole: sensual, earthy, yet loving and virginal. She no longer runs from him as she did in earlier encounters, when things became too intimate with the prince.

This is also a moment of recognition for Cinderella. She has discovered a unity of both female forces within her. There were clues previously as to the wholeness of her nature, but she ignored them. She managed to overlook the times when she was sensual, at the ball, and was still kind to her family, generously giving them jewelry. She failed to see her true nature when she was beautiful and yet very humble in the presence of nobility. Now she can no longer hide herself. The prince has seen her spiritual, virginal, and sensual facets and her true nature is revealed to all, including her astonished family. She has found strength in her wholeness, and the prince is both her aid in discovering herself and her reward for being discovered.

**59.** This passage asserts that:

    I. only those versions of the story that are American can be used to illustrate Horney's theories.

    II. regardless of the version of the Cinderella tale, the story tells of a young girl's passage into womanhood.

    III. the concept of the evil stepmother or foster mother is a main ingredient in the Cinderella story.

    IV. Cinderella's sisters typically are older than she and less attractive.

    V. the prince finally sees only one facet of Cinderella.

**A.** I, II, and III    **C.** II, III, and IV
**B.** I and IV       **D.** IV only

**60.** According to this passage, Cinderella:

**A.** contemplates revenge on her sisters and mother but doesn't carry through with it.
**B.** does not seek revenge at all.
**C.** gives up her need for revenge after she marries the prince.
**D.** cannot bring herself to completely forgive her persecutors.

**61.** The author of this passage concludes the following from the fact that in at least three versions of the story, Cinderella is made to wear animal skins.

**A.** She needs the warmth that these skins provide.
**B.** The animal skins have nothing to do with the rites of passage that she is going through.
**C.** The animal skins symbolize the profane animal world that she figuratively is leaving.
**D.** She may decide to keep the animal skins.

**62.** Throughout the essay, but especially in the concluding paragraphs, the author suggests that Cinderella:

**A.** is less complex than she had originally thought herself to be.
**B.** is moving psychologically toward a condition of wholeness.
**C.** intentionally exploits the prince to bring about her own growth.
**D.** is weakened by her newly discovered wholeness.

**63.** One might draw the following conclusions from this passage:

**A.** Horney probably had the Cinderella story in mind when she formulated her theories.
**B.** Folktales and fairy tales such as Cinderella can be useful in illustrating aspects of psychological theories such as those of Horney.
**C.** Horney's theories are valid because the plots of the various versions of the Cinderella story bear them out.
**D.** Horney altered the story to make it fit her theories.

**64.** An appropriate title for this essay would be:

**A.** "If the Shoe Fits": Horney's Theories and the Cinderella Story.
**B.** The Narcissism of Cinderella.
**C.** The Stepmother as Heroine.
**D.** The Varieties of Magical Experience: The Shoe that Fits.

## Passage III (Questions 65–69)

Probably most people enter medical school driven in large measure by their desire to help their fellow humankind. Although the prospects of achieving substantial wealth and reasonably high public esteem may be related motives, most consider that the search to live some form of the Golden Rule is an important reason for entering medical school. There is a growing perception among the general public, however, that many physicians are more interested in themselves and their families than in their patients. An understanding of the role conflicts experienced in medical school, residency training, and professional practice must begin in the earliest days of medical education.

The sociologist, Wendy Carlton, studied the development of medical students and concluded that three rather distinct perspectives, the moral, clinical, and legal, directly affect decision making by physicians. Her extensive observation suggested to her that "medical students are being socialized into using the clinical perspective to resolve clinical problems with little or no regard for the ethical aspects of their professional behavior. In particular there is a striking absence of both discussion of and concern with ethical issues, despite a growing body of literature that argues for the relevance of training in ethics for physicians in an age of technological medicine." The clinical perspective, to Carlton, meant the traditional evaluation of the patient to create a "clinical picture" and, indeed, she entitled her book *In Our Professional Opinion.*

Carlton found that medical students upon entering medical school use the moral, clinical, and legal perspectives in that order. After acquiring clinical experience they apply the ranking used by physicians: clinical, legal, and then the moral. Hospital administrators invoke the legal, the clinical, and then the moral. "Laypersons," she contended, "use the moral perspective and depend on professionals to provide the clinical and legal perspectives, though they may use information from the media in an attempt to address the clinical and legal aspects of problem solution."

There is considerable concern on the part of many that the clinical perspective described by Carlton can degenerate into a callous disregard for

---

Adapted from addresses of Dr. Stephen M. Ayres, Dean, School of Medicine, Medical College of Virginia, Virginia Commonwealth University, 1990.

patient interest. Shem, in 1978, presented a satirical view of the brutal world of the intern in his book, *The House of God.* Terry Mizrahi, a sociologist who observed medical house staff behavior in a large urban teaching center, felt that Dr. Shem's book "verified the overall detachment and dehumanizing resulting from the training process." Her book, *Getting Rid of Patients,* "substantiated a world of contradictions wherein the patient was oppressed while being characterized as the oppressor."

Melvin Konner, an anthropologist who entered medical school in his mid-thirties after a variety of experiences (including a two-year stint with faith healers from the hunter-gatherers of the Kalahari desert in Africa), described his educational experiences in *Becoming A Doctor.* He characterized physicians as "tough, brilliant, knowledgable, hardworking, and hard on themselves. They are reliable and competent in situations ranging from 18-month-long management of cancer chemotherapy through 18-hour-long brain surgery to emergencies in which life may hinge on what they can do in 18 seconds. They have experienced many things that are closed to others. With very few exceptions, they are professionals."

"Perhaps they have earned the right to arrogance; they certainly feel that they have. But one wonders if they can see the self-serving aspects of their behavior." Konner goes on to emphasize the importance of "a nonphysical aspect to healing, which I am prepared to call spiritual. It relates to heart and mind, hope and will, love and courage, values and ideas, social and cultural—including religious—life. In the hospital, I learned to keep my thoughts to myself about all such matters. There, the pretense is that everyone knows about them, and it is unnecessary to talk of them. In reality, everyone 'knows' about them but practically nobody cares, except insofar as finding them the source of a good laugh. Such cynicism, which increases during the medical school years, deeply affects the young physicians' view of life—not just of illness but of the whole human experience. They have trained themselves to participate just so far and no farther with, say, a terminal cancer patient in his or her search for personal meaning; but then they cannot simply slough off this habit of diffidence when it comes to their own search for meaning, when they contemplate the course of their own lives. It is less than appealing, what this makes of them; yet I love them in some crazy way . . . I would not want my daughter or son to be one or to marry one . . . Yet of course, when I am in trouble—and notice that I do not say 'if'—I will go to them, and they will improve my chances."

The life of the medical student is challenging and at times frustrating. Although intelligence and good undergraduate preparation are essential, they are not enough. Medicine is really the study of the human condition. What was once called "bedside manner" or "attitude" really means an understanding of the ingredients of human happiness. Although good health seems essential for the enjoyment of life, it is clearly not enough. And the advantages of good health frequently must be tempered by the need for reasonable diet, reasonable shelter, and love and understanding. The practice of medicine is a calling, not a business. Physician-healers must know the science of health and disease but must also know what comprises the total experience that generally is called "being human." The first year of medical education, and part of the second, emphasizes the science of medicine. The patient experience toward the end of the first year of medical education, and the remaining years of education, are designed to help the student internalize the view that the practice of medicine must be based on the broadest possible understanding of the human condition. "The secret of the care of the patient is in caring for the patient."

65. The author could have chosen as a title for this passage:

A. Professional Growth of the Practicing Physician.
B. The Development of Medical Students.
C. The Life of the Medical Student.
D. The Development of the Physician.

66. The medical student of today:

A. is greatly concerned with achieving high public esteem.
B. needs only superior intelligence and good undergraduate education to succeed.
C. hopes to marry a classmate in order to have a more congenial marriage.
D. is concerned and wants to serve humanity.

67. Carlton suggests that as medical students undergo their training:

A. the ethical and moral issues predominate their decision-making process.
B. socialization elevates clinical decision making as a predominant force.
C. they are greatly influenced by hospital administrators who concentrate on legal issues.
D. they soon feel that they have earned the right to arrogance because of their thorough training.

68. In its discussion of the balance between the science of medical practice and what could be termed the art of dealing with patients, the passage implies that:

A. good health is enough for the enjoyment of life.
B. love and understanding of human emotions are not serious considerations in the overall scheme of a human being.
C. bedside manner can be learned.
D. medicine must use as its basis for practice a broad appreciation of life and humankind.

69. Which of the following statement(s) is/are *contradicted by* the passage?

A. Medical education should not consider the role conflicts experienced by students of medicine.
B. Laypersons focus quickly on the clinical and legal perspectives.
C. Physicians concentrate on their own happiness and are not hard on themselves.
D. All of the above.

## Passage IV (Questions 70–75)

Throughout the various phyla of the plant and animal kingdom, numerous species have evolved. It is apparent that sexual reproduction plays an important role in the continuation of the species and in the expression of different phenotypes within the species. This mode of reproduction is accomplished by the fusion of two gametes that will give rise to a zygote. In order for future generations to maintain the same number of chromosomes as their parents, the gametes must undergo a reduction in chromosome number. If the offspring express phenotypic traits that are different from those of their parents, there must be a rearrangement of the DNA within the chromosomes. The reduction of the number of chromosomes and mixing of the gene pool are accomplished by the process of meiosis.

The process of meiosis is characterized by a naturally occurring sequence of events that are usually artificially subdivided into ten different stages. The first five stages constitute the first or reductional division of meiosis. At the end of the reductional division, the chromosomes are reduced to one-half their original number (haploid). The last five stages constitute the second or equatorial division of meiosis. Germ cells undergoing meiosis give rise to haploid gametes that contain one representative of each type of chromosome. The chromosomes of the gametes may also demonstrate variations in genetic composition due to crossing over that takes place during the first prophase.

Replication of DNA occurs during interphase before the process of meiosis begins. The condensation and coiling of chromatin to form chromosomes marks the beginning of prophase 1, the first stage of meiosis. Homologous chromosomes pair with one another to form a structure called a bivalent. Next, each chromosome splits lengthwise to form two chromatids. The homologous pairs of chromosomes are now composed of four chromatids that are referred to as a tetrad. The chromatids of tetrads become short and thick and breaks may occur in them. The breaks are eventually repaired but segments of different chromatids may be joined together. This process, referred to as crossing-over, enables segments of two different chromatids to be joined together. This enables the gametes to receive chromosomes derived from segments of both homologous chromosomes. In the second stage of meiosis or metaphase 1, the nuclear membrane disappears, a spindle apparatus forms, and the homologous pairs align along the equatorial plate of the cell. In anaphase 1, the homologous chromosomes migrate to opposite poles of the cell. Telophase 1 is characterized by the complete separation of the homologous pairs, and the spindle apparatus disappears. The nuclear membrane begins to reform and in many organisms a cytoplasmic division may occur at this stage.

After a brief interphase, prophase II begins. Prophase II is the first stage in the second or equatorial division of meiosis. It is characterized by the condensing of chromatin to form the chromosomes. During metaphase II, the spindle apparatus forms and the chromosomes line up along the equatorial plate. In anaphase II, the daughter chromosomes migrate to opposite poles of the cell. Anaphase II differs from the first anaphase in that the centromere divides and the two chromatids now become the daughter chromosomes. The daughter chromosomes separate completely and reach opposite poles of the cell in telophase II. Subsequent divisions of the cytoplasm result in the formation of two daughter cells that have a haploid number of chromosomes.

The two divisions of the germ cell during meiosis produce four gametes with one-half the original number of chromosomes.

From Hugo R. Seibel and Kenneth E. Guyer. *How to Prepare for the Medical College Admission Test*, 6th ed. Hauppauge, New York: Barron's Educational Series, Inc., 1990.

70. According to this passage, at the end of the reductional division of meiosis:

    A. four haploid sets of chromosomes are produced.
    B. the homologous pairs of chromosomes are completely separated.
    C. the chromatin duplicates and coils.
    D. the centromeres divide and daughter chromosomes move to opposite poles of the cell.

71. At which state or phase does the process known as "crossing-over" occur?

    A. during the equatorial division
    B. before the tetrad separates
    C. during anaphase I
    D. during prophase II

**72.** The phase during which there is a duplication of the chromatin is known as:

    **A.** metaphase I.
    **B.** anaphase II.
    **C.** telophase I.
    **D.** interphase.

**73.** Which process from the list below makes variation in genetic composition possible?

    **A.** the formation of homologous pairs
    **B.** mitotic division of germ cells
    **C.** crossing over
    **D.** random mutations

**74.** Using information provided in the passage, one could reasonably conclude that:

    **A.** all species in both the plant and animal kingdom are capable of sexual reproduction.
    **B.** haploid cells are found only in animals.
    **C.** four functional gametes are always formed by the process of meiosis.
    **D.** zygote formation may produce an offspring that has the same number of chromosomes as its parents.

**75.** Which of the following statement(s) is/are *supported by* the passage?

    **A.** Meiosis is artificially subdivided into ten stages.
    **B.** Reproduction results in phenotypic expression.
    **C.** DNA duplicates before meiosis starts.
    **D.** All of the above.

## Passage V (Questions 76–80)

Does the order of a child's birth in a family have a bearing on the type of adult he/she will grow up to be, or is the theory of ordinal position simply an interesting topic of cocktail party conversation? Although it has been the highlight of numerous debates and the subject of various studies, ordinal position remains a little-understood personality variable.

From Hugo R. Seibel and Kenneth E. Guyer. *How to Prepare for the Medical College Admission Test*, 6th ed. Hauppauge, New York: Barron's Educational Series, Inc., 1990.

Consider the oldest child in a family of three children. Parents often claim that their firstborn has a solid head on his/her shoulders, behaves in a mature manner, and is capable of getting along with adults. This important family member often exhibits a quiet front, yet is able to take the lead, care for his/her siblings, and act like a miniature adult. Parents view the firstborn as an intelligent individual who will grow up to be a pillar of the community. A perfect illustration of the importance of being firstborn can be seen in the old custom of primogeniture that was particularly popular during the feudal period in Europe.

Primogeniture allowed the oldest member of a family, in most situations oldest male, to inherit all lands and possessions of his parents, to the exclusion of his siblings. The ordinal position of being the firstborn male therefore carried much power, as the firstborn was considered to be intelligent, level-headed, and capable of taking over as family protector and landlord once the father died. Theoretically the oldest would be unselfish and see to the care of the younger family members, but in actuality this was often not the case. Outlawed in the United States and no longer the mode of inheritance in Europe for today's population as a whole, primogeniture was in evidence as late as the 1920s and can still be seen in degree with some of Europe's royal families.

The second-born child in a family of three is pictured quite differently from the oldest. This child is much more lively, less willing to take orders, does not show the same interest in adults, and often has difficulty communicating with them. He/she may even become a "problem" child in school. Teachers have been heard to complain that "B is not in the least like A was . . . ." Could it be that the second born is striking out in an attempt to find his/her own place? The problems of the second child in a family seem to intensify even more when the "baby" comes along and moves him/her into the "middle child" position. Now he/she has to contend not only with a successful older brother or sister, but also with the youngest who seems to be the favorite.

The youngest child appears not to feel the need to measure up to anyone and goes along his/her own way to develop into an often exuberant, well-rounded individual. Because he/she is the baby, the mother doesn't expect this third sibling to function like a miniature adult, and she considers "cute" a great number of the actions that were viewed as unsatisfactory in the case of the other children.

Personality traits are not the only topic of interest in the ordinal position arena. The academic ability of children in various birth positions has also received attention. One interesting study reported a comparison of mathematics grades between women who were separated into three groups: (1) firstborn, (2) at least second born but not last born, and (3) last born in a family. Women without siblings were excluded from the study. The results indicate a statistical difference in mathematics grades between groups (1) and (3) but no other significant differences. Group (1) achieved higher mathematics grades than group (3).

Theories of motivation and anxiety have been advanced to explain the difference in achievement. The motivation theory states that the oldest child receives more encouragement from the parents than is given to other children. For a time, the first child is the only child, an experience not shared by the other children. Particularly during this early period the parents may try very hard to help the child, thus striving to experience vicariously their own unfulfilled expectations. The anxiety theory adds another factor to try to explain the lower achievement of the youngest child. Not only is the youngest child not pushed, as was the case with his/her older siblings, but this lack of parental pushing may be interpreted as lack of parental interest. The youngest child may develop feelings of anxiety, and these may interfere with performance. Thus, the youngest child may suffer as a result of less parental pressure and expectations as well as suffering from self-imposed anxiety, both contributing to lower performance.

76. The central thesis of the passage is that:

    **A.** the motivational drive (as well as the anxiety level of children) is directly linked to the order in which they are born.

    **B.** the development of a child's personality may be affected by the ordinal position he/she holds in his/her family.

    **C.** primogeniture, which is the custom of passing on property to the oldest male member of a family, is the vehicle used by the royal families of Europe to ensure that their fortunes will remain intact.

    **D.** ordinal position remains a little understood personality variable despite the fact that it is a popular topic both at the research and at the debate level.

77. Based on the information given in the passage, it is reasonable to conclude that:

    **A.** the oldest child in a family is the child best equipped to handle stressful situations.

    **B.** more research needs to be conducted before any concrete judgments can be made regarding the effect that birth order has on an individual's personality.

    **C.** academically, the youngest child tends to be lazy because he/she has been babied by parents and siblings.

    **D.** married couples should become well versed in ordinal position literature so that they will have a guide to follow when they are ready to have children.

78. What is the probable reason that the author used the paragraph on primogeniture in this passage?

    **A.** As a means of making the passage more interesting for the reader by introducing a historical topic.

    **B.** In order to make the reader aware of the fact that the firstborn was expected to share his inheritance with his younger siblings.

    **C.** To make the reader aware of the fact that the custom was outlawed in the United States around 1920.

    **D.** As a means of illustrating that ordinal position, especially the place of the firstborn, has been a topic of interest for a long period of time.

79. Which of the following statements is/are *supported by* the information in the passage?

    I. Parents often claim that firstborn children behave in a more mature manner than laterborn.

    II. The "baby" of the family is often a child with an outgoing personality.

    III. By the time the third child comes along, mothers no longer seem to put the same emphasis on certain aspects of behavior that they did when raising their first.

    **A.** I only     **C.** I and II only
    **B.** II only     **D.** I, II, and III

**80.** Which of the following statements is *contradicted by* the information given in the passage?

**A.** Comparison to older siblings, by teachers and other adults, is the best method for stimulating the middle child to work harder.

**B.** Second-born children who later move into the "middle child" position achieve on a higher plane in school than do second born who remain in the same position.

**C.** The youngest child does not feel the need to measure up to anyone.

**D.** The second-born child sometimes has a problem communicating with adults.

## Passage VI (Questions 81–87)

Performance appraisals—"Who needs them? I'm doing a good job, so why does someone need to sit and put it in writing, then waste my time and theirs talking about it? If I'm doing something that they don't like, let them tell me about it when it happens." This is a typical comment heard from many employees.

The performance appraisal, if completed properly, can be one of the most useful tools a manager can use in developing and training subordinates regardless of what some employees may express. It is a compilation of the employee's strengths and weakness in one concise form. It serves to show the employee the areas in which a good job is being done and also indicates which areas need improvement. The appraisal serves as a permanent record that documents the employee's growth and progress or shows why a promotion is not offered. A performance appraisal forces a manager to discuss an employee's performance on a one-to-one basis and find out more about what the employee's opinions and aspirations might be. This area is often overlooked in the busy day-in and day-out routine of business. It gives the employee a chance to see what the boss really thinks about his or her work.

An interesting and often very beneficial way of handling a performance appraisal is to give employees a blank evaluation form a few days before the appraisal interview and ask that they

From Hugo R. Seibel and Kenneth E. Guyer. *How to Prepare for the Medical College Admission Test*, 6th ed. Hauppauge, New York: Barron's Educational Series, Inc., 1990.

rate themselves. When the appraisal takes place, the manager and employee compare their evaluations and work out the areas of disagreement so that each understands the other's position. An unusual result often takes place. Not only do the manager and employee end up with a better knowledge of each other, but they often find that their evaluations are very close to being in agreement. If anything, the employees usually find that they have underrated themselves. An exception to this result, which the manager must be alert to recognize, is that an unsatisfactory performer may evaluate his or her performance higher than does the manager. The appraisal interview in this situation can often be more valuable than that of the satisfactory performer. It gives the manager an opportunity to counsel an already trained employee and turn around the performance rather than having to seek out and train a replacement. The manager must evaluate the time expense, and attitude of the present employee against the time and expense of hiring and training a new employee.

Performance appraisals, properly administered, can cut down on turnover and greatly increase the morale of a department. The result is increased productivity, which is really what we are all striving to accomplish.

Although standard procedure in industry for many years, performance appraisals have also reached higher education. In recent years college students have come to see themselves as purchasing a service, specifically that of education. They have demanded greater accountability, asking that the remuneration of faculty members be tied to teaching effectiveness. Many faculty members agree with the concept in theory but feel that measurement of teaching effectiveness is flawed.

Teaching effectiveness is often determined through evaluations by administrators, faculty colleagues, or students, or by a combination of two or more of these evaluations. Students are usually most interested in evaluations by students, believing that they are the "consumers" who are most directly affected by the quality of the "product" called teaching. Faculty members counter that evaluations by students are flawed, in that they are affected by the charisma (or lack of it) of the instructor, the level of difficulty of the subject matter, and the grades given in the course.

A more objective method has been suggested by various groups—the student performance at the end of the course. All students taking a particular course could be given a standard test; mean scores in sections taught by different instructors could then be compared and related to each instructor's teaching effectiveness. The results could be affected, of course, by the students' IQs, motivation, and prior instruction in the material covered by the course.

81. Of the positive aspects pertaining to the use of performance appraisals, which of those listed below is/are directly alluded to in the passage?

    A. The performance appraisal gives the employee and the manager a time to discuss the employee's future in private.
    B. Employees and managers usually can work out their differences during the appraisal interview.
    C. Performance appraisals often lead to a better understanding between managers and employees and eventually can lead to increased productivity.
    D. All of the above.

82. Which of the following statement(s) is/are NOT *supported nor contradicted by* the information in the passage?

    A. Most large companies are now using the performance appraisal method because it has been proven a highly effective tool for dismissing unsatisfactory employees.
    B. All performance appraisals are preceded by giving employees blank forms to rate themselves.
    C. Managers feel that performance appraisals are a waste of time.
    D. All of the above.

83. Which of the following statements is/are *contradicted by* the information in the passage?

    A. A satisfactorily performing employee will rate himself or herself higher than the manager.
    B. A performance appraisal points out only the weak areas of performance.
    C. A performance appraisal is the most useful tool a manager uses in developing and training subordinates.
    D. All of the above.

84. Some faculty members, addressing concerns about the accuracy and validity of student evaluations of teaching, caution that:

    A. all suggested methods of evaluation of teaching effectiveness are quite subjective.
    B. the charisma of the instructor is a factor in evaluation of teaching effectiveness.
    C. evaluations of an instructor's teaching effectiveness are unaffected by student grades.
    D. evaluations of an instructor's teaching effectiveness are affected by the time of day when lectures are given.

85. According to the passage, greater difficulty of the course would have what effect on student ratings of teacher effectiveness?

    A. lower ratings
    B. higher ratings
    C. no effect
    D. the passage does not say

86. The author indicates that students are most interested in ratings of teaching effectiveness when determined by:

    A. evaluation by faculty colleagues.
    B. evaluation by administrators.
    C. evaluation by students.
    D. objectively determined progress of the performance of the class.

87. Regarding performance appraisals in industry and student evaluations of teaching, the passage asserts that:

    A. students view themselves as consumers.
    B. performance evaluations benefit the parties involved.
    C. performance appraisals can lead to increased productivity.
    D. all of the above are true statements.

## Passage VII (Questions 88–92)

Paul Tillich, in his article "The Lost Dimension in Religion," asserts that in contemporary Western society there is an absence of spirituality; moreover, that in spite of a growing interest in religion, and because of it, the religious element as Tillich defines it has all but vanished. The popularity of "go-to-church-every-Sunday" and the televangelism of the '80s belong to the "concrete religion" of literal hermeneutics (the science of interpreting an author's words or scriptures), rituals, and institutions.

The lost dimension as Tillich describes it is the loss of each individual's asking himself or herself basic and important existential questions such as: "What is the meaning of life? Where do we come from, where do we go to? What shall we do, what should we become in the short stretch between birth and death?" This spiritual "dimension of depth" is lost to modern man, he says, and "religion as the state of being grasped by an infinite concern" is absent.

Though written 30 years ago, this observation is still insightful today, perhaps even more so. Tillich explains how spiritual depth has become lost to contemporary Man. He traces the causes to Man's relationship with Nature and with himself, a relationship in which Nature is "subjected scientifically and technically" by the whims of Man, and self-knowledge is nearly nonexistent.

But, Tillich claims that, though today's generations lack the courage to ask themselves weighty eschatological questions (dealing with final matters, such as death), previous generations had the courage to do so. On this point, Tillich is slightly evasive. Does he mean that, say, a rise in materialism and technology parallels a drop in spirituality, and that previous generations who were less materialistic and technologically oriented were more spiritual? Perhaps, but he seems to rely heavily on our technologically oriented lives as evidence of a decline in spirituality. One might agree with him on this point but still believe that the roots go much deeper, and that our technology-based living and subsequent relationship with Nature is indeed an effect of something else as much as it is a cause of a loss of spirituality. Might not the dualistic perspective implicit in our own philosophical heritage, which seeks to divide the whole into parts, be called into question, along with the scientific method and "value-free" science? The present-day relationship between Man and Nature may well be a cause of the "loss of the dimension of depth"; but one could also argue that the seeds were sown a long time ago, so long ago that a more appropriate discussion of the loss of spiritual depth would include Man's relationship to technology as well.

The true religion, according to Tillich, moves vertically, hence "depth." It involves a personal dimension as well; personal existential questions ask for personal existential answers. And what Tillich sees in present-day religion (institutional and literalistic) is a horizontal aspect, a dimension that denies itself "basic and universal meaning" and the symbolic interpretation of sacred texts. This "horizontal" religion goes hand-in-hand with contemporary horizontal living, where technological/industrial society makes things " 'better and better,' 'bigger and bigger,' " there is "movement ahead without end," and "every moment is filled with something" whether it be television or a 40-hour-a-week job. In the horizontal dimension, "no one can experience depth . . . [or start] becoming aware of himself." Symptomatic of this kind of life is the question of whether or not God exists, a "discussion in which both sides are wrong, because the discussion itself is wrong and possible only after the loss of the dimension of depth."

Tillich advocates a kind of personal inquiry, a soul-searching "in spite of the loss of the dimension of depth"; an asking of questions such as "What is the meaning of Life?" But Tillich, for all his discussion of spirituality, makes no reference to the intuitive side of Man's nature. Tillich seems to imply that existential questions and any answers they might find are rational in their relationship to one another, and that the latter follows logically from the former; that there is indeed an answer that can be articulated. I suspect that this perspective is still inside the cultural context that gave rise to the loss of the dimension of depth in the first place— perhaps Tillich needs to step out of that context and into a context that is intuitive and in which personal existential questions are acknowledged from a source much deeper than the rational mind. It is perhaps the intuitive/spiritual that is the true religious character that, as Tillich says, "in spite of the loss of dimension of depth, its power is present, and is most present in those who are aware of the loss . . . ."

Adapted from Taylor Fleet, "A Critique of Paul Tillich," VCU, 1989.

88. The author of this passage observes that according to Tillich, contemporary society:

    A. is no longer interested in religion.
    B. suffers from a loss of spirituality.
    C. is more than willing to ask itself weighty existential questions.
    D. none of the above.

89. Which of the following, according to the passage, accurately reflects Tillich's view?

    A. True religion moves vertically.
    B. True religion is the same as present-day (institutional and literalistic) religion.
    C. Present-day society encourages individuals to ask deep questions about human existence.
    D. True religion asks questions addressing whether or not God exists.

90. Although the passage reflects general agreement with Tillich on many points, the author disagrees with Tillich on which of the following?

    A. his assertion that modern man lacks true religion
    B. his belief that people are more materialistic today than in the past
    C. his definition of spirituality
    D. his failure to take into account the intuitive side of human nature in discussing ways by which individuals can find answers to spiritual questions

91. The author finds Tillich's ideas about the lost dimension in religion:

    A. less valid than they were when Tillich wrote them 30 years ago.
    B. at least as insightful as they were 30 years ago.
    C. interesting but too theoretical to be applied to actual human beings.
    D. illustrative of T. S. Eliot's idea that modern man lives in a spiritual wasteland.

92. An appropriate title for this essay might be:

    A. The Relevance of Tillich's Ideas Thirty Years Later.
    B. The Optimism of Paul Tillich.
    C. Tillich as Champion of Man's Intuition.
    D. The Tillich that No One Knows.

# WRITING SAMPLE

2 ESSAYS
60 MINUTES (30 MINUTES/TOPIC)

*DIRECTIONS:*   This is a test of your writing skills. The test consists of two parts. You will have 30 minutes to complete each part. Use your time efficiently. Before you begin writing each of your responses, read the assignment carefully to understand exactly what you are being asked to do. Because this is a test of your writing skills, your response to each part should be as well organized and clearly written as you can make it in the time allotted.

**93.** Consider this statement:

**Men are dependent on circumstances, not circumstances on men.**

**Herodotus**

Write a unified essay in which you perform the following tasks. Explain the meaning of the above statement. Describe a specific situation where circumstances might be dependent on individuals. Discuss what you think determines whether or not individuals are dependent on circumstances or vice versa.

**94.** Consider this statement:

**The voluntary death by which a man puts an end to intolerable suffering is really an act of redemption.**

**Ernst Heinrich Haeckel
(German biologist)**

Write a unified essay in which you perform the following tasks. Explain what you think the above statement means. Describe a specific situation in which the voluntary death by which a person put an end to intolerable suffering would not be an act of redemption. Discuss what you think determines the choice of voluntary death in the face of human suffering.

# BIOLOGICAL SCIENCES

52 QUESTIONS
70 MINUTES

*DIRECTIONS:* The following questions or incomplete statements are in groups. Preceding each series of questions or statements is a paragraph or a short explanatory statement, a formula or set of formulas, or a definition. Read the written material and then answer the questions or complete the statements. Select the ONE BEST ANSWER for each question and indicate your selection by marking the corresponding letter of your choice on the Answer Form. Eliminate those alternatives you know to be incorrect and then select an answer from among the remaining alternatives.

## Passage I (Questions 95–99)

The function of the thyroid gland is to produce colloidal material containing the thyroid hormones $T_3$ (triiodothyronine) and $T_4$ (thyroxin), which affect the rate of metabolism of all tissues.

The iodides consumed by the body are absorbed and carried to the iodide pool in the extracellular fluid via the circulatory system. Five basic events occur during the production of thyroid hormone: (a) trapping iodide; (b) oxidation of iodide to iodine; (c) synthesis of hormone; (d) storage of hormone in the thyroid follicle; and (e) release of hormone into the circulation. TSH (thyroid stimulating hormone) from the anterior pituitary influences the trapping mechanism. It can be stated that thyroid hormone: (a) controls the rate of metabolism; (b) controls growth, maturation, and differentiation of the organism; and (c) influences nervous system activity.

Problems associated with thyroid function are:

1. **Cretinism** — a congenital failure of proper development. The cretin is a dwarf physically and mentally.

2. **Myxedema** — an acquired thyroid deficiency in the adult. This deficiency can be due to thyroidectomy, neoplasms, or a pituitary deficiency in TSH secretion. The clinical picture is the presentation of a patient who is fairly heavy, phlegmatic, and devoid of expression; the skin is rough and dry and sensitive to cold. The patient is sluggish mentally and physically. Laboratory tests show a low basal metabolic rate, low protein-bound iodine, and a high serum cholesterol level.

3. **Graves' disease** — an increased activity of the thyroid gland. The patient exhibits loss of weight, nervousness, irritability, increased metabolic rate, rapid heart rate, and sweating.

A patient is brought into the emergency room and, upon examination, a thyroid goiter is discovered. You suspect that he is suffering from a thyroid disorder, and you ask the intern for a definition of *hypothyroidism.*

95. He responds that *hypothyroidism* is the general term for syndromes that reflect:

   A. increased secretion of thyroid hormones.
   B. decreased secretion of thyroid hormones.
   C. no change in secretion of thyroid hormones.
   D. increased secretion of thyroid stimulating hormone releasing factor.

96. A basal metabolism rate test is ordered that measures the rate of oxidative metabolism. In hypothyroidism, this rate is:

   A. above normal.
   B. normal.
   C. below normal.
   D. not significant in your diagnosis.

97. Because of the hypothyroidism that you suspect, you would also consider that this patient:

    I. has gained weight.
    II. converts less food into energy.
    III. stores more food as fat.
    IV. has an accelerated metabolic rate.

    A. I, III, and IV only
    B. II, III, and IV only
    C. I, II, and III only
    D. all of the above

98. The physical examination in this patient would also yield the following:

    A. The patient is mentally sluggish.
    B. The patient's skin is rough and dry.
    C. The patient's serum cholesterol level would be elevated.
    D. All of the above.

99. If hyperthyroidism were the diagnosis you would reason and find:

    A. a pituitary deficiency in TSH.
    B. a block in the oxidation of iodide to iodine.
    C. a phlegmatic patient.
    D. irritability.

## Passage II (Questions 100–107)

The ABO blood grouping system is explained on the basis of a single triallelic system with genes A, B, and O operating at a single genetic locus. Phenotypic and genotypic characteristics may be expressed as follows:

| Phenotype | Genotype |
|-----------|----------|
| A | A/A; A/O |
| B | B/B; B/O |
| O | O/O |
| AB | A/B |

The A and B genes appear to be codominant; they are dominant over O; which is recessive.

Paternity will be excluded if the child (a) has an antigen that is present in neither the mother nor the putative father, and (b) does not have an antigen that the putative father has and would have had to give to his progeny (e.g., a type O child and a type AB putative father).

Correct reassignment of infants misassigned to parents in a hospital is often achieved by looking for any of the following kinds of incompatibilities between the infants and the couples and then assigning each infant to a couple with which only compatibilities exist:

1. The child has an antigen that is present in neither spouse.

2. The child lacks one or more antigens that either spouse or both spouses would have had to give him/her.

Increased probability of exclusion of alleged paternity or of a correct parental reassignment of misassigned infants results in several kinds of blood groups, HLA, and the following kinds of genetically determined proteins are also included in the studies: hemoglobin, serum proteins, red cell enzymes, and several other enzymes.

The ABO blood group is transmitted in humans as alleles A and B that are codominant, occurring at the same autosomal locus as a recessive allele O. In some cases it may be utilized to assist in determining paternity or in reuniting a lost child with his or her biological parents.

100. A woman of blood type O claims a child of blood type AB, and alleges that the father is a man of blood type B. The most likely explanation is that:

    A. these are the biological parents.
    B. she is the mother but the man is not the father.
    C. neither is a possible parent of the child.
    D. she is not the mother but the man's blood type does not rule him out as the father.

101. If the man in question 100 is found to have previously fathered a child of blood type O, the chance that a child of the man and the woman in this question would be blood type O is:

    A. zero.          C. 33%.
    B. 25%.           D. 50%.

102. With the information from the above question, the chance that any child of the man and woman would be a girl with blood type B is

    A. zero.          C. 33%.
    B. 25%.           D. 50%.

103. The above man with a phenotype B will possess which of the following genotypes?

    A. A/O          C. O/O
    B. B/O          D. A/B

104. Phenotype may be defined as:

    A. genetic makeup of an individual.
    B. hidden traits of an individual.
    C. unrelated characteristics.
    D. visible expression of genotype.

105. Alleles are genes that:

    A. arise during the cross-over process.
    B. are linked to one chromosome only.
    C. are always sex-linked and are transmitted from mothers to their sons.
    D. occupy corresponding positions on homologous chromosomes.

106. Rh-related hemolytic anemia of the newborn (erythroblastosis foetalis) may result when the:

    A. father, mother, and fetus are all Rh negative.
    B. father and mother are Rh positive, but the fetus is Rh negative.
    C. mother is Rh negative and the fetus is Rh positive.
    D. mother is Rh positive and the fetus is Rh negative.

107. The czarina of Russia and Queen Victoria of England were normal women who produced sons suffering from hemophilia, a disease that is caused by a sex-linked recessive gene, h. The more common dominant gene, H, produces normal blood clotting. The genotype of these women must have been:

    A. HH.           C. hh.
    B. Hh.           D. none of the above.

**Questions 108–112 are NOT based on a descriptive passage.**

108. Which of the following catalyzes synthesis of messenger RNA in eukaryotes?

    A. RNA polymerase I
    B. RNA polymerase II
    C. RNA polymerase III
    D. RNA polymerase IV

109. Which of the following organelles are involved in the synthesis of proteins that will be secreted from a eukaryotic cell?

    A. free ribosomes
    B. mitochondria
    C. ribosomes on rough endoplasmic reticulum
    D. Golgi bodies

110. A normal vertebrate skeletal muscle fiber (cell) is:

    A. uninucleate and striated.
    B. multinucleate and striated.
    C. uninucleate and nonstriated (or unstriated).
    D. multinucleate and nonstriated (or unstriated).

111. The proximal convoluted tubule in the human kidney is primarily involved in:

    A. filtration of material from blood to urine.
    B. establishment of a high salt concentration in the kidney.
    C. reabsorption of useful solutes from urine.
    D. hormonally controlled water reabsorption from urine.

112. The two cerebral hemispheres in the mammalian brain are connected by the:

    A. corpus callosum.
    B. pons.
    C. medulla oblongata.
    D. cerebellum.

**Passage III** (Questions 113–119)

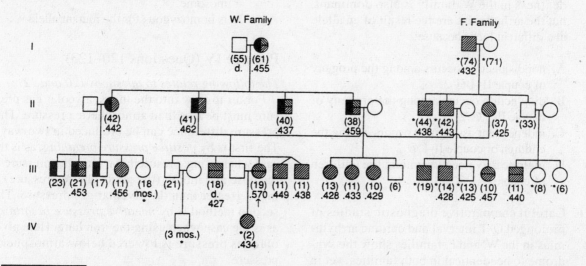

Study of *W* and *F* families showing presence of syncope, electrocardiographic evidence of prolonged Q-T interval and abnormal audiogram. The propositus (Case 1) is III-10 (**arrow**). Case 2 is her cousin (III-2). Figures in parentheses indicate subject's age. Intervals (in hundredths of a second) appear directly below each subject's age. **Black** symbols indicate abnormal audiogram; hatched symbols indicate prolonged QTc interval (0.425 second) (////) or syncope (\\\\); d = died. A history, physical examination and one or more electrocardiograms were obtained in all patients. An audiogram was obtained in all cases, except those marked by a star, in which hearing was only examined clinically.

Inheritance of Q-T prolongation (≥ 0.425 sec) and cardiac arrhythmias in the W. and F. families is shown in the above pedigree, which was ascertained through the proposita, III-10, who suffered cardiac arrest and had to be resuscitated 12 hours after her first delivery following an uneventful pregnancy. A major objective of the study was the determination of whether prolonged Q-T interval in these families was (1) the autosomal recessive form, Jervell, Lang-Nielsen syndrome, also characterized by high-frequency perceptive deafness, (2) Ward-Romano syndrome, an autosomal dominant form, not associated with deafness, or (3) perhaps a third type, inherited in some other fashion.*

**113.** Prolonged Q-T interval and cardiac arrhythmias appear to be phenotypic manifestations of the same allele, a phenomenon known as:

A. genetic heterogeneity.
B. genetic polymorphism.
C. pleiotropism.
D. phenocopies.

**114.** The pedigree clearly shows that the arrhythmias in the W. family are dominant because they:

A. affect both monozygotic twins in the third generation.
B. are sometimes associated with deafness.
C. show unbroken lineal descent.
D. are transmitted by both sexes.

*Adapted by Dr. J. I. Townsend, Virginia Commonwealth University, from "Q-T Prolongation and Ventricular Arrhythmias With and Without Deafness in the Same Family"; E. C. Mathews, A. W. Blount, and J. I. Townsend. *The American Journal of Cardiology*, (1972): 29:702.

115. Likewise, the pedigree clearly shows that deafness in the W. family is also dominant, but the arrhythmias are the result of an allele at a different locus because:

    A. nondisjunction occurs among the progeny of couple II- I @ 2.
    B. disjunction occurs among the progeny of couple II-1 @ 2.
    C. independent assortment occurs among the children of couple II-1 @ 2.
    D. meiotic drive occurs among the children of couple II-1 @ 2.

116. Careful comparative diagnostic studies of prolonged Q-T interval and cardiac arrhythmias in the W. and F. families show the syndrome to be identical in both families, yet in the F. family this dominant trait skips a generation (II-11). This skipping is a phenomenon known as:

    A. reduced penetrance.
    B. unequal crossing-over.
    C. transversion.
    D. variable expressivity.

117. That prolonged Q-T interval and the arrhythmias are autosomal is shown by:

    A. female to male transmission in both families.
    B. male to male transmission in the F. family.
    C. lack of male to male transmission.
    D. male to female transmission.

118. That deafness is autosomal is shown by:

    A. male to male transmission.
    B. lack of male to male transmission.
    C. two affected males (II-3 and II-5) have daughters whose hearing is normal.
    D. an affected female (II-2) has a daughter whose hearing is normal.

119. The proposita (III-10) has by far the greatest prolonged Q-T interval (0:570 sec) in this extended pedigree. The likely explanation is that she:

    A. is an example of genetic anticipation.
    B. has a deletion of the locus on one chromosome.

    C. has a duplication of the locus on one chromosome.
    D. is homozygous for the mutant allele.

## Passage IV (Questions 120–123)

*The following relates to questions 120 and 121:*

For air to flow into the lungs, alveolar gas pressure must be less than atmospheric pressure. This pressure difference can be produced in two ways. The first is by *positive pressure breathing*, as is the case when using a resuscitator. Here the pressure at the nose and mouth (the atmospheric pressure) is made greater than the alveolar gas pressure. The second method is by *negative pressure breathing*, as is the case when using the iron lung. Here alveolar gas pressure is lowered below atmospheric pressure.

Normal breathing is a form of negative pressure breathing. If intra-alveolar pressure (also called intrapulmonary pressure) is plotted while breathing, we see that during inspiration the enlarging thorax and lungs expand the alveolar gas and its pressure transiently drops below atmospheric pressure (i.e., it becomes negative). This pressure difference causes air to flow into the lungs. Expiration involves transiently elevating the intra-alveolar pressure above atmospheric pressure. This occurs as the collapsing chest-lung system compresses the alveolar gas. Gas then flows out of the lungs.

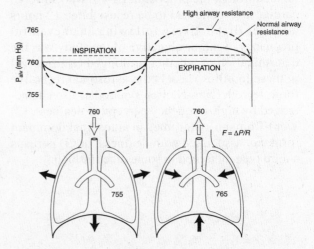

Air flow is directly proportional to the pressure difference between alveolar gas and the atmosphere, and inversely proportional to airway resistance:

$$Flow\ (F) = \frac{P_{atm} - P_{alv}}{\text{Airway Resistance (R)}}$$

Thus, the greater the airway resistance, the greater the pressure difference required to produce any given flow. High airway resistance will produce greater fluctuations in intra-alveolar pressure during inspiration and expiration.

The severity of airway resistance is reflected in the *intrapleural pressure* as well as the intra-alveolar pressure during the breathing cycle. Before inspiration begins, the intrapleural pressure reflects the elastic strength with which the lungs are tending to collapse. Of course, at this volume (the FRC) the elastic force of the lungs is balanced by the elastic strength of the chest wall tending to expand. The intrapleural pressure is slightly negative (i.e., below atmospheric pressure).

During inspiration, the elastic recoil strength of the lungs progressively increases as the lungs are stretched. This alone would lower the intrapleural pressure (i.e., make it more negative). In addition, the lowered intra-alveolar pressure (reflecting airway resistance during inspiration) and tissue viscous resistance (which opposes the inflation effort) lower the intrapleural pressure even more. Thus, during inspiration the intrapleural pressure becomes even lower (more negative) than it would if the elastic forces existed alone. Of this additional decrease in intrapleural pressure from nonelastic resistances, 80% is due to pressure needed to overcome airway resistance; tissue viscous resistance accounts for only 20% of the nonelastic resistance.

At the end of inspiration, flow stops as intra-alveolar pressure equilibrates with atmospheric pressure. At this volume (FRC + TV), functional residual capacity (FRC) plus the tidal volume (TV), the intrapleural pressure reflects the elastic strength of the lungs tending to collapse. Since the lungs are stretched more during inspiration, the intrapleural pressure is lower (more negative) following inspiration than before. The functional residual capacity is the (tidal volume–anatomical dead space) × frequency of breathing. During normal breathing, the volume of air inspired (expired) is called the tidal volume.

During expiration, the elastic recoil strength of the lungs progressively decreases as the lungs deflate, and the intrapleural pressure rises (becomes less negative) accordingly. In addition, the elevated intra-alveolar pressure and the tissue viscous resistance oppose deflation and act outward against the intrapleural space. Therefore, the intrapleural pressure during expiration is higher (less negative) than it would be if the elastic forces were unopposed.

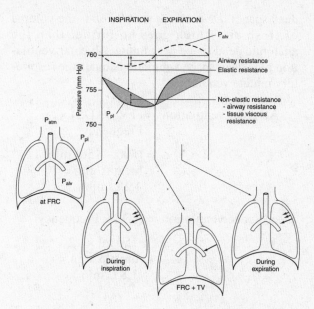

With a tidal volume of 500 ml, only 350 ml goes to the respiratory unit and 150 ml goes no further than the anatomic dead space. Most of the 350 ml that reaches the alveoli is involved in gas exchange, but some is a *"wasted volume"* — meaning it is a volume in excess of that needed to equilibrate with the blood passing through the capillaries of that area. A wasted volume occurs to some extent even in a healthy individual and will be produced when there is an elevated ventilation-perfusion ratio. An elevated ventilation-perfusion ratio occurs when either the blood flow is reduced or ventilation is in excess of that needed to equilibrate the volume of blood perfusing the area. Alveolar gas in an area with a high ventilation-perfusion ratio will exhibit increased oxygen and decreased carbon dioxide concentrations because of the excess oxygen delivery and carbon dioxide removal. The wasted volume plus the anatomic dead space equals the *physiologic dead space*. Even in a healthy individual the physiologic dead space is slightly larger than the anatomic dead space.

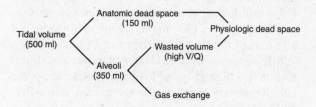

*Alveolar ventilation* refers to the volume of fresh air, which reaches the respiratory unit per minute and is equal to the rate of breathing times the volume of fresh air reaching the respiratory unit per breath (i.e., the tidal volume minus the anatomic dead space). *Dead space ventilation* is the volume of fresh air, which goes no further than the anatomic dead space per minute. Alveolar ventilation plus dead space ventilation equals the respiratory minute ventilation.

$$\text{Alveolar ventilation} = (TV - ADS) \times \text{Frequency}$$
$$= (500 - 150) \text{ ml} \times 12 \text{ breaths/min} = 4.2 \text{ L/min}$$

$$\text{Dead space ventilation} = ADS \times \text{Frequency}$$
$$= 150 \text{ ml} \times 12 \text{ breaths/min} = 1.8 \text{ L/min}$$

The composition of alveolar air, reflecting the oxygen uptake by blood and carbon dioxide release from blood, has a lower $PO_2$ (100 mm Hg) and a higher $PCO_2$ (40 mm Hg) than that of atmospheric or moist tracheal air. Both alveolar air and atmospheric air have the same total pressures, since these compartments are connected by open tubes of the anatomic dead space.

Alveolar air is typically represented as having a constant composition. This is justified because the fluctuations which occur in $PO_2$ and $PCO_2$ with each breathing cycle are very slight. Because the volume of fresh air entering the alveoli (350 ml) is very small compared with the "pool" of alveolar air already in the lungs (FRC = 2,200 ml), the inspired fresh air is so diluted that the $PO_2$ will increase and the $PCO_2$ will decrease by only 1 or 2 mm Hg.

Assuming a constant oxygen uptake and carbon dioxide release by the body, the content of alveolar air will reflect the ventilatory rate of the lungs. Hyperventilation makes alveolar air more like fresh air, raising alveolar $PO_2$ and lowering $PCO_2$. Hypoventilation, in contrast, produces a lower $PO_2$ and an elevated $PCO_2$ in the alveoli. Similarly, not all areas of the lung have the same $PO_2$ and $PCO_2$. While some areas are relatively hyperventilated and have a high $PO_2$ and low $PCO_2$, other areas are simultaneously hypoventilated and have a low $PO_2$ and high $PCO_2$.

120. The driving pressure ($\Delta P$) in breathing which causes air to flow into the lungs is:

   A. atmospheric pressure ($P_{atm}$).
   B. the intra-alveolar (intrapulmonary) pressure ($P_{alv}$).
   C. atmospheric pressure minus the intra-alveolar pressure.
   D. the intrapleural pressure ($P_{pl}$).

121. During inspiration, intra-alveolar pressure ($P_{alv}$):

   A. transiently goes below atmospheric pressure ($P_{atm}$).
   B. transiently goes above atmospheric pressure.
   C. equals atmospheric pressure.
   D. equals intrapleural pressure.

122. The alveolar ventilation per minute refers to the amount of fresh air that reaches the alveoli of the lungs per minute. Alveolar ventilation per minute equals the:

   A. functional residual capacity × frequency of breathing.
   B. physiologic dead space × frequency of breathing.
   C. anatomic dead space × frequency of breathing.
   D. (tidal volume – anatomic dead space) × frequency of breathing.

123. Hypoventilation produces which of the following changes in alveolar gas composition?

   A. The partial pressure of oxygen increases and the partial pressure of carbon dioxide decreases.
   B. The partial pressures of both oxygen and carbon dioxide increase.
   C. The partial pressure of oxygen decreases and the partial pressure of carbon dioxide increases.
   D. The partial pressures of both oxygen and carbon dioxide decrease.

**Questions 124–126 are NOT based on a descriptive passage.**

124. In an inducible operon such as the lac operon in *E. coli*, the repressor protein coded by the regulator gene binds to the _____ to inactivate the operon.

    A. regulator gene
    B. first structural gene in the operon
    C. promoter
    D. operator sequence

125. Ectoderm, mesoderm, and endoderm form as distinct layers during _____ in most animal embryos.

    A. fertilization
    B. organogenesis
    C. cleavage
    D. gastrulation

126. In humans, antibodies are synthesized by:

    A. B lymphocytes and plasma cells.
    B. granulocytes (neutrophils and eosinophils).
    C. platelets.
    D. the liver.

## Passage V (Questions 127–131)

Toluene or methylbenzene is an important starting material for the synthesis of many aromatic compounds. The methyl group activates all unsubstituted carbons of the benzene ring for attack by electrophilic reagents, leading to substitution at one or more additional carbons. The *ortho, meta,* and *para* positions are substituted at different rates, depending on the capacity of the electron-donating methyl group to stabilize positively charged intermediates generated by the electrophilic attack. Unlike larger alkyl groups, the methyl group is too small to have a significant steric effect on the rate of substitution at the *ortho* position. Under appropriate conditions, the methyl group itself is often modified or derivatized, in which case, subsequent substitutions in the ring will be directed by the character of the modified group. Many different substituted products and positional isomers can be produced by manipulating reagents, reaction conditions, and the order of the various reactions. The *ortho, meta,* and *para* isomers usually differ sufficiently in properties to permit separation by standard physical methods. In any of the reactions of toluene, assume that ortho and para isomers can be separated.

127. The reaction of toluene with $Br_2$ in the presence of $FeBr_3$ would be expected to produce primarily:

    A. benzyl bromide, $C_6H_5CH_2Br$.
    B. *m*-bromotoluene.
    C. *o* and *p*-bromotoluene.
    D. an equimolar mixture of *m, o,* and *p*-bromotoluene.

128. The compound that undergoes electrophilic aromatic substitution more readily than toluene is:

    A. chlorobenzene.
    B. nitrobenzene.
    C. acetophenone.
    D. phenol.

129. The best sequence of reagents for conversion of toluene to *m*-nitrobenzoic acid is:

    A. $HNO_3$-$H_2SO_4$, then oxidation with hot $KMnO_4$ or $K_2Cr_2O_7$.
    B. Oxidation with hot $KMnO_4$ or $K_2Cr_2O_7$, followed by $HNO_3$-$H_2SO_4$.
    C. Bromination of toluene with $Br_2$-$FeBr_3$, followed by displacement with $NaNO_2$.
    D. Reaction of toluene with $Br_2$-$FeBr_3$, followed by oxidation with $KMnO_4$, or $K_2Cr_2O_7$, and then displacement of Br by $NaNO_2$.

130. The major product of the reaction of *p*-nitrotoluene with $Br_2$-$FeBr_3$ is:

    A. 2-bromo-4-nitrotoluene.
    B. 3-bromo-4-nitrotoluene.
    C. *p*-nitrobenzyl bromide, *p*-$NO_2C_6H_4CH_2Br$.
    D. 2, 6-dibromo-4-nitrotoluene.

**131.** Which of the following resonance structures is a contributor to the intermediate formed in the nitration of toluene to form *p*-nitro-toluene?

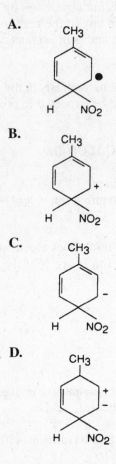

**A.**

**B.**

**C.**

**D.**

## Passage VI (Questions 132–139)

The categories of necessary dietary nutrients include the essential amino acids, essential fatty acids, essential elements, and the vitamins. The nine essential amino acids for humans are found in all dietary proteins. They are called: phenylalanine, valine, threonine, tryptophan, isoleucine, methionine, histidine, leucine, and lysine. All other amino acids that are found in proteins are nonessential and can be synthesized in the body from other dietary sources. The one true essential fatty acid is linoleic. However, linoleic and arachidonic acids can help meet the nutritional requirement for this category of nutrients. Because generally all of these essential fatty acids are found in combinations of oils and fats, all three can be viewed as "essential" in a practical sense. Along with carbohydrates, we obtain both essential amino acid and fatty acids from the macronutrients (i.e., large quantities) of protein and fat respectively in our diet.

The essential elements are subcategorized as the electrolytes sodium, potassium, and chloride; the bulk essential minerals—calcium, phosphorus, and magnesium and the trace essential minerals—iron, zinc, selenium, iodine, cobalt, molybdenum, manganese, copper, chromium, and fluoride. All of these are needed, but the amount we need each day varies from micrograms to hundreds of milligrams. Vitamins are found in foods in water-soluble or fat soluble forms. The former includes vitamin C, thiamine, riboflavin, niacin, vitamin $B_6$, folacin, vitamin $B_{12}$, biotin, and pantothenic acid. The fat-soluble vitamins are vitamins A, D, E, and K. These are all required in the diet in trace amounts (i.e., micrograms to milligrams).

Choose the *one best* answer for each of the following:

**132.** Which of the following is *not* an essential nutrient?

**A.** valine      **C.** glucose
**B.** linoleic acid      **D.** vitamin E

**133.** Which of the following is *not* a vitamin?

**A.** thiamine      **C.** niacin
**B.** biotin      **D.** arachidonic acid

**134.** Which of the following is *not* a fat-soluble vitamin?

**A.** vitamin A      **C.** vitamin D
**B.** vitamin $B_{12}$      **D.** vitamin E

**135.** Which of the following is a bulk essential element?

A. selenium     C. iron
B. copper       D. calcium

**136.** A macronutrient is:

I. a carbohydrate.
II. a protein.
III a fat.
IV. a vitamin.

A. I only       C. I, II, and III
B. II only      D. I, II, III, and IV

**137.** Regulation of the resorption of calcium from bone is controlled by the:

A. thyroid gland.
B. parathyroid glands.
C. thymus.
D. adrenal glands.

**138.** Undigested food is eliminated from the body by the process of:

A. exocytosis.     C. egestion.
B. excretion.      D. catabolism.

**139.** The energy released from the anaerobic respiration of a glucose molecule is less than that released from the aerobic respiration of a glucose molecule because:

A. aerobic respiration forms many more new, strong bonds than anaerobic respiration.
B. more enzymes are required for anaerobic respiration than for aerobic respiration.
C. anaerobic respiration occurs 24 hours a day, while aerobic respiration can occur only at night.
D. anaerobic respiration requires oxygen but aerobic respiration does not require oxygen.

## Passage VII (Questions 140–142)

Blood samples from two groups of rats were assayed for luteinizing hormone (LH) in two separate radioimmunoassays. Half the rats were intact and half were orchidectomized. Some samples in each group were collected in the morning and some were collected in the afternoon. The data are summarized in the following table:

| | Intact or Orchid X | Sampled AM or PM | LH ng/ml |
|---|---|---|---|
| | **Assay I** | | |
| 1 | I | AM | 5.0 |
| 2 | O | AM | 50 |
| 3 | I | PM | 4.8 |
| 4 | O | PM | 480 |
| 5 | I | AM | 5.2 |
| 6 | O | AM | 52 |
| 7 | I | PM | 5.1 |
| 8 | O | PM | 350 |
| 9 | I | AM | 4.9 |
| 10 | O | AM | 100 |
| | **Assay 2** | | |
| 11 | I | PM | 7.5 |
| 12 | O | PM | 75 |
| 13 | I | AM | 7.7 |
| 14 | O | AM | 770 |
| 15 | I | PM | 7.3 |
| 16 | O | PM | 250 |
| 17 | I | AM | 7.4 |
| 18 | O | AM | 100 |
| 19 | I | PM | 7.6 |
| 20 | O | PM | 640 |

**140.** Based on the above table, which of the following statements is *not supported by* the information given?

A. Orchidectomy is followed by increased levels of LH in the blood.
B. Blood LH levels are higher in the afternoon than in the morning.
C. The differences between LH values in these two assays are probably explained by interassay variations because the ratios between intact and orchidectomized levels are similar.
D. LH release in the orchidectomized rats may be occurring episodically.

141. Which of the following conclusions is supported by the data?

A. The presence of the gonad inhibits LH secretion.
B. LH levels are higher in the morning than in the afternoon.
C. LH stimulates one or more functions in the gonad.
D. LH stimulates gamete production in the gonad.

142. The relationship between assay 1 and assay 2 is best explained by which of the following?

A. Values in assay 1 are higher than in assay 2.
B. Values in assay 2 are higher than in assay 1.
C. A systematic error occurred in assay 2.
D. A systematic error occurred in assay 1.

**Questions 143–146 are NOT based on a descriptive passage.**

143. Which hydrocarbon is a member of the series with the general formula $C_nH_{2n-2}$?

A. butane        C. benzene
B. ethene        D. ethyne

144. Which class of compounds has the general formula R–O–R'?

A. esters        C. ethers
B. alcohols      D. aldehydes

145. Of the functional groups listed below, which is incorrectly identified?

A. $-NH_2$ amino group
B. $-\overset{\|}{\underset{O}{C}} - CH_3$ acetyl group
C. $-\overset{\|}{\underset{O}{C}} - NH_2$ amide group
D. $-\overset{\|}{\underset{O}{C}} - OH$ hydroxyl group

146. An individual has at his disposal benzyl chloride, benzene, aluminum chloride, and sodium, and he wishes to synthesize diphenylmethane. He should react:

A. all four compounds.
B. benzyl chloride and sodium.
C. benzyl chloride, benzene, and aluminum chloride.
D. benzyl chloride, benzene, and sodium.

# Model Examination Answer Key

## Physical Sciences

| | | | |
|---|---|---|---|
| 1. **B** | 12. **D** | 23. **C** | 34. **D** | 45. **C** |
| 2. **D** | 13. **C** | 24. **A** | 35. **A** | 46. **D** |
| 3. **D** | 14. **A** | 25. **A** | 36. **A** | 47. **D** |
| 4. **A** | 15. **D** | 26. **C** | 37. **A** | 48. **C** |
| 5. **A** | 16. **B** | 27. **B** | 38. **D** | 49. **B** |
| 6. **B** | 17. **D** | 28. **D** | 39. **A** | 50. **B** |
| 7. **C** | 18. **C** | 29. **C** | 40. **B** | 51. **C** |
| 8. **B** | 19. **C** | 30. **C** | 41. **C** | 52. **B** |
| 9. **C** | 20. **D** | 31. **B** | 42. **A** | |
| 10. **B** | 21. **B** | 32. **B** | 43. **B** | |
| 11. **C** | 22. **A** | 33. **C** | 44. **A** | |

## Verbal Reasoning

| | | | | |
|---|---|---|---|---|
| 53. **C** | 61. **C** | 69. **D** | 77. **B** | 85. **D** |
| 54. **D** | 62. **B** | 70. **B** | 78. **D** | 86. **C** |
| 55. **A** | 63. **B** | 71. **B** | 79. **D** | 87. **D** |
| 56. **D** | 64. **A** | 72. **D** | 80. **A** | 88. **B** |
| 57. **D** | 65. **D** | 73. **C** | 81. **D** | 89. **A** |
| 58. **B** | 66. **D** | 74. **D** | 82. **D** | 90. **D** |
| 59. **C** | 67. **B** | 75. **D** | 83. **D** | 91. **B** |
| 60. **B** | 68. **D** | 76. **D** | 84. **B** | 92. **A** |

## Writing Sample

93. See page 222 for a sample essay.
94. See page 223 for a sample essay.

## Biological Sciences

| | | | | |
|---|---|---|---|---|
| 95. **B** | 106. **C** | 117. **B** | 128. **D** | 139. **A** |
| 96. **C** | 107. **B** | 118. **C** | 129. **B** | 140. **B** |
| 97. **C** | 108. **B** | 119. **D** | 130. **A** | 141. **A** |
| 98. **D** | 109. **C** | 120. **C** | 131. **B** | 142. **B** |
| 99. **D** | 110. **B** | 121. **A** | 132. **C** | 143. **D** |
| 100. **D** | 111. **C** | 122. **D** | 133. **D** | 144. **C** |
| 101. **D** | 112. **A** | 123. **C** | 134. **B** | 145. **D** |
| 102. **B** | 113. **C** | 124. **D** | 135. **D** | 146. **C** |
| 103. **B** | 114. **C** | 125. **D** | 136. **C** | |
| 104. **D** | 115. **C** | 126. **A** | 137. **B** | |
| 105. **D** | 116. **A** | 127. **C** | 138. **C** | |

# Explanation of Answers for Model Examination

## Physical Sciences

1. **B.** The shortest wavelength corresponds to the highest photon energy, according to E = hc/λ. The maximum energy available occurs when the incident high-speed electron gives up all its energy at one time (in a bremsstrahlung process). If 80,000 volts is used to accelerate the electrons, the most energetic x-ray photon can have 80,000 eV of energy (but only a very small number of 80 keV photons will occur).

2. **D.** The $K_\beta$ transition is more energetic. This is shown by the shorter wavelength. The photon energy is $E = hf = hc/\lambda$. The $K_\alpha$ transitions are more probable. This is shown by the higher peak, which corresponds to a greater intensity due to a higher number of emitted photons.

3. **D.** The minimum wavelength depends only on the accelerating voltage. The electrical work done in accelerating the electrons is equal to the maximum photon energy:

$$eV_0 = hc/\lambda_{min}$$

4. **A.** The peaks are characteristic of the *target* material. The photon energy emitted (say for an $n = 3$ to $n = 1$ transition) never changes. If $V_0$ is increased, the height of the peaks (intensity) will increase. (If the voltage is decreased to a very *low* value the peaks may not be seen because the incident electrons do not have enough energy to eject an inner shelf electron on the target. Thus a continuous spectrum can occur without the peaks.)

5. **A.** The photon energy formula, $E = hc/\lambda$, shows that the photons of shortest (minimum) wavelength are the most energetic. Only a few of the incident electrons give up *all* their 35,000 eV of energy to create the photons of minimum wavelength (and maximum energy).

6. **B.** The frictional work uses up all the kinetic energy. Frictional force is μmg, and frictional work is μmgs. Thus:

$$W_f = KE_i - o = KE_i \quad \text{or} \quad \mu mgs = 1/2 \, mv^2$$

thus solving for skid length, s: $s = v^2/(2\,\mu g)$, and the skid length is proportional to the *square of the speed*. The mass drops out of the equation.

7. **C.** Because the skid length depends on speed squared, a car with twice the speed of another will slide *four* times as far.

8. **B.** The forces during the collision *are* equal and opposite according to Newton's third law of motion. Each of the other responses is incorrect for the following reasons: **A.** The more massive van has *greater* momentum at the same speed. **C.** The forces are actually *equal* and opposite. **D.** It would require *more* mechanical work to stop the van because it has larger mass. In this case, the vehicles do not stop. The large van would actually reverse the velocity of the small car and "drive" the car backwards.

9. **C.** As in the explanation for question 8, the forces during collision are equal and opposite. The other responses are incorrect because: **A.** The forces are always equal and opposite according to Newton's Third Law. **B.** Untrue, since the forces are actually equal and opposite. **D.** This is a true statement but it has nothing to do with the question asked, and does not explain why the car would suffer more damage in a head-on collision.

10. **B.** In this particular experiment, the paint marks are three times farther apart when the speed (60 mph) is three times greater. Thus the times to travel between paint marks, which is the reaction time, remain the same. (The reaction times could vary from one test to another. Here the two times happened to be identical.)

11. **C.** The reaction of calcium carbonate to form calcium bicarbonate requires water and carbon dioxide. Pure carbon dioxide gas is used. Therefore, no water enters the system and no reaction occurs.

12. **D.** The passage states that calcium oxide is used to neutralize acidic soils. Therefore, the solution must be basic (pH > 7.0). Also, oxides of the alkaline earth metals are basic.

13. **C.** Calcium chloride dissociates completely in water to form $Ca^{2+}$ and $2Cl^-$. The resulting solution conducts electricity and is a strong electrolyte.

14. **A.** Dissolved particles, calcium bicarbonate in this case, lower the freezing point of a solution.

15. **D.** Calcium is a Group 2 element and forms ions with +2 charge.

16. **B.** 56.1 g CaO corresponds to 1 mole of CaO (56.1 g CaO/56.1 g CaO = 1 mole CaO). According to the reaction stoichiometry in the passage, 1 mole of carbon dioxide is produced for each mole of CaO. One mole of gas at STP always occupies 22.4 L.

17. **D.** The Archimedes Principle states that the buoyant force exerted on an object by a fluid is equal to the weight of the fluid displaced by the object. When an object floats, it displaces a volume of water the weight of which equals the weight of the floating object.

18. **C.** A submerged object displaces a fluid volume equal to the volume of the submerged object.

19. **C.** The buoyant force on the submerged block equals the weight of water displaced. This latter is greater than the weight of the block because the water density is greater than that of the wooden block.

20. **D.** The speeds are the same because there is the same "pressure head," $\rho g y$, to force the water out of the stopcocks where $y$ is the 2 m depth, the same in both tanks. One can formally show this and find the actual speed by using Bernoulli's equation.

21. **B.** Use conservation of mechanical energy. Let the initial gravitational potential energy equal the final kinetic energy at the bottom:

$$\frac{1}{2}mv^2 = mgh$$

where $h = 0.8$ meters.
The mass, $m$, cancels and:

$$v = \sqrt{2gh} = \sqrt{2(10 \text{ m/s}^2)(0.8 \text{ m})}$$
$$= 4.0 \text{ m/s}$$

22. **A.** The period for any small angle of swing is given by the formula:

$$T = 2\pi\sqrt{L / g} = 2\pi\sqrt{0.8 / 10}$$
$$= 1.8 \text{ s}$$

23. **C.** The period does not depend on the angle of swing (as long as the angle is small enough, less than about 10°).

24. **A.** L can be found by squaring the equation for the period:

$$T^2 = 4\pi^2(L/g) = 4\pi^2(L/10) = 4 \text{ s}^2$$

Then:

$$L = 1.0 \text{ m}.$$

25. **A.** $T$ increases. The moon's force of gravity is $\frac{1}{6}$ that of Earth, so $g_{moon} = 1.6$ m/s$^2$.
When used in the formula, the period will be longer by $\sqrt{6}$. ($T_{moon} = 4.9$ s). Video of the astronauts on the moon clearly showed the weaker force of gravity. They appeared to be moving in slow motion if they leaped upward.

26. **C.** The equation of continuity for fluid flow is:

$$Av = \text{a constant value}$$
$$A_1v_1 = A_2v_2 = A_3v_3$$

Thus: $\quad v_3 = A_1v_1/A_3$

$$v_3 = (3 \text{ m}^2)(2 \text{ m/s})/2 \text{ m}^2 = 3.0 \text{ m/s}$$

27. **B.** Conservation of charge and mass requires the sum of the subscript (charge) numbers to be equal on both sides of the reaction as well as the sum of the superscript (mass) numbers to be equal. We must have then: $2 + 7 = 8 + 1$ and $4 + 14 = 17 + 1$. The missing subscript is 1, as is the missing superscript. The object is

actually a proton initially, but we write the symbol for neutral hydrogen, since the proton will "grab" an electron to become hydrogen.

28. **D.** The Coulomb force between two charged particles is given by: $F = kq_1q_2/r^2$. In this case, the ratio of the new force to the old force is:

$$\frac{F_2/F_1 = k(3q_Aq_B)/(3r)^2}{kq_Aq_B/r^2} = 1/3$$

29. **C.** The current through the 2-ohm resistor must split up with the larger portion going through the smaller resistor in the parallel branch. The 3-ohm and 6-ohm resistors are in the ratio of 1 to 2, so the 3-ampere current will split into the ratio of 2 to 1 — that is, 2 amperes through the 3-ohm resistor and 1 ampere through the 6-ohm resistor.

30. **C.** Since air friction is present, the ball will reach a "terminal velocity" shown as the value of $v$ corresponding to the horizontal dotted line.

31. **B.** Using Conservation of Mechanical Energy, $PE_A = PE_C + KE_C$. Then: $mgh_A = mgh_C + 1/2mv^2$ where $v$ is the speed at point C. Cancel the mass $m$ and solve for $v$. Note that we need not solve for the energies at B because the total mechanical energy is always constant.

32. **B.** A real image is formed, so the focal length is positive. The lens is midway between the object and the screen, so the object and image distance are both equal to 30 cm and are positive. The thin lens equation gives the focal length:

$$1/f = 1/d_o + 1/d_i$$
$$= 1/30 + 1/30$$
$$1/f = 2/30$$
$$f = +15 \text{ cm.}$$

33. **C.** The transmittance is the fraction of incident light that passes through the sample. This fraction is $72/81 = 0.889$.

34. **D.** The absorbance is defined as the negative logarithm of transmittance. $-\log 0.889 = 0.051$.

35. **A.** The Beer-Lambert Law states that $A = -\log T = EMl$ where

$A$ = absorbance
$T$ = transmittance
$E$ = a constant for the particular solute and wavelength of light
$M$ = molarity of solution
$l$ = path length of light

Thus absorbance varies directly with path length and with molar concentration; and decreasing the concentration by half will also halve the absorbance.

36. **A.** In the above statement of the Beer-Lambert Law it is seen that absorbance varies directly with path length. Thus, halving the path length will halve the absorbance.

37. **A.** The absorbance was 0.051. Doubling the concentration will double the absorbance to 0.102. Since absorbance = −log transmittance, and

$$\text{transmittance} = \frac{\text{reading with transmitted light}}{\text{reading with incident light}}$$

antilog (0.102) = 0.791
(0.791)(81) = 64

38. **D.** The reading, the transmittance, and the absorbance will be affected by the wavelength of light, but the direction and magnitude cannot be readily predicted.

39. **A.** HCl in water is expected to be virtually 100% ionized into $H^+$ (or $H_3O^+$) and $Cl^-$. $pH = -\log [H^+] = -\log (1 \times 10^{-2}) = 2$

40. **B.** Because the volume has doubled, [HCl] = 0.005 molar = $5 \times 10^{-3}$.

Because HCl is virtually completely ionized,

$$[H^+] = 5 \times 10^{-3} \text{ molar}$$
$$pH = -\log (5 \times 10^{-3})$$
$$\log 10^{-3} = -3$$
$$\log 5 = \underline{0.6990}$$
$$\text{sum} = -2.3010$$
$$-(-2.3010) = 2.3010$$

You should recognize that the answer must be between 2 and 3 because log (5) is a positive number between zero and one.

41. **C.** The Henderson-Hasselbalch equation states

$$pH = pK_a + \log \frac{[salt]}{[acid]}$$

The strongly ionized HCl will react with sodium propionate to yield propionic acid. Thus 0.01 moles of HCl will react with 0.01 moles of sodium propionate to yield 0.01 moles of propionic acid (HPr). An additional 0.01 moles of NaPr will remain unreacted.

$$pH = pK_a + \log \frac{[salt]}{[acid]} = 4.89 + \log \frac{(0.01)}{(0.01)} = 4.89$$

When the concentrations of weak acid and salt are equal,

$$\frac{[Salt]}{[Acid]} = 1 \text{ and } \log 1 = 0$$

At these concentrations, pH = $pK_a$. (The concentrations should be expressed in molarities rather than simply total moles. Reflection allows us to recognize that the end result will be the same as long as we are consistent in a single set of computations.)

42. **A.** Hydrochloric acid is a strong acid; the other acids are weak acids.

43. **B.** Look again at the Henderson-Hasselbalch equation. We have diluted [salt] and [acid] equally. Thus the pH remains at the $pK_a$.

44. **A.** The stronger the acid, the lower its $pK_a$. Thus, pyruvic acid is the strongest acid among the three.

45. **C.** Percent ionization = 100 (degree of ionization)

$$100 \times 0.12 = 12$$

46. **D.** Remember Graham's Law:

$$\frac{V_1}{V_2} = \sqrt{\frac{m_2}{m_1}}$$

$$\frac{1}{0.5} = \sqrt{\frac{m_2}{m_1}}$$

Squaring $\frac{1}{0.25} = \frac{m_2}{20} = 4$

$$m_2 = 80$$

47. **D.** $V_1 \times N_1 = V_2 \times N_2$
$$(20.0)(0.200) = (40.0)(0.100) = 4$$

This tells us nothing about the structure of the acid. Remember that the normality deals only with the available protons in solution rather than the molarity. The acid could be monoprotic, diprotic, or triprotic, but we have been given no information to allow us to decide.

48. **C.** $pK_w = pH + pOH = 14$
$4.5 + pOH = 14$
$pOH = 14 - 4.5 = 9.5$

49. **B.** $pH = pK_a + \log \frac{[salt]}{[acid]}$

When the salt (dissociated anion) and acid concentrations are equal, $\log 1 = 0$. Thus, pH = $pK_a$ or 4.2 in this case.

50. **B.** Buffering is always best at the $pK_a$.

51. **C.** $\frac{P_1 V_1}{T_1} = \frac{P_2 V_2}{T_2}$

Since $T_1 = T_2$, they will cancel out.

$$(1)(1) = 2V \text{ and } V = \frac{1}{2} \text{ or } 0.50$$

52. **B.** The step involved is a precipitation step. Increasing the $Cl^-$ concentration will reduce the concentration of $Ag^+$ in solution. Remember $K_{sp} = [Ag^+][Cl^-]$ and the source of the $Cl^-$ is irrelevant. Thus increased concentration of $Cl^-$ must result in decreased concentration of $Ag^+$ in order to maintain the solubility product constant. Addition of $Ag_2 SO_4$ would probably be counterproductive, since additional $Ag^+$ is being added, and probably all will not be recovered.

## Verbal Reasoning

53. **C.** The central theme of the passage deals with the monumental amounts of research that have been done in the field of public education over the past 20 years. Mention of the vast research effort is made in paragraphs three, four, and five, whereas paragraph six makes it clear that research will continue.

54. **D.** Paragraph two states that the outcry was created in part by declining economic conditions, as well as the publication of exhaustive studies of school resources and their impact.

55. **A.** Paragraph one makes it clear that the reform in question for this passage deals with the nation's public school systems.

56. **D.** All three statements are included in the answer. In education "the field" is considered the classroom (I). "Researchers" going into the field indicates that they are observing teachers and students in action (II). The fact that researchers have gone into the field in great numbers indicates that there is much interest in educational reform research (III).

57. **D.** The combination of **B** and **C** encompasses educators who are researchers as well as those who are practicing in the field at all levels, and names three specific sets of practitioners who are closest to school settings. The question asks, what groups, and a choice is provided to include all the combinations.

58. **B.** Paragraphs four and five discuss researchers in the field and some progress that has been made as a result of their efforts. The "tone" that the author sets in these paragraphs allows one to assume that she feels hands-on research is beneficial.

59. **C.** Paragraph two traces the story back to seventh century China and goes on to state that the plot is universal. The central thesis of the passage is that all versions of the story share many ingredients, and the first paragraph asserts that one of these chronicles the transformation into womanhood. Paragraph three notes the evil stepmother as a feature common to various versions of the story.

60. **B.** A main point of the passage is that a consistent aspect of Cinderella's character is her loving and forgiving spirit.

61. **C.** No mention is made of Cinderella's need for warmth (**A** is incorrect). The skins clearly are important in a ritual sense (**B** is incorrect). Cinderella always returns to a clean, well-dressed state; and because it symbolically is essential that she give up the skins and there is no mention that she keeps them, **D** is incorrect.

62. **B.** Cinderella, as the author notes in the final paragraph, is moving toward a condition of wholeness. There is nothing to suggest that she is less complex than she had thought (**A** is incorrect), that she exploits the prince (**C** is incorrect), or that her wholeness weakens her (**D** is incorrect).

63. **B.** A central purpose of the essay is to show how various versions of this tale make concrete various aspects of Horney's theories. Nowhere is there a suggestion that Horney had in mind the Cinderella story or that Horney altered the story in any way, thus **A** and **D** are incorrect. And, though one might find that the parallel between Horney's theories and the fairy tale provide one illustration of how the theories appear to be supported by their presence in a given story like *Cinderella,* nowhere is there a suggestion that the validity of a theory could be based on a single story application such as this one. Thus **C** is incorrect.

64. **A.** Although the first part of the title is a clever play on words, it also prepares the reader for the "fit" between Horney's theories and the Cinderella tale. The three other titles are not descriptive of the pattern of argument in the essay, and in the cases of **B** and **C**, contradict information in the text.

65. **D.** The best and most encompassing title would be The Development of the Physician. The passage does not deal with professional growth and the development and training of the medical student exclusively. Although it is mentioned that the first two years of the study of medicine focus on the scientific aspects and thereafter the clinical practice

predominates the life of the students, it is not examined specifically.

66. **D.** The passage makes it clear that most students enter this profession because they care for their fellow man and want to serve him; in fact the passage ends on the note that "the secret of the care of the patient is in caring for the patient." Achieving public esteem is a part of becoming a physician and certainly although intelligence and a good background help, they are not enough in the making of a physician. Marriage among classmates is not discussed.

67. **B.** Moral, clinical, and legal perspectives affect decision making and are in the order used upon first entrance into school. Socialization, however, elevates the clinical perspective to resolve the myriad of clinical situations. The issue of the influence of hospital administrators is not debated in the passage. The author quotes from Konner in respect to arrogance, but no conclusion is reached in respect to the statement that their extensive training gives anyone that right.

68. **D.** Good health, although essential, is not enough for medical practice; the article stresses continuously that the overall, the broad, the human, the appreciation of life, love, and mankind must be considered and held in focus in order to serve appropriately.

69. **D.** All the statements presented in this question are definitely contradicted by the information in the passage.

70. **B.** The passage makes it clear that at the end of the reductional division the chromosomes are reduced to one-half their original number. Meiosis results in four gametes that possess one-half the chromosomal number of an adult. The production of gametes, or sex cells—egg and sperm—is known as gametogenesis. Because an individual possesses an equal amount of genetic material from both parents and the same number of chromosomes as either parent, a reduction to one-half that number must be accomplished in the development of the egg and sperm.

71. **B.** During the process of meiosis, a recombination of genetic material is possible; this is effected through crossing-over, as noted in paragraph three. In crossing-over, comparable portions of chromatids are exchanged; crossing-over is more the rule than the exception. Replication results during the first part of meiosis in four chromatids and two of them may exchange materials. This exchange occurs before the tetrads separate.

72. **D.** The third paragraph indicates that replication of DNA occurs during interphase before meiosis starts. Interphase is the time during which the cell grows and prepares itself for meiosis.

73. **C.** See the explanation for previous questions dealing with this passage.

74. **D.** Eggs and sperm are haploid; a fertilized egg (zygote) possesses the diploid number of the parent again. Also see explanations for previous questions.

75. **D.** The first sentence of paragraph two mentions ten stages. Paragraph one states that sexual reproduction plays an important role in the expression of different phenotypes, and paragraph three indicates that replication of DNA occurs during interphase before meiosis begins.

76. **D.** The fact that ordinal position remains a little understood personality variable is stated in the opening paragraph and sets the tone for the passage.

77. **B.** Although much research has been done on birth order, it is not possible to make *absolute* statements about any of the ordinal positions. It has not been proven, for example, that the oldest is *always* the most mature. The opening paragraph implies that more studies need to be conducted.

78. **D.** The author states that primogeniture is "a perfect illustration of the importance of being first born." Because the custom began in feudal times, it is reasonable for the reader to conclude that the paragraph was inserted to provide a sense that the subject of ordinal birth has been the subject of study for some time.

79. **D.** All statements made in the question are correct. Parents attach to their firstborn such characteristics as a solid head on his/her shoulders, a mature behavior, and the ability to associate with adults, to be able to lead, to care for siblings, and to grow up as a pillar of the community. The youngest child is freer to develop into an exuberant and free-spirited individual because mothers do not expect the youngest to function in an adultlike manner. Many actions that were frowned upon previously are now considered cute in nature.

80. **A.** Although a comparison of the middle child to the older child is made, no direct comment or evidence is presented that this helps him/her reach higher levels of achievement; in fact because of the comparison and the desire of the child to establish his own identity, he may even become a problem student. The passage makes it clear that the firstborn usually performs better, and that the youngest feels the least need to excel. It is also stated in the passage that communication with adults is typically a problem of the second born.

81. **D.** All the statements are supported by the information in the passage.

82. **D.** The author of the passage neither supports nor contradicts the statements presented in the question.

83. **D.** All three statements are clearly contradicted by the information presented in the passage.

84. **B.** The charisma of the instructor is a factor in the evaluation of teaching effectiveness. There are objective methods available and grades do play a role in student ratings. Time of day is not discussed in the passage.

85. **D.** The difficulty of subject matter material and its effect on student ratings is not discussed in the passage.

86. **C.** Students are usually most interested in evaluations by students, believing that they are the "consumers" who are most directly affected by the quality of the "product" called teaching.

87. **D.** Paragraph five visualizes students as purchasers. Paragraph two points out that employers and employees benefit from evaluations, and paragraph four states that the end result is increased productivity.

88. **B.** In paragraph one, the author plainly asserts that Tillich believes contemporary society is characterized by an absence of spirituality, whereas, ironically, there is a growing interest in religion.

89. **A.** Tillich, according to the author, sees true religion as moving vertically, and thus being characterized by "depth." Tillich's main thesis deals with the ways in which (1) present-day religion runs counter to true religion and (2) present-day society discourages people from asking weighty eschatological questions.

90. **D.** Although the author agrees with Tillich's assertions that modern man lacks true religion and is more materialistic now than in the past, he questions in his final paragraph the strictly "rational" ways that Tillich implies are the only ways of knowing spiritual truth. Nowhere in the essay does the author quarrel with Tillich's definition of spirituality.

91. **B.** In paragraph three, the author states plainly that Tillich's ideas are perhaps even more insightful or relevant than they were 30 years ago.

92. **A.** Though the author clarifies and qualifies Tillich's positions, he asserts that Tillich is still as relevant as he was "30 years ago."

## Writing Sample

93. **Essay**

Herodotus's viewpoint here is clearly a fatalistic one. It is easy to see the logic behind it. Because mankind does not exist separately from either the rest of existence or the past, then every time that a person acts, she is in some ways also reacting to that surrounding existence and to the history that preceded that act. It is a frustrating point of view; and, in spite of its strange truth, it is probably a viewpoint best left without too much rumination. It is the given in life and the unchangeable. A resignation to this point of view would in some ways also be a voluntary denial of one's autonomy, of one's existence.

I say "voluntary" because I believe that the opposite viewpoint is, paradoxically, just as true. If I turn my head while driving in order to check my radio dial and in doing so also slightly turn my steering wheel causing an accident with an oncoming school bus, did not my act of turning my head create a circumstance whereby that accident occurred? Of course, it did. If I had not turned my head, then I would have not turned the wheel; and if I had not turned the wheel then the bus would not have hit my car. However, from Herodotus's viewpoint, my act did not exist by itself. Had the radio not been in the car, had a different song even been on the station, then I would perhaps not have turned my head to adjust the dial. Had the bus driver waited longer at her last stop or had she not stopped for a cup of coffee on her way to work, then perhaps she would not have been at that place at that specific time. The issue is as puzzling as the issue of whether the chicken appeared first or the egg. It is the question of the identification of an original cause in a long line of causes.

What a thinking person is most likely to conclude is that individuals and their circumstances are mutually interdependent rather than mutually exclusive and that therefore a statement like that of Herodotus is, in a sense, meaningless. His is only a statement of perspective and, further, a rather negative one. But to say the opposite, that circumstances are dependent on individuals and not vice versa, would be naive and ignorant. A rational person would have to accept interdependence of individuals and circumstances in order to live realistically and effectively in the world. She would then act carefully, remaining aware both that there are circumstances over which she has no control and that her act will be part of the circumstances to come.

### 93. Explanation of Response: 6

The paper focuses sharply on the statement and addresses each of the three writing tasks. Paragraph one explains what the statement means, paragraph two gives a specific situation in which individuals do, in fact, determine circumstances (a reversal of the assertion that "men are dependent on circumstances, not circumstances on men"), and paragraph three reconciles the statement and the situation that illustrates that the opposite of the statement may also be true.

The paper provides an analysis of the potential dangers of all-or-none statements like the one in question. It does so by examining the logical extension of the idea that individuals are dependent on circumstances and by characterizing the implications of this assertion as "fatalistic." The logic of the paper's argument is sophisticated, on the one hand agreeing with the "strange truth" of Herodotus's point in paragraph one, but in paragraph two illustrating with a series of circumstances "dependent on individuals" that the reverse is also true. The final paragraph presents a balanced consideration of the interdependent relationship between individuals and the circumstances that they create and by which they are shaped.

The writing is clear and nicely controlled. The sentences are varied, containing simple (e.g., sentence one), compound (e.g., sentence four), and complex structures (e.g., sentence three). The first sentence of each paragraph serves as a topic sentence and gives unity to the paragraph that follows. Transitions, such as "however" in sentence five of paragraph two, provide coherence within the paragraph.

### 94. Essay

Haeckel's quotation is an enigma because its meaning depends upon the interpretation of ambiguous words, "voluntary death," "intolerable suffering," and of course, "redemption." It is not clear whether the "voluntary death" is a suicide or a murder or any of the possibilities between these two extremes. So, even at the outset, the reader steps onto a shaky platform on which rests the remainder of Haeckel's statement. This "voluntary death" would specifically be the one that would put "an end to intolerable suffering." Because to "suffer" something is, in a sense, to "tolerate" it, then "intolerable suffering" would be an impossibility by definition. Finally, this enigmatic but "voluntary death," voluntary perhaps only because it is caused by a human act, is "an act of redemption." Naturally, one's thoughts might turn to the religious connotations of the word. In this case, it would mean a sort of act of deliverance from evil by sacrifice. If, however, you strip the mystery of religious aura from the word, it means simply a payback. Perhaps the redemption is the cashing in of the mortal life for freedom from human suffering. Keeping all of this in mind, Haeckel's statement, though, still a puzzle of sorts, must mean that for a person to cause or to allow death in order to discontinue the suffering of pain (of one sort or another) is an exchange of the body, which is only loaned for the duration of mortality, in exchange for the freedom of the human spirit.

Now, one could argue (and people certainly have argued) endlessly about the moral right and/or wrong of this idea because it is at the core of the controversies over euthanasia, abortion, and the execution of criminals. The argument is over, the "right" or "wrong" of this "redemption." Because "'right" and "wrong" cannot really be defined but only agreed upon tentatively (as with laws), perhaps the literal meaning of the quote might be a better target for thought. The problem here is that it is not clear whose "intolerable suffering" is being referred to in the statement. For example, if I refuse to tolerate or to suffer the presence of my annoying little brother, is my killing him or allowing him to die an act of redemption? The thought is appalling, of course, but, according to Haeckel, it would, in fact, be a redemptive act (even if the sacrifice entailed is only that of my own innocence). The way that Haeckel's quotation is worded, there are no real exceptions.

Haeckel's quotation could be used to try to justify morally the act of taking a human life. But the statement does not morally justify anything; it merely defines a type of "voluntary death" as a sort of exchange. The end of a human's life is always an exchange of one state for another. So the moral question, the "choice" perhaps, is a personal one (or a legal one). Morality is not defined by absolute natural laws; it is rather defined personally (or, in a social situation, legally). What governs the choice maker or the potential actor consists of nothing more absolute and nothing less vague than his or her conscience and personal beliefs. Haeckel's quote could be used loosely to justify an act that results in death. But "used" is the key word

here. Moral decision, decisions about right and wrong, are not that easy. Ultimately, the choice of a *"voluntary* death" in "the face of intolerable suffering" is determined only by the judgment and conscience of the individual, the mysterious "volunteer."

## 94. **Explanation of Response: 4**

The paper focuses on the topic defined by the statement and addresses the three writing tasks. The first paragraph responds to the task of explaining the statement, in this case a task complicated by the need to clarify definitions of words that have multiple meanings. In the second paragraph, the paper provides what is clearly one of the most extreme examples imaginable to demonstrate that, given the phrasing of the quotation, there are no specific situations in which "voluntary death" would not be an act of redemption. Paragraph three explores the factors that determine the choice of voluntary death in the face of intolerable suffering.

There is no question that Haeckel's statement raises difficult problems, and it is clear that this essay constructs a sophisticated argument that explores the complexity of these problems. The strategy of defining ambiguous terms in paragraph one is a good one; the choice to explore the connotations of these words also is effective, though anyone who chooses to spend this much time on definition in the first paragraph should be aware of the danger of overdoing it. This essay stops just short of this. The reason that this essay received a 4 rather than a 5 or 6 is that the second task ("Describe a specific situation in which the voluntary death by which a person puts an end to intolerable suffering would not be an act of redemption") is not confronted as directly as it might be. The paper maintains that "there are no real exceptions," virtually by definition. The writer might have used his or her skill with definition clearly demonstrated in paragraph one to construct at least one hypothetical situation that would provide a conceivable exception to Haeckel's statement. In addition to the need for a specific "exceptional" situation in paragraph two, the paper could be strengthened by the use of other examples to illustrate the major points in paragraphs one and three. This paper in general, however, is tightly reasoned, and it moves logically toward the conclusion that the choice of voluntary death in the face of intolerable suffering is ultimately a moral decision, one based on conscience.

# Biological Sciences

95. **B.** The thyroid hormones affect the rate of metabolism of all the tissues of the body; they control the growth, maturation, and differentiation of the organism. A goiter is any enlargement of the gland due to neoplasm or inflammatory disease. Endemic goiters are due to lack of iodine intake; this results in the increased production of TSH, compensatory hypertrophy and eventual exhaustion of the gland. Thyroxin deficiency leads to goiter; if the deficiency is not corrected, cretinism in the young and myxedema in the adult may be a consequence.

96. **C.** Hypothyroidism would result in a patient who is fairly heavy, phlegmatic, is devoid of expression, and has rough and dry skin and laboratory tests would show a low basal metabolic rate, low protein bound iodine, and a high serum cholesterol level.

97. **C.** The hypothyroid patient would have shown weight gain since less food is converted into energy and more food is stored as fat.

98. **D.** See explanations for questions 95–97.

99. **D.** A hyperthyroid patient would exhibit weight loss, nervousness, irritability, increased metabolic rate, rapid heart rate, sweating, and a protrusion of the eyeballs.

100. **D.** This woman is not the mother. She can contribute only the O gene, and this child must receive an A gene from one parent and a B gene from the other parent. The man cannot be ruled out as the father with the limited information given, since he can contribute a B gene to a child.

101. **D.** If the man previously fathered a child with blood type O, then the man must have a genotype of BO. The woman can contribute only the O gene. Since the man has an equal chance of contributing the B or the O gene,

there is a 50% chance of the child being type O (genotype OO) or type B (genotype BO).

102. **B.** The chance of any child of this couple being type B is 50% (see explanation for question 99). The chance that any child will be a girl is 50%. Since the blood type and the sex are independent of each other, multiply their individual chances (50% × 50% = 25%).

103. **B.** Phenotypic and genotypic characteristics may be expressed as follows:

| Phenotype | Genotype |
|-----------|----------|
| A | A/O |
| B | B/O |
| O | O/O |
| AB | A/B |

104. **D.** Genotype refers to the genetic makeup of the organism. The genotype is expressed via phenotypic characteristics that are visible and observable under normal circumstances.

105. **D.** An allele is one of a pair of genes that occupies the same locus on homologous chromosomes.

106. **C.** Rhesus (Rh) agglutinogen is present in humans and is represented by a dominant gene R. The agglutinogen of an Rh positive fetus passes across the placenta, enters the maternal blood stream, and elicits the production of an agglutinin (antibody) by the mother. The agglutinin passes into the circulation of the fetus and if present in sufficient concentration can produce agglutination, at times fatal to the developing fetus.

107. **B.** Hemophilia, a frequent disease of the royal houses of Europe, is a bleeding disorder transmitted through a sex-linked recessive gene. It results in abnormal coagulation; hemophilia A is the classical true hemophilia resulting from a deficiency of factor VIII. Both sexes carry a complete complement of sex-linked genes. A female, with the XX arrangement, will only exhibit a recessive gene if she has received it from both parents (a rare event with an uncommon gene), whereas in the XY male the recessive gene cannot be masked because there is no partner X and so a larger number of recessive genes

are expressed. A man receives his X from his mother and passes it on to his daughters. His daughters are the carriers of sex-linked traits and their sons may be affected.

108. **B.** Synthesis of mRNA is catalyzed by RNA polymerase II.

109. **C.** Proteins for secretion are made by ribosomes on rough endoplasmic reticulum and then modified in Golgi bodies.

110. **B.** Skeletal muscle cells are striated due to the highly organized thick (myosin) and thin (actin) myofilaments and contain numerous nuclei.

111. **C.** Reabsorption of useful solutes is the primary function of the proximal convoluted tubule.

112. **A.** The corpus callosum connects the cerebral hemispheres.

113. **C.** Pleiotropism is defined as multiple phenotypic effects of a gene (allele).

114. **C.** 1-2, who manifests prolonged Q-T interval, has 14 descendants who are also affected and six who are not. Each of the 14 affected descendants has an affected parent; both parents (II-3&10) of four are affected. The trait thus shows unbroken lineal descent and is, therefore, *dominant*.

115. **C.** *Deafness is not a pleiotropic affect of the gene producing prolonged Q-T*, for these abnormalities are observed *assorting* among the progeny of a male (II-1), who is doubly homozygous normal, and his wife (II-2), who is heterozygous for both abnormalities, that is, doubly heterozygous. Alleles segregate (Mendel's first law) from each other; nonalleles may assort. In the absence of linkage, *independent assortment* (Mendel's second law) of nonalleles occurs. Although the sample is not large enough to rule out weak linkage, it does rule out allelism.

116. **A.** Every affected descendant of the affected progenitor (I-3) of the F. family has at least one parent affected, except III-21, a son of II-11, who marks the only break in lineal descent of the trait. If the trait were recessive,

the three normal mothers (I-4, II-9, and II-12) of affected children would have to be carriers. Because of the rarity of the defect and the lack of biological kinship between these women and their spouses, it is highly unlikely that they are carriers. It is probable that the trait is dominant and that the allele has slightly reduced penetrance and failed to manifest itself phenotypically in II-11.

117. **B.** If one were limited to the data on the W. family, it would be impossible to distinguish whether the defect is autosomal or X-linked. That is because we could not then rule out male-to-male transmission among the progeny of couple II-3&10, who have three arrhythmic sons. Nonetheless, prolonged Q-T and the arrhythmias are clinically indistinguishable and almost certainly determined by the same *autosomal dominant* allele as in the F. family, where male-to-male transmission shows that this dominant trait is autosomal. X-linked traits cannot be transmitted from father to son (male-to-male) because sons can receive their X chromosome (in which X-linked traits are transmitted) from only their mother, *not* from their father.

118. **C.** All of the daughters of affected males would be affected if the trait were X-linked because they received their father's X chromosome which would have contained the (dominant) mutant allele had it been X-linked. None of the daughters of the affected fathers (II-3 and II-5) are affected, thus the mutant allele is *not* in the X chromosome; the trait is autosomal.

119. **D.** Many autosomal dominant genes that produce rather mild phenotypic effects in the heterozygote produce much more extreme effects—in some cases, even lethality—in homozygotes. It is likely that *the propista (III-10) is homozygous* for the prolonged Q-T allele and demonstrates the more extreme phenotype frequently manifested by homozygotes for rare autosomal dominant traits.

120. **C.** The driving force ($\Delta P$) causing air to flow into or out of the lungs is the pressure difference between the atmospheric pressure ($P_{atm}$) and the intra-alveolar pressure ($P_{alv}$). The absolute atmospheric or intra-alveolar pressures do not dictate air flow, it is the pressure

difference that is important. Intrapleural pressure reflects lung elastic forces as well plus any smaller pressure difference between $P_{atm}$ and $P_{alv}$ while breathing. Thus, the absolute value of the intrapleural pressure has no bearing on inspiration.

121. **A.** During inspiration the chest wall enlarges, expanding the lungs and the intra-alveolar air. Thus, the intra-alveolar pressure transiently drops below atmospheric pressure, pulling air into the lungs. During expiration the chest wall collapses causing the intra-alveolar pressure to transiently go above atmospheric pressure and air flows out of the lungs. When intra-alveolar pressure equals atmospheric pressure, no air will flow into or out of the lungs. The intrapleural pressure will always be lower than the intra-alveolar pressure by an amount equal to the elastic forces of the lungs. Thus, intra-alveolar pressure never goes below intrapleural pressure.

122. **D.** As defined, the alveolar ventilation equals the amount of fresh air which reaches the alveoli per minute. Thus, alveolar ventilation is the amount of fresh air reaching the alveoli per breath times the number of breaths per minute. Because part of the fresh air inspired gets no farther than the anatomic dead space (i.e. it doesn't reach the alveoli), the fresh air actually reaching the alveoli equals the tidal volume minus the volume of the anatomic dead space. The frequency of breathing times any other lung volume equals something other than the alveolar ventilation.

123. **C.** With hypoventilation, oxygen delivery to the alveolar gas is less than normal and the partial pressure of oxygen will decrease. Concurrently, the removal of carbon dioxide from the alveolar compartment is less than normal and the partial pressure of carbon dioxide will increase.

124. **D.** The repressor protein binds to the operator sequence to block access to the promoter.

125. **D.** The three germ layers become apparent during gastrulation.

126. **A.** B lymphocytes and plasma cells are the only cells in humans that can form antibodies.

127. **C.** The methyl group of toluene is an $o, p$-directing group.

128. **D.** The hydroxyl group is a highly activating group, whereas the chloro, nitro, and acetyl groups deactivate the ring towards electrophilic aromatic substitutions.

129. **B.** Oxidation of toluene yields benzoic acid. Nitration would yield the meta isomer because the carboxyl group is meta directing.

130. **A.** The methyl group activates the $o, p$-positions and directs the Br to the ortho position. The nitro group is a meta directing deactivating group.

131. **B.** The nitration of benzene involves the attack of a nitronium ion, $NO^+_2$, on toluene to form a cyclohexadienyl cation as the intermediate.

132. **C.** Valine is one of the nine essential amino acids, whereas linoleic acid is the only true essential fatty acid. Vitamin E is fat soluble and found in foods. Glucose is essential, but is obtained in other forms, such as polysaccharides. Polysaccharides contain many monosaccharide units joined in long chains and among the most important are starch and cellulose. Starch is the reserve carbohydrate in plants and on complete hydrolysis it yields glucose.

133. **D.** Linoleic, linolenic, and arachidonic acids (polyunsaturated) are listed as essential fatty acids, because they cannot be synthesized by the animal and must therefore be provided in the diet. Among the water soluble vitamins are thiamine, biotin, and niacin.

134. **B.** The fat-soluble vitamins are vitamins A, D, E, and K. The water-soluble vitamins are vitamin C, thiamine, riboflavin, niacin, vitamin $B_6$, folacin, vitamin $B_{12}$, biotin, and pantothenic acid.

135. **D.** The bulk essential minerals are calcium, phosphorus, and magnesium, whereas the trace essential minerals are iron, zinc, selenium, iodine, cobalt, molybdenum, manganese, copper, chromium, and fluoride.

136. **C.** Amino acids are derived from proteins; carbohydrates that are polyhydroxy aldehydes and the simplest carbohydrate units are known as monosaccharides. The most important monosaccharide is glucose; it is obtained by the hydrolysis of starch. Fat and oil constitute one of the three main classes of food. Fats and oils are esters of glycerol with carboxylic acids.

137. **B.** Parathyroid hormone acts upon bone, eliciting changes in calcium and phosphorus. Osteoclasts are the cells stimulated by parathyroid hormone to facilitate the resorption of calcium and phosphorus from bone. Administration of parathyroid hormone to animals without parathyroids results in an increase of phosphorus excretion in the urine, a fall in serum inorgamic phosphorus levels, an increase in serum calcium, and an increase of calcium excretion in the urine.

138. **C.** Excretion concerns itself with the elimination of water (fluid) and metabolic wastes, whereas egestion is the process of eliminating undigested food materials. Catabolism is the chemical breakdown of molecules.

139. **A.** In anaerobic respiration glucose is converted to two molecules of the 3-carbon compound pyruvic acid. In aerobic respiration, glucose is converted to six molecules each of carbon dioxide and water. Anaerobic respiration is only about 3% as efficient as aerobic respiration. The anaerobic pathway is the same as the aerobic to the pyruvic acid stage.

140. **B.** LH (luteinizing hormone) is secreted by the pituitary gland. In the male, it is also called ICSH (interstitial, cell stimulating, hormone) from its effects on the testes. In our case, half of each group had its testes removed. This eliminates the feedback from testes to pituitary. Comparison of AM and PM readings for intact rats shows no significant

differences in LH levels. For orchidectomized rats, levels vary widely, with no consistent AM-PM relationship.

141. **A.** The strongest pattern in the data is higher LH values in orchidectomized rats. Choice B is not true. Choices C and D, although true, are not directly supported by the data given.

142. **B.** Values are higher on average in each category in assay 2. This may be due to a systematic error in either assay, but that cannot be determined from the data given.

143. **D.** The general formula $C_nH_{2n-2}$ applies to all members of the alkyne series. The suffix for names in this series is "yne." Ethyne is the only choice that has the correct ending.

144. **C.** Ethers have the general formula R–O–R′. The other compounds have the following general formulas:

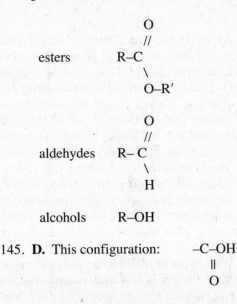

$$\text{esters} \qquad R-C \begin{matrix} O \\ \parallel \\ \\ \diagdown \\ O-R' \end{matrix}$$

$$\text{aldehydes} \qquad R-C \begin{matrix} O \\ \parallel \\ \\ \diagdown \\ H \end{matrix}$$

alcohols     R–OH

145. **D.** This configuration:

$$-\underset{\underset{O}{\parallel}}{C}-OH$$

is characteristic of carboxyl groups. A hydroxyl group is identified by –OH.

146. **C.** $\varnothing CH_2Cl + \varnothing \xrightarrow{AlCl_3} \varnothing-CH_2-\varnothing$

Friedel-Crafts Reaction

$\varnothing CH_2Cl + Na \longrightarrow \varnothing-CH_2CH_2-\varnothing$

Wurtz Reaction

# SCORING OF THE MCAT

A report of the results of your performance on the MCAT is sent to you, to the medical schools selected, and, with your agreement, to your Premedical Advisor, usually within six to eight weeks of taking the exam.

The score sheet will list the results of each of the four subtests. The score for the three multiple-choice subtests (but not the Writing Sample) is based on the number of correct answers. (Thus, guessing wrong will not induce a lowering of the score.)

The scores for three of the subtests—physical sciences, biological sciences, and verbal reasoning—are reported on a 1 to 15 scale. These *scaled scores* when reported are converted from *raw* scores. (The conversion factor varies with different exams and compensates for minor variations in difficulty between exams.)

The scaled scores earned are best interpreted in relation to the performance of other examinees by means of three data sheets, namely, means (and standard deviations) for each subtest, percentile rank ranges, and percentages of students receiving each scaled score, which are sent along with your scores.

# FUTURE MCAT PLANS

The MCAT is undergoing a multiyear comprehensive review. This project is intended to increase its value to medical school admissions committees. The text evaluation is expected to continue until 2012.

The anticipated extensive changes include: a section dealing with biochemistry, genetics, and a new "culture of medicine." The updated exam is expected to evaluate those skills on top of its established testing of general science knowledge, problem solving, critical thinking, and other skills.

The culture of medicine focus will include testing cultural competence and effective communicatin skills, crucial to the future of the physician workforce. This may be done by the use of an essay, and possibly videos.

The motive behind the program review is that, as the medical profession continues to undergo rapid changes, it's critical that the tools we use to select future doctors also evolve. Consequently, the comprehensive MCAT review seeks to ensure that the MCAT has the most current and effective content to assist medical school admissions officers in their efforts to select the best qualified applicants.

The changes in the MCAT are not aimed at weighing more heavily in the admission process. Medical schools will continue to evaluate applicants on traditional measures like transcripts, personal interviews, essays, volunteer service, medical activity exposure, and research work.

The last revision of the MCAT in 1990 sought to test for a wider range of knowledge than just the sciences. Indications are that the planned revised MCAT will not change radically the existing test. When the changes have been formulated, they will be publicized along with advice and how to study for them.

# 8 Medical Schools

## Basic data on medical schools

In this chapter you will find Table 8.1, Basic Data on the Medical Schools, which provides numerical data dealing with many school characteristics and serves as a quick source of information and a means for easily comparing features of schools you may be interested in.

## BASIC DATA ON MEDICAL SCHOOLS _____

Table 8.1, Basic Data on the Medical Schools, contains the kind of information that will be useful in helping you decide which schools to apply to. At a glance you can see and compare application data, admissions statistics, academic statistics, and expenses.

Please note that while the information in this table is as up to date and accurate as possible, it is recommended that you check the individual medical school catalogs prior to applying.

For a very small number of schools, data for the 2008–2009 year could not be secured. In such cases, which are identified by the symbol # after the school name, earlier data are used. This fact should be borne in mind when using data for these schools.

It should be noted that the bottom segment of each data capsule has a series of six bar graphs. These provide information on tuition and fees for residents and nonresidents. These figures can at a glance be compared with average general figures in both categories.

### How to Use This Table

This comprehensive table can help you formulate the initial and final list of medical schools to which you may wish to apply for admission. It will guide you at the outset to the schools located in your own and adjacent states where you may have a special priority (Column 1). It will also provide you with a ready means of identifying those schools that accept large numbers of out-of-state applicants (Column 8), which merit being placed on your list. If you are a woman or a minority group member, you can learn whether you should apply to a particular school by noting Columns 7 and 14, respectively. Assessing your potential academic suitability merely requires checking GPA (Column 11), and MCAT score averages (Column 16). Finally, affordability of a school will be indicated by Columns 17 and 18, which list tuition and other expenses, respectively.

After preparing your preliminary list based on geographical and residency considerations, you should then amend your list by taking into consideration such other factors as GPA, MCAT scores, and tuition. You should be cautioned not to automatically drop schools from the list merely because they are unsuitable in only one respect. In other words, if your GPA is 3.4 and the acceptance mean is 3.6, this by itself does not eliminate you from consideration since the 3.6 represents a mean, indicating that there probably was a range that included the 3.4 level. Similarly, the percentages of women and minorities accepted has to be taken in the context of total class size. Thus, 10% minorities accepted out of a class of 150 is 15, while 20% of a class of only 50 is 10. Finally, what you can afford to spend on the costly interview process needs to come into play when you are finalizing your list. It should prove very helpful when making up your list to refer to the profiles of the schools in Chapter 9.

# Definitions

The following are explanations and definitions of the column headings in Table 8.1.

### Application Fee

In most cases, this fee is required after your application has passed the initial screening by the medical school. This fee is sent at the time you submit your supplementary application. The preliminary application fee is usually the AMCAS application fee that is paid when submitting the form.

### Earliest and Latest Filing Dates

These are usually firm dates.

### Number of Applicants

This column gives an idea of how many applications were received for the 2008–2009 class.

### Applicants Enrolled

The columns indicate the men, women, and out-of-state students accepted for the 2008–2009 class. The ratio of the total number of men and women accepted to the total number of applicants gives an indication of the competitive nature of admission at each school.

### Class Size

The figures in this column refer to the 2008–2009 class.

### Percentage with Four Years of College

This shows the relative chances of a third-year student gaining admission.

### Percent Interviewed

This indicates the relative importance of being granted an interview at a specific school.

### Percent Residents

This indicates the desirability of a student to apply to a specific out-of-state school.

### Percent Minorities

This column shows what percentage of the first-year class were members of a minority group.

### Mean MCAT Scores

The mean MCAT scores for the three subtests for the 2008 entering class are listed in this column. The subtest abbreviations are P–physical sciences, B–biological sciences, and V–verbal reasoning.

### Deposit

This column shows the amount of money that must be sent in to hold a place in the class. It may be applied toward eventual tuition cost and in some cases is refundable.

### Tuition

2008–2009 tuition costs (annual) for first-year students are given.

### Other Expenses

This estimate covers the minimum room and board, fees, and other expenses, excluding microscope costs, for the first year.

### Financial Aid

This column indicates the percentage of students receiving financial aid. This is awarded on the basis of demonstrated need in the form of grants, loans, and scholarships. Such financial support is usually available each year for the four-year study sequence. More information is available in Chapter 12.

## Table 8.1. BASIC DATA ON THE MEDICAL SCHOOLS (2008–2009)

| School | Application Data | | | Admission Statistics | | | | | |
| | Fee | Filing Dates | | Number of Applicants | Applicants Enrolled | | | Class Profile | |
| | | Earliest | Latest | | Men | Women | Out of State | Class Size | % with 4 Years College |
|---|---|---|---|---|---|---|---|---|---|
| **Alabama** | | | | | | | | | |
| University of South Alabama College of Medicine | 75 | 6/1 | 11/15 | 997 | 42 | 32 | 8 | 74 | |
| University of Alabama School of Medicine | 75 | 6/1 | 11/15 | 1960 | 104 | 72 | 16 | 176 | 100 |
| **Arizona** | | | | | | | | | |
| University of Arizona College of Medicine | 75 | 6/1 | 11/15 | 814 | 51 | 83 | 0 | 134 | n/a |
| **Arkansas** | | | | | | | | | |
| University of Arkansas College of Medicine | 100 | 7/1 | 11/1 | 1230 | 100 | 55 | 6 | 155 | n/a |
| **California** | | | | | | | | | |
| Loma Linda University School of Medicine | 75 | 6/1 | 11/1 | 4327 | 97 | 75 | 84 | 172 | n/a |
| Stanford University School of Medicine | 80 | 6/1 | 11/1 | 6567 | 40 | 46 | 54 | 86 | 100 |
| University of California—Davis School of Medicine | 60 | 6/1 | 10/1 | 4861 | 43 | 62 | 3 | 105 | 100 |
| University of California—Irvine School of Medicine | 60 | 6/1 | 11/1 | 4536 | 53 | 51 | 3 | 104 | 100 |
| University of California—Los Angeles, David Geffen | 60 | 6/1 | 11/1 | 7824 | 94 | 75 | 23 | 169 | n/a |
| University of California—San Diego School of Medicine | 60 | 6/1 | 11/1 | 5500 | 66 | 68 | 10 | 134 | n/a |
| University of California—San Francisco School of Medicine | 60 | 6/1 | 10/15 | 6303 | 67 | 96 | 17 | 163 | 100 |
| Keck School of Medicine University of Southern Cal. | 90 | 7/1 | 11/1 | 6618 | 86 | 73 | 39 | 168 | 100 |
| **Colorado** | | | | | | | | | |
| University of Colorado School of Medicine | 100 | 6/1 | 11/1 | 2953 | 83 | 74 | 35 | 159 | n/a |

n/a    data not available

| | Admission Statistics | | | Academic Statistics | Expenses | | | | |
| | Class Profile | | | | | Tuition | | | |
| Mean GPA | Interviewed | % Residents | % Minorities | Mean MCAT | Deposit | Resident | Nonresident | Other | Financial Aid |
|---|---|---|---|---|---|---|---|---|---|
| 3.7 | 21 | 95 | 7 | P-10,0 B-11.0 V-10.1 | $50 | 16,082 | 29,562 | n/a | 90 |
| 3.8 | 19 | 90 | 6 | P-10 B-10.4 V-10 | $50 | 16,608 | 43,848 | 11,540 | 79 |
| 3.8 | 8 | 100 | 4 | P-10 B-10 V-10 | n/a | 17,767 | 0 | n/a | 93 |
| 3.7 | 3 | 90 | 3 | P-10 B-10 V-10 | n/a | 16,430 | 31,962 | n/a | 93 |
| 3.7 | 9 | 51 | 49 | P-10 B-10 V-10 | n/a | 35,506 | 35,506 | n/a | 89 |
| 3.8 | 62 | 40 | 17 | P-12 B-12 V-10.9 | 0 | 43,589 | 43,789 | 27.599 | 74 |
| 3.7 | 10 | 97 | 3 | P-11 B-11 V-10 | 0 | 36,544 | 36,544 | 13,500 | 93 |
| 3.7 | 10 | 97 | 3 | P-11 B-11 V-10 | n/a | 21,823 | 34,068 | n/a | 90 |
| 3.8 | 9 | 86 | 9 | P-11 B-12 V-10 | n/a | 22,551 | 34,596 | n/a | 86 |
| 3.8 | 10 | 93 | 1 | P-11 B-11 V-10 | n/a | 21,465 | 33,710 | n/a | 91 |
| 3.8 | 10 | 83 | 13 | P-11 B-11 V-10 | n/a | 21,218 | 33,463 | n/a | 86 |
| 3.6 | 106 | 76 | 25 | P-10.1 B-10.1 V-10.1 | $100 | 43,556 | 43,556 | 20.62 | 89 |
| 3.8 | 19 | 78 | 8 | P-11 B-11 V-11 | $200 | 24,828 | 48,030 | n/a | 93 |

## Table 8.1. BASIC DATA ON THE MEDICAL SCHOOLS (2008–2009)

| School | Fee | Earliest | Latest | Number of Applicants | Men | Women | Out of State | Class Size | % with 4 Years College |
|---|---|---|---|---|---|---|---|---|---|
| | | Application Data | | | Admission Statistics | | | | |
| | | Filing Dates | | | | Applicants Enrolled | | Class Profile | |
| **Connecticut** | | | | | | | | | |
| University of Connecticut School of Medicine | 85 | 6/1 | 12/15 | 2950 | 40 | 45 | 21 | 85 | 100 |
| Yale University School of Medicine | 85 | 6/1 | 10/15 | 5021 | 53 | 47 | 86 | 100 | n/a |
| **DC Washington** | | | | | | | | | |
| Georgetown University School of Medicine | 130 | 6/1 | 10/31 | 11237 | 101 | 93 | 193 | 194 | 100 |
| Howard University College of Medicine | 45 | 6/1 | 12/15 | 5310 | 66 | 64 | 88 | 130 | n/a |
| George Washington University Sch. of Med. | 125 | 6/1 | 1/1 | 13082 | 77 | 100 | n/a | 177 | 100 |
| **Florida** | | | | | | | | | |
| Florida International University College of Medicine | | | | | | | | | |
| University of Central Florida College of Medicine | | 6/1 | 12/1 | | | | | | |
| University of Florida College of Medicine | 30 | 6/1 | 12/1 | 2847 | 70 | 65 | 8 | 135 | 91 |
| University of Miami School of Medicine | 75 | 6/15 | 1/31 | 4638 | 103 | 91 | 57 | 194 | 90 |
| University of South Florida College of Medicine | 30 | 7/6 | 12/1 | 2494 | 57 | 63 | 11 | 1120 | 100 |
| **Georgia** | | | | | | | | | |
| Emory University School of Medicine | 100 | 6/15 | 10/15 | 4014 | 62 | 70 | 83 | 132 | 100 |
| Medical College of Georgia School of Medicine | no | 6/1 | 11/1 | 1950 | 110 | 80 | 2 | 190 | 100 |
| Mercer University School of Medicine | 50 | 6/1 | 11/1 | 784 | 46 | 44 | 0 | 90 | 100 |
| Morehouse School of Medicine | 50 | 6/1 | 12/1 | 3623 | 21 | 31 | 31 | 52 | n/a |

n/a    data not available

| | Admission Statistics | | | Academic Statistics | | Expenses | | | | |
|---|---|---|---|---|---|---|---|---|---|---|
| | | Class Profile | | | | | | Tuition | | |
| Mean GPA | Interviewed | % Residents | % Minorities | Mean MCAT | Deposit | Resident | Nonresident | Other | Financial Aid |
| 3.7 | 13 | 75 | 15 | P-10.4 B-10.9 V-10 | $100 | 24,142 | 46,678 | n/a | 88 |
| 3.8 | 20 | 14 | 13 | P-11 B-11 V-10 | n/a | 41,220 | 41,220 | n/a | 87 |
| 3.7 | 10 | 1 | 7 | P-10.7 B-11.0 V-10.1 | $100 | 41,356 | 41,356 | 26,029 | 90 |
| 3.4 | 7 | 32 | 49 | P-8 B-8 V-9 | n/a | 29,846 | 29,846 | n/a | 92 |
| 3.6 | 8 | 100 | 19 | P-9.7 B-10.1 V-9.6 | $100 | 45,892 | 45,892 | 22,418 | 82 |
| | | | | | | 4,136 | 70,786 | | |
| | | | | | | 22,500 | 42,500 | 17,500 | |
| 3.7 | 13 | 94 | 16 | P-10.8 B-11.1 V-9.9 | $200 | 23,929 | 51,777 | 6,485 | 85 |
| 3.7 | 104 | 706 | 26 | P-10 B-11 V-11 | $100 | 30,048 | 39,254 | 22,770 | 92 |
| 3.7 | 16 | 91 | 13 | P-10 B-11 V-9.7 | 0 | 21,000 | 53,000 | 19,771 | 80 |
| 3.7 | 17 | 37 | 25 | P-11.6 B-11.6 V-10.8 | n/a | 40,700 | 40,700 | 9,492 | 87 |
| 3.8 | 9 | 89 | 6 | P-10 B-11 V-10 | n/a | 14,237 | 31,663 | n/a | 78 |
| 3.6 | 37 | 100 | 2 | P-8.7 B-9.0 V-9.3 | $100 | 37,200 | 37,200 | 15,840 | 92 |
| 3.4 | 9 | 40 | 75 | P-9 B-8 V-8 | n/a | 29,248 | 29,248 | n/a | 94 |

## Table 8.1. BASIC DATA ON THE MEDICAL SCHOOLS (2008–2009)

| School | Fee | Application Data — Filing Dates — Earliest | Latest | Admission Statistics — Number of Applicants | Applicants Enrolled — Men | Women | Out of State | Class Profile — Class Size | % with 4 Years College |
|---|---|---|---|---|---|---|---|---|---|
| **Hawaii** | | | | | | | | | |
| University of Hawaii John A. Burns, Sch. Med. | 50 | 6/1 | 11/1 | 1895 | 28 | 34 | 6 | 62 | n/a |
| **Illinois** | | | | | | | | | |
| Southern Illinois University School of Medicine | 50 | 6/1 | 11/15 | 1173 | 40 | 32 | 0 | 72 | 100 |
| Rush Medical College Rush University | 75 | 6/1 | 11/1 | 6475 | 60 | 70 | 34 | 130 | 100 |
| University of Illinois, College of Medicine | 70 | 6/1 | 11/15 | 7692 | 170 | 131 | 63 | 307 | n/a |
| Northwestern University Medical School | 75 | 6/1 | 10/15 | 7527 | 85 | 84 | 130 | 169 | n/a |
| Chicago Medical School R. Franklin University of Medicine and Science | 100 | 6/1 | 11/1 | 6447 | 100 | 90 | 140 | 190 | n/a |
| Loyola University Chicago Stritch School of Medicine | 70 | 6/1 | 11/15 | 9487 | 70 | 76 | 75 | 146 | n/a |
| University of Chicago, Pritzker School of Medicine | 75 | 6/1 | 10/15 | 7787 | 53 | 59 | 68 | 112 | n/a |
| **Indiana** | | | | | | | | | |
| Indiana University, School of Medicine | 50 | 6/1 | 12/15 | 3369 | 173 | 135 | 262 | 308 | n/a |
| **Iowa** | | | | | | | | | |
| University of Iowa, College of Medicine | 60 | 6/1 | 11/1 | 2895 | 77 | 71 | 50 | 148 | n/a |
| **Kansas** | | | | | | | | | |
| University of Kansas School of Medicine | 50 | 6/1 | 10/15 | 1918 | 83 | 93 | 28 | 176 | n/a |

n/a    data not available

| Mean GPA | Admission Statistics | | | Academic Statistics | Expenses | | | | |
| | Class Profile | | | | | Tuition | | | |
| | Interviewed | % Residents | % Minorities | Mean MCAT | Deposit | Resident | Nonresident | Other | Financial Aid |
|---|---|---|---|---|---|---|---|---|---|
| 3.8 | 12 | 90 | 42 | P-10 B-10 V-9 | n/a | 22,632 | 46,624 | 24,357 | 80 |
| 3.5 | 23 | 100 | 18 | P-9.0 B-10.0 V-9.0 | $100 | 22,210 | n/a | 11,704 | 96 |
| 3.6 | 6 | 26 | 15 | P-10.4 B-10.5 V-9.9 | $100 | 44,928 | 44,928 | 2,739 | 90 |
| 3.7 | 12 | 21 | 11 | P-10 B-11 V-10 | n/a | 27,828 | 56,724 | n/a | 89 |
| 3.8 | 11 | 23 | 5 | P-11 B-11 V-10 | n/a | 40,313 | 40,313 | n/a | 77 |
| 3.7 | 11 | 22 | 5 | P-10 B-11 V-9.7 | n/a | 39,472 | 39,472 | n/a | 79 |
| 3.7 | 6 | 49 | n/a | P-10 B-11 V-10 | n/a | 37,620 | 37,620 | n/a | 89 |
| 3.8 | 10 | 39 | 12 | P-12 B-12 V-11 | n/a | 35,985 | 35,985 | n/a | 87 |
| 3.7 | 28 | 85 | 11 | P-9.4 B-10.3 V-10.3 | $50 | 27,151 | 42,130 | n/a | 92 |
| 3.7 | 23 | 34 | 24 | P-10.5 B-11.0 V-10.2 | $60 | 26,113 | 41,927 | 34,984 | 92 |
| 3.7 | 24 | 84 | 8 | P-9 B-10 V-10 | n/a | 22,976 | 40,367 | n/a | 93 |

## Table 8.1. BASIC DATA ON THE MEDICAL SCHOOLS (2008–2009)

| School | Fee | Filing Dates Earliest | Filing Dates Latest | Number of Applicants | Men | Women | Out of State | Class Size | % with 4 Years College |
|---|---|---|---|---|---|---|---|---|---|
| **Kentucky** | | | | | | | | | |
| University of Kentucky College of Medicine | 50 | 6/1 | 11/1 | 2259 | 67 | 46 | 22 | 113 | n/a |
| University of Louisville School of Medicine | 75 | 6/1 | 10/15 | 2348 | 87 | 108 | 35 | 155 | 78 |
| **Louisiana** | | | | | | | | | |
| Louisiana State University, Shreveport | 50 | 6/1 | 11/1 | 1004 | 71 | 46 | 2 | 117 | n/a |
| Tulane University School of Medicine | 95 | 6/1 | 12/15 | 6800 | 94 | 81 | 108 | 175 | n/a |
| Louisiana State University School of Medicine— New Orleans | 50 | 6/1 | 11/30 | 1414 | 98 | 81 | 6 | 179 | n/a |
| **Maryland** | | | | | | | | | |
| Johns Hopkins University School of Medicine | 75 | 6/1 | 10/15 | 6149 | 59 | 59 | 105 | 118 | n/a |
| Uniformed Services University of the Health Sciences | 0 | 6/1 | 11/15 | 1950 | 120 | 51 | 165 | 171 | 100 |
| University of Maryland School of Medicine | 70 | 6/1 | 11/1 | 4503 | 67 | 93 | 27 | 160 | n/a |
| **Massachusetts** | | | | | | | | | |
| Boston University School of Medicine | 100 | 6/1 | 11/1 | 10870 | 87 | 90 | 150 | 177 | 90 |
| University of Massachusetts Medical School | 75 | 6/1 | 11/1 | 830 | 46 | 57 | 2 | 103 | n/a |
| Harvard Medical School | 85 | 6/1 | 10/15 | 6642 | 88 | 77 | 147 | 165 | n/a |
| Tufts University School of Medicine | 105 | 6/1 | 1/15 | 9103 | 97 | 81 | 126 | 178 | 100 |

n/a    data not available

| Mean GPA | Admission Statistics | | | | Academic Statistics | Expenses | | | | |
| | Class Profile | | | | | | Tuition | | | |
| | Interviewed | % Residents | % Minorities | Mean MCAT | | Deposit | Resident | Nonresident | Other | Financial Aid |
|---|---|---|---|---|---|---|---|---|---|---|
| n/a | 13 | 81 | 6 | n/a | | $100 | 26,600 | 49,670 | n/a | n/a |
| 3.6 | 16 | 77 | 9 | P-9.4 B-10 V-9.5 | | $100 | 24,498 | 42,820 | 19,018 | 92 |
| 3.8 | 23 | 98 | 6 | P-9 B-10 V-9 | | n/a | 10,458 | 24,606 | n/a | 87 |
| 3.5 | 17 | 38 | 3 | P-10 B-11 V-10 | | n/a | 45,080 | 45,080 | n/a | 84 |
| 3.7 | 29 | 96 | 6 | P-9 B-9 V-10 | | n/a | 12,866 | 27,014 | n/a | 89 |
| 3.9 | 13 | 12 | 11 | P-10 B-11 V-10 | | n/a | 37,579 | 37,579 | n/a | 88 |
| 3.5 | 29 | 4 | 6 | P-10 B-10 V-10 | | 0 | n/a | n/a | n/a | n/a |
| 3.7 | 11 | 82 | 12 | P-11 B-11 V-10 | | n/a | 21,998 | 40,233 | n/a | 84 |
| 3.6 | 95 | 12 | 19 | P-11 B-11 V-10 | | $500 | 44,786 | 44,786 | 22,446 | 82 |
| 3.7 | 6 | 98 | 10 | P-11 B-11 V-11 | | n/a | 13,424 | n/a | n/a | 96 |
| 3.8 | 16 | 11 | 11 | P-11 B-11 V-10 | | n/a | 40,499 | 40,499 | n/a | 81 |
| 3.6 | 9 | 29 | 11 | P-10.9 B-11.1 V-10.3 | | $100 | 47,116 | 47,116 | n/a | 80 |

**Table 8.1. BASIC DATA ON THE MEDICAL SCHOOLS (2008–2009)**

| School | Application Data | | | Admission Statistics | | | | | |
|---|---|---|---|---|---|---|---|---|---|
| | | Filing Dates | | | Applicants Enrolled | | | Class Profile | |
| | Fee | Earliest | Latest | Number of Applicants | Men | Women | Out of State | Class Size | % with 4 Years College |
| **Michigan** | | | | | | | | | |
| Michigan State University College of Human Medicine | 60 | 6/1 | 11/15 | 5001 | 73 | 83 | 23 | 158 | n/a |
| University of Michigan Medical School | 85 | 6/1 | 11/15 | 5669 | 77 | 93 | 86 | 170 | n/a |
| Wayne State University School of Medicine | 50 | 6/1 | 12/15 | 3968 | 181 | 121 | 25 | 302 | n/a |
| **Minnesota** | | | | | | | | | |
| Mayo Medical School | 85 | 6/1 | 11/1 | 3429 | 23 | 19 | 32 | 42 | n/a |
| University of Minnesota— Duluth School of Medicine | 75 | 6/1 | 11/15 | 1413 | 26 | 33 | 8 | 59 | 93 |
| University of Minnesota Medical School— Minneapolis | 75 | 6/1 | 11/15 | 3212 | 92 | 78 | 30 | 170 | 100 |
| **Mississippi** | | | | | | | | | |
| University of Mississippi School of Medicine | 50 | 6/1 | 10/15 | 272 | 55 | 50 | 0 | 110 | 100 |
| **Missouri** | | | | | | | | | |
| St. Louis University, School of Medicine | 100 | 4/1 | 12/15 | 5176 | 98 | 78 | 135 | 176 | 100 |
| University of Missouri— Columbia School of Medicine | 75 | 6/1 | 11/1 | 1264 | 52 | 44 | 10 | 96 | n/a |
| University of Missouri— Kansas City School of Medicine | no | 8/1 | 11/15 | 940 | 38 | 56 | 39 | 94 | n/a |
| Washington University School of Medicine | 50 | 6/15 | 11/30 | 4058 | 63 | 59 | 113 | 122 | 100 |
| **Nebraska** | | | | | | | | | |
| University of Nebraska Medical Center | 45 | 6/1 | 11/1 | 1415 | 51 | 73 | 15 | 124 | 100 |
| Creighton University Medical School | 95 | 7/1 | 11/1 | 5718 | 63 | 63 | 110 | 126 | 100 |

n/a    data not available

| | Admission Statistics | | | Academic Statistics | | Expenses | | | | |
|---|---|---|---|---|---|---|---|---|---|---|
| | Class Profile | | | | | | Tuition | | | |
| Mean GPA | Interviewed | % Residents | % Minorities | Mean MCAT | Deposit | Resident | Nonresident | Other | Financial Aid |
| 3.6 | 9 | 85 | 5 | P-10 B-10 V-10 | n/a | 28,010 | 60,850 | n/a | 95 |
| 3.8 | 14 | 49 | 7 | P-11 B-11 V-10 | n/a | 24,755 | 39,119 | n/a | 94 |
| 3.7 | 24 | 92 | 8 | P-10 B-11 V-10 | n/a | 28,668 | 56,656 | n/a | 90 |
| 3.9 | 9 | 24 | 10 | P-11 B-11 V-10 | n/a | 29,700 | 29,700 | n/a | 100 |
| 3.7 | 10 | 87 | 12 | P-9.4 B-9.7 V-9.3 | $100 | 29,073 | 36,606 | 19,528 | 98 |
| 3.7 | 14 | 82 | 24 | P-11 B-11.25 V-10.55 | $100 | 29,975 | 37,508 | 20,994 | 95 |
| 3.7 | 71 | 100 | 17 | P-8.5 B-9.3 V-10.5 | $100 | 11,649 | 27,142 | 12,616 | 86 |
| 3.7 | 18 | 76 | 6 | P-10.5 B-11 V-10.5 | $100 | 43,830 | 43,830 | 22,423 | 84 |
| 3.8 | 22 | 90 | 0 | P-10 B-11 V-10 | n/a | 23,846 | 46,432 | n/a | 96 |
| n/a | 26 | 67 | 0 | n/a | n/a | 28,228 | 55,161 | n/a | 83 |
| 3.9 | 29 | 7.4 | 11.5 | P-12.8 B-12.8 V-11.7 | n/a | 45,500 | 45,500 | 9,572 | 84 |
| n/a | 27 | 88 | 6 | P-9.5 B-10.2 V-9.5 | $100 | 21,988 | 51,560 | 17,990 | 100 |
| 3.7 | 10 | 12.7 | 7.9 | P-10 B-10 V-10 | $100 | 42,612 | 42,612 | 39,485 | 87 |

## Table 8.1. BASIC DATA ON THE MEDICAL SCHOOLS (2008–2009)

| School | Application Data | Filing Dates | | Admission Statistics | Applicants Enrolled | | | Class Profile | |
|---|---|---|---|---|---|---|---|---|---|
| | Fee | Earliest | Latest | Number of Applicants | Men | Women | Out of State | Class Size | % with 4 Years College |
| **Nevada** | | | | | | | | | |
| University of Nevada School of Medicine | 45 | 6/1 | 11/1 | 1221 | 29 | 33 | 5 | 62 | 100 |
| **New Hampshire** | | | | | | | | | |
| Dartmouth Medical School | 75 | 7/1 | 1/2 | 5586 | 44 | 34 | 70 | 78 | 100 |
| **New Jersey** | | | | | | | | | |
| New Jersey Medical School University of Medicine | 75 | 6/1 | 12/1 | 4695 | 95 | 83 | 23 | 178 | n/a |
| Robert Wood Johnson Medical School Univ. of Med. and Dent. | 75 | 6/1 | 12/1 | 3551 | 68 | 98 | 1 | 166 | n/a |
| **New Mexico** | | | | | | | | | |
| University of New Mexico School of Medicine | 50 | 6/1 | 11/15 | 589 | 33 | 42 | 2 | 75 | 100 |
| **New York** | | | | | | | | | |
| SUNY Health Science Ctr. at Syracuse College of Medicine | 100 | 6/1 | 10/15 | 5321 | 83 | 77 | 30 | 160 | 100 |
| University of Rochester School of Medicine | 75 | 6/1 | 11/15 | 4222 | 50 | 54 | 58 | 104 | 100 |
| SUNY at Stoney Brook School of Medicine | 75 | 6/1 | 12/15 | 3699 | 67 | 59 | 17 | 126 | 100 |
| SUNY of Buffalo School of Medicine and Biomed. Science | 65 | 6/1 | 11/15 | 3839 | 60 | 75 | 32 | 135 | 100 |
| SUNY Downstate Medical Center College of Medicine | 80 | 6/1 | 12/15 | 4565 | 85 | 85 | 24 | 170 | n/a |
| New York University School of Medicine | 100 | 6/1 | 10/15 | 7573 | 80 | 80 | 94 | 160 | n/a |
| Mount Sinai School of Medicine of New York University | 105 | 6/1 | 11/1 | 6745 | 72 | 68 | 85 | 140 | 100 |
| Weill Medical College of Cornell University | 75 | 6/1 | 10/15 | 5853 | 48 | 53 | 67 | 101 | n/a |
| Columbia University College of Physicians and Surgeons | 85 | 6/1 | 10/15 | 7014 | 78 | 76 | 111 | 153 | 100 |

n/a     data not available

| | Admission Statistics | | | Academic Statistics | | Expenses | | | | |
| Mean GPA | Class Profile | | | | | | Tuition | | | |
| | Interviewed | % Residents | % Minorities | Mean MCAT | Deposit | Resident | Nonresident | Other | Financial Aid |
|---|---|---|---|---|---|---|---|---|---|
| 3.6 | 22 | 88 | 24 | P-9.9 B-10.5 V-9.4 | 0 | 13,520 | 33,885 | 2,961 | 77 |
| 3.7 | 12 | 10 | 22 | P-11 B-11 V-11 | 0 | 40,120 | 40,120 | 12,860 | 90 |
| 3.7 | 18 | 87 | 9 | P-11 B-11 V-10 | n/a | 24,121 | 37,188 | n/a | 84 |
| 3.7 | 15 | 99 | 8 | P-11 B-11 V-10 | n/a | 24,296 | 37,363 | n/a | 86 |
| 3.6 | 38 | 98 | 40 | P-9 B-10 V-9.5 | $100 | 14,671 | 42,043 | 5,514 | 95 |
| 3.5 | 17 | 81 | 27 | P-10.8 B-10.5 V-9.5 | $100 | 18,800 | 33,500 | 19,711 | 84 |
| 3.7 | | 44 | 19 | P-10.8 B-11.3 V-10.3 | $100 | 38,700 | 38,700 | 19,639 | 85 |
| 3.76 | 17 | 86 | 17 | P-11 B-11 V-10 | $100 | 18,800 | 33,500 | 24,683 | 83 |
| 3.7 | 20 | 76 | 5 | P-10.1 B-10.5 V-10.0 | $100 | 18,800 | 36,000 | 1,500 | 90 |
| 3.7 | 22 | 86 | 10 | P-11 B-11 V-10 | n/a | 19,370 | 34,070 | n/a | 89 |
| 3.7 | 13 | 41 | 5 | P-12 B-12 V-11 | n/a | 40,729 | 40,729 | n/a | 75 |
| 3.7 | 13 | 39 | 10 | P-11.9 B-11.9 V-11.0 | 0 | 35,250 | 35,250 | 15,345 | 90 |
| 3.8 | 13 | 34 | 18 | P-12 B-12 V-11 | n/a | 40,890 | 40,890 | n/a | 84 |
| 3.8 | 15.7 | 27 | 21 | P-12.2 B-12.4 V-11.9 | 0 | 43,140 | 43,140 | 18,548 | 85 |

## Table 8.1. BASIC DATA ON THE MEDICAL SCHOOLS (2008–2009)

| School | Application Data | | | Admission Statistics | | | | | |
| | Fee | Filing Dates | | Number of Applicants | Applicants Enrolled | | | Class Profile | |
| | | Earliest | Latest | | Men | Women | Out of State | Class Size | % with 4 Years College |
|---|---|---|---|---|---|---|---|---|---|
| Albany Medical College | 105 | 6/1 | 11/15 | 6834 | 71 | 73 | 76 | 144 | n/a |
| Albert Einstein College of Med. of Yesh. Univ. | 115 | 6/1 | 3/15 | 7383 | 96 | 88 | 111 | 180 | 100 |
| New York Medical College | 100 | 6/1 | 12/15 | 11250 | 94 | 94 | 140 | 188 | 100 |
| **North Carolina** | | | | | | | | | |
| Duke University School of Medicine | 80 | 6/1 | 11/15 | 5309 | 51 | 49 | 79 | 100 | n/a |
| East Carolina University School of Medicine | 60 | 6/1 | 11/15 | 878 | 37 | 39 | 0 | 76 | 95 |
| University of North Carolina School of Medicine | 65 | 6/1 | 11/15 | 3965 | 79 | 82 | 24 | 161 | n/a |
| Wake Forest School of Medicine | 55 | 6/1 | 11/1 | 7502 | 75 | 47 | 75 | 122 | 100 |
| **North Dakota** | | | | | | | | | |
| University of North Dakota School of Medicine | 50 | 7/1 | 11/1 | 303 | 26 | 36 | 17 | 62 | 100 |
| **Ohio** | | | | | | | | | |
| Wright State University School of Medicine | 45 | 6/1 | 11/15 | 3097 | 52 | 48 | 8 | 100 | 100 |
| University of Cincinnati College of Medicine | 25 | 6/1 | 11/15 | 3349 | 107 | 52 | 61 | 159 | 100 |
| Ohio State University College of Medicine | | 6/1 | 11/1 | 4446 | 120 | 92 | 106 | 212 | 100 |
| Northeastern Ohio Univ. | 50 | 6/1 | 11/1 | 2040 | 51 | 58 | 4 | 115 | 100 |
| Case Western Reserve University School of Medicine | 85 | 6/1 | 11/1 | 6028 | 101 | 84 | 123 | 185 | n/a |
| University of Toledo | 80 | 6/15 | 11/1 | 3431 | 98 | 78 | 58 | 176 | 100 |
| **Oklahoma** | | | | | | | | | |
| University of Oklahoma College of Medicine | 65 | 6/1 | 10/15 | 1487 | 102 | 64 | 17 | 166 | 99 |

n/a    data not available

| | Admission Statistics | | | Academic Statistics | | Expenses | | | | |
|---|---|---|---|---|---|---|---|---|---|---|
| | | Class Profile | | | | | | Tuition | | |
| Mean GPA | Interviewed | % Residents | % Minorities | Mean MCAT | Deposit | Resident | Nonresident | Other | Financial Aid |
| 3.6 | 10 | 47 | 3 | P-10 B-11 V-10 | n/a | 43,008 | 43,008 | n/a | 88 |
| 3.7 | 16 | 43 | 13 | P-10.8 B-11.3 V-10 | $100 | 42,364 | 42,364 | 17,116 | 73 |
| 3.6 | 12 | 26 | 37 | P-10.2 B-10.5 V-9.3 | $100 | 41,500 | 41,500 | 14,270 | 86 |
| 3.8 | 15 | 21 | 22 | P-11 B-11 V-11 | n/a | 41,839 | 41,839 | n/a | 75 |
| 3.6 | 51 | 100 | 32 | P-9.1 B-9.7 V-9.4 | $100 | 7,144 | 0 | 22,909 | 84 |
| 3.8 | 15 | 85 | 12 | P-11 B-11 V-11 | n/a | 11,964 | 35,630 | n/a | 84 |
| 3.7 | 8 | 38 | 12 | P-10.4 B-10.4 V-10.4 | $100 | 38,248 | 38,248 | 17,500 | 73 |
| 3.7 | 52 | 73 | 21 | P-8.7 B-9.5 V-8.9 | $100 | 22,515 | 41,675 | 20,340 | 95 |
| 3.6 | 7 | 92 | 10 | P-9.4 B-9.8 V-9.4 | 0 | 29,781 | 40,251 | 15,943 | 95 |
| 3.6 | 19 | 62 | 9 | P-10.8 B-11.3 V-10.2 | n/a | 27,987 | 42,457 | 18,405 | 85 |
| 3.7 | 15 | 50 | 10 | P-11.4 B-11.5 V-10.4 | $10 | 28,809 | 44,091 | 21,356 | 93 |
| 3.7 | 74 | 96.5 | 6 | P-9.0 B-9.6 V-9.4 | $100 | 27,861 | 55,722 | 4,925 | 77 |
| 3.7 | 22 | 34 | 10 | P-12 B-12 V-11 | n/a | 41,966 | 41,966 | n/a | 80 |
| 3.6 | 15 | 12 | 9 | P-10 B-10 V-10 | 0 | 24,072 | 51,508 | 30,000 | 95 |
| 3.8 | 21 | 90 | 18 | P-9.8 B-10 V-10 | $100 | 17,945 | 42,063 | 25,750 | 90 |

## Table 8.1. BASIC DATA ON THE MEDICAL SCHOOLS (2008–2009)

| School | Fee | Earliest | Latest | Number of Applicants | Men | Women | Out of State | Class Size | % with 4 Years College |
|---|---|---|---|---|---|---|---|---|---|
| **Oregon** | | | | | | | | | |
| Oregon Health and Science University School of Medicine | 100 | 6/1 | 10/15 | 4371 | 56 | 62 | 44 | 118 | n/a |
| **Pennsylvania** | | | | | | | | | |
| Temple University School of Medicine | 70 | 6/1 | 12/15 | 9715 | 95 | 83 | 83 | 178 | n/a |
| University of Pittsburgh School of Medicine | 75 | 6/1 | 11/1 | 5413 | 88 | 59 | 101 | 147 | 100 |
| University of Pennsylvania School of Medicine | 80 | 6/1 | 10/15 | 6344 | 74 | 79 | 115 | 153 | n/a |
| Drexel University College of Medicine | 75 | 6/1 | 12/1 | 12006 | 127 | 128 | 177 | 255 | 88 |
| Jefferson Medical College Thomas Jefferson University | 80 | 6/1 | 11/15 | 9323 | 132 | 123 | 156 | 255 | 88 |
| Pennsylvania State University College of Medicine | 70 | 6/1 | 11/15 | 6691 | 77 | 77 | 74 | 154 | n/a |
| **Puerto Rico** | | | | | | | | | |
| Universidad Central del Caribe | 100 | 6/1 | 12/15 | 1021 | 36 | 29 | 16 | 65 | n/a |
| Ponce School of Med. | 100 | 6/15 | 12/15 | 1306 | 34 | 34 | 15 | 68 | 98 |
| San Juan Bautista Medical School | 75 | 6/1 | 12/15 | 204 | 22 | 38 | 21 | 60 | n/a |
| **Rhode Island** | | | | | | | | | |
| Brown University, School of Medicine | 95 | 6/1 | 11/1 | 6016 | 42 | 53 | 62 | 95 | n/a |
| **South Carolina** | | | | | | | | | |
| Medical University of South Carolina College of Medicine | 75 | 6/1 | 12/1 | 2043 | 97 | 61 | n/a | 158 | n/a |

n/a    data not available

| | Admission Statistics | | | Academic Statistics | Expenses | | | | |
| | | Class Profile | | | | | Tuition | | | |
| Mean GPA | Interviewed | % Residents | % Minorities | Mean MCAT | Deposit | Resident | Nonresident | Other | Financial Aid |
|---|---|---|---|---|---|---|---|---|---|
| 3.8 | 12 | 63 | 3 | P-10 B-11 V-11 | n/a | 29,665 | 40,480 | n/a | 91 |
| 3.7 | 8 | 53 | 7 | P-10 B-11 V-10 | n/a | 38,502 | 47,004 | n/a | 88 |
| 3.6 | 19 | 31 | 16 | P-11.8 B-11.9 V-10.9 | $100 | 36,752 | 40,772 | 14,650 | 90 |
| 3.8 | 15 | 25 | 10 | P-12 B-12 V-11 | n/a | 42,873 | 42,873 | n/a | 83 |
| 3.5 | 11 | 318 | 9 | P-10.2 B-10.6 V-9.6 | $100 | 42,430 | 42,430 | 11,505 | 87 |
| 3.6 | 9 | 39 | 11 | P-10.4 B-10.8 V-10.2 | $100 | 43,033 | 43,033 | 20,700 | 84 |
| 3.7 | 14 | 52 | 6 | P-10 B-11 V-10 | n/a | 33,058 | 44,920 | n/a | 93 |
| 3.5 | 18 | 55 | 15 | P-11 B-11 V-10 | $100 | 24,890 | 31,890 | 16,675 | 87 |
| 3.5 | 14 | 78 | 99 | P-11 B-11 V-10 | $1,000 | 19,352 | 28,850 | 20,524 | 86 |
| 3.3. | 6 | n/a | 0 | P-11 B-11 V-10 | $300 | 18,770 | 34,801 | 25 | 92 |
| 3.8 | 5 | 35 | 7 | P-12 B-12 V-11 | n/a | 38,672 | 38,672 | n/a | 73 |
| 3.7 | 19 | n/a | 20 | P-10 B-10 V-10 | n/a | 24,367 | 67,166 | n/a | 88 |

## Table 8.1. BASIC DATA ON THE MEDICAL SCHOOLS (2008–2009)

| School | Fee | Earliest | Latest | Number of Applicants | Men | Women | Out of State | Class Size | % with 4 Years College |
|---|---|---|---|---|---|---|---|---|---|
| | | Application Data | | | Admission Statistics | | | | |
| | | Filing Dates | | | | Applicants Enrolled | | Class Profile | |
| University of South Carolina School of Medicine | 75 | 6/1 | 1/15 | 1960 | 43 | 43 | 14 | 86 | 100 |
| **South Dakota** | | | | | | | | | |
| University of South Dakota School of Medicine | 35 | 6/1 | 11/15 | 650 | 29 | 25 | 37 | 54 | 100 |
| **Tennessee** | | | | | | | | | |
| East Tennessee State University James H. Quillen | 50 | 6/1 | 11/15 | 1449 | 27 | 33 | 6 | 60 | n/a |
| Meharry Medical College School of Medicine | 65 | 6/1 | 12/15 | 4529 | 48 | 52 | 90 | 100 | 100 |
| University of Tennessee— Memphis College of Medicine | 50 | 6/1 | 11/15 | 1424 | 88 | 62 | 9 | 150 | n/a |
| Vanderbilt University School of Medicine | 50 | 6/1 | 11/15 | 5032 | 54 | 51 | 91 | 105 | 100 |
| **Texas** | | | | | | | | | |
| Texas Tech University School of Medicine | 50 | 5/1 | 10/1 | 2954 | 84 | 56 | 6 | 219 | 100 |
| Paul Foster School of Medicine at Texas Tech | | 5/1 | 10/1 | | | | | | |
| University of Texas Southwestern Medical School | | 5/1 | 10/1 | 3299 | 109 | 111 | 20 | 219 | 100 |
| University of Texas Medical School at San Antonio | 55 | 5/1 | 10/1 | 3529 | 111 | 110 | 20 | 221 | n/a |
| University of Texas Med. Branch at Galveston | no | 5/1 | 10/1 | 3642 | 122 | 105 | 12 | 227 | n/a |
| Texas A&M University College of Medicine | 45 | 5/1 | 10/15 | 3133 | 45 | 60 | 1 | 105 | n/a |
| Baylor College of Medicine | 80 | 6/1 | 11/1 | 4879 | 90 | 86 | 38 | 176 | 100 |
| University of Texas—Houston Medical School | 55 | 5/1 | 10/1 | 3598 | 137 | 93 | 18 | 230 | 100 |

n/a     data not available

| Mean GPA | Admission Statistics | | | Academic Statistics | Expenses | | | | | |
| | Class Profile | | | | | Tuition | | | |
| | Interviewed | % Residents | % Minorities | Mean MCAT | Deposit | Resident | Nonresident | Other | Financial Aid |
|---|---|---|---|---|---|---|---|---|---|
| 3.5 | 17 | 95 | 23 | P-8.7 B-9.7 V-9.8 | $100 | 24,776 | 60,458 | 8,096 | 90 |
| 3.8 | 25 | 80 | 4 | P-9.6 B-10.4 V-9.5 | $100 | 15,281 | 36,603 | 24,940 | 97 |
| 3.7 | 17 | 90 | 5 | P-10 B-10 V-10 | n/a | 21,043 | 41,993 | n/a | 93 |
| 3.5 | 10 | 10 | 83 | P-8 B-9 V-8 | $300 | 32,336 | 32,336 | 27,321 | 84 |
| 3.6 | 34 | 94 | 13 | P-10 B-10 V-10 | n/a | 19,385 | 37,297 | n/a | 90 |
| 3.8 | 18 | 13 | 19 | P-11.9 B-11.6 V-10.4 | n/a | 38,400 | 38,400 | 20,520 | 88 |
| 3.7 | 26 | 90 | 10 | P-9.5 B-10.11 V-9.5 | $100 | 11,350 | 26,000 | 2,864 | 100 |
| | | | | | | 11,700 | 18,500 | | |
| 3.8 | 27 | 91 | 49 | P-11.3 B-11.5 V-10.5 | n/a | 12,100 | 25,200 | 18,009 | 83 |
| | 30 | 80 | 23 | P-10 B-10 V-10 | 0 | 11,970 | 21,157 | 29,076 | 89 |
| 3.8 | 27 | 95 | 10 | P-11 B-11 V-11 | n/a | 6,550 | 19,650 | n/a | 83 |
| 3.8 | 23 | 96 | 4 | P-10 B-10 V-10 | n/a | 10,682 | 23,782 | n/a | 92 |
| 3.85 | 14 | 78 | 22 | P-12 B-12 V-11 | $300 | 6,550 | 25,882 | 32,893 | 87 |
| 3.7 | 12 | 92 | 21 | P-10.3 B-10.8 V-9.9 | 0 | 9,775 | 22,815 | 6,167 | 85 |

### Table 8.1. BASIC DATA ON THE MEDICAL SCHOOLS (2008–2009)

| School | Fee | Application Data — Filing Dates — Earliest | Latest | Admission Statistics — Number of Applicants | Applicants Enrolled — Men | Women | Out of State | Class Profile — Class Size | % with 4 Years College |
|---|---|---|---|---|---|---|---|---|---|
| **Utah** | | | | | | | | | |
| University of Utah Medical School | 100 | 6/1 | 11/1 | 1270 | 70 | 32 | 27 | 102 | n/a |
| **Vermont** | | | | | | | | | |
| University of Vermont College of Medicine | 85 | 6/1 | 11/1 | 5772 | 56 | 58 | 67 | 114 | 100 |
| **Virginia** | | | | | | | | | |
| Eastern Virginia Medical School | 95 | 6/1 | 11/15 | 4997 | 65 | 50 | 41 | 115 | n/a |
| Medical College of Virginia Commonwealth University | 80 | 6/1 | 10/15 | 6154 | 104 | 88 | 81 | 192 | 100 |
| University of Virginia School of Medicine | 80 | 10/15 | n/a | 4302 | | | | 145 | |
| **Washington** | | | | | | | | | |
| University of Washington School of Medicine | 35 | 6/1 | 11/3 | 4598 | 89 | 102 | 16 | 191 | n/a |
| **West Virginia** | | | | | | | | | |
| Marshall University School of Medicine | 50 | 6/1 | 10/15 | 1316 | 35 | 43 | 21 | 78 | 95 |
| West Virginia University School of Medicine | 100 | 6/1 | 11/1 | 2881 | 55 | 53 | 47 | 108 | n/a |
| **Wisconsin** | | | | | | | | | |
| University of Wisconsin Medical School | 56 | 6/1 | 11/1 | 3264 | 76 | 87 | 38 | 163 | 98 |
| Medical College of Wisconsin | 70 | 6/1 | 11/1 | 6429 | 116 | 96 | 138 | 212 | 100 |
| **Canada** | | | | | | | | | |
| Faculty of Medicine University of Alberta | 100 | 7/2 | 11/1 | 1150 | 85 | 70 | 70 | 155 | n/a |
| University of Calgary Faculty of Medicine | 120 | 7/1 | 10/15 | 1405 | 74 | 76 | n/a | 150 | 89 |

n/a    data not available

| | Admission Statistics | | | Academic Statistics | | Expenses | | | | |
| --- | --- | --- | --- | --- | --- | --- | --- | --- | --- | --- |
| | | Class Profile | | | | | Tuition | | | |
| Mean GPA | Interviewed | % Residents | % Minorities | Mean MCAT | Deposit | Resident | Nonresident | Other | Financial Aid |
| 3.7 | 37 | 74 | 0 | P-9 B-10 V-10 | n/a | 20,692 | 38,528 | n/a | 96 |
| 3.7 | 17 | 0 | 24 | P-10 B-10 V-10 | $100 | 26,280 | 46,700 | 13,149 | 87 |
| 3.5 | 136 | 64 | 8.7 | P-10 B-10 V-10 | $100 | 23,980 | 44,328 | n/a | 95 |
| 3.6 | 14 | 58 | 6.25 | P-10 B-10 V-9.7 | $100 | 25,644 | 39,281 | 24,678 | 89 |
| 3.7 | 24 | | 54 | P-11.2 B-11.55 V-10.6 | | 32,650 | 2,650 | n/a | |
| 3.7 | 18 | 92 | 1 | P-11 B-11 V-10 | n/a | 17,425 | 41,429 | n/a | 90 |
| 3.5 | 19 | 73 | 22 | P-8.5 B-9.4 V-9 | 0 | 16,738 | 42,328 | n/a | 91 |
| 3.8 | 12 | 66 | 3 | P-10 B-10 V-10 | n/a | 19,204 | 41,866 | n/a | 93 |
| 3.7 | 14 | 77 | 11 | P-10.3 B-11.4 V-10.0 | n/a | 23,060 | 34,190 | 16,477 | 96 |
| 3.7 | 10 | 35 | 11 | P-10 B-10 V-10 | $100 | 38,940 | 38,940 | 12,095 | 84 |
| 3.9 | 377 | 85 | 3 | P-11.9 B-12.0 V-10.43 | $1,000 | 11,086 | 11,086 | 2,857 | n/a |
| 3.7 | 31 | 85 | n/a | P-11 B-11.4 V-10.3 | $500 | 13,818 | 13,818 | 5,020 | n/a |

**Table 8.1. BASIC DATA ON THE MEDICAL SCHOOLS (2008–2009)**

| School | Application Data | | | Admission Statistics | | | | | |
|---|---|---|---|---|---|---|---|---|---|
| | | Filing Dates | | | Applicants Enrolled | | | Class Profile | |
| | Fee | Earliest | Latest | Number of Applicants | Men | Women | Out of State | Class Size | % with 4 Years College |
| University of Saskatchewan Faculty of Medicine | 50 | 7/1 | 11/1 | 591 | 33 | 51 | 6 | 84 | 65 |
| University of British Columbia | 105 | 8/1 | 10/2 | 1006 | 108 | 148 | 12 | 256 | n/a |
| University of Laval Faculty of Medicine | n/a | 11/15 | 3/1 | 1713 | 59 | 149 | n/a | 208 | n/a |
| Memorial University of New Foundland | 75 | 7/2 | 10/15 | 700 | 24 | 40 | 17 | 64 | 100 |
| Queens University Faculty of Medicine | n/a | 7/1 | 9/15 | 1614 | 54 | 46 | n/a | 100 | n/a |
| McMaster University Faculty of Medicine | 175 | 7/1 | 9/15 | 4848 | 68 | 96 | n/a | 164 | n/a |
| University of Western Ontario | no | 7/1 | 9/1 | 2300 | 75 | 72 | n/a | 147 | n/a |
| University of Toronto | 75 | 7/1 | 12/1 | 3165 | 97 | 127 | n/a | 224 | n/a |
| Universite of Montreal | no | 12/1 | 1/15 | 2116 | 88 | 182 | 1 | 270 | n/a |
| University of Ottawa Faculty of Medicine | n/a | 7/6 | 9/15 | 3356 | 53 | 86 | 12 | 139 | n/a |
| Dalhousie University Faculty of Medicine | n/a | 9/1 | 10/31 | 295 | 32 | 58 | 0 | 90 | n/a |
| McGill University | 85 | 9/1 | 11/15 | 1400 | 78 | 98 | 16 | 176 | 56 |
| Universite de Sherbrooke | 70 | 11/1 | 3/1 | 1849 | 80 | 121 | 34 | 201 | n/a |
| University of Manitoba | 90 | 8/15 | 10/10 | 957 | 50 | 50 | 9 | 100 | n/a |

n/a     data not available

| Mean GPA | Admission Statistics | | | Academic Statistics | Expenses | | | | | |
| --- | --- | --- | --- | --- | --- | --- | --- | --- | --- | --- |
| | Class Profile | | | | | Tuition | | | | |
| | Interviewed | % Residents | % Minorities | Mean MCAT | Deposit | Resident | Nonresident | Other | Financial Aid |
| 87.5 | 12 | 93 | 7 | P-9.1 B-9.6 V-9.3 | $500 | 11,470 | n/a | n/a | n/a |
| 83 | 36 | 95 | n/a | P-10.3 B-11.0 V-9.3 | $300 | 14,800 | n/a | 700 | n/a |
| n/a | n/a | n/a | n/a | n/a | n/a | 2,000 | 13,750 | n/a | n/a |
| 100 | 71 | 72 | n/a | P-10 B-10 V-10 | $200 | 6,250 | 30,000 | 9,630 | 80 |
| 3.6 | 29 | n/a | n/a | P-10 B-10 V-10 | n/a | 14,175 | n/a | n/a | 69 |
| 3.7 | 11 | n/a | n/a | n/a | n/a | 17,396 | 91,137 | n/a | 90 |
| 3.7 | 19 | n/a | n/a | P-10 B-10 V-10 | n/a | 16,527 | n/a | n/a | 50 |
| 3.9 | 15 | n/a | n/a | P-11 B-12 V-10 | n/a | 18,145 | 45,383 | n/a | 81 |
| 3.7 | 38 | 96 | n/a | n/a | n/a | 4,000 | 23,000 | n/a | n/a |
| n/a | 15 | n/a | n/a | n/a | n/a | 15,286 | n/a | n/a | |
| 3.7 | 8 | 0 | 2 | P-10 B-9 V-9 | n/a | 12,270 | 17,100 | n/a | n/a |
| 3.7 | 32 | 91 | n/a | P-11 B-12 V-10 | $500 | 4,893 | 24,825 | n/a | n/a |
| n/a | 42 | 83 | n/a | n/a | $200 | 2,829 | 8,225 | n/a | n/a |
| 4.0 | 32 | 91 | n/a | P-11 B-12 V-10 | n/a | 7,595 | 7,595 | n/a | n/a |

# 9 Medical School Profiles

**In-depth medical school profiles**

This chapter consists of in-depth medical school profiles that provide detailed information on various elements distinguishing individual schools.

## IN-DEPTH MEDICAL SCHOOL PROFILES

The following profiles consist of in-depth descriptions of all fully accredited U.S. medical schools and the 16 Canadian medical schools. Each school profile consists of three distinct components: (1) a box containing the school name, address, phone, fax, e-mail and World Wide Web numbers, (2) a data capsule containing a summary of vital statistics for the first year class (for more details, see Chapter 8), and (3) the school's specific descriptive characteristics, which are identified in the next paragraph and are defined below.

### How to Use These Profiles

No two medical schools are the same. They differ in many ways, including their origins, admissions procedures and requirements, curriculum, grading policies, facilities, and special programs; each school is unique in what it has to offer.

After making a tentative list of schools to which you would consider applying (using the data in Table 8.1 in the preceding chapter), you should review each school's qualities in the profiles presented here to see if you qualify for admission and if the school will meet your personal needs.

The admissions requirements will let you know if you can meet the school's specific requirements beyond those mandated for all medical school applicants. If you cannot meet these requirements, applying is an exercise in futility. For instance, if a school limits its students exclusively to state residents, it is pointless to apply unless you meet this criterion. This section also suggests elective courses that may be advisable for you to take in your junior or senior years to make you more eligible for admission to specific schools.

Students should become familiar with the curriculum of the schools to which they are interested in applying. It is also recommended that, when visiting school campuses for an interview, you inquire from current students what their reaction is to the existing curriculum. Specific information on the performance under this curriculum on both parts of the USMLE can be of special value in assessing its impact. Also, the faculty's attitude toward the curriculum and any prospective modifications that will be introduced may be solicited from your interviewer (near the end of the session). You may wish to evaluate your findings with fellow premeds who have visited the same school, to determine how factual your data is. It may even prove worthwhile to secure information in advance of your visit about the curriculum from previous interviewees, so that you can then obtain specific information that you feel needs elaboration.

Familiarity with information regarding grading and promotion policies, facilities, and special programs will provide you with source material for making further inquires at the time of your interview and help make your visits more meaningful.

# Definitions

Following are definitions of terms pertaining to the various features used in outlining each school's characteristics:

## *Introduction*

A brief historical overview for the school is provided. It will usually also indicate other schools for the health professions that are affiliated with the university, as well as some geographical features that are of special importance.

## *Admissions*

Though the minimum requirement for most schools is at least three years (90 credit hours) of undergraduate study at an accredited college, the percentage of those accepted with only this background is small. *The MCAT is required by almost all schools*, although in exceptional circumstances admission can be secured without having taken this exam, or it may be made contingent on securing satisfactory scores when taken at a later date. *Basic or minimum premedical science courses* means one year of biology, inorganic chemistry, organic chemistry, and physics plus appropriate laboratory work. Some schools have additional requirements such as English, mathematics, or certain advanced science courses especially biochemistry. These are indicated along with any recommended courses. Since an interview is almost always by invitation, it is not indicated in each entry as a prerequisite for admission. *Transfer and advanced standing:* Transferring from one American medical school to another may present problems because of variations in curricula and length of programs. When these issues present no problem and space is available, transfer can be made at the end of the academic year. American citizens studying at foreign medical schools may be considered for admission to advanced standing, usually into the third-year class, at some schools. Generally, they must have completed their basic science courses and have taken the Medical Sciences Knowledge Profile examination.

## *Curriculum*

Each curriculum is indicated as to length and type. The classifications used (except where a school preferred not to be identified in this manner) are: *traditional* (basic sciences are taught during first two years using a departmental or nonintegrated format. The last two years consist of clerkships in major and minor clinical specialties with little or no time allotted for electives); *semitraditional* (basic sciences are taught in traditional manner. The third year is devoted to clerkships in major specialties. The fourth year is mainly devoted to electives. Clinical correlation with basic sciences is usually provided); *semimodern* (one of the two years devoted to basic sciences is presented using a core or organ systems approach. The third year is devoted to clerkships in major specialties and the fourth year is mainly for electives. Clinical correlation with basic sciences is emphasized and the student is introduced to patients early in the preclinical program); *modern* (both basic science years are presented using core or organ systems approach. The third year is devoted to clerkships in major clinical specialties and the fourth year consists mainly of electives. Clinical correlation with basic sciences is strongly emphasized and the student is introduced to patients very early in the preclinical program). The following terms will be useful in understanding the various school curricula:

### Introductory basic medical science courses

generally means anatomy, physiology, and biochemistry.

### Advanced basic medical science courses

generally means microbiology, pharmacology, and pathology.

### Clerkships

service on a hospital ward where the medical student works under direct supervision of a physician and becomes directly involved in the care of patients.

### Major clinical specialties

usually medicine, surgery, pediatrics, obstetrics-gynecology, and psychiatry-neurology.

### Minor clinical specialties

generally anesthesiology, dermatology, otolaryngology, ophthalmology, radiology, and public health-preventive medicine.

### Subspecialty

specialized area of major specialty; for example, subspecialties of surgery are orthopedic surgery, neurosurgery, thoracic surgery, cardiac surgery, pediatric surgery, etc.

### Preceptorship

service in a medical office or home situation where the student works under supervision of a family physician and becomes initiated into patient care in a nonhospital format.

### Electives

unassigned time is usually provided during the fourth year. This permits students to select from a variety of educational options that can enhance that student's career.

## Grading and Promotion Policies

The system used is not the same in all schools, so it is specifically identified for each school. Promotion usually is determined by a faculty committee and specific details concerning the policy of individual schools is outlined. Some schools require students to take only Steps 1 and 2 of the USMLE. Others may require a passing total score for promotion to the third year and graduation.

## Facilities

### Teaching

Facilities are of two kinds: those used for basic sciences and those used in clinical instruction. The former usually contain teaching and research laboratories, lecture rooms, and departmental and faculty offices. Clinical teaching occurs in hospitals with major facilities usually located on campus adjacent to the basic science building. Other hospitals in the city or area may be affiliated with the school (for example, have a contractual arrangement whereby the medical school faculty partly or completely staffs the hospital and uses its beds in teaching). Campus hospitals are frequently owned by the school and are then referred to as university hospitals. Major teaching and affiliated hospitals are noted in the description and the number of beds indicated. *Other:* Facilities concern the research and library facilities associated with the medical school. *Housing:* Facilities include information for single and married students. Off-campus accommodations are available near most schools and the Office of Student Affairs of the school may be able to assist students in securing such facilities. Details as to size, furnishings, and rental costs may be given in the school catalog.

## Special Features

This section deals with two topics, *minority admissions* and *other degree programs*. In the former, the extent of a school's recruiting efforts of underrepresented students is identified and special summer programs are noted. Under the latter heading, combined programs (especially MD-PhD programs) are identified, and any unique areas of graduate training that are not part of the traditional basic sciences are mentioned.

## Prospective New Medical Schools

Three schools currently are seeking approval from relevant medical and governmental agencies in order to establish and develop schools of medicine. This is expected to take place in the next few years. The schools are:

Touro University
School of Medicine
Hackensack, New Jersey
*http://touro.edu*

Hofstra University
School of Medicine
Hempstead, NY
*http://hofstra.edu/Home*

The Commonwealth Medical School
Scranton, PA 18503
*WWW:thecommonwealthmedical.com*

## ALABAMA

# University of Alabama School of Medicine

University Station
A-100, Volker Hall
Birmingham, Alabama    35294

*Phone:* 205-934-2433          *Fax:* 205-934-8740
*E-mail:* medschool@uab.edu
*WWW:* uab.edu/uasom

| Application Filing | | Accreditation | |
|---|---|---|---|
| Earliest: | June 1 | LCME | |
| Latest: | November 1 | | |
| Fee: | $75 | **Degrees Granted** | |
| AMCAS: | yes | MD, MD-PhD | |

### Enrollment: 2008–2009 First-Year Class

| Men: | 104 | 59% | Applied: | 1960 |
|---|---|---|---|---|
| Women: | 72 | 41% | Interviewed: | 373 |
| Minorities: | 11 | 6% | Enrolled: | 176 |
| Out of State: | 16 | 10% | | |

### 2008–2009 Class Profile

| *Mean MCAT Scores* | | *Mean GPA* |
|---|---|---|
| Physical Sciences: | 10.0 | 3.8 |
| Biological Sciences: | 10.4 | |
| Verbal Reasoning: | 10.0 | *Mean Science* |
| | | 3.7 |

**Tuition and Fees**

| | |
|---|---|
| **Resident** | 16,608 |
| Average (public) | 25,100 |
| Average (private) | 42,600 |
| **Nonresident** | 43,848 |
| Average (public) | 43,900 |
| Average (private) | 43,500 |

0    10    20    30    40    50
(in thousands of dollars)

Percentage receiving financial aid: 79%

Above data applies to 2007–2008 academic year.

## Introduction

The School of Medicine began in Mobile in 1859. After several relocations, its main Medical Center campus was established in Birmingham in 1945. Branch campuses are also present in Huntsville and Tuscaloosa. The first 2 years of the educational program take place at the main campus, while clinical teaching occurs on all 3 campuses. The School of Medicine is one of the 6 health schools making up the University of Alabama Medical Center. The others are schools of Dentistry, Optometry, Nursing, Health-Related Professions, and Public Health.

## Admissions (AMCAS)

Additional courses beyond the basic premedical science requirements are one year each of mathematics and English on all three campuses.

## Curriculum

4-year semitraditional. *First and second years:* Consist of education in the basic medical science as related to human biology and pathology. This is followed by an integrated study of organ system function and disorders. The humanities as related to medicine are also studied, and the skills necessary for physical diagnosis are developed. *Third and fourth years:* Consist of required rotations through clinical science disciplines, including participation in the cases of patients in both hospital and ambulatory settings (under faculty supervision). The clinical training curriculum requirements are similar.

## Grading and Promotion Policies

A quartile system is used that distributes student performance across an upper, lower, and middle two quartiles. Obtaining a total passing score on Steps 1 and 2 of the USMLE is required for promotion to the third year and graduation after the fourth, respectively.

## Facilities

*Teaching:* The school is part of the university's Medical Center. The Basic Science Building contains teaching facilities and administrative and faculty offices. The major clinical teaching facility is the University Hospital (817 beds) in Birmingham. Other facilities utilized are the VA Hospital (479 beds), the Children's Hospital, the Cooper Green Hospital, the Eye Foundation Hospital, and various community hospitals. *Other:* The Lyons-Harrison Research Building, Tinsley Harrison Tower, and basic science research and education buildings are the primary research facilities. Clinical facilities utilized in Tuscaloosa are the Druid City Hospital, the VA Medical Center, and the Capstone Medical Center. The Huntsville Hospital and the Ambulatory Care Center in Huntsville are also used. *Libraries:* The Lister Hill Library of the Health Sciences in Birmingham is a 4-story structure that contains more than 150,000 volumes. The Health Sciences Library at Tuscaloosa has about 10,000 volumes and subscribes to 475 journals. The library at Huntsville has about 9000 volumes. *Housing:* There are 178 modern apartment units in the Medical Center consisting of 28 efficiency, 84 one-bedroom, 62 two-bedroom, and 4 three-bedroom apartments. Preference is given to married students but consideration is given to single students for occupancy of the smaller units.

## Special Features

*Minority admissions:* Minority Student Program to discover and encourage study of medicine among minority group members. *Other degree programs:* Dual MD-PhD and MD-MPH programs.

# University of South Alabama College of Medicine

Mobile, Alabama   36688

*Phone:* 251-460-7176        *Fax:* 251-460-6278
*WWW:* southalabama.edu/com

| Application Filing | | Accreditation |
|---|---|---|
| Earliest: | June 1 | LCME |
| Latest: | November 15 | |
| Fee: | $75 | **Degrees Granted** |
| AMCAS: | yes | MD, MD-PhD |

### Enrollment: 2008–2009 First-Year Class

| | | | | |
|---|---|---|---|---|
| Men: | 42 | 57% | Applied: | 997 |
| Women: | 32 | 43% | Interviewed: | 210 |
| Minorities: | 5 | 7% | Enrolled: | 74 |
| Out of State: | 8 | 5% | | |

### 2008–2009 Class Profile

| *Mean MCAT Scores* | | *Mean GPA* |
|---|---|---|
| Physical Sciences: | 10.0 | 3.7 |
| Biological Sciences: | 11.0 | |
| Verbal Reasoning: | 10.1 | *Mean Science* |
| | | 3.7 |

### Tuition and Fees

| | (in thousands of dollars) |
|---|---|
| **Resident** | 16,082 |
| Average (public) | 25,100 |
| Average (private) | 42,600 |
| **Nonresident** | 29,562 |
| Average (public) | 43,900 |
| Average (private) | 43,500 |

Percentage receiving financial aid: 90%

Above data applies to 2007–2008 academic year.

## Introduction

This public, state-sponsored medical school is located on the university's 1200 acre campus in the Springhill section of Mobile. It occupies 13 buildings, including a 400-bed Medical Center, which contains a Level I trauma center. The first class was admitted in 1973 and 64 applicants are enrolled annually. A 150-acre park containing recreational facilities lies adjacent to the campus. The first 2 years are taught in the main campus in the Medical Sciences Building; the last 2 clinical years are spent the University of South Alabama hospitals and clinics.

## Admissions (AMCAS)

Required courses include the basic premedical sciences, English, 1 year of college mathematics, and 1 year of humanities. Highly recommended is a course in calcu-

lus. Three years of college is required, but a bachelor's is preferred. Nonresidents should have competitive MCAT and grade point averages to be considered for an interview. Applicants are urged to take the MCAT in the spring of the year of the application and to have a basic science requirement completed when applying. This will facilitate prompt processing of the application. *Transfer and advanced standing:* None.

## Curriculum

4-year semimodern. *First and second years:* The student is primarily concerned with the basic biomedical sciences. To give these studies more meaning, provision is made for student contact with patients during these preclinical years. *Third year:* Clerkships provide training in most of the basic problems with which patients present themselves. Students learn to apply scientific principles to the examination, diagnosis, and treatment of human disease. Seminars, conferences, and clinical rounds with members of the teaching staff are important in giving the student a rounded perspective of human illness. *Fourth year:* Mostly elective in order to provide each student the opportunity to choose a program best suited to his or her individual needs. Each department makes available to the student a spectrum of general and special courses from which the student selects a minimum of 36 weeks of study, with the advice and approval of a faculty advisor. Research may be carried as an elective. Off-campus studies (local, elsewhere in the United States, and in other countries) may be elected with the prior approval of the Associate Dean for Student Affairs, a departmental chair, and faculty advisor. Elective work need not be confined to the senior year, but may be carried out for no credit whenever possible during prior academic years.

## Facilities

*Teaching:* The basic sciences are housed in the Medical Sciences Building on the 1200-acre university campus in the western section of Mobile. Clinical teaching is conducted at the University of South Alabama Medical Center, USA Knollwood, and USA Doctors Children's and Women's Hospital. *Other:* Other facilities include the Moorer Clinical Sciences Building, University of South Alabama Cancer Center, Primate Research Laboratory, Laboratory of Molecular Biology, Family Practice Center, Mastin Building, Pediatric Outpatient Clinic, and Psychiatric Building. *Library:* The Biomedical Library contains more than 65,000 volumes and receives about 2500 periodicals. *Housing:* Furnished residence halls on campus are available for unmarried students. A university-owned subdivision immediately adjacent to campus offers housing for both married and single students.

## Special Features

*Minority admissions:* An active recruitment program is coordinated by the Office of Student Affairs. *Other degree programs:* Combined MD-PhD degree programs are offered in the basic medical sciences.

# ARIZONA

# University of Arizona College of Medicine

P.O. Box 245075
Tucson, Arizona   85724

*Phone:* 520-626-6214        *Fax:* 520-626-3777
*E-mail:* medapp@email.arizona.edu
*WWW:* medicine.arizona.edu

| Application Filing | | Accreditation | |
|---|---|---|---|
| Earliest: | June 1 | LCME | |
| Latest: | November 1 | | |
| Fee: | $75 | **Degrees Granted** | |
| AMCAS: | yes | MD, MD-PhD | |

### Enrollment: 2008–2009 First-Year Class

| Men: | 51 | 38% | Applied: | 814 |
|---|---|---|---|---|
| Women: | 83 | 62% | Interviewed: | 616 |
| Minorities: | 5 | 4% | Enrolled: | 134 |
| Out of State: | 0 | 0% | | |

### 2008–2009 Class Profile

| *Mean MCAT Scores* | | *Mean GPA* |
|---|---|---|
| Physical Sciences: | 10 | 3.8 |
| Biological Sciences: | 10 | |
| Verbal Reasoning: | 10 | *Mean Science* |
| | | 3.70 |

### Tuition and Fees

| Resident | 17,767 |
|---|---|
| Average (public) | 25,100 |
| Average (private) | 42,600 |
| Nonresident | n/app |

(in thousands of dollars)

Percentage receiving financial aid: 93%

Above data applies to 2007–2008 academic year.

## Introduction

Authorization for establishment of the College of Medicine was granted in 1962 and the first class was initiated in 1967. The University Medical Center, completed in 1971, was expanded in 1994. The new Arizona Health Sciences Library and Learning Resource Center was completed in 1992.

## Admissions (AMCAS)

Basic premedical science courses plus 2 semesters of English are required for admission. Applicants for both entering and transfer openings will be considered only from Arizona residents and certified and funded WICHE applicants. Selection of candidates for admission is based on ability, motivation, maturity, integrity, interpersonal skills, and exposure to medicine. *Transfer and advanced standing:* Applicants must be matriculated in WHO-listed foreign medical schools, 2-year or 4-year U.S. LCME-accredited medical schools, or accredited schools of osteopathy and must have completed the basic sciences. All applicants must take the USMLE.

## Curriculum

4-year semimodern. *First year:* A 40-week period when the basic sciences are presented. Patient contact is provided and behavioral sciences are emphasized. *Second year:* A 36-week period consisting of advanced basic science courses, behavioral sciences, and a continuation of the introduction to clinical sciences. *Third year:* A 48-week period when the clinical sciences are presented with at least 6 weeks of clerkships in each of the principal departments. *Fourth year:* A 33-week period for electives in the student's career path.

Biologic, cultural, psychosocial, economic, and sociologic concepts and data are provided in the core curriculum. Increasing emphasis is placed on problem-solving ability, beginning with initial instruction and carried through to graduation. Excellence in performance is encouraged and facilitated. Awareness of the milieu in which medicine is practiced is also encouraged. The learning environment encompasses lectures, small-group instruction, independent study, clinical clerkships, practice in physical diagnosis, computer-based instruction, and a variety of other modes for the learner. The Patient Instructor Program in the second year uses a unique method of clinical instruction. Real patients are trained to help students fine-tune their physical examination and history-taking skills. Students receive immediate feedback on their performance from the patient instructors, which helps to develop and improve the skills needed during the clinical years. Students learn in various settings at the University Medical Center, and a variety of community inpatient and outpatient settings.

## Grading and Promotion Policies

An Honors/Pass/Fail system is in operation. A written evaluation that characterizes specific student performance is also recorded with the Office of Student Affairs. The major criterion for promotion is that the student passes all required courses in the curriculum during each academic year. The student may repeat a course only once. A passing score must be recorded for both Steps 1 and 2 of the USMLE in order to graduate.

## Facilities

*Teaching:* The Health Sciences Center complex is located adjacent to the university campus and consists of several interconnected buildings: Basic Science, Clinical Sciences, Outpatient Clinic, University Medical Center, Children's Research Center, the Health Sciences Library, and Cancer Center. *Other:* Additional facilities used are the Tucson VA Hospital and Tucson and Phoenix hospitals. *Library:* The Health Sciences Center Library houses 176,000 volumes and 3600 medical journals. It is the only major biomedical library in the area. *Housing:* Some rooms are available for single students in the residence halls and for married students at the Family Housing Project.

## Special Features

*Minority admissions:* Disadvantaged, rural, and minority residents of Arizona are urged to apply for admission. *Other degree programs:* A combined MD-PhD program of study is also offered.

# ARKANSAS

# University of Arkansas College of Medicine

4301 West Markham Street
Little Rock, Arkansas 72205

*Phone:* 501-686-5354          *Fax:* 501-686-5873
*E-mail:* southtomg@umas.edu
*WWW:* uams.edu

| Application Filing | Accreditation |
|---|---|
| Earliest: July 1 | LCME |
| Latest: November 1 | |
| Fee: 100 | **Degrees Granted** |
| AMCAS: yes | MD, MD-PhD, MD-MS |

### Enrollment: 2008–2009 First-Year Class

| | | | | |
|---|---|---|---|---|
| Men: | 100 | 65% | Applied: | 1230 |
| Women: | 55 | 35% | Interviewed: | 392 |
| Minorities: | 5 | 3% | Enrolled: | 155 |
| Out of State: | 6 | 4% | | |

### 2008–2009 Class Profile

| *Mean MCAT Scores* | | *Mean GPA* |
|---|---|---|
| Physical Sciences: | 10 | 3.7 |
| Biological Sciences: | 10 | |
| Verbal Reasoning: | 10 | *Mean Science* |
| | | 3.6 |

### Tuition and Fees

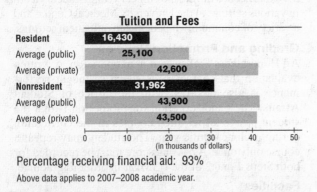

| | |
|---|---|
| **Resident** | 16,430 |
| Average (public) | 25,100 |
| Average (private) | 42,600 |
| **Nonresident** | 31,962 |
| Average (public) | 43,900 |
| Average (private) | 43,500 |

(in thousands of dollars)

Percentage receiving financial aid: 93%

Above data applies to 2007–2008 academic year.

## Introduction

In 1879 the Arkansas Industrial University established a medical department. This component became part of the University of Arkansas for Medical Sciences in 1975. The latter incorporates 5 colleges, training physicians, nurses, pharmacists, health-related professionals, and graduate students.

## Admissions (AMCAS)

Prerequisites include the minimum premedical science courses plus 3 semesters of English and 2 semesters of mathematics. Recommended courses include genetics, embryology, genetics, quantitative analysis, statistics, cell biology, psychology, anthropology, logic, history, and literature. Nonresidents should have a GPA above

3.5 and an MCAT score of 9 or higher in each subtest. Graduate students applying need an advisor's letter assuring graduation by August. *Transfer and advanced standing:* For the third year only, with very limited places available. Applicants are considered on a case-by-case basis and must demonstrate strong ties to the state of Arkansas.

## Curriculum

4-year semitraditional. *First year:* (36 weeks) Introductory basic sciences as well as opportunity for patient contact by means of the introduction to the medical profession course. *Second year:* (32 weeks) Consists of the advanced basic sciences and courses in behavioral science, physical diagnosis, and mechanism of disease. *Third year:* (48 weeks) Consists of clerkship rotations through the major clinical specialties. *Fourth year:* (from 36 to 48 weeks) Open to more than 200 electives selected with advice of a faculty advisor. Research may be carried out as part of elective. Off-campus study locally or elsewhere in U.S. or abroad may be selected.

## Grading and Promotion Policies

A letter grading system is used in basic sciences and required clinical rotations; a Pass/Fail system is used in electives. Subjective assessments are used by a Promotions Committee in determining a student's eligibility for promotion. A passing grade must be recorded on Step 1 of the USMLE for promotion to the third year.

## Facilities

*Teaching:* Medical Center includes a 9-story Educational Building that provides basic science facilities. University Hospital (400 beds) is the principal site for clinical training. This facility is augmented by the Ambulatory Care Center and the Arkansas Cancer Research Center. The school is affiliated with the Arkansas Children's Hospital and VA Hospitals in Little Rock and North Little Rock. It cooperates with other Little Rock hospitals in its training programs. *Other:* T. H. Barton Institute of Medical Research, Arkansas State Hospital for Nervous Diseases, Arkansas Rehabilitation Institute, Biomedical Research Center, Jones Eye Institute, and the Central Arkansas Radiation Therapy Institute. *Housing:* All single freshman and sophomore students are required to live in the residence hall unless special exemption is received. Approximately 35 one-bedroom furnished apartments are available for married students.

## Special Features

*Minority admissions:* The college's Office of Minority Student Affairs conducts programs designed to identify and assist prospective admission candidates among minority and disadvantaged students in the state. *Other degree programs:* Dual MD-PhD and MD-MS programs available, offered in conjunction with the Graduate School of the university. Medical Student Research Program enables students to work in selected areas of research. Work done under this program may be applied toward a PhD degree.

# CALIFORNIA

## Keck School of Medicine of the University of Southern California

1975 Zonal Avenue
Los Angeles, California   90089

*Phone:* 323-442-2552      *Fax:* 323-442-2433
*WWW:* usc.edu/keck

**Application Filing**
Earliest:   July 1
Latest:     November 1
Fee:        $90
AMCAS:   yes

**Accreditation**
LCME

**Degrees Granted**
MD, MD-PhD, BS-MD
MD-MPH, MD-MBA

### Enrollment: 2008–2009 First-Year Class

| | | | | | |
|---|---|---|---|---|---|
| Men: | 86 | 54% | Applied: | 6618 |
| Women: | 73 | 46% | Interviewed: | 622 |
| Minorities: | 40 | 25% | Enrolled: | 168 |
| Out of State: | 39 | 24% | | |

### 2008–2009 Class Profile

*Mean MCAT Scores*
Physical Sciences:   10.11
Biological Sciences: 10.11
Verbal Reasoning:    10.11

*Mean GPA*
3.61

*Mean Science*
3.6

### Tuition and Fees

| | |
|---|---|
| Resident | 43,536 |
| Average (public) | 25,100 |
| Average (private) | 42,600 |
| Nonresident | 43,536 |
| Average (public) | 43,900 |
| Average (private) | 43,500 |

(in thousands of dollars)

Percentage receiving financial aid: 89%

## Introduction

This medical school was founded in 1885 and is part of a privately supported, nondenominational university. Its 31-acre campus is located in northeast Los Angeles, directly across from its major teaching hospital, which is one of the largest in the country. It is located 7 miles from the University Park campus and 3 miles from the Los Angeles Civic Center.

## Admissions (AMCAS)

Minimum premedical science courses are required. A 1-semester course in molecular biology is also required as are 30 semester hours of social sciences, humanities, and English composition. Computer literacy, college mathematics, or calculus are strongly recommended. The student body comes from all parts of the United States, as well as from several foreign countries. *Transfer and advanced standing:* Only second-year students enrolled and in good standing at LCME-approved medical schools may be considered for admission for the third

year. Such students must pass Step 1 of the USMLE.

## Curriculum

4-year modern. *First year:* Students are progressively involved in patient care beginning with the first semester of the first year. An introduction to clinical medicine course begins in the freshman year and runs through the sophomore year. Doctor-patient relationships and interviewing are presented during the first year, and physical diagnosis and history-taking are discussed in the second. Groups of approximately 6 to 7 students are led by a faculty member who serves as a clinical tutor for their first 2 years. Basic sciences are taught largely in an organ system approach. Appropriate material in the basic sciences is presented during the study of these systems; patients are observed and examined for clinical illustration of the subject under discussion. *Second year:* The student studies the pathologic aspects of medicine, also predominantly in organ system approach. In addition, a student may begin an investigative project. *Third year:* Student participation is required in the clinical clerkships, such as internal medicine and general surgery. Elective study is provided in the third and fourth years. *Fourth year:* Consists almost entirely of work chosen by the student. In addition, students have an opportunity to engage in clinical or basic research through voluntary participation in a summer fellowship program between the freshman and sophomore years.

## Grading and Promotion Policies

First two years—pass, fail. Final two years—honors, high pass, pass, fail. Grading basis is Honors, Satisfactory, Unsatisfactory.

## Facilities

*Teaching:* Instruction is conducted on campus, in the Medical Center, and in affiliated hospitals, community clinics, and institutions. Through the elective program, instruction is also provided at medical schools and hospitals in other states and countries. The 30-acre campus is located across the street from its chief teaching hospital, the Los Angeles County-USC Medical Center (2105 beds). A 284-bed USC Hospital located on the Health Sciences Campus opened in 1991. *Other:* Additional clinical facilities include Norris Cancer Hospital and Research Institute, Doheny Eye Institute, Hospital of the Good Samaritan, Eisenhower Medical Center, and Barlow, California Huntington Memorial, and Presbyterian Inter-Community Hospitals. *Library:* The library can house 300,000 volumes and seat 250 readers. *Housing:* Information is not available.

## Special Features

*Other degree programs:* Several components of the school provide direct support to students, including the Student Health Service, the Offices of Curriculum, Minority Affairs, and Student Affairs. Services include tutorial assistance, health and counseling services, extensive extracurricular academic and nonacademic programs, school and university student government, services for students with disabilities, sophisticated library and electronic resources, and various other services. *Other degree programs:* The school sponsors an MD-PhD and a Research Scholar program. Apply during the first or second year of medical school. An 8-year Baccalaureate-MD program is offered to high school seniors.

# Loma Linda University School of Medicine

Loma Linda, California   92350

*Phone:* 909-558-4467     *Fax:* 909-558-0359
*E-mail:* admissions@sm.llu.edu
*WWW:* llu.edu/medicine

| Application Filing | | Accreditation |
|---|---|---|
| Earliest: | June 1 | LCME |
| Latest: | November 1 | |
| Fee: | $75 | **Degrees Granted** |
| AMCAS: | yes | MD, MD-PhD, MD-MS |

### Enrollment: 2008–2009 First-Year Class

| Men: | 97 | 56% | Applied: | 4327 |
|---|---|---|---|---|
| Women: | 75 | 44% | Interviewed: | 391 |
| Minorities: | 10 | 6% | Enrolled: | 172 |
| Out of State: | 84 | 49% | | |

### 2008–2009 Class Profile

| *Mean MCAT Scores* | | *Mean GPA* |
|---|---|---|
| Physical Sciences: | 10 | 3.72 |
| Biological Sciences: | 10 | |
| Verbal Reasoning: | 10 | *Mean Science* |
| | | 3.7 |

**Tuition and Fees**

| | |
|---|---|
| Resident | 35,506 |
| Average (public) | 25,100 |
| Average (private) | 42,600 |
| Nonresident | 35,506 |
| Average (public) | 43,900 |
| Average (private) | 43,500 |

0   10   20   30   40   50
(in thousands of dollars)

Percentage receiving financial aid: 89%

Above data applies to 2007–2008 academic year.

## Introduction

This medical school, like its parent body, Loma Linda University, is owned and operated by the Seventh-Day Adventist Church. It was founded in 1909. The campus includes basic science facilities and a Medical Center. The school is located inland not far from Los Angeles. The curriculum of the university is approved by LCME.

## Admissions (AMCAS)

Required are the minimum premedical science courses plus English. The MCAT also is required. Preference is shown to members of the Seventh-Day Adventist Church, but it is a firm policy of the admissions committee to admit each year a number of non-church-related applicants who have demonstrated a strong commitment to Christian principles. Applicants are sought who have critical judgment, demonstrate problem-solving skills, and are independent thinkers. After receipt of the AMCAS application, each applicant is requested to submit a supplementary application and arrange that the medical school receive a preprofessional evaluation and/or letters of recommendation from their undergraduate college. Invitations for an interview are extended to selected applicants both at the medical school campus and various sites throughout the country. *Transfer and advanced standing:* Accepted into the junior year if space is available, compelling reasons exist, and Step 1 of the USMLE has been successfully completed.

## Curriculum

4-year semitraditional. *First year:* Consists of gross anatomy, courses entitled You and Your Patient, Information Science and Population-based Medicine, neuroscience, physical diagnosis, Cell Structure and Function, Medical Applications of the Basic Sciences. Students take biochemistry, molecular biology, and genetics. *Second year:* Consists of physiology, microbiology, pathology, psychopathology, and physical diagnosis. *Third year:* Consists of 4- to 12-week rotations through the standard required clerkships plus family medicine, as well as a 4-week orientation to clinical medicine. *Fourth year:* This year includes 2 major specialty subinternships plus experience in emergency medicine, intensive care, neurology, and preventive medicine, as well as up to 22 weeks of electives. A unique feature of this school is the special interest in the student's professional growth. This approach to "whole-person" development involves both the faculty of medicine and religion.

## Grading and Promotion Policies

Students are evaluated on a Pass/Fail basis; however, class ranks are determined on a percentile system. Passing Step 1 of the USMLE is required for promotion to clinical clerkships. Obtaining a total passing score on Steps 1 and 2 of the USMLE is required for promotion to the third year and graduation after the fourth year, respectively.

## Facilities

*Teaching:* School is located on the university campus. Clinical teaching takes place at University Hospital (500 beds) and several affiliated hospitals. *Other:* A medium-scale, general-purpose computer facility serves the students and faculty of the university in instructional and research functions. *Library:* Medical and related fields make up more than half of the holdings of the Del Webb Memorial Library located on campus.

## Special Features

*Minority admissions:* The school does not discriminate on the basis of race, age, sex, or handicap. *Other degree programs:* MD-MS and MD-PhD programs are available.

# Stanford University School of Medicine

251 Campus Drive
Stanford, California   94305

*Phone:* 650-723-6861          *Fax:* 650-725-7855
*E-mail:* admissions@stanford.edu
*WWW:* med.stanford.edu

| Application Filing | | Accreditation | |
|---|---|---|---|
| Earliest: | June 1 | LCME | |
| Latest: | October 15 | | |
| Fee: | $80 | **Degrees Granted** | |
| AMCAS: | yes | MD, MD-PhD | |

### Enrollment: 2008–2009 First-Year Class

| Men: | 40 | 47% | Applied: | 6567 |
|---|---|---|---|---|
| Women: | 46 | 53% | Interviewed: | 407 |
| Minorities: | 15 | 17% | Enrolled: | 86 |
| Out of State: | 54 | 63% | | |

### 2008–2009 Class Profile

| *Mean MCAT Scores* | | *Mean GPA* |
|---|---|---|
| Physical Sciences: | 12 | 3.75 |
| Biological Sciences: | 12 | |
| Verbal Reasoning: | 10.7 | *Mean Science* |
| | | 3.70 |

**Tuition and Fees**

| | |
|---|---|
| **Resident** | 43,389 |
| Average (public) | 25,100 |
| Average (private) | 42,600 |
| **Nonresident** | 43,789 |
| Average (public) | 43,900 |
| Average (private) | 43,500 |

0    10    20    30    40    50
(in thousands of dollars)

Percentage receiving financial aid: 74%

## Introduction

The School of Medicine was founded in 1858 as the medical department of the College of the Pacific. It later became affiliated with the University City College, and subsequently, in 1882, was given the name Cooper Medical College in honor of the original founder. In 1908 it was adopted by Leland Stanford Junior University and relocated to outside San Francisco. Stanford University School of Medicine was established in 1958. A new Medical Center was opened in 1959 and is located on an 8800-acre campus.

## Admissions (AMCAS)

The standard premedical courses are required. Strongly recommended, but not required, are knowledge of a modern foreign language. Spanish is especially useful. Courses in calculus, biochemistry, physical chemistry, and behavioral sciences are strongly encouraged. No preference is shown to California residents. Foreign applicants must have completed a minimum of 1 year of study in a U.S., Canadian, or United Kingdom accredited college or university. *Transfer and advanced standing:* Transfer students are not accepted.

## Curriculum

4-year modern. The goals of the curriculum are to develop outstanding clinical skills and the capacity for leadership in the practice of scientific medicine, and to prepare as many students as possible for careers in research and teaching. Stanford's flexible curriculum is its major innovative approach to medical education. It was designed to create an environment that encourages intellectual diversity and to provide opportunities for students to develop as individuals. While traditional courses and clerkships are required for graduation, the duration of study leading to the MD degree may vary from 4 to 6 years. Students have flexibility in sequencing courses by demonstrating competency through examination. This curriculum stimulates self-directed learning, and provides students time to pursue an investigative project, obtain teaching experience, perform community service, explore special interests, or obtain advanced degrees.

## Grading and Promotion Policies

The grading system is Pass/Fail/Marginal Performance in the basic sciences and clinical clerkships. Narrative evaluations are used in the clerkships. Step 1 and Step 2 of the USMLE must be passed in order to graduate.

## Facilities

*Teaching:* The school is part of the Stanford University Medical Center and consists of 26 departments. The major clinical teaching facilities are Stanford University Hospital (663 beds), Lucile Packard Children's Hospital (152 beds), Santa Clara Valley Medical Center (791 beds), and the Palo Alto Veterans Administration Hospital (1000 beds). *Library:* The Lane Medical Library contains more than 280,000 volumes and more than 3000 periodicals. The Fleischmann Learning Resource Center is an independent study center offering media and computer-based programs. SUMMIT (Stanford University Medical Media and Information Technologies) produces faculty- and student-authored programs. *Housing:* Apartments are available for single and married students.

## Special Features

*Minority admissions:* The school believes that a student body that is both highly qualified and diverse in terms of culture, class, gender, race, ethnicity, background, work and life experiences, skills, and interests is essential to the education of physicians. Because of its strongly belief in the value of diversity, the school especially encourages applications from African Americans, Mexican Americans, Native Americans, and mainland Puerto Ricans, as well as from others whose backgrounds and experience provide additional dimensions that will enhance the school's program. An early matriculation program, which includes preclinical coursework and research opportunities, has been developed for students from disadvantaged backgrounds. *Other degree programs:* Combined MD-PhD programs are offered in most basic medical sciences as well as in cancer biology, epidemiology, immunology, neurobiology, and medical information sciences.

# University of California—Davis School of Medicine

4610 X Street
Sacramento, California   95817

*Phone:* 916-734-4800          *Fax:* 530-754-6252
*E-mail:* medadmsinfo@ucdavis.edu
*WWW:* som.ucdavis.edu

| Application Filing | | Accreditation | |
|---|---|---|---|
| Earliest: | June 1 | LCME | |
| Latest: | October 1 | | |
| Fee: | $60 | **Degrees Granted** | |
| AMCAS: | yes | MD, MD-PhD, | |
| | | MD-MPH, MD-MBA | |

### Enrollment: 2008–2009 First-Year Class

| | | | | | |
|---|---|---|---|---|---|
| Men: | 43 | 41% | Applied: | 4861 |
| Women: | 62 | 59% | Interviewed: | 470 |
| Minorities: | 3 | 3% | Enrolled: | 105 |
| Out of State: | 3 | 3% | | |

### 2008–2009 Class Profile

| Mean MCAT Scores | | Mean GPA |
|---|---|---|
| Physical Sciences: | 11.0 | 3.7 |
| Biological Sciences: | 11.0 | |
| Verbal Reasoning: | 10.0 | Mean Science |
| | | 3.6 |

### Tuition and Fees

| | |
|---|---|
| Resident | **n/av** |
| Average (public) | **n/av** |
| Average (private) | **n/av** |
| Nonresident | 36.544 |
| Average (public) | 43,900 |
| Average (private) | 43,500 |

0    10    20    30    40    50
(in thousands of dollars)

Percentage receiving financial aid:  93%

Above data applies to 2007–2008 academic year.

## Introduction

This medical school admitted its first class in 1968. Its educational goal is to provide students with a medical knowledge base that enables them to choose to pursue a career in primary care, specialty practice, public health, research, or administration. While most of the facilities necessary for earning the medical degree are located on the University of California Davis campus, most of the school's clinical space is at the UC Davis Medical Center in Sacramento.

## Admissions (AMCAS)

Requirements include the basic premedical science courses plus 1 year each of English and mathematics that includes integral calculus. First preference goes to residents and next to WICHE applicants. *Transfer and advanced standing:* Currently enrolled students in good standing at U.S. or Canadian medical schools may apply for admission to the third year of study. Applications are considered on a space available basis.

## Curriculum

4-year semimodern. The curriculum seeks to provide a balanced blend of basic and clinical sciences. *First year:* Consists of the introductory basic medical sciences, immunology, and general pathology. These are combined with social sciences, an introduction to the art of communicating with patients, and clinical medicine. *Second year:* Provides for a transition between basic and clinical sciences with the presentation of pathology, nutrition, pharmacology, microbiology, human sexuality, pathological basis of disease, and physical diagnosis, as well as laboratory diagnostic techniques and community health. *Third year:* Consists of clerkship rotations in the major specialties, maternal and child health, and psychiatry. *Fourth year:* Electives and elective clerkships, with required courses in medical ethics, medical economics, and medical jurisprudence.

## Grading and Promotion Policies

Pass/Not Pass first 2 years; Honors, Pass, Fail 3rd and 4th years. Satisfactory/Unsatisfactory in elective courses. At the end of each year, the medical school's Promotion Board evaluates each student's record. Students must record a passing total score on Step 1 of the USMLE for promotion to the third year and record a score on Step 2 to graduate.

## Facilities

*Teaching:* The basic sciences are taught at the Medical Sciences I complex in Davis. Clinical facilities are provided by the University Medical Center (523 beds), which has over 100 specialty clinics. *Other:* Clinical instruction also takes place at a number of affiliated hospitals and family practice centers. In 2006 the medical school will relocate to a new single campus in Sacramento opposite UC Medical Center. *Library:* The Health Sciences Library is located adjacent to the School of Medicine and has more than 142,000 volumes and 3700 periodicals. The library has terminal access to MEDLINE, an on-line retrieval system for medical periodical information. A branch library is operated at the Sacramento Medical Center. *Housing:* Some on-campus housing is available at residence halls for unmarried students; a number of 1- and 2-bedroom units are available for married students.

## Special Features

*Minority admissions:* An active recruitment program is coordinated by the Medical Education Student Services. A 2-week summer prematriculation program is offered. *Other degree programs:* Combined MD-PhD programs are offered in a wide variety of disciplines including biomedical engineering, biophysics, endocrinology, genetics, nutrition, and psychology. The MD-MPH degree program is offered through the UC Berkeley School of Public Health, the UC School of Medicine–Davis, and an MD-MBA through the UC, Graduate School of Management.

# University of California—Irvine School of Medicine

Irvine, California   92697

*Phone:* 949-824-5388          *Fax:* 949-824-2485
*E-mail:* medadmit@uci-edu
*WWW:* ucrhs.uci.edu/com

| Application Filing | | Accreditation | |
|---|---|---|---|
| Earliest: | June 1 | LCME | |
| Latest: | November 1 | | |
| Fee: | $60 | **Degrees Granted** | |
| AMCAS: | yes | MD, MD-PhD | |

### Enrollment: 2008–2009 First-Year Class

| Men: | 58 | 51% | Applied: | 4536 |
|---|---|---|---|---|
| Women: | 51 | 49% | Interviewed: | 473 |
| Minorities: | 3 | 3% | Enrolled: | 104 |
| Out of State: | 2 | 3% | | |

### 2008–2009 Class Profile

| *Mean MCAT Scores* | | *Mean GPA* |
|---|---|---|
| Physical Sciences: | 11 | 3.7 |
| Biological Sciences: | 11 | |
| Verbal Reasoning: | 10 | *Mean Science* |
| | | 3.7 |

**Tuition and Fees**

| | |
|---|---|
| **Resident** | 21,823 |
| Average (public) | 25,100 |
| Average (private) | 42,600 |
| **Nonresident** | 34,068 |
| Average (public) | 43,900 |
| Average (private) | 43,500 |

0     10     20     30     40     50
(in thousands of dollars)

Percentage receiving financial aid:  90%

Above data applies to 2007–2008 academic year.

## Introduction

The school became part of the University of California in 1965. Prior to this time it was known as the California College of Medicine, which traces its roots to a private institution founded in 1896. The school is located between Los Angeles and San Diego. Approximately 425 medical students are enrolled.

## Admissions

The Admissions Committee screens for applicants whose record indicates the potential to meet the rigorous demands of the curriculum. In addition to scholastic achievement, attributes deemed desirable include leadership and participation in extracurricular activities, evidence of exposure to clinical medicine, research and community service. Consideration is given to applicants from disadvantaged backgrounds.

Preference is given to California residents. *Transfer and advanced standing:* The school does not accept transfer students.

## Curriculum

4-year modern. The school is dedicated to the nurturing of humanistic, caring physicians with state-of-the-art clinical expertise and skills. In additon to the basic sciences in the first two years, substantial clinical material has been integrated into the curriculum through the development of a series of "Patient–Doctor" courses. These courses are longitudinal multidisciplinary experiences broadly designed to prepare students for their medical careers. In the first year, students work with standardized patients to develop interview and physical examination skills. These clinical skills are further strengthened in the second year by working in the community with patients. In addition, clinically oriented courses are designed to complement the material covered in the basic science courses. During the clinical years, students go through the core clinical services of internal medicine, family medicine, surgery, obstetrics and gynecology, psychiatry, pediatrics, emergency medicine, radiology, and neurology. Clinical advisors guide students in the selection of 20 weeks of electives tailored to the students' career goals and educational needs. The content themes are ethics, humanities, communication skills, physical diagnosis, and medical economics.

## Grading and Promotional Policies

The School of Medicine uses an Honors/Pass/Fail grading system. To satisfy the requirement for the MD degree, students must also pass both Step 1 and Step 2 of the United States Medical Licensing Examination (USMLE) and successfully pass a Clinical Practice Examination (CPX) prior to graduation.

## Facilities

UCI Medical Center offers a full scope of acute and general care. The Medical Center houses: a most sophisticated neonatal unit, University Children's Hospital, an Emergency Department, a Neuropsychiatric Center, and the Chao Family Comprehensive Cancer Center. The Medical Center has five neighborhood health centers located throughout Orange County.

## Special Features

*Minority admissions:* The school has a multicultural community, composed of individuals from diverse backgrounds. Programs, classes, workshops, lectures, and everyday interactions are enriched by acceptance of one another.

# University of California— Los Angeles, David Geffen School of Medicine

Le Conte Avenue
Los Angeles, California   90095

*Phone:* 310-825-6081          *Fax:* 310-206-5046
*E-mail:* somadmiss@mednet.ucla.edu
*WWW:* dgsem.healthsciences.ucla.edu/ms-resources

| Application Filing | | Accreditation |
|---|---|---|
| Earliest: | June 1 | LCME |
| Latest: | November 1 | |
| Fee: | $60 | **Degrees Granted** |
| AMCAS: | yes | MD, MD-PhD, MD-MPH |

### Enrollment: 2008–2009 First-Year Class

| Men: | 94 | 56% | Applied: | 7824 |
|---|---|---|---|---|
| Women: | 75 | 44% | Interviewed: | 717 |
| Minorities: | 15 | 9% | Enrolled: | 169 |
| Out of State: | 23 | 14% | | |

### 2008–2009 Class Profile

| *Mean MCAT Scores* | | *Mean GPA* |
|---|---|---|
| Physical Sciences: | 11 | 3.8 |
| Biological Sciences: | 12 | |
| Verbal Reasoning: | 10 | *Mean Science* |
| | | 3.8 |

### Tuition and Fees

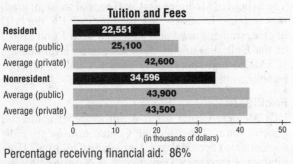

| | |
|---|---|
| Resident | 22,551 |
| Average (public) | 25,100 |
| Average (private) | 42,600 |
| Nonresident | 34,596 |
| Average (public) | 43,900 |
| Average (private) | 43,500 |

(in thousands of dollars)

Percentage receiving financial aid: 86%

Above data applies to 2007–2008 academic year.

## Introduction

This was the first University of California Medical School in Southern California, enrolling its charter class in 1951. The school is located on the UCLA campus and is closely connected with the University Medical Center. Both the School of Medicine and Medical Center have expanded along with the growth of Los Angeles into a major metropolitan urban center.

## Admissions (AMCAS)

Prerequisites are the basic premedical science courses (if possible, including quantitative analysis as part of inorganic chemistry), 1 year of mathematics (including introductory calculus and statistics), and 1 year of English (including composition). Spanish, humanities, and computer skills are highly recommended. Completing courses overlapping those in medical school, such as

human anatomy, is not advisable. Taking the spring MCAT is recommended. Applicants are favored who have a broad training and high achievement in their college education. Applicants are initially screened on the basis of their personal essay, letters of recommendation, their GPA, and MCAT scores. Selected applicants will be scheduled to have a personal interview by members of the faculty. About 25 of the students admitted each year are accepted into the Drew/UCLA Joint Medical Program, designed for students with an interest in caring for underserved populations. *Transfer and advanced standing:* From U.S. medical schools only, into the third-year class.

## Curriculum

4-year semitraditional. Stress is on the holistic approach in medicine. *First year:* Introductory basic sciences and patient contact and experience in history and physical examination as well as an elective program and a preceptorship program. *Second year:* Study of the process of disease through advanced basic science courses using an organ-system approach; diagnosis and treatment through courses in clinical surgery, clinical neurology, outpatient psychiatry, radiology, and obstetrics. *Third year:* Clerkships in clinical sciences and work in wards and outpatient clinics. *Fourth year:* Consists of electives—advanced elective clinical clerkships with primary patient responsibility, and in-depth elective courses that can be centered on major area of clinical interest or a combination of related or diverse disciplines.

## Grading and Promotion Policies

Letter grading in basic sciences, clinical sciences, and electives. Promotion is contingent upon satisfactory completion of required work each year. Completion of Steps 1 and 2 of the USMLE is required.

## Facilities

*Teaching:* The School of Medicine is located in the Center for Health Sciences, which is the largest building in California. The University Hospital (517 beds) is the major clinical training center. Many other hospitals, including Harbor General (800 beds), are affiliated with the medical school. *Other:* The Brain Research Institute is a 10-story wing, connected to the Neuropsychiatric Institute and also houses the Los Angeles County Cardiovascular Research Laboratory. The Reed Neurological Research Center is an 8-story unit devoted to clinical research in neuromuscular disease. *Library:* The Biomedical Library is an 8-level facility in the northeast corner of the campus. *Housing:* Living accommodations are available in the university's residence halls or married students' housing.

## Special Features

*Minority admissions:* The school has an active recruitment program and offers a 4-week summer prologue to medicine program for accepted students. *Other degree programs:* Combined MD-PhD degree programs are offered in a variety of disciplines including medical physics, biomathematics, engineering, and experimental pathology. An MD-MPH program is also offered.

# University of California—San Diego School of Medicine

9500 Gilman Drive
La Jolla, California    92093

*Phone:* 858-534-3880        *Fax:* 858-534-5282
*E-mail:* somadmissions@ucsd.edu
*WWW:* meded-portal.ucsd.edu

| Application Filing | Accreditation |
|---|---|
| Earliest: June 1 | LCME |
| Latest: November 1 | |
| Fee: $60 | **Degrees Granted** |
| AMCAS: yes | MD, MD-PhD, MD-MPH |

### Enrollment: 2008–2009 First-Year Class

| | | | | |
|---|---|---|---|---|
| Men: | 66 | 49% | Applied: | 5500 |
| Women: | 68 | 51% | Interviewed: | 569 |
| Minorities: | 2 | 1% | Enrolled: | 134 |
| Out of State: | 10 | 7% | | |

### 2008–2009 Class Profile

| *Mean MCAT Scores* | | *Mean GPA* |
|---|---|---|
| Physical Sciences: | 11.0 | 3.8 |
| Biological Sciences: | 11.0 | |
| Verbal Reasoning: | 10.0 | *Mean Science* |
| | | 3.8 |

### Tuition and Fees

| | |
|---|---|
| **Resident** | 21,465 |
| Average (public) | 25,100 |
| Average (private) | 42,600 |
| **Nonresident** | 33,710 |
| Average (public) | 43,900 |
| Average (private) | 43,500 |

(in thousands of dollars)

Percentage receiving financial aid: 91%

Above data applies to 2007–2008 academic year.

## Introduction
This school is located on the main campus of the University at La Jolla, making it accessible to a wide variety of educational opportunities. Its scenic location is unique, affording students special opportunities for both educational and cultural advancement.

## Admissions (AMCAS)
It is recommended that students enter medical school after 4 years of undergraduate study; the absolute minimum requirement is attendance for 3 academic years at an approved college of arts and sciences. Students who have attended a foreign school must have completed at least 1 year of undergraduate study at an accredited 4-year college or university in the United States prior to application. Applicants are required to have completed the minimum premedical science courses and 1 year of mathematics (only calculus, statistics, or computer sci-

ence is considered). The ability to express oneself clearly in both oral and written English is essential. A broad base of knowledge is advantageous in preparing for the many roles of a physician and may include courses in behavioral sciences, the biology of cells and development, genetics, biochemistry, English, social sciences, or conversational Spanish. Applicants are advised to take the MCAT. Only permanent residents or U.S. citizens will be considered for admission and preference is given to California state residents. *Transfer and advanced standing:* Transfer students from either foreign or domestic medical schools are not accepted.

## Curriculum
4-year modern. Program places emphasis upon human disease with aim of expanding scientific knowledge and in the context of social applicability. The curriculum is divided into 2 major components: the core curriculum and the elective programs. Both are pursued concurrently, with the core predominating in the early years and the elective in the latter. Elective programs offer students a set of choices suited to their unique background, ability, and career objectives. *Preclinical phase:* The first year includes social and behavioral sciences, biostatistics, and an introduction to clinical medicine as well as some introductory and advanced basic science courses. The second year includes anatomy as well as advanced electives. *Clinical phase:* An extended continuum consisting of rotation through the major clinical specialties and electives (which take up about half of the total time of these 2 years).

## Grading and Promotion Policies
Grading is either Pass or Fail, and a narrative of each student's performance in his/her individual courses is prepared. These narratives are collated yearly and summarized, with a copy of the summary made available to students and their main advisor.

## Facilities
*Teaching:* The school is located on the university campus in La Jolla. The primary teaching hospitals include the Veterans Administration Medical Center, UCSD Medical Center, and Balboa Naval Hospital. *Other:* Clinical teaching is also done at Mercy Hospital, Sharp Hospital, Children's Health Center, and the Kaiser Permanente Health Maintenance Organization as well as a wide spectrum of front-line, outpatient clinics, ranging from tiny Indian reservation facilities in east San Diego County, to the Clinica de Campesinos to the south. *Library:* The Biomedical Library is located on the UCSD medical school campus and houses a large collection of books and journals. *Housing:* Limited on-campus housing is available.

## Special Features
*Minority admissions:* The school conducts an active recruitment program and offers a summer preparatory program for disadvantaged students who have been accepted. *Other degree programs:* Combined MD-PhD programs available in a variety of disciplines, including biology, bioengineering, and chemistry. Also available is an MD-MPH program in conjunction with San Diego State University.

# University of California— San Francisco School of Medicine

San Francisco, California   94143

*Phone:* 415-476-4044
*E-mail:* admissions@medsch.ucsf.edu
*WWW:* medschool.ucsf.edu

| Application Filing | | Accreditation | |
|---|---|---|---|
| Earliest: | June 1 | LCME | |
| Latest: | October 15 | | |
| Fee: | $60 | **Degrees Granted** | |
| AMCAS: | yes | MD, MD-PhD | |

### Enrollment: 2008–2009 First-Year Class

| | | | | | |
|---|---|---|---|---|---|
| Men: | 67 | 41% | Applied: | 6303 | |
| Women: | 96 | 59% | Interviewed: | 601 | |
| Minorities: | 22 | 13% | Enrolled: | 163 | |
| Out of State: | 27 | 17% | | | |

### 2008–2009 Class Profile

| *Mean MCAT Scores* | | *Mean GPA* |
|---|---|---|
| Physical Sciences: | 11.0 | 3.8 |
| Biological Sciences: | 11 | |
| Verbal Reasoning: | 10 | *Mean Science* |
| | | 3.8 |

**Tuition and Fees**

| | |
|---|---|
| **Resident** | 21,218 |
| Average (public) | 25,100 |
| Average (private) | 42,600 |
| **Nonresident** | 33,463 |
| Average (public) | 43,900 |
| Average (private) | 43,500 |

0   10   20   30   40   50
(in thousands of dollars)

Percentage receiving financial aid: 86%

Above data applies to 2007–2008 academic year.

## Introduction

The University of California—San Francisco School of Medicine can trace its roots back to Toland Medical College, founded in 1864. UCSF became affiliated with the state university system in 1873.

## Admissions (AMCAS)

Minimum premedical science courses are required; biology should include vertebrate zoology. Mathematics, upper-division biological sciences, and humanities courses are recommended. *Transfer and advanced standing:* No students are accepted at any level.

## Curriculum

4-year modern. *First and second years:* A series of interdisciplinary block courses is offered. Basic, clinical, social, and behavioral sciences are integrated. Emphasis is placed on student-directed, active learning in small groups. Students have patient contact, learn physical exam skills, and explore issues of ethics and professionalism in the longitudinal Foundations of Patient Care course. *Third and fourth years:* In the last 2 years, various clinical departments provide 46 weeks of core clerkships, which teach students the basic techniques of clinical medicine. Also, in the third year, students participate in 22 one-half-day longitudinal clinic sessions. An additional 34 weeks of clinical and basic science courses must be elected from a wide range of offerings. There are numerous opportunities for students to engage in research.

## Grading and Promotion Policies

The grading system used is Honors/Pass/Not Pass. Honors are not awarded in the first-year courses. The Student Screening Committee on Student Promotions assesses the performance of all students at the end of each quarter and recommends one of the following: promotion to the next quarter; promotion to the next quarter, subject to certain conditions; formal repetition of one or more quarters of work; or consideration of dismissal from the school. A passing total score must be recorded in Step 1 of the USMLE for promotion to the third year; Step 2 must be taken only to record a score.

## Facilities

*Teaching:* The first and second year essential core courses are offered at the Medical Sciences Building and the Health Sciences Instruction and Research Building. Core clinical instruction utilizes the UCSF Medical Center, which comprises the Herbert C. Moffitt/Joseph M. Long Hospital, the UCSF/Mount Zion Medical Center, and the UCSF Children's Hospital; Langley Porter Psychiatric Institute; San Francisco General Hospital; and the San Francisco Veterans Affairs Medical Center, as well as other area hospitals. *Other:* There are 16 major research centers within the school: AIDS Research Institute, Cancer Research Institute, Cardiovascular Research Institute, Center for Health and Community, Center for Reproductive Sciences, Center for Tobacco Control Research and Education, Comprehensive Cancer Center, Hooper Foundation, Hormone Research Institute, Institute for Global Health, Institute for Health Policy Studies, Institute for Neurodegenerative Diseases, and others. *Library:* The major portions of the library are housed in the Paul and Lydia Kalmanovitz Library; there are nearly 800,000 volumes and nearly 9000 periodicals. *Housing:* The university operates Turk Boulevard Apartments and Avenue Houses for single students, and Aldea San Miguel for families.

## Special Features

*Minority admissions:* UCSF's multifaceted program seeks to identify, recruit, and prepare disadvantaged students for careers in the health sciences. Included in these efforts are academic support services and counseling opportunities. *Other degree programs:* Dual-degree programs offering MS, MPH, and PhD degrees are offered for this purpose. MD-PhD programs are offered in a variety of disciplines.

## COLORADO

# University of Colorado School of Medicine

4200 East Ninth Avenue
Aurora, Colorado   80045

*Phone:* 303-724-8025          *Fax:* 303-724-8028
*E-mail:* somaolmin@uchsc.edu
*WWW:* uchsc.edu/sm/sm/mddgree.htm

| Application Filing | | Accreditation |
|---|---|---|
| Earliest: | June 1 | LCME |
| Latest: | November 1 | |
| Fee: | $100 | **Degrees Granted** |
| AMCAS: | yes | MD, MD-PhD, MD-MBA |

### Enrollment: 2008–2009 First-Year Class

| Men: | 83 | 53% | Applied: | 2953 |
|---|---|---|---|---|
| Women: | 74 | 47% | Interviewed: | 569 |
| Minorities: | 5 | 3% | Enrolled: | 157 |
| Out of State: | 35 | 22% | | |

### 2008–2009 Class Profile

| *Mean MCAT Scores* | | *Mean GPA* |
|---|---|---|
| Physical Sciences: | 11.0 | 3.8 |
| Biological Sciences: | 11.0 | |
| Verbal Reasoning: | 11.0 | *Mean Science* |
| | | 3.8 |

**Tuition and Fees**

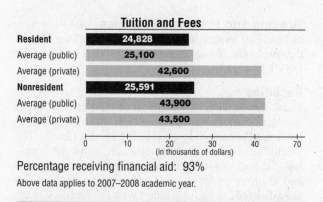

| | |
|---|---|
| **Resident** | 24,828 |
| Average (public) | 25,100 |
| Average (private) | 42,600 |
| **Nonresident** | 25,591 |
| Average (public) | 43,900 |
| Average (private) | 43,500 |

0   10   20   30   40   70
(in thousands of dollars)

Percentage receiving financial aid: 93%

Above data applies to 2007–2008 academic year.

## Introduction

The School of Medicine is one of the 4 components of the University of Colorado Health Sciences Center. The others are the schools of Dentistry and Nursing, and their Graduate School. The School of Medicine began in 1883 in Boulder. The first University Hospital was a 30-bed facility contracted in 1885, then relocated in 1911 to Denver, a city that offers many cultural and recreational facilities.

## Admissions (AMCAS)

Required courses include the minimum premedical science courses plus 1 year of college-level mathematics and English literature, and 1 semester of English composition. About 85% of the approximately 125 first-year openings are awarded to residents. *Transfer and advanced standing:* Applicants in good standing from approved U.S. medical schools will be considered, when openings occur, for admission to sophomore classes. Preference is given to Colorado residents. Colorado residents who have completed their basic sciences at nonaccredited medical schools must have successfully passed Step 1 of the USMLE before being considered for openings in the sophomore class.

## Curriculum

4-year semimodern. *First year:* Introductory basic sciences and courses in genetics and biometrics, as well as the first of a 3-year longitudinal course in primary care. *Second year:* Advanced basic sciences and courses in physical examination and preclerkship, pathophysiology of disease, clinical neurosciences, basic cardiac life support and primary care. *Third and fourth years:* Clerkship rotations through the major clinical specialties, electives, and free time. Seminars in minor clinical specialties are held throughout the school year. A large number of clinical and basic science opportunities are offered for the elective quarters. This allows students to major in certain specialties or subspecialties or to have experience in programs in community medicine, family medicine, or rural practice. It also provides for additional work in basic sciences or in laboratory research. An elective rural preceptorship is available, and participation in independent research during vacation is strongly encouraged. Among electives offered are courses in alcoholism, drug abuse, community medicine, ethical problems in medicine, geriatrics, health care delivery systems, human sexuality, occupational medicine, and environmental health hazards.

## Grading and Promotion Policies

System used is Honors/Pass/Fail. The performance of each student is considered by curriculum and promotion committees, which determine when students have satisfactorily completed appropriate coursework.

## Facilities

*Teaching:* Basic sciences are taught in the School of Medicine Building, which also has space for faculty offices and research laboratories. Clinical teaching takes place at the University Hospital (386 beds), at Colorado General Hospital (450 beds), at the VA Hospital (500 beds), and at Denver General Hospital (340 beds). *Other:* The Sabin Building for Cellular Research, the Webb-Waring Institute for Medical Research, the Clinical Research Wing of the Colorado General Hospital. *Library:* Denison Memorial Library is located in a building bearing the same name. The collection includes more than 150,000 volumes, and 2000 periodicals are received regularly. *Housing:* No residence halls available.

## Special Features

*Minority admissions:* A minority-group students program gives special consideration to the applicants, provides advisory and tutoring services, and grants financial aid for eligible students. The school also offers an 8-week summer course, Introduction to Medical Science, for some students. *Other degree programs:* Combined MD-PhD programs are offered in the basic medical sciences and in biometrics, biophysics, and genetics; there is a combined MD-MBA program.

# CONNECTICUT

# University of Connecticut School of Medicine

263 Farmington Avenue
Farmington, Connecticut    06030

*Phone:* 860-679-3874          *Fax:* 860-679-1282
*E-mail:* sanford@nso1.uchc.edu
*WWW:* www.uchc.edu

| Application Filing | | Accreditation | |
|---|---|---|---|
| Earliest: | June 1 | LCME | |
| Latest: | December 15 | | |
| Fee: | $95 | **Degrees Granted** | |
| AMCAS: | yes | MD, MD-PhD, | |
| | | MD-MPH, MD-MBA | |

### Enrollment: 2008–2009 First-Year Class

| Men: | 40 | 47% | Applied: | 2950 |
|---|---|---|---|---|
| Women: | 45 | 53% | Interviewed: | 384 |
| Minorities: | 13 | 15% | Enrolled: | 95 |
| Out of State: | 21 | 25% | | |

### 2008–2009 Class Profile

| *Mean MCAT Scores* | | *Mean GPA* |
|---|---|---|
| Physical Sciences: | 10.4 | 3.6 |
| Biological Sciences: | 10.2 | |
| Verbal Reasoning: | 10 | *Mean Science* |
| | | 3.6 |

**Tuition and Fees**

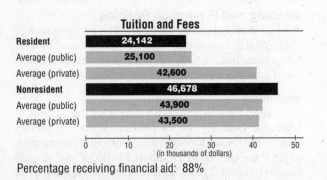

| | (in thousands of dollars) |
|---|---|
| Resident | 24,142 |
| Average (public) | 25,100 |
| Average (private) | 42,600 |
| Nonresident | 46,678 |
| Average (public) | 43,900 |
| Average (private) | 43,500 |

Percentage receiving financial aid: 88%

## Introduction

The University of Connecticut has been in existence since 1881. The School of Medicine was activated in 1968 and together with the School of Dental Medicine research facilities and the University Hospital and Ambulatory Unit forms the University of Connecticut Health Center. The campus is located on 162 wooded acres, 7 miles west of Hartford in scenic Farmington. Boston and New York are each about 2 hours away.

## Admissions (AMCAS)

Required courses include the basic premedical sciences. Applicants must demonstrate facility in quantitative and communicative skills. The faculty believes a broad liberal arts education provides the best preparation for those entering the medical profession. Strong preference is given to residents. *Transfer and advanced standing:* Third-year U.S. medical school transfers only.

## Curriculum

4-year modern. It consists of 3 phases: *Phase 1:* Extends for 2 years. The didactic portion requires 20 hours per week devoted to the basic concepts and facts of medicine. It will involve lectures, laboratories, and seminars. Problem-based learning sessions will lead to an understanding of the material in a clinical context. Areas to be covered include: human system, human development in its environment, mechanism of disease, student practice, introduction to clinical medicine, Elective 1, and practical clinical experiences. *Phase 2:* Extends over 1 year. It is divided into 3 months of required experiences, 2 months of selectives, and 6 months of electives. A student practice preceptorship extends over the entire 4 years. This curriculum is characterized by early clinical exposure, integrated and interdisciplinary relationships in the basic sciences and between the basic sciences and clinical disciplines, and clinical experiences in ambulatory and hospital settings. This approach is aimed at preparing professionals entering the evolving new health care system. The principal goal is to provide a fund of knowledge that will enable students to pursue postgraduate training needed in their future careers. By attaining basic competency, the graduate will ultimately be able to provide high-quality, cost-effective clinical care.

## Grading and Promotion Policies

A Pass/Fail system is used, with Honors/Pass/Fail in the third year. Students must pass Steps 1 and 2 of the USMLE.

## Facilities

*Teaching:* Students obtain most of their clinical experience in hospitals in the greater Hartford area and at the John Dempsey Hospital at the Health Center. The Health Center is a member of a consortium of hospitals that seeks to strengthen health education programs and improve patient care. Ten health care institutions are affiliated, and 11 are allied with the Health Center. *Library:* Lyman Maynard Stowe Library is centrally located in the Health Sciences Center. *Housing:* Provision for both single and married student housing is coordinated by the Office of Student Affairs.

## Special Features

*Minority admissions:* The school actively recruits disadvantaged applicants by visits to area institutions and participation in informational programs. The Medical/Dental Preparatory Program is an 8-week summer program that simulates the first year of basic medical sciences. Minority enrollment has averaged 15% or more in recent years. *Other degree programs:* MD-PhD programs are offered in a variety of disciplines including molecular biology and immunology.

# Yale University School of Medicine

367 Cedar Street
New Haven, Connecticut   06510

*Phone:* 203-785-2696          *Fax:* 203-785-3234
*E-mail:* medical.admissions@Yale.edu
*WWW:* info.med.Yale.edu

| Application Filing | | Accreditation | |
|---|---|---|---|
| Earliest: | June 1 | LCME | |
| Latest: | October 15 | | |
| Fee: | $85 | **Degrees Granted** | |
| AMCAS: | no | MD, MD-PhD, MD-JD | |
| | | MD-MPH, MD-MBA | |

### Enrollment: 2008–2009 First-Year Class

| | | | | | |
|---|---|---|---|---|---|
| Men: | 53 | 53% | Applied: | | 5021 |
| Women: | 47 | 47% | Interviewed: | | 998 |
| Minorities: | 13 | 13% | Enrolled: | | 100 |
| Out of State: | 86 | 86% | | | |

### 2008–2009 Class Profile

| *Mean MCAT Scores* | | *Mean GPA* |
|---|---|---|
| Physical Sciences: | 11 | 3.8 |
| Biological Sciences: | 11 | |
| Verbal Reasoning: | 10 | *Mean Science* |
| | | 3.8 |

**Tuition and Fees**

| | |
|---|---|
| Resident | 35,865 |
| Average (public) | 25,100 |
| Average (private) | 42,600 |
| Nonresident | 35,865 |
| Average (public) | 43,900 |
| Average (private) | 43,500 |

0    10    20    30    40    50
(in thousands of dollars)

Percentage receiving financial aid: 87%

Above data applies to 2007–2008 academic year.

## Introduction

This medical school was established by a state charter granted to Yale College in 1810. Subsequently, faculty members, local physicians, and other citizens raised funds that resulted in the New Haven Hospital, which served as a place to train medical students. In 1965 the hospital and the university became affiliated. The School of Medicine is a component of the Yale-New Haven Medical Center that also contains the School of Nursing and Yale-New Haven Hospital.

## Admissions

Courses in the basic premedical sciences are required. Students demonstrating proficiency in science by AP scores should substitute advanced courses. *Transfer and advanced standing:* Students studying at other medical schools, domestic or foreign, are not encouraged to apply. In a few cases, students are accepted into second or third year.

## Curriculum

*First year:* Four-year semimodern. The curriculum emphasizes normal biological form and function, and has been designed to coordinate information from various disciplines. It features a development approach to human behavior as related to health and illness. Anatomy and physiology are taught intensively two-thirds of the academic year. The first year includes a medicine, society, and public health series. Students are introduced to the principles and skills in medical interviewing and physical examination. *Second year:* The emphasis is on the disease process. A special feature is a series of all-day colloquia investigating diseases in an in-depth format. Basic principles of diagnostic radiology and laboratory medicine are included during the first 14 weeks. There are opportunities to enhance skills in history-taking and physical examination. The remaining 18 weeks feature modules in cardiovascular, clinical neuroscience and psychiatry, endocrine, female reproductive, GI/liver, lung/respiratory, musculoskeletal, renal/urinary tract, general oncology, and hematology. The medicine, society, and public health series continues. *Third and fourth years:* The clinical experience consists of direct patient care. Rotations include internal medicine and 3 subspecialties of surgery. There are clerkships in obstetrics and gynecology, psychiatry, pediatrics, clinical neuroscience, and primary care.

## Grading and Promotion Policies

It is not the policy of this school to grade its students, and numerical standings are not determined. The performance of the students is carefully evaluated and reported by the faculty. All students must also pass Step 1 and Step 2 of the USMLE as a threshold requirement for graduation.

## Facilities

*Teaching:* The school occupies several city blocks about one-half mile southwest of the University Center. Basic sciences are taught at the Jane Ellen Hope Building, Lander Hall, and Brady Memorial Laboratory. Clinical instruction takes place primarily at Yale-New Haven Hospital (900 beds) and the VA Hospital (513 beds) in West Haven. *Library:* Yale Medical Library is located in Sterling Hall and contains more than 380,000 volumes, receives 2600 journals, and has more than 90,000 other books of the last 2 centuries. The library is one of the country's largest medical libraries. *Housing:* Edward S. Harkness Memorial Hall provides living accommodations for single men and women and married students.

## Special Features

*Minority admissions:* The school receives a substantial number of minority group applications even though it does not have a special recruitment program. *Other degree programs:* Combined degree programs are available for an MD-PhD in a variety of disciplines including anthropology, biology, chemistry, economics, engineering, genetics, biophysics, and psychology. MD-MBA, MD-MPH, and MD-JD programs are also offered.

## DISTRICT OF COLUMBIA

# The George Washington University School of Medicine and Health Sciences

2300 Eye Street, N.W.
Washington, D.C.   20037

*Phone:* 202-994-3506          *Fax:* 202-994-1753
*E-mail:* medadmit@gwu.edu
*WWW:* www.gwumc.edu/admis/

| Application Filing | | Accreditation | |
|---|---|---|---|
| Earliest: | June 1 | LCME | |
| Latest: | January 1 | | |
| Fee: | $125 | **Degrees Granted** | |
| AMCAS: | yes | MD, MD-PhD, MD-MPH | |

### Enrollment: 2008–2009 First-Year Class

| Men: | 77 | 43% | Applied: | 13,082 |
|---|---|---|---|---|
| Women: | 100 | 57% | Interviewed: | 1046 |
| Minorities: | 34 | 19% | Enrolled: | 177 |
| Out of State: | | n/a | | |

### 2008–2009 Class Profile

| *Mean MCAT Scores* | | *Mean GPA* |
|---|---|---|
| Physical Sciences: | 9.7 | 3.6 |
| Biological Sciences: | 10.1 | |
| Verbal Reasoning: | 9.6 | *Mean Science* |
| | | 3.5 |

**Tuition and Fees**

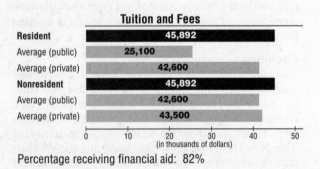

| | |
|---|---|
| **Resident** | 45,892 |
| Average (public) | 25,100 |
| Average (private) | 42,600 |
| **Nonresident** | 45,892 |
| Average (public) | 42,600 |
| Average (private) | 43,500 |

0   10   20   30   40   50
(in thousands of dollars)

Percentage receiving financial aid: 82%

## Introduction

The School of Medicine was established in 1825. In 1844 Congress granted it the use of the Washington Infirmary, establishing one the earliest general teaching hospitals in the country. The School of Medicine and Health Sciences is a component of the George Washington Medical Center, which includes the University Hospital, a Health Sciences Library, Medical Faculty Associates, and the School of Public Health and Health Services.

## Admissions (AMCAS)

Courses in English composition and literature are required in addition to the basic premedical science courses. Being a private institution, the school accepts students from almost every state. An early selection program for second-year GW undergraduates and other select schools is available. *Transfer and advanced standing:* Transfer students are accepted into the second- and third-year classes.

## Curriculum

4-year semitraditional. A course, Practice of Medicine (POM), in the first and second year introduces students to the clinical setting while also teaching the basic sciences. In the final two years, POM reinforces and reintegrates the basic sciences as students' clinical experience progresses. *First year:* Introduction to normal human biology and function, by means of the basic medical science courses. *Second year:* Focus on abnormal human biology with the introduction of pharmacology, pathology, microbiology, psychopathology taught initially in a core curriculum and then progressing to an interdisciplinary, organ-system-organized discussion of the pathology, pharmacology, and the natural history of disease. *Third year:* 8-week clerkships through the 5 major clinical disciplines and a 6-week primary care clerkship. *Fourth year:* Includes 37 weeks of course work and must include a 4-week "acting internship" in medicine, pediatrics, or family practice; three 2-week courses in anesthesiology, emergency medicine, and neuroscience; two 2-week courses to be selected from urology, orthopedics, otolaryngology, pediatric surgery, and ophthalmology; a course in medical decision making; and at least one didactic course offering. Students may spend some elective time at other institutions in the U.S. and abroad.

## Grading and Promotion Policies

System used is Honors/Pass/Conditional/Fail. Students must pass Step 1 and Step 2 of the USMLE.

## Facilities

*Teaching:* Walter G. Ross Hall is the basic science building. Clinical instruction takes place at the 371-bed University Hospital, as well as at numerous affiliated hospitals. The new GW Hospital opened in August 2002. The top floor of the new facility boasts an Educational Center for medical student and resident use. The Educational Center contains highly technical patient simulators, expanded standardized patient examination rooms, a computer resource center, and lounge/conference areas. *Library:* The Himmelfarb Health Sciences Library is expanding, with a capacity for 80,000 volumes. *Housing:* Limited university housing is available.

## Special Features

*Minority admissions:* Admissions committee members visit selected schools to discuss the school's program with minority students. *Other degree programs:* Combined MD-PhD degree programs are offered in the basic sciences as well as an MD-MPH program. There is a 7-year GW BA-MD. In addition, an 8-year BS-MD program is available through St. Bonaventure University.

# Georgetown University School of Medicine

Box 571421
Washington, D.C.  20057

*Phone:* 202-687-1154     *Fax:* 202-687-3079
*E-mail:* medicaladmissions@georgetown.edu
*WWW:* som.georgetown.edu

| Application Filing | | Accreditation |
|---|---|---|
| Earliest: | June 1 | LCME |
| Latest: | October 31 | |
| Fee: | $130 | **Degrees Granted** |
| AMCAS: | yes | MD, MD-PhD, MD/MS, MD-MBA |

### Enrollment: 2008–2009 First-Year Class

| Men: | 101 | 52% | Applied: | 11,237 |
|---|---|---|---|---|
| Women: | 93 | 48% | Interviewed: | 1124 |
| Minorities: | 14 | 7% | Enrolled: | 194 |
| Out of State: | 193 | 99% | | |

### 2008–2009 Class Profile

| *Mean MCAT Scores* | | *Mean GPA* |
|---|---|---|
| Physical Sciences: | 10.8 | 3.67 |
| Biological Sciences: | 11.0 | |
| Verbal Reasoning: | 10.2 | *Mean Science* |
| | | 3.7 |

**Tuition and Fees**

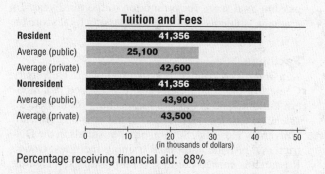

| | |
|---|---|
| Resident | 41,356 |
| Average (public) | 25,100 |
| Average (private) | 42,600 |
| Nonresident | 41,356 |
| Average (public) | 43,900 |
| Average (private) | 43,500 |

(in thousands of dollars)

Percentage receiving financial aid: 88%

## Introduction

Founded in 1851, this school is the oldest Jesuit and Catholic medical school in the United States. It is guided by the philosophy of "cura personalis," care for the whole person. Georgetown's mission is to educate knowledgeable, skillful, ethical, and compassionate physicians and biomedical scientists dedicated to the care of others and the health needs of society.

## Admissions (AMCAS)

Applicants are selected based on academics, character, maturity, and motivation. Evaluation of the applicants includes academics, MCAT scores, community service, medical and volunteer experiences, as well as the AMCAS scores, secondary essays, and comments from recommenders. Personal interviews are required and conducted on campus. *Transfer and advanced standing:* Students in good standing from LCME-accredited schools may apply to transfer into either the second or the third year. They are required to pass Step 1 of the USMLE.

## Curriculum

The curriculum offers a general professional, integrated education in medicine. The curriculum for the first two years uses a multidisciplinary approach to both the normal and abnormal human biological processes. The approach is a series of modular courses that grow in complexity. The first 2 years also provide students with an early introduction to the care of the patient. The third year provides a comprehensive introduction to the care of and responsibility for patients through clerkships in the major medical specialties. The fourth year offers a wide range of experiences giving each student substantial responsibility for the management of patient care. Students are required to complete an independent study project and to assist the underserved in community-based, or school-based, situations.

## Grading and Promotion Policies

The grading system consists of Honors, High Pass, Pass, and Fail. A student who receives a Fail in any course is considered academically deficient and has his or her status reviewed. A failure could lead to dismissal, repeating a year, or doing remedial work in a specific course. Passing Step 1 is required prior to entering the third year. Passing of both components of Step 2 is required for graduation.

## Facilities

*Teaching:* Basic sciences are taught in the School of Medicine Building, the Preclinical Science Building, the Basic Science Building, and the New Research Building. Clinical teaching and research takes place at the University Hospital and the 11 affiliates providing access to over 7,000 beds. Other students have access to all the federal libraries, museums, and agencies. Multiple free recreational activities are available including but not limited to biking, running, rock climbing, and canoeing. *Library:* Dahlgren Memorial Library, the Library of Congress, the National Library of Medicine, and the National Institutes of Health Library are available to faculty, staff, and students.

## Special Features

*Programs:* Georgetown offers a special admissions program for underrepresented and economically disadvantaged students, including a prematriculation year of study. An MD/PhD, MD/MBA, MD/MS program is also available. The Health Justice Scholar Track is an elective course designed to provide for medical students who have an interest in social justice and health advocacy.

# Howard University College of Medicine

520 W Street, N.W.
Washington, D.C.   20059

*Phone:* 202-806-6270        *Fax:* 202-265-0048
*E-mail:* hucmadmissions@howard.edu
*WWW:* med.howard.edu/

| Application Filing | | Accreditation |
|---|---|---|
| Earliest: | June 1 | LCME |
| Latest: | December 15 | |
| Fee: | $45 | **Degrees Granted** |
| AMCAS: | yes | MD, MD-PhD, BS-MD |

### Enrollment: 2008–2009 First-Year Class

| | | | | |
|---|---|---|---|---|
| Men: | 66 | 50% | Applied: | 5310 |
| Women: | 64 | 59% | Interviewed: | 328 |
| Minorities: | 96 | 49% | Enrolled: | 130 |
| Out of State: | 88 | 68% | | |

### 2008–2009 Class Profile

| *Mean MCAT Scores* | | *Mean GPA* |
|---|---|---|
| Physical Sciences: | 8 | 3.4 |
| Biological Sciences: | 8 | |
| Verbal Reasoning: | 9 | *Mean Science* |
| | | 3.4 |

### Tuition and Fees

| | |
|---|---|
| **Resident** | 29,846 |
| Average (public) | 25,100 |
| Average (private) | 42,600 |
| **Nonresident** | 29,846 |
| Average (public) | 43,900 |
| Average (private) | 43,500 |

0    10    20    30    40    50
(in thousands of dollars)

Percentage receiving financial aid: 92%

Above data applies to 2007–2008 academic year.

## Introduction

This is the oldest and largest African-American medical school in the country. It began in 1868 as the university's medical department, with the goal of training physicians in medically underserved areas. Its students come from all over the world and its alumni make up a significant segment of the nation's minority physicians.

## Admissions (AMCAS)

Requirements include a minimum of 62 credits (2 years) of undergraduate work, plus minimum premedical science courses and 1 year of English and college mathematics. There are no residence restrictions; 70% of the students are African-American; about 50% are women. Selection is based not only on academic achievements and personal qualities, but also on the likelihood of practice in communities or facilities needing physician services. *Transfer and advanced standing:* Placement is infrequent, and usually at the end of the second year. Foreign transfers are not accepted.

## Curriculum

4-year modern. Program is flexible in order to produce the physician-scientist. *First year:* Core concept presentation of introductory basic sciences and interdisciplinary courses, plus optional electives. *Second year:* Continued core concept presentation of advanced basic sciences plus interdisciplinary courses in pathophysiology of organ systems, infectious diseases, and physical diagnosis. Elective courses are offered. *Third year:* A series of clerkships through the major clinical specialties. Possibility for involvement in community health care is also provided. *Fourth year:* A 9-month program similar to junior year, except that periods of specialization are increased by allotment of 24 weeks of elective time (4 of which can be used for vacation). A 5-year curriculum is offered to students who demonstrate academic difficulty during the first semester. This curriculum does not require taking additional courses, but it extends the standard one over a 5-year period.

## Grading and Promotion Policies

System used is the Honors/Satisfactory/Unsatisfactory. Students must take Step 1 of the USMLE and obtain a passing total score for promotion to the third year. To graduate, students must record a passing total score on Step 2.

## Facilities

*Teaching:* The college is part of Howard University Center for the Health Sciences. It is housed in a modern building and is the site for teaching basic medical sciences. Clinical teaching is at the 300-bed Howard University Hospital. Several other hospitals in the District area provide additional training facilities. *Other:* Research is carried out in several buildings, including a Cancer Center. *Library:* The Health Sciences Library contains more than 265,000 volumes, and 1750 periodicals. National Institutes of Health and National Library of Medicine are available to students. *Housing:* Professional students are not usually allocated accommodations on campus, but a university-owned apartment complex is nearby.

## Special Features

*Minority admissions:* The college is dedicated to training minority applicants and has a strong recruitment program that includes early admission and academic reinforcement for admitted students. *Other degree programs:* A dual-degree program is available for the MD-PhD in most of the basic sciences; a BS-MD program is also offered. Both degrees may be obtained in a 6-year period. Continuing education is available for graduates.

# FLORIDA

# Florida International University College of Medicine

1200 SW 8th Street
Miami, Florida   33199

*Phone:* 305-348-0644          *Fax:* 305-348-0650
*E-mail:* med.admission@fiu.edu
*WWW:* medicine.fiu.edu/admissions

| Application Filing | | Accreditation |
|---|---|---|
| Earliest: | June 1 | n/a |
| Latest: | October 15 | **Degrees Granted** |
| Fee: | $30 | n/a |
| AMCAS: | yes | |

### Enrollment: 2008–2009 First-Year Class

| Men: | n/a | Applied: | n/a |
|---|---|---|---|
| Women: | n/a | Interviewed: | n/a |
| Minorities: | n/a | Enrolled: | n/a |
| Out-of-State: | n/a | | |

### 2008–2009 Class Profile

| *Mean MCAT Scores* | | *Mean GPA* |
|---|---|---|
| Physical Sciences: | n/a | n/a |
| Biological Sciences: | n/a | *Mean Science* |
| Verbal Reasoning: | n/a | n/a |

**Tuition and Fees**

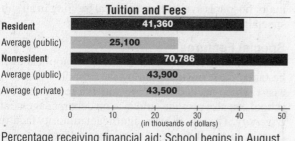

| | |
|---|---|
| Resident | 41,360 |
| Average (public) | 25,100 |
| Nonresident | 70,786 |
| Average (public) | 43,900 |
| Average (private) | 43,500 |

0    10    20    30    40    50
(in thousands of dollars)

Percentage receiving financial aid: School begins in August 2009. No data available yet.

## Introduction

The medical school is part of a multicampus university serving South Florida in general and Miami in particular. The school is housed in the 544-acre University Park Campus, offering ready access to the international airport, cultural centers, and social outlets. The inaugural class for this school will initiate studies in August 2009, with a class of 40 students. The four-year educational and training program is designed to provide in-depth exposure to all major areas of medicine. The specific focus of the program will be on family and community medicine. The aim of the College of Medicine will be to have a positive impact on medical education as well as to elevate the level of patient care for the Florida community.

## Admissions (AMCAS)

Selection will be based on the secondary (AMCAS) application, letters of recommendation, and interview assessment as viewed by the Admissions Committee. The school will seek individuals whose academic background has been rigorous and who have high moral and ethical standards. The applicants should be able to demonstrate clear evidence of their interest in medicine as reflected by their degree of and participation in one or more medical assistance settings, being altruistic and having a genuine interest in learning. Evidence of and a desire for communal service are valuable, as is strong interpersonal skills. Essentially, what is sought are acceptable candidates, young people with the intellectual potential and personal attributes to develop into competent and compassionate physicians.

## Curriculum

The educational program is organized as a 4-year program of integrated studies. The curriculum has 5 pathways: (1) Clinical Medicine, Disease, Illness, and Injury, (2) Human Biology as reflected in the basic medical sciences, (3) Medicine and Society, (4) Professional Development, and (5) Statistical and Evidence-based Medicine. Curricular innovations include a goal of enabling students to understand the factors that affect personal and community health care. To attain relevant exposure, students will work with families and communities as part of interdisciplinary teams involving representatives from public health, nursing and social work schools. Community service will be required. Thesis-based research is optional.

## Grading and Promotion Policies
Information not available.

## Facilities
Information not available.

## Special Features
*Financial aid:* Demonstrated need on the part of the accepted applicant for financial aid; must be provided in the form of scholarships, low-interest loans. *Housing:* There exists state-of-the-art on-campus housing, available to students. This is supplemented by a residential counseling program. Necessary forms to apply for campus housing are available. Off-campus housing is also available.

# University of Central Florida College of Medicine

2201 Research Parkway
P.O. Box 60116
Orlando, Florida   32816

*Phone:* 407-823-4244          *Fax:* 407-823-4048
*E-mail:* mdadmissions@mail.ucf.edu

| Application Filing | | Accreditation |
|---|---|---|
| Earliest: | June 1 | n/a |
| Latest: | December 1 | **Degrees Granted** |
| Fee: | yes | n/a |
| AMCAS: | yes | |

### Enrollment: 2008–2009 First-Year Class

| Men: | n/a | Applied: | n/a |
|---|---|---|---|
| Women: | n/a | Interviewed: | n/a |
| Minorities: | n/a | Enrolled: | n/a |
| Out-of-State: | n/a | | |

### 2008–2009 Class Profile

| *Mean MCAT Scores* | | *Mean GPA* |
|---|---|---|
| Physical Sciences: | n/a | n/a |
| Biological Sciences: | n/a | *Mean Science* |
| Verbal Reasoning: | n/a | n/a |

### Tuition and Fees

| | |
|---|---|
| Resident | 22,500 |
| Average (public) | 25,100 |
| Nonresident | 42,500 |
| Average (public) | 43,500 |
| Average (private) | 43,900 |

0    10    20    30    40    50
(in thousands of dollars)

Percentage receiving financial aid: n/a

## Introduction

This school will initiate its program of medical education with its charter class in August 2009. The school will strive for excellence in education, health care delivery, and research. It will also seek to promote public health. To attain these goals, the school will utilize the services of prominent physicians and scholars in research and technology as well as distinguished educators.

## Admissions (AMCAS)

Completing an AMCAS or supplementary application is essential. The Interview Committee members will seek to identify prospective students who are highly motivated, academically proven, and compassionate, and have diverse skills and experiences relevant to the medical profession.

## Curriculum

The program involves a blending of state-of-the-art technology, utilization of virtual patients, both clinical and laboratory experiences, directed small-group sessions, interactive didactic lectures, and research. The first 2 years of the curriculum are structured into modules. The initial year of basic sciences focuses on the relationship between the human body and disease. The second year uses an organ system-based approach in relation to the study of pathological processes and clinical diseases, in terms of diagnosis and treatment. Substantial clinical exposure will be provided during the first 2 years. The third and fourth years are devoted essentially to clinical experience and core clerkships. The program has required community service activities and research obligations.

## Grading and Promotion Policies

Information not available.

## Facilities

Students will have training opportunities at Orlando Regional Hospital and Florida Hospital Systems, as well as the Veteran Affairs Hospital. There will be other major hospitals available for clinical training in all subspecialties.

## Special Features

*Financial aid:* The financial status of the applicant will be taken into consideration by the school, which will assist where needed to secure suitable resources. The school can also provide guidance on debt management.
*Diversity:* The school has a significant minority faculty. It seeks to enroll qualified minority students.

# University of Florida College of Medicine

Gainesville, Florida    32610

*Phone:* 352-392-4569          *Fax:* 352-392-1307
*E-mail:* robyn@dean.medufl.edu
*WWW:* med.ufl.edu

| Application Filing | | Accreditation | |
|---|---|---|---|
| Earliest: | June 1 | LCME | |
| Latest: | December 1 | | |
| Fee: | 30 | **Degrees Granted** | |
| AMCAS: | yes | MD, MD-PhD, | |
| | | BS-MD, MD-MBA, | |
| | | MD-MPH, MD-JD | |

### Enrollment: 2008–2009 First-Year Class

| Men: | 70 | 52% | Applied: | 2847 |
|---|---|---|---|---|
| Women: | 65 | 48% | Interviewed: | 360 |
| Minorities: | 21 | 16% | Enrolled: | 135 |
| Out of State: | 8 | 23% | | |

### 2008–2009 Class Profile

| *Mean MCAT Scores* | | *Mean GPA* |
|---|---|---|
| Physical Sciences: | 10.8 | 3.73 |
| Biological Sciences: | 11.1 | |
| Verbal Reasoning: | 9.9 | *Mean Science* |
| | | 3.66 |

### Tuition and Fees

| | |
|---|---|
| **Resident** | 23,930 |
| Average (public) | 25,100 |
| Average (private) | 42,600 |
| **Nonresident** | 51,777 |
| Average (public) | 43,900 |
| Average (private) | 43,500 |

0    10    20    30    40    50
(in thousands of dollars)

Percentage receiving financial aid: 85%

## Introduction

This medical school began in 1956 and occupies the southeast corner of the 2000-acre University of Florida campus. It is a component of the University of Florida Health Sciences Center, which also consists of colleges of Dentistry, Veterinary Medicine, Nursing, Pharmacy, and Public Health and Health Professions.

## Admissions (AMCAS)

Only the minimum premedical science courses plus biochemistry (with lab) are required. The college gives preference to those who have completed the requirements for a bachelor's degree and who are state residents. Very few of the class are nonresidents; out-of-state applicants should have a 3.9 or better GPA. Selection is based on academic record, MCAT scores, letters of recommendation, and personal attributes. *Transfer and advanced standing:* Transfer is rarely possible.

## Curriculum

4-year semitraditional. *First year:* In addition to the basic sciences, courses in diagnostic imaging, patient care, human behavior, and molecular genetics are presented. *Second year:* Advanced basic sciences, courses in ophthalmology, radiology, physical diagnosis, and ethics are offered. *Third year:* Eight clinical clerkships extending over 52 weeks. *Fourth year:* Surgical and medical clerkships, coursework, and electives in selected categorical areas related to medicine within the medical school or at 2 nonuniversity settings. During the first summer and elective period, students may become involved in research. The option also exists for extending the preclinical basic science program courses over a 3-year period.

## Grading and Promotion Policies

The system used is letter/number but some courses use a Pass/Fail system. At the end of each quarter the Committee on Academic Status reviews each student's performance on the basis of grades and comments by faculty and recommends suitable action to the dean. Students who receive Fs in 2 major courses in one semester will be dropped automatically. In order to graduate, the student must pass Step 1 and take Step 2 of the USMLE.

## Facilities

*Teaching:* Basic sciences are taught in J. Hillis Miller Health Center, which includes the Shands Teaching Hospital (850 beds). Clinical teaching also takes place at the nearby VA Hospital (450 beds). *Other:* Research facilities are present in the Health Center, VA Hospital, and Academic Research Building, Genetic Institutes. *Library:* The Health Center Library has a collection of more than 193,000 books and periodicals. Computer-based retrieval services are available. *Housing:* Accommodations are available for single students in Beaty Towers and Schucht Village, and for married students in Cory, University, Maguire, and Diamond Memorial Villages. The latter contain 1-, 2-, and some 3-bedroom apartments.

## Special Features

*Minority admissions:* The college encourages underrepresented applicants from minority groups. A summer workshop for new minority matriculants is sponsored annually. It is an orientation and academic preparation program. *Other degree programs:* The school offers a Junior Honors Medical Program that allows college juniors to enroll in basic medical science seminars and undergraduate courses. During their senior year they become full-time medical students and receive their baccalaureate at year's end. Several dual-degree programs are also offered, including a funded MD/PhD track for those desiring academic careers.

# University of Miami Miller School of Medicine

P.O. Box 016159
Miami, Florida  33101

*Phone:* 305-243-6791          *Fax:* 305-243-6548
*E-mail:* med.admissions@miami.edu
*WWW:* http://www.miami.edu/medical-admissions

| Application Filing | | Accreditation |
|---|---|---|
| Earliest: | June 1 | LCME |
| Latest: | December 1 | |
| Fee: | $65 | **Degrees Granted** |
| AMCAS: | yes | MD, MD-PhD |

### Enrollment: 2008–2009 First-Year Class

| | | | | |
|---|---|---|---|---|
| Men: | 101 | 57% | Applied: | 4426 |
| Women: | 75 | 43% | Interviewed: | 494 |
| Minorities: | 11 | 6% | Enrolled: | 176 |
| Out of State: | 32 | 18% | | |

### 2008–2009 Class Profile

| *Mean MCAT Scores* | | *Mean GPA* |
|---|---|---|
| Physical Sciences: | 11.0 | 3.8 |
| Biological Sciences: | 11.0 | |
| Verbal Reasoning: | 10.0 | *Mean Science* |
| | | 3.7 |

**Tuition and Fees**

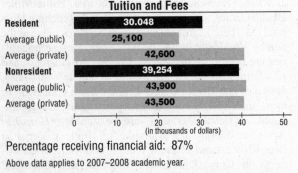

| | |
|---|---|
| Resident | 30.048 |
| Average (public) | 25,100 |
| Average (private) | 42,600 |
| Nonresident | 39,254 |
| Average (public) | 43,900 |
| Average (private) | 43,500 |

0   10   20   30   40   50
(in thousands of dollars)

Percentage receiving financial aid: 87%
Above data applies to 2007–2008 academic year.

## Introduction

This is the oldest and largest medical school in Florida and was established in 1952. The School of Medicine is located next to Jackson Memorial Hospital in the Civic Center area of Miami. The school has undergone considerable growth and is especially noted for its extensive research. As a result of its growth, this medical school has developed into one of the largest and most comprehensive medical centers nationwide. The school has a large full-time faculty and receives numerous research grants. The school's affiliated hospitals provide upper-class students with excellent clinical training experiences because of their large number of admissions and the broad spectrum of cases seen.

## Admissions (AMCAS)

Required courses include minimum premedical science courses plus 2 semesters of English. Biochemistry is recommended. The school gives preference to residents. Those nonresidents who have especially attractive academic records and MCAT scores should consider applying. In addition to one's undergraduate scholastic record and aptitude test scores, such considerations as interpersonal skills, motivation, maturity, and leadership ability are considered. Selected individuals are invited to the medical campus for an interview in order to complete the admissions process. Acceptances are sent out on a rolling admission basis until the class of about 182 is filled. *Transfer and advanced standing:* Not available.

## Curriculum

4-year modern. *First year:* Designed to provide the student with a background of normal structure, function, and behavior. Basic sciences are integrated into study of organ systems. These courses include gross anatomy, cell biophysics, neuroscience, biochemistry, and systemic physiology. The latter is an interdisciplinary course dealing with structure and function of organ systems. The Community Clinical Experience runs throughout the first and second years. It provides a setting in which students acquire clinical skills through direct patient contact from the beginning of the freshman year. *Second year:* Initial weeks are devoted to general concepts of advanced basic sciences. A major course in mechanisms of disease emphasizes the disease processes that affect various organ systems. The transition to third-year work is prepared for by physical diagnosis. *Third year:* Consists of clerkship rotations through the major clinical specialties. *Fourth year:* Consists of electives. Students may select from a number of programs at the school and at other institutions, if approved. Students may choose from clinical (direct patient care and consultative care), academic, and research electives.

## Facilities

*Teaching:* Basic sciences are taught in the Rosenstiel Medical Sciences Building. Clinical teaching takes place at Jackson Memorial Hospital (1500 beds) and the VA hospital (900 beds). *Other:* Bascom Palmer Eye Institute, Sylvester Comprehensive Cancer Center, Diabetes Research Institute, Ryder Trauma (Level 1) Center, Miami Project to Cure Paralysis. *Library:* The Calder Memorial Library houses more than 180,000 volumes and more than 2100 periodicals. *Housing:* No student housing exists at present.

## Special Features

*Minority admissions:* Applications from women and socioeconomically disadvantaged candidates are encouraged, as are those from older applicants. *Other degree programs:* MD-PhD program for qualified applicants with extensive prior research experience.

# University of South Florida College of Medicine

12901 Bruce B. Downs Boulevard
Tampa, Florida    33612

*Phone:* 813-974-2229          *Fax:* 813-974-4990
*E-mail:* md-admissions@health.usf.edu
*WWW:* hsc.usf.edu

| Application Filing | | Accreditation |
|---|---|---|
| Earliest: | July 6 | LCME |
| Latest: | December 1 | |
| Fee: | $30 | **Degrees Granted** |
| AMCAS: | yes | MD, MD-PhD, MD-MPH, |
| | | MD-MBA, MD-JD |

### Enrollment: 2008–2009 First-Year Class

| Men: | 57 | 48% | Applied: | 2494 |
|---|---|---|---|---|
| Women: | 63 | 52% | Interviewed: | 400 |
| Minorities: | 16 | 13% | Enrolled: | 120 |
| Out of State: | 11 | 9% | | |

### 2008–2009 Class Profile

| *Mean MCAT Scores* | | *Mean GPA* |
|---|---|---|
| Physical Sciences: | 10.0 | 3.7 |
| Biological Sciences: | 11.0 | |
| Verbal Reasoning: | 9.7 | *Mean Science* |
| | | 3.6 |

**Tuition and Fees**

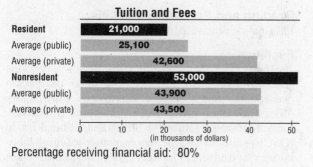

| | |
|---|---|
| **Resident** | 21,000 |
| Average (public) | 25,100 |
| Average (private) | 42,600 |
| **Nonresident** | 53,000 |
| Average (public) | 43,900 |
| Average (private) | 43,500 |

(in thousands of dollars)

Percentage receiving financial aid: 80%

## Introduction

This school, established in 1971, is one of the 3 colleges of the University of South Florida Health Sciences Center. Its location on a 1600-acre site of the northeast section of Tampa, which is an expanding metropolitan area of over 3 million people, has enhanced the rapid growth of the institution.

## Admissions (AMCAS)

Required courses include the minimum premedical science courses plus 2 semesters of English and mathematics. It is recommended that the MCAT be taken in the spring of the year of application and that the required sciences be completed at the time of application. Coursework in communication, arts, humanities, and natural sciences is encouraged. Applicants who present a bachelor's degree from a liberal arts college are preferred. A 3-year applicant must present a superior academic record and demonstrated maturity. To be competitive, Florida residents should have a GPA of 3.0 or better on a 4.0 scale and score at a minimum of 24 on the MCAT. *Transfer and advanced standing:* Information is available on the Web site.

## Curriculum

4-year semitraditional. The 4-year curriculum is designed to permit the student to learn the fundamental principles of medicine, to acquire skills of critical judgment based on evidence and experience, and to develop an ability to use principles and skills wisely in solving problems in health and disease. It includes the sciences basic to medicine, the major clinical disciplines, and other significant elements such as behavioral science, medical ethics, and human values. The intent is to foster in students the ability to learn through self-directed, independent study throughout their professional lives. Using both ambulatory and hospital settings, students are given increasing responsibility for patient care in preparation to enter graduate medical education residencies.

## Grading and Promotion Policies

Students' performance in academic coursework will be evaluated by assignment of grades of Honors (H), Pass with Commendation (PC), Pass (P), Fail (F), or Incomplete (I). Passing grades are H, PC, and P in order of excellence. Deficient grades are F or I. The F or I grade may be given to a student who fails to complete course requirements or who fails to attend or participate in required course activities.

## Facilities

The USF Health Sciences Center offers hospital educational opportunities at facilities with more than 3500 patient beds. The primary teaching facilities are H.L. Moffitt Cancer Center and Research Institute, James A. Haley Veterans' Hospital, and Tampa General Hospital. The university's 538 College of Medicine faculty members work both on and off campus. Health Sciences Center affiliates for clinical education also include the following: USF Medical Clinic, University Diagnostic Clinic, University Psychiatry Center, All Childrens' Hospital, Bayfront Medical Center, Bay Pines Veterans' Hospital, and the Shriner Hospital for Crippled Children.

## Special Features

*Minority admissions:* Special efforts are made to encourage qualified minority students to apply. *Other degree programs:* The school has an MD-PhD program for a select few students interested in a research career. Likewise, students interested in public health, preventive medicine, epidemiology, health care systems, or related areas can secure an MD-MPH degree. This degree requires minimal additional time and is awarded by The College of Public Health. Special programs are available for those interested in primary care. An MD-MBA degree is awarded in concert with the College of Business.

## GEORGIA

# Emory University School of Medicine

1440 Clifton Road, NE
Atlanta, Georgia   30322

*Phone:* 404-727-5655          *Fax:* 404-727-0045
*E-mail:* medadmiss@emory.edu
*WWW:* med.emory.edu

| Application Filing | | Accreditation |
|---|---|---|
| Earliest: | June 15 | LCME |
| Latest: | October 15 | |
| Fee: | $100 | **Degrees Granted** |
| AMCAS: | yes | MD, MD-PhD, |
| | | MD-MSCR |

### Enrollment: 2008–2009 First-Year Class

| | | | | | |
|---|---|---|---|---|---|
| Men: | 62 | 47% | Applied: | 4014 |
| Women: | 70 | 53% | Interviewed: | 682 |
| Minorities: | 83 | 63% | Enrolled: | 132 |
| Out of State: | 32 | 24% | | |

### 2008–2009 Class Profile

| *Mean MCAT Scores* | | *Mean GPA* |
|---|---|---|
| Physical Sciences: | 11.6 | 3.7 |
| Biological Sciences: | 11.6 | |
| Verbal Reasoning: | 10.8 | *Mean Science* |
| | | 3.74 |

### Tuition and Fees

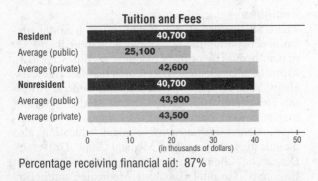

| | |
|---|---|
| **Resident** | 40,700 |
| Average (public) | 25,100 |
| Average (private) | 42,600 |
| **Nonresident** | 40,700 |
| Average (public) | 43,900 |
| Average (private) | 43,500 |

(in thousands of dollars)

Percentage receiving financial aid: 87%

## Introduction

Emory is a privately controlled university affiliated with the Methodist Church. The Emory University School of Medicine was established in 1915. The forerunner of this school was the Atlanta Medical College, which was established in 1856. This school was merged with Southern Medical College to form the Atlantic College of Physicians and Surgeons and a subsequent merger took place with the Atlanta School of Medicine in 1905. In 1915 the name was changed to Emory University School of Medicine. It is located on 620 acres in the Druid Hills section of Atlanta.

## Admissions (AMCAS)

In addition to the traditional requirements of one year each of biology, chemistry, physics, and organic chem-

istry, Emory also requires 6 semester hours of English and 18 semester hours of humanities and behavioral/social science course work. The MCAT is required. For applicants who have retaken the exam, the best set of scores is typically weighted most heavily. Emory operates a rolling admissions process.

## Curriculum

The curriculum is divided into four phases: *Phase 1:* Foundations of Medicine (18 months). This phase provides students with the core knowledge of basic and clinical sciences. *Phase 2:* Applications of Medical Sciences (12 months). This phase provides students with core knowledge of the basic clinical medical specialties. *Phase 3:* Discovery (5 months). This phase is a structured time for students to concentrate in a specific area of interest, such as basic or clinical research, public health, community development, medical ethics, or other areas. *Phase 4:* Translation of Medical Sciences (9 months). This phase prepares the student for the transition to physician. Rotations as a subintern; advanced clinical work in an ICU; experience in the Emergency Department; and a final capstone course prior to graduation are required. An integral part of the curriculum involves expansion of the current Society System. There are four clinician advisors in each one of four societies. Every student is assigned to a society and has a society advisor. These faculty members are teachers of clinical skills and small group mentors. The society advisor-student role continues until a student graduates.

## Grading and Promotion Policies

Information not available.

## Facilities

*Teaching:* The Medical Education Building contains state-of-the-art facilities including three 160-person classrooms, four 40-person classrooms with faculty offices, 19 small group rooms, a 4-room Simulation Suite, a 16-room Objective Structured Clinical Exam (OSCE) suite, two 75-person computer-teaching laboratories, and a student lounge. Clinical instruction takes place at Emory University Hospital, Grady Memorial Hospital, the VA Hospital, Crawford Long Hospital, Children's Hospital, and Children's Health of Atlanta at Egleston ambulatory primary care and outpatient facilities throughout the metropolitan area. *Library:* The Woodruff Health Sciences Center Library has more than 250,000 volumes and 1,800 periodicals. Other clinical libraries are located in Emory University, as well as Crawford Long and Grady hospitals. *Housing:* Opportunities to rent or own close to the campus are affordable and abundant. A new graduate housing facility is scheduled to open in 2009.

## Special Features

MD-PhD, MD-MPH, and MD-MSCR programs are available to students accepted to the MD program.

# Medical College of Georgia School of Medicine

1120 15th Street
Augusta, Georgia 30912

*Phone:* 706-721-3186 *Fax:* 706-721-0959
*E-mail:* stdadmin@mail.mcg.edu
*WWW:* www.mcg.edu

| Application Filing | | Accreditation | |
|---|---|---|---|
| Earliest: | June 1 | LCME | |
| Latest: | November 1 | | |
| Fee: | no | **Degrees Granted** | |
| AMCAS: | yes | MD, MD-PhD | |

### Enrollment: 2008–2009 First-Year Class

| | | | | | |
|---|---|---|---|---|---|
| Men: | 110 | 58% | Applied: | 1950 | |
| Women: | 80 | 42% | Interviewed: | 482 | |
| Minorities: | 11 | 6% | Enrolled: | 190 | |
| Out of State: | 2 | 11% | | | |

### 2008–2009 Class Profile

| *Mean MCAT Scores* | | *Mean GPA* |
|---|---|---|
| Physical Sciences: | 10 | 3.8 |
| Biological Sciences: | 11 | |
| Verbal Reasoning: | 10 | *Mean Science* |
| | | 3.7 |

**Tuition and Fees**

| | |
|---|---|
| **Resident** | 14,237 |
| Average (public) | 25,100 |
| Average (private) | 42,600 |
| **Nonresident** | 31,663 |
| Average (public) | 43,900 |
| Average (private) | 43,500 |

(in thousands of dollars)

Percentage receiving financial aid: 78%

Above data applies to 2007–2008 academic year.

## Introduction

The University System of Georgia includes all state-operated institutions of higher education. The school is part of this system. The medical school, founded in 1828, is located in Augusta, which is on the south bank of the Savannah River, midway between the Great Smoky Mountains and the Atlantic Coast.

## Admissions (AMCAS)

The basic premedical science courses are required as well as courses in English sufficient to satisfy baccalaureate degree requirements. Biochemistry is recommended. Very strong preference is given to state residents, as well as to candidates with 4 years of undergraduate work. Only up to 5% of nonresidents will be admitted in any given year. Potential nonresident applicants need to have especially strong credentials to be given serious consideration. Selection is made on the basis of an assessment of the applicant's achievements and potential based on credentials and recommendations received, MCAT scores, and interview performance. *Transfer and advanced standing:* Applicants from other MD programs are considered on a space-available basis.

## Curriculum

4-year modern. *First and second years:* During the preclinical years, students acquire the building blocks of basic science and the skills required for clinical decision making and patient interaction. The modular content of the curriculum is taught in lectures, labs with integrated clinical conferences, and small-group activities. The year begins with the cellular and Systems Processes Module and a Brain and Behavior Module. Offered concurrently with the basic science modules, the yearlong Essentials and Clinical Medicine course emphasizes family, cultural, and population aspects of health care, communication skills, information retrieval and analysis, health promotion/disease prevention, ethics, history taking with children and adults, and a community project. The Essentials of Clinical Medicine course is a 2-year sequence that emphasizes those skills needed to prepare students for the third year. *Second year:* Essentials of Clinical Medicine addresses interviewing and physical examination, common medical problems, and interdisciplinary topics such as ethics, nutrition, and the impact of behavior on health while highlighting principles of patient care for each stage of life. Cellular and Systems Disease States is a yearlong module divided into 5 systems-based blocks. In this module, students are exposed to the topics of medical microbiology, pathology, and pharmacology in the context of clinical medicine. *Third year:* The required core clerkships: in internal medicine, pediatrics, family medicine, ob/gyn, surgery, psychiatry, and neurology. *Fourth year:* Students must complete 4-week rotations in emergency medicine, critical care, and an acting internship in medicine, family medicine, or pediatrics. The remainder of the fourth year is for elective study, which can include both clinical and research courses.

## Grading and Promotion Policies

Letter grades are used. Steps 1 and 2 of the USMLE are required of all students.

## Facilities

*Teaching:* Basic sciences are taught primarily in the Research and Education Building. Clinical teaching takes place at the Medical College of Georgia Hospital and Clinics (540 beds) and affiliated hospitals and practice sites in the city and across the state. *Library:* The library houses more than 164,000 volumes and 1230 periodicals. Access to electronic databases and interlibrary loan is available. *Housing:* Accommodations are available in 4 residence halls for single students. One- and 2-bedroom apartments are available for married students.

## Special Features

*Minority admissions:* The college conducts an intensive recruitment program and is committed to increasing minority representation in the student body. *Other degree programs:* MD-PhD programs are offered in a variety of disciplines including endocrinology.

# Mercer University School of Medicine

1550 College Street
Macon, Georgia    31207

*Phone:* 478-301-2524      *Fax:* 478-301-2547
*E-mail:* admissions@mercer.edu
*WWW:* medicine.mercer.edu/

| Application Filing | | Accreditation |
|---|---|---|
| Earliest: | June 1 | LCME |
| Latest: | November 1 | |
| Fee: | $50 | **Degrees Granted** |
| AMCAS: | yes | MD |

## Enrollment: 2008–2009 First-Year Class

| | | | | |
|---|---|---|---|---|
| Men: | 46 | 51% | Applied: | 784 |
| Women: | 40 | 49% | Interviewed: | 290 |
| Minorities: | 14 | 15% | Enrolled: | 90 |
| Out of State: | 0 | 0% | | |

## 2008–2009 Class Profile

| *Mean MCAT Scores* | | *Mean GPA* |
|---|---|---|
| Physical Sciences: | 8.7 | 3.6 |
| Biological Sciences: | 9.4 | |
| Verbal Reasoning: | 9.3 | *Mean Science* |
| | | 3.5 |

**Tuition and Fees**

| | (in thousands of dollars) |
|---|---|
| Resident | 37,200 |
| Average (public) | 25,100 |
| Average (private) | 42,600 |
| Nonresident | 37,200 |
| Average (public) | 43,900 |
| Average (private) | 43,500 |

Percentage receiving financial aid: 87%

## Introduction

This school, founded in 1982, has the special mission of training physicians whose service will help meet the health care needs of rural and other underserved areas of Georgia. Located in Macon, in the heart of central Georgia, it is within driving distance of both Atlanta and Savannah.

## Admissions (AMCAS)

The basic premedical science courses are required. Biochemistry is highly recommended. Applicants with rural backgrounds are encouraged to apply. To date, only legal residents of Georgia have been allowed to apply. Selection is based on demonstrated academic achievement and evidence of potential. Applicants are sought who share the school's mission of seeking to serve the health care needs of rural and other underserved areas of Georgia. The school requires a supplementary application in addition to the AMCAS application, as well as a minimum of 2 letters of reference. *Transfer and advanced standing:* Transfer students from LCME-accredited medical schools are considered for admission into the junior year. Applicants must be legal residents of Georgia.

## Curriculum

4-year problem-based. A 4-program educational scheme is used to train physicians for service in rural and/or medically underserved areas of Georgia. *Program 1 (Biomedical Problems):* During this 74-week program groups of 6 to 7 students work with faculty in a tutorial setting to study the basic medical and behavioral science concepts that underlie medical problems. The array and the sequence of problems are chosen to ensure that students acquire the basic medical and behavioral science knowledge requisite to medical practice. *Program 2 (Fundamentals of Clinical Practice):* This occurs throughout the first 2 years during which students learn the skills basic for interaction with patients. Students interview and examine actual and standardized patients and have opportunities to practice their skills in the offices of supervising community physicians. *Program 3 (Community Medicine):* This program spans 4 years. Initially, students attend seminars and group discussions on biostatistics, epidemiology, and public health. Each student is assigned to a rural community and makes site visits to learn about medical practice and the health care needs of the area. In the fourth year this culminates in a 4-week community-based primary care clerkship during which the student lives in the community and participates in the practice of the supervising physician. *Program 4 (Clerkships-Electives):* The third year contains rotations in internal medicine, surgery, ambulatory family medicine, pediatrics, obstetrics/gynecology, and psychiatry. During year 4, critical care and emergency medicine, in addition to 22 weeks of electives, are required.

## Grading and Promotion Policies

A Pass/Fail system is used.

## Facilities

*Teaching:* The basic sciences are taught at the Education Building, and clinical training is offered at the Medical Center of Central Georgia in Macon and the Memorial Health University Medical Center in Savannah and regional hospitals. *Library:* A comprehensive medical library is available for student and faculty use. *Housing:* Apartments are available on campus and within a 15-minute drive of the school.

## Special Features

*Minority admissions:* There is a program that involves strong recruiting efforts directed toward traditionally black colleges in Georgia. *Other degree programs:* MPH, MFT, MSA.

# Morehouse School of Medicine

720 Westview Drive, S.W.
Atlanta, Georgia    30310

*Phone:* 404-752-1650          *Fax:* 404-752-1512
*E-mail:* mdadmissions@msm.edu
*WWW:* www.msm.edu/

| Application Filing | | | Accreditation | |
|---|---|---|---|---|
| Earliest: | June 1 | | LCME | |
| Latest: | December 1 | | | |
| Fee: | $50 | | **Degrees Granted** | |
| AMCAS: | yes | | MD, MD-PhD | |

### Enrollment: 2008–2009 First-Year Class

| Men: | 21 | 40% | Applied: | 3623 |
|---|---|---|---|---|
| Women: | 31 | 60% | Interviewed: | 248 |
| Minorities: | 39 | 75% | Enrolled: | 52 |
| Out of State: | 31 | 60% | | |

### 2008–2009 Class Profile

| *Mean MCAT Scores* | | *Mean GPA* |
|---|---|---|
| Physical Sciences: | 9 | 3.4 |
| Biological Sciences: | 9 | |
| Verbal Reasoning: | 9 | *Mean Science* |
| | | 3.3 |

**Tuition and Fees**

| | |
|---|---|
| Resident | 29,248 |
| Average (public) | 25,100 |
| Average (private) | 42,600 |
| Nonresident | 43,900 |
| Average (public) | 29,248 |
| Average (private) | 43,500 |

0    10    20    30    40    50
(in thousands of dollars)

Percentage receiving financial aid: 94%

Above data applies to 2007–2008 academic year.

## Introduction

Morehouse School of Medicine is independent of its parent school Morehouse College. Morehouse School of Medicine is the most recent member of the Atlanta University Center, which is an organization of 6 independent institutions making up the largest predominantly African-American private educational structure in the world. It is one of 3 medical schools in the nation founded by historically African-American institutions. It began as a 2-year school in 1978 and was later transformed into a 4-year institution, graduating its first class in 1985.

## Admissions (AMCAS)

The basic premedical science courses plus 1 year of college mathematics and English are required. Courses in biochemistry, embryology, and genetics are recommended. Selection is determined by consideration of multiple factors, including the undergraduate record, the quality of the academic program, MCAT scores, extracurricular activities, and evidence of determination in completing meaningful projects. The applicants will be judged based on recommendations, an interview, their sense of compassion, integrity, and perseverance. A desire to serve in a rural or underserved area is also a meaningful consideration. *Transfer and advanced standing:* Into second year only, provided space is available. The student must be in good standing at an LCME-accredited medical school.

## Curriculum

4-year traditional. *First and second years:* Devoted to the basic medical sciences as well as courses in human behavior and psychopathology, nutrition, community medicine, and biostatistics, along with human values in medicine and introduction to clinical medicine courses. After completing the first 2 years, students are expected to have a solid understanding of the principles, concepts, and fundamental facts of the basic sciences. During the first year, exposure to clinical medicine is provided by means of assigning each student a preceptor. The school's strengths lie in its diversified faculty, small class size, and the fact that courses are taught both by departmental and interdepartmental faculty. *Third and fourth years:* These 2 years involve rotation through the clinical specialties plus 20 weeks of electives. The curriculum is geared to train students as public health practitioners who are committed to meeting the primary health care needs of underserved inner city and rural patients. To this end the philosophy of viewing the patient as a whole person is emphasized. This is done by means of a variety of teaching experiences that relate medical conditions to emotional, social, cultural, and environmental considerations.

## Grading and Promotion Policies

Letter grades are used. Students must obtain passing total scores on Steps 1 and 2 of the USMLE for promotion to the third year and graduation, respectively.

## Facilities

*Teaching:* The first 2 years are taught at the Basic Medical Sciences Building. Clinical training is available at a number of affiliated hospitals in Atlanta and surrounding areas. *Library:* The medical library collection meets both student and faculty needs. *Housing:* Not available on campus.

## Special Features

*Minority admissions:* The school's recruitment officer is actively involved in identifying, informing, and encouraging potential applicants. *Other degree programs:* The school offers a PhD program in biomedical sciences as well as a Master of Public Health degree program. Interested MD students may apply to either program.

# University of Hawaii at Maanoa
# John A. Burns School of Medicine

651 Ilalo Street
Honolulu, Hawaii    96813

*Phone:* 808-692-1000          *Fax:* 808-692-1251
*E-mail:* mnishik@hawaii.edu
*WWW:* hawaiimed.hawaii.edu

| Application Filing | | Accreditation | |
|---|---|---|---|
| Earliest: | June 1 | LCME | |
| Latest: | November 1 | | |
| Fee: | $50 | **Degrees Granted** | |
| AMCAS: | yes | MD, MD-PhD, MD-MS | |

### Enrollment: 2008–2009 First-Year Class

| | | | | | |
|---|---|---|---|---|---|
| Men: | 28 | 45% | Applied: | 1895 | |
| Women: | 34 | 55% | Interviewed: | 231 | |
| Minorities: | 42 | 68% | Enrolled: | 62 | |
| Out of State: | 6 | 10% | | | |

### 2008–2009 Class Profile

| *Mean MCAT Scores* | | *Mean GPA* |
|---|---|---|
| Physical Sciences: | 10.0 | 3.65 |
| Biological Sciences: | 10.0 | |
| Verbal Reasoning: | 9.0 | *Mean Science* |
| | | 3.51 |

**Tuition and Fees**

| | |
|---|---|
| **Resident** | 22,632 |
| Average (public) | 18,500 |
| Average (private) | 35,000 |
| **Nonresident** | 45,624 |
| Average (public) | 34,500 |
| Average (private) | 36,750 |

0    10    20    30    40    50
(in thousands of dollars)

Percentage receiving financial aid: 77%

Above data applies to 2007–2008 academic year.

## Introduction

The University of Hawaii is located in Honolulu. In 1961 the John A. Burns School of Medicine was founded as a 2-year program and expanded in 1973 to 4 years. The medical school is one of the components of the College of Health Science and Social Welfare, which includes schools of Nursing, Public Health, and Social Work.

## Admissions (AMCAS)

Specific work required for entrance consists of the minimum premedical science courses. Courses should be of the type acceptable for majors. One semester of biochemistry as well as molecular and cell biology and one year of mathematics and English are advised; behavioral sciences are recommended. Residents of Hawaii and the Pacific Islands are given preference.

## Curriculum

4-year modern. The case-based curriculum, which involves active student participation, is characterized by the following features: the use of problem-based modules to acquire knowledge, small group tutorials to enhance self-directed learning, the basic sciences presented in the context of solving clinical problems, students being taught to think critically and to evaluate new information and research data with group leaders serving as educational facilitators, and content experts who function as information resources. For the learning process, the laboratory exercises, demonstrations, the library and audiovisual and computer centers supplement faculty input. *First and second years:* These are divided into MD 1–8 and provide opportunities for electives in the basic sciences, a primary care and a community medicine course. Toward the end of the first year, primary care experience and a project begins. Patient contact begins with MD1 and extends throughout the program. The scientific background for understanding patients' problems are studied most intensively in earlier units, but will also be considered later, since it is relevant to the care of any patient in any clinical situation. *Third year:* Begins with clinical clerkships in surgery, obstetrics-gynecology and women's health, family practice and community medicine, pediatrics, psychiatry, and internal medicine. The integration of the basic sciences and clinical medicine is continued during these rotations. Simultaneously, the concept of learning in the context of health care problems in small group tutorials is continued. *Fourth year:* It includes a required 4 weeks in emergency medicine, 3 weeks of seminars dealing with medical ethics, decision analysis, medical economics, and diagnostic imaging. The balance of the time is for electives. The school's emphasis is on training primary care physicians. Moreover, it is hoped that as physicians, they will spend at least part of their career in the underserved areas of Hawaii and the Pacific.

## Grading and Promotion Policies

Grades are recorded as satisfactory/unsatisfactory during the first, second, and fourth years, and honors/satisfactory/unsatisfactory in the third year. The student must obtain passing total scores on Steps 1 and 2 of the USMLE for graduation.

## Facilities

*Teaching:* The Medical School's Medical Education Building and Biomedical Sciences Building are located in Kaka'ako. The clinical departments are based in affiliated community hospitals, where clinical teaching takes place. *Library:* The Health Sciences Library is located in the Medical School's Medical Education Building in Kaka'ako. *Housing:* Students are expected to make their own living arrangements.

## Special Features

*Minority admissions:* A special program provides students from socioeconomically and academically underprivileged areas with the opportunity to study medicine. *Other degree programs:* Dual MD-MS and MD-PhD programs are offered in a variety of disciplines.

## ILLINOIS

# Chicago Medical School
# Rosalind Franklin University of Medicine and Science

3333 Green Bay Road
North Chicago, Illinois   60064

*Phone:* 847-578-3204          *Fax:* 847-578-3284
*E-mail:* cms.admissions@rosalindfranklin.edu
*WWW:* rosalindfranklin.edu/cms

| Application Filing | | Accreditation | |
|---|---|---|---|
| Earliest: | June 1 | LCME | |
| Latest: | November 1 | | |
| Fee: | $100 | **Degrees Granted** | |
| AMCAS: | yes | MD, MD-PhD | |

### Enrollment: 2008–2009 First-Year Class

| Men: | 100 | 53% | Applied: | 6447 |
|---|---|---|---|---|
| Women: | 90 | 47% | Interviewed: | 693 |
| Minorities: | 10 | 5% | Enrolled: | 190 |
| Out of State: | 149 | 78% | | |

### 2008–2009 Class Profile

| *Mean MCAT Scores* | | *Mean GPA* |
|---|---|---|
| Physical Sciences: | 10 | 3.7 |
| Biological Sciences: | 11 | |
| Verbal Reasoning: | 9.0 | *Mean Science* |
| | | 3.7 |

**Tuition and Fees**

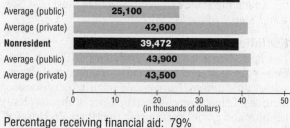

| | |
|---|---|
| Resident | 39,472 |
| Average (public) | 25,100 |
| Average (private) | 42,600 |
| Nonresident | 39,472 |
| Average (public) | 43,900 |
| Average (private) | 43,500 |

(in thousands of dollars)

Percentage receiving financial aid: 79%

Above data applies to 2007–2008 academic year.

## Introduction

This school was established in 1912 with the goal of enabling men and women to study medicine at night, a common practice at that time. It attracted a staff of excellent teachers and practitioners in 1917 when an older medical school in Chicago closed and its faculty transferred to the Chicago Medical School. In 1930 the school moved to a complex located west of downtown Chicago, and in 1967 the University of Health Sciences was established. The university consists of the Chicago Medical School, the Dr. William M. Schell College of Podiatric Medicine, and the School of Graduate and Postdoctoral Studies.

## Admissions (AMCAS)

Only the basic premedical science courses are required plus 1 year of mathematics and English. Completion of a baccalaureate degree is preferred. The school does not impose geographical restrictions. Students are selected on the basis of their potential to study and practice medicine. This is determined by their academic achievement, MCAT scores, appraisals received, and the personal interview (when granted). Qualities assessed are scholastic ability, motivation, educational background, and character. *Transfer and advanced standing:* Limited to filling spaces in the second or third year classes, vacated by attrition.

## Curriculum

4-year semitraditional. Students may be permitted to finish requirements in 5 years, if they choose. *Year 1:* 30 weeks of class time in the basic sciences. *Year 2:* A clinically oriented introduction to medicine begins in the first quarter and increases progressively. Interdepartmental cooperation between clinical and basic science departments is emphasized. Overall, 30 weeks devoted to the advanced basic sciences. *Year 3:* 50 weeks devoted to clerkships in major specialties. Correlation of clinical instruction with basic sciences in conferences and seminars. *Year 4:* 36 weeks devoted to electives and selectives in affiliated hospitals and extramural institutions, along with a medical subinternship rotation. With approval, some students may be permitted to complete all requirements in $5^{1}/_{2}$ years. Under this option, students are required to complete the first 2 years within 3 academic years. Clinical clerkships and electives must be completed in $2^{1}/_{2}$ years. The 4-year curriculum consists of 13 terms, with the first 6 devoted to the basic sciences.

## Grading and Promotion Policies

Letter grades are used in required courses and Pass/Fail in electives. There is a monthly review of performance by departments and a quarterly review by an evaluation committee. Students must record passing scores on Steps 1 and 2 of the USMLE in order to graduate.

## Facilities

*Teaching:* The basic science instruction takes place in the classroom and administration building in North Chicago. Primary clinical teaching occurs in affiliated hospitals: Cook County Hospital, Edward Hines Veterans Affairs Medical Center, North Chicago Veterans Medical Center, Illinois Masonic Center, Lutheran General Hospital, Mount Sinai Hospital Medical Center, Norwalk Hospital, Swedish Covenant Hospital, Highland Park Hospital, and Great Lakes Naval Hospital. *Library:* The library contains 75,000 volumes and subscribes to 1200 periodicals. *Housing:* None available on campus.

## Special Features

*Minority admissions:* The school is actively involved in the recruitment of disadvantaged students and participates in the Chicago Area Health and Medical Careers Program. *Other degree programs:* MD-PhD programs are offered in basic science disciplines.

# Loyola University Chicago Stritch School of Medicine

2160 South First Avenue
Maywood, Illinois   60153

*Phone:* 708-216-3229
*WWW:* http://www.meddean.luc.edu/

| Application Filing | | Accreditation |
|---|---|---|
| Earliest: | June 1 | LCME |
| Latest: | November 15 | |
| Fee: | $70 | **Degrees Granted** |
| AMCAS: | yes | MD, MD-PhD |

### Enrollment: 2008–2009 First-Year Class

| | | | | | |
|---|---|---|---|---|---|
| Men: | 70 | 48% | Applied: | 9487 |
| Women: | 76 | 52% | Interviewed: | 528 |
| Minorities: | 5 | 3% | Enrolled: | 146 |
| Out of State: | 75 | 51% | | |

### 2008–2009 Class Profile

| *Mean MCAT Scores* | | *Mean GPA* |
|---|---|---|
| Physical Sciences: | 10 | 3.7 |
| Biological Sciences: | 11.0 | |
| Verbal Reasoning: | 10 | *Mean Science* |
| | | 3.6 |

### Tuition and Fees

| | |
|---|---|
| Resident | 37,620 |
| Average (public) | 25,100 |
| Average (private) | 42,600 |
| Nonresident | 37,620 |
| Average (public) | 43,900 |
| Average (private) | 43,500 |

0   10   20   30   40   50
(in thousands of dollars)

Percentage receiving financial aid: 89%

Above data applies to 2007–2008 academic year.

## Introduction

Loyola is a private school with a Jesuit Catholic heritage. The Stritch School of Medicine was founded in 1870. It was located in Chicago until 1969 when Loyola opened its medical center campus in Maywood, a suburban community located about 12 miles from downtown Chicago. The medical school is affiliated with a number of hospitals in and around Chicago that offer clinical training sites for medical students.

## Admissions (AMCAS)

This school requires satisfactory completion of the basic premedical science courses, all with laboratory. A semester or quarter of biochemistry can be substituted for part of the organic chemistry requirements. About half of the first-year openings are generally filled by Illinois residents. A preliminary screening of the AMCAS Application is done to determine applications considered competitive. *Transfer and advanced standing:* Space for transfers from domestic schools are based upon attrition.

## Curriculum

4-year semitraditional. *First and second years:* The first year familiarizes the students with the science basic to normal structure and function of the body from cell to organ. The Patient-Centered Medicine I course provides students with skills and experiences crucial in the patient-doctor relationship. The second year familiarizes students with the mechanisms of human disease and the therapeutic approach. The Patient-Centered Medicine course expands the clinical skills and reasoning to allow transition to the third year. It is devoted to developing an understanding of the sciences basic to the practice of medicine. During the early clinical experience course, students are provided training in clinical skills and experiences in ambulatory medicine settings. *Third and fourth years:* Organized into clinical clerkships. The core curriculum includes medicine (12 weeks), surgery (12 weeks), pediatrics (6 weeks), psychiatry (6 weeks), family medicine (6 weeks), neurology (4 weeks), obstetrics and gynecology (6 weeks), and subinternship experiences in medicine or pediatrics including critical care experience (8 weeks). Students also take between 32 and 40 weeks of electives during these 2 years. Through these electives, they anticipate their residency training and prepare for careers in medicine suited to their particular interests and talents.

## Grading and Promotion Policies

The system used is Honors/High Pass/Pass/Fail. Student performance is regularly reviewed by the Office of Student Affairs in accordance with the provision of the Academic Policy Manual. Students must pass Step 1 and Step 2 of the USMLE.

## Facilities

*Teaching:* Teaching spaces, including a Clinical Skills Center, are designed to support curriculum that emphasizes problem-based learning and small-group discussion methods. Clinical teaching takes place at the university hospital and ambulatory center, the Hines VA Hospital, and affiliated hospitals. *Other:* Research facilities are available at the medical center. *Library:* The Health Sciences Library has 1420 electronic journals, 188,431 serial volumes and 57,727 books. *Housing:* There is no on-campus housing.

## Special Features

*Minority admissions:* The school sponsors a summer enrichment program for premedical students. The program combines academic and clinical experiences that are designed to prepare students for physician careers in medicine. *Other degree program:* MD-PhD dual degree program.

# Northwestern University Feinberg School of Medicine

303 East Chicago Avenue
Chicago, Illinois 60611

*Phone:* 312-503-8206    *Fax:* 312-503-0550
*E-mail:* med-admissions@northwestern.edu
*WWW:* medschool.northwestern.edu

| Application Filing | | Accreditation | |
|---|---|---|---|
| Earliest: | June 1 | LCME | |
| Latest: | October 15 | | |
| Fee: | $75 | **Degrees Granted** | |
| AMCAS: | yes | MD, MD-PhD, MD-MS | |

### Enrollment: 2008–2009 First-Year Class

| | | | | | |
|---|---|---|---|---|---|
| Men: | 85 | 50% | Applied: | 7527 | |
| Women: | 84 | 50% | Interviewed: | 863 | |
| Minorities: | 8 | 5% | Enrolled: | 169 | |
| Out of State: | 130 | 77% | | | |

### 2008–2009 Class Profile

| *Mean MCAT Scores* | | *Mean GPA* |
|---|---|---|
| Physical Sciences: | 11.0 | 3.8 |
| Biological Sciences: | 11.3 | |
| Verbal Reasoning: | 10.0 | *Mean Science* |
| | | 3.8 |

### Tuition and Fees

| | |
|---|---|
| **Resident** | 40,313 |
| Average (public) | 25,100 |
| Average (private) | 42,600 |
| **Nonresident** | 40,313 |
| Average (public) | 43,900 |
| Average (private) | 43,500 |

(in thousands of dollars)

Percentage receiving financial aid: 77%

Above data applies to 2007–2008 academic year.

## Introduction

Northwestern University is a private university established in 1851. The medical school was opened in 1859 and is located on the university's lakefront Chicago campus.

## Admissions (AMCAS)

Admission requirements include the MCAT, 90 college credits, plus the basic premedical sciences. For admission no consideration is given to the state of residence, race, creed, color, or sexual orientation. *Transfer and advanced standing:* A small number of applications are considered only for the third year on the basis of academic excellence and personal needs.

## Curriculum

4-year semimodern. *First and second years:* Cover the basic sciences in an organ-based, integrated fashion. Each day consists of 2 hours of lecture and 2 hours of problem-based learning or other small-group sessions. The afternoon course deals with the relationships of the patient, physician, and society. During both years, patient interaction is part of the instruction to prepare the student for their clerkships. *Third year:* Consists of required clerkships in internal medicine, surgery, primary care, pediatrics, obstetrics/gynecology, psychiatry, and neurology. *Fourth year:* Students take an acting internship in medicine, pediatrics, or surgery, and 16 weeks of electives. Research experience is encouraged throughout the 4 years.

## Grading and Promotion Policies

The first 2 years are Pass/Fail. The clerkships and rotations are graded on an Honors/Pass/Fail basis. A Committee on Promotion reviews student records at the end of each academic year to determine those qualified for promotion. Although not required, all students take the USMLE examinations.

## Facilities

*Teaching:* The first 2 years take place in the Montgomery Ward, Searle, Tarry, and Wiebolt Buildings on the Chicago campus. Clinical facilities are provided by 5 independent area hospitals that comprise the Northwestern-McGraw Medical Center. These are the new Northwestern Memorial Hospital, including the inpatient Feinberg Pavilion, the outpatient Galter Pavilion and the Prentice Women's Hospital, the Evanston Northwestern Health Care Center, the Rehabilitation Institute of Chicago, and the Veterans Administration Chicago Health Care System-Lakeside Division. Outpatient experience is provided through both the full-time faculty clinics and individual offices of private practice physicians. *Library:* The Galter Health Sciences Library houses 285,175 volumes, more than 1865 periodicals, 330 on-line journals, and 8 on-line databases. *Housing:* Single rooms for men and women are available in Abbott Hall and Lakeshore Center. There is limited housing for married students without children. Apartments may be rented by students in 2 buildings belonging to Northwestern Memorial Hospital.

## Special Features

*Minority admissions:* Underrepresented minorities are encouraged to apply, and recruitment is conducted on high school and college campuses. The school participates in the summer program of the Chicago Area Health Careers Opportunity Program and the Robert Wood Johnson Medical Minority Enrichment Program. *Other degree programs:* A combined MD-PhD program is available for students interested in a research career in academic medicine. MD-MPH and MD-MS programs (with Kellogg School Business) are also available.

# Rush Medical College of Rush University

600 South Paulina Street
Chicago, Illinois   60612

*Phone:* 312-942-6913      *Fax:* 312-942-2333
*E-mail:* RMC_admissions@rush.edu
*WWW:* rushu.rush.edu/medical

| Application Filing | | Accreditation |
|---|---|---|
| Earliest: | June 1 | LCME |
| Latest: | November 1 | |
| Fee: | $75 | **Degrees Granted** |
| AMCAS: | yes | MD, MD-PhD |

### Enrollment: 2008–2009 First-Year Class

| Men: | 60 | 46% | Applied: | 6475 |
|---|---|---|---|---|
| Women: | 70 | 54% | Interviewed: | 399 |
| Minorities: | 15 | 12% | Enrolled: | 130 |
| Out of State: | 34 | 26% | | |

### 2008–2009 Class Profile

| *Mean MCAT Scores* | | *Mean GPA* |
|---|---|---|
| Physical Sciences: | 10.4 | 3.6 |
| Biological Sciences: | 10.5 | |
| Verbal Reasoning: | 9.9 | *Mean Science* |
| | | 3.5 |

**Tuition and Fees**

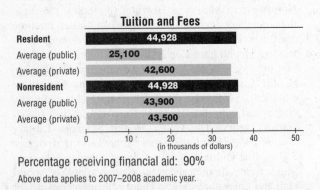

| | |
|---|---|
| Resident | 44,928 |
| Average (public) | 25,100 |
| Average (private) | 42,600 |
| Nonresident | 44,928 |
| Average (public) | 43,900 |
| Average (private) | 43,500 |

0      10      20      30      40      50
(in thousands of dollars)

Percentage receiving financial aid: 90%

Above data applies to 2007–2008 academic year.

## Introduction

Rush Medical College, founded in 1837, is the oldest component of Rush University. Through an academic and health care network of more than a dozen affiliated hospitals and a neighborhood health center, Rush University Medical Center serves 1.5 to 2 million people annually; students train in urban and suburban areas in a variety of socioeconomic and ethnic settings.

## Admissions (AMCAS)

The Committee on Admissions considers both the academic and nonacademic qualifications of applicants in making its decisions and places strong emphasis on the applicant's humanistic concerns, unique experiences, and demonstrated motivation for a career in medicine. All applicants are invited to complete the supplemental application and submit letters of recommendation.

The committee looks for objective evidence that the applicant will be able to handle the academic demands of the curriculum. Healthcare-related experiences and social service activities are measures of how an applicant pursues values, engages in activities that move outside of the applicant's usual boundaries, and expands his or her horizons. Academic achievement, letters of recommendation, MCAT performance, health care experience, and interviews are considered in the final evaluation of all applicants. Only U.S. citizens or permanent residents are considered for admission.

## Curriculum

*Preclinical curriculum:* The primary objective of the first year (M-1) is to provide students with exposure to the vocabulary and the fundamental concepts upon which clinical medicine is based. The courses utilize lecture, laboratory, small group, and workshop formats. The M-2 curriculum centers on the causes and effects of disease and therapeutics. Several courses utilize a case-based approach integrating basic sciences into the context of clinical medicine. The Physicianship Program is an integrated and multidisciplinary program that spans the M1 and M2 years and is designed to provide students with a foundation of clinical knowledge, skills, attitudes, and behaviors so students are prepared for clinical experiences where physician skills are practiced in the context of patient care.

*Clinical Curriculum:* The third and fourth years provide students with training in clinical skills, diagnosis, and patient management in a variety of clinical settings. The third year is comprised of required core clerkships, while the fourth year provides students with the opportunity to pursue areas of special interest. Students complete the majority of their required clinical rotations at Rush University Medical Center or the John H. Stroger, Jr. Hospital.

## Grading and Promotion Policies

The final evaluation in coursework is recorded as Honors, Pass, or Fail. An additional grade of High Pass is utilized in the clinical years. The Committee on Student Evaluation and Promotion receives evaluations of each clinical period and determines when students are eligible for promotion. A total passing score must be obtained on Step 1 of the USMLE and a score recorded on Step 2.

## Facilities

Rush Medical College is located on the near west side of Chicago. The John H. Stroger, Jr. Hospital of Cook County, a major teaching affiliate, is two blocks away. The community is thriving and culturally diverse, with easy access by public transportation.

## Special Features

The Rush Community Service Initiatives Program creates a network of community programs that matches students' interest and initiative with the social and healthcare needs of Chicago's underserved population. Students have the opportunity to participate in clinical and nonclinical programs.

# Southern Illinois University School of Medicine

P.O. Box 19624
Springfield, Illinois   62794

*Phone:* 217-545-6013          *Fax:* 217-545-5538
*E-mail:* admissions@siumed.edu
*WWW:* http://siumed.edu

| Application Filing | | Accreditation | |
|---|---|---|---|
| Earliest: | June 1 | LCME | |
| Latest: | November 15 | | |
| Fee: | $50 | **Degrees Granted** | |
| AMCAS: | yes | MD, MD-JD | |

### Enrollment: 2008–2009 First-Year Class

| | | | | | |
|---|---|---|---|---|---|
| Men: | 40 | 55% | Applied: | | 1173 |
| Women: | 32 | 45% | Interviewed: | | 270 |
| Minorities: | 13 | 18% | Enrolled: | | 72 |
| Out of State: | 0 | 0% | | | |

### 2008–2009 Class Profile

| *Mean MCAT Scores* | | *Mean GPA* |
|---|---|---|
| Physical Sciences: | 9 | 3.50 |
| Biological Sciences: | 10 | |
| Verbal Reasoning: | 9 | *Mean Science* |
| | | 3.4 |

### Tuition and Fees

| | |
|---|---|
| **Resident** | 22,210 |
| Average (public) | 25,100 |
| Average (private) | 42,600 |
| **Nonresident** | 22,210 |
| Average (public) | 43,900 |
| Average (private) | 43,500 |

(in thousands of dollars) 0 10 20 30 40 50

Percentage receiving financial aid: 95.8%

## Introduction

The Southern Illinois University School of Medicine at Springfield is one of 5 campuses in the Southern Illinois University system. Southern Illinois University began as a teachers' college in the late 1800s, and the School of Medicine was opened in 1969. The first year of medical school is spent on the Carbondale campus; the remaining 3 years are spent on the Springfield campus. The Carbondale campus is located in a rural residence setting; the Springfield campus is located in the state capital.

## Admissions (AMCAS)

The minimum premedical science courses plus English and mathematics are recommended. An interview is a prerequisite to acceptance. Invitations for an interview are extended to those whose record indicates achieve-

ment in academics, extracurricular activities, and employment and volunteer experiences. Preference is shown to Southern and Central Illinois residents. Interviews take place in Springfield. *Transfer and advanced standing:* School will consider applications from students in good standing at other U.S. LCME-accredited allopathic medical colleges. For requirements contact the Office of Student Affairs.

## Curriculum

4-year modern. Academic year begins in August. *First year:* Designed to develop competence in several disciplines basic to medicine, such as physiology, biochemistry, anatomy, behavioral sciences, humanities, and clinical medicine, the curriculum is organized around organ systems, focuses on the normal organism, and is taught in Carbondale. *Second year:* Presented in Springfield, instruction is integrated and organized around organ systems, but the focus is on abnormalities associated with disease. The major academic disciplines include gastrointestinal diseases and clinical medicine. *Third year:* Clinical clerkships are provided in the following major specialties: internal medicine, surgery, obstetrics/gynecology, pediatrics, family practice, psychiatry, and physician-patient relationships. *Fourth year:* Multiple weeks of elective study that may include advanced clinical clerkships, basic science research, and medical application of ancillary disciplines. Fourth year clerkships in medical humanities and neurology are mandatory.

## Grading and Promotion Policies

An Honors/Pass/Fail system is used. Students must pass Step 1 of the USMLE before graduation. Students must take Step 2 CS and CK before graduation.

## Facilities

*Teaching:* The educational program is conducted at both the medical education facilities in Carbondale and the medical center in Springfield. The split campus allows the School of Medicine to maximize the existing resources of a major university and the long-established clinical facilities in Springfield: Memorial Medical Center and St. John's Hospital. *Libraries:* One library is located within Carbondale's Morris Library Science Division, consists of more than 100,000 bound volumes, and subscribes to 1000 periodicals. In Springfield, the library is located in the Medical Instruction Facility, contains 113,000 bound volumes and subscribes to 1600 periodicals. *Housing:* Married housing units are available in Carbondale. In Springfield, only off-campus housing is available.

## Special Features

*Minority admissions:* The school sponsors a non-degree-granting Medical-Dental Education Preparatory Program (MED-PREP) for disadvantaged students. *Other degree programs:* The 6-year MD-JD program is open to all in-state and out-of-state applicants. This type of combined program is offered by only a limited number of medical schools.

# University of Chicago
# Pritzker School of Medicine

924 East 57th Street, BLSC 104
Chicago, Illinois    60637

*Phone:* 773-702-1937          *Fax:* 773-834-5412
*E-mail:* pritzkeradmissions@bsd.uchicago.edu
*WWW:* http://www.pritzker.bsd.uchicago.edu

| Application Filing | | Accreditation | |
|---|---|---|---|
| Earliest: | June 1 | LCME | |
| Latest: | October 15 | | |
| Fee: | $75 | **Degrees Granted** | |
| AMCAS: | yes | MD, MD-PhD | |

### Enrollment: 2008–2009 First-Year Class

| Men: | 53 | 47% | Applied: | 7787 |
|---|---|---|---|---|
| Women: | 59 | 53% | Interviewed: | 749 |
| Minorities: | 13 | 12% | Enrolled: | 112 |
| Out of State: | 68 | 61% | | |

### 2008–2009 Class Profile

| *Mean MCAT Scores* | | *Mean GPA* |
|---|---|---|
| Physical Sciences: | 12.0 | 3.8 |
| Biological Sciences: | 12.0 | |
| Verbal Reasoning: | 11.0 | *Mean Science* |
| | | 3.8 |

**Tuition and Fees**

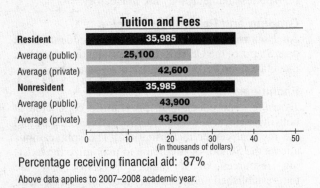

| Resident | 35,985 |
|---|---|
| Average (public) | 25,100 |
| Average (private) | 42,600 |
| Nonresident | 35,985 |
| Average (public) | 43,900 |
| Average (private) | 43,500 |

0      10      20      30      40      50
(in thousands of dollars)

Percentage receiving financial aid: 87%

Above data applies to 2007–2008 academic year.

## Introduction

The University of Chicago is located approximately 7 miles from downtown Chicago in the Hyde Park section. The Pritzker School of Medicine, established in 1927, is part of the Division of Biological Sciences of the University of Chicago.

## Admissions (AMCAS)

The minimum premedical science courses are required, but 1 semester of biochemistry (with lab) may be substituted for the second semester of organic chemistry. Studies in the social sciences, humanities, English composition, and mathematics are recommended but not required. *Transfer and advanced standing:* If space is available, students from LCME-accredited institutions may be considered for transfer into second- or third-year openings on the basis of compelling personal reasons.

## Curriculum

4-year semimodern. *First year:* Consists of courses in the basic sciences. A 2-quarter clinical medicine course introduces students to patients with diseases illustrating the medical correlates of the subjects taught concurrently. The summer is available for research or other activities. *Second year:* Consists of advanced courses. Clinical medicine, including physical diagnosis, continues through the second year. *Third year:* Consists of 5 major clinical clerkships (internal medicine, surgery, pediatrics, psychiatry, and obstetrics and gynecology) with 1 month of the pediatrics rotation and 1 month of the surgery rotation offering opportunities to experience subspecialties. Students also attend departmental seminars and conferences. *Fourth year:* The fourth year is entirely elective and normally consists of consult electives, research, basic science coursework, reading courses, subinternships, ambulatory experiences, and away rotations in other countries.

## Grading and Promotion Policies

Courses in the first 2 years and most electives and research are graded on the Pass/Fail basis. Clinical clerkships use internal designators of Honors/High Pass/Pass/Low Pass/Fail. Research is required to graduate with honors. Promotion and continuance of students is in accordance with published guidelines and recommendations made by the Committee on Promotions. Students are not required to pass the USMLE Steps 1 and 2 to progress through the medical school.

## Facilities

*Teaching:* Basic sciences are taught in the Biological Sciences Learning Center. Clinical teaching takes place in the university hospitals, including the new Comer Children's Hospital. Students are also taught in 2 other major off-site community-based hospitals. *Other:* Research laboratories are located throughout the medical center and in other nearby facilities. A new Center for Integrative Research opened in 2005 that allows for shared research spaces between the physical and biological sciences. *Library:* The Crerar Library houses more than 996,000 volumes and 7000 periodicals, constituting one of the largest science holdings in the United States. *Housing:* 1100 apartments are available.

## Special Features

*Minority admissions:* The medical school actively seeks minority students through city-wide and national recruitment efforts. *Other degree programs:* The Medical Scientist Training Program is offered for a combined MD/PhD degree. The Medicine in the Social Sciences and Humanities program is a fully-funded program allowing for the completion of an MD-PhD degree where the PhD is in a social science or humanities discipline. Students may also pursue a joint program to earn their MBA, JD, MPP, or MPH.

# University of Illinois at Chicago College of Medicine

808 South Wood Street m/c 783
Chicago, Illinois    60612

*Phone:* 312-996-5635          *Fax:* 312-996-6693
*E-mail:* medadmit@uic.edu
*WWW:* medicine.uic.edu

| Application Filing | | Accreditation | |
|---|---|---|---|
| Earliest: | June 1 | LCME | |
| Latest: | November 15 | | |
| Fee: | $70 | **Degrees Granted** | |
| AMCAS: | yes | MD, MD-PhD, MD-MS | |

### Enrollment: 2008–2009 First-Year Class

| | | | | | |
|---|---|---|---|---|---|
| Men: | 170 | 55% | Applied: | | 7093 |
| Women: | 137 | 45% | Interviewed: | | 874 |
| Minorities: | 26 | 11% | Enrolled: | | 307 |
| Out of State: | 63 | 21% | | | |

### 2008–2009 Class Profile

| *Mean MCAT Scores* | | *Mean GPA* |
|---|---|---|
| Physical Sciences: | 10 | 3.7 |
| Biological Sciences: | 11.0 | |
| Verbal Reasoning: | 10 | *Mean Science* |
| | | 3.6 |

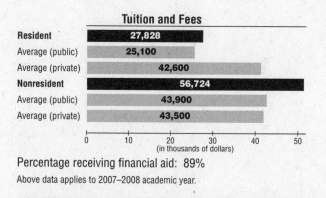

**Tuition and Fees**

| | |
|---|---|
| Resident | 27,828 |
| Average (public) | 25,100 |
| Average (private) | 42,600 |
| Nonresident | 56,724 |
| Average (public) | 43,900 |
| Average (private) | 43,500 |

(in thousands of dollars)

Percentage receiving financial aid: 89%

Above data applies to 2007–2008 academic year.

## Introduction

In 1867 the University of Illinois was chartered as a land grant institution. The medical school was founded in 1881 as the College of Physicians and Surgeons of Chicago. The College of Medicine has 4 campuses: Chicago, Urbana-Champaign, Peoria, and Rockford. The University of Illinois College of Medicine at Chicago is located in the west side medical center district.

## Admissions (AMCAS)

The minimum premedical science courses are required and mathematics and behavioral science are recommended. Strong preference is given to state residents. The College of Medicine consists of 4 geographic sites, located in Chicago, Peoria, Rockford, and Urbana-

Champaign, and 2 educational tracks. Students enrolled on the Chicago Track attend there all 4 years. Students enrolled on the Urbana, Peoria, or Rockford (UPR) Track spend the first year at Urbana-Champaign for basic science study and will remain there (mainly students enrolled in the combined degree Medical Scholars Program [MSP]) or move to Peoria or Rockford for the next 3 years. *Transfer and advanced standing:* A limited number of students who pass the school's qualifying exam may be admitted to the second year on a space-available basis. Third-year transfers are considered only from among students currently enrolled in the second year of an out-of-state U.S. or Canadian allopathic medical school, with preference given to state residents with compelling reasons to return to Illinois.

## College of Medicine at Chicago

This site is located about 2 miles west of downtown Chicago and is the largest of the 4 geographic sites. The College of Medicine at Chicago offers a 4-year program providing a solid foundation in the basic and clinical sciences leading to the MD degree. The curriculum consists of 2 years of basic and preclinical sciences followed by 2 years of clinical work. *First year:* This covers the introductory basic sciences. Clinical conferences are offered to reinforce basic science principles relevant to the practice of medicine. *Second year:* In addition to the advanced basic sciences, LPC courses are offered in medical ethics and human sexuality as well as physical diagnosis and problem solving. *Third year:* Rotation through 6 major clinical specialties. *Fourth year:* Involves rotations. The balance of the time is devoted to electives.

## College of Medicine at Peoria

The college is located a few blocks west of downtown Peoria. This site includes basic science facilities and is affiliated with the Methodist Medical Center of Illinois and St. Francis Medical Center, allowing access to 1100 beds. Only the upper 3 years are taught, including advanced basic sciences and clinical studies. *Second year:* This serves as an introduction to clinical medicine, using a systemic pathophysiological teaching approach. *Third year:* The basic required clerkship rotations are taught, with the emphasis on the clinical practice of medicine and the delivery of health care. *Fourth year:* Consists of at least 36 weeks of instruction.

## College of Medicine at Rockford

Located near the northeast side of the city, the college consists of a teaching center and 3 associated hospitals—Rockford Memorial, St. Anthony Medical Center, and Swedish-American Hospital. The program at Rockford includes a unique experience in primary health care delivery at one of 3 Community Health Centers (CHC). This experience continues for 2 half days per week during the M-3 and M-4 years. *Second year:* This consists of pathology, pharmacology, issues in contemporary medicine, and clinical medicine skills, as well as a systemic-oriented introduction to clinical medicine. *Third year:* This consists of the required core clerkships in the CHC experience. *Fourth year:* This consists of a 4-week clerkship in neurology, and additional work in the CHC experience.

## College of Medicine at Urbana-Champaign

Located on the university campus, the college has, in addition to its basic science facilities, affiliations for clinical training with almost all the hospitals in the east-central region of Illinois. The college offers a complete 4-year medical education program leading to an MD degree. The first-year basic medical science program at Urbana-Champaign also serves those students who complete the last 3 years of medical school in Peoria or Rockford. *First year:* All the basic sciences except pharmacology, pathology, and epidemiology are taught and are organized into learning units distributed among 8 clinical problem themes directly relating basic medical science to human disease. First-year students have an option to participate in the Medical Doctor Adviser (MDA) Program, which enables them to meet with practicing physicians for advisement and instruction. *Second year:* The remaining basic sciences are offered as well as introduction to clinical medicine in the second semester of the sophomore year, which includes direct student contact with hospitalized patients. *Third and fourth years:* The core clinical clerkships, medical electives, and in-depth individual study experiences comprise the last 2 years.

## Grading and Promotion Policies

A Pass/Fail system is used for the first year with a 5-item grading system for the clinical portion of the curriculum. Students must record passing total grades on Step 1 and Step 2 of the USMLE for graduation.

## Special Features

*Minority admissions:* Recruitment is conducted through the Urban Health Program, and a 6-week summer prematriculation program is offered for accepted students. *Other degree programs:* Combined MD-MS and MD-PhD programs are offered by the College of Medicine at Chicago in the basic sciences and public health and at Urbana-Champaign in over 40 disciplines including the basic sciences. A special decompressed first-year program is available. An opportunity to engage in an Independent Study Program is available at the Chicago, Rockford, and Peoria sites for students interested in this type of curriculum.

## INDIANA

# Indiana University School of Medicine

1120 South Drive, Fesler Hall 213
Indianapolis, Indiana  46202

*Phone:* 317-274-3772          *Fax:* 317-278-0211
*E-mail:* kabaxter@iupui.edu
*WWW:* medicine.iu.edu

| Application Filing | | Accreditation |
|---|---|---|
| Earliest: | June 1 | LCME |
| Latest: | December 15 | |
| Fee: | $50 | **Degrees Granted** |
| AMCAS: | yes | MD, MD-PhD, MD-MS |

### Enrollment: 2008–2009 First-Year Class

| | | | | |
|---|---|---|---|---|
| Men: | 173 | 56% | Applied: | 3569 |
| Women: | 135 | 44% | Interviewed: | 999 |
| Minorities: | 32 | 10% | Enrolled: | 308 |
| Out of State: | 262 | 85% | | |

### 2008–2009 Class Profile

| *Mean MCAT Scores* | | *Mean GPA* |
|---|---|---|
| Physical Sciences: | 10.3 | 3.7 |
| Biological Sciences: | 10.3 | |
| Verbal Reasoning: | 10.3 | *Mean Science* |
| | | 3.7 |

**Tuition and Fees**

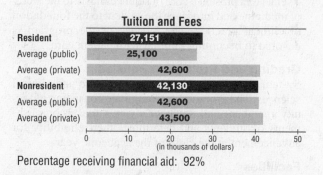

| | |
|---|---|
| Resident | 27,151 |
| Average (public) | 25,100 |
| Average (private) | 42,600 |
| Nonresident | 42,130 |
| Average (public) | 42,600 |
| Average (private) | 43,500 |

0  10  20  30  40  50
(in thousands of dollars)

Percentage receiving financial aid: 92%

## Introduction

The Indiana University School of Medicine began in 1907 on the Bloomington campus. In 1908 Indiana University became responsible for all medical education in the state of Indiana, and in 1971 the Indiana Statewide Medical Education System was put into effect. It has teaching centers in all major cities in Indiana. The Indiana University Medical Center includes schools of Medicine, Dentistry, Nursing, and Allied Health Sciences, as well as university hospitals, and research laboratories.

## Admissions (AMCAS)

Only minimum premedical science courses are required. Preference is given to residents; a number of out-of-state residents are accepted yearly. The application of nonresidents who have significant ties to Indiana may be given greater consideration than to others in this category. The basis for selection is the school's own technical standards judged essential, as well as scholarship, references, personality, and character. *Transfer and advanced standing:* Only transfers of Indiana residents from American or foreign medical schools are considered.

## Curriculum

4-year semimodern. The major objectives of the curriculum are the concentration of core material in both preclinical and clinical years, early exposure to patients, and extensive elective time. The *first year* is devoted to core basic science courses and introduction to clinical medicine. *Second year* to core basic science courses and continuing patient contact through the introduction to medicine courses. *Third year* (12 months) is devoted to clinical experience in pediatrics, obstetrics, gynecology, psychiatry, medicine, and surgery. *Fourth year* (9 months). Experience in a variety of clinical specialties and the remainder is reserved exclusively for electives.

## Grading and Promotion Policies

System used is Honors/High Pass/Pass/Fail. Students must pass Steps 1 and 2 of the USMLE to graduate.

## Facilities

The Medical Center is located in Indianapolis; the School of Medicine has students on 8 other campuses. *Teaching:* In Indianapolis, preclinical teaching takes place in the Medical Sciences Building. Clinical facilities are provided by the University Hospital, Robert W. Long Hospital, William H. Coleman Hospital for Women, and James Whitcomb Riley Hospital for Children. *Other:* Emerson Hall accommodates clinical departments; Fesler Hall houses clinical laboratories and offices. Riley Hospital has connecting wings for pediatric and cancer research. A psychiatric research unit is also located at the center. Combined hospitals of the medical center contain 2000 beds. Neighboring hospitals provide some additional experience. *Library:* The medical library and nursing library combined house more than 125,000 volumes and subscribe to 2500 periodicals. *Housing:* Very limited on-campus housing.

## Special Features

*Minority admissions:* The school has an active program to identify, advise, and recruit disadvantaged students. *Other degree programs:* Students interested in medical science can work to combine an MD degree with either an MS or a PhD in biomedical disciplines. The combined MD-PhD may also be earned in other sciences, and law, social and behavioral sciences, and the humanities on the Bloomington campus.

# IOWA

# University of Iowa Roy J. and Lucille A. Carver College of Medicine

Iowa City, Iowa   52242-1101

*Phone:* 319-335-8052          *Fax:* 319-335-8049
*E-mail:* medical-admission@uiowa.edu
*WWW:* medicine.uiowa.edu/osac

| Application Filing | | Accreditation | |
|---|---|---|---|
| Earliest: | June 1 | LCME | |
| Latest: | November 1 | | |
| Fee: | $60 | **Degrees Granted** | |
| AMCAS: | yes | MD, MD-PhD, MD-MPH | |

### Enrollment: 2008–2009 First-Year Class

| Men: | 77 | 52% | Applied: | 3895 |
|---|---|---|---|---|
| Women: | 71 | 48% | Interviewed: | 665 |
| Minorities: | 36 | 24% | Enrolled: | 148 |
| Out of State: | 50 | 34% | | |

### 2008–2009 Class Profile

| *Mean MCAT Scores* | | *Mean GPA* |
|---|---|---|
| Physical Sciences: | 10.5 | 3.73 |
| Biological Sciences: | 11 | |
| Verbal Reasoning: | 10.2 | *Mean Science* |
| | | 3.67 |

### Tuition and Fees

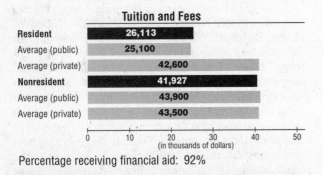

| Resident | 26,113 |
| Average (public) | 25,100 |
| Average (private) | 42,600 |
| Nonresident | 41,927 |
| Average (public) | 43,900 |
| Average (private) | 43,500 |

(in thousands of dollars)

Percentage receiving financial aid: 92%

## Introduction

The University of Iowa is located in Iowa City, and includes the College of Medicine, which was founded in 1850. This school has evolved into the state's major health center. It includes a large University Hospital and clinics. The Health Science Center also contains schools of Nursing, Dentistry, Pharmacy, and Public Health, and is located on a 900-acre campus.

## Admissions (AMCAS)

College requires minimum premedical science courses plus 1 advanced biology course and college algebra and trigonometry or higher math. Iowa residents are given strong preference, and excellent nonresidents are admit-

ted. The school seeks candidates with academic ability, and skills in problem solving. Manual dexterity and interpersonal relations, overall attractive GPA, science courses, and MCAT scores are essential features used to indicate scholarly proficiency. Applicants must submit an advising committee report or 3 letters of reference of which 2 should be academic. Finally, the interview is an integral part of the admission process, which helps finalize the decision. It is granted by invitation only. *Transfer and advanced standing:* Not available.

## Curriculum

4-year semitraditional. *First and second years:* The first 4 semesters cover the basic medical science courses and introduce the student's foundations of clinical practice through a special course each semester. *Third year:* Comprises summer session and 2 semesters of rotating clinical clerkships in major specialties, in which student participates in patient care. *Fourth year:* Devoted in part to 3 electives in which students focus on whatever facet of medical education best relates to their professional interests. During the clinical years, required subspecialty clerkships need to be completed in anesthesia, dermatology, neurology, ophthalmology, orthopedics, otolaryngology, psychiatry, radiology, and urology, as well as courses in laboratory medicine and electrocardiography. Also required is a subinternship in 1 of a number of medical disciplines, in which the student assumes responsibility for managing patients on inpatient units supervised by a senior resident and a faculty physician. In summary, the first 4 semesters present a core of sciences basic to the study of medicine and introduce the student to the foundation of clinical practice. The balance of the program is devoted to becoming familiar with patient care.

## Grading and Promotion Policies

System used is Honors/Pass/Fail in basic and clinical sciences. The Promotions Committee consisting of faculty members and students reviews the accomplishments of students and determines their eligibility for advancement at the close of the academic year.

## Facilities

*Teaching:* Preclinical sciences are taught at the Medical Education and Biomedical Research Facility and the Bowen Science Building. Clinical teaching primarily takes place at the University Hospital (800 beds), and VA Hospital (100 beds). *Other:* The major research facilities include the Medical Research Center, Eckstein Medical Research Building, and Medical Education and Biomedical Research Facility. *Library:* The Hardin Library for Health Sciences houses 350,000 volumes. *Housing:* Information not available.

## Special Features

*Other degree programs:* Combined MD-PhD programs are offered in a variety of disciplines. The college also offers combined MD-MPH, MD-MBA, and MD-JD degrees.

# KANSAS

## University of Kansas School of Medicine

3901 Rainbow Boulevard
Kansas City, Kansas   66160

*Phone:* 913-588-5245        *Fax:* 913-588-5259
*E-mail:* premedinfo@kumc.edu
*WWW:* kumc.edu/som.html

| Application Filing | | Accreditation | |
|---|---|---|---|
| Earliest: | June 1 | LCME | |
| Latest: | October 15 | | |
| Fee: | $50 | **Degrees Granted** | |
| AMCAS: | yes | MD, MD-PhD | |

### Enrollment: 2008–2009 First-Year Class

| Men: | 83 | 47% | Applied: | 1918 |
|---|---|---|---|---|
| Women: | 93 | 53% | Interviewed: | 465 |
| Minorities: | 14 | 8% | Enrolled: | 176 |
| Out of State: | 28 | 16% | | |

### 2008–2009 Class Profile

| *Mean MCAT Scores* | | *Mean GPA* |
|---|---|---|
| Physical Sciences: | 9 | 3.7 |
| Biological Sciences: | 10 | |
| Verbal Reasoning: | 10 | *Mean Science* |
| | | 3.7 |

**Tuition and Fees**

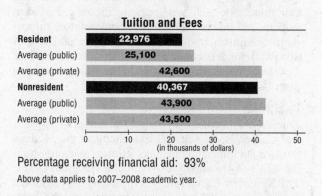

| | (in thousands of dollars) |
|---|---|
| Resident | 22,976 |
| Average (public) | 25,100 |
| Average (private) | 42,600 |
| Nonresident | 40,367 |
| Average (public) | 43,900 |
| Average (private) | 43,500 |

Percentage receiving financial aid: 93%

Above data applies to 2007–2008 academic year.

## Introduction

The University of Kansas opened in 1866. In 1899 a 1-year preparatory course for medical school was initiated. Students who completed the course then transferred to other medical schools. In 1906 clinical training began at Bell Memorial Hospital and graduating with a medical degree became possible. In 1924 the medical school and hospital expanded and moved to its present location. The Medical Center now consists of schools of Medicine, Nursing, Allied Health, and Office of Graduate Studies.

## Admissions (AMCAS)

The school requires a bachelor's degree and minimum premedical science courses. One semester of college-level mathematics and 1 year of English are also required. The school is a state-supported institution. Preference is given to residents, but nonresidents are accepted. *Transfer and advanced standing:* If vacancies exist, candidates for the third-year class are considered from other U.S. medical schools. Applicants must be Kansas residents currently enrolled and in good standing.

## Curriculum

4-year semimodern. The curriculum integrates normal human structure and function with alterations caused by disease. Clinical experiences that are provided during all 4 years reinforce the biomedical sciences. They also provide students with an opportunity to learn the essential principles of patient assessment, preventive and behavioral medicine, and medical ethics. Training is provided in community and ambulatory settings including rural sites. Among the teaching methods used are case-based instruction and small-group and computer-assisted learning. A generalist approach is used that emphasizes the evaluation of patients with differentiated problems. *First year:* Focuses on the introductory basic sciences using an organ system approach. After a presentation of cellular and molecular biology, the other three 4-week segments of the first semester are devoted to the cardiovascular, respiratory, and musculoskeletal systems. The 4 segments of the second semester are devoted to the gastrointestinal and endocrine system as well as neuroscience. An Introduction to Clinical Medicine course extends throughout the year. *Second year:* Devoted to disease pathogenesis, pathogenic agents, pharmacotherapeutics, and subjects covering the advanced basic sciences. The Introduction to Clinical Medicine extends throughout the year. *Third year:* Provides for basic experience by means of rotations through major clinical sciences as well as ambulatory medicine and geriatrics. *Fourth year:* Consists of a subinternship, rural preceptorship, ambulatory specialties, and public health, as well as 16 weeks of electives.

## Grading and Promotion Policies

A passing total score is required on Step 1 of the USMLE for promotion to the third year and on Step 2 for graduation. There is a 5-level grading system: Superior/High Satisfactory/Satisfactory/Low Satisfactory/Unsatisfactory.

## Facilities

*Teaching:* The school is part of the university's Medical Center. Orr-Major Hall provides classrooms and labs for teaching basic science courses as well as space for individual research and departmental offices. The University Hospital provides facilities used in clinical training. *Library:* Dykes Medical Library contains more than 110,000 volumes. *Housing:* There is no on-campus housing.

## Special Features

*Minority admissions:* An active recruitment program exists. *Other degree programs:* A combined MD-PhD program is offered in a variety of disciplines.

# KENTUCKY

# University of Kentucky College of Medicine

800 Rose Street
Lexington, Kentucky   40506

*Phone:* 859-323-6161          *Fax:* 859-257-3633
*E-mail:* kymedap@uky.edu
*WWW:* www.mc.uky.edu/medicine

| Application Filing | | Accreditation | |
|---|---|---|---|
| Earliest: | June 1 | LCME | |
| Latest: | November 1 | | |
| Fee: | $50 | **Degrees Granted** | |
| AMCAS: | yes | MD, MD-PhD, MD-MS, MD-MPH, MD-MBA | |

### Enrollment: 2008–2009 First-Year Class

| | | | | | |
|---|---|---|---|---|---|
| Men: | 67 | 59% | Applied: | 2259 | |
| Women: | 46 | 41% | Interviewed: | 597 | |
| Minorities: | 7 | 6% | Enrolled: | 113 | |
| Out of State: | 22 | 19% | | | |

### 2008–2009 Class Profile

| *Mean MCAT Scores* | | *Mean GPA* |
|---|---|---|
| Physical Sciences: | 9.7 | 3.6 |
| Biological Sciences: | 9.9 | |
| Verbal Reasoning: | 9.8 | *Mean Science* |
| | | 3.6 |

### Tuition and Fees

| | |
|---|---|
| **Resident** | 26,600 |
| Average (public) | 25,100 |
| Average (private) | 42,600 |
| **Nonresident** | 49,670 |
| Average (public) | 43,900 |
| Average (private) | 43,500 |

(in thousands of dollars)

Percentage receiving financial aid: 85%

## Introduction

In 1956 the University of Kentucky Medical Center was established. The College of Medicine is one of the programs offered at the University of Kentucky Medical Center campus in Lexington. The College of Medicine is part of the University of Kentucky Chandler Medical Center, which also contains schools of Dentistry, Nursing, Pharmacy, and Allied Health profession, as well as the University Hospital and Ambulatory Care Center.

## Admissions (AMCAS)

In addition to the basic premedical science courses, 1 year of English is required. Courses in mathematics and in the psychological and social sciences are recommended. Preference is given to residents, but a small number of nonresidents who have a clear interest in pursuing their medical education in Kentucky are accepted each year. Secondary applications are sent to all Kentucky residents and to nonresidents having attractive GPAs and MCAT scores (3.75 or higher and at least 10 on each sub-test, respectively). Admission decisions are made upon review of academic and nonacademic criteria. The latter include interpersonal skills, leadership abilities, and evidence of service to others. *Transfer and advanced standing:* Transfer is possible for selected students with compelling reasons for transferring and strong Kentucky ties.

## Curriculum

4-year semimodern. *First and second years:* Consist of 48 and 36 weeks, respectively, of scheduled class work in the basic sciences. Each week has about 23 hours of scheduled activities. *Third year:* Clerkship rotations through the major clinical specialties and primary care are required. *Fourth year:* Selection of specialty and electives. One rotation is required in a surgery and medical active internship, one emergency medicine rotation, one advanced clinical pharmacology and anesthesiology course, one gerontology elective, a dean's colloquium, a selective in primary care or rural medicine, and a selective rotation in a rural setting.

## Grading and Promotion Policies

Grades are A, B, C, E (Failure), P (Pass), W (Withdrawal), U (Unsatisfactory), and I (Incomplete). A student who is doing unsatisfactorily in 2 or more classes in one academic year may be dropped. At regular intervals the Student Progress and Promotions Committee for each class reviews the record of each student and makes recommendations relative to promotion, adjustment of academic load, remediation, or dismissal. Students must record passing scores on Step 1 of the USMLE for promotion to the third year and on Step 2CK and Step 2CS for graduation.

## Facilities

*Teaching:* The college is part of the university's Medical Center. Basic sciences are taught at the Medical Science Building and the major clinical teaching site is the 473-bed University of Kentucky Hospital. *Other:* The Kentucky Clinic offers comprehensive outpatient medical services. The Sander-Brown Research Center on Aging is a national gerontology resource facility. The Lucille Parker Markey Cancer Center includes a patient care facility and the Combs Research Building. *Library:* The Medical Center Library houses more than 160,000 volumes and 2000 periodicals. The newly constructed W.T. Young Library has more than one million volumes in its collection. *Housing:* University housing is available.

## Special Features

*Minority admissions:* The college has an active recruitment program and offers a summer prematriculation program for accepted students. *Other degree programs:* Combined MD-PhD degree programs are offered in the basic medical sciences. MD-MBA and MD-MPH programs are also offered.

# University of Louisville School of Medicine

Health Sciences Center
Louisville, Kentucky    40202

*Phone:* 502-852-5193          *Fax:* 502-852-0302
*E-mail:* medadm@louisville.edu
*WWW:* louisville.edu/medschool

| Application Filing | | Accreditation | |
|---|---|---|---|
| Earliest: | June 1 | LCME | |
| Latest: | October 15 | | |
| Fee: | $75 | **Degrees Granted** | |
| AMCAS: | yes | MD, MD-PhD, | |
| | | MD-MBA, MD-MPH, | |
| | | MD-MA, MD-MSc | |

### Enrollment: 2008–2009 First-Year Class

| Men: | 87 | 56% | Applied: | 2348 |
|---|---|---|---|---|
| Women: | 68 | 44% | Interviewed: | 386 |
| Minorities: | 14 | 9% | Enrolled: | 155 |
| Out of State: | 35 | 23% | | |

### 2008–2009 Class Profile

| *Mean MCAT Scores* | | *Mean GPA* |
|---|---|---|
| Physical Sciences: | 9.3 | 3.6 |
| Biological Sciences: | 10.0 | |
| Verbal Reasoning: | 9.5 | *Mean Science* |
| | | 3.5 |

### Tuition and Fees

| | |
|---|---|
| **Resident** | 27,330 |
| Average (public) | 25,100 |
| Average (private) | 42,600 |
| **Nonresident** | 46,652 |
| Average (public) | 43,900 |
| Average (private) | 43,500 |

(in thousands of dollars) 0 10 20 30 40 50

Percentage receiving financial aid: 92%

## Introduction

The University of Louisville School of Medicine was originally part of the Louisville Medical Institute when it was established in 1833. In 1846 it became part of the University of Louisville, which is part of the state university system. In 1908 the school merged with 4 others and adopted its present name. In the late 1980s the school embarked on a comprehensive building program, which included the construction of the University of Louisville Hospital. The Health Science Center consists of the schools of Medicine, Dentistry, Nursing, and Public Health and Information Services.

## Admissions (AMCAS)

Requirements include minimum premedical science courses plus 1 semester of calculus (or 2 semesters of other college mathematics courses) and 2 semesters of English. Preference is given to state residents. Selection is determined by academic achievement and potential as reflected by the applicant's college record, MCAT scores, recommendations of the premedical advisory committee, extracurricular activities, personality, and motivation. The latter qualities are determined by a personal interview granted only to candidates for admission whose academic credentials merit comprehensive review. *Transfer:* Applicants from LCME-accredited schools with documented circumstances necessitating the need to return to Kentucky will be considered on a limited basis.

## Curriculum

4-year semitraditional with an introduction to clinical medicine. *First and second years:* Consist of basic science courses. Humanities in Medicine requirement in second year for 4 weeks; The Intersection of Medicine and Religion. *Third year:* Devoted to required clerkships. *Fourth year:* 4 required clinical rotations and a Rural/ Urban rotation in specified disciplines/ specialties, and 14 weeks of clinical electives. Humanities in Medicine requirement in fourth year is weekly for 12 weeks online. Students choose 1 of 2 courses; History of Medicine or Literature in Medicine.

## Grading and Promotion Policies

A grade of Pass or Fail is submitted at the completion of each course. The Committee on Student Promotions approves the scholastic activities of the individual or may recommend one of several courses of action if work is unsatisfactory. A passing total score on Step 1 of the USMLE is needed for promotion to the third year. Taking Step 2 is required.

## Facilities

*Teaching:* Basic sciences are taught in the Instructional Building at the Health Science Center near downtown Louisville. Primary clinical facilities are University of Louisville, Kosair-Children's Hospital, and Veterans Administration Medical Center. Other clinical affiliates are the Bingham Clinic, Norton Audubon Hospital, Frazier Rehab Institute, Jewish Hospital, James Graham Brown Cancer Center, and Trover Clinic (Madisonville, KY). *Other:* 2 Baxter Biomedical Research Buildings are devoted entirely to scientific investigation by all departments of the school. A commons building houses the Health Sciences library, auditorium, and cafe. *Housing:* Medical-Dental dormitory located near the Health Sciences Center, and numerous affordable apartment complexes within 10–15 minutes of the medical school.

## Special Features

*Minority admissions:* Aids in recruitment and retention of minorities. *Other degree programs:* A combined MD-PhD program is available in a variety of disciplines including biophysics, immunology, and toxicology. *Other dual degrees offered are:* MD/MA in Bioethics and Medical Humanities, MD/MBA, MD/MSc in Clinical Investigation Sciences, and MD/MPH.

# LOUISIANA

## Louisiana State University* School of Medicine in New Orleans

1901 Perdido Street
New Orleans, Louisiana   70112

*Phone:* 504-568-6262          *Fax:* 504-568-7701
*E-mail:* ms-admissions@suhsc.edu
*WWW:* medschool.suhsc.edu

| Application Filing | | Accreditation | |
|---|---|---|---|
| Earliest: | June 1 | LCME | |
| Latest: | November 30 | | |
| Fee: | $50 | **Degrees Granted** | |
| AMCAS: | yes | MD, MD-PhD, | |
| | | MD-MPH | |

### Enrollment: 2008–2009 First-Year Class

| Men: | 98 | 55% | Applied: | 1414 |
|---|---|---|---|---|
| Women: | 81 | 45% | Interviewed: | 403 |
| Minorities: | 11 | 6% | Enrolled: | 179 |
| Out of State: | 6 | 4% | | |

### 2008–2009 Class Profile

| *Mean MCAT Scores* | | *Mean GPA* |
|---|---|---|
| Physical Sciences: | 9 | 3.7 |
| Biological Sciences: | 9 | |
| Verbal Reasoning: | 10 | *Mean Science* |
| | | 3.7 |

### Tuition and Fees

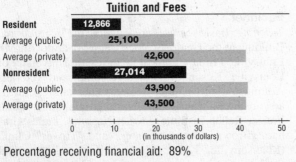

| | (in thousands of dollars) |
|---|---|
| **Resident** | 12,866 |
| Average (public) | 25,100 |
| Average (private) | 42,600 |
| **Nonresident** | 27,014 |
| Average (public) | 43,900 |
| Average (private) | 43,500 |

Percentage receiving financial aid: 89%

Above data applies to 2007–2008 academic year.

### Introduction

The Louisiana State University School of Medicine in New Orleans was founded in 1931. The School of Medicine is located next to Charity Hospital, adjacent to the city's central business district. It is a major component of the Louisiana State University Medical Center, which includes schools of Dentistry, Nursing, Allied Health Sciences, and Graduate Studies.

### Admissions (AMCAS)

The basic premedical science courses and taking the MCAT are required. Only state residents are accepted into the first-year class. *Transfer and advanced standing:* Information not available.

_____

*School affected by 2005 hurricane.

### Curriculum

4-year semimodern. *First and second years:* Emphasize several basic sciences and their relevancy to clinical medicine. Clinical experiences begin in the first year in courses such as Introduction to Clinical Medicine. In the second year, an integrated approach to the teaching of basic science and preclinical courses is used. *Third year:* Clerkships begin where students rotate through the various clinical disciplines. *Fourth year:* Students are given several months for electives in addition to required rotations in Ambulatory Medicine, Acting Internships, etc. Some of these rotations can be completed at institutions associated with the school or at other approved institutions outside the state or country. Computer-assisted instruction is an important component of the curriculum. Although major emphasis is placed on training primary care physicians, there are opportunities for research and the pursuit of more specialized training.

### Grading and Promotion Policies

Grades are Honors, High Pass, Pass, Fail, Withdrew Passing, and Withdrew Failing. Periodic reviews are made of student performance by means of exams, staff reports, and other forms of appraisal. Eligibility for promotion rests on completion of all coursework and requirements and approval by the Promotions Committee. A passing score must be recorded for Step 1 of the USMLE prior to entering the third year. Step 2 must be passed prior to graduation.

### Facilities

*Teaching:* The Medical Education Building is the site for basic science instruction. The school is located near the center of the New Orleans business district. The two main teaching hospitals are the Medical Center of Louisiana at New Orleans and University Hospital. Ten other hospitals are affiliated with LSU. An auditorium equipped with the most up-to-date audiovisual facilities provides space for medical meetings and faculty/student assemblies and lectures. *Library:* The library is located in the Resource Center. It services all professional schools in the Medical Center with more than 176,000 volumes and current periodicals in excess of 1500 titles. *Housing:* University-controlled housing is provided for 300 married and single students. Located 3 blocks from the school, the residence hall provides 1-, 2-, or 3-bedroom apartments for married students and double rooms for single men and women. Recreational facilities are located in the dormitory.

### Special Features

*Minority admissions:* The Office of Minority Affairs coordinates recruitment. The school offers a Minority Summer Prematriculation Program for accepted first-year students to facilitate adjustment to medical school. *Other degree programs:* Combined MD-PhD programs are offered in a variety of disciplines, as is an MD-MPH degree. The school offers an Honors program for exceptional students. It involves independent research on a problem of scientific interest.

# Louisiana State University*
# School of Medicine in Shreveport

1501 Kings Highway, P.O. Box 33932
Shreveport, Louisiana   71130

*Phone:* 318-675-5190          *Fax:* 318-675-8690
*E-mail:* shvadm@lsumc.edu
*WWW:* shilsuhsc.edu/medschool/index/html

| Application Filing | | Accreditation | |
|---|---|---|---|
| Earliest: | June 1 | LCME | |
| Latest: | November 1 | | |
| Fee: | $50 | **Degrees Granted** | |
| AMCAS: | yes | MD, MD-PhD | |

### Enrollment: 2008–2009 First-Year Class

| | | | | | |
|---|---|---|---|---|---|
| Men: | 71 | 61% | Applied: | 1004 | |
| Women: | 46 | 39% | Interviewed: | 226 | |
| Minorities: | 7 | 6% | Enrolled: | 117 | |
| Out of State: | 2 | 2% | | | |

### 2008–2009 Class Profile

| *Mean MCAT Scores* | | *Mean GPA* |
|---|---|---|
| Physical Sciences: | 9 | 3.8 |
| Biological Sciences: | 10 | |
| Verbal Reasoning: | 9 | *Mean Science* |
| | | 3.7 |

**Tuition and Fees**

| | |
|---|---|
| Resident | 10,458 |
| Average (public) | 25,100 |
| Average (private) | 42,600 |
| Nonresident | 24,606 |
| Average (public) | 43,900 |
| Average (private) | 43,500 |

0    10    20    30    40    50
(in thousands of dollars)

Percentage receiving financial aid: 87%

Above data applies to 2007–2008 academic year.

## Introduction

The Louisiana State University School of Medicine in Shreveport was founded in 1966. The medical school facilities are located next to the Louisiana State University Hospital. The permanent medical facilities were occupied in 1975, 2 years after the first MD degrees were awarded by the school. The medical school is part of the Louisana State University Medical Center. This entity is involved in education, research, patient care services, and community outreach activities. The medical center consists of 6 professional schools. In addition to 2 medical schools, there is a dental school, nursing school, school of allied health professions, and graduate school. Health care services are provided to hospitals and medical clinics in Shreveport and New Orleans as well as through dental, nursing, and allied health clinics in these 2 cities and by means of the

*School affected by 2005 hurricane.

numerous affiliated hospitals and clinics throughout Louisiana. The system therefore is involved in providing acute and primary health care services to insured as well as for indigent and uninsured.

## Admissions (AMCAS)

Required courses, in addition to the minimum premedical sciences, include English (6 semester hours). MCAT scores within 3 years are also required. Since the number of highly qualified state residents exceeds the number of places available, there are no places available for nonresidents. Selection is determined by academic performance, MCAT scores, the letter of recommendation from the premedical advisory committee, and when granted, the personal interview with the faculty. *Transfer and advanced standing:* Information not available.

## Curriculum

4-year semitraditional. The curriculum is characterized by providing early contact with patients, a firm grounding in the basic sciences, exposure to clinical correlation experiences, and opportunities electives during the first, second, and fourth years, and a program of comprehensive care in each of the 4 years of medical school. *First year:* Courses include introductory basic sciences plus introductory classes in comprehensive health care, genetics, radiology, psychiatry, and biometry. *Second year:* Advanced basic sciences with a major course in clinical diagnosis to prepare students for clinical years and neurology, perspectives in medicine II and comprehensive care are also offered. *Third and fourth years:* Emphasis on supervised experience in patient care, especially in the development of clinical skills. All of the fourth year is electives with opportunities for extramural and intramural work in family practice, other clinical specialties, basic sciences, and research.

## Grading and Promotion Policies

A letter system is used for coursework and Pass/Fail for electives.

## Facilities

*Teaching:* Louisiana State University Hospital (675 beds) is the principal teaching facility. The ten-story medical school adjoining the University Hospital houses lecture halls and laboratories used for most didactic teaching and basic science research. A separate ambulatory care facility is used for a multi-year course in ambulatory and family medicine. *Other:* Shreveport VA Hospital (450 beds) and E. A. Conway Hospital in nearby Monroe are affiliated with the school. *Library:* A fully modern library houses more than 90,000 volumes and subscribes to more than 1300 periodicals. A local network of terminals accesses several national data bases for study and research. *Housing:* None.

## Special Features

*Minority admissions:* Recruitment of disadvantaged students is facilitated by visits to Louisiana colleges and communications with other educational institutions. *Other degree programs:* Combined MD-PhD programs are offered in a variety of disciplines.

# Tulane University*
# School of Medicine

1430 Tulane Avenue
New Orleans, Louisiana   70112

*Phone:* 504-988-5187          *Fax:* 504-988-6735
*E-mail:* medsch@tulane.edu
*WWW:* www.tmc.tulane.edu/departments/admissions/
index/html

| Application Filing | | Accreditation | |
|---|---|---|---|
| Earliest: | June 1 | LCME | |
| Latest: | December 15 | | |
| Fee: | $95 | **Degrees Granted** | |
| AMCAS: | yes | MD, MD-PhD, | |
| | | MD-MPH, MD-MS | |

### Enrollment: 2008–2009 First-Year Class

| Men: | 94 | 54% | Applied: | 6800 |
|---|---|---|---|---|
| Women: | 81 | 46% | Interviewed: | 1176 |
| Minorities: | 6 | 3% | Enrolled: | 175 |
| Out of State: | 108 | 62% | | |

### 2008–2009 Class Profile

| *Mean MCAT Scores* | | *Mean GPA* |
|---|---|---|
| Physical Sciences: | 10.0 | 3.5 |
| Biological Sciences: | 11 | |
| Verbal Reasoning: | 10.0 | *Mean Science* |
| | | 3.4 |

**Tuition and Fees**

| | (in thousands of dollars) |
|---|---|
| Resident | 45,080 |
| Average (public) | 25,100 |
| Average (private) | 42,600 |
| Nonresident | 45,080 |
| Average (public) | 43,900 |
| Average (private) | 43,500 |

Percentage receiving financial aid: 84%

Above data applies to 2007–2008 academic year.

## Introduction

The Tulane University School of Medicine was established in 1834 as the Medical College of Louisiana. In 1845 the school became the Medical Department of the University of Louisiana. The school was closed during the Civil War, reopening with the termination of that conflict but struggling financially for survival until 1884 when a local merchant, Paul Tulane, provided funds for what became Tulane University. A major multidisciplinary medical center was later established incorporating the School of Medicine, School of Public Health and Tropical Medicine, the Tulane University Hospital and Clinic, and other units.

## Admissions (AMCAS)

Prerequisite courses are the basic premedical sciences and English. Because Tulane is a private institution, there are no residency requirements and, thus, large numbers

*School affected by 2005 hurricane.

of out-of-state students are accepted. *Transfer and advanced standing:* A few students will be accepted into the second and third year classes if space is available.

## Curriculum

4-year semimodern. The curriculum is under continuous evaluation and improvement. It provides the necessary foundation for graduates to be well prepared to enter any field of medicine. An emphasis has been placed upon self-directed learning, integration of basic and clinical sciences, and more active forms of learning. *First and second years:* Students take the basic sciences courses that form the foundation for clinical application. In the second semester of the first year, and continuing through the second year, students participate in the elective program, which allows each student to supplement the curriculum according to his/her own goals and ambitions. Along with lectures, courses incorporate problem-based learning sessions, small group discussions, laboratories, and clinical correlations. Throughout the first 2 years, the course in Foundations in Medicine provides clinical experience both on campus and in community-based settings. *Third year:* Consists of 48 weeks devoted to basic core clerkships in the major clinical areas. Students have direct responsibility for the diagnosis and management of clinical problems presented by the patients in the various hospitals affiliated with the medical school. *Fourth year:* Consists of both required clerkships and electives.

## Grading and Promotion Policies

Grades are Honors/High Pass/Pass/Condition/Fail. Any grade of below Pass constitutes an academic deficiency that must be removed by remedial work and/or examination in order to advance to the succeeding year. Students are required to record a score in Step I of the USMLE.

## Facilities

Located in downtown New Orleans, the medical center occupies several full city blocks. While classroom activities are held, for the most part, at 1430 Tulane Avenue, clinical teaching takes place primarily at the Tulane University Hospital and Clinic, Charity Hospital, and the New Orleans Veteran's Administration Hospital. Other hospitals in New Orleans and beyond provide supplementary teaching facilities. *Library:* The Rudolph Matas Library houses more than 150,000 volumes, and has subscriptions to all major medical periodicals. *Housing:* An apartment complex for student housing is located adjacent to the Tulane University Hospital and Clinic.

## Special Features

*Minority admissions:* The school has an active recruitment program targeted at the southeastern and southwestern parts of the country. A Summer Reinforcement and Enrichment Program is available for minority undergraduate premedical students. *Other degree programs:* Combined MD-PhD programs are offered in a variety of disciplines. MD-MS and MD-MPH programs are also available.

# MARYLAND

# Johns Hopkins University School of Medicine

733 North Broadway
Baltimore, Maryland   21205

*Phone:* 410-955-3182      *Fax:* 410-955-7494
*E-mail:* somaddmiss@jhmi.edu
*WWW:* hopkinsmedicine.org/som

| Application Filing | | Accreditation | |
|---|---|---|---|
| Earliest: | June 1 | LCME | |
| Latest: | October 15 | | |
| Fee: | $75 | **Degrees Granted** | |
| AMCAS: | yes | MD, MD-PhD, MD-MPH | |

### Enrollment: 2008–2009 First-Year Class

| Men: | 59 | 50% | Applied: | 6149 |
|---|---|---|---|---|
| Women: | 59 | 50% | Interviewed: | 774 |
| Minorities: | 13 | 11% | Enrolled: | 118 |
| Out of State: | 105 | 88% | | |

### 2008–2009 Class Profile

| *Mean MCAT Scores* | | *Mean GPA* |
|---|---|---|
| Physical Sciences: | 10 | 3.9 |
| Biological Sciences: | 11 | |
| Verbal Reasoning: | 10.0 | *Mean Science* |
| | | 3.9 |

**Tuition and Fees**

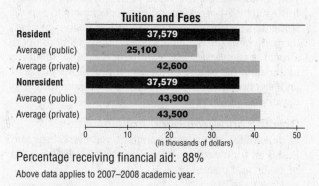

| | (in thousands of dollars) |
|---|---|
| **Resident** | 37,579 |
| Average (public) | 25,100 |
| Average (private) | 42,600 |
| **Nonresident** | 37,579 |
| Average (public) | 43,900 |
| Average (private) | 43,500 |

Percentage receiving financial aid: 88%

Above data applies to 2007–2008 academic year.

## Introduction

Johns Hopkins University was established in 1876 after Johns Hopkins provided 7 million dollars to establish a university, hospital, and teaching center. The School of Medicine opened in 1893. The main School of Medicine campus is located in eastern Baltimore.

## Admissions

Bachelor's degree or its equivalent required, minimum premedical science course requirements plus 2 semesters of calculus or statistics and 24 semester hours of social and behavioral sciences and humanities. Courses in biochemistry and advanced biology are recommended. There are no residence requirements and no preference is shown in selection of applicants, and candidates from all sections of the country are invited to apply. Selection is based on demonstrated academic achievement, unusual talents, strong humanistic and leadership qualities, and creative potential. *Transfer and advanced standing:* Transfer applications are considered for the second- or third-year class, and are accepted only into the standard 4-year curriculum. Places are rarely available.

## Curriculum

4-year semimodern. The program includes the integration of basic sciences and clinical experiences and the expanded use of case-based, small group learning sessions. Students have early contact with clinical medicine by working with community-based physicians. The physician and society course spans the 4-year program and covers a wide range of topics. *First year:* Integrated coverage of introductory basic sciences, neuroscience, and epidemiology. *Second year:* Devoted to advanced basic sciences, clinical skills, and start of clerkships. *Third and fourth years:* Required clerkships in major clinical areas and electives.

## Grading and Promotion Policies

Honors, High, Pass, Fail grades are used in required courses and clerkships and for electives. Grades are based on the composite judgment of responsible instructors, and not solely upon results of examinations. At the end of each academic year, the Committee on Student Promotions decides what actions will be taken regarding student status. The USMLE is not used to evaluate students for promotion or graduation.

## Facilities

*Teaching:* Most of the preclinical departments are situated in the W. Barry Wood Basic Science Building. The Johns Hopkins Hospital (1100 beds) occupies 14 acres of land adjacent to buildings that house the preclinical departments. Separate buildings contain specialty clinics such as the new oncology and outpatient center. The school is also affiliated with Bayview Medical Center (665 beds), Good Samaritan Hospital (277 beds), and Sinai Hospital of Baltimore (516 beds), and is associated with other institutions. *Other:* Research facilities for the preclinical sciences and clinical investigation are located in the Basic Science and Traylor Research Buildings. The Ross Research Building contains 240 modern laboratory suites. *Library:* The Welch Medical Library is located in a separate building adjacent to the other buildings of the School of Medicine and houses more than 354,000 volumes and 3600 periodicals. *Housing:* Reed Residence Hall is available for single students. A housing office assists other students in finding off-campus housing.

## Special Features

*Minority admissions:* The school has an active admissions program. *Other degree programs:* Combined MD-PhD programs are available in all the basic sciences as well as in biomedical engineering, biophysics, history of medicine, human genetics, molecular biology, epidemiology, cellular and molecular medicine. The school also offers combined MD-MPH and MD-DSc in Public Health programs.

# Uniformed Services University of the Health Sciences F. Edward Hebert School of Medicine

4301 Jones Bridge Road
Bethesda, Maryland    20814

*Phone:* 301-295-3101        *Fax:* 301-295-3545
*E-mail:* admissions@usuhs.mil
*WWW:* www.usuhs.mil

## Application Filing
Earliest:    June 1
Latest:      November 15
Fee:         none
AMCAS:       yes

## Accreditation
LCME

## Degrees Granted
MD

## Enrollment: 2008–2009 First-Year Class

| | | | | | |
|---|---|---|---|---|---|
| Men: | 120 | 70% | Applied: | | 1950 |
| Women: | 51 | 30% | Interviewed: | | 570 |
| Minorities: | 10 | 6% | Enrolled: | | 171 |
| Out of State: | 165 | 96% | | | |

## 2008–2009 Class Profile

| *Mean MCAT Scores* | | *Mean GPA* |
|---|---|---|
| Physical Sciences: | 10 | 3.50 |
| Biological Sciences: | 10 | |
| Verbal Reasoning: | 10 | *Mean Science* |
| | | 3.5 |

## Tuition and Fees

**Resident**            0
Average (public)   0
Average (private)  0
**Nonresident**        0
Average (public)   0
Average (private)  0

| | | | | | |
|---|---|---|---|---|---|
| 0 | 10 | 20 | 30 | 40 | 50 |

(in thousands of dollars)

Percentage receiving financial aid: n/app

## Introduction
The Uniformed Services University of the Health Sciences is located at the National Naval Medical Center. The university was created by the Department of Defense in 1972 to train career medical officers. The establishment of the school was sponsored by the late congressman F. Edward Hebert, whose initiative secured congressional approval for the creation of the Uniformed Services University. This is a tuition-free school, whose graduates provide medical services to the military.

## Admissions (AMCAS)
The basic premedical science courses plus 1 semester of calculus and 1 year of college English are required.

Selection for admission proceeds along 3 screening phases. The first involves review of the AMCAS application; the second phase mandates submission of supplementary material (an essay on choosing a medical service career and premedical recommendations) and its review; the third phase is the interview. Progress through these phases is competitive and selection is made on a rolling admission basis. *Transfer and advanced standing:* None.

## Curriculum
4-year semitraditional. *First year:* After a 4-week officer orientation program, the introductory basic sciences are taught. In addition, courses are offered in epidemiology and biometrics, human context in health care, military studies and medical history, diagnostic parisitology and medical zoology, medical psychology, and introduction to Clinical Medicine I. *Second year:* In addition to the advanced basic sciences, courses presented include clinical concepts, preventive medicine, radiographic interpretation, and introduction to Clinical Medicine II. *Third year:* A 48-week period of rotations through the major clinical specialties including family practice. *Fourth year:* Consists of medical, surgical, and psychiatric selective blocks, neurology, military preventive medicine, contingency and emergency medicine, subinternships, and elective clerkships. Note that since military medicine is in a sense a specialty, its unique hazards must be understood. This is provided by a course entitled Military Medicine Field Studies, offered during the summer following the freshman year. Students spend 1 week in field training exercise followed by a 4-week operational assignment to expose students to a typical real-world military environment, its medical hazards, and the potential intensity of operational exercises. This will better enable them to understand the nature of the environment, its physical and psychological stresses, and the personnel they will be serving in the future.

## Grading and Promotion Policies
Letter grades are used for courses and clerkships and Pass/Fail for electives. Both steps of the USMLE must be taken and passed.

## Facilities
*Teaching:* The school is located on the grounds of the Naval Hospital. Five buildings contain faculty offices, classrooms, student multidisciplinary and other laboratories and various support units. Thirteen affiliated hospitals provide clinical teaching facilities. *Library:* The Learning Resources Center possesses about 75,000 volumes and receives about 1500 medical periodicals. *Housing:* None available on campus.

## Special Features
Recruitment for the School of Medicine is sponsored by the Office of Recruitment and Admissions. For further information, call 800-772-1343, or visit *www.usuhs.mil*. *Other degree programs:* PhD and MPH programs are offered.

# University of Maryland School of Medicine

655 West Baltimore Street, Suite 190
Baltimore, Maryland    21201

*Phone:* 410-706-7478         *Fax:* 410-706-0467
*E-mail:* mfoxwell@som.umaryland.edu
*WWW:* medschool.umaryland.edu

| Application Filing | Accreditation |
|---|---|
| Earliest:  June 1 | LCME |
| Latest:    November 1 | |
| Fee:       $70 | **Degrees Granted** |
| AMCAS:     yes | MD, MD-PhD, MD-MS, MPH |

### Enrollment: 2008–2009 First-Year Class

| Men: | 67 | 42% | Applied: | 4503 |
|---|---|---|---|---|
| Women: | 93 | 58% | Interviewed: | 474 |
| Minorities: | 19 | 12% | Enrolled: | 160 |
| Out of State: | 27 | 18% | | |

### 2008–2009 Class Profile

| *Mean MCAT Scores* | | *Mean GPA* |
|---|---|---|
| Physical Sciences: | 11 | 3.7 |
| Biological Sciences: | 11 | |
| Verbal Reasoning: | 10 | *Mean Science* |
| | | 3.7 |

**Tuition and Fees**

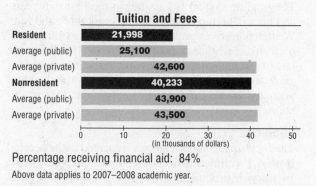

| | |
|---|---|
| Resident | 21,998 |
| Average (public) | 25,100 |
| Average (private) | 42,600 |
| Nonresident | 40,233 |
| Average (public) | 43,900 |
| Average (private) | 43,500 |

(in thousands of dollars)

Percentage receiving financial aid: 84%

Above data applies to 2007–2008 academic year.

## Introduction

The University of Maryland School of Medicine is located on the Baltimore City Campus, and is the fifth oldest medical school in the United States. The first class graduated in 1810. It was one of the first colleges to build its own hospital for clinical instruction. The school is part of the 11 campuses of the University of Maryland system. The School of Medicine at the Baltimore Campus is the central component of a large academic Health Center that provides for medical education, patient care, biomedical research, and community service.

## Admissions (AMCAS)

In addition to the minimum premedical science courses, requirements include 1 year of English. Applicants must also have completed a minimum of 90 semester hours at an accredited college or university. Preference is given to Maryland residents. The application process has several stages. All AMCAS applicants now receive a second-stage application. From those in Stage 2, applicants are selected for interviews, which are conducted on campus. *Transfer and advanced standing:* Information not available. Transfers into the third year limited only by attrition.

## Curriculum

*First and second years:* The basic sciences are integrated and taught as systems, using interdisciplinary teaching with both basic and clinical science faculty. Contact hours have been reduced, with an emphasis on independent study. A half-day course in introduction to clinical practice is dedicated to the instruction of interviewing, physical examination, intimate human behavior, ethics, and the dynamics of ambulatory care. *Third year:* Clerkships through major medical specialties. A mandatory rotation in family medicine is included. There is emphasis on ambulatory teaching in all other disciplines and a longitudinal half-day experience in a clinical setting in which the student will have continuity of care for patients and families. *Fourth year:* Devoted to ambulatory care, student subinternships, and electives.

## Grading and Promotion Policies

A letter grade system is used. Step 1 of the USMLE is required, and promotion to the third year is dependent on passing.

## Facilities

*Teaching:* The school is located a short distance from the newly developed Inner Harbor. University Hospital and affiliated hospitals around Baltimore have more than 1400 beds for teaching purposes. *Other:* The school also is affiliated with the Shock Trauma Center, Cancer Center, Institute of Psychiatric and Human Behavior, and the Sudden Infant Death Syndrome Institute. *Library:* The Health Sciences Library houses more than 240,000 volumes and subscribes to 3100 periodicals. It also provides access to a wide range of data bases. *Housing:* Dormitory rooms are available on campus in the apartments and town houses are available a short distance from the campus.

## Special Features

*Minority admissions:* The school has an active recruitment program that involves visits to colleges, seminars, and workshops. A prematriculation summer program is available to all students for those accepted into the first year. *Other degree programs:* Combined MD-PhD programs are available in all the basic sciences and in epidemiology, human genetics, and preventive medicine. An MD-MS degree in biomedical ethics is available. An MPH program is available to students after matriculation.

## MASSACHUSETTS

# Boston University School of Medicine

715 Albany Street
Boston, Massachusetts    02118

*Phone:* 617-638-4630          *Fax:* 617-638-4718
*E-mail:* medadms@bu.edu
*WWW:* www.bumc.bu.edu

| Application Filing | | Accreditation |
|---|---|---|
| Earliest: | June 1 | LCME |
| Latest: | November 1 | |
| Fee: | $100 | **Degrees Granted** |
| AMCAS: | yes | MD, MD-PhD, MD-MPH |

### Enrollment: 2008–2009 First-Year Class

| | | | | |
|---|---|---|---|---|
| Men: | 87 | 49% | Applied: | 10,870 |
| Women: | 90 | 51% | Interviewed: | 1033 |
| Minorities: | 150 | 85% | Enrolled: | 177 |
| Out of State: | 34 | 17% | | |

### 2008–2009 Class Profile

| *Mean MCAT Scores* | | *Mean GPA* |
|---|---|---|
| Physical Sciences: | 11.0 | 3.6 |
| Biological Sciences: | 11.0 | |
| Verbal Reasoning: | 10.0 | *Mean Science* |
| | | 3.5 |

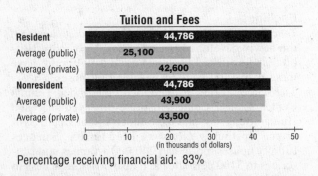

**Tuition and Fees**

| | |
|---|---|
| Resident | 44,786 |
| Average (public) | 25,100 |
| Average (private) | 42,600 |
| Nonresident | 44,786 |
| Average (public) | 43,900 |
| Average (private) | 43,500 |

0    10    20    30    40    50
(in thousands of dollars)

Percentage receiving financial aid: 83%

## Introduction

The New England Female Medical College was founded in 1848. In 1873, the college became the Boston University School of Medicine, the first coeducational medical school in the U.S. The medical campus includes the Schools of Medicine, Dental Medicine, and Public Health, as well as the hospital, Boston Medical Center.

## Admissions

Applicants are selected not only on the basis of academic record, recommendations, research experience, and involvement in community activities and service, but also on qualities of personality, character, and resilience. A personal interview is an integral part of the admissions process. Minimum premedical school coursework, as well as courses in two semesters of both English and humanities are required. Coursework in behavioral sciences, biochemistry, genetics, social sciences, molecular biology, and biostatistics or other college level mathematics is recommended.

## Curriculum

*First year:* Introduction to Clinical Medicine: students interview and evaluate patients beginning in the first week of school. The basic sciences are linked to applications in clinical practice, emphasizing multidisciplinary learning. *Second year:* The full-year systems-based Diagnosis and Therapy course focuses on pathophysiology with an integrated, multidisciplinary format led by basic science and clinical faculty. *Third year:* Core clinical training includes clerkships in all the major disciplines, with ambulatory and inpatient experience in generalist and subspecialty venues. *Fourth year:* Surgical subspecialties, ambulatory internal medicine, and subinternships are among the advanced rotations. A wide range of electives are available.

## Grading and Promotion Policies

The grading system is pass/fail in the first two years, and honors/high pass/pass/fail in years three and four. Written narratives provide supplemental evaluation of performance. Students take Step 1 of the USMLE at the end of the second year; a passing grade is required for graduation. Students take USMLE Step 2 after the third year, and record the grade as a requirement for graduation.

## Facilities

The four-square-block campus is located in the heart of Boston. Preclinical instruction is held principally in the 14-story Instructional Building. Students complete most of their clinical training at Boston Medical Center Hospital. Students may also do clinical work in the school's network of affiliated hospitals and community health centers.

## Special Features

*Minority admissions:* BUSM is committed to diversity in the faculty and student body. *Other degree programs:* Combined degree programs include BA-MD, MD/MPH, MD/PhD, and MD/MBA.

# Harvard Medical School

25 Shattuck Street
Boston, Massachusetts   02115

*Phone:* 617-432-1550          *Fax:* 617-432-3307
*E-mail:* admissions-office@hms.harvard.edu
*WWW:* hms.harvard.edu/hms/hms.asp

| Application Filing | | Accreditation | |
|---|---|---|---|
| Earliest: | June 1 | LCME | |
| Latest: | October 15 | | |
| Fee: | $85 | **Degrees Granted** | |
| AMCAS: | yes | MD, MD-PhD | |

### Enrollment: 2008–2009 First-Year Class

| | | | | | |
|---|---|---|---|---|---|
| Men: | 88 | 53% | Applied: | 6642 | |
| Women: | 77 | 47% | Interviewed: | 1049 | |
| Minorities: | 18 | 11% | Enrolled: | 165 | |
| Out of State: | 147 | 89% | | | |

### 2008–2009 Class Profile

| *Mean MCAT Scores* | | *Mean GPA* |
|---|---|---|
| Physical Sciences: | 11 | 3.8 |
| Biological Sciences: | 11 | |
| Verbal Reasoning: | 10 | *Mean Science* |
| | | 3.8 |

**Tuition and Fees**

| | (in thousands of dollars) |
|---|---|
| **Resident** | 40,499 |
| Average (public) | 25,100 |
| Average (private) | 42,600 |
| **Nonresident** | 40,499 |
| Average (public) | 43,900 |
| Average (private) | 43,500 |

Percentage receiving financial aid: 81%

Above data applies to 2007–2008 academic year.

## Introduction

The Harvard Medical School was founded in 1782. It has been located on the Longwood Avenue Quadrangle since 1906. In 1987 the Medical Education Center was opened next to the Medical School. It is a diverse academic medical center and has cooperative links to 18 independent medical institutions.

## Admissions

Minimum premedical science courses are required in addition to 1 year of calculus and 1 year of expository writing. Recommended courses include 16 hours in these areas: literature, languages, the arts, humanities, and social sciences. Selection is not based on residence. Selection is based on academic excellence as reflected by an applicant's GPA, MCAT scores, and recommendations. Other considerations are the personal essay, life experiences, community service activities, and research work. *Transfer and advanced standing:* Occasionally students are admitted to third-year class.

## Curriculum

4-year modern. Two programs are offered. The New Pathway Program is designed to accommodate the variety of interests, educational backgrounds, and career goals that characterize the student body. Basic science and clinical content are interwoven throughout the 4 years. *First and second years:* Uses a problem-based approach that emphasizes small-group tutorials and self-directed learning, complemented by laboratories, conferences, and lectures. Students are expected to analyze problems, locate relevant material in library and computer-based resources, and develop habits of life-long learning and independent study. *Third and fourth years:* Core clinical clerkships; advance science or independent project; patient-doctor III; and electives. The second MD Pathway is the Harvard-MIT-sponsored Health Sciences and Technology Program (HST). The curriculum of this program is designed for the student with a strong interest and background in quantitative science. The curriculum is in a semester format. HST students join students of the New Pathway Program for their clinical rotation. Thirty students are admitted each year. The school and its affiliated hospitals offer an extraordinary variety of courses. In addition, students have excess courses offered in other faculties at Harvard University and at Massachusetts Institute of Technology. Courses at these schools can be utilized in formulating an elective program.

## Grading and Promotion Policies

System used is Honors/Pass/Fail. Promotion Boards for each of the first 3 years determine those qualified to be promoted. Students must record total passing scores on Steps 1 and 2 of the USMLE for promotion and graduation, respectively.

## Facilities

*Teaching:* Preclinical courses are taught in the buildings that compose Longwood Avenue Quadrangle. Clinical instruction takes place in Beth Israel Hospital (368 beds), Brigham and Women's Hospital (650 beds), Massachusetts General Hospital (1060 beds), and others. *Other:* Research facilities available in most of the medical school buildings. *Library:* The Countway Library of Medicine is one of the largest in the country. *Housing:* Dormitory housing is available for men and women; apartments for married students are nearby.

## Special Features

*Minority admissions:* A full-time administrator coordinates the active minority recruitment program, which is geared to enroll students having academic strength, community commitment, and leadership ability. An 8-week prematriculation summer program is offered for a limited number of disadvantaged students to enhance their academic preparation and provide exposure to research. *Other degree programs:* The MD-PhD program exists for qualified applicants who wish to integrate medical school and intensive scientific training. A collaborative program exists with the Harvard School of Public Health.

# Tufts University School of Medicine

136 Harrison Avenue
Boston, Massachusetts   02111

*Phone:* 617-636-6571
*E-mail:* medadmissions@tufts.edu
*WWW:* tufts.edu/med

| Application Filing | | Accreditation | |
|---|---|---|---|
| Earliest: | June 1 | LCME | |
| Latest: | January 15 | | |
| Fee: | $105 | **Degrees Granted** | |
| AMCAS: | yes | MD, MD-PhD, MD-MPH | |
| | | MD-MBA | |

### Enrollment: 2008–2009 First-Year Class

| Men: | 97 | 54% | Applied: | 9103 |
|---|---|---|---|---|
| Women: | 81 | 46% | Interviewed: | 819 |
| Minorities: | 21 | 12% | Enrolled: | 178 |
| Out of State: | 126 | 70% | | |

### 2008–2009 Class Profile

| *Mean MCAT Scores* | | *Mean GPA* |
|---|---|---|
| Physical Sciences: | 10.9 | 3.6 |
| Biological Sciences: | 11.1 | |
| Verbal Reasoning: | 10.3 | *Mean Science* |
| | | 3.5 |

**Tuition and Fees**

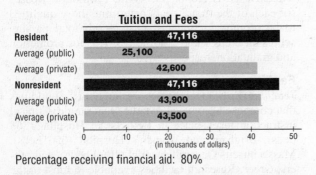

| | |
|---|---|
| Resident | 47,116 |
| Average (public) | 25,100 |
| Average (private) | 42,600 |
| Nonresident | 47,116 |
| Average (public) | 43,900 |
| Average (private) | 43,500 |

(in thousands of dollars)

Percentage receiving financial aid: 80%

## Introduction

Tufts University was established in 1850 as the Tufts Institute of Learning. In 1872 the name was changed to Tufts College, and in 1953 it became Tufts University. This reflects transition from the small liberal arts college to a complex multi-campus university. The School of Medicine was established in 1893. Because of the diverse hospitals affiliated with the school, students are provided with clinical experiences that range from inner-city tertiary-level hospitals to rural-based individual preceptorships.

## Admissions (AMCAS)

Minimum premedical science courses are required, as is proficiency in written and spoken English. Courses in calculus, statistics, and computers are desirable. There is no preference for state residents. *Transfer and*

*advanced standing:* Acceptance into the second or third year is possible as places become available.

## Curriculum

4-year modern. The program emphasizes, problem solving and critical, analytical discussion in small groups and case-based learning. *First and second years:* Focuses on the biology of cells and molecules followed by a segment dealing with the structure and development of tissues and organs, then the functions of the organs and the organism and its environment. The biology of normal cells, tissues, and organs is presented prior to exposure to the pathological manifestations of these components. The curriculum also covers such topics as nutrition, health care economics, family medicine, ethics, socioeconomics, physician-patient relationship, and history of medicine. The Preclinical Elective Program is designed to encourage students to pursue outside interests and talents as well as to foster meaningful faculty-student relationships. Students can explore opportunities in basic science, clinical medicine, or community aspects of medicine. In addition, the faculty is able to work more closely with students and to serve as role models, mentors, and informal advisors. *Third year:* Consists of rotations through the major clinical specialties and an elective period. *Fourth year:* Consists of a minimum of eight 4-week rotations. Five of these 8 must be taken at Tufts-affiliated hospitals; of these, 2 must be ward service rotations and 1 must be the clinical specialties rotation. Beyond these requirements, students are free to schedule approved learning experiences as part of their elective rotations at the Tufts-associated hospitals or elsewhere in the United States or abroad.

## Grading and Promotion Policies

The system used is Honors/High Pass/Pass/Low Pass/Fail. Passing Steps 1 and 2 of the USMLE is required for graduation.

## Facilities

*Teaching:* The major school structure is the Sackler Center. Clinical teaching facilities are provided by the New England Center Hospital (452 beds) and off campus by St. Elizabeth's Hospital (385 beds), Bayside Medical Center (950 beds), VA Hospital (769 beds), Lemuel Shattick Hospital (250 beds), and others. *Other:* Clinical research is carried out in the Ziskind Research Building of New England Medical Center Hospital. *Library:* The Health Sciences Library houses 92,000 volumes and subscribes to 1400 periodicals. *Housing:* A residence hall for men and women is located 1 block from the main building.

## Special Features

*Minority admissions:* Recruitment of minority applicants is directed primarily to the Boston, New England, and New York areas. A preadmission summer program is offered for accepted applicants. *Other degree programs:* Combined MD-PhD programs are offered in a variety of disciplines including immunology and molecular biology. A combined MD-MPH program is also offered. A combined MD-MBA degree in health management is also offered in collaboration with adjacent schools.

# University of Massachusetts Medical School

55 Lake Avenue, North
Worcester, Massachusetts 01655

*Phone:* 508-856-2323 *Fax:* 508-856-3629
*E-mail:* admissions@umassmed.edu
*WWW:* umassmed.edu

| Application Filing | | Accreditation | |
|---|---|---|---|
| Earliest: | June 1 | LCME | |
| Latest: | November 1 | | |
| Fee: | $75 | **Degrees Granted** | |
| AMCAS: | yes | MD, MD-PhD | |

### Enrollment: 2008–2009 First-Year Class

| Men: | 46 | 45% | Applied: | 830 |
|---|---|---|---|---|
| Women: | 57 | 55% | Interviewed: | 470 |
| Minorities: | 10 | 10% | Enrolled: | 103 |
| Out of State: | 2 | 2% | | |

### 2008–2009 Class Profile

| *Mean MCAT Scores* | | *Mean GPA* |
|---|---|---|
| Physical Sciences: | 11 | 3.7 |
| Biological Sciences: | 11 | |
| Verbal Reasoning: | 11 | *Mean Science* |
| | | 3.7 |

### Tuition and Fees

| Resident | 13,414 |
|---|---|
| Average (public) | 25,100 |
| Average (private) | 42,600 |
| Nonresident | n/app |
| Average (public) | |
| Average (private) | |

0 10 20 30 40 50
(in thousands of dollars)

Percentage receiving financial aid: 96%

Above data applies to 2007–2008 academic year.

## Introduction

The University of Massachusetts Medical School opened in 1970 and is located in Worcester. The school seeks to train residents of Massachusetts for service in the state, especially underserved areas. The school is affiliated with the University of Massachusetts Medical Center, which encompasses a regional trauma center as well as an air ambulance reception area. The school is located on the banks of Lake Quinsigamond.

## Admissions (AMCAS)

The basic premedical science courses and 1 year of English are required. Courses in calculus, psychology, sociology, and statistics are recommended. *Transfer and advanced standing:* Applicants will be accepted, provided there are vacancies in the class.

## Curriculum

4-year semimodern. *First and second years:* The cur-riculum in the preclinical sciences emphasizes thought-ful coordination across disciplines and inter-disciplinary courses. Throughout the first 2 years, stu-dents also participate in twice-weekly sessions consisting of The Patient, Physician, and Society (PPS) and the Longitudinal Preceptorship Program (LPP). Both courses are tightly integrated and coordinated with concurrent basic science disciplines. *Third and fourth years:* The clerkship years comprise the third and fourth years of study. Required clerkships consist of clinical rotations in internal medicine, family prac-tice, pediatrics, obstetrics and gynecology, psychiatry, neurology, and surgery. The medicine clerkship includes 4 weeks in an internist's office. The surgery clerkship consists of a hospital-based, 8-week compo-nent and a 4-week ambulatory component. The fourth year consists of a required 4-week clerkship in neurol-ogy and a 4-week subinternship in medicine plus a minimum of an additional 24 weeks of electives. With the guidance and counsel of faculty members, students plan a balanced program of study appropriate to their field of interest, combining work in both basic science and clinical medicine. The Senior Scholars Program also exists for selected students who desire intensive study in a field of special interest or research. Under the guidance of a faculty mentor, a unique program of at least 3 months combining both basic science and clinical experience in a given discipline is arranged.

## Grading and Promotion Policies

System used is Honors/Satisfactory/Marginal/Unsatis-factory/ Incomplete. Students are required to take USMLE Step 1 and Step 2. Promotion from one phase of the curriculum to the next will be determined by the Committee on Promotions, consisting of instructors from each department involved in the curriculum of a given period of study.

## Facilities

*Teaching:* A 10-story Basic and Clinical Sciences Building was completed in 1973. A 400-bed teaching hospital that adjoins the Sciences Building opened in 1976. The Medical Center is the designated regional trauma center for Central Massachusetts as well as the base of operation for New England Life Flight. *Other:* Among the affiliated hospitals for clinical teaching are the St. Vincent Hospital (600 beds), Worcester City Hospital (250 beds), Worcester Memorial Hospital (379 beds), and Berkshire Medical Center (365 beds). *Library:* The Medical School Library is housed in the Sciences Building and includes the capacity for more than 100,000 volumes. *Housing:* The school has no facilities to house students; they have to find places in the community.

## Special Features

*Minority admissions:* Minority students who are legal residents of Massachusetts are invited to apply for admission. A 4-week Summer Enrichment Program (SEP) is available for sophomore and higher level col-lege students. *Other degree programs:* Combined MD-PhD programs are offered in all the basic medical sciences and in immunology and molecular genetics.

# MICHIGAN

# Michigan State University College of Human Medicine

East Lansing, Michigan   48824

*Phone:* 517-353-9620       *Fax:* 517-432-0021
*E-mail:* mdadmissions@ msu.edu
*WWW:* MDadmissions.msu.edu

| Application Filing | | Accreditation | |
|---|---|---|---|
| Earliest: | June 1 | LCME | |
| Latest: | November 15 | | |
| Fee: | $60 | **Degrees Granted** | |
| AMCAS: | yes | MD, MD-PhD, MD-MA | |

### Enrollment: 2008–2009 First-Year Class

| Men: | 73 | 46% | Applied: | 5001 |
|---|---|---|---|---|
| Women: | 83 | 54% | Interviewed: | 440 |
| Minorities: | 8 | 5% | Enrolled: | 158 |
| Out of State: | 23 | 15% | | |

### 2008–2009 Class Profile

| *Mean MCAT Scores* | | *Mean GPA* |
|---|---|---|
| Physical Sciences: | 10 | 3.6 |
| Biological Sciences: | 10 | |
| Verbal Reasoning: | 10 | *Mean Science* |
| | | 3.5 |

### Tuition and Fees

| | |
|---|---|
| Resident | 28,010 |
| Average (public) | 25,100 |
| Average (private) | 42,600 |
| Nonresident | 60,890 |
| Average (public) | 43,900 |
| Average (private) | 43,500 |

(in thousands of dollars) 0 10 20 30 40 50

Percentage receiving financial aid: 95%

Above data applies to 2007–2008 academic year.

## Introduction

The aim of the College of Human Medicine at Michigan State University is to train primary care physicians in order to provide superior health care for everyone. To this end, the school seeks to educate and train competent physicians who are sensitive to the needs of the medically underserved residents of Michigan and who will respectfully and tactfully deal with patients and their families. It is essentially a large university operating in a small college setting. The university's health care educational complex incorporates, in addition, an Allopathic Medical School, a College of Osteopathic Medicine, and a College of Veterinary Medicine.

## Admissions (AMCAS)

Requirements include the basic premedical science courses, 1 year of English and college algebra plus 8 credits of nonscience courses. Preference is given to applicants from Michigan. Enrollment of nonresidents is limited to no more than 20%. Selection based on GPA, MCAT scores, relevant work experience, and compatibility with the school's primary care mission. Applicants who are highly motivated, have a good ability to communicate, manifest problem-solving skills, and demonstrate maturity are considered with favor. The class makeup is sought to be diverse in terms of background, talents and personalities. An interview is an essential component of the admission process. *Transfer and advanced standing:* Considered when vacancies exist.

## Curriculum

4-year semimodern. The curriculum is divided into 3 blocks integrating the basic biological and behavioral sciences with clinical training and problem-solving skills. *Block I:* A 1-year discipline-based experience that provides an introduction to the fundamentals of the basic biological and psychological/social sciences, along with mentor group and early clinical skills training that includes patient contact. *Block II:* A 1-year experience in the second year that is problem-based and learner-centered with the majority of learning occurring in the small group setting. An extended curricular option for both Blocks I and II is offered at no extra cost. *Block III:* An 84-week experience that includes the traditional clinical clerkships plus core competency and primary care experiences. This period is spent in 1 of the 6 communities affiliated with the university. Students live in their assigned community for the total period of required clinical training. Electives may be taken elsewhere. The community physicians work closely with community-based faculty members of the college to provide a unique and highly relevant learning environment.

## Grading and Promotion Policies

All grading in the school is Honors/Pass/Fail. A total passing score on Steps 1 and 2 of the USMLE is required for promotion to the third year and graduation, respectively.

## Facilities

*Teaching:* The primary facilities utilized in basic science instruction are Life Sciences Building, Fee Hall, and Giltner Hall. The Clinical Center is an ambulatory care facility where students are trained in clinical sciences during the first 2 years of the curriculum. Students receive their formal clinical training during the last 2 years in community settings in 18 hospitals in 6 Michigan communities. *Library:* Information not available. *Housing:* On-campus dormitory rooms and apartments for both single and married students. There is also a large selection of off-campus housing.

## Special Features

*Minority admissions:* A major effort is made to include applicants from inadequately represented geographic, economic, and ethnic groups. *Other degree programs:* Combined MD-MA and MD-PhD programs available in basic and behavioral science departments by individual arrangement.

# University of Michigan Medical School

1301 Catherine Street
Ann Arbor, Michigan    48109-0010

*Phone:* 734-764-6317          *Fax:* 734-763-0453
*E-mail:* umichmedadmiss@umich.edu
*WWW:* http://www.med.umich.edu/medschool/

| Application Filing | | Accreditation | |
|---|---|---|---|
| Earliest: | June 1 | LCME | |
| Latest: | November 15 | | |
| Fee: | $85 | **Degrees Granted** | |
| AMCAS: | yes | MD, MD-PhD, BA-MD | |

### Enrollment: 2008–2009 First-Year Class

| | | | | | |
|---|---|---|---|---|---|
| Men: | 77 | 45% | Applied: | | 5669 |
| Women: | 93 | 55% | Interviewed: | | 801 |
| Minorities: | 12 | 7% | Enrolled: | | 170 |
| Out of State: | 86 | 51% | | | |

### 2008–2009 Class Profile

| *Mean MCAT Scores* | | *Mean GPA* |
|---|---|---|
| Physical Sciences: | 11 | 3.8 |
| Biological Sciences: | 11 | |
| Verbal Reasoning: | 10 | *Mean Science* |
| | | 3.8 |

**Tuition and Fees**

| | |
|---|---|
| **Resident** | 24,755 |
| Average (public) | 25,100 |
| Average (private) | 42,600 |
| **Nonresident** | 39,119 |
| Average (public) | 43,900 |
| Average (private) | 43,500 |

(in thousands of dollars)

Percentage receiving financial aid: 94%

Above data applies to 2007–2008 academic year.

## Introduction

The University of Michigan Medical School is located in the University of Michigan Medical Center in Ann Arbor along with the University of Michigan hospitals. Its origin can be traced back to the establishment of the university in 1817. The first class graduated in 1851. The beginning of the modern Medical School came in 1869 when it replaced the proprietary school. The quality of the new school was already praised in the famous Flexner Report. The University Hospital, the most modern in the world at that time, was opened up in 1925. The school is located on an 84-acre campus and provides large city facilities with a small city atmosphere.

## Admissions (AMCAS)

In addition to the basic premedical science courses plus biochemistry, 6 credits of English and 18 credits of nonscience subjects are required. A biochemistry course is also required. Advanced courses in biology and/or chemistry are recommended. Preference is given to residents, but a significant number of nonresidents are admitted. Thirty-five highly qualified high school graduates who have been accepted by the University of Michigan College of Literature, Science and the Arts will be admitted to the 8-year Integrated Premedical-Medical Program. They earn their BA degree after the fourth year. *Transfer and advanced standing:* None.

## Curriculum

4-year semimodern. *First year:* Provides a foundation in the basic biomedical sciences. It consists of 2 units, namely, Introduction to the Patient and Multidisciplinary Conferences, which extends throughout the year. During the fall term, gross anatomy and pathology are covered, and in the winter term, embryology, histology, host defense, microbiology, pharmacology and physiology are presented. *Second year:* Organized into 12 organ system and disease-based sequences, taught in an integrated multidisciplinary manner. *Third year:* Consists of four 12-week blocks, that are spent on required major clerkships plus medicine and neurology. *Fourth year:* Consists of eleven 4-week periods. Students are encouraged to pursue fields of personal interest.

## Grading and Promotion Policies

The first year is Pass/Fail only; in the second, third, and fourth years, a modified system comprised of Honors, High Pass, Pass, and Fail. Clinical clerkship grades are usually accompanied by a narrative description of student performance. Students are required to pass Step 1 of the USMLE for promotion to the third year, and are required to pass Step 2 for graduation.

## Facilities

*Teaching:* Basic sciences are taught in Medical Sciences Buildings Unit I and II in the Medical Center. Clinical instruction takes place at the University Hospitals (888 beds) supplemented by the use of St. Joseph Mercy Hospital (522 beds) and the VA Hospital (486 beds). The University Hospital was opened in 1986. *Other:* Medical Center includes: Simpson Memorial Institute devoted to cancer research and diseases of the blood; 3 Kresge buildings for clinical research; and the Buhl Research Center for Human Genetics. Two new Medical Sciences Research Buildings were opened in 1986 and 1988 and a third in 1994. *Library:* The A. Alfred Taubman Medical Library houses more than 200,000 volumes and 3000 periodicals; the Learning Resource Center is housed in the library building and includes computers, laser printers, and an extensive audiovisual collection for student use. *Housing:* Some facilities available.

## Special Features

*Minority admissions:* The school has an active minority-student recruitment program. Some scholarships for underrepresented minority students are available. *Other degree programs:* School offers combination MD-PhD programs in a variety of disciplines including human genetics.

# Wayne State University School of Medicine

540 East Canfield Avenue
Detroit, Michigan    48201

*Phone:* 313-577-1466          *Fax:* 313-577-9420
*E-mail:* admissions@med.wayne.edu
*WWW:* med.wayne.edu/

| Application Filing | | Accreditation |
|---|---|---|
| Earliest: | June 1 | LCME |
| Latest: | December 15 | |
| Fee: | $50 | **Degrees Granted** |
| AMCAS: | yes | MD, MD-PhD |

### Enrollment: 2008–2009 First-Year Class

| Men: | 181 | 60% | Applied: | 3968 |
|---|---|---|---|---|
| Women: | 121 | 40% | Interviewed: | 842 |
| Minorities: | 24 | 8% | Enrolled: | 302 |
| Out of State: | 25 | 8% | | |

### 2008–2009 Class Profile

| *Mean MCAT Scores* | | *Mean GPA* |
|---|---|---|
| Physical Sciences: | 10 | 3.7 |
| Biological Sciences: | 11 | |
| Verbal Reasoning: | 10 | *Mean Science* |
| | | 3.7 |

**Tuition and Fees**

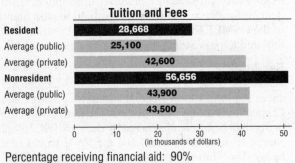

| | |
|---|---|
| Resident | 28,668 |
| Average (public) | 25,100 |
| Average (private) | 42,600 |
| Nonresident | 56,656 |
| Average (public) | 43,900 |
| Average (private) | 43,500 |

(in thousands of dollars)

Percentage receiving financial aid: 90%

Above data applies to 2007–2008 academic year.

## Introduction

The Wayne State University School of Medicine was established in 1868. It is associated with the Detroit Medical Center, which contains 6 health care institutions. It is located in the northcentral area of Detroit. The facilities of the School of Medicine are relatively modern, having been completed in the last 25 years.

## Admissions (AMCAS)

Applicants should have taken the basic premedical courses plus a biology course and 1 year of English. The school does consider nonresidents for admission but state residents, as defined by university regulations, are given preference. In addition to residency, selection is based on the standard considerations, namely, college record, MCAT scores, recommendations/evaluations, and interview results. *Transfer and advanced standing:* Applicants from U.S. or Canadian schools will be considered for second- and third-year classes.

## Curriculum

4-year semi-modern. *First year:* Begins with an introductory clinical course, which runs through all four years, including Introduction to the Patient, human sexuality, medical interviewing, physical diagnosis, public health and prevention, and evidence-based medicine. Year 1 is organized around the disciplines of structure (anatomy, histology, embryology, and radiology), function (biochemistry, physiology, genetics, and nutrition), and ends with an integrated neuroscience course. *Second year:* A completely integrated year focusing on pathophysiology, including immunology/microbiology and pharmacology. *Third year:* Consists of a series of clinical clerkships including medicine, surgery, pediatrics, family medicine, psychiatry, neurology, and obstetrics/gynecology. During the third year all students have a 6-month continuity clerkship. *Fourth year:* This is an elective year and includes emergency medicine, a subinternship, and an ambulatory block month. The school uses traditional lectures, small group and panel discussions, computer assisted instruction, and multimedia in its teaching program.

## Grading and Promotion Policies

System used is Honors/Pass/Fail. In order to qualify for promotion to the next class, a student must demonstrate competency on all subject examinations. All students will be required to pass Step 1 of the USMLE in order to be promoted into the third year.

## Facilities

*Teaching:* The School of Medicine is located in the heart of the 236-acre Detroit Medical Center. Gordon Scott Hall houses the school's basic science departments, as well as administrative and service offices. Clinical teaching takes place at the Harper Hospital (557 beds), Children's Hospital (320 beds), Grace Hospital (957 beds), Hutzel Hospital (360 beds). *Other:* Clinical teaching also takes place off campus at the Detroit Receiving Hospital (700 beds) and VA Hospital (890 beds). *Library:* Shiffman Medical Library houses more than 150,000 volumes. *Housing:* Available in the campus area.

## Special Features

*Minority admissions:* The school's Office of Recruitment is actively engaged in furthering minority-student enrollment. Entering students can participate in a summer program designed to facilitate the transition to medical school. *Other degree programs:* Combined MD-PhD degree programs are offered in a variety of basic science disciplines.

## MINNESOTA

# Mayo Clinic College of Medicine Mayo Medical School

200 First Street, S.W.
Rochester, Minnesota   55905

*Phone:* 507-284-3671          *Fax:* 507-284-2634
*E-mail:* MedSchoolAdmissions@mayo.edu
*WWW:* mayo.edu/mms

| Application Filing | | Accreditation | |
|---|---|---|---|
| Earliest: | June 1 | LCME | |
| Latest: | November 1 | | |
| Fee: | $85 | **Degrees Granted** | |
| AMCAS: | yes | MD, MD-PhD | |

### Enrollment: 2008–2009 First-Year Class

| Men: | 23 | 54% | Applied: | 3429 |
|---|---|---|---|---|
| Women: | 19 | 46% | Interviewed: | 295 |
| Minorities: | 4 | 10% | Enrolled: | 42 |
| Out of State: | 32 | 76% | | |

### 2008–2009 Class Profile

| *Mean MCAT Scores* | | *Mean GPA* |
|---|---|---|
| Physical Sciences: | 11 | 3.9 |
| Biological Sciences: | 11 | |
| Verbal Reasoning: | 10.0 | *Mean Science* |
| | | 3.8 |

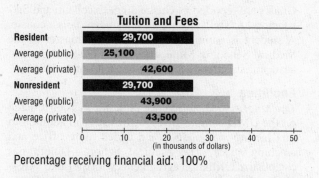

**Tuition and Fees**

| Resident | 29,700 |
| Average (public) | 25,100 |
| Average (private) | 42,600 |
| Nonresident | 29,700 |
| Average (public) | 43,900 |
| Average (private) | 43,500 |

(in thousands of dollars)

Percentage receiving financial aid: 100%

## Introduction

The Mayo Medical School is part of the Mayo Clinic. Its origin goes back to 1863, when Dr. William Worrall Mayo settled in Rochester. He was joined 20 years later by his two physician sons who set up a private integrated group practice in which they were joined by other respected physicians. This led to the formation of the renowned Mayo Clinic. The faculty of the Medical School is associated with the Clinic and hospitals. The school was founded in 1972.

## Admissions (AMCAS)

Only the minimum premedical science courses are required. A course in biochemistry is also required. Forty-two students comprise each class. The initial screening involves a review of the contents of the AMCAS application. Those being considered further will receive a standardized phone interview instead of a supplementary application. *Transfer and advanced standing:* Not available.

## Curriculum

4-year modern. The small class size facilitates a personalized course of instruction characterized by extensive clinical interaction and the integration of basic and clinical sciences throughout all segments of the curriculum. Patient contact begins early in the first year and increases commensurate with student progress. The integration of basic and clinical sciences occurs in a manner that strengthens basic science concepts, stresses the patient orientation appropriate for an undergraduate medical school, and utilizes a variety of active, problem-oriented, faculty-guided and self-learning techniques to aid student comprehension. Integration of the various components of the curriculum is promoted by organization of course material into broad functional units that span several curricular years. The curricular units are: the cell; the organ; the patient, physician, and society; the scientific foundations of medical practice; clinical experiences; and the research trimester. This type of curricular organization enables content integration of the basic and clinical sciences and between basic and clinical science.

## Grading and Promotion Policies

An Honors/Pass/Fail system is used. Students are required to take Steps 1 and 2 of the USMLE. Promotion will be based on evidence of behavior and maturation, consonant with the student's talents and defined professional goals.

## Facilities

*Teaching:* Located in Rochester, the school makes use of the facilities of the Mayo Clinic in its preclinical program. The Guggenheim Building houses the facilities for education and research in most of the basic sciences; the Plummer Building houses the library and Biomedical Communications; and the Hilton Building houses clinical laboratories of the Department of Laboratory Medicine, Microbiology, and Endocrine Research. Clinical teaching takes place at 2 hospitals: Rochester Methodist Hospital and St. Mary's Hospital, which provide 2000 beds and several clinical research facilities. *Other:* Facilities for research are located in the Medical Sciences Building, Guggenheim Building, and Rochester Methodist and St. Mary's Hospitals. *Library:* Information not available. *Housing:* Students are responsible for finding their own housing in the area.

## Special Features

*Minority admissions:* The school actively seeks minority students and welcomes their application for admission. *Other degree programs:* Combined MD-PhD programs are offered in several disciplines including immunology and pathology. A combined MD-Oral Maxillofacial Surgery program is also offered to candidates who have completed the DDS degree.

# University of Minnesota Medical School—Duluth Campus

10 University Drive
Duluth, Minnesota   55812

*Phone:* 218-726-8511          *Fax:* 218-726-7057
*E-mail:* medadmis@d.umn.edu
*WWW:* semd.d.umn.edu

| Application Filing | | Accreditation |
|---|---|---|
| Earliest: | June 1 | LCME |
| Latest: | November 15 | |
| Fee: | $75 | **Degrees Granted** |
| AMCAS: | yes | None |

### Enrollment: 2008–2009 First-Year Class

| | | | | |
|---|---|---|---|---|
| Men: | 26 | 44% | Applied: | 1413 |
| Women: | 33 | 56% | Interviewed: | 141 |
| Minorities: | 7 | 12% | Enrolled: | 59 |
| Out of State: | 8 | 14% | | |

### 2008–2009 Class Profile

| *Mean MCAT Scores* | | *Mean GPA* |
|---|---|---|
| Physical Sciences: | 9.4 | 3.7 |
| Biological Sciences: | 9.7 | |
| Verbal Reasoning: | 9.3 | *Mean Science* |
| | | 3.6 |

### Tuition and Fees

| | (in thousands of dollars) |
|---|---|
| **Resident** | 29,073 |
| Average (public) | 25,100 |
| Average (private) | 42,600 |
| **Nonresident** | 36,606 |
| Average (public) | 43,900 |
| Average (private) | 43,500 |

Percentage receiving financial aid: 98%

## Introduction

In 1947 the University of Minnesota—Duluth became an associate campus of the University of Minnesota. This school provides the first 2 years of medical education, after which students automatically transfer to the parent school in Minneapolis for the completion of their training. The school seeks to provide primary care practitioners for rural communities throughout Minnesota and American Indian communities nationwide.

## Admissions (AMCAS)

Prerequisite courses are: 1 semester biology, biochemistry, 4 additional science courses (2 being upper level), and 1 upper-level non-science course. Applicants must be U.S. citizens or permanent residents. Strong preference is given to Minnesota residents. A mechanism has also been established for transfer to the University of Minnesota Medical School in Minneapolis on a non-competitive basis for completion of MD requirements.

## Curriculum

2-year semimodern. The curriculum exposes the students to basic behavioral and clinical sciences to prepare them for continuing their studies in Minneapolis. *First year:* Following the applied anatomy course and principles of basic medical science, clinical material is correlated with the basic sciences in integrated courses including nervous system, hematopoiesis and host defenses, histopathology, dermatology, and the musculoskeletal system. Students also participate in the Family Practice Preceptorship Program. Each student is assigned to a family physician within the immediate area and is introduced to medicine as practiced in that setting. *Second year:* Integrated courses in the respiratory, cardiovascular, gastrointestinal, and endocrine systems, as well as integrated clinical medicine are presented. Students spend more time in the clinical setting and receive more intensive instruction in clinical medicine. The preceptorship program in the second year involves the student with physicians who practice in rural areas of Minnesota. This interaction occurs three times per year for a 3-day period each time. Additional courses in the behavioral sciences are offered throughout both years of medical school. Therefore, in the first 2 years of medical school, the students acquire the necessary knowledge of the scientific basis for medical practice while reinforcing this knowledge by active participation in the patient care setting.

## Grading and Promotion Policies

Grades are reported as Oustanding, Excellent, and Satisfactory. A No Pass is given if a student fails a course. A student is automatically allowed to transfer to the Medical School in Minneapolis if he or she is in good academic standing and has passed Step 1 of the USMLE.

## Facilities

*Teaching:* A medical science building was constructed on the UMD campus in 1979. In 1997, an addition to this facility was opened and added more office and teaching space. The Medical School—Duluth has established affiliation agreements with St. Luke's Hospital, Miller-Dwan, and St. Mary's Duluth Clinic Health Care System. These facilities provide students with access to an extremely diverse patient population in the clinical setting. *Library:* In 2000, all contents of the Health Science Library were transferred to the newly constructed UMC Library Building. The health sciences have strengthened considerably due to the acquisition of full-text electronic resources and a full-service library with new study rooms, computers, and connections for laptop computers. *Housing:* Most students live in houses and apartments in Duluth and surrounding areas. No on-campus housing is available.

## Special Features

*Minority admissions:* Applicants from minority groups are underrepresented in the health professions, particularly Native Americans; they are encouraged to apply.

# University of Minnesota Medical School—Minneapolis

420 Delaware Street, S.E.
Minneapolis, Minnesota  55455

*Phone:* 612-625-7977          *Fax:* 612-625-8228
*E-mail:* meded@umn.edu
*WWW:* med.umn.edu/

| Application Filing | | Accreditation | |
|---|---|---|---|
| Earliest: | June 1 | LCME | |
| Latest: | November 15 | | |
| Fee: | $75 | **Degrees Granted** | |
| AMCAS: | yes | MD, MD-PhD, | |
| | | MD-MBA, MD-MPH | |
| | | MD-MS (BME) | |

### Enrollment: 2008–2009 First-Year Class

| | | | | | |
|---|---|---|---|---|---|
| Men: | 92 | 54% | Applied: | | 3212 |
| Women: | 78 | 46% | Interviewed: | | 464 |
| Minorities: | 42 | 24% | Enrolled: | | 170 |
| Out of State: | 30 | 18% | | | |

### 2008–2009 Class Profile

| *Mean MCAT Scores* | | *Mean GPA* |
|---|---|---|
| Physical Sciences: | 11.2 | 3.71 |
| Biological Sciences: | 11.25 | |
| Verbal Reasoning: | 10.55 | *Mean Science* |
| | | 3.74 |

**Tuition and Fees**

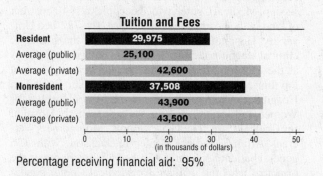

| | |
|---|---|
| Resident | 29,975 |
| Average (public) | 25,100 |
| Average (private) | 42,600 |
| Nonresident | 37,508 |
| Average (public) | 43,900 |
| Average (private) | 43,500 |

(in thousands of dollars)

Percentage receiving financial aid: 95%

## Introduction

The University of Minnesota Medical School was established in 1888 when 3 of the 4 proprietary medical schools in the area joined together; a fourth joined later. By 1911 the first unit of the University Hospital was dedicated. The school has a long tradition of research and clinical achievement and is characterized by strong departments in the basic medical sciences.

## Admissions (AMCAS)

Requirements include a bachelor's degree, 1 semester each of biology and chemistry plus labs, 4 other life sciences of which 2 must be upper-level and 1 upper-level writing, humanities, or social sciences course. Courses in genetics and statistics are highly recommended. Preference for admission is given to legal residents of Minnesota. *Transfer and advanced standing:* Transfer students are accepted into the third year and usually only from the 2-year University of Minnesota Medical School—Duluth.

## Curriculum

4-year semitraditional. *First year:* Includes coursework in the basic medical sciences, behavioral science, and introductory experiences with patients. *Second year:* Consists of both department and integrated interdisciplinary courses organized and taught along organ system and topical lines. *Third and fourth years:* Consist of a total of 76 weeks of academic requirements, 56 weeks of required clerkships, and 24 weeks of electives. Before beginning this phase of the program, the student selects a faculty advisor and develops a plan for these 2 academic years. For most students, this period begins in June following the second year and ends in May of the senior year, with graduation and awarding of the MD degree. The 56 weeks of required clinical courses include: 12 weeks of internal medicine; 6 weeks each of surgery, obstetrics-gynecology, pediatrics, and psychiatry; 4 weeks of neurology, 4 weeks of a surgical subspecialty, 4 weeks of energy medicine, and an 8-week outpatient clinical primary care experience. Students may also elect to participate in research, rural medicine, and international medicine experiences as part of their Third Year/Fourth Year curriculum.

## Grading and Promotion Policies

Grading in the two years is on a P-N (Pass-Fail) system, with Honors designation for students in the top 20% of each of the First-year and Second-year classes. Students receive evaluations as Satisfactory, Excellent, and Honors for clinical coursework. Students who receive I or N grades are reviewed by the Student Scholastic Standing Committee. Students must pass Steps 1 and 2 of the USMLE as a requirement for graduation and the MD degree. Students must pass the USMLE Step 1 to continue full-time work in the Third Year.

## Facilities

*Teaching:* The University Hospital and most of the major hospitals in the Minneapolis-St. Paul area are affiliated with the medical school and provide clinical training facilities. *Other:* Facilities for research are located in the Health Sciences Center. *Library:* A comprehensive medical library that contains many books and subscribes to numerous periodicals is available for student use. *Housing:* Information is not available.

## Special Features

*Minority admissions:* Minority applicants are encouraged to apply. *Other degree programs:* A 7-year MD-PhD program is available for superior students planning academic medicine careers. The school also offers programs leading to MD-MBA, MD-MPH, ID-MD, and MD-MHI degrees.

# MISSISSIPPI

## University of Mississippi School of Medicine

2500 North State Street
Jackson, Mississippi   39216

*Phone:* 601-984-5010          *Fax:* 601-984-1079
*E-mail:* AdmitMD@som.umsmed.edu
*WWW:* http:som.umc.edu

| Application Filing | | Accreditation |
|---|---|---|
| Earliest: | June 1 | LCME |
| Latest: | October 15 | |
| Fee: | $50 | **Degrees Granted** |
| AMCAS: | yes | MD |

### Enrollment: 2008–2009 First-Year Class

| | | | | |
|---|---|---|---|---|
| Men: | 55 | 50% | Applied: | 272 |
| Women: | 55 | 50% | Interviewed: | 193 |
| Minorities: | 19 | 17% | Enrolled: | 110 |
| Out of State: | 0 | 0% | | |

### 2008–2009 Class Profile

| *Mean MCAT Scores* | | *Mean GPA* |
|---|---|---|
| Physical Sciences: | 8.5 | 3.64 |
| Biological Sciences: | 9.3 | |
| Verbal Reasoning: | 9.0 | *Mean Science* |
| | | 3.58 |

### Tuition and Fees

| | |
|---|---|
| **Resident** | 11,649 |
| Average (public) | 25,100 |
| Average (private) | 42,600 |
| **Nonresident** | 27,142 |
| Average (public) | 43,900 |
| Average (private) | 43,500 |

(in thousands of dollars)

Percentage receiving financial aid:  86%

## Introduction

The University of Mississippi School of Medicine, located in Jackson, is part of the University of Mississippi Medical Center. The Medical Center also includes Schools of Dentistry, Nursing, Health-Related Professions, Graduate Studies in the Medical Sciences, and the University Hospitals and Clinics. The School of Medicine opened in 1903 and operated as a 2-year institution until 1955 when it expanded to a 4-year program and relocated in Jackson.

## Admissions (AMCAS)

In addition to the basic premedical sciences, required courses include 1 year of mathematics, 1 year of English, and 1 of advanced science. High priority is given to state residents. *Transfers and advanced standing:* Applications are considered from those who are in good standing at their previous school.

## Curriculum

4-year traditional. *First year:* Introductory basic sciences plus psychiatry and cardiopulmonary resuscitation. *Second year:* Advanced basic sciences as well as courses in parasitology, genetics, psychiatry, epidemiology, and biostatistics, all of which are covered in the first 2 quarters. The third quarter is devoted to multidepartmental introduction to clinical medicine, which provides classroom instruction in history taking and physical examination. This is supplemented by weekly tutorial sessions conducted by members of the faculty and is correlated with instruction in clinical laboratory diagnosis. *Third year:* Rotating clerkships in major clinical specialties as well as in family medicine and radiology. *Fourth year:* Consists of 9 required calendar-month blocks of clinical subjects. One block must come from 2 of the 3 major clinical specialties. Two courses must be taken in an ambulatory setting and 1 block in neuroscience, medicine, and surgery is required. The goal of the curriculum is to provide students with an opportunity to acquire a knowledge base, clinical skills, and personal qualities desirable for a practitioner.

## Grading and Promotion Policies

A numerical grading system is used. Students must achieve not less than 70 in each course and a weighted average of not less than 75 each year. Students must record scores in specific individual exams of Steps 1 and 2 of the USMLE.

## Facilities

*Teaching:* The school is part of the University of Mississippi Medical Center, which occupies a 164-acre tract of land in the heart of the capital city. The 722-bed University Hospitals and Clinics serve as the principal clinical teaching facility. It includes ambulatory clinics at the Jackson Medical Mall, the University Medical Pavilion, the University Hospital, the Blair E. Batson Hospital for Children, the Winfred L. Wiser Hospital for Women and Infants, and the Wallace Conerly Hospital for Critical Care. The G.V. "Sonny" Montgomery Veterans Affairs Medical Center of Jackson, with 136 general patient beds and a 120-bed nursing home, is the principal teaching affiliate for Medical Center educational programs. The McBryde Rehabilitation Center for the Blind adjoins the University Hospital, as does the Mississippi Methodist Hospital and Rehabilitation Center. *Library:* The Rowland Medical Library is a part of the Verner Smith Holmes Learning Resource Center. It contains more than 307,115 items and receives 2368 current periodicals and serial publications.

## Special Features

*Minority admissions:* The school has a strong commitment to enrolling and retaining minority and/or disadvantaged students. Its efforts are coordinated by its Division of Multicultural Affairs. It offers a 9-week preparatory reinforcement and enrichment program and a preentry summer program for accepted minority students. *Other degree programs:* Combined MD-PhD programs are offered in the basic sciences and preventive medicine and a postbaccalaureate Professional Portal Track program offers an MS degree.

## MISSOURI

# Saint Louis University School of Medicine

1402 South Grand Boulevard
St. Louis, Missouri   63104

*Phone:* 314-977-9870          *Fax:* 314-977-9825
*E-mail:* slumd@slu.edu
*WWW:* http://medschool.slu.edu

| Application Filing | Accreditation |
|---|---|
| Earliest:   June 1 | LCME |
| Latest:    December 15 | |
| Fee:     $100 | **Degrees Granted** |
| AMCAS:  yes | MD, MD-PhD, |
| | MD-MPH, MD-MBA |

### Enrollment: 2008–2009 First-Year Class

| | | | | | |
|---|---|---|---|---|---|
| Men: | 98 | 56% | Applied: | 5176 |
| Women: | 78 | 44% | Interviewed: | 942 |
| Minorities: | 11 | 6% | Enrolled: | 176 |
| Out of State: | 135 | 76% | | |

### 2008–2009 Class Profile

| *Mean MCAT Scores* | | *Mean GPA* |
|---|---|---|
| Physical Sciences: | 10.5 | 3.7 |
| Biological Sciences: | 11 | |
| Verbal Reasoning: | 10.5 | *Mean Science* |
| | | 3.6 |

**Tuition and Fees**

| | |
|---|---|
| **Resident** | 43,830 |
| Average (public) | 25,100 |
| Average (private) | 42,600 |
| **Nonresident** | 43,830 |
| Average (public) | 43,900 |
| Average (private) | 43,500 |

(in thousands of dollars)

Percentage receiving financial aid: 84%

## Introduction

St. Louis University, established by the Jesuits in 1818, was the first university chartered west of the Mississippi. The School of Medicine was opened in 1836. It is one of the university's 6 professional schools, the others being Business, Law, Nursing, Public Health, Doisy College of Health Professions, and Social Service. During the last half of the nineteenth century, political developments forced the separation of the medical school from the university. Reintegration took place in 1963. It was at that time that many distinguished physicians also joined the faculty.

## Admissions (AMCAS)

In addition to the basic premedical science courses, requirements include 1 year of English and 12 credits of humanities and behavioral science courses. Recommended courses include calculus and biochemistry. Seventy-five percent of each class are nonresidents. *Transfer and advanced standing:* Applicants from accredited U.S. medical schools are considered for the third-year classes.

## Curriculum

4-year semimodern. The curriculum consists of 3 phases. *Phase 1:* Consists of a Fundamental or a Biomedical Sciences course, a Health Information Resources course to develop computer skills and proficiency in gathering information on various aspects of human disease and patient care, and a Patient, Physician, and Society course that includes such units as ethics, communication skills, and physical diagnosis. *Phase 2:* Includes an organ and systems approach. *Phase 3:* Incorporates year III and year IV with an added clerkship in Family Medicine and opportunities to design individualized programs, including electives. Ambulatory care activities have been significantly expanded.

## Grading and Promotion Policies

The system used is Honors/Pass/Fail. Overall achievement and the promise of students is taken into consideration in deciding promotion. Students must record a passing total score on Step 1 of the USMLE for promotion to the third year and on Step 2 CK for graduation.

## Facilities

*Teaching:* The school consists of a medical sciences building, Doisy Hall, Caroline Building, Doisy Research Center, Anheuser Busch Institute, and Doisy Learning Resources Center. *Clinical* facilities consist of: Saint Louis University Hospital, Cardinal Glennon Memorial Hospital for Children, Bethesda Cancer Research Center, St. Mary's Health Center, and Wohl Memorial Mental Health Institute. Several other hospitals are affiliated with the school. *Other:* Laboratory facilities are available at: The University Hospital, School of Medicine, Doisy Research Center, Pediatric Research Institute, and Institute for Molecular Virology. *Library:* The Medical Center Library has a collection of 112,109 volumes and receives 1421 periodicals. *Housing:* A medical fraternity offers housing.

## Special Features

*Minority admissions:* The School of Medicine is committed to diversity in the classroom and in the clinics so that all of our students understand and learn from each other about the practice of medicine in a diversified environment. *Other degree programs:* Combined MD-PhD programs are available in the basic medical sciences and in molecular virology. Combined MD-MPH and MD-MBA programs are available.

# University of Missouri—Columbia School of Medicine

One Hospital Drive
Columbia, Missouri    65212

*Phone:* 573-882-9219        *Fax:* 573-884-2988
*E-mail:* mizzoumed@missouri.edu
*WWW:* muhealth.org~medicine

| Application Filing | | Accreditation | |
|---|---|---|---|
| Earliest: | June 1 | LCME | |
| Latest: | November 1 | | |
| Fee: | $75 | **Degrees Granted** | |
| AMCAS: | yes | MD, MD-PhD, MD-MS | |

### Enrollment: 2008–2009 First-Year Class

| Men: | 52 | 54% | Applied: | 1264 |
|---|---|---|---|---|
| Women: | 44 | 46% | Interviewed: | 283 |
| Minorities: | 0 | | Enrolled: | 96 |
| Out of State: | 10 | 10% | | |

### 2008–2009 Class Profile

| *Mean MCAT Scores* | | *Mean GPA* |
|---|---|---|
| Physical Sciences: | 10 | 3.8 |
| Biological Sciences: | 11 | |
| Verbal Reasoning: | 10 | *Mean Science* |
| | | 3.8 |

### Tuition and Fees

| | (in thousands of dollars) |
|---|---|
| **Resident** | 23,846 |
| Average (public) | 25,100 |
| Average (private) | 42,600 |
| **Nonresident** | 46,432 |
| Average (public) | 43,900 |
| Average (private) | 43,500 |

Percentage receiving financial aid: 96%

Above data applies to 2007–2008 academic year.

## Introduction

The University of Missouri has 4 campuses: Columbia, Kansas City, Rolla, and St. Louis. The Columbia campus, the oldest and largest, is the site of the university's Columbia School of Medicine. This institution, established in 1872 as a 2-year medical school, expanded in 1956 into its present 4-year program. The University of Missouri Health Sciences Center includes the School of Medicine, University Hospital, Columbia Regional Hospital, VA Hospital, and other satellite facilities.

## Admissions (AMCAS)

In addition to the basic premedical science courses, mathematics and English composition (one year) are required. State residents are given very strong preference, especially those from small cities, towns, and rural areas. *Transfer and advanced standing:* Limited number admitted into third year. Applicants to the third year must post passing USMLE scores. Missouri residency is required for advanced standing positions.

## Curriculum

4-year semimodern. *First and second years:* Preclinical training is in eight 10-week blocks, each block consisting of 8 weeks of instruction followed by a week of evaluation and a week of vacation. A 10-week summer vacation falls between blocks 4 and 5. Each learning block is comprised of 2 components—the Basic Science Problem-based Learning (PBL) component and the Introduction to Patient Care (IPC) component. Using a clinical case format, the PBL component integrates the traditional basic sciences. Students work together to gather and organize information and then to generate and test hypotheses. In the IPC component, students explore a variety of content and skill-building experiences, including the physical exam skills, interviewing, health care/health policy, epidemiology, use of diagnostic tests and psychosocial aspects of medicine. Beginning in their first semester, students work with physician mentors and with standardized patients. Students also are assigned to a weekly clinic for an ambulatory care experience. *Third and fourth years:* The third year features 7-week required clerkships in child health, family medicine, internal medicine, obstetrics and gynecology, psychiatry/neurology, and surgery. The fourth year has three 8-week required advanced clinical selectives from a medical area, a surgical area, and one other selective. Also required in the fourth year are 6 weeks of advanced biomedical sciences and 16 weeks of general electives.

## Grading and Promotion Policies

The School of Medicine uses a multilevel grading system with Satisfactory/Unsatisfactory in the first year, Honors/Satisfactory/Unsatisfactory in the second year, and Honors/Letter of Commendation/Satisfactory/Unsatisfactory in the third and fourth years. Students must pass USMLE Step 1 prior to their fourth year and Step 2CK and Step 2C5 to graduate.

## Facilities

*Teaching:* The School of Medicine is located on the main, or Columbia, campus of the university and is connected to the University Hospital and Clinics. Basic sciences are taught in the Medical Sciences Building; newly renovated student "labs" are rooms designed for PBL sessions, small-group discussions, and home base study rooms. Clinical teaching takes place at the University Hospital (495 beds), Mid-Missouri Mental Health Center (87 beds), the VA Hospital (480 beds), and other affiliated off-campus hospitals. *Other:* The Ellis Fischell Cancer Center and Children's Hospital are part of the Health Sciences Center complex. *Library:* The Medical Library is located in the new Medical Annex and has more than 196,000 volumes. About 2000 periodicals are received regularly.

## Special Features

*Minority admissions:* The school has an active program and offers special summer programs for high school minority, rural and/or disadvantaged students. *Other degree programs:* Combined MD-MS program, as well as MD-PhD in the basic sciences, is offered.

# University of Missouri— Kansas City School of Medicine

2411 Holmes
Kansas City, Missouri    64108

*Phone:* 816-235-1870          *Fax:* 816-235-6579
*E-mail:* umkcmedweb@umkc.edu
*WWW:* umkc.edu/medicine

| Application Filing | | Accreditation | |
|---|---|---|---|
| Earliest: | August 1 | LCME | |
| Latest: | November 15 | | |
| Fee: | no | **Degrees Granted** | |
| AMCAS: | no | BA-MD, MD | |

### Enrollment: 2008–2009 First-Year Class

| | | | | | |
|---|---|---|---|---|---|
| Men: | 38 | 40% | Applied: | 940 | |
| Women: | 56 | 60% | Interviewed: | 241 | |
| Minorities: | 0 | 0% | Enrolled: | 94 | |
| Out of State: | 33 | 33% | | | |

### 2008–2009 Class Profile

| *Mean MCAT Scores* | | *Mean GPA* |
|---|---|---|
| Physical Sciences: | n/av | n/av |
| Biological Sciences: | n/av | |
| Verbal Reasoning: | n/av | |

**Tuition and Fees**

| | |
|---|---|
| **Resident** | 28,228 |
| Average (public) | 25,100 |
| Average (private) | 42,600 |
| **Nonresident** | 55,161 |
| Average (public) | 43,900 |
| Average (private) | 43,500 |

0    10    20    30    40    50
(in thousands of dollars)

Percentage receiving financial aid: 83%

Above data applies to 2007–2008 academic year.

## Introduction

In 1971 a combined 6-year undergraduate and graduate program of study was offered at the University of Missouri Kansas City School of Medicine for the first time; thus, rather than being patterned after the traditional program of 4 years of undergraduate study followed by 4 years of medical school, the program at this school is designed to accept high school graduates, who will spend 6 years and receive combined baccalaureate-medical degrees at the completion of their studies. The school is located on a 135-acre campus.

## Admissions

Major emphasis of school is the combined 6-year BA-MD program for graduating high school seniors. Only limited number of places will be open for Missouri residents completing the usual premedical college program. *For year 1:* High school students should have strong science background and take other courses that will prepare them for a medical school education that is community oriented. *For year 3:* Minimum of a baccalaureate degree is required. Selection is based on an applicant's academic potential as reflected by high school performance and scores on the ACT. Personal qualities sought are maturity, proper motivation, interpersonal skills, reliability, sense of compassion, and interests. Potentially qualified applicants are invited for interviews at the medical school campus. *Transfer and advanced standing:* Not applicable.

## Curriculum

6-year modern. Program operates on a 48-week year and has the objective of preparing physicians committed to comprehensive health care. *Years 1 and 2:* These years comprise liberal arts and introductory medical courses. Emphasis is on team approach and courses integrate patient interviews and examinations with basic medical sciences, psychology, and sociology. *Years 3 through 6:* A clinical scholar is assigned for each small group of students and will act as their guide during the balance of study. Clinical sciences are taught in the affiliate hospitals, with a problem-centered approach. Student attains a specific set of clinical competencies as a precondition to attaining degree. Each student is given the opportunity to acquire a broad base of information in the basic, clinical, and behavioral sciences. The program also provides the students with a realistic knowledge of community health problems and resources. Education is provided in a positive learning environment, enhanced by strong student support services. An alternative extended study program is also available. The graduate should be prepared for advanced training, should qualify for medical licensure, and should be stimulated for a career involving lifelong learning.

## Grading and Promotion Policies

A Pass/Fail system is used, and obtaining a total passing score on Steps 1 and 2 of the USMLE is required for promotion and graduation, respectively.

## Facilities

*Teaching:* A new medical school building has been completed. Clinical facilities include Children's Mercy Hospital, a major acute Psychiatric Center, St. Luke's Hospital, and Truman Medical Center, the primary adult care teaching hospital. *Other:* Several community hospitals are associated with the school and provide beds for teaching. *Library:* The Health Sciences Library is located on the second floor of the medical school building. *Housing:* Students are expected to live in the university residence hall on the main campus for the first year.

## Special Features

*Minority admissions:* A Minority Recruitment Committee works to identify and recruit health science students early in their secondary schooling. *Other degree programs:* None.

# Washington University School of Medicine

660 South Euclid Avenue
St. Louis, Missouri 63110

*Phone:* 314-362-6858          *Fax:* 314-362-4658
*E-mail:* wumscoa@wustl.edu
*WWW:* medschool.wustl.edu

| Application Filing | | Accreditation |
|---|---|---|
| Earliest: | June 15 | LCME |
| Latest: | November 30 | |
| Fee: | $50 | **Degrees Granted** |
| AMCAS: | yes | MD, MD-PhD, MD-MA |

### Enrollment: 2008–2009 First-Year Class

| Men: | 63 | 52% | Applied: | 4058 |
|---|---|---|---|---|
| Women: | 49 | 48% | Interviewed: | 116 |
| Minorities: | 11 | 11% | Enrolled: | 122 |
| Out of State: | 117 | 94% | | |

### 2008–2009 Class Profile

| *Mean MCAT Scores* | | *Mean GPA* |
|---|---|---|
| Physical Sciences: | 12.8 | 3.87 |
| Biological Sciences: | 12.8 | |
| Verbal Reasoning: | 11.7 | *Mean Science* |
| | | 3.87 |

### Tuition and Fees

| | |
|---|---|
| **Resident** | 45,550 |
| Average (public) | 25,100 |
| Average (private) | 42,600 |
| **Nonresident** | 45,550 |
| Average (public) | 43,900 |
| Average (private) | 43,500 |

(in thousands of dollars)

Percentage receiving financial aid: 86.9%

## Introduction

The St. Louis Medical College was established as an independent school in 1842 and became the medical division of Washington University in 1891. In 1899 the Missouri Medical College became part of Washington University as well. The Medical Center is located on the eastern edge of Forrest Park in St. Louis and includes the School of Medicine and a number of teaching hospitals.

## Admissions (AMCAS)

Required courses include the basic premedical sciences and differential and integral calculus. *Transfer and advanced standing:* Third-year class positions are available to well-qualified individuals enrolled in U.S. medical schools who have compelling personal reasons for transfer.

## Curriculum

4-year modern. The goal of the curriculum is to provide students having diverse backgrounds and interest with the basic knowledge and skills essential for further professional development. The education is through lectures, small group sessions, problem-based exercises, and self-directed learning. Students must learn the interrelationship between the basic and clinical sciences and how old knowledge is reevaluated and new knowledge acquired. The curriculum includes a core experience based upon a sequence of courses during the first and second year that introduce the panorama of medicine. The major medical disciplines are presented in the third year in a way that allows all students to select the career most suited for them. The fourth year consists of electives. It provides students an opportunity to expand their knowledge in a wide range of specialties. The extent of their exploration into specific areas is determined by their depth of interest.

## Grading and Promotion Policies

A Pass/Fail grading system is used for the first year. Thereafter, the grades are Honors, High Pass, Pass, and Fail. In the third and fourth years, grades are accompanied by comments characterizing each student's performance. Promotions are made by committees on academic evaluation of students. Taking Steps 1 and 2 of the USMLE is recommended.

## Facilities

*Teaching:* The Farrell Learning and Teaching Center provides state-of-the-art facilities introducing formal lecture halls and wet and dry labs. Every workstation in the Center is equipped with power and data connections, and for after-hours learning, the building also includes computer rooms and study carrels. Enclosed walkways connect Farrell to the Medical School-affiliated hospitals Barnes-Jewish and St. Louis Children's Hospital, which together provide 1624 hospital beds. Patient-centered outpatient care takes place in the multispecialty Center for Advanced Medicine. *Library:* The 8-level Library and Biomedical Communication Center houses more than 290,000 volumes including more than 5400 journal titles, and provides on-line links to more than 2600 journals. *Housing:* Available in the Olin Residence Hall for approximately 250 students; abundant, reasonably priced apartments are within easy walking distance.

## Special Features

Recruitment of underrepresented minority students is facilitated by the school's Associate Dean for Diversity Programs. *Other degree programs:* 5-year MD-MA program offering a year of research training, and 8-year combined MD-PhD program in various basic sciences.

# NEBRASKA

# Creighton University School of Medicine

2500 California Plaza
Omaha, Nebraska   68178

*Phone:* 402-280-2799          *Fax:* 402-280-1241
*E-mail:* medschadm@creighton.edu
*WWW:* medicine.creighton.edu

| Application Filing | | Accreditation | |
|---|---|---|---|
| Earliest: | July 1 | LCME | |
| Latest: | November 1 | | |
| Fee: | $95 | **Degrees Granted** | |
| AMCAS: | yes | MD, MD-PhD, MD-MS | |

### Enrollment: 2008–2009 First-Year Class

| Men: | 63 | 50% | Applied: | 5718 |
|---|---|---|---|---|
| Women: | 63 | 50% | Interviewed: | 578 |
| Minorities: | 10 | 8% | Enrolled: | 126 |
| Out of State: | 110 | 87% | | |

### 2008–2009 Class Profile

| *Mean MCAT Scores* | | *Mean GPA* |
|---|---|---|
| Physical Sciences: | 10 | 3.72 |
| Biological Sciences: | 10 | |
| Verbal Reasoning: | 10 | *Mean Science* |
| | | 3.65 |

**Tuition and Fees**

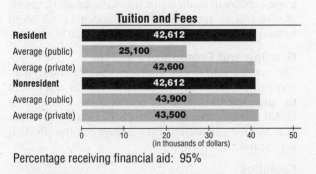

| Resident | 42,612 |
| Average (public) | 25,100 |
| Average (private) | 42,600 |
| Nonresident | 42,612 |
| Average (public) | 43,900 |
| Average (private) | 43,500 |

(in thousands of dollars)

Percentage receiving financial aid: 95%

## Introduction

Creighton University, a Jesuit institution, has 4 health science schools. The School of Medicine was established in 1892. Clinical instruction is carried out in several institutions.

## Admissions (AMCAS)

The basic premedical science courses and 1 year of English are required. A course in biochemistry and/or genetics is recommended. There are no restrictions on residence. *Transfer and advanced standing:* Possible to the second or third year for qualified applicants when spaces are available. Admission restricted to those who have a Creighton University affiliation.

## Curriculum

4-year semimodern. A new curriculum has been intro-
duced, divided into 4 components. *Component one:* The biomedical fundamentals serves as the foundation of the educational program. *Component two:* Comprised of more complex basic science information presented in a clinically relevant context consisting of a series of organ-based and disease-based courses. *Component three:* Consists of six required core clerkships emphasizing basic medical principles, primary care, and preventive medicine. *Component four:* Provides additional responsibilities for patient care. A 12-week block of critical care medicine and the 24 weeks of electives provide subinternship experience. Clinical experience is a prominent part of the curriculum in all components, beginning with the physical diagnosis instruction in the first year and with students assigned to longitudinal clinics in the second year. The curriculum also integrates ethical and societal issues into all 4 components. Instructional methodology includes case-based small-group sessions and computer-assisted instruction in all components.

## Grading and Promotion Policies

This school uses a Pass/Fail/Honors Evaluation system. Students are evaluated individually against curriculum standards and are not ranked among their peers. A Fail grade will not be accepted for graduation credit. Promotion to the next higher class depends upon a record of acceptable conduct and satisfactory completion of the entire year's work with a minimum of Pass in each course. All students are required to pass Step 1 of the USMLE before promotion into the clinical years of the curriculum and to take Step 2 of the USMLE in their senior year. Successful completion is not required for promotion but is necessary for licensure to practice.

## Facilities

*Teaching:* Basic medical sciences are taught in the Criss Medical Center. This 3-unit center houses the School of Medicine offices, research facilities, laboratories, lecture halls, extensive television teaching classrooms, and other facilities for Medicine. Saint Joseph Hospital is the principal site for Creighton medical instruction. Creighton students also participate in clinical instruction at Alegent Health Immanuel Medical Center Behavioral Sciences Center, Children's Hospital, Omaha Veterans Medical Center, Bergan Mercy Medical Center, and some clinical services at other area hospitals. *Library:* The library is part of the Creighton University Bioinformation Center. Over 200,000 volumes of print and non-print material are available. Access is provided to many bibliographic databases such as MEDLINE, Micromedex, etc. *Housing:* Creighton University has limited space in the apartment-style Towers residence hall for families. The Department of Residence Life, 104 Swanson Hall, posts information on rentals in the area of campus. Arrangements are left to individual students.

## Special Features

*Minority admissions:* The Office of Minority Affairs coordinates an active recruitment program.

# University of Nebraska Medical Center

85517 Nebraska Medical Center
Omaha, Nebraska    68198

*Phone:* 402-559-2259          *Fax:* 402-559-6840
*E-mail:* johara@unmc.edu
*WWW:* unmc.edu/uncom/

| Application Filing | | Accreditation | |
|---|---|---|---|
| Earliest: | June 1 | LCME | |
| Latest: | November 1 | | |
| Fee: | $45 | **Degrees Granted** | |
| AMCAS: | yes | MD, MD-PhD, MD-MPH | |

## Enrollment: 2008–2009 First-Year Class

| | | | | | |
|---|---|---|---|---|---|
| Men: | 51 | 41% | Applied: | 1415 |
| Women: | 73 | 59% | Interviewed: | 382 |
| Minorities: | 6 | 4% | Enrolled: | 124 |
| Out of State: | 15 | 12% | | |

## 2008–2009 Class Profile

| *Mean MCAT Scores* | | *Mean GPA* |
|---|---|---|
| Physical Sciences: | 9.5 | 3.7 |
| Biological Sciences: | 10.2 | |
| Verbal Reasoning: | 9.5 | *Mean Science* |
| | | 3.7 |

### Tuition and Fees

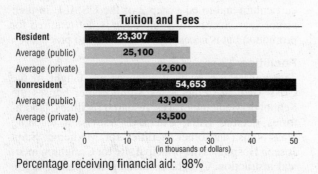

| | |
|---|---|
| Resident | 23,307 |
| Average (public) | 25,100 |
| Average (private) | 42,600 |
| Nonresident | 54,653 |
| Average (public) | 43,900 |
| Average (private) | 43,500 |

0    10    20    30    40    50
(in thousands of dollars)

Percentage receiving financial aid: 98%

## Introduction

The University of Nebraska College of Medicine was established in 1902 when Omaha Medical College joined the University of Nebraska. The latter was established in 1880. Currently, the University of Nebraska Medical Center includes the colleges of Medicine, Nursing, and Pharmacy, School of Allied Health Professions, University Hospital, and several other facilities. Omaha is located in the western part of the state and is its largest city.

## Admissions (AMCAS)

The basic premedical science courses, introductory calculus or statistics, 4 courses in social sciences and/or humanities, and courses in writing, biochemistry, and genetics are also required. Few out-of-state residents are accepted. *Transfer and advanced standing:* No transfers from non-LCME-approved schools or from non-medical professional schools are accepted.

## Curriculum

4-year semimodern. The school seeks to provide its graduates with superior skills in problem solving and clinical reasoning, extensive knowledge of the biomedical and psychosocial sciences, and skills needed for lifelong learning of medicine. *First and second years:* Students are exposed to the basic medical sciences. During these years students also begin to learn clinical skills and reasoning. In the third and fourth years students apply their knowledge on the hospital wards and clinical offices. *Third year:* Students take clinical clerkships in Family Medicine, Internal Medicine, Obstetrics and Gynecology, Pediatrics, Psychiatry, and Surgery. *Fourth year:* Students select from a variety of clinical and basic science experience. In order to graduate, students must show that they have acquired the knowledge, skills, and attitudes necessary for residency training. Students get early experience in medical problem solving through preceptorships and clinical case study in groups. At the beginning of medical school, students work in small groups with a faculty member to solve clinical cases. This initial exercise helps develop the library and information retrieval skills they will need in their medical studies. Case study and small group teaching emphasizing problem-based learning are becoming more prominent features of all of the basic science courses. Clinical experience provided to the students is supplemented by the availability of simulated patients to learn history taking and physical examination skills. These innovative changes in medical education provide greater relevance to patient care in medical practice. Consequently, graduates should be more qualified to undertake advanced training regardless of the specialty they plan to enter.

## Grading and Promotion Policies

The system used is Honors/High Pass/Pass/Marginal, and Fail. Students are limited to 5 years of enrollment to complete the medical curriculum. Passage of USMLE Step 1 is required for promotion to the senior year and for graduation. Taking Step 2 of the USMLE is required.

## Facilities

*Teaching:* Basic sciences are taught in the Michael F. Sorrell Center for Health Science Education. Clinical teaching takes place at University Hospital (434 beds). Nebraska Medical Center serves various affiliated hospitals. *Library:* The McGoogan Library of Medicine is situated in Wittson Hall and houses more than 234,000 volumes and 2200 periodicals. *Housing:* Student Services has a listing of private off-campus housing available to students.

## Special Features

*Minority admissions:* The school has an active recruitment program for disadvantaged and rural students. It also offers summer enrichment programs for college juniors and seniors, depending on availability of grant funds. *Other degree programs:* Combined MD-PhD programs available in all the basic sciences, and an MD-MPH program is also available.

# NEVADA

## University of Nevada School of Medicine

Mail Stop 357
Reno, Nevada  89557

*Phone:* 775-784-6063          *Fax:* 775-784-6194
*E-mail:* asa@med.unr.edu
*WWW:* medicine.nevada.edu

| Application Filing | | Accreditation | |
|---|---|---|---|
| Earliest: | June 1 | LCME | |
| Latest: | November 1 | | |
| Fee: | $45 | **Degrees Granted** | |
| AMCAS: | yes | MD, MD-PhD | |

### Enrollment: 2008–2009 First-Year Class

| Men: | 29 | 47% | Applied: | 1221 |
|---|---|---|---|---|
| Women: | 33 | 53% | Interviewed: | 177 |
| Minorities: | 15 | 24% | Enrolled: | 62 |
| Out of State: | 5 | 7% | | |

### 2008–2009 Class Profile

| *Mean MCAT Scores* | | *Mean GPA* |
|---|---|---|
| Physical Sciences: | 9.9 | 3.6 |
| Biological Sciences: | 10.6 | |
| Verbal Reasoning: | 9.4 | *Mean Science* |
| | | 3.5 |

**Tuition and Fees**

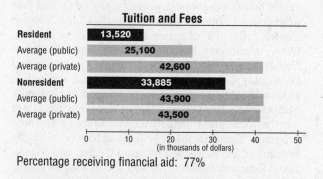

| | |
|---|---|
| Resident | 13,520 |
| Average (public) | 25,100 |
| Average (private) | 42,600 |
| Nonresident | 33,885 |
| Average (public) | 43,900 |
| Average (private) | 43,500 |

0    10    20    30    40    50
(in thousands of dollars)

Percentage receiving financial aid: 77%

### Introduction

The University of Nevada School of Medicine is a community-oriented medical school that was founded in 1969. Supplementing university-based faculty, community physicians serve as teachers. The goal is to train physicians in primary care to be able to provide both rural health care delivery and treatment in an office or hospital setting. This school is one of a small group of community-based institutions.

### Admissions (AMCAS)

In addition to the basic premedical science courses, 1 additional semester of biology, and 2 behavioral science courses are required. There is no quota for out-of-state residents, but few are accepted into the second and third years. High priority for admission is given to Nevada residents. A very small number of nonresidents from Alaska, Idaho, Montana, and Wyoming or those with residential ties with Nevada are considered for admission. Applicants are evaluated on the basis of the level of their achievement, MCAT scores, extracurricular and health-care related activities, and letters of recommendation. Selected applicants are invited for interviews in either Reno or Las Vegas. *Transfer and advanced standing:* Possible from U.S. schools only.

### Curriculum

4-year semimodern. *First and second years:* The curriculum emphasizes the biomedical and behavioral sciences basic to medicine. Basic science disciplines are integrated with each other and with clinical problems to promote the learning of problem-solving skills. A clinical correlation course exploring the basics of biomedical ethics, is taught. Early clinical training is provided for students to learn patient interviewing, doctor-patient relationship skills, and the basics of physical examination and diagnosis. Students spend time with a physician to observe medical practice in the office setting and clinic settings. There are also opportunities to participate in basic and clinical science research throughout the curriculum. *Third and fourth years:* These emphasize a balance of ambulatory and inpatient medical education designed to better prepare students for residency in all specialties. Third- and fourth-year students study clinical medicine in Reno, Las Vegas, and rural Nevada.

### Grading and Promotion Policies

Letters and numbers are used in addition to a Pass/Fail system. Both steps of the USMLE must be taken.

### Facilities

*Teaching:* Five buildings at the north end of the Reno campus house classrooms, office space, the library, and research labs. Clinical facilities are the Veterans Administration Medical Center, Washoe Medical Center, and the University Medical Center, which provide some 2000 beds. *Library:* A Life and Health Sciences Library holds a significant number of books and subscribes to a wide variety of journals.

### Special Features

*Minority admissions:* The school is committed to the recruitment, selection, and retention of individuals who are members of groups traditionally underrepresented. The University of Nevada, Reno does not discriminate on the basis of race, color, religion, sex, age, creed, national origin, or physical disability.

# NEW HAMPSHIRE

# Dartmouth Medical School

3 Rope Ferry Road
Hanover, New Hampshire    03755

*Phone:* 603-650-1505          *Fax:* 603-650-1560
*E-mail:* dms.admissions.@dartmouth.edu
*WWW:* dms.dartmouth.edu/

| Application Filing | | Accreditation |
|---|---|---|
| Earliest: | July 1 | LCME |
| Latest: | January 2 | |
| Fee: | $75 | **Degrees Granted** |
| AMCAS: | yes | MD, MD-PhD, MD-MBA, MD-MPH |

### Enrollment: 2008–2009 First-Year Class

| Men: | 44 | 56% | Applied: | 5586 |
|---|---|---|---|---|
| Women: | 34 | 44% | Interviewed: | 670 |
| Minorities: | 17 | 22% | Enrolled: | 78 |
| Out of State: | 70 | 90% | | |

### 2008–2009 Class Profile

| *Mean MCAT Scores* | | *Mean GPA* |
|---|---|---|
| Physical Sciences: | 11.0 | 3.7 |
| Biological Sciences: | 11.0 | |
| Verbal Reasoning: | 11.0 | *Mean Science* |
| | | 3.7 |

**Tuition and Fees**

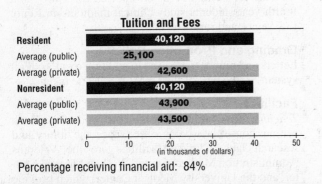

| Resident | 40,120 |
| Average (public) | 25,100 |
| Average (private) | 42,600 |
| Nonresident | 40,120 |
| Average (public) | 43,900 |
| Average (private) | 43,500 |

(in thousands of dollars)

Percentage receiving financial aid: 84%

## Introduction

Dartmouth Medical School, located in Hanover, New Hampshire, is the fourth oldest medical school in the United States. Founded in 1797, the school is a component of the Dartmouth Hitchcock Medical Center. The school is located in the heart of Hanover approximately 3 miles from the medical center.

## Admissions (AMCAS)

The basic premedical science courses and a course in calculus are required. There are no residence restrictions, but special consideration is given to applicants from New Hampshire and Maine. *Transfer and advanced standing:* Transfers are considered only when places are available; preference is given to students from other U.S. schools with compelling needs to be in Hanover.

## Curriculum

4-year. The New Directions curriculum is designed to integrate the study of basic and clinical sciences throughout medical school while supporting close working relationships between students and the faculty. *First and second years:* The first and second years include a course entitled "On Doctoring," which pairs students with faculty practitioners in local communities and alternates with biweekly, small group tutorials on campus. The first year also emphasizes basic science courses. *Third year:* Clerkships in many disciplines are scheduled in six 8-week blocks of the third year. *Fourth year:* Students take advanced courses that complete their clerkships in neurology and women's health, a subinternship, and many electives.

## Grading and Promotion Policies

System used is Honors/ High Pass/Pass/Fail. Promotion is by vote of the faculty and no student will be promoted who has not passed all courses. Taking Steps 1 and 2 of the USMLE is required; passing it is not.

## Facilities

*Teaching:* The primary clinical teaching site is Dartmouth-Hitchcock Medical Center. The center serves a very large patient population. As a Level 1 Trauma Center, it treats many acute emergency cases. The Medical Center itself is a partnership of four organizations: Dartmouth Medical School, Mary Hitchcock Memorial Hospital, the Dartmouth-Hitchcock Clinic, and the VT Veterans Affairs Medical Center. It is a major center of transitional "bench to bedside" research. The center boasts a higher-than-average rate of patient participation in clinical trials. At Norris Cotton Cancer Center, fully 17% of patients enter into clinical trials. *Other:* Children's Hospital at Dartmouth, the Spine Center, Cardiology, Gastroenterology, Obstetrics and Gynecology, and Neurology. The flow of research is enhanced by two major research sites on the Lebanon campus. The Borwell and Rubin Research Buildings are the focal point of the Medical School's research program. These facilities will be enhanced with the opening of the Advanced Imaging Center, and Transitional Research Building, as well as a new home for the Center. *Libraries:* The Dana Biomedical Library at the Medical School's Hanover Campus, and the Matthews-Fuller Health Sciences Library at the Medical Center have printed and digital books and journals, databases, indexes, computer programs, and audiovisual materials. *Housing:* Graduate housing is available. Most students live in off-campus housing.

## Special Features

*Minority admissions:* The school actively encourages applications from qualified minority students. *Other degree programs:* Combined MD-PhD programs are offered in several disciplines. An MD-MBA program is offered in conjunction with Dartmouth's Amos Tuck School. The medical school's Dartmouth Institute for Health Policy and Clinical Practice offers graduate degrees.

# New Jersey Medical School University of Medicine and Dentistry of New Jersey

185 South Orange Avenue
Newark, New Jersey   07109

*Phone:* 973-972-4631          *Fax:* 973-972-7986
*E-mail:* njmsadmiss@umdnj.edu
*WWW:* njms.umdnj.edu

| Application Filing | | Accreditation | |
|---|---|---|---|
| Earliest: | June 1 | LCME | |
| Latest: | December 1 | | |
| Fee: | $75 | **Degrees Granted** | |
| AMCAS: | yes | MD, MD-PhD, BA-MD | |

### Enrollment: 2008–2009 First-Year Class

| Men: | 95 | 53% | Applied: | 4695 |
|---|---|---|---|---|
| Women: | 83 | 47% | Interviewed: | 840 |
| Minorities: | 16 | 9% | Enrolled: | 178 |
| Out of State: | 23 | 13% | | |

### 2008–2009 Class Profile

| *Mean MCAT Scores* | | *Mean GPA* |
|---|---|---|
| Physical Sciences: | 11 | 3.7 |
| Biological Sciences: | 11 | |
| Verbal Reasoning: | 10 | *Mean Science* |
| | | 3.6 |

### Tuition and Fees

| | |
|---|---|
| **Resident** | 24,121 |
| Average (public) | 25,100 |
| Average (private) | 42,600 |
| **Nonresident** | 37,188 |
| Average (public) | 43,900 |
| Average (private) | 43,500 |

0    10    20    30    40    50
(in thousands of dollars)

Percentage receiving financial aid: 84%

Above data applies to 2007–2008 academic year.

## Introduction

As part of the University of Medicine and Dentistry of New Jersey, the New Jersey Medical School is located in Newark and the current facilities were established in 1977. The University of Medicine and Dentistry of New Jersey also includes a second Medical School in Piscataway, a School of Osteopathic Medicine in Stratford, a Dental School in Newark, a Graduate School for Biomedical Sciences in Newark, as well as a Health-Related, Professional School of Public Health, and School of Nursing.

## Admissions (AMCAS)

Minimum premedical science courses plus lab and 1 year of English are required. A course in college mathematics is recommended. Applications from nonresidents are encouraged. Consideration for admission includes scholastic accomplishments, motivation, perseverance, and mechanical skills. Highest priority for acceptance is given to those excelling in such attributes.

## Curriculum

*4-year semitraditional. First and second years:* Consists of basic science courses correlated with problem-based learning and clinical experiences. Part of the second year is devoted to an introduction to the clinical sciences, during which the student receives instruction in history taking, physical diagnosis, and pathophysiology. In addition, courses in preventive medicine and community health, behavioral science, and psychiatry are offered. *Third year:* Spent in rotations through core clinical departments. This is a closely supervised, hands-on, comprehensive learning experience in which the student acquires the basic knowledge and techniques of clinical medicine. Instruction is carried out mainly in small groups and is individualized. *Fourth year:* Devoted to advanced required work and elective programs. The required courses are emergency medicine, neurology, surgical subspecialties, physical medicine and rehabilitation, and an acting internship, all of which bring together the ethical, legal, and social factors that are part of total patient care. Sixteen weeks of electives are available.

## Grading and Promotion Policies

An Honors/High Pass/Pass/Fail system is used. Decisions on promotion are made by executive faculty on recommendation of a Promotions Committee. Decisions are based upon a comprehensive evaluation of accomplishments. Students must pass Step 1 and Step 2 of the USMLE for graduation.

## Facilities

*Teaching:* A campus on a 58-acre site in Newark is the hub of a major medical educational complex, including the Biomedical Science Building, the University Hospital, and a library. *Other:* Clinical teaching facilities include University Hospital, Hackensack University Medical Center, Veterans Affairs Medical Center in East Orange, Morristown Memorial Hospital, and Kessler Institute for Rehabilitation. *Library:* Library of Medicine houses 70,000 volumes and 2000 periodicals. *Housing:* No housing facilities are available on campus, but there are many rooms or apartments in the local area, and a Housing Office provides support.

## Special Features

*Minority admissions:* The school conducts an extensive recruitment program. Accepted minority students attend a 7-week summer pre-enrollment enrichment program. *Other degree programs:* Combined MD-PhD, MD-JD, MD-MBA programs are offered, and a 7-year BA-MD program with 7 undergraduate colleges. A limited number of Academic Excellence scholarships for entering first-year students are offered.

# Robert Wood Johnson Medical School
# University of Medicine and Dentistry of New Jersey

675 Hoes Lane
Piscataway, New Jersey   08854

*Phone:* 732-235-4576        *Fax:* 732-235-5078
*E-mail:* rwjapdmterregca@umdnj.edu
*WWW:* rwlms.umdnj.edu

| Application Filing | | Accreditation | |
|---|---|---|---|
| Earliest: | June 1 | LCME | |
| Latest: | December 1 | | |
| Fee: | $75 | **Degrees Granted** | |
| AMCAS: | yes | MD, MD-PhD, | |
| | | MD/MBA, MD-MPH | |

### Enrollment: 2008–2009 First-Year Class

| | | | | | |
|---|---|---|---|---|---|
| Men: | 68 | 41% | Applied: | 3551 |
| Women: | 98 | 59% | Interviewed: | 515 |
| Minorities: | 14 | 8% | Enrolled: | 166 |
| Out of State: | 1 | 1% | | |

### 2008–2009 Class Profile

| *Mean MCAT Scores* | | *Mean GPA* |
|---|---|---|
| Physical Sciences: | 11 | 3.7 |
| Biological Sciences: | 11 | |
| Verbal Reasoning: | 10 | *Mean Science* |
| | | 3.7 |

**Tuition and Fees**

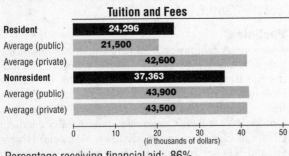

| | |
|---|---|
| **Resident** | 24,296 |
| Average (public) | 21,500 |
| Average (private) | 42,600 |
| **Nonresident** | 37,363 |
| Average (public) | 43,900 |
| Average (private) | 43,500 |

(in thousands of dollars)

Percentage receiving financial aid: 86%

Above data applies to 2007–2008 academic year.

## Introduction

Robert Wood Johnson Medical School has 3 campuses. All students receive their basic science education on the Piscataway campus. Students complete their clinical training on either the New Brunswick or the Camden campus. The school originally was known as Rutgers Medical School when it began in 1961 as a 2-year medical school. It became part of the University of Medicine and Dentistry in 1970.

## Admissions (AMCAS)

The basic premedical science courses as well as 1 semester of mathematics and 1 year of English are required. Priority is given to state residents but nonresidents are accepted. Selection is based on academic achievements, MCAT scores, preprofessional evaluations, and a personal interview, which is by invitation only. Applicants must be citizens or hold permanent residence status at the time the application is submitted to be eligible for admission. *Transfer and advance standing:* Applicants to the third-year class are considered.

## Curriculum

4-year semitraditional. *First and second year:* Basic and clinical sciences are integrated in the first 2 years with emphasis on clinical skills and an opportunity for self-directed learning. *Third year:* The clinical year consists of rotations through the major specialties and a 2-year patient-centered medicine course, having integrated topics such as professionalism, humanism, multiculturalism, and medical ethics. *Fourth year:* Consists of electives as well as a subinternship, neurology, emergency medicine, and critical care clerkships as well as outpatient subspecialties.

## Grading and Promotion Policies

System used is Honors/High Pass/Pass/Low Pass/Fail. A passing score on the USMLE Step 1 is required for promotion into the third year, and passage of Step 2 is required for graduation.

## Facilities

*Teaching:* The Medical Science Complex in Piscataway includes the Medical Sciences Tower, Kessler Teaching Laboratories, Center for Advanced Biotechnology and Medicine, Environmental and Occupational Health Sciences Institute, and a research tower and School of Public Health. Clinical teaching takes place at the Robert Wood Johnson University Hospital and other affiliated hospitals in central New Jersey. In Camden, clinical teaching takes place principally at Cooper University Hospital. *Library:* The Rutgers University Library of Science and Medicine adjoins the Medical Science Complex in Piscataway, and clinical libraries are available in Camden and New Brunswick. *Housing:* Students are assisted in finding nearby housing.

## Special Features

*Minority admissions:* The school has an active recruitment program and offers a 10-week summer enrichment program for incoming minority students. *Other degree programs:* Combined MD-PhD (RWJMS, Rutgers, Princeton) programs are offered in the basic medical sciences, as well as MD-MBA, MD-MPH, MD-JD, MD-MS in biomedical informatics, and MD-MS in jurisprudence.

# University of New Mexico School of Medicine

Albuquerque, New Mexico   87131

*Phone:* 505-272-4766          *Fax:* 505-925-6031
*E-mail:* somadmissions@salud.unm.edu
*WWW:* http://hsc.unm.edu/som/admissions

| Application Filing | | Accreditation |
|---|---|---|
| Earliest: | July 1 | LCME |
| Latest: | November 15 | |
| Fee: | $50 | **Degrees Granted** |
| AMCAS: | yes | MD, MD-PhD |

### Enrollment: 2008–2009 First-Year Class

| Men: | 33 | 44% | Applied: | 589 |
|---|---|---|---|---|
| Women: | 42 | 56% | Interviewed: | 224 |
| Minorities: | 30 | 40% | Enrolled: | 75 |
| Out of State: | 2 | 27% | | |

### 2008–2009 Class Profile

| *Mean MCAT Scores* | | *Mean GPA* |
|---|---|---|
| Physical Sciences: | 8.8 | 3.6 |
| Biological Sciences: | 10.0 | |
| Verbal Reasoning: | 9.5 | *Mean Science* |
| | | 3.47 |

**Tuition and Fees**

| | (in thousands of dollars) |
|---|---|
| **Resident** | 14,671 |
| Average (public) | 18,500 |
| Average (private) | 35,000 |
| **Nonresident** | 42,043 |
| Average (public) | 34,500 |
| Average (private) | 36,750 |

0    10    20    30    40    50
(in thousands of dollars)

Percentage receiving financial aid: 95%

## Introduction

The University of New Mexico School of Medicine was established in 1961 and admitted its first class in 1964. The medical school is located on the north campus of The University of New Mexico, which allows students and faculty easy access to the educational, recreational, and cultural offerings of the university.

## Admissions (AMCAS)

The school encourages application from all interested students, regardless of their areas of academic study. To be considered for admission, applicants must be residents of New Mexico for at least one year at the time of application or have strong ties to New Mexico. Strong ties include graduating from a New Mexico high

school attended for at least one year or being financially dependent on a New Mexico resident. Consideration is also given to members of the Navajo Tribe who reside on the Navajo Reservation and to residents of Montana and Wyoming. The applicants must apply through the Early Decision Program and must also have at least the same average MCAT/GPA as the last year entering class in order to receive consideration. The minimum requirements are: meet residency requirement, a Bachelor's degree, an MCAT score of 22 or better, a GPA score of 3.0 or better on a 4.0 scale. Prerequisites include the basic premedical courses, one course in biochemistry that includes proteins, nucleic acids, enzymes, and intermediary metabolism.

## Curriculum

Current educational initiatives are aimed at improving the integration of the basic sciences and clinical medicine, shifting teaching and learning to ambulatory and community settings, integrating problem-based learning throughout the curriculum and emphasizing computer literacy and information management skills. The School of Medicine's four-year curriculum includes: problem-based and student-centered learning, the incorporation of a population and behavior perspective into the clinical skills learning coupled with sustained, community-based learning, the incorporation of a population and behavioral perspective into the clinical years, peer teaching, computer-assisted instruction, and biweekly seminars on professional responsibility.

## Grading and Promotion Policies

Phase I grades are based on competency examinations given at the end of each curricular unit that assess knowledge, skills, and abilities learned across lectures, tutorials, labs, clinical skills, and a continuity clinic. Grades for the "blocks" are on a 4 point scale: outstanding, good, satisfactory, unsatisfactory (fail). Grades for tutorials are pass–fail, although a student must pass tutorial in order to pass the corresponding competency exam. Grades for autopsies are credit–no credit.

## Facilities

The campus includes many facilities such as the state-of-the-art Domenici Education Center and Barbra and Bill Richardson Pavilion. Medical students are taught in the Basic Medical Science Building and the Domenici Education Auditorium and the University of New Mexico Hospital. Numerous other clinical facilities are also available.

## Special Features

The campus maintains a diverse student population. *Other degree programs:* the combined MD-PhD program, the combined BA/MD program, Prep (Premedical Enrichment Program) and the MPH/MD program.

## NEW YORK

# Albany Medical College
Office of Admissions
47 New Scotland Avenue
Albany, New York   12208

*Phone:* 518-262-5521          *Fax:* 518-262-5887
*E-mail:* admissions@mail.amc.edu
*WWW:* amc.edu

| Application Filing | | Accreditation |
|---|---|---|
| Earliest: | June 1 | LCME |
| Latest: | November 15 | |
| Fee: | $105 | **Degrees Granted** |
| AMCAS: | yes | MD, MD-PhD, BS-MD, BS-MS-MD |

### Enrollment: 2008–2009 First-Year Class

| | | | | |
|---|---|---|---|---|
| Men: | 71 | 49% | Applied: | 6834 |
| Women: | 73 | 51% | Interviewed: | 663 |
| Minorities: | 5 | 3% | Enrolled: | 144 |
| Out of State: | 76 | 53% | | |

### 2008–2009 Class Profile

| *Mean MCAT Scores* | | *Mean GPA* |
|---|---|---|
| Physical Sciences: | 10 | 3.6 |
| Biological Sciences: | 11 | |
| Verbal Reasoning: | 10 | *Mean Science* |
| | | 3.5 |

**Tuition and Fees**

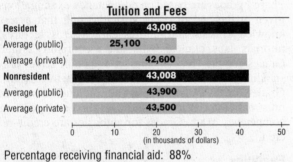

| | |
|---|---|
| **Resident** | 43,008 |
| Average (public) | 25,100 |
| Average (private) | 42,600 |
| **Nonresident** | 43,008 |
| Average (public) | 43,900 |
| Average (private) | 43,500 |

(in thousands of dollars)

Percentage receiving financial aid: 88%

Above data applies to 2007–2008 academic year.

## Introduction
This private medical school has been in existence since 1839. It is a coeducational and nondenominational school. In 1873 Albany Medical College joined with Union College and Albany Law School to form Union University.

## Admissions (AMCAS)
Applicants must have completed a minimum of 3 years of college work in an accredited college or university. Required courses include 1 year of the basic premedical sciences plus proficiency in oral and written English. Applicants for first-year admission are also required to take the Medical College Admission Test and submit official scores. *Transfer and advanced standing:* No opportunities exist.

## Curriculum
4-year semitraditional. *First year:* Basic science instruction is combined with clinical cases to focus on normal function. *Second year:* Focuses primarily on abnormal function and the disease state. *Third year:* Clinical clerkships offered emphasize ambulatory care in varied settings: rural, urban, managed care, and private practice. *Fourth year:* Required experiences are hospital based, preparing students for residency and practice. Additional elective time allows students to round out their education and further explore specific areas of interest. During both the third and fourth years, basic science material is revisited within the context of a student's clinical experience. Several other modules span the entire 4-year experience. Health Care and Society introduces students to the psychosocial, humanistic, ethical, and legal aspects of care. Comprehensive Care Case Study emphasizes primary care, systems of care, comparisons of care in different settings, issues related to the epidemiology of disease, prevention and wellness, geriatrics, AIDS, and substance abuse. This module focuses students' attention on the concept of health care delivered by a team rather than an individual.

## Grading and Promotion Policies
Students are graded on a modified Pass/Fail system. Grades assigned are Honors, Excellent, Good, Marginal, and Unsatisfactory. Students must take Steps 1 and 2 of the USMLE as candidates and record scores.

## Facilities
*Teaching:* The Albany Medical College is located in the state's capital. The school consists of a 7-floor Medical Education Building and a 5-story Medical Research Building, which together provide teaching facilities, research laboratories, faculty and administrative offices, clinic areas, a bookstore, student lounge, and library. The Albany Medical College and the Albany Medical Center Hospital are physically joined in 1 large complex. The Albany Medical Center Hospital, the nearby Veterans Administration Medical Center, and other affiliated hospitals provide facilities for clinical instruction. *Library:* The library possesses about 111,300 volumes, 1500 audiovisual programs (including computer programs), and receives 1250 medical periodicals on a regular basis. *Housing:* A residence hall accommodating 168 single students is located within easy walking distance.

## Special Features
*Minority admissions:* The school conducts an active minority recruitment program. A Minority Affairs Office provides academic, social, and cultural support services for enrolled students. *Other degree programs:* Joint programs with undergraduate schools at Rensselaer Polytechnic Institute, Union College, and Siena College. Selected high school applicants are admitted to these highly competitive special focus, combined-degree programs. A combined MD-PhD program exists.

# Albert Einstein College of Medicine of Yeshiva University

1300 Morris Park Avenue
Bronx, New York    10461

*Phone:* 718-430-2106          *Fax:* 718-430-8840
*E-mail:* admissions@aecom.yu.edu
*WWW:* aecom.yu.edu

| Application Filing | | Accreditation | |
|---|---|---|---|
| Earliest: | June 1 | LCME | |
| Latest: | March 15 | | |
| Fee: | $115 | **Degrees Granted** | |
| AMCAS: | yes | MD, MD-PhD | |

### Enrollment: 2008–2009 First-Year Class

| Men: | 88 | 46% | Applied: | 7383 |
|---|---|---|---|---|
| Women: | 92 | 54% | Interviewed: | 1181 |
| Minorities: | 13 | 13% | Enrolled: | 180 |
| Out of State: | 104 | 58% | | |

### 2008–2009 Class Profile

| *Mean MCAT Scores* | | *Mean GPA* |
|---|---|---|
| Physical Sciences: | 10.8 | 3.7 |
| Biological Sciences: | 11.3 | |
| Verbal Reasoning: | 10 | *Mean Science* |
| | | 3.7 |

**Tuition and Fees**

| | |
|---|---|
| Resident | 42,364 |
| Average (public) | 25,100 |
| Average (private) | 42,600 |
| Nonresident | 42,364 |
| Average (public) | 43,900 |
| Average (private) | 43,500 |

0    10    20    30    40    50
(in thousands of dollars)

Percentage receiving financial aid: 99%

## Introduction

A part of Yeshiva University, Albert Einstein College of Medicine was established in 1955. It is a privately endowed coeducational institution. Affiliated with the school are 2 postgraduate divisions, the Sue Goldberg Graduate Division of Medical Sciences and the Belfer Institute for Advance Biomedical Studies, making the school a major center for medical education, clinical care (through its affiliated hospitals), and biomedical research.

## Admissions (AMCAS)

Required courses include the basic premedical sciences and 1 year each of mathematics and English. Recommended courses are those in the humanities and social science. *Transfer and advanced standing:* None.

## Curriculum

4-year modern. The preclinical curriculum consists largely of interdisciplinary courses designed to enable students to acquire an integrated understanding of the biomedical sciences, become effective in applying knowledge to the solution of clinical problems, and become successful self-directed learners with excellent information retrieval skills. Running parallel with these courses is an extensive Introduction to Clinical Medicine program in which students interact with patients in clinical settings and engage in small-group discussions about illness and health care from psychosocial, cultural, ethical, and health policy perspectives. Case-based small-group conferences emphasizing preparation, collaboration, and participation constitute a major educational strategy throughout the preclinical curriculum. *Third year:* Clerkship rotations in all major disciplines, including family medicine, geriatrics, and ambulatory care in community-based settings. *Fourth year:* Includes a subinternship in medicine, pediatrics, or adolescent medicine. There is also a 6-month elective period.

## Grading and Promotion Policies

Grades in preclerkship courses are Pass/Fail in the first year and Honors/Pass/Fail in the second year. Grades in clinical courses are Honors/High Pass/Pass/Low Pass/Fail. There is also a narrative evaluation in each clerkship. A student must pass all preclerkship courses in order to be promoted to the clerkship year. Passing total test scores on Step 1 and 2 of the USMLE examination must be recorded prior to graduation.

## Facilities

*Teaching:* The Albert Einstein College of Medicine has extensive research and teaching facilities located in buildings spread over a 17-acre campus in the Westchester Heights section of the Bronx, New York. Clinical teaching is carried out at Jacobi Medical Center, Montefiore Medical Center, and at ambulatory care centers located throughout New York City and lower Westchester County. *Library:* Gottesman Library houses more than 250,000 volumes and 2400 periodicals. *Housing:* The college operates 2 apartment complexes that provide apartments for single as well as married students. A modern, fully equipped athletic center with a swimming pool is located on campus.

## Special Features

*Minority admissions:* The college's director of the Office of Minority Student Affairs is in charge of minority student recruitment. A 2-week prematriculation summer preparatory course is offered to students with relatively weak science backgrounds. *Other degree programs:* A combined MD-PhD program is offered for those interested in a teaching and a research career in either the basic biomedical or clinical sciences. Students are expected to prepare a reference report of scholarly substance prior to graduation.

# Columbia University College of Physicians and Surgeons

630 West 168th Street
New York, New York    10032

*Phone:* 212-305-3595          *Fax:* 212-305-3601
*E-mail:* psadmissions@columbia.edu
*WWW:* cumc.columbia.edu/dept/ps

| Application Filing | | Accreditation | |
|---|---|---|---|
| Earliest: | June 1 | LCME | |
| Latest: | October 15 | | |
| Fee: | $85 | **Degrees Granted** | |
| AMCAS: | yes | MD, MD-PhD, MD-MPH | |

### Enrollment: 2008–2009 First-Year Class

| | | | | | |
|---|---|---|---|---|---|
| Men: | 78 | 50% | Applied: | 6839 | |
| Women: | 77 | 50% | Interviewed: | 1194 | |
| Minorities: | 14 | 9% | Enrolled: | 155 | |
| Out of State: | 117 | 75% | | | |

### 2008–2009 Class Profile

| *Mean MCAT Scores* | | *Mean GPA* |
|---|---|---|
| Physical Sciences: | 12 | 3.8 |
| Biological Sciences: | 12 | |
| Verbal Reasoning: | 11 | *Mean Science* |
| | | 3.8 |

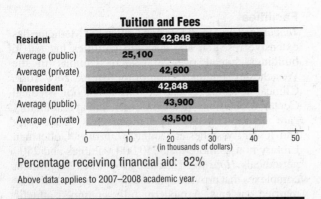

**Tuition and Fees**

| | (in thousands of dollars) |
|---|---|
| Resident | 42,848 |
| Average (public) | 25,100 |
| Average (private) | 42,600 |
| Nonresident | 42,848 |
| Average (public) | 43,900 |
| Average (private) | 43,500 |

Percentage receiving financial aid: 82%
Above data applies to 2007–2008 academic year.

## Introduction

Columbia University was established in 1754 and by 1767 it had its own medical instructors. Originally known as King's College, the school's name was changed to Columbia University in the City of New York in 1912. In 1814 the medical faculty of Columbia College merged with the College of Physicians and Surgeons. The Columbia-Presbyterian Medical Center was opened in 1928. Seven years later a permanent alliance was established with the university, and the college is now part of the Columbia-Presbyterian Medical Center, incorporating the Medical School, a Dental School, Presbyterian Hospital, and its subdivisions.

## Admissions

Requirements include the basic premedical science courses (with mammalian biology preferred) and 1 year of English. The college welcomes applications from candidates in all geographical areas. *Transfer and advanced standing:* Transfer students from colleges in the United States or Canada are considered. Relatively few candidates whose previous education was not obtained in this country or in Canada are admitted to an entering class or with advanced standing.

## Curriculum

4-year semitraditional. *First year:* Basic science courses with frequent correlation clinics through which basic science material may be related to medical problems. An introduction to medical practice course is also offered. *Second year:* One semester of advanced basic science course with the addition of interdepartmental courses in abnormal human biology and an introduction to the evaluation of patients and their problems. *Third year:* Consists of a rotation in or clerkships in the clinical discipline. *Fourth year:* Clinical and basic science electives. An elective in medicine in the tropics is available to fourth-year students who serve for 3 months in hospitals in South America, Africa, or Asia. An elective in the ambulatory care area is required.

## Grading and Promotion Policies

The system used is Honors/Pass/Fail. Students may be advanced to the next academic year or be allowed to repeat a year only upon the recommendation of the faculty members under whom they studied during the previous year.

## Facilities

*Teaching:* The College of Physicians and Surgeons is in a 17-story building, each floor of which connects with the wards and service of the Presbyterian Hospital. A 10-story ultramodern hospital located adjacent to Presbyterian Hospital was opened in 1989. In addition to the Presbyterian Hospital, 7 other hospitals are affiliated with the college. The William Black Medical Research Building is a 20-story building connected with the college building. The Hammer Health Sciences Center contains multidisciplinary teaching laboratories, classrooms, and research laboratories and the Psychiatric Institute is housed in a new research building. Other facilities include a Clinical Cancer Center and a General Clinical Research Center. *Library:* The medical library occupies the first 4 floors of the Hammer Health Sciences Center. In addition to its large collection of books and periodicals, the library contains extensive and comfortable areas for study. *Housing:* Bard Hall is the residence for men and women, and there are a limited number of apartments for married students available at Bard Haven.

## Special Features

*Minority admissions:* The school has designated its Office of Special Projects to coordinate its minority recruitment program. This office offers a 6-week summer MCAT preparation course. *Other degree programs:* Hospital residencies for the training of specialists and continuing education courses offer medical training beyond the MD degree. Combined MD-PhD programs are available in a variety of disciplines. An MD-MPH program is also available.

# Mount Sinai School of Medicine of New York University

One Gustave L. Levy Place
New York, New York   10029

*Phone:* 212-241-6696          *Fax:* 212-828-4135
*E-mail:* admissions@mssm.edu
*WWW:* mssm.edu

| Application Filing | | Accreditation |
|---|---|---|
| Earliest: | June 1 | LCME |
| Latest: | November 1 | |
| Fee: | $105 | **Degrees Granted** |
| AMCAS: | yes | MD, MD-PhD, |
| | | MD-MPH, MD-MBA |

### Enrollment: 2008–2009 First-Year Class

| | | | | |
|---|---|---|---|---|
| Men: | 72 | 51% | Applied: | 6745 |
| Women: | 68 | 49% | Interviewed: | 850 |
| Minorities: | 26 | 19% | Enrolled: | 140 |
| Out of State: | 26 | 19% | | |

### 2008–2009 Class Profile

| *Mean MCAT Scores* | | *Mean GPA* |
|---|---|---|
| Physical Sciences: | 11.9 | 3.65 |
| Biological Sciences: | 11.9 | |
| Verbal Reasoning: | 11.0 | *Mean Science* |
| | | 3.58 |

### Tuition and Fees

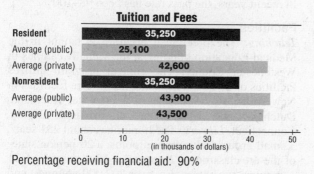

| | |
|---|---|
| **Resident** | 35,250 |
| Average (public) | 25,100 |
| Average (private) | 42,600 |
| **Nonresident** | 35,250 |
| Average (public) | 43,900 |
| Average (private) | 43,500 |

0    10    20    30    40    50
(in thousands of dollars)

Percentage receiving financial aid: 90%

## Introduction

Mount Sinai School of Medicine is a privately endowed, nondenominational institution. Developed from the 150-year tradition of patient care, professional education, and research of the Mount Sinai Hospital, it enrolled its first students in 1968, and is now officially affiliated with New York University.

## Admissions (AMCAS)

A minimum of 3 years of college and the MCATs are required. Most students have earned the bachelor's degree. Students are required to complete the basic premedical science courses and 1 year of English. Non-science majors who meet all of the admissions criteria are considered on an equal basis. Selection is based on scholastic achievement, integrity, maturity, motivation, and creativity. *Transfer and advanced standing:* Transfer students are not accepted.

## Curriculum

4-year semimodern. *First and second years:* Student-patient interactions begin in the first month of school with introduction to clinical medicine, and continue throughout. In addition to 3 introductory courses—student well-being, introduction to emergency medicine, and ethics—the first year focuses on an integrated approach to the study of molecules and cells, structure and function, and pathogenesis and host defense mechanisms. A case-based sequence is used to provide clinical relevance for the basic science that is being learned. Case-based integration and intro to clinical medicine continue during the second year, along with a focus on epidemiology and biostatistics. These are accompanied by a year-long study of mechanisms of disease and pharmacology. *Third year:* Clinical rotations include new and innovative clerkships that combine the disciplines of medicine and geriatrics, and pediatrics and obstetrics/gynecology. An integrated seminar series spans the year. *Fourth year:* Provides the student an increasing degree of patient care responsibility, and allows for extended electives. An emergency medicine rotation and a subinternship in medicine and pediatrics are required. A clinical translational fellowship combines the clinical practice of medicine with the relevant basic science. The year-end post-match integrated selective focuses on mastering the skills that are necessary to ensure a productive and educational internship experience.

## Grading and Promotion Policies

Courses are graded Pass/Fail during the first 2 years, Honors/High Pass/Pass/Fail in the last 2. Passing Step 1 and 2 of the USMLE is required.

## Facilities

The medical campus's 22 buildings include a hospital, research and service laboratories, teaching facilities, the Postgraduate School of Medicine, and the Graduate School of Biological Sciences. The Mount Sinai Hospital, a 1200-bed facility, constitutes the basic resource for clinical education. Additional clinical training sites extend throughout New York City, New Jersey, Westchester County, and Long Island. They include municipal hospitals, a Veteran's Affairs Medical Center, and private community hospitals, as well as private practitioners' offices. *Library:* The Levy Library occupies one and a half floors of the Annenberg Building. *Housing:* Housing is provided for single students in an on-campus residence hall. Housing is available for married couples and families in other Mount Sinai-owned buildings in the neighborhood.

## Special Features

*Minority admissions:* Strongly motivated students from minority backgrounds are encouraged to apply. A pre-entrance summer enrichment program is available for accepted students. *Other degree programs:* The school also offers a Medical Scientist Training Program for those interested in obtaining an MD/PhD, a Public Health (MD-MPH) and an MD-MBA in conjunction with Baruch College at CUNY.

# New York Medical College
Valhalla, New York    10595

*Phone:* 914-594-4507          *Fax:* 914-594-4976
*E-mail:* mdadmit@nymed.edu
*WWW:* nymc.edu

| Application Filing | | Accreditation |
|---|---|---|
| Earliest: | June 1 | LCME |
| Latest: | December 15 | |
| Fee: | $100 | **Degrees Granted** |
| AMCAS: | yes | MD, MD-PhD, |
| | | MD-MPH |

### Enrollment: 2008–2009 First-Year Class

| Men: | 94 | 50% | Applied: | 11,250 |
|---|---|---|---|---|
| Women: | 94 | 50% | Interviewed: | 1383 |
| Minorities: | 69 | 37% | Enrolled: | 188 |
| Out of State: | 140 | 74% | | |

### 2008–2009 Class Profile

| *Mean MCAT Scores* | | *Mean GPA* |
|---|---|---|
| Physical Sciences: | 10.2 | 3.5 |
| Biological Sciences: | 10.5 | |
| Verbal Reasoning: | 9.8 | *Mean Science* |
| | | 3.4 |

### Tuition and Fees

| | |
|---|---|
| **Resident** | 41,500 |
| Average (public) | 25,100 |
| Average (private) | 42,600 |
| **Nonresident** | 41,500 |
| Average (public) | 43,900 |
| Average (private) | 43,500 |

0    10    20    30    40    50
(in thousands of dollars)

Percentage receiving financial aid: 86%

## Introduction
New York Medical College is located in Valhalla, New York, in suburban Westchester County, within the nation's largest metropolitan region. Founded in 1860, the School of Medicine has a long-standing reputation for producing both generalists and specialists. The university's wide range of affiliated hospitals provide extensive resources and educational opportunities.

## Admissions (AMCAS)
Applicants must have taken the MCAT exam within the last 3 years and must have completed the basic premedical courses. Each of these must have been completed with lab work. Two semesters of English are also required. *Transfer and advanced standing:* In rare instance from U.S. or Canadian schools to the third-year class.

## Curriculum
4-year semitraditional. *First year:* The traditional core of the first-year curriculum—sciences and behavioral science—is supplemented by clinical case correlations and courses in epidemiology and biostatistics. All first-year students take an Introduction to Primary Care course where they have regular patient contact working in the office of a primary care physician. *Second year:* Focus on pathology/pathophysiology; emphasizes small-group discussion, problem-based learning, and self-study. Clinical skills training, pharmacology, and medical microbiology prepare students for entry into the clerkship experience of the next 2 years. *Third year:* Students complete clerkships in conventional disciplines. *Fourth year:* Consists of required clinical rotations taken at affiliated hospitals and electives at medical institutions across the country and around the world. About 20 fourth-year students take international electives each year.

## Grading and Promotion Policies
Grading is Honors/High Pass/Pass/Fail. Passing Step 1 and Step 2 of the USMLE is a graduation requirement. In recent years, the pass rate has been 98–100%.

## Facilities
*Teaching:* The preclinical program is taught in the Medical Education building at the Valhalla campus in Westchester County. The clinical program utilizes facilities of 26 hospitals in and health care facilities in New York City, the counties of Westchester, Rockland, Dutchess, and Ulster, and in Fairfield County, Connecticut. *Library:* The library has about 231 seats, 3 small group multipurpose rooms, a 20-person state-of-the-art classroom, 2 computer labs, a total of 21 computers for library use, over 207,000 volumes, and approximately 13,000 electronic journals.

## Special Features
*Minority admissions:* NYMC seeks to admit a diverse class, including diversity of gender, race, ethnicity, cultural and economic background, and life experience. *Other degree programs:* Students have an opportunity to earn joint degrees, combining the MD with an MPH in the School of Public Health or a PhD in the Graduate School of Basic Medical Sciences.

# New York University School of Medicine

550 First Avenue
New York, New York   10016

*Phone:* 212-263-5290          *Fax:* 212-263-0720
*E-mail:* admissions@med.NYU.edu
*WWW:* med.nyu.edu

| Application Filing | | Accreditation | |
|---|---|---|---|
| Earliest: | June 1 | LCME | |
| Latest: | October 15 | | |
| Fee: | $100 | **Degrees Granted** | |
| AMCAS: | no | MD, MD-PhD | |

### Enrollment: 2008–2009 First-Year Class

| Men: | 80 | 50% | Applied: | 7573 |
|---|---|---|---|---|
| Women: | 80 | 50% | Interviewed: | 960 |
| Minorities: | 8 | 5% | Enrolled: | 160 |
| Out of State: | 94 | 59% | | |

### 2008–2009 Class Profile

| *Mean MCAT Scores* | | *Mean GPA* |
|---|---|---|
| Physical Sciences: | 12 | 3.7 |
| Biological Sciences: | 12 | |
| Verbal Reasoning: | 11 | *Mean Science* |
| | | 3.7 |

**Tuition and Fees**

| | |
|---|---|
| Resident | 40,729 |
| Average (public) | 25,100 |
| Average (private) | 42,600 |
| Nonresident | 40,729 |
| Average (public) | 43,900 |
| Average (private) | 43,500 |

(in thousands of dollars)

Percentage receiving financial aid: 75%

Above data applies to 2007–2008 academic year.

## Introduction

New York University, a nondenominational private institution was established in 1831; the School of Medicine was founded in 1841. The Bellevue Hospital Medical College, established in 1861, merged in 1898 with New York University to form the University and Bellevue Hospital Medical College, which became New York University College of Medicine in 1935. The present name was adopted in 1960. The School of Medicine boasts a host of distinguished alumni including Walter Reed, William Gorgas, Jonas Salk, and Albert Sabin.

## Admissions

Requirements include the premedical science courses and 1 year of English. Recommended courses are biochemistry, genetics, and molecular biology. *Transfer and advanced standing:* Not available.

## Curriculum

4-year traditional. Basic sciences are introduced with interdepartmental correlations. *First year:* Concerned with the normal pattern of cellular and organ dynamics. An introduction to the physiologic and pathologic basis of human disease is provided that sets the stage for principles of clinical science and psychiatry. *Second year:* Devoted to general and organ pathology and neurological sciences. Continuation of the introduction to clinical science is correlated closely with studies in special pathology. Advanced basic sciences and principles of physical diagnosis provide the basis for clinical clerkships. *Third year:* Clinical clerkships in the major areas of medicine. *Fourth year:* A subinternship in a clinical area of interest for 6 weeks. An elective program of approved research or clinical studies at the school, at another U.S. school, or at a school abroad makes up the balance of the year. In recent years some changes have been introduced into the curriculum. These changes are designed to encourage independent learning by the use of small group seminars, problem-solving exercises, and computer-assisted learning. Critical facts and concepts of scientific principles are acquired in the basic science program. These provide the foundation for clinical training. An honors program and independent research opportunities enhance the basic science program.

## Grading and Promotion Policies

A Pass/Fail system is used in the basic sciences and a letter or number in required clinical sciences. Advancement from 1 year to the next is made by a Faculty Committee that can approve advancement or require the student to repeat. Taking Steps 1 and 2 of the USMLE is optional.

## Facilities

*Teaching:* The School of Medicine is located adjacent to the East River, between 30th and 34th Streets in Manhattan. The preclinical program is carried out in the Medical Science Building. Clinical teaching facilities are provided by the University Hospital (622 beds), Bellevue Hospital (3000 beds), and New York Veterans Hospital (1218 beds). *Other:* The off-campus Goldwater Memorial Hospital (1250 beds) and the Hospital of Joint Disease are also affiliated. *Library:* The library houses more than 100,000 volumes and 1600 periodicals. In addition, the Institute of Environmental Medicine at Sterling Forest offers another reference library. *Housing:* Residence halls on campus provide single rooms or shared apartments for all students.

## Special Features

*Minority admissions:* The school has an active recruitment program. *Other degree programs:* The school offers the Medical Scientist Training Program for an MD-PhD in all basic science disciplines. Opportunities are enhanced by the Honors Research Program of Independent Study and Masters Scholars Program in areas such as bioethics, public health, and medical informatics.

# University of Buffalo School of Medicine and Biomedical Sciences

131 Biomedical Education Building
3435 Main Street
Buffalo, New York    14214

*Phone:* 716-829-3466          *Fax:* 716-829-3849
*E-mail:* jjrosso@buffalo.edu
*WWW:* smbs.buffalo.edu

| Application Filing | | Accreditation | |
|---|---|---|---|
| Earliest: | June 1 | LCME | |
| Latest: | November 15 | | |
| Fee: | $65 | **Degrees Granted** | |
| AMCAS: | yes | MD, MD-PhD, | |
| | | MD-MBA, MD-MPH | |

### Enrollment: 2008–2009 First-Year Class

| | | | | | |
|---|---|---|---|---|---|
| Men: | 60 | 44% | Applied: | 3839 | |
| Women: | 75 | 56% | Interviewed: | 768 | |
| Minorities: | 7 | 5.2% | Enrolled: | 135 | |
| Out of State: | 32 | 24% | | | |

### 2008–2009 Class Profile

| *Mean MCAT Scores* | | *Mean GPA* |
|---|---|---|
| Physical Sciences: | 10.10 | 3.67 |
| Biological Sciences: | 10.47 | |
| Verbal Reasoning: | 9.98 | *Mean Science* |
| | | 3.60 |

**Tuition and Fees**

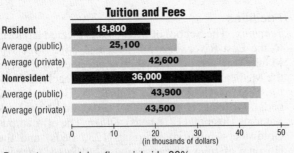

| | |
|---|---|
| Resident | 18,800 |
| Average (public) | 25,100 |
| Average (private) | 42,600 |
| Nonresident | 36,000 |
| Average (public) | 43,900 |
| Average (private) | 43,500 |

(in thousands of dollars)

Percentage receiving financial aid: 90%

## Introduction

The School of Medicine and Biomedical Sciences of the State University of Buffalo was a private institution when it was established in 1846; it merged with the SUNY system in 1962. Instrumental in organizing the medical school was Millard Fillmore, the first chancellor, who later became the thirteenth president of the United States. The University of Buffalo has the most comprehensive campus in the SUNY system.

## Admissions (AMCAS)

Requirements include the basic premedical science courses and 1 year of English. A baccalaureate degree from an accredited college or university is desirable. The choice of a major is optional; however, beyond securing a solid foundation in the sciences by means of the prerequisites, students should seek to develop a background in the social sciences and humanities. Some preference is given to qualified residents of New York State. Competitive out-of-state applicants are encouraged to apply. Applications are accepted from children of alumni regardless of state of residence, but no preferential priority is accorded.

## Curriculum

4-year semimodern. The curriculum is designed to teach students in the fundamentals of medicine. It seeks to demonstrate the interrelationships between the basic and clinical sciences, allow early exposure to patient care, and provide ample opportunities to explore both primary care and medical specialties. Integrated organ system-based modules are used to teach the basic sciences. In addition to traditional lectures and laboratories, students participate in small-group problem-based learning. An active learning style is encouraged. The third year offers the traditional clerkships and elective opportunities. Students may take as many as 4 elective experiences away from Buffalo in the fourth year.

## Grading and Promotion Policies

An Honors/Pass/Fail system is used. A Promotion Committee reviews the progress of students at the end of each year and is responsible for recommendations based on all aspects of the student's work and departmental appraisals. Successful completion of Step 1 of the USMLE in 3 attempts is required before matriculating to the third year.

## Facilities

*Teaching:* The preclinical years are taught in totally modern facilities completed in 1986, which provide an environment conductive to informal experiences, small group teaching, and student enrichment. A modern computer-assisted learning laboratory, together with study carrels, is located in the school and the Health Science Library. The library is "world class" with a fine collection of textbooks and journals, an excellent reading room, and a history of medicine collection. Clinical teaching is coordinated in 9 hospitals located in Buffalo and the suburbs of Amherst, and at rural sites in the Buffalo area.

## Special Features

*Minority admissions:* The school is committed to the educational preparation of students from underrepresented population groups in medicine. *Other degree programs:* The medical school offers early-assurance guarantees to exceptional students at the end of the third semester of college. The school offers an integrated 7-year MD-PhD program limited to a maximum of 4 students per year. The school also offers a combined MD/MBA 5-year program limited to 4 students per year, and an MD/MPH program also limited to 4 students per year.

# SUNY Downstate Medical Center College of Medicine

450 Clarkson Avenue
Brooklyn, New York    11203

*Phone:* 718-270-2446        *Fax:* 718-270-4775
*E-mail:* admissions@downstate.edu
*WWW:* http://www.downstate.edu/College-of-Medicine

| Application Filing | | Accreditation | |
|---|---|---|---|
| Earliest: | June 2 | LCME | |
| Latest: | December 15 | | |
| Fee: | $80 | **Degrees Granted** | |
| AMCAS: | yes | MD, MD-PhD | |

### Enrollment: 2008–2009 First-Year Class

| | | | | | |
|---|---|---|---|---|---|
| Men: | 85 | 50% | Applied: | 4565 | |
| Women: | 85 | 50% | Interviewed: | 997 | |
| Minorities: | 17 | 10% | Enrolled: | 170 | |
| Out of State: | 24 | 14% | | | |

### 2008–2009 Class Profile

| *Mean MCAT Scores* | | *Mean GPA* |
|---|---|---|
| Physical Sciences: | 11 | 3.7 |
| Biological Sciences: | 11 | |
| Verbal Reasoning: | 10 | *Mean Science* |
| | | 3.7 |

**Tuition and Fees**

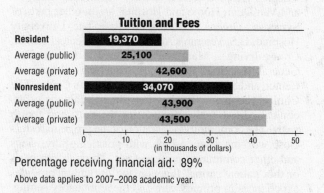

| | |
|---|---|
| Resident | 19,370 |
| Average (public) | 25,100 |
| Average (private) | 42,600 |
| Nonresident | 34,070 |
| Average (public) | 43,900 |
| Average (private) | 43,500 |

0  10  20  30  40  50
(in thousands of dollars)

Percentage receiving financial aid: 89%

Above data applies to 2007–2008 academic year.

## Introduction

In 1860 the Long Island College Hospital became the Health Science Center at Brooklyn. It subsequently was called the Downstate Medical Center because of its role as a major provider of health care in the downstate New York region. It is located on a 13-acre urban campus in Brooklyn. The medical school is now part of SUNY Health Science Center of Brooklyn, which also includes colleges of Nursing, Health-Related Professions, School of Graduate Studies, and University Hospital.

## Admissions (AMCAS)

In addition to the basic premedical sciences, requirements include 1 year of English. One year of college mathematics and a course in biochemistry and in advanced science are recommended. Admissions preference is given to New York State residents. *Transfer and advanced standing:* Students are considered for admission to the third-year class. Those wishing to transfer must take Step 1 of the USMLE.

## Curriculum

4-year semitraditional. *First and second years:* Cover the basic medical sciences and include free half-days throughout the first 2 years for electives, correlation clinics in the second year to show relationships of basic sciences to clinical work, and introduction to patients during second-year Problem-Based Learning (PBL) Track. Second-year curriculum organized into organ system approach. *Third year:* Clerkship rotation in the major clinical specialties. *Fourth year:* Individualized selective programs making available a variety of courses and clinical experiences. The primary goal of the curriculum is to prepare competent physicians as general or specialty practitioners, researchers, or medical administrators or academicians. Students are expected to gain an understanding of health and its promotion and of disease prevention. The students will become proficient in basic clinical skills such as history taking, the performance of comprehensive physical and mental health examinations, and interpreting the findings. Competence in the performance of basic procedures is also expected. The curriculum is undergoing a major revision stimulated by the change in the organization and practice of medicine, the explosion of new scientific and clinical information, the desire to integrate basic and clinical sciences throughout the four years of medical training, and the need for an earlier exposure to patient care.

## Grading and Promotion Policies

A Honors/High Pass/Pass/Conditional/Fail system is used; the USMLE Step 1 is required for promotion to third year.

## Facilities

*Teaching:* The Health Science Education Building houses state-of-the-art classrooms, laboratories, an auditorium, and 2 floors of study carrels. Clinical teaching takes place at University Hospital (350 beds), Kings County Hospital (1234 beds), and several other affiliated institutions. *Other:* Facilities for research are located in the Basic Sciences Building. *Library:* The Medical Research Library, one of the largest medical school libraries in the country, occupies 3 floors of the Health Science Education Building. The Bibliographic Retrieval Service has 150 data bases. *Housing:* Two 11-story residence halls provide housing for both single and married students.

## Special Features

*Minority admissions:* The school has an active recruitment program aimed at the Northeast. It offers a summer enrichment program for college sophomores and one for prematriculating students. *Other degree programs:* Combined MD-PhD programs are available in some of the basic sciences.

# State University of New York Upstate Medical University

766 Irving Avenue
Syracuse, New York    13210

*Phone:* 315-464-4570          *Fax:* 315-464-8867
*E-mail:* admiss@upstate.edu
*WWW:* upstate.edu/com

| Application Filing | | Accreditation |
|---|---|---|
| Earliest: | June 1 | LCME |
| Latest: | October 15 | |
| Fee: | $100 | **Degrees Granted** |
| AMCAS: | yes | MD, MD-PhD |

### Enrollment: 2008–2009 First-Year Class

| | | | | |
|---|---|---|---|---|
| Men: | 83 | 51% | Applied: | 5321 |
| Women: | 77 | 49% | Interviewed: | 904 |
| Minorities: | 4 | 26% | Enrolled: | 160 |
| Out of State: | 30 | 26% | | |

### 2008–2009 Class Profile

| *Mean MCAT Scores* | | *Mean GPA* |
|---|---|---|
| Physical Sciences: | 11 | 3.8 |
| Biological Sciences: | 11 | |
| Verbal Reasoning: | 10 | *Mean Science* |
| | | 3.7 |

**Tuition and Fees**

| | |
|---|---|
| Resident | 19,956 |
| Average (public) | 25,100 |
| Average (private) | 42,600 |
| Nonresident | 34,656 |
| Average (public) | 43,900 |
| Average (private) | 43,500 |

0    10    20    30    40    50
(in thousands of dollars)

Percentage receiving financial aid: 90%

## Introduction

The Upstate Medical University can trace its origin to the establishment in 1834 of the General Medical School which joined the newly formed Syracuse University in 1871. Expansion of the facilities took place in the 1930s and in 1950 the College of Medicine was transferred to the then newly organized State University of New York.

## Admissions (AMCAS)

Required courses include the premedical sciences and 1 year of English. Preference will be given to New York State residents. Applications are accepted from U.S. citizens and from permanent residents who have completed at least 3 years of college study (90 semester hours) in the United States or Canada. Achieving excellence in the sciences is essential; however, academic work in the humanities and social sciences is equally important.

## Curriculum

4-year semimodern. *First and second years:* The curriculum integrates the basic and clinical sciences, with basic science courses teaching the clinical implications of the material, and provides clinical experience starting in the first semester. All courses are aligned by organ systems. *Third and fourth years:* The third and fourth years are considered a single unit. Every student is required to complete 50 weeks of clerkships and 26 weeks of electives. Forty-two weeks of required clerkship and 6 weeks of electives are included in the third year; 8 weeks of required time and 20 weeks of electives are included in the fourth year. Required courses are: medicine, general surgery, ophthalmology, otorhinolaryngology, radiology, anesthesiology, and orthopedic surgery, psychiatry, obstetrics and gynecology, neuroscience, and preventive medicine and neurology.

## Grading and Promotion Policies

The grading system used is Honors/High Pass/Pass/Fail. Taking Steps 1 and 2 of the USMLE is required.

## Facilities

*Teaching:* Facilities for instruction and research are in Weiskotten Hall. Most of the hospital affiliates are adjacent to the basic science building at Weiskotten Hall. St. Joseph's Hospital Health Center, Community General, and Van Duyn Home and Hospital are in other parts of Syracuse. *Other:* Affiliates are the State University Hospital, U.S. Veteran's Administration Medical Center, Crouse-Irving Memorial Hospital, Community-General Hospital, Richard H. Hutchings Psychiatric Center, and St. Joseph's Hospital and Health Center. The Clinical Campus at Binghamton, a branch campus, offers clinical educational programs for the third and fourth years. The community orientation of the program fosters close working relationships with practicing physicians and other community professionals. Through emphasis on the "patient caring" function, the curriculum provides experiences in primary care and the ambulatory setting. *Library:* The library's collection numbers more than 130,000 volumes and about 2200 rare books. The library also has access to 2 large online bibliographic services. *Housing:* Two modern 10-story residence halls on campus provide dormitory rooms, studios, and one-bedroom apartments for single and married students.

## Special Features

*Minority admissions:* The school is committed to having student enrollment reflect the diverse population of the state. *Other degree programs:* Research is an important aspect of medical education; four common options are MD-PhD Program, Research Electives, Summer Research, and MSRP.

# Stony Brook University School of Medicine

Health Sciences Center
Stony Brook, New York    11794

*Phone:* 631-444-2113          *Fax:* 631-444-6032
*E-mail:* somadmissions@stonybrook.edu
*WWW:* hscsunysb.edu/som

| Application Filing | | Accreditation | |
|---|---|---|---|
| Earliest: | June 1 | LCME | |
| Latest: | December 15 | | |
| Fee: | $75 | **Degrees Granted** | |
| AMCAS: | yes | MD, MD-PhD | |

### Enrollment: 2008–2009 First-Year Class

| | | | | | |
|---|---|---|---|---|---|
| Men: | 67 | 53% | Applied: | 3699 | |
| Women: | 59 | 47% | Interviewed: | 629 | |
| Minorities: | 22 | 17% | Enrolled: | 126 | |
| Out of State: | 17 | 13% | | | |

### 2008–2009 Class Profile

| *Mean MCAT Scores* | | *Mean GPA* |
|---|---|---|
| Physical Sciences: | 11.0 | 3.65 |
| Biological Sciences: | 11.0 | |
| Verbal Reasoning: | 10 | *Mean Science* |
| | | 3.6 |

**Tuition and Fees**

| | |
|---|---|
| Resident | 18,800 |
| Average (public) | 18,500 |
| Average (private) | 35,000 |
| Nonresident | 33,500 |
| Average (public) | 34,500 |
| Average (private) | 36,750 |

0    10    20    30    40    50
(in thousands of dollars)

Percentage receiving financial aid: 83%

## Introduction

The School of Medicine opened in 1971 and is one of 5 professional schools, in addition to the hospital, that make up the Health Sciences Center at Stony Brook. The school aims to achieve excellence in preparing students for careers in medical practice or research through its curriculum and through activities that are designed to provide students with the skills that are appropriate for success in all fields of medicine. The school is located 60 miles east of Manhattan on Long Island's wooded north shore.

## Admissions (AMCAS)

The basic premedical science courses plus one year of English are required. *Transfer and advanced standing:* Transfers to the third-year class are considered for stu-dents from other LCME-accredited schools only if a place is available.

## Curriculum

4-year semimodern. *First year:* Consists of basic science courses and introductory courses related to patient care. Courses include: molecules, genes, and cells; the body; neurosciences; the organs; and pathology plus additional minor courses. *Second year:* Continues with the systems approach. It focuses on an integrated presentation of courses in pharmacology and microbiology. *Third year:* Consists of clerkships in medicine, surgery, pediatrics, obstetrics-gynecology, and reproductive medicine, psychiatry, and primary care, as well as a 4-week elective. Incorporated in each clerkship is a segment entitled Medicine in Contemporary Society. *Fourth year:* The student assumes greater patient-care responsibilities and continues to acquire clinical and laboratory skills. This is attained during a 1-month subinternship in either medicine, family medicine, pediatrics, or general surgery. Another requirement is a 1-month didactic course in emergency medicine, laboratory medicine, or therapeutics. Other requirements are the completion of a 1-month primary care clerkship at one of the school's affiliated institutions or elsewhere and also 1 month of neurology experience. All students must successfully complete an exercise with standardized patients designed to evaluate clinical competency. The system's approach to medicine that forms the core of the curriculum has been favorably received by the students. It reduces the amount of lecture time by strengthening the organization of course material, and decreases the burden imposed by competing examinations.

## Grading and Promotion Policies

Honors/Pass/Fail system is used. Students take Step 1 of the USMLE in the second year and must pass in order to advance to the clinical year of study. Students have to pass USMLE Step 2 to graduate.

## Facilities

*Teaching:* Clinical teaching takes place at the University Hospital (534 beds), Nassau University Medical Center (800 beds), Northport VA Hospital (480 beds), Winthrop University Hospital (591 beds), and other institutions. *Library:* The Health Sciences Library is located in the Health Science Center. *Housing:* Residence halls are arranged in quadrangles, each having single and double rooms and 4- or 6-person suites.

## Special Features

*Minority admissions:* Stony Brook University encourages applications from members of groups that have historically been underrepresented in medicine. *Other degree programs:* The Medical Scientist Training Program (MSTP) is a fully funded MD-PhD program. Students must complete a 1-month deductive course in emergency medicine, laboratory medicine, 1 month of neurology, and 2 weeks of radiology. The remainder of the 4th year is devoted to elective time.

# University of Rochester School of Medicine

601 Elmwood Avenue
Rochester, New York    14642

*Phone:* 585-275-4339        *Fax:* 585-756-5479
*E-mail:* mdadmish@urmc.rochester.edu
*WWW:* urmc.rochester.edu/smd

| Application Filing | | Accreditation | |
|---|---|---|---|
| Earliest: | June 1 | LCME | |
| Latest: | October 15 | | |
| Fee: | $75 | **Degrees Granted** | |
| AMCAS: | yes | MD, MD-PhD, MD-MS, | |
| | | MD-MBA, MD-MPH | |

### Enrollment: 2008–2009 First-Year Class

| | | | | | |
|---|---|---|---|---|---|
| Men: | 50 | 48% | Applied: | 4222 |
| Women: | 54 | 52% | Interviewed: | 680 |
| Minorities: | 28 | 19% | Enrolled: | 104 |
| Out of State: | 58 | 56% | | |

### 2008–2009 Class Profile

| *Mean MCAT Scores* | | *Mean GPA* |
|---|---|---|
| Physical Sciences: | 10.8 | 3.7 |
| Biological Sciences: | 11.3 | |
| Verbal Reasoning: | 10.3 | *Mean Science* |
| | | 3.7 |

**Tuition and Fees**

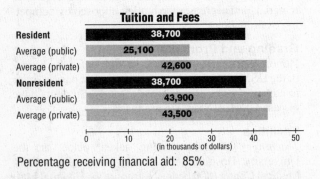

| | |
|---|---|
| Resident | 38,700 |
| Average (public) | 25,100 |
| Average (private) | 42,600 |
| Nonresident | 38,700 |
| Average (public) | 43,900 |
| Average (private) | 43,500 |

(in thousands of dollars)

Percentage receiving financial aid: 85%

## Introduction

The University of Rochester, founded in 1850, is an independently supported, nonsectarian institution. The University of Rochester Medical Center consists of the School of Medicine and Dentistry, School of Nursing, Strong Memorial Hospital, Golisano Children's Hospital, and Eastman Dental Center.

## Admissions

Required courses include the basic premedical sciences, 1 year of English, and courses in the humanities and/or social sciences. The MCAT is required. *Transfer and advanced standing:* None. International students, unless they are Rochester graduates, are not considered.

## Curriculum

4-year modern. Rochester's Double Helix Curriculum captures the integrated strands of basic science and clinical medicine as they are woven throughout the 4-year curriculum. The focus of our educational program is not merely the transfer of information but the transformation of the learner in a culture providing that ingenious combination of support and challenge that leads to education. Every course is interdisciplinary and, unlike most medical schools, clinical skills training from the beginning leads not to shadowing, but to the start of real clinical work as part of the health care team. Actual clinical cases drive the learning of science. Students return to increasingly advanced basic science in the second, third, and fourth years through an integrated series of problem-based learning exercises. Multidisciplinary PBL cases are used in all courses with usually 3 PBL tutorials per week and an average of 14 lecture hours per week. Clinical exposure begins during the first week of school with an introduction to clinical medicine in the fall semester and the start of the primary care/ambulatory longitudinal clerkship beginning during the first spring semester. This experience includes all the ambulatory components of family medicine, pediatrics, internal medicine, women's health, psychiatry, and ambulatory surgery, and is completed by the end of the second year. Inpatient clerkships are completed by December of the fourth year and focus on acute care experiences in adult medicine, women's and children's health, mind/brain/behavior, and emergency care.

## Grading and Promotion Policies

Pass/Fail is the current system. The USMLE is not used in promotion decisions.

## Facilities

*Teaching:* The basic sciences are taught in the Medical Education Wing; clinical teaching takes place in Strong Memorial Hospital (750 beds), at 3 affiliated community hospitals, in an Ambulatory Care Center, and in the offices of many practicing physician-teachers. *Other:* Research laboratory space for basic science departments is in the Medical Education Wing. *Library:* The Edward G. Miner Library houses more than 200,000 volumes and subscribes to 3000 periodicals. *Housing:* 1 to 2 bedroom apartments are available near the Medical Center.

## Special Features

*Minority admissions:* The Center for Advocacy, Community Health, and Education and Diversity coordinates an active recruitment program involving a Summer Research Fellowship Program for upper-level students. *Other degree programs:* A BA-MD program is offered. Combined degree programs are available for MD-MS and MD-PhD candidates. An MD-MPH combined degree program is available through Community and Preventive Medicine. MPH-MS programs are offered, and an MBA program is available in the Simon School of Business Administration.

# Weill Medical College of Cornell University

445 East 69th Street
New York, New York    10021

*Phone:* 212-746-1067          *Fax:* 212-746-8052
*E-mail:* wcumc-admissions@med.cornell.edu
*WWW:* med.cornell.edu/education

| Application Filing | | Accreditation | |
|---|---|---|---|
| Earliest: | June 1 | LCME | |
| Latest: | October 15 | | |
| Fee: | $75 | **Degrees Granted** | |
| AMCAS: | yes | MD, MD-PhD, | |
| | | MD-MBA | |

### Enrollment: 2008–2009 First-Year Class

| Men: | 48 | 48% | Applied: | 5853 |
|---|---|---|---|---|
| Women: | 53 | 52% | Interviewed: | 753 |
| Minorities: | 18 | 18% | Enrolled: | 101 |
| Out of State: | 67 | 66% | | |

### 2008–2009 Class Profile

| *Mean MCAT Scores* | | *Mean GPA* |
|---|---|---|
| Physical Sciences: | 12 | 3.8 |
| Biological Sciences: | 12 | |
| Verbal Reasoning: | 11 | *Mean Science* |
| | | 3.9 |

**Tuition and Fees**

| | (in thousands of dollars) |
|---|---|
| Resident | 40,890 |
| Average (public) | 25,100 |
| Average (private) | 42,600 |
| Nonresident | 40,890 |
| Average (public) | 43,900 |
| Average (private) | 43,500 |

Percentage receiving financial aid: 84%

Above data applies to 2007–2008 academic year.

## Introduction

The Weill Medical College of Cornell University was established in 1898 and is situated on the upper east side of New York City. Although the university is located in Ithaca, New York, the medical school was established in New York City to provide students with clinical experience and laboratory-oriented instruction. An academic medical center was established in 1962 that affiliated Cornell Medical School with New York Hospital. With the relocation, both these components became part of a common campus—the New York Hospital-Cornell Medical Center. The school name was changed in 1998 to the Joan and Sanford I. Weill Medical College of Cornell University.

## Admissions (AMCAS)

A solid background in science is important. Required courses include the basic premedical science courses and 1 year of English. *Transfer and advanced standing:* When vacancies occur, students are considered for admission to the third year. Candidates must furnish evidence of satisfactorily completed work and must present a letter of current good standing from their U.S.-accredited school.

## Curriculum

4-year modern. The curriculum integrates the basic sciences, the clinical sciences, and clinical practice by offering interdisciplinary basic science courses, early exposure to clinical concepts, and clinical experiences. The curriculum emphasizes problem-solving skills and aims to develop the students' ability and motivation for continued self-study. In keeping with developments in the health care delivery system, it has expanded clinical education in the ambulatory setting by offering office-based preceptorships in years 1 and 2 and a primary care clerkship in year 3. Upon completion of the second year of medical school, students take 3 introductory clinical courses: Clinical Pharmacology, Anesthesia, and the Introductory Clerkship. The third and fourth years have a combined clinical curriculum with required clinical clerkships, a subinternship, Medicine, Patients and Society III, Health Care Systems, and elective courses. This educational continuum ends with 8 weeks of required credits in advanced basic sciences.

## Grading and Promotion Policies

Performance is graded by an Honors/Pass/Fail system, in the first 2 years and Honors/High Pass/Pass/Fail in the last 2.

## Facilities

*Teaching:* Most of the instruction for the first 2 years takes place at the Weill Educational Center, a multipurpose teaching complex. It consists of an auditorium and 21 modular teaching laboratories. Designed for maximum flexibility, it accommodates teaching formats and methodology. The medical school campus enbraces one of the most advanced centers in the world for biomedical sciences, including Rockefeller University, Memorial Sloan-Kettering Cancer Center, New York Presbyterian Medical Center and Hospital for Special Surgery, and other affiliated institutions.

## Special Features

*Minority admissions:* The school makes a nationwide effort to enroll qualified members of groups underrepresented in medicine. It conducts a research fellowship program for college premedical students who have completed their junior year and have a major interest in the medical problems of the underserved. *Other degree programs:* The school offers a fully funded combined MD-PhD program, which is coordinated with the Rockefeller University, Memorial Sloan-Kettering Cancer Center, and the Cornell University Graduate School of Medical Sciences. An MD-MBA program is offered in conjunction with the Johnson School of Management of Cornell University.

# NORTH CAROLINA

# Brody School of Medicine at East Carolina University

Greenville, North Carolina 27834

*Phone:* 252-744-2202  *Fax:* 252-744-1926
*E-mail:* somadmissions@ecu.edu
*WWW:* ecu.edu/somadmissions/

| Application Filing | | Accreditation |
|---|---|---|
| Earliest: | June 1 | LCME |
| Latest: | November 15 | |
| Fee: | $60 | **Degrees Granted** |
| AMCAS: | yes | MD, MD-PhD, |
| | | MD-MBA, MD-MPH |

### Enrollment: 2008–2009 First-Year Class

| | | | | |
|---|---|---|---|---|
| Men: | 37 | 49% | Applied: | 878 |
| Women: | 39 | 51% | Interviewed: | 450 |
| Minorities: | 24 | 32% | Enrolled: | 76 |
| Out of State: | 0 | 0% | | |

### 2008–2009 Class Profile

| *Mean MCAT Scores* | | *Mean GPA* |
|---|---|---|
| Physical Sciences: | 9.1 | 3.6 |
| Biological Sciences: | 9.7 | |
| Verbal Reasoning: | 9.4 | *Mean Science* |
| | | 3.5 |

### Tuition and Fees

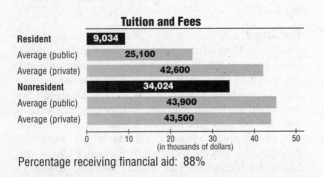

| | |
|---|---|
| Resident | 9,034 |
| Average (public) | 25,100 |
| Average (private) | 42,600 |
| Nonresident | 34,024 |
| Average (public) | 43,900 |
| Average (private) | 43,500 |

0   10   20   30   40   50
(in thousands of dollars)

Percentage receiving financial aid: 88%

## Introduction

The School of Medicine at East Carolina University, located in the Health Sciences Center in Greenville, enrolled its first 4-year class in 1977. Educational facilities are located on a 100-acre Health Science Center Campus. The school has a 3-fold mission: training physicians for primary care, recruiting and educating minority students, and community service.

## Admissions (AMCAS)

Only the basic premedical science courses and 1 year of English are required. A second year of English and humanities/social science courses are recommended. Strong preference for admission is given to qualified residents of North Carolina. The school seeks qualified students from a variety of backgrounds who have diverse personalities. Thus in the selection process the intellectual, personal, and social characteristics of each applicant are considered. These features are reflected in data such as college record, MCAT scores, and letters of recommendation/evaluation. This information is supplemented by the impression gained from 2 personal interviews, conducted at the medical school campus by 2 members of the Admissions Committee. *Transfer and advanced standing:* Considered only if vacant positions exist.

## Curriculum

4-year semitraditional. *First year:* In addition to the introductory basic sciences of anatomy, biochemistry, and physiology, courses in microbiology, genetics, psychosocial basis of medical practice, medical ethics, and a primary care preceptorship are offered. The 2-year clinical skills course begins early in the first semester. *Second year:* In addition to the advanced basic sciences of immunology, pathology, and pharmacology, courses are offered in substance abuse, human sexuality, clinical pathophysiology, and social issues in medicine. Primary care preceptorships and the clinical skills course continue throughout the second year. *Third year:* There are 6 major clinical rotations that last 8 weeks each, and together include at least 10 weeks of ambulatory experience. *Fourth year:* There are 36 weeks of clinical and basic science selectives. Of these, 2 months must be spent in primary care, and 1 month each in a surgical selective and an internal medicine selective.

## Grading and Promotion Policies

Letter grades are used in evaluating students. Both steps of the USMLE must be taken and students must pass Part I prior to promotion into the third year.

## Facilities

*Teaching:* The Brody Medical Science Building contains lecture halls, classrooms, conference rooms, and well-equipped laboratories, and an auditorium. The primary affiliated clinical teaching institution is the 725-bed Pitt County Memorial Hospital. *Other:* The Regional Cancer Center, Heart Center, Radiation Therapy Center, Eastern Carolina Family Practice Center, Biotechnology Building, Life Sciences Building, and various other clinical and technological facilities are all located on the medical school campus. *Library:* The Health Sciences Library has 300,000 volumes and receives more than 1800 periodicals. *Housing:* Ample private housing is available in the area.

## Special Features

*Minority admissions:* An active recruitment program is coordinated by the Academic Support and Enrichment Center (ASEC). *Other degree programs:* MD-PhD programs can be arranged on an individual basis, and MD-MBA and MD-MPH are also available.

# Duke University School of Medicine

Box 3710, Medical Center
Durham, North Carolina   27710

*Phone:* 919-684-2985          *Fax:* 919-684-8893
*E-mail:* medadm@ mc.duke.edu
*WWW:* http://www.dukemed.duke.edu

| Application Filing | | Accreditation | |
|---|---|---|---|
| Earliest: | June 1 | LCME | |
| Latest: | November 15 | | |
| Fee: | $80 | **Degrees Granted** | |
| AMCAS: | yes | MD, MD-PhD, MD-MPH | |

### Enrollment: 2008–2009 First-Year Class

| | | | | | |
|---|---|---|---|---|---|
| Men: | 51 | 51% | Applied: | | 5309 |
| Women: | 49 | 49% | Interviewed: | | 780 |
| Minorities: | 22 | 22% | Enrolled: | | 100 |
| Out of State: | 79 | 79% | | | |

### 2008–2009 Class Profile

| *Mean MCAT Scores* | | *Mean GPA* |
|---|---|---|
| Physical Sciences: | 11 | 3.8 |
| Biological Sciences: | 11 | |
| Verbal Reasoning: | 11 | *Mean Science* |
| | | 3.8 |

### Tuition and Fees

| | |
|---|---|
| **Resident** | 41,839 |
| Average (public) | 25,100 |
| Average (private) | 42,600 |
| **Nonresident** | 41,839 |
| Average (public) | 43,900 |
| Average (private) | 43,500 |

0    10    20    30    40    50
(in thousands of dollars)

Percentage receiving financial aid: 75%

Above data applies to 2007–2008 academic year.

## Introduction

The School of Medicine at Duke University was founded in 1930. The Medical Center, which includes the School of Medicine, the School of Nursing, and a hospital, is located on Duke's west campus. These health care facilities are all part of Duke University, an institution established in 1924 by James Buchanan Duke, industrialist and philanthropist. His original endowment served to transform Trinity College in Durham, North Carolina into Duke University.

## Admissions (AMCAS)

Required courses include the basic premedical science courses, 1 year of calculus, and 1 year of English (consisting primarily of expository English composition). An introductory course in biochemistry is suggested during the senior year. Residence does not influence admissions decision. *Transfer and advanced standing:* None, except in unusual circumstances.

## Curriculum

4-year modern. *First year:* This year introduces students to the basic sciences, which are the building units of medicine. The subjects are condensed into the essentials necessary for medical practice and serve as the basis for clinical studies, which begin in the following year. Courses are taught in blocks, so that students need to concentrate on no more than 3 major areas at a time. The lecture-based courses are integrated within the same block, so that relevant material is taught together. *Second year:* During this year students begin seeing patients full-time. An intense 3-week preparatory period enables them to undertake clinical clerkships in internal medicine, surgery, obstetrics/gynecology, and pediatrics. The basic science principles learned become meaningful and are reinforced in the course of working with patients. The clinical exposure permits the student to become familiar with the major patient-care disciplines and thus facilitates making thoughtful decisions concerning the path to pursue during the elective third and fourth years. *Third year:* This year provides an opportunity for significant personal growth. The opportunity is given to study an area of particular interest in depth. Each student chooses an independent scholarship project and enrolls in the appropriate general study program. All third-year projects last 8½ months. Faculty advisors help the student design a study program that best meets the individual's needs. The program serves to encourage a lifelong commitment to scholarship and enhances one's medical education regardless of their ultimate goal. *Fourth year:* This very flexible year rounds out the student's education. It offers opportunities for sampling areas of interest, becoming more comfortable with patients, mastering the core competencies that have not yet been achieved, and deciding on one's postgraduate training.

## Grading and Promotion Policies

The Honors/Pass/Fail system is used. The USMLE is not required for promotion or graduation. Records of students are reviewed periodically by promotion committees consisting of course directors.

## Facilities

*Teaching:* Preclinical teaching takes place in the Thomas D. Kinney Central Teaching Laboratory. Clinical instruction takes place at Duke Hospital (1008 beds), and at the Durham VA Hospital (489 beds). *Library:* The Medical Center Library houses more than 200,000 volumes and subscribes to 5000 periodicals. The Trent Collection includes books on the history of medicine, and is considered noteworthy for the Southeast. *Housing:* Off-campus housing is easily available and affordable.

## Special Features

*Minority admissions:* The school has an active minority recruitment program. *Other degree programs:* Combined-degree programs include the Medical Scientist Training Program for the MD-PhD, the Medical Historian Training Program for the MD-PhD, the MD-JD program for a joint medical and legal degree, and the MD-MPH for a medical degree and a degree of Masters in Public Health.

# University of North Carolina at Chapel Hill School of Medicine

CB 9500 121 McNider Bldg.
Chapel Hill, North Carolina  27599

*Phone:* 919-962-8331          *Fax:* 919-966-9930
*E-mail:* randee_alston@med.unc.edu
*WWW:* med.unc.edu/

| Application Filing | | Accreditation |
|---|---|---|
| Earliest: | June 1 | LCME |
| Latest: | November 15 | |
| Fee: | $65 | **Degrees Granted** |
| AMCAS: | yes | MD, MD-PhD, MD-MPH |

### Enrollment: 2008–2009 First-Year Class

| | | | | |
|---|---|---|---|---|
| Men: | 79 | 49% | Applied: | 3965 |
| Women: | 82 | 51% | Interviewed: | 581 |
| Minorities: | 20 | 12% | Enrolled: | 161 |
| Out of State: | 24 | 15% | | |

### 2008–2009 Class Profile

| *Mean MCAT Scores* | | *Mean GPA* |
|---|---|---|
| Physical Sciences: | 11 | 3.8 |
| Biological Sciences: | 11 | |
| Verbal Reasoning: | 11 | *Mean Science* |
| | | 3.7 |

**Tuition and Fees**

| | |
|---|---|
| Resident | 11,964 |
| Average (public) | 25,100 |
| Average (private) | 42,600 |
| Nonresident | 35,630 |
| Average (public) | 43,900 |
| Average (private) | 43,500 |

(in thousands of dollars) 0–50

Percentage receiving financial aid: 84%

Above data applies to 2007–2008 academic year.

## Introduction

Located on the Chapel Hill campus of the University of North Carolina, the School of Medicine was founded in 1879. It did not become a 4-year school until 1952. Adjacent to the School of Medicine on the university campus are: schools of Dentistry, Pharmacy, and Public Health. Clinical training is provided by several major, on-campus facilities, as well as health education centers located in community settings throughout the state.

## Admissions (AMCAS)

The basic premedical courses plus 1 year of English are required. Recommended are courses in cell and molecular biology and biochemistry. There are a limited number of places available to nonresidents, since preference is given to residents. Selection involves choosing those with the greatest potential, who are sent supplementary applications. These are screened and appropriate candidates are invited for an interview prior to final selection. Qualities sought are maturity, leadership, motivation, integrity, and an academic record of accomplishment. *Transfer and advanced standing:* A very limited number of places are available for transfer to the third year. Students in good standing at accredited U.S. medical schools are considered.

## Curriculum

4-year modern. The goals of the curriculum are to build problem-solving and communicative skills and to develop habits of self-assessment and continual learning that will remain with the physician throughout his/her professional life. *First year:* Consists of the introductory basic sciences and microbiology-virology, immunology, neurobiology, introduction to medicine, and social and cultural issues in medical practice, as well as a selective seminars program. *Second year:* Consists of several major courses: mechanisms of disease (includes 11 organ systems courses), pathology, pharmacology, epidemiology, psychiatry, and physical diagnosis, as well as selective seminars. *Third year:* Rotation through clerkship of major clinical specialties extending over 48-week period. *Fourth year:* A 4-week acting internship and a 4-week ambulatory care selective are 2 required selectives of the senior year. In addition, there are 24 weeks divided into 6 periods of electives. Opportunities for specialized clinical activities are offered as well as opportunities for in-depth study and investigation in special areas of interest to the student.

## Grading and Promotion Policies

The system used is Honors/Pass/Fail. The Student Promotions Committee recommends promotion or dismissal to the dean.

## Facilities

*Teaching:* The school is part of the medical center located on campus. Berryhill Basic Medical Sciences Building and preclinical Education Facilities Building provide facilities for the basic sciences. Clinical teaching takes place at the North Carolina Memorial Hospital (607 beds) and AHEC facilities throughout the state. Affiliation for teaching purposes has been established with a number of community hospitals. *Other:* The Medical Sciences Research Building provides facilities for research. *Library:* The Health Sciences Library houses more than 202,000 volumes and 4000 periodicals. *Housing:* Residence halls are available on campus for single as well as some married students.

## Special Features

*Minority admissions:* The school has an active recruitment program and sponsors an 8-week Medical Education Development program for college students. *Other degree programs:* Combined MD-PhD programs are available in a variety of disciplines including biomedical engineering, genetics, mathematics, neurobiology, and toxicology. MD-MPH programs are also offered.

# Wake Forest University School of Medicine

Winston-Salem, North Carolina   27157

*Phone:* 336-716-4264   *Fax:* 336-716-9593
*E-mail:* medadmit@wfubmc.edu
*WWW:* wfubmc.edu

| Application Filing | | Accreditation | |
|---|---|---|---|
| Earliest: | June 1 | LCME | |
| Latest: | November 1 | | |
| Fee: | $55 | **Degrees Granted** | |
| AMCAS: | yes | MD, MD-PhD, MD-MBA | |

### Enrollment: 2008–2009 First-Year Class

| | | | | | |
|---|---|---|---|---|---|
| Men: | 75 | 61% | Applied: | | 7502 |
| Women: | 47 | 39% | Interviewed: | | 600 |
| Minorities: | 14 | 11% | Enrolled: | | 122 |
| Out of State: | 75 | 61% | | | |

### 2008–2009 Class Profile

| *Mean MCAT Scores* | | *Mean GPA* |
|---|---|---|
| Physical Sciences: | 10.4 | 3.7 |
| Biological Sciences: | 10.4 | |
| Verbal Reasoning: | 10.4 | *Mean Science* |
| | | 3.7 |

**Tuition and Fees**

| | |
|---|---|
| **Resident** | 38,248 |
| Average (public) | 18,500 |
| Average (private) | 35,000 |
| **Nonresident** | 38,248 |
| Average (public) | 34,500 |
| Average (private) | 36,750 |

(in thousands of dollars)

Percentage receiving financial aid: 73%

## Introduction

In 1834 the Wake Forest Institute opened, and became a university in 1967. The Bowman Gray School of Medicine originally opened in 1902 as the Wake Forest Medical School. It was renamed the School of Medical Sciences in 1937 and operated as a 2-year medical school until 1941, when it was moved from Wake County to Winston-Salem as a 4-year medical school in association with the North Carolina Baptist Hospitals, Inc., and named Bowman Grey School of Medicine, which now constitutes the Wake Forest University Baptist Medical Center. In 1997 the medical school was renamed Wake Forest University School of Medicine.

## Admissions (AMCAS)

The basic premedical courses are required. English and history are strongly recommended. Completion of 90 semester hours is necessary, but 120 are advised. A total of 108 students enter annually. Admission is without regard to race, creed, sex, religion, age, physical handicap, marital status, or national origin. *Transfer and advanced standing:* Transfer to third-year class is dependent upon vacancies.

## Curriculum

4-year modern. The medical student education program is aimed at achieving 9 specific goals, namely, self-directed learning and stimulating the desire for life-long learning, securing a science core biomedical knowledge, as well as gaining proficiency in clinical skills, problem solving, clinical reasoning skills, interviewing and communication skills, information management skills, and professional behavior and attitudes. Students master the basic and clinical medical sciences in an integrated manner throughout the entire program. They utilize small-group, case centered learning and other educational methods. This approach involves close integration through a computer network. Early community exposure and attention to population healthcare are distinguishing features of the program. Professionalism issues are considered at all phases to provide prospective physicians with a better understanding of their role in society.

## Grading and Promotion Policies

Grading is on a 0 to 3 scale. Students are provided with progress evaluations at the end of each course or rotation. The Promotion Committee meets regularly to evaluate student performance and make evaluations. Students must record total passing scores on Step 1 of the USMLE for promotion and on Step 2 for graduation.

## Facilities

*Teaching:* Much of the basic science instruction takes place in the renovated James A. Gray Building and Hanes Research Building. The main teaching hospital is the North Carolina Baptist Hospital (880 beds). *Other:* Affiliated institutions include Forsyth Memorial Hospital (896 beds), and the Northwest Area Health Education Center. *Library:* The Coy C. Carpenter Library contains more than 150,000 volumes including approximately 2300 medical and scientific journals. It has on-line access to various computerized bibliographic services. *Housing:* The school maintains no housing facilities, but apartments, rooms, and houses are available in the surrounding residential area.

## Special Features

*Minority admissions:* A recruitment program is sponsored by the school through its Office of Minority Affairs. There is a tuition-free postbaccalaureate program through Wake Forest University for students who have not achieved admission to medical school. *Other degree programs:* MD-MBA, MD-PhD, and MD-MS Health Sciences Research are offered.

# NORTH DAKOTA

## University of North Dakota School of Medicine and Health Sciences

501 North Columbia Road
Box 9037
Grand Forks, North Dakota    58202

*Phone:* 701-777-4221          *Fax:* 701-777-4942
*E-mail:* jdheit@med.nodak.edu
*WWW:* www.med.und.nodak.edu/

| Application Filing | | Accreditation | |
|---|---|---|---|
| Earliest: | July 1 | LCME | |
| Latest: | November 1 | | |
| Fee: | $50 | **Degrees Granted** | |
| AMCAS: | no | MD, MD-PhD | |

### Enrollment: 2008–2009 First-Year Class

| Men: | 26 | 42% | Applied: | 303 |
|---|---|---|---|---|
| Women: | 36 | 58% | Interviewed: | 156 |
| Minorities: | 13 | 27% | Enrolled: | 62 |
| Out of State: | 17 | 21% | | |

### 2008–2009 Class Profile

| *Mean MCAT Scores* | | *Mean GPA* |
|---|---|---|
| Physical Sciences: | 8.7 | 3.7 |
| Biological Sciences: | 9.5 | |
| Verbal Reasoning: | 8.9 | *Mean Science* |
| | | 3.7 |

### Tuition and Fees

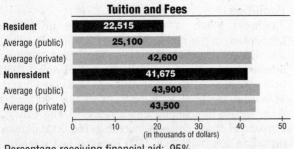

| | |
|---|---|
| Resident | 22,515 |
| Average (public) | 25,100 |
| Average (private) | 42,600 |
| Nonresident | 41,675 |
| Average (public) | 43,900 |
| Average (private) | 43,500 |

(in thousands of dollars)

Percentage receiving financial aid: 95%

## Introduction

Established in 1884, the University of North Dakota includes 8 colleges. The School of Medicine at the University of North Dakota was opened in 1905. Until 1973, it offered only the first 2 years of medical education with arrangements made with other schools for the last 2 years of clinical training. The school emphasizes the training for providing primary care in a rural setting.

## Admissions

The equivalent of 4 academic years or a minimum of 90 semester hours from an approved college is required for admission. Preference is given to applicants who have earned a bachelor's degree. Required coursework includes the basic premedical science courses and courses in college algebra, psychology or sociology, and English composition and literature. Students should be computer literate. The only out-of-state students admitted in recent years are through the minority program INMED (Indians-into-Medicine), through the Professional Exchange Program of WICHE, or through the reciprocity agreement with the state of Minnesota.

## Curriculum

4-year modern. This school's curriculum features an early introduction to clinical medicine, a patient-centered learning curriculum, and an emphasis on rural medicine. Blocks I-IV and Blocks V-VIII, each 40 weeks long, are the framework for the first and second years. Using the Patient-Centered Learning (PCL) format, small-group sessions are designed to facilitate the integration of the basic sciences with clinically relevant cases. The cases utilize a multidisciplinary approach to learning the basic sciences. The PCL sessions are supported by laboratory exercises, interactive question and answer sessions, demonstration, and concept-anchoring lectures. Students begin interacting with patients during the first semester of medical school. Skill development in patient communication and physical examination is stressed, as well as understanding ethical, socioeconomic, population, and statistical issues. Students take six 8-week clerkships during the third year (Internal Medicine, Family Medicine, General Surgery, Obstetrics and Gynecology, Psychiatry, and Pediatrics), or they may complete the majority of the third year in a rural setting through the school's Rural Opportunities in Medical Education (ROME) program. Students take 6 or more electives during the senior year as well as acting internships in medicine and in surgery.

## Grading and Promotion Policies

The grading system is Satisfactory-Unsatisfactory. The student must satisfactorily complete all of the coursework in a given year before beginning the required courses for the next year.

## Facilities

*Teaching:* The school is part of the North Dakota Medical Center. Courses in the first 2 years are taught in Grand Forks in the Medical Sciences North building that contains classrooms, laboratories, administrative offices, and the library. Clinical teaching is coordinated through the 4 regional campuses in Bismarck, Fargo, Grand Forks, and Minot. *Other:* Community hospitals throughout the state are affiliated with the school as well as the VA Medical Center in Fargo, the USAF Hospitals in Grand Forks and Minot, and the PHS Hospitals and Clinics that are part of the Indian Health Service. *Library:* The Health Sciences Library houses more than 50,000 volumes and about 1000 periodicals. Specialized biomedical research is conducted in the Edwin C. James Research Facility and the USDA Human Nutrition Research Center. *Housing:* A variety of on-campus housing is available.

## Special Features

*Minority admissions:* The INMED (Indians-into-Medicine) program admits up to 7 fully qualified American Indian students to medical school each year. The Center for Rural Health serves both the school and rural communities throughout the state. *Other degree programs:* A combined MD-PhD program is offered.

## OHIO

# Case Western Reserve University School of Medicine

10900 Euclid Avenue
Cleveland, Ohio   44106

*Phone:* 216-368-3450          *Fax:* 216-368-6011
*E-mail:* casemedadmissions@case.edu
*WWW:* medisnew.cwru.edu

| Application Filing | | Accreditation | |
|---|---|---|---|
| Earliest: | June 1 | LCME | |
| Latest: | November 1 | | |
| Fee: | $85 | **Degrees Granted** | |
| AMCAS: | yes | MD, MD-PhD | |

### Enrollment: 2008–2009 First-Year Class

| Men: | 101 | 55% | Applied: | 6028 |
|---|---|---|---|---|
| Women: | 84 | 45% | Interviewed: | 1340 |
| Minorities: | 18 | 10% | Enrolled: | 185 |
| Out of State: | 123 | 66% | | |

### 2008–2009 Class Profile

| *Mean MCAT Scores* | | *Mean GPA* |
|---|---|---|
| Physical Sciences: | 12 | 3.7 |
| Biological Sciences: | 12 | |
| Verbal Reasoning: | 11.0 | *Mean Science* |
| | | 3.7 |

### Tuition and Fees

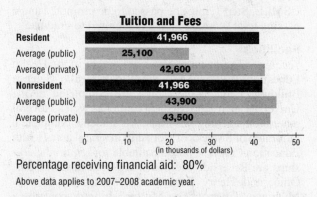

| | |
|---|---|
| Resident | 41,966 |
| Average (public) | 25,100 |
| Average (private) | 42,600 |
| Nonresident | 41,966 |
| Average (public) | 43,900 |
| Average (private) | 43,500 |

0   10   20   30   40   50
(in thousands of dollars)

Percentage receiving financial aid: 80%

Above data applies to 2007–2008 academic year.

## Introduction

Case Western Reserve University originated in 1967, when Western Reserve College and Case Institute of Technology combined to form the largest biomedical research institution in Ohio. The School of Medicine was established in 1943, when a medical department was added to Western Reserve College. In 1952 the school pioneered the introduction of an integrated, multidisciplinary, and problem-based innovative medical curriculum that was adopted by many other institutions, in part or in whole.

## Admissions (AMCAS)

The basic premedical science courses and 1 semester of English composition is required. More than half the places are filled by residents. Applicants from minor-

ity groups are encouraged. The selection process is influenced by the goal of generating a divergent student population both geographically and in the terms of undergraduate school represented. For this reason, academic qualifications such as grades, MCAT scores, and letters of recommendation are not the sole criteria used in the selection process. Successful applicants are those who have an attractive set of credentials demonstrating both achievement and potential. An interview is granted to candidates being seriously considered for admission. *Transfer and advanced standing:* Each candidate is considered individually.

## Curriculum

4-year modern. *First year:* Consists of instruction in subject areas of cell biology, differentiated cell, metabolism, biostatistics, cardiovascular-respiratory and renal systems, tissue injury, and mechanisms of infection. *Second year:* Consists of instruction in the organ systems as well as biometry and legal medicine. *Third year:* Consists of clerkship rotation through the major clinical specialties. *Fourth year:* Consists of neurosciences, surgical subspecialties, primary care, and 5 months of electives selected by the student.

## Grading and Promotion Policies

Evaluation of a student is based on interim examinations, comprehensive examinations at the end of the year, and instructor's observations of performance in laboratory and clinical work. Grading is Pass/Fail in the basic sciences and Honors/Pass/Fail in the required clinical sciences. The Committee on Students determines whether or not it is desirable to refuse further registration to any student. Taking Step 1 of the USMLE is required. A passing total score must be obtained on Step 2 to graduate.

## Facilities

*Teaching:* The school is located on the university campus about 5 miles east of the center of Cleveland. The Health Science Center is the site of teaching of the basic sciences. Clinical teaching is done at University Hospitals of Cleveland, Metro Health Medical Center, the Cleveland Veterans Administration Hospital, St. Luke's Hospital, and Mt. Sinai Hospital. *Other:* The Mather Memorial Building, the East Wing and Sears Administration Tower provide space for research facilities. *Library:* The collections of the schools of Medicine, Dentistry, and Nursing are located in the Health Center Library. The collection totals more than 150,000 volumes and 3000 periodicals. *Housing:* A graduate residence hall for single men and women is located within a 10-minute walk of the central campus.

## Special Features

*Minority admissions:* The school's active recruitment program is conducted by its Office of Minority Student Affairs. A 6-week summer enrichment program is offered to incoming students. *Other degree programs:* Combined MD-PhD degree programs are offered in a variety of disciplines. An affiliated medical school, the Cleveland Clinic of Medicine, opened in 2004.

# University of Toledo College of Medicine

3045 Arlington Avenue
Toledo, Ohio 43614

*Phone:* 419-383-4229 *Fax:* 419-383-3222
*E-mail:* medadmissions@utuet.utoledo.edu
*WWW:* usc.utoledo.edu

| Application Filing | | Accreditation |
|---|---|---|
| Earliest: | June 15 | LCME |
| Latest: | November 1 | |
| Fee: | $80 | **Degrees Granted** |
| AMCAS: | yes | MD, MD-PhD, MD-MSBS, MD-MPH |

### Enrollment: 2008–2009 First-Year Class

| | | | | |
|---|---|---|---|---|
| Men: | 98 | 63% | Applied: | 3431 |
| Women: | 78 | 37% | Interviewed: | 515 |
| Minorities: | 15 | 5% | Enrolled: | 176 |
| Out of State: | 58 | 34% | | |

### 2008–2009 Class Profile

| *Mean MCAT Scores* | | *Mean GPA* |
|---|---|---|
| Physical Sciences: | 10.0 | 3.6 |
| Biological Sciences: | 10.0 | |
| Verbal Reasoning: | 10.0 | *Mean Science* |
| | | 3.5 |

### Tuition and Fees

| | |
|---|---|
| **Resident** | 24,072 |
| Average (public) | 25,100 |
| Average (private) | 42,600 |
| **Nonresident** | 51,508 |
| Average (public) | 43,900 |
| Average (private) | 43,500 |

0 10 20 30 40 50
(in thousands of dollars)

Percentage receiving financial aid: 95%

## Introduction

On July 1, 2006 the Medical University of Ohio merged with the University of Toledo to become the University of Toledo College of Medicine. The 475-acre Health Science Campus includes the College of Medicine, College of Graduate Studies, College of Nursing, College of Health Science and Human Service, and the University Medical Center.

## Admissions (AMCAS)

The basic premedical science courses, including 1 year of biology, 1 year of physics, 1 year of general chemistry, 1 year of organic chemistry, in addition to 1 year of English and mathematics, are required. Additional courses in biology are recommended. The school requires all applicants to take the MCAT and to have a baccalaureate degree at the time of admission. Beyond the required courses, the choice of a major is optional. Ohio residents are given priority in admissions. Nonresidents with a superior background are considered for acceptance. *Transfer and advanced standing:* Ohio residents from LCME-accredited schools are considered.

## Curriculum

*First and second years:* During the preclinical years science content is integrated into the following interdisciplinary instructional units: Cellular and Molecular Biology, Human Structure and Development, Neuroscience/Behavioral Science and Organ systems. All students also participate in a Clinical Decision Making course, which spans the first 2 years. This course uses the range of instructional experiences designed to provide medical students with the fundamental knowledge and skills necessary for clinical decision making. *Third year:* Devoted to clinical clerkships in internal medicine, surgery, pediatrics, obstetrics and gynecology, psychiatry, and family medicine. *Fourth year:* Includes clerkships in nerulogy, as well as a number of electives. Fourth-year students can schedule elective rotations in all parts of the country or internationally. Some students use elective time to conduct research in an area of special interest.

## Grading and Promotion Policies

The system uses Honors, High Pass, Pass, Fail. The USMLE, Step 1, must be passed to be promoted and a passing total score on Step 2 is required to graduate.

## Facilities

*Teaching:* The basic sciences are taught in the Health Education Building and the Block Health Science Building. Clinical clerkships are completed at the University of Toledo Medical Center as well as several other area teaching hospitals. All students complete a minimum of 8 weeks of clerkship in a rural area Health Education Center. *Other:* Available for required clerkships are Riverside Methodist Hospital in Columbus, Ohio, and Henry Ford Health System in Detroit, Michigan. *Library:* The Mulford Library contains a large collection of bound books and journals. *Housing:* Available on the Main Campus.

## Special Features

*Minority admissions:* The university has an active recruitment program. The Admissions Office works in cooperation with the Office for Institutional Diversity and the Office of Student Affairs in the recruitment, selection, and retention of qualified students. *Other degree programs:* A combined MD-PhD program, MD-MSBS program, and MD-MPH program are available.

# Northeastern Ohio Universities Colleges of Medicine and Pharmacy

4209 State Route 44
P.O. Box 95
Rootstown, Ohio    44272

*Phone:* 330-325-6270          *Fax:* 330-325-8372
*E-mail:* admission@neoucom.edu
*WWW:* neoucom.edu

| Application Filing | | Accreditation | |
|---|---|---|---|
| Earliest: | June 1 | LCME | |
| Latest: | November 1 | | |
| Fee: | $50 | **Degrees Granted** | |
| AMCAS: | yes | MD, MD-PhD | |

### Enrollment: 2008–2009 First-Year Class

| Men: | 57 | 50% | Applied: | 2040 |
|---|---|---|---|---|
| Women: | 58 | 50% | Interviewed: | 151 |
| Minorities: | 7 | 6% | Enrolled: | 115 |
| Out of State: | 4 | 3% | | |

### 2008–2009 Class Profile

| *Mean MCAT Scores* | | *Mean GPA* |
|---|---|---|
| Physical Sciences: | 9.2 | 3.73 |
| Biological Sciences: | 9.6 | |
| Verbal Reasoning: | 9.4 | *Mean Science* |
| | | 3.63 |

**Tuition and Fees**

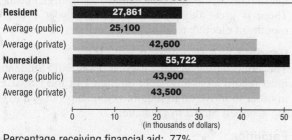

| | |
|---|---|
| Resident | 27,861 |
| Average (public) | 25,100 |
| Average (private) | 42,600 |
| Nonresident | 55,722 |
| Average (public) | 43,900 |
| Average (private) | 43,500 |

(in thousands of dollars)

Percentage receiving financial aid: 77%

## Introduction

The Northeastern Ohio University College of Medicine was established in 1973, and received full accreditation in 1981. The goal of the school is to train physicians to have knowledge of principles and practices of primary care in a community setting as well as the potential for specialization. Graduates receive a BS degree from the consortium university and an MD degree from the College of Medicine. The principal teaching site is in Rootstown on a 55-acre site in northeastern Ohio, located 35 miles southeast of Cleveland.

## Admissions (AMCAS)

A BS-MD program is available to students entering directly from high school. The MD program is available to students who already have a premedical background. For the MD program, the required courses are 1 year of organic chemistry and 1 year of physics at the college level. The number of spaces available for MD degree program candidates varies with the amount of attrition in years 2 and 3 of the BS-MD degree program. Very strong preference is given to Ohio residents. Usually no more than 10% non-Ohio residents are admitted annually, and the admission criteria for these applicants is more stringent. Applicants should demonstrate strong academic preparation as reflected by their GPA and MCAT scores. They should also give indication of personal characteristics and motivation to practice medicine. *Transfer and advanced standing:* A small number of places are available for applicants entering the sophomore year of the MD (4-year) portion of the program based on attrition from the freshman year.

## Curriculum

6-year semitraditional. Students spend the first 2 years at several possible undergraduate institutions completing premedical studies. The first year of medical studies involves the basic sciences and is completed at the Rootstown campus. The second year involves a study of pathophysiologic processes underlying clinical signs and symptoms of disease. Some teaching during the first 2 years takes place at ambulatory care centers of teaching hospitals. The third year consists of the standard clinical clerkships including family medicine and a primary care preceptorship. The latter takes place at hospitals in Akron, Canton, and Youngstown. The fourth year consists of electives and specially designed selectives in the medical humanities as well as a community health clerkship. There is a problem-based learning program that extends across the first 3 years. It is available as a distinct course or within core clerkships.

## Grading and Promotion Policies

The system used is Honors/Satisfactory/Conditional-Unsatisfactory/Unsatisfactory. Steps 1 and 2 of the USMLE must be taken and a total passing score recorded to be promoted into the clerkship years and to graduate, respectively.

## Facilities

*Teaching:* The academic base consists of the University of Akron, Kent State University, and Youngstown State University, with the Basic Medical Sciences campus in Rootstown. Clinical facilities are utilized at 18 associated community hospitals in Akron, Canton, and Youngstown. *Library:* Located at the Basic Medical Sciences Center. *Housing:* Available for first- and second-year medical students on all 3 campuses.

## Special Features

*Minority admissions:* Qualified minority and disadvantaged rural students are encouraged to apply. *Other degree programs:* Combined MD-PhD programs are offered in the basic sciences and in biomedical engineering.

# Ohio State University College of Medicine

370 West Ninth Avenue
Columbus, Ohio   43210

*Phone:* 614-292-7137          *Fax:* 614-247-7959
*E-mail:* medicine@osu.edu
*WWW:* http://medicine.osu.edu

| Application Filing | | Accreditation |
|---|---|---|
| Earliest: | June 1 | LCME |
| Latest: | November 1 | |
| Fee: | $60 | **Degrees Granted** |
| AMCAS: | yes | MD, MD-PhD, MD-MS |
| | | MD-MBA, MD-MPH, |
| | | MD-JD |

### Enrollment: 2008–2009 First-Year Class

| | | | | |
|---|---|---|---|---|
| Men: | 120 | 57% | Applied: | 4446 |
| Women: | 92 | 43% | Interviewed: | 655 |
| Minorities: | 22 | 10% | Enrolled: | 212 |
| Out of State: | 106 | 50% | | |

### 2008–2009 Class Profile

| *Mean MCAT Scores* | | *Mean GPA* |
|---|---|---|
| Physical Sciences: | 11.4 | 3.7 |
| Biological Sciences: | 11.5 | |
| Verbal Reasoning: | 10.4 | *Mean Science* |
| | | 3.7 |

**Tuition and Fees**

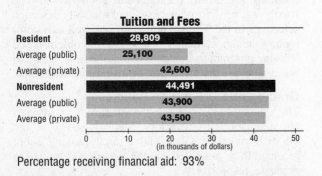

| | |
|---|---|
| Resident | 28,809 |
| Average (public) | 25,100 |
| Average (private) | 42,600 |
| Nonresident | 44,491 |
| Average (public) | 43,900 |
| Average (private) | 43,500 |

0   10   20   30   40   50
(in thousands of dollars)

Percentage receiving financial aid: 93%

## Introduction

The Ohio State University College of Medicine was established in 1914; it began with the Starling-Ohio Medical College and its predecessors. The college is located on the south edge of the main university campus.

## Admissions (AMCAS)

A baccalaureate degree is expected, but 3-year candidates are considered. Application is made through AMCAS. The MCAT test is required. Prerequisite courses include the basic premedical sciences. Recommended courses are biochemistry, physiology, and molecular genetics. Transfer applicants are considered for entrance into the third year, from LCME-accredited, MD-granting institutions in the United States.

## Curriculum

4-year modern. Med 1 and Med 2 students have their choice of 2 curricular pathways: Integrated Pathway or Independent Study Pathway. The Integrated Pathway features body systems-oriented content that fuses the basic and clinical sciences. It combines the proven educational methods of student-centered active learning, small-group case-based discussion, and lectures. The Independent Study Pathway allows students to utilize highly structured objectives, resource guides, and web- and computer-based materials to learn on their own. *First year:* Study of gross anatomy and embryology as part of a 6-member student team for the first 12 weeks of medical school. Critical analysis and problem-solving skills will be developed as students learn about the body systems. Patient-centered medicine and physician development courses take place weekly, combining small group role-playing settings, lectures, and experiences with senior citizens and physicians in the community. *Second year:* Students continue in their selected pathways, further strengthening clinical interviewing skills, learning how to do a comprehensive physical examination, and building diagnostic abilities. Working with real and standardized patients, students gain an appreciation for the pathophysiology of disease. *Third year:* Begins with a 2-week Introduction to Clinical Medicine. The next 12 months are spent in a range of experiences, including ambulatory primary care medicine, obstetrics and gynecology, surgery, itnernal medicine, psychiatry, neurology, pediatrics, and surgery. *Fourth year:* This year features 4 Diffentiation of Care selectives covering the undifferentiated patient, chronic care, a subinternship in internal medicine, and a subinternship in surgical care. There is great flexibility in the fourth year, with 3 months of elective rotations and 3 months of vacation.

## Grading and Promotion Policies

The non-grading system used is Pass/Fail. Students must record a passing score on Step 1 of the USMLE in order to move on to required clerkships and a passing score on Step 2 to graduate.

## Facilities

The Ohio State University Medical Center includes: James Cancer Hospital and Solove Research Institute, Comprehensive Cancer Center, Ross Heart Hospital, and many other facilities for treating physical and behavioral illnesses. *Library:* The John A. Prior Health Sciences Library maintains nearly 200,000 volumes and receives more than 3000 electronic journals and 2800 print titles.

## Special Features

*Minority admissions:* The college conducts an active minority recruitment program. *Other degree programs:* Combined Degrees, BS-MD, MD-MBA, MD-PhD, MD-MHA, and MD-JD are offered.

# University of Cincinnati College of Medicine

P.O. Box 670552
Cincinnati, Ohio    45267

*Phone:* 513-558-7314          *Fax:* 513-558-1165
*E-mail:* com.admis@ucmail.uc.edu
*WWW:* med.uc.edu

| Application Filing | | Accreditation | |
|---|---|---|---|
| Earliest: | June 1 | LCME | |
| Latest: | November 15 | | |
| Fee: | $25 | **Degrees Granted** | |
| AMCAS: | yes | MD, MD-PhD, MD-MBA | |

### Enrollment: 2008–2009 First-Year Class

| Men: | 107 | 67% | Applied: | 3349 |
|---|---|---|---|---|
| Women: | 52 | 33% | Interviewed: | 636 |
| Minorities: | 15 | 9% | Enrolled: | 159 |
| Out of State: | 61 | 38% | | |

### 2008–2009 Class Profile

| *Mean MCAT Scores* | | *Mean GPA* |
|---|---|---|
| Physical Sciences: | 10.8 | 3.6 |
| Biological Sciences: | 11.3 | |
| Verbal Reasoning: | 10.2 | *Mean Science* |
| | | 3.5 |

**Tuition and Fees**

| | |
|---|---|
| Resident | 27,987 |
| Average (public) | 25,100 |
| Average (private) | 42,600 |
| Nonresident | 42,987 |
| Average (public) | 43,900 |
| Average (private) | 43,500 |

0    10    20    30    40    50
(in thousands of dollars)

Percentage receiving financial aid: 85%

## Introduction

The University of Cincinnati College of Medicine was established in 1819. It is part of the university's Medical Center, which also includes colleges of Pharmacy, Nursing, and Health. Graduates choose careers in a broad range of primary care and medical subspecialties. Research opportunities for students are extensive and the school receives NIH research funding.

## Admissions (AMCAS)

All applicants should have the knowledge obtained in premedical basic science courses and mathematics. In addition, the undergraduate program should provide an understanding of the social, cultural, and behavioral factors that influence our society. Regardless of the area of concentration, the applicant should have acquired effective learning, communication, and problem-solving skills. A knowledge of the basic principles of statistics and computer literacy are recommended. As a state-supported university, priority will be given to Ohio residents. *Transfer and advanced standing:* Possible only into the third year.

## Curriculum

4-year semitraditional. *First year:* Focuses on the normal structure, function, and development of the human body, using an integrated systems approach to basic and clinical science topics. It includes an introduction to doctor/patient relationships and physical diagnosis skills. *Second year:* Continues the integrated systems approach focusing on the disease processes, prevention, and the further development of physical diagnosis skills. *Third year:* Clerkships include 8-week rotations each in internal medicine, obstetrics-gynecology, pediatrics, and surgery; a 6-week rotation in psychiatry; a 4-week rotation in family medicine; a 2-week rotation in radiology; and 4 weeks of electives. *Fourth year:* Requirements are an 8-week acting internship in internal medicine, a 4-week clinical neuroscience selective, and 24 weeks of electives which must include a 4-week internal medical elective, a 4-week outpatient elective, and a 4-week clinical experience. Portions of the elective time may be taken at other U.S. medical centers or abroad.

## Grading and Promotion Policies

Grades of Honors, High Pass, Pass, Remediate, or Fail are used. Students must pass USMLE Step 1 before advancement to the third year. Students must pass the USMLE Step 2 before graduating.

## Facilities

*Teaching:* The majority of the school is housed in the Medical Sciences Building. Clinical training takes place at the University Hospital, Children's Hospital Medical Center, VA Medical Center, and ambulatory care sites. *Other:* Three associated teaching hospitals are located within a mile of the Medical Center. *Housing:* A limited number of on-campus apartments are available for single and married students. A variety of proximate off-campus housing is available.

## Special Features

*Minority admissions:* The school actively recruits minority, disadvantaged, and other nontraditional applicants. *Other degree programs:* Combined MD-PhD program of any of the basic sciences and a 5-year MD-MBA program are available.

# Wright State University Boonshaft School of Medicine

P.O. Box 1751
Dayton, Ohio    45401

*Phone:* 937-775-2934          *Fax:* 937-775-3322
*E-mail:* somSQQ@wright.edu
*WWW:* http://www.med.wright.edu/

| Application Filing | | Accreditation | |
|---|---|---|---|
| Earliest: | June 1 | LCME | |
| Latest: | October 15 | | |
| Fee: | $45 | **Degrees Granted** | |
| AMCAS: | yes | MD, MD-PhD, | |
| | | MD-MBA, MD-MPH | |

### Enrollment: 2008–2009 First-Year Class

| Men: | 52 | 50% | Applied: | 3097 |
|---|---|---|---|---|
| Women: | 48 | 48% | Interviewed: | 217 |
| Minorities: | 20 | 20% | Enrolled: | 100 |
| Out of State: | 8 | 8% | | |

### 2008–2009 Class Profile

| *Mean MCAT Scores* | | *Mean GPA* |
|---|---|---|
| Physical Sciences: | 9.4 | 3.58 |
| Biological Sciences: | 9.8 | |
| Verbal Reasoning: | 9.4 | *Mean Science* |
| | | 3.47 |

### Tuition and Fees

| | |
|---|---|
| **Resident** | 25,190 |
| Average (public) | 25,100 |
| Average (private) | 42,600 |
| **Nonresident** | 35,660 |
| Average (public) | 43,900 |
| Average (private) | 43,500 |

0    10    20    30    40    50
(in thousands of dollars)

Percentage receiving financial aid: 94%

## Introduction

Wright State University, located in Dayton, was founded in 1964; the School of Medicine was founded 10 years later. It is located on the main university campus in the city of Fairborn, a community within the metropolitan area of Dayton. The school's goal is to provide physicians with a strong foundation in primary care and comprehensive training in critical, acute, and chronic care as well as preventive medicine. A very substantial percentage of the school's graduates enter family medicine.

## Admissions (AMCAS)

The basic premedical science courses are required plus 1 year each of English and mathematics. The school seeks students with diverse social, ethnic, and educational backgrounds. Secondary applications and letters of recommendation are requested upon receipt of the AMCAS application. Dedication to human concerns, communication skills, maturity, motivation, letters of recommendation, and academic qualifications are considered when reviewing applications. One-on-one interviews are by invitation only with Ohio residents receiving very strong preference. Women, minorities, and applicants from rural Ohio are particularly encouraged to apply. *Transfer and advance standing:* Students may transfer from LCME accredited schools at the third year level.

## Curriculum

4-year modern. Major courses are designed to prepare students for lifelong learning and service in primary care fields. *Biennium I:* Students are taught in an interdisciplinary fashion using didactic teaching, large group lectures, small group discussions, computer-based instruction, and case-based/problem-based learning. Throughout the first 2 years, normal structure and functioning, behavioral sciences, health promotion, and disease prevention are integrated into the curriculum. Students are introduced to basic principles and mechanisms of disease in the spring of the first year. Instruction progresses through various organizational levels from molecular to organ systems. From the beginning of the freshman year, students acquire clinical skills through direct patient contact and interaction with clinical faculty preceptors. To provide additional opportunities for clinical exposure and enrichment, clinically based electives are offered as immersion experiences between academic periods in the first 2 years. Students rotate through 6 core clerkships during the third year. Individualized electives, mandatory clerkships, junior internships, and time for board study complete the fourth year.

## Grading and Promotion Policies

Information not available.

## Facilities

*Teaching:* Educational programs are conducted in the Medical Sciences, Biological Sciences, and Health Sciences buildings on the main campus. Clinical instruction takes place in the 8 local affiliated teaching hospitals and institutions, in free-standing ambulatory health centers, and in physicians' offices. *Library:* The Fordham Health Sciences Library contains a large collection of books and journals, audiovisual and computer programs, access to on-line data base searching, quiet study areas, and after-hour study space.

## Special Features

*Minority Admissions:* The school has a stated policy of providing educational opportunities to students from underrepresented minority groups. An Office of Minority Affairs is coordinated by an Assistant Dean for Minority Affairs. A 4-week prematriculation program, minority physician mentoring, big brother/big sister peer tutoring, board preparation courses, and assistance in development of critical thinking and learning are available. Resident and nonresident minority students are strongly encouraged to apply. *Other degree programs:* After matriculation students may apply for admission to the biomedical sciences PhD program, the MBA program, and the MPH program.

# OKLAHOMA

## University of Oklahoma College of Medicine

P.O. Box 26901
Oklahoma City, Oklahoma   73126

*Phone:* 405-271-2331          *Fax:* 405-271-3032
*E-mail:* adminmed@uohsc.edu
*WWW:* medicine.uohsc.edu/admissions

| Application Filing | | Accreditation |
|---|---|---|
| Earliest: | June 1 | LCME |
| Latest: | October 15 | |
| Fee: | $65 | **Degrees Granted** |
| AMCAS: | yes | MD, MD-PhD |

### Enrollment: 2008–2009 First-Year Class

| Men: | 102 | 61% | Applied: | 1487 |
|---|---|---|---|---|
| Women: | 64 | 30% | Interviewed: | 312 |
| Minorities: | 35 | 21% | Enrolled: | 166 |
| Out of State: | 17 | 10% | | |

### 2008–2009 Class Profile

| *Mean MCAT Scores* | | *Mean GPA* |
|---|---|---|
| Physical Sciences: | 9.8 | 3.8 |
| Biological Sciences: | 10.2 | |
| Verbal Reasoning: | 10 | *Mean Science* |
| | | 3.8 |

### Tuition and Fees

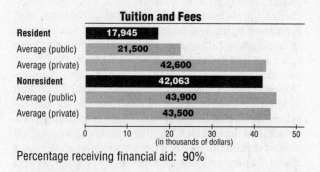

| Resident | 17,945 |
| Average (public) | 21,500 |
| Average (private) | 42,600 |
| Nonresident | 42,063 |
| Average (public) | 43,900 |
| Average (private) | 43,500 |

(in thousands of dollars)

Percentage receiving financial aid: 90%

## Introduction

Established in 1900 the University of Oklahoma College of Medicine combined with Epworth Medical College in 1910. The College of Medicine is one of 7 colleges belonging to the Health Sciences Center. The other schools are the colleges of Dentistry, Nursing, Pharmacy, Public Health, Allied Health, and the Graduate College. The College of Medicine offers programs in Oklahoma City and Tulsa. In Oklahoma City it is situated on the 200-acre Oklahoma Health Center.

## Admissions (AMCAS)

Requirements include 3 semesters of English; 1 semester of general zoology with lab; 1 semester (any

one) of cell biology, histology, embryology, genetics, or comparative anatomy; 3 semesters (any combination) of anthropology, psychology, sociology, philosophy, humanities, or foreign language; 2 semesters of physics; 2 semesters of general chemistry; and 2 semesters of organic chemistry. Strong preference is given to residents. Nonresidents can make up no more than 15% of each class. Acceptance is based on the applicant's GPA, MCAT scores, recommendations, and interview. Emphasis is placed on health care experience, maturity, commitment, and community service. *Transfer and advanced standing:* Applicants from other medical schools may be admitted with advanced standing.

## Curriculum

*4-year. First and second years:* Each of these years is 36 weeks. The program provides an integrated overview of the basic sciences and is accented by clinical correlation demonstrations. Patient contact begins in the first year in a wide variety of settings, including physicians' private offices. Interdepartmental courses in clinical medicine are offered. *Third and fourth years:* These make up a 23-month continuum; 10 months in the third year are devoted to required clerkships in major clinical specialties; 5 months in the fourth year are devoted to required internships in major clinical specialties. Six months must be utilized for elective coursework.

## Grading and Promotion Policies

The letter grading system is used. All courses must be completed with a grade of C or better (D or better in courses of fewer than 30 clock hours). Students are required to take and pass Step 1 of the USMLE prior to beginning third-year clinical rotations. Step 2 must be taken to record a score.

## Facilities

*Teaching:* The college is located on the university's Oklahoma City and Tulsa campuses. Basic sciences are taught in Oklahoma City. Clinical teaching takes place at 5 hospitals and numerous clinics located on campus and at 14 affiliated hospitals. In the beginning of the third year, 25% of the class may transfer to the Tulsa campus. *Library:* The Health Sciences Library in Oklahoma City contains more than 156,000 books, journals, and audiovisual material. *Housing:* The Oklahoma campus has 86 units.

## Special Features

*Minority admissions:* The university seeks to identify and recruit underrepresented minorities, and applicants from this group or candidates with a disadvantaged background are encouraged to apply. *Other degree programs:* The university offers an MD-PhD degree.

# OREGON

# Oregon Health and Science University School of Medicine

3181 S. W. Sam Jackson Park Road
Portland, Oregon    97239

*Phone:* 503-494-2998        *Fax:* 503-494-3400
*WWW:* http://www.ohsu.edu/som-dean/admit.html

| Application Filing | | Accreditation | |
|---|---|---|---|
| Earliest: | June 1 | LCME | |
| Latest: | October 15 | | |
| Fee: | $100 | **Degrees Granted** | |
| AMCAS: | yes | MD, MD-PhD, MD-MPH | |

### Enrollment: 2008–2009 First-Year Class

| | | | | | |
|---|---|---|---|---|---|
| Men: | 56 | 47% | Applied: | 4371 | |
| Women: | 62 | 53% | Interviewed: | 513 | |
| Minorities: | 3 | 3% | Enrolled: | 118 | |
| Out of State: | 44 | 37% | | | |

### 2008–2009 Class Profile

| *Mean MCAT Scores* | | *Mean GPA* |
|---|---|---|
| Physical Sciences: | 10.0 | 3.8 |
| Biological Sciences: | 11 | |
| Verbal Reasoning: | 11 | *Mean Science* |
| | | 3.7 |

**Tuition and Fees**

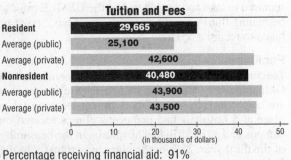

| | |
|---|---|
| **Resident** | 29,665 |
| Average (public) | 25,100 |
| Average (private) | 42,600 |
| **Nonresident** | 40,480 |
| Average (public) | 43,900 |
| Average (private) | 43,500 |

0   10   20   30   40   50
(in thousands of dollars)

Percentage receiving financial aid: 91%

Above data applies to 2007–2008 academic year.

## Introduction

As part of the Oregon State System of Higher Education, Oregon Health Sciences University is an independent collegiate health center. It was established in 1887 as the University of Oregon Medical School. Reorganization took place in 1974 when the schools of Medicine, Dentistry, and Nursing joined together to form the University of Oregon Health Science Center. The university is located on a 101-acre campus in Sam Jackson Park, a short distance from downtown Portland.

## Admissions (AMCAS)

A bachelor's degree is required prior to matriculation. The basic premedical science courses, 1 college level course in mathematics, and 1 year each of humanities, social sciences, and English (including 1 semester of composition) are required. Courses in biochemistry and genetics are required. A course in statistics is strongly recommended. *Transfer and advanced standing:* Availability decided yearly. Preference is given to Oregon residents.

## Curriculum

4-year semitraditional. *First and second years:* Primarily devoted to the sciences basic to medicine, focusing initially on the normal structure and function of the human body and continuing with the study of the pathological basis of disease and its treatment. The course principles of clinical medicine is presented concurrently to develop fundamental knowledge and skills in patient interviewing and physical diagnosis. Socioeconomic, behavioral population health issues are also introduced during this period. *Third and fourth years:* Consist of clinical clerkships. A 6-week rural primary care experience is required and there are opportunities to pursue elective courses in clinical and basic sciences.

## Grading and Promotion Policies

Grades are Honors, Near Honors, Marginal, or Fail. Students must take Step 1 and Step 2 of the USMLE to graduate.

## Facilities

*Teaching:* The Oregon Health and Science University includes more than 20 buildings used for medical education, research, and patient care. The preclinical curriculum is provided in the Basic Sciences and Education buildings, which are designed for teaching in small group settings, as well as containing adequate space for lectures and laboratories. Clinical teaching is provided at the University Hospital and Clinics, Doernbecher Children's Hospital, and Portland Veteran's Administration Medical Center, as well as several affiliated hospitals and clinical teaching sites. In addition to research facilities, teaching space, and patient care facilities, the campus includes a computer center, library, and a fitness and sports center. *Library:* The library and auditorium afford facilities for lectures and scientific meetings. The library contains about 150,000 volumes of books and periodicals and subscribes to 2500 current periodicals. *Housing:* Information not available.

## Special Features

*Minority admissions:* The School of Medicine Admissions Committee seeks diversity in its student body and in the physician workforce to enhance the effective delivery of health care. *Other degree programs:* Combined MD-PhD degree programs are offered in a variety of disciplines including medical genetics, medical psychology, and pathology. An MD-MPH program is also available.

# Drexel University College of Medicine

2900 Queen Lane
Philadelphia, Pennsylvania  19129

*Phone:* 215-991-8202          *Fax:* 215-843-1766
*E-mail:* medadmis@drexel.edu
*WWW:* drexelmed.edu

| Application Filing | Accreditation |
|---|---|
| Earliest:  June 1 | LCME |
| Latest:  December 1 | |
| Fee:  $75 | **Degrees Granted** |
| AMCAS:  yes | MD, MD-PhD, BA-MD, |
| | MD-MPH, MD-MBA |

### Enrollment: 2008–2009 First-Year Class

| | | | | | |
|---|---|---|---|---|---|
| Men: | 127 | 50% | Applied: | 12,006 |
| Women: | 128 | 50% | Interviewed: | 1320 |
| Minorities: | 49 | 19% | Enrolled: | 255 |
| Out of State: | 177 | 69% | | |

### 2008–2009 Class Profile

| *Mean MCAT Scores* | | *Mean GPA* |
|---|---|---|
| Physical Sciences: | 10.2 | 3.5 |
| Biological Sciences: | 10.6 | |
| Verbal Reasoning: | 10 | *Mean Science* |
| | | 3.4 |

**Tuition and Fees**

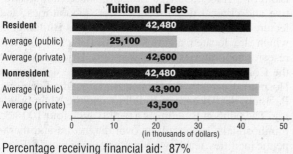

| | |
|---|---|
| Resident | 42,480 |
| Average (public) | 25,100 |
| Average (private) | 42,600 |
| Nonresident | 42,480 |
| Average (public) | 43,900 |
| Average (private) | 43,500 |

(in thousands of dollars)

Percentage receiving financial aid: 87%

## Introduction

Drexel University's approach to medical education is consistent with the school's 2 centuries of health care history. In 1848 the founders of Hahnemann University (then named the Homeopathic Medical College of Pennsylvania) thought that there were better ways to treat patients than the harsh medical practices of the time. In 1850 the founders of the Medical College of Pennsylvania established the nation's first medical school for women. In 1993 the Medical College of Pennsylvania and Hahnemann University consolidated into 1 institution—MCP Hahnemann University. The school offers undergraduate and graduate programs in health professions, nursing, public health, medicine, and biomedical graduate studies.

## Admissions

In addition to the basic premedical science courses, 1 year of English is required. *Transfer and advanced standing:* Applications are considered for the second and third years if openings are available.

## Curriculum

4-year semimodern. Recognizing that different students have different ways of learning, Drexel University offers a choice between 2 innovative academic curricula for their first years of study. Interdisciplinary Foundations of Medicine (IFM) integrates basic science courses and presents them through clinical symptom-based modules. IFM is faculty driven; students learn in lectures, labs, and small groups. The Program for Integrated Learning (PIL), a problem-based curriculum, is student driven, supervised and facilitated by faculty. Students learn in small groups, labs, and resource sessions by focusing on case studies. Both options focus on professional medical education, preparing students to pursue careers in either a generalist or a specialist discipline. Both stress problem solving, lifelong learning skills, and the coordinated teaching of basic science with clinical medicine. In the third year, students take clinical clerkships, covering 6 key medical and surgical subjects. Academic, clinical, and professional skills are emphasized and integrated in both inpatient and ambulatory clinical settings. In the fourth year, the "pathway" program lets students gain career experience in a general professional pathway or a discipline-specific pathway of their choice.

## Grading and Promotion Policies

A Pass/Fail system is used.

## Facilities

*Teaching:* The Educational and Research Building includes state-of-the-art research labs, modern teaching facilities, including two 175-seat auditoriums, a learning resource center, a clinical learning lab, a computer center, and high-tech audiovisual linkages between various locations. Hospitals providing clinical training include Hahnemann Hospital, MCP Hospital, St. Christopher's Hospital for Children, and Graduate Hospital. *Other:* Affiliate hospitals include Allegheny General Hospital in Pittsburgh, Lehigh Valley Hospital in Allentown, Monmouth Medical Center in Monmouth, and Pinnacle Health Hospital in Harrisburg. *Library:* The Florence A. Moor Library of Medicine contains more than 37,000 volumes and more than 1050 serial publications are received regularly. *Housing:* The Office of Student Affairs assists students in finding local housing.

## Special Features

*Minority admissions:* The school has an active recruitment program. *Other degree programs:* The school offers a combined MD-MPH program, and an MD-MBA program with Drexel University's Executive MBA program, and an MD-PhD program with the School of Biomedical Sciences. There is a BA-MD program with Villanova University and a BA or BS-MD program with Drexel University.

# Jefferson Medical College
# Thomas Jefferson University

1015 Walnut Street
Philadelphia, Pennsylvania   19107

*Phone:* 215-955-6983          *Fax:* 215-955-5151
*E-mail:* jmc.admissions@jefferson.edu
*WWW:* jefferson.edu/jmc/admissions

| Application Filing | | Accreditation | |
|---|---|---|---|
| Earliest: | June 1 | LCME | |
| Latest: | November 15 | | |
| Fee: | $80 | **Degrees Granted** | |
| AMCAS: | yes | MD, MD-PhD, MD-MBA | |
| | | MD-MPH | |

### Enrollment: 2008–2009 First-Year Class

| Men: | 132 | 52% | Applied: | 9323 |
|---|---|---|---|---|
| Women: | 123 | 48% | Interviewed: | 802 |
| Minorities: | 29 | 11% | Enrolled: | 255 |
| Out of State: | 156 | 61% | | |

### 2008–2009 Class Profile

| *Mean MCAT Scores* | | *Mean GPA* |
|---|---|---|
| Physical Sciences: | 10.4 | 3.63 |
| Biological Sciences: | 10.8 | |
| Verbal Reasoning: | 10.2 | *Mean Science* |
| | | 3.58 |

**Tuition and Fees**

| | |
|---|---|
| Resident | 43,033 |
| Average (public) | 25,100 |
| Average (private) | 42,600 |
| Nonresident | 43,033 |
| Average (public) | 43,900 |
| Average (private) | 43,500 |

0   10   20   30   40   50
(in thousands of dollars)

Percentage receiving financial aid: 84%

## Introduction

Jefferson Medical College was established in 1824, almost 150 years before Thomas Jefferson University was founded. Located in Philadelphia, Jefferson Medical College is the second largest private medical school in the United States. A Postgraduate College of Graduate Studies is affiliated with the university. The Medical College is located on a 13-acre urban campus in Philadelphia. In recent years there has been a significant expansion in research programs at the school.

## Admissions (AMCAS)

The basic premedical science courses are required. *Transfer and advanced standing:* A very limited number of applications for transfer into the third year may be considered if compelling reasons exist.

## Curriculum

4-year semimodern. The aim of the curriculum is to acquire basic knowledge and skills and to develop appropriate professional behavior. *First year:* Focuses on the function of the human organism in its physical and psychosocial context. Clinical coursework emphasizes the importance of the physician-patient relationship, medical interviewing and history taking, human development, behavioral science, and principles, as well as core clinical skills and reasoning. *Second year:* There is a shift to pathophysiology and disease. Small-group sessions focus on problem-solving, evidence-based medicine and service-based learning. *Third year:* Made up of a 42-week period that covers the required clerkships, advanced basic science courses, and rehabilitation medicine. *Fourth year:* Consists of medical and surgical subspecialties and in-and-out patient subinternship in medicine or surgery.

## Grading and Promotion Policies

*First and second years:* Courses in the basic medical sciences are given Honors, Pass, or Fail; 70 is passing. *Third and fourth years:* Clinical courses for all Phase I and Phase II required courses and all electives will be recorded as High Honors, Above Expected Competence, Expected Competence, Marginal Competence, Incomplete—I, Failure—F. An examination grade will also be recorded for all required Phase I courses. A written evaluation report is made a part of a student's permanent academic record. Students must record passing total scores on Steps 1 and 2 CK. Students must sit for Step 2 CS before graduation.

## Facilities

*Teaching:* The Jefferson Alumni Hall houses all basic science departments (and recreational facilities). The new Dorrance H. Hamilton building includes a new state-of-the-art auditorium and a small-group teaching room of 3 floors. College Building houses administrative and clinical department offices, laboratories, and lecture rooms and connects with the Curtis Building, in which are located additional clinical faculty offices, research laboratories, and classrooms. Bridges connect the College and Curtis buildings with the 4 Jefferson Hospital structures: the Gibbon Building, the Foerderer Pavilion, the Thompson Building, and the Main building. The Gibbon Building is a facility with four 100-bed minihospitals, each with its own diagnostic and therapeutic facilities, teaching rooms, and physicians' offices, and the Bodine Center for Radiation Therapy. The outpatient Surgical Center contains physicians' offices, operating rooms, and surgical facilities for same-day surgery. *Other:* The college is affiliated with 19 hospitals. *Library:* The Scott Library Building contains 170,000 volumes and receives 2300 periodicals. *Housing:* Orlowitz, Barringer, and Martin buildings provide apartment rentals.

## Special Features

*Minority admissions:* The college encourages applications from minority and other disadvantaged students. *Other degree programs:* Selected students can earn BS and MD degrees in 6 or 7 calendar years from Jefferson Medical College in cooperation with Pennsylvania State University. There is a combined MD-PhD program with the College of Graduate Studies, Thomas Jefferson University, a joint 5-year MD-MBA (and MHA) program with Widener University, and an MPH program.

# Pennsylvania State University College of Medicine

P.O. Box 850, 500 University Drive
Hershey, Pennsylvania    17033

*Phone:* 717-531-8755          *Fax:* 717-531-6225
*E-mail:* studentadmissions@hmc.psu.edu
*WWW:* hmc.psu.edu/md/

| Application Filing | | Accreditation | |
|---|---|---|---|
| Earliest: | June 1 | LCME | |
| Latest: | November 15 | | |
| Fee: | $70 | **Degrees Granted** | |
| AMCAS: | yes | MD, MD-PhD | |

### Enrollment: 2008–2009 First-Year Class

| Men: | 77 | 50% | Applied: | 6691 |
|---|---|---|---|---|
| Women: | 77 | 50% | Interviewed: | 942 |
| Minorities: | 10 | 6% | Enrolled: | 154 |
| Out of State: | 74 | 48% | | |

### 2008–2009 Class Profile

| *Mean MCAT Scores* | | *Mean GPA* |
|---|---|---|
| Physical Sciences: | 10 | 3.7 |
| Biological Sciences: | 11 | |
| Verbal Reasoning: | 10 | *Mean Science* |
| | | 3.7 |

**Tuition and Fees**

| | (in thousands of dollars) |
|---|---|
| Resident | 33,058 |
| Average (public) | 25,100 |
| Average (private) | 42,600 |
| Nonresident | 44,920 |
| Average (public) | 43,900 |
| Average (private) | 43,500 |

Percentage receiving financial aid: 93%

Above data applies to 2007–2008 academic year.

## Introduction

Pennsylvania State's Milton S. Hershey Medical Center opened its doors to the first class of medical students in 1967. It became the first medical school in the nation to establish a Department of Humanity, introducing humanistic disciplines into the required medical curriculum. The school was also the first to start an independent Department of Family and Community Medicine. From its beginning, medical education and patient care have been guided by the institution's commitment to be innovative in providing patient care.

## Admissions (AMCAS)

Three years of college and the basic premedical science courses plus 1 year of mathematics and 1 semester each of humanities and behavioral science are required. Recommended courses include calculus, statistics, genetics, and sociology. Additional courses in the humanities and social sciences are also encouraged. *Transfer and advanced standing:* Transfer is possible from LCME-accredited institutions.

## Curriculum

4-year semimodern. *First year:* The curriculum combines elements of traditional medical teaching and case-based, student-centered learning with strategic lectures, laboratories, and small-group discussions. *Second year:* More heavily oriented to case-based learning in organ/system approach to human health, pathophysiology, and disease. *Third year:* Includes a sequence of required core clinical clerkships in internal medicine, general surgery, pediatrics, obstetrics and gynecology, psychiatry, family and community medicine, and primary care. These are supplemented by available selectives, as well as week-long sessions in Advanced Clinical Diagnostic and Therapeutics, Communications and Professionalism, and Improving Healthcare. *Fourth year:* The school offers a wide variety of both clinical and research electives. All students participate in an individualized research program.

## Grading and Promotion Policies

Examinations may be written, oral, or practical. Grades of Honors, High Pass, Pass or Fail are determined by the faculty. The faculty is also responsible for recommendations for promotion and graduation. Students must take Steps 1 and 2 of the USMLE and have a score reported in order to graduate.

## Facilities

*Teaching:* The principal structure is the 9-story Medical Sciences Building and Hospital, which contains basic teaching facilities, clinical sciences facilities, the teaching hospital, and research laboratories. *Other:* The Animal Research Farm is used for both teaching and research. The Central Animal Quarters, located in the Medical Sciences Building, is designed for teaching and experimentation. A Biomedical Research Building provides space for faculty and students. *Library:* The Harrell Library serves the Medical Sciences Building and the teaching hospital. Holdings total more than 100,000 volumes. This includes more than 3200 medical history, humanities, and rare books. About 2000 journal titles are currently received. The library also contains a Library Learning Center and individual student study carrels. *Housing:* There are 1-, 2-, and 3-bedroom apartments.

## Special Features

*Minority admissions:* The school is strongly committed to and actively involved in the recruitment of minority applicants. *Other degree programs:* Combined MD-PhD programs are available in a number of disciplines. An overseas study program is available to selected applicants.

# Temple University School of Medicine

3340 North Broad Street
Philadelphia, Pennsylvania    19140

*Phone:* 215-707-3656          *Fax:* 215-707-6932
*E-mail:* medadmissions@temple.edu
*WWW:* medschool.temple.edu

| Application Filing | | Accreditation |
|---|---|---|
| Earliest: | June 1 | LCME |
| Latest: | December 15 | |
| Fee: | $70 | **Degrees Granted** |
| AMCAS: | yes | MD, MD-PhD, |
| | | MD-MPH |

### Enrollment: 2008–2009 First-Year Class

| | | | | |
|---|---|---|---|---|
| Men: | 95 | 53% | Applied: | 9715 |
| Women: | 83 | 47% | Interviewed: | 817 |
| Minorities: | 13 | 7% | Enrolled: | 178 |
| Out of State: | 83 | 47% | | |

### 2008–2009 Class Profile

| *Mean MCAT Scores* | | *Mean GPA* |
|---|---|---|
| Physical Sciences: | 10.0 | 3.7 |
| Biological Sciences: | 11 | |
| Verbal Reasoning: | 10 | *Mean Science* |
| | | 3.7 |

### Tuition and Fees

| | (in thousands of dollars) |
|---|---|
| **Resident** | 38,502 |
| Average (public) | 25,100 |
| Average (private) | 42,600 |
| **Nonresident** | 47,004 |
| Average (public) | 43,900 |
| Average (private) | 43,500 |

Percentage receiving financial aid: 88%

Above data applies to 2007–2008 academic year.

## Introduction

Temple University School of Medicine originated as the College of Temple University in 1901.

## Admissions (AMCAS)

Only the basic premedical courses plus 6 credits of humanities are required. Preference is given to Pennsylvania residents, but about 35% of the class are nonresidents. Strong preference is given also to students with 4 years of college. *Transfer and advanced standing:* In selecting applicants for acceptance, objective considerations such as academic record and MCAT scores are used. In addition, subjective variables such as recommendations, extracurricular activities, and work experience are considered. Those selected for further evaluation are invited for an interview. Transfer is accepted for the third year on a space-available basis to qualified candidates from other LCME-approved schools.

## Curriculum

4-year semimodern. *First and second years:* Will be divided into a number of interdisciplinary blocks, each organized according to body or organ systems and taught by faculty from several basic science and clinical academic departments. *Third and fourth years:* Provide exposure to a variety of clinical experiences, both inpatient and ambulatory, with enhanced emphasis on integration with the basic sciences, evidence-based medicine, and professionalism. The integrated curriculum more closely reflects the way in which students will be expected to identify and address clinical problems in both their educational and professional careers. It will penetrate the somewhat artificial barriers inherent in basic science discipline-based courses and demonstrate the close linkage between the basic sciences and clinical medicine, inculcating into students those fundamental skills that will provide an excellent foundation for their careers in medicine.

## Grading and Promotion Policies

Honors/High Pass/Pass/Conditional/Fail. A written evaluation of each student is required for each clinical clerkship and is encouraged for each basic science course. Steps 1 and 2 of the USMLE must be taken and passed.

## Facilities

*Teaching:* Medical school activities during the first 2 years are housed in the School of Medicine and Kresge Science Hall. The latter is a teaching structure with student laboratories, demonstration classrooms, and a library. Clinical teaching takes place at Temple University Hospital, Temple University Children's Medical Center, Fox Chase Cancer Center, Western Pennsylvania Hospital, Croser Chester Medical Center, Reading Hospital, St. Luke's Hospital, and Abington Hospital. The Clinical Simulation Center features simulated operating room and exam suites, and "SimMan" and "SimBaby," robotic mannequins programmed to "present" myocardial infarctions and dozens of other events. The large learning laboratory teaches medical students and residents clinical skills through a combination of high-tech and traditional methods. *Other:* There are formal agreements of affiliation with other general and specialty hospitals and letters of agreement with a number of institutions in Philadelphia, other parts of Pennsylvania, and New Jersey. The Fels Research Institute and Thrombosis Research Center are integral parts of the school. *Library:* A modern library is available to students and faculty. It houses a large number of books and periodicals and a computer center. *Housing:* No university-related dormitories are available.

## Special Features

*Minority admissions:* The school has an active recruitment program and offers an 8-week summer enrichment program for incoming students from minority and disadvantaged backgrounds. *Other degree programs:* Combined MD-PhD, MD-MPH, and MD-MBA programs are available.

# University of Pennsylvania School of Medicine

Suite 100, Stemmler Hall
3450 Hamilton Walk
Philadelphia, Pennsylvania   19104

*Phone:* 215-898-8001          *Fax:* 215-573-6645
*E-mail:* admiss@mail.med.upenn.edu
*WWW:* med.upenn.edu

| Application Filing | | Accreditation | |
| --- | --- | --- | --- |
| Earliest: | June 1 | LCME | |
| Latest: | October 15 | | |
| Fee: | $80 | **Degrees Granted** | |
| AMCAS: | yes | MD, MD-PhD, MD-MBA | |

### Enrollment: 2008–2009 First-Year Class

| Men: | 74 | 48% | Applied: | 6344 |
| --- | --- | --- | --- | --- |
| Women: | 79 | 52% | Interviewed: | 938 |
| Minorities: | 16 | 10% | Enrolled: | 153 |
| Out of State: | 115 | 75% | | |

### 2008–2009 Class Profile

| *Mean MCAT Scores* | | *Mean GPA* |
| --- | --- | --- |
| Physical Sciences: | 12 | 3.8 |
| Biological Sciences: | 12 | |
| Verbal Reasoning: | 11 | *Mean Science* |
| | | 3.8 |

**Tuition and Fees**

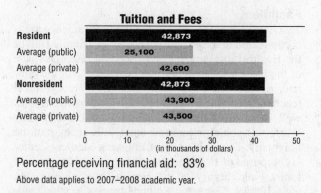

| | |
| --- | --- |
| Resident | 42,873 |
| Average (public) | 25,100 |
| Average (private) | 42,600 |
| Nonresident | 42,873 |
| Average (public) | 43,900 |
| Average (private) | 43,500 |

0    10    20    30    40    50
(in thousands of dollars)

Percentage receiving financial aid: 83%

Above data applies to 2007–2008 academic year.

## Introduction

The University of Pennsylvania School of Medicine was originally known as the College of Philadelphia. Founded in 1765, it was the first medical school established in the United States. It is a private, nondenominational school, located on the Irwin campus of the University of Pennsylvania in Philadelphia. The clinical training facilities such as the Hospital of the University of Pennsylvania and Children's Hospital of Philadelphia are located adjacent to the school.

## Admissions (AMCAS)

Suggested courses are the basic premedical science courses. It is recommended that in addition to acquiring a foundation in the basic sciences plus mathematics, the student should have appropriate competence in English and communication. Some preference is given to Pennsylvania

students. *Transfer and advanced standing:* Information is not available.

## Curriculum

4-year. *First year:* Consists of 40 weeks of basic sciences emphasizing normal form and function and an integrated clinical program. *Second year:* Begins with 6 months of coordinated teaching of pharmacology, pathophysiology, infectious disease, and continuation of the clinical program. This is followed by clinical clerkships. *Third and fourth years:* Programs consist of a mixture of required and elective courses chosen from over 100 offered which cover all basic and clinical sciences. New programs using seminars and minicourses help the student learn psychosocial and behavioral aspects of medicine, reinforce the student's knowledge of basic science, and reinforce an attitude favorable to later continuing self-education.

## Grading and Promotion Policies

Each department submits a grade of Honors, Pass, or Fail for a student along with a description of the student's characteristics. The additional grade of High Pass is used by clinical departments. At the end of 3 academic years, the student's performance is evaluated and recommendations for postgraduate training are made. Students must obtain total passing scores on Steps 1 and 2 of the USMLE in order to graduate.

## Facilities

*Teaching:* Students receive clinical instruction and experience in the hospitals of the University of Pennsylvania Medical Center as well as in other hospitals in Philadelphia and its vicinity. The chief source of clinical experience is the Hospital of the University of Pennsylvania. Besides teaching facilities, it houses research institutions and laboratories. Students serve clerkships and preceptorships at the Graduate Hospital of the University of Pennsylvania. A program for teaching and training has been established at Philadelphia General Hospital. Teaching privileges at Pennsylvania Hospital are reserved for clerkships in medicine, obstetrics, and surgery and for certain electives. Services at the Children's Hospital of Philadelphia are used for pediatric and surgical teaching. Students are assigned to the services of medicine and surgery at Presbyterian-University of Pennsylvania Medical Center. In addition, certain elective courses are offered there. *Other:* Courses, clerkships, and research facilities are offered at several other closely affiliated hospitals in the vicinity and at the Alfred Newton Richards Medical Research Building. *Library:* The library, which is housed in the Johnson Pavilion, contains more than 100,000 volumes and receives more than 2000 periodicals and other publications. *Housing:* On campus, Graduate Towers and High Rise North offers apartments and suites on a 12-month basis.

## Special Features

*Minority admissions:* The school has short- and long-term recruitment programs to recruit underrepresented minority groups. *Other degree programs:* Combined MD-PhD programs are available in the basic medical sciences; MD-JD and MD-MBA programs are also offered.

# University of Pittsburgh School of Medicine

Pittsburgh, Pennsylvania   15261

*Phone:* 412-648-9891          *Fax:* 412-648-8768
*E-mail:* admissions@medschool.pitt.edu
*WWW:* medschool.pitt.edu

| Application Filing | | Accreditation |
|---|---|---|
| Earliest: | June 1 | LCME |
| Latest: | November 1 | |
| Fee: | $25 | **Degrees Granted** |
| AMCAS: | yes | MD, MD-PhD, MD-MA, MD-MS |

### Enrollment: 2008–2009 First-Year Class

| | | | | |
|---|---|---|---|---|
| Men: | 88 | 60% | Applied: | 5413 |
| Women: | 59 | 40% | Interviewed: | 1028 |
| Minorities: | 24 | 16% | Enrolled: | 147 |
| Out of State: | 101 | 69% | | |

### 2008–2009 Class Profile

| *Mean MCAT Scores* | | *Mean GPA* |
|---|---|---|
| Physical Sciences: | 11.8 | 3.7 |
| Biological Sciences: | 11.9 | |
| Verbal Reasoning: | 10.9 | *Mean Science* |
| | | 3.7 |

**Tuition and Fees**

| | (in thousands of dollars) |
|---|---|
| Resident | 36,752 |
| Average (public) | 25,100 |
| Average (private) | 42,600 |
| Nonresident | 40,772 |
| Average (public) | 43,900 |
| Average (private) | 43,500 |

Percentage receiving financial aid: 90%

## Introduction

In 1886 a charter was granted for the establishment of the Western Pennsylvania Medical College. In 1892 this school became affiliated with the Western University of Pennsylvania, which later became the University of Pittsburgh. The School of Medicine is located in the Oakland district of Pittsburgh and has extensive research facilities.

## Admissions (AMCAS)

Applicants must have completed the basic premedical science courses including 1 year of English composition. Courses in the behavioral sciences, biostatistics, calculus, computer sciences, humanities and social sciences are recommended. Gaining a background in the social and behavioral sciences and humanities is encouraged. In the evaluation process, consideration is given to the applicant's academic record, MCAT performance, preprofessional evaluations, faculty recommendations, extracurricular undergraduate activities, and personal interview. Various personal characteristics such as integrity and motivation are considered. Transfer students are considered when vacancies occur.

## Curriculum

4-year semimodern. The curriculum emphasizes general principles and self-learning based on actual cases. *First and second years:* A multidisciplinary approach organized by organ system is used. Its aim is to develop communication and problem-solving skills; learning in small groups, rather than in large lectures. The curriculum mainstreams social, cultural, and ethical issues, and introduces the student to clinical medicine in the first year. *Third year:* Covers the major clinical specialties in the form of clerkships as well as ambulatory subspecialties. *Fourth year:* Consists of electives and a required subinternship. All students complete a longitudinal scholarly project.

## Grading and Promotion Policies

Students are graded on the basis of their practical work and oral and written examinations. The system used is Honors/Pass/Fail. Students must record total passing scores on Step 1 and Step 2 of the USMLE for graduation.

## Facilities

*Teaching:* All of the teaching in the basic science areas is conducted in the 12-story Alan Magee Scaife Hall of the Health Professions. The office and research space of the basic science departments and some of the clinical departments are also located there. Clinical teaching is conducted in the Health Center Hospitals as well as in hospitals in other parts of the city. The Western Psychiatric Institute and Clinic is a part of the university. The University of Pittsburg Medical Center is composed of 19 hospitals. *Library:* The Maurice and Laura Falk Library of the Health Professions is the main library. There are 8 other libraries in which students have full privileges. *Housing:* On-campus housing is available.

## Special Features

*Minority admissions:* The school has an active recruitment program and offers an 8-week Summer Research Program for undergraduate college students. *Other degree programs:* Students selected for academic promise will be admitted to joint MD-PhD study programs in a variety of disciplines. Also offered is a joint MD-MA Ethics degree and an MD-MS in clinical research.

# PUERTO RICO

## Ponce School of Medicine

P.O. Box 7004
Ponce, Puerto Rico    00752

*Phone:* 787-840-2575          *Fax:* 787-842-0461
*E-mail:* admissions@psm.edu
*WWW:* psm.edu/student Affairs/

| Application Filing | | Accreditation |
|---|---|---|
| Earliest: | June 15 | n/a |
| Latest: | December 15 | **Degrees Granted** |
| Fee: | yes | n/a |
| AMCAS: | yes | |

### Enrollment: 2008–2009 First-Year Class

| | | | | | |
|---|---|---|---|---|---|
| Men: | 34 | 50% | Applied: | | n/a |
| Women: | 34 | 50% | Interviewed: | | n/a |
| Minorities: | 67 | 99% | Enrolled: | | 68 |
| Out of State: | 15 | 22% | | | |

### 2008–2009 Class Profile

| *Mean MCAT Scores* | | *Mean GPA* |
|---|---|---|
| Physical Sciences: | 7 | 3.5 |
| Biological Sciences: | 8 | *Mean Science* |
| Verbal Reasoning: | 7 | 3.4 |

### Tuition and Fees

| | |
|---|---|
| **Resident** | 19,352 |
| Average (public) | 25,100 |
| **Nonresident** | 28,850 |
| Average (public) | 42,600 |
| Average (private) | 43,500 |

0    10    20    30    40    50
(in thousands of dollars)

Percentage receiving financial aid:
School begins in August 2009. No data available yet.

## Introduction

The school graduated its first class in 1981. It seeks to develop professionals who have been exposed to a high quality of medical education, while strengthening their moral and ethical standards, and to prepare them for providing quality health care in a changing medical delivery environment.

## Admissions

Selection is carried out by an Admissions Committee on the basis of the applicants' Academic Achievement, MCAT scores, letters of evaluation, and a personal interview. Equal consideration is given regardless of race, religion, ethnic background, or origin. Puerto Rico residents are given preference, but limited numbers of mainland Americans are selected. Candidates with a functional knowledge of English and Spanish are encouraged to apply, since instruction is given in both these languages.

## Curriculum

The goal of the curriculum is to produce primary physicians. The curriculum is designed to provide students with early exposure to family and community health issues. During the first 2 years, the primary focus is the basic sciences, while the third and fourth years provide clinical experience, in a multidisciplinary context. During the fourth year, primary care courses on direct patient contact are offered. Emphasis is especially given, whenever possible, to include the family; a program-based earning program is part of the clinical correlation sessions in the first year of studies, as well as a pathophysiology course in the second year. During the basic science program, integrative exercises and small-group discussions are scheduled. Both community service and thesis research requirements are optional.

## Grading and Promotion Policies

Student performance is graded based on an Honors, Pass/Fail system.

## Facilities

The Playa Diagnostic Center is the main site for training in community medicine and family practice. In addition, the following facilities are available as part of the school's education and training program: Damas Hospital (356 beds), Dr. Pila Hospital (160 beds), St. Luke's Hospital (1550 beds), Conception Hospital (188 beds), and Yauco Regional Hospital (140 beds). *Housing:* On-campus housing is not available. The school provides a list of suitable apartments within a 10-mile radius. Rents at these locations are on average $700 per month.

## Special Features

*Financial aid:* Admission is not based on the financial status of the student. Upon acceptance, applicants are provided with the necessary forms and advice on securing financial aid.

# San Juan Bautista School of Medicine

Caguas, Puerto Rico
P.O. Box 4968
Caguas, Puerto Rico    00725

*Phone:* 787-743-3038          *Fax:* 787-746-3093
*E-mail:* admissions@sanjuanbautista.edu
*WWW:* sanjuanbautista.edu/admissions.aspx

| Application Filing | | Accreditation | |
|---|---|---|---|
| Earliest: | June 1 | n/a | |
| Latest: | April 1 | **Degrees Granted** | |
| Fee: | $75 | n/a | |
| AMCAS: | yes | | |

### Enrollment: 2008–2009 First-Year Class

| | | | | | |
|---|---|---|---|---|---|
| Men: | 29 | 43% | Applied: | n/a | |
| Women: | 38 | 57% | Interviewed: | n/a | |
| Minorities: | 58 | 87% | Enrolled: | n/a | |
| Out of State: | 21 | 31% | | | |

### 2008–2009 Class Profile

| *Mean MCAT Scores* | | *Mean GPA* |
|---|---|---|
| Physical Sciences: | 11 | 3.3 |
| Biological Sciences: | 11 | *Mean Science* |
| Verbal Reasoning: | 10 | 3.1 |

### Tuition and Fees

| | |
|---|---|
| **Resident** | 17,000 |
| Average (public) | 25,100 |
| **Nonresident** | 43,500 |
| Average (public) | 43,900 |
| Average (private) | 42,600 |

(in thousands of dollars)

Percentage receiving financial aid: 96%

School begins in August 2009.

## Introduction

This school has been in existence for more than 3 decades. The LCME granted accreditation to its academic program in 2007. The school is located in an important urban center in Puerto Rico. The goal of this institution is to educate and train primary care physicians for service to the community.

## Admissions

Students are evaluated on the basis of both their academic and personal qualifications. These include academic achievement in the premedical courses, and MCAT scores. In addition, notice is taken of the applicant's motivation to pursue a medical career, leadership abilities, interpersonal skills, and the extent of participation in community affairs. Appropriate students are asked to appear for a personal interview where a more in-depth evaluation can be secured for consideration by the Admission Committee.

## Curriculum

The curriculum is organized so that the preclinical courses are offered during the first 2 years. The third year is devoted to core clinical clerkships, both in-patient and out-patient; this includes a research clerkship. The fourth year serves to reinforce clinical exposure with core and elective clerkships as well as subspecialty clerkships. A number of innovations have been included in the curriculum aimed at strengthening the earning process. These involve multi-disciplinary exercises and various different community experiences. The latter involve about 150 hours of exposure during the first 3 years.

## Grading and Promotion Policies

Steps 1 and 2 of the USMLE are required.

## Facilities

The school and its affiliated hospital, the San Bautista Medical Center, are located on a 52-acre campus. The school houses administrative offices, the library, and a Learning Resources Center, in addition to classrooms and laboratories. *Housing:* Campus housing is unavailable. The school provides information about available housing in the city.

## Special Features

*Financial aid:* The school provides counseling on financial aid resources and advice on filing applications for assistance.

# Universidad Central del Caribe School of Medicine

P.O. Box 60-327
Bayamon, Puerto Rico    00960

*Phone:* 787-798-3001          *Fax:* 787-269-7550
*E-mail:* icordero@uccaribe.edu
*WWW:* uccaribe.edu

| Application Filing | | Accreditation |
|---|---|---|
| Earliest: | June 1 | n/a |
| Latest: | December 15 | **Degrees Granted** |
| Fee: | $100 | n/a |
| AMCAS: | yes | |

### Enrollment: 2008–2009 First-Year Class

| Men: | 33 | 50% | Applied: | n/a |
|---|---|---|---|---|
| Women: | 33 | 50% | Interviewed: | n/a |
| Minorities: | 3 | 5% | Enrolled: | n/a |
| Out of State: | n/a | | | |

### 2008–2009 Class Profile

| *Mean MCAT Scores* | | *Mean GPA* |
|---|---|---|
| Physical Sciences: | 11 | 3.5 |
| Biological Sciences: | 11 | *Mean Science* |
| Verbal Reasoning: | 10 | n/a |

**Tuition and Fees**

| | (in thousands of dollars) |
|---|---|
| Resident | 24,500 |
| Average (public) | 25,100 |
| Nonresident | 31,890 |
| Average (public) | 42,600 |
| Average (private) | 43,500 |

Percentage receiving financial aid: n/a

## Introduction

This nonprofit private institution was founded in 1976. The goal of the school is to instill in its students an intense sense of professionalism, together with a commitment to the health and social well-being of the residents of the island.

## Admissions

The Admissions Committee has a nondiscriminatory policy regarding age, race, religion, sex, economic status, or political philosophy. It is necessary for applicants to demonstrate linguistic proficiency in both Spanish and English. Spanish is the predominant language used at the institution, but instruction may also be given in English. The principal selection factors are the applicant's academic record, namely, the overall GPA, science GPA, MCAT scores, recommendations and evaluation, letters on behalf of the applicant, as well as interview performance.

## Curriculum

The school program is organized into an initial 2 years of preclinical and 2 years of clinical studies. The schedule incorporates a longitudinal program of bioethics and humanities that will help strengthen professional behavior. Clinical correlations are included with the basic sciences. Students are exposed to patients starting in the first year. In the next year students participate in a problem-based course that is structured around relevant medical issues for the entire year. The third year is dedicated essentially to required clerkships in internal medicine, pediatrics, obstetrics-gynecology, general surgery, and family medicine. These take place for the most part in an ambulatory care setting. In addition, students enroll in a psychiatric clerkship. The senior year includes required courses in neurology, ambulatory medicine, bioethics, and humanities in medicine. This year includes 18 weeks of electives. Both community service and a research program are available.

## Grading and Promotion Policies

Students are evaluated in both the basic and clinical sciences on the basis of later grade and Pass/Fail systems. Steps 1 and 2 of the USMLE are required.

## Facilities

In 1990 a building was opened to teach the basic sciences and to house the school library. This building is located adjacent to the Dr. Ramon Ruiz Arman University Hospital, which serves as the municipal teaching hospital. The school is located on a 56-acre academic health center in the city of Bayamon. *Housing:* On-campus housing is unavailable; however, the school maintains a list of affordable apartments in its vicinity.

## Special Features

*Financial aid:* All applicants can receive counseling from the school's Office of Student Affairs. Students who have been accepted can apply for appropriate federal and commonwealth scholarships and loan programs.

# University of Puerto Rico School of Medicine

P.O. Box 365067
San Juan, Puerto Rico    00936

*Phone:* 787-743-3038          *Fax:* 787-746-3093
*WWW:* md.rcm.upr.edu

| Application Filing | | Accreditation |
|---|---|---|
| Earliest: | June 1 | n/a |
| Latest: | December 15 | **Degrees Granted** |
| Fee: | $75 | n/a |
| AMCAS: | | |

### Enrollment: 2008–2009 First-Year Class

| | | | | |
|---|---|---|---|---|
| Men: | 22 | 37% | Applied: | n/a |
| Women: | 38 | 63% | Interviewed: | n/a |
| Minorities: | 0 | 0% | Enrolled: | n/a |
| Out of State: | n/a | | | |

### 2008–2009 Class Profile

| *Mean MCAT Scores* | | *Mean GPA* |
|---|---|---|
| Physical Sciences: | n/a | n/a |
| Biological Sciences: | n/a | *Mean Science* |
| Verbal Reasoning: | n/a | n/a |

### Tuition and Fees

| | |
|---|---|
| **Resident** | 18,770 |
| Average (public) | n/a |
| **Nonresident** | 34,801 |
| Average (public) | n/a |
| Average (private) | n/a |

0    10    20    30    40    50
(in thousands of dollars)

Percentage receiving financial aid: 92%

School begins in August 2009.

## Introduction

This is the oldest medical school in Puerto Rico, having been established in 1949. The school seeks to achieve academic excellence by interdisciplinary teaching as well as by providing superior clinical training and research experience. The school seeks to generate a favorable environment for both personal and professional growth. In addition, the school's aim is not only to transmit, but also to increase, medical knowledge.

## Admissions

Being a state-supported institution, preference for admission will be given to qualified applicants who are legal residents of Puerto Rico. Foreign national applicants who have an established residence in Puerto Rico will be considered only if, at the time of application, they are US citizens, or have been granted a permanent residence visa in the United States. Student selection by the Admissions Committee is based on academic achievement, MCAT scores, letters of recommendation from institutions, personal interview performance, and extracurricular activities. Interviews are granted only by the Admissions Office. The school has its specific formula in assessing the weight given to the various admissions criteria. Rejected applicants have the option of reapplying.

## Curriculum

The curriculum is designed to extend over a 4-year period. The first 2 years largely cover the basic sciences. They introduce students to the prerequisites for the clinical sciences including its behavioral aspects. Part of the second year is devoted to pathophysiology, physical diagnosis, and basic clerkships, which are taught by a multidisciplinary faculty. There are small-group sessions, utilizing the problem-based learning approach. This educational method is introduced early in the medical curriculum. Human behavior, environmental factors, and public health concepts are integrated into the curriculum. The third and fourth years are devoted to clinical clerkship experiences and elective courses. The main focus of the curriculum is devoted to primary community health care exposure. The school will supply support services and educational counseling to students in order to facilitate retention.

## Grading and Promotion Policies

Students are graded on a letter grade basis throughout the 4 years. Steps 1 and 2 of the USMLE are required for promotion and graduation. Both community service and a research thesis are optional.

## Facilities

The clinical training occurs at the hospitals affiliated with the Puerto Rican Medical Consortium. This includes facilities outside of San Juan. The location of the medical school is near the District Hospital. This facilitates integration of the basic and clinical science departments and allows for better utilization of available services. *Housing:* Information not available.

## Special Features

*Financial aid:* This is provided to accepted applicants on the basis of confidential applications they can submit. The major criteria is the extent of financial need. Forms for scholarships are available at the Financial Aid Office. Scholarship aid can be applied for at the time the student seeks admission, since it will not influence the outcome of the process. Foreign students are not eligible for financial aid.

# The Warren Albert Medical School of Brown University

97 Waterman Street, Box GA 213
Providence, Rhode Island   02912

*Phone:* 401-863-2149            *Fax:* 401-863-2660
*E-mail:* medschool_admissions@brown.edu
*WWW:* med.brown.edu

| Application Filing | | Accreditation | |
|---|---|---|---|
| Earliest: | June 1 | LCME | |
| Latest: | November 1 | | |
| Fee: | $95 | **Degrees Granted** | |
| AMCAS: | yes | MD, MD-PhD | |

### Enrollment: 2008–2009 First-Year Class

| Men: | 42 | 44% | Applied: | 6016 |
|---|---|---|---|---|
| Women: | 53 | 56% | Interviewed: | 279 |
| Minorities: | 7 | 7% | Enrolled: | 95 |
| Out of State: | 62 | 65% | | |

### 2008–2009 Class Profile

| *Mean MCAT Scores* | | *Mean GPA* |
|---|---|---|
| Physical Sciences: | 12 | 3.8 |
| Biological Sciences: | 12 | |
| Verbal Reasoning: | 11 | *Mean Science* |
| | | 3.8 |

**Tuition and Fees**

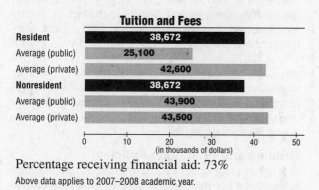

| | |
|---|---|
| Resident | 38,672 |
| Average (public) | 25,100 |
| Average (private) | 42,600 |
| Nonresident | 38,672 |
| Average (public) | 43,900 |
| Average (private) | 43,500 |

(in thousands of dollars)

Percentage receiving financial aid: 73%

Above data applies to 2007–2008 academic year.

## Introduction

Brown University was founded in 1764 in Providence, Rhode Island. Brown's medical education program began in 1963, with a 2-year program. In 1975 a program leading to the MD degree was accredited. The Program in Liberal Medical Education (PLME) combines premedical and medical education in a 7- to 8-year course of study.

## Admissions

In 2004 Brown began accepting applications from qualified college graduates through AMCAS. However, the majority of students in each MD entering class enter via the LME program. Other routes of admission include the Early Identification Program for students enrolled at Providence College, Rhode Island College, the University of Rhode Island, Tougaloo College, and the postbaccalaureate premedical programs at Bryn Mawr, Columbia, and Goucher Colleges. *Transfer and advanced standing:* Students who are enrolled at LCME-accredited U.S. or Canadian medical schools or Rhode Island residents attending WHO-accredited foreign medical schools may apply for advanced standing. Students admitted to Brown Medical School must demonstrate competence in the sciences basic to medicine and must have successfully completed the basic premedical sciences and calculus.

## Curriculum

4 years semitraditional. *First and second years:* During the fall semester of the first year, students take physiology, anatomy, histology, and "Doctoring," a new, 2-year course training at community sites. During the spring semester of the first year, some of the advanced basic sciences and Doctoring are offered. Pathophysiology provides the structure for the second year, which is organized around organ systems or concepts. Additional advanced basic sciences are also part of the second year. *Third year:* Students must satisfactorily complete 50 weeks of traditional clinical clerkships and 32 weeks of electives. *Fourth year:* An advanced clinical clerkship (subinternship) in medicine, pediatrics, or surgery and a longitudinal, ambulatory clerkship are also required.

## Grading and Promotion Policies

The evaluation of format is on an Honors/Pass/Fail scale; clinical evaluations are supplemented by narratives. Step 1 and Step 2/2B must be taken prior to graduation.

## Facilities

*Teaching:* Preclinical classroom instruction takes place primarily in the Biomedical Center, which also houses research laboratories and computer and audiovisual resources for students. Clinical training takes place at 7 affiliated teaching hospitals in the Providence area. *Other:* Laboratories for Molecular Medicine are located in Providence's Jewelry District. *Library:* Sciences Library on campus houses a collection of 660,000 print volumes and subscribes to more than 13,000 on-line journals and 250 databases. *Housing:* Information not available.

## Special Features

*Minority admissions:* The objective of the school is the recruitment, retention, and graduation of students from groups underrepresented in medicine. *Other degree programs:* A combined MD-PhD program is offered in a variety of disciplines. Medical students may also obtain masters degrees in Public Health or Medical Science.

# SOUTH CAROLINA

# Medical University of South Carolina College of Medicine

171 Ashley Avenue
Charleston, South Carolina    29464

*Phone:* 843-792-3283          *Fax:* 843-792-0204
*E-mail:* taylorwl@musc.edu
*WWW:* musc.edu/com/com/html

| Application Filing | | Accreditation | |
|---|---|---|---|
| Earliest: | June 1 | LCME | |
| Latest: | December 1 | | |
| Fee: | $75 | **Degrees Granted** | |
| AMCAS: | yes | MD, MD-PhD, | |
| | | MD-MHA, MD-MBA, | |
| | | MD-MPH | |

### Enrollment: 2008–2009 First-Year Class

| | | | | | |
|---|---|---|---|---|---|
| Men: | 70 | 52% | Applied: | | 1501 |
| Women: | 65 | 48% | Interviewed: | | 355 |
| Minorities: | 14 | 10% | Enrolled: | | 135 |
| Out of State: | 4 | 3% | | | |

### 2008–2009 Class Profile

| *Mean MCAT Scores* | | *Mean GPA* |
|---|---|---|
| Physical Sciences: | 9 | 3.63 |
| Biological Sciences: | 10 | |
| Verbal Reasoning: | 10 | *Mean Science* |
| | | n/av |

**Tuition and Fees**

| | |
|---|---|
| Resident | 20,566 |
| Average (public) | 25,100 |
| Average (private) | 42,600 |
| Nonresident | 56,618 |
| Average (public) | 43,900 |
| Average (private) | 43,500 |

0    10    20    30    40    50
(in thousands of dollars)

Percentage receiving financial aid:  81%

## Introduction

The University of South Carolina School of Medicine (USCSM) was established in 1977 and is located in the state's capital city. The school offers a wide range of educational and professional opportunities to its students, featuring a small class size, a nationally recognized Senior Mentor Program, and a state-of-the-art ultrasound curriculum. The school works closely with its 3 major affiliated hospitals to provide students valuable clinical experience.

## Admissions (AMCAS)

Basic premedical science courses (biology, inorganic and organic chemistry), and a year of English (composition and literature) are required. A semester of biochemistry is highly recommended. No specific major is preferred. The preliminary screening of applicants is by means of the AMCAS application, letters of recommendation, and the USCSM supplementary application. The selection of candidates for admission is based on a review of undergraduate academic performance, MCAT scores, letters of recommendation, and, when granted, the assessment of a personal interview at the medical school. Legal residents of South Carolina are given priority, but some nonresidents with superior credentials and ties to the state may gain admission. *Transfer and advanced standing:* Transfer from other accredited U.S. medical schools into the second or third year is possible if space is available.

## Curriculum

4-year semitraditional. *First and second years:* These 2 years are devoted to introductory and advanced basic sciences. The Introduction to Clinical Medicine course spans all 4 semesters of the basic science years and is a transitional, multidisciplinary course designed to facilitate moving students from preclinical (basic science) preparation and thinking to readiness to enter the clinical arena. A variety of instructional formats is utilized in the preclinical curriculum, including lectures, small-group activities, and standardized patient exercises. First- and second-year students may take non-credit elective courses to gain supplemental educational experiences in areas of personal interest. In addition, interdisciplinary material on nutrition, substance abuse, ultrasound, ethics and professionalism, genetics, and geriatrics is presented over the 4-year period. *Third year:* Consists of 8-week clerkships in internal medicine, surgery, pediatrics, and psychiatry/neurology and 6-week clerkships in family medicine and obstetrics/gynecology. Two 2-week electives periods are also included in the third year. *Fourth year:* Consists of 4-week rotations in internal medicine, surgical subspecialties, and an acting internship, with the remainder of the year devoted to a selective/elective program and a 2-week capstone experience. Students strengthen their clinical skills and pursue individual academic interests during this year.

## Grading and Promotion Policies

A letter grading system is used. Students are required to pass Step 1 of the USMLE before being promoted to the third year and Step 2 CS and CK before graduation.

## Facilities

*Teaching:* During the first 2 years, all courses are taught on the basic science campus, which is completely wireless and adjoins the VA Medical Center. Clinical training takes place at the VA Medical Center, Palmetto Health Richland, Greenville Hospital Systems University Medical Centers, and other affiliated hospitals. *Library:* The medical school library is located on the basic science campus. It has a strong collection of 28,208 electronic journals, 420 electronic books, 83 databases, 33,150 print books, and 340 print journals.

## Special Features

*Minority admissions:* The school has an active minority recruitment program. *Regional campus:* Students may choose to do their third and fourth years in Greenville, South Carolina. *Other degree programs:* Combined MD-PhD and MD-MPH programs are offered.

# University of South Carolina School of Medicine

Columbia, South Carolina   29208

*Phone:* 803-733-3325        *Fax:* 803-733-3328
*E-mail:* jeanette@gw.med.sc.edu
*WWW:* med.sc.edu

| Application Filing | | Accreditation | |
|---|---|---|---|
| Earliest: | June 1 | LCME | |
| Latest: | January 15 | | |
| Fee: | $75 | **Degrees Granted** | |
| AMCAS: | yes | MD, MD-PhD, | |
| | | MD-MPH | |

### Enrollment: 2008–2009 First-Year Class

| | | | | | |
|---|---|---|---|---|---|
| Men: | 43 | 50% | Applied: | | 1960 |
| Women: | 43 | 50% | Interviewed: | | 336 |
| Minorities: | 6 | 5% | Enrolled: | | 84 |
| Out of State: | 10 | 7% | | | |

### 2008–2009 Class Profile

| *Mean MCAT Scores* | | *Mean GPA* |
|---|---|---|
| Physical Sciences: | 8.7 | 3.5 |
| Biological Sciences: | 9.7 | |
| Verbal Reasoning: | 9.8 | *Mean Science* |
| | | 3.7 |

**Tuition and Fees**

| | |
|---|---|
| Resident | 24,776 |
| Average (public) | 25,100 |
| Average (private) | 42,600 |
| Nonresident | 60,458 |
| Average (public) | 43,900 |
| Average (private) | 43,500 |

0   10   20   30   40   50
(in thousands of dollars)

Percentage receiving financial aid: 90%

## Introduction

As the most recent school at the University of South Carolina, the School of Medicine was not established until 1977. Located in the state capital, the school offers a wide range of educational and professional opportunities to its students. This includes small class size and an emphasis on the correlation between basic science and clinical science training. The school works closely with its 7 affiliated hospitals to provide students valuable clinical experience.

## Admissions (AMCAS)

The basic premedical science courses plus 1 year of English (composition and literature) and 1 year of mathematics are required. Courses in integral and differential calculus are recommended and no specific major is preferred. The selection of candidates for admission is based on a review of undergraduate academic performance, MCAT scores, comments provided in faculty evaluation, and, when granted, the assessment of a personal interview at the medical school. Legal residents of South Carolina are given priority, but some nonresidents with superior credentials may gain admission. The preliminary screening is by means of the AMCAS application and a request for supplementary material may follow. This includes letters of recommendation. *Transfer and advanced standing:* Transfer from other accredited U.S. medical schools into the second or third year is possible if space is available.

## Curriculum

4-year semitraditional. *First and second years:* These 2 years are devoted to the introductory and advanced basic sciences that are integrated with clinical correlations. An Introduction to Clinical Medicine includes family medicine, clinical medicine, preventive medicine, psychiatry, and behavioral science components in a small-group format. In addition, interdisciplinary material on nutrition, substance abuse, human values, genetics, and geriatrics are presented over the 4-year period. An Introduction to Clinical Medicine course provides the background and skills needed for the last 2 years. This course emphasizes independent and cooperative learning and includes components devoted to case-based education. First- and second-year students may take certain non-credit elective courses that provide supplemental educational experiences in areas of personal interest. *Third year:* This consists of 8-week clerkships in the major clinical sciences. *Fourth year:* Consists of rotations in medicine and surgery subspecialties and neurology with the remainder of the year devoted to a selective/elective program. Students can strengthen their clinical skills and pursue individual academic interests during this year.

## Grading and Promotion Policies

A letter grading system is used. Students are required to pass Step 1 of the USMLE before being promoted to the third year, and Step 2 before graduation.

## Facilities

*Teaching:* The courses during the first 2 years are taught in the Medical Sciences Building, which also houses various departmental offices. Clinical training takes place at the VA Medical Center, Palmetto Richland Memorial Hospital, Hall Psychiatric Institute, Greenville Memorial Hospital, and other affiliated hospitals. *Library:* The Medical School library is located on the grounds of the VA Center and has a collection of more than 90,000 volumes and subscribes to more than 1200 periodicals. *Housing:* On-campus housing is available to married students only.

## Special Features

*Minority admissions:* The school has an active minority recruitment program. *Other degree programs:* Combined MD-PhD and MD-MPH programs are offered.

# SOUTH DAKOTA

# University of South Dakota Sanford School of Medicine

414 East Clark Street
Vermillion, South Dakota   57069

*Phone:* 605-677-5233          *Fax:* 605-677-5109
*E-mail:* sdmadmissions@usd.edu
*WWW:* http://usd.edu/med/md

| Application Filing | | Accreditation |
|---|---|---|
| Earliest: | June 1 | LCME |
| Latest: | November 15 | |
| Fee: | $35 | **Degrees Granted** |
| AMCAS: | yes | MD |

### Enrollment: 2008–2009 First-Year Class

| | | | | |
|---|---|---|---|---|
| Men: | 29 | 54% | Applied: | 650 |
| Women: | 25 | 46% | Interviewed: | 163 |
| Minorities: | 2 | 1% | Enrolled: | 54 |
| Out of State: | 7 | 20% | | |

### 2008–2009 Class Profile

| *Mean MCAT Scores* | | *Mean GPA* |
|---|---|---|
| Physical Sciences: | 9.6 | 3.8 |
| Biological Sciences: | 10.4 | |
| Verbal Reasoning: | 9.5 | *Mean Science* |
| | | 3.7 |

**Tuition and Fees**

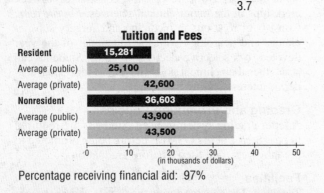

| | |
|---|---|
| **Resident** | 15,281 |
| Average (public) | 25,100 |
| Average (private) | 42,600 |
| **Nonresident** | 36,603 |
| Average (public) | 43,900 |
| Average (private) | 43,500 |

(in thousands of dollars)

Percentage receiving financial aid: 97%

## Introduction

The School of Medicine was established as a 2-year basic sciences institution in 1907. In the 1970s it converted to an MD degree-granting program, graduating its first class of MDs in 1977. The mission of the school is to provide the opportunity for South Dakota residents to receive a broad-based medical education with an emphasis on family practice.

## Admissions (AMCAS)

The school requires the basic premedical sciences plus one year of mathematics, courses in English composition, genetics, statistics, behavioral sciences, Microbiology/Immunology, and biochemistry. Taking the MCAT is required and must be within 3 years of the application year. Although a baccalaureate degree is desirable, students with 90 semester credits may matriculate if accepted.  Interviews are granted to South Dakota residents and to selected nonresidents with strong ties to the state such as graduating from a South Dakota high school. *Transfer and advanced standing:* Candidates for advanced standing/transfer are considered only from students in good standing at an LCME-accredited medical school, only when potential openings are available in the class and only if transfer is requested into either Year Two or Three.

## Curriculum

4-year semitraditional. The program blends a traditional curriculum with problem-based learning, case-based learning, clinical correlations in the basic sciences, and a significant ambulatory component during the third year. *First year:* The basic medical sciences and Introduction to Clinical Medicine. *Second year:* The advanced basic medical sciences including Microbiology and Pharmacology, as well as Laboratory Medicine, Introduction to Clinical Medicine, and Advanced Behavioral Sciences. At the end of year two, students have a one-month preceptorship in a primary care clinic. *Third year:* 48 weeks of required clerkships, plus 3 weeks of Clinical Colloquium. *Fourth year:* Rural Family Medicine, Emergency Medicine, subinternship and surgical specialties. Twenty-two weeks remaining for electives.

## Grading and Promotion Policies

Grading system is A to F with D or F being unsatisfactory and resulting in review by the Student Progress and Conduct Committee. Students must pass USMLE Rep 1, UMLE Step 2, CK, and a school-administered OSCE to graduate and must also take USMLE Step 2-CS to graduate.

## Facilities

*Teaching:* Preclinical instruction is based in the Lee Medical Building in Vermillion. Clinical teaching takes place at 3 clinical campuses based in Sioux Falls, Rapid City, and Yankton. *Library:* The Christian P. Lommen Health Science Library is located in Vermillion and the Karl and Mary Jo Wegner Health Sciences Information Center is located in Sioux Falls. *Housing:* On-campus housing resources are available on the Vermillion campus.

## Special Features

*Diversity:* The Medical School has several programs for identifying and assisting Native Americans who are interested in a medical career. *Other advanced degree programs:* There is a PhD program in Basic Biomedical Sciences. In 2006 the first students were accepted into the new Physician Scientist Program—a combined degree program including the MD and PhD degrees.

## TENNESSEE

# East Tennessee State University James H. Quillen College of Medicine

P.O. Box 70580
Johnson City, Tennessee   37614

*Phone:* 423-439-2033          *Fax:* 423-439-2110
*E-mail:* sacom@etsu.edu
*WWW:* http://com.etsu.edu

| Application Filing | | Accreditation | |
|---|---|---|---|
| Earliest: | June 1 | LCME | |
| Latest: | November 15 | | |
| Fee: | $50 | **Degrees Granted** | |
| AMCAS: | yes | MD, MD-PhD, MD-MS | |
| | | MD-BS | |

### Enrollment: 2008–2009 First-Year Class

| Men: | 27 | 45% | Applied: | 1449 |
|---|---|---|---|---|
| Women: | 33 | 55% | Interviewed: | 253 |
| Minorities: | 3 | 5% | Enrolled: | 60 |
| Out of State: | 6 | 10% | | |

### 2008–2009 Class Profile

| *Mean MCAT Scores* | | *Mean GPA* |
|---|---|---|
| Physical Sciences: | 10 | 3.73 |
| Biological Sciences: | 10 | |
| Verbal Reasoning: | 10 | *Mean Science* |
| | | 3.7 |

**Tuition and Fees**

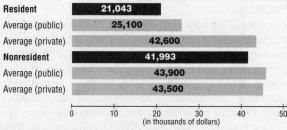

| Resident | 21,043 |
| Average (public) | 25,100 |
| Average (private) | 42,600 |
| Nonresident | 41,993 |
| Average (public) | 43,900 |
| Average (private) | 43,500 |

0   10   20   30   40   50
(in thousands of dollars)

Percentage receiving financial aid: 93%

Above data applies to 2007–2008 academic year.

## Introduction

James H. Quillen College of Medicine is situated on the main campus of East Tennessee State University and it is one of the most recent fully accredited medical schools in the country. It graduated its first class in 1982. The school provides a community-based program with an emphasis on the education of primary care physicians. Small class size is another characteristic of this school. The College of Medicine is located in a naturally beautiful environment adjacent to 3 small rural communities in East Tennessee: Johnson City, Kingsport, and Bristol.

## Admissions (AMCAS)

The basic premedical sciences plus 3 communications skills courses are required. Preference is given to residents of Tennessee. Admission is based upon a competitive selection process. Applicants are screened on the basis of academic achievement, MCAT scores, recommendations, extracurricular activities, and work experience. The school may request supplementary information and a personal interview on the VA campus from applicants they are seriously considering. *Transfer and advanced standing:* Transfer to the second or third year is possible but extremely rare.

## Curriculum

Two major curricular options are available: a Generalist Track and a Rural Primary Care Track. First- and second-year courses include: the human body, human developmental biology and genetics, psychiatry, biostatistics, epidemiology, cell and tissue biology, biochemistry, physiology, microbiology, pathology, immunology, clinical neuroscience, pharmacology, and practicing medicine. The third year of the curriculum is largely devoted to full-time clerkship experiences on the medical services of the affiliated hospitals and in physician's offices. The third year has required clerkships of 8 weeks each in internal medicine, surgery, pediatrics, obstetrics/ gynecology, psychiatry, and family medicine. The fourth year consists of a choice of 4 four-week selectives, to include an intensive care experience, an inpatient subinternship, a specialty/subspecialty subinternship, and an ambulatory care subinternship, and a minimum of 16 weeks of electives.

## Grading and Promotion Policies

Letter grades are predominant, except for clinical electives, where a Pass/Fail system is used.

## Facilities

*Teaching:* The basic science building, in the heart of Johnson City, contains all of the medical school's administration as well as many classrooms, lecture rooms, labs, and offices. Many of the basic science faculty and research labs are also housed within this facility. *Other:* The school maintains a close relationship with other teaching hospitals, which includes 2 Level I trauma centers and 1 Level II trauma center, and more than 3000 patient beds for clinical teaching. *Library:* The medical library has a seating capacity of 113 and houses more than 100,000 books and journals. *Housing:* Available on and near the campus.

## Special Features

*Minority admissions:* The school participates in a summer Premedical Enrichment Program and the Tennessee Preprofessional Program for minorities. *Other degree programs:* An integrated MD-BS program is available to ETSU students. A combined MD-PhD as well as MD-MS program are offered.

# Meharry Medical College School of Medicine

1005 D. B. Todd Jr. Boulevard
Nashville, Tennessee   37208

*Phone:* 615-327-6223          *Fax:* 615-327-6228
*E-mail:* admissions@mmc.edu
*WWW:* mmc.edu

| Application Filing | | Accreditation | |
|---|---|---|---|
| Earliest: | June 1 | LCME | |
| Latest: | December 15 | | |
| Fee: | $65 | **Degrees Granted** | |
| AMCAS: | yes | MD, MD-PhD | |

### Enrollment: 2008–2009 First-Year Class

| Men: | 48 | 48% | Applied: | 4529 |
|---|---|---|---|---|
| Women: | 52 | 52% | Interviewed: | 451 |
| Minorities: | 40 | 40% | Enrolled: | 100 |
| Out of State: | 90 | 78% | | |

### 2008–2009 Class Profile

| *Mean MCAT Scores* | | *Mean GPA* |
|---|---|---|
| Physical Sciences: | 8 | 3.5 |
| Biological Sciences: | 9 | |
| Verbal Reasoning: | 8 | *Mean Science* |
| | | 3.4 |

**Tuition and Fees**

| | |
|---|---|
| Resident | 32,336 |
| Average (public) | 25,100 |
| Average (private) | 42,600 |
| Nonresident | 32,336 |
| Average (public) | 43,900 |
| Average (private) | 43,500 |

0   10   20   30   40   50
(in thousands of dollars)

Percentage receiving financial aid: 84%

## Introduction

Established in 1876, Meharry Medical College educates about half of all African-American doctors and dentists in the United States. It was founded as the medical department of Central Tennessee College of Nashville, which later became Walden University. In 1915 a new charter was granted to the school from the state, establishing Meharry as an independent institution. Presently it includes schools of Medicine, Dentistry, Graduate Study and Research, and Allied Health. Its mission is the education of primary care physicians, for service in medically underserved areas.

## Admissions (AMCAS)

Requirements include 1 year of English in addition to the basic premedical science courses. Preference given to those students who have more than 3 years of premedical training. The selection process is based on consideration of both the cognitive and noncognitive skills of the applicant, related to their potential for success as medical students. Indicators for academic achievement are the performance in the standard premedical science courses and on the MCAT. These along with the GPA and recommendations provide a screening mechanism for extending an interview invitation. At the interview, noncognitive elements are assessed. The school accepts students from throughout the country. Special consideration is given to disadvantaged students. *Transfer and advanced standing:* Yes.

## Curriculum

4-year semitraditional. *First year:* An introduction to cell biology is followed by a progression from the cell through organ systems in the teaching of biochemistry, anatomy, and physiology. *Second year:* Includes courses in family and community health, genetics, and physical diagnosis. *Third and fourth years:* The clinical clerkships, beginning in the junior year and extending into the senior year, consist of six 8-week blocks in each of the following: internal medicine, pediatrics, surgery, obstetrics-gynecology, family and preventive medicine, and psychiatry. The fourth-year students take three 4-week blocks of surgery, Area Health Education Center, and radiology; two 4-week blocks in internal medicine; and three 4-week blocks of guided electives. The school offers students a 5-year curriculum, in which the first year of the standard curriculum is extended over a 2-year period.

## Grading and Promotion Policies

Grades of A, B, C, and F and a summary of the student's work are issued. Receiving total passing scores on Steps 1 and 2 of the USMLE is required for promotion to the third year and graduation, respectively.

## Facilities

*Teaching:* The School of Medicine is housed primarily in a building that contains basic science departments and teaching laboratories, a teaching hospital with clinical departments, and research facilities. Hubbard Hospital houses the basic and clinical sciences departments including laboratories, classrooms, an amphitheater, teaching laboratories, and other facilities. *Library:* The library contains more than 50,000 volumes and 1000 journal titles and is located in the Learning Resources Center. *Housing:* Dorothy Brown Hall houses co-ed students, and the Student-Faculty Apartment Complex contains 1- and 2-bedroom apartments.

## Special Features

*Minority admissions:* The college, which over the years has turned out nearly half of the 7000 African-American physicians graduated from American medical schools, is offering through the Kresge Learning Resources Center an opportunity for alumni and other physicians to continue their education. Several 8-week summer programs are available for undergraduates. *Other degree programs:* Combined MD-PhD programs in a variety of disciplines.

# University of Tennessee Health Science Center College of Medicine

910 Madison Avenue
Memphis, Tennessee    38163

*Phone:* 901-448-5559          *Fax:* 901-448-1740
*E-mail:* nstroter@utmem.edu
*WWW:* utmem.edu/medicine

| Application Filing | Accreditation |
|---|---|
| Earliest:  June 1 | LCME |
| Latest:  November 15 | |
| Fee:  $50 | **Degrees Granted** |
| AMCAS:  yes | MD, MD-PhD, MD-MS |

### Enrollment: 2008–2009 First-Year Class

| | | | | |
|---|---|---|---|---|
| Men: | 88 | 59% | Applied: | 1424 |
| Women: | 62 | 41% | Interviewed: | 488 |
| Minorities: | 19 | 13% | Enrolled: | 150 |
| Out of State: | 9 | 6% | | |

### 2008–2009 Class Profile

| *Mean MCAT Scores* | | *Mean GPA* |
|---|---|---|
| Physical Sciences: | 10 | 3.6 |
| Biological Sciences: | 10 | |
| Verbal Reasoning: | 10 | *Mean Science* |
| | | 3.58 |

### Tuition and Fees

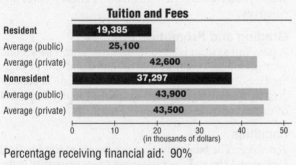

| | (in thousands of dollars) |
|---|---|
| Resident | 19,385 |
| Average (public) | 25,100 |
| Average (private) | 42,600 |
| Nonresident | 37,297 |
| Average (public) | 43,900 |
| Average (private) | 43,500 |

Percentage receiving financial aid: 90%

Above data applies to 2007–2008 academic year.

## Introduction

Established in 1851, the University of Tennessee at Memphis has a complete health science center that includes the colleges of Medicine, Graduate School of Health Sciences, Dentistry, Nursing, Pharmacy, and Allied Health Sciences. The school originated from the Medical Department of the University of Nashville, which in 1909 consolidated with the Medical Department of the University of Tennessee to form the University of Tennessee Department of Medicine. Further mergers took place with other institutions resulting in the formation of the present College of Medicine.

## Admissions (AMCAS)

The basic premedical science courses as well as courses in English composition and literature (6 credits) are required. Preference is given to state residents; very few nonresidents are accepted. A minimum of 3 years of college and taking the MCAT are required, but securing the degree is generally expected. The major selected is optional, but there should be some balance between the science and nonscience coursework. Applicants are considered from a region consisting of Tennessee and its contiguous states. Nonresidents are accepted in limited numbers (usually 10%) and most have especially attractive records. Selection is based on academic record, MCAT scores, preprofessional recommendations, and personal interviews. The latter when granted allow for in-depth evaluation of the candidate. *Transfer and advanced standing:* Students are accepted only into the third year of the curriculum. They must be residents of Tennessee at the time they enter medical school or be children of alumni, must pass the USMLE Step 1, and must have completed the biomedical science portion of the curriculum.

## Curriculum

4-year semimodern. *First and second years:* Courses are offered in prevention, community and culture, doctoring (recognizing signs and symptoms), interprofessional health practice, molecular basis of disease, physiology, gross anatomy, microbiology, pathology, pathophysiology, pharmacology, neuro-sciences. *Third year:* Consists of clerkships in family medicine, internal medicine, obstetrics and gynecology, pediatrics, psychiatry, neurology, and surgery. *Fourth year:* Ambulatory medicine, required clerkships in medicine and surgical specialties, other specialty clerkships, patient/safety quality improvement, clerkship in optional electives.

## Grading and Promotion Policies

An A to F grading policy is used. Students must achieve a 2.0 GPA for promotion, and must record total passing scores on Step 1 of the USMLE for promotion to the third year, and on Step 2 for graduation.

## Facilities

*Teaching:* The college is part of the University of Tennessee Memphis Health Science Center. Students may spend 10 of the 20 clinical months at the units in Knoxville and Chattanooga. No more than 2 months may be spent at other institutions. *Library:* The C.P.J. Mooney Memorial Library holds more than 172,000 bound volumes. *Housing:* Two on-campus dormitories are available.

## Special Features

*Minority admissions:* The school maintains a long-term program for recruiting disadvantaged students. It also sponsors 3 summer enrichment programs for undergraduate college as well as high school students. Scholarships for African-American students are available. *Other degree programs:* Combined MD-PhD programs are offered in the basic medical sciences.

# Vanderbilt University School of Medicine

21st Avenue South at Garland Avenue
Nashville, Tennessee    37232

*Phone:* 615-322-2145          *Fax:* 615-343-8397
*E-mail:* pat.sageh@vanderbilt.edu
*WWW:* mc.vanderbilt.edu/medschool/

| Application Filing | | Accreditation |
|---|---|---|
| Earliest: | June 1 | LCME |
| Latest: | November 15 | |
| Fee: | $50 | **Degrees Granted** |
| AMCAS: | yes | MD, MD-PhD |

### Enrollment: 2008–2009 First-Year Class

| | | | | |
|---|---|---|---|---|
| Men: | 54 | 51% | Applied: | 5032 |
| Women: | 51 | 49% | Interviewed: | 906 |
| Minorities: | 20 | 19% | Enrolled: | 105 |
| Out of State: | 91 | 86% | | |

### 2008–2009 Class Profile

| *Mean MCAT Scores* | | *Mean GPA* |
|---|---|---|
| Physical Sciences: | 11.7 | 3.78 |
| Biological Sciences: | 11.6 | |
| Verbal Reasoning: | 10.4 | *Mean Science* |
| | | 3.8 |

**Tuition and Fees**

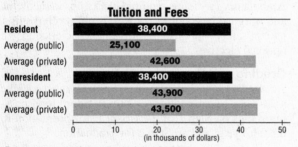

| | |
|---|---|
| **Resident** | 38,400 |
| Average (public) | 25,100 |
| Average (private) | 42,600 |
| **Nonresident** | 38,400 |
| Average (public) | 43,900 |
| Average (private) | 43,500 |

0    10    20    30    40    50
(in thousands of dollars)

Percentage receiving financial aid: 88%

## Introduction

Vanderbilt University was established in the late 1800s. The School of Medicine has been part of Vanderbilt University since it opened. This private university is located 1 1/2 miles from the business center of Nashville; it consists of 10 schools. The School of Medicine is part of the Vanderbilt University Medical Center whose affiliated hospitals provide students with an opportunity for comprehensive, diversified clinical training.

## Admissions (AMCAS)

The basic premedical science courses and 6 semester hours of English are required. Advanced Placement (CLEP) and pass/fail credits are not considered for required courses. A bachelor's degree is required/ acceptable. The present student body comes from a wide variety of states. *Transfer and advanced standing:* Only for the third year. Selection is a 2-step process. The first involves screening AMCAS applications with a focus on a candidate's educational background and potential for a medical career. Favorable individuals receive supplemental applications and an invitation for an interview, preferably on campus. Regional interviews, however, are possible.

## Curriculum

4-year semitraditional curriculum integrates clinical experiences beginning in the first year. *First year:* The molecular foundations of medicine and the structure, function, and development of the human body. Outpatient preceptorships begin, as does a 2-year research experience, pairing students and faculty members. Courses include microbiology and immunology. *Second year:* Disease diagnosis and therapeutics, brain and behavior. The physical diagnosis course utilizes a state-of-the-art center. Electives continue as does research. Patient, Profession, and Society tackles additional topics, such as mental health, health law, and health care policy. *Third year:* Four 11-week blocks of internal medicine, surgery, pediatrics, OB-GYN, and neurology and psychiatry. Each 11-week block is followed by a 1-week intersession where the basic sciences relevant to the anticipated clerkship are reviewed. *Fourth year:* Subinternships in medicine and surgery, and emergency medicine, primary care, and electives.

## Grading and Promotion Policies

A pass/fail system is used in the first year. The second year is Honors/Pass/Fail and the third and fourth years are Honors/High Pass/ Pass/Fail. Promotion is considered by a committee composed of the faculty at the end of each academic year.

## Facilities

*Teaching:* The basic sciences are taught at the Medical Center and clinical teaching takes place primarily at the Vanderbilt University Hospital, the Nashville VA Medical Center, The Vanderbilt Children's Hospital, and the Psychiatric Hospital. *Library:* The Medical Center Library contains more than 201,000 volumes.

## Special Features

*Minority admissions:* The school conducts an active recruitment program matriculating increasing numbers of minority applicants. *Other degree programs:* Combined MD-PhD degree programs are offered in the basic sciences and biomedical engineering. A number of dual degrees are available including, MD-MBA, MD-JD, MD-MPH, and MD-Divinity.

## TEXAS

# Baylor College of Medicine

One Baylor Plaza
Houston, Texas    77030

*Phone:* 713-798-4842          *Fax:* 713-798-5563
*E-mail:* admissions@bcm.edu
*WWW:* bcm.edu

| Application Filing | | Accreditation | |
| --- | --- | --- | --- |
| Earliest: | June 1 | LCME | |
| Latest: | November 1 | | |
| Fee: | $80 | **Degrees Granted** | |
| AMCAS: | no | MD, MD-PhD, | |
| | | MD-MBA | |

### Enrollment: 2008–2009 First-Year Class

| Men: | 90 | 51% | Applied: | 4879 |
| --- | --- | --- | --- | --- |
| Women: | 86 | 49% | Interviewed: | 683 |
| Minorities: | 38 | 22% | Enrolled: | 176 |
| Out of State: | 33 | 22% | | |

### 2008–2009 Class Profile

| *Mean MCAT Scores* | | *Mean GPA* |
| --- | --- | --- |
| Physical Sciences: | 12 | 3.9 |
| Biological Sciences: | 12 | |
| Verbal Reasoning: | 11 | *Mean Science* |
| | | 3.9 |

### Tuition and Fees

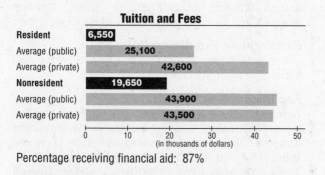

| Resident | 6,550 |
| --- | --- |
| Average (public) | 25,100 |
| Average (private) | 42,600 |
| Nonresident | 19,650 |
| Average (public) | 43,900 |
| Average (private) | 43,500 |

0    10    20    30    40    50
(in thousands of dollars)

Percentage receiving financial aid: 87%

## Introduction

Baylor College of Medicine was chartered by the state of Texas and organized in 1900 as an independent, non-sectarian institution in Dallas. In 1903 it became affiliated with Baylor University and in 1943 the school relocated to Houston and became the medical school for the newly formed Texas Medical Center. The college separated from Baylor University in 1969.

## Admissions (TMDSAS)

To be considered for admission, an applicant must have satisfactorily completed, by the time of enrollment in medical school, not less than 90 semester hours (or an equivalent number of quarter hours) at a fully accredited college in the United States. The following courses must have been completed satisfactorily: the basic premedical science courses and 1 year of English. *Transfer and advanced standing:* Admission into the first clini-cal year from fully accredited medical colleges in the U.S. is on a competitive basis, and the number admitted depends upon the availability of adequate faculty and facilities. No specific number of spaces is set aside.

## Curriculum

4-year semimodern. *First year:* Basic medical sciences, and patient, physicians, and society and integrated problem solving. *Second year:* Finish basic sciences in December; begin clinical rotations in January. *Third year:* Required rotations through clinical science disciplines; patient care in both hospital and ambulatory settings; electives; clerkships in the major and some minor specialities, as well as primary care. *Fourth year:* Required rotations through clinical science disciplines; patient care in both hospital and ambulatory settings; electives; clerkships in the major and some minor specialties, as well as primary care and management of disease.

## Grading and Promotion Policies

Grades for the basic science courses and basic science electives are recorded as Honors, Pass, Marginal Pass, and Fail; required clinical clerkships and clinical electives are recorded as Honors, High Pass, Pass, Marginal Pass, and Fail. Students may not begin clinical clerkships until they have completed all the basic science courses. Steps 1 and 2 of the USMLE is optional.

## Facilities

*Teaching:* The basic sciences are taught at the DeBakey Biomedical Research Building, which also contains auditoriums with a seating capacity of about 735. Five more buildings, the Jesse H. Jones Building for Clinical Research, the M. D. Anderson Basic Science and Research Building, the Jewish Institute for Medical Research, the Roy and Lillie Cullen Building, and the Ben Taub Research Center, provide additional space for the basic science departments. Clinical teaching and research take place in 8 general and specialized hospitals in the area. *Library:* The Jesse H. Jones Library includes an audiovisual resource center from which medical educational broadcasts are received. The library contains more than 180,000 volumes and receives a wide variety of periodicals. *Housing:* A student dormitory, belonging to the Texas Medical Center, offers accommodations for single and married students without children and is located across the street from the college. Women students can seek housing in the Nurses' Dormitory of Texas Women's University.

## Special Features

*Minority admissions:* The school has an active recruitment program for minority students. *Other degree programs:* Combined MD-PhD degree HSTP is offered in a variety of disciplines: audiology and bioacoustics, biochemistry, biotechnology, cell biology, cell and molecular biology, developmental biology, microbiology and immunology, molecular genetics, neurosciences, physiology, cardiovascular sciences, and molecular biophysics, pharmacology, virology and epidemiology. A combined MD-PhD degree in biomedical engineering is also offered with Rice University.

# Texas A&M University System Health Science Center College of Medicine

159 Joe Reynolds Medical Building
College Station, Texas    77843

*Phone:* 979-845-2634        *Fax:* 979-845-5533
*E-mail:* watkins-.orths@medicine.tamhsc.edu
*WWW:* medicine.tamhsc.edu

| Application Filing | | Accreditation | |
|---|---|---|---|
| Earliest: | May 1 | LCME | |
| Latest: | October 15 | | |
| Fee: | $45 | **Degrees Granted** | |
| AMCAS: | yes | MD, MD-PhD | |

### Enrollment: 2008–2009 First-Year Class

| Men: | 45 | 42% | Applied: | 3133 |
|---|---|---|---|---|
| Women: | 60 | 58% | Interviewed: | 727 |
| Minorities: | 4 | 4% | Enrolled: | 105 |
| Out of State: | 4 | 4% | | |

### 2008–2009 Class Profile

| *Mean MCAT Scores* | | *Mean GPA* |
|---|---|---|
| Physical Sciences: | 10 | 3.8 |
| Biological Sciences: | 10 | |
| Verbal Reasoning: | 10 | *Mean Science* |
| | | 3.8 |

**Tuition and Fees**

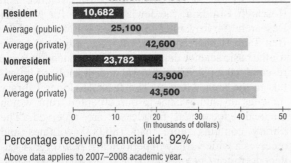

| | |
|---|---|
| Resident | 10,682 |
| Average (public) | 25,100 |
| Average (private) | 42,600 |
| Nonresident | 23,782 |
| Average (public) | 43,900 |
| Average (private) | 43,500 |

(in thousands of dollars)

Percentage receiving financial aid: 92%

Above data applies to 2007–2008 academic year.

## Introduction

Established in 1973 and enrolling its first class in 1977, the College of Medicine has evolved into The Texas A&M University System Health Science Center College of Medicine. The college is the result of the affiliation between Texas A&M University and several clinical facilities. The college is located on the university campus at College Station. The clinical campus is located in Temple, Texas.

## Admissions (TMDSAS)

The college considers individuals who have completed their undergraduate coursework at an accredited college or university. By state mandate, enrollment of individuals who are residents of states other than Texas may not exceed 10%. Most entering students have completed a baccalaureate degree before enrolling. The basic premedical sciences plus 2 courses in English and 1 in calculus are required. Students are required to take the MCAT. In the selection process, academic ability and potential is determined from the applicant's scholastic record and MCAT scores. Considerable weight is given to characteristics such as motivation, maturity, and interpersonal skills. Experiences that reveal leadership, determination, and a sense of service are of special significance. Some realistic familiarity with medicine is very desirable. Applicants with suitable credentials may be invited for a campus interview. *Transferred and advanced standing:* Dependent on the availability. Applicants must apply through the Texas Medical and Dental Schools Application Service by contacting http//dpwebldp.utexas.edu/mdac.

## Curriculum

4-year semitraditional. *First and second years:* These are spent studying the basic medical sciences. Each course includes clinical correlation experiences and small group conferences; therefore, students begin acquiring clinical skills in their first year. During the second year, students spend half a day each week for 36 weeks learning fundamental clinical skills under the supervision of practicing physician faculty members. The ethical and social aspects of medical practice receive special emphasis in the curriculum. *Third and fourth years:* These are devoted to clinical training in several different patient settings. Small clerkship groups allow for intimate clinical training experiences.

## Grading and Promotion Policies

Letter grades are used for the first 3 years and Satisfactory/Unsatisfactory for the fourth.

## Facilities

*Teaching:* The basic sciences are taught at the Joe Reynolds Medical Building located on the university campus. Clinical training is obtained at the Scott and White Hospital and Clinic (486 beds), and Olin E. Teague Veterans Center (200 beds). *Other:* Darnall Army Community Hospital (264 beds) and Driscoll Children's Hospital (188 beds). *Library:* The Medical Library has 104,000 books and subscribes to 1700 journals. The clinical campus library contains 15,000 books and receives 1600 journals. *Housing:* Medical students will find housing options in the Bryan/College Station Community. On the Temple campus, 62 one and two-bedroom apartments are subsidized by the college for medical students.

## Special Features

*Minority admissions:* Recruitment is coordinated by the School Relations Office (Admissions), and a summer research program is offered for minority high school students. *Other degree programs:* Combined MD-PhD degree programs are available.

# Texas Tech University Health Sciences Center School of Medicine

3601 4th Street
Lubbock, Texas 79430

*Phone:* 806-743-2297 *Fax:* 806-743-2725
*E-mail:* somadm@ttuhsc.edu
*WWW:* ttuhsc.edu

| Application Filing | | Accreditation | |
|---|---|---|---|
| Earliest: | May 1 | LCME | |
| Latest: | October 15 | | |
| Fee: | $50 | **Degrees Granted** | |
| AMCAS: | no | MD, MD-PhD, MD-MBA | |

### Enrollment: 2008–2009 First-Year Class

| Men: | 75 | 54% | Applied: | 2655 |
|---|---|---|---|---|
| Women: | 65 | 46% | Interviewed: | 770 |
| Minorities: | 35 | 25% | Enrolled: | 140 |
| Out of State: | 7 | 5% | | |

### 2008–2009 Class Profile

| *Mean MCAT Scores* | | *Mean GPA* |
|---|---|---|
| Physical Sciences: | 9.3 | 3.57 |
| Biological Sciences: | 10.0 | |
| Verbal Reasoning: | 9.1 | *Mean Science* |
| | | 3.48 |

### Tuition and Fees

| | |
|---|---|
| Resident | 9,762 |
| Average (public) | 25,100 |
| Average (private) | 42,600 |
| Nonresident | 22,862 |
| Average (public) | 43,900 |
| Average (private) | 43,500 |

(in thousands of dollars)

Percentage receiving financial aid: 91%

## Introduction

The School of Medicine was opened in 1972 as a multi-campus regional institution with Lubbock as the administrative center and Amarillo and Permian Basin as regional centers. The School of Medicine is one of 5 schools in the Health Sciences Center, the other 4 being schools of Nursing, Pharmacy, Allied Health, and Graduate School of Bio-Medical Sciences. The major objective of the School of Medicine is to provide quality medical education and develop programs to meet health care needs for about 100 counties of West Texas.

## Admissions (TMDSAS)

The basic premedical science courses plus 1 year of upper-level biology and English are required. Residents of Texas are given priority. Out-of-state applications are considered only if the candidate has an overall grade point average of 3.60 or higher and a composite MCAT score of 30 or higher. *Transfer and advanced standing:* Applicants who have passed the USMLE Step 1 will be considered for third-year placement when vacancies are available.

## Curriculum

*First year:* Divided into 4 interdisciplinary blocks: clinical oriented anatomy, biology of cells, structure and function of major organ systems, and host defense. Running throughout this year is a block for clinical experience. *Second year:* Features an interdisciplinary organ-based systems approach, combining microbiology, pathology, neurosciences, and clinical medicine running continually through this year. Additional early clinical experience is provided. *Third year:* Students move to the clinical arena. Each student focuses on 1 clinical discipline and rotates through the 6 standard clinical areas. Third-year students participate in a continuity clinical experience twice a month where they follow their own patients in an office setting under faculty supervision. *Fourth year:* Each of the regional campuses offer both required and elective rotations. There are a variety of required rotations, a subinternship, and elective experiences.

## Grading and Promotion Policies

The grading system is Honors/High Pass/Pass/Marginal/Fail. Students are required to take USMLE Step 1 at the end of the 2nd year. Passage is required for promotion to the 3rd year.

## Facilities

*Teaching:* Basic sciences are taught in the first two years at the Health Sciences Center in Lubbock. The clinical sciences are taught in Lubbock and at the regional centers in Amarillo and Permian Basin. *Library:* The Library contains more than 100,000 volumes and receives more than 1,600 periodicals regularly, with facilities on all teaching campuses.

## Special Features

*Minority admissions:* The institution seeks to recruit a diverse medical class, thus race and ethnicity will be among the factors considered in the admission process. A summer premedical program is offered to some qualified applicants. *Other degree programs:* Combined MD-PhD, MD-MBA, and JD/MD programs are offered.

# Paul L. Foster School of Medicine at Texas Tech University Health Science Center at El Paso

4800 Alberta Avenue
El Paso, Texas    79905

*Phone:* 915-545-6551          *Fax:* 915-545-6548
*WWW:* ttuhsc.edu

| Application Filing | | Accreditation | |
|---|---|---|---|
| Earliest: | May 1 | n/a | |
| Latest: | October 1 | **Degrees Granted** | |
| Fee: | n/a | n/a | |
| AMCAS: | yes | | |

### Enrollment: 2008–2009 First-Year Class

| Men: | n/a | Applied: | n/a |
|---|---|---|---|
| Women: | n/a | Interviewed: | n/a |
| Minorities: | n/a | Enrolled: | n/a |
| Out of State: | n/a | | |

### 2008–2009 Class Profile

| *Mean MCAT Scores* | | *Mean GPA* |
|---|---|---|
| Physical Sciences: | n/a | n/a |
| Biological Sciences: | n/a | *Mean Science* |
| Verbal Reasoning: | n/a | n/a |

### Tuition and Fees

| Resident | 11,700 |
|---|---|
| Average (public) | n/a |
| Nonresident | 18,500 |
| Average (public) | n/a |
| Average (private) | n/a |

0    10    20    30    40    50
(in thousands of dollars)

Percentage receiving financial aid: n/a
School begins in August 2009.

## Introduction

Until 2003, students from El Paso secured their basic science medical education at another facility of the Texas medical education system. In that year, a plan initiated a number of years earlier was realized and a full-fledged medical school was inaugurated. A unique feature of this medical school is the fact that students at this institution can gain exposure to relatively rare diseases, seen by only a small number of medical school students. These diseases still exist so this program will help ensure that there will be competent medical personnel capable of diagnosing and treating patients who develop such illnesses. The school will also seek to provide training opportunities to its students by providing them with exposure to a variety and diversity of patients beyond those described in the standard textbooks. The goal is to develop highly qualified physicians for both the El Paso and broader Texas communities.

## Admissions

Selection is processed by the TMDSAS system and is competitive. Factors considered are MCAT scores, academic performance, as reflected in the overall and science GPA, the intensity of the applicants' undergraduate curriculum, level of extracurricular activities, extent of medical and nonmedical work preferences, recommendations from faculty and premedical advisor, the personal statement, and evidence of leadership skills. Also taken into consideration is one's status as a disadvantageous or minority student.

## Curriculum

The school provides an integrated curriculum that replaces conventional clinical presentations with the reality of patient-physician interaction. The clinical exposure will be based on relevant groundwork in anatomy, biochemistry, and other basic sciences. This approach has been found to be a valuable teaching method that provides for (1) improvement in the comprehension of the knowledge presented, (2) retention of the information, and (3) the student's acqusition of his/her critical diagnostic reasoning skills. During the last 2 clinical years the curriculum is arranged so that students are actively learning diverse aspects of essential clinical education.

## Grading and Promotion Policies

Steps 1 and 2 of the USMLE are required. A community service requirement is obligatory.

## Facilities

The structural entities needed for research and student housing have opened up. Facilities are utilized for research in diabetes, infectious diseases, environmental health, and other subjects. The Medical Educational Building was completed at the end of 2007. It houses the library, classrooms, small-group rooms, and laboratories.

## Special Features

*Financial aid:* Once accepted, prospective students are eligible to secure assistance from the Office of Student Financial Aid. Some funds can be secured by working in the summers. *Diversity programs:* The school seeks to recruit qualified applicants who reflect the population. The socioeconomic background of applicants is one of the factors considered in the admission process.

# University of Texas Medical Branch at Galveston

301 University Boulevard
Galveston, Texas 77555

*Phone:* 409-772-6958 *Fax:* 409-747-2909
*E-mail:* tsilva@utmb.edu
*WWW:* www.som.utmb.edu

| Application Filing | | Accreditation | |
|---|---|---|---|
| Earliest: | May 1 | LCME | |
| Latest: | October 1 | | |
| Fee: | no | **Degrees Granted** | |
| AMCAS: | no | MD, MD-PhD | |

### Enrollment: 2008–2009 First-Year Class

| | | | | | |
|---|---|---|---|---|---|
| Men: | 122 | 54% | Applied: | | 3642 |
| Women: | 125 | 46% | Interviewed: | | 990 |
| Minorities: | 23 | 10% | Enrolled: | | 227 |
| Out of State: | 12 | 5% | | | |

### 2008–2009 Class Profile

| *Mean MCAT Scores* | | *Mean GPA* |
|---|---|---|
| Physical Sciences: | 11 | 3.8 |
| Biological Sciences: | 11 | |
| Verbal Reasoning: | 11 | *Mean Science* |
| | | 3.8 |

### Tuition and Fees

| | |
|---|---|
| **Resident** | 6,550 |
| Average (public) | 25,100 |
| Average (private) | 42,600 |
| **Nonresident** | 19,650 |
| Average (public) | 43,900 |
| Average (private) | 43,500 |

(in thousands of dollars)

Percentage receiving financial aid: 83%

Above data applies to 2007–2008 academic year.

## Introduction

The University of Texas Medical Branch-Galveston was established in 1891. It is a state-owned medical center and the Medical Branch has nearly 100 campus- and community-based clinics.

## Admissions (TMDSAS)

The MCAT and a minimum of 90 semester hours of college work, including 1 year of English, the basic premedical science courses, and 1 semester of calculus are required. The most significant selection factors are intellect, achievement, character, interpersonal skills, and motivation. In evaluating candidates, consideration is given to the academic record, MCAT scores, preprofessional committee evaluations, and the personal interview. Only American citizens or applicants with permanent visas are considered. Preference is given to residents of Texas.

## Curriculum

4-year semimodern. *First and second years:* The Integrated Medical Curriculum (IMC), in which 197 students are enrolled, utilizes a fully integrated basic science core followed by a multidisciplinary approach organized by organ systems. This tract emphasizes self-directed active learning, stimulated by actual clinical cases. Various educational methods are utilized including small-group, problem-based learning, formal lectures, laboratories, demonstrations, and computer-assisted education. Early community-based clinical experiences are provided. The social, cultural, and ethical issues of the medical profession and the introduction of the student to clinical medicine are addressed across the curriculum in the Practice of Medicine course in Years I and II. The final weeks of the second year are devoted to the great syndromes, which are integrated case studies of complex multi-organ problems. *Third year:* All students have to complete the standard clinical rotations plus 1 in family medicine. *Fourth year:* Required clerkships are neurology, senior surgery, emergency medicine and advanced cardiac life support, radiology, dermatology, and an acting internship selective. The remaining 20 weeks are electives and are taken at approved U.S. or international sites. Students apply to the ILT and are selected at random.

## Grading and Promotion Policies

The grading systems for the required core courses are Honors, High Pass, Pass, and Fail. For elective courses the system is Pass/Satisfactory/Fail.

## Facilities

*Teaching:* The basic sciences are taught at the Clinical Sciences Buildings. John Sealy Hospital (the principal clinical service and teaching facility), 6 other hospitals, and 2 outpatient clinics make up the Medical Branch Hospitals Complex. *Other:* Many other institutions including the Shriners Burn Institute and the Marine Biomedical Institute are available for teaching and research. *Library:* The Moody Medical Library houses about 250,000 books and subscribes to biomedical journals. *Housing:* Limited dormitory rooms are available.

## Special Features

*Minority admissions:* The school has an active recruitment program, a postbaccalaureate program, and a summer medical school familiarization program. *Other degree programs:* Combined MD-PhD programs are available in the basic sciences and medical humanities.

# University of Texas Medical School at Houston

P.O. Box 20708
Houston, Texas 77030

*Phone:* 713-500-5116 *Fax:* 713-500-0604
*E-mail:* msadmissions@uth.tmc.edu
*WWW:* http://www.med.uth.tmc.edu

| Application Filing | | Accreditation |
|---|---|---|
| Earliest: | May 1 | LCME |
| Latest: | October 1 | |
| Fee: | $55 | **Degrees Granted** |
| AMCAS: | no | MD, MD-PhD, MD-MPH |

### Enrollment: 2008–2009 First-Year Class

| | | | | |
|---|---|---|---|---|
| Men: | 137 | 60% | Applied: | 3598 |
| Women: | 93 | 40% | Interviewed: | 432 |
| Minorities: | 49 | 21% | Enrolled: | 230 |
| Out of State: | 18 | 8% | | |

### 2008–2009 Class Profile

| *Mean MCAT Scores* | | *Mean GPA* |
|---|---|---|
| Physical Sciences: | 10.3 | 3.7 |
| Biological Sciences: | 10.8 | |
| Verbal Reasoning: | 9.9 | *Mean Science* |
| | | 3.53 |

### Tuition and Fees

| | |
|---|---|
| **Resident** | 9,775 |
| Average (public) | 25,100 |
| Average (private) | 42,600 |
| **Nonresident** | 22,875 |
| Average (public) | 43,900 |
| Average (private) | 43,500 |

(in thousands of dollars)

Percentage receiving financial aid: 88%

## Introduction
This school was established in 1972. It serves as a center of education, patient care, and research. It is one of 6 schools belonging to the University of Texas Health Science Center at Houston.

## Admissions
This is processed by the Texas Medical School Application Service. The MCAT and at least 90 college credit hours are required in addition to the premedical courses. See website for details.

## Curriculum
In the first year, there is a coordinated effort to cover the basic science material using a systems-based approach. There are also many ways in which the curriculum is enhanced. These include team learning, problem-based learning, and clinical correlations. All classes use streaming video, a valuable study tool. Early patient encounters are achieved through the medical school's standardized Patient Program, one of the largest and oldest in the country. Primary care and preceptorships also assist the medical student in gaining exposure to patient care early in his/her education. The clinical years provide an extremely strong educational experience. Medical students learn from a large percentage of the more than 5½ million patient visits to the Texas Medical Center each year. The clinical rotations also provide a very interactive experience. At the end of them each medical student is well equipped to enter an internship year with confidence. During the fourth year, each student has faculty and staff support to develop an educational plan for his/her career goals. Students at UTH are very successful in gaining the residence of their choice, facilitated by a larger Graduate Medical Education program, and experienced faculty.

## Grading and Promotion Policies
The grading system used is 5 cohorts: Honors/High Pass/Pass/Marginal Performance/Fail. There is no GPA calculated, and no class rank assigned, which augments the highly supportive and collegial environment. The parameters for achievement are outlined at the beginning of each class, and a competent-based system is used for grading, not a curve-based system. USMLE Step 1 is taken at the end of the second year, with ample time for study, and USMLE Step 2 is usually taken during the senior year.

## Facilities
*Teaching:* The facilities provided at the University of Texas Medical School at Houston are state-of-the-art. There is wireless access for students throughout the campus. The Learning Resource Center houses 150 study carrels and group study rooms. The Surgical and Clinical Skills Center has 2 fully operational operating arenas, advanced training simulators, a virtual reality surgical center, and a microsurgical training center. Students have access to most of the hospitals in the Texas Medical Center for rotations and electives. The Houston Academy of Medicine/Jesse Jones Library is adjacent to the campus. Student housing consists of 2 extensive complexes.

## Special Features
There are numerous student organizations that foster the cohesive environment, including an Alliance for Diversity and Culture, specialty clubs, and elective credit courses such as Medical Spanish. There is a free tutoring program and a USMLE preparation program.

# University of Texas Medical School at San Antonio

7703 Floyd Curl Drive
San Antonio, Texas    78229

*Phone:* 210-567-6080          *Fax:* 210-567-6962
*E-mail:* medadmissions@uthscsa.edu
*WWW:* som.uthscsa.edu

| Application Filing | | Accreditation | |
|---|---|---|---|
| Earliest: | May 1 | LCME | |
| Latest: | October 1 | | |
| Fee: | $55 | **Degrees Granted** | |
| AMCAS: | no | MD | |

### Enrollment: 2008–2009 First-Year Class

| | | | | | |
|---|---|---|---|---|---|
| Men: | 111 | 50% | Applied: | 3529 | |
| Women: | 110 | 50% | Interviewed: | 1069 | |
| Minorities: | 51 | 23% | Enrolled: | 221 | |
| Out of State: | 10 | 3% | | | |

### 2008–2009 Class Profile

| *Mean MCAT Scores* | | *Mean GPA* |
|---|---|---|
| Physical Sciences: | 10 | 3.5 |
| Biological Sciences: | 10 | |
| Verbal Reasoning: | 10 | *Mean Science* |
| | | 3.46 |

### Tuition and Fees

| | |
|---|---|
| **Resident** | 11,970 |
| Average (public) | 25,100 |
| Average (private) | 42,600 |
| **Nonresident** | 27,157 |
| Average (public) | 43,900 |
| Average (private) | 43,500 |

(in thousands of dollars)

Percentage receiving financial aid: 89%

## Introduction

The University of Texas School of Medicine is part of the University of Texas Health Science Center at San Antonio, which is located within the South Texas Medical Center. The Health Science Center consists of the school of medicine, Dental School, Graduate School of Biomedical Sciences, and Nursing School. The school is located in the northwest section of the city in an area preserved to provide a rural-type setting.

## Admissions (TMDSAS)

Aside from the basic premedical science courses, 1 additional year of biology, 1 year of English, 1 semester of calculus, and 1 semester of biochemistry are required. A few nonresidents are admitted. Applicants must take the MCAT and have at least 3 years of college. Securing a broad humanities background is desirable. While strong preference is given to Texas residents, up to 10% of the entering class may come from out of state. Applicants for admission are ranked and selected on the basis of their GPA, individual components of their MCAT scores, and undergraduate school evaluation. Receiving thoughtful consideration are personal characteristics such as motivation, maturity, responsibility, and integrity. Coupled with these is the record of the candidate's achievements in extracurricular activities.

## Curriculum

4-year, semimodern. *First year:* Covers the introductory basic medical sciences in an organ system-based approach. *Second year:* The key course is pathology with other subjects such as pharmacology, pediatrics, obstetrics/gynecology, and surgery, using an organ system approach. In addition, a course in the behavioral sciences/psychiatry is offered. *Third year:* Devoted exclusively to 8 clerkship rotations of 6 weeks each in the major clinical specialties, as well as family medicine and medical and surgical subspecialties. *Fourth year:* Consists of a 2-month didactic period with the balance being devoted to electives. Some time is allotted for interviews for postgraduate training and/or vacation.

## Grading and Promotion Policies

All final grades are reported as letter grades. Any student encountering academic difficulty shall be provided an opportunity to make up deficiencies and improve performance.

## Facilities

The basic sciences are taught in the Medical School Building. Clinical teaching takes place at the University Hospital, the Brady/Green Community Health Center, the VA Hospital, and 3 other affiliated institutions. The latter includes the Santa Rosa Medical Center, Wilford Hall USAF Hospital, Brook Army Hospital, the Aerospace Medical Division of USAF, and the Baptist Memorial Hospital System. The Regional Academic Health Center, located in the Rio Grande Valley in Harlingen, Texas, is a second clinical educational campus. It is a training site for 24 third- and fourth-year students. Research laboratories are located in the Medical School Building. *Library:* The library is also located in the Medical School Building. *Housing:* Information not available.

## Special Features

*Minority admissions:* The school is very interested in the recruitment, retention, and graduation of qualified minority applicants. *Other degree programs:* None.

# University of Texas Southwestern Medical School at Dallas

5323 Harry Hines Boulevard
Dallas, Texas   75390

*Phone:* 214-648-5617          *Fax:* 214-648-3289
*E-mail:* admissions@utsouthwestern.edu
*WWW:* utsouthwestern.edu

| Application Filing | | Accreditation |
|---|---|---|
| Earliest: | May 1 | LCME |
| Latest: | October 1 | |
| Fee: | $65 | **Degrees Granted** |
| AMCAS: | no | MD, MD-PhD |

### Enrollment: 2008–2009 First-Year Class

| | | | | |
|---|---|---|---|---|
| Men: | 109 | 49% | Applied: | 3279 |
| Women: | 111 | 51% | Interviewed: | 819 |
| Minorities: | 97 | 49% | Enrolled: | 219 |
| Out of State: | 20 | 9% | | |

### 2008–2009 Class Profile

| *Mean MCAT Scores* | | *Mean GPA* |
|---|---|---|
| Physical Sciences: | 11.3 | 3.81 |
| Biological Sciences: | 11.5 | |
| Verbal Reasoning: | 10.3 | *Mean Science* |
| | | 3.77 |

### Tuition and Fees

| | |
|---|---|
| **Resident** | 12,100 |
| Average (public) | 25,100 |
| Average (private) | 42,600 |
| **Nonresident** | 25,200 |
| Average (public) | 43,900 |
| Average (private) | 43,500 |

0   10   20   30   40   50
(in thousands of dollars)

Percentage receiving financial aid: 83%

## Introduction

UT Southwestern Medical School was founded in 1943 as a part of the University of Texas Southwestern Medical Center at Dallas. Located just north of downtown Dallas, the 150-acre campus includes modern classrooms and laboratories and an extensive medical library, as well as a variety of athletic facilities. An important focus of the educational effort of UT Southwestern is training primary care physicians and preparing doctors who will practice in underserved areas of Texas, as well as those interested in careers in academic medicine and research.

## Admissions (TMDSAS)

In addition to the basic premedical science courses, an extra year of biology (or zoology), 1 semester of calculus, and 1 year of English are required. *Transfer and advanced standing:* Transfer students are accommodated only in the third year and must be currently in good standing at another LCME-accredited school.

## Curriculum

4-year semitraditional. *First year:* Medical biochemistry, biology of cells and tissues, human anatomy, medical embryology, human behavior and psychopathology, medical genetics, physiology, medical neuroscience, and immunology. *Second year:* Clinical medicine, principles and practice, immunology and medical microbiology, anatomic and clinical pathology, and medical pharmacology are integrated and covered by body systems. *Third and fourth years:* Divided into blocks and allocated to internal medicine, surgery, obstetrics/gynecology, pediatrics, neurology, family practice, and psychiatry. All instruction pertaining to these departments is given within its own block of time. About half of the fourth year is open to electives.

## Grading and Promotion Policies

Traditional letter grading system within which D and F are failing grades in years 1 through 3. Year 4 grades are Pass/Fail. Each student's performance is computed on the basis of a system of quantitative and qualitative weighting. A student incurring a failing grade may be asked by the Promotions Committee to withdraw from school, to repeat the year's work, or to remove the deficiency by some other means. Satisfactory performance on Step 1 and Step 2 of the USMLE are required prior to graduation.

## Facilities

*Teaching:* The 70-acre main campus serves as the focus of a large medical complex that includes Parkland Memorial Hospital, Children's Medical Center, University Hospitals at St. Paul, Zale Zipshy, City of Dallas Health Department, and Southwestern Institute of Forensic Sciences. *Other:* James W. Aston Ambulatory Care Center and Fred F. Florence Bioinformation Center. The 30-acre north campus has been developed providing abundant research space. It is directly connected to the south campus. Affiliated teaching facilities include Baylor University Medical Center, John Peter Smith Hospital (Fort Worth), Charlton Methodist Hospital, Presbyterian Hospital of Dallas, Timberlawn Psychiatric Hospital, University of Texas Health Science Center at Tyler, and Veterans' Administration Medical Center. *Library:* The library has a collection of 175,000 volumes and receives 2400 serials annually. *Housing:* A student apartment complex is available.

## Special Features

*Minority admissions:* The school has an active minority student recruitment program. *Other degree programs:* Combined MD-PhD programs are offered in a variety of disciplines including molecular biophysics, cell regulation, genetics and development, molecular microbiology, neuroscience, biochemistry and molecular biology and immunology. Coordinated MD-MBA, MD-MPH, and MD-MS Clinical Science programs are also available.

# University of Utah School of Medicine

30 North 1900 East
Room 1C029
Salt Lake City, Utah    84132

*Phone:* 801-581-7498          *Fax:* 801-585-2931
*E-mail:* deans.admissions@hsc.utah.edu
*WWW:* http://www.uuhsc.utah.edu/som

| Application Filing | | Accreditation |
|---|---|---|
| Earliest: | June 1 | LCME |
| Latest: | November 1 | |
| Fee: | $100 | **Degrees Granted** |
| AMCAS: | yes | MD, MD-PhD, |
| | | MD-MPH |

### Enrollment: 2008–2009 First-Year Class

| Men: | 70 | 69% | Applied: | 1270 |
|---|---|---|---|---|
| Women: | 32 | 31% | Interviewed: | 474 |
| Minorities: | 0 | 0% | Enrolled: | 102 |
| Out of State: | 27 | 26% | | |

### 2008–2009 Class Profile

| *Mean MCAT Scores* | | *Mean GPA* |
|---|---|---|
| Physical Sciences: | 9 | 3.7 |
| Biological Sciences: | 10.1 | |
| Verbal Reasoning: | 10 | *Mean Science* |
| | | 3.7 |

### Tuition and Fees

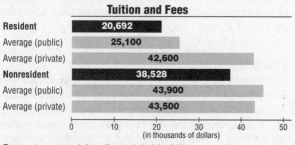

| | |
|---|---|
| **Resident** | 20,692 |
| Average (public) | 25,100 |
| Average (private) | 42,600 |
| **Nonresident** | 38,528 |
| Average (public) | 43,900 |
| Average (private) | 43,500 |

0    10    20    30    40    50
(in thousands of dollars)

Percentage receiving financial aid: 96%

Above data applies to 2007–2008 academic year.

## Introduction

The University of Utah School of Medicine is part of the University of Utah Health Sciences Center along with the University of Utah Hospital, the College of Pharmacy, the College of Nursing and Health, and the Spencer S. Eccles Health Sciences Library. The School of Medicine was originally founded as a 2-year school in 1905, and expanded to a 4-year program in 1943.

## Admissions (AMCAS)

Requirements include the basic premedical science courses. Inorganic chemistry should include work in qualitative and quantitative analysis and 1 of the biology courses should be cell biology or biochemistry, plus 1 semester of social sciences and humanities. Nonresident applicants are required to apply through the Early Decision Program. Competition for the very limited number of places available for non-WTCHE residents is very intense. The MCAT must be taken. Completing 4 years of college and receiving the baccalaureate degree is required. *Transfer and advanced standing:* This is only possible when the transferring student's spouse is a member of the medical school faculty or holds a postgraduate residency training program.

## Curriculum

4-year semitraditional. *First and second years:* These 2 years focus on establishing a strong foundation in the basic sciences. Courses are offered dealing with health-care financing and delivery, community and public health, research methadology and medical literature analysis, biostatistics, and epidemiology. There is in-depth coverage of patient evaluation skills. Problem-based learning sessions are utilized in many courses and standardized patients are employed to enhance clinical skills training. Web-based learning tools have been developed for many courses. *Third year:* Consists of clerkships in the standard major clinical areas of training. *Fourth year:* Consists of a subinternship and a neurology clerkship, as well as public health and medical ethics courses and electives in areas of the individual student's personal interest.

## Grading and Promotion Policies

Evaluation using an Honors/Pass/Fail system plus faculty narratives is utilized. Students must take and record a passing score on the USMLE Step 1 and Step 2 for matriculation into the third year and graduation, respectively.

## Facilities

*Teaching:* All preclinical instruction can be received within the Medical Center. Most of the clinical training is obtained in the University Hospital and the VA Hospital. *Other:* Five hospitals in Salt Lake City and 2 in Ogden are affiliated. *Library:* The library contains more than 100,000 volumes and 1750 current medical journal subscriptions. *Housing:* Board and room are available in residence halls for single students; there are also apartments for married students.

## Special Features

*Minority admissions:* The school has an active recruitment program and is prepared to provide financial and academic support for Native American, Mexican-American, and African-American students from economically disadvantaged communities who are likely to complete the medical curriculum successfully. *Other degree programs:* Combined MD-PhD degree programs are offered in the basic medical sciences as well as biophysics, and an MD-MPH also is available.

# VERMONT

## University of Vermont College of Medicine

89 Beaumont Avenue
Burlington, Vermont    05405

*Phone:* 802-656-2154         *Fax:* 802-656-9663
*E-mail:* medadmissions@uvm.edu
*WWW:* med.uvm.edu

| Application Filing | | Accreditation | |
|---|---|---|---|
| Earliest: | June 1 | LCME | |
| Latest: | November 1 | | |
| Fee: | $85 | **Degrees Granted** | |
| AMCAS: | yes | MD, MD-PhD | |

### Enrollment: 2008–2009 First-Year Class

| Men: | 56 | 49% | Applied: | 5772 |
|---|---|---|---|---|
| Women: | 58 | 51% | Interviewed: | 981 |
| Minorities: | 11 | 10% | Enrolled: | 114 |
| Out of State: | 67 | 59% | | |

### 2008–2009 Class Profile

| *Mean MCAT Scores* | | *Mean GPA* |
|---|---|---|
| Physical Sciences: | 10 | 3.7 |
| Biological Sciences: | 10 | |
| Verbal Reasoning: | 10 | *Mean Science* |
| | | 3.6 |

**Tuition and Fees**

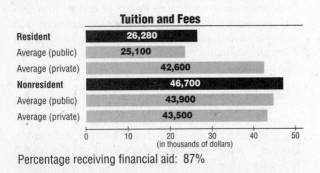

| | |
|---|---|
| Resident | 26,280 |
| Average (public) | 25,100 |
| Average (private) | 42,600 |
| Nonresident | 46,700 |
| Average (public) | 43,900 |
| Average (private) | 43,500 |

(in thousands of dollars)

Percentage receiving financial aid: 87%

## Introduction

Established in 1822, the University of Vermont College of Medicine has a long-standing approach to medical education that reinforces the centrality of the doctor-patient relationship, and the caring values of medicine. The college offers students early access to broad clinical experience, a firm grounding in the basic sciences, access to research facilities, and an emphasis on community service.

## Admissions (AMCAS)

Applicants must have completed at least 3 years of undergraduate study, but a baccalaureate degree is strongly encouraged. An applicant's undergraduate studies must include the basic premedical science courses. A course in biochemistry or molecular genetics is also recommended. Students are encouraged to secure a broad and balanced educational background. College work must demonstrate intellectual drive, independent thinking, curiosity, and self-discipline. Applicants should seek out opportunities to develop oral and written communication skills. Successful applicants often have demonstrated service to the community. Highly qualified students are accepted from Vermont, and a number of Maine applicants are offered seats through the Maine Access Program. Approximately 60% of the student body come from other states.

## Curriculum

4-year modern. *Level one:* Extending over 18 months, this segment seeks to have students develop a fundamental understanding of health and illness. *Level two:* Clinical clerkships progressively improve the skills of students through daily care of patients. The clerkships provide structured experience and didactic instruction within different medical specialties, in both ambulatory and hospital environments. Interdisciplinary sessions contribute to development of technical skills and competency in physician-patient decision-making. *Level three:* During the 15 months, the student applies prior competencies to the supervised management of patients and to the teaching of peers, patients, and more junior students.

## Grading and Promotion Policies

Students are regularly evaluated, and are required to satisfactorily pass each course and clerkship, and to fulfill the requirements of the Advanced Integration year. Comprehensive examinations are required to be taken at appropriate intervals. Students must take and pass the USMLE Step I and Step II, prior to January 1 of the year of graduation.

## Facilities

*Teaching:* There is a new medical education center and 600,000 sq. ft. of teaching and research space at Fletcher Allen, a 562-bed teaching hospital, that is the largest in the state. *Other:* Research facilities are located within the medical school complex and off campus. *Library:* Medical students use the Dana Medical Library to study in and to conduct research. *Housing:* On-campus choices include UVM's married student housing, about 4 miles from campus, and nearby apartments and residence halls. Group houses or shared apartments in walking or biking distance from school are popular off-campus choices.

## Special Features

*Minority admissions:* The College of Medicine is committed to increasing cultural diversity in the academic community. *Other degree programs:* The MD-PhD program is designed to train future physician-scientists through a curriculum that integrates clinical care with basic research.

## VIRGINIA

# Eastern Virginia Medical School

700 Woluey Road
Norfolk, Virginia   23507

*Phone:* 757-446-5812          *Fax:* 757-446-5896
*E-mail:* nanezki@evms.edu
*WWW:* http://www.evms.edu

| Application Filing | | Accreditation |
|---|---|---|
| Earliest: | June 1 | LCME |
| Latest: | November 15 | |
| Fee: | $100 | **Degrees Granted** |
| AMCAS: | yes | MD |

### Enrollment: 2008–2009 First-Year Class

| Men: | 53 | 46% | Applied: | 4895 |
|---|---|---|---|---|
| Women: | 62 | 54% | Interviewed: | 624 |
| Minorities: | 6 | 5% | Enrolled: | 115 |
| Out of State: | 37 | 32% | | |

### 2008–2009 Class Profile

| *Mean MCAT Scores* | | *Mean GPA* |
|---|---|---|
| Physical Sciences: | 10 | 3.6 |
| Biological Sciences: | 11 | |
| Verbal Reasoning: | 10 | *Mean Science* |
| | | 3.5 |

**Tuition and Fees**

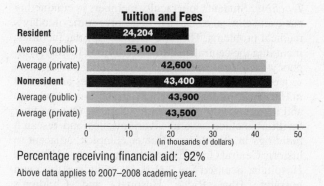

| | |
|---|---|
| Resident | 24,204 |
| Average (public) | 25,100 |
| Average (private) | 42,600 |
| Nonresident | 43,400 |
| Average (public) | 43,900 |
| Average (private) | 43,500 |

(in thousands of dollars)

Percentage receiving financial aid: 92%

Above data applies to 2007–2008 academic year.

## Introduction

The Eastern Virginia Medical School's purpose was to provide the Hampton Roads community with health care and offer students a quality medical education; consequently, major focus has been on the training of potential primary care physicians. This goal is achieved by the school's affiliations with more than 35 community-based health care facilities in the area. The school's mission has been enhanced by a series of innovative programs established through the Center for Generalist Medicine.

## Admissions (AMCAS)

Applicants must have a minimum of 100 semester hours from an accredited American or Canadian college or university, which must include the basic premedical science courses. Applicants are expected to have grades of C or better in all required courses. Credits earned in advanced placement programs or CLEP are acceptable. No application will be considered complete without scores of the MCAT taken within 2 years prior to application. *Transfer and advanced standing:* Transfer students for second and third years are considered. Applicant must be currently enrolled in an LCME-approved medical school. Applicants are considered to fill any places vacated by attrition.

## Curriculum

4-year semimodern. *Years 1 and 2:* The basic sciences are presented as a basis for the practice of medicine. Small-group, problem-based sessions with basic and clinical scientists as facilitators are utilized. Students receive introductory education in clinical and interpersonal skills and attend preceptorships with a physician in private practice. *Years 3 and 4:* Students rotate through clinical clerkships in family medicine, internal medicine, obstetrics and gynecology, pediatrics, psychiatry, and surgery, and through selectives designed to meet special interests and career goals. A significant portion of the clinical clerkships are devoted to ambulatory care, but as expected, the major portion is associated with inpatient care. In addition to the standard required clerkships, there are rotations in surgical subspecialties, geriatrics, and substance abuse. For students planning generalist careers, opportunities are available for taking electives in rural health care and an honors tract. Electives may occupy up to 6 months and provide a significant opportunity for subspecialty and/or research experience.

## Grading and Promotion Policies

Students are promoted on the basis of their ability to complete required objectives satisfactorily, with achievement being designated as Honors, High Pass, Pass, Fail, or Incomplete.

## Facilities

*Teaching:* The school's primary teaching and research facilities are housed in buildings that are part of the 33-acre Eastern Virginia Medical Center. Clinical experience is provided through affiliation with 29 medical health care facilities located within Hampton Roads. *Other:* Research facilities are located in Lewis Hall, Hofheimer Hall, and South Campus. *Library:* The library has a large collection of books and receives a wide range of serial periodicals. *Housing:* Limited college-owned housing is available for students.

## Special Features

*Minority admissions:* Educationally disadvantaged students are encouraged to apply and scholarships are available. *Special programs:* No combined programs are currently available.

# University of Virginia School of Medicine

P.O. Box 800725
Charlottesville, Virginia   22908

*Phone:* 434-924-5571        *Fax:* 434-982-2586
*E-mail:* bab7g@virginia.edu
*WWW:* http://www.med.virginia.edu/home.html

| Application Filing | | Accreditation |
|---|---|---|
| Earliest: | June 1 | LCME |
| Latest: | November 1 | |
| Fee: | $75 | **Degrees Granted** |
| AMCAS: | yes | MD, MD-PhD |

### Enrollment: 2008–2009 First-Year Class

| Men: | 76 | 55% | Applied: | 4302 |
|---|---|---|---|---|
| Women: | 66 | 45% | Interviewed: | 548 |
| Minorities: | 27 | 19% | Enrolled: | 145 |
| Out of State: | 65 | 45% | | |

### 2008–2009 Class Profile

| *Mean MCAT Scores* | | *Mean GPA* |
|---|---|---|
| Physical Sciences: | 11.55 | 3.73 |
| Biological Sciences: | 11.26 | |
| Verbal Reasoning: | 10.59 | *Mean Science* |
| | | 3.7 |

**Tuition and Fees**

| | (in thousands of dollars) |
|---|---|
| Resident | 32,650 |
| Average (public) | 25,100 |
| Average (private) | 42,600 |
| Nonresident | 42,650 |
| Average (public) | 43,900 |
| Average (private) | 43,500 |

0   10   20   30   40   50
(in thousands of dollars)

Percentage receiving financial aid: 85%

## Introduction

Thomas Jefferson established the University of Virginia in 1819. As one of the 8 original schools, the School of Medicine was established in 1900 with a full 4-year instructional plan. The School of Medicine and the University of Virginia Hospital are both located on the same campus in Charlottesville. Its location is within driving distance of Richmond and Washington, D.C. The university ranks high in published surveys.

## Admissions (AMCAS)

The basic premedical science courses are required. Preference is given to residents. A minimum 3 years of college is required, as is taking the MCAT. Choice of a major is optional but gaining a broad educational background is encouraged. Selection is determined by evaluation of academic performance, extracurricular volunteer and work experience, letters of recommendation, and interview performance. Interviews are granted by invitation only and take place only on campus. *Transfer and advanced standing:* State residents receive preference for transfer into the third year if any vacancies exist.

## Curriculum

4-year modern. The curriculum is divided into 4 major components. *Basic sciences:* (18 months) Provides a basic knowledge, both psychological and physical, of the structure of the normal and diseased human. *Clinical clerkships:* (11 months) Provides a learning experience by direct contact with patients. *Electives:* (8 months) Offers clinical rotations, graduate courses, or research activities.

## Grading and Promotion Policies

A Pass/Fail grading system is used except in the third year. Students who have satisfactorily completed all the work of the session are eligible for promotion. Those who have incurred deficiencies that can be reasonably removed by the opening of the next session may be provisionally promoted. Students with serious deficiencies may be required to repeat the session's work. Students who are not considered competent to continue training in medicine may be required to withdraw. Students must record a passing total score on USMLE Step 1 and Step 2 to graduate.

## Facilities

*Teaching:* Students join faculty members in conducting basic and clinical research to help solve some of today's medical problems. They are aided by special facilities, including the central electron microscope facility, lymphocyte culture center, and protein and nucleic acid sequencing center. Many of these facilities are located in Harvey E. Jordan Hall, which also houses classrooms and laboratories for the 5 basic sciences. *Other:* Other facilities include several vivarium sites and research buildings in the Medical Center complex, adjacent to historic Central Grounds, and the University of Virginia Hospitals, licensed for 900 beds, including the main hospital, Blue Ridge Hospital, and Children's Rehabilitation Center. Students also receive clinical training at other hospitals in Virginia. *Library:* The Claude Moore Health Sciences Library contains 140,000 volumes and receives approximately 3000 publications. *Housing:* Limited housing is available for married students who may or may not have children.

## Special Features

*Minority admissions:* The school has an active recruitment program. It also offers a Summer Enrichment Program for senior college students and graduates and applicants who have been accepted for admission. *Other degree programs:* Combined MD-PhD degree programs are offered in the basic sciences and jointly with other departments of the Graduate School or School of Engineering.

# Virginia Commonwealth University School of Medicine

P.O. Box 980565
Richmond, Virginia 23298

*Phone:* 804-828-9629 *Fax:* 804-828-1246
*E-mail:* somadm@hsc.vcu.edu
*WWW:* medschool.vcu.edu

## Application Filing
Earliest: June 1
Latest: October 15
Fee: $80
AMCAS: yes

## Accreditation
LCME

## Degrees Granted
MD, MD-PhD,
MD-MPH, MD-MHA

### Enrollment: 2008–2009 First-Year Class

| | | | | | |
|---|---|---|---|---|---|
| Men: | 104 | 52% | Applied: | 6154 |
| Women: | 88 | 48% | Interviewed: | 856 |
| Minorities: | 12 | 6.25% | Enrolled: | 192 |
| Out of State: | 81 | 43% | | |

### 2008–2009 Class Profile

| *Mean MCAT Scores* | | *Mean GPA* |
|---|---|---|
| Physical Sciences: | 10 | 3.6 |
| Biological Sciences: | 10 | |
| Verbal Reasoning: | 9.7 | *Mean Science* |
| | | 3.5 |

### Tuition and Fees

| | |
|---|---|
| **Resident** | 25,644 |
| Average (public) | 21,500 |
| Average (private) | 42,600 |
| **Nonresident** | 39,281 |
| Average (public) | 43,900 |
| Average (private) | 43,500 |

(in thousands of dollars) 0 10 20 30 40 50

Percentage receiving financial aid: 89%

## Introduction

This school originated when Hampden-Sydney College created a medical department in Richmond in 1837, which in 1854 became the Medical College of Virginia. In 1893 the College of Physicians and Surgeons was established, which consolidated with Medical College of Virginia in 1913.

## Admissions (AMCAS)

Requirements include the basic premedical science courses, 1 year of mathematics, and 1 year of English. Preference is given to those with baccalaureate degrees; residents preferred. *Transfer and advanced standing:* Transfer students are considered only into the third year when vacancies occur. Residents are given preference.

## Curriculum

4-year semimodern. *First and second years:* The basic sciences are covered in the first 2 years. The body is divided into organ systems to permit integration of the basic science disciplines with one another and with clinical medicine. Ethics are also taught during this period. *Third year:* This year is devoted to rotation through the major clinical specialties, also including community practice and neurology. *Fourth year:* Consists of 4-week periods for an acting internship, a family practice acting internship, and urgent care. A 3-week update course in clinical science is offered at the end of the year. The balance of the year consists of 4-week rotations in various electives.

## Grading and Promotion Policies

Grades of Honors/High Pass/Pass Marginal/Fail are determined by the faculty. Passing Steps 1 and 2 of the USMLE is required for graduation.

## Facilities

*Teaching:* Classrooms and laboratories for the basic medical sciences are in Sanger Hall, the Medical Sciences Building, and the Egyptian Building. Clinical teaching is done at the Medical Center, which consists of the West, Main, North, and Critical Care hospitals, at the A.D. Williams Memorial Clinic, and at the VA Hospital. *Other:* Students in their third year spend a month in 1 of 5 community hospitals. *Library:* The comprehensive collections of Tompkins-McCaw Library support study and research needs. *Housing:* Cabaniss Hall, a 432-bed dormitory, and 4 residence halls provide for student housing needs.

## Special Features

*Minority admissions:* The Director of the Student Outreach and the Director of the Diversity Access Program are actively involved in recruitment of minority students. The college also offers a Preadmissions Study Skills Workshop. *Other degree programs:* Combined MD-PhD programs are available in a variety of disciplines including biometry, biophysics, and genetics. The school also offers coordinated MD-MPH, MD-MHA, and MD-MS degree programs.

## WASHINGTON

# University of Washington School of Medicine

Seattle, Washington    98195

*Phone:* 206-543-7212          *Fax:* 206-616-3341
*E-mail:* askuwsom@u.washington.edu
*WWW:* uw.medicine.org/education/mdprogram/

| Application Filing | | Accreditation | |
|---|---|---|---|
| Earliest: | June 1 | LCME | |
| Latest: | November 3 | | |
| Fee: | $35 | **Degrees Granted** | |
| AMCAS: | yes | MD, MD-PhD | |

### Enrollment: 2008–2009 First-Year Class

| Men: | 89 | 47% | Applied: | 4598 |
|---|---|---|---|---|
| Women: | 102 | 53% | Interviewed: | 838 |
| Minorities: | 2 | 1% | Enrolled: | 191 |
| Out of State: | 16 | 8% | | |

### 2008–2009 Class Profile

| *Mean MCAT Scores* | | *Mean GPA* |
|---|---|---|
| Physical Sciences: | 11 | 3.7 |
| Biological Sciences: | 11 | |
| Verbal Reasoning: | 10 | *Mean Science* |
| | | 3.7 |

**Tuition and Fees**

| | |
|---|---|
| **Resident** | 17,425 |
| Average (public) | 25,100 |
| Average (private) | 42,600 |
| **Nonresident** | 41,429 |
| Average (public) | 43,900 |
| Average (private) | 43,500 |

0    10    20    30    40    50
(in thousands of dollars)

Percentage receiving financial aid: 90%

Above data applies to 2007–2008 academic year.

## Introduction

As the only medical school that directly provides educational service to Washington, Wyoming, Alaska, Montana, and Idaho (WWAMI), the University of Washington School of Medicine was established in 1945. In 1971 the School of Medicine instituted a program to provide a decentralized medical education and a variety of educational opportunities. Through the WWAMI program, basic science education and clinical training is offered in sites throughout the 5 states.

## Admissions (AMCAS)

The basic premedical science courses and proficiency in mathematics and English are required. Preference is given to legal residents of the states of Washington, Wyoming, Alaska, Montana, and Idaho (WWAMI Program). In addition, basic knowledge of biochemistry/molecular biology concepts is recommended. Applicants who are being seriously considered will be asked to file supplementary information, which includes appropriate recommendations, as well as meeting other technical requirements, namely, confirmation of likelihood of graduation and authorization for a background check. Selection for admission is determined on the basis of prior undergraduate work and on the MCAT, which the applicant must take. This is supplemented by such information as the candidate's motivation, maturity, work experience, evidence of public service, and research experience. *Transfer and advanced standing:* None.

## Curriculum

4-year modern. *First year:* The introductory basic sciences are taught in relation to their clinical relevance. Courses in epidemiology, psychology, and molecular and cellular biology are offered as well as an introduction to clinical medicine course. *Second year:* The advanced basic sciences are taught within a systems context. In addition, courses are offered in genetics, hematology, and health care systems. *Third and fourth years:* Students select from a variety of elective clerkships after completing the prescribed clerkships. Additional requirements during these years are: neurology, surgical subspecialties, rehabilitation medicine, emergency medicine, and an elective clinical clerkship. There is also an Independent Investigative Inquiry requirement. The WWAMI program provides for decentralized medical education; therefore, students at this school may receive a portion of their training at sites away from the University of Washington campus. This arrangement is a component of the agreement to participate in the WWAMI program.

## Grading and Promotion Policies

A system of Pass/Fail is used the first year, Honors, Pass, Fail in the second year, and Honors, High Pass, Pass, and Fail during the clinical years.

## Facilities

*Teaching:* Clinical teaching programs are conducted in the Health Sciences Building and in the University Hospital. *Other:* Other affiliated hospitals in the city and throughout the Pacific Northwest provide opportunities for clinical training. *Library:* A comprehensive medical library is available for students and staff. *Housing:* Information not available.

## Special Features

*Minority admissions:* No students are admitted to the medical school on a preferential basis, but the school is interested in considering as many qualified applicants as it can from minority groups regardless of residence. *Other degree programs:* Combined MD-PhD programs are available in the basic sciences.

## WEST VIRGINIA

# Marshall University Joan Edwards School of Medicine

1600 Medical Center Drive
Huntington, West Virginia   25701

*Phone:* 304-691-1738      *Fax:* 304-691-1744
*E-mail:* warren@marshall.edu
*WWW:* musom.marshall.edu/

| Application Filing | | Accreditation |
|---|---|---|
| Earliest: | June 1 | LCME |
| Latest: | November 15 | |
| Fee: | $50 Resident, $100 NR | **Degrees Granted** |
| AMCAS: | yes | MD, MD-PhD, MD-MS |

### Enrollment: 2008–2009 First-Year Class

| Men: | 35 | 45% | Applied: | 1316 |
|---|---|---|---|---|
| Women: | 43 | 55% | Interviewed: | 250 |
| Minorities: | 21 | 27% | Enrolled: | 78 |
| Out of State: | 17 | 22% | | |

### 2008–2009 Class Profile

| *Mean MCAT Scores* | | *Mean GPA* |
|---|---|---|
| Physical Sciences: | 8.5 | 3.5 |
| Biological Sciences: | 9.4 | |
| Verbal Reasoning: | 9.0 | *Mean Science* |
| | | 3.4 |

### Tuition and Fees

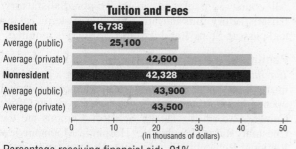

| Resident | 16,738 |
| Average (public) | 25,100 |
| Average (private) | 42,600 |
| Nonresident | 42,328 |
| Average (public) | 43,900 |
| Average (private) | 43,500 |

(in thousands of dollars)

Percentage receiving financial aid: 91%

## Introduction

Marshall University was founded in 1837, but the School of Medicine was not established until 1978. The Marshall University Joan C. Edwards School of Medicine was established under the Veteran's Administration Medical School Assistance and Health Training Act. The school offers a community-based program with emphasis on the education of primary care physicians.

## Admissions (AMCAS)

The basic premedical science courses, English composition and rhetoric, and social or behavioral sciences are required. Preference is given to state residents. Some positions may be available to well-qualified nonresidents from states contiguous to West Virginia or to nonresidents who have strong ties to West Virginia. Other nonresidents are not considered. Regardless of their state of residency, applicants are considered only if they are U.S. citizens or have permanent visas. Evaluation of candidates for admission involves a review of a candidate's academic records and test scores, although this by itself is not decisive. An insight into the applicant's character is sought by review of letters of recommendation and an assessment at an interview. Features of interest to the Admission Committee are motivation, integrity, sensitivity, and judgment. *Transfer and advanced standing:* The School of Medicine considers for transfer admissions those applicants who are currently in good standing at an allopathic medical school. Positions are limited by attrition and are rarely available. The residency policy for regular admissions also applies to transfer admissions with one exception—only U.S. citizens are considered.

## Curriculum

4-year semitraditional. Students integrate basic science information with clinical medicine the first 2 years. *First year:* Consists of the traditional foundational disciplines of medicine. *Second year:* Consists of an integrated Systems Curriculum, made up of blocks: Core Principals, Infectious Agents and Antimicrobials, Neoplasia and Hematology, and Dermatology, Toxicology, and Eye. Throughout both years students have direct patient contact. During both years students learn the fundamental principles of patient care, including the skills of history taking and the physical exam. *Third and fourth years:* Students rotate through clerkships at participating community hospitals and other locations in the clinical fields of medicine, surgery, pediatrics, psychiatry, family practice, obstetrics-gynecology, and emergency medicine. Two months of rural health care at approved sites are required of all students. Twenty-three weeks are devoted to electives in the senior year.

## Grading and Promotion Policies

A letter grading system (A, B, C, F) is utilized. **USMLE Step 1:** Required. Students must record a passing score for promotion. **Step 2:** Clinical Skills (CS): Required. Students must record a passing score to graduate. **Step 2:** Clinical knowledge (CK): Required. Students must record a passing total score to graduate.

## Facilities

*Teaching:* The school is affiliated with the Cabell Huntington Hospital (363 beds), St. Mary's Hospital (440 beds), VA Medical Center, and hospitals and clinics in other communities. A new comprehensive cancer center, a classroom research facility and education/outpatient facility recently opened. *Library:* The medical library collection is available to students as well as faculty and is constantly expanding its holdings. *Housing:* Housing is available in university dormitories and in furnished family dwelling units.

## Special Features

*Minority admissions:* No special recruitment program is available. *Other degree programs:* MD-MS and MD-PhD programs are available.

# West Virginia University School of Medicine

P.O. Box 9111
Morgantown, West Virginia 26506

*Phone:* 304-293-2408 *Fax:* 304-293-7814
*E-mail:* medadmissions@hsc.wvu.edu
*WWW:* hsc.wvu.edu/som

| Application Filing | | Accreditation |
|---|---|---|
| Earliest: | June 1 | LCME |
| Latest: | November 1 | |
| Fee: | $100 | **Degrees Granted** |
| AMCAS: | yes | MD, MD-PhD |

### Enrollment: 2008–2009 First-Year Class

| | | | | |
|---|---|---|---|---|
| Men: | 55 | 51% | Applied: | 2881 |
| Women: | 53 | 49% | Interviewed: | 356 |
| Minorities: | 3 | 3% | Enrolled: | 108 |
| Out of State: | 47 | 44% | | |

### 2008–2009 Class Profile

| *Mean MCAT Scores* | | *Mean GPA* |
|---|---|---|
| Physical Sciences: | 10 | 3.8 |
| Biological Sciences: | 10 | |
| Verbal Reasoning: | 10 | *Mean Science* |
| | | 3.7 |

**Tuition and Fees**

| | |
|---|---|
| Resident | 19,204 |
| Average (public) | 25,100 |
| Average (private) | 42,600 |
| Nonresident | 41,866 |
| Average (public) | 43,900 |
| Average (private) | 43,500 |

(in thousands of dollars)

Percentage receiving financial aid: 93%

Above data applies to 2007–2008 academic year.

## Introduction

The West Virginia School of Medicine first opened in 1902, but did not begin to provide a 4-year program until 1960 when the University Hospital opened. The school became known as the West Virginia University Health Sciences Center, Charleston Division, in 1972 when the Charleston Area Medical Center joined the university. In 1974 the Wheeling Division of the Health Sciences Center was established. It is currently known as the Robert C. Byrd Sciences Center of West Virginia University. Beside the School of Medicine, the Center contains schools of Dentistry, Nursing, and Pharmacy.

## Admissions

Requirements include the basic premedical science courses and 1 year each of English and of behavioral or social sciences. Courses in biochemistry and molecular biology are very desirable. Computer literacy is required. Minimum of 90 hours of college work is required at a grade of C or higher from an accredited U.S. or Canadian school. *Transfer and advanced standing:* Transfer applications for admission to the third-year class are accepted.

## Curriculum

4-year semitraditional. *First and second years:* Introductory and advanced basic sciences. Student is introduced to community medicine and clinical medicine, including the foundations for histories and physicals. The first-year basic science courses are integrated, and have common test methods and problem-based learning clinical applications. *Third year:* The traditional clerkships, including neurology and family medicine. *Fourth year:* This year is partially structured and partially elective. Five months are devoted to a required rotation, 2 months involve rural primary care, 1 month in critical care/anesthesia, 1 month in surgery or a surgical subspecialty, and 1 month in internal medicine, family medicine, or a pediatric subinternship. The balance of the program is elective. Each student, in consultation with an advisor, develops the program best suited to attain his or her goals. The Office of Student Services has a list of approved electives. Third- and fourth-year experiences are primarily based in Ruby Memorial Hospital or Eastern Charleston Division, with some approved rotations at other institutions. During the third and fourth years, students spend a minimum total of 3 months in rural clinic locations.

## Grading and Promotion Policies

All courses are graded on an Honors/Satisfactory/ Unsatisfactory plus narrative grading system. Taking and passing Steps 1 and 2 of the USMLE is required.

## Facilities

*Teaching:* The Health Sciences Building opened for instructional purposes in 1957. Ruby Memorial Hospital opened in 1988; adjoining is the new Physician Office Center. Also on the Health Sciences Campus are the Chestnut Ridge Psychiatric Hospital, Mountainview Regional Rehabilitation Hospital, an outpatient center, and a cancer center. *Library:* The Health Sciences Center Library has more than 265,000 bound volumes and 60,000 monograph titles, and receives 2227 journals. The Library and Health Sciences Center provide free internet access to National Library of Medicine data bases for affiliated students, faculty, and staff. Special services are offered to support medical students on rural rotations. *Housing:* A new addition was completed in early 2007.

## Special Features

*Minority admissions:* The school has a minority recruitment program and offers a 1-month summer enrichment program. *Other degree programs:* Combined MD-PhD programs are offered in the basic medical sciences and other disciplines.

# WISCONSIN

## Medical College of Wisconsin

8701 Watertown Plank Road
Milwaukee, Wisconsin 53226

*Phone:* 414-456-8246          *Fax:* 414-456-6506
*E-mail:* mcwms@mcw.edu
*WWW:* mcw.edu/acad/admission

| Application Filing | | Accreditation | |
|---|---|---|---|
| Earliest: | June 1 | LCME | |
| Latest: | November 1 | | |
| Fee: | $70 | **Degrees Granted** | |
| AMCAS: | yes | MD, MD-PhD | |

### Enrollment: 2008–2009 First-Year Class

| Men: | 116 | 55% | Applied: | 6429 |
|---|---|---|---|---|
| Women: | 96 | 45% | Interviewed: | 643 |
| Minorities: | 23 | 11% | Enrolled: | 212 |
| Out of State: | 138 | 65% | | |

### 2008–2009 Class Profile

| *Mean MCAT Scores* | | *Mean GPA* |
|---|---|---|
| Physical Sciences: | 10.0 | 3.72 |
| Biological Sciences: | 10.0 | |
| Verbal Reasoning: | 10.0 | *Mean Science* |
| | | 3.65 |

### Tuition and Fees

| | |
|---|---|
| **Resident** | 38,940 |
| Average (public) | 25,100 |
| Average (private) | 42,600 |
| **Nonresident** | 38,940 |
| Average (public) | 43,900 |
| Average (private) | 43,500 |

(in thousands of dollars) — scale 0 to 50

Percentage receiving financial aid: 84%

## Introduction

The Medical College of Wisconsin, originally part of Marquette University, was founded in the 1890s. It is the educational division of the Milwaukee Regional Medical Center, which also contains 6 other health care institutions. The college relocated its educational facilities in 1978, from downtown Milwaukee to the Medical Center campus in the west suburban section of the city.

## Admissions (AMCAS)

Required courses include the basic premedical science courses plus a 1-year course in English and in algebra (if not taken in high school). Applicants are evaluated on the basis of their college record and MCAT scores, as well as subjective elements such as their recommendations, personal statement, activities, and interview. The personal statement is given considerable weight. A significant number of nonresidents are accepted.

*Transfer:* May be considered based on space availability.

## Curriculum

*4-year semitraditional. First and second years:* Basic medical sciences, in addition to a new course that provides first- and second-year students with integrated early generalist experiences, the foundation skills and attitudes of professional development, and knowledge in the following disciplines: human behavior, bioethics and care of the terminally ill, information management, physical diagnosis, and health care systems. *Third and fourth years:* This time is devoted to rotating clerkships in major and some minor specialties. Six months of electives, including study at another school, are offered during senior year. This school offers a five-year program and an Extended Curriculum Option for students needing more time to complete the requirement for the MD degree. In the five-year program, the standard first-year coursework is expanded over a 2-year interval. In the Extended Curriculum Option the choice is given to expand the first or the second year. The third clinical clerkship year and fourth elective course year must be completed over the usual time. Full tuition and fees are charged during the first four years of the program and reduced tuition and fees are charged in the fifth year. The Extended Curriculum Option was designed for students who wish to expand either of the first 2 years for nonacademic reasons. This may include a commitment to an ongoing research project or to help meet the demands of family life. Special permission needs to be granted in order to participate in either of these programs.

## Grading and Promotion Policies

A 5.0 grading system (Honors/High Pass/Pass/Low Pass/Fail) is used. Students must take Step 1 of the USMLE and record a passing total score for promotion to the fourth year. Step 2 must be taken and a score reported.

## Facilities

*Teaching:* Clinical instruction takes place at 4 major hospitals: Froedtert Hospital, VA Hospital, Children's Hospital of Wisconsin, and Milwaukee Psychiatric Hospital. *Library:* A comprehensive medical library is available for student and staff use. *Housing:* On-campus housing is not offered.

## Special Features

*Minority admissions:* The school encourages students belonging to underrepresented groups to apply. The Admissions Committee, in addition to considering the applicant's credentials, evaluates motivation and cultural and educational background. The Office of Academic Affairs/Diversity offers various programs to assist such students. *Other degree programs:* The school has combined MD-PhD programs in the basic medical sciences, including biophysics. MS programs in biostatistics and epidemiology, as well as an MA in bioethics are also offered.

# University of Wisconsin— Madison School of Medicine and Public Health

750 Highland Avenue
Madison, Wisconsin 53705

*Phone:* 608-263-4925 *Fax:* 608-262-4226
*E-mail:* jyshepard@wisc.edu
*WWW:* med.wisc.edu

| Application Filing | | Accreditation | |
|---|---|---|---|
| Earliest: | June 1 | LCME | |
| Latest: | November 1 | | |
| Fee: | $56 | **Degrees Granted** | |
| AMCAS: | yes | MD, MD-PhD, | |
| | | MD-MPH | |

### Enrollment: 2008–2009 First-Year Class

| | | | | | |
|---|---|---|---|---|---|
| Men: | 76 | 47% | Applied: | 3264 | |
| Women: | 87 | 53% | Interviewed: | 450 | |
| Minorities: | 18 | 11% | Enrolled: | 163 | |
| Out of State: | 38 | 23% | | | |

### 2008–2009 Class Profile

| *Mean MCAT Scores* | | *Mean GPA* |
|---|---|---|
| Physical Sciences: | 10.3 | 3.7 |
| Biological Sciences: | 11.1 | |
| Verbal Reasoning: | 10 | *Mean Science* |
| | | 3.7 |

**Tuition and Fees**

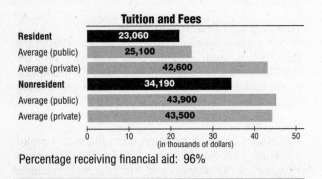

| | |
|---|---|
| Resident | 23,060 |
| Average (public) | 25,100 |
| Average (private) | 42,600 |
| Nonresident | 34,190 |
| Average (public) | 43,900 |
| Average (private) | 43,500 |

0 10 20 30 40 50
(in thousands of dollars)

Percentage receiving financial aid: 96%

## Introduction

The University of Wisconsin School of Medicine and Public Health has had a 4-year program in medicine since 1925 and has the largest research commitment of any school or college on campus, receiving substantial extramural research support. National surveys consistently rank UW Hospital and Clinics among the finest academic medical centers in the United States.

## Admissions (AMCAS)

Admission requires having a bachelor's degree prior to entering the program, except for outstanding students. The degree may be earned in any discipline. Courses that meet the premedical science prerequisites, must be the same as those required of science majors and must be 1 academic year in length. Entering students must also have 1 semester each of advanced biology, organic chemistry, biochemistry, mathematics (calculus is recommended), and statistics. Few nonresidents are accepted. A variety of factors are considered in the admission process. *Transfer and advanced standing:* Very few transfers are accepted into the third-year class.

## Curriculum

*First year:* Courses are organized into 2 semesters, each containing 3 blocks. The block structure is comprised of regular cycles of teaching and learning experiences, followed by an integrated week of review, assessment, integration activities, and independent study. Topics best related to one another are presented in the same semester. *Second year:* Continuing with the integrated block system, students focus on the pathophysiology of systems, pharmacology, and neoplasia. *Third year:* Students rotate through clinical clerkships in a variety of settings. *Fourth year:* In addition to clinical electives in a specialty area, students participate in a subinternship in internal medicine, electives in a surgical area, and a preceptorship. Students choose elective courses throughout the 4-year program.

## Grading and Promotion Policies

First-year students are graded on a Pass/Fail system. Second- and third-year students are given letter grades. Students must obtain a passing total score on Step 1 of the USMLE for promotion to the third year and on Step 2 for graduation.

## Facilities

*Teaching:* The school's Health Science Learning Center features advanced instructional technologies in its lecture halls, classrooms, clinical training, assessment areas, and computing labs. The student body is divided into 5 learning communities, allowing for individual and small-group problem solving. Students gain valuable experience on-site at the UW Hospital and Clinics, and throughout our statewide campus. *Library:* The Ebling Library is conveniently located in the Learning Center, and features group study rooms, scanner usage, wireless network capability, and 32 research workstations. The library can provide electronic access to virtually any type of medical publication, and has developed an extensive video library. *Housing:* A variety of student housing options are available, for single and married students.

## Special Features

*Minority admissions:* The school is committed to increasing the number of physicians from groups underrepresented in medicine. *Other degree programs:* These are the Wisconsin Academy for Rural Medicine (WARM) and the Medical Scientist Training Program (MSTP), which offers a joint MD/PhD program.

# CANADA

# Dalhousie University
# Faculty of Medicine

Halifax, Nova Scotia, Canada    B3H 4H7

*Phone:* 902-494-1874        *Fax:* 902-494-6369
*E-mail:* medicine.admissions@dal.ca
*WWW:* medicine.dal.ca/

| Application Filing | | Accreditation | |
|---|---|---|---|
| Earliest: | September 1 | LCME, CACMS | |
| Latest: | October 31 | | |
| Fee: | n/av | **Degrees Granted** | |
| AMCAS: | no | MD, MD-PhD | |

### Enrollment: 2008–2009 First-Year Class

| | | | | | |
|---|---|---|---|---|---|
| Men: | 32 | 36% | Applied: | 295 | |
| Women: | 58 | 64% | Interviewed: | 250 | |
| Minorities: | 2 | 2% | Enrolled: | 90 | |
| Out of State: | 0 | 0% | | | |

### 2008–2009 Class Profile

| *Mean MCAT Scores* | | *Mean GPA* |
|---|---|---|
| Physical Sciences: | 10.0 | 3.7 |
| Biological Sciences: | 9.0 | |
| Verbal Reasoning: | 9.0 | *Mean Science* |
| | | n/av |

**Tuition and Fees**

| | |
|---|---|
| Resident | 12,270 |
| Average (public) | 25,100 |
| Average (private) | 42,600 |
| Nonresident | 17,100 |
| Average (public) | 43,900 |
| Average (private) | 43,500 |

0   10   20   30   40   50
(in thousands of dollars)

Percentage receiving financial aid: n/av

Average tuition shown is for U.S. schools.

## Introduction

Dalhousie University is a nondenominational, privately endowed, coeducational university that was founded in 1818. It is located in a residential area of Halifax on the Atlantic coast of Canada. The Faculty of Medicine was established in 1868 and is responsible for providing physicians for the 3 maritime provinces of Nova Scotia, New Brunswick, and Prince Edward Island.

## Admissions

Dalhousie University Faculty of Medicine admits 82 students annually. Admission preference for 74 seats is given to Canadian citizens (landed immigrants) whose place of residence is in Nova Scotia, New Brunswick, or Prince Edward Island. The remaining 8 seats are reserved for applicants from other parts of Canada and the world. The minimum requirements for entry are a bachelor's degree and the Medical College Admission Test. There are no prerequisite courses required. Broad study of the life, physical, and social sciences, and humanities is desirable. *Transfer and advanced standing:* Students are accepted only under special circumstances.

## Curriculum

4-year semimodern. Students follow an innovative Case-Oriented, Problem-Stimulated learning approach to their curriculum (or COPS, as it is known). During the first 2 years, student learning is organized predominately in small groups. The final 2 years involve clinical clerkships, with the majority of learning organized on hospital wards. The goal of the curriculum is to provide the medical education foundation essential to permit a graduate to undertake training in any specialty branch. Emphasis is placed on small group teaching and on independent learning. The development of clinical skills is a critical component of the education process.

## Grading and Promotion Policies

All grading is at the level of Pass or Fail for all 4 years. Several types of evaluations are held throughout the 4 years of study, including learning exams, which help the student to self-evaluate areas already covered. Formal exams are held at the end of each unit/clerkship and students must pass all examinations in each year to be promoted to the next. Students are also evaluated on their performance in all small group sessions, including clinical.

## Facilities

*Teaching:* Dalhousie has a wide variety of hospitals and other clinical settings for patient-oriented teaching. The school is affiliated with 4 major teaching hospitals in the Maritime provinces: The Queen Elizabeth II Health Sciences Center, the IWK Health Center, the Nova Scotia Hospital, and the Atlantic Health Sciences Corporation. *Other:* The Sir Charles Tupper Medical Building also houses research facilities in basic and clinical sciences. *Library:* The W. K. Kellogg Health Science Library has a collection of approximately 158,000 volumes, and yearly receives 2400 current serials. The collection also includes over 2900 audiovisual programs. *Housing:* University housing is available for students on and off campus as single rooms or shared apartments.

## Special Features

The faculty of medicine offers a combined MD-PhD program as well as a BSC (medicine) program and a medical Undergraduate Student Advisor Program.

# McGill University Faculty of Medicine

3655 Promenada Sir William Osler
Montreal, Quebec, Canada H3G 1Y6

*Phone:* 514-398-3517    *Fax:* 514-398-4631
*E-mail:* admissions@med.mcgill.ca
*WWW:* med.mcgill.ca

| Application Filing | | Accreditation | |
|---|---|---|---|
| Earliest: | September 1 | LCME, CACMS | |
| Latest: | November 15 | | |
| Fee: | $85 | **Degrees Granted** | |
| AMCAS: | no | MD, CM | |

### Enrollment: 2008–2009 First-Year Class

| Men: | 78 | 44% | Applied: | 1400 |
|---|---|---|---|---|
| Women: | 98 | 56% | Interviewed: | 448 |
| Minorities: | n/av | n/av | Enrolled: | 178 |
| Out of State: | 16 | 9% | | |

### 2008–2009 Class Profile

| *Mean MCAT Scores* | | *Mean GPA* |
|---|---|---|
| Physical Sciences: | 11 | 3.77 |
| Biological Sciences: | 12 | |
| Verbal Reasoning: | 10 | *Mean Science* |
| | | 3.7 |

### Tuition and Fees

| | |
|---|---|
| **Resident** | 12,066 |
| Average (public) | 25,100 |
| Average (private) | 42,600 |
| **Nonresident** | 24,825 |
| Average (public) | 43,900 |
| Average (private) | 43,500 |

(in thousands of dollars) 0 10 20 30 40 50

Percentage receiving financial aid: 35%

Average tuition shown is for U.S. schools.

## Introduction

In 1823, 4 staff members of the recently opened Montreal General Hospital founded the Montreal Medical Institution where they gave lectures for medical students. The Faculty of Medicine was established in 1829. World-renowned physician William Osler taught from 1874 to 1884. McGill is located in the heart of Montreal.

## Admissions

Requirement includes: A 4-year bachelor's degree: Basic undergraduate-level sciences (1 year biology, 1 year chemistry, 1 year physics, ½ year organic chemistry), MCAT. The degree must be conducted with a full course load in each semester and can be in the discipline of your choice. There are no geographical restrictions for entrance into the program and about 20 non-Canadian students are accepted each year.

## Curriculum

The objective of the curriculum aims to equip the student to meet the most stringent standards of medical practice and professionalism to ensure career-long excellence in whole-person care. Upon completion of the program, the graduate will be able to function responsibly, in a supervised clinical setting, at the level of an "undifferentiated" physician. The program emphasizes the fundamental sciences and scientific methodology as pillars of medical knowledge. It provides traditional lectures and small-group teaching, as well as laboratory and computer teaching. There are 5 components to the curriculum: (1) The Basis of Medicine, which provides a system-based, integrated approach to normal functions of the body. The students have extensive opportunities for hands-on laboratory sessions and have patient contact sessions. (2) The physicianship and physician apprenticeship component consists of small groups that meet throughout the 4 years of the program. The focus is on the roles of the physician as a professional and healer, to the knowledge, skills, attitudes, and behaviors required of professionalism and healing. (3) The Introduction to Clinical Medicine provides a clinical experience, using both in-patient and ambulatory settings and utilizes our Medical Simulation Center. (4, 5) The Core and Senior Clerkships are the last 2 components that involve many rotations in both urban and rural environments, along with plenty of opportunity for electives.

## Grading and Promotion Policies

The evaluation system is multifaceted and includes small-group assessments of written examinations, oral clinical examinations, assessment of written case reports, and others. The grading system is Pass/Fail.

## Facilities

*Teaching:* There are 5 university teaching hospitals, 3 specialty teaching hospitals, and 13 special research centers and units. All patients are available for the teaching of medical students. Research opportunities, available at the undergraduate and graduate levels, are provided in all of the basic medical sciences and in many fields of clinical medicine. The language of instruction is English. *Library:* The Life Sciences Library contains hundreds of thousands of specialized volumes and an excellent journal collection. The Osler Library has a collection in medical history and biography. *Housing:* Housing for approximately 1000 students is available.

## Special Features

*Other degree programs:* An MD-MBA program provides management skills that are unique to health care. A combined MD-PhD program is offered for those interested in a career in academic medicine.

# McMaster University School of Medicine

1200 Main Street West
Hamilton, Ontario, Canada    L8N 3Z5

*Phone:* 905-525-9140          *Fax:* 905-546-0349
*E-mail:* mdadmit@mcmaster.ca
*WWW:* fhs.mcmaster.ca/mdprog

| Application Filing | | Accreditation | |
|---|---|---|---|
| Earliest: | July 1 | LCME, CACMS | |
| Latest: | September 15 | | |
| Fee: | $175 | **Degrees Granted** | |
| AMCAS: | yes | MD | |

### Enrollment: 2008–2009 First-Year Class

| Men: | 68 | 34% | Applied: | 4848 |
|---|---|---|---|---|
| Women: | 96 | 66% | Interviewed: | 546 |
| Minorities: | n/a | n/a | Enrolled: | 164 |
| Out of State: | n/a | n/a | | |

### 2008–2009 Class Profile

| *Mean MCAT Scores* | | *Mean GPA* |
|---|---|---|
| Physical Sciences: | n/app | 3.73 |
| Biological Sciences: | n/app | |
| Verbal Reasoning: | n/app | *Mean Science* |
| | | n/a |

**Tuition and Fees**

| | |
|---|---|
| Resident | 17,396 |
| Average (public) | 25,100 |
| Average (private) | 42,600 |
| Nonresident | 11,137 |
| Average (public) | 43,900 |
| Average (private) | 43,500 |

(in thousands of dollars) — scale 0 to 50

Percentage receiving financial aid: 90%

Average tuition shown is for U.S. schools.

Above data applies to 2007–2008 academic year.

## Introduction

The School of Medicine at McMaster University admitted its first student in 1969. It offers both undergraduate and postgraduate medical education programs. The McMaster University Health Sciences Center provides extensive hospital and ambulatory facilities for the clinical training of its students.

## Admissions

Completion of at least 3 years of university degree credit work and an overall B average are required, but no prerequisite courses. Priority is given to Ontario, out-of-province, and then out-of-country applicants in determining those to be interviewed. Applicants need not take the MCAT. Nonbiology majors are given the same consideration as students with a more scientific orientation. Selection is determined by an Admissions Committee consisting of faculty, students, and community members. Their criteria involve an assessment of academic achievement in college and of personal qualities based on letters of recommendation, an autobiographical sketch, a personal interview, and the outcome of a personal tutorial. Beyond demonstrating adequate intellectual capability, the sensitivity to the varied personal needs of patients is necessary. In addition, candidates should be comfortable with the contents of the school's educational program. Those who appear to have these assets and skills are invited for an interview. Applicants who are not Canadian citizens or landed immigrants in Canada are invited for an interview only when they are considered clearly more suitable in all criteria than Canadian candidates. *Transfer or advanced standing:* Not available.

## Curriculum

3-year (130 weeks) semimodern. Small-group tutorials, self-directed problem-based learning. The curriculum is divided into 6 units as follows: *Unit 1* (16 weeks): Introduction. *Units 2, 3, 4* (39 weeks): Comprehensive analysis of human structure, function, and behavior organized around the organ systems of the body. *Unit 5* (12 weeks): Life cycle dealing with health care problems along the conception to death continuum. *Unit 6* (48 weeks): The clerkships. There is also a 6-week period of revision at the end of the programs. *Electives:* The program includes 26 weeks of electives designed to encourage in-depth study in portions of the medical program. The program also includes horizontal electives that run concurrently with the 3-year program. The entire program works on a full-year schedule.

## Grading and Promotion Policies

A Pass/Fail system is used. Taking the USMLE is optional.

## Facilities

*Teaching:* The Health Sciences Centre provides classroom area for basic sciences instruction and contains a 371-bed teaching hospital. The major hospitals in Hamilton also provide clinical teaching for the McMaster program. *Other:* The Health Sciences Centre also houses research facilities. *Library:* The Health Science Library provides a large number of periodicals, clinical science references, and audiovisual materials for student use. *Housing:* Information not available.

## Special Features

No combined programs are currently available.

# Memorial University of Newfoundland Faculty of Medicine

Prince Phillip Drive
St. John's, Newfoundland, Canada   A1B 3V6

*Phone:* 709-777-6615           *Fax:* 709-777-8422
*E-mail:* munmed@mun.ca
*WWW:* med.mun.ca/admissions

| Application Filing | | Accreditation | |
|---|---|---|---|
| Earliest: | July 1 | LCME, CACMS | |
| Latest: | October 15 | | |
| Fee: | $75 | **Degrees Granted** | |
| AMCAS: | no | MD, MD-PhD | |

### Enrollment: 2008–2009 First-Year Class

| Men: | 24 | 38% | Applied: | 700 |
|---|---|---|---|---|
| Women: | 40 | 65% | Interviewed: | 219 |
| Minorities: | n/a | n/a | Enrolled: | 64 |
| Out of State: | 17 | 27% | | |

### 2008–2009 Class Profile

| *Mean MCAT Scores* | | *Mean GPA* |
|---|---|---|
| Physical Sciences: | 10 | 84% |
| Biological Sciences: | 10 | |
| Verbal Reasoning: | 10 | *Mean Science* |
| | | n/a |

### Tuition and Fees

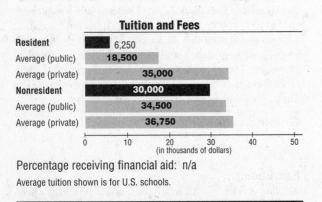

| Resident | 6,250 |
| Average (public) | 18,500 |
| Average (private) | 35,000 |
| Nonresident | 30,000 |
| Average (public) | 34,500 |
| Average (private) | 36,750 |

(in thousands of dollars)

Percentage receiving financial aid: n/a
Average tuition shown is for U.S. schools.

## Introduction

Memorial University of Newfoundland was established in St. John's, Newfoundland in 1925; it was granted full university status in 1949. The campus extends over 220 acres and the university offers a broad range of programs.

The Faculty of Medicine awarded its first degrees in 1973. It is located in the Health Sciences Centre, on the northwest corner of the main university campus along with the schools of Nursing and Pharmacy, and St. John's General Hospital.

## Admissions

A bachelor's degree is required. In exceptional circumstances, an applicant may be considered who does not hold a bachelor's degree; such an applicant must have completed at least 60 credit hours and have had work-related or other experience acceptable to the admissions committee. The course of study must include 6 credit hours in English. All applicants must take the MCAT prior to the application deadline. Preference is given to residents of Newfoundland and Labrador; however, a number of places are available for residents of other parts of Canada as well as non-Canadians. *Transfer and advanced standing:* Normally, the medical school does not acccept transfer students from other medical schools. In rare circumstances, a transfer may be considered if there is space available.

## Curriculum

4-year traditional. The curriculum, the physical structure, and the administrative organization of the school were planned to allow for maximum cooperation among the various basic science and clinical disciplines. The MD degree is granted upon completion of the fourth year, at which time Medical Council of Canada Examinations may be taken. *First year:* During the first year of the medical program, students take introductory courses in cell structure and functions, biochemistry, physiology, molecular genetics, pharmacology, microbiology, anatomy, behavioral science, ethics, interviewing skills, and community medicine. These opportunities are provided in a wide range of medical settings, family practice, and general hospital, rural hospital, and public health programs. *Second half of the first year and second year:* At this time teaching has a systems approach; material from anatomy, physiology, pathology, and clinical medicine is presented in an integrated manner. *Third year:* Structured clinical clerkship that includes 8 weeks of electives. *Fourth year:* Clinical clerkships, electives, and selectives. Rotations for Rural Medicine take place in the first, third, and fourth years.

## Grading and Promotion Policies

A Pass/Fail system is used. Taking the USMLE is optional.

## Facilities

*Teaching:* The medical school complex includes the Health Sciences Centre with its medical sciences teaching facilities and the General Hospital (531 beds). Affiliated hospitals in St. John's and other areas of Newfoundland participate in the school's clinical teaching programs. *Library:* A biomedical library and research facilities are also part of the medical complex. *Housing:* Accommodations on campus are limited. Residences for single and married students are provided on the campus, and the university maintains a list of approved off-campus accommodations. A health service is open to all students.

# Queen's University Faculty of Health Sciences School of Medicine

68 Barrie St
Kingston, Ontario, Canada    K7L 3N6

*Phone:* 613-533-3307          *Fax:* 613-533-3190
*E-mail:* queensmd@queensu.ca
*WWW:* http://meds.queensu.ca

| Application Filing | | Accreditation | |
|---|---|---|---|
| Earliest: | July 1 | LCME, CACMS | |
| Latest: | September 15 | | |
| Fee: | n/av | **Degrees Granted** | |
| AMCAS: | yes | MD | |

### Enrollment: 2008–2009 First-Year Class

| Men: | 54 | 52% | Applied: | 1614 |
|---|---|---|---|---|
| Women: | 46 | 48% | Interviewed: | 467 |
| Minorities: | n/a | n/a | Enrolled: | 100 |
| Out of State: | n/a | n/a | | |

### 2008–2009 Class Profile

| *Mean MCAT Scores* | | *Mean GPA* |
|---|---|---|
| Physical Sciences: | 10.0 | 3.59 |
| Biological Sciences: | 10.0 | |
| Verbal Reasoning: | 10.0 | *Mean Science* |
| | | n/a |

### Tuition and Fees

| | |
|---|---|
| Resident | 14,175 |
| Average (public) | 25,100 |
| Average (private) | 42,600 |
| Nonresident | n/a |

0    10    20    30    40    50
(in thousands of dollars)

Percentage receiving financial aid: 69%

Average tuition shown is for U.S. schools.

Above data applies to 2007–2008 academic year.

## Introduction

One of the integral components of this university is the Faculty of Medicine, established in 1954. The city of Kingston, in which the campus is located, is on Lake Ontario at the origin of the St. Lawrence River. The goal of the school is to provide a broad medical education and to train medical students for specialized postgraduate education.

## Admissions

Candidates must be Canadian citizens, Canadian landed immigrants prior to the closing date for receipt of applications, or the children of Queen's University alumni who reside outside Canada. Each year, 100 students are admitted. Selection is based on a superior academic record and the personal characteristics considered desirable in a future medical practitioner. These are determined at an interview. Invitations are extended for an interview on the basis of the applicant's GPA and MCAT scores. Consideration is given to mitigating circumstances to those whose academic level may lie beneath the cut-off point for an interview. The MCAT and completing 2 semesters of biological and physical sciences and humanities or social studies are required.

## Curriculum

4-year semimodern. The curriculum emphasizes a great degree of self-education and the promotion of the art and the science of medicine in order to prepare the student for a changing healthcare system. A system-based approach integrating biomedicine and clinical sciences is used in order to emphasize relevance and avoid undue repetition. There is a decreased emphasis on lectures and an increase in independent study time and electives. Students are introduced in their first year to doctor-patient communication and physical examination procedures. Clinical skills are taught throughout the curriculum. There is an 8-week Critical Enquiry elective at the end of the second year, which provides an opportunity for students to investigate a medical question in depth. Learning formats include lectures, tutorials, seminars, symposia, and problem-based learning. Intensive clinical exposure and training is provided to ensure securing diagnostic and treatment experience. Responsibility for patient care is delegated on a graduated basis.

## Facilities

*Teaching:* Botterell Hall is the major facility, housing the library, some student facilities, and major classrooms; the departments of anatomy, biochemistry, microbiology and immunology, pharmacology and toxicology, and physiology; a national cancer institute research group of the department of pathology; and animal facilities. The department of pathology has its major facility in the Richardson Laboratory, which is connected to Kingston General Hospital. Etherington Hall, devoted to clinical teaching and research, is also connected to KGH and contains a major auditorium. *Other:* Other major facilities include Abramsky Hall, major research space in the Hotel Dieu Hospital, and in the LaSalle Building. *Library:* The Health Sciences Library contains about 100,000 volumes and more than 1400 serials, and offers interlibrary loan service. *Housing:* Information not available.

## Special Features

There are no combined degree programs at this time.

# Université de Sherbrooke Faculté de Médecine

Sherbrooke, Quebec, Canada    J1H 5N4

*Phone:* 819-564-5208          *Fax:* 819-820-6809
*E-mail:* Admission-Med@USherbrooke.ca
*WWW:* usherbrooke.ca/doctoral_medecine/

| Application Filing | | Accreditation | |
|---|---|---|---|
| Earliest: | November 1 | LCME, CACMS | |
| Latest: | March 1 | | |
| Fee: | $70 | **Degrees Granted** | |
| AMCAS: | no | MD, MD-MS, MD-PhD | |

### Enrollment: 2008–2009 First-Year Class

| | | | | |
|---|---|---|---|---|
| Men: | 121 | 40% | Applied: | 1849 |
| Women: | 80 | 60% | Interviewed: | 777 |
| Minorities: | n/a | n/a | Enrolled: | 201 |
| Out of State: | 34 | 17% | | |

### 2008–2009 Class Profile

| *Mean MCAT Scores* | | *Mean GPA* |
|---|---|---|
| Physical Sciences: | n/a | n/a |
| Biological Sciences: | n/a | |
| Verbal Reasoning: | n/a | |

### Tuition and Fees

| | |
|---|---|
| **Resident** | 2,829 |
| Average (public) | 25,100 |
| Average (private) | 42,600 |
| **Nonresident** | 8,225 |
| Average (public) | 43,900 |
| Average (private) | 43,500 |

0    10    20    30    40    50
(in thousands of dollars)

Percentage receiving financial aid: 50%

Average tuition shown is for U.S. schools.

## Introduction

Admitting its first class in 1966, this French-speaking institution is part of the developing Health Sciences Centre, which includes a modern teaching hospital and a department of nursing.

## Admissions

Admission to the Faculté de Médecine is primarily based on ability and premedical achievement, as demonstrated by students' academic records. Learning skills tests are included in the selection. Candidates from the province of Quebec are required to participate in multiple mini interviews, in addition to the Test d'aptitudes à l'apprentissage de la médecine à l'Université de Sherbrooke. There are 170 places reserved for applicants from the province of Quebec; positions may be filled by French-speaking students from Western Canadian provinces and territories. In addition, 24 places are reserved for applicants from New Brunswick. One place is available for an applicant from Prince Edward Island; one place is available for an applicant from Newfoundland; and 3 places are available for applicants from Nova Scotia. One to 6 places are available for Canadian Forces candidates. One to 4 places are available for applicants from First Nations and Inuits from Quebec, and one place is available for a qualified foreign applicant with a student visa. Applicants must be fluent in both written and spoken French.

## Curriculum

The form of teaching is a problem-based learning program. Formal lecturing has been reduced to a minimum. Audiovisual facilities, seminars, small group discussions, panels, field work, and case studies are used extensively. Most learning sessions integrate many disciplines representing various departments. Students work in the hospital from the beginning of their first year.

## Grading and Promotion Policies

Grading is on a 4-point basis, A = 4. Evaluations are made by examination results and reports of professors on student progress. A grade of C, based on these exams and evaluation reports, must be obtained for promotion at fourth year's end. Taking the USMLE is optional.

## Facilities

As required by modern medical teaching, the Faculté de Médecine is integrated into a developing Health Sciences Centre to serve all members of the health team. This centre includes a modern 682-bed teaching hospital. Sixteen hospitals, many health centers, and CLSC are affiliated with the Faculté de Médecine. *Library:* An on-campus biomedical library containing a large number of bound volumes and periodicals is available for use by students and faculty. *Housing:* On campus housing is available.

## Special Features

Combined degree programs are available at the MD-MS and MD-PhD levels to students with outstanding academic records.

# Université Laval
# Faculté de Médecine

Sainte-Foy, Quebec, Canada    G1K 7P4

*Phone:* 418-656-2131          *Fax:* 418-656-2733
*E-mail:* admission@fmedulaval.ca
*WWW:* ulaval.ca

| **Application Filing** | | **Accreditation** |
|---|---|---|
| Earliest: | November 15 | LCME, CACMS |
| Latest: | March 1 | |
| Fee: | n/av | **Degrees Granted** |
| AMCAS: | no | MD, MD-PhD |

### Enrollment: 2008–2009 First-Year Class

| Men: | 59 | 28% | Applied: | 1713 |
|---|---|---|---|---|
| Women: | 149 | 72% | Interviewed: | n/a |
| Minorities: | n/a | n/a | Enrolled: | 208 |
| Out of State: | n/a | n/a | | |

### 2008–2009 Class Profile

| *Mean MCAT Scores* | | *Mean GPA* |
|---|---|---|
| Physical Sciences: | n/a | n/a |
| Biological Sciences: | n/a | |
| Verbal Reasoning: | n/a | |

### Tuition and Fees

| | |
|---|---|
| **Resident** | 2,500 |
| Average (public) | 25,100 |
| Average (private) | 42,600 |
| **Nonresident** | 13,750 |
| Average (public) | 43,900 |
| Average (private) | 43,500 |

0    10    20    30    40    50
(in thousands of dollars)

Percentage receiving financial aid: n/a

Average tuition shown is for U.S. schools.

Above data applies to 2007–2008 academic year.

## Introduction

Named after the first Bishop of Quebec, this private institution was established in 1852, after being granted a royal charter by Queen Victoria. Teaching instruction is in French.

## Admissions

The basic premedical science courses plus mathematics through calculus are required. Applicants should have a good command of the French language as it is the language of instruction. Priority is given to residents of Quebec, but outstanding French-speaking students from other provinces and countries are considered. The MCAT is not required, but if taken, its results are considered. Applicants from Quebec College and other Canadian universities are required to submit a standardized curriculum vitae and participate in a session known as the Assessment by Stimulation, which extends over 3 hours. Gifted French-speaking students from other provinces and the United States are evaluated on the basis of scholastic achievement, their CVs, and letters of recommendation. *Transfer and advanced standing:* Applications for transfer are not accepted.

## Curriculum

4-year nontraditional. *First and second years:* One trimester of basic sciences, followed by 3 trimesters with an organ system-integrated approach plus courses in ethics, epidemiology, and the psychosocial aspects of medicine. Most teaching is done through small group discussion. *Third and fourth years:* Eleven weeks of primary clerkship followed by 18 months of clerkship rotation through the major clinical specialties including family medicine and social and preventive medicine. During this period, 3 months are devoted to electives.

## Grading and Promotion Policies

Letter grades in basic sciences, required clinical sciences, and electives. Taking the USMLE is optional.

## Facilities

*Teaching:* Clinical instruction takes place at 1 academic health center, 1 affiliated hospital, and 1 institute. Research facilities in most fields are available. *Library:* A comprehensive medical library is at the disposal of students and faculty. *Housing:* Accommodations are available for many students.

## Special Features

An MD-PhD program is available.

# University of Alberta
# Faculty of Medicine & Dentistry

2-45 Medical Sciences Building
Edmonton, Alberta, Canada   T6G 2H7

*Phone:* 780-492-6350          *Fax:* 780-492-9531
*E-mail:* admissions@med.ualberta.ca
*WWW:* med.ualberta.ca

| Application Filing | | Accreditation | |
|---|---|---|---|
| Earliest: | July 1 | LCME, CACMS | |
| Latest: | November 1 | | |
| Fee: | $100 | **Degrees Granted** | |
| AMCAS: | no | MD, MD-MS, MD-PhD | |

### Enrollment: 2008–2009 First-Year Class

| | | | | | |
|---|---|---|---|---|---|
| Men: | 85 | 52% | Applied: | 1150 | |
| Women: | 70 | 48% | Interviewed: | 434 | |
| Minorities: | n/a | n/a | Enrolled: | 155 | |
| Out of State: | 15 | 2% | | | |

### 2008–2009 Class Profile

| *Mean MCAT Scores* | | *Mean GPA* |
|---|---|---|
| Physical Sciences: | 11.95 | 3.89 |
| Biological Sciences: | 12.09 | |
| Verbal Reasoning: | 10.43 | *Mean MCAT* |
| | | 3.88 |

**Tuition and Fees**

| | |
|---|---|
| Resident | 11,086 |
| Average (public) | 25,100 |
| Average (private) | 42,600 |
| Nonresident | 11,086 |
| Average (public) | 43,900 |
| Average (private) | 43,500 |

0   10   20   30   40   50
(in thousands of dollars)

Percentage receiving financial aid: n/a
Average tuition shown is for U.S. schools.

## Introduction

The university, established in 1908, is located in Edmonton, the capital of the province of Alberta. The Faculty of Medicine was founded in 1913 with a 3-year program. It subsequently became a 4-year MD degree program whose first class was graduated in 1925. In addition to the Medical School, the university has professional programs in dentistry, law, and library science.

## Admissions

Requirements include the basic premedical sciences and courses in biochemistry, statistics, and English.

Preference is given to Alberta residents. About 15% of all first-year places are available to out-of-province students. Three places beyond the total class size are allocated to Aboriginal applicants. Selection is determined by an assessment of scholastic achievement, performance on the MCAT, and evidence of personal suitability for a career in medicine. This information is secured from college transcripts, letters of recommendation, and an interview. *Transfer and advanced standing:* School accepts transfer students only under exceptional circumstances and only from LCME-accredited Canadian institutions.

## Curriculum

4-year semimodern. The first 2 years consist of instruction from September to May, while the last 2 years are a combined 86-week program with a 4-week vacation break. *Year I:* One academic year of instruction covering most of the basic sciences and an introduction to clinical skills. *Year II:* A 1-year program of interdepartmental teaching in a clinical setting relating clinical and basic medical sciences to human diseases. *Year III:* Consists of rotating clerkships in affiliated hospitals with 10 weeks devoted to electives in a wide range of fields, also an elective in either geriatrics or rural family medicine. Students are encouraged to organize individual programs with career and special interests in mind.

## Grading and Promotion Policies

Evaluations of student work are made at the conclusion of each phase of the program on the basis of performance on final, course, and interdisciplinary examinations. A Pass/Fail grading system is used. Each student must attain a GPA of at least 5.0 to progress to the next level of study. Taking both or any steps of the USMLE is optional.

## Facilities

*Teaching:* The Faculty of Medicine is located on the campus of the University of Alberta. The Basic Sciences Building houses facilities for the teaching of basic science, and the 843-bed W. C. MacKenzie Health Sciences Centre provides for most of the clinical instruction. There are also several other hospitals affiliated with the school. *Other:* Facilities for research in experimental medicine are available at the Surgical-Medical Research Institute. The Cancer Research Institute is housed at the McEachern Cancer Research Laboratory. *Library:* A comprehensive medical library contains a large number of bound volumes and periodicals. *Housing:* There are residence halls available for single students and a 299-unit apartment building for married students.

## Special Features

Combined MD-PhD programs are available in a variety of disciplines including immunology and pathology. An MD-MS program is also offered.

# University of British Columbia Faculty of Medicine

2194 Health Sciences Mall
Vancouver, British Columbia, Canada   V6T 1Z3

*Phone:* 604-822-4482          *Fax:* 604-822-6061
*E-mail:* mark@medd.med.ubc.ca
*WWW:* http://www.med.ubc.ca

| Application Filing | | Accreditation | |
|---|---|---|---|
| Earliest: | June 15 | LCME, CACMS | |
| Latest: | October 1 | | |
| Fee: | $105 | **Degrees Granted** | |
| AMCAS: | no | MD, MD-PhD | |

### Enrollment: 2008–2009 First-Year Class

| Men: | 108 | 42% | Applied: | 1006 |
|---|---|---|---|---|
| Women: | 148 | 58% | Interviewed: | 362 |
| Minorities: | n/a | n/a | Enrolled: | 256 |
| Out of State: | 12 | 5% | | |

### 2008–2009 Class Profile

| *Mean MCAT Scores* | | *Mean GPA* |
|---|---|---|
| Physical Sciences: | 10.3 | 3.5 |
| Biological Sciences: | 11.0 | |
| Verbal Reasoning: | 9.3 | *Mean Science* |
| | | n/a |

### Tuition and Fees

| | |
|---|---|
| Resident | 14,800 |
| Average (public) | 25,100 |
| Average (private) | 42,600 |
| Nonresident | n/a |

(in thousands of dollars)

Percentage receiving financial aid: n/a
Average tuition shown is for U.S. schools.

## Introduction

The University of British Columbia was initiated in 1950 and is one component of the university, which has a variety of faculties and schools. The Health Sciences Center is located on the university campus, which contains an instructional resources center, and acute care as well as psychiatric hospitals. The medical school is an integral part of a large provincial university.

## Admissions

Required courses include the basic premedical sciences, 1 year of English composition and literature, and 1 year of general biochemistry. Residents of British Columbia are given priority. Applicants must have 90 university credits minimum and take the MCAT. A personal interview is advisable. The selection of candidates for admission to UBC's medical school is governed by guidelines established by the school's Senate and is the responsibility of the Faculty of Medicine Admissions Selection Committee.

## Curriculum

4-year semimodern. The program is built on principles of student self-directed learning, integration of biomedical and social sciences, early clinical contact, information management, professional development, and social responsibility.

## Grading and Promotion Policies

Grades are letter or percentage. Promotion is determined by the Faculty Committee at the end of each session. The committee also decides whether unsatisfactory work can be corrected by a special examination or by repeating the course, or if the failing student must withdraw from studies completely. Taking the USMLE is optional.

## Facilities

The BC provincial government has funded the building of new facilities at UBC, to accommodate the new program and foster the study of life sciences across the province. State-of-the-art technology will be used in the delivery of education from one site to another. In addition, technology-enabled learning will make expertise from around the globe available to UBC medical students. *Library:* On-campus library facilities exist at the Woodward Biomedical Library and a branch library is maintained at Vancouver Hospital. *Housing:* For detailed information regarding housing, contact the Island Medical Program, the Northern Medical Program, and the Vancouver Fraser Medical Program directly. *Other:* The Island Medical Program at Uvic, the Northern Medical Program at Uvic, and the UBC-based Vancouver Fraser Medical Program.

## Special Features

The UBC Faculty of Medicine's Associate Dean of Equity oversees the selection process to ensure that all applicants are given careful consideration without regard to age, gender, sexual orientation, race, ancestry, color, place of origin, family status, physical or mental disability, political belief, religion, or marital or economic status. *Other degree programs:* MD-PhD program offered. Distributed program with geographic sites in Prince George, Vancouver, and Victoria.

# University of Calgary Faculty of Medicine

3330 Hospital Drive, N.W.
Calgary, Alberta, Canada   T2N 4N1

*Phone:* 403-220-4262        *Fax:* 403-210-8148
*E-mail:* ucmedapp@ucalgary.ca
*WWW:* http://www.med.ucalgary.ca/admissions

| Application Filing | | Accreditation | |
|---|---|---|---|
| Earliest: | July 1 | LCME, CACMS | |
| Latest: | October 15 | | |
| Fee: | $120 | **Degrees Granted** | |
| AMCAS: | no | MD | |

### Enrollment: 2008–2009 First-Year Class

| Men: | 74 | 49% | Applied: | 1405 |
|---|---|---|---|---|
| Women: | 76 | 51% | Interviewed: | 432 |
| Minorities: | n/a | n/a | Enrolled: | 150 |
| Out of State: | n/a | n/a | | |

### 2008–2009 Class Profile

| *Mean MCAT Scores* | | *Mean GPA* |
|---|---|---|
| Physical Sciences: | 11.0 | 3.66 |
| Biological Sciences: | 11.4 | |
| Verbal Reasoning: | 10.3 | *Mean Science* |
| | | n/a |

### Tuition and Fees

| | |
|---|---|
| **Resident** | 13,818 |
| Average (public) | 25,100 |
| Average (private) | 42,600 |
| **Nonresident** | 13,818 |
| Average (public) | 43,900 |
| Average (private) | 43,500 |

0   10   20   30   40   50
(in thousands of dollars)

Percentage receiving financial aid: n/a
Average tuition shown is for U.S. schools.

## Introduction

The University of Calgary began in 1945 when the Calgary Normal School became a branch of the University of Alberta's Education Faculty. It moved to its current campus in northwest Calgary in 1960 and gained full autonomy as a degree-granting institution in 1966. The Faculty of Medicine was initiated in 1970 and established its facilities in the Calgary Health Science Centre in 1972.

## Admissions

Priority is given to residents of Alberta, and non-Canadian citizens are not considered. Applicants need not have a strict premedical background if their academic record is superior. The basic premedical science courses and biochemistry, cell biology, physiology, English, calculus, psychology, sociology, or anthropology are recommended. The MCAT must be taken. Final applicants will be required to attend an interview at Calgary. *Transfer and advanced standing:* Because the 3-year MD program is regarded as a continuum of coursework, transfers cannot be considered.

## Curriculum

3-year (11 months) each. After graduation, the student usually takes at least 2 years of postgraduate work. The initial program provides a basic education, while the graduate work furnishes opportunity for specialization. The main emphasis is on problem solving, with patient contact and responsibility throughout the entire program. *First and second years:* The core of the curriculum is based on clinical presentation. These are categorized by their degree of complexity, body system, and human development. An independent study program of 16 hours per week is time set aside secure from encroachment by scheduled curricular activities. Four hours a week are allotted for electives. *Third year:* Consists of clinical clerkships where the concepts taught in the first 2 years are applied. Elective programs are available. The core of the curriculum is based on clinical presentation of patients. These are categorized by their degree of complexity, body system, and human developmental relationship.

## Grading and Promotion Policies

Evaluation is made on a multidisciplinary basis and will test the student's factual knowledge and his/her ability to solve problems. Grading is on a Pass/Fail basis.

## Facilities

*Teaching:* The Calgary Health Sciences Centre provides a model of health care services, teaching and research areas, an audiovisual center, and space for labs, lecture halls, and study areas. Clinical teaching takes place at Foothills Hospital, Peter Longhead Hospital, and Alberta Children's Hospital. *Library:* The Health Sciences Library contains about 130,000 volumes and subscribes to about 2000 periodicals. An interlibrary loan service also exists. *Housing:* Both single and married student housing is available.

## Special Features

A combined degree program is offered.

# University of Manitoba Faculty of Medicine

270-727 McDermot Avenue
Winnipeg, Manitoba, Canada    R3E 3PS

*Phone:* 204-789-3499          *Fax:* 204-789-3929
*E-mail:* registrar_med@umanitoba.ca
*WWW:* umanitoba.ca/medicine

| Application Filing | | Accreditation | |
|---|---|---|---|
| Earliest: | August 15 | LCME | |
| Latest: | Ocotber 10 | | |
| Fee: | $90 | **Degrees Granted** | |
| AMCAS: | no | MD, MD-PhD | |

### Enrollment: 2008–2009 First-Year Class

| | | | | | |
|---|---|---|---|---|---|
| Men: | 60 | 55% | Applied: | 948 | |
| Women: | 50 | 45% | Interviewed: | 317 | |
| Minorities: | 6 | 5% | Enrolled: | 110 | |
| Out of State: | 11 | 10% | | | |

### 2008–2009 Class Profile

| *Mean MCAT Scores* | | *Mean GPA* |
|---|---|---|
| Physical Sciences: | 11 | 4.00 |
| Biological Sciences: | 11 | |
| Verbal Reasoning: | 10 | *Mean Science* |
| | | n/a |

**Tuition and Fees**

| | |
|---|---|
| **Resident** | 7,595 |
| Average (public) | 25,100 |
| Average (private) | 42,600 |
| **Nonresident** | 7,595 |
| Average (public) | 43,900 |
| Average (private) | 43,500 |

0    10    20    30    40    50
(in thousands of dollars)

Percentage receiving financial aid: n/a

Average tuition shown is for U.S. schools.

Above data applies to 2007–2008 academic year.

## Introduction

Medical education in Manitoba is designed to provide students with the knowledge and experience they need to practice medicine in a profession where new developments in science and public health policy create an ever-changing environment.

## Admissions

The Faculty of Medicine restricts enrollment to Canadian citizens and permanent residents. All applicants must have completed a bachelor's degree, and prerequisites in biochemistry and humanities or social science. At the University of Manitoba, these are Biochemistry 2360 and 2370. Applicants should be aware that there are course prerequisites for biochemistry at University of Manitoba and should obtain this information from their faculty student advisors. It is recommended that students consider taking courses in the life sciences, particularly biology and physiology. All applicants must take the Medical College Admission Test (MCAT). Applicants are assessed in part on their adjusted grade point average (AGPA). A personal Assessment Score is based on written information provided by the applicant and referees and an interview.

## Curriculum

In the first two years of the program, the subject matter is divided into blocks that cover core concepts in health and medicine, human development, and body systems. Clinical Skills, Problem-Solving, Medical Humanities, Law, Laboratory and Investigative Medicine, Health Equity and Survival Tactics are integrated into the six blocks. The final two years, called the "clerkship," are spent in direct contact with patients and doctors in a clinical setting in which students gain experience with increasing responsibility for patient care and management.

## Grading and Promotion Policies

The Pass/Fail system is used. Taking the USMLE is optional.

## Facilities

The Faculty of Medicine is located at the Bannatyne Campus. Facilities for instruction are provided there, including the Clinical Learning and Simulation Facility. In addition to the affiliated teaching hospitals, students also have access to the institutes and centers of Cell Biology, Health Policy, Child Health, Cancer Care Manitoba, Cardiovascular Sciences, Spinal Cord Research, St. Boniface General Hospital Research Centre, the national Microbiology Laboratory, and the Institute of Biodiagnostics (NRC). The varied settings in which medicine is practiced in Winnipeg and in rural and northern Manitoba provide students with the opportunity to study community medicine outside the major teaching institutions.

## Special Features

Combined MD-PhD and MD-BS medicine programs offered.

# Université de Montreal School of Medicine

P.O. Box 6128, Station Centre-Ville
Montreal, Quebec, Canada    H3C 3J7

*Phone:* 514-343-6265          *Fax:* 514-343-6629
*E-mail:* admmed@ere.umontreal.ca
*WWW:* med.umontreal.ca

| Application Filing | | Accreditation |
|---|---|---|
| Earliest: | December 1 | LCME, CACMS |
| Latest: | January 15 | |
| Fee: | no | **Degrees Granted** |
| AMCAS: | yes | MD |

### Enrollment: 2008–2009 First-Year Class

| Men: | 88 | 33% | Applied: | 2116 |
|---|---|---|---|---|
| Women: | 182 | 67% | Interviewed: | 796 |
| Minorities: | n/a | n/a | Enrolled: | 270 |
| Out of State: | 1 | 4% | | |

### 2008–2009 Class Profile

| *Mean MCAT Scores* | | *Mean GPA* |
|---|---|---|
| Physical Sciences: | n/a | 3.7 |
| Biological Sciences: | n/a | |
| Verbal Reasoning: | n/a | *Mean Science* |
| | | 3.7 |

**Tuition and Fees**

| | |
|---|---|
| **Resident** | 4,000 |
| Average (public) | 25,100 |
| Average (private) | 42,600 |
| **Nonresident** | 23,000 |
| Average (public) | 43,900 |
| Average (private) | 43,500 |

(in thousands of dollars) — scale 0 to 50

Percentage receiving financial aid: n/a

Average tuition shown is for U.S. schools.

Above data applies to 2007–2008 academic year.

## Introduction

The Faculty of Medicine was established in 1843. In 1891 the school merged with the Faculty of Medicine of the Montreal branch of Laval University. In 1920 the latter institution was granted independent status and the school became known by its present name. Instruction in the medical school is in French.

## Admissions

A thorough knowledge of the French language is required. All candidates accepted must be either Canadian citizens or landed immigrants. To be eligible, all applicants must have successfully completed college or university courses in mathematics, physics, chemistry, and biology. Students having just graduated from the provincial colleges of general and professional education, as well as those with a bachelor's degree nonrelated to biological health sciences, are accepted in a premedical year devoted to basic biological and behavioral sciences. Selection of candidates is competitive and based on a global score derived from scholastic records and interviews. About a quarter of applicants are invited for interviews that take place on the site of the medical school.

## Curriculum

4-year. Consists of 2 preclinical and 2 clinical years. *First and second years:* Formal lecturing is reduced to a minimum and replaced by active methods, especially problem-based learning and small-group discussions. Introduction to clinical medicine takes place in a continuous and progressive fashion and 2 elective courses are mandatory throughout these 2 preclinical years. *Third and fourth years:* Consists of a clerkship of 80 weeks duration with 4 one-month elective stages including one in a regional community setting.

## Facilities

*Teaching:* Clinical instruction is carried out at 14 affiliated teaching hospitals and research centers. *Library:* A comprehensive medical library containing numerous bound volumes and periodicals is at the disposal of students and faculty. *Housing:* Information not available.

## Special Features

Residency training in the teaching hospitals is under the direction of the Faculty of Medicine. Various courses and symposia are organized by the continuing medical education division.

# University of Ottawa Faculty of Medicine

451 Smyth Road
Ottawa, Ontario, Canada   K1H 8M5

*Phone:* 613-562-5409          *Fax:* 613-562-5651
*E-mail:* admissmd@uottawa.ca
*WWW:* medicine.uottawa.ca/eng

| **Application Filing** | | **Accreditation** |
|---|---|---|
| Earliest: | July 6 | LCME, CACMS |
| Latest: | September 15 | |
| Fee: | n/a | **Degrees Granted** |
| AMCAS: | yes | MD, BSc-MD |

### Enrollment: 2008–2009 First-Year Class

| | | | | |
|---|---|---|---|---|
| Men: | 53 | 38% | Applied: | 3356 |
| Women: | 86 | 62% | Interviewed: | 516 |
| Minorities: | n/a | n/a | Enrolled: | 139 |
| Out of State: | 12 | 9% | | |

### 2008–2009 Class Profile

| *Mean MCAT Scores* | | *Mean GPA* |
|---|---|---|
| Physical Sciences: | n/a | n/a |
| Biological Sciences: | n/a | |
| Verbal Reasoning: | n/a | *Mean Science* |
| | | n/a |

### Tuition and Fees

| | |
|---|---|
| Resident | 15,286 |
| Average (public) | 25,100 |
| Average (private) | 42,600 |
| Nonresident | n/app |

0   10   20   30   40   50
(in thousands of dollars)

Percentage receiving financial aid: n/a

Average tuition shown is for U.S. schools.

Above data applies to 2007–2008 academic year.

## Introduction

This school began as a 2-year medical science program in 1926; a 4-year curriculum was introduced in 1953. In 1988 a 6-year curriculum was initiated, which includes a 2-year premedical program. The school prepares its students for careers in family medicine, specialty practice, and research.

## Admissions (OMSAS)

Successful completion of the 3 full-time years of a university program and of the basic premedical science courses and 1 year of humanities is required. Taking the MCAT is no longer obligatory. Only Canadian citizens or landed immigrants are considered for admission except in the case of children of alumni. *Transfer and advanced standing:* Not possible. Criteria for selection are: academic excellence, evaluation of the detailed autobiographical essay submitted, and results of the interview with representatives of the admissions committee.

## Curriculum

4-year semitraditional. *First and second years:* Stage 1 includes 70 weeks of study of essential biomedical principles and consists of 13 multidisciplinary blocks. The students learn clinical skills in an integrated fashion with the study of body systems. Stage 2, also 2 years, is devoted to clinical clerkships, and 16 weeks are available for elective study. During their undergraduate medical training, the students acquire the knowledge, skills, and attitudes they need to recognize, understand, and apply effective and efficient strategies for the prevention and management of the most common and most severe health problems. The program integrates the basic and clinical sciences throughout the 4 years. It also emphasizes health promotion and disease prevention; it is responsive to individual needs and abilities and to the changes occurring in society and the health care system. Emphasis is placed on self-learning; principles and facts are learned in a multidisciplinary way in the context of clinical problems. Whole-class lectures and seminars are used to discuss basic concepts, explore new developments, and provide overviews of the biomedical sciences fundamental to the practice of medicine. Training occurs in ambulatory, primary, secondary, and tertiary settings, and the students function as members of the medical team in collaboration with other health professionals. The training fosters trust and compassion, communication skills, ethical professional conduct, and patient advocacy.

## Grading and Promotion Policies

An Honors/Pass/Fail system is used. Taking the USMLE is optional.

## Facilities

*Teaching:* The university's Health Science Building houses the facilities for basic science instruction. Clinical instruction takes place at Ottawa General Hospital (450 beds) and Ottawa Civic Hospital (900 beds). *Other:* Other facilities include Children's Hospital of Eastern Ontario (300 beds), Royal Ottawa Hospital (150 beds), and several smaller institutions. *Library:* The Health Sciences Library has 40,000 volumes and subscribes to about 2000 journals. *Housing:* Information is not available.

## Special Features

A combined BSc-MD program is available.

# University of Saskatchewan College of Medicine

Saskatoon, Saskatchewan, Canada    S7N 5E5

*Phone:* 306–966-6143          *Fax:* 306-966-2601
*E-mail:* heather.mandeville@usask.ca
*WWW:* medicine.usask.ca

| Application Filing | | Accreditation | |
|---|---|---|---|
| Earliest: | July 1 | LCME, CACMS | |
| Latest: | November 1 | | |
| Fee: | $55 | **Degrees Granted** | |
| AMCAS: | no | MD, MSC-MD, | |
| | | PhD-MD | |

### Enrollment: 2008–2009 First-Year Class

| Men: | 33 | 39% | Applied: | 591 |
|---|---|---|---|---|
| Women: | 51 | 61% | Interviewed: | 195 |
| Minorities: | 6 | 6% | Enrolled: | 84 |
| Out of State: | 6 | 6% | | |

### 2008–2009 Class Profile

| *Mean MCAT Scores* | | *Mean GPA* |
|---|---|---|
| Physical Sciences: | 9.1 | 87.48% |
| Biological Sciences: | 9.6 | |
| Verbal Reasoning: | 9.3 | |

**Tuition and Fees**

| | |
|---|---|
| Resident | 11,490 |
| Average (public) | 25,100 |
| Average (private) | 42,600 |
| Nonresident | n/a |
| Average (public) | 43,900 |
| Average (private) | 43,500 |

(in thousands of dollars)

Percentage receiving financial aid: n/a

Average tuition shown is for U.S. schools.

## Introduction

The University of Saskatchewan began teaching medical students in a 2-year medical sciences program in 1926. The present college was introduced in 1953 with a 4-year curriculum leading to the MD degree. In 1968 the curriculum changed to 4 years with a 1-year premedical university requirement. The curriculum reverted to a 4-year program in 1988 with a minimum 2-year premedical requirement.

## Admissions

Requirements include 2 full premedical years and the basic premedical science courses, biochemistry, English, and 2 electives in the social sciences or humanities. Priority is given to residents of Saskatchewan; however, 6 positions may be offered to out-of-province students. All applicants must be Canadian citizens or landed immigrants and have lived in Canada for at least 3 years. Applicants are required to take the MCAT. *Transfer and advanced standing:* Not applicable at this college. For detailed information, contact the Admissions Secretary at the above address.

## Curriculum

4-year. The curriculum is aimed at educating doctors for entrance into any phase of the medical profession. *First year:* Largely devoted to basic sciences and introductory clinical sciences. *Second year:* Includes bridging sciences—pathology, microbiology, immunology, pharmacology, and nutrition—and systems, clinical sciences, and concurrent courses. *Third year:* Continuation of systems, clinical sciences, and concurrent courses. *Fourth year:* Rotation clerkship through internal medicine, surgery, obstetrics/gynecology, pediatrics, psychiatry, family medicine, anesthesia, neurology, geriatric medicine, and electives.

## Grading and Promotion Policies

Percentage grades are assigned for most courses; Pass/Fail for the others.

## Facilities

*Teaching:* Basic sciences are taught in the Medical Building. Clinical instruction takes place at the University Hospital, connected with the Medical Building. *Other:* Other affiliated hospitals are St. Paul's, Saskatoon City Hospital, Regina General Hospital, and Pasqua Hospital. *Library:* The Medical Building also houses the school library. *Housing:* Information not available.

## Special Features

MSC-MD, PhD-MD combined program is available.

# University of Toronto Faculty of Medicine

1 King's College Circle
Toronto, Ontario, Canada    M5S 1A8

*Phone:* 416-978-2717          *Fax:* 416-971-2163
*E-mail:* id.taylor@utoronto.ca.
*WWW:* facmed.utoronto.ca

| Application Filing | | Accreditation | |
|---|---|---|---|
| Earliest: | July 1 | LCME, CACMS | |
| Latest: | October 1 | | |
| Fee: | $75 | **Degrees Granted** | |
| AMCAS: | no | MD, MD-PhD | |

### Enrollment: 2008–2009 First-Year Class

| | | | | |
|---|---|---|---|---|
| Men: | 97 | 43% | Applied: | 3165 |
| Women: | 127 | 57% | Interviewed: | 487 |
| Minorities: | n/a | n/a | Enrolled: | 224 |
| Out of State: | n/a | n/a | | |

### 2008–2009 Class Profile

| *Mean MCAT Scores* | | *Mean GPA* |
|---|---|---|
| Physical Sciences: | 11 | 3.9 |
| Biological Sciences: | 12 | |
| Verbal Reasoning: | 10 | *Mean Science* |
| | | n/a |

**Tuition and Fees**

| | |
|---|---|
| Resident | 18,145 |
| Average (public) | 25,100 |
| Average (private) | 42,600 |
| Nonresident | 45,383 |
| Average (public) | 43,900 |
| Average (private) | 43,500 |

0    10    20    30    40    50
(in thousands of dollars)

Percentage receiving financial aid: 81%

Average tuition shown is for U.S. schools.

Above data applies to 2007–2008 academic year.

## Introduction

The Faculty of Medicine is the largest in all of Canada. It belongs to a university that can trace its origin back to Kings College, which was founded in 1843. The school is affiliated with 10 teaching hospitals. It was a site of several major medical breakthroughs that have had a profound impact on society. This includes the discovery of insulin, which facilitated the management of diabetes, and the development of the cardiac pacemaker, which permits an artificial regulation of the heart rate.

## Admissions (OMSAS)

Requirements include completion of 3 years at a Canadian university or, for applicants registered in a non-Canadian university, a recognized bachelor's degree.

All applicants must have the following prerequisites: 2 full courses in the life sciences and 1 full course in humanities, social science, or language. Preference is given to residents of Ontario. Applicants must take the MCAT and have a personal interview. No preference for admission is given to science majors. *Transfer and advanced standing:* Transfer students from other medical schools are not considered because of enrollment limitations.

## Curriculum

4-year semimodern. The curriculum is focused on student-centered learning. The preclerkship phase consists of 6 multidisciplinary courses, each of which is built upon a series of patient-based cases. Selected lectures, seminars, and laboratory exercises will complement small-group, problem-based learning sessions. The remainder of the 4 years is dedicated to the clinical clerkship, which will include a basic or junior component and specialty or senior component. During the clerkship phase, education occurs on the wards, in the laboratories, and in ambulatory care units of affiliated teaching hospitals. The curriculum is based on 4 guidelines: patient-centered learning, integrated and multidisciplinary content, student-motivated learning, and structured problem-based education. Students are placed in hospital and community settings from the beginning of their training. The emphasis on patient contact enables students to apply basic medical knowledge as they acquire it. Early involvement in various health-care settings exposes them to the roles and responsibilities of the health-care team and other health professionals. Each course provides students with relevant basic science, clinical medicine, and community health prospectives.

## Grading and Promotion Policies

An Honors, Pass, Fail grading system is in effect. Honors, Pass, Fail standing in a course is based on a summation of evaluations within the course using the weightings given within the curriculum directory for individual course evaluative components. All evaluation must be passed for promotion to the next year of study. No grades can be considered final until approved by the Board of Examiners.

## Facilities

*Teaching:* The basic courses for the first 2 years are given at the Medical Sciences Building. The university is associated with 11 hospitals, the largest being Toronto Hospital with over 1400 beds. *Other:* Research facilities are housed in the Medical Sciences Building. *Library:* The medical library contains a large volume of books and subscribes to many periodicals. *Housing:* Some university housing is available. For students unable to find accommodations on campus, the school maintains a list of local housing.

## Special Features

A combined MD-PhD program is offered by the Faculty of Medicine and the School of Graduate Studies.

# University of Western Ontario Schulich School of Medicine and Dentistry

London, Ontario, Canada   N6A 5C1

*Phone:* 519-661-3744          *Fax:* 519-850-2958
*E-mail:* admissions@schulich.u.wo.ca
*WWW:* schulich.uwo.ca

| Application Filing | | Accreditation | |
|---|---|---|---|
| Earliest: | July 1 | LCME, CACMS | |
| Latest: | September 1 | | |
| Fee: | no | **Degrees Granted** | |
| AMCAS: | yes | MD, MD-PhD | |

### Enrollment: 2008–2009 First-Year Class

| Men: | 75 | 51% | Applied: | 2300 |
|---|---|---|---|---|
| Women: | 72 | 49% | Interviewed: | 445 |
| Minorities: | n/a | n/a | Enrolled: | 147 |
| Out of State: | n/a | n/a | | |

### 2008–2009 Class Profile

| *Mean MCAT Scores* | | *Mean GPA* |
|---|---|---|
| Physical Sciences: | 10 | 3.7 |
| Biological Sciences: | 10 | |
| Verbal Reasoning: | 10 | *Mean Science* |
| | | 3.7 |

### Tuition and Fees

| Resident | 16,527 |
|---|---|
| Average (public) | 25,100 |
| Average (private) | 42,600 |
| Nonresident | n/app |

0    10    20    30    40    50
(in thousands of dollars)

Percentage receiving financial aid: 50%

Average tuition shown is for U.S. schools.

Above data applies to 2007–2008 academic year.

## Introduction

The Faculty of Medicine was initiated in 1882 and became affiliated with the university in 1912. The Medical School underwent various stages of growth and became closely associated with the Dental School, which was established in 1965. The university is a private school.

## Admissions (OMSAS)

Applicants are considered only from Canadian citizens or permanent residents. Requirements include MCAT scores. To be eligible to apply students must have completed or be currently enrolled in a program leading to an undergraduate degree at a recognized university and expect to have completed a minimum of 15 full or equivalent courses by the end of the academic year (September–April) in which application is being made. Selection is based on academic achievement, MCAT scores, and a personal interview. The latter are granted by invitation. The basic premedical courses are required.

## Curriculum

4-year modern. *Years 1 and 2:* Provide the student with a solid grounding in the basic and clinical sciences. These 2 years are each divided into a series of blocks: Introduction to Medicine, The Thorax, The Abdomen, Head and Neck, Back and Limbs, and Systems. Within each block, various subject areas are presented that integrate the basic and clinical sciences. The weekly timetable is structured around a presenting case that is introduced at the beginning of each week. The case provides the stimulus for instruction, and is designed to highlight a number of objectives of the MD program. Throughout the week, the student is exposed to a variety of teaching methods including small group tutorials, problem-based learning, lectures and large group discussions, self-instructional materials, and laboratories. Time is also provided in the curriculum for students to explore career opportunities. Students participate in early patient contact that emphasizes a patient-centered approach to medicine, beginning in Year 1. Part of being a good physician is understanding the community in which patients live, and the first 2 years of the program provide a variety of opportunities for student involvement in the community. At the end of the first year, all medical students participate in Rural Week to gain clinical experience and exposure to rural medicine in a southwestern Ontario community hospital. *Years 3 and 4:* Include a 52-week integrated clerkship, clinical electives, and advanced basic science electives. During the third year clerkship, the student becomes an active member of clinical care teams in the following medical disciplines: family medicine, medicine, obstetrics and gynecology, pediatrics, psychiatry, and surgery. All students in the third year are required to complete a community clinical clerkship for a minimum of 4 weeks outside of London. Beginning in Year 4, clinical electives are arranged entirely by the student in any area of medicine, at Western or in other centers. After completion of the clinical electives, students return to Western in February for the Transition Period, which includes: advanced basic sciences, advanced communication skills, general review, ecosystem health, and health care systems.

## Grading and Promotion Policies

An Honors/Pass/Fail grading system is used, and taking the USMLE is optional.

## Facilities

*Teaching:* Clinical teaching facilities exist at London Health Science Center, Joseph Health Center, and several other affiliated institutions. *Library:* A comprehensive medical library is available for student and staff use. *Housing:* Information not available.

## Special Features

Three positions in the class will be set aside each year for applicants to the MD-PhD program. If these positions are not filled they would revert to the general pool of slots in the first-year class. The MD-PhD program is an option available to outstanding individuals, both academically and in research potential.

# 10 Opportunities for Women

Historical overview
Women's health issues
Medicine: a career for women
Doors are open
Admission to medical school
The woman physician: a status report
Unique challenges for women in medicine
Financial aid and support sources

## HISTORICAL OVERVIEW

A summary of the history of medical education in the United States reveals the surprising observation that, in terms of acceptance of women into medical school, there is no consistent pattern.

Acceptances of women fluctuated widely until 1970 when a sustained increase ensued. That the road to women gaining admission into medical school has been long and hard may not always be evident. For example, Johns Hopkins School of Medicine accepted women with its first medical school class in 1893 and had more women than men in their entering class. It should be noted, however, that this situation is not as straightforward as it seems. The initial establishment of this school involved a substantial endowment from a group of Baltimore-area women who made their contribution dependent upon the acceptance of women into the school. However, for the most part, during the nineteenth century women primarily participated in health care professions as nurses.

The first American woman medical graduate was Elizabeth Blackwell, who received her degree from (the now defunct) Geneva Medical College in New York in 1849. Prior to that, Harriet Hunt began to practice medicine in 1835 after gaining professional training by serving as an apprentice to a Boston physician. She had been repeatedly denied admission into all of the exclusively male medical schools.

Blackwell's acceptance was followed by a handful of other women. Those women who succeeded in getting into medical school seldom received clinical experience, as hospitals did not want women treating their patients. On the other hand, homeopathic and other nontraditional schools were more liberal regarding admission of women.

The educational opportunities for women improved somewhat when Philadelphia's Quakers established a school in 1850 exclusively for women, Medical College of Pennsylvania (which became coeducational in 1969). This event probably motivated some eminent and enlightened male physicians in New York, Boston, and Chicago to contribute money and use their influence to establish all-women institutions in those three cities.

Unable to gain admission to U.S. schools, starting in the 1880s, women in large numbers went to such European cities as Paris and Zurich to secure a first-rate medical education. However, the struggle was far from over after they completed their medical studies because hospitals would not hire them. Therefore, Elizabeth Blackwell and her sister opened a 24-bed infirmary. (She also opened a medical school, as she was dissatisfied with the caliber of some of the graduates of women's colleges who were working for her.) Some women doctors went west, where they were welcomed because of the rough lifestyle in which circumstances often required prompt treatment of many trauma cases.

After the turn of the century, financial problems as well as the 1910 Flexner report resulted in the closing of some of the all-women medical schools and the merger of others. By 1919 only the original Philadelphia Medical School for Women remained.

When Johns Hopkins introduced coeducational medical training in 1893, other medical schools were encouraged to do the same. However, the door to the admission of women opened only a crack and unofficial quotas existed that kept the numbers of women down to an insignificant amount.

The reduction of male manpower during World War I resulted in a small increase in the number of women accepted into American schools (from 5 to 6%, as compared with 4.4% in 1900).

The longstanding problem for women to secure hospital experience remained. Thus, by the 1920s more than 90% of U.S. hospitals did not accept women and women did not attend institutions run by men.

World War II temporarily lowered the barriers to women gaining admission, since the number of qualified male applicants was limited. After the war, the numbers were once again made smaller so that women were making up only 5 to 8% of entering classes.

Since 1970 there has been a dramatic increase in the enrollment of women due to court decisions and the intense impact of the feminist movement, which swept aside the unofficial quota system.

# WOMEN'S HEALTH ISSUES

A slow but gradual increase in interest in women's health issues is currently taking place. This is due to three factors:

1. women are demanding more from their health care providers;

2. a record number of women are being admitted to medical school;

3. more women have risen to positions where they can influence health policy.

The standard reference patient, used in medical school until recently, was the 70 kilogram male. The special health needs of women, (except for female reproductive organs) were not addressed. Now the NIH has an Office of Research on Women's Health (ORWH) and has funded a more than half-billion-dollar 15-year Women's Health Initiative. Increasing numbers of physicians are taking continuing education courses dealing with woman's health, and medical schools are slowly introducing women's health issues into their curricula.

At one time, it was common practice for research projects to omit women from research trials. This was encouraged by the thalidomide and DES tragedies of the 1960s and 1970s, which resulted in pregnant women and those with childbearing potential being prohibited by the FDA from participating in most drug trials. Moreover, the belief that the monthly hormonal changes in women could destabilize research results further served to restrict research studies to males.

In the early 1980s it was noted that the death rate from heart disease and cancer was the same for both sexes. Nevertheless, the 1982 landmark study of coronary artery disease was restricted to 15,000 males. As a result of intervention by some women in Congress, a task force was established in 1983 to examine the status of American women's health. In 1985 the task force reported, among other things, that the lack of attention to women's health issues had indeed "compromised the quality" of women's health care. Subsequently it was learned that only 13.5% of NIH funds went for research on women's health issues. Although NIH issued new guidelines to include women in clinical research study pools, even by 1990 the situation had not significantly changed. The appointment of the first female NIH director in 1992 led to the establishment of the Office of Research on Women's Health, whose permanency was confirmed by being included in the 1993 NIH Revitalization Act. This act mandated the inclusion of subpopulations (women and minorities) in all NIH-funded studies.

In 1992 the Council on Graduate Medical Education (COGME) identified 42 training components considered essential to preparing physicians to provide comprehensive health care for women. Internists and ob/gyn specialists are currently the principal health care providers for women. Both groups are fully trained to provide all these components. This has prompted self-education on women's health issues by physicians through continuing education courses. The American Medical Women's Association (AMWA) has sponsored development of a two-part course based on the life phases of women, rather than on organs.

While universities in the 1960s and 1970s integrated women's studies into their curricula, medical schools are only now just beginning to focus on women's health issues. Several residency programs have also undertaken initiatives in this area.

One reason to feel there will be improvement in the area of women's health is the fact that it is easier to introduce these issues into problem-based curricula. Because this educational approach is becoming increasingly popular, the trend may impact favorably on helping resolve the question of women's health during the present decade.

Medical College of Pennsylvania (MCP), in cooperation with Hannemann Medical College, is doing the pioneering work in this area. Undoubtedly, as women become increasingly represented on medical school faculties, there will be an acceleration of interest in, and attempts to remedy the absence of, medical education on women's health issues at both the undergraduate and graduate levels. The fact that women now make up about half of each entering class will presumably also impact positively. These efforts will also be furthered by the National Academy on Women's Health Medical Education that was jointly formed by the MCP and AMWA.

There are some who advocate establishing a women's health specialty. Others argue that this would be a mistake, since it would suggest that only those specialists would then be knowledgeable about women's health needs and problems. This debate will ultimately be settled by the wishes of women medical students in terms of merely getting an education or wanting specialty training in the area of women's health, and by the choice of women patients.

In summary, there is a consensus that the time is right to introduce women's health education into the general curriculum but the process may take some time to achieve.

# MEDICINE: A CAREER FOR WOMEN

The large number of women applying to medical school demonstrates how attractive this profession is for them. This career presents them with many opportunities. Women accepted to medical school are as likely to complete their studies as men and will also probably make a lifetime career in the profession.

The special attraction of medicine for women may stem from the following:

1. *Satisfaction*. Practicing medicine provides an opportunity to render a service.

2. *Opportunities*. A broad spectrum of possible roles are offered, such as patient care, teaching, laboratory research, community service, and administration.

3. *Independence*. Convenient hours and distribution of effort among multiple activities can be arranged.

4. *Flexibility*. There is an opportunity to change careers during different phases of life, such as additional educational opportunities, receiving a master's degree in public health, moving into the area of public policy by working for a state or federal agency, or serving in a health-care management position.

5. *Stimulation*. The continuing challenge of practicing medicine provides for lifetime learning and is reinforced by the high prestige of the social role of a physician and the satisfaction of achievements attained through one's intellectual and physical efforts.

## DOORS ARE OPEN _____

By 1975, enrollment of women in medical schools increased to 20%, and by 1980 to 29% of the total number of medical students. For the 2005–06 academic year, first-year women made up more than 40% of the entering class (see Table 10.1). About 50% of the women and (men) who applied since 2005-2006 were admitted to medical school. Of the 126 U.S. medical schools, more than 50 currently have a total female enrollment greater than 50%, and less than 15 schools have a total female enrollment of 40% or less. Consequently, all the other medical schools (about 60), have an enrollment of 40 to 50% women, a dramatic change over the past several decades.

The impact of increased enrollment of women is shown by the fact that in the 40-year span between 1930 and 1970 only 14,000 women graduated from medical school, while over the 10-year period between 1970 and 1980 more than 20,000 women graduated.

The increase in total enrollment that has taken place is not due to an improved aptitude on the part of women students applying or an increase in the number of women obtaining their baccalaureate degree. Rather the increase is probably due to the following reasons: (1) a perceptible change in society's attitude toward women in medicine, particularly in the educational climate; (2) the realization that women make up a vast and untapped source of medical talent; (3) the obvious difference between the proportion of female doctors in this country as against other countries; and (4) the increase in the trend for women to become wage earners, reflecting a changing cultural pattern.

## ADMISSION TO MEDICAL SCHOOL _____

The dramatic change in the admission picture for women is reflected in two major ways. The first manifestation is evident in the number of women being accepted (currently more than 50%) and the number of women in recent graduation classes (presently more than 40%). Second is the sustained character of the positive enrollment picture for women, which has extended for more than 25 years. Thus, while the year-to-year increases have been small over the last few years, they have maintained the forward momentum to the point where an average 40% enrollment level for women in U.S. medical schools becomes a realistic expectation. This is especially true since the white male segment of the applicant pool has decreased sharply over the past 25 years, from nearly 80% to less than 50%, while female applicants constitute well over 40% of the pool, a threefold increase over the same period.

The prospects for women in medicine are more encouraging now than at any other time in the past century. This is clearly evident from a review of the percentages of women accepted in recent years, which establishes that an equal percentage of women to men were accepted from their respective applicant pools. Therefore, it can be anticipated that women will continue to make up a large part of medical school classes in the coming years.

The obvious conclusion is that women now make up a major, permanent segment of the available freshman places.

## THE WOMAN PHYSICIAN: A STATUS REPORT _____

The status of women will be discussed from three perspectives: (1) an overview, (2) residency choices, and (3) faculty appointments.

### An Overview

The initial profile of the typical woman physician emerged from an extensive study that was conducted in 1957 covering graduates from a 15-year period. In terms of their personal life, it showed that 57% of all female doctors were married and that these women had, on the average, 1.8 children (as against the national average of 2.3 children in all medical families). Other findings were that half of the married physicians were part of a husband-wife doctor team and that women doctors were slightly more likely to be divorced than females in the general population. Recent studies updated this profile and showed that

## Table 10.1 PERCENTAGE OF WOMEN IN THE 2008–2009 FIRST-YEAR CLASS

| School | % | School | % |
|---|---|---|---|
| Albany Medical College | 51 | Morehouse School of Medicine | 60 |
| Albert Einstein College of Medicine | 54 | Mount Sinai School of Medicine of New York University | 49 |
| Baylor College of Medicine | 45 | | |
| Boston University School of Medicine | 53 | New Jersey Medical School, University of Medicine and Dentistry | 47 |
| Brody School of Medicine at East Carolina University | 51 | New York Medical College | 50 |
| Case Western Reserve University School of Medicine | 45 | New York University School of Medicine | 50 |
| Chicago Medical School, University of Medicine and Science | 47 | Northeastern Ohio Universities College of Medicine | 51 |
| Columbia University College of Physicians and Surgeons | 50 | Northwestern University Feinberg School of Medicine | 50 |
| Creighton University School of Medicine | 50 | Ohio State University College of Medicine | 43 |
| Dartmouth Medical School | 44 | Oregon Health & Science University | 53 |
| Drexel University College of Medicine | 50 | Pennsylvania State University College of Medicine | 50 |
| Duke University School of Medicine | 49 | Ponce School of Medicine | 50 |
| East Tennessee State University, James H. Quillen College of Medicine | 45 | Robert Wood Johnson Medical School, University of Medicine and Dentistry of New Jersey | 59 |
| Eastern Virginia Medical School | 54 | | |
| Emory University School of Medicine | 53 | Rush Medical College | 60 |
| George Washington University School of Medicine and Health Sciences | 47 | San Juan Bautista Sch. of Med. | 55 |
| | | St. Louis University School of Medicine | 44 |
| Georgetown University School of Medicine | 48 | Southern Illinois University School of Medicine | 45 |
| Harvard Medical School | 47 | Stanford University School of Medicine | 53 |
| Howard University College of Medicine | 50 | State University of New York Upstate Medical University | 51 |
| Indiana University School of Medicine | 44 | | |
| Jefferson Medical College, Thomas Jefferson University | 48 | Stony Brook University School of Medicine | 45 |
| | | SUNY at Buffalo School of Medicine and Biomedical Sciences | 56 |
| Johns Hopkins University School of Medicine | 50 | | |
| Keck School of Medicine of the University of Southern California | 45 | SUNY Downstate Medical Center | 50 |
| | | Temple University School of Medicine | 47 |
| Loma Linda University School of Medicine | 44 | Texas A&M University System, Health Science Center, College of Medicine | 58 |
| Louisiana State University School of Medicine in New Orleans | 45 | | |
| | | Texas Tech University School of Medicine | 40 |
| Louisiana State University School of Medicine in Shreveport | 39 | Tufts University School of Medicine | 46 |
| | | Tulane University School of Medicine | 46 |
| Loyola University Chicago, Stritch School of Medicine | 52 | Uniformed Services University, F. Edward Hebert School of Medicine | 30 |
| Marshall University School of Medicine | 55 | | |
| Mayo Medical School | 46 | Universidad Central del Caribe | 45 |
| Medical College of Georgia | 42 | University of Alabama School of Medicine | 41 |
| Medical College of Wisconsin | 45 | University of Arizona College of Medicine | 62 |
| Medical University of South Carolina College of Medicine | 50 | University of Arkansas College of Medicine | 35 |
| Meharry Medical College School of Medicine | 52 | University of Buffalo School of Medicine and Biomedical Sciences | 56 |
| Mercer University School of Medicine | 50 | University of California — Davis, School of Medicine | 59 |
| Michigan State University College of Human Medicine | 54 | University of California — Irvine, School of Medicine | 49 |

**Table 10.1 PERCENTAGE OF WOMEN IN THE 2008–2009 FIRST-YEAR CLASS (Continued)**

| School | % | School | % |
|---|---|---|---|
| University of California — Los Angeles, David Geffen School of Medicine | 44 | University of Pittsburgh School of Medicine | 40 |
| University of California—San Diego, School of Medicine | 51 | University of Rochester School of Medicine | 52 |
| University of California—San Francisco, School of Medicine | 59 | University of South Alabama College of Medicine | 51 |
| University of Chicago, Pritzker School of Medicine | 53 | University of South Carolina School of Medicine | 50 |
| University of Cincinnati College of Medicine | 33 | University of South Dakota Sanford School of Medicine | 46 |
| University of Colorado School of Medicine | 47 | University of South Florida College of Medicine | 52 |
| University of Connecticut School of Medicine | 53 | University of Tennessee College of Medicine | 41 |
| University of Florida College of Medicine | 48 | University of Texas Medical Branch at Galveston | 54 |
| University of Hawaii at Maanoa, John A. Burns School of Medicine | 48 | University of Texas Medical School at Houston | 40 |
| University of Illinois at Chicago, College of Medicine | 45 | University of Texas Medical School at San Antonio | 50 |
| University of Iowa College of Medicine | 48 | University of Texas, Southwestern Medical School at Dallas | 51 |
| University of Kansas School of Medicine | 53 | University of Toledo | 44 |
| University of Kentucky College of Medicine | 41 | University of Utah School of Medicine | 31 |
| University of Louisville School of Medicine | 44 | University of Vermont College of Medicine | 51 |
| University of Maryland School of Medicine | 55 | University of Virginia School of Medicine | 45 |
| University of Massachusetts Medical School | 55 | University of Washington School of Medicine | 53 |
| University of Miami School of Medicine | 43 | University of Wisconsin School of Medicine | 53 |
| University of Michigan Medical School | 55 | Vanderbilt University School of Medicine | 49 |
| University of Minnesota — Duluth, School of Medicine | 56 | Virginia Commonwealth University School of Medicine | 46 |
| University of Minnesota Medical School — Minneapolis | 46 | Wake Forest University School of Medicine | 50 |
| University of Mississippi School of Medicine | 50 | The Warren Albert Medical School of Brown University | 56 |
| University of Missouri — Columbia, School of Medicine | 46 | Washington University School of Medicine | 48 |
| University of Missouri — Kansas City, School of Medicine | 60 | Wayne State University School of Medicine | 40 |
| University of Nebraska Medical Center | 40 | Weill Medical College of Cornell University | 52 |
| University of Nevada School of Medicine | 53 | West Virginia University School of Medicine | 49 |
| University of New Mexico School of Medicine | 60 | Wright State University School of Medicine | 48 |
| University of North Carolina School of Medicine | 51 | Yale University School of Medicine | 47 |
| University of North Dakota School of Medicine | 58 | | |
| University of Oklahoma College of Medicine | 40 | | |
| University of Pennsylvania School of Medicine | 52 | | |

female doctors married in the same proportion as nonphysicians and that nearly 70% of them had children. Moreover, female physicians were much more likely to have had working mothers than male doctors, indicating the importance of role models in developing career decisions.

In terms of their professional lives, it was found that women tended to practice in larger cities and that a large number (over one-third) worked either on a fixed salary or in what could be characterized as "fixed-hours" positions. Also, women had a slightly higher tendency to specialize than men, with the most popular fields being pediatrics, psychiatry, anesthesiology, and pathology. Other fields having significant appeal to women were obstetrics-gynecology, internal medicine, family practice, and public health. About half were found to have been in full-time practice all of their professional lives and 87% in full- and part-time practice.

Since the 1957 study was conducted, it is clear that extensive changes have occurred. Opinions about the importance of a career for a woman have changed, as well as attitudes concerning traditional family patterns.

Group practice and part- or full-salaried positions with hospitals, health departments, medical schools, or pharmaceutical companies are but some of the ways in which women can enjoy medical careers with regular and reasonable hours. With the increase in the number and size of Health Maintenance Organizations (HMOs) and the possibility of some form of national health insurance plan, the number of these positions most assuredly will increase.

A significant impact that will improve the status of women in medicine is the fact that many women physician leaders say that they feel a responsibility to mentor young women, because they have found that good mentors helped them excel in their own careers. Mentors can be a valuable asset during training. They advise and encourage and can provide inside information. Mentors can serve to nominate their proteges for committee assignments, awards, grants, and competitive positions, and facilitate research and publication. It is not unique to utilize mentoring as a device for professional advancement, since it has long been a primary career tool in medicine. Seeking guidance from a mentor should be a route to follow, even when there are obstacles to establishing such a relationship.

## Residency Choices

With the doors being opened to women, they have moved out of the traditional fields of postgraduate training into all major specialty areas, to differing degrees. A recent survey of the distribution of women in the major residences shows that they can be grouped into six groups, which we categorize as a percentage of all residents:

1. above 50%: pediatrics, geriatric medicine, dermatology, obstetrics/gynecology;
2. 40–50%: preventive medicine, psychiatry;
3. 30–40% family practice, internal medicine, pathology, pediatric subspecialties;
4. 20–30%: anesthesiology, emergency medicine, internal medicine subspecialties, diagnostic radiology;
5. 10–20%: surgery and its subspecialties; and
6. under 10%: orthopedic surgery, urology.

## Faculty Appointments

With women assuming a larger role in medical practice, it is natural that some should elect to enter the field of medical education or academic medicine. They represent about 20% of the basic and clinical science faculties and make up more than 30% in such departments as family practice, obstetrician/gynecology, pediatrics, physical medicine, psychiatry, and public health. This matches the representation in residency training areas, as is indicated in the preceding section.

# UNIQUE CHALLENGES FOR WOMEN IN MEDICINE

There are three major issues facing women in medicine today, namely (1) professional acceptance, (2) gender bias, and (3) family.

## Professional Acceptance

A significant conference entitled "Woman MD" was held at Johns Hopkins University School of Medicine. In attendance were 200 female doctors from across the country who met to study the impact of the increase in the number of women entering medicine. Among the major issues raised were that:

1. Women physicians were looked down upon for showing feelings of tenderness and sadness toward patients and their families, thereby violating what is considered implicit medical standards of behavior. It was pointed out, however, that demonstrating sensitivity and compassion is not incompatible with the need for the doctor to also demonstrate strength.

2. Women physicians often enter specialties they did not originally want because of various family obligations.

3. Women physicians, especially young ones, were concerned that they would not be able to have both a career and a family unless they found a mate who would help with the housework and child rearing—or unless they were untiring "superwomen."

In a summary of the symposium, the women doctors were warned of two separate "pitfalls": an intolerance of the emotional responses of the other sex in times of stress and possible discrimination if they tried to change the medical system too much.

In general, the attitude of young women physicians toward their professional futures is optimistic. The forces responsible for changes have been the trail-blazing efforts of older women, together with changes in societal values and laws. Having become firmly convinced that medicine is a suitable career choice, more and more women are applying to medical schools and discriminatory barriers are falling.

## Gender Bias

In the early 1990s several medical journals published the results of surveys among female medical students and residents regarding harassment. The results indicate that between 50 and 75% experienced some form of gender discrimination. The offensive behavior took the form of denied professional opportunities, malicious gossip, sexist slurs, and even sexual advances. Surprisingly, harassment varied with different fields, being most prevalent in general surgery and least in pediatrics. Students were reportedly harassed by both faculty and residents. While harassment during medical training is quite common, women face this issue more intensely because of their gender. The hierarchical nature of the medical power structure, with men in the upper echelons, is thought to contribute to this problem.

Gender bias impacts on women negatively, both directly and indirectly. It may slow their advancement, thereby keeping them in a lower pay scale, and may also be psychologically damaging enough to lower self-confidence and sometimes work performance.

Efforts are being made to curtail harassment. This includes periodic publication by the medical school of its policy against discrimination, presenting "Gender Neutral Awards" to faculty who are especially sensitive to gender issues, establishing workshops where the relationship between genders are discussed, sponsoring lectures, publishing newsletters, and providing support groups.

## Family

A recent survey indicated that about 10% of female medical graduates had one or more dependents. This represents about 3,000 medical school students. While the issue of childbearing during medical training years has long been known to educators, little progress has been made to satisfactorily resolve it. The problem is being addressed on an *ad hoc* basis, which may in some cases provide for flexibility, rather than by having written institutional policies addressing maternity leave. As the percentage of women medical students increases, this issue will probably be brought to the forefront.

There is conflicting advice being offered on preparing for parenting, with some advocating preparation, while others emphasizing the importance of the need to adapt as problems arise. Certainly, medical residents, who frequently are guaranteed about six weeks of parental leave, should advise their program directors well in advance so that adequate coverage during their absence can be provided. It should be noted that a substantial number of residency programs do not have written parental leave policies and that those that do vary.

Of special significance are the child-care arrangements that are made prior to delivery. In most cases where a day-care center or other facility has to be used, the availability of a backup care provider is still essential. A supportive spouse is a key element in the quest to attain successful parenting.

There appears to be no ideal time for a woman physician to have a child. Young children may make it difficult to pursue her studies and training, and she may be at a financial disadvantage during that part of her life. Conversely, delaying child bearing may result in infertility as a result of normal age-related changes. This is a highly personal choice, and individual circumstances will influence it. Young women, perhaps, should seek the advice of older women physicians as they make their plans.

For additional information see:

*Journal of the American Medical Women's Association*, May/June 1992.

*Working and Parenting* by B. Brazelton, Addison-Wesley, 1985.

*Day-Care: Finding the Best Child Care for Your Family*, American Academy of Pediatrics, Dept. C/H, 141 NW Point Blvd, Elk Grove, IL 60007.

*Medicine and Parenting*, 1991, and *Building a Stronger Women's Program*, 1993, AAMC Publication Sales, 2450 N Street NW, Washington, DC 20037.

## Bottom Line

- Currently at least 50% of all applicants to medical school are women.

- Currently, almost 50% of all those admitted are women.

- Given the above situation, it is anticipated that half of all prospective residents will be women, but their distribution among the specialties will vary greatly.

- Women are admitted to all U.S. medical schools. The last remaining all-women medical school accepted its first male students in 1970.

- Women tend to not do as well as men on the basic science segment of the licensing exam. In the second and third parts, which are clinically oriented, the gender gap apparently disappears.

- Women medical students appear to experience more stress than males, which may be manifested as depression, increased alcohol use, and personal problems.

- More than half the women specialists are board certified.

- The number of married women entering medical school is low (about 15%). By graduation this number usually doubles.

- Women predominantly favor specialization in pediatrics, psychiatry, family practice, and obstetrics/gynecology. Only very limited numbers are seeking postgraduate training in general surgery and consequently, any of its subspecialties.

# FINANCIAL AID AND SUPPORT SOURCES

The following are financial aid sources specifically for women students. Additional details are available from the organizations listed below:

1. American Association of University Women Educational Foundation. Contact: Director, Fellowships Office, American Association of University Women, 1111 16th Street, NW, Washington, DC 20036.

2. American Medical Women's Association Loan Fund. Contact: American Medical Women's Association, Inc., 801 North Fairfax Street, Alexandria, VA 22314.

3. Educational Financial Aid Sources for Women. Contact: Clairol Loving Care Scholarship Program, 345 Park Avenue, New York, NY 10022.

In the past several years a number of groups have become active with an aim to facilitate women's adaptation to the demands of residency. They include:

American Medical Student Association, Women in Medicine Task Force, 1902 Association Drive, Reston, VA 22091.

American Medical Women's Association, 2302 East Speedway #206A, Tucson, AZ 85719.

Association of American Medical Colleges, Special Assistant to the President on Women's Issues, 2450 N Street NW, Washington, DC 20037.

# Opportunities for Minorities

Minorities in medicine: historical perspective
Doors are open for minorities
Admission of minorities: a status report
Current challenges
Financial aid for minority students
Summer enrichment programs

## MINORITIES IN MEDICINE: HISTORICAL PERSPECTIVE

Currently, a very substantial number of practicing African-American physicians are graduates of one medical school, Howard University College of Medicine, Washington, DC, one of the three predominantly black schools. At one time, virtually all African-American medical students attended these schools. By the end of World War II, one-third of medical schools were exclusively white and, as late as 1960, African-Americans were unable to gain admission to 12 schools. In 1968 the AAMC strongly urged medical schools to begin to admit increased numbers of minority students.

The three medical schools, Howard (Washington, DC), Meharry (Nashville, Tennessee), and Morehouse (Atlanta, Georgia), continue to play a major role in training the pool of minority medical students, admitting about 15% of all such students. From the other 123 allopathic schools, six account for another 15%. Thus, nine schools currently accept about one-third of all underrepresented students.

The three traditionally black medical schools remain attractive to minority students for a variety of reasons. Such schools tend to cost less than many predominantly white institutions. They also provide more role models, having many African-Americans on their faculties. Socialization problems, so common at nonminority schools, obviously do not exist. These schools seem to carefully monitor academic performance and provide assistance to their students, even those not at risk to fail. Thus, the three historically black schools have retained their pivotal position in the education of underrepresented minority physicians (even though they now contain a significant number of white students among their student bodies).

## DOORS ARE OPEN FOR MINORITIES

The academic medical community has responded in a positive manner to provide greater opportunities for members of minority groups to secure admission. There are intensive efforts to enroll minority group members: African-Americans, Native Americans/Alaskan natives, Mexican Americans, mainland Puerto Ricans, Asians, or Pacific Islanders. This policy has been effective, as reflected by the fact that, for example, from 1990–95, minority group members, making up the first-year class, increased to 2,000, or about 12%. This represents a significant increase over the less than 5% representation about two decades earlier. Facilitating this process is the fact that many schools have a specific person to deal with minority affairs. Thus, if you are a member of a minority group, you should often address your inquiries to "Director of Minority Affairs."

A special service that has been initiated to assist such students is the Medical

Minority Applicant Registry (Med-MAR). This service enables any minority student applying to medical school to have his or her basic biography (except GPA and MCAT scores) circulated to all U.S. medical schools without charge. A list of such students is published two times a year. To be put on this list, you should identify yourself on the questionnaire as a member of a minority group at the time you take the MCAT, or contact the Minority Student Information Clearing House, Association of American Medical Colleges, One Dupont Circle, NW, Suite 200, Washington, DC 20036.

You should also consider that some medical schools may waive their application fee for minority group students with economic need. The AMCAS fee can also be waived because of financial need, but the MCAT fee is never waived.

The increase in the number of African-Americans being admitted to medical school has had an impact on their total enrollment and on the number of African-Americans graduating. As expected, the number of African-Americans undertaking graduate education, that is, securing special training by means of residencies, has increased significantly over the past decade. The majority of African-Americans initiating residency training do so at hospitals located in California, Maryland, New Jersey, New York, and Pennsylvania. The majority of African-Americans in residency programs are being trained in five specialties: family practice, internal medicine, obstetrics-gynecology, pediatrics, and surgery.

To help disadvantaged or minority group students, some schools arrange special summer programs prior to the formal beginning of medical school for candidates already admitted. In addition, a variety of flexible curricular alternatives are available in some schools for such students as they progress through medical school. For specific information on these programs, contact the Office of Minority Students Affairs at the individual schools.

Summaries of special minority admissions programs are outlined for individual schools in the special features section of the medical school profiles, which are found in Chapter 9.

## ADMISSION OF MINORITIES: A STATUS REPORT

The number of applicants from underrepresented minorities has decreased since 1996. Between 1992 and 1998 minority applicants had a statistically better chance of being accepted to medical school than others. Since then, however, the trend has been reversed for black applicants (but not for other minority group members). In recent years, minority students have made up less than 11% of first-year classes.

The reason for the decline in minority enrollment may be due to the elimination or modification of affirmative action policies. The conflict over medical school admissions policies and minority representation stems from a 1978 case of a student, Alan Bakke, who sued a medical school because he was rejected when his credentials were superior to those of several African-American students who were accepted. He argued that the medical school turned him down on the basis of race in order to achieve a minimum racial quota of minority students. The Supreme Court supported Mr. Bakke's contention and disallowed reverse discrimination but permitted race to be considered one of the factors in the admissions decision. The second part of this decision was reversed in 1996 and in subsequent rulings by the Court of Appeals for the Fifth Circuit. Civil rights groups are seeking to overturn the appeal court's action.

Attempts to overturn affirmative action at the ballot box are also being opposed by a variety of professional health care organizations. The educational and legal systems have yet to find a balanced formula that takes into account the needs of white students with good grades and high MCAT scores who may not be admitted to medical school in favor of minority students who are competing to fill the same openings.

On the positive side, the minority applicant pool has remained significant, and the chances of admission are 50%, as compared with 40% a decade ago. The mean MCAT scores for minority applicants have also improved. There remains, though, a

## Table 11.1 PERCENTAGE OF MINORITY STUDENTS IN THE 2008–2009 FIRST-YEAR CLASS

| School | % | School | % |
|---|---|---|---|
| Albany Medical College | 3 | Morehouse School of Medicine | 75 |
| Albert Einstein College of Medicine | 13 | Mount Sinai School of Medicine of New York University | 19 |
| Baylor College of Medicine | 11 | New Jersey Medical School, University of Medicine and Dentistry | 16 |
| Boston University School of Medicine | 18 | New York Medical College | 37 |
| Brody School of Medicine at East Carolina University | 32 | New York University School of Medicine | 5 |
| Brown Medical School | 7 | Northeastern Ohio Universities College of Medicine | 6 |
| Case Western Reserve University School of Medicine | 10 | Northwestern University Feinberg School of Medicine | 5 |
| Chicago Medical School, University of Medicine and Science | 5 | Ohio State University College of Medicine | 10 |
| Columbia University College of Physicians and Surgeons | 9 | Oregon Health & Science University | 3 |
| Creighton University School of Medicine | 8 | Pennsylvania State University College of Medicine | 10 |
| Dartmouth Medical School | 22 | Ponce School of Medicine | 99 |
| Drexel University College of Medicine | 19 | Robert Wood Johnson Medical School, University of Medicine and Dentistry of New Jersey | 8 |
| Duke University School of Medicine | 22 | |  |
| East Tennessee State University, James H. Quillen College of Medicine | 5 | Rush Medical College | 2 |
| Eastern Virginia Medical School | 5 | San Juan Bautista, Sch. of Med. | 10 |
| Emory University School of Medicine | 25 | St. Louis University School of Medicine | 6 |
| George Washington University School of Medicine and Health Sciences | 19 | Southern Illinois University School of Medicine | 18 |
| Georgetown University School of Medicine | 7 | Stanford University School of Medicine | 17 |
| Harvard Medical School | 11 | State University of New York Upstate Medical University | 11 |
| Howard University College of Medicine | 49 | Stony Brook University School of Medicine | 17 |
| Indiana University School of Medicine | 11 | SUNY at Buffalo School of Medicine and Biomedical Sciences | 5 |
| Jefferson Medical College, Thomas Jefferson University | 11 | SUNY Downstate Medical Center | 10 |
| Johns Hopkins University School of Medicine | 11 | Temple University School of Medicine | 7 |
| Keck School of Medicine of the University of Southern California | 25 | Texas A&M University System, Health Science Center, College of Medicine | 4 |
| Loma Linda University School of Medicine | 6 | Texas Tech University School of Medicine | 10 |
| Louisiana State University School of Medicine in New Orleans | 4 | Tufts University School of Medicine | 11 |
| Louisiana State University School of Medicine in Shreveport | 6 | Tulane University School of Medicine | 3 |
| Loyola University Chicago, Stritch School of Medicine | 3 | Uniformed Services University, F. Edward Hebert School of Medicine | 6 |
| Marshall University School of Medicine | 22 | Universidad Central del Caribe | 15 |
| Mayo Medical School | 10 | University of Alabama School of Medicine | 6 |
| Medical College of Georgia | 6 | University of Arizona College of Medicine | 4 |
| Medical College of Wisconsin | 11 | University of Arkansas for Medical Sciences, College of Medicine | 3 |
| Medical University of South Carolina College of Medicine | 7 | University of California — Davis, School of Medicine | 59 |
| Meharry Medical College School of Medicine | 40 | University of California — Irvine, School of Medicine | 3 |
| Mercer University School of Medicine | 2 | University of California — Los Angeles, David Geffen School of Medicine | 9 |
| Michigan State University College of Human Medicine | 5 | University of California — San Diego, School of Medicine | 1 |

**Table 11.1  PERCENTAGE OF MINORITY STUDENTS IN THE 2008–2009 FIRST-YEAR CLASS (Continued)**

| School | % | School | % |
|---|---|---|---|
| University of California — San Francisco, School of Medicine | 13 | University of Pittsburgh School of Medicine | 16 |
| University of Chicago, Pritzker School of Medicine | 12 | University of Rochester School of Medicine | 19 |
| University of Cincinnati College of Medicine | 9 | University of South Alabama College of Medicine | 7 |
| University of Colorado School of Medicine | 3 | University of South Carolina School of Medicine | 7 |
| University of Connecticut School of Medicine | 15 | University of South Dakota Sanford School of Medicine | 1 |
| University of Florida College of Medicine | 16 | University of South Florida College of Medicine | 13 |
| University of Hawaii at Maanoa, John A. Burns School of Medicine | 42 | University of Tennessee College of Medicine | 13 |
| University of Illinois at Chicago College of Medicine | 11 | University of Texas Medical Branch at Galveston | 10 |
| University of Iowa College of Medicine | 48 | University of Texas Medical School at Houston | 21 |
| University of Kansas School of Medicine | 8 | University of Texas Medical School at San Antonio | 23 |
| University of Kentucky College of Medicine | 6 | University of Texas, Southwestern Medical School at Dallas | 49 |
| University of Louisville School of Medicine | 9 | University of Toledo | 9 |
| University of Maryland School of Medicine | 12 | University of Utah School of Medicine | 0 |
| University of Massachusetts Medical School | 10 | University of Vermont College of Medicine | 24 |
| University of Miami School of Medicine | 6 | University of Virginia School of Medicine | 19 |
| University of Michigan Medical School | 7 | University of Washington School of Medicine | 1 |
| University of Minnesota — Duluth, School of Medicine | 12 | University of Wisconsin School of Medicine | 11 |
| University of Minnesota Medical School— Minneapolis | 24 | Vanderbilt University School of Medicine | 19 |
| University of Mississippi School of Medicine | 17 | Virginia Commonwealth University School of Medicine | 6.3 |
| University of Missouri — Columbia, School of Medicine | 0 | Wake Forest University School of Medicine | 8 |
| University of Missouri — Kansas City, School of Medicine | 0 | Washington University School of Medicine | 11 |
| University of Nebraska Medical Center | 18 | Wayne State University School of Medicine | 8 |
| University of Nevada School of Medicine | 24 | Weill Medical College of Cornell University | 18 |
| University of New Mexico School of Medicine | 40 | West Virginia University School of Medicine | 3 |
| University of North Carolina at Chapel Hill School of Medicine | 12 | Wright State University School of Medicine | 20 |
| University of North Dakota School of Medicine | 21 | Yale University School of Medicine | 13 |
| University of Oklahoma College of Medicine | 18 | | |
| University of Pennsylvania School of Medicine | 10 | | |

discrepancy when compared with the acceptance rate for majority applicants, which currently stands at 55%. Also, the attrition rate among minority medical students has doubled over the past decade to 12%.

The cutback in educational funding has made acceptance into medical school a formidable challenge for underprivileged students; the dropout rate along the way is high from completion of elementary school through college. In addition, these students are being discouraged by the same factors that have generated a negative climate relative to choosing medicine as a career. These include talk of an oversupply of physicians, malpractice litigation publicity, rising tuition costs, and (for some) the need to treat AIDS patients.

# CURRENT CHALLENGES

This subject will be considered from two perspectives, enrollment and retention.

## Enrollment

Over the past decade, the overall composition of the entering medical school classes has changed from predominantly white male to a very substantial number of women and a modest, yet significant, number of minority members. This radical change is in response to the drastic alteration in the social climate of the United States.

Currently, although African-Americans make up 12% of the population, they account for only 3% of the physicians in the United States and 8% of the medical students in the country. Similarly, Hispanic-Americans comprise 9% of the population and 4% of the nation's physicians. Native Americans fare worse, making up 0.8% of the public and 0.1% of its doctors. These three groups are thus considered underrepresented minorities. The medical education establishment responds to these facts by maintaining an ambitious recruitment campaign.

## Retention

Many medical schools make special efforts to assist disadvantaged students. They provide summer enrichment programs for premeds to help prepare for MCATs, as well as an experience in basic premed science coursework and research. This is usually the first opportunity for premeds to meet an academic physician. Enrichment programs were found to improve subsequent academic performance. Many schools also offer postbaccalaureate and prematriculation programs to accepted minority students in order to prepare them academically before they must face the pressures of their first year in medical school. These programs are attractive because they have a small faculty-student ratio and provide early exposure to the basic medical sciences. In some schools, students are permitted to lighten the load of the first year by satisfactorily completing part of it in advance. Flexible curricula and five-year programs are becoming more common in medical schools. Many schools also make special efforts to prepare minority students for the USMLE. All of the aforementioned strategies enhance both recruitment and retention of disadvantaged students. In addition, such students have access to the wide variety of academic and social support services offered to all students.

The cost of medical education remains high and can reach $150,000 for four years of tuition and fees at some schools. This can be especially burdensome for minority students. The average debt of African-American students after college and medical school exceeds $55,000. Yet the dropout rate does not seem to have been heavily influenced by the financial demands of medical education. A potentially disturbing issue is the possibility that federally funded minority scholarships may be in danger of being curtailed.

Recognizing the demographic shift toward a multiethnic and multiracial society, the AAMC established a special recruitment campaign—Project 3000 by 2000—to enhance science education in public schools, thus helping to nurture the potential pool of minority applicants.

Minority applicants can now explore the opportunities that are offered to them at the schools to which they are considering applying and can determine if they will feel comfortable there for four years.

While enrollment efforts have had a positive impact on increasing minority class representation, it is now recognized that these efforts need to be strengthened to encourage students to endure the rigors of the training process and to complete their medical studies. This is indicated by the fact that the dropout rate for freshman minority students is close to 10%, as compared with 3% for all other students.

The cause of the increased dropout rate among minority students may not be exclusively academic, but, rather, due to cultural conflicts and lack of social adjustment. Many minority students are the first members of their family to have reached such an educational level and are under intense pressure to succeed. Many minority students have attained admission to medical school without encouragement, and may even have been advised against pursuing higher education or a professional career. Therefore, for most of them, medical school is a pioneering experience in a not too supportive environment. This makes the process an extremely challenging one. A major element influencing this situation is a lack of role models, since few minority members come from physician families. Moreover, only about 3% of all medical school faculty are minority physicians. (Included in this figure are those at predominantly black institutions.) There is the perception that minority faculty are more approachable and responsive to disadvantaged students. Such support can be critical to a student's progress. The number of minority residents is unfortunately not large enough to have them serve as role models. In all, the lack of role models is considered a critical issue in the retention of minority students.

Medical schools that have been successful in recruitment and retention of minorities have made use of mentoring programs. A mentor can provide a direct vision of what it means to be a physician. The mentor can not only offer support during difficult intervals, but also can help students make pivotal career choices relative to such issues as choosing electives, specialization, and where to do one's residency training. At some institutions, white faculty members have been used to serve as mentors, due to the shortage of minority faculty.

A lack of social interaction in medical school leads to a sense of isolation among minority students. This leads them to form their own networks, which helps to a degree. Having a chapter of a national minority student organization on campus also can be useful as a form of protection against social isolation.

Because of alienation early in their education, minority students frequently do not acquire desirable skills for group learning. Also, they often are not prepared for the demanding workload in medical school. For some minority students who lack adequate academic preparedness, improvement in study skills is essential.

Success in handling standardized tests—the SAT I or ACT exam, MCAT, or USMLE—is especially challenging for minority students. Hispanic students, who frequently speak English as a second language, are at a special disadvantage. Remaining in medical school is often closely tied to performance on Step 1 of the USMLE.

# FINANCIAL AID FOR MINORITY STUDENTS

The following listing gives a brief idea of the scholarships and loans available for minority group students. Additional information is available from each of the sources cited:

1. National Medical Fellowships, Inc. For minority group students. Contact: Executive Secretary, 110 West 32nd Street, New York, NY 10001.

2. American Medical Association and Research Foundation. Contact: Foundation, 535 North Dearborn, Chicago, IL 60610.

3. National Scholarship Service and Fund for Negro Students. Contact: Executive Director, NSSFNS Application Department, 250 Auburn Avenue, Suite 500, Atlanta, GA 30303.

4. United Student Aid Funds, Inc. For low-income families. Contact: Executive Director, 11100 USA Parkway, Fishers, IN 46038.

5. Emergency Scholarships. For American Indian students. Contact: Association on American Indian Affairs, P.O. Box 268, Sisseton, SD 57262

6. Bureau of Indian Affairs. For American Indians and Eskimos. Contact: Director, Higher Education Program, 500 Gold, S.W., Albuquerque, NM 87103.

Additional information is available from the AAMC by writing to the Minority Student Opportunities in U.S. Medical Schools, AAMC, 2450 N Street NW, Washington, DC 20037.

Information on financial aid is also available from the following sources:

1. *Financial Aid for Minorities in Health Fields*, published by Garrett Park Press, PO Box 190, Garrett Park, MD 20896, 1993. It contains references to fellowships, loans, grants, and awards.

2. Office of Statewide Health Planning and Development, Health Profession Career Opportunity Program, 1600 Ninth Street, Sacramento, CA 95814. Upon request, you will receive a free copy of *Financial Advice for Minority Students Seeking an Education in the Health Professions*.

3. Office of the Associate Dean for Student Affairs, Boston University, School of Medicine, 80 East Concord Street, Boston, MA 02118. Ask for *Financing Medical Education*.

# SUMMER ENRICHMENT PROGRAMS

Summer enrichment programs are designed to increase the minority applicant pool in medical schools. Participants obtain a variety of assistance, including concentrated science review courses. They also receive help in improving test taking, study and writing skills, and clinical research lab exposure.

**California**
*Student Research Program*
American Heart Association
1710 Gilbreth Road
Burlingame, CA 94010
(415) 259-6700

*Minority Access to Health Careers Program*
MAHC Program
California Polytechnic State University
San Luis Obispo, CA 93407
(805) 756-2840

*HCOP Summer Enrichment Program*
Program Coordinator
San Jose State University
College of Applied Arts and Sciences
One Washington Square
San Jose, CA 95192
(408) 924-2911

*Collegiate Union for Health-Related Education (CUHRE)*
Aztec Center, 305A
San Diego State University
San Diego, CA 92182
(619) 594-4793

*Summer Academic Study Program (SASP)*
Office of Minority Affairs
School of Medicine
University of California, Davis
Davis, CA 95616
(916) 752-4808

*Summer Premedical Program*
Office of Educational and Community Programs
College of Medicine
University of California, Irvine
PO Box 4089
Irvine, CA 92717
(714) 824-4603

*Enrichment Program*
Office of Student Support Services, B-154 CHS
School of Medicine
University of California, Los Angeles
Los Angeles, CA 90024
(310) 825-3575

*HePP Consortium for Health Care Preparation*
Office of Minority Affairs
School of Medicine
University of Southern California
1333 San Pablo St., MCH 51-C
Los Angeles, CA 90033
(213) 342-1050

*Summer Research Training Program for College Students*
Graduate Division
513 Parnassus, S-140, Box 0404
University of California, San Francisco
San Francisco, CA 94143
(415) 476-8134

*Summer MCAT Preparation Program*
Center for Educational Achievement
Charles R. Drew University
School of Medicine and Science
1621 East 120th Street
Los Angeles, CA 90059
(213) 563-4926

*Summer Interships*
Hispanic Center of Excellence
University of California, San Francisco
145 Irving Street, Rm. 106
San Francisco, CA 94143
(415) 476-3667

*Project Prepare*
Medical Center
University of Southern California
1975 Zonal Avenue, KAM B-29
Los Angeles, CA 90033
(213) 342-1328

**Connecticut**
*Medical/Dental Preparatory Program*
Office of Student Affairs, MC 3905
Health Center
University of Connecticut
Farmington, CT 06030
(203) 679-3483

**District of Columbia**
*Summer Health Careers Advanced Enrichment Program*
Director, Center for Preprofessional Education
Box 473, Administrative Building
Howard University
Washington, DC 20059
(202) 806-7231

**Iowa**
*Summer Enrichment Program*
Associate for Student Affairs
University of Iowa
College of Medicine
124 Medicine Administration Building
Iowa City, IA 52242
(319) 335-8056

**Louisiana**
*Summer Reinforcement and Enrichment Program (SREP)*
Office of MEDREP
Tulane Medical Center
1430 Tulane Avenue-SL 40
New Orleans, LA 70112
(504) 588-5327

**Massachusetts**
*Summer Honors Undergraduate Research Program*
Division of Medical Science
Harvard Medical School
260 Longwood Avenue
Boston, MA 02115
(617) 432-4980

*Minority Summer Research Program*
MIT Summer Research Program
Graduate School Office, Rm. 3-138
Cambridge, MA 02139
(617) 253-4869

*Summer Enrichment Program*
Office of Outreach Programs
University of Massachusetts
55 Lake Avenue N
Worchester, MA 01655
(508) 856-5541

## Michigan

*Summer Enrichment Program in Health Administration for Undergraduate Minority Students*
Department of Health Services, Management and Policy
M 3031 School of Public Health II
University of Michigan
Ann Arbor, MI 48109
(313) 763-9900

## Minnesota

*Summer Inorganic Chemistry and Precalculus Program*
*Summer Biology Program*
*Summer Organic Chemistry and Calculus Program*
*Summer Physics Program*
515 Delaware Street SE
1-125 Moos Tower
Minneapolis, MN 55455
(612) 624-5904

## Nebraska

*Summer Research Enrichment Program*
Director, Multicultural Affairs Office
600 South 42nd Street
Omaha, NE 68198
(402) 559-4437

## New York

*Summer Student Program*
Science Education Center, Bldg. 438
Brookhaven National Laboratory
Upton (Long Island), NY 11973
(631) 282-4503

*Travelers Summer Research Fellowship for Minority Premedical Students*
Cornell University Medical College
1300 York Avenue, D-119
New York, NY 10021
(212) 746-1057

*Summer Research Fellowship (SURF) Program*
Director, Ethnic and Multicultural Affairs
School of Medicine and Dentistry
University of Rochester
601 Elmwood Avenue
Rochester, NY 14642
(716) 272-2175

## North Carolina

*College Phase Summer Program*
Office of Minority Affairs
Bowman Gray School of Medicine
Medical Center Boulevard
Winston-Salem, NC 27157
(910) 716-4201

**Ohio**
*Pre-Entry Program*
MEDPATH
1178 Graves Hall
College of Medicine
Ohio State University
Columbus, OH 43210
(614) 292-3161
Fax (614) 688-4041

*Summer Scholars Program*
College of Osteopathic Medicine
Ohio University
Center for Excellence
930 Grosvenor Hall
Athens, OH 45701
(614) 593-0917

*Summer Premedical Enrichment Program*
Office of Student Affairs and Admissions
College of Medicine
University of Cincinnati
231 Bethesda Avenue
Cincinnati, OH 45267
(513) 538-7212

**Oklahoma**
*Headlands Indian Health Careers Summer Program*
Headlands Indian Health Careers
BSEB Rm 200
University of Oklahoma
Health Sciences Center
PO Box 26901
Oklahoma City, OK 73126
(405) 271-2250

**Pennsylvania**
*Summer Premedical Academic Enrichment Program*
Director of Minority Programs
School of Medicine
University of Pittsburgh
M-247 Scaife Hall
Pittsburgh, PA 15261
(412) 648-8987

**Texas**
*Honors Premedical Academy*
Project Coordinator
Division of School Based Programs
Baylor College of Medicine
1709 Dryden, Suite 545
Houston, TX 77030
(800) 798-8244

*Bridge to Medicine Summer Program for Minority Disadvantaged College Students*
Office of Student Affairs and Admissions
College of Medicine
Texas A&M University
106 Reynolds Medical Building
College Station, TX 77843
(409) 862-4065

**Virginia**
*Medical Academic Advancement Program*
Office of Student Academic Support
School of Medicine, Box 446
University of Virginia
Charlottesville, VA 22908
(804) 924-2189

**Washington**
*Northwest Consortium Minority Medical Education Program (MMEP)*
School of Medicine SM-22
University of Washington
Seattle, WA 98195
(206) 685-2489

**Wisconsin**
*Summer Science Enrichment Program*
School of Dentistry
Marquette University
PO Box 1881
Milwaukee, WI 53201
(414) 288-1533

## Bottom Line

The medical education establishment is committed to increasing the number of under-represented minorities in medical school. To this end, it is to your advantage to:

- Visit the AAMC site considering Career in Medicine and Applying to Medical School (*www.aamc.org*).

- Seek a **Summer Medical Education Program (SMEP)** sponsored by the AAMC. It provides full tuition, housing and meals, over a six-week **summer preparatory medical school program**. Awards are made to highly motivated students seeking admission to medical schools. Also, a list of Summer Enrichment Programs is provided.

- **Medical Careers** are another source of information that should be made use of.

- For those with extreme financial limitations, there is assistance available through the AAMC's **Free Assistant Program (FAP)**. If approved, you can reduce the MCAT from $180 to $75 and receive transmission of 10 free medical school applications.

- During the MCAT exam, students from racial and ethnic groups that are underrepresented in medicine or are economically disadvantaged may choose to take part in a self-identification registry, the **Minority Medical Applicant Registry (Med-Mar)**. This free listing provides basic biographical information and MCAT scores to all AAMC member medical colleges for their consideration.

# 12 Financing Your Medical Education

Introduction
Financial aid primer
The current financial aid crisis
Successfully managing educational indebtedness
Scholarships and loans
Useful financial definitions

## INTRODUCTION

A medical education can be extremely expensive. The annual tuition at the costliest school has exceeded $28,000, and the national mean for private schools is more than $16,000 per academic year.

The reason for high tuition is many-faceted. Many schools are burdened with the major expense of sustaining commitments—from tenured faculty to capital improvements. Research, which requires a physical plant and equipment, is no longer as heavily subsidized by the federal government. Medical technology has created increasingly costly instrumentation that must be updated to maintain the state-of-the-art performance.

Essentially, tuition constitutes only a very small part of the school's income. The bulk of the income comes from research grants, government funding, endowments, and medical practice fees. For most private schools the critical factor is the endowment. For public medical schools the allotment by the state legislature is the determining factor, with the state's economy and demographics being the key factors.

The only bright spot in the financial picture is that there is evidence that tuition levels may have peaked and recently, in a few cases, tuition reductions have taken place, perhaps in response to the decline in applicants during the late 1980s.

The high cost of medical education raises problems for many students. Various sources of financial assistance are presently available, so that, once accepted, a student can feel relatively assured that adequate financial support will be forthcoming, if not in scholarships, then in loans. Recent proposed cuts in the federal aid to medical schools have included mostly attempts to cut back on research and building grants. These cuts in funding would affect the research being done primarily by staff professors and would threaten the future of research and the training of research scientists. In addition, other proposals include the substitution of a loan program instead of scholarships for students. Needless to say, educators have been decrying these cuts and have been urging a reassessment of financial allocations.

How do medical students meet their expenses? Usually from multiple sources including gifts and loans from families, their own earnings, and, if married, their spouses' earnings. Scholarships and loans form another major source of financial assistance, with about 50% of all students currently being helped by either of these means. Employment during medical school is not advisable, but work during the summers is possible. In light of this situation, it is important that prospective medical students anticipating the need for financial assistance undertake long term planning early in their careers. Once the student has been accepted and has decided to attend a school, the financial aid office should be contacted for information and assistance. In most cases, financial aid is provided solely on the basis of need.

In determining how to finance your medical education, keep the following points in mind:

1. The most important sources of current financial information are the individual schools.

2. Students who are planning to apply to medical school should obtain current information as to tuition and fees (and any projected increases), room and board, and other expenses (see specific school catalog Table 8.1, Chapter 8).

3. Students who have been accepted and are considering enrolling at a school should request relevant information from the school's Financial Aid Office.

4. Students who have decided to enroll at a school should arrange to obtain specific information about a personal aid package by requesting an interview with the school's financial aid officer.

5. Some federally funded programs exist (see Scholarships and Loans section) that provide financial aid for medical school students in return for a specified number of years of service.

6. Students should realize that the financial aid picture is a changing one and that the general pattern of aid has been toward a declining level of support.

7. Financial aid awards are usually made on the basis of demonstrated need established by a financial analysis system. There are three national organizations that analyze the information provided by the students and their families. The results are sent to the individual medical schools. The schools then determine the award to be made.

8. Public medical schools are less expensive for residents and, generally, for non-residents also than private schools. This applies to both tuition and fees as well as all other expenses.

9. In 2005–2006, the *average* cost of tuition and fees for freshman medical students will be about $12,399 for residents and $27,297 for nonresidents at a *public* school, and $32,000 at a *private* school.

10. The total *average* expenses (tuition, fees, living) for 2005–2006 for a freshman thus can be estimated as $20,800 for a resident attending a state school and $34,000 for a nonresident. For a student attending a private school, the average total expenses were about $37,000.

Note that there is a range on both sides of all the above figures.

## FINANCIAL AID PRIMER

Financial support during one's medical education is dependent upon personal need; a brief discussion of financial management is therefore in order.

The basic challenge facing most medical students is how to be able to maintain one's life style while avoiding falling into excessive debt. The key is to determine how far you need to go into debt in order to maintain an adequate standard of life, while meeting your educational obligations and also securing a loan at the lowest cost.

It is essential to maintain a good credit rating to insure that you earn the loans you will need to cover your substantial expenses. Be aware that *a poor credit rating can jeopardize your acceptance into medical school*. Schools may question the desirability of granting an acceptance if they are unconvinced that the applicant will obtain essential loans. Your credit standing in most states can be secured for a small fee (around $15) from one of the following:

- Equifax Credit Information Services, Inc. 1-800-997-2493
- Experian 1-800-397-3742
- Transunion 1-800-888-4213

You should be reminded that credit card interest rates can be very high, can accumulate quickly, and can overwhelm an individual to the point of damaging one's credit rating. Using a debit card, which immediately deducts from your bank account upon making a purchase, can help keep matters under control.

The key to remaining financially solvent is to live within one's budget. While schools' financial aid offices will help develop a budget for their students to determine the extent of their need for scholarships and loans, it is desirable that they prepare their own draft.

### Table 12-1
### ONE-YEAR DRAFT BUDGET

| Income | |
| --- | --- |
| **Sources** | **Amount** |
| Family | |
| Spouse (net earnings) | |
| Savings (available) | |
| Assets income (if any) | |
| Other income | |
| **Total Income** | **Expenses** |
| Tuition | |
| School fees | |
| Rent or mortgage | |
| Heating (oil) | |
| Utilities (electric, gas, water) | |
| Food (in and out of home) | |
| Household supplies | |
| Medical insurance | |
| Medical expenses (ongoing) | |
| Clothing (including laundry) | |
| Car (other transportation) | |
| Auto insurance | |
| **Total Expenses** | |

Total income minus total expenses will provide an estimate of financial aid needed. When using relatively accurate information in completing the above table you can arrive at a reasonably good estimate of how much financial aid you will need for each year.

It is quite reasonable for most students to expect to need financial aid to close the fiscal gap between income and expenses; as a matter of fact, more than three-fourths of medical students require financial assistance. Funds are commonly secured by completing a financial aid application for each school and should be returned promptly. This should be done even *prior* to acceptance for it ensures that your financial aid application can be considered promptly when your admission is confirmed.

Financial aid can be provided from a variety of sources and come in several forms. These include

- Scholarships with and without service obligations
- Loans subsidized and not subsidized by the government

- Other sources such as family or veteran benefits
- You need to anticipate substantial paperwork, which is time consuming and tedious, but the results it can bring make it worthwhile. The sooner you act on this matter, the more likely it is that you will see a favorable outcome. It is also in your best interest to apply for both scholarships and loans. You need to work with the school's financial aid office. Also, Web sites relative to scholarships should be consulted. This search needs to be done carefully because of the myriad of options available.

## THE CURRENT FINANCIAL AID CRISIS

During the 1990s, there was a marked escalation in tuition and other costs related to medical education. This inflationary spiral may continue for the foreseeable future but at a slower pace. It is taking place unfortunately at a time when financial aid programs are being cut. This situation has caused a rising deficit between what funds are needed by medical students and what financial aid is available to them. To aggravate the situation, legislation reducing federal grants to medical and osteopathy schools was approved. In addition, it has become increasingly difficult to receive bank loans through the Federally Insured Student Loan Program, and private sources of support to medical students are also on the decline. All this strongly suggests that very careful consideration be given to financing one's medical education well before one considers applying for admission. In 1976 a Health Manpower bill was passed that requires almost every recipient of a federally supported medical scholarship to serve at least two years with the National Health Service Corps in areas of need.

It is essential for prospective medical students to be fully aware of the high cost of a medical education and its possible consequences. With proper planning this challenge can be met.

Medical school tuition and fees are the largest expense facing a medical student. The current average cost of tuition represents an increase of more than 400% for private schools and 275% for public schools over the past 25 years. Thus, for a typical private school, the cost of four years of medical school (tuition, fees, and living expenses) can run as high as $150,000 or more.

If the reasonable assumption is made that half of the total expenses are covered by borrowed money, loan repayment, which begins five years after graduation, will exceed $1,000 a month. In addition, interest, which begins at the time of borrowing and is due as "interest only" payments as early as two years after graduation, when added to the principal of the loan, would increase considerably the monthly repayment cost beyond $1,000 per month. Parenthetically, this interest is not tax deductible.

The next question then is, at what income level must one be in order to be able to comfortably repay a debt of approximately $75,000? Such a debt repayment level is estimated as 8% of one's *gross* income per year. This would require an income of $145,000, while an income of $97,000 would make repayment difficult, and an income of $70,000 would not allow for repayment. These income levels are to take place five years after graduation, namely at the time of completion of postgraduate (residency) training. To achieve the desirable upper income level at the initial stage of one's professional career is quite difficult.

These debt prospects suggest that, as time goes on, premedical students from less affluent backgrounds will find themselves unable to pursue medical careers or, if choosing to do so, will shun such lower remunerative specialties as family medicine, pediatrics, or general internal medicine. Particularly severe pressure would be felt under these conditions by qualified minority students who do not have access to special financial assistance.

In the light of this situation, prospective medical students should do as much research as possible about financing their education, debt service, and available resources. The apparent leveling off of tuition will also be helpful, even though the cost of living will continue to increase. If, as some anticipate, there are massive loan defaults, the impetus for aggressive governmental action to solve the financial aid crisis will be necessary.

An example of the direction that the issue of loan default is taking is the action by the Health Resources and Services Administration (HRSA) against the several thousand individuals who have not repaid federal Health Education Assistance Loans (HEAL). Hoping to pressure them into repayment, they have published their names and last known addresses in the *Federal Register*, the official government listing of federal actions and regulations. HRSA, in an effort to recover funds, can go further and alert credit bureaus, request that IRS withhold tax refunds, and bar defaulters from being eligible for Medicare or Medicaid reimbursement for their services. They can even arrange for the Department of Justice to litigate and withhold wages and property. They are also seeking to secure the cooperation of state agencies in getting them to withhold licenses to practice to such individuals until their loans are paid up.

# SUCCESSFULLY MANAGING EDUCATIONAL INDEBTEDNESS

Most medical students take out loans to pay for the cost of their education. Borrowing means that they benefit by having access to someone else's money now because they agree to pay it back with interest later. This reimbursement is a legal obligation that they assume. Those defaulting on repayment can face serious financial and legal consequences, which can impact negatively on borrowers, both personally and professionally.

The majority of students are able to repay their loans. The two major ways to succeed in handling debt repayment is to participate in a loan repayment program (usually sponsored by the federal government), and or practice prudent debt management. The latter is outlined in the following five advisory tips.

### TIP 1    Avoid overspending
It is essential that you live within your budget so that your need to borrow will be under control and ultimately your debt load will be restricted to an absolute minimum.

### TIP 2    Avoid using credit cards
You must recognize that this form of payment represents an expensive loan. Credit cards should certainly not be used to purchase items that you cannot afford; you should restrict yourself to one credit card and it should be held for identification purposes or emergency use.

### TIP 3    Understand your loan
The terms of all loans are different. From the outset you should be aware of the interest rate, duration of your loan, deferment options, and consolidation conditions. You will then know how to handle your loan and avoid under- or overpayments and possible default.

### TIP 4    Check your mail
Psychologically, some students try to avoid opening mail from lenders because they do not like to read "bad news." This attitude obviously can backfire and payments can be missed. Your loan is then passed on to another lender for collection. Also, you may be sending your payments to a wrong address and over a period of time this may result in loan default.

### TIP 5   Keep accurate records

To be sure that your payment is properly credited to your account, it is obviously in your best interest to maintain a complete and up-to-date record of all your payments. You should also note the remaining balances and see if they correspond to that indicated on the lender's statement. If there is a discrepancy, contact the lender promptly and call their attention to the apparent possible error.

# SCHOLARSHIPS AND LOANS

Scholarships largely come from two sources: medical schools and the federal government. All medical schools have some scholarships or tuition-remission grants available that are awarded on the basis of financial need and scholastic performance. The school catalogs usually give the necessary details. The federal government provides most of the funds that the medical schools, as well as banks and other lending institutions, make available to students.

## Bottom Line

The following issues should be taken into consideration when financing your professional education:

- *Educational costs.* Medical school has become incredibly expensive over past decades. On average, students pay an annual tuition of around $12,000 at medical schools in their home state, while out-of-staters pay around $30,000. Private schools obviously have far higher tuition levels. When estimating your total expenses, you need to consider costs beyond tuition, such items as administrative and laboratory fees, textbooks, and instruments, all of which can be substantial. Additionally, a variety of expenses that are part of living expenses must be included.

- *Strategic planning.* The understandable goal of most students attending medical school is to maintain a desirable lifestyle while simultaneously repaying their debt. Although this is an ideal situation, in reality, to avoid excessive debt, one may need to adjust one's lifestyle downward to some extent. The key element is staying within a budget that is designed to keep your debt manageable. This will serve to diminish unnecessary stress and strain, and let you focus better on your education.

- *Good credit.* Having a favorable credit record prior to applying for financial aid is essential. Medical schools will check it and they have the prerogative of canceling an acceptance if they feel the applicant will be unable to secure loans to pay for their education due to a poor credit history.

- *Formulate a budget.* This is a most critical element in maintaining financial stability. It is done by determining income from all sources, estimating all anticipated expenses, and then subtracting the latter from the former. This will reveal the extent of supplementary financial support that is necessary to meet one's needs.

- *Financial aid sources.* Students should not feel uncomfortable about the need to obtain financial aid from outside sources. More than two-thirds of medical students are in this position.

- *Financial aid.* This may be secured as:
  (a) Scholarships without a service obligation to repay.
  (b) Scholarships with a service obligation.
  (c) Loans subsidized by the government.
  (d) Loans not subsidized by the government.
  (e) Other financial sources.

*Seeking financial aid.* It is in your best interest to apply for scholarships and loans. Seek your librarian's assistance in uncovering suitable scholarship sources. When you apply through the school's Financial Aid Office, your eligibility for need-based funding will be evaluated. It is important that you understand your scholarship/loan terms and obligations. If you are unclear about them, clarify the issue with your school's Financial Aid Officer. Be aware that some financial aid programs are subject to change at the discretion of the funding agency. Each loan has different rules about when and exactly how it must be paid back.

## Scholarships

### Scholarships for First-year Students of Exceptional Financial Need

U.S. citizens or permanent residents who have been accepted and are planning to enroll as freshmen in medical school, and have exceptional financial need, can apply for such a scholarship. While funds under this program are very limited, they do provide for tuition as well as a stipend (currently about $6,000) for all other educational expenses. No service payback is required. School financial aid officers are the best sources of information concerning these scholarships.

### Armed Forces Health Professions Scholarship Program

All three armed forces offer scholarships to U.S. citizens who have been accepted or are already enrolled at a medical school in the United States or Puerto Rico. These scholarships provide full tuition and payment of educational expenses, plus a substantial stipend (currently in excess of $6,000). Recipients must serve one year of active military duty for each year they receive support, with the usual minimum being three years. Premedical advisors generally have, or can secure, information concerning the individual programs sponsored by the Army, Navy, and Air Force. (See *Other loan sources, #2*, on page 432.)

### National Health Service Corps Scholarship Programs (NHSC)

These scholarships are provided by the U.S. Public Health Service, on a competitive basis, to students enrolled at U.S. medical schools. They provide for tuition, educational expenses, and a substantial stipend (currently about $6,000). Support may be provided for up to four years, and the stipend is subject to annual cost-of-living adjustments. Recipients of such a scholarship, usually upon completion of postgraduate training, must provide one year of service in health manpower shortage areas for each year of financial support provided (two years minimum). The service may be fulfilled as salaried federal employees of the National Health Service Corps, or as self-employed private practitioners.

## Loans

### Health Education Assistance Loan Program (HEAL)

This program provides insured loans of up to $20,000 a year (with a maximum of $80,000 for four years). Interest is not to exceed 12% during the life of the loan, and the principal is repayable over a 10- to 25-year period starting nine months after completion of postgraduate training. It is also possible (if funds are available) to repay the loan in part or in whole by arranging a service contract through the Department of Health and Human Services.

### Federal Stafford Loan

These loans are provided in two forms: subsidized and unsubsidized. For the former, the government pays the interest while the student is in school. The latter requires that the student pay interest throughout the life of the loan. These loans have a variable interest rate with 2.5% cap and provide a maximum of $8,500 (subsidized) and $10,000 (unsubsidized) annually. Repayment begins six to nine months after completing studies. Repayment can be extended up to ten years.

### Health Professions Student Loan Program (HPSL)

This program is administered by the medical schools and gives a student who has exceptional need the opportunity to borrow the cost of tuition and up to $2,500 for other expenses per year. The interest rate is 5% and is applied after completion of residency training. The loan is repayable over a ten-year period.

### Perkins Loans

Formerly known as the National Direct Student Loan Program (NDSL), it is administered by the U.S. Office of Education. This program enables a student to borrow up to $440,000 (including loans received as an undergraduate). The interest rate is 5% and repayment can extend over a ten-year period. Repayment begins six months after completing school.

### Guaranteed Student Loan Program (GSL)

This program is also administered by the U.S. Office of Education. It permits a student to borrow up to $5,000 per year, the maximum not to exceed $25,000 (including undergraduate loans). The sources of these guaranteed funds are banks, savings and loan associations, or other participating lending institutions. Interest is at 9% and repayment begins 6 to 12 months after completing one's studies.

### National Health Service Corps: Federal Loan Repayment Program

This program provides payment toward both government and commercial education loans. This can amount to $25,000 per year for the first two years and up to $35,000 for every year thereafter with a minimum two-year commitment.

### Other loan sources

Medical schools have loan funds provided by philanthropic foundations, industry, or alumni. Interest rates and repayment policies are determined by the individual schools.

Funds in the form of scholarships and loans in varying amounts are available from many other sources. There are, however, restrictions as to eligibility based on residence, ethnic group, or other requirements. Sources of some of these programs are:

1. National Medical Fellowships, Inc., 250 West 57th Street, New York, NY 10019

2. Armed Forces Health Professions Scholarship Program. Commander, US Army Health Professions Support Agency SGPS-PD, 5109 Lessburg Pike, Falls Church, VA 22041; Commander, Navy Recruiting Command, 801 North Randolph, Arlington, VA 22203; United States Air Force, Recruiting Service, Medical Recruiting Division, Randolph Air Force Base, TX 78148

3. American Medical Association, Education and Research Foundation, 535 North Dearborn Street, Chicago, IL 60610

4. Educational and Scientific Trust of the Pennsylvania Medical Society, P.O. Box 8820, 777 East York Drive, Harrisburg, PA 17105

5. USA Funds Loan Information Services 8349, P.O. Box 6180, Indianapolis, IN 46209

6. National Health Service Corps Scholarship Program, U.S. Public Health Recruitment, 8201 Greensboro Drive, McLean, VA 22102

7. Robert Wood Johnson Student Loan Guarantee Program, 675 Hoes Lane, Piscataway, NJ 08854

There are many sources of information regarding specialized financial aid programs that are offered to state residents or to those entering particular specialty fields. For additional information on such programs, consult the following publications:

1. *Medical Scholarship and Loan Fund Program,* published by the AMA, 535 North Dearborn Street, Chicago, IL 60610.

2. *FIND: Financial Information National Directory—Health Careers,* published by the AMA, 535 North Dearborn Street, Chicago, IL 60610.

3. "The Health Education Assistance Loan Program: A New Way to Help Finance Your Health Professions Education." HEAL, 5600 Fishers Lane, Rockville, MD 20857.

4. "The Health Field Needs You! Sources of Financial Aid Information," published by the Bureau of Health Professions, Health Resources and Service Administration, DHHS, Parklawn Building, 5600 Fishers Lane, Rockville, MD 20857.

In addition, there are several programs for women and minority group students. Information on these programs is included in Chapters 10 and 11.

## Bottom Line

With regard to financing your medical education, the following additional information should be borne in mind:

- It is important that prospective medical students become knowledgeable about financial aid resources in order to be able to secure adequate funding.

- One can anticipate that the cost of medical education, which is quite high, will continue to increase, so begin investigating potential financial aid resources as early as possible when planning your career.

- One should recognize that outside employment is not a viable option for most medical students and individual school sources of funds are often limited.

- Accepted applicants should contact their school's Financial Aid Office early on, in order to explore and become familiar with the procedures for obtaining assistance.

- With most of the financial aid coming from outside sources, applicants should become familiar with all scholarship and loan resources available (see above).

## USEFUL FINANCIAL DEFINITIONS

The following are some definitions that may prove helpful in understanding financial aid issues:

*Actual interest rate.* The annual interest rate charged by the lender (see next definition).

*Applicable interest rate.* The maximum statutory interest rate that may be legally charged. (This may be equal or less than the actual interest rate.)

*Award letter.* This refers to the school's mode of advising an applicant of his/her available financial aid. It indicates both the type and amount.

*Base year.* The calendar year prior to the year for which financial aid is being sought.

*Credit rating.* An evaluation of the applicant's potential for repaying a loan, reflecting an individual creditability or risk as a borrower.

*Free Application for Federal Student Aid form (AFSA).* The form required to be completed by most financial aid programs in order to determine one's eligibility.

*Financial aid package.* The total amount of aid awarded to a student as reflected in the award letter.

*Forbearance.* The period of time provided by the lender during which loan payments need not be made but interest rate accrues.

*Grace period.* The interlude before graduation when debt repayments are not obligatory.

*Loan service.* The organization holding the loan or a third-party provider that deals with its activities.

*Loan transfer.* A change in the identity of the loan holder or services.

*Principal.* The amount originally borrowed but not including any accrued interest.

*Payment period.* The period, or clearance interlude, during which a loan needs to be repaid.

*Sallie Mae.* The organization that holds a substantial portion of educational loans acquired from the original lender.

*Subsidized loan.* A loan on which the federal government pays the accumulated interest.

*Variable interest rate.* An agreement that calls for changes in the interest rate at set time interludes.

# 13 Medical Education

**Evolution of the medical curriculum**
**The traditional curriculum**
**The curriculum in transition**
**The new medical school curricula**
**Attrition in medical school**
**Preparing for medical school**
**The making of a physician**
**United States Medical Licensing Examination**

Until the early 1900s, medical education in the United States was unstructured and unregulated. A person wishing to become a doctor would usually seek some didactic training at a medical school and/or spend time as an apprentice with one or more physicians. Since a license to practice was not needed, many unqualified individuals were engaged in the healing arts. The caliber of many medical schools was also open to serious question.

In 1910, after an investigation into the state of affairs existing in medical education, Abraham Flexner proposed a program of reorganizing medical education in a way that would ensure that only qualified individuals would enter the profession. With the adoption of the Flexner report, many medical schools of borderline quality became defunct while others significantly improved their standards. Another result was that medical education became a structured four-year program consisting of two years of basic sciences or preclinical training followed by two years of clinical experience. This educational program was essentially the same in all medical schools.

To ensure the maintenance of high standards, today all medical schools must obtain and maintain legal accreditation. The status of their educational programs is periodically evaluated by the Liaison Committee on Medical Education (LCME) of the Association of American Medical Colleges. This has not restricted medical schools, however, from introducing modifications in their traditional programs. The two-phase traditional program, nonetheless, still strongly influences the medical education process.

## EVOLUTION OF THE MEDICAL CURRICULUM

The curriculum for educating physicians in the United States has evolved through four phases since the first medical school was established in Philadelphia in 1765.

- *Phase I—The apprenticeship era (1765–1871).* During this period a student's ability to pay tuition and not his or her academic qualifications was the sole criterion for admission into medical school. The program involved two four-month semesters of classroom attendance, with no patient contact. This critical educational gap was followed by a one- to three-year apprenticeship with a private general practitioner, chosen by each student. Upon completion of this interlude the individual embarked upon a career as a medical practitioner.

- *Phase II—Discipline-centered era (1872–1951).* During this lengthy period, which was the traditional curriculum for many decades, the faculty was organized into discipline-specific departments. Both generalists and specialists conducted class-room and clinical instruction. Over time a changed learning environment developed that encouraged students to become independent thinkers, develop medical problem-solving skills, and become active short- and long-term, self-directed learners. Ultimately, a traditional four-year curriculum developed, consisting of two years of basic science and two of clinical training. After the fallout from the Flexner report, this arrangement became the standard for all U.S. medical schools.

- *Phase III—Organ system era (1951–present).* In this curriculum, the basic and clinical sciences are integrated within an organ-system framework. The appeal of this program, which remains a component of many current curricula, is due to the belief in the independent integration of information during clinical training, and the utilization of learning objectives. It involves program design by curriculum topic, which is a more effective tool than the rigid disciple-based approach.

- *Phase IV—Problem-based era (1968–present).* This program seeks to view the patient from the perspective of a whole person rather than as an individual with some organ system dysfunction. This curriculum is structured within the context of clinical problems. Students are exposed to small-group, problem-based learning. Thus, the educational approach involves a student-centered, active setting, minimizing attendance at large group lectures. Discussions of clinical problems serve as vehicles for integrating the basic and clinical sciences into coherent and clinically relevant learning experiences.

The consequences of the curricular changes that have taken place during Phases III and IV are discussed under The New Medical School Curricula. As this title implies, curriculum modification and innovation is, as it should be, an ongoing process.

Recent reports suggest that we may soon be entering Phase V, with the development of a Clinical Presentation Curriculum. This approach focuses on the manner of patient presentation, which serves as the context for imparting to students relevant basic and clinical science information.

# THE TRADITIONAL CURRICULUM

## The First Year

This introductory phase is devoted to the study of normal human biology, which includes anatomy, biochemistry, and physiology. The scope and emphasis within each of these areas are gradually being altered as new experimental approaches result in fresh data. Thus, for example, while the time allotted to gross anatomy is being diminished, the time spent on histology (microscopic anatomy) is being increased, and more emphasis is being placed on ultrastructural and histochemical findings. Most schools incorporate clinical demonstrations within basic science lectures so as to relate subject matter to actual medical problems. Many schools offer some introductory lectures in the behavioral sciences and genetics during the first year.

The first year is about 35 weeks long, with about 35 hours of required class work per week. Half or more of the class time is spent in lectures; the rest is spent in the laboratory.

## The Second Year

The second year is the bridge between the preclinical sciences and the clinical subjects that occupy the bulk of the final two years of study. This year establishes the scientific basis for understanding abnormal states of human biology. The standard courses taken during the sophomore year are pathology, microbiology, pharmacology, physical diagnosis, clinical laboratory procedures, and introductions to certain specialty fields such as public health and psychiatry.

Pathology is probably the keystone course of the sophomore year. It provides an introduction to the essential nature of disease and, in particular, the structural and functional changes that cause or are caused by disease. During the second semester, the more common diseases of each organ system and each organ are studied. The teaching process in pathology involves formal lectures, clinical pathological conferences, and laboratory exercises in pathological histology.

Microbiology provides an introduction to disease processes. It involves a study of the microorganisms that invade the body. The basis of mechanisms of infection and immunity is analyzed. One of the most effective means of combating disease is through drugs. Pharmacology concerns itself with the chemistry of the natural and synthetic drugs and their action in the healthy and diseased human body. The full impact of this subject comes to the forefront during the lengthy laboratory exercises in which experimental animals are frequently used to measure the effects of drugs.

The groundwork provided by the aforementioned courses, together with those completed during the first year, provide a great deal of fundamental information about the human body in illness and in health. The next step is to become familiar with the practical techniques required to determine the nature of a patient's illness. An introduction to this procedure is provided by the course in physical diagnosis. This phase of preclinical study gives one a strong psychological lift. The student learns the art of taking a medical history and examining a sick patient. The sophomore year ends with a framework for the clinical years well established.

## The Third Year

While the junior year is highlighted by considerable exposure to clinical experience, the formal educational process continues during this period with lectures, conferences, and seminars in medicine, surgery, pediatrics, obstetrics, and gynecology, as well as other specialties and subspecialties. The educational process is usually closely integrated with presentation of relevant patient cases. The emphasis in this early clinical training period is on the diagnosis of disease. The principles of treatment noted will be emphasized later.

Juniors are assigned various patients for a "workup," obtaining a history and physical examination. To carry out the former, the junior medical student learns to interrogate the patient so as to elicit and organize the chronological story of his or her present illness, obtain information as to the general state of his or her past and present health, secure vital data concerning the patient's family history, occupation, and social life. Supplementing this is a physical examination using manual manipulative and instrumental aids (stethoscope and ophthalmoscope). All the information is then integrated to provide preliminary diagnosis. The student then decides whether laboratory tests, X-rays, or special studies are needed. A faculty member reviews the entire "workup" and makes adjustments or confirms the order for diagnostic tests. This preliminary stage of clinical training, like all initial educational experiences, is of special importance. It helps develop a critical approach that tends to avoid the hazards that result from insufficient gathering of information, careless observation, or improper evaluation of the obtained data.

The initial diagnostic training is provided as part of service in the outpatient clinics and in the hospital wards. Later in the year, having attained proficiency in working up new patients, the student serves as a full-time clinical clerk in various clinical departments and in their outpatient clinics. As an apprenticing diagnostician, he or she is introduced to a variety of specialties. The aim of these experiences is not only to introduce the student to possible areas of specialization, but to teach the techniques of detecting all kinds of illness, regardless of specialization. Generally, the student will spend one quarter on medicine, another on surgery, a third on obstetrics-gynecology and pediatrics, and a fourth on electives.

As a clerk in medicine the student will rotate among various outpatient clinics and become familiar with groups of diseases that are classified as cardiovascular, allergic, infectious, rheumatic, neurological, gastrointestinal, and dermatological. Teaching clinics in these subspecialties are conducted by members of the medical school's faculty.

Short periods of time (several weeks each) are usually allotted to otolaryngology (diseases of the ear and throat) and ophthalmology. The student learns the basic diagnostic techniques in these specialties and has an opportunity to study the medical and surgical treatments used in these areas.

The clerkship in surgery enables the student to apply their newly acquired diagnostical training. The student gains insight into the process of determining when an operation is required as well as the need for pre- and post-surgical care. If assigned to the emergency room, he or she may have an opportunity to perform, under supervision, minor surgery such as treatment for infections of fingers, draining of abscesses, or suturing of lacerations. Many institutions offer as an elective a course in operative surgery where animals are treated as patients. Participation by the third-year student in such a program provides him or her with an opportunity for training as a surgeon, first assistant, scrub nurse, and anesthetist.

The student develops a foundation in the physiology of the human female in the first year and in pathology of diseases of the female urogenital system in the second year; he or she is now prepared for clinical work in gynecological diseases, and during the third year, the student participates in conferences, ward rounds, lectures, surgery, and outpatient clinics. It is quite common for the student to deliver about a half dozen babies. These deliveries are naturally performed under the close supervision of a resident in obstetrics. Aside from the training in childbirth, the student learns about the medical and emotional problems of prenatal care. In the outpatient obstetric clinic the student has the opportunity to examine and counsel women in pregnancy. This provides an especially favorable opportunity to develop skills in doctor-patient relationships.

The clerkship in pediatrics is devoted to the study of children and their diseases. The life span covered is from shortly after birth to adolescence. The student is taught to recognize the need not only for diagnosis of the pediatric diseases but to anticipate them and thus better help to ensure that the child will develop into a healthy adult. The preparation for the pediatric clerkship is frequently initiated in the latter part of the second year with lectures and some clinical experience in the fundamentals, such as heart sounds, X-rays, and EEGs of infants and children. Work in the clinics and wards becomes more intensive in the third year when the student is exposed to varied medical and surgical problems of children's diseases. The fourth year provides additional opportunity for pediatric training along with greater responsibility.

During the third year, the student-instructor relationship becomes more personalized and an exchange of views begins to take place; the student assumes the status of a junior colleague. The junior medical student's responsibilities are carefully demarcated and essentially restricted to taking medical history and carrying out a physical examination. The acute illnesses students see in the wards and the explicit problems they handle in the clinics are often "classical," and therefore students are free from the necessity of coping with diagnostic and therapeutic uncertainties that fall outside their limited area of knowledge.

## The Fourth Year

In the fourth year, the student's activities are frequently divided into four quarters. One is devoted to surgery (including general, orthopedic, and urological), another to medicine, a third to pediatrics, psychiatry, neurology, and radiology, and a fourth to elective study. There is usually considerable latitude in the arrangement of the order in which the program may be carried out.

In the surgical clerkship, seniors may frequently be assigned their own cases. They will, under careful supervision, be responsible for the patient workup, help arrange for laboratory tests, and contribute to discussions involving the diagnosis. Students will participate in preparing the patient for surgery, and, in the operating room, can expect to serve as third or fourth surgical assistant. They may be assigned to keep watch over the patient in the recovery room and be responsible for routine postoperative check-ups until the patient is discharged. The aim of the limited surgical experience for the senior student is not to secure specialized training, but to gain diagnostic experience so as to have a balanced insight into the usefulness of surgical intervention in the process of healing the sick. The exposure in surgery will be very broad, ranging from tonsillec-tomies to cardiac surgery.

In the block of surgical time devoted to orthopedics, the senior is exposed to the diagnosis and treatment of diseases of the joints and vertebral column, as well as frac-tures and deformities of the bones of the body. In urology some surgical and medical experience is gained by coming into contact with patients suffering from diseases of the kidney, bladder, prostate gland, and reproductive organs.

The quarter devoted to clinical clerkship in medicine is rather similar to that in surgery; naturally, the nature of the patient's illness and the method of treatment differ. Nevertheless, for the fourth-year student, there are workups to be made, tests to be ordered, and diagnoses to be reached. Several times a week students and their supervi-sors will go on rounds and students will participate in the discussions about the patients' conditions, treatments, and prognoses. During the clerkship period, seniors will be on call 24 hours a day and must be ready to assist in emergencies and to comfort patients through periods of stress. Naturally, throughout this period, the house staff—the residents—will bear the direct responsibilities for prescribing treatment and direct-ing emergency care. But senior medical students nevertheless gain firsthand insight into the responsibilities that must be assumed by them during postgraduate training.

# THE CURRICULUM IN TRANSITION

Since the mid-1960s, there has been increased pressure from medical students to intro-duce greater flexibility into their courses of study. In response to this criticism, most schools have established committees (sometimes including students) to periodically reevaluate and update their curricula. In many schools, new curricula have been intro-duced that have modified the traditional program using one or more of several different approaches:

1. Determination of a core curriculum. This approach places the emphasis on prin-ciples rather than only on facts.

2. Greater correlation between basic and clinical sciences. In the first year, the stu-dent is exposed to some clinical experience by seeing patients having illnesses related to the subject being studied.

3. Greater emphasis placed on function than structure. This approach is reflected by a decrease in the amount of time allotted to morphological studies (anatomy, for example) and by an integration of material presented by different departments.

4. Introduction of multiple-track systems. This offers students who have com-pleted the core curriculum, which is the required common experience of all stu-dents, to choose one of several pathways having different emphases, depending upon their ultimate career goals. Thus, there is a differentiation of exposure depending upon interest, need, and ability.

5. Use of interdisciplinary and interdepartmental courses. These frequently replace departmental offerings, especially in the basic sciences. The combined view-points of several basic medical sciences are presented in an integrated fashion as each organ system is discussed, rather than being taught in the classical manner at varied times through separate courses. The organ systems are muscular, skeletal, nervous, cardiovascular, respiratory, gastrointestinal, hematopoetic, genitourinary,

integumentary, endocrine, and reproductive. This type of teaching is known as "back to back"; that is, the normal aspects of the anatomy, chemistry, physiology, and pharmacology are considered in relation to abnormal or pathological principles.

6. Use of visual aids. These and other modern methods of instruction are much more widely used, although their effectiveness cannot yet be evaluated.

7. Taking qualifying examinations. In many schools students are encouraged to take such examinations before beginning certain basic science courses. If successful, they may proceed to other areas or disciplines without further coursework in the subject they demonstrated competence in.

8. Introduction of more elective time. This permits the student to spend additional time in areas of special interest, thus facilitating the choice of and preparation for a specialty or becoming more proficient in a selected area.

9. A slow national trend toward sweeping curricular change with an emphasis on communication skills. Thus far these changes have taken place at Harvard University, University of Pittsburgh, Johns Hopkins University, University of Michigan, University of Toronto, and Northwestern University. Consistent with national trends, the new curriculum emphasizes active self-directed learning rather than rote memorization. The supporters of this change feel that medical "facts" become obsolete so quickly that it is pointless to force students to memorize them. Rather, they believe students should be trained to be "lifelong learners."

10. Accelerating the program of studies. A very small number of schools have offered their most promising students opportunities to complete their studies in less than four years. The schools listed below have standard four-year programs and may offer an accelerated three-year option.

Baylor College of Medicine
Johns Hopkins University
Northwestern University
Ohio State University
SUNY at Buffalo
University of Illinois at Chicago
University of North Carolina
University of Texas Medical School at Galveston
University of Washington

A number of schools shortened their standard curriculum during World War II as well as in the early 1970s. However, the enthusiasm for the three-year program diminished markedly, and all schools now offer a four-year program as a requirement for all students.

A recent accelerated program has been introduced that incorporates the first year of post graduate training (PGY1) in the standard four-year MD program into a single unit. The goal of this program, which is so far offered only in a limited number of schools, is to encourage medical students to elect to enter primary care careers through family practice or internal medicine. You should inquire at your school of interest whether such a program is offered there.

11. Lengthening the program of studies. If it proves necessary, some medical schools permit students to extend their educational program for a year. Among such schools are:

Boston University
Creighton University
Howard University
Medical College of Wisconsin

Stanford University
University of California, San Diego
University of California, San Francisco
University of Hawaii

12. Arts and medicine. Many medical schools have arranged for their students, especially those considering a career in pediatrics, to participate in an Arts for Children in Hospitals program. It employs hands-on arts activities one on one or through music or dance sessions. The goal is to help medical students learn how to become comfortable with young patients.

Since there now exists a diversity of curricula because of the many possible variations, it is advisable for the prospective applicant to become familiar with the programs offered by the school in which they are interested (see individual school profiles, Chapter 9).

# THE NEW MEDICAL SCHOOL CURRICULA

A major consequence of the introduction of new medical curricula is the individualization of medical schools. From the time of the Flexner report in 1910 until Case Western Reserve University introduced organ-based learning in 1952, all medical schools were essentially the same in following the traditional two-year basic science courses plus a two-year clinical science curriculum. They differed only in the size, facilities, and quality of their teaching staff. With the introduction by McMaster University of problem-based learning in 1975, the option for wide-ranging curricula variations became feasible and has, in fact, taken place.

The major nontraditional approach to medical education in the basic and clinical sciences involves incorporating fact-intensive courses into an integrated curriculum. In this approach the focus is on general principles that usually cut across traditional disciplines, resulting in blocks of time devoted to a particular organ system in the context of various relevant sciences. Frequently coupled with this educational format is a technique known as problem-based learning, in which small groups of medical students analyze clinical case histories with the participation of a faculty member. Each student selects an aspect of the case to research and at the next session each discusses what was uncovered, thereby generating a collaborative learning system. This system is currently in effect on a limited basis in about 60 medical schools, about half the medical programs in the United States. While fully assessing the effectiveness of this approach is premature, preliminary findings indicate that students educated under the nontraditional system had overall lower scores on Step 1 of the USMLE, but generally scored higher on Step 2. Students seem to like the new system, perhaps because it is less demanding. A full day of lectures along with tedious lab work has been eliminated in favor of only a few lecture hours daily with streamlined labs.

There are some stresses in small group learning situations, such as one-upmanship to impress teachers and classmates by students who enjoy demonstrating their substantial pool of knowledge. Another problem is that some students do not pull their weight in meeting their assignments, making it more difficult for others. In addition, this new approach requires readjustment away from the competitive isolated learning experience. Approaching a problem in a "holistic" manner, rather than memorizing a mass of facts as was done during the premed years, involves drastic change, but may prove very worthwhile in the end.

## Alternative Medicine

Over the past few decades many alternative practitioners of healing have gradually gained some acceptance. In a recent survey it was found that about one-third of all Americans use some form of unconventional therapy, spending close to $14 billion annually on treatments.

U.S. medical schools have responded slowly to this change. Thus far, about half include information about alternative medicine in their curriculum. These include Georgetown, Harvard, Tufts, University of California in San Francisco, and the Universities of Arizona, Louisville, and Virginia. Among the reasons offered for doing so is that nontraditional medicine can benefit patients, especially those suffering from chronic pain. Physicians may sometimes find using a holistic approach more stimulating than merely treating diseases.

The momentum behind the drive for alternatives to conventional medicine may have its roots in the longstanding undercurrent of unorthodox practices existing in medicine. The assertive spirit of social movements in our society, where the call is to take hold of one's destiny, has probably also impacted on the practice of medicine.

Within the medical community, there is strong opposition by some to alternative medical approaches, with the argument that their claims are not subject to rigorous scientific testing. Thus, physicians who desire to include alternative therapies in their practice run the risk of ostracism. However, intense public interest in alternative medicine is gradually forcing a change. In mid-1992, the National Institutes of Health opened an office for the study of unconventional medical practices, which will provide research grants. Establishing good clinical trials to test unorthodox treatments is not easy. When definitive positive results emerge, the possibility of including some alternative medical practice into the mainstream of allopathic medicine will become more likely. (For definitions of alternative medical practices, see Appendix F.)

In view of the large number of individuals using alternative modalities, it is desirable that future physicians be aware of the nontraditional practitioners and be sympathetic to patients who have sought help outside of conventional medicine.

## Elective Programs

Almost all schools now offer opportunities for students to pursue such activities as independent study, honors programs, and special research projects, either at home or elsewhere during the academic year or in the summer.

Elective time may be offered any year but, it is especially common in the fourth year. In most schools the students have the option of consulting a faculty advisor when selecting electives. The extent of elective time may vary from a number of weeks to the entire fourth academic year. The choice of electives will depend on a student's personal interests and talents. Clinical electives may include additional clerkships in primary care and in many specialties and subspecialties. Electives may, at the medical school's discretion, be taken at academic centers or nonacademic centers away from one's institution of matriculation. Thus, some choose to become involved in a research project, while others may select a preceptorship, practicing with a physician in a rural community. Some students even decide to go overseas for a period of service (see below). In addition to clinical electives, the option may exist for electives in the basic of behavioral sciences.

## Overseas Study

In the pre-World War II decades, it was common for U.S. physicians to travel overseas, usually to Europe, for specialty training. With the dramatic advances in U.S. medical education, this is no longer necessary. During the 1980s, however, it was noted that there was an increase in the number of U.S. medical students taking clinical electives abroad, especially in developing countries. It is thought that currently more than 15% of medical students participate in international health projects.

Overseas study is essentially a student-motivated undertaking. Finding an appropriate place abroad that has adequate funding can be quite difficult. The initiative to secure a position rests with students, although they may find a sympathetic faculty member to assist them.

The desire to have a unique life adventure while also serving as a goodwill ambassador is one of the motivating factors for overseas work-study endeavors. A more pragmatic motive is the desire by some students to determine which area of international health they should pursue. However, most of those who feel compelled to undertake such a project do so in order to contribute to improving health care resources of underserved people.

Medical students considering an overseas stint should be prepared to be flexible so far as living conditions are concerned, both in terms of accommodations and diet. Also, they should not consider their project a sight-seeing trip and they need to take time to learn about the culture of the elective country. They must be aware that there are negative aspects to service abroad. Some residency program directors view such an activity as time off from medicine. Frustrated by the inability to improve conditions in underdeveloped areas, some individuals may fail in their efforts to study and help overseas health care providers.

Obtaining permission from a medical school to study abroad should, in most cases, not prove difficult, since more than 90% of the schools allow third- or fourth-year students to do so for up to two months. However, only about 25% of the schools provide training in international health. This is regrettable, since preparation is the key to a successful overseas stay and typical university-based clinical training is inadequate for preparing students for service in underdeveloped areas. The University of Arizona Health Sciences Center in Tucson, Arizona, offers a free summer international health course that is held in high regard.

Medical Assistance Program International, Brunswick, Georgia, funded by the Reader's Digest International Fellowships, provides funding for 50 senior medical students to serve in overseas missions. It is one of the few programs offering overseas study support.

The following additional advice can be useful in trying to secure an overseas elective:

1. Seek an established program to ensure that it will be well organized.

2. Start the search for an elective country early; overseas correspondence is time consuming.

3. Get to know people in your elective country, since this can provide for meaningful future relationships.

4. Be prepared to deal with communication problems, loneliness, and frustration.

5. Consider yourself a collaborator for health improvement, rather than a savior.

6. Travel lightly, but be sure to take pure chlorine for water purification and a non-leaking water bottle in which to store it.

7. Respect the ways of the people you are visiting; in all likelihood, they will then reciprocate.

8. Before departing, read *Cross-cultural Medicine: What to Know Before You Go* (AMSA International Health Task Force) and *Where There Is No Doctor: A Village Health Care Handbook* (Chesperian Foundation, Palo Alto, California).

For an in-depth discussion of foreign medical study, see Chapter 15.

## Community Service Activities

In the 1950s medicine emphasized the patient as an individual, rather than as part of a larger group. In the 1960s patients were introduced to students early in the educational process and medical ethics became a part of the curriculum. Currently, new concerns have emerged, such as the impact of technology on the terminally ill and the spiraling cost of and accessibility to health care.

In recent years there has been a growing awareness among health care professionals of the needs of the disadvantaged, which include nearly 40 million uninsured Americans. This has resulted in students volunteering their services, and some of these activities are gaining medical school recognition.

Service programs that students have initiated and led involve a very wide range of activities such as work in soup kitchens for the homeless, helping to build low-income housing, serving as health educators in local grade schools, or assisting in medical clinics.

Increasing numbers of medical school administrators are beginning to view such activities as an integral component of medical education, rather than merely an extracurricular activity. Medical schools are starting to support such programs both financially and by granting academic credit for community service. Some schools are engaged in formally integrating community service into their curricula. Schools such as Dartmouth, University of California (Davis), and the University of Miami have large numbers of their first-year students participating in community service projects. Thousands of fourth-year students are involved in service as community health educators or as volunteers in clinics for underserved populations.

Community service is also reflected in the activities of medical students (and physicians) at the hundreds of free clinics located in urban and rural areas across the country. Medical students can thus gain hands-on experience under supervision in primary care. Both this and nonmedical-oriented service projects offer students an opportunity for a brief respite from the rigors of formal lectures, labs, and exams. It also serves as a reminder about the humanitarian goals of medicine as a caring profession.

Legislation that is part of the National Community Service Trust Act supports the award of grants to schools to facilitate service learning. The extent of funding for this and similar programs remains uncertain in an era of budget tightening.

## ATTRITION IN MEDICAL SCHOOL

If you have been accepted to a U.S. medical school, you are one of a select group of students who have survived the successive academic prunings of elementary school, high school, college, and medical school selection procedures. In addition, you rank in the upper 50% of all students entering graduate and professional schools. Medical schools seek to graduate as many of their entrants as possible; therefore you stand a better chance of successfully completing your medical education than students in other professional schools in the United States or medical students in practically every other country. While the attrition rate in American professional schools is relatively high, that for medicine has consistently been relatively low. Nevertheless, any loss of medical students is a loss to society and is especially painful when one considers the many qualified applicants who were rejected and thus denied an opportunity to study medicine.

It is therefore encouraging to report that the overall dropout rate has remained very low over the years. The withdrawals from the total student enrollment in a recent year were 751, or 1.85% of the enrollment. Moreover, even this figure may in reality be artificially high because one-fifth of the students (143, or 0.35%) withdrew to pursue advanced study and are expected to return to medical school. In addition, less than one-third of the withdrawals or dismissals (223) were for academic reasons, the remainder (385, or 1%), for other reasons, making, in actuality, the true attrition rate closer to 0.5%. This means that admissions committees have been able to select from the large pool of qualified applicants those most likely to succeed. If accepted, you should feel confident that with consistent hard work you will most likely complete your course of studies.

An analysis of student records over an extended period has provided significant information regarding the relationship of various student characteristics to attrition that can help you assess your own chances for success and indicate when extra care and effort may be called for. Successful students are more likely to have attended an undergraduate college with a sizable premedical program that they found to be both difficult and competitive. The premedical grades of academic dropouts are substantially lower than are the grades of both successful students and nonacademic dropouts. The average test scores for dropouts are much lower than those of successful students. Unsuccessful students report almost twice as many personal problems as do successful students. Older students have a much higher dropout rate than do younger ones. Women have a somewhat higher attrition rate than men have. It should be noted, however, that studies have shown that the academic dropout rate was the same for both sexes but the dropout rate for nonacademic reasons (marriage or pregnancy) was almost three times higher in women. The dropout rate did not differ significantly for married students or for those reporting similar time allocations to study, part-time employment, or extracurricular activities. Successful students tend to be influenced by a desire for independence and for prestige, whereas unsuccessful students are most likely to be influenced in their career choice by such additional factors as reading and by religious and service motivation.

The following are some specific suggestions that can reduce your changes of dropping out of medical school. Prior to entering medical school you should obtain a strong background of fundamental knowledge in the sciences and develop good study habits; seek opportunities to test your motivation for a career in medicine by exposure to health science-related work (lab assistant, hospital aide, volunteer work with handicapped, visiting hospitals and medical schools); and seek admission to medical schools where you can most likely gain admission and that are most suited to your abilities and interests.

If you fail at the end of a year and are offered a chance to repeat, accept the opportunity to do so if you still want to study medicine. The chances are high that you, like many previous repeaters, will successfully complete your studies. Should you decide to withdraw voluntarily, do so only after consultation with appropriate faculty and administrative members of your school.

# PREPARING FOR MEDICAL SCHOOL

## The Transition

There are significant differences between attending college, especially a small one, and being enrolled in a medical school. It is thus desirable to first enumerate some of the characteristics of the learning environment in medical school so as to provide a better perspective as to what is involved in making the transition.

Medical school is characterized by:

1. a fast-paced, fact-oriented, and highly impersonal environment, especially during the first two years;

2. the keen competition that usually exists because the students have similar backgrounds as high achievers and are all taking the same required courses. The competition usually involves staying above the median class level, although striving for superior grades obviously exists;

3. the staggering amount of material that is usually presented and must be assimilated in a short amount of time;

4. multi-instructor course teaching, which inherently does not favor the establishment of meaningful student-faculty relationships; and

5. early exposure to human cadaver dissection, and subsequently to dying and death, without adequate preparation.

## Retaining Idealism

The special challenge of medical school is retaining the sense of idealism premedical students usually bring with them at the outset of their studies. Medical school is an especially stressful interlude in a young person's life. It is not uncommon to find third- or fourth-year students speaking of the negative impact of the pressures of the first years. Cynicism and apathy appear to be replacing much of the idealism that was present at the beginning of a student's education.

Medical students frequently begin their education with many idealistic interests, strong views on the need for political and economic change, constructive thoughts on increasing the number of general practitioners, and positive attitudes toward medical ethics and eliminating bias. When their studies begin, stress also builds up. During the initial years, students are expected to learn vast amounts of information, besides taking the regular school exams. Students face taking Step 1 of the USMLE, long clinical rotations, and, finally, the challenge of finding a suitable residency. Heightening the existing burden is the anxiety brought on by student loan debt. Consequently, students begin to feel overwhelmed and start to prioritize the distribution of their interest and energy, with little idealism remaining for work to bring about change and progress.

In order to be maintained, idealistic beliefs need encouragement or they dissipate. In theory, sustaining altruism should be a shared responsibility of student, school, and profession. Unfortunately, important fiscal concern for their institution or their constituents distracts school administrators or profession leaders from focusing on this issue. In reality, the responsibility for retaining idealism falls essentially on the students. While some feel that it is impossible to do, many have successfully accomplished it.

The key to nurturing one's sense of idealism as a medical student is to reinforce it. This can perhaps best be done by establishing close relationships with like-minded classmates. In addition, participation in the activities of student organizations, such as the American Medical Student Association, Student National Medical Association, American Medical Women's Association, or the Student Section of the American Medical Association, can be stimulating. The ideals generated and contacts made can serve to sustain one's altruistic impulses.

Domestic or overseas volunteer work in typical social settings can provide another opportunity for enhancing idealistic motives. Taking electives at rural community or similar locations can prove to be an enriching experience that will nourish service attitudes.

## Thinking Positively

During the long period of medical school and postgraduate training, many challenges must be faced, the results of which may be quite disappointing. They may include poor results on a major test, an unfavorable evaluation of a clerkship performance by one's superior, a severe reprimand by an attending physician for inappropriate patient treatment, or totally negative patient outcome of therapy. Such disappointments coming on the heels of a time already filled with intense professional and personal demands can, if prolonged, negatively influence your mental health and, in the long run, possibly your physical well-being. We are beginning to gather scientific evidence that suggests that there may be a link between chronic stress and depression with suppression of the immune response and possibly even with some chronic diseases. Cross-disciplinary research is leading to the development of the field of psychoneuroimmunology, which studies the influence of mental attitude on physical health.

There are many individuals who naturally lend to think negatively. For these people there is a need to learn how to reverse such patterns by steering their thoughts in a positive direction. Strategies are available to view expectations in a more favorable light. Maladaptive thought habits are not easily corrected, but attaining lasting results requires a constructive program for thinking and viewing events differently.

By enlisting our conscious mind as an ally in strengthening our immunological status, we can, in turn, protect our physical well-being. Thus, one should operate on the premise that because of the connection between body and mind, positive thoughts can induce positive biochemical changes that enhance the body's well-being and therefore serve as a deterrent to illness.

Negative thought patterns should be promptly challenged by subjecting them to a reality check. Failure in one or even more issues is not a true predictor of a future lack of success. Rather, a lack of success should be taken in the context of the many and consistent patterns of success over one's lifetime. There is a reason to believe that the power of positive thinking can in time deflect negative thought habits and thus protect one's health by enhancing resistance to physical illness. Obviously, sustained negative thinking and repetitive depressive episodes require professional attention.

# Coping with Stress

The inherent characteristics of medical school listed earlier clearly lend themselves to stimulating a stressful life for the medical student. This potential is enhanced by the natural insecurity that a major new phase in life can engender. Thus, a significant element in achieving success by a medical student is knowing how to cope with stress.

The ability to cope with stress is dependent upon your personality as well as your prior life experiences. Some people can withstand very intense stress before they feel the pressure, while others have a lower stress tolerance threshold. Mastering the art of coping with stress is essential in order to succeed in medical school.

Coping with stress is also essential in helping you maintain your health. Under stress, your breathing becomes shallow and uneven, your pulse speeds up, and your senses sharpen. Consequently, a stressful day frequently results in a feeling of tiredness. Prolonged stress has been demonstrated to contribute to headaches, skin rashes, or even more serious illness such as ulcers and asthma.

If you have any problems coping with stress, you should seek information about deep breathing, stretching, or regular aerobic exercises that can help you control the feelings generated by pressure. Consulting a physician can also prove useful, especially in severely stressful situations where medication may be indicated.

At the very outset, it should be recognized that, if you have been admitted to medical school, you have already proven that you can probably cope rather effectively with stress induced by educational demands. A successful premedical phase clearly included getting superior grades in college, especially in the science courses, as well as on the MCAT exam, completing an application that was impressive, and effectively facing the challenge of admission interviews. These achievements should serve to strongly reinforce your sense of confidence in being able to cope with stress while attending medical school.

The goal in coping with stress should be twofold: (1) to control the extent of your exposure to stressful situations; and (2) to learn how to respond to stress.

The following seven suggestions may be useful in coping with stress:

1. Maintain your health as optimally as possible. This includes following an appropriate diet and a suitable exercise regimen.

2. Try to meet pending responsibilities one at a time. Tasks and problems should be prioritized and addressed accordingly. When possible, subdivide large problems into small manageable tasks, which in turn should also be solved in a prioritized manner.

3. Utilize your time efficiently. This means budgeting time in an appropriate manner. Don't overextend yourself with an excessive number of scheduled activities, or underestimate the time they may require. Be flexible in meeting needed changes in planned activities.

4. Realize that some stressful situations are unavoidable. These include scheduled examinations, traffic delays, and so on. Since you cannot exercise control over certain potential stress-inducing problems, try to accept them calmly and matter-of-factly.

5. Find a wholesome outlet for stress and frustrations. This can include participation in some sports activities, or the use of a close friend to whom you can verbalize your frustrations and fears.

6. Avoid situations that you know will be stressful. Thus, if last-minute cramming for an exam generates stress, schedule your study time so that you are fully prepared in advance of the test deadline and therefore can avoid cramming. Similarly, if getting to school is an erratic experience time-wise, schedule an adequate amount of time in order to avoid the frustration and stress created by the fear of arriving late.

7. Allow for several short periods of relaxation during the day. These can be taken at mealtimes and for more extended periods on weekends. Periodic holiday vacations can help you to recover from long spells of intense activity.

## Looking Ahead

While at the outset of your medical school career it is natural to focus on the courses at hand, it is also important to have a longer-term perspective on your education. One needs to recognize that in its essence the first two years are the essential preparation for the last two-year clerkship training years. It is thus important to master a number of skills during the preclinical phase of your education to be able to satisfactorily cope with the challenges you will face when undertaking clinical service on the wards.

In this regard, a recent report indicated that a significant number of medical students may have an uphill battle during their clinical training. This is suggested from a study that found that between 30 and 50% of clerkship directors reported that medical students are unprepared in six competency areas.

A survey of a significant number of clerkship directors indicates that they believe that improvement is necessary in communication, interviewing, and examination skills, professionalism, and understandings of systems of care and life cycle stages. As a consequence of this situation, some clerkship directors have been forced to provide remediation in one or more of these areas of professionalism, communication, interviewing, and examination skills, because of a deficiency in preclinical preparation. It is thought that preparation for the clinical skills component of the USMLE Step 2 may prove helpful in this area when working on the wards.

## First-year Guidelines

Special emphasis deserves to be placed on the freshman year of medical school, where attrition, if it will occur at all, is most likely. Like the first year of high school or college, it marks a year of transition from the triumph of graduation to the lowest rung of the school's hierarchical ladder. It frequently involves relocating and having a new group of peers.

The average freshman begins medical school with unresolved feelings about his or her level of achievement attainable in a new and unproven milieu. The nature of the academic environment, with its large volume of work and the presence of bright and hard-working classmates, makes it difficult to prove oneself and attain one's inner expectations. Students with a high degree of self-worth and those who can gain gratification from intrinsic rewards, such as the satisfaction derived by keeping up with and passing through the curriculum, will best respond emotionally to the existing stressful situation. Providing self-praise rather than seeking external sources of encouragement is helpful.

The special features of the freshman year that deserve to be brought to the attention of prospective medical students are as follows:

1. Students frequently have a wide range of emotional experiences during the course of the year, ranging from exhilaration to anxiety, frustration, and, at times, depression.

2. The academic program offered is usually uneven, with some courses being exciting and others dull. Taken as a whole, the program is exhausting.

3. A key to success is to organize one's time most effectively to meet your specific needs. Allowance should be made in your schedule for a reasonably fulfilling personal and social life.

4. Upperclass students may provide useful insights into the pressures to be faced and methods of coping, as well as helpful study tips. The advice given should not always be taken at face value, but must be adjusted to one's specific needs.

5. While attaining high grades is commendable, developing a competent grasp of the material presented should be the prime goal. This involves developing a priority system of study of the wide-ranging subject matter and the various topics, focusing on understanding concepts, and fitting the details into the conceptual framework so as to facilitate their retention.

6. Development of an objective approach to clinical problems should begin during the first year. This involves beginning to establish a flexible emotional balance between excessive sympathy for patients and exaggerated detachment.

7. It is important to avoid a feeling of complete isolation in an endless sea of information, some of which is esoteric and apparently irrelevant to your specific career activities. To avoid losing one's perspective, it is useful to set aside some free time for clinical observation, such as attending rounds or conferences.

8. Although difficulties and setbacks may occur, they need not necessarily lead to failure. They should be placed in the context of your many successes.

9. Emotional self-care, using such methods as having planned breaks and regular exercise, utilizing preventive stress management techniques, and maintaining personal relationships, as well as providing oneself with rewards, is important.

10. Prompt help should be sought if signs of trouble, in the form of depression, relationship problems, and increased use of alcohol or drugs, become evident.

11. To offset the decrease in overall physical activity due to the considerable time spent in the classroom and laboratory, an exercise schedule, even if at quite a limited level, should be maintained.

12. To help ensure good physical, mental, and emotional health and stamina, proper attention should be paid to nutrition, diet, and getting enough sleep.

Finally, it should be kept in mind that, while there frequently is an increase in stress as the freshman year progresses, there is also a tendency for the ability to cope effectively to improve. Associated with this improvement is a betterment in health and mood. Along with these changes comes a heightened enjoyment of medical school, with feelings of greater competence and reduced uncertainty about entering a medical career.

## Second-year Guidelines

The second year marks a turning point on the student's road to becoming a physician. The focus is drastically altered, from what heretofore has been almost exclusively the normal state of the human body, to a consideration of the disease process, its consequences, and modes of therapy. While conceptual thinking continues to be required, the volume and the content of the information presented place a heavy premium on memorization. This year represents an equalization in potential between premeds and nonscience majors.

For obvious reasons, pathology represents the key transitional course from the normal to the diseased. It is usually taught by means of formal lectures, exercises in the laboratory, seminars in clinical problem solving, and autopsy exposure. The interplay of anatomy, biochemistry, and physiology with pathology provides the intellectual challenge inherent in this subject. The linkage of clinical observations with autopsy findings as revealed in clinicopathologic conferences (CPCs) provides dramatic insights into the effects of the disease process.

Pharmacology complements pathology, since the actions of individual drugs and drug families can be learned in the context of the diseases they treat. This course stimulates a review of relevant basic science topics and, while heavy on memorization, also demands conceptual understanding.

A significant course of the upper sophomore semester is physical diagnosis. This is usually taught by formal lectures, at hospital teaching rounds, and by individual hospital assignments. This course provides an invaluable base upon which to build for the coming clinical medical school years and postgraduate training.

The major challenge of the second year is to balance all its demands, namely multiple-coursework, patient responsibilities, and preparation for tests and Step 1 of USMLE in June. The second year thus has all the components to generate a great deal of physical and emotional stress, and it usually does. The advice given as to stress management in the preceding section is obviously applicable for preventing and/or meeting this year's challenges. The survival skills developed during the first year should help ensure satisfactory completion of the second.

## Third-year Guidelines

The beginning of the third year marks a major turning point in professional medical education. It represents the onset of a lifelong involvement with the realities of clinical medicine.

The initial impact is reflected by the need to learn how to develop a relationship with patients. In this regard, medical students should clarify to the patient and/or the patient's family their position as being on the first rung in the medical hierarchy. This may preferably be reinforced by referring to oneself as "student Doctor Smith." This will limit the student's responsibilities to their appropriate level and permit unanswerable patient questions to be referred to the appropriate authority without embarrassment.

Concomitant with the introduction to patient care is the impact it has on the attitude of the medical student toward patients. There generally (and unfortunately) is a change in attitude from being service oriented to being self-education oriented. The goal that should be sought is the ability to view the patient simultaneously as a human being and as a source of biomedical knowledge.

Another special feature of the junior year is the development of a relationship with the house staff. There will be substantial learning opportunities as well as exposure to menial routine or "scut" work. Thus the results can be both exhilarating and rewarding, and frustrating and depressing. The key to a meaningful experience is to determine what the patient's diagnostic or therapeutic plan is so that you can interact as intelligently as possible with the other members of the medical team.

During this year the opportunity to view the bedside manners of different attending physicians will be available, perhaps for the first time. Each will be found to have a distinctive style that can be instructive to the doctor-in-training.

Learning to chart, that is, to prepare a current, clear, concise, and complete record of the patient's progress, is a significant part of the educational experience. Finally, a central element of medical school experience, namely the "workup," taking a history and performing a physical examination, will be introduced during the junior year. Developing a positive attitude toward hospital work routine and critical skills in achieving a differential diagnosis is the key to professional success. To master the art of diagnosis, one must work out the rationale for every question and organize questions into logical groups. Leads should be followed up by additional questions and a search for specific physical findings. Thoroughness in working up the patient will prove most rewarding for both the practitioner and the patient.

In summary, the junior year represents a relearning of the basic sciences in a clinical setting. Learning the biochemical and physiological bases of disease mechanisms in the context of living patients will facilitate developing the skills to provide therapeutic relief.

The onset of the clinical years is the appropriate time to learn how to avoid making mistakes. The three basic rules in this regard are:

1. Recognize your own limitations. Be prepared to admit when you feel unqualified to undertake an assigned task. Do not try to bluff your way through a challenge or develop an air of bravado that you can do anything.

2. Don't be afraid of new challenges, so long as you feel assured you are being adequately supervised during the course of carrying them out.

3. Do not ignore the advice of residents and nurses. Their experience and judgment can be very helpful in avoiding costly errors or embarassing situations.

A number of schools offer formal training in technical skills such as venipuncture. Such introductory courses most frequently teach "universal precautions," such as handling needles and wearing protective gear. Existing programs, however, vary from a five-day intensive course to ad hoc training at the hospital.

## Fourth-year Guidelines

The fourth year represents the final stages before assuming the responsibilities of postgraduate education. The knowledge and experience acquired during the first three years will be put to use during this year of intensive clinical training.

A number of admonitions are in order as the student now proceeds toward the practice of medicine.

1. The principal goal in practicing medicine should be the satisfaction gained through service to others.

2. The essence of good medicine is to reach a diagnosis on the basis of a carefully secured, complete history and physical examination, supplemented, where necessary, by laboratory findings. The lab results should not be used, however, to negate the results of a good "workup," nor should they serve per se as a diagnostic tool.

3. Patients tend to place physicians on a pedestal. By recognizing that the majority of illnesses are self-limiting, physicians should realize that often the services they render only provide reassurance and make the patient comfortable. This should promote an attitude of humility that can counteract the ego-stimulating factor inherent in the practice of medicine.

4. While medicine is an inexact science, its practice nevertheless requires one to be as exact as possible. Nothing should be taken for granted; otherwise, unforeseen complications can ensue.

5. It should always be recognized that it is the patient who is ill, and that it is the patient, not the disease, that should be treated.

6. There is a critical need to remain up to date by reading the current literature and attending meetings. This will ensure quality health care and maintenance of an intellectually stimulating quality in the practice of medicine.

7. Responsibility to the profession calls for the practitioner to set the best possible example in appearance, speech, and behavior.

8. The goal should not be solely to gain an education by isolating oneself from world affairs and one's community. By remaining alert to what is transpiring and being as active as possible, one meets the broader responsibilities associated with the title "Doctor."

## Goals to Strive for in Medical School

The premedical college years can, in some cases, have a negative impact because of the competition for a place in the entering class. Those gaining admission are usually achievers of high grades that have been attained by intensive studying. This generates an attitude where learning becomes a chore rather than a pleasure.

The goals in medical school should be associated with the learning process. They should be to:

1. learn how to develop and maintain a love for knowledge;

2. learn to develop and maintain a balanced lifestyle incorporating work, relaxation, rewarding relationships, and varying interests;

3. learn to be receptive to new concepts while at the same time being reserved in making definitive judgments, since not all that appears logical is proved correct in the end;

4. learn to develop a genuine interest in finding out more about people and the best ways to care for them as individuals;

5. learn to use one's imagination and not be overwhelmed by the mountain of information ingested;

6. learn how to acquire a serviceable foundation in the biomedical sciences during the preclinical years and how to secure additional information in each area when needed;

7. learn how to attain a secure knowledge base during the clinical years upon which to build during postgraduate training;

8. learn to accept the fact that practicing medicine requires some personal sacrifice in terms of one's private life, time off, and in other areas;

9. learn that one's goals are not only to acquire knowledge and skill, but also to retain an interest in society and the world; and

10. learn to accept the fact that medicine is a continual challenge and that it brings with it both the joy of triumph and the sorrow of defeat.

# THE MAKING OF A PHYSICIAN

The premedical and medical school preparation and training intervals usually extend over an eight-year period. During this time, the student is, for the most part, preoccupied with coursework and then clinical training. The concerns are essentially with the mechanics of climbing from one rung to the next on the ladder of professional status. Little time is thus available to reflect upon the nature of the nonacademic aspects of medical education and medical practice, although these may be subtly realized as one journeys along the educational route. By enunciating them at this point and bringing them to the attention of prospective physicians, the metamorphosis from layperson to healer may be better understood and appreciated.

Two fundamental interpersonal characteristics must be understood to develop a proper perspective about the practice of medicine.

## Physician-Patient Relationship

The basic strength of medicine has been, and undoubtedly will remain, the highly personalized one-to-one relationship between the patient and the physician. It involves establishing and maintaining a bond of trust and faith between an individual in pain and the doctor selected to diagnose and cure, or at least alleviate, the suffering. The interaction between these two human beings seeking a common goal is the cornerstone of the practice of medicine. Maintaining this unique interpersonal bond between patient and doctor, even if other members of the health team are interposed in the diagnostic and therapeutic phases, is one of the most essential elements of medical practice.

## Physician-Patient Responsibility

The second key element in the care of, as well as in caring about, the patient is providing appropriate care. The trust placed in the hands of a physician needs to be reciprocated by his or her genuine concern for the patient. This involves the proper application of both the science and the art of medicine so that one achieves the goal of the maintenance of health, or easing of pain.

To meet one's responsibilities as a physician involves absorbing and assimilating a sound basis in human biology and acquiring and maintaining a high level of clinical expertise. Only a sound scientific basis for critical evaluation will enable the physician to incorporate or reject various items in the large volume of data obtained during the course of a patient's "workup" and thereby arrive at an appropriate diagnosis.

A better relationship may be facilitated if one has a view of what the patient seeks in a physician. A survey has shown that priority is given to: (1) being knowledgeable, (2) being competent, (3) answering questions honestly and completely, (4) providing clear explanations to medical problems, (5) making sure that patients understand what they have been told, (6) spending adequate time with them, and (7) demonstrating a genuine interest in the patient's health and welfare.

# UNITED STATES MEDICAL LICENSING EXAMINATION

There is no national medical licensing body in the United States. It is the function of the individual states to determine who shall practice within their borders and to maintain high standards of medical practice in accordance with their own rules and regulations. In recognition of the thoroughness and widely accepted standards of the USML examinations, its certificate is accepted by the medical licensing authorities of the District of Columbia, Puerto Rico, and all states except Louisiana and Texas.

The National Board of Medical Examiners (NBME) has established three qualifying examinations which are referred to as Steps 1, 2, and 3 of the United States Medical Licensing Examination (USMLE). Step 1 is given all year round, over an eight-hour day, and is a multiple-choice test. It seeks to assess the ability to apply knowledge and understanding of key concepts of basic biomedical science, with an emphasis on the principles and mechanisms of disease and modes of therapy. Step 2 is given in March and September and has a similar format to Step 1. It seeks to assess the ability to apply the medical knowledge and understanding of clinical science considered essential for the provision of patient care under supervision, including emphasis on health care and disease prevention. A clinical skills component has been incorporated in Step 2 of the USMLE; a fee of around $1,000 has been set for it. There is also a charge for exam review questions, which can serve as a self-assessment exam program. Step 3 seeks to assess the ability to apply the medical knowledge and understanding of biomedical and clinical science considered essential for the supervised practice of medicine with emphasis on patient management in ambulatory settings. To be eligible to take Step 3, the individual must (a) have obtained the MD degree (or its equivalent) or the DO degree, (b) have successfully completed both Steps 1 and 2, (c) if a foreign medical school graduate, have successfully completed a Fifth Pathway Program, and (d) have met the requirements for taking Step 3 imposed by the medical licensing authority that is administering the examination, such as the completion of any postgraduate requirements. The latter generally is the near completion or completion of one full postgraduate training year in an accredited graduate program.

All three steps of the USMLE are offered in a computerized format and need to be taken at Sylvan Technology Centers, which are responsible for scheduling. Registration information is provided by the Office of Student Affairs at each of the medical schools and from the National Board of Medical Examiners (NBME), Department of Licensing Examination Services, 3750 Market Street, Philadelphia, PA 19104. This organization's Web site address is *www.nbme.org*.

# Postgraduate Medical Education

Incorporating the residency and internship
Resident matching program
Residency training
Medical specialties
Fellowship training
Improving postgraduate training
Challenges in training
New trends in medical specialties
Physician employment opportunities

## INCORPORATING THE RESIDENCY AND INTERNSHIP

When the internship first became an established part of postgraduate medical education in the early part of this century, its purpose was straightforward and uniform: a *rotating* internship, with nearly equal portions devoted to medicine, surgery, pediatrics, and obstetrics-gynecology, which provided the first extended clinical experience and the first supervised responsibility for the welfare of patients. These experiences were deemed essential and usually sufficient to complete the preparation of a younger physician for independent practice.

With advances in medicine, the purpose of an internship was no longer obvious nor uniform. The internship did not provide the student's first practical experience with problems of diagnosis and treatment; that function is served by undergraduate clinical clerkships. Nor was it adequate to provide the final educational experience preceding independent practice; the additional training of a residency is generally considered necessary to fulfill that purpose.

The nature of the internship also changed over the years. Aside from the original rotating format, in time two other types came into use: *mixed* internships—providing training in two or three fields with prolonged concentration in one of them; and *straight* internships—devoting time entirely to single areas, such as medicine, surgery, or pediatrics.

While medical school curricula are the corporate responsibilities of faculties, internship programs were not the corporate responsibilities of hospitals. The responsibility of ensuring a truly educational internship was usually that of an individual head of a service or heads of several independent services. An inevitable result of such highly individualized and fragmented responsibility was that internship programs varied widely in the extent to which they duplicated the experience already gained in the clinical clerkship, in the amount of routine and sometimes menial service required, and in their educational quality.

As a result of the highly questionable value of the internship in the educational process and the very high percentage of physicians taking residencies, its usefulness as a distinct program came into serious question. At its annual convention in December 1968, the AMA adopted a resolution that "an ultimate goal is unification of the internship and residency years into a coordinated whole." Further steps toward implementation of this resolution were subsequently adopted and the goal was set that by July 1, 1978 all internship programs would be integrated with residency training to form a unified program of graduate medical education which has taken place. This means that the internship year now is the first year of residency and that one person, who is assigned as program director in a specialty at a given institution, is responsible for the entire program. That person has the option of requiring or recommending a specific type of first year program (rotating, mixed, or straight) acceptable as part of the residency program, or even assigning trainees to an outside hospital for their first residency year. A significant amount of flexibility has been introduced so as to permit the graduating physician to secure postgraduate training that is specifically designed for individual interests and career goals. It will also facilitate long-term plans and ensure a more stable personal life.

# RESIDENT MATCHING PROGRAM

Almost all graduates of U.S. and Canadian medical schools secure internship appointments in U.S. hospitals through the National Resident Matching Program (NRMP). More specifically, in a recent year, 93% of about 14,300 U.S. senior medical students who participated in the NRMP received a first-year residency position. This reverses the trend for placement in proceeding years. Foreign medical graduates are eligible to participate if they have passed the USMLE in September or earlier. In recent years, the number of foreign medical graduates participating in the Matching Program significantly increased. They filled almost all of the 500 residency slots that were offered.

Currently, about 50,000 residents are training at U.S. civilian hospitals. The number of residency slots has increased slightly in recent years, particularly in the fields of anesthesiology, internal medicine, and, to a lesser degree, psychiatry and emergency medicine. There were decreases in positions for residents in the fields of pathology and plastic surgery.

In the fall of the senior year, all medical students apply to the hospitals to which they would like an appointment. Sometime during the winter, after the students' marks have been submitted to the hospital residency program director, they may be invited to visit the hospital where they will be interviewed by one or several attending physicians as well as the director of the training program. After the interviews are completed in the early spring, prospective interns make up a list of hospitals to which they have applied, with the number one choice at the top, the last choice at the bottom. All the participating hospitals submit similar lists of the students they have interviewed. The lists are gathered in a central office and fed into a computer, and pairings are made. The seniors' preferences are then matched with the hospitals' preferences. This program, which was instituted in 1952, avoids a great deal of chaos and anguish, since previously neither students nor hospitals knew where they were until the last moment. The match rate for U.S. medical graduates is usually higher than 90%.

All specialty boards have made significant modifications in their requirements to adjust to the plan for integrated postgraduate training; senior medical students may now apply for a first year of graduate medical education (PGYI), either in one of the existing types of "internships" or in a first year of residency in most specialties. For additional information contact: National Resident Matching Program, 2450 N Street NW, Suite 201, Washington, DC 20037.

The current average salaries for residents are in the $25,000 to $50,000 range. However, as a result of the deterioration of their financial status because their salaries have not kept up with inflation and their education indebtedness has increased, many residents hold second jobs. Married people, especially those with children, are the most likely to be forced to supplement their incomes by "moonlighting"—working at outside jobs.

The rate of annual increase in house staff (resident) salaries has been growing slowly over the past few years. Some hospitals have not increased their stipends at all, and a number have even decreased them. In general, pay increases are higher at hospitals located in the Northeast and lowest for those in the South. Also, the pay for house staff at university-owned hospitals, because of their higher status as teaching institutions, tends to be lower than the national average, while that for hospitals with limited university affiliation tends to be higher.

Most hospitals offer health insurance for house staff and their dependents as part of the benefit package. Vacation time varies from one to four weeks annually with the amount increasing by the number of years of training.

Currently, somewhat more than half the hospitals have maternity leave policies but the types of programs vary considerably. One-third of the hospitals treat maternity leave as sick leave, another third have specific guidelines, and the others consider it as short-term disability leave, without pay or vacation.

# RESIDENCY TRAINING

After the first postgraduate year comes specialization. The function of this extended period of training has changed greatly since its start a century ago. At that time a residency was a special period of additional clinical education for a few promising and scholarly young physicians who wished to become the teachers or leaders in medicine. Residency training since the period after World War II has become standard for the average physician and more than 1,500 American hospitals offer such programs. Completing an approved residency and passing a written and/or oral examination given by a specialty board are the basic requirements for certification as a specialist.

In the early 1900s, nearly half of all medical school graduates entered general practice. By the 1960s this figure had shrunk to about 20%. A recent study concerning medical specialization showed that there has been a significant increase in interest in primary care/family practice over the past several decades. Economic factors are comparatively minor in determining medical specialization, while up to 87% of the sampling indicated intellectual interests to be a major determining factor. Most recruits are entering internal medicine, surgery, psychiatry, obstetrics/gynecology, and pediatrics. Women physicians have generally favored fixed-schedule specialties (anesthesiology, radiology, psychiatry, pediatrics, public health) and work settings (state hospitals and industry).

The length of residency training varies among the different specialties and is indicated in Table 14.1.

It is possible to apply for a residency in a manner comparable to AMCAS. This is by means of the AAMC-sponsored Electronic Residency Application Service (ERAS). Offices of Deans of Students at medical schools (both allopathic and osteopathic) can provide the necessary material needed to apply. Canadians can also use ERAS.

It should be noted that many of the specialties listed have subspecialties that may require two to three years additional fellowship training beyond that listed in Table 14.1.

## Securing a Residency

Appointments to residency positions are competitive and usually made through the Resident Matching Program. Your ranking by the Resident Program Director largely depends on three considerations:

1. medical school performance;

2. summary of recommendations from clinical clerkship supervisors; and,

3. residency interview performance.

The success of the interview can impact decisively on your future career. For this reason, we offer advice on preparing for your residency interview in this section.

Obtaining a residency appointment is not a hit-or-miss affair. Careful planning can avoid many pitfalls and improves your chances for success. Medical students frequently underestimate the importance of residency selection. The training program determines the specialty tract, and within the program, the curriculum and its monitoring staff can profoundly influence your career path. In addition, each program has its own philosophy and work environment. In selecting a program, a determination is made as to the amount of time that you will have to devote to meet the program's requirements over a period of several years. The residency interview provides a possible means of enhancing your chances for securing a house staff appointment as well as finding out if it is the right one for you.

## Table 14.1 RESIDENCY TRAINING FOR VARIOUS SPECIALTIES AND SUBSPECIALTIES

| Specialty | Nature of Work | Prerequisite Year(s) | Training Area | Training Period (years) Minimum | Maximum |
|---|---|---|---|---|---|
| Aerospace Medicine | Care for individuals involved in space travel | One | Preventive Medicine | Two | Two |
| Allergy and Immunology | Treatment of illness due to hypersensitivity to a specific substance or condition | Three | Medicine | Two | Three |
| Anesthesiology | Producing a partial or total loss of pain by use of drugs, gases, or other means | One | Clinical Base | Three | Four |
| Cardiovascular Disease | Diagnosis and treatment of heart and blood vessel diseases | Three | Medicine | Three | Three |
| Child and Adolescent Psychiatry | Treatment of emotional disorders of children and adolescents | One | General Psychiatry | Four | Four |
| Colon and Rectal Surgery | Treatment of diseases of the lower bowel | Three | General Surgery | Two | Two |
| Dermatology | Treatment of skin diseases | One | Medicine | Three | Three |
| Diagnostic Radiology | Use of specialized X-ray techniques for diagnosis | One | Clinical Base | Four | Five |
| Emergency Medicine | Diagnosis and treatment of acute and life-threatening illnesses | One | Medicine | Two | Three |
| Family Practice (Primary Care) | Evaluating total health needs and providing routine treatment | — | — | Three | Three |
| Forensic Pathology | Use of pathological methods in criminal investigations | Three | Pathology | One | Two |
| Gastroenterology | Diagnosis and treatment of disease of the digestive tract | Three | Medicine | Two | Three |
| Hand Surgery | Treatment of injuries to the hand | Five | General Surgery | One | One |
| Internal Medicine | Treatment of diseases and organs with medications | — | — | Three | Three |
| Neonatal-Perinatal Medicine | Treatment of infants and high-risk newborns | Three | Pediatrics | Three | Three |
| Nephrology | Diseases of the kidneys | Three | Medicine | Two | Three |
| Neurosurgery | Surgery of the nervous system | One | General Surgery | Five | Five |
| Neurology | Treatment of nervous system with medications | One | Clinical Base | Three | Four |
| Neuropathology | Diagnosis of pathological conditions of the nervous system | Four | Pathology | One | Two |
| Nuclear Medicine | Use of radioactive substances in the diagnosis and treatment of diseases | Three | Medicine, Pathology, or Radiology | Two | Three |
| Obstetrics and Gynecology | Care during pregnancy and labor and treatment of diseases of genital and reproductive system | One | Clinical Base | Three | Four |

**Table 14.1 RESIDENCY TRAINING FOR VARIOUS SPECIALTIES AND SUBSPECIALTIES (Continued)**

| Specialty | Nature of Work | Prerequisite Year(s) | Training Area | Training Period (years) Minimum | Maximum |
|---|---|---|---|---|---|
| Ophthalmology | Care and treatment of eye diseases | One | Optional | Three | Four |
| Orthopedic Surgery | Treatment of skeletal deformities and injuries of the bones and joints | One | General Surgery | Three | Four |
| Otolaryngology | Treatment of ear, nose, and throat diseases | One | General Surgery | Three | Four |
| Pathology | Diagnosis of structural and functional changes in the body tissues due to diseases | One | Optional | Four | Four |
| Pediatrics | Care of infants and children and treatment of their diseases | — | — | Three | Four |
| Pediatric Cardiology | Treatment of heart diseases in children | Three | Pediatrics | Two | Two |
| Pediatric Nephrology | Treatment of kidney disease in children | Three | Pediatrics | Two | Two |
| Physical Medicine and Rehabilitation | Treatment by physical and mechanical means to permit maximum restoration of function | One | Medicine and Surgery | Three | Three |
| Plastic Surgery | Surgery to repair or restore injured, deformed or destroyed parts of the body, especially by transferring tissue | Four | General Surgery | Two | Three |
| Preventive Medicine | Prevention of disease for individuals and the public | One | Public Health | Two | Two |
| Primary Care | [See Family Practice] | | | | |
| Psychiatry | Treatment of mental disease | One | Clinical Base | Four | Four |
| Pulmonary Disease | Disease of the respiratory tract | Three | Medicine | Two | Three |
| Radiology | Diagnosis of disease by radioactive means | One | Clinical Base | Four | Four |
| Rheumatology | Diagnosis and treatment of arthritic diseases | Three | Medicine | Two | Three |
| Sports Medicine | Treatment of sports-related injuries | Three | Emergency Medicine | One | One |
| Surgery | Treatment of diseases by surgical intervention | One | — | Four | Seven |
| Therapeutic Radiology | Treatment of diseases by radiation therapy | One | Clinical Base | Four | Four |
| Thoracic Surgery | Surgical treatment of chest diseases | Four | General Surgery | Two | Two |
| Urology | Treatment of kidney and bladder diseases | Three | General Surgery | Two | Two |
| Vascular Surgery | Surgery of blood vessels | Five | General Surgery | One | One |

The following are important suggestions to help you secure a suitable position. Many of the pointers noted in the premed interview discussion are relevant here as well.

### Do Your Homework

Familiarize yourself with the program for which you are being offered an interview. It is risky to go unprepared, since you can make poor choices of places to visit and appear uninformed at the interview. Carefully study published residency program material that was sent to you or a classmate or is on file at your medical school. Such material could provide information concerning facilities, faculty-resident ratio, and the philosophy, curriculum, work hours, and support staff at the teaching hospital.

Setting up a card file on all prospective interview sites is useful. It will help you refresh your memory just prior to a visit. Add new information and your impressions after each visit for possible future reference. Sequence your interview schedule so that the interviews are not so close that you do not have time to recover from one before you present yourself for another and you can arrive fresh and enthusiastic for each interview. A "practice" interview at a program low on your acceptance list is a good way to develop self-confidence. Your highest priority interview should be scheduled in the middle of your interview cycle. By that time you should have an adequate amount of experience and will not be physically drained by this demanding process. Remember that making a good initial impression can be enhanced by a firm handshake and proper grooming.

### Know Yourself

It is important at the outset of the entire interview process to define your goals career-wise. Completion of a personality test and discussion with faculty members with whom you are close about your goals, interests, and strengths can be helpful. After this process you should be able to clearly articulate your career plans and defend your choices. This should include knowledge of your choice of a clinical or academic career and the type of the residency you are seeking.

### Anticipate Obvious Questions

Although interviews vary widely, many questions asked are standard ones. Among the most favorite ones are:

1. What are your short- and long-range goals?

2. What are your strengths and weaknesses?

3. Why do you seek admission to this program?

4. What do you want out of life?

5. Why did you choose medicine as a career?

6. What have been your most important accomplishments so far?

Practicing answers to these questions is advisable so long as they do not sound rehearsed when you deliver them. Mock interviews with fellow students can prove useful in preparing for the real ones.

### Ask Tactful Questions About the Program

You should seek to learn about the program in the context of the interview session by inquiring as to the program's commitments to education versus service obligation. Tactful questions are appropriate; therefore, rather than asking about a program's weakness, phrase your question as an inquiry. You may wish to ask the interviewer if the program has received an unrestricted grant, what areas it would be invested in. The most appropriate questions to ask are those relevant to education and the quality of patient care. In any case, the questions you ask should be determined by the position of the person to whom you are speaking. In other words, when being interviewed by a department head, an inquiry relevant to salary or housing would not be appropriate but should be directed to a resident. Questions about the philosophy and curriculum of a program should obviously be presented to the program director and would suggest a more meaningful interest. Try to leave a positive and memorable impression on your interviewer.

### Sample the Residency
The best way to evaluate a program is to spend a senior year rotation at the hospital in which you might consider doing your residency. When this is not feasible, you may be able to spend a day as an observer with residents, following them on rounds (if possible, dressed in whites). First-hand observation on the wards and in the clinics will provide a good window to assess the value of the program. Questioning residents is useful.

### Present a Team Player Image
The residency is quite different from medical school; therefore, it is desirable to leave an impression that you can make the transition from working independently to being part of a team. Projecting the sense that you will fit well into the existing team will enhance your chance of securing the residency appointment you are interested in.

### Be Yourself
While making a strong effort to project a favorable image, you should also strive to be sure that it is a realistic one. You must balance your desire to get the appointment with a candid assessment of whether the position will fill your own needs. When you leave the interview, you should go away with a positive feeling that this is the place you would like to spend the next several years training, to attain the proficiency you will require in order to succeed in your profession.

# MEDICAL SPECIALTIES

One of medicine's attractions is the numerous and wide variety of career options it offers. These options range from allergy to women's health, and incorporate an intense work style, from emergency or critical care medicine to a more dispassionate approach such as psychiatry. Medicine may involve actively seeing patients or dealing primarily with one's peers (pathology or radiology). A practice can require superior manipulative skills such as surgery or primarily diagnosis and prescribing medications (family practice) or both (urology). Because of this disparity of options, individuals having a broad range of interests, talents, and personalities can usually find an appropriate outlet for them.

Once you succeed in getting into medical school, within the span of a little more than two years you will be faced with the challenge of selecting a residency. Competition for appointments varies depending on the area in question.

The characteristics of the common specialties are identified in Table 14.1 and will be elaborated upon somewhat below so as to familiarize prospective medical students with the array of choices they face. Details can be obtained from the specialty organizations whose addresses and Web sites are given in Appendix D.

**Allergy and Immunology.** This is a subspecialty of both pediatrics and internal medicine. It is concerned with the diagnosis and treatment of allergic, asthmatic, and immunologic diseases. Patients are seen largely by referral. This is largely an office-based practice with few night calls. Practices are located primarily in metropolitan areas. Although there is competition from nonspecialists, opportunities are increasing.
*Contact Organization:* American Academy of Allergy, Asthma, and Immunology.

**Anesthesiology.** Specialists in this area are qualified to provide general or regional anesthesia during a variety of procedures. These include both surgical and diagnostic as well as obstetric activities. They may also be involved in critical care and pain management. This is largely a hospital-based practice, but some specialists may be involved in office-based activities when some routine procedures need to be performed (endoscopies). Night call is common for hospital-affiliated specialists.
*Contact Organization:* American Society of Anesthesiologists.

**Cardiovascular Diseases.** These specialists diagnose and treat patients who have heart or circulatory system problems. Cardiology is a subspecialty of internal medicine and its practice has both noninvasive and invasive components. In the former, the history, physical examination, and appropriate tests serve as the standard approach to patient care. Invasive cardiologists perform angiographies to evaluate the status of the coronary or other arteries or insert "stents" to maintain their function as an open blood pathway. Noninvasive cardiologists are usually hospital-based and night call is quite common.

*Contact Organization:* American College of Cardiology.

**Child and Adolescent Psychiatry.** This is a subspecialty of psychiatry. It involves the diagnosis and treatment of children and adolescents having emotional, behavioral, and mental problems. These specialists operate private practices and work in both in- and out-patient care. They get referrals from pediatricians and social service agencies.

*Contact Organization:* American Academy of Child and Adolescent Psychiatry.

**Colon and Rectal Surgery.** This is a subspecialty of general surgery. It involves the diagnosis and surgical treatment of disorders of the colon, rectum, anal canal, and peri-anal region. Colonoscopy and more limited endoscopy procedures are the standard diagnostic techniques employed in this specialty.

*Contact Organization:* American Society of Colon and Rectal Surgeons.

**Critical Care Medicine.** This hospital-based specialty is concerned with the care of critically ill medical and surgical patients. It requires a broad medical background with special knowledge of fluid, cardiovascular, and respiratory management in order to stabilize such patients. Specialists in this area commonly tend to be pulmonary medicine specialists.

*Contact Organization:* Society of Critical Care Medicine.

**Dermatology.** This specialty deals with the diagnosis and treatment of acute and chronic diseases of the skin of individuals of all ages. Both medical and surgical modalities are used in this specialty.

*Contact Organization:* American Academy of Dermatology.

**Diagnostic Radiology.** This diagnostic specialty utilizes X-rays, ultrasounds, magnetic fields, and other energy source. Consequently, aside from interpreting basic radiographs, diagnostic radiologists must learn to interpret scans and images. There is also a need to learn a variety of diagnostic interventional procedures.

*Contact Organization:* American College of Radiology.

**Emergency Medicine.** This is a hospital-based specialty. These physicians treat a broad spectrum of illnesses and injuries for individuals in all age groups. They seek to stabilize patients with critical illnesses and injuries, and work on a fixed schedule.

*Contact Organization:* American College of Emergency Physicians.

**Family Practice.** These specialists are qualified to provide general medical care to all members of the family. The exact nature of an individual's practice depends on his or her own special qualifications and interests as well as location and affiliated hospitals. The services provided are mostly in an office setting and involve seeing patients of varying ages and a broad spectrum of illnesses. Their patients may include both children and seniors. Family practice physicians are even involved in providing counseling for psychological issues that are part of life such as childbirth, stress, and grief.

*Contact Organization:* American Academy of Family Physicians.

**Gastroenterology.** This is a subspecialty of internal medicine. Practitioners diagnose and treat diseases of the digestive tract, liver, and gallbladder. Technical improvements in directly inspecting the GI tract have expanded the procedures that can now be performed.

*Contact Organization:* American College of Gastroenterology.

*Geriatric Medicine.* This is a relatively new subspecialty of medicine that involves primary medical and psychosocial care of senior citizens. There is an increasing demand for such specialists as the population rapidly ages. The demand will be accelerated as the current small group of certified gerontologists retires. Geriatric physicians usually work in conjunction with a multispecialty team of medical and nonmedical professionals. There also are opportunities aside from private practice in the academic community or corporate medicine.

*Contact Organization:* American Geriatric Society.

*Hand Surgery.* This is a subspecialty of general orthopedic or plastic surgery. It deals with diseases of or injuries to the hand or forearm. This specialty utilizes the many developed microsurgical techniques derived from the fields of plastic and orthopedic surgery. The surgical procedures used can usually be performed on an outpatient basis.

*Contact Organization:* American Association of Hand Surgery.

*Hematology-Oncology.* These two distinct subspecialties are linked together by both training and practice. Hematology involves the diagnosis and treatment of blood diseases, while oncology is associated with cancer-type illnesses. Advances in these two fields have allowed for therapeutic results that can provide for the extension of life. Preliminary specialization in internal medicine is required in this office-based specialty, but significant in-patient service and night calls can be anticipated.

*Contact Organizations:* American Society of Hematology and The American Society of Clinical Oncology.

*Infectious Diseases.* Another subspecialty of internal medicine, this involves the diagnosis and treatment of infectious diseases. The status of this subspecialty initially was revitalized due to the introduction of antibiotics. It now flourishes because of the HIV/AIDS epidemic, the bioterrorism threat, and development of drug-resistant bacteria. The physicians may be involved in internal medicine practice in addition to working in this area directly or as a consultant.

*Contact Organization:* Infectious Disease Society of America.

*Internal Medicine.* This specialty provides training for those interested in becoming general internists as well as for a large variety of potential medical subspecialists. It can also be combined in an internal medicine-pediatric residency. The general internist treats adults suffering from both acute and chronic diseases and also provides primary care facilitating health maintenance. The status of this specialty has become elevated with the flourishing of HMOs.

*Contact Organization:* American College of Physicians–American Society of Internal Medicine.

*Neonatal-Perinatal Medicine.* These pediatric subspecialists provide medical care to newborns in the intensive care unit who usually are placed there because they are born prematurely. They are qualified to provide the medical intervention that is so essential for survival. They direct a team of ancillary professionals needed to provide a variety of services.

*Contact Organization:* American Academy of Pediatrics.

*Nephrology.* This subspecialty of internal medicine is involved in the diagnosis and nonsurgical treatment of kidney and urinary tract diseases. It is essentially an office-based practice, usually treating older adults suffering from chronic kidney disease who require long-term care. The service provided usually is associated with managing dialysis and providing care for kidney transplant patients.

*Contact Organization:* American Society of Nephrology.

*Neurological Surgery.* This surgical subspecialty deals with the management of lesions of the brain, spinal cord, peripheral nerves, and their supporting structures. While commonly a surgical approach is the treatment of choice, it need not always be so. This is a very challenging surgical subspecialty; it can produce both dramatic success and dismal failures with tragic consequences. A broad range of patients, from newborn to the elderly are seen and treated.

*Contact Organization:* American Association of Neurological Surgeons.

**Neurology.** Practitioners in this area are involved in the diagnosis and treatment of brain, spinal cord, peripheral nerve, and neuromuscular diseases. They frequently attend patients suffering from stroke, seizure, and a severe headache. This is primarily an office-based specialty whose demand is increasing as the number of its elderly in the population increases.

*Contact Organization:* American Neurological Association.

**Nuclear Medicine.** Specialists in this field use radioactive materials for both diagnostic and treatment purposes. A variety of aspects of physics, statistics, computer science, and math are used in conjunction with medicine. The radioactive material is introduced into the bloodstream to provide imaging of selected body organ systems. Practitioners are hospital-based and secure their initial training in internal medicine, radiology, or pathology.

*Contact Organization:* American College of Nuclear Medicine.

**Obstetrics and Gynecology.** This dual specialty deals with the female reproductive tract both in health and illnesses. The former involves providing medical and, when necessary, surgical care to pregnant women. Gynecologists apply the same two approaches to diseases of the reproductive tract and also deal with problems of infertility. Specialists commonly work in both areas, but as they advance in years they tend to remain only in gynecology. This specialty is considered part primary care because of a broader interest in women's health.

*Contact Organization:* American College of Obstetricians and Gynecologists.

**Occupational Medicine.** A subspecialty of preventive medicine, it focuses on the effects of certain potentially hazardous occupations on the worker's health. Occupational physicians, therefore, work for the government, industry, academic institutions, and specialized clinics.

*Contact Organization:* American College of Occupational and Environmental Medicine.

**Ophthalmology.** This specialty is concerned with the diagnosis and treatment of diseases of the eye and periocular area. It is largely office-based, but involves medical and surgical components and thus is very popular. Patients of all ages are seen and subspecialization is common due to the technological and medical advances made in this field.

*Contact Organization:* American Academy of Ophthalmology.

**Orthopedic Surgery.** Specialists are engaged in diagnosing diseases and injuries to the bones of the extremities and the vertebral column. Aiming to preserve maximal musculoskeletal function, surgical, medical, and physical therapy approaches are used. This specialty is appealing to those who have superior manual dexterity and like to work with their hands. It commonly involves emergency and night calls.

*Contact Organization:* American Academy of Orthopedic Surgeons.

**Pediatrics.** These specialists are concerned with the general well-being of children and adolescents and even adults. They provide routine, preventive care and treat acute and many chronic illnesses for those in the lower age range, with whom they establish long-term relationships. This is, for the most part, an office-based specialty, with currently more females entering than men practicing.

*Contact Organization:* American Academy of Pediatrics.

**Physical Medicine and Rehabilitation.** Specialists in this field are known as physiatrists. They are involved in the diagnosis and location and treatment of individuals with impaired musculoskeletal, neurological, and other body system disabilities. Patients of all ages are treated. Their problem may have originated due to brain or spinal cord damage or as the result of accidents. Physiatrists seek to positively impact upon patients' physical, psychosocial, and career-related activities as well as seek remission of pain.

*Contact Organization:* American Academy of Physical Medicine and Rehabilitation.

**Plastic Surgery.** These specialists apply their surgical skills to rectify body disfigurements. The source of the impaired area may be due to a birth defect, injury, disease, or aging process. Aside from being surgically highly skilled, one needs a strong aesthetic sense to achieve the desirable results in both reconstructive and cosmetic undertakings. Much of the procedures are carried out on an ambulatory basis.

*Contact Organization:* American Academy of Plastic and Reconstructive Surgery.

**Preventive Medicine.** This field is involved in population-based approaches to environmental health promotion and disease prevention. Physicians in this field are employed by government agencies, managed care organizations, industry, and academic institutions. It involves, in addition to knowledge of general preventive medicine, a background in epidemiology, informatics, and biostatistics.

*Contact Organization:* American College of Preventive Medicine.

**Psychiatry.** Specialists in this area diagnose diseases of the mind. They treat a very broad spectrum of mental illness. While usually practicing in an office-based setting, they also see patients in psychiatric hospitals and community health and substance abuse centers. The impressive development in potent psychotropic medications has broadened this field potential for treatment.

*Contact Organization:* American Psychiatric Association.

**Public Health.** This is a subspecialty of preventive medicine. It deals with health issues capable of or affecting entire communities, in addition to individuals. To promote health and understand the possible danger of disease or risky situations, these specialists evaluate relevant community information, develop suitable protective public health policies, and seek to facilitate achieving set goals. Those in this field work for government agencies and private health organizations, as well as academic and research institutions.

*Contact Organization:* American College of Preventive Medicine.

**Surgery.** The area of general surgery covers the diagnosis and treatment of diseases of and injuries to the abdominal organs and the soft tissues of the trunk. It forms the basis for subspecialization in a wide variety of areas. General surgeons require five years of training and usually have a short-term contract with their patients.

*Contact Organization:* American College of Surgeons.

**Thoracic Surgery.** These subspecialists apply their surgical skills to treat diseases of and injuries to the heart and lungs as well as other components of the chest. Common procedures are coronary artery bypass, heart valve repair, and lung lesions. This is a very stressful specialty, given the physical and emotional demands involved. It requires lengthy training of up to six years.

*Contact Organization:* American College of Surgeons.

**Urology.** In males, these specialists treat diseases of and injuries to the urethras, bladder, prostate, and genitals. In females they are concerned with the first two of these organs.

*Contact Organization:* American College of Urologists.

**Vascular Surgery.** This subspecialty of general surgery is associated with the diagnosis and treatment of diseases of the arterial, venous, and lymphatic systems. To maintain an active practice, many of these specialists combine their practice with that of general surgery.

*Contact Organization:* American Association for Vascular Surgery.

# FELLOWSHIP TRAINING

After completing four years of medical school and several years of residency, many physicians consider seeking a fellowship for training in a subspecialty. While still in medical school, additional training beyond the residency is considered remote but this attitude is reversed in the course of time. By gaining an awareness of the advantages of subspecialization, trends in various medical disciplines, and the challenge involved in securing a suitable fellowship, one can more easily decide if this is an appropriate course to follow.

Motivating factors influencing residents to pursue fellowship training vary. For some, the issue is to enhance the marketability of their own specialty. Others are concerned with the issue of variety of work experience, while some seek the special challenge that certain subspecialties present, such as critical care, neonatology, etc.

Financial remuneration is also significant when considering subspecialization. While primary care physicians are now in increasing demand, specialty practices are financially more rewarding, as specialists perform more billable procedures. In addition, their patients are more likely to have medical insurance.

Subspecialization is also attractive to some because of its implied higher status within the medical community. Being interested in a limited area makes it easier to keep abreast of new information and technological advances in a particular field. A subspecialist also usually has a more routine work schedule. Thus, all the aforementioned features have resulted in the increased attractiveness of subspecialization in recent years. While the number of medical school graduates choosing an internal medicine residency has declined somewhat, the number of those electing to subspecialize in this field has remained high. Some subspecialties are attracting more candidates than others. There has been some decline in interest in hematology, rheumatology, endocrinology, geriatrics, and infectious diseases. On the other hand, the fastest growing subspecialty within internal medicine is critical care, due to the fact that it is an action-oriented area. The demand for this type of subspecialty will continue to grow as more hospitals offer high tech procedures such as open heart surgery and organ transplants.

Another very popular field is pediatric emergency medicine, with a substantial increase in the number of fellowships available. Orthopedic surgery is still another area where subspecialization is very common. Areas of special interest include orthopedic oncology, knee reconstruction, and hand and spine surgery. Subspecialization is also increasingly common among radiology residents.

During medical school and residency, the individual has to focus on the clinical side of medicine. After the residency, research becomes important. This includes developing a suitable project, collecting data, and analyzing and reporting the results. Potential fellows should determine in advance where research funding will come from or if they must secure it on their own. Candidates should determine the extent of interest of the fellowship program in generating publications, especially if the program is academically oriented. This can be ascertained by inquiring about the program's publication record and if it supports fellows in presenting abstracts of their research at academic meetings. Fellowship candidates should try to determine the strength of the director's commitment to the program, so as to judge the extent of support they can anticipate.

It is useful to determine in advance the role of the fellow in the program to find out if the staff position, while an important one, does not place an excessive burden on the individual. Knowing the number of attendings and residents available to assist can help determine if the fellowship will merely serve to fill a resident gap, or if it will be a genuine advanced training position. Obtaining a current copy of the conference and call schedule can provide a good insight into the nature of the position. The number of fellows in a program is also important, because the environment is more stimulating when a group that is on a similar educational level is working together.

Accreditation of fellowship programs varies. It usually takes place after being established at a large hospital that has an adequate number of fellowships. When a program is not accredited, it is important that the program director have a strong enough reputation to compensate for this liability. This is especially relevant in less traditional subspecialties, such as fertility.

Currently, there is increasing pressure to standardize subspecialty educational programs and create a matching process in this area, as for residencies. This effort is geared to enhance the overall quality control of fellowship offerings. It already exists in some of the internal medicine subspecialties and is now impacting on other areas, such as radiology and pediatrics. Gradually, the number of free-standing programs will be reduced as accreditation of fellowship programs increases.

## Obtaining a Fellowship

To obtain an attractive fellowship requires careful strategic planning. Standards for fellowship applicants vary. Program directors are quite selective and competition for an appointment is keen. Completing a residency at an institution where the fellowship is offered can usually give the applicant an edge. The disadvantage in continuing at the same institution is that the fellow receives rather narrow training, since the fellow is in contact with the same attending as in the residency, and the opportunity to expand contacts is limited. If one anticipates ultimately seeking a fellowship, the residency training should at least be at an institution that has a good track record of its residents securing fellowships. Thus, the site of one's residency training is one major critical factor in the process of finding suitable subspecialty training.

A second strategic consideration is selecting appropriate faculty to provide letters of recommendation. The goal is to receive these from the people you worked with and who are prepared to write as strongly as possible in your behalf. The impact of a favorable letter is significantly influenced by the stature of the author of the letter. Obviously, a department chair's letter has greater credibility than one from a junior faculty member. Similarly, a positive impact can be made by a letter from a prominent person in the specialty or a known acquaintance of the fellowship program director. Completing an elective in the prospective area of subspecialization can facilitate obtaining helpful letters of recommendation.

Of special importance is the interview and interpersonal and communication skills that the candidate demonstrates. Showing that you are open-minded, flexible, and enthusiastic, and that you are amenable to open discussion of issues will enhance your chances to secure a fellowship.

# IMPROVING POSTGRADUATE TRAINING

The long-established system of clinical education is one in which senior physicians serve as instructors to their junior colleagues. This apprentice system may be flawed by the fact that mentor physicians often lack formal training as educators. This weakness impacts directly on the atmosphere and ultimate success of the learning process. As a result of the increased awareness that many physicians are deficient in teaching skills, a few medical schools, residency programs, and continuing education seminars are providing opportunities to remedy this situation. Physicians are learning the basics of good teaching, such as how to create a positive learning climate, how to enhance learner retention, and how to evaluate learner performance.

There are many skeptics, especially among older physicians, who question the need and value of teaching physicians how to teach. Some of the younger doctors believe that clinical teaching is a basic medical skill that is as valuable as physical diagnosis or history taking.

Providing teaching skills to physicians is hampered by the fact that it is not a grant-funded area and does not generate patient revenue. In addition, it is not formally encouraged by the medical establishment but is the driving force of some individual medical school faculty members. While not yet widespread, support for their efforts is gaining momentum.

One of the approaches used, in addition to a discussion of teaching skills, is video-taped role-play exercises. Each role-play is a sort of skit that is designed to demonstrate common, yet troublesome, scenarios in clinical teaching. After the role-play is completed, participants review the tape and analyze their performance.

Since the majority of physicians-in-training do not yet have access to teaching skills training, they are forced to learn how to teach on their own. While this is difficult to accomplish, they can seek help at the Office of Medical Education at their hospital or school. Also, information on clinical teaching may be available in a medical library. The best sources are the following short books: *The Physician as Teacher and Residents as Teachers* by T. L. Schweml and N. Whitman and *Teaching during Rounds: A Handbook for Attending Physicians and Residents*, by J. Edwards and D. Weonholtz.

Finally, improvement in teaching skills can even be obtained by so simple an approach as identifying and listing the attributes of the most skilled clinical teachers one has been exposed to and trying to emulate them. Similarly, the weaknesses of poor clinical teachers can be identified so that those deficiencies can be avoided.

## CHALLENGES IN TRAINING

For many years the postgraduate training interlude was looked upon as an initiation rite into the exclusive world of medical practice. Stress and a heavy workload have long been accepted as part of this process. Recently, a growing number of educators, as well as many trainees, have emphasized the negative aspects of this process.

A key problem is that most physicians, including young attendings, consider the troubling environment of postgraduate training a "rite of passage," and they forget some of the most traumatic interactions of their careers. It is important not to block out one's memories of the stress and trauma of the apprenticeship years in order to avoid repeating inflicting the injustices on others further down in the hierarchy. Unfortunately, it appears that the abuse phenomenon may still be perpetuated nationwide in the most rigid training programs.

Already, competition, rather than team effort, may be fostered in medical school. The emphasis is strong on the science of medicine, with the human aspects of medical care often being neglected. In the residency, the heavy workload and its associated responsibilities overshadow educational goals. A further impact of these conditions is the tendency toward physician desensitivation, but reforms over the past few years have improved both the education and training systems. Nevertheless, unhealthy demands are still being placed upon prospective practitioners. It took a fatal error in judgment by a sleep-starved resident to bring about the 80-hour work week for New York State residents, which has also been adopted in other areas. Those outside the system are still astounded by such conditions, while some within the system regret that changes have been made.

The dehumanization effect may be initiated in medical school when patients are presented merely as abstract cases. Standardization of patients to 150-pound white male stereotypes makes it harder to think in terms of patient differences.

The negative impact of stress and long work hours was ignored for a long time. When its effects in human terms became evident, such as substance abuse or increased divorce rate, more attention was given to the problem. A number of approaches have been developed to cope with this problem, including formation of support groups. The consensus is that, while progress has been made, it will take time to alter long-entrenched attitudes.

## NEW TRENDS IN MEDICAL SPECIALTIES

Discoveries in research and changes in society have resulted in changes within established medical specialties, as well as the evolution of new specialties. A brief overview of several specialties that have taken new directions follows.

## Primary Care/Family Practice

Public demand for a single, competent physician for the entire family has grown as the availability of such physicians continues to diminish. To meet this need, the specialty of family practice evolved. This specialty differs from the others in that it is defined in terms of functions performed rather than limited by treatment of certain diseases or parts of the body or on the basis of the patient's chronological age.

The specialist in family practice must acquire a basic core of knowledge in all areas of medicine. Being the physician of first contact, he or she is responsible for evaluating the patient's total health needs over an extended period of time. Family practice is thus a specialty in breadth rather than a specialty in depth.

The family practice specialty will become especially important as the U.S. health care system undergoes changes. A suitable balance between specialists and generalists will be one of the ultimate goals to ensure the success of a new system. An overabundance of specialists makes the health care system more expensive, less accessible, and less focused on prevention. The imbalance is a principal cause of the high cost of health care.

Suggestions are being made for ways to shift the trend away from specialization by limiting funding for training in subspecialalties and by creating incentives for entering the field of primary care. Among the attractive features of a primary care practice is the opportunity to treat patients ranging in age from children to the elderly. A primary care physician also sees a great variety of cases, from cardiology to rheumatology, and is responsible for providing continual care, creating a special bond between the patient and the physician.

Many physicians are becoming convinced of the value of preventive primary care. Health care reforms, emphasis on primary care, and the demand by women for more comprehensive health care have motivated obstetricians/gynecologists to seek recognition as primary care providers. Some groups, such as the American Academy of Family Physicians, strongly oppose granting such recognition, believing that it should be used for specially trained practitioners. Women frequently use ob/gyn specialists who sometimes also provide a general medical check-up. The American College of Obstetricians and Gynecologists has redefined its mission to include health care of women throughout their lifetime. They have even encouraged their members to subscribe to a journal containing generalist information.

Considerable efforts are being made to encourage medical students to choose primary care as their specialty, but there is some uncertainty about the most effective means of achieving this goal. Some feel that having generalists serve as student mentors is the best approach but a medical school survey found that faculty can do little to influence student specialty choice. A different study, however, demonstrated that, where required family practice clerkships exist, the number of students electing to become primary care physicians has significantly increased. This should be of interest to those premedical students considering primary care as their career choice.

Interest in family practice over the past few years has risen significantly, with the number of fourth year students matched with this specialty at high levels, second only to internal medicine. There has been a concerted and successful effort by the American Academy of Family Physicians to market this specialty. They have targeted medical schools to set up departments of family practice, and most now have them. Students are encouraged to take primary care clerkships within family practice settings. Such exposure, as noted above, can profoundly alter one's career goals. When the number of physicians entering family practice, internal medicine, and pediatrics for residency training—namely the primary care specialties—combined, it makes up about half of all physicians receiving postgraduate training. Of these three groups, the overwhelming majority of those entering family practice will remain in primary care, while, of the other two segments, a portion go into subspecialty training.

While the federal government is interested in reforming medical education as part of altering the health care system, these efforts are slowed down by political in-fighting. A somewhat more meaningful effort in being made by state legislatures. Their focus is to encourage the training of more primary care physicians so as to promote cost-effective medicine and to encourage physicians to practice in underserved areas. Thus, 13 (out of 21) states succeeded in enacting legislation that offers medical students financial aid or scholarships as incentives to practice in remote areas or inner city ghettos. These states include Maryland, Rhode Island, North Carolina, and Nebraska. Some states, such as Pennsylvania, have increased their funding directly for programs in family practice training. Mandating the training of primary care physicians can be successful in a state like Washington, which serves a largely rural population locally, and in adjacent states. Most other states turned down quota systems. Some schools are voluntarily setting goals of steering students to become primary care physicians in the hope of avoiding legislative coercion later on.

## Pediatrics

Although some serious infectious diseases of childhood have been conquered, children will always need care for the usual viral illnesses. Now, however, more attention is being focused on the patient as a whole, especially his or her behavioral problems. Thus such issues as child abuse, drug addiction, and suicide prevention are emerging areas of concern for pediatricians.

A developing subspecialty is pediatric emergency care. Increasing recognition of the need for specialists in this area is reflected by the fact that one-third of all emergency room visits involve children. They frequently present different problems than adults. Those specializing in pediatric emergency care usually complete a pediatric residency and an emergency medicine fellowship. A special five-year program for certification is under consideration.

The next frontier to become open to pediatricians will undoubtedly involve the treatment of genetic diseases with drugs that will become common because of advances in genetic engineering technology that are expected to take place in the near future.

## Psychiatry

The field of psychiatry is undergoing "remedicalization" in that the emphasis is now on using medical therapy in the context of hospital practice and closer affiliations with other specialties. In addition, a strong move toward subspecialization is developing, and such areas as geriatric psychiatry, clinical psychopharmacology, and forensic psychiatry are emerging.

## Diagnostic Radiology

New patterns of health care delivery coupled with advances in imaging technology are altering the professional schedules of radiologists. They are now more frequently on call, and more of them are practicing in outpatient settings.

The expanded use of magnetic resonance imaging (MRI), ultrasound, CAT scans, and other technologies has brought radiologists more intimately into the core of medical practice. Nevertheless, radiological techniques are used by other specialists as well, and an intense jurisdictional debate is in progress.

Subspecialization by means of fellowship training in such areas as ultrasound or pediatric radiology is increasing.

## Emergency Medicine

The relatively new specialty is emerging as a distinct entity, as indicated by the fact that board certification now requires specialized training in this area rather than merely passing the qualifying examinations.

Academic emergency medicine centers are now aiming at securing high-quality physicians with four years of training. As more medical students are exposed to this area, a very substantial upswing in the numbers seeking admission to residency programs is expected.

## Physical Medicine and Rehabilitation

War injuries and polio epidemics led to the development of physicians especially trained in treating pain and in rehabilitation therapy. Although debilitating diseases such as polio have been eradicated, accident and stroke victims and paralytics live much longer today, and thus the need for the services of physiatrists has increased.

Physiatrists are largely hospital based in terms of their practice, but more are moving into part-time private practice. Moreover, the approach of customizing treatment plans within the context of the patient's quality of life and maximal potential is becoming the norm. This specialty continues to use the multidisciplinary approach in patient care, which is an especially attractive feature for those who choose training in this area.

## Sports Medicine

This specialty is still in its infancy, and there are as yet no formal residency programs. Nevertheless an increasing number of physicians, including those trained in orthopedics and family practice, are entering full-time sports medicine. This field is developing because of the dramatic increase in popularity of physical fitness. In addition, the field is expanding beyond treatment to an understanding of the disease process and to prevention. In time, certification and a clearer definition of this specialty will evolve.

## Cosmetic Surgery

This developing field is an offshoot of reconstructive surgery. It comes in response to a more affluent society and the desire to obtain a greater degree of self-worth. Technical advances have also promoted cosmetic surgery as a distinct area of specialization. Breast reconstruction, liposuction, and certain kinds of laser surgery are but a few of the more recent developments that are encompassed by this field. In 1979 the American Board of Cosmetic Surgery was established; it certifies physicians from varying specialties who are primarily involved in cosmetic surgery.

## Geriatrics

This emerging specialty deals with medical care of the aged, usually defined as being over 65. It involves review of a patient's medical and social history, marital status, and functional ability. The geriatrician aims to address the patient as a whole.

The need for geriatricians is great and will increase as the percentage of the aged in the population gradually increases. The aged spend more than double the nation's health care dollars in proportion to their group size.

Geriatricians are usually initially trained in a specialty such as internal medicine or other relevant area and spend a two-year fellowship training period. Standards for fellowships are being developed.

## Career Placement

National trends in career placement are not directly available, and specialty imbalances change from year to year as well. The activities of the AMA Physician's Placement Service for the past few years do provide an insight into what is happening. The AMA's statistics show that there is a general pattern of undersupply of physicians for general and family practice and an oversupply of anesthesiologists, dermatologists, pediatricians, psychiatrists, radiologists, surgeons, and urologists. The only area other than general practice in which there currently seems to be a shortage is otolaryngology, with fewer specialists in this field in proportion to the opportunities available. Note, however, that the oversupply of particular specialists reflects the desires for prime locations, rather than a national oversupply.

Perhaps a good indicator of the current specialty trends is the residency choices of medical school graduates. For a very recent year these choices were approximately as follows:

Internal medicine, 27%
Pediatrics, 11%
Family practice, 12%
Surgery, 10%
Obstetrics and gynecology, 8%
Psychiatry, 6%
Orthopedic surgery, 5%
Radiology, 4%
Anesthesiology, 3%
Emergency medicine, 3%
Others, 11%

## PHYSICIAN EMPLOYMENT OPPORTUNITIES

Because of the shortage of physicians in rural and inner city areas, it was decided in the late 1960s to increase the number of practicing physicians. It was assumed that this would bring about a surplus of urban physicians and induce a better geographical distribution of health professionals. This has not come about and the underserved areas have had only modest improvement in spite of a higher ratio of specialists to generalists of 70:30. Projections of a surplus of over 100,000 specialists and a shortage of 30,000 generalists by the year 2000 have been reported.

In partial response to this situation, the number of allotted residency slots have diminished from 135% to 100%. Medical schools are beginning to focus on training primary care physicians by giving students an opportunity to complete ambulatory clerkships. Nevertheless, greater emphasis on the changing health care scene has to be brought to the attention of prospective physicians so that they can find their appropriate place in the professional world.

# 15 Foreign Medical Study

**Admission**
**Transfer to U.S. schools**
**Internship and residency**
**Fifth Pathway opportunities**
**Requirements for residency and/or practice**
**Selecting a foreign medical school**
**Foreign medical schools**

During the early decades of this century it was relatively common to find Americans going to Europe for postgraduate medical training. Since World War II, significant numbers of Americans have gone overseas for their undergraduate medical education. At the peak of this trend, it was roughly estimated that as many as 10,000 were enrolled in foreign medical schools. Approximately 1,000 new students are thought to matriculate each year and this figure is only an estimate.

The fact that a significant number of Americans are studying medicine abroad should not be taken to mean that if you fail to gain acceptance in the United States, you should automatically seek admission to a foreign school. You should first determine if rejection by American schools means that you genuinely lack the ability to complete your medical studies. You should realize that *only* well qualified and highly motivated students stand a good chance of overcoming the many obstacles of studying medicine in a foreign medical school. They then face the difficulties of securing suitable postgraduate training and a license to practice in the United States. The obstacles to be faced in overseas medical study are reflected by the findings of a study that indicates that, of all the American students entering foreign medical schools, one-third will complete their studies after many years but cannot qualify to practice in the United States, and one-third will finish their studies within the standard period (five to eight years) and eventually enter the U.S. physician manpower pool (although they may not end up practicing in the state of their choice).

Current estimates are that several hundred foreign-trained American physicians become practitioners each year; that is, less than half of those who have gone overseas. If you are contemplating overseas study you should ask yourself if you really want to become a physician so much that you are willing to do so by this long and very arduous means, if you have a chance of gaining acceptance to a U.S. school if you reapply, and if you could be happy in some health science career other than medicine.

## ADMISSION

The process of securing admission to a foreign medical school is cumbersome because there are no standard application procedures or forms, no standard documents required for submission, and no central clearing service for foreign schools. In spite of these difficulties, it is still advisable to avoid private placement agencies that advertise that they can get you into a foreign school. They provide their services at a high fee and you can gain admission on your own if you are qualified. The following sources of information will be of help:

1. *Foreign embassies and consulates.* They usually have catalogs of the medical schools in their countries. They frequently have staff members who are familiar

with the current admission policies and procedures and whose advice should be sought. This source may have applications and descriptive literature or may provide the names and addresses of admissions officers.

2. *Institute of International Education,* 809 United Nations Plaza, NY 10017, maintains a library of foreign university catalogs.

3. *World Directory of Medical Schools* published by the World Health Organization, Geneva. This publication, while providing some helpful data, is not written especially for the potential American applicant and lacks such useful information as how to initiate an application, who is responsible for admissions at a particular school, and how many Americans are enrolled at the school. Therefore, this volume may not be worth purchasing but should nevertheless be examined at a reference library.

Most German, Austrian, and Belgian schools have relatively high admission standards and strict scholastic requirements. As many as from 30 to 50% of the students fail the basic science examination that is taken prior to beginning clinical studies. However, graduates from schools in these three countries have some of the best records for passing the ECFMG examination. Italian, Mexican, and Spanish schools have relatively low admissions requirements and accept and graduate relatively large numbers of students. Graduates from schools in these countries have had the most difficulty passing the ECFMG examination. (This possibly may be due to the poor quality of the students and not necessarily the standards of education at the schools.)

The course of studies in foreign medical schools varies from four to six years. At some schools, examinations are usually taken voluntarily at the end of one- or two-year periods and can be retaken a number of times. This system of academic freedom adds to the existing problem of studying medicine in a foreign language.

# TRANSFER TO U.S. SCHOOLS

In 1970 the Coordinated Transfer Application System (COTRANS) was established on an experimental basis to facilitate the transfer of students studying abroad to U.S. medical schools. In the past, this system involved taking Part 1 of the National Board Examinations at a U.S. or foreign test center, a program terminated in 1979. During the decade of COTRANS's existence, less than half of those who took Part 1 of the NBME passed and only about half of those who passed managed to transfer to U.S. medical schools. This points up the inherent difficulties associated with overseas medical study.

In June 1980 a special examination was developed by the NBME for U.S. citizens enrolled in foreign medical schools who wish to apply for transfer with advanced standing to a U.S. medical school. It was known as the Medical Sciences Knowledge Profile (MSKP). This examination was designed to provide medical schools with a method of evaluating such an applicant's knowledge in the basic medical sciences and in introductory clinical diagnoses. No total score or pass or fail was reported, but the difficulty of transferring to a U.S. medical school is reflected in the fact that less than 40% of students have succeeded in doing so each year. Moreover, the numbers transferring have declined. The MSKP was replaced by the USMLE Step 1 in June 1992. The grade on this exam is now used to evaluate U.S. applicants who wish to transfer.

# INTERNSHIP AND RESIDENCY

There are five pathways for foreign graduates to follow in securing AMA-approved internship and residency appointments: (1) transferring with advanced standing to a U.S. medical school and repeating one or more years (the policies of U.S. medical schools regarding transfer and advanced standing are given in the profiles for the individual schools in Chapter 8); (2) certification by ECFMG on the basis of satisfying the ECFMG educational requirements as well as passing the ECFMG examination; (3)

obtaining a full and unrestricted license to practice medicine, issued by a state or other U.S. jurisdiction authorized to license physicians; (4) successfully passing the complete licensure examination in any state or licensing jurisdiction where a full and unrestricted license is issued upon satisfactory completion of internship or residency without further examination; and (5) an approach that is especially popular among one segment of foreign medical students, and is for obvious reasons known as the Fifth Pathway, which is discussed in the next section.

Among the drawbacks of attending a foreign medical school is the difficulty in securing a residency appointment at a U.S. hospital upon graduation. A substantial number of Americans, after investing much effort, time, and money, are unable to secure a residency in this country due to a variety of reasons. First, they may have received a poor medical education at the school they elected to attend, which seriously weakens their candidacy for postgraduate training. Second, they are competing against other foreign graduates for the very limited number of places not filled by graduates of U.S. schools. Finally, the total number of residency openings is diminishing in response to the perceived over-supply of physicians that is anticipated. Consequently, the awareness of this potential problem in the educational program of foreign medical students should stimulate careful consideration of this career pathway.

## FIFTH PATHWAY OPPORTUNITIES

Students who have completed all of the formal requirements of the foreign medical school except internship and/or social service may substitute a year of supervised clinical training for the required foreign internship (that is, clinical clerkship or junior internship) under the direction of an AMA-approved medical school. Upon successful completion, students may enter the first year of an approved residency program without having to complete the social service requirement of the foreign country. Before beginning the supervised clinical training, students must have their academic records reviewed and approved by the school supervising the clinical training and must pass a screening examination acceptable to the Council on Medical Education. The ECFMG examination and/or Step 1 of the USMLE are used for this purpose.

Currently only mainland U.S. medical schools offer Fifth Pathway clerkships. This option applies primarily to students in Mexican medical schools and is open only to physicians who have completed their undergraduate premedical studies in an acceptable manner at an accredited American college or university. The Fifth Pathway program allows U.S. students who have completed the requirements for a medical degree in Mexico to be eligible for a continuous academic year of supervised clinical training under the direction of a medical school approved by the Liaison Committee on Medical Education. The students who complete this supervised clinical training are then able to enter an AMA-approved graduate training program without completing the Mexican-required internship or social science obligation. This program facilitates graduates of Mexican medical schools to pass into graduate medical programs in this country. The following schools are associated with this Fifth Pathway program. They give preference to state residents. Inquiries should be addressed to the directors of these programs.

University of Arizona
College of Medicine
Tucson, AZ 85724
(Arizona residents only)

University of California, Irvine
California College of Medicine
Irvine, CA 92717
(Preference for California Residents)

Loma Linda University
School of Medicine
Loma Linda, CA 92354
(Out of state residents discouraged)

University of Colorado
School of Medicine
Denver, CO 80262
(Colorado residents only)

University of Illinois
College of Medicine
1737 West Polk, Room 204
Chicago, IL 60612
(Preference for Illinois residents)

Albert Einstein College of Medicine
The Bronx Lebanon Hospital Center
Fulton Avenue at 169th Street
Bronx, NY 10456

New York University
School of Medicine
Booth Memorial Medical Center
56-45 Main Street
Flushing, NY 11355
(New York residents only)

State University of New York
Downstate Medical Center
College of Medicine
The Brooklyn Hospital
121 Dekalb Avenue
Brooklyn, NY 11201

Mount Sinai School of Medicine
Fifth Ave. & 100 St.
New York, NY 10029

New York Medical College
Valhalla, NY 10595

Brown University
Division of Biology and Medicine
Providence, RI 02912

It should be noted that additional hospitals in California, Illinois, New Jersey, and Texas may also offer Fifth Pathway opportunities, and additional information can be obtained from the Council on Medical Education of the American Medical Association. Securing a Fifth Pathway appointment presents a significant challenge, because their numbers are very limited and competition is intense.

# REQUIREMENTS FOR RESIDENCY AND/OR PRACTICE _____

### CSA Examination

Effective July 1, 1998, IMGs seeking to enter U.S. residency programs must pass the Clinical Skills Assessment Examination (CSA) if they did not pass Steps 1 and 2 of the USMLE and an English Proficiency examination. This test, developed by the ECFMG, is a measure of clinical and interpersonal abilities using "standardized" patients. The aim is to gauge a doctor's ability to communicate with and examine patients, reach a diagnosis on the basis of a detailed physical exam, and formulate a written record of the findings. It is anticipated that a similar requirement will go into effect for U.S. medical graduates in a few years.

### FLEX Examination

The Federation Licensing Examination (FLEX), which has been replaced by the USMLE, was prepared by the Federation of State Medical Boards for administration by the state medical boards of examiners, which participate in the program. Admission to the examination for medical graduates, including foreign medical graduates, depended upon the statutory regulatory requirements of the individual states. All states and the District of Columbia participated in the program except for Florida and Texas.

### ECFMG Examination

Students from the United States who are graduates of foreign medical schools and wish to practice or to secure an internship or residency in the United States must pass an examination given by the Educational Council for Foreign Medical Graduates (3930 Chestnut St., Philadelphia, PA 19104). This examination, which is given twice a year in many centers throughout the world, consists of 360 multiple-choice questions selected from a pool of questions previously used in Steps 1 and 2 of the USMLE. To pass, a student must attain a score of 75.

### State Board Requirements

While the AMA recognizes a graduate of any foreign medical school who has been certified by the ECFMG as eligible for internship and residency training, licensure to practice in the United States is under the jurisdiction of state governments, each of which establishes its own standards. Some states accept no foreign graduates while others accept only graduates from certain foreign schools. Information on the requirements in each state can be secured from the Secretary of each State Board of Medical Examiners. (Graduates of Canadian medical schools are considered equivalent to U.S. graduates but must meet the requirements for citizenship and internship.)

# SELECTING A FOREIGN MEDICAL SCHOOL _____

In deciding to attend a foreign medical school, which presents an awesome challenge, you should be very certain that (1) you cannot gain admission to a U.S. allopathic or osteopathic school, (2) you are not interested in an alternative career in the health sciences, and (3) you have adequate financial support. Electing to study outside of this country is a major decision and selecting a school to attend represents another critical hurdle.

Careful planning and investigation of *all* the issues should be made *before* you make any commitments. As a component of your planning, you should determine how best to meet the foreign language requirements (where necessary) that will enable you to properly secure your medical education and training. Only a few schools that accept foreign students teach in English (such as those in the Philippines, Israel, and the Caribbean). By examining catalogs, you should seek to determine how the course of studies at an overseas school compares with that at a typical U.S. school. There should be an attempt to secure information about the quality of the education and the adequacy of the clinical facilities, which are critical to be able to succeed in a residency. This information may come from students who have been or are currently in attendance at the school in question. They (or their families) can provide useful information concerning the nature of the housing and cost of living expenses at their particular foreign school. A key piece of information is how well U.S. students perform after attending the foreign medical schools in question. Also, insight can be secured by finding out how U.S. citizens perform on the ECFMG. It should be realized that this data cannot be taken without allowing for a number of variables, such as the quality of the students in each country, the number of times the exam was taken, the time lapse between taking the exam and completing one's education, and other factors, such as the total number of applicants taking the exam.

## FOREIGN MEDICAL SCHOOLS

Traveling overseas for several years to develop specialty expertise after one's internship was very popular during the first half of the twentieth century. Thus, many Americans, for example, were trained in surgery in prominent German and Austrian medical centers. In the second half of the same century, there no longer was a need to be trained overseas, since adequate postgraduate programs were established at hospitals throughout the United States.

However, there has been a continuous migration of Americans to overseas medical schools for their education. Most popular were the medical schools in such West European countries as France, Germany, Switzerland, Italy, and Spain. These countries have now become inaccessible to most prospective American premeds (except those with dual citizenship) as they are interested in training their own citizens to meet existing and future healthcare needs.

There are still some overseas schools accepting applicants but one needs to be extremely careful when making a decision to attend an overseas institution. Several of these schools are of higher caliber and are identified by an asterisk.

### Australia

The following three schools have begun accepting a number of U.S. and Canadian students. They follow the basic curriculum used in this country and utilize the problem-based educational approach.

*Flinders University, School of Medicine
G.P.O. Box 2100, Adelaide, Australia 5001
Tel: 461-8-8204-4162
Fax: 61-8-8204-5845

*Sydney University Medical School
Faculty Office and Medical Program Administration
Faculty of Medicine
Edward Ford Building (A27),
University of Sydney
NSW 2006, Australia
Phone: 61-2-9351-3132
Fax: 61-2-9351-3196

*Queensland University School of Medicine
University of Queensland,
Maine Medical School
Herston Road, Herston
QLD, 4066, Australia
Phone: +61-7-3365-5278
Fax: +61-7-3365-5433

## Caribbean Schools

These medical schools were set up specifically to serve the needs of Americans unable to gain admission to U.S. schools. Some of these schools have disbanded over the past decades, resulting in students being left "high and dry" in the midst of their studies. This has tarnished the reputation of the off-shore schools as a whole, thus, special care needs to be used when considering these schools.

St. George's University, Grenada
Office of Admissions, c/o The North American Correspondent
University Services, Ltd.
1 East Main Street
Bay Shore, NY 11706
Tel: (from US) (631) 665-8500 or (800) 899-6337
Grenada (473) 444-4175;
Fax: (631) 665-5590

SABA University
School of Medicine
The Bottom, Saba, Netherlands–Antilles
Information/Admission Office
Educational International Committee, LLC
P.O. Box 386
Qadnen, MA 01140
(978) 630-5122
Fax: (978) 332-2168

Ross University, Dominica
Main US Admission Office
499 Thornhall Street, 10th Floor
Edison, NJ 08837
Tel: (732) 978-5300, (888) 404-7677

American University of the Caribbean, St. Martin
Medical Education Information Office, Inc. (MEOI)
901 Ponce de Leon Boulevard, 401, Coral Gables, FL 33134
Tel: (305) 446-006

## Ireland

The school listed below accepts overseas applicants, and Americans have a good track record of successfully completing their education there. Nevertheless, general obstacles relative to facing an IMG still await them.

*Royal College of Surgeons, Dublin, Ireland
Admission Office, 123 St. Stephen's Green, Dublin 2, Ireland
Tel: (353) 1-403-2451
Fax: (353) 1-403-2451

The Atlantic Bridge Program
3419 Via Lido, PMB #629, Newport Beach, CA 92663, USA
Tel: (949) 723-6318
Fax: (949) 723-4436

## Israel

The following two schools have medical school programs designed for Americans with English as the language of instruction. While they are superior educational programs, upon graduation IMG obstacles to securing a residency and certification still remain.

*Sackler School of Medicine, Tel-Aviv, Israel
Office of Admissions, Sackler School of Medicine
17 East 62nd Street
New York, NY 10021
Tel: (212) 688-8811
Fax: (212) 223-0368

Touro College/Faculty of Medicine of the Technion—Israel
Institute of Technology, Haifa, Israel
*Touro College School of Health Sciences
1700 Union Boulevard, Bay Shore, NY 11706
Tel: (516) 665-1600
Fax: (516) 665-4986

## Mexico

The school listed below also has a program for international students. It has graduated a large number of Americans and thus has proven to be very popular.

Universidad Autonoma de Guadalajara, Mexico
San Antonio Office: 4715 Fredericksburg Road, 3rd Floor
San Antonio, TX 78229
Tel: (210) 366-1611; (800) 531-5494
Fax: (210) 377-2975

or

Albany Office: 20 Corporate Woods Boulevard, Suite 205,
Albany, NY 12211
Tel: (518) 434-7392, (866) 434-7392
Fax: (518) 434-7393

## Philippines

The two schools below have served as education and training sites for the most successful American students who came to this country. The language of instruction is English and the program extends four years divided into two semesters each.

There are many more medical schools in the Philippines that Americans have attended in smaller numbers. The Philippine consulate can provide names and addresses for these institutions.

University of the Philippines, Manila
Chair, Admission Committee, College of Medicine
University of the Philippines, Manila
547 Pedro Gil Street, Ermita, PO Box 593, Manila 1000, Philippines
Tel: +63-2-526-4170
Fax: +63-2-526-0371

University of the East, Quezon City, Santo Thomas
Office of the Registrar, University of the East,
Ramon Magsaysay Medical Center
College of Medicine, Aurora Boulevard, Sta. Mesa,
Quezon City 1105, Philippines
Tel: +63-2-715-0861

## Bottom Line

- Graduates of foreign medical schools are known as International Medical Graduates (IMG).

- Attending a foreign medical school is a major challenge, financially, intellectually, culturally, and emotionally.

- When considering attending a foreign medical school, you need to make a comprehensive assessment of your ability to succeed. This is because many foreign schools accept *all* applicants who have the minimum requirements for admission, thus, acceptance should not be taken as a vote of confidence in your abilities.

- The most suitable candidates for attending foreign medical schools are those who are capable of being able to adapt to a different culture and lifestyle, who are determined to succeed, have solid long-term financial support, and are very flexible about their future specialty choice.

- An important educational asset for every candidate contemplating studying medicine overseas is that they are well qualified to handle multiple-choice tests. This type of test will be the determinant for securing a residency and then passing required licensing examinations. The USMLE Steps 1 and 2 are major obstacles to securing ECFMG certification for about half of the IMGs. An average or better MCAT score in the high 20s is indicative of a likelihood of a favorable outcome on this issue. Those with MCATs in the low 20s are poor candidates for an acceptance at foreign medical schools.

- There are special rules for an IMG to secure a U.S. residency and in most states to become licensed.

- It is desirable, if at all possible, to visit the foreign medical school before you commit yourself. This is costly but worthwhile in determining how you will fit into the new milieu. During your visit you should thoroughly evaluate the school's teaching (lecture and lab) and clinical facilities, library, and prospective living conditions. You should come back with a realistic sense of judging your future prospects for success if you enroll. This judgment should materialize from what you see and from conversations with Americans currently enrolled in the school. When you get back you should be able to answer two questions: Will I fit in and can I make it in spite of all prospective obstacles?

- Before considering a visit, secure information about foreign medical schools from their Web sites and obtain literature from advising offices. All such information should, however, be viewed with the understanding that you are receiving a sales pitch.

- If you have what it takes, pick the right school and have the perseverance to stick it out—it can be done. Good luck!

# 16 Osteopathic Medicine

Basic philosophy
Choosing osteopathic medicine
Osteopathic education, training, and certification
Educational data
Admission update
Relationship between osteopathic and allopathic medicine
Financial assistance
The osteopathic scene in a nutshell
Osteopathic medical school profiles

Aside from the 124 standard, or allopathic, medical schools, there are 19 osteopathic schools in the United States, which, in a recent year, had an enrollment of 10,300 students. There were more than 50,000 osteopathic physicians listed in the directory published by the American Osteopathic Association. Thus, this branch of medicine contributes a significant number of professionals to the physicians' pool. Over the past several years, interest in osteopathy has intensified significantly. This is reflected by an overall increase in enrollment, including women and minority students, and a new school—the nineteenth. For this reason, the philosophy, educational data, admission prospects, and training program leading to the Doctor of Osteopathy, or DO degree, are outlined.

## BASIC PHILOSOPHY

The osteopathic approach was developed by a physician, Dr. Andrew Taylor Sill, in 1874 and is based upon a holistic view of the function of the human body. Osteopathic medicine is structured on the principles that the human body is an integrated organism and therefore abnormal function in one part of the body exerts unfavorable influences on other parts and on the body as a whole; a complex system exists in the body that tends to provide for self-regulation and self-healing in the face of stress; adequate function of all body organs and systems depends on the integrating forces of the nervous and circulatory system; the body's musculoskeletal system (such as bones, joints, connective tissues, skeletal muscles, and tendons) plays an important role in the body's continuous effort to resist and overcome illness and disease. Based on these principles, osteopathic medicine postulates that any stress—physical, mechanical, or emotional—that causes muscles to become tense (referred pain) intensifies the constant stream of sensory nerve impulses being sent *to* the central nervous system (CNS) by receptors in the muscles and tendons. If this neural barrage is severe enough, it may spill over and initiate an excessive volley of autonomic nerve impulses that pass *away* from the CNS to segmentally related organs and tissues. As a result, muscular responses to referred pain may trigger a neural feedback that can become a secondary source of irritation and pain. This, in turn, may induce responses by the internal organs that are referred back to the musculoskeletal system and a vicious cycle of sensory-motor nerve excitation can be created. Unless this cycle is interrupted, it may perpetuate itself until the somatic response to referred pain becomes more severe than the original visceral disease. The somatic response in effect becomes a secondary disease.

The musculoskeletal system is easily accessible and it is believed that the treatment of it may be beneficial in altering the disease process by interrupting the vicious cycle of neural exchange. In practice, osteopathic medicine involves the application of manipulative procedures to help tense muscles, tendons, and connective tissues to relax. The increase in muscle-fiber length resulting from the relaxation eases the tension on the impulse receptors in the muscles and tendons, reducing sensory bombardment to the spinal cord. This reduction may allow the entire body to return to more normal homeostatic levels and permit segmentally related visceral structures to repair themselves under more normal conditions. It is important to note that *the osteopathic system of diagnosis and therapy is used in conjunction with the standard medical procedures of drug and surgical therapy*. As part of the educational program, osteopathic colleges train their students in the standard medical diagnostic and therapeutic methods as well as those associated with osteopathic medicine. For additional information write the American Osteopathic Association, 142 E. Ontario Street, Chicago, IL 60611.

## Bottom Line

Dr. Still, founder of osteopathy, postulated the following cardinal principals for his new approach to the art of healing, namely:

- The body is a unit that operates as an integrated structural and functional entity.
- The body systems are intrinsically capable of self-healing in the event of disease.
- Integration of activities within the body is the responsibility of the circulatory and nervous systems.
- The combined musculoskeletal systems have a functional capacity beyond that of serving as a structural framework and for support. When these systems are healthy, they help maintain vital blood and nerve supply to the body and vice-versa; if unhealthy the supply is impeded.
- The diseased part of the body can be challenged by another healthy segment to restore the normal state.

## CHOOSING OSTEOPATHIC MEDICINE

There currently are 23 functioning osteopathic medical schools. The increasing popularity of osteopathic medical education is reflected in the fact that about six schools have opened over the past number of years, while no new allopathic schools opened in recent decades.

The question arises, why should premeds elect to apply to a DO-granting institution over a school awarding an MD degree? At least four reasons can be offered in response:

*Easier admission.* It is well known that gaining admission into medical school in general, and into allopathic schools in particular, is very challenging. It has been established that all the major parameters for admission, namely, GPA, science cumulative average, and MCAT scores are *on average* significantly lower for osteopathic applicants who are admitted. Also, older applicants stand a better chance of gaining admission into an allopathic school. Similarly, those with a strong interest in primary care as well as those coming from rural backgrounds are more likely to gain admission. With the popularity of osteopathic medical schools increasing, it is likely that it will become more difficult to secure admission as the number of applicants increase. More women have become applicants to DO-granting schools, to the point where they form about half of each entering class (as is the case in allopathic schools). Underrepresented minorities currently represent less than 9% of the total student body of osteopathic schools.

*Role model.* One of the strong influences on career choices of young people are older role models. They can impact not only on their choice of a medical career, but also can influence even the selection of a specific specialty. Thus, students can be profoundly influenced by contacts with DOs at some point in their lives. Contact with an osteopathic physician is essential when applying for admission, since a letter from such a professional is usually a requirement for admission.

*Primary care focus.* The basic philosophical concept of osteopathy and the focus of its education has always been on treating the whole patient rather than concentrating only on the disease. This longstanding view has been incorporated in the allopathic medical specialty of family practice. Consequently, about half of osteopathic medical school graduates end up basically as old-fashioned GPs, while for allopathic school graduates the number is merely 15%. Nevertheless, half of all DOs do seek specialty training and osteopathic specialty organizations exist (see Appendix E). Thus, for those whose convictions about the value of primary care is strong, their attraction to osteopathy is understandable, and the basis of their motivation is obvious.

*Manipulative therapy.* This therapeutic approach is a unique feature of osteopathy. It stems from the firmly held conviction that the musculoskeletal system is the key to the disease process. Thus osteopathic manipulative therapy, when applied to the vertebral column to relieve pain, can be quite effective, and thus may be of special appeal to some individuals, helping motivate them toward a career as an osteopathic physician.

It should be noted, however, that in nonprimary care osteopathic residencies (as, obviously, in allopathic ones), musculoskeletal therapy is not considered a first-line therapeutic approach. As a matter of fact, some in the osteopathic profession advocate doing away with this approach entirely, so the lines between both branches of medicine, while already blurred, would be eliminated. Therefore, interest in this unique form of therapy should not be the sole motivation for anyone choosing osteopathy, although it can be an ancillary one.

## OSTEOPATHIC EDUCATION, TRAINING, AND CERTIFICATION

It is important to be cognizant about the nature of osteopathic education and certification when considering a career in this branch of medicine.

**Education.** Basically, the same curriculum is in effect at both allopathic and osteopathic schools. Naturally, there are variations in emphasis among different osteopathic schools. Medical school curricula are discussed in Chapter 13. Initially courses are given in the basic sciences, which particularly stand out because of their depth. The clinical sciences at osteopathic schools are weaker, especially at schools whose teaching hospital affiliations are limited.

Naturally, a unique feature of osteopathic schools to a varying degree, are the courses in osteopathic manipulative medicine and treatment. Nevertheless, DO graduates can feel secure that by applying themselves conscientiously and securing meaningful postgraduate training, competency to practice medicine is assured.

**Postgraduate training.** Training as residents can be secured at osteopathic hospitals and at many, but not all, MD teaching centers. As the list of osteopathic specialty organizations (Appendix E) indicates, training can be secured in specialties ranging from anesthesiology to vascular surgery.

As indicated earlier, we can anticipate a dramatic increase in the number of osteopathic medical school graduates. The number of first-year or entry-level allopathic residency positions, both regular and transitional, is in excess of what can be filled. Thus, significant numbers of places are available to be filled by DO graduates. It is commonplace to find osteopathic graduates as physicians-in-training at many allopathic teaching hospitals. There, they secure higher salaries and quality training, and can specialize in areas not open at osteopathic hospitals. This is especially true for surgical specialties. There are, however, problems associated with certification for DOs who complete training in MD-approved positions (see discussion below).

Finally, it should be noted that an internship matching program for osteopathic graduates does exist. While increasing numbers of DOs are entering MD-approved specialties, some are still closed. These are general surgery and its subspecialties. However, one can get such training in some osteopathic programs and professional osteopathic organizations in these fields exist.

*Certification.* In recent years, a significant number of internal medicine and family practice residency programs (currently about 60), engaged in training MDs have been granted AOA accreditation. This provides assurance that all primary care DO physicians graduating from such programs are automatically eligible for AOA board certification and licensure.

Aside from jointly recognized programs, DO graduates planning to secure training at MD-accredited programs have dual hurdles to face, from both the program and the AOA. Completion of such a program makes you eligible to take the AMA's specialty board examination. However, to take the AOA's exam in the same field, you will need to pay this organization a high fee for a residency program site visit to evaluate its status. Moreover, arranging for such a visit does not necessarily guarantee approval of the program. Should a negative report result, some osteopathic hospitals will not grant these physicians a staff appointment, allowing them to practice there, in spite of AMA certification.

Another obstacle arises in cases where a DO is completing a PGY-1 at an MD-approved program. He or she cannot receive internship credit, allowing further postgraduate training at an osteopathic residency program.

*Licensure.* In a very few states, such as Florida and Michigan, DOs are still unable to secure a license to practice medicine, unless they complete an internship approved by the AOA. However, an AOA-approved PGY-1 internship, does not count as meeting the prerequisite for admission to an allopathic residency (but only has value at some osteopathic specialty programs). Thus completing a DO internship is fraught with problems. Those who want to enter an MD-approved residency program must repeat the PGY-1 year at an AMA-approved program in order to be eligible.

## Bottom Line

When looking at a career as an osteopathic physician, consideration should be given to the following potential pitfalls:

- There still exists on the part of some MDs an antiosteopathic hostility that under certain circumstances may induce discriminatory action.

- There may be difficulties in securing a residency appointment in general and a surgical residency in particular. However, DOs frequently are welcomed in MD residency programs where vacancies exist.

- There also are distinct hardships for DOs in securing appointments at those non-surgical allopathic programs that are highly competitive. In some specialties, residencies are unobtainable because positions for DOs are simply unavailable.

- Many prospective patients lack an understanding of the status of DOs and what services they are capable of providing. Some people may be totally unaware that osteopaths are physicians who are fully qualified and entitled to practice medicine.

- There are potential certification and licensure impediments for DOs.

## Future Prospects

Members of this profession look upon it from a different viewpoint. Osteopathic medicine is seen as a system of assessment and treatment of health problems through a biomechanical approach. DOs work with the hands, using a variety of treatment techniques, such as soft-tissue stretching and dynamic passive joint mobilization in addition to conventional medical methods.

The medical school curriculum and state licensing requirements for DOs is basically the same as for MDs. DOs are also provided with instruction in hands-on osteopathic diagnosis and osteopathic manipulative treatment. Training is provided at about 25 osteopathic medical schools, and there are more than 200 exclusive osteopathic hospitals nationwide. Most osteopathic physicians are in primary care practice. They are eligible for Medicare and Medicaid reimbursement the same way as their MD counterparts.

For many decades, osteopathy had a stigma, which has very markedly diminished over the past 20 years. Osteopathic and allopathic physicians frequently work side by side in a spirit of mutual respect. While acceptance is still not universal, the marked improvement in the relationship between the two branches of medicine is reflected by the fact that some traditional physicians are attending seminars in osteopathic manipulative techniques. The changing situation is evidence that osteopathy will not be looked upon as belonging to alternative medicine, but is assuming its natural position in mainline medicine.

## EDUCATIONAL DATA

In the United States, there are presently 19 osteopathic colleges. The establishment of colleges of osteopathic medicine is being discussed in other areas of the country. In a recent year, the present 19 colleges admitted about 2,500 freshmen out of an applicant pool of about 9,500. Students from six states—Pennsylvania, Michigan, Ohio, Missouri, Texas, and Iowa—made up the largest segment of the enrollment of the first-year classes. The grade point average of the class was about 3.3 (where 4.0 = A). This is a somewhat lower average than that for the entering class at conventional medical schools. Thus borderline premedical students who are intrinsically qualified should seek to secure places in osteopathic medical schools.

Admissions committees are putting increased emphasis on grade point average, recommendations, and interviews, and less emphasis on test scores. The committees seek the same general characteristics in prospective students as allopathic medical schools (such as dependability, maturity, integrity), but they also look for special interest in and motivation to study osteopathic medicine. Letters of recommendation from osteopathic physicians (and even students) adequately acquainted with applicants can be helpful.

The number of women in a recent freshman class was about 40% of the total enrollment. This is relatively similar to the proportion of women enrolled in allopathic medical school. The number of entering students having less than four years of undergraduate education was a small percentage of the total entering class. This clearly reflects the fact that both osteopathic and allopathic medical schools still feel that the fourth year in the undergraduate college is desirable.

The average age of entering osteopathic students has been 24 years (range: 20–42); this is somewhat higher than for those accepted in allopathic medical schools. It may be because many matriculants were motivated to enter this field after exposure to related community service careers. Among the older freshmen, many have backgrounds in teaching, allied health fields, and research. As with the allopathic schools, applicants over 28 need not expect to have special difficulties in gaining admission. The basic science course requirements for admission to osteopathic schools are the same as those for allopathic schools. The majority of freshmen, as would be expected, were biology or chemistry majors and almost all of them took the MCAT.

The curriculum at an osteopathic school is almost identical with that offered at the allopathic schools. Study is divided into basic science and clinical science training. There is a required course in the basic theory and practice of osteopathic medicine. The philosophy of osteopathic medicine, with its emphasis on total health care, is incorporated where appropriate into the standard courses. Curriculum revision in line with that taking place at allopathic schools is also occurring at osteopathic schools.

# ADMISSION UPDATE

As with allopathic schools, the number of applicants to osteopathic medical schools varies widely over time. In 1997 the number peaked to well over 10,000 and then bottomed out in 2002 at about 6,000. Since then the numbers increased significantly each year, to where it currently has surpassed the 1997 level.

Complementing the rise in the number of applicants in the recent past is a parallel increase in the number of available first-year places at osteopathic colleges. This is the result of both the expansion of class size at existing institutions and the opening of several new schools. As a consequence of the increase in enrollment, it is anticipated that the number of graduates will double over a five-year period. Consequently, there will be a significant increase in the proportion of physician population made up of osteopaths, leading to a wider acceptance of the profession, especially in the area of primary medical care.

Along with an increased applicant pool, the academic credentials of those seeking admission to osteopathic colleges over the past several years gradually increased. This applies to all three components of the MCAT examination—the verbal, biological, and physical sciences. This holds true also for the GPAs, namely, the overall science and nonscience grades.

Students who are interested in attending an osteopathic medical school should be aware that osteopathic medical schools, like many allopathic schools, utilize a centralized application service for processing student applications. To obtain the application packet, which contains an application form for the AACOMAS and procedures for applying as well as materials describing each college and its fees, write to the American Association of Colleges of Osteopathic Medicine Application Service, 5550 Friendship Boulevard, Suite 310, Chevy Chase, MD 20815-7231.

## Bottom Line

While more places are available, competition is increasing since more qualified applicants are applying for admission; therefore, the challenge of gaining admission to osteopathic medical school is increasing.

# RELATIONSHIP BETWEEN OSTEOPATHIC AND ALLOPATHIC MEDICINE

The AMA recommends that AMA-approved internship and residency programs be opened to qualified graduates of schools of osteopathy; that American boards for medical specialties accept for examination for certification those osteopaths who have completed AMA-approved internships and residency programs and have met the other regular requirements applicable to all board candidates; that accredited hospitals accept qualified osteopaths for appointment to the medical staffs of hospitals; and that determination of qualification be made at the level of the medical staff of a hospital, or the review committees and boards having appropriate jurisdiction.

The aforementioned recommendations have opened the way for wider acceptance of DOs into the mainstream of medical training and practice. Twenty-four specialty boards have agreed to examine for certification osteopathic graduates who have completed AMA-approved internships and residency programs. Among the 24 are the American Boards of Pathology, Pediatrics, Physical Medicine and Rehabilitation, Preventive Medicine, Radiology, Anesthesiology, Dermatology, Internal Medicine, Obstetrics and Gynecology, Orthopedic Surgery, Psychiatry, and Neurology.

The application of the AMA proposals is indicated by the fact that in a recent year about 300 hospitals had appointed some 2,000 osteopathic physicians to their attending staff as house officers. These appointments were spread over 25 states with the largest number in Pennsylvania, New Jersey, California, Michigan, and Washington. These figures will probably rise steadily during the next few years.

# FINANCIAL ASSISTANCE

1. *National Osteopathic Scholarships.* Annually 25 scholarships of $1,500 are awarded to entering osteopathic students. These will be applied to tuition at the rate of $750 per year for the first two years. (Information is available from the Office of Education, American Osteopathic Association, 142 East Ontario Street, Chicago, IL 60611.)

2. *Canadian Osteopathic Scholarships.* A $3,000 scholarship is available to a first- or second-year Canadian student enrolled in an osteopathic school. (Information is obtainable from Canadian Osteopathic Education Trust Fund, Suite 126, 3545 Cote des Neiges Road, Montreal 25, Quebec.)

3. *New Jersey Association of Osteopathic Physicians and Surgeons Scholarships.* Scholarships are awarded to assist in paying tuition for first-year students who are New Jersey residents. (Information is obtainable from the Executive Director, New Jersey Association of Osteopathic Physicians and Surgeons, 1 Distribution Way, Monmouth Junction, NJ 08852-3001.)

4. *National Osteopathic Foundation Student Loan Fund.* An approved candidate may borrow a sum not exceeding $1,000 annually. (Information is obtainable from the National Osteopathic Foundation, 5775G Peachtree-Dunwoody Road, Suite 500, Atlanta, GA 30342.)

# THE OSTEOPATHIC SCENE IN A NUTSHELL

Table 16.1 reflects the admissions picture at the osteopathic medical schools presently in operation.

Note: Applications for most osteopathic schools are processed by a centralized application service, the American Association of Colleges of Osteopathic Medicine Application Service (AACOMAS). To secure an application, write to AACOMAS, 5550 Friendship Boulevard, Suite 310, Chevy Chase, MD 20815-7231.

# OSTEOPATHIC MEDICAL SCHOOL PROFILES

In these school descriptions, the admissions requirement of the basic premedical science courses refers to one year each of inorganic and organic chemistry, biology, and physics, plus laboratory work.

## Definitions

The following are explanations and definitions of the column headings on Table 16.1.

## Application Fee

In most cases this fee is usually required after your application has passed its initial screening.

## Earliest and Latest Filing Dates

These are usually firm dates.

## Total Number of Applicants

This figure is relevant when compared with the total of all women enrolled in the entering class (shown in the next two columns). It indicates how competitive admission may be.

## Enrollment

This refers to the 2008–2009 first-year class.

## Expenses

This refers to the 2008–2009 academic year.

## Table 16.1. BASIC DATA FOR OSTEOPATHIC SCHOOLS (2008–2009)*

| School | Application Data | | | Admission Statistics | | | | |
| | Fee | Filing Dates | | Number of Applicants | Entering Class | | | |
| | | Earliest | Latest | | Men | Women | Minority | Out of State |
|---|---|---|---|---|---|---|---|---|
| Arizona College of Osteopathic Medicine of Midwestern University | 50 | 6/1 | 1/1 | n/a | 155 | 95 | 30 | 34 |
| Touro University— California College of Osteopathic Medicine | 100 | 6/1 | 3/15 | 3243 | 70 | 65 | 39 | 33 |
| Western University of Health Sciences College of Osteopathic Medicine of the Pacific | 65 | 2/15 | 4/15 | 3222 | 123 | 98 | 99 | 6 |
| Nova Southeastern University College of Osteopathic Medicine | 50 | 6/1 | 3/1 | 5000 | 125 | 105 | 90 | 111 |
| Chicago College of Osteopathic Medicine Midwestern University | 40 | 6/1 | 1/1 | 5000 | 85 | 81 | 40 | 68 |
| Des Moines University, College of Osteopathic Medicine | 50 | 6/1 | 2/1 | 3273 | 106 | 115 | 35 | n/a |
| Pikeville College, School of Osteopathic Medicine | 75 | 6/1 | 2/1 | 1949 | 49 | 34 | 6 | 43 |
| University of New England College of Osteopathic Medicine | 55 | 2/1 | 3/15 | n/a | 56 | 75 | 2 | 95 |
| Michigan State University College of Osteopathic Medicine | 75 | 6/1 | 12/1 | n/a | 112 | 119 | 4 | 5 |
| Kirksville College of Osteopathic Medicine | 60 | 6/1 | 2/1 | 3174 | 102 | 72 | 9 | 134 |
| University of Health Sciences College of Osteopathic Medicine | 50 | 6/1 | 2/1 | 3000 | 146 | 120 | 13 | 196 |
| New Jersey School of Osteopathic Medicine | 90 | 5/1 | 2/1 | 3296 | 59 | 51 | 50 | 22 |
| New York College of Osteopathic Medicine | 60 | 4/15 | 2/1 | 4500 | 154 | 144 | 35 | 43 |
| Ohio University College of Osteopathic Medicine | 40 | 5/1 | 2/15 | 3167 | 52 | 65 | 31 | 18 |
| Oklahoma State University College of Osteopathic Medicine | 40 | 6/1 | 2/1 | 1708 | 42 | 46 | 30 | 15 |
| Philadelphia College of Osteopathic Medicine | 250 | 9/30 | 2/1 | 3541 | 137 | 130 | 49 | 105 |
| Lake Erie College of Osteopathic Medicine | n/a | 6/1 | 4/1 | 6563 | 234 | 202 | 397 | 2 |
| University of North Texas Texas College of Osteopathic Medicine | n/a | 6/1 | 10/1 | 1986 | 92 | 83 | 26 | 13 |
| West Virginia School of Osteopathic Medicine | 115 | 6/1 | 2/15 | 2879 | 119 | 92 | 47 | 146 |

*Note: Recently established schools not included in Table 16.1 (see profiles).

| Expenses | | |
|---|---|---|
| Tuition | | |
| Resident | Nonresident | Other |
| 41,242 | n/a | |
| 35,000 | n/a | 97 |
| 41,350 | 41,350 | 87 |
| 29,030 | 35,545 | |
| 40,122 | 44,643 | 24,000 |
| 34,140 | n/a | 99 |
| 32,800 | n/a | 93 |
| 41,260 | | |
| 28,011 | 60,891 | |
| 38,980 | 725 | 88 |
| 39,436 | 39,436 | 97 |
| 25,218 | 39,461 | 92 |
| 39,985 | 39,985 | 92 |
| 24,111 | 35,031 | 4,777 |
| 18,545 | 36,467 | 1,426 |
| 36,984 | 36,984 | n/a |
| 25,900 | 27,250 | 90 |
| 13,598 | 29,348 | 91 |
| 20,426 | 50,546 | 29,348 |

**Table 16.1. BASIC DATA FOR OSTEOPATHIC SCHOOLS (2008–2009)***

| School | Fee | Application Data | | Admission Statistics | | | | |
| | | Filing Dates | | Number of Applicants | Entering Class | | | |
| | | Earliest | Latest | | Men | Women | Minority | Out of State |
|---|---|---|---|---|---|---|---|---|
| Ga-campus PCOM | 250 | 6/1 | 2/1 | 1327 | 47 | 39 | 32 | 51 |
| Touro University Nevada | 100 | 6/1 | 5/15 | n/a | 80 | 54 | 7 | n/a |
| Edward Via Virginia College | 85 | 5/1 | 2/1 | 2725 | 91 | 97 | 50 | 131 |
| Rocky Vista University College of Osteopathic Medicine | | 3/15 | 4/15 | 2104 | 80 | 80 | 15 | 98 |
| Lincoln Memorial University DeBusk College | | 3/15 | 4/1 | 2039 | 84 | 76 | 10 | 105 |
| Touro College, NY | n/a | 2/15 | 4/15 | 3243 | 70 | 65 | 39 | 32 |
| Pacific Northwest University of Osteopathic Medicine | 250 | 6/1 | 4/1 | n/a | 49 | 51 | 7.5 | n/a |

*Note: Recently established schools not included in Table 16.1 (see profiles).

| Expenses | | |
|---|---|---|
| Tuition | | |
| Resident | Nonresident | Other |
| 36,984 | 36,984 | n/a |
| 36,786 | same | |
| 32,900 | 32,900 | 95 |
| 34,200 | 38,000 | 90 |
| 31,500 | 31,500 | 3,630 |
| 36,500 | 36,500 | 31,662 |
| 30,000 | n/a | 80 |

## ARIZONA

# Arizona College of Osteopathic Medicine of Midwestern University

19555 North 59th Avenue
Glendale, Arizona   85308

*Phone:* 632-572-3215
*Fax:* 623-572-3229
*E-mail:* admissaz@midwestern.edu
*WWW:* midwestern.edu

| Application Filing | | Accreditation | |
|---|---|---|---|
| Earliest: | June 1 | AOA (provisional) | |
| Latest: | January 1 | **Degrees Granted** | |
| Fee: | $50 | DO | |

### Enrollment: 2008–2009 First-Year Class

| Men: | 155 | 62% | Applied: | 703 |
|---|---|---|---|---|
| Women: | 95 | 38% | Enrolled: | 250 |
| Out of State: | 34 | 14% | Minorities: | 24 |

### Tuition and Fees

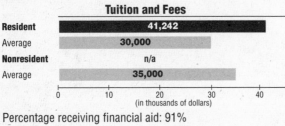

| Resident | 41,242 |
|---|---|
| Average | 30,000 |
| Nonresident | n/a |
| Average | 35,000 |

(in thousands of dollars)

Percentage receiving financial aid: 91%

Above data applies to 2007–2008 academic year.

## Introduction

Founded in 1995, this is the newest of the colleges of osteopathic medicine. With its sister college, the Chicago College of Osteopathic Medicine, it is part of Midwestern University. The school is located on a 122-acre site in Glendale, Arizona, a suburb of Phoenix. Midwestern University also includes a College of Pharmacy and a College of Allied Health Professions.

## Admissions (AACOMAS)

Completion of a minimum of 3 years of college including the basic premedical science courses plus 2 courses in English. Students are encouraged to take additional courses in the humanities, as well as the social and behavioral sciences. Applicants must have a minimum GPA and science cum of 2.75, but, more realistically, they should be closer to 3.4, with MCAT grades of 8 and 9s (total around 26). A rolling admission process is used by the committee, which makes periodic decisions. Approximately 145 students will be accepted for the incoming class. To facilitate the admissions process, applicants will be expected to complete a supplemental application provided by the osteopathic college after receipt of the AACOMAS application. These are sent only to those meeting the minimum admission requirements. In addition, it is recommended that an evaluation from the preprofessional advisory committee and a letter of recommendation from an osteopathic physician be sent in the applicant's behalf.

## Supplementary Requirements

The MCAT scores must be from an exam taken within three years of applying. Two letters of recommendation are required. One letter must be from a premedical advisory committee or science professor who taught the student. The second letter must be from an DO or MD, with the former preferred.

## Curriculum

*First and second years:* Includes a strong basic science core coupled with an early introduction to clinical medicine. Courses in Clinical Correlates/Case Presentation clarifies the connections between didactic teachings and clinical findings and foster the development of critical thinking and problem-solving skills. Through the Preceptor Program beginning in the first year, students spend an afternoon every other week shadowing a physician at community and ambulatory practice sites. *Third and fourth years:* Students rotate through a variety of clinical departments at ambulatory and hospital sites. Required rotations include family medicine, internal medicine, surgery, pediatrics, obstetrics/gynecology, psychiatry, expanded primary care, geriatrics, critical care, and emergency medicine. Students also complete 16 weeks of elective rotations.

## Facilities

Information not available.

## Affiliated Teaching Hospitals

Hospital affiliations in the valley and throughout the state are extensive and include: Arrowhead Community Hospital, Boswell Memorial, Charter Behavioral, Phoenix Regional Medical Center, Paradise Valley Hospital, Sierra Vista Community, Ft. Huachuca U.S. Army Medical Facility, John C. Lincoln (North Mountain and Deer Valley), Kingman Regional, Luke Air Force Base, Mesa General, Tempe St. Lukes, Parker Community, Scottsdale Healthcare, Thunderbird Samaritan, and Maryvale Hospital.

## Housing

About 200 on-campus, student apartments, consisting of 1- and 2-bedrooms, are available. Athletic facilities are nearby.

## CALIFORNIA

# Touro University—California
# College of Osteopathic Medicine

Vallejo, California    94592

*Phone:* 888-880-7336 or 707-638-5227
*Fax:* 707-638-5250
*E-mail:* admit@touro.edu
*WWW:* tu.edu

| Application Filing | | Accreditation | |
|---|---|---|---|
| Earliest: | June 1 | ADA | |
| Latest: | March 15 | **Degrees Granted** | |
| Fee: | $100 | DO | |

### Enrollment: 2008–2009 First-Year Class

| Men: | 70 | 52% | Applied: | 3243 |
|---|---|---|---|---|
| Women: | 45 | 48% | Enrolled: | 135 |
| Out of State: | 33 | 24% | Minorities: | 39 |

**Tuition and Fees**

| | |
|---|---|
| Resident | 35,000 |
| Average | 30,000 |
| Nonresident | 35,000 |
| Average | 35,000 |

0    10    20    30    40
(in thousands of dollars)

Percentage receiving financial aid: 97%

## Introduction

Touro University—California is located in the northeast part of San Francisco Bay on Mare Island and includes the College of Osteopathic Medicine, College of Health Sciences, College of Pharmacy, and the College of Education. The focus of the College of Osteopathic Medicine is on preparing competent osteopathic physicians through classroom and clinical teaching, service to the community, and research. Emphasis is placed on the primary care disciplines, while not ignoring the need for highly qualified physicians in other specialties, including surgery, ER, obstetrics/gynecology, psychiatry, sports medicine, orthopedics, radiology, cardiology, and others. All of this is accomplished within the framework of an institution that is committed to providing a quality education in the best traditions of the Jewish heritage.

## Admissions (AACOMAS)

4-year. All candidates for admission to the College of Osteopathic Medicine are required to submit a primary application through the AACOMAS. Qualified candidates will be invited to submit a supplemental application and various letters of recommendation. Touro University operates on a rolling admissions basis. Applicants are encouraged to apply early to enhance their admission potential.

## Supplementary Requirements

Applicants must submit supplemental applications, which are available on line. It is necessary to secure letters of recommendation from a premedical advisory committee or 2 from science professors as well as 1 from a physician (preferably a DO). In addition, a signed standard technical certification form must be submitted.

## Curriculum

TUCOM students take courses in all of the subject areas one would expect any physician to master, including anatomy, pathology, microbiology, histology, osteopathic principles and practices, pharmacology, immunology, clinical skills, doctor-patient communications, and systems courses that focus on each major system of the body. The goal is to prepare students for the realities of medicine as it exists, as well as how it is likely to be in the future. Practice in problem solving is part of the daily classroom clinic experience as the school strives to provide an educational program consistent with emerging directions of healthcare.

## Housing

Limited on-campus housing is available and off-campus housing assistance is provided.

## Special Programs

This school has a branch campus:
Henderson, Nevada.

# Western University of Health Sciences College of Osteopathic Medicine of the Pacific

309 East Second Street
Pomona, California   91766

*Phone:* 909-469-5335          *Fax:* 909-469-5570
*E-mail:* admissions@westernu.edu
*WWW:* westernu.edu

| Application Filing | | Accreditation | |
|---|---|---|---|
| Earliest: | February 15 | AOA | |
| Latest: | April 15 | **Degrees Granted** | |
| Fee: | $60 | DO | |

### Enrollment: 2008–2009 First-Year Class

| Men: | 123 | 58% | Applied: | 3222 |
|---|---|---|---|---|
| Women: | 88 | 42% | Enrolled: | 225 |
| Out of State: | 6 | 1% | Minorities: | 99 |

**Tuition and Fees**

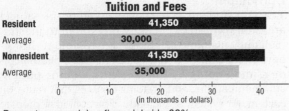

| Resident | 41,350 |
| Average | 30,000 |
| Nonresident | 41,350 |
| Average | 35,000 |

(in thousands of dollars)

Percentage receiving financial aid: 88%

## Introduction

The College of Osteopathic Medicine of the Pacific was established in 1977. It is the only osteopathic medical school in the far West and is an independent, nonprofit institution, accredited by the state of California. The Western University of Health Sciences became its parent institution in 1996. In the vicinity of the college are many hospitals, clinics, colleges, and universities. Pomona is a multiethnic community in southern California known for its pleasant climate.

## Admissions (AACOMAS)

Candidates for admission must have a minimum science GPA of 3.30, a minimum overall GPA of 3.30, and a minimum average MCAT score of 9. All prerequisite coursework must be completed at the time of application. The AACOMAS application must be filed prior to June 15. The Western University/COMP supplementary application and all supporting docu-ments must be filed prior to August 1. Interviews and decisions are granted August through September. If you apply as an Early Admission Decision candidate, you must apply only to Western University/COMP. Qualified applicants may take advantage of the Early Admission Decision Program if they apply only to Western University/COMP and submit their application to AACOMAS prior to June 15. Highly qualified candidates who have a strong preference for Western University/COMP are eligible for an Early Admission Decision.

## Supplementary Requirements

A supplemental application is required. The average scores for accepted applications is a GPA of 3.5, Science 3.4, and an MCAT score of 9. In addition, supporting letters of recommendation from a premedical advisory committee, or 3 classroom professors, 2 of whom must be in the sciences, and a letter of recommendation from an osteopathic physician, preferably a DO. The MCAT scores should not be more than 3 years old.

## Curriculum

4-year. In addition to the standard medical school curriculum, there is a strong emphasis on nutrition, prevention wellness, and osteopathic manipulative medicine. The curriculum is organized in semesters and stresses the interdependence of the biological, clinical, behavioral, and social sciences. *First and second years:* Taught in the Health Sciences Center in Pomona, California, with clinical instruction and field experiences on campus and in the surrounding area. *Third and fourth years:* Utilized for the clerkship program in osteopathic and mixed staff hospitals and other clinical facilities in California and other states throughout the country. The school also operates a family practice outpatient clinic in Pomona, which helps serve the health needs of the community and also provides clinical training for its students. The school provides students with state-of-the-art on-campus facilities for the first two years of the didactic curriculum. The entire campus has a broad-based fiber optic infrastructure, with the capacity to connect thousands of computer and laptop notebooks to the Internet.

## Affiliated Teaching Hospitals

The school is affiliated with many hospitals, physicians' offices, and ambulatory health care centers throughout the United States.

## Housing

There is no on-campus housing. A housing referral system is available.

# Rocky Vista University
# College of Osteopathic Medicine

8401 Chambers Road
Parker, Colorado 80134

*Phone:* (303) 373-2008          *Fax:* (720) 875-2875
*E-mail:* admissions@rockyvistauniversity.org
*WWW:* rockyvistauniversity.org

| Application Filing | | Accreditation |
|---|---|---|
| Earliest: | May 1 | Pending |
| Latest: | March 15 | **Degrees Granted** |
| Fee: | n/a | DO |

### Enrollment: 2008–2009 First-Year Class

| | | | | |
|---|---|---|---|---|
| Men: | 80 | 50% | Applied: | n/a |
| Women: | 80 | 50% | Enrolled: | 160 |
| Out of State: | 98 | 61% | Minorities: | 15 |

**Tuition and Fees**

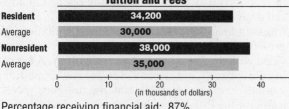

| | |
|---|---|
| Resident | 34,200 |
| Average | 30,000 |
| Nonresident | 38,000 |
| Average | 35,000 |

(in thousands of dollars)

Percentage receiving financial aid: 87%

## Introduction

In March 2007 there was the ground-breaking ceremony for this new osteopathic medical school. It is scheduled to be opened in August 2008. The school has received provisional accreditation.

## Admission (AACOMAS)

4-year. Applicant must complete the AACOMAS application. Selected applicants who meet minimal requirements will be invited to complete a supplemental application. Also required: a minimum 90 semester hours of accepted work from an accredited institution, including 1 year of biology, general and organic chemistry, and physics. A course in English composition and 1 in literature is required. The *minimal* requirements for consideration for admission are an overall as well as science GPA of 2.50. It should be recognized that chances of admission for students with minimal GPA are limited. Thus, significantly higher academic achievement is expected in order to gain admission. The most recent MCAT scores must be submitted.

## Curriculum

The school's aim is to provide a state-of-the-art, scientifically based education for its students. It aims to stimulate personal and professional growth and develop its students' professional potential.

## Affiliated Teaching Hospitals

The school administration has obtained community partnerships that will ensure that clinical sites and facility resources needed for student organization are available in the state of Colorado. The core clinical education of the students will be conducted under the supervision and guidance of college-appointed faculty to ensure that students have the maximum opportunity to acquire the foundation of knowledge, skills, and competencies they will need to be prepared and competitive for entry to any graduate medical education program.

## Housing

Information not available.

## FLORIDA

# Lake Erie College of Osteopathic Medicine, Bradenton Campus

5000 Lakewood Branch Boulevard
Bradenton, Florida 34211

*Phone:* 941-756-0690
*E-mail:* Bradenton@lecom.edu
*WWW:* lecom.edu

| Application Filing | | Accreditation |
|---|---|---|
| Earliest: | June 1 | AOA |
| Latest: | March 1 | **Degrees Granted** |
| Fee: | $50 | DO |

### Enrollment: 2008–2009 First-Year Class

| Men: | n/a | Applied: | n/a |
|---|---|---|---|
| Women: | n/a | Enrolled: | n/a |
| Out of State: | n/a | Minorities: | n/a |

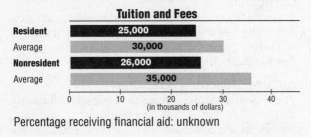

**Tuition and Fees**

| | |
|---|---|
| **Resident** | 25,000 |
| Average | 30,000 |
| **Nonresident** | 26,000 |
| Average | 35,000 |

(in thousands of dollars)

Percentage receiving financial aid: unknown

## Introduction

This school is part of a master planned community involved in training physicians to help meet the growing and aging population in Florida and surrounding states. The school was founded in 2004 and has a branch in Erie, Pennsylvania.

## Admission (AACOMAS)

The college seeks to admit students who will excel in academic, clinical care, research, and community service. Selection favors those applicants who show awareness of osteopathic medicine, recognizing the importance of total health care for the individual and the community. Requirements include a minimum GPA of 3.3 and science GPA of 2.7

## Supplementary Requirements

MCAT scores not older than 3 years must be submitted. A supplemental application has to be completed, and a letter of recommendation from the premedical advisory committee or 2 letters from science professors needs to be submitted.

## Curriculum

The school has designed a student-centered curriculum, while recognizing that there are different learning styles. The students at this branch campus follow a problem-based learning pathway (PBL). This is a self-directed learning program. Each group of 8 students meets with a faculty facilitator 3 times a week. Students work independently and in small groups developing learning issues and discussing new information relative to factual patient cases. Groups will request additional history and physical results and an EKG or MRI, as needed. As students begin formulating differing diagnoses, they also progress through basic and clinical science, which helps them in diagnosing patient cases.

## Facilities

Instruction takes place in a building opened in 2004 and designed with problem-based learning in mind. It was built to accommodate 600 students with room for growth. The lecture halls and classrooms are provided with the latest in wireless technology. A Learning Resource Center provides access to medical journals, texts, and learning material designed specifically for the PBL curriculum.

## Affiliated Teaching Hospitals

Hospitals and clinics in 10 states provide clinical training in the third and fourth years. The hospitals include the Lakewood Branch and the Manatee Medical Centers.

## Special Programs

There are preceptors and clinical osteopathic assessment programs designed for first- and second-year students that take place in association with local physicians for clinical exposure. Opportunities such as student monitoring and community service are available.

# Nova Southeastern University College of Osteopathic Medicine

3301 College Ave. P.O. Box 299000
Fort Lauderdale, Florida   33329

*Phone:* 954-262-1101          *Fax:* 954-262-2282
*E-mail:* com@nsu.nova.edu
*WWW:* medicinenova.edu

| Application Filing | | Accreditation |
|---|---|---|
| Earliest: | June 1 | AOA |
| Latest: | March 1 | **Degrees Granted** |
| Fee: | $50 | DO |

### Enrollment: 2008–2009 First-Year Class

| | | | | |
|---|---|---|---|---|
| Men: | 125 | 54% | Applied: | 917 |
| Women: | 105 | 46% | Enrolled: | 230 |
| Out of State: | 111 | 48% | Minorities: | 90 |

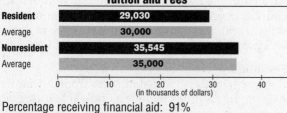

**Tuition and Fees**

| | |
|---|---|
| Resident | 29,030 |
| Average | 30,000 |
| Nonresident | 35,545 |
| Average | 35,000 |

(in thousands of dollars)

Percentage receiving financial aid: 91%

Above data applies to 2007–2008 academic year.

## Introduction

Nova University was established in 1964. It is a private school offering both undergraduate and graduate degrees. The Health Professions Division was created when Nova University joined Southeastern University to become Nova Southeastern University. The College of Osteopathic Medicine is part of this division, which includes colleges of Pharmacy, Optometry, Allied Health, and Medical Sciences. In 1996 the Health Professions Divisions relocated from North Miami Beach to a 220-acre campus in Fort Lauderdale.

## Admissions (AACOMAS)

The basic premedical science courses, plus courses in English composition and literature, a bachelor's degree, and the MCAT are required. Students are encouraged to take additional courses in behavioral sciences, cultural subjects, and the humanities. The entering class consists of 236 students. The school uses a rolling admissions policy, selecting applicants for admission from those already interviewed. Invitations for interviews are issued after review of the initical AACOMAS and supplementary applications, the evaluation from the student's college, and from an osteopathic physician. It is essential that the Admissions Office receive a letter of evaluation from a premedical committee and an osteopathic physician on the student's behalf.

## Supplementary Requirements

Completion of a bachelor's degree at an accredited college or university is required. Students with only 90 semester hours of acceptable course work will be considered. A supplemental application needs to be submitted. A letter of recommendation from the school's preprofessional committee, or if unavailable, three letters, two of them from science professors, are acceptable. A letter of evaluation from an osteopathic physician is also required.

## Curriculum

4-year. *Years 1 and 2:* Two years are spent on campus and include the basic sciences and didactic clinical sciences. During this part of their training, students also are introduced to patient evaluation and the technology of medicine, and special emphasis is placed on manipulative medicine. Students receive early clinical teaching with other doctors during their first and second year. *Years 3 and 4:* Students spend 22 months in clinical training, including teaching rotations in affiliated hospitals and experience in ambulatory care facilities. They then return to campus for a pre-internship seminar, just prior to graduation, in preparation for internship, residency, and board exams. The curriculum emphasizes family medicine, internal medicine, ob/gyn, and pediatrics. A rotation in rural medicine is also required.

## Facilities

The school is a component of the University's Health Professions Division. In developing the structures for 20 acres of campus, the division sought advice from a wide range of individuals, including students and faculty. It has been designed to enhance the learning experience.

## Affiliated Teaching Hospitals

Twenty Florida hospitals and 16 other medical centers serve as teaching hospitals.

## Housing

All students are required to secure their own housing accommodations. The school does have some limited on-campus housing facilities within a 2-block radius of the school.

## Special Programs

The interdisciplinary generalist program exposes students to primary care clinical settings from the beginning of the first year. The goal is to increase the number of graduates entering family medicine, general pediatrics, and general internal medicine.

# GEORGIA

## Georgia Campus—Philadelphia College of Osteopathic Medicine

625 Old Peachtree Road NW
Suwanee, Georgia    30024

*Phone:* 678-225-7500          *Fax:* 678-225-7509
*E-mail:* admissions@pcom.edu
*WWW:* pcom.edu

| Application Filing | | Accreditation | |
|---|---|---|---|
| Earliest: | May 1 | Pending | |
| Latest: | February 1 | **Degrees Granted** | |
| Fee: | $50 | DO | |

### Enrollment: 2008–2009 First-Year Class

| | | | | | |
|---|---|---|---|---|---|
| Men: | 47 | 55% | Applied: | 1327 | |
| Women: | 39 | 45% | Enrolled: | 86 | |
| Out of State: | 51 | 59% | Minorities: | 32 | |

**Tuition and Fees**

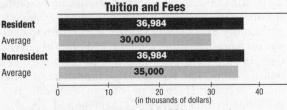

| | |
|---|---|
| Resident | 36,984 |
| Average | 30,000 |
| Nonresident | 36,984 |
| Average | 35,000 |

0    10    20    30    40
(in thousands of dollars)

Percentage receiving financial aid: 98%

## Introduction

This school is a branch campus of the same-named institution in Philadelphia, Pennsylvania. It is scheduled to begin operations in the 2005-2006 academic year. It will be located in Gwinnett County, a short distance from Atlanta. It has received approval from the Osteopathic Association Commission on Osteopathic College Accreditation to accept students for admission. The college will house modern classrooms and extensive computer resources.

## Admissions (AACOMAS)

Admission requirements are the same as those of the parent school. The first class will be made up of 80 students. Interviews will be held in Atlanta. It will focus on training students from Georgia and other southern states to practice osteopathic medicine. They will be encouraged to establish their practices in cities and rural areas experiencing a shortage of physicians.

## Supplementary Requirements

A supplemental application is required. In addition, a letter of recommendation from your school's premedical committee, premedical advisor, or Dean is essential. Faculty letters are not a suitable substitute. MCAT scores, not older than 3 years, must be submitted.

## Curriculum

The curriculum and academic calendar will mirror that of the Philadelphia campus. Its focus will be on training for primary and preventive health care. An integrated systems approach provides first- and second-year students with a general clinical education. The Day One program offers students clinical exposure from the beginning of medical school with courses in primary patient care and manipulative skills. Third- and fourth-year students work in ambulatory care sites, and in doctors' offices and hospitals.

## Facilities

Georgia campus is located minutes from downtown Atlanta. Its facilities include a clinical learning lab providing standardized and simulated patient experience, and an information commons with extensive digital reference and textbook resources connected to a wireless network. It also has 2 large classrooms, numerous small-group teaching classrooms, a large anatomy laboratory, and individual study areas. In addition, there is available a well-equipped fitness center and lounge areas as student amenities to enhance and provide a well-rounded learning experience.

## Affiliated Teaching Hospitals

Information not available.

## Housing

Information not available.

## Special Programs

This school has a branch campus in Philadelphia, Pennsylvania.

# ILLINOIS

## Chicago College of Osteopathic Medicine Midwestern University

555 31st Street
Downers Grove, Illinois   60515

*Phone:* 630-515-7200          *Fax:* 630-971-6086
*E-mail:* admissil@midwestern.edu
*WWW:* midwestern.edu

| Application Filing | | Accreditation |
|---|---|---|
| Earliest: | June 15 | AOA, NCA |
| Latest: | March 2 | |
| Fee: | $40 | |

### Enrollment: 2008–2009 First-Year Class

| | | | | |
|---|---|---|---|---|
| Men: | 93 | 54% | Applied: | 675 |
| Women: | 80 | 46% | Enrolled: | 173 |
| Out of State: | 68 | 39% | Minorities: | 40 |

**Tuition and Fees**

| | |
|---|---|
| Resident | 40,122 |
| Average | 30,000 |
| Nonresident | 44,643 |
| Average | 35,000 |

0   10   20   30   40
(in thousands of dollars)

Percentage receiving financial aid: 90%

## Introduction

The Chicago College of Osteopathic Medicine originally opened in 1900. It later merged with another osteopathic school, and in 1970 it assumed its present name. The school later changed its name again by adding Midwestern University when it expanded beyond the osteopathic program. The basic sciences are taught on the 103-acre Downers Grove Campus in a western suburb of Chicago. In 1995, the Arizona College of Osteopathic Medicine was founded as a part of Midwestern University. The University also houses a College of Pharmacy and a College of Health Sciences.

## Admissions (AACOMAS)

Completion of a bachelor's degree with miminum 2.75 overall and science GPA and the  MCAT are necessary. The basic premedical science courses are required. A total of 200 students are admitted each August. Approximately one half of the class comes from Illinois.

## Supplementary Requirements

A supplementary application is necessary. Also needed are two letters of recommendation, one of which should come from a physician (preferably a DO) and one from the premedical advisory committee or a science faculty member.

## Curriculum

4-year. The school has developed and continues to refine its curriculum that educates students in the basic medical arts and sciences; they also spend their first 2 years completing a rigorous basic science curriculum and preparing for their clinical studies. During their third and fourth years, students rotate through a variety of clinical departments accruing an impressive 92 weeks of direct patient care experience.

## Facilities

The large, attractive campus is located in a suburban setting. The lecture hall is comfortable and high tech. A Library Technology Center and Academic Laboratory Center are present. Recreational facilities include an indoor swimming pool, workout amenities, complete gymnasium, volley ball court, and outdoor athletic fields.

## Affiliated Teaching Hospitals

Students rotate through numerous hospitals throughout the Chicago area.

## Housing

On-campus housing features one and two bedroom suite-style residence hall rooms and family apartments.

## Special Programs

The school offers a dual DO-PhD program.

# IOWA

# Des Moines University College of Osteopathic Medicine

3200 Grand Avenue
Des Moines, Iowa   50312

*Phone:* 515-271-1499          *Fax:* 515-271-7085
*E-mail:* doadmit@dmu.edu
*WWW:* dmu.edu

| Application Filing | Accreditation |
|---|---|
| Earliest: June 1 | AOA |
| Latest: February 1 | **Degrees Granted** |
| Fee: $50 | DO, DO/MPH, DO/MHA |

### Enrollment: 2008–2009 First-Year Class

| | | | | |
|---|---|---|---|---|
| Men: | 106 | 48% | Applied: | 3273 |
| Women: | 115 | 52% | Enrolled: | 221 |
| Out of State: | 150 | 73% | Minorities: | 35 |

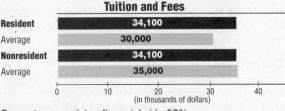

**Tuition and Fees**

| | |
|---|---|
| Resident | 34,100 |
| Average | 30,000 |
| Nonresident | 34,100 |
| Average | 35,000 |

(in thousands of dollars)

Percentage receiving financial aid: 99%

## Introduction

Des Moines University's College of Osteopathic Medicine was established in 1898. It is the second oldest osteopathic school in the United States. The institution has undergone changes several times in name and location to accommodate expanding enrollment and programs of study. In 1972 the college relocated to its present 22-acre site in Des Moines, Iowa and in the 1980s the university enlarged by opening up a College of Podiatric Medicine and Surgery and a College of Health Sciences, which trains physicians' assistants, physical therapists, and health care administrators.

## Admissions (AACOMAS)

Bachelor's degree and the MCAT are required. The basic premedical science courses plus 6 hours of English composition, speech, or language are required. Recommended courses include genetics, comparative anatomy, and psychology. A supplementary application is sent to all applicants who meet the minimum academic requirements, after completion of which they are reviewed for interview consideration. Only selected individuals are invited for an interview. A final decision is made on the basis of the AACOMAS and supplemental applications, the letters of recommendation, and the interview.

## Supplementary Requirements

Completion of a supplemental application is required. A minimum cumulative and science GPA of 3.0 is recommended. In addition, 2 letters of recommendation from members of the science faculty who have been the applicant's instructors or 1 premedical committee letter (including the names of committee members), as well as a letter by a physician (MD or DO), nurse, or volunteer coordinator, describing the applicant's medical exposure, are required.

## Curriculum

4-year. For the major part of the first year, students take core courses in the basic sciences. This is followed by the study of basic sciences and clinical medicine using an integrated organ system approach. The third and fourth year are devoted to preceptorships, clinical clerkships, and hospital clerkships in medicine, surgery, pediatrics, obstetrics-gynecology, and psychiatry. History and physical diagnosis are introduced in the first year. The principles, practices, and theory of osteopathic manipulative medicine are taught during the entire curriculum and are interwoven with the didactic, laboratory, and clerkship experiences.

## Facilities

The school is located on a 125-acre site in the downtown, metropolitan Des Moines area, near the art center and Governor's Mansion.

## Affiliated Teaching Hospitals

The university operates several on-site clinics and is affiliated with selected rural and urban clinics throughout Iowa and the United States.

## Housing

The university is a nonresidential campus. Housing is available in nearby apartments and homes.

## Special Programs

Extensive research opportunities for student research are offered; in addition, a master's degree program with a Certificate in Gerontology can be acquired.

## KENTUCKY

# Pikeville College, School of Osteopathic Medicine

214 Sycamore Street
Pikeville, Kentucky 41501

*Phone:* 606-218-5400          *Fax:* 606-218-5405
*E-mail:* pcsem@pc.ledu
*WWW:* pc.edu

| Application Filing | | Accreditation |
|---|---|---|
| Earliest: | June 1 | AOA |
| Latest: | February 1 | **Degrees Granted** |
| Fee: | $75 | DO |

### Enrollment: 2008–2009 First-Year Class

| | | | | |
|---|---|---|---|---|
| Men: | 49 | 59% | Applied: | 1949 |
| Women: | 34 | 41% | Enrolled: | 83 |
| Out of State: | 38 | 54% | Minorities: | 6 |

**Tuition and Fees**

| | |
|---|---|
| **Resident** | 32,800 |
| Average | 30,000 |
| **Nonresident** | 32,800 |
| Average | 35,000 |

(in thousands of dollars)

0  10  20  30  40

Percentage receiving financial aid: 93%

## Introduction

Pikeville College, School of Osteopathic Medicine (PCSOM) offers a 4-year program that results in the degree of Doctor of Osteopathic Medicine. Osteopathic physicians trained at Pikeville provide a full range of specialties and subspecialties services as practiced in tertiary hospitals; however, many DOs go into primary care in medically underserved areas.

## Admissions (AACOMAS)

To be considered for admission, students must have a baccalaureate degree, completed specific required science courses, take the MCAT, and apply through AACOMAS.

PCSOM's curriculum and coursework is very similar to other medical school programs. The school places special emphasis on the following 3 critical areas: manual medicine, community and behavior medicine, and ambulatory care.

## Supplementary Requirements

A supplementary application is required. Also necessary is a letter of recommendation from the school's premedical committee or 2 letters from science faculty members familiar with the applicant.

## Curriculum

*First and second years:* Teaching takes place mostly in the lecture hall and laboratory, covering the standard medical school disciplines, plus our special topics. Tuesday and Friday afternoons are spent in doctors' offices, learning to take patient histories and carrying out physical examinations. During the summer of their second year, the students take 2 major full-time courses: medicine and surgery. These are intensive courses, which will prepare the student to interact fully at the bedside or in various settings during the final 2 years of their medical school education. *Third and fourth years:* Consist of clinical clerkships. The student will rotate and work in various disciplines including family practice, rural clinic, ER, general internal medicine, general surgery, pediatrics, obstetrics/gynecology, psychiatry, and osteopathic practice. The student will spend from 1 to 4 months in each of these areas, depending on PCSOM's requirements and the student's interest. Most of the extensive clinical training will be completed in the Appalachian region.

## Facilities

The existing facility has modernized classrooms, labs, and an up-to-date telemedicine/medical library. The facilities were expanded allowing for additional biomedical research facilities and offices.

## Affiliated Teaching Hospitals

Numerous hospitals in Kentucky and surrounding areas provide clinical facilities for training.

## Housing

Students must secure their own housing but they will be assisted in their search for appropriate affordable housing.

## Special Programs

Each student is supplied with a Pentium laptop computer equipped with Windows MS Office, a modem, ROM's free Internet access, as well as all required textbooks, all necessary dissection equipment, microscopes, and ophthalmoscopes. In addition, lab coats and scrub suits are provided.

## MAINE

# University of New England College of Osteopathic Medicine

11 Hills Beach Road
Biddeford, Maine    04005

*Phone:* 207-602-2329          *Fax:* 207-602-5967
*E-mail:* unecomadmissions@une.edu
*WWW:* http://www.une.edu/com/admissions

| Application Filing | | Accreditation |
|---|---|---|
| Earliest: | February 1 | AOA |
| Latest: | March 15 | **Degrees Granted** |
| Fee: | $55 | DO-MPH |

### Enrollment: 2008–2009 First-Year Class

| | | | | |
|---|---|---|---|---|
| Men: | 61 | 57% | Applied: | 3369 |
| Women: | 72 | 54% | Enrolled: | 133 |
| Out of State: | 98 | 79% | Minorities: | 17 |

**Tuition and Fees**

| | |
|---|---|
| Resident | 41,260 |
| Average | 25,500 |
| Nonresident | 41,260 |
| Average | 30,200 |

0      10      20      30      40
(in thousands of dollars)

Percentage receiving financial aid: 93%

## Introduction

The University of New England was created in 1979 through the merger of the New England College of Osteopathic Medicine (NECOM) and St. Francis College. The University is located in Biddeford, Maine, on the Atlantic Ocean, 15 miles south of Portland and 90 miles north of Boston. UNECOM is committed to serving the people of New England, and its mission is educating primary care physicians.

## Admissions (AACOMAS)

Academic requirements include ninety (90) semester hours or 75 percent credit toward a baccalaureate degree. Any academic major is acceptable from a regionally accredited college or university. Prerequisites include the basic premed courses and one year of English composition and/or literature; biochemistry is also required for matriculation, but not for application. Successful completion of all prerequisite courses and MCAT are required prior to being offered a supplemental application. Prospective students are encouraged to take additional courses in anatomy, calculus, genetics, microbiology, and/or physiology as well as coursework in arts and letters, communication, humanities, and social sciences. Letters of recommendation from a prehealth committee, prehealth advisor, or two faculty members are required, along with at least one letter from a professional reference. A letter from an osteopathic physician is strongly recommended. Select candidates are invited to campus for an interview with faculty, clinicians, and current students. Applicants are evaluated on their demonstration of scholastic abilities, exposure to and experience in health care and human services, leadership, community service and/or research experience, and other factors.

## Curriculum

*Preclinical:* The first year begins with a focus on basic sciences and an exposure to the physician–patient relationship through early clinical experiences. *Second year:* System-based modules are taught by a cadre of practicing clinicians and basic scientists who bring the real world into the classroom. Students' clinical skills are enhanced in the Experiences in Doctoring courses, with community placements and practice with standardized patients at the Clinical Performance Center, as well as the differential diagnoses classes. The year concludes with a capstone course and Advanced Cardiac Life Support. *Clinical:* The *third year* is devoted to clerkships in core disciplines of internal medicine, family medicine, obstetrics, pediatrics, psychiatry, surgery, and community health at clinical campuses throughout the northeast. Students are involved in patient care and didactic sessions in ambulatory, hospital, and rural settings. The third year concludes with a student colloquium for the assessment of acquired skills in the simulated patient program. *Year four:* requires clerkships in osteopathic manipulative medicine, emergency medicine, internal medicine, and surgery while providing an opportunity for electives.

## Affiliated Teaching Hospitals:

In addition to the information presented, UNECOM's third-year clinical training centers (noted above) are located throughout New England, New York, New Jersey, and Pennsylvania. Fourth-year students complete selective and elective rotations around the country.

## Housing

There is no on-campus housing available for medical students. Most students live in the cities of Biddeford and Saco.

# Michigan State University College of Osteopathic Medicine

A136 East Fee Hall
East Lansing, Michigan   48824

*Phone:* 517-353-7740          *Fax:* 517-355-3296
*E-mail:* com.admission
*WWW:* com.msu.edu/hc.msu.edu

| Application Filing | | Accreditation |
|---|---|---|
| Earliest: | June 1 | AOA |
| Latest: | December 1 | **Degrees Granted** |
| Fee: | $75 | DO, DO-PhD |

**Enrollment: 2008–2009 First-Year Class**

| | | | | |
|---|---|---|---|---|
| Men: | 112 | 47% | Applied: | 787 |
| Women: | 119 | 53% | Enrolled: | 211 |
| Out of State: | 5 | 24% | Minorities: | 4 |

**Tuition and Fees**

| | |
|---|---|
| **Resident** | 28,011 |
| Average | 30,000 |
| **Nonresident** | 60,891 |
| Average | 35,000 |

(in thousands of dollars)

Percentage receiving financial aid: 92%

Above data applies to 2007–2008 academic year.

## Introduction

In 1855 Michigan State University was instituted. There are 11 undergraduate and 13 graduate schools. The school began as a private institution, the Michigan College of Osteopathic Medicine, in Pontiac. By an act of the Michigan legislature in 1969, it gained its current affiliation. The College of Osteopathic Medicine opened in 1971.

## Admissions (AACOMAS)

Completion of the MCAT and a minimum of 3 years of college (but virtually all students have bachelor's degree by enrollment). The basic premedical science courses are required as well as 2 courses (6 credits) in English and in the behavioral sciences (psychology, sociology, anthropology). A grade point average minimum of C (2.5) is required, but a near B is recommended. An MCAT total around 25 is also desirable. Courses in biochemistry and genetics are strongly recommended. Additional courses in biology such as anatomy, cell biology, histology, and microbiology are also recommended. A supplementary application

will be sent only to selected applicants. It may include a request for an essay, nonacademic information, and evaluation forms. Decisions are made after an applicant has been interviewed. There is an Early Decision Program (EDP) for exceptional students seeking admission only to this school. An entering class of 125 students is anticipated and in-state students will predominate.

## Supplementary Requirements

A minimum cumulative of 2.7 and science average and MCAS total score of 18 is needed. A supplemental application is also required.

## Curriculum

4-year. Focuses on principles of normal and abnormal structure and function, which are necessary to an understanding of dysfunction in body systems of all age groups. Clinical training and problem solving are included at every level, progressing in difficulty, adding topical information and reinforcing concepts. The curriculum includes 1 year of integrated basic science courses, 1 year of systems biology courses, and 2 years of clinical clerkships that include ambulatory and inpatient care in community hospitals and health care agencies. The theories and applications of osteopathic manipulative medicine and osteopathic principles and practice are included at all levels of curriculum. In support of the school's mission, the curriculum is designed to increase the number of graduates prepared to practice community-integrated primary care medicine to address the health care needs of the people of Michigan. This is accomplished by providing a broader scope and greater depth of practice in the ambulatory setting, by an increased emphasis on practicing medicine as part of an interdisciplinary team, and by using technology for communication, information retrieval, and education.

## Facilities

The large university campus includes gardens, museums, performing arts, and sports activities, and space is available for small groups or individual study.

## Affiliated Teaching Hospitals

Several throughout the state, including many in the Detroit metropolitan area.

## Housing

University housing is available on campus and in the Lansing/East Lansing area.

## Special Programs

The college offers a variety of advanced degree programs. A dual DO-PhD program, Master's in Health and Humanities, Masters in Epidemiology, and a Master's in Public Health are offered by the University.

## MISSOURI

# A.T. Still University Kirksville College of Osteopathic Medicine

800 West Jefferson
Kirksville, Missouri 63501

*Phone:* 866-626-2878, ext. 2237   *Fax:* 866-626-2969
*E-mail:* admissions@atsu.edu
*WWW:* www.atsu.edu

| Application Filing | | Accreditation | |
|---|---|---|---|
| Earliest: | June 1 | AOA, NCA | |
| Latest: | February 1 | **Degrees Granted** | |
| Fee: | $60 | DO | |

### Enrollment: 2008–2009 First-Year Class

| | | | | | |
|---|---|---|---|---|---|
| Men: | 102 | 60% | Applied: | 3174 |
| Women: | 72 | 40% | Enrolled: | 174 |
| Out of State: | 134 | 84% | Minorities: | 9 |

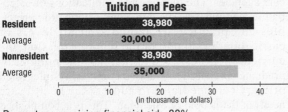

**Tuition and Fees**

| | |
|---|---|
| Resident | 38,980 |
| Average | 30,000 |
| Nonresident | 38,980 |
| Average | 35,000 |

(in thousands of dollars)

Percentage receiving financial aid: 88%

## Introduction

The Kirksville College of Osteopathic Medicine was established in 1892. It was the first school of its type, originating as the American School of Osteopathy. The school's goal is the preparation of osteopathic physicians for primary care and specialty training. The school is located on a 60-acre campus in Kirksville, which is in northeastern Missouri.

## Admissions (AACOMAS)

This school has a branch campus in Mesa, Arizona; however, applications for admission are processed in Kirksville, Missouri. A bachelor's degree and the MCAT are required. The basic premedical science courses plus 1 year of English are necessary. A minimum of cumulative and a science GPA of 2.50 is required. Also needed are 2 letters of recommendation, 1 from a premedical advisor or premedical committee or science faculty member and 1 from an MD or DO or one's present employer. A secondary application is sent to all applicants who meet minimum admission standards. Those reaching the final phase of the selection process will be invited for an interview, after which a decision will be made.

## Curriculum

Students spend the first year on the Mesa, Arizona campus learning together via small groups, real-life patient interactions, and simulated clinical experiences. The second year is spent in small-group settings learning from additional clinical presentations at a Community Health Center campus. Community Health Centers are independent organizations serving as the nation's high-quality health care safety net. These health centers provide comprehensive, coordinated primary care services through 6,000 clinics in the United States and its territories. Third- and fourth-year students will complete their clinical rotations at Community Health Center campuses, associated hospitals, health care providers, and other select health care institutions. Osteopathic principles and practices are integrated throughout the curriculum, and the osteopathic manipulative treatment program is designed for primary care applications. This provides distinctive training in the value of the healing touch in patient care.

## Affiliated Teaching Hospitals

The university has a modern campus in: Arizona, which contains extensive simulation laboratories, digital learning resources, and group problem-solving venues that will serve as a campus for students their first year of the program. Approximately 10 learners will move to each of the Community Health Centers campuses in Missouri for years 2 to 4 of the program.

## Housing

There are 44 student apartments on campus and numerous private residences throughout the city.

## Special Programs

The school offers a student wellness program. The School Health Management has a variety of master's degree programs.

# Kansas City University of Medicine and Biosciences College of Osteopathic Medicine

1750 Independence Avenue
Kansas City, Missouri    64106

*Toll free:* 800-234-4847
*Phone:* 818-283-2352
*E-mail:* admissions@kcumb.edu
*WWW:* kcumb.edu

| Application Filing | | Accreditation |
|---|---|---|
| Earliest: | June 1 | AOA |
| Latest: | February 1 | **Degrees Granted** |
| Fee: | $50 | DO |

### Enrollment: 2008–2009 First-Year Class

| | | | |
|---|---|---|---|
| Men: | 146 | | |
| Women: | 120 | Enrolled: | 266 |
| Out of State: | 196 | Minorities: | 13 |

**Tuition and Fees**

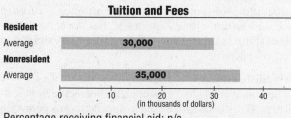

Resident
Average  30,000
Nonresident
Average  35,000

(in thousands of dollars)

Percentage receiving financial aid: n/a

## Introduction

This school was founded in 1916. It has undergone several name changes over the years. Today it is one of the oldest and largest colleges of osteopathic medicine with a student body of more than 900 students. This accredited college of osteopathic medicine seeks to provide its students with a meaningful quality education that will ensure their future success as practitioners. This is done by exposing them to highly competent mentors and facilitating their getting valuable hands-on experience. The focus will also be to build lasting relationships with their peers. The educational program is carried out in state-of-the-art facilities and involves the community in the training program. Upon graduation, the school offers a wide range of postdoctoral training programs.

## Admissions

A bachelor's degree and scores from the MCAT within the last 3 years are required. The standard premedical science courses plus 1-year courses are required.

## Supplementary Requirements

A supplementary application is needed as are letters of recommendation from the premedical advisory committee, a science faculty member, and a physician (preferably a DO).

## Curriculum

The goal of the school's curriculum is to integrate the basic and clinical sciences. It seeks to unify all essential concepts and information in a continuum of clinical presentations. The foundations of anatomy, biochemistry, epidemiology, genetics, immunology, medical ethics, microbiology, osteopathic principles and practices, pathology, pharmacology, physiology, pediatrics, family medicine, surgery, and psychiatry are incorporated into clinical presentations covering all diseases physicians will encounter in day-to-day practice. New concepts as well as health care policy, medical informatics, and health and wellness are integrated into the curricular structure.

## Facilities

The Educational Pavilion features an auditorium with a sophisticated audiovisual system, an anatomy lab with networked camera equipment, a library with an extensive print and multimedia collection, a student fitness center, a cafeteria, meeting rooms, and a library. A special site serves as an academic resource center, and the Center for Clinical Competence provides students with the latest in simulated emergency services.

## Affiliated Teaching Hospitals

Clinical teaching is provided at Lakeside Osteopathic Hospital, Conley Hospital, The Osteopathic Hospital, and the University Hospital.

## Housing

Information not available.

## Special Programs

An MS in Biomedical Science and a 4-year dual DO-MBA in Health Care Leadership are available.

## NEVADA

# Touro University—Nevada College of Osteopathic Medicine

874 American Pacific Drive
Henderson, Nevada    89014

*Phone:* 702-777-1751          *Fax:* 702-777-1752
*E-mail:* rcorbman@touro.edu
*WWW:* tu.edu

| Application Filing | Accreditation |
|---|---|
| Earliest: June 1 | AOA |
| Latest: May 15 | **Degrees Granted** |
| Fee: $100 | DO |

### Enrollment: 2008–2009 First-Year Class

| | | | | |
|---|---|---|---|---|
| Men: | 80 | 60% | Applied: | 439 |
| Women: | 54 | 40% | Enrolled: | 134 |
| Out of State: | n/a | | Minorities: | 1% |

**Tuition and Fees**

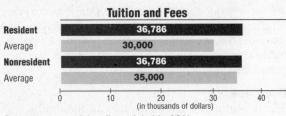

| | |
|---|---|
| Resident | 36,786 |
| Average | 30,000 |
| Nonresident | 36,786 |
| Average | 35,000 |

0    10    20    30    40
(in thousands of dollars)

Percentage receiving financial aid: 98%
Above data applies to 2007–2008 academic year.

## Introduction

This is one of the newest colleges of Osteopathic Medicine and is the only one in Nevada. The school is located in Henderson, in the southeastern part of the valley adjacent to Las Vegas and close to McCarren International Airport. It is a branch of the same-named school on Mare Island located in the San Francisco Bay area. The school occupies a 70,000-square-foot remodeled facility. It aims to train osteopathic physicians who are committed to primary care and the holistic approach to the patient.

## Admissions (AACOMAS)

Requirements for admission include having a bachelor's degree from an accredited institution of higher education prior to enrollment. Applicants must have completed 2 courses of inorganic chemistry, organic chemistry (a semester of biochemistry can be substituted for organic chemistry), and 2 semesters of physics. The MCAT must be taken and the scores should not be older than 3 years.

After receipt of the primary application (AACOMAS), qualified candidates are sent a supplemental application. With the request, they submit an evaluation form from a preprofessional advisory committee or letters of recommendation from 2 science faculty members familiar with the applicant, in addition, a letter of recommendation from a physician (DO or MD). Selected candidates are invited for interviews that usually are conducted at the Nevada campus.

## Supplementary Requirements

A supplemental application is required. Application status inquiries should to be made by e-mail.

## Curriculum

Students are taught the essential science and clinical science courses. These include anatomy, histology, microbiology, pathology, pharmacology, immunology, clinical skills, osteopathic principles and practice, doctor-patient communication, and courses that focus on each of the major systems of the body. Practice and problem solving are components of both classroom and clinic experience, but the school realizes there is a need for highly trained physicians in other specialties.

## Facilities

The college has a large osteopathic medicine man-ipulative skills lab with 78 tables. Special rooms equipped with closed-circuit TV capability are designed for monitoring and recording student-patient interaction. Lecture halls contain full intra/internet access at all seats. A large gross anatomy bed is also available. The library is equipped with access to most databases, electronic journals, and other educational resources.

## Affiliated Teaching Hospitals

Information not available.

## Housing

Information not available.

## NEW JERSEY

# University of Medicine and Dentistry of New Jersey School of Osteopathic Medicine

1 Medical Center Drive
Stratford, New Jersey    08084

*Phone:* 856-566-7050          *Fax:* 856-566-6895
*E-mail:* somadm@umduj.edu
*WWW:* som.umduj.edu/

| Application Filing | | Accreditation | |
|---|---|---|---|
| Earliest: | May 1 | AOA | |
| Latest: | February 1 | **Degrees Granded** | |
| Fee: | $90 | DO, DO-PhD, | |
| | | DO-JD | |

### Enrollment: 2008–2009 First-Year Class

| Men: | 59 | 55% | Applied: | 3296 |
|---|---|---|---|---|
| Women: | 51 | 45% | Enrolled: | 110 |
| Out of State: | 22 | 20% | Minorities: | 52 |

**Tuition and Fees**

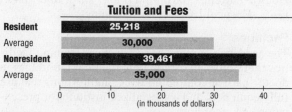

| | |
|---|---|
| Resident | 25,218 |
| Average | 30,000 |
| Nonresident | 39,461 |
| Average | 35,000 |

(in thousands of dollars)

Percentage receiving financial aid: 92%

## Introduction

In 1976 the School of Osteopathic Medicine was founded as a division of the University of Medicine and Dentistry in New Jersey. The school is located in Stratford, in southern New Jersey, and within driving distance of both New York City and Philadelphia.

## Admissions (AACOMAS)

Completion of the MCAT and a baccalaureate degree are necessary. The basic premedical science courses are required as is 1 year each of English, mathematics, and behavioral science (psychology, sociology, or anthropology). One semester of the mathematics requirement can be satisfied by a course in computer science or statistics. An entering class of 108 is anticipated and it is filled on a rolling admissions basis. Selected applicants will be asked for a letter of recommendation and will be invited for an interview prior to the committee's decision. When the class is filled, an alternate list is established.

## Supplementary Requirements

The desirable cumulative and science GPA is 3.00 and a supplemental application is required. A letter of recommendation from the premedical committee or 2 science professors familiar with the applicant are necessary, as are the MCAT scores.

## Curriculum

4-year. Committed to an emphasis on primary patient care, the school provides a medical education that fully trains students in the principles of scientific medicine, while emphasizing the interrelation between structure and function in explaining the disease process.

## Facilities

A 3-story Academic Center houses the library, basic science and anatomy labs, classrooms, lounge, student services, cafeteria, and wellness center. The school has a large Science Center and Research Center. The University Doctors' Pavilion houses the clinical departments and outpatient services.

## Affiliated Teaching Hospitals

Kennedy Memorial Hospitals-University Medical Center (607 beds), Our Lady of Lourdes Medical Center (201 beds), and St. Francis Hospital (200 beds).

## Housing

Students are assisted in obtaining housing near the school. There is no housing for students on campus.

## Special Programs

The dual programs include DO-PhD, DO-MBA, and DO-MPA.

## NEW YORK

# New York College of Osteopathic Medicine of New York Institute of Technology

Old Westbury, New York   11568

*Phone:* 516-686-3747          *Fax:* 516-686-3831
*E-mail:* comader@nyit.edu
*WWW:* nyit.edu/nycom

| Application Filing | | Accreditation |
|---|---|---|
| Earliest: | April 15 | AOA |
| Latest: | February 1 | **Degrees Granted** |
| Fee: | $60 | DO, DO-MS, |
| | | DO-MBA |

### Enrollment: 2008–2009 First-Year Class

| Men: | 154 | 51% | Applied: | 4500 |
|---|---|---|---|---|
| Women: | 144 | 49% | Enrolled: | 298 |
| Out of State: | 43 | 14% | Minorities: | 35 |

**Tuition and Fees**

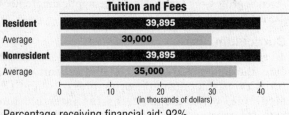

| | |
|---|---|
| Resident | 39,895 |
| Average | 30,000 |
| Nonresident | 39,895 |
| Average | 35,000 |

(in thousands of dollars)

Percentage receiving financial aid: 92%

## Introduction
New York College of Osteopathic Medicine was established in 1977 as one of the 8 schools of New York Institute of Technology, a private college founded in 1955 offering care-oriented, professional education. NYCOM is located on the Old Westbury campus of NYIT, approximately 25 miles from NYC on Nassau County's historic Gold Coast.

## Admissions
Both a prospective bachelor's degree and taking the MCAT are necessary to be considered for admission. All required premedical prerequisites, and 1 year of English must be met. Selected applicants are asked to complete a supplemental application and submit pre-professional evaluations from their undergraduate advisory office. The anticipated class size is 260 students and is filled on a rolling basis.

## Supplementary Requirements
A supplemental application is necessary.

## Curriculum
4-years. *First and second years:* Students may select from 2 curricular tracks: the Traditional Integrated Lecture-Based track or the small-group case-based Doctor-Patient Continuum track. *Third and fourth years:* Hospital-based clinical training.

## Facilities
The academic campus has 3 advanced training facilities that house an osteopathic medical laboratory, a doctor-patient continuum wing, auditoriums that are fully equipped, and a specialized institute for presentation and recording.

## Affiliated Teaching Hospitals
St. Barnabas Hospital (Bronx), St. Barnabas Medical Center (NJ), North Shore University/LIU, Good Samaritan Hospital, Maimonides Medical Center, Lutheran Medical Center, Nassau University Medical Center, St. Vincent Midtown, Wilson Memorial, Union Hospital (NJ), Mid-Hudson (Kingston, NY), Long Beach Hospital, Jamaica Hospital, Queens Hospital, Peninsula Hospital, Wyckoff Heights Medical Center, and others.

## Housing
No on-campus housing available. The school provides off-campus housing information to assist first-year students.

## Special Programs
Combined DO-MBA, DO-MS in clinical Nutrition, and Predoctoral Academic, Medicine Fellowships are offered.

# Touro College, New York
# School of Osteopathic Medicine
230 West 125th Street
New York, NY  10027

*Phone:* 646-981-4556       *Fax:* 212-678-1784
*E-mail:* obedf@touro.edu
*WWW:* touro edu/med/

| Application Filing | Accreditation |
|---|---|
| Earliest: June 1 | Pending |
| Latest: January 2 | **Degrees Granted** |
| Fee: $50 | DO–DOMS |

### Enrollment: 2008–2009 First-Year Class
| | | | | |
|---|---|---|---|---|
| Men: | 68 | 50% | Applied: | n/a |
| Women: | 67 | 50% | Enrolled: | 135 |
| Out-of-State: | n/a | | Minorities: | 66 |

**Tuition and Fees**

Resident: 32,625
Average: 30,000
Nonresident: 32,625
Average: 35,000

(in thousands of dollars)

Percentage receiving financial aid: 85%

## Introduction
In October 2007 the first new medical school in New York State in 30 years was inaugurated in Harlem with a class of 135 students.

The mission of the school is aimed at improving medical care for the Harlem community as well as increasing the number of minorities practicing medicine. Most clinical training will take place in Harlem and other underserved areas. The school will be an integral part of the community in which it is located. It will work with local educational institutions to promote the increased availability of medical services in Harlem and the delivery there of osteopathic medical services in a variety of settings.

## Admissions (AACOMAS)
4-year. All candidates for admission are required to submit a primary application through AACOMAS. Qualified candidates will be invited to submit a supplemental application and appropriate letters of recommendation. The school operates on a rolling admission basis. Applicants are encouraged to apply early to enhance their admission potential.

## Supplementary Requirements
A supplementary application is required, as is a letter of recommendation from the premedical committee or letters from 2 science faculty who know the applicant. A letter of recommendation is also needed from a DO or MD.

## Curriculum
Students take courses in all of the basic subject areas such as anatomy, pathology, microbiology, histology, as well as practice-oriented courses, such as ostheopatic principles and procedures, pharmacology, immunology, clinical skills, and doctor-patient communications. In addition, systems courses that focus on each major system of the body will be offered. The school's mission is to prepare students for the realities of medicine as it exists, as well as how it is likely to be in the future. Practice in problem solving is part of daily classroom experience. The school will strive to provide an educational program consistent with emerging directions of health care.

## Facilities
These include two large amphitheaters with desks having laptop computer accommodations. Also present are an osteopathic medicine manipulation lab accommodating 27 electric tables, a modern library with computer stations, a comfortable student lounge, and an entire floor devoted to research.

## Affiliated Teaching Hospitals
Information not available.

## Housing
Off-campus housing assistance is provided.

# OHIO

# Ohio University College of Osteopathic Medicine

102 Grosvernor Hall
Athens, Ohio    45701

*Phone:* 740-593-4313          *Fax:* 740-593-2256
*E-mail:* admissions@exchange.oucom.ohiou.edu
*WWW:* http://www.oucom.ohiou.edu

| Application Filing | | Accreditation | |
|---|---|---|---|
| Earliest: | June 1 | AOA | |
| Latest: | January 2 | **Degrees Granted** | |
| Fee: | $30 | DO, DO-PhD, | |
| | | DO-MPH, DO-MBA, | |
| | | DO-MHA, DO-MS | |

### Enrollment: 2008–2009 First-Year Class

| Men: | 51 | 44% | Applied: | 3167 |
|---|---|---|---|---|
| Women: | 65 | 56% | Enrolled: | 117 |
| Out of State: | 18 | 13% | Minorities: | 31 |

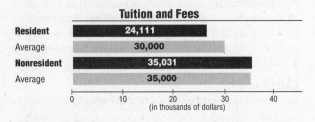

**Tuition and Fees**

| | |
|---|---|
| **Resident** | 24,111 |
| Average | 30,000 |
| **Nonresident** | 35,031 |
| Average | 35,000 |

(in thousands of dollars)

## Introduction

Ohio University was established in 1804. It is a public school with 9 undergraduate and 8 graduate schools. The College of Osteopathic Medicine was established in 1975. The school focuses on training in primary care including family medicine, internal medicine, and pediatrics. More than half of its graduates practice primary care medicine.

## Admissions (AACOMAS)

Completion of a baccalaureate degree and the MCAT are necessary. The basic premedical science courses plus 1 year each of English and behavioral science are required. Additional courses in the biological sciences are highly recommended. Students with 3 years of exceptional college work are considered. After a review of the AACOMAS application, completion of a supplemental application and supporting material will be requested from those receiving further consid-

eration. This will include submission of preprofessional advisory committee evaluations. A letter of evaluation from an osteopathic physician is highly recommended. The size of the entering class is expected to be 120 students. It will be filled on a rolling basis.

## Supplementary Requirements

A supplementing application is needed as well as a letter of recommendation from the premedical advisory committee or recommendations from 2 natural science members of the faculty who know the applicant. A letter of recommendation from an osteopathic physician is highly recommended.

## Curriculum

4-year. The focus of instruction is on the holistic approach to practicing primary care medicine, with the realization that even the medical specialist needs a firm understanding of these disciplines. The curricula involves a combination of learning activities including case-based learning, computer-based programs, independent and group study, early clinical contact, and traditional lectures and laboratories. The college offers 2 curricular options to accommodate students with different learning styles. The Clinical Presentation Continuum (CPC) curriculum integrates letures, small group, self-directed learning, and early clinical contact into its structure. In addition to the CPC track, the Patient Case Continuum (PCC), a problem-based learning curriculum, utilizes self-directed learning, working in small groups, and early clinical activities. Due to the limited number of positions in the PCC program, students wishing to be considered for the PCC curriculum must go through a second selection process after having been admitted to the school.

## Facilities

A learning resources center contains classroom technology, as well as a student affairs complex.

## Affiliated Teaching Hospitals

The school provides clinical training at 16 hospitals that form regional training centers in 4 different regions of Ohio.

## Housing

Student housing is available in off-campus apartments and houses.

## Special Features

The school offers combined degree programs leading to a DO-PhD, DO-MBA, DO-MHA, DO-MPH, and DO-MS.

# OKLAHOMA

## Oklahoma State University College of Osteopathic Medicine

1111 West 17th Street
Tulsa, Oklahoma 74107

*Phone:* 800-677-1972
918-561-8421 *Fax:* 918-561-8243
*E-mail:* lindsey.kirkpatrick@chs.okstate.edu
*WWW:* healthsciences.okstate.edu

| Application Filing | | Accreditation |
|---|---|---|
| Earliest: | June 1 | AOA |
| Latest: | February 1 | **Degrees Granted** |
| Fee: | $40 | DO/MS |
| | | DO/PhD, DO/MBA |

### Enrollment: 2008–2009 First-Year Class

| Men: | 42 | 48% | Applied: | 1708 |
|---|---|---|---|---|
| Women: | 46 | 52% | Enrolled: | 88 |
| Out of State: | 15 | 17% | Minorities: | 30 |

**Tuition and Fees**

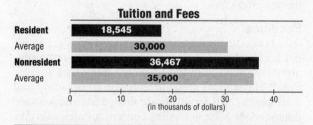

| Resident | 18,545 |
| Average | 30,000 |
| Nonresident | 36,467 |
| Average | 35,000 |

(in thousands of dollars)

### Introduction

Oklahoma State University was established in 1890. It is a public school with 6 undergraduate schools, and 1 graduate school. The College of Osteopathic Medicine originally opened in 1972 and enrolled its first class in 1974, which graduated in 1977. That year the college moved to its permanent campus on the west bank of the Arkansas River, near downtown Tulsa. In 1988, the College of Osteopathic Medicine joined Oklahoma State University.

### Admissions (AACOMAS)

Completion of 4 years of college preferred, the MCAT and at least a 3.0 grade point average and 2.75 science cumulative average are necessary. English and the basic premedical science courses are required plus at least 1 upper division science course, including lab. Examples include: biochemistry, histology, embryology, comparative anatomy, and microbiology. An entering class size of 88 students is anticipated. Selected applicants may be asked to submit a supplemental application form from their preprofessional advisory committee and a recommendation from an osteopathic physician. The AACOMAS and supplemental applications, recommendations, and interview assessment will form the basis of a decision on suitability for admission.

### Supplementary Requirements

A minimum GPA of 3.0 is needed as is a minimum average MCAT score of 7 or a total of 21. A supplementary application is also necessary. A letter of recommendation from the premedical advisory committee or 3 letters from faculty, 2 of which are from the natural sciences, are also required. Also needed is a letter from an osteopathic physician.

### Curriculum

4-year. Divided into basic and clinical sciences, and emphasizes primary care. The program uses a coordinated, spiraling systems approach in which subject matter is continuously reintroduced in greater depth and complexity. *First year:* Concentrates on the basic sciences and preliminary clinical concepts. Preparation of the student for early patient contact requires a foundation in anatomy, physiology, behavioral science, techniques of physical examination, diagnosis and patient interview, and recognition of normal and abnormal patterns of physical conditions and disease. *Second year:* Emphasizes the interdisciplinary study of the structure and function of body systems. In addition, students are introduced to specialized clinical care and medical procedures related to each body system and receive continuing instruction in osteopathic principles and practices. *Third and fourth years:* Devoted exclusively to clinical rotations, where students work with patients under physician-faculty supervision. Students rotate through basic hospital services, including general medicine, surgery, obstetrics/gynecology, pediatrics, internal medicine, and emergency medicine. Other clinical training occurs at a small rural hospital, a primary care clinic, a psychiatric facility, a community health facility, and offices of private physicians. The curriculum is based on the semester system, with summers off, except the last year and one half, which is continuous.

### Facilities

The college is located only minutes from downtown Tulsa and is part of a four-building complex. The tutorial entity contains classrooms, a medical library, and bookstore. The Health Care Center is located somewhat south of the main campus. It serves as a teaching clinic and health care resource for the community.

### Affiliated Teaching Hospitals

Tulsa Regional Medical Center (521 beds), Enid Regional Hospital (101 beds), Hillcrest Health Center, St. Anthony Medical Center, Medical Center of Southeast Oklahoma, and 30 other rural community hospitals in Oklahoma and Arkansas.

### Housing

Not offered.

### Special Programs

The college also offers DO-MBA, DO-PhD, MS in biological sciences, MS in forensic science, and MFSA in forensic science administration degree programs.

# PENNSYLVANIA

# Philadelphia College of Osteopathic Medicine

4170 City Avenue
Philadelphia, Pennsylvania   19131

*Phone:* 215-871-6700          *Fax:* 215-871-6719
*E-mail:* admissions@pcom.edu
*WWW:* pcom.edu

| Application Filing | | Accreditation | |
|---|---|---|---|
| Earliest: | June 1 | AOA, Middle States | |
| Latest: | February 1 | **Degrees Granted** | |
| Fee: | $50 | DO, DO-MBA, | |
| | | DO-MPH, DO-PhD | |

### Enrollment: 2008–2009 First-Year Class

| | | | | | |
|---|---|---|---|---|---|
| Men: | 137 | 55% | Applied: | 3541 | |
| Women: | 130 | 49% | Enrolled: | 267 | |
| Out of State: | 105 | 39% | Minorities: | 49 | |

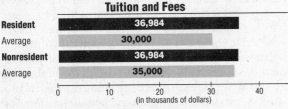

**Tuition and Fees**

| | |
|---|---|
| **Resident** | 36,984 |
| Average | 30,000 |
| **Nonresident** | 36,984 |
| Average | 35,000 |

(in thousands of dollars)

Percentage receiving financial aid: 93%

## Introduction

The school was founded in 1899. The college emphasizes training primary care practitioners with almost 65% of graduates choosing careers in family practice, general internal medicine, obstetrics/gynecology, and pediatrics.

## Admissions

A bachelor's degree or 3 years of college work with a minimum 3.2 average, the basic premedical science courses, and the MCAT are required. The size of the incoming class is expected to be 250 students. After receipt of the AACOMAS application, a supplemental application is sent to the candidate for admission. This must be completed and returned and arrangements should be made for a recommendation from the college's preprofessional advisory committee to be sent. A letter of evaluation from an osteopathic physician is advisable but not required. Qualified applicants are invited for an interview and they are usually notified within one month after this has taken place.

### Supplementary Requirements

A supplementary application is necessary as are MCAT scores, which should not be more than 3 years old.

### Curriculum

4-year. Students embark on an intensive program that provides a blend of classroom teaching, clinical experience, and research. The curriculum combines basic science and clinical course content with integrated courses such as the Fundamentals of Biomedicine and clinical and basic neurosciences, as well as an integrated approach to pharmacology, pathology, and oncology. During third- and fourth-year clinical clerkships, students become directly involved in patient care under the guidance of primary care and specialty-trained physicians.

### Facilities

All classroom and study areas support wireless Internet access. Instruction takes place in two amphitheaters equipped with the latest teaching technology. Small classrooms are available for group study and conferences. All facilities are designed to accommodate students; the activities center includes exercise equipment, student lounges, and recreation areas, and places for a variety of competitive sports activities.

### Affiliated Teaching Hospitals

Information not available.

### Housing

Two fraternity houses accommodating 60 men, private rooming houses, and apartments are available in the vicinity.

### Special Programs

The dual degree programs add one or two years to the regular medical school program. A branch campus is located in Swanee, Georgia.

# Lake Erie College of Osteopathic Medicine

LECOM at Seton Hill
One Seton Hill Drive
Greensburg, Pennsylvania    15601

*Phone:* 724-261-2020        *Fax:* 724-261-2021
*E-mail:* admissions@lecom.edu

| Application Filing | | Accreditation | |
|---|---|---|---|
| Earliest: | June 1 | AOA | |
| Latest: | March 1 | **Degrees Granted** | |
| Fee: | $50 | DO | |

### Enrollment: 2008–2009 First-Year Class

| | | | | | |
|---|---|---|---|---|---|
| Men: | 234 | 59% | Applied: | 6563 | |
| Women: | 202 | 41% | Enrolled: | 436 | |
| Out of State: | 2 | 1% | Minorities: | 397 | |

**Tuition and Fees**

| | |
|---|---|
| Resident | 25,900 |
| Average | 30,000 |
| Nonresident | 27,250 |
| Average | 35,000 |

0    10    20    30    40
(in thousands of dollars)

Percentage receiving financial aid: 90%

## Introduction

The College of Medicine was founded in 1992 with the goal of preparing students to become osteopathic physicians. A branch campus is located in Brandenton, Florida. The first 2 years of the educational program are offered on the main campus or branch campus, while clinical training is offered at many clinical training sites.

## Admissions (AACOMAS)

4-year. A bachelors' degree is required for admissions. The basic premedical science courses are required with additional requirements in English and behavioral sciences. Applicants are required to complete the AACOMAS and supplemental applications as well as to submit recent MCAT scores. The applicant should arrange for the submission of a preprofessional advisory committee evaluation and a recommendation from an osteopathic physician. Selected applicants will be invited for an interview.

## Curriculum

The school has designed student-centered curricula that recognize that medical students have different learning styles. Students can enroll in the traditional Lecture-Discussion Pathway, small-group, Problem-Based Learning Pathway, or the individually directed, self-learning Independent Pathway. The main campus in Erie, Pennsylvania, offers all 3 learning pathways. Brandenton campus enrolls all students in the Problem-Based Learning Pathway. All educational pathways begin with 12 weeks of gross anatomy. The school requires students to complete 2 years of Osteopathic Manipulative Medicine Training. The Lecture-Discussion Pathway starts with the core curriculum of basic sciences and introduction to clinical education. After gross anatomy, courses are offered in microbiology, immunology, physiology, biochemistry, pathology, health care management, and spirituality, medicine, and ethics. In the second semester of the first year, the curriculum integrates the basic and clinical science components of each particular human organ system through classroom and small-group instruction/discussion. Lectures offer clinical perspectives from the point of view of both the primary care physician and as the specialist. Students begin clinical experience during the first year working with physician preceptors and learning to take patient histories and conduct physical examinations through the Clinical Osteopathic Diagnostic Applications Course taught by local physicians. The Problem-Based Learning Pathway emphasizes student-centered, self-directed learning. Groups of 8 students meet with the faculty facilitator 3 times per week. A series of cases focus on learning the basic and clinical sciences involved in solving patient problems. Students work independently and in small groups on learning issues at each session. Cases are based on actual patients. Students initially learn only the name, age, gender, and chief complaint. Following discussions, the group will request additional information, such as the results of a history and physical. Additional discussion follows and the students begin to form differential diagnoses requesting additional clinical data such as the results of an EKG or an MRI as needed. Students progress through basic science and onto clinical science as they become better at solving patients' cases at the end of the second year. The Independent Study Pathway provides significant flexibility for students during their first 2 years of medical school. The Pathway requires the student to have excellent organizational and time management skills in order to proceed through the curriculum and meet strict examination deadlines. Modules are divided into Core and Systems. Core modules deal with fundamentals of basic science, while Systems modules integrate basic science and clinical disciplines in an organ systems approach to learning.

## Affiliated Teaching Hospitals

The school is affiliated with more than 80 clinical training sites including hospitals, medical centers, clinics, and physician practices.

## TENNESSEE

# Lincoln Memorial University DeBusk College of Osteopathic Medicine

6965 Cumberland Gap Parkway
Harrogate, Tennessee 37752

*Phone:* 800-325-0900, Ext. 7090 423-869-7090
*Fax:* 423-869-7172
*E-mail:* jonathan.leo@lmunet.edu
*WWW:* lmunet.edu

| Application Filing | | Accreditation |
|---|---|---|
| Earliest: | June 1 | Pending |
| Latest: | February 15 | **Degrees Granted** |
| Fee: | $50 | DO |

### Enrollment: 2008–2009 First-Year Class

| | | | | |
|---|---|---|---|---|
| Men: | 84 | 53% | Applied: | 2039 |
| Women: | 76 | 47% | Enrolled: | 160 |
| Out of State: | 105 | 66% | Minorities: | 10 |

### Tuition and Fees

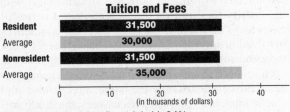

| | |
|---|---|
| **Resident** | 31,500 |
| Average | 30,000 |
| **Nonresident** | 31,500 |
| Average | 35,000 |

(in thousands of dollars)

Percentage receiving financial aid: 94%

## Introduction

4-year. In May 2006, Lincoln Memorial University broke ground on the facility that will house the DeBusk College of Osteopathic Medicine. The state-of-the-art, 4-story building will house lecture halls, laboratories, administrative and faculty offices, classroom space, and a space for research. The building was opened to the inagural class of osteopathic medical students in August 2007.

## Admissions

The school seeks to attract future practitioners to help serve the need for medicine for the southern Appalachian region. It aims also to provide highly qualified phsysicians to underserved communities. The school seeks individuals who are inquisitive, highly compassionate, and eager to serve.

## Supplementary Requirements

A premedical committee letter of recommendation or 2 letters from science professors are required. Also a letter of evaluation from an osteopathic physician is needed.

## Curriculum

The academic program emphasizes the musculoskeletal system in the total body organization. Students will be trained to recognize the inherent capacity within the person to overcome disease and maintain health and to educate physicians to incorporate this therapeutic capacity in their methods of treatment. The program will also seek to provide sufficient academic training to make students recognize health situations that must be referred to a consultant. The curriculum will be divided into 2 phases: a preclinical phase (years 1 and 2) and a clinical phase (years 2 and 3). The goal will be to provide training in problem solving and expertise in diagnosis. The curriculum will also emphasize the integration of the basic and clinical sciences in medical practice. In summary, the curriculum is a system-based approach to learning, formulated on the current state-of-the-arts expanding base.

## Facilities

The campus is a 1-hour drive north of Knoxville. It is housed in a 4-story building, which contains 2 large auditoriums, a learning resource telemedicine/distance learning center, an osteopathic medicine manipulative laboratory, clinic examination rooms, stimulation laboratories, an anatomy laboratory, a library, and a large student lounge. Also available to students is a sports arena and cafeterias.

## Affiliated Teaching Hospitals

Information not available.

## Housing

On-campus housing is available.

## Special Programs

Available graduate programs to osteopathic students are MBA, MED, MS-DS, EDS degrees and teacher licensure certification.

# University of North Texas
# Texas College of Osteopathic Medicine

3500 Camp Bowie Boulevard
Fort Worth, Texas   76107

*Phone:* 817-735-2204          *Fax:* 817-735-2225
*E-mail:* tcomadmissions@hsc.unt.edu
*WWW:* hsc.unt.edu

| Application Filing | | Accreditation |
|---|---|---|
| Earliest: | June 1 | AOA |
| Latest: | November 1 | **Degrees Granted** |
| Fee: | $55 | DO, DO-MPH, DO-PhD |

**Enrollment: 2008–2009 First-Year Class**

| | | | | |
|---|---|---|---|---|
| Men: | 92 | 53% | Applied: | 1986 |
| Women: | 83 | 47% | Enrolled: | 175 |
| Out of State: | 13 | 10% | Minorities: | 26 |

**Tuition and Fees**

| | |
|---|---|
| Resident | 18,598 |
| Average | 30,000 |
| Nonresident | 29,348 |
| Average | 35,000 |

(in thousands of dollars)

Percentage receiving financial aid: 91%

## Introduction
In 1970 the Texas College of Osteopathic Medicine was established. The first class of students graduated in 1974. The next year, the Texas College of Osteopathic Medicine became a state-funded medical school, affiliated with the University of North Texas. Students are encouraged to become family medicine or primary care physicians and to practice in communities where medical practice is most needed. However, some graduates enter specialties outside of primary care.

## Admissions
Each year, TCOM admits approximately 135 students who have demonstrated both the academic ability and personal characteristics to become skilled osteopathic physicians. Applicants are required to submit their application for admission to the Texas Medical and Dental Schools Application Service (TMDSAS) on or before October 15 of the year prior to matriculation. Selected applicants are invited to campus for an interview. TCOM admits applicants through the TMDSAS match. The match is a coordinated admissions process between the state's 7 state-supported medical schools. Application decisions are distributed beginning on February 1 for the next incoming fall class.

## Supplementary Requirements
A supplemental application must be submitted as well as MCAT scores taken within the last 3 years. At least 2 faculty letters of evaluation need to be submitted on the applicant's behalf to the TMDSAS. A letter of recommendation from the applicant's health professions committee may be used as a substitute for faculty evaluations.

## Curriculum
4-year. TCOM utilizes an integrated systems curriculum for the first 2 years. Students learn the scientific fundamentals of medicine through body systems. During the first year, courses such as anatomy, pharmacology, and manipulative medicine are taught simultaneously, so students have an integrated understanding of how the nervous system works or how the cardiovascular system works. Second-year students are introduced to clinical problems related to each body system such as asthma in the respiratory system or arterial disease in the cardiovascular system. Students are exposed to clinical care in the first year. Third-year medical students are required to complete the following core clinical rotations: clinical skills, emergency medicine, family medicine, internal medicine, interal medicine subspecialty, manipulative medicine, mental health, obstetrics and gynecology, pediatrics, primary care partnership, and surgery. Fourth-year medical students have the option to pursue 24 weeks of elective clinical rotations in hospitals and clinics throughout the United States.

## Facilities
The Health Science Center Campus is located in the cultural district of downtown Fort Worth. The gross anatomy laboratory utilizes computers with specialized software packages designed to maximize student awareness of the application of this subject and clinical care. The school has also pioneered the use of simulators in clinical instruction. A large medical library holding prints and electronic materials is available.

## Affiliated Teaching Hospitals
Agreements were made with 20 Texas clinics and hospitals in the state.

## Housing
Apartments or rooms in private homes.

## Special Programs
Dual-degree programs being offered are: DO-PhD, DO-MS. Other dual-degree programs are offered in conjunction with different university divisions.

# VIRGINIA

# Edward Via Virginia College of Osteopathic Medicine

2265 Kraft Drive
Blacksburg, VA   24060

*Phone:* 541-231-6138          *Fax:* 540-231-5252
*E-mail:* admissions@vcom.vt.edu
*WWW:* vcom.vt.edu

| Application Filing | | Accreditation |
|---|---|---|
| Earliest: | May 1 | COCA |
| Latest: | February 1 | **Degrees Granted** |
| Fee: | $85 | DO |

### Enrollment: 2008–2009 First-Year Class

| Men: | 91 | 48% | Applied: | 2725 |
|---|---|---|---|---|
| Women: | 97 | 52% | Enrolled: | 188 |
| Out of State: | 131 | 66% | Minorities: | 50 |

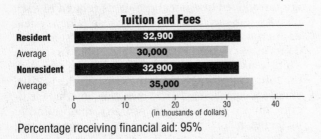

**Tuition and Fees**

- Resident: 32,900
- Average: 30,000
- Nonresident: 32,900
- Average: 35,000

(in thousands of dollars)

Percentage receiving financial aid: 95%

## Introduction

This school is located in the heart of the Blue Ridge and Appalachian mountains. Blacksburg is about 28 miles from Roanoke, Virginia. The school's facilities are in the Corporate Research Center of Virginia Tech. It has state-of-the-art classrooms and learning labs, electronic libraries, and telecommunication facilities. Students enjoy all the amenities of a large campus, including sports, recreation, theater, and music facilities. The school is accredited through the Commission on Osteopathic Accreditation.

The college's mission is to prepare primary care osteopathic physicians, to serve in medically underserved areas of Virginia, North Carolina, the Appalachian region, and adjacent states. It seeks students who are underrepresented in health care and those interested in mission medicine.

## Admissions (AACOMAS)

Completion of a baccalaureate degree is very desirable and the MCAT examination is required. The basic premedical science courses plus courses in English are essential. In addition, letters of recommendation from your college Premedical Advisory Committee, as well as an osteopathic physician who knows you are necessary. An applicant's academic achievement (GPA) and potential, as well as his or her sense of compassion and commitment to primary patient care in a rural setting are critical factors in the admission process. Applicants receiving supplementary forms should return them as soon as possible, no later than March 15.

Applicants deemed qualified will be invited for an interview, after which a decision will be made on their application for admission. Residents of Virginia, North Carolina, and the Appalachian region are encouraged to apply.

## Supplementary Requirements

A supplementary application is necessary. Letters of evaluation from the premedical committee or premedical advisor or, if not available, from 1 or more science faculty is required; in addition, a letter of recommendation from an osteopathic physician is needed.

## Curriculum

The school aims to prepare osteopathic primary care physicians to serve in rural and medically underserved areas of Appalachia. Aside from a strong teaching program in primary care, the school affords students clinical exposure as early as the first year, VCOM has a strong research orientation, which is focused on areas of health and wellness, cardiopulmonary medicine, bones and joints, cancer, neurological problems, and the biology of aging.

## Facilities

The large building housing the college contains 2 separate lecture halls and there are 6 clinical examination rooms where osteopathic manipulation and physical simulation skills are taught. The gross anatomy laboratory is equipped with computers using anatomy software.

## Affiliated Teaching Hospitals

Clinical training is available at numerous hospitals throughout Virginia, including those in the cities of Blacksburg, Salem, and many others.

## Housing

Housing not available, but assistance in securing it is provided.

## Special Programs

The college offers dual-degree programs on both the master's and PhD levels. It also has a special tract for students interested in a career in medical missions as well as a collaborative agreement with Virginia Tech that provides for unique educational experiences in research and sports medicine.

## WASHINGTON

# Pacific Northwest University of Health Sciences College of Osteopathic Medicine

111 South 3rd Street
Yakima, Washington    98901

*Phone:* 509-452-5100          *Fax:* 509-452-5101
*E-mail:* admissions@pnwu
*WWW*.pnwu.org

| Application Filing | | Accreditation |
|---|---|---|
| Earliest: | June 1 | n/a |
| Latest: | April 1 | **Degrees Granted** |
| Fee: | n/a | DO |

### Enrollment: 2008–2009 First-Year Class

| | | | | |
|---|---|---|---|---|
| Men: | 49 | 49% | Applied: | n/a |
| Women: | 51 | 51% | Enrolled: | 100 |
| Out of State: | n/a | | | |

### Tuition and Fees

| | |
|---|---|
| **Resident** | 30,000 |
| Average | n/a |
| **Nonresident** | 2,500 |
| Average | 30,000 |

(in thousands of dollars) 0 — 10 — 20 — 30 — 40

Percentage receiving financial aid: 80%

## Introduction

Pacific Northwest University's College of Osteopathic Medicine was founded in 2005 to provide students with a medical education and training in osteopathic principles, to encourage and promote lifelong intellectual activity, and to obtain in the 5-state region of the Pacific Northwest educational experiences, and increase the number of osteopathic physicians practicing in rural and underserved areas.

## Admissions (AACOMAS)

The minimum academic requirements for admission to the first-year class are a baccalaureate degree from a regionally accredited college or university, MCAT test scores (taken within the last 3 years), and satisfactory completion of courses (1 semester each in English Composition and Literature, and 1 year of general and organic chemistry, physics, and the biological sciences). Letters of recommendation should be sent on the applicant's behalf by a physician (preferably a DO who is a member of AOA), a science faculty member, and a premedical advisor of the premedical committee.

## Supplementary Requirements

A supplementary application, which can be downloaded from the school website, is required.

## Curriculum

The curriculum has been designed to prepare graduates to practice in any setting or specialty. However, the school's educational program is tailored to meet the unique needs of patients in rural underserved areas. Years 1 and 2 will be taught at the Yakima campus and will integrate the basic science curriculum with early clinical exposure. Years 3 and 4 will be spent in the Pacific Northwest 5-state region. The school is constructing an 80,000-square-foot, state-of-the-art facility on its 12-acre campus in the Terrace Heights area of Yakima.

## Affiliated Teaching Hospitals

Information is not available.

## Housing

Students must secure their own housing but the school will assist students in their search for appropriate, affordable housing.

## WEST VIRGINIA

# West Virginia School of Osteopathic Medicine

400 North Lee Street
Lewisburg, West Virginia 24901

*Phone:* 304-647-6373 *Fax:* 304-645-4859
*E-mail:* admissions@wvsom.edu
*WWW:* wvsom.edu

| Application Filing | | Accreditation |
|---|---|---|
| Earliest: | June 1 | AOA |
| Latest: | February 15 | **Degrees Granted** |
| Fee: | $50 | DO |

### Enrollment: 2008–2009 First-Year Class

| | | | | | |
|---|---|---|---|---|---|
| Men: | 119 | 56% | Applied: | 2879 |
| Women: | 92 | 47% | Enrolled: | 211 |
| Out of State: | 146 | 69% | Minorities: | 47 |

**Tuition and Fees**

| | |
|---|---|
| **Resident** | 20,426 |
| Average | 30,000 |
| **Nonresident** | 50,546 |
| Average | 35,000 |

(in thousands of dollars)

Percentage receiving financial aid: 95%

## Introduction

The West Virginia School of Osteopathic Medicine was founded in 1974 as Greenbrier College of Osteopathic Medicine. It became part of the West Virginia system of higher education in 1976. Its 43-acre campus is located in rural Appalachia. Its focus is on training primary care physicians for service in rural communities of West Virginia.

## Admissions (AACOMAS)

Completion of a minimum of 3 years of college, the MCAT, and at least a C+ grade point average are necessary. The basic premedical science courses plus 1 year of English are required. Additional courses in molecular and organic biology are strongly recommended. A CPR certificate is required prior to matriculation. It is expected that a class size of 200 will be selected from the applicant pool. First preference is given to West Virginia applicants. A supplementary application, recommendations from a preprofessional advisory committee and a physician, as well as an interview, are essential elements of the admission process.

## Supplementary Requirements

A supplemental application is required. Also needed is a letter of recommendation from a premedical committee or advisor or approved basic sciences professor. A letter is also required from an osteopathic physician.

## Curriculum

4-year. The curriculum has been designed with the special medical needs of the population of Appalachia in mind. The program emphasizes both the basic and clinical sciences and extensive training in diagnostic skills, including early clinical experiences. Students are prepared for the challenges of a rural practice through exposure to family medicine clerkships. The school has 2 curricular tracts for its students during the first 2 years of the program. *First year and second years:* The System-Based Learning approach has both a classroom and laboratory focus in teaching the basic medical sciences. Integrated with these studies are the principles and practices of osteopathy, physical diagnosis, and physician skills. The Problem-Based Learning approach involves small-group and student-oriented education and involves case studies and structural exercises. Courses in osteopathic manipulative treatment, physical diagnosis, physician skills, and anatomy are taught. *Third and fourth years:* Involves providing students an opportunity to gain direct primary care clinical experience with patients in various settings in the major areas of general medicine, while assuming graduated responsibility. Training sites are distributed statewide in West Virginia.

## Facilities

The Center for Medicine and Technology is the most recent addition to the facilities. It contains 2 modern, 200-seat lecture halls. Other facilities include an expanded gross anatomy lab and Admission Center. An on-campus primary care clinic provides convenient and varied clinical training opportunities for students.

## Affiliated Teaching Hospitals

The college has contractual arrangements with off-campus hospitals and clinics that provide training in the clinical years.

## Housing

There is no on-campus housing, but ample rentals are available in the immediate vicinity.

## Special Programs

Student organizations are active in many civic and health-related activities in the community.

# Medical Practice

Many years of study, a long interval of training, and a lifetime of dedicated service are required in order to become a good physician. It is therefore essential that a premedical student have an overview of the nature of the medical profession. This can be accomplished in a number of different ways, including (1) reading about the activities of medical students, physicians-in-training, and those in practice (see bibliography); (2) talking with medical students and doctors; and (3) performing volunteer work in a hospital.

This chapter seeks to supplement the aforementioned approaches by discussing the most basic elements of medical practice.

The practice of medicine is a combination of both science and art. The scientific component involves the application of technological modalities in solving clinical problems. This requires the judicious use of (1) biochemical methods, (2) biophysical imaging techniques, and (3) therapeutic modalities—areas that have seen remarkable advances over the past decade. Competence in utilizing these areas, while essential, does not meet all the requirements of a good practitioner. What is needed, in addition to the aforementioned elements, is the ability to extract vital information from a mass of contradictory signs and computer-generated data in order to arrive at a tentative diagnosis and determine an appropriate course of action. This involves deciding whether to actively pursue a clinical clue or merely to continue observing as well as judging, if treating the condition involves a greater risk than not treating it at all. This combination of knowledge, judgment, and intuition is the key to the art of medicine.

Medical practice requires scientific knowledge, technical skill, and human understanding. The last quality involves treating the patient with tact and sympathy and realizing that a patient is a human being, not merely a collection of symptoms, damaged organs, and/or disturbed emotions. The physician must recognize that the patient is, at the same time, fearful and hopeful, and in need of relief, assistance, and reassurance. To meet this challenge, the physician must genuinely care for people.

## PHYSICIAN-PATIENT RELATIONSHIP

As stated above, physicians must recognize that patients are not the equivalent of cases or diseases; they are individuals, whose problems often transcend the complaints they are verbalizing. They frequently are anxious and frightened when they visit their physicians and may try to convince themselves that their illness does not exist. They may even try unconsciously to divert attention from the real problem that they perceive to be threatening. At times, illness is used as a means to gain attention or as a way to extricate themselves from a difficult emotional situation. With this in mind, physicians need to view their clinical findings in a broader context involving not only the patient but the patient's family and social background.

Knowledge of the patient's origin, education, home, family, job, and goals is very desirable. It provides useful information that permits the physician to establish rapport with the patient and to develop a good insight into the patient's illness. Under these circumstances, mutual trust is developed and an open channel of communication is established.

The traditional one-on-one patient-physician relationship is changing due to the change in the setting in which medicine is practiced today. Frequently, when dealing with a serious illness, patient care involves a variety of allied health professionals, in addition to several medical specialists. A health team effort is therefore commonly mandated, which can prove especially beneficial if the primary care physician asserts a leadership position and maintains a special status in the patient's eyes. The primary care physician needs to retain the ultimate decision-making authority in the areas of diagnosis and treatment. This arrangement should also be in effect when medicine is practiced in a group setting, for it is the primary care physician who has an overview of the patient's problems and reaction to medications, as well as knowing the patient's response to his or her illness and to the challenges that must be faced.

The modern hospital can be an intimidating environment for most patients. Being confined to bed, surrounded by buttons, air jets, and lights, with one's body invaded by tubes and wires, visited randomly and at all hours of the day and night by members of the health care team—physicians, nurses, technicians, therapists, and aides—often stimulates a loss of a patient's sense of reality. This negative situation may be further reinforced by transporting the patient to X-ray departments or special testing and/or therapy facilities.

The primary care physician frequently serves as the pivotal link between the patient and reality. The stressful hospital situation can be somewhat ameliorated by a strong doctor-patient relationship.

There are a number of factors that lead to impersonalization of medical care. These include:

1. strong efforts to reduce the cost of health care;
2. heavy reliance on computerization and technological advances for diagnosis and treatment;
3. growth of health maintenance organizations (HMOs), which may not allow patients to select their physician;
4. need for more than one physician to be involved in the care of seriously ill patients;
5. increased mobility of physicians and patients;
6. increased frequency of litigation by patients to express their dissatisfaction with their physicians or treatment or results.

In the light of this medical climate, it is especially challenging for physicians to maintain a humanistic attitude. It is now even more essential that each patient, regardless of personal circumstances, be treated carefully and courteously. This means that the physician-patient relationship needs to be built on a foundation of respect, integrity, and compassion. The level of communication between both sides should allow the patient, to the fullest possible extent, to gain an understanding of the nature of the illness, the treatment protocol, and prognosis.

In dealing with patients, the physician should avoid being judgmental of their values and lifestyles unless it is medically relevant (for example, smoking and alcohol or substance abuse, which should be firmly discouraged). In the course of one's practice, every physician can anticipate meeting patients who evoke negative, as well as positive, emotional reactions. Physicians need to be aware of this possibility and should not allow their judgment or actions to interfere with their patients' best interests.

In order to treat a patient effectively, a good relationship between physician and patient must be established. This mainly depends on the empathetic response on the part of the physician and recognition of the physician's caring attitude by the patient.

## CLINICAL SKILLS

The basic three-step approach used by physicians in diagnosing disease involves taking a patient's history, performing a physical examination, and ordering laboratory tests and/or imaging procedures. These steps are discussed in-depth below:

### History Taking

All the facts in the patient's medical history should be noted in the written record. The history can be recorded in one of two ways: (1) it can be recorded in chronological order, in which case recent events should be emphasized most; or (2) if a problem-oriented approach is used, the problems that are clinically most pronounced should be noted first. The nature of the symptoms should be in the patient's own words. In eliciting the history, the physician needs to be careful to avoid suggesting answers in the course of guiding the patient through the interview. It is important that careful attention be given to all the details of the interview, no matter how minor, since a seemingly small detail may be important in making the diagnosis.

More than an organized listing of symptoms, a well-written history, elicited during the interview, should also reveal something about the patient, in addition to the nature of the patient's disease. This information may be extracted from facial expressions, voice inflections, and the attitude that is evident during the discussion of the illness. Taking a history is a challenge since patients are highly subjective in their presentation and may also be affected by their past experience. In addition, there is a fear of disability or even death, as the impact of illness on one's family inevitably influences a person's account of the problem. Unfortunately, language or sociological obstacles, as well as failing mental recall, can, in some cases, very significantly interfere with the patient giving an adequate history. In such cases, the physician may have to seek the help of an interpreter or a member of the patient's family in order to obtain an accurate history. The physician's skill, knowledge, patience, and experience will greatly influence the quality of the history taken.

Obtaining a family medical history can be very helpful in short-term care and preventive health. The process of history taking also serves to establish or strengthen the physician-patient relationship. Patients should be put at ease and should be allowed to express their thoughts. The confidential nature of the information should be emphasized.

### Physical Examination

Physical signs are objective and verifiable evidence of disease. Their significance is enhanced when these signs confirm a structural or functional change indicated by the patient's history. On occasion, the physical signs may be the only evidence of disease, especially if the history is not informative.

The physical exam should be carried out methodically and thoroughly. While the focus of the exam may be on the diseased area or organ, in a new patient the exam should cover the entire body. The results should be recorded at the time they are obtained. Skill in this area is required and comes with time.

## Laboratory Tests

The increase in the number, type, and availability of laboratory tests has resulted in the increased reliance on this approach for the solution of clinical problems. It is essential to bear in mind that laboratory tests are often believed by physicians to be the final authority, regardless of possible fallibility of the tests, the individuals handling or interpreting them, or of the instruments. Laboratory data cannot replace observation of the patient. Both the expense and possibilities of misinterpretation of the lab tests ordered should be taken into account by the physician. Laboratory tests are rarely done individually, but rather as batteries (24 up to 40). The various combinations of lab tests are frequently quite useful. The thoughtful use of screening tests should not be confused with indiscriminate lab testing. Screening tests are useful because they enable the physician to obtain a group of lab results conveniently, utilizing a single specimen of blood, at relatively low cost. Biochemical measurements, together with simple lab tests, such as blood counts, urine analyses, and sedimentation rate often provide the principle clue to the presence of a pathological process. The physician must be alert for abnormalities in screening test results that may not indicate significant disease. An isolated laboratory abnormality on an otherwise well patient should not provoke an in-depth medical workup. The lab test itself may bear repeating to see if the results are reproducible. The physician can then determine whether the results are significant. Clinical judgment will determine how to proceed if this occurs.

## Imaging Techniques

Over the past quarter of a century, the use of imaging techniques as a diagnostic method has become well established. This includes ultrasonography, a method of examination using soundwaves to visualize internal organs; computerized axial tomography (CAT); magnetic resonance imaging (MRI); and position emission tomography (PET). This major new diagnostic approach has frequently replaced invasive techniques that require insertion into the body of tubes, wires, or catheters or surgical biopsy. The latter are frequently painful and at times quite risky to the patient. While very valuable, imaging technique results need validation and are often extremely expensive. Therefore, this approach should be used judiciously, but not as a supplement to invasive techniques.

# DIAGNOSING DISEASE

Arriving at a diagnosis involves analysis and synthesis—two aspects of logic. The physician identifies all the problems raised after hearing the patient's complaints, performing a physical exam, and receiving lab findings. Most physicians try to place the medical problem they are dealing with into one of several syndromes. A syndrome is a group of symptoms associated with any disease process, which constitutes together a picture of the disease.

The syndrome incorporates a hypothesis concerning a tissue, organ, or organ system. For example, congestive heart failure will produce a wide variety of symptoms, all of which are connected to the single pathophysiological mechanism, namely inadequacy of the heart muscle. Similarly, identifying a syndrome usually narrows down the number of possibilities for an illness and suggests ordering relevant clinical and lab studies.

Making a diagnosis is more difficult if one cannot categorize the patient's signs and symptoms. Nevertheless, the same logical approach, starting with the symptoms, proceeding to the physical findings, and lab results will usually lead to a diagnosis.

Diagnosing disease can prove at times very challenging and require considerable intellectual and physical effort. With the advances in laboratory and imaging technology, the task has been made much easier, but there are times when even these modalities do not provide satisfying answers. The physician should not hesitate to consult a specialist to help establish a probable diagnosis.

# PATIENT CARE

This issue is initiated with the establishment of a personal relationship between the physician and patient. The effectiveness of therapeutic measures prescribed is enhanced in the presence of a sense of confidence and trust. Reassurance by the physician under these conditions may be all that is necessary to improve the patient's well-being. Similarly, for illnesses that are not easily treatable, a sense by the patient that the physician is doing everything possible is an essential therapeutic approach.

Clinical decision making should involve the patient, especially where quality of life issues are concerned. In such cases, a determination of what the patient values most should be made after lengthy conversation between physician and patient. When it is not medically possible to eliminate the disease and its consequences, improving the quality of life should of course be the treatment goal.

# ASSESSING TREATMENT

Objective standards are usually used in judging the effectiveness of treatment. The patient measures the outcome in terms of relief of pain and preservation of or regaining lost function. Although subjective, a patient's state of health can be divided into a number of components: bodily comfort; physical, social, professional, and personal activities; sexual and cognitive functions; sleep; overall view of one's health; and general sense of well-being. Relative to these components, the patients' views of their disabilities can be obtained by verbal exchanges. Proper medical practice requires the consideration of both the objective and subjective aspects of treatment outcome.

## Drug Therapy

New drugs are introduced every year. While it is hoped that they are significantly better than their predecessors, many have only a marginal advantage. With this in mind, a cautious approach should be used in dealing with a new medication, unless it is established with certainty to be a real advance. Otherwise, it is preferable to continue to use established drugs whose benefits and side-effects are known to the treating physician.

Over the next few decades, the practice of medicine will be greatly influenced by the health care needs of the elderly. It is estimated that the number of individuals over 65 will triple in the next 30 years. For this reason it is important for the physician to be familiar with the different responses of the elderly patient to disease. The physician must also be knowledgeable about common disorders that occur with aging and altered response of the elderly patient to medication.

## Iatrogenic Disorders

These disorders refer to those generated by a testing or treatment modality and are not connected to the existing medical condition.

The judicious use of powerful medical tools requires that the physician consider their action, potential dangers, and costs. Every medical procedure carries certain risks; however, to benefit from the advances of modern medicine, reasonable risks need to be taken. Reasonable means considering both positive and negative aspects of a procedure and determining what is more desirable under the circumstances. Special attention must be given to the use of medications, which in some instances can generate more harm than good.

The physician's use of language and behavior can at times lead to needless anxiety if the patient is given a misleading impression of his or her condition. Being involved with treating the disease should not shift the physician's concern from the overall well-being and economic welfare of the patient.

# ACCOUNTABILITY

Over the past several decades, there have been increased demands that physicians account for the way in which they practice by meeting certain federal and state standards. The hospitalization of patients whose care is funded by the government is subject to utilization review. This procedure requires the physician to defend the reason for the patient's hospital stay if it extends beyond the established average standard. Elective surgery, in some cases, requires a second opinion. The purpose of these regulations is to try to limit the high cost of health care. Probably, all aspects of medical practice will in time be subjected to this type of review, which will profoundly alter medical practice.

Other approaches that may be used to judge continuing competence of physicians are an assessment of continuing education, auditing patients' records, reexamination for recertification, and time-limited certification as a prerequisite for relicensing. Such requirements clearly improve a physician's factual knowledge, but it is uncertain if they similarly effect the quality of practice.

# GUIDELINES TO PRACTICING MEDICINE

Physicians have at their disposal a large number of diagnostic techniques and therapeutic modalities. The challenge is to select the most appropriate and cost-effective approach for the specific patient and that clinical condition. Formal clinical practice guidelines are being developed by government and professional organizations. These guidelines ensure that no patient, regardless of financial status, receives substandard care; protection is provided to the physician against inappropriate malpractice charges; and the insurance company is protected against excessive use of medical resources. There are, however, negative aspects to the use of guidelines. There may be major differences of opinion on the routine use of certain procedures, such as mammography. Guidelines, by being broadly applicable, cannot take into account the genetic and environmental effects on individuals. Therefore, the key is to utilize the guidelines as a meaningful framework while maintaining the flexibility to judge each case in the overall context of the reasonable standards set by knowledgeable clinicians. Under these circumstances, medicine will remain a learned profession rather than a mere technical vocation.

## Cost Effectiveness in Medical Care

With the spiraling cost of health care, it is necessary to establish priorities as to how money is allocated. There is a greater emphasis today on the prevention of diseases. There is much that physicians can do to foster cost control but socioeconomic concerns should not interfere with the welfare of the patient.

# TEACHING AND RESEARCH

It is obligatory for physicians to share their knowledge with colleagues, medical students, and members of the allied professions. Advances in medical knowledge depend on acquiring new information from various types of research, both basic and clinical. Publicizing this information can bring about improved medical care. Where appropriate, physicians should encourage participation in ethical clinical investigations.

Examples of preventive health measures include immunization for a variety of childhood diseases, mammography and Pap smears for women to screen for breast and uterine cancer, colonoscopy and PSA testing (for men) to screen for colon cancer and prostate cancer, and influenza immunization for all patients over 50 as well as those patients with chronic diseases such as diabetes and hypertension. Such an approach can be most beneficial to long-term health, however, many private health insurers are not yet promoting this approach to health care, in spite of its undeniable benefits.

# TYPES OF PRACTICES

In the final year of postgraduate medical training (unless you are enrolled in the armed forces), planning ahead for opening a practice is essential. This involves determining the location as well as the nature of your practice. Many considerations are involved in both issues. They need to be carefully considered before making a final decision.

Location considerations include not only personal preferences regarding the type of community—rural or urban—but also how strong will be the demand for your services and for how long. In other words, a pediatrician obviously would not consider an area where the predominant population is made up of retirees. Even if you plan to join an older physician and ultimately take over his or her practice, you need to assess the likelihood of demand for your services down the line if the neighborhood changes.

As to the nature of your practice, it is important to determine if you prefer to start on your own or work for others. There are several options in each of three major categories, solo, group and salaried practice. These will be explored below.

## Solo Practitioners

Solo practitioners currently still remain the largest group of practicing physicians, but their numbers are diminishing as the health care system changes. These physicians have direct contact with each one of their patients as the provider of professional services. In exchange for remuneration they are personally responsible for their patients' health. They operate out of their own office or time-share one with others.

There are several advantages to this traditional form of practice, particularly for primary care physicians, internists, pediatricians, and obstetricians/gynecologists. These include establishing long-term relationships, in most cases. (People do move out of the area or are dissatisfied and select someone else.) Another consideration is the independence that solo practice permits. Solo practitioners determine the location of their practice, arrange their office to their liking, hire the personnel they think they need and who they want to employ, select the laboratories that will perform their tests, set their own office hours, fees, and all the many other elements associated with a practice. To a large extent, therefore, they determine the extent of the success of their own practice.

On the negative side, there is the factor of uncertainty of how rapidly their practice will grow and how frequently they will get referrals from others; consequently, the rate of growth of their income will be unpredictable. Initially their income may be less than that of salaried practitioners whose expenses are paid for by their employers. Another major consideration is that solo practitioners assume full liability for the unavoidable overhead associated with such a practice. Another factor is the need to have coverage on days off or during vacations.

With the marked increase in paperwork required for Medicare, Medicaid, and insurance reimbursement, an additional heavy burden and expense has been placed on physicians. This issue adds to the already restricted autonomy of physicians due to federal, state, and insurance company regulations that evaluate the appropriateness of patient treatment and tests and set guidelines for the length of hospitalization.

There are a number of variations to solo practice that try to reduce some of its negative features. The following are some examples:

### Solo-HMO Practice

Many established solo practitioners seeking to maintain this form of patient care that they have long been accustomed to, but realizing the changing situation in health care economics, have made a significant adjustment. They have decided to keep their solo practice, but at the same time be linked to an HMO accepting their lower levels of reimbursement and making up for it with a large volume of patients, for each of whom they receive a monthly stipend, if in a capitated HMO, or a reduced fee-for-service payment if in a noncapitated HMO.

### Associateship

For younger physicians, establishing an expense-sharing relationship with another physician in the same specialty can be mutually rewarding. In such an arrangement both physicians agree to maintain their own solo practice and to share office expenses (rent, staff, etc.) in a proportionately acceptable way. The details of this relationship do not necessarily require a formal legal contract, but a written outline in the form of a memorandum of understanding should be signed by both associates. In the case of an association with a senior physician, the benefits for the younger practitioner being in practice with an established physician include an opportunity to obtain easier community recognition, a chance to learn the management aspects of a medical practice, a readily available consultant, and a way to keep operating costs down at a time when income levels are just building up. For the senior associate, such a relationship provides the benefit of having a covering physician readily available, providing an opportunity for more leisure time. It also lowers operating costs at a time when income may be declining, since it occurs in the last phase of professional life. Very often, an associateship can lead to a partnership; in such a case, a contract providing full details of the nature of the arrangement concerning the division of both income and expenses is essential.

### Acquiring a Practice

Another way to establish a solo practice is to purchase one from a retiring or relocating physician. One can secure a practice in which the potential can be estimated based upon the practice's past performance. It is important to get an accurate assessment of the value of such a practice, which calls for an analysis of income, assets, and liabilities.

## Group Practice

This is the second most popular form of practice. It is defined as three or more physicians, who provide medical care, jointly using the same facility and personnel and dividing the income as agreed to by the group. A group practice may be a corporation, a partnership, or an association of solo practitioners, but the majority of group practices are corporations. This arrangement provides a legal mechanism to protect the assets of the corporation from being seized in the event a member of the group is sued for malpractice and loses and cannot make full restitution from personal assets.

The number of group practices is increasing because they provide several advantages. They allow for a pooling of expenses for facilities, technical support services, and equipment, all of which come from a common revenue base. In other words, where the purchase of a piece of expensive equipment, such as an MRI machine, by an individual radiologist may well be prohibitive, a group can more readily afford it. This is because groups have the financial resources and space, and can use expensive equipment more fully to make it pay off. In addition, patient loads can be juggled easier so that, when one group member is occupied, another can be made available to the patient. The group members can easily schedule night coverage, vacation time, and emergency care.

Members of a group work shorter and more regular hours than solo practitioners. When a group has five or more members, income is on a par with that of physicians who are self-employed. In a successful group, a business manager may be hired to handle the many time-consuming bureaucratic aspects of an active practice and also supervise and coordinate personnel activities. Also, in a group practice, each physician has colleagues available to consult when necessary.

There are some negative aspects to group practice, such as the loss of independence by being a member of a group. Also, major business decisions regarding purchasing equipment, hiring or firing personnel, renovating, relocating, or expanding facilities require a consensus. For a group to practice successfully requires a compatibility of personalities and professional outlooks. Also, as implied above, in groups that are smaller than five—which is very common—income levels may well be lower than those of solo practitioners, since the number of patients may be restricted to space and personnel limitations.

As with most issues, therefore, there are both positive and negative sides to being a member of a group practice. If you are considering it, you need to be cautious and thoroughly evaluate the nature of the practice and determine if you would be compatible with the group members. Certainly you should be the type of person who is a team player before you enter any group practice; however, the rewards of being a member of a successful group practice can readily outweigh its disadvantages.

## Salaried Practitioners

These are physicians who work under contract for private hospitals, governmental institutions (hospitals, clinics, or agencies), commercial, industrial, or insurance companies or HMOs (see below), and receive a fixed remuneration for their services rendered over a given amount of time. This type of practice is especially appealing to those just beginning their practice. Over half of those completing their postgraduate training begin this way and many move on to solo or group practices.

The advantages to those starting a medical practice as a salaried employee are clear. The principle reason given by many is to avoid the financial strain of having to cope with a relatively low income for many months when beginning a new solo practice and taking the gamble of succeeding, especially at a time when the new practitioner is perhaps still burdened by heavy student loans. It is extremely challenging under these conditions to have to sign an office lease, order furniture and equipment, engage a staff, and arrange for the many other requirements a new solo practice mandates.

A further element influencing a physician's career planning at an early stage is the knowledge that national economic trends, such as inflation and depression, as well as such issues as personal and professional contacts, can markedly impact on the degree of success in private practice. Achieving an active practice depends on more than one's technical skills as a physician.

Being a salaried physician provides a means of avoiding the aforementioned risks while at the same time realizing many benefits. These include a secure position with reasonably good remuneration and an attractive benefit package that includes health care coverage (medical and dental for both physician and their family), paid vacations, holidays, sick leave, and shorter, defined working hours.

On the other hand, there are significant disadvantages to being a salaried practitioner, including a limit on one's income, which is generally less than that of successful solo practitioners (unless maintaining a limited outside practice is allowed). In addition, there is a loss of autonomy as a salaried practitioner. The latter includes having to respond to directives of the administration for whom one works and having to satisfy one's immediate supervisor. As a result of these liabilities, there is a marked tendency for physicians to undertake salaried appointments initially and, after a few years, move on to solo or group practices. Within six to eight years of beginning practice, therefore, the number of salaried physicians diminishes from well above half to under a third. In addition, the decline in the number of salaried employees varies for different specialties: Naturally, pathologists are 100% salaried with surgeons and psychiatrists being under 50%.

## Health Maintenance Organization (HMO) Practitioners

Practitioners working for HMOs can be found in all of the employment options discussed above, depending on the organization's structure. Increasingly, HMOs are becoming a major source of employment for physicians and will undoubtedly become even more important as the health care system changes over the next several decades. Three types of arrangements are possible:

### *Staff Position*

This is a salaried appointment under contract. It is a very common position for a new physician who intends, in a relatively short period of time, to go into solo practice or join a group. It provides an opportunity to improve one's skills, develop self-confidence, and earn enough money to begin paying off debts. Physicians employed under such an arrangement do not share in the HMO's profits (or losses).

### Group Member Position

In this case the physician members sign on as partners and as such have a direct interest in the success of the organization whose profits they share. This arrangement is an option for those physicians for whom salaried or solo practices are not attractive because they prefer fixed hours and wish to avoid all the other burdens that a private practice involves, even if it means possibly having a lower income.

### Affiliated Position

This is an arrangement where physicians who belong to a group known as an Independent Practitioners Association (IPA) are contracted to serve a segment of an HMO's patient load. The primary activities of such physicians are outside of the HMO and not involved in the organization's business success.

## Locum Tenens

After completing residency training, some physicians, albeit a minority, have opted to defer their decision for a while and have elected a more mobile form of practice. They have chosen to serve as substitutes in areas where there is a shortage of doctors. They are called *locum tenens*, the Latin name for place holder. They usually obtain their position through a placement agency, but some freelance. The *locum tenens* concept was developed to entice physicians to come to rural areas and to keep them there. They were used to substitute for physicians who wanted time off for vacations and continuing education, or who were ill. To replace them during such intervals, a network of temporary physicians was organized.

Currently, it is estimated that 12,000 physicians in every age group and specialty are working as *locum tenens*. While the majority of them are over 50 and semiretired, the fastest growing group are recent residency graduates. The reasons for engaging in this work are the desire to travel and the opportunity to explore a variety of different practices. In addition, since this is a way to keep living expenses down, new physicians can use their savings to more rapidly pay off their medical school loans.

For some new practitioners this may prove to be a good transitional phase but they need to be aware of all of the ramifications. An assignment may last for a few days or several months and may vary from steady work in one area to practicing in widely separated locations. In addition, practitioners are responsible for their own health insurance. A major consideration is the impact of relocating one's family, both in physical and psychological terms, and it can prove costly in view of the need to store some belongings and ship others. Naturally, for single people, these problems are less troublesome.

There are currently about 25 agencies placing physicians, with CompHealth-Kron being the largest, but some prefer the freelance route. The key to success using this approach is to arrange a steady flow of assignments using an organized marketing plan. In addition to this substantial challenge, the freelancers must handle all the administrative details, such as obtaining and paying for medical licenses and malpractice insurance, travel and housing arrangements, etc., normally taken care of by the booking agency for a fee, which may be up to 40% of the client's income.

## Practicing Abroad

Physicians seeking opportunities to serve overseas can contact the following sources for information:

National Council for International Health
1701 K Street NW Suite 600
Washington, DC 20006
(202) 833-5900

Health Volunteers Overseas
P.O. Box 65157
Washington Station
Washington, DC 20035-5157
(202) 296-0928

St. Joseph Medical Center
P.O. Box 1935
South Bend, Indiana 46634
(219) 237-7637

## Volunteerism

Free clinics came into being in the 1960s. They primarily served the homeless and the underprivileged. While many still cater to indigent populations, numerous clinics serve working people who lack insurance coverage. What was originally begun as a fringe movement has evolved into a significant—if only partial—way to alleviate the health care crisis.

Free clinics provide physicians a chance to serve patients unencumbered by red tape and insurance regulations. They offer quality medical care that would otherwise not be available, because they operate on the principle that health care is a right and not a privilege. At most free clinics, part-time volunteer physicians (and medical students) offer out-patient primary care assisted by volunteer lay people. Administrative chores may be handled by salaried personnel and care is usually provided on the basis of genuine need. Many patients earn too much to qualify for public assistance, but too little to pay for medical benefits through insurance coverage.

To accommodate their working clientele, free clinics are usually open during the evenings. Most consist of an examining room, a small lab, and a dispensary, and can usually have some lab and X-ray work performed at local facilities. The sites of free clinics vary, some being in donated church basements; others in better facilities. In most cases, clinics need to be accessible to public transportation and an area considered safe by the volunteers. Since clinics usually do not receive governmental support, they are free from paper work and needed funds are supplied by grants, donations, and fund-raising events.

Physicians donate their time in varying amounts ranging from once a week to once every several months. Interns and residents—whose time is extremely limited—offer their services out of a desire to contribute to the welfare of the community. Some volunteer physicians are retirees.

Perhaps one of the considerations causing physicians to be reluctant to donate time is the malpractice liability issue. All states have Good Samaritan laws, but they vary, and not all offer free clinics immunity from negligence suits.

The high cost of prescription drugs presents a special problem: Free clinics try to secure samples donated by physicians or pharmaceutical companies or they distribute generic drugs that they purchase.

At this time free clinics offer a much-needed outlet for worthwhile services that the medical community can provide.

# PROFESSIONAL HAZARDS

The practice of medicine, like other professions, has inherent occupational hazards, such as becoming infected with a bacterium or virus, and the very real risk of being sued for malpractice. Physicians take precautions for such problems by being careful in their management techniques and treatment and securing adequate liability insurance coverage. In addition, there is a more subtle way in which physicians can be severely impaired. In the intense drive to achieve professional success, they may ignore their own families, fail to form abiding personal friendships, never develop hobbies or find the time for relaxation and introspection. As in other professions, the obsession with success can lead to one becoming a workaholic and, in all too many cases, to the abuse of alcohol or drugs.

Work-related problems may stem from the combination of long working hours and the pursuit of excellence, causing physicians to lose sight of their own personal needs. They may repress and deny the strains, stresses, fatigue, and disappointments that are inevitable with the practice of medicine.

Patients can make enormous demands on their physicians, while the physicians themselves sometimes come to believe that they are invincible. This feeling is reinforced by the fact that they have successfully surmounted a vigorous and lengthy training regimen, replete with intense challenges and often demeaning activities. Further strengthening the all-powerful feeling is the success of becoming part of an elite group where their egos are enlarged by the adulation of patients, subordinates, and even colleagues. Maintaining this status demands enormous dedication and at times calls for others to "slow down and take it easy." Holding onto and even increasing one's monetary rewards can become a major driving force in professional life and being part of a "team" or medical group can increase the pressure for intensive activity.

After many years in active practice, physicians may find it difficult to retire; the respect and gratitude of patients can become an important element of their life. Retirement may therefore be delayed out of fear of boredom, the loss of personal satisfaction and financial rewards, or simply the fear of finding a new lifestyle. Physicians who continue to practice after their skills have begun to diminish risk making decisions that could be detrimental to themselves, their associates, and, most of all, their patients. However, with the changes in the practice of medicine today, more and more physicians are retiring at an early age rather than deal with the bureaucracy, mountains of paper work, and drop in income.

The changing climate in health care will have significant impact on the practice and rewards of the medical profession. It will challenge physicians to be even more alert to the potential dangers and require that they consider their own basic needs and periodically reevaluate the demands that they place on themselves and the toll that it takes.

## PHYSICIAN REMUNERATION

It is thought by many that the recession of the 1980s contributed significantly to the substantial increase in the medical school applicant pool during the following decade. This is due to the perception that a career as a physician can ensure economic security.

The prospective physician needs to recognize that, while the income of physicians-in-training during post-graduate years has gone up over the past decade, in reality, other considerations come into play. New physicians starting their own practice need to be concerned with the unknown impact that the approaching changes in the health care system will have. They also need to take into consideration major overhead costs, such as those associated with purchasing medical equipment, malpractice insurance, office rental, employee salaries, etc. It is therefore more meaningful to deal with median net income, as shown in the accompanying graph. It demonstrates, over the past 25 years, a similar income pattern for each of the five-year periods, except at a higher overall level. We therefore find that there is a steep rise in income for the first dozen years. It rises less sharply over the next five years and peaks between 20 and 25 years, when the physician is about 50 years old. After a quarter of a century of practice, income gradually declines.

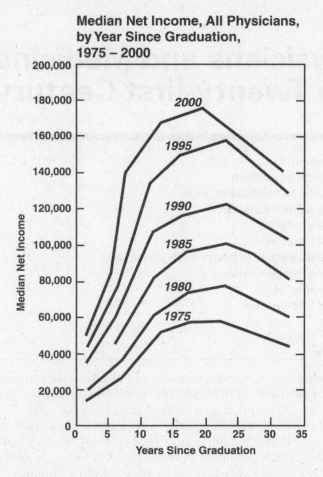

**Median Net Income, All Physicians, by Year Since Graduation, 1975 – 2000**

Median Net Income (vertical axis): 0 to 200,000
Years Since Graduation (horizontal axis): 0 to 35

Lines labeled: 2000, 1995, 1990, 1985, 1980, 1975

## Remuneration in the Future

During the next century, it is quite questionable whether the pattern of the last 25 years as outlined above will be maintained. Indicators suggest that a leveling off or even possible decrease may be taking place from a peak median net annual income of nearly $175,000. This is particularly true for salaried physicians employed in group practices, hospitals, and health maintenance organizations. This potential trend reversal in the remuneration pattern will result from the steadily increasing power of managed care providers that are gaining dominance in a market containing an abundance of physicians who are seeking to tap into the patient pool.

Among physician employers, HMOs pay less since they feel they provide regular working hours and assume the expenses for office and malpractice insurance. Within this market, indications are that primary care physicians (family physicians, internists, and pediatricians) may be in a more favorable position in terms of remuneration. Their salaries may actually increase as a result of the fact that they are assuming the vital role of "gatekeeper" to the medical care establishment.

A relatively recent study indicates that physician income is not rising as fast as other professional practices. For example, the average net income for primary care physicians, after adjusting for inflation, declined 10% from 1993 to 2003 to around to $121,600, while the average adjusted net income for medical specialists slipped 2% during this period.

# Physicians and Medicine in the Twenty-first Century

The challenge
Premedical education
Admission to medical school
Medical school education
Medical students
Medical practice
Specialists versus primary care physicians
Medical litigation crisis
Cybermedicine
Medical informatics

## THE CHALLENGE

The description of the unfortunate state of physician training published in 1910 in the Flexner report served to revolutionize medical education in the United States. As this century nears its end, a new crisis seems to be looming. U.S. schools are producing some of the most technologically well-trained physicians in the world; nevertheless, critics argue that while our educational system is readily meeting the challenges of our technological advancement in medicine, it is failing in other respects. Physicians-in-training are being overwhelmed by the exploding volume of scientific knowledge and are not equipped to face the oncoming changing health care environment.

The planned reforms in the health care system will probably alter it dramatically and it is therefore essential that students be kept informed of the needs and opportunities that emerge. It is believed that one of the most significant needs will be for primary care physicians, and a surplus of specialists is predicted early in the twenty-first century. Thus, health care reform is linked to medical education reform, because overreliance on specialists results in excessive costs and reduced access to health care. Additionally, market factors have not served to equalize distribution and specialists are less likely to practice in rural areas.

The decade between 1980 and 1990 saw a drop in the percentage of primary care physicians from 40% to about 30%. Some believe that medical education contributed to this downward trend, due to the fact that the first two years of medical school usually provides little clinical exposure and, in the last two years, student role models are subspecialists. In addition, many schools still do not require clerkships in family medicine. Some students are told by their teachers that general practice is not challenging enough. Others are dissuaded by the heavy debt loads that they have built up in medical school. Primary care is less remunerative than specialties; therefore, eliminating this debt is more difficult for a primary care physician than a specialist.

The response to demographic shifts in population has also been slow on the part of the medical education establishment. Minority groups are the fastest growing population segment, mandating an awareness of the impact of socioeconomic conditions that are specific to them. There is an increasing call for education in *population medicine,* considering the impact of social and economic factors on health. In addition, there is a belief that medical students are not taught disease prevention or how to encourage good health habits.

Preparing medical students to work in the new managed health care environment is another major challenge. In such settings, a health care team effort involves such allied health care professionals as physician assistants or advanced practice nurses, but this experience does not usually occur while one is a student.

There are those who feel that interpersonal and communication skills are not adequately emphasized during the educational phase. In addition, the system tends to diminish the students' sense of altruism during the course of their demanding education but some efforts to improve this situation have been initiated.

Educators argue that the curriculum is presently full and will become overloaded as biomedical information expands into new areas. Incorporating new information presents another challenge. Problem-based learning is an approach being tried in order to address this issue. The supporters of this educational method believe that the teaching under this system is more relevant and the students are therefore more inclined to become lifelong learners. Many are using actors as standardized patients to present certain symptoms and thus better evaluate clinical competence. Increased use of computers can prove beneficial in the learning process.

Impeding better integration of the basic and clinical sciences is thought by some to be the timing of the USMLE, with Step 1 covering the basics and Step 2 the clinical sciences. Some have urged combining them, with both steps taken at the end of the medical education program, thus eliminating the focus of teaching solely for board preparation. Reforms that involve providing students with earlier clinical experience are difficult and costly to bring about. Translating sound ideas into practice presents major problems. In addition, central curriculum planning is frequently opposed at the departmental level.

There are those who call for reexamining the mission of medical schools, especially at state institutions. The reassessment, if undertaken, can result in significant reforms.

Another problem is the lack of continuity between undergraduate and graduate education. Several schools are initiating programs that serve to combine both of these phases, with the usual aim being to encourage primary care.

More radical suggestions being heard are related to shortening medical education by accepting students into medical schools after their junior year in college and to eliminating the last year of medical school, which is in significant part devoted to securing a residency appointment. Thus, the undergraduate process would be reduced to six years, which is an option offered by a number of schools and is standard in Europe. Shortening the educational process would lower the debt obligations of medical students and, consequently, may reduce the pressures to seek training in higher paid subspecialties so as to wipe out such debt sooner and easier. This debt problem and its impact has prompted calls to make medical school tuition-free, an approach that in some quarters is being seriously considered. Supporters of this goal feel that it reinforces the concept that medicine is a profession with social obligations. Behind this approach is the desire to mandate that half of the residency appointments should be in primary care. Tuition relief, if elected, would be traded off by future professional choice limitation. There are even calls for a national program of mandatory service obligation. While it is quite unlikely that it will be introduced, some schools are requiring that their students perform community activities.

To graduate more socially responsible physicians, some schools are reviewing admission criteria and are looking beyond grades and MCAT scores to such factors as altruism and community involvement. To better judge this, some have appointed lay people to their admissions committee. One of the reasons for increasing minority representation is the fact that such students may be more responsive to community needs.

While medical schools can contribute to the increase in the number of primary care physicians, it is hoped that market forces will impact on this issue so that an overabundance of subspecialists will be translated into more primary care physicians.

An awareness of the future needs of society, which should be provided by medical schools, can influence residency choices. Health care reform may impact significantly on medical education. Schools will need to be offered the means of gaining a broad enough experience to train students to meet the needs of the coming century. Ideas for reforms are under active discussion and some have been made over the years. The prospects are favorable for significant progress in the foreseeable future.

While recognizing the need to develop a new type of physician, there is a realization that medical schools can't, on their own, generate more primary care M.D.s. The market forces seem now to be slowly reversing the equation, making subspecialists less in demand, while generalists are becoming more attractive. As the impact of these forces become known to medical students, their career goals may better fall in line with prospects for employment.

Medicine is a very dynamic profession. It changes not only as a result of advances in medical knowledge and technology, but also because of changes in the way medical care is offered. For the past number of years, health care has been the subject of a national debate. The reforms that will take place in the U.S. health system will significantly impact on all aspects of medicine including premedical education, admission to medical school, medical education, medical students, health care delivery, and physicians' specialties. The effect on each of these the components will be discussed in the rest of this chapter.

## PREMEDICAL EDUCATION

The practice of medicine, as it has been evolving over the past decade, suggests that in the twenty-first century it will differ significantly from medical practice in the twentieth century. It is therefore reasonable to assume that premedical education goals will also need to be refocused appropriately. The basic learning goals to be emphasized in college are as follows:

1. Become familiar with the rapid advances in medicine that preclude the possibility of being able to rely indefinitely on knowledge solely gained in medical school and postgraduate training. One should pursue subjects of interest in either general or specialized areas for the sake of constantly acquiring more knowledge.

2. Develop skills in computer technology, especially with regard to communication skills. Accessing and sharing available information will be essential for making critical judgments.

## ADMISSION TO MEDICAL SCHOOL

The AAMC's Council on General Professional Education of the Physician (GPEP), after a three-year study involving leading medical educators issued a report whose recommendations are believed to be of such import, that they could impact very significantly on the training of physicians for practice in the twenty-first century. The GPEP recommendations are relevant to both premedical and medical students. For those planning a medical career, the following recommendations are of special interest:

1. College faculties should require that the education of all students encompass broad study in the natural and social sciences and in humanities.

2. Medical schools should require only essential courses for admission; these should be part of the core curriculum that all college students must take.

3. Medical school admissions committees' practice of recommending additional courses beyond those required for admission should cease.

4. Medical schools should modify their admissions requirements, so that college students who apply and have successfully pursued a wide range of study may be viewed as highly as the students who have concentrated in the sciences.

5. Medical schools should devote more attention to selecting students who have the values and attitudes that are essential for members of a caring profession, who have critical analytical abilities, and who have the ability to learn independently.

Along with these recommendations, admissions criteria will be developed that are focused at increasing the proportion of students likely to enter primary care fields. Therefore, some priority will likely be given to women and married applicants and those from public colleges and rural backgrounds, as well as applicants with impressive evidence of community service.

# MEDICAL SCHOOL EDUCATION

The AAMC's GPEP report was a comprehensive document that dealt with all aspects of medical education. As far as the curriculum is concerned, some of the recommendations by the panel of experts were:

1. Medical schools should develop procedures and adopt explicit criteria for the systematic evaluation of student performance.

2. Medical schools should emphasize the development of independent learning and problem-solving skills.

3. The level of skills and knowledge that a student should reach in order to enter graduate medical education (residency training) should be defined more clearly.

4. Medical schools should encourage their students to concentrate their elective programs on the advancement of their general professional education rather than on pursuit of a residency position.

5. Medical students' general professional education should include an emphasis on the physician's responsibility to work with individual patients and communities to promote health and prevent disease.

Obviously, each medical school will interpret these guidelines for curriculum changes according to its own philosophy of education. This will add greater variability to the learning experiences one can have at different institutions. It will obviously be another significant factor to consider when selecting a medical school.

Medical education will place less emphasis on mastery of content and greater emphasis on the learning process. The latter will include critical thinking, problem-solving skills, and the retrieval of information. In addition, attention will be focused on independent, self-directed learning skills. Medical school curricular time will increase for topics related to preventive medicine, public and community health, nutrition, geriatrics, behavioral sciences, and medical ethics. There will be greater educational opportunities in community health centers and out-patient clinics. Medical schools will place more emphasis on primary care and seek to channel a very substantial part of each graduating class into such residency programs. Thus, physician training will emphasize the health care needs of the community and nation, rather than being self-determined or determined by institutional agencies. Medical students will become better prepared for team-oriented practices.

# MEDICAL STUDENTS

Medical students will probably consist of nearly equal numbers of men and women. It is likely that, while in medical school, students will be provided with increased opportunities for community service. While financial aid will be available, it will be more difficult to obtain. Close to graduation, students may find reduced residency opportunities; after graduation, they will find that they will have to repay their student loans earlier, since deferral time will be reduced.

# MEDICAL PRACTICE

The changes in the overall health care scene that are taking place will have a profound impact on prospective medical students who will be the practitioners of the twenty-first century. These changes will be reflected in the three areas discussed separately below.

## Physician Status

• In the twenty-first century most physicians will be salaried employees rather than fee-for-service practitioners. They will work in or for group practices, hospitals, insurance companies, medical schools, or health maintenance organizations (HMOs). Medical care will be provided to patients as a result of contractual agreements between business and governmental units and medical providing groups, with solo practitioners usually not having access to enrollees of such plans. As a result of this restructuring, competition will increase among individual health care providers.

• It is anticipated that there will be fewer specialists and a greater number of primary care physicians. Some subspecialists may have to retrain in order to also serve as primary care physicians.

• Practicing physicians will be held more accountable for their performance.

• Business managers will have more input into how medical services will be provided.

• On the positive side, there will be less paper work imposed on physicians and thus they will have more time to see patients. It is anticipated that primary care physicians will be reimbursed at a higher level while specialist remuneration will decrease. The working schedule of physicians will be more predictable. This will provide them with greater leisure time.

• Medical care in the next century will focus much more on prevention and patient education in order to both extend life and also reduce long-term medical costs. Physicians will experience reduced per-patient revenue, but with an increased number of patients having access to medical care, they will be forced to see more patients in order to maintain their income.

## Physician-Patient Relationships

Today, the depersonalization of medical care due to the interference of administrative personnel has had a dehumanizing effect upon patients. The disease, rather than the patient, is being treated. A positive doctor-patient relationship can be restored by providing a more sympathetic and attentive attitude. Medical treatment is not always essential or even necessary, but the patient's psychological and emotional needs should always be addressed.

## Physician Reimbursement

The focus in health care over the past several decades has changed from one aimed at increasing access to medical care to an emphasis on decreasing costs. Both public and private insurers have been seeking ways to significantly lower expenditures. Most current health care proposals have the following features in common. They would (1) insure access to health care of most, if not all, citizens, especially those in the central cities and rural areas (who are frequently uninsured); (2) establish cost controls; (3) establish defined criteria for quality; (4) require preventive care (such as immunizations, mammograms, etc.); and (5) introduce medical malpractice reform (see below).

### Managed Care

Proposals for managed care fall into three major categories. The first is a national system (modeled on that in Canada) that is completely under government control. The second is diametrically opposite and is a "free market" approach, which allows the principle of supply and demand to control the health care system. The third, a middle of the road approach, is known as "play or pay." This involves businesses either purchasing insurance for their employees or paying into a health insurance pool for use in governmental pools.

All managed care is not government sponsored. Managed care is in effect, in the private sector, run by businesses that contract to provide comprehensive health care for their employees with group providers for specified time periods and preestablished costs for each employee. As a result, physicians have, in increasing numbers, become part of corporate medicine. They have been engaged as salaried employees of Health Maintenance Organizations (HMOs), which sometimes own hospitals. These organizations hospitalize patients much less frequently, and therefore are less expensive than traditional fee-for-service practitioners. HMOs have become increasingly successful. They have stimulated the formation of Independent Practice Associations (IPAs), in which groups of physicians treat patients in their own offices, and Preferred Provider Organizations (PPOs), which contract with companies to provide health care to employees.

Group providers seek to offer internally as much needed medical care as possible. Highly specialized care that the group cannot offer is supplied by outside specialists, who are reimbursed by the group. If the cost to the group at the end of the contract period is less than that guaranteed in the contract, the group will turn a profit. If the cost is more, it will incur a loss. In managed care under private control, physicians must make critical medical and ethical judgments about providing patients with access to diagnostic and therapeutic medical services. In contrast, in a fee-for-service relationship, the physician is paid to provide the patient with services that also necessitate making professional judgments about what medical tests and procedures are medically mandated, for it passes over into the area of "defensive" medicine.

All of these developments clearly indicate that increasing numbers of physicians will elect to become salaried employees rather than traditional fee-for-service doctors. The prediction has been made that more than 75% of newly graduated physicians will eventually work this way.

There are concerns that too much time is being spent by physicians on the business aspects of conducting a medical practice, especially dealing with HMOs. A recent innovation is the formation of Practice Management Companies (PMCs), which purchase practices and then assume responsibility for running the business end of them.

Having the office managed by a professional company provides for greater leverage when negotiating contracts with third-party payers or managed-care firms. Physicians are then free to devote themselves to providing patient care and avoid the distractions of the business phase of a practice for which they usually lack training and skills.

Physicians are also taking courses in business administration. This provides them with a grounding in the fundamentals of running their practice like a business.

## SPECIALISTS VERSUS PRIMARY CARE PHYSICIANS

In the course of the past half century, the number of specialists has increased dramatically. At the same time, the number of primary care physicians (general practitioners or family physicians) has declined substantially.

As noted above, primary care is becoming especially important as the health care system is being revamped. Because of the over-abundance of specialists, it is believed that health care is excessively expensive and less focused on prevention. The goal, therefore, is to establish a suitable balance between specialists and primary care physicians. To shift the trend away from specialization, there is a move on to restrict funding for subspecialization and to create incentives for those entering primary care.

Among the attractive features of primary care is the opportunity for treating patients of all ages. Another appealing element for a primary care physician is the wide variety of cases one is able to treat. A third feature is that of providing continuing care and the development of a special bond between the patient and the physician.

A survey of nearly 300 fourth year medical students was conducted to determine what factors played a role in choosing primary care careers. It was found that this group was more likely to be motivated by: (1) the opportunity to provide direct patient care in an ambulatory setting; (2) the fact that there is continuity of care; and (3) the possibility of being involved in the psychological aspects of medical care. Those electing high-tech specialties were more likely to be motivated by a desire for a large income, greater prestige, regular hours, and more leisure and family time. Furthermore, this study indicated that the significant factors involved in the choice did not include any of the following: student age; race; sex; marital status and level of indebtedness; concern about the increasing regulation of medical practice, malpractice, and health manpower reports; or the increasing number of elderly and chronically ill patients.

A developing challenge to primary care, whose impact can't as yet be measured, comes from proponents seeking to offer such care by nonphysician providers. Thus, primary care is currently available at offices where nurse practitioners, physician assistants, or other similar personnel work under the supervision of a physician. Their message to the public and the government is that there are less expensive alternatives available as sources of primary medical service. It remains to be seen how serious a threat this option will prove to be to primary care physicians.

## MEDICAL LITIGATION CRISIS

The technological revolution in medicine, which has dramatically increased life expectancy, has raised patient expectations, in some cases unrealistically, resulting in an explosion of malpractice litigation. This in turn has caused insurance premiums to rise to such an extent as to motivate some doctors to curtail or even completely give up their practices. Others have taken up "defensive" medicine, which can result in overtesting and consequently contributes to the alarming increase in health care costs.

An unfortunate side effect of "litigation fever" has been a decrease in the production of vaccines because of a fear of lawsuits arising from adverse reactions. Pharmaceutical companies apparently prefer to give up this aspect of their business rather than risk the cost of litigation.

## CYBERMEDICINE

The Internet is a conglomerate of computer networks that encircles the world. As of a few years ago there were upwards of 50,000 networks with about 10 million computers serving approximately 150 million users. The Internet or "information superhighway" is a spin-off from a project that was initiated in 1969 linking the computers of the government's military research centers to protect data in the event of a nuclear attack.

The public can access the Internet directly through universities, scientific organizations, and public libraries. The Internet is popular and busy because, for the most part, it is basically free. Your university or medical school is most likely to have an account and be online.

Using your own home computer you need a modem to access the Internet over your phone line and a communications program to communicate with the computer at the other end of the line. Using a university account has a major disadvantage for it requires technical skill to work through a maze without the help of a customer service department. Time has to be invested to learn how to proceed and find what you are looking for; nevertheless, there is a substantial savings using a university account rather than a commercial one.

On the other hand, if you feel overwhelmed by such chores you have the option of gaining Internet access through a commercial company (such as America Online, Compuserve, Prodigy, etc.). You may also use an ISP (Internet Service Provider), which is a company that provides direct access to the Internet for a low monthly fee. It is important to learn which features you will have access to and how much it will cost. This should be weighed against your specific needs and budget limitations. Once you have adjusted to the Internet and find it essential, you may decide to move over to a university account and drastically lower your costs.

While the Internet is expanding, its basic types of services are:

1. **E-Mail.** With this system, you prepare a communication using a text editor, and then send it to an e-mail address, which is in the form of a code, containing the symbol @. To the left of the symbol is the recipient's name or assigned code number, and on the right are letters and numbers separated by dots. These serve to identify the recipient's department and institution ("domains"). The last three letters indicate the type of institution (such as educational, edu.; commercial, com.; governmental, gov., etc.) (A two-letter overseas code may be used instead of the three-letter institutional code when appropriate.)

   Dialing your Internet account via a local phone number permits you to send your message locally, cross-country, or overseas, at no extra cost. It should be noted that with e-mail you lose the privacy provided by the postal service, but you gain in speed and delivery reliability.

2. **Internet "chat."** This is similar to e-mail, but involves "talking" to the recipient by typing messages back and forth. It provides instant access and prompt response but requires some degree of rapid typing skill. Internet books provide pointers on "computer-etiquette."

3. **Projecting.** There are networks that enable you to link up with "news-groups" and provide access to mailing lists of computerized meetings.

   After mastering e-mail and news-groups technique, the basis has been set to move out and access computers located in distant places with the assistance of available commercial services, such as Gopher, Tel-net, ftp (file transfer protocol), etc.

For the medical student, the Internet provides a means for a break from the isolation of study and tension of exams and rounds. It allows one to communicate with old or new friends by e-mail or "chatting."

The Internet provides students with the ability to access numerous medical information sites and, as computer skills improve, more medical students and physicians will take advantage of it and benefit from it.

# MEDICAL INFORMATICS

Access to medical information by computer is constantly increasing. To facilitate the orderly acquisition of such data, the field of medical informatics, the application of information technology to medicine, has emerged. Medical Informatics is a new developing discipline that is geared to play a role in the critical realm of decision support. This involves helping physicians obtain the essential data that enables them to make medical decisions. Other areas impacted by this new field are medical education, electronic medical records, natural language processing, telemedicine, and artificial intelligence. Physicians may be involved in this field on a full- or part-time basis.

Prerequisites for entering the area of Medical Informatics are a strong interest in computers, an ability to collaborate with others, a strong sense of curiosity, and a desire to experiment and teach. Fellowships are available through the National Library of Medicine, Biomedical Information Support Branch, Extramural Program, 8600 Rockville Pike, Bethesda, MD 20894 (Web site: http://www.N/m.nih.gov./).

The University of Missouri—Columbia School of Medicine has established a department of health management and informatics. It will offer graduate degrees in health informatics and health administration.

# PART TWO

# DENTISTRY

# 19 | Dentistry as a Career

Why study dentistry?
The need for dentists
Today's trends in dentistry
Dental specialties
Is dentistry for you?
Dentistry as an alternative to medicine

Dentistry is a profession dealing with the prevention, diagnosis, and treatment of oral diseases and disorders, with primary emphasis on the health of teeth and gums. In a sense, dentistry is a medical subspecialty. Good oral health is critical to human psychological and physical well-being since the state of the teeth affect speech and expression, and, also, systemic diseases frequently manifest themselves in the oral cavity.

There are more than 150,000 active dentists in the United States; most of them are in private practice with the remainder working as salaried professionals. Of those in private practice, 80% are general practitioners who are contributing to the improvement of their communities' health standards and are rewarded by having favorable working conditions and ample financial remuneration.

Many thousands of dentists hold positions as commissioned officers in the armed forces. Others are employed by the Veterans Administration and in public health dentistry at the state or local level. There are also several thousand full- or part-time teachers, administrators, and investigators in dental schools and in dental research laboratories.

## WHY STUDY DENTISTRY?

Dentistry provides young men and women of talent and dedication with an opportunity for a lifetime of professional satisfaction. The following are some of the attractive attributes of the dental profession:

1. It provides a strong sense of inner satisfaction derived from the knowledge that one is contributing to the physical well-being of one's patients.

2. It provides a personal feeling of achievement that comes from the successful application of one's judgmental and manual skills in resolving problems.

3. It provides an opportunity for group leadership as the head of a dental care team, making use of one's managerial and organizational skills.

4. It provides a basis for economic security and long-term financial stability.

5. It provides an opportunity to gain status in the community and thereby serve one's neighbors outside of one's professional capacity.

## THE NEED FOR DENTISTS

The demands for dental care by the public have increased annually. The three factors responsible for this situation are greater affluence, better education, and increased population growth. (Nevertheless, only about 50% of the general population sees a dentist with any regularity.) The response to the demand for increased dental care has been an increase in the number of patients handled by dentists. Nevertheless, it should be realized that the demand for dental services tends to fluctuate with changes in economic conditions. In any case, the national need for dental care will not only be maintained, but will probably be increased, thus suggesting an attractive future for most prospective members of the dental profession.

A note of caution is necessary, for in a recent report on employment prospects for dentists, the U.S. Department of Labor has said: "employment prospects to grow about as fast as average. . . . Increasingly abundant supply of practitioners will make it more difficult to start a practice. Competition for patients is likely to be intense in some localities, which could adversely affect earnings."

## TODAY'S TRENDS IN DENTISTRY

Over the past half century a gradual reevaluation of both the philosophy and the practice of dentistry has taken place. Whereas around World War II it was estimated that half of all Americans over 65 had lost all their teeth, by the end of this century, this figure for the same age group will have been reduced dramatically. The reason for this is that there has been a profound improvement in the oral health of recent generations of Americans caused by water fluoridation and the associated change in the role of dentistry, from one of treatment to one of prevention of tooth decay and gum diseases.

In terms of dental practice, an arsenal of new tools, techniques, drugs, and restorative materials has been developed over the past 30 years. These have dramatically expanded and improved the dentist's capacity for providing care in all areas. Among these developments are: (1) the high-speed air drill that minimizes the pain, time, and noise associated with drilling; (2) a variety of materials, both metal and plastic, that can now make up crowns and bridges; (3) plastic sealants that can be applied as a coating film over children's teeth to prevent decay-causing bacteria from attacking them for up to two years; (4) an alternative to bridges and dentures whereby one or more teeth can be set over metal implants inserted into the jaw bone; (5) a new technique called bonding in which a composite material that is undetectable can be glued onto the tooth, enabling chipped teeth to be repaired, spaces between teeth to be filled, and worn-down teeth to be restored, all with aesthetically appealing results.

Advances have also been made in diagnostic techniques, and research is continuing with the focus on preventive dentistry. The prospects for better oral health, therefore, are much higher, provided that increasing numbers of people practice good oral hygiene and avail themselves regularly of competent dental care.

Another major change that may be in the offing is the way dental services will be delivered. The traditional approach since the development of modern dentistry has been to have services provided by the individual practitioner. During the last decade, groups of specialists in a particular specialty area have joined together to utilize a common facility on a rotation basis, thereby cutting down significantly on operating expenses. Thus group practices devoted exclusively to endodontics, for example, have developed.

Multipractitioner dental clinics, that is, clinics that offer primarily general but also specialty services, have sprung up in department stores and shopping centers. Their expansion from only a handful in 1978 has primarily been stimulated by legal decisions allowing dentists to advertise. Other contributing factors are the high cost of quality dental care at private offices and the unequal distribution of dentists in some areas.

In 1979 about 125 million Americans spent more than $13 billion for dental treatment, 90% of which was provided by individual practitioners. It is certain that the trend is away from private care and toward multipractitioner clinics. This will have enormous implications both for patients and for dentists already in practice and those planning careers in dentistry. The new approach to dental care delivery holds the promise of offering less expensive and more convenient care.

# DENTAL SPECIALTIES

With advances in a variety of dental techniques and with the current focus on preventive and restorative dentistry, the need for special expertise in the various branches of dentistry has significantly increased. While general practitioners have training in and frequently do work in specialty areas, there are currently about 20,000 dentists whose practice is limited exclusively to one specialty. These dentists have had from one to four years of additional training (depending on the specialty), during which time their diagnostic and operative skills were further developed to achieve a superior degree of competence.

The following eight areas of specialization are recognized by the American Dental Association. (They are listed in order of the number of practitioners in each specialty.)

### Orthodontics

This specialty has about 6,500 practitioners. It is concerned with correcting irregular and abnormal dental development. Orthodontic procedures are applicable to patients in any age group, but treatment is more easily and effectively achieved on youngsters. The goal is not only to improve appearance, but to correct the functioning of the teeth by altering the bite. Correcting a bad bite, or malocclusion, will aid in eating and speaking, and will prevent eventual loosening or even loss of teeth, in addition to having a positive cosmetic effect. A bad bite is generally the result of an incorrect relationship that developed during childhood between jaw shape and teeth size. It may also result from habits such as thumb-sucking, nail-biting, or night grinding. Since teeth are moved to improper positions by forces that are out of balance in the mouth, they can be moved back by opposing forces. This is done by the use of various fixed orthodontic appliances such as metal braces, rubber bands, or plastic brackets. Removable appliances may also be used on occasion.

### Oral Surgery

There are more than 3,600 practitioners in this specialty. They use surgical procedures to deal with defects and diseases of the entire maxillofacial region—the middle and lower face. Their work encompasses the jaws, cheekbones, and other skeletal elements and their surrounding structures. In addition, the oral surgeon diagnoses and treats injuries, deformities, and growths in and around the jaw. When a tooth (or teeth) must be extracted, the procedure is usually carried out in an oral surgeon's office. Another common surgical procedure is apicoectomy, or surgical removal of a tooth's root tip. Reemplanting teeth knocked out in an accident and treating simple or compound jaw fractures are types of traumatic-injury treatments requiring an oral surgeon's skills.

### Periodontics

This specialty has about 2,000 practitioners. It is concerned with the diagnosis and treatment of diseases affecting the periodontal tissues that support the teeth, namely the gum, periodontal membrane, and surrounding bone. These diseases are very insidious and become increasingly prevalent with age. The earlier treatment is instituted, the more likely it is that teeth loss can be prevented. Periodontal diseases are diagnosed by several procedures; probing the depth of the space around a tooth, comparing bone level as reflected in X-rays taken at two different dates, and examining for tooth mobility. Slight or somewhat moderate disease can be readily treated by scaling—the removal of plaque or tartar, or root planing—a fine smoothing of the surface of the root. More advanced cases require curettage—scraping of the tissues lining the infected tooth pocket. In severe cases, surgical intervention to expose teeth, or even bone grafting, may be necessary. Various splinting techniques that join loose teeth to firm ones are also utilized.

### Pedodontics

The specialty also has about 2,000 practitioners. It is concerned with the treatment of children, adolescents, and young adults exclusively. Pedodontists are in a sense equivalent to pediatricians. In their special facilities and in the approach they use, they strive to establish in the child a positive attitude towards dentistry and a disposition to develop good oral hygiene habits. It is essential to maintain the health of the primary ("baby") teeth for, if decay sets in or premature loss occurs, the health and shape of the permanent teeth could be adversely affected. Also, the overall health of a child will be influenced by the condition of the primary teeth. Undetected decaying teeth can cause poor eating and chewing habits and thereby influence the overall state of a child's health.

### Endodontics

There are about 1,000 specialists in the field. It deals with the diagnosis and treatment of diseases of the pulp (nerve) of the tooth. With the current emphasis on saving teeth and utilizing extraction only as a last resort, root canal therapy is a vitally important dental specialty. A tooth needs endodontic treatment if the nerve has been damaged by decay, infection, irritation, or trauma. In such cases, the endodontist cleans out the nerve canal(s), removing the degenerated pulp. When the tooth is asymptomatic and has stabilized, the canal(s) can be filled. The complexity of the treatment is determined by how many canals the tooth may have. Also, a live (vital) tooth is more readily treated than a dead (non-vital) tooth, especially if the latter has abscessed.

### Prosthodontics

There are about 750 dentists in this field. Only several decades ago it was a common assumption that as one grew older, teeth would have to be lost, and a partial or even full set of dentures was thought to be unavoidable. While the current philosophy is that with good oral hygiene and prompt and competent treatment extraction can be minimized, there are nevertheless patients who will lose teeth and require a replacement for them. Replacement of even a single (non-wisdom) tooth is desirable, since if it is not replaced the teeth on either side of the gap may move. To replace missing or extracted teeth, a fixed or removable bridge can be attached to one or both adjacent teeth, or, in some situations, removable partial or full dentures may be required.

### Oral Pathology

There are currently about 100 specialists in oral pathology. They are concerned with diseases of the mouth, studying their causes, processes, and effects. Essentially a diagnostician, an oral pathologist usually serves as a consultant to other specialists, as well as a teacher of dental students.

### Dental Public Health

This field also has about 100 specialists. They are involved in promoting the oral health of communities by stimulating development of programs that aid in the prevention and control of dental diseases. Such specialists also gather and analyze data that are useful in determining the effectiveness of the oral health methods being used in a community.

## IS DENTISTRY FOR YOU?

In evaluating whether dentistry is a suitable career for you, consider the following:

1. Do you have adequate native manual dexterity?
2. Do your teachers and faculty advisor feel that dentistry is a desirable career for you, and do you have the support of your family?
3. After speaking with and observing one or more dentists at work, do you find their profession attractive?
4. After visiting a dental school and/or clinic and speaking with administrators, faculty, and students, are you still strongly in favor of pursuing a dental career?

# DENTISTRY AS AN ALTERNATIVE TO MEDICINE _____

Dentistry offers an attractive alternative career for *borderline* premedical and preosteopathic juniors. In such circumstances you should carefully evaluate whether dentistry is of sufficient interest to you as an alternative career. If this is the case, you should consider applying for admission to both medical and dental schools simultaneously at the end of your junior year in college (although obviously not to both types of schools at the same university). This can be done because admission requirements are almost identical and the medical and dental aptitude tests are very similar. Students who apply to medical and dental schools should inform their preprofessional advisory office of this fact so that appropriate evaluations can be prepared.

Trying to gain admission to dental school with the intent of using this as an avenue or lever to get into medical school, however, is self-defeating. Medical schools will not be favorably impressed by an applicant who is taking a valuable dental class place and is obviously using it primarily to aid his or her transfer from one professional school to another. When such a student lacks a genuine interest in dentistry, he or she may also end up wasting time and money in dental school.

If you fail to gain admission to medical school and did not apply to dental school in your junior year, you can consider doing so in the senior year or even later. Dental school admission committees are well aware that premedical or former premedical students will also apply for admission to dental school. While they naturally prefer "straight" predental majors, they know that many able and successful practicing dentists were former premedical students.

# 20 Preparing for and Applying to Dental School

Educational preparation
Application procedures
Admissions criteria

## EDUCATIONAL PREPARATION

The discussion in Chapter 2 concerning high school and college education is generally applicable to predental students and should be reviewed.

### High School

While in high school, you should acquire a broad liberal arts education and at the same time demonstrate that you have a genuine interest and good ability in the sciences, especially biology. Taking an advanced course in biology (if available) and/or undertaking a special science project may be particularly useful. In addition, completing a course in art, sculpture, mechanical drawing, or machine shop work will help determine and improve your manual dexterity. Active participation in a variety of extracurricular activities, such as a dramatic society or sports team, will assist you in judging your interest in and ability to work with people.

### Undergraduate Studies

The criteria for selecting a college noted on page 20 are fully applicable to predental students.

The overwhelming majority of students entering dental school have completed four years of college. Thus you should plan your program on this basis (unless you have valid reasons for applying earlier). There is no specific required major for predental students, although most quite naturally select biology or chemistry. It is essential that your college studies:

1. include the minimum science course requirements, namely, inorganic chemistry—1 year, biology—1 year, physics—1 year, and organic chemistry—1 year;

2. demonstrate that you have solid abilities in the sciences by satisfactorily completing the aforementioned required courses and any science electives you take;

3. provide you with a well-rounded background in the social sciences and humanities by completing courses in English composition, history, and psychology;

4. reinforce your manual dexterity by taking courses that require use of your hands (such as art, sculpture, drafting). If this is not possible, then an extracurricular program involving such activities as model building, chalk carving, or playing a musical instrument can substitute for formal experience.

## APPLICATION PROCEDURES

### General Considerations

The initial step in the application process is to select the schools to which you will seek admission. The selection process should take into consideration the following:

1. *School requirements*. Dental schools have varying requirements for organic chemistry, elective science courses, and even some nonscience courses. School catalogs should be consulted to ensure that you will be able to meet all the requirements prior to enrolling.

2. *Financial status*. The cost of dental education is high. The best means of keeping costs down is to attend a state school in the state where you are a legal resident. Also, transportation costs will be less if you go to school as close to your permanent home as possible.

3. *School curriculum*. There are different perspectives in dental education as reflected in the various types of curricula currently in use. These are defined in Chapter 25, and the individual school curriculum is identified as part of the profiles given for each dental school in that chapter.

4. *Alumni admission ratio*. Admissions Committees give careful consideration to the undergraduate school the applicant attends, and this can influence the chance of acceptance. By applying to schools that have consistently accepted a significant number of students from your college, you will automatically improve your chances.

5. *Admissions criteria*. The four factors determining admission are academic performance (both overall and in science), recommendations, DAT scores, and interview performance. Schools place varying degrees of emphasis on these factors, as shown in Tables 20.1 and 20.2. By applying to schools where your weaknesses may be less significant, you can possibly improve your chances for admission. As to the total number of schools to which one should apply, this depends on your basic admission potential (academic average and DAT scores) and the amount of money you are prepared to spend as part of the admissions process. It should be realized that being called for out-of-town interviews can substantially increase the costs of applying. Generally, the number of applications can vary from 5 to 15 for A to C students, respectively.

## How to Apply

There are two methods of applying: either directly to the school or through an application service. In the former case, the application must be secured from the dental school and the applicant will have to have all transcripts and recommendations sent to each dental school he or she is applying to. When applying to one of the 50 (out of 54) schools participating in the American Association of Dental Schools Application Service (AADSAS), the Application Booklet of the AADSAS must be used. This can be secured from your predental advisor or from AADSAS, 1625 Massachusetts Avenue, NW, Washington, DC 20036.

As part of the AADSAS application, an essay dealing with your career motivation is expected. A sample essay is reproduced on the following page, to give you an idea of what may be submitted.

In addition to the completed Application Booklet, AADSAS receives copies of all transcripts and the processing fee ($95 for the first school and $15 for each additional school). AADSAS processes the information provided, computes GPAs, and sends a screening copy to the applicant for approval or correction. AADSAS then sends each of the dental schools selected a copy of the approved screening copy and copies of transcripts. Also, the applicant is sent a confirmation copy. Thus only one set of transcripts is needed when applying through AADSAS, but letters of recommendation and photographs must be sent directly to each of the schools. The school usually will have its own application fee that may be required either at the time you apply through AADSAS or at a later date.

### Sample Essay for AADSAS Application

*My interest in dentistry is the result of the inspiration of two people: my maternal grandfather and my family dentist. My late grandfather lived in our home and thus was personally aware of my ability, already as a child, to assemble kits and, more generally, to fix things around the house. He graduated from the New York School of Mechanical Dentistry in 1941, and understandably channeled my interest toward the dental profession.*

*When I entered college, I enrolled as a pre-dentistry major. Nevertheless, I wanted to be certain that dentistry was the profession to which I wanted to devote my life. My family dentist allowed me to watch him at work. He patiently explained to me the basic problem of each patient and how he went about treating it. Each patient required a different type of therapy and the variety of cases thoroughly fascinated me.*

*My reason for preferring dentistry above any other health profession is that the former allows me more eye contact and friendliness between doctor and patient. A good dentist must be concerned with more than just the patient's oral health; he must consider the patient's physical appearance, comfort, and ability to properly maneuver his teeth. The teenager's teeth must be straightened for esthetic reasons. The older patient must be fitted with dentures that will serve him well in both speech and mastication. And the young child whose permanent teeth are now appearing must be observed, to prevent the development of speech impediments, as a result of abnormal tooth growth.*

*The first year of college represented, for me, an induction period in my academic growth. Since I entered college on early admission at the age of 16, I have gotten progressively better adjusted to the work load. This change is reflected in my gradually improving index. The transition from only three years of high school (which I finished with a 94 average) to the more intense pressure and heavier workload, on the college level, explains my unimpressive performance in my freshman year. This is despite the fact that I was as conscientious then as I am now and as I have always been.*

*Besides understating my scholastic potential, my college transcript cannot reflect my interest in a highly specialized area of chemistry. During the Spring Semester of 2002, I presented a seminar on catenanes and knots (i.e., cyclic molecules that are mechanically linked or interlocked), which have been shown to be the basis of certain viral infections and cancers. I am currently investigating the possible role of catenanes in oral pathology.*

*As a result of my consistently improving academic performance, I was named to the Dean's list with high honor at my college. In an effort to gain experience toward my intended profession, I worked at a local dental hospital in New York, during the 2001–2002 academic year. The preceding year, I worked as a volunteer dental assistant at a dental clinic affiliated with a New York dental school. I am currently volunteering at another local dental clinic, while completing my undergraduate studies. My extensive dental exposure and academic work has provided me with both the motivation and background to successfully complete a program of dental studies and develop into a competent and empathic practitioner.*

## ADMISSIONS CRITERIA

Aside from the applicant's personal qualifications as reflected in the grade point average, DAT scores, recommendations, and interview rating, the most important factor in determining admission to dental school is the number of people making up the pool of applicants from which the entering class is selected. Therefore this consideration will be discussed first and then the personal attributes next.

### Applicant Pool

In 2000 there were 7,772 applicants for admission to dental schools in the United States. Of these, approximately 4,327 were admitted to the freshman class, giving about a 1.7:1 applicant/acceptance ratio. Each of the applicants filed an average of 6 applications to secure a place.

The number of dental school applicants has tended to follow a pattern of cycles. During the post-World War II period (1945–57) there was an abundance of applicants.

From 1958 to 1963 there was a sharp decline. Subsequently, from 1964 to 1974 a steady increase in the applicant pool was recorded. Since 1974, there has been a dramatic decrease (about 50%) in the number of male applicants. This has been reflected in the change in the applicant/acceptance ratios from 3.0:1 to 1.2:1 over the past five years. It seems likely that at least for the immediate future the favorable acceptance ratio (from the applicant's point of view) will be maintained since the number of first-year places is projected to remain basically unchanged.

## Grade Point Average (GPA)

The applicant's overall and science grade point averages (especially at a school where grade inflation is not a factor) along with the DAT scores (see below) will provide admissions committees with the screening factors necessary to determine if an interview should be granted. Obviously, your college's reputation is an important consideration in assessing the credibility of the applicant's GPA. During recent years, the mean GPA was c. 3.2 (and the mean science GPA was c. 3.1).

## DAT Scores

As indicated in Table 20.1, most dental schools place considerable emphasis on the DAT scores. However, the importance of the individual subtest scores varies considerably, as shown in Table 20.2.

The DAT is designed to predict capabilities in two areas, academic and manual. Thus in addition to the nine subtest scores, average scores are reported in both of these categories. The academic average represents the average of all but the two perception ability test (PAT) scores, while the manual ability is summarized by the average of the two- and three-dimensional PAT scores. Table 20.2 suggests that more importance is given to the academic average than to the PAT average.

## Recommendations

These are usually provided by a committee and/or the predental advisor. The recommendations may be submitted in the form of a letter incorporating faculty comments and/or an evaluation form. This material serves to provide a personalized evaluation that makes your transcript more meaningful. Recommendations can serve to enhance your chances for admission by bringing to the admissions committee's attention information about your personality, motivation, and innate abilities, as well as clarifying any uncertain aspects relative to your credentials.

Letters of recommendation from former employers (especially dentists, research laboratories, and/or dental clinics) can provide useful information to the admissions committee. However, personal recommendations from your family dentist or religious leader are not especially meaningful.

## Interview

Most dental schools require a personal interview as part of the admission procedure. Being granted one implies that the school is seriously considering your application. The interview provides an opportunity for you to "sell yourself" as well as to explain any discrepancies or weaknesses, and to elaborate on your strengths. The discussion of "The Interview" in Chapter 6 is, for the most part, relevant to predental students as well and should be reviewed. It also contains a list of typical and atypical questions.

## Table 20.1. THE IMPORTANCE GIVEN TO VARIOUS SOURCES OF INFORMATION CONCERNING THE DENTAL SCHOOL APPLICANT

| ST | DENTAL SCHOOL | PRE-DENTAL GRADE POINT AVERAGE | | | INTERVIEW | LETTERS OF RECOMMEND-ATION | MANUAL DEXTERITY TEST | REQUIRED YEARS OF PRE-DENTAL EDUCATION |
|---|---|---|---|---|---|---|---|---|
| | | SCIENCE | NON-SCIENCE | OVERALL | | | | |
| AL | UNIVERSITY OF ALABAMA | VI | VI | VI | VI | VI | N/A | 3 YEARS |
| AZ | ARIZONA SCHOOL OF DENTISTRY AND ORAL HEALTH | VI | SI | SI | VI | SI | SU | 3 YEARS |
| CA | UNIVERSITY OF THE PACIFIC | VI | SI | VI | VI | VI | SI | 3 YEARS |
| | UNIVERSITY OF CALIFORNIA, SAN FRANCISCO | VI | SI | VI | VI | SI | N/A | 3 YEARS |
| | UNIVERSITY OF CALIFORNIA, LOS ANGELES | VI | VI | VI | VI | VI | N/A | 3 YEARS |
| | UNIVERSITY OF SOUTHERN CALIFORNIA | VI | SI | VI | VI | VI | NI | 2 YEARS |
| | LOMA LINDA UNIVERSITY | VI | SI | VI | VI | SI | VI | 3 YEARS |
| CO | UNIVERSITY OF COLORADO | VI | SI | VI | VI | SI | N/A | 3 YEARS |
| CT | UNIVERSITY OF CONNECTICUT | VI | SU | SI | VI | VI | SU | 3 YEARS |
| DC | HOWARD UNIVERSITY | VI | SI | VI | VI | VI | N/A | 4 YEARS |
| FL | UNIVERSITY OF FLORIDA | SI | SU | VI | SU | VI | SU | BA/BS |
| | NOVA SOUTHEASTERN UNIVERSITY | VI | SI | VI | VI | SI | N/A | 3 YEARS |
| GA | MEDICAL COLLEGE OF GEORGIA | VI | N/A | VI | VI | SI | N/A | 3 YEARS |
| IL | SOUTHERN ILLINOIS UNIVERSITY | VI | SI | VI | VI | VI | N/A | 2 YEARS |
| | UNIVERSITY OF ILLINOIS, CHICAGO | VI | VI | VI | VI | VI | SI | 3 YEARS |
| IN | INDIANA UNIVERSITY | VI | SU | SI | VI | SI | N/A | 3 YEARS |
| IA | UNIVERSITY OF IOWA | VI | SI | VI | VI | VI | NI | 3 YEARS |
| KY | UNIVERSITY OF KENTUCKY | VI | SI | VI | VI | VI | SI | 2 YEARS |
| | UNIVERSITY OF LOUISVILLE | VI | SI | VI | VI | VI | SI | OTHER[1] |
| LA | LOUISIANA STATE UNIVERSITY | VI | SI | VI | VI | VI | VI | 3 YEARS |
| MD | UNIVERSITY OF MARYLAND | VI | SI | VI | VI | VI | N/A | OTHER[2] |
| MA | HARVARD UNIVERSITY | VI | VI | N/A | VI | VI | VI | BA/BS |
| | BOSTON UNIVERSITY | VI | VI | VI | VI | VI | N/A | 3 YEARS |
| | TUFTS UNIVERSITY | VI | SI | VI | VI | SI | N/A | 2 YEARS |
| MI | UNIVERSITY OF DETROIT - MERCY | VI | SI | VI | VI | SI | SI | 2 YEARS |
| | UNIVERSITY OF MICHIGAN | VI | SI | VI | VI | VI | VI | 2 YEARS |
| MN | UNIVERSITY OF MINNESOTA | VI | SI | VI | VI | SI | SI | 3 YEARS |
| MS | UNIVERSITY OF MISSISSIPPI | VI | SU | VI | VI | SI | N/A | 3 YEARS |
| MO | UNIVERSITY OF MISSOURI, KANSAS CITY | VI | SU | VI | VI | SI | N/A | 3 YEARS |
| NE | CREIGHTON UNIVERSITY | VI | VI | VI | VI | VI | SI | 2 YEARS |
| | UNIVERSITY OF NEBRASKA | VI | N/A | VI | VI | SU | SU | 3 YEARS |
| NV | UNIVERSITY OF NEVADA, LAS VEGAS | VI | NI | VI | VI | VI | VI | 3 YEARS |
| NJ | U. OF MEDICINE & DENTISTRY OF NEW JERSEY | VI | SI | VI | VI | VI | SI | 3 YEARS |
| NY | COLUMBIA UNIVERSITY | VI | NI | VI | VI | SI | N/A | 3 YEARS |
| | NEW YORK UNIVERSITY | VI | VI | VI | VI | SI | N/A | 3 YEARS |
| | STATE UNIVERSITY OF NEW YORK, STONY BROOK | VI | SI | VI | SI | SI | N/A | 2 YEARS |
| | STATE UNIVERSITY OF NEW YORK, BUFFALO | VI | SI | VI | VI | VI | N/A | 3 YEARS |
| NC | UNIVERSITY OF NORTH CAROLINA | VI | SI | SI | VI | VI | N/A | 3 YEARS |
| OH | OHIO STATE UNIVERSITY | VI | SU | SI | VI | VI | SI | 2 YEARS |
| | CASE WESTERN RESERVE UNIVERSITY | VI | SI | VI | VI | SI | N/A | 2 YEARS |
| OK | UNIVERSITY OF OKLAHOMA | VI | NI | VI | VI | SI | SU | 2 YEARS |
| OR | OREGON HEALTH & SCIENCE UNIVERSITY | VI | SI | VI | VI | SI | N/A | 3 YEARS |
| PA | TEMPLE UNIVERSITY | VI | SI | VI | SI | SI | VI | 3 YEARS |
| | UNIVERSITY OF PENNSYLVANIA | VI | SI | VI | VI | SI | SI | 3 YEARS |
| | UNIVERSITY OF PITTSBURGH | VI | VI | VI | VI | SI | SI | 3 YEARS |
| SC | MEDICAL UNIVERSITY OF SOUTH CAROLINA | VI | SI | VI | VI | SI | N/A | BA/BS |
| TN | MEHARRY MEDICAL COLLEGE | N/A | N/A | N/A | N/A | N/A | N/A | 2 YEARS |
| | UNIVERSITY OF TENNESSEE | VI | SI | VI | SI | NI | SI | 3 YEARS |
| TX | TEXAS A&M UNIVERSITY - BAYLOR COLLEGE | VI | SU | VI | VI | VI | SU | 2 YEARS |
| | UNIVERSITY OF TEXAS, HOUSTON | SI | SU | SI | VI | SI | SU | 3 YEARS |
| | UNIVERSITY OF TEXAS, SAN ANTONIO | VI | SU | VI | VI | VI | SU | 3 YEARS |
| VA | VIRGINIA COMMONWEALTH UNIVERSITY | VI | SI | VI | VI | VI | VI | 3 YEARS |
| WA | UNIVERSITY OF WASHINGTON | VI | SI | SI | VI | SI | VI | 3 YEARS |
| WV | WEST VIRGINIA UNIVERSITY | VI | SI | VI | VI | SI | SI | 3 YEARS |
| WI | MARQUETTE UNIVERSITY | VI | SI | VI | SI | SI | SI | 3 YEARS |
| PR | UNIVERSITY OF PUERTO RICO | SI | SI | VI | VI | SI | SI | 3 YEARS |
| | UNITED STATES TOTAL "VI" ANSWERS | 52 | 8 | 47 | 50 | 26 | 8 | - - |
| SK | UNIVERSITY OF SASKATCHEWAN | N/A | N/A | VI | SI | SI | VI | 2 YEARS |
| AB | UNIVERSITY OF ALBERTA | N/A | N/A | VI | VI | N/A | N/A | 2 YEARS |
| BC | UNIVERSITY OF BRITISH COLUMBIA | N/A | N/A | N/A | N/A | N/A | N/A | 3 YEARS |
| MB | UNIVERSITY OF MANITOBA | VI | SI | SI | VI | N/A | N/A | 2 YEARS |
| NS | DALHOUSIE UNIVERSITY | VI | SI | SI | VI | SI | SI | OTHER |
| ON | UNIVERSITY OF TORONTO | N/A | N/A | VI | VI | N/A | N/A | 3 YEARS |
| | UNIVERSITY OF WESTERN ONTARIO | N/A | N/A | N/A | N/A | N/A | N/A | N/A |
| PQ | MCGILL UNIVERSITY | VI | SI | VI | VI | VI | SI | BA/BS |
| | UNIVERSITÉ DE MONTRÉAL | SU | SU | VI | N/A | N/A | SI | 2 YEARS |
| | UNIVERSITÉ LAVAL | N/A | N/A | VI | SI | N/A | N/A | 2 YEARS |
| | CANADA TOTAL "VI" ANSWERS | 3 | 0 | 6 | 5 | 1 | 1 | - - |

[1] MINIMUM OF 90 HOURS TO APPLY.
[2] MINIMUM OF 90 SEMESTER HOURS; BACHELOR'S DEGREE PREFERRED.

VI = VERY IMPORTANT    SU = SOMEWHAT UNIMPORTANT    SI = SOMEWHAT IMPORTANT    NI = NOT IMPORTANT    N/A = NOT AVAILABLE

Source: American Dental Association, Survey Center, 2003-04 Survey of Predoctoral Dental Education.

## Table 20.2. THE IMPORTANCE GIVEN TO DENTAL ADMISSION TEST SCORES

| ST | DENTAL SCHOOL | ACADEMIC AVERAGE | PERCEPTUAL ABILITY | TOTAL SCIENCE | QUANTI-TATIVE | READING COMP | BIOLOGY | INORGANIC CHEMISTRY | ORGANIC CHEMISTRY |
|----|---------------|------------------|--------------------|---------------|---------------|--------------|---------|--------------------|--------------------|
| AL | UNIVERSITY OF ALABAMA | VI | SI | VI | SI | VI | VI | VI | VI |
| AZ | ARIZONA SCHOOL OF DENTISTRY AND ORAL | SI | SI | SI | SI | SI | VI | VI | VI |
| CA | UNIVERSITY OF THE PACIFIC | VI | VI | VI | SU | VI | SI | SI | SI |
| | UNIVERSITY OF CALIFORNIA, SAN FRANCISCO | VI | VI | SI | SU | VI | SI | SI | SI |
| | UNIVERSITY OF CALIFORNIA, LOS ANGELES | VI | VI | VI | VI | VI | VI | VI | VI |
| | UNIVERSITY OF SOUTHERN CALIFORNIA | VI | VI | SI | NI | NI | SI | SI | SI |
| | LOMA LINDA UNIVERSITY | VI | VI | SI | SU | SI | SI | SI | SI |
| CO | UNIVERSITY OF COLORADO | SI | VI | SI | SI | VI | VI | SI | SI |
| CT | UNIVERSITY OF CONNECTICUT | SI | SI | VI | SU | SI | VI | SI | SI |
| DC | HOWARD UNIVERSITY | VI | VI | VI | SI | VI | VI | VI | VI |
| FL | UNIVERSITY OF FLORIDA | VI | SU | VI | SU | SI | SI | SI | VI |
| | NOVA SOUTHEASTERN UNIVERSITY | VI | SU | VI | NI | VI | VI | VI | VI |
| GA | MEDICAL COLLEGE OF GEORGIA | VI | VI | N/A | N/A | SI | N/A | N/A | N/A |
| IL | SOUTHERN ILLINOIS UNIVERSITY | VI | VI | VI | SU | SI | SI | SI | SU |
| | UNIVERSITY OF ILLINOIS, CHICAGO | VI | VI | VI | SI | SI | VI | VI | VI |
| IN | INDIANA UNIVERSITY | VI | VI | VI | NI | SU | SI | SI | SI |
| IA | UNIVERSITY OF IOWA | SI | SU | VI | SI | SI | VI | VI | VI |
| KY | UNIVERSITY OF KENTUCKY | VI | SU | VI | SU | VI | VI | VI | VI |
| | UNIVERSITY OF LOUISVILLE | VI | SI | VI | SI | VI | VI | SI | SI |
| LA | LOUISIANA STATE UNIVERSITY | VI | VI | VI | VI | VI | VI | VI | VI |
| MD | UNIVERSITY OF MARYLAND | VI | SI | VI | SI | VI | VI | SI | VI |
| MA | HARVARD UNIVERSITY | VI | VI | VI | VI | VI | VI | VI | VI |
| | BOSTON UNIVERSITY | VI | VI | VI | SI | VI | SI | SI | SI |
| | TUFTS UNIVERSITY | VI | VI | VI | SI | SI | SI | SI | SI |
| MI | UNIVERSITY OF DETROIT - MERCY | VI | SI | VI | NI | VI | VI | SI | SI |
| | UNIVERSITY OF MICHIGAN | VI | VI | VI | SI | VI | VI | VI | VI |
| MN | UNIVERSITY OF MINNESOTA | VI | VI | VI | SI | VI | VI | VI | VI |
| MS | UNIVERSITY OF MISSISSIPPI | VI | VI | VI | VI | SI | SI | SI | SI |
| MO | UNIVERSITY OF MISSOURI, KANSAS CITY | VI | SI | SI | SU | VI | SI | SI | SI |
| NE | CREIGHTON UNIVERSITY | VI | VI | VI | VI | VI | VI | VI | VI |
| | UNIVERSITY OF NEBRASKA | SI | SI | SI | SI | SI | SI | SI | SI |
| NV | UNIVERSITY OF NEVADA, LAS VEGAS | VI | VI | NI | NI | NI | NI | NI | NI |
| NJ | U. OF MEDICINE & DENTISTRY OF NEW JERSEY | VI | SI | VI | VI | VI | VI | VI | VI |
| NY | COLUMBIA UNIVERSITY | VI | SI | SI | NI | SI | SI | SU | VI |
| | NEW YORK UNIVERSITY | VI | VI | VI | VI | VI | VI | VI | VI |
| | STATE UNIVERSITY OF NEW YORK, STONY BROOK | VI | VI | VI | SI | SI | SI | SI | SI |
| | STATE UNIVERSITY OF NEW YORK, BUFFALO | VI | VI | VI | VI | VI | SI | SI | SI |
| NC | UNIVERSITY OF NORTH CAROLINA | SI | VI | VI | SI | SI | VI | SI | VI |
| OH | OHIO STATE UNIVERSITY | VI | VI | VI | SU | VI | VI | VI | VI |
| | CASE WESTERN RESERVE UNIVERSITY | VI | SI | VI | SU | VI | VI | VI | VI |
| OK | UNIVERSITY OF OKLAHOMA | VI | SU | VI | SU | VI | SI | SI | SI |
| OR | OREGON HEALTH & SCIENCE UNIVERSITY | VI | SI | VI | VI | SI | VI | VI | VI |
| PA | TEMPLE UNIVERSITY | VI | VI | VI | SI | VI | VI | VI | VI |
| | UNIVERSITY OF PENNSYLVANIA | SI | SU | SI | SU | SI | SU | SU | SU |
| | UNIVERSITY OF PITTSBURGH | VI | SI | VI | SI | VI | VI | VI | SI |
| SC | MEDICAL UNIVERSITY OF SOUTH CAROLINA | VI | VI | VI | VI | VI | VI | VI | VI |
| TN | MEHARRY MEDICAL COLLEGE | N/A | N/A | N/A | N/A | N/A | N/A | N/A | N/A |
| | UNIVERSITY OF TENNESSEE | VI | SI | VI | SI | SI | SI | SI | SI |
| TX | TEXAS A&M UNIVERSITY - BAYLOR COLLEGE | VI | SU | SI | SI | VI | VI | VI | VI |
| | UNIVERSITY OF TEXAS, HOUSTON | SI | SU | SI | SU | SI | SI | SI | SI |
| | UNIVERSITY OF TEXAS, SAN ANTONIO | VI | SU | SI | SI | SI | VI | VI | VI |
| VA | VIRGINIA COMMONWEALTH UNIVERSITY | VI | VI | VI | SI | SI | VI | VI | VI |
| WA | UNIVERSITY OF WASHINGTON | VI | VI | SI | SI | VI | SI | SI | SI |
| WV | WEST VIRGINIA UNIVERSITY | VI | VI | VI | SI | VI | VI | VI | VI |
| WI | MARQUETTE UNIVERSITY | VI | SI | VI | SI | SI | SI | SI | SI |
| PR | UNIVERSITY OF PUERTO RICO | VI | VI | SI | SI | SI | SI | SI | SI |
| | UNITED STATES TOTAL "VI" ANSWERS | 47 | 31 | 40 | 10 | 30 | 31 | 25 | 28 |
| SK | UNIVERSITY OF SASKATCHEWAN | N/A | SI | N/A | N/A | VI | N/A | N/A | N/A |
| AB | UNIVERSITY OF ALBERTA | N/A | VI | N/A | N/A | VI | N/A | N/A | N/A |
| BC | UNIVERSITY OF BRITISH COLUMBIA | N/A | N/A | N/A | N/A | N/A | N/A | N/A | N/A |
| MB | UNIVERSITY OF MANITOBA | VI | SI | N/A | N/A | N/A | N/A | N/A | N/A |
| NS | DALHOUSIE UNIVERSITY | SI | SI | SI | SI | SI | SI | SI | N/A |
| ON | UNIVERSITY OF TORONTO | VI | VI | N/A | N/A | N/A | N/A | N/A | N/A |
| | UNIVERSITY OF WESTERN ONTARIO | N/A | N/A | N/A | N/A | N/A | N/A | N/A | N/A |
| PQ | MCGILL UNIVERSITY | VI | VI | SI | SI | VI | SI | SI | N/A |
| | UNIVERSITÉ DE MONTRÉAL | VI | SU | SI | SU | VI | SI | SI | N/A |
| | UNIVERSITÉ LAVAL | N/A | VI | N/A | N/A | N/A | N/A | N/A | N/A |
| | CANADA TOTAL "VI" ANSWERS | 4 | 4 | 0 | 0 | 4 | 0 | 0 | N/A |

VI = VERY IMPORTANT  SU = SOMEWHAT UNIMPORTANT  N/A = NOT AVAILABLE
SI = SOMEWHAT IMPORTANT  NI = NOT IMPORTANT

Source: American Dental Association, Survey Center, 2003-04 Survey of Predoctoral Dental Education.

# 21 The Dental Admission Test (DAT)

**Importance of the DAT**
**Contents of the DAT**
**Preparing for the DAT**
**Taking the DAT**
**Sample DAT questions**
**Scoring of the DAT**
**Canadian DAT**

This test is conducted two times a year (October and April) and is sponsored by the Division of Educational Measurements, American Dental Association, 211 East Chicago Avenue, Chicago, IL 60611. Students planning to enter in the fall of the following year should take the examination in the preceding April or October. The choice between these two dates is dependent on your state of preparedness (since admission announcements are not made before December 1). If you plan to use the summer to study, the DAT should be taken in October; otherwise, it should be taken earlier and gotten out of the way (as well as ensure an opportunity to repeat it if necessary).

An application for the DAT can be obtained from the Division of Educational Measurements at the address above, or from the predental advisor. The application should include a recent photo and the $150 fee. This fee covers the cost of sending five official transcripts of scores to selected dental schools, as well as a copy for the applicant and the predental advisor, and DAT preparation materials. Additional official transcripts of scores can be sent if requested. The charge is $5 each if ordered at the time of applying or if requested later.

Testing centers for the Saturday administration are located in one or more cities in each state, as well as in the District of Columbia. Sunday (or Monday) administrations are provided in about 10 states and require a letter from a religious leader confirming the applicant's affiliation with a Sabbath-observing religious group. Foreign testing centers are set up as needed, but require special arrangements. The additional fee for a test administered in a foreign country is $25.

## IMPORTANCE OF THE DAT

About six weeks after taking the DAT, each applicant will receive a personal copy of the scores (with an explanation of them) at the permanent address listed on the original application form. DAT scores are based on the number of correct answers recorded. The scores are reported to the dental schools requested by the applicant as standard scores rather than raw scores. The conversion of raw scores to standard scores is based on the distribution of applicant performances. Scores used in the testing program range from 1 to 30. There is no passing or failing score, but a standard score of 15 signifies average performance on a national basis.

By the use of standard rather than raw scores it is possible to compare the performance of one applicant with the performance of all applicants. Also, since the DAT is designed to predict performance in both academic and technical areas, two average scores are included in the test report—the academic average and the Perceptual Ability

Test (PAT) average. The former is an average of quantitative reasoning, verbal reasoning, reading comprehension, biology, and inorganic and organic chemistry test scores; the latter is an average of the two- and three-dimensional Perceptual Ability Test scores.

Dental schools place varying degrees of emphasis on the two average scores and the individual subtest scores (see Tables 20.1 and 20.2). In any case the DAT scores are not taken out of context, but rather they represent one of the four major elements considered by admissions committees. The other elements are the grade point and science averages, letters of recommendation and evaluations, and the dental school interview. Good DAT scores will reinforce a strong applicant's chances for admission and help a weak candidate get in-depth consideration and possibly an interview. Poor DAT scores will raise doubts about a strong candidate's true abilities and serve to defeat a weak candidate's chances completely.

## CONTENTS OF THE DAT

There are four examinations included in the Dental Admission Testing Program. The entire program requires one half day for administration. The examinations included are:

I.    Survey of Natural Sciences

BIOLOGY — Origin of Life. Cell Metabolism (including photosynthesis). Enzymology. Thermodynamics. Organelle Structure and Function. Biological Organization and Relationship of Major Taxa (monera, angiosperms, arthropods, chordates, etc.) using the five-kingdom system. Structure and function of the following vertebrate systems: integumentary, skeletal, muscular, circulatory, immunological, digestive, respiratory, urinary, nervous, endocrine, and reproductive. Fertilization, Descriptive Embryology, and Developmental Mechanics. Mendelian Inheritance, Chromosomal Genetics, Meiosis, Molecular and Human Genetics. Natural Selection, Population Genetics, Speciation, Population and Community Ecology, Animal Behavior (including social behavior).

GENERAL CHEMISTRY — Stoichiometry (percent of composition, empirical formulas from percent of composition, balancing equations, weight/weight, weight/volume, density problems). Gases (kinetic molecular theory of gases, Graham's, Dalton's, Boyle's, Charles', and ideal gas laws). Liquids and Solids. Solutions (colligative properties, concentration calculations). Acids and Bases. Chemical Equilibrium (molecular, acid/base, precipitation, equilibria calculations). Thermodynamics and Thermochemistry (laws of thermodynamics, Hess's law, spontaneity prediction). Chemical Kinetics (rate laws, activation energy, half life). Oxidation-Reduction Reactions (balancing equations, determination of oxidation numbers, electro-chemical concepts and calculations). Atomic and Molecular Structure (electron configuration, orbital types, Lewis-Dot diagrams, atomic theories, molecular geometry, bond types, quantum mechanics). Periodic Properties (include categories of nonmetals, transition metals, and non-transition metals). Nuclear Reactions.

ORGANIC CHEMISTRY — Bonding (atomic orbitals, molecular orbitals, hybridization, Lewis structures, bond angles, bond lengths). Mechanisms (energetics, structure & stability of intermediates: $S_N1$, $S_N2$, elimination, addition, free radical and substitution mechanisms. Chemical & Physical Properties of Molecules (stability, solubility, polarity, inter- and intra-molecular forces: separation techniques). Organic Analysis (introductory infrared and H NMR spectroscopy, simple chemical tests). Stereochemistry (conformational analysis, optical activity, chirality, chiral centers, places of symmetry, enantiomers, diastereomers, meso compounds). Nomenclature (IUPAC rules, identification of functional groups in molecules). Reaction of the Major Functional Groups (prediction of reaction products and important mechanistic generalties). Acid-Base Chemistry (resonance effects, inductive effects, prediction of products and equilibria). Aromatic (concept of aromaticity, electrophilic aromatic substitution).

Synthesis (identification of the product of, or the reagents used in, a simple sequence of reactions).

II.    Reading Comprehension

Ability to read, organize, and remember new information in dental and basic sciences. Ability to comprehend thoroughly when studying scientific information. Reading materials are typical of materials encountered in the first year of dental school and require no prior knowledge of the topic other than a basic undergraduate preparation in science. The Reading Comprehension test will contain three reading passages.

III.    Quantitative Reasoning

Algebraic Equations, Fractions, Conversions (pounds and ounces; inches and feet), Percentage, Exponential Notation, Probability and Statistics, Geometry, Trigonometry, and Applied Mathematics Problems.

IV.    Perceptual Ability

Angle Discrimination, Form Development, Block Counting, Orthographic Projections, and Object Visualization.

(Reprinted with permission of the American Dental Association.)

# PREPARING FOR THE DAT

To do well on the DAT you should start preparing for the test two to three months prior to the test date. Preparation should be done on a regular basis, devoting a set number of hours each week exclusively to reviewing the necessary material. A study plan that takes into consideration your strong and weak areas of knowledge should be thoughtfully prepared prior to initiating your study program. Special emphasis should be placed on learning facts that are organized around principles and concepts, rather than on isolated details, since the former will be retained longer. Frequent review at regular intervals will be of special help in retaining details that are not of primary importance. Study and review sessions should be terminated as soon as signs of mental fatigue become evident.

Since the DAT is a multiple-choice test, some general considerations may prove helpful. Too much should not be read into a question; it is best to take the questions at face value. Avoid the impulse to change answers when some uncertainty develops. Look for the general principle involved in the question and try to recall specific details you have memorized.

When taking the DAT make certain that you

1. have a good night's sleep before the day of the exam. Also, try to relax between the various parts of the exam;

2. avoid taking medications that will inhibit your performance (such as antihistamines or tranquilizers);

3. use regular reading glasses rather than contact lenses;

4. carefully read all directions before you start to answer the questions;

5. answer the questions in the exact manner and the exact place specified;

6. concentrate exclusively on the question under consideration;

7. determine how much time you have for each question (divide the number of questions in the subtest by the time allotted for that subtest);

8. respond first to all questions you are sure of the answers to;

9. next, answer those questions that require guessing (since the test score is based on the total number of questions answered correctly);

10. finally, answer questions that are time consuming. (Coding these and "guessing" questions for identification at the outset may save time later.)

The exam will usually begin at 8:00 A.M. and will last until 1:30 P.M. For individual tests the time limit is indicated on the cover of each of the four exam booklets.

The Survey of Natural Sciences and the Perceptual Ability tests are administered first. The Reading Comprehension and the Quantitative Reasoning tests are administered after a 15-minute break. A confidential biographical questionnaire accompanies the test and is used for studies on test validity and test usage.

The test scores for the DAT are reported to the dental schools upon the written request of the test candidates in terms of standard scores rather than raw scores. Through the use of standard scores it is possible to compare the performance of one applicant with the performance of all applicants on any or all of the topics included in the DAT.

# TAKING THE DAT

The following five Steps provide guidelines relative to the DAT:

*Step 1*. Apply to take the DAT
The fee for taking the DAT is $190, payable only by credit card. Registration for the test can be done electronically (see www.ada.org/ada/testing).

*Step 2*. Electronic notification of eligibility
Processing your DAT eligibility request involves securing by e-mail confirmation of electronic eligibility and instructions requesting your appointment and scheduling of the test.

*Step 3*. Schedule a time to take the DAT
Once you receive your DAT eligibility notification, you can schedule your test appointment at a Prometric Tests Center. Tests are administered year-round in the United States. It is advisable to schedule your test two to three months in advance.

*Step 4*. Take the DAT
Next you will complete the DAT at one of the Prometric Test Centers, on the date that was scheduled.

*Step 5*. Scores on the test
Promptly after completion of the DAT, a score report and explanation will be provided to the test takers at the testing center. This *official* copy is the only one that you will receive. However, the unofficial score is subject to review and audit, prior to reporting the official result, which is sent to dental schools. Transmission of your scores takes place within three to four weeks after taking the test. Scores are sent to all schools listed on your application. The fee for this service was included in the payment made when you applied to take the test.

Additional information regarding taking the DAT can be secured from: Dental Aptitude Test, Department of Testing Services, 211 East Chicago, Suite 600, Chicago, IL 60611. Their phone number is 800-232-1694.

# SAMPLE DAT QUESTIONS

The following are examples of typical DAT questions covering all four categories on this examination:

## PART 1 Survey of Natural Sciences

100 QUESTIONS; TIME LIMIT: 90 minutes

### Biology (40 questions on test)

1.  Exocytosis occurs when this organelle's membrane fuses with the plasma membrane.
    A.  Secretory vesicle
    B.  Nucleus
    C.  Mitochondrion
    D.  Ribosome
    E.  Golgi body

2.  NAD and FAD are important molecules in living systems because they
    A.  cause the synthesis of ATP from ADP and phosphate.
    B.  serve as oxidation-reduction coenzymes.
    C.  can reduce the activation energy of a biological reaction.
    D.  control the level of acetyl Co-A in the cell.
    E.  are essential reactants in those reactions called dehydration reactions.

3.  The addition of potassium iodide as a nutritional supplement to common table salt would most directly affect the function of which of these glands?
    A.  Thyroid
    B.  Sweat glands
    C.  Adrenal cortex
    D.  Kidneys
    E.  Parathyroid

4.  The outer layer of cells, the ectoderm, in a developing embryo gives rise to the
    A.  muscle system.
    B.  reproductive system.
    C.  circulatory system.
    D.  skeletal system.
    E.  nervous system.

5.  Removal of the gallbladder makes it more difficult to digest foods high in
    A.  carbohydrates.
    B.  nucleic acids.
    C.  proteins.
    D.  fats.
    E.  vitamins.

### Inorganic Chemistry (30 questions on test)

**6.** Supercooled water at –10°C can spontaneously warm to 0°C in a perfectly insulated container. This is possible because
   **A.** supercooled materials do not obey energy conservation laws.
   **B.** supercooled water needs less energy for change of temperature than ordinary water.
   **C.** a small amount of energy is given to the surroundings.
   **D.** some of the water freezes and this provides energy.
   **E.** ice is unusual in that it is less dense than liquid water.

**7.** How many grams of NaOH (40.0 g/mol) are required to make 250 ml of a 0.500 M solution?

   **A.** $(250)(0.500)$

   **B.** $\dfrac{(250)(500)}{1000}$

   **C.** $\dfrac{(250)(0.500)(40.0)}{1000}$

   **D.** $\dfrac{1000}{(250)(0.500)(40.0)}$

   **E.** $(250)(0.500)(40.0)$

**8.** What is the percentage of oxygen by weight in $Zn(H_2PO_4)_2$ (259g/mol)?
   **A.** 53.3%
   **B.** 24.7%
   **C.** 39.5%
   **D.** 6.18%
   **E.** 49.4%

**9.** At 0°C and 1.0 atmosphere pressure (STP) 22.0 grams of gas occupies 11.2 liters. The gas could be which of the following?
   **A.** $CO_2 = 44g/mol$
   **B.** $CO = 28g/mol$
   **C.** $NH_3 = 17g/mol$
   **D.** $CH_4 = 16g/mol$
   **E.** $C_4H_{10} = 58g/mol$

**10.** When the following equation is properly balanced, the coefficient of $H_2O$ is
$$Mg_3N_2 + H_2O \rightarrow Mg(OH)_2 + NH_3$$
   **A.** 9
   **B.** 6
   **C.** 4
   **D.** 3
   **E.** 2

**Organic Chemistry (30 questions on test)**

11.   In the reaction, $CH_3$—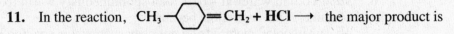=$CH_2$ + HCl ⟶   the major product is

A.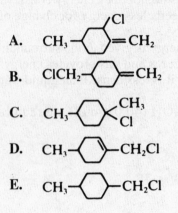

B.   $ClCH_2$—◯=$CH_2$

C.   $CH_3$—◯〈$^{CH_3}_{Cl}$

D.   $CH_3$—◯—$CH_2Cl$

E.   $CH_3$—◯—$CH_2Cl$

12.   Which reaction below is a possible termination step in the free radical chlorination of $CH_3CH_2CH_2CH_3$ by $Cl_2$?

A.   $CH_3CH_2CH_2CH_3 + Cl \rightarrow CH_3CH_2\overset{.}{C}HCH_3 + HCl$
B.   $CL_2 \rightarrow Cl\bullet + Cl\bullet$
C.   $CH_3CH_2CH_2CH_2\bullet + Cl\bullet \rightarrow CH_3CH_2CH_2CH_2Cl$
D.   $CH_3CH_2CH_2CH_3 + Cl\bullet \rightarrow CH_3CH_2CH_2CH_2\bullet + HCl$
E.   $CH_3CH_2\overset{.}{C}HCH_3 + CL_2 \rightarrow CH_3CH_2CHCH_3 + Cl\bullet$

13.   Which is the correct structure of *para*-aminobenzoic acid, PABA, a common ingredient in sunscreens?

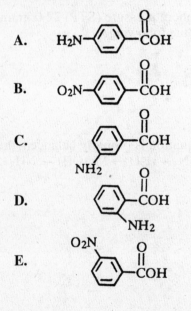

**14.** What is the product of the following reaction?

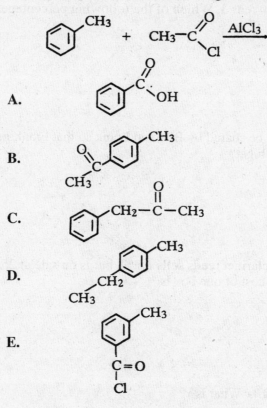

**A.**

**B.**

**C.**

**D.**

**E.**

**15.** The IUPAC name for the compound shown below is:

$$CH_3-CH_2-CH-CH_2-\underset{\underset{CH_3}{|}}{\overset{\overset{CH_2-CH_3}{|}}{C}}-CH_3$$

$$\quad\quad\quad\quad\quad\quad CH_3$$

**A.** 3,5-Dimethyl-3-ethylhexane
**B.** 4,4-Dimethyl-2-ethylhexane
**C.** Trimethylheptane
**D.** 3,3,5-Trimethylheptane
**E.** 3,5-Trimethylheptane

# PART 2  Quantitative Reasoning

**16.** $1/4 + 2/5 - 1/6 = ?$
  **A.** $-1/60$
  **B.** $2/15$
  **C.** $29/60$
  **D.** $8/15$
  **E.** $49/60$

**17.** A person's earnings increased by 10% from Year 1 to Year 2, and decreased 10% from Year 2 to Year 3. Which of the following percentages represents the change from Year 1 to Year 3?

    **A.** +20
    **B.** +1
    **C.** 0
    **D.** –1
    **E.** –11

**18.** $180 is to be shared by Bob and Frank so that Frank gets 25% more than Bob. How much does Bob get?

    **A.** $72
    **B.** $80
    **C.** $100
    **D.** $108
    **E.** $144

**19.** A box of clarinet reeds sells for $8 but is on sale at 25% off. If there is a sales tax of 6%, the total cost of one box is

    **A.** $5.52
    **B.** $5.65
    **C.** $6
    **D.** $6.36
    **E.** $6.48

**20.** $42\text{-}1/6 = 0.1x$ What is $x$?

    **A.** 7
    **B.** 25.2
    **C.** 70
    **D.** 252
    **E.** 2520

## PART 3 Perceptual Ability

**21.** Examine the four INTERIOR angles and rank each in terms of degrees from SMALL TO LARGE. Choose the alternative that has the correct ranking.

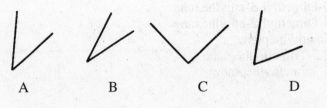

  A        B        C        D

ALTERNATIVES
    **(A)** A—B—C—D
    **(B)** B—A—D—C
    **(C)** A—C—B—D
    **(D)** C—D—A—B

**22.**  The pictures that follow are top, front, and end views of various solid objects. The views are without perspective. That is, the points in the viewed surface are viewed along parallel lines of vision. The projection of the object looking DOWN on it is shown in the upper left-hand corner (TOP VIEW). The projection looking at the object from the FRONT is shown in the lower left-hand corner (FRONT VIEW). The projection looking at the object from the END is shown in the lower right-hand corner (END VIEW). These views are ALWAYS in the same positions and are labeled accordingly.

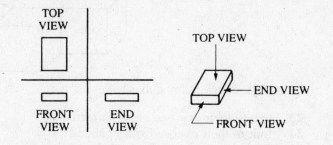

If there were a hole in the block, the views would look like this:

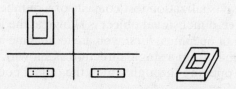

Note that lines that cannot be seen on the surface in some particular view are DOTTED in that view.

In the problems that follow, two views will be shown, with four alternatives to complete the set. You are to select the correct one and mark its number on the answer sheet.

EXAMPLE:  Choose the correct END VIEW.

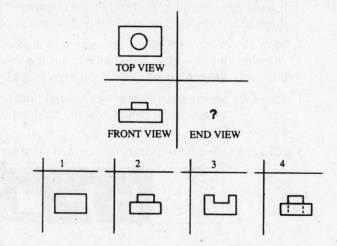

**23–25.** This group of cubes has been made by cementing together cubes of the same size. After being cemented together, each group was PAINTED ON ALL EXPOSED SIDES EXCEPT THE BOTTOM ON WHICH IT IS RESTING.

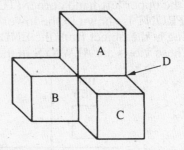

In the figure how many cubes have

**23.** two of their exposed sides painted?
**24.** four of their exposed sides painted?
**25.** five of their exposed sides painted?

**26.** This visualization test consists of a number of items similar to the following sample. A three-dimensional object is shown at the left. This is followed by outlines of five apertures or openings. *First*, you are to imagine how the object looks from *all* directions (rather than from a single direction as shown). *Then*, pick from the five apertures outlined, the opening through which the object could pass directly if the proper side were inserted first.

Here are the rules:

1. Prior to passing through the aperture, the irregular solid object may be turned in any direction. It may be started through the aperture on a side not shown.

2. Once the object is started through the aperture, it may not be twisted or turned. It must pass completely through the opening. The opening is always the exact shape of the appropriate external outline of the object.

3. Both objects and apertures are drawn to the same scale. Thus it is possible for an opening to be the correct shape but too small for the object. In all cases, however, differences are large enough to judge by eye.

4. There are no irregularities in any hidden portion of the object. However, if the figure has symmetric indentations, the hidden portion is symmetric with the part shown.

5. For each object there is only one correct aperture.

A     B     C     D     E

**27.** A flat pattern will be presented. This pattern is to be folded into a three-dimensional figure. The correct figure is one of the four given at the right of the pattern. There is only one correct figure in each set. The outside of the pattern is what is seen at the left.

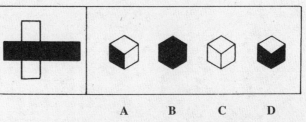

A     B     C     D

# Answers to Sample Questions

## Part 1  Survey of Natural Science

| BIOLOGY | INORGANIC CHEMISTRY | ORGANIC CHEMISTRY |
|---|---|---|
| 1. **A** | 6. **D** | 11. **C** |
| 2. **B** | 7. **C** | 12. **C** |
| 3. **A** | 8. **E** | 13. **A** |
| 4. **E** | 9. **A** | 14. **B** |
| 5. **D** | 10. **B** | 15. **D** |

## Part 2  Quantitative Reasoning

16. **C**
17. **D**
18. **B**
19. **D**
20. **E**

## Part 3  Perceptual Ability

21. **B**
22. **B**
23. **A**
24. **B**
25. **A**
26. **C**
27. **D**

## Explanation of Perceptual Ability Questions

**21.**   The correct ranking of the angles from small to large is B-A-D-C; therefore, alternative **B** is correct.

**22.**   The front view shows that there is a smaller block on the base and that there is no hole. The top view shows that the block is round and in the center of the base. The answer, therefore, must be **B**.

**23–25.** We are determining the number of exposed and painted sides for each of the four cubes. A cube by definition has six sides. Because the bottom of these four cubes are unpainted, there can be a maximum of five painted sides. In addition, where cubes are cemented together, the number of possible unpainted sides is diminished.

Cube A has five painted sides: its bottom is unpainted and is glued to the top of cube D, thus answering question 25.

Cubes B and C each have four painted sides, because their bottoms are unpainted and one of their sides is cemented to cube D. This answers question 24.

Cube D, which is hidden below cube A and behind cube C, has two painted sides. Its bottom (all the cubes) is unpainted, and two of its sides and its top are cemented to cubes A, B, and C, respectively. This answers question 23.

**26.**   The correct answer is **C** since the object would pass through this aperture if the side at the left were introduced first.

**27.**   One of the figures (A,B,C,D) can be formed from the flat pattern at the left. The only figure that corresponds to the pattern is **D**. If the shaded surfaces are looked at as the sides of the box, then all four sides must be shaded, while the top and bottom are white.

## SCORING OF THE DAT

DAT test scores are determined on the basis of the number of correct answers on your scoring sheet. Thus, there is no penalty for guessing wrong, and you should record an answer to every question rather than leave any blank.

The comparison of raw scores to standard scores is based on distribution of the performances of all those who took the exam. A standard score of 15 is considered average, within the program range of 1 to 30. As with comparable aptitude tests, there is no passing or failing grade. Examinees will receive a copy of their test scores as well as a detailed explanation of their meaning.

## CANADIAN DAT

A Canadian Dental Aptitude Test has been developed by the Canadian Dental Association and the Association of Canadian Faculties. For information on this test contact the Canadian Dental Association (l'Association Dental Canadienne), 1815 Alta Vista Drive, Ottawa, Ontario K1G 3Y6.

# 22 Opportunities in Dentistry for Women and Minorities

**Doors are open for women**
**Minorities in dentistry**

## DOORS ARE OPEN FOR WOMEN

In many respects the United States is clearly a world leader; yet the number of women in professional life in this country is disproportionate to the population as a whole. Less than 10% of dentists here are women. This figure stands in marked contrast to that of Russia or Finland, where about 80% of the dentists are women. It is also very different from other nations, such as Greece, France, Sweden, and Holland, where 25% to 50% of the dentists are women.

While the reasons for the sparsity of women dentists in this country are not positively known, one of the significant factors probably has been the belief that the profession is too physically demanding for women. While this widely held assumption is questionable to begin with, it has lost any possible validity in light of the drastic change in dentistry from a two-hand, stand-up profession to a four-hand, sit-down one.

Over the past decade, whatever barriers may have existed to prevent women from entering the field of dentistry have certainly fallen. This is evident from the dental school enrollment figures for women, which show a 400% increase since 1970. Women have responded to favorable opportunities in dentistry. Thus, even though the pool of male applicants decreased dramatically from 1985 to 1990, the pool of female applicants held constant or increased somewhat during this same period. Since 1990, the number of males and females enrolled has basically been stable, with about 2,700 males and 1,600 females making up each first-year class. For 2000, however, the number of women enrolled was 1,721 or 39% of all enrollees. This percentage is somewhat higher than that of women enrolled in the past five years. No evidence of sex bias is suggested from the application data of the past five years. Thus it is clear that motivated and qualified women can readily find a place in dental school. The profession is receptive to their admittance and it is likely that women will play a significant role in oral health care in the years to come.

## MINORITIES IN DENTISTRY

While there has been a substantial decrease in the total applicant pool to dental school, the minority applicant pool, on the other hand, has increased. Thus, for 1996–97, a total of 5,470 out of 16,570, or about 33% of all students enrolled in dental schools in the United States were minority group members. The breakdown among minority groups for first-year enrollees is about 24% Asian, 4.9% Hispanic, 5.9% African-American, and 0.6% Native American. Within these four groups, the enrollment of the first three has gone down a little over the past year and that of Asian students has increased slightly. This suggests that minority enrollment may be leveling off. The minority enrollment for freshmen for 2000–01 in each of the dental schools is given in Table 22.1.

## Minority Recruitment in Dental Schools

To help improve the proportion of minority students represented in the dental schools, special recruitment and retention efforts are employed by many schools. The following are some of the approaches used by dental schools to enhance recruitment and retention of minority and disadvantaged students.

1. Recruitment extends into high schools and community centers, using seminars and workshops to inform prospective students of the opportunities that are available.

2. Contacts are developed and maintained with prospective applicants by means of college campus visits and communicating with predental advisors and other relevant faculty members.

3. In some cases application fees are waived.

4. Prematriculation orientation programs are frequently offered for from two to ten weeks during the summer. As part of such a program, learning skills, test-taking methods, and training to improve study habits and note-taking abilities may be offered.

5. Prematriculation summer programs in dental anatomy, histology, or biochemistry are offered by some schools to lighten the freshman-year load.

6. Students may be assigned special faculty and/or upper-class student advisors. Personal professional counseling may also be offered.

7. Students may be provided with tutorial assistance when necessary.

8. Students may be permitted to extend their educational program to five instead of four years, thereby lightening their load each semester by one or two courses.

9. Individual teaching utilizing audiovisual learning modules may be offered.

10. Special scholarship and loan funds may be provided.

## Table 22.1. FIRST-YEAR DENTAL SCHOOL MINORITY ENROLLMENT

| ST | DENTAL SCHOOL | AFRICAN-AMERICAN | | HISPANIC | | NATIVE AMERICAN | | ASIAN | | NOT SPECIFIED | |
|---|---|---|---|---|---|---|---|---|---|---|---|
| | | MALE | FEMALE | MALE | FEMALE | MALE | FEMALE | MALE | FEMALE | MALE | FEMALE |
| AL | UNIVERSITY OF ALABAMA | - | 5 | - | 1 | - | - | 2 | - | - | - |
| AZ | ARIZONA SCHOOL OF DENTISTRY AND DENTAL HEALTH | - | 1 | - | 2 | 2 | 2 | 1 | 2 | - | 3 |
| CA | UNIVERSITY OF THE PACIFIC | 1 | 1 | 1 | 7 | - | - | 27 | 21 | 5 | 5 |
| | UNIVERSITY OF CALIFORNIA, SAN FRANCISCO | 3 | 2 | 3 | 4 | - | - | 18 | 21 | - | - |
| | UNIVERSITY OF CALIFORNIA, LOS ANGELES | - | 1 | 1 | 2 | - | - | 18 | 28 | - | - |
| | UNIVERSITY OF SOUTHERN CALIFORNIA | - | 1 | 2 | 1 | - | - | 38 | 24 | 2 | 1 |
| | LOMA LINDA UNIVERSITY | 2 | 1 | 4 | - | - | - | 25 | 25 | - | - |
| CO | UNIVERSITY OF COLORADO | - | - | 1 | 2 | - | 1 | 1 | 1 | - | 1 |
| CT | UNIVERSITY OF CONNECTICUT | - | 2 | 1 | - | - | - | 4 | 3 | - | - |
| DC | HOWARD UNIVERSITY | 31 | 44 | 1 | - | - | - | - | 3 | - | - |
| FL | UNIVERSITY OF FLORIDA | - | 1 | 4 | 5 | - | - | 6 | 11 | - | - |
| | NOVA SOUTHEASTERN UNIVERSITY | - | 3 | 1 | 4 | - | - | 13 | 11 | 2 | 3 |
| GA | MEDICAL COLLEGE OF GEORGIA | - | 6 | 1 | - | - | - | 3 | - | - | 1 |
| IL | SOUTHERN ILLINOIS UNIVERSITY | 1 | 2 | 1 | - | - | - | 3 | 1 | - | 1 |
| | UNIVERSITY OF ILLINOIS, CHICAGO | 1 | - | 3 | 2 | - | - | 12 | 9 | - | - |
| IN | INDIANA UNIVERSITY | - | 1 | - | - | 1 | - | 4 | 8 | - | - |
| IA | UNIVERSITY OF IOWA | - | 3 | 2 | 1 | - | - | 1 | 1 | 2 | - |
| KY | UNIVERSITY OF KENTUCKY | - | 2 | 1 | 1 | - | - | - | 2 | - | - |
| | UNIVERSITY OF LOUISVILLE | - | 3 | - | - | - | - | 4 | 2 | - | - |
| LA | LOUISIANA STATE UNIVERSITY | - | - | - | 1 | - | - | 1 | 5 | - | - |
| MD | UNIVERSITY OF MARYLAND | 2 | 4 | 3 | - | - | 1 | 9 | 17 | - | 2 |
| MA | HARVARD UNIVERSITY | 1 | 1 | - | 3 | - | - | 3 | 11 | 2 | - |
| | BOSTON UNIVERSITY | - | - | 2 | 5 | - | - | 30 | 20 | 15 | 6 |
| | TUFTS UNIVERSITY | - | 4 | 7 | 2 | - | - | 23 | 31 | - | - |
| MI | UNIVERSITY OF DETROIT - MERCY | 1 | 1 | 1 | 2 | - | - | 4 | 3 | - | - |
| | UNIVERSITY OF MICHIGAN | 5 | 3 | 1 | 2 | - | 1 | 10 | 16 | - | - |
| MN | UNIVERSITY OF MINNESOTA | 1 | - | 1 | - | - | - | 1 | 2 | 13 | 4 |
| MS | UNIVERSITY OF MISSISSIPPI | 3 | 2 | - | - | - | - | 1 | - | - | - |
| MO | UNIVERSITY OF MISSOURI, KANSAS CITY | 1 | 1 | - | 1 | - | 1 | 4 | 8 | - | - |
| NE | CREIGHTON UNIVERSITY | 1 | 1 | 4 | - | - | - | 4 | 6 | - | - |
| | UNIVERSITY OF NEBRASKA | - | - | 2 | 1 | - | - | 1 | - | - | - |
| NV | UNIVERSITY OF NEVADA, LAS VEGAS | - | - | 5 | - | 1 | 1 | 4 | 5 | 1 | - |
| NJ | U. OF MEDICINE & DENTISTRY OF NEW JERSEY | 1 | - | 1 | 2 | - | - | 9 | 11 | - | - |
| NY | COLUMBIA UNIVERSITY | 2 | 1 | - | 1 | - | - | 15 | 16 | 6 | 3 |
| | NEW YORK UNIVERSITY | 4 | 5 | 2 | 7 | - | - | 60 | 48 | 24 | 19 |
| | STATE UNIVERSITY OF NEW YORK, STONY BROOK | - | 1 | - | - | - | - | 2 | 3 | 4 | 1 |
| | STATE UNIVERSITY OF NEW YORK, BUFFALO | - | - | 2 | 1 | - | - | 9 | 6 | 1 | 1 |
| NC | UNIVERSITY OF NORTH CAROLINA | 4 | 9 | 1 | 1 | - | - | 5 | 4 | 1 | 1 |
| OH | OHIO STATE UNIVERSITY | 1 | 5 | - | - | - | - | 7 | 4 | 2 | - |
| | CASE WESTERN RESERVE UNIVERSITY | - | 1 | 1 | - | - | - | 4 | 6 | 3 | - |
| OK | UNIVERSITY OF OKLAHOMA | 1 | - | 1 | - | 6 | 3 | 2 | 4 | - | - |
| OR | OREGON HEALTH & SCIENCE UNIVERSITY | 1 | 1 | 1 | - | - | - | 1 | 5 | 11 | 2 |
| PA | TEMPLE UNIVERSITY | 3 | 4 | 3 | 2 | - | - | 14 | 13 | - | 1 |
| | UNIVERSITY OF PENNSYLVANIA | 2 | 9 | 1 | 4 | - | - | 16 | 20 | - | - |
| | UNIVERSITY OF PITTSBURGH | 1 | 1 | 2 | 7 | - | - | 10 | 7 | - | - |
| SC | MEDICAL UNIVERSITY OF SOUTH CAROLINA | 1 | 2 | 2 | 1 | - | - | 2 | - | - | - |
| TN | MEHARRY MEDICAL COLLEGE | 15 | 22 | - | 2 | - | - | 3 | 4 | - | - |
| | UNIVERSITY OF TENNESSEE | 4 | 9 | 3 | - | - | - | 4 | 3 | - | - |
| TX | TEXAS A&M UNIVERSITY - BAYLOR COLLEGE | 1 | 3 | 9 | 7 | - | - | 11 | 13 | - | - |
| | UNIVERSITY OF TEXAS, HOUSTON | - | 3 | 6 | 4 | - | - | 6 | 9 | - | - |
| | UNIVERSITY OF TEXAS, SAN ANTONIO | - | 1 | 6 | 6 | 1 | - | 2 | 7 | 2 | 2 |
| VA | VIRGINIA COMMONWEALTH UNIVERSITY | 3 | - | 2 | 1 | - | - | 5 | 6 | - | - |
| WA | UNIVERSITY OF WASHINGTON | 1 | 1 | - | 1 | - | - | 9 | 7 | - | - |
| WV | WEST VIRGINIA UNIVERSITY | - | 1 | - | - | - | - | 1 | - | - | 1 |
| WI | MARQUETTE UNIVERSITY | 1 | 3 | 3 | 1 | - | - | 3 | 3 | - | - |
| PR | UNIVERSITY OF PUERTO RICO | - | - | 11 | 29 | - | - | - | - | - | - |
| | TOTAL OF NON-ZERO ENTRIES | 100 | 178 | 110 | 126 | 11 | 11 | 478 | 493 | 96 | 58 |
| | UNITED STATES TOTAL BY ETHNICITY/RACE | | 278 | | 236 | | 22 | | 971 | | 154 |
| | PERCENT OF FIRST-YEAR ENROLLMENT | | 6.0 | | 5.1 | | 0.5 | | 21.0 | | 3.3 |

Source; American Dental Association, Survey Center, 2003-04 Survey of Predoctoral Dental Education.

Data reprinted with permission.

# 23 Financing Your Dental Education

The current financial aid crisis
Scholarships and loans

The total cost of a dental education depends on a number of factors, such as: (1) whether the dental school is a public or private institution; (2) whether the student is a state resident; (3) whether the student is single or married; (4) the location of the school; and (5) the student's lifestyle. Obviously, there can be wide differences in total costs. For most students, selecting a school involves not only its reputation, location, and educational program, but, first and foremost, its costs. A reliable estimate of costs for the freshman year can be readily ascertained by examining the last two columns of Table 25.1 in Chapter 25 and then multiplying by four to get an estimate of the total costs for all four years.

## THE CURRENT FINANCIAL AID CRISIS

Most students applying to dental school can expect to incur high educational costs. Moreover, with the inflation rate slowly continuing to escalate, these costs can be expected to continue to rise. Unfortunately, while costs are rising dramatically, federal aid, which is the major source of scholarships and loans awarded to students in the health professions, is being cut back. This has had a strong negative impact on prospective applicants and their families and may be one of the most significant factors in the decline in the applicant pool.

## SCHOLARSHIPS AND LOANS

The major portion of financial support that is made available to dental students is provided, either directly or indirectly, by the federal government. These funds are channeled through such programs as:

1. Scholarships for Health Professions Students of Exceptional Financial Need
2. Armed Forces Health Professions Scholarship Programs
3. National Health Corps Scholarship Program

These three scholarship programs and loan programs are discussed in detail in Chapter 12. Financial aid officers at the dental schools should be consulted regarding these and all other forms of support.

There are also regional groups that provide support for students living in certain states. These are:

### Western Interstate Commission for Higher Education (WICHE)

Students who are residents of western states that do not have dental schools (Alaska, Arizona, Hawaii, Montana, Nevada, Utah, and Wyoming) may apply to the WICHE Student Exchange Programs. The home state contributes a support fee to the dental school to offset part of the educational costs of its resident. The student then has to pay resident's tuition at a public or reduced tuition at a private school. For more information, contact The Professional Student Exchange Program, Western Interstate Commission for Higher Education, PO Box 9752, Boulder, CO 80301-9752.

### Southern Regional Education Board (SREB)

Students who are residents of southern states (Alabama, Arkansas, North Carolina, and Tennessee) some of which do not have dental schools, are eligible to participate in SREB's Regional Contract Program. Each home state contributes a fixed fee, while the student pays the resident's tuition at a public school and receives a reduction in tuition at a private school. For more information contact: Ann H. Creech, Southern Regional Education Board, 592 Tenth Street NW, Atlanta, GA 30318-5790, Phone: (404) 875-9211.

### United Student Aid Funds

This fund endorses loans up to $5,000 per year for a total of $15,000 for all guaranteed loan programs. Repayment begins ten months after leaving school, with interest not exceeding 7%. For additional information contact: USA Funds Endorsement Center, 1100 USA Parkway, Fishers, IN 46038.

Two restricted sources of financial aid are:

### American Fund for Dental Health Minority Scholarship Program

This program provides recipients with scholarships of up to $2,000 per year for the first two years of dental school. One must be accepted by a dental school and be a member of an underrepresented minority (African-American, Native American, Mexican-American, or Puerto Rican) to apply. For information contact: American Fund for Dental Health, 211 East Chicago Avenue, Suite 1630, Chicago, IL 60611.

### Dentistry Canada Fund

This program provides information concerning scholarships and loans. For information contact: Dentistry Canada Fund, 1815 Promenade Alta Vista Drive, Ottawa, ON, Canada, K1G 3Y6.

Financial aid on a state level is also available for some state residents. These sources are listed below by state:

**Indiana**
*Student Loan Fund Program*
Indiana Dental Association
PO Box 2467
Indianapolis, IN 46202-2467

**Kansas**
*Loan Fund*
Kansas State Dental Auxiliary
School of Dentistry
University of Missouri at Kansas City
Kansas City, MO 64108

**Louisiana**
*Dental Student Loan Fund*
Women's Auxiliary to the Louisiana Dental Association
10 Stilt Street
New Orleans, LA 70124

**Minnesota**
*Student Loan Fund*
Minnesota State Dental Association
2236 Marshall Avenue
St. Paul, MN 55104

*Loan Funds*
School of Dentistry
University of Minnesota
Washington Avenue and Union Street, S.E.
Minneapolis, MN 55455

**New Mexico**
*Student Loan Fund*
New Mexico Dental Association
2917 Santa Cruz Avenue, S.E.
Albuquerque, NM 87106

**Virginia**
*Rural Scholarship/Loan*
Virginia Commonwealth University
520 North 12th Street, Room 309
Richmond, VA 23298

**West Virginia**
*Dental School General Loan Fund*
School of Dentistry
West Virginia University
Morgantown, WV 26506

# 24 Dental Education

**Dental curriculum**
**Other educational programs**
**Postgraduate training**

## DENTAL CURRICULUM

Dental schools are located within or close to medical and hospital facilities. The traditional four-year program of studies corresponds to that of medicine and consists of two preclinical years of basic sciences and two years of clinical study. The basic sciences (anatomy, physiology, biochemistry, etc.) are taken by dental students in some schools together with medical students; in others, instruction is given exclusively in dental school. While most work consists of lecture and laboratory experiments, preclinical study also includes learning the basic techniques of dental restoration and treatment through practice on inanimate models.

The two clinical years are spent treating patients having a variety of oral diseases and disorders, while working under the supervision of clinical instructors. A variety of clinical procedures and dental care for special patients (for example, the old and infirm) are mastered during this period. Making use of dental auxiliary personnel is outlined.

Beginning in the 1960s, the traditional curriculum in dentistry underwent change; the nature of this change was two fold. First there was a new approach that involved integration of the basic and clinical sciences with emphasis on relevance, and thus students were introduced to the patient earlier. Also, greater emphasis was placed on preventive dentistry, public health dentistry, practice management, and hospital dentistry. The curricula of almost all dental schools have been updated to a greater or lesser extent along these lines.

A second major change that was attempted was the shortening of the curriculum to three years. This experiment, however, appears not to have been successful and, as of this time, all dental schools have a four-year program leading to the D.D.S. or D.M.D. degree except the University of the Pacific, which has a three-year program, and Harvard, which has a five-year program.

To provide an insight into the various dental school courses and the approximate amount of time devoted to each, a summary is presented in Table 24.1.

**Table 24.1**
**DENTAL SCHOOL COURSES AND HOURS ALLOTTED**

| Course | Average number of hours |
|---|---|
| **Basic Sciences** | |
| Anatomy (gross) | 200 |
| Anatomy (histology, general and oral) | 135 |
| Biochemistry | 100 |
| Microbiology | 100 |
| Pathology (general and oral) | 185 |
| Pharmacology | 75 |
| Physiology | 100 |
| subtotal | 895 |
| **Clinical Sciences** | |
| Anesthesiology | 50 |
| Auxiliary Utilization | 140 |
| Dental Materials | 70 |
| Diagnosis | 120 |
| Emergency Treatment | 50 |
| Endodontics | 150 |
| Hospital Dentistry | 40 |
| Nutrition | 25 |
| Occlusion | 115 |
| Operative Dentistry | 475 |
| Oral Surgery | 140 |
| Orthodontics | 125 |
| Pedodontics | 150 |
| Periodontics | 220 |
| Physical Evaluation | 60 |
| Prosthodontics (fixed and removable) | 800 |
| Special Care | 70 |
| Tooth Morphology | 85 |
| subtotal | 2885 |
| Total hours of training | 3780 |

A sample breakdown of the major courses by year is shown in Table 24.2. Schools will allot varying amounts of time to the different courses and some courses may appear under different titles.

**Table 24.2**
**MAJOR COURSES IN THE DENTAL CURRICULUM—BY YEAR**

| First Year | Second Year | Third Year | Fourth Year |
|---|---|---|---|
| Biochemistry | Endodontics | Endodontics | Endodontics |
| Dental Anatomy | Complete Dentures | Crown and Bridge | Oral Surgery |
| Dental Materials | Removable Prosthodontics | Operative Dentistry | Operative Dentistry |
| Gross Anatomy | Pathology | Pharmacology | Periodontics |
| Histology | Partial Dentures | Oral Diagnosis | Partial Dentures |
| Physiology | Operative Dentistry | Periodontics | Pedodontics |
| Microbiology | | | |

To clarify the nature of the major courses taken in dental school, a brief description of their content follows. (Courses are listed alphabetically.)

### Biochemistry

The course covers the biochemical processes that occur at the cellular and subcellular levels, and with tissue and organ metabolism and function. Emphasis is placed on the molecular basis of oral and other human disease.

### Complete Dentures

Both the theoretical and practical aspects related to the construction of complete dentures are considered during this second-year course. A complete denture is constructed for a mannequin.

### Crown and Bridge (Fixed Prosthodontics)

This course extends over the last three years. In the second year the student is introduced to the principles and basic techniques of fixed prosthodontics. Included are such topics as articulation, tooth preparation, impressions, working cast construction, waxing, casting, soldering, and finishing. The third year focuses on the research aspects, evaluating comparative studies of materials and techniques used in prosthodontics. The fourth year is devoted to seminars on current problems in the field and to clinical procedures for more complex problems.

### Dental Anatomy

This freshman course deals with the anatomical structure, individual characteristics, and the functional arrangement of teeth and their development.

### Dental Materials

This first-year course serves to introduce the student to the basic principles and properties of materials used in dental treatment. Experience to gain and improve manipulative skills with selected materials is provided.

### Endodontics

This subject is usually taught starting in the sophomore year. The differential diagnosis of dental pain is taught. Emphasis is placed on the technique used for preparing access cavities, preparing the root canal, obliterating the canal space, and utilizing endodontic instruments. The periodontal diseases and the use of surgical techniques in their treatment are discussed. The fourth year emphasizes clinical work such as surgical treatment of pathological disorders of tissues and all phases of root canal therapy.

### Gross Anatomy

The goal of this course is to familiarize the student with the anatomical basis for the study of the basic sciences and the clinical practice of dentistry. Emphasis is placed on the functional significance of various organ systems and regions by means of integrating the lectures and laboratory sessions. The latter use predissected cadavers, skeletons, models, X-rays, and movies.

### Histology

A study of the microscopic structure of tissues with special reference to the morphology of the oral cavity, particularly the teeth. Both light and electron microscopic levels of organization of tissues are analyzed.

### Microbiology

The course introduces the student to bacteriology, virology, parasitology, immunology, and mycology as related to the oral cavity. The student learns the microbial diagnostic techniques and studies the bacteria of the nasopharynx and the processes of antibiotic resistance.

### Operative Dentistry

In the second year, the basic concepts and procedures of tooth restoration are presented. Cavity preparation and restoration are taught in the laboratory. All types of cavities and the use of various restorative materials are covered. An anatomical mannequin is used to obtain experience. After a transition period from mannequin to patient, students are provided with an opportunity, over the last two years, to apply their theoretical knowledge in the clinic under supervision. Lectures, demonstrations, and seminars provide the opportunity to evaluate progress and receive individual guidance.

### Oral Diagnosis

This course extends over the last two years. In the third year, students are taught how to take a history and carry out a clinical examination in light of the patient's complaint. The course serves to correlate the basic and clinical information by focusing on diseases and abnormalities of the oral cavity. Clinical work involving oral diagnosis is required. The fourth year consists of a seminar course devoted to diagnosis and treatment planning of specially selected cases that provide valuable learning experiences.

### Oral Surgery

Having had courses in anesthesiology, radiology, and exodontics in the first through third years, the student is prepared for this fourth-year course in oral surgery. The course is devoted to the diagnosis and surgical treatment of diseases, injuries, and defects of the jaws and related structures.

### Partial Dentures

The student is taught partial denture concepts and techniques. Technical experience is gained by fabricating dentures, using a mannequin as a patient.

### Pathology

Taught during the second and third years, this course stresses the recognition and treatment of oral diseases based on their clinical characteristics and an understanding of the disease process.

### Pharmacology

Taught in the second or third year, this course aims to acquaint students with drugs currently in use, and to prepare them for the rational application of the drugs in dental practice.

### Physiology

Taught in the first year, the course deals first with cell physiology and then with the function of the organ system. The physiological basis of dentistry and its application to clinical practice are emphasized.

### Pedodontics

This subject is taught from the second to the fourth years. In the second year, the emphasis is on the procedures used with children of primary and mixed dentition ages, related to child management, oral pathology, preventive orthodontics, and operative techniques. The laboratory deals with restorative dentistry in the primary dentition. In the third year, the lectures deal with the procedures utilized, etiology, prognosis, and treatment of the dental problems of children. Supervised clinical experience is provided to learn the art of teaching dental hygiene to children and to develop the skills to diagnose and treat them. The fourth year is a continuation of the third-year course.

### Periodontics

This subject is usually taught during the last two years. The course includes a study of periodontal diseases, incorporating clinical and histopathological findings, etiological factors, and methods of prevention. The techniques of periodontal therapy are taught and clinical experience is provided.

## OTHER EDUCATIONAL PROGRAMS

A small number of students enter dental school prior to completion of their undergraduate studies. In many such cases a bachelor's degree can be earned while completing the dental curriculum, but only if the college at which the individual did undergraduate work offers such a program and awards the degree independently.

Some schools provide the opportunity for selected students to earn their dental degree together with one of the following advanced degrees:

### Master of Science (M.S.)

This degree is usually offered in oral biology or a basic science. It usually requires about one additional year of study.

### Masters in Public Health (M.P.H.)

This is a program designed for those especially interested in dental public health. It requires from one summer to one year of additional study.

### Doctor of Philosophy (Ph.D.)

This degree is usually awarded for work completed in one of the basic sciences. It requires at least two additional years of study and is designed for those planning careers in academic dentistry.

**Table 24.3**
**DENTAL SCHOOLS PROVIDING OPPORTUNITIES TO EARN OTHER DEGREES CONCURRENTLY**

| MS | MPH | PhD |
|---|---|---|
| Alabama | Alabama | Alabama |
| California, Los Angeles | California, Los Angeles | California, Los Angeles |
| California, San Francisco | Connecticut | Case Western Reserve |
| Case Western Reserve | Columbia | Connecticut |
| Columbia | Harvard | Harvard |
| Illinois | Illinois | Illinois |
| Louisville | Loma Linda | Iowa |
| Medical College of Georgia | North Carolina | Loma Linda |
| Medical College of Virginia | Northwestern | Maryland |
| Ohio State | | Medical College of Georgia |
| Oregon | | Medical College of Virginia |
| Pennsylvania | | New Jersey |
| Tennessee | | North Carolina |
| Washington | | Northwestern |
| West Virginia | | Pennsylvania |
| | | South Carolina |
| | | Southern California |
| | | SUNY at Buffalo |
| | | Tennessee |
| | | Texas, San Antonio |
| | | Washington |
| | | West Virginia |

# POSTGRADUATE TRAINING

There are eight dental specialties that are recognized by the American Dental Association. Becoming a specialist usually requires from one to four additional years of training beyond the dental degree and, in most instances, practical experience in the field.

Specialty training is offered at some dental schools and at many hospitals and medical centers. Further information on institutions offering postgraduate training can be secured from: The Commission on Dental Accreditation, American Dental Association, 211 East Chicago Avenue, Chicago, IL 60611.

# 25 Dental Schools

The dental scene in a nutshell
In-depth dental school profiles

This chapter consists of two components: a table and school profiles. Table 25.1 in "The Dental Scene in a Nutshell" provides numerical data dealing with various items and serves as a quick source of information and a means for comparing elements of various schools. The "In-Depth Dental School Profiles" offer detailed information that distinguishes the individual schools.

## THE DENTAL SCENE IN A NUTSHELL

Table 25.1, "Basic Data on the Dental Schools," contains the kind of data that should be useful in helping you decide which schools to apply to. At a glance you can see and compare application data, admission statistics, academic statistics, and expenses.

Please note that while the information in this table is as up to date and accurate as possible, it is recommended that you check with the individual dental schools before applying.

## How to Use This Table

The following list explains the column headings in Table 25.1.

### Application Fee
In many cases, this fee is required only at the time of final application. The preliminary application is usually the AADSAS application, for which a fee is paid when submitting the form.

### Earliest and Latest Filling Dates
These are usually firm dates.

### Number of Applicants
This column gives an idea of how many applications were received for the 2008–2009 class.

### Entering Class
The columns indicate the men, women, minority, and out-of-state students who enrolled in the 2008–2009 entering class.* The ratio of the total number of men and women accepted to the total number of applicants gives an indication of the competitive nature of admissions at each school.

### Two Years College
This shows the relative chances of a second-year student gaining admission.

### Three Years College
This shows the relative chances of a third-year student gaining admission.

### Mean GPA
The mean grade point average. It is usually somewhat lower for residents.

### Mean Science

The mean science grade point average. It also is usually somewhat lower for residents.

### DAT Academic Average

The mean academic average test score for entering first-year students.

### DAT PAT Average

The mean perceptual ability test score for entering first-year students. This and the preceding score can serve as a guide for the standards and competitive nature of each school.

### Tuition

2008–2009 tuition costs (annual) for first-year students, unless otherwise indicated.

### Other

This estimate covers fees, books, instruments, and other supplies and materials for the first year.

## Table 25.1  BASIC DATA ON THE DENTAL SCHOOLS (2008–2009 ACADEMIC YEAR)

| | Application Data | | | | Admission Statistics | | | |
| | | Filing Dates | | | | Entering Class | | |
| School | Fee | Earliest | Latest | Number of Applicants | Men | Women | Minority | Out of State |
|---|---|---|---|---|---|---|---|---|
| **ALABAMA** | | | | | | | | |
| University of Alabama School of Dentistry | 75 | 5/1 | 12/1 | 805 | 36 | 22 | 6 | 7 |
| **ARIZONA** | | | | | | | | |
| Arizona School of Dentistry & Oral Health | 60 | | 12/1 | 2929 | 29 | 39 | 16 | 46 |
| Midwestern University School of Dentistry | 50 | 6/1 | 3/1 | 1680 | 57 | 53 | 30 | 80 |
| **CALIFORNIA** | | | | | | | | |
| Loma Linda University School of Dentistry | 75 | 5/15 | 12/1 | 2059 | 60 | 29 | 29 | 75 |
| University of California—Los Angeles School of Dentistry | 60 | 6/1 | 1/1 | 1987 | 15 | 12 | 48 | 14 |
| University of California—San Francisco School of Dentistry | 60 | 5/15 | 10/15 | 1761 | 52 | 34 | 9 | 16 |
| University of Southern California School of Dentistry | 85 | 6/1 | 2/1 | 3200 | 79 | 65 | 17 | 55 |
| University of the Pacific School of Dentistry | 75 | 6/1 | 12/1 | 3115 | 141 | 72 | 69 | 12 |
| **COLORADO** | | | | | | | | |
| University of Colorado at Denver School of Dental Medicine | 50 | 5/15 | 12/31 | 1500 | 32 | 18 | 2 | 21 |
| **CONNECTICUT** | | | | | | | | |
| University of Connecticut School of Dentistry | 75 | 6/1 | 1/1 | 1515 | 21 | 23 | 8 | 20 |
| **WASHINGTON, D.C.** | | | | | | | | |
| Howard University College of Dentistry | 45 | 5/1 | 1/15 | 2546 | 41 | 44 | 39 | n/a |
| **FLORIDA** | | | | | | | | |
| Nova Southeastern Univ. College of Dentistry | 50 | 6/1 | 3/1 | 2750 | 65 | 9 | 96 | 45 |
| University of Florida College of Dentistry | 30 | 5/1 | 12/1 | 1472 | 33 | 50 | 27 | 11 |
| **GEORGIA** | | | | | | | | |
| Medical College of Georgia School of Dentistry | 30 | 6/1 | 10/15 | 311 | 32 | 34 | 11 | 0 |

n/a    not available

| % With | | Mean GPA | Admission Statistics | | | | Expenses | | |
| | | | Accepted Out of State | | Entering Class | | Tuition | | |
| 2 Years of College | 3 Years of College | Mean GPA | Mean Total GPA | Mean Science GPA | DAT Academic Average | DAT PAT Average | Resident | Non-Resident | Other |
|---|---|---|---|---|---|---|---|---|---|
| 0 | 100 | 3.7 | | 3.6 | 19 | 19 | 16,647 | 43,199 | 9,028 |
| 5 | 95 | 3.4 | | | 18 | 18 | 44,160 | 44,160 | n/a |
| n/a | 100 | 3.4 | | 3.4 | 18 | 19 | 49,231 | 49,231 | 8,650 |
| n/a | n/a | 3.5 | | 3.4 | 19 | 19 | 40,367 | 40,367 | n/a |
| n/a | n/a | 3.7 | | 3.7 | 22 | 20 | 24,250 | 24,250 | n/a |
| 0 | 0 | 3.5 | | 3.5 | 20 | 20 | 27,925 | 40,170 | n/a |
| 0 | 100 | 3.4 | | 3.5 | 21 | 19 | 71,620 | 71,620 | n/a |
| 1,4 | 97 | 3.4 | | 3.5 | 19 | 19 | 68,835 | 68,835 | 0 |
| 2 | 98 | 3.6 | | 3.6 | 19 | 20 | 31,950 | 57,253 | n/a |
| 0 | 100 | 3.6 | | 3.5 | 20 | 20 | 25,108 | 50,151 | 29,700 |
| n/a | n/a | 3.19 | | 2.9 | 16 | 15 | 21,065 | 21,065 | n/a |
| n/a | n/a | 3.5 | | 3.6 | 19 | 18 | 40,045 | 42,750 | n/a |
| 0 | 100 | 3.6 | | 3.5 | 19 | 19 | 24,524 | 51,004 | 23,577 |
| 0 | 100 | 3.6 | | 3.6 | 18 | 19 | 25,807 | 22,784 | 8,444 |

## Table 25.1  BASIC DATA ON THE DENTAL SCHOOLS (2008–2009 ACADEMIC YEAR)

| School | Application Data | | | | Admission Statistics | | | |
| | Fee | Filing Dates | | Number of Applicants | Entering Class | | | |
| | | Earliest | Latest | | Men | Women | Minority | Out of State |
|---|---|---|---|---|---|---|---|---|
| **ILLINOIS** | | | | | | | | |
| Southern Illinios University School of Dental Medicine | 20 | 5/15 | 2/1 | 678 | 30 | 20 | 5 | 0 |
| University of Illinois, Chicago College of Dentistry | 65 | 6/1 | 12/1 | 1670 | 43 | 26 | 14 | 5 |
| **INDIANA** | | | | | | | | |
| Indiana University School of Dentistry | 50 | 5/15 | 2/1 | 1787 | 67 | 34 | 2 | 31 |
| **IOWA** | | | | | | | | |
| University of Iowa College of Dentistry | 60 | 6/1 | 11/1 | 1087 | 49 | 31 | 11 | 23 |
| **KENTUCKY** | | | | | | | | |
| University of Kentucky College of Dentistry | 65 | 12/1 | | 1464 | 32 | 24 | 6 | 16 |
| University of Louisville School of Dentistry | 50 | 6/1 | 1/1 | 2721 | 36 | 49 | 17 | 41 |
| **LOUISIANA** | | | | | | | | |
| Louisiana State University School of Dentistry | 50 | 9/1 | 2/28 | 250 | 37 | 23 | 13 | 7 |
| **MARYLAND** | | | | | | | | |
| University of Maryland Baltimore College of Dental Surgery | 75 | 5/1 | 1/1 | 2806 | 64 | 66 | 18 | 57 |
| **MASSACHUSETTS** | | | | | | | | |
| Boston University, Goldman School of Dental Medicine | 70 | 6/1 | 2/1 | 4387 | 63 | 52 | 31 | 91 |
| Harvard School of Dental Medicine | 70 | 6/1 | 12/15 | 1186 | 12 | 10 | 1 | 11 |
| Tufts University School of Dental Medicine | 70 | 5/15 | 2/1 | 4344 | 83 | 84 | 69 | 118 |
| **MICHIGAN** | | | | | | | | |
| University of Detriot—Mercy School of Dentistry | 75 | 5/15 | 2/1 | 1843 | 50 | 37 | 36 | 27 |
| University of Michigan School of Dentistry | 50 | 5/15 | 12/1 | 2144 | 56 | 49 | 23 | 38 |

n/a    not available

| % With | | Mean GPA | Admission Statistics | | | | | Expenses | | |
|---|---|---|---|---|---|---|---|---|---|---|
| | | | Accepted Out of State | | Entering Class | | | Tuition | | |
| 2 Years of College | 3 Years of College | | Mean Total GPA | Mean Science GPA | DAT Academic Average | DAT PAT Average | | Resident | Non-Resident | Other |
| 14 | 86 | 3.7 | | 3.6 | 18 | 18.4 | | 26,090 | 35,362 | n/a |
| 0 | 100 | 3.3 | | 3.3 | 19 | 19 | | 38,082 | 65,722 | n/a |
| 0 | 99 | 3.5 | | 3.5 | 19 | 20 | | 35,947 | 65,328 | n/a |
| 2 | 95 | 3.7 | | 3.6 | 19 | 19 | | 26,681 | 44,871 | n/a |
| 0 | 100 | 3.6 | | 3.5 | 19 | 19 | | 22,780 | 46,474 | n/a |
| 0 | 100 | 3.5 | | 3.3 | 17 | 16 | | 18,850 | 45,094 | n/a |
| 0 | 100 | 3.6 | | 3.5 | 19 | 20 | | 5,865 | 9,200 | n/a |
| 99 | 1 | 3.5 | | 3.4 | 19 | 19 | | 19,998 | 43,378 | n/a |
| 0 | 100 | 3.3 | | 3.2 | 19 | 19 | | 53,097 | 53,097 | 30,272 |
| n/a | n/a | 3.7 | | 3.8 | 21 | 22 | | 38,600 | 38,600 | n/a |
| 0 | 100 | 3.4 | | 3.4 | 19 | 19 | | 62,475 | 62,475 | 20,250 |
| 1 | 2 | 3.6 | | 3.6 | 19 | 20 | | 45,734 | 57,342 | 11,442 |
| 0 | 100 | 3.5 | | 3.3 | 19 | 18 | | 28,354 | 43,272 | n/a |

## Table 25.1 BASIC DATA ON THE DENTAL SCHOOLS (2008–2009 ACADEMIC YEAR)

| School | | Application Data | | | Admission Statistics | | | |
|---|---|---|---|---|---|---|---|---|
| | | | Filing Dates | | | Entering Class | | |
| | Fee | Earliest | Latest | Number of Applicants | Men | Women | Minority | Out of State |
| **MINNESOTA** | | | | | | | | |
| University of Minnesota School of Dentistry | 75 | 5/15 | 12/1 | 1073 | 55 | 42 | 15 | 31 |
| **MISSISSIPPI** | | | | | | | | |
| University of Mississippi School of Dentistry | 50 | 7/1 | 11/1 | 129 | 21 | 16 | 6 | 0 |
| **MISSOURI** | | | | | | | | |
| University of Missouri— Kansas City School of Dentistry | 45 | 9/1 | 10/1 | 1095 | 63 | 39 | 6 | 28 |
| **NEBRASKA** | | | | | | | | |
| Creighton University School of Dentistry | 45 | 7/1 | 2/1 | 3185 | 47 | 38 | 7 | 79 |
| University of Nebraska College of Dentistry | 50 | 5/15 | 2/1 | 940 | 15 | 23 | 0 | 11 |
| **NEVADA** | | | | | | | | |
| University of Nevada, Las Vegas   School of Dentistry | 50 | 5/15 | 1/15 | 2918 | 48 | 34 | 21 | 24 |
| **NEW JERSEY** | | | | | | | | |
| University of Medicine and Dentistry of New Jersey | 75 | 6/1 | 12/1 | 1946 | 27 | 25 | 4 | 2 |
| **NEW YORK** | | | | | | | | |
| Columbia University School of Dental and Oral Surgery | 70 | 6/1 | 2/15 | 2169 | 17 | 16 | 5 | n/a |
| New York University College of Dentistry | 75 | 6/1 | 2/1 | 3500 | 65 | 38 | 3 | 159 |
| State University of New York at Buffalo, School of Dental Medicine | 50 | 5/15 | 1/1 | 2001 | 39 | 23 | 0 | 26 |
| Stoney Brook University, School of Dental Medicine | 75 | 7/1 | 1/15 | 1445 | 25 | 14 | 14 | 1 |
| **NORTH CAROLINA** | | | | | | | | |
| University of North Carolina School of Dentistry | 78 | 6/30 | 12/1 | 960 | 49 | 51 | 21 | 10 |

n/a    not available

| % With | | | Admission Statistics | | | | Expenses | | |
| | | | Accepted Out of State | | Entering Class | | Tuition | | |
| 2 Years of College | 3 Years of College | Mean GPA | Mean Total GPA | Mean Science GPA | DAT Academic Average | DAT PAT Average | Resident | Non-Resident | Other |
|---|---|---|---|---|---|---|---|---|---|
| n/a | n/a | n/a | | 3.6 | 19 | 20 | 22,228 | 39,598 | n/a |
| 0 | 100 | 3.6 | | 3.6 | 18 | 19 | 11,530 | 11,530 | 8,157 |
| 100 | 100 | 3.6 | | 3.6 | 18 | 18 | 27,813 | 27,813 | n/a |
| 5 | 95 | 3.6 | | 3.5 | 18 | 20 | 46,962 | 46,962 | n/a |
| n/a | n/a | 3.8 | | 3.6 | 19 | 18 | 14,207 | 52,135 | n/a |
| 24 | 76 | 3.5 | | 3.3 | 19 | 19 | 30,837 | 53,337 | n/a |
| 3 | 8 | 3.6 | | 3.3 | 19 | 18 | 23,136 | 36,203 | n/a |
| 0 | 0 | 3.6 | | 3.4 | 22 | 19 | 45,760 | 45,760 | n/a |
| 0 | 4 | 3.4 | | 3.3 | 19 | 18 | 50,490 | 50,490 | n/a |
| 1 | 2 | 3.6 | | 3.6 | 19 | 18 | 16,200 | 32,000 | n/a |
| 0 | 100 | 3.7 | | 3.7 | 21 | 19 | 22,723 | 39,023 | n/a |
| 2 | 93 | 3.6 | | 3.5 | 19 | 19 | 19,730 | 32,790 | 5,700 |

## Table 25.1  BASIC DATA ON THE DENTAL SCHOOLS (2008–2009 ACADEMIC YEAR)

| School | Fee | Earliest | Latest | Number of Applicants | Men | Women | Minority | Out of State |
|---|---|---|---|---|---|---|---|---|
| | | **Application Data** | | | **Admission Statistics** | | | |
| | | **Filing Dates** | | | **Entering Class** | | | |
| **OHIO** | | | | | | | | |
| Case Western Reserve<br>   Univ. School of Dentistry | 45 | 5/15 | 1/1 | 3326 | 44 | 26 | 22 | 57 |
| Ohio State University<br>   College of Dentistry | 30 | 6/1 | 11/15 | 1179 | 54 | 31 | 3 | 20 |
| **OKLAHOMA** | | | | | | | | |
| University of Oklahoma<br>   College of Dentistry | 65 | 5/15 | 9/1 | 648 | 43 | 15 | 12 | 11 |
| **OREGON** | | | | | | | | |
| Oregon Health Science Univ.<br>   School of Dentistry | 75 | 6/1 | 11/1 | 1071 | 58 | 17 | 13 | 30 |
| **PENNSLYVANIA** | | | | | | | | |
| Temple University<br>   Maurice H. Kornberg<br>   School of Dentistry | 30 | 5/15 | 2/1 | 4438 | 68 | 57 | 18 | 74 |
| University of Pennsylvania<br>   School of Dental Medicine | 50 | 6/1 | 1/1 | 2445 | 115 | 50 | 65 | 97 |
| University of Pittsburgh<br>   School of Dental Medicine | 35 | 6/1 | 11/30 | 2114 | 39 | 14 | 1 | 56 |
| **SOUTH CAROLINA** | | | | | | | | |
| Medical University of<br>   South Carolina,<br>   College of Dental Medicine | 75 | 5/15 | 12/1 | 634 | 40 | 12 | 1 | 13 |
| **TENNESSEE** | | | | | | | | |
| Meharry Medical College<br>   School of Dentistry | 60 | 5/15 | 1/15 | 1976 | 28 | 23 | 49 | 43 |
| University of Tennessee<br>   College of Dentistry | 50 | 6/1 | 11/30 | 544 | 58 | 22 | 10 | 26 |
| **TEXAS** | | | | | | | | |
| Baylor College of Dentistry | 35 | 5/1 | 10/1 | 1400 | 26 | 14 | 13 | 2 |
| University of Texas<br>   Health Science Center<br>   Houston Dental Branch | 55 | 5/1 | 10/1 | 1182 | 39 | 45 | 12 | 1 |
| University of Texas<br>   Health Science Center<br>   San Antonio Dental School | 55 | 10/1 | n/a | 1056 | 44 | 53 | 15 | 4 |

n/a    not available

| % With | | Mean GPA | Admission Statistics | | | | Expenses | | |
| --- | --- | --- | --- | --- | --- | --- | --- | --- | --- |
| | | | Accepted Out of State | | Entering Class | | Tuition | | |
| 2 Years of College | 3 Years of College | Mean GPA | Mean Total GPA | Mean Science GPA | DAT Academic Average | DAT PAT Average | Resident | Non-Resident | Other |
| 4 | 90 | 3.6 | | 3.6 | 19 | 20 | 48,830 | 48,830 | 12,572 |
| 0 | 1 | 3.6 | | 3.5 | 19 | 18 | 24,663 | 53,724 | n/a |
| 0 | 100 | 3.65 | | 3.7 | 19 | 17 | 14,865 | 36,645 | n/a |
| 0 | 0 | 3.6 | | 3.6 | 19 | 20 | 26,962 | 40,252 | 14,524 |
| 1 | 99 | 3.4 | | 3.4 | 19 | 19 | 35,390 | 48,902 | 6,207 |
| 0 | 3 | 3.7 | | 3.6 | 20 | 20 | 53,990 | 53,990 | 28,938 |
| 0 | 10 | 3.6 | | 3.4 | 19 | 18 | 32,460 | 39,788 | n/a |
| 0 | 0 | 3.5 | | 3.5 | 19 | 18 | 25,430 | 72,944 | n/a |
| 1 | 99 | 3.2 | | 3.2 | 16 | 16 | 38,367 | 38,367 | n/a |
| 0 | 100 | 3.5 | | 3.5 | 18 | 19 | 18,368 | 18,368 | n/a |
| 0 | 0 | 3.6 | | 3.5 | 20 | 17 | 5,400 | 16,200 | n/a |
| 4 | 92 | 3.6 | | 3.5 | 19 | 19 | 16,531 | 27,331 | 5,793 |
| 0 | 100 | 3.8 | | 3.6 | 19 | 19 | 11,125 | 21,925 | n/a |

## Table 25.1 BASIC DATA ON THE DENTAL SCHOOLS (2008–2009 ACADEMIC YEAR)

| School | Fee | Application Data | | Number of Applicants | Admission Statistics | | | |
|---|---|---|---|---|---|---|---|---|
| | | Filing Dates | | | Entering Class | | | |
| | | Earliest | Latest | | Men | Women | Minority | Out of State |
| **VIRGINIA** | | | | | | | | |
| Virginia Commonwealth Univ. School of Dentistry | 70 | 5/15 | 11/1 | 2600 | 65 | 35 | 7 | 45 |
| **WASHINGTON** | | | | | | | | |
| University of Washington School of Dentistry | 35 | 11/5 | n/a | 1076 | 35 | 27 | 7 | 5 |
| **WEST VIRGINIA** | | | | | | | | |
| West Virginia University School of Dentistry | 50 | 6/1 | 11/1 | 1554 | 23 | 27 | 10 | 11 |
| **WISCONSIN** | | | | | | | | |
| Marquette University School of Dentistry | 45 | 5/15 | 1/1 | 3134 | 80 | 47 | 33 | 17 |
| **CANADA** | | | | | | | | |
| Dalhousie University Faculty of Dentistry | 75 | 9/1 | 12/1 | 324 | 23 | 5 | n/a | 7 |
| McGill University Faculty of Dentistry | 80 | 11/15 | 1/15 | 450 | 10 | 20 | n/a | n/a |
| Université de Montréal Faculté de Médecine Dentaire | 30 | 1/1 | 3/1 | n/a | 26 | 59 | n/a | n/a |
| Université Laval Faculté Medecine Dentaire | 62 | n/a | n/a | 643 | 16 | 32 | n/a | n/a |
| University of Alberta Faculty of Dentistry | 115 | 7/1 | 11/1 | 383 | 35 | 23 | 12 | n/a |
| University of British Columbia Faculty of Dentistry | 200 | 6/1 | 11/1 | 332 | 22 | 17 | n/a | n/a |
| University of Manitoba Faculty of Dentistry | 75 | 11/15 | 1/22 | 304 | 16 | 14 | n/a | 5 |
| University of Saskatchewan College of Dentistry | 125 | 8/1 | 1/15 | 303 | 20 | 8 | n/a | 2 |
| University of Toronto Faculty of Dentistry | 230 | 7/1 | 12/1 | 484 | 24 | 41 | n/a | 4 |
| University of Western Ontario Faculty of Dentistry | 250 | n/a | 12/1 | 620 | 27 | 26 | n/a | 5 |

n/a     not available

| % With | | | Admission Statistics | | | | Expenses | | |
| --- | --- | --- | --- | --- | --- | --- | --- | --- | --- |
| | | | Accepted Out of State | | Entering Class | | Tuition | | |
| 2 Years of College | 3 Years of College | Mean GPA | Mean Total GPA | Mean Science GPA | DAT Academic Average | DAT PAT Average | Resident | Non-Resident | Other |
| 2 | 98 | 3.5 | | 3.5 | 19 | 20 | 19,656 | 38,965 | n/a |
| 0 | 98 | 3.5 | | 3.6 | n/a | n/a | 17,425 | 41,429 | n/a |
| 2 | 98 | 3.5 | | 3.4 | 17 | 18 | 14,455 | 36,337 | 12,735 |
| 11 | 89 | 3.6 | | 3.5 | 18 | 19 | 34,330 | 43,080 | n/a |
| n/a | 100 | 3.7 | | 3.7 | 18 | 16 | 14,074 | 35,000 | n/a |
| 33 | 7 | 3.7 | | 3.7 | 22 | 21 | 3,985 | 11,474 | n/a |
| 100 | n/a | n/a | | n/a | n/a | n/a | 2,650 | 2,000 | n/a |
| 50 | 25 | n/a | | n/a | n/a | 15 | 3,860 | 3,860 | n/a |
| 23 | 51 | 3.9 | | 3.8 | n/a | 21 | 13,579 | 13,579 | 18,000 |
| 10 | 82 | 85 | | n/a | 21 | 22 | 15,000 | 36,000 | n/a |
| 17 | 23 | 3.8 | | 3.6 | 20 | 19 | 13,595 | 13,595 | n/a |
| 32 | 25 | 89.1 | | n/a | 18.56 | 21.64 | 32,741 | 32,741 | 6,919 |
| 22 | 59 | 3.8 | | n/a | 20 | 20 | 28,901 | 57,004 | n/a |
| n/a | 75 | 88.5 | | n/a | 20 | n/a | 32,900 | 53,130 | n/a |

# IN-DEPTH DENTAL SCHOOL PROFILES

The dental school profiles consist of in-depth descriptions of all the accredited U.S. dental schools and Canadian dental schools. The profiles include an introductory paragraph, admission procedures and requirements, curriculum, grading and promotion policies, facilities, and special features as described below.

## Capsule

Each profile is preceded by a capsule featuring the essential information that defines each school. It includes communication addresses and numbers; facts on application deadlines, accreditation, and degrees; enrollment figures and test scores; and a graphic display of tuition, broken out by residents and nonresidents as compared with average nationwide costs.

## Introduction

The background of the dental school as well as the parent institution (if any) is described in this section.

## Admissions

Although the minimum requirement for most U.S. schools is at least three years (90 semester hours) of undergraduate study at an accredited college or university, the percentage of those accepted with only this background is quite small. Most students hold a baccalaureate degree at the time they begin their dental school studies. (Some Canadian schools have a one- or two-year college prerequisite.) *The DAT is required for admission by essentially all U.S. schools* (but not by those in Canada). The basic or minimum predental science course requirements referred to in this section consist of one year each of biology, inorganic chemistry, organic chemistry, and physics along with their appropriate laboratory work. Any additional required or recommended courses are indicated. Most other required courses include those covered by any regular general education program at an undergraduate college. An interview may or may not be required but it is given only at the invitation of the school. Since residence is in some cases a significant element in the admission process, the general policy is noted. (For an overall picture of this factor, see Table 23.1, which lists the number of nonresidents accepted.)

## Transfer and Advanced Standing

The level to which transfer is possible varies from school to school. Foreign dental school graduates may be accepted at some undergraduate level at institutions that grant advanced standing (usually only into the second year).

## Curriculum

The curriculum is described as to length and type. The classifications used are: *traditional* (basic science taught during the first two years, although some clinical exposure may be provided. Last two years consist of clerkships in major and minor clinical specialties with little or no time allotted for electives); *diagonal curriculum* (phases in clinical experience to significant extent beginning in the first year, but the bulk of the clinics are still scheduled for the last two years); *flexible curriculum* (no rigid course curriculum and students complete the program in varying amounts of time).

## Grading Policy

Where known, the grading policy is described. These policies may be different in the basic and clinical sciences.

## Facilities

The facilities utilized both in the basic sciences and for clinical training are described.

## Special Features

Other degree programs or special programs for recruiting and retaining disadvantaged students are described in this section.

## ALABAMA

# University of Alabama at Birmingham School of Dentistry

1919 Seventh Avenue, South
University Station, SDA 125
Birmingham, Alabama   35294

*Phone:* 205-934-3387         *Fax:* 205-934-0209
*E-mail:* admissions@csl.dental.uab.edu
*WWW:* dental.uab.edu

| Application Filing | | Accreditation |
|---|---|---|
| Earliest: | June 1 | CODA |
| Latest: | December 1 | |
| Fee: | $75 | **Degrees Granted** |
| AADSAS: | yes | DMD, DMD-MS, DMD-PhD |

### Enrollment: 2005–2006 First-Year Class

| | | | | |
|---|---|---|---|---|
| Men: | 36 | 61% | *Mean* | |
| Women: | 12 | 25% | total GPA: | 3.7 |
| Minorities: | 6 | 10% | science: | 3.6 |
| Out of State: | 7 | 12% | | |
| With 2 years of college: | 0% | | *Average* | |
| With 3 years of college: | 0% | | DAT academic: | 19 |
| | | | DAT-PAT: | 19 |

### Tuition and Fees

| | |
|---|---|
| **Resident** | 16,647 |
| Average | 24,250 |
| **Nonresident** | 43,199 |
| Average | 37,850 |

(in thousands of dollars)

Percentage receiving financial aid:  79%

## Introduction

The University of Alabama was first established in 1831. After the Civil War, the school was rebuilt and reopened in 1869. In 1969 the University of Alabama system was established, and included 3 universities. The Birmingham campus of the University of Alabama holds the Medical Center, the University College, and the Graduate School. The 2 other campuses are located in Tuscaloosa and Huntsville. The School of Dentistry is part of the Medical Center at Birmingham, and was established in 1945. It admitted its first class of students in 1948. In addition to offering a program leading to the DMD degree, the School of Dentistry has accredited programs in all the specialties as well as dental assisting. This school pioneered the development of "four-handed dentistry" and the expanded utilization of trained auxiliary personnel.

## Admissions (AADSAS)

In addition to the basic predental science courses, 1 year each of mathematics and English are required. Recommended electives may be from biology (embryology, genetics, comparative anatomy, cell physiology), chemistry (quantitative analysis), calculus, literature, foreign languages, business, art, and sculpting. Preference is given to residents of Alabama and neighboring states. *Transfer and advanced standing:* Not available.

## Information for Special Applicants

The school conducts a program designed to interest, recruit, and retain disadvantaged minority students and other individuals from groups traditionally underrepresented in the profession. Advice and special counseling are given to these individuals, once identified, in the application procedure. Several faculty members sharing responsibility in this area are also members of the Admissions Committee and are therefore able to contribute to the total evaluation of these special applicants.

## Curriculum

4-year traditional. The curriculum incorporates innovative interdisciplinary programs that emphasize the application of the basic sciences to various clinical problems. Initial clinical experience is provided during the latter part of the first year, at intervals during the second year, and intensively during the third and fourth years. Elective programs are offered to fourth-year students. They cover a wide variety of topics and experiences.

## Facilities

The School of Dentistry Building is located within the medical facilities campus in downtown Birmingham. Off-campus clinical experience is also provided as an elective experience during the senior year at underserved areas throughout the state.

## Special Features

A program exists that is designed to interest, recruit, and retain minority students and women. Programs leading to the DMD-MS or PhD in one of the basic sciences are available.

## Special Programs

Academic and personal counseling is available to all students through assignment to faculty advisors in the School of Dentistry or through the University Counseling Service. It is anticipated that problems the student might experience can be identified and confronted before they become compounded. Tutorial assistance is available if necessary. This institution has the capability to graduate every student accepted into the freshman class and makes every effort to do so. Faculty and students alike are committed to this mutual goal. Students accepted into the school should be prepared to support the entire expense of their dental education. The Student Loan Committee will strive to equitably distribute all available funds.

# ARIZONA

# Arizona School of Dentistry & Oral Health

5850 East Still Circle
Mesa, Arizona    85206

*Phone:* 866-626-2878          *Fax:* 660-626-2960
*E-mail:* admissions@atsu.edu
*WWW:* atsu.edu/

| Application Filing | | Accreditation | |
|---|---|---|---|
| Earliest: | June 1 | CDA | |
| Latest: | December 15 | | |
| Fee: | $60 | **Degrees Granted** | |
| AADSAS: | yes | DMD | |

### Enrollment: 2008–2009 First-Year Class

| | | | | |
|---|---|---|---|---|
| Men: | 29 | 43% | *Mean* | |
| Women: | 39 | 57% | total GPA: | 18 |
| Minorities: | 16 | 24% | science: | 3.3 |
| Out of State: | 46 | 68% | | |
| | | | *Average* | |
| | | | DAT academic: | 18 |
| | | | DAT-PAT: | 18 |

### Tuition and Fees

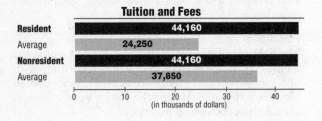

| | |
|---|---|
| Resident | 44,160 |
| Average | 24,250 |
| Nonresident | 44,160 |
| Average | 37,850 |

0    10    20    30    40
(in thousands of dollars)

## Introduction

This school initiated its dental program in September 2003 and graduated its first class in 2007. The school is situated on a 23-acre campus, in the east valley of Arizona's Phoenix metropolitan area. The school shares a campus with the Arizona School of Health Sciences, which also offers programs in audiology, occupational therapy, physician assistant studies, physical therapy, athletic training, human movement, and doctorate of health sciences, as well as the School of Osteopathic Medicine in Arizona and third- and fourth-year training for Kirksville College of Osteopathic Medicine's Arizona Region medical students. The school is under the A.T. Still University umbrella.

## Admissions (AADSAS)

A minimum of 3 years (90 credits) of undergraduate studies is required, but a baccalaureate degree is preferred. Required courses are 1 year biology, general chemistry, organic chemistry, and physics, 1 class of human physiology, biochemistry, and English. Recommended additional courses are anatomy and microbiology. Computer literacy is required. Applicants must submit DAT scores. A minimum GPA of 2.5 is necessary. There are no specific residency requirements. Transfer applications are reviewed on a case-by-case basis. Advanced standing is not available.

## Curriculum

4-year. *First year:* Integrated Human Sciences with preclinical dental simulation. *Second year:* Integrated clinical sciences with preclinical didactic courses and clinical experiences. *Third year:* Mentored on-site clinical experience with clinical didactic courses. *Fourth year:* Community-based clinical experiences with community clinical partners.

## Facilities

The campus is located in East Mesa at Recker/Baseline Roads. It comprises a 3-story classroom/lab building and a 2-story 81-chair dental clinic. In addition, a 6-chair clinic is located on the west side of the Phoenix metropolitan area in Glendale, Arizona. A temporary orthodontic clinic is located in the current dental clinic but will expand to a separate building in 2009. Plans are to build a YMCA, intergenerational village, and hospital on campus.

# Arizona College of Dental Medicine of Midwestern University

19555 North 59th Avenue
Glendale, Arizona    85308

*Phone:* 623-572-3215
*E-mail:* admissaz@midwestern.edu
*WWW:* midwestern.edu

| Application Filing | | Accreditation |
|---|---|---|
| Earliest: | June 1 | CDA |
| Latest: | March 1 | |
| Fee: | $50 | **Degrees Granted** |
| AADAS: | yes | DMD |

### Enrollment: 2008–2009 First-Year Class

| | | | | |
|---|---|---|---|---|
| Men: | 57 | 52% | *Mean* | |
| Women: | 53 | 48% | total GPA: | 3.3 |
| Minorities: | 30 | 27% | science: | 3.4 |
| Out of State: | 80 | 72% | *Average* | |
| With 3 years of college: | n/a | | DAT academic: | 18.0 |
| With 4 years of college: | 100% | | DAT-PAT: | 19.0 |

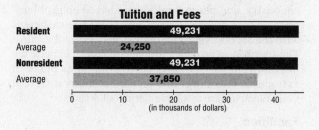

**Tuition and Fees**

| | |
|---|---|
| Resident | 49,231 |
| Average | 24,250 |
| Nonresident | 49,231 |
| Average | 37,850 |

(in thousands of dollars)

## Introduction

This dental school is the most recent addition to the university's health care programs of study. There already are colleges of osteopathic medicine and of pharmacy. The dental program is in the process of becoming accredited by the American Dental Association. The school is located on the Glendale, Arizona campus. The inaugural class was admitted in fall 2008.

## Admissions (AADSAS)

Within the competitive admissions framework, the college uses multiple criteria to select the most qualified, diverse group of candidates from an applicant pool that greatly exceeds the number of seats available. Applicants are evaluated on academic coursework, performance on the Dental Aptitude Test (DAT), their application (AADSAS) essay, letters of evaluation, and interviews. Demonstrated community service through volunteerism or service-oriented employment is preferred.

To be competitive, an applicant should have earned a bachelor's degree from an accredited college or university. Course requirements include: 1 year general chemistry, biology, and physics, 1-semester courses in anatomy, physiology, microbiology, a quarter semester biochemistry, plus a course in English.

## Curriculum

4-year. The program of study leading to the Doctor of Dental Medicine degree includes basic academic work in the basic sciences, the behavioral sciences and the clinical sciences, preclinical simulation studies, practical clinical dentistry, and community clinical rotations that follow the guidelines of the American Dental Association and the Commission on Dental Education. Upon completion of the program student doctors will be eligible for licensing in the state of Arizona and the southwestern United States through the Western Region Board Examination and throughout the country upon passing regional examinations.

## Grading Policy

Information not available.

## Facilities

Information not available.

## Special Features

The school's development is in response to the fact that current nationwide statistics indicate a shortage of dentists. For every 3 dentists that retire, only 2 enter the profession. The school is also cognizant of the advances in dental care, rising interest in cosmetic dentistry, and the ever-increasing understanding of the relationship between oral and systemic health. These 3 factors have also contributed an increased demand for dental services.

## CALIFORNIA

# Loma Linda University School of Dentistry

Loma Linda, California   92350

*Phone:* 909-558-4621          *Fax:* 909-558-4211
*E-mail:* admissions@sd.llu.edu
*WWW:* dentistry.llu.edu

| Application Filing | | Accreditation | |
|---|---|---|---|
| Earliest: | May 15 | CDA | |
| Latest: | December 1 | | |
| Fee: | $75 | **Degrees Granted** | |
| AADSAS: | yes | DDS, DDS-PhD | |

### Enrollment: 2008–2009 First-Year Class

| | | | |
|---|---|---|---|
| Men: | 66 | 69% | *Mean* |
| Women: | 29 | 31% | total GPA: 3.5 |
| Minorities: | 29 | 31% | science: 3.4 |
| Out of State: | 75 | 79% | |
| With 2 years of college: | 0% | *Average* |
| With 3 years of college: | 4% | DAT academic: 19 |
| | | | DAT-PAT: 19 |

**Tuition and Fees**

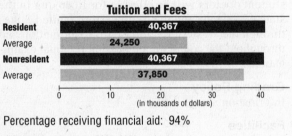

| | |
|---|---|
| Resident | 40,367 |
| Average | 24,250 |
| Nonresident | 40,367 |
| Average | 37,850 |

(in thousands of dollars)

Percentage receiving financial aid: 94%

Above data applicable to 2007–2008 academic year.

## Introduction

In 1905 Seventh-Day Adventists established Loma Linda University. In 1953 the School of Dentistry at Loma Linda University was founded. Located 60 miles east of Los Angeles, the university consists of 7 health science schools including schools of Dentistry, Medicine, Pharmacy, Nursing, Health-Related Professions, and a Graduate School. Besides offering a DDS program, the school has advanced educational programs in a variety of specialties and also offers a BS in dental hygiene. An International Dental Program trains dentists from other countries according to the standards of American dental medicine.

## Admissions (AADSAS)

In addition to the basic predental science courses, a semester course in English composition and in literature are required. It is recommended that upper level science courses be selected from biochemistry, histology, anatomy, physiology, and immunology. Other useful courses are algebra, calculus, psychology, sociology, principles of management, accounting, sculpture, and ceramics. A minimum GPA of 2.7 is required.

## Curriculum

4-year traditional. The courses in anatomy have clinical applications, and the laboratories in physiology, biochemistry, and pharmacology are based on problem-oriented case presentations. Clinical experience begins with the second year and intensifies during the third. The fourth year provides for the delivery of experience in comprehensive dental care. This takes place in extracurricular programs located at many different sites. Electives are available during all 4 years.

## Facilities

The school is located on the university's campus in Loma Linda along with the university's other health profession training schools.

## Special Features

Remedial and tutorial programs are available for all students. Placement services for locating and evaluating practice opportunities are available at no cost to the student. Outreach programs are carried out for underserved population groups locally, in Mexico, and other foreign countries.

# University of California— Los Angeles School of Dentistry

10833 LeConte Avenue
Los Angeles, California 90095

*Phone:* 310-794-7971 *Fax:* 310-825-9808
*E-mail:* dols_admissions@dentistry.ucla.edu
*WWW:* dent.ucla.edu

| Application Filing | | | Accreditation |
|---|---|---|---|
| Earliest: | June 1 | | CDA |
| Latest: | January 1 | | |
| Fee: | $60 | | **Degrees Granted** |
| AADSAS: | yes | | DDS, DDS-MS |

### Enrollment: 2008–2009 First-Year Class

| | | | |
|---|---|---|---|
| Men: | 15 | 51% | *Mean* |
| Women: | 14 | 49% | total GPA: 3.7 |
| Minorities: | 8 | 28% | science: 3.7 |
| Out of State: | 14 | 49% | |
| With 2 years of college: | | 0% | *Average* |
| With 3 years of college: | | n/a | DAT academic: 22 |
| | | | DAT-PAT: 20 |

**Tuition and Fees**

| | |
|---|---|
| Resident | 24,704 |
| Average | 24,250 |
| Nonresident | 12,245 |
| Average | 37,850 |

0    10    20    30    40
(in thousands of dollars)

Percentage receiving financial aid: 95%

Above data applicable to 2007–2008 academic year.

## Introduction

The University of California at Los Angeles, an undergraduate and a graduate school, was established in 1919. In 1960 the University of California Los Angeles School of Dentistry was founded. The initial class was enrolled in 1965. The school is located in the Center of Health Sciences on the UCLA campus in west Los Angeles, along with the schools of Medicine, Nursing, and Public Health. The school has expanded by developing postdoctoral programs, establishing a research institute, organizing a satellite clinic in Venice, California, and downtown Los Angeles, and collaborating with adjacent colleges in training dental hygienists and dental assistants.

## Admissions (AADSAS)

In addition to the basic predental science courses, a 1-year course in English composition and a 1-semester course in biochemistry and introductory psychology are required. Additional recommended courses that can be selected are human or comparative anatomy, histology, physiology, microbiology, English composition, fine arts, drafting, communication, and business. There are no residency restrictions. Minority and underprivileged students are encouraged to apply. *Transfer and advanced standing:* Not available.

## Curriculum

4-year. In addition to the basic sciences, students are trained in the use of clinical preventive measures during the first year. They are also exposed to an integrated basic-clinical sciences program section on oral biology that begins in the first year and continues into the third. Clinical experience in comprehensive patient care begins in the first year. Numerous elective programs are available that cover a wide variety of topics, such as the clinical management of patients, and experiences, such as hospital service rotations.

## Grading Policy

The grading system used is a modification of the Pass/Not Pass rating system.

## Facilities

The Dental School Building is located in the Center for Health Sciences on the UCLA campus. Off-campus clinical instruction is also provided.

## Special Features

A combined DDS-MS program requires 1 additional year to complete.

# University of California— San Francisco School of Dentistry

513 Parnassus Avenue  S–630
San Francisco, California    94143

*Phone:* 415-514-0770          *Fax:* 415-476-4226
*E-mail:* admissionsbetbeze@dentistry.ucsf.edu
*WWW:* dentistry.ucsf.edu

| Application Filing | | Accreditation | |
|---|---|---|---|
| Earliest: | May 15 | CODA | |
| Latest: | October 15 | | |
| Fee: | $60 | **Degrees Granted** | |
| AADSAS: | yes | DDS, DDS-MS, DDS-PhD | |

### Enrollment: 2008–2009 First-Year Class

| | | | |
|---|---|---|---|
| Men: | 52 | 60% | *Mean* |
| Women: | 34 | 39% | total GPA: 3.52 |
| Minorities: | 9 | 10% | science: 3.48 |
| Out of State: | 16 | 18% | |
| With 2 years of college: | | n/a | *Average* |
| With 3 years of college: | | n/a | DAT academic: 20 |
| | | | DAT-PAT: 20 |

**Tuition and Fees**

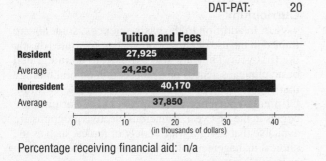

| Resident | 27,925 |
| Average | 24,250 |
| Nonresident | 40,170 |
| Average | 37,850 |

(in thousands of dollars)

Percentage receiving financial aid: n/a

## Introduction
The San Francisco campus of the University of California is dedicated to the health sciences and consists of schools of Dentistry, Medicine, Nursing, and Pharmacy, and their teaching hospitals. No undergraduate degrees can be obtained there. The University of California in San Francisco was established in 1873; the School of Dentistry was founded in 1881. In addition to offering a DDS degree, the School of Dentistry has a graduate program leading to a PhD in oral biology and postgraduate programs in specialties.

## Admissions (AADSAS)
Completion of 139 quarter units or 93 semester units of college work at an accredited institution is a minimum requirement for admission to the UCSF School of Dentistry. A minimum of 30 quarter units or 20 semester units must be completed at an accredited 4-year institution. California residents must have a min-imum overall and science college grade point average of 2.7. Non-California residents must have a minimum overall and science college grade point average of 3.0

## Information for Special Applicants
The school offers a number of activities to help disadvantaged and/or underrepresented minority students prepare for a career in dentistry. The recruitment program sponsors activities such as DAT reviews, summer programs, preview days, and admission/interview workshops. In addition, the school provides preadmission counseling, informal transcript evaluation, and mentorship opportunities.

## Curriculum
The predoctoral curriculum was revised at the School of Dentistry in 2004. The concept of the new curriculum is to organize material into 5 thematic streams that emphasize and reinforce the integration of basic sciences and clinical sciences in dental education: biomedical science, dental science, patient-centered care, preventive and restorative dental sciences, and scientific methods. This will better enable graduates to provide the best patient care, to translate science into practice, and to follow a variety of career paths.

## Grading Policy
All courses in the predoctoral curriculum are graded Pass (P), No Pass (NP). Courses in the third and fourth years have Honors designation for outstanding performance. Courses that extend over more than 1 quarter are graded Satisfactory Pass (SP) or Unsatisfactory Pass (UP) until the last quarter, when the P/NP grades are awarded for the entire course.

## Facilities
The school is part of the Health Science campus. The School of Dentistry facilities, including its newly renovated clinics on Parnassus Avenue and in the community, its research laboratories, campus facilities, and library make it a well-equipped setting in which to conduct education, patient care, and research.

## Special Features
The school offers academic assistance in the form of tutorials. It also conducts a wide variety of outreach activities. A joint DDS-MD oral and maxillofacial program is sponsored by the schools of Dentistry and Medicine. Applicants must hold the DDS degree from an accredited school and must be accepted into the UCSF School of Dentistry's oral and maxillofacial surgery program before seeking admission to the School of Medicine. Several scholarships and other non-repayable funds, as well as federal and university loans, are available to entering dental students with financial need. Financial aid applications for entering students should be submitted to student Financial Services at the time of the applicant's admission. A student's need for financial aid while in dental school may be reviewed at any time during the year.

# University of Southern California Norris Dental Science Center School of Dentistry

1925 West 34th Street
Los Angeles, California    90089

*Phone:* 213-740-2851          *Fax:* 213-740-8109
*E-mail:* uscsdadm@usc.edu
*WWW:* usc.edu/dental

| Application Filing | | Accreditation | |
|---|---|---|---|
| Earliest: | June 1 | CDA | |
| Latest: | March 1 | | |
| Fee: | $65 | **Degrees Granted** | |
| AADSAS: | yes | DDS, DDS-MBA, | |
| | | DDS-MS | |

### Enrollment: 2008–2009 First-Year Class

| | | | | | |
|---|---|---|---|---|---|
| Men: | 79 | 55% | *Mean* | | |
| Women: | 65 | 45% | total GPA: | 3.4 | |
| Minorities: | 11 | 12% | science: | 3.45 | |
| Out of State: | 55 | 38% | | | |
| With 2 years of college: | 0% | | *Average* | | |
| With 4 years of college: | 100% | | DAT academic: | 18 | |
| | | | DAT-PAT: | 19 | |

**Tuition and Fees**

| | |
|---|---|
| **Resident** | 71,620 |
| Average | 24,250 |
| **Nonresident** | 71,620 |
| Average | 37,850 |

0    10    20    30    40
(in thousands of dollars)

Percentage receiving financial aid: 90%

## Introduction

Established in 1880, the University of Southern California is a private school. The University of Southern California School of Dentistry was founded in 1897. The goal of the school is the education of highly trained general practitioners. Its faculty have contributed significantly to advances in dental medicine, particularly in the area of the use of semiprecious metal alloys and tooth restorative materials. The school offers a DDS and BS in dental hygiene.

## Admissions (AADSAS)

The school requires the basic predental science courses and 1 year of English composition, as well as 1 year of philosophy, history, or fine arts. Additional recommended courses that can be selected are biochemistry, human or comparative anatomy, embryology, histology, genetics, physiology, psychology, sociology, and economics. Nonresidents are evaluated and selected based on the same criteria as California residents. A personal interview may be required. *Transfer and advanced standing:* Transfers from American and Canadian schools may be considered on a space-available basis. Acceptance with advanced standing is rare.

## Curriculum

4-years. The problem-based learning curriculum is an educational approach, that provides a vertical integration of basic sciences and clinical content over all 4 years of the program. This approach to education is of a student-centered and inquiry based nature, which integrates all aspects of the fundamental basic and clinical sciences from the onset of the learning experience. Its objective is to educate students who will be committed to lifelong, self-motivated learning, skilled in the techniques of problem solving in the clinical setting. Furthermore, it seeks to ensure that students are well prepared to deal with the future advances in dental therapy and dental care delivery, able to deal with the medical presentations of dental patients, and effective in-group learning/accomplishment environments, and highly skilled in the delivery of quality dental health.

## Facilities

The school is located on the USC campus and is housed in the Norris Dental Science Center. Other teaching resources include affiliated hospitals and a mobile clinic.

## Special Features

An Office of Admissions coordinates all recruitment and retention programs. This office also coordinates other student services, including tutorial, financial aid, and job placement.

# University of the Pacific
# Arthur A. Dugoni
# School of Dentistry

2155 Webster Street
San Francisco, California 94115

*Phone:* 415-929-6491 *Fax:* 415-749-3363
*WWW:* dental.pacific.edu

| Application Filing | | Accreditation |
|---|---|---|
| Earliest: | June 1 | CDA |
| Latest: | December 1 | |
| Fee: | $75 | **Degrees Granted** |
| AADSAS: | yes | DDS |

### Enrollment: 2008–2009 First-Year Class

| | | | |
|---|---|---|---|
| Men: | 141 | 66% | *Mean* |
| Women: | 72 | 34% | total GPA: 3.4 |
| Minorities: | 69 | 32% | science: 3.5 |
| Out of State: | 12 | 6% | |
| With 3 years of college: | 1.5% | | *Average* |
| With 4 years of college: | 97% | | DAT academic: 21 |
| | | | DAT-PAT: 19 |

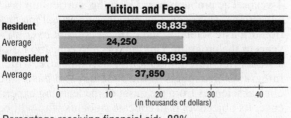

**Tuition and Fees**

| | |
|---|---|
| **Resident** | 68,835 |
| Average | 24,250 |
| **Nonresident** | 68,835 |
| Average | 37,850 |

(in thousands of dollars)

Percentage receiving financial aid: 88%

## Introduction
San Francisco has been the home of the School of Dentistry since its incorporation in 1896 as the College of Physicians and Surgeons. In 1962 the College of Physicians and Surgeons combined with the University of the Pacific.

## Admissions (AADSAS)
At least 3 years of college work, 90 semester credits, is recommended. Courses taken at a community college are acceptable if they are transferable as equivalent to predental courses at a 4-year college. Required courses in predental education must include the following: 4 semesters of biological sciences; comparative anatomy, physiology, or histology are strongly recommended; 2 semesters of general physics, 2 semesters of organic chemistry, or 1 semester each of organic chemistry and biochemistry and 2 semesters of English composition or speech. Additional recommended courses are cell biology, physiology, genetics, business, accounting, and economics, as well as fine arts, humanities, and social science courses. The admissions committee carefully considers each applicant's scholastic record, scores on the DAT, the AADSAS essay, and letters of evaluation. Other personal attributes and qualities as well as demonstration of the applicant's understanding of a career in the dental profession are also reviewed. Applicants who are offered the opportunity to enroll must complete planned coursework at a specified performance level. Acceptance to the School of Dentistry is provisional until all required admissions materials have been received and verified to be consistent with the information available at the time of a provisional acceptance.

## Curriculum
The curriculum emphasizes early initiation of clinical experience and integration of biomedical and clinical excellence. Students with research interests and ability are encouraged to undertake projects under the guidance of experienced faculty members. Student progress in the program is evaluated by academic performance committees and carefully monitored by the Academic Advisory Committees that serve to identify any problems (such as undiagnosed learning disabilities) and recommend tutorial and other support. The highest standards are maintained in preparation for National Dental Examining Boards and licensure for practice. Very few students are delayed in their progress toward graduation. The curriculum combines basic biomedical, preclinical, and clinical science subjects with applied behavioral sciences.

## Facilities
A 9-story building was completed in 1967 for functional teaching of clinical dentistry and to conduct dental research. A 12-operatory dental clinic has served as the school's major extended campus in southern Alameda County. The university also renovated a building near the school to help meet students' needs for housing. The facility houses 126 residents in 66 apartments and also provides a contemporary dental technical laboratory, a physical fitness center, and study rooms for use by the residents.

## Special Features
The school has a program for the admission of qualified ethnic minorities, women, and members of underrepresented groups.

## COLORADO

# University of Colorado at Denver School of Dental Medicine

Mail Stop F 833
Aurora, Colorado    80045

*Phone:* 303-724-7122          *Fax:* 303-724-7109
*E-mail:* barbara.swedansky@uchsc.edu
*WWW:* uchsc.edu/sod

| Application Filing | | Accreditation | |
|---|---|---|---|
| Earliest: | May 15 | CDA | |
| Latest: | December 31 | | |
| Fee: | $50 | **Degrees Granted** | |
| AADSAS: | yes | DDS | |

### Enrollment: 2008–2009 First-Year Class

| | | | |
|---|---|---|---|
| Men: | 32 | 64% | *Mean* |
| Women: | 18 | 36% | total GPA: | 3.6 |
| Minorities: | 2 | 4% | science: | 3.6 |
| Out of State: | 21 | 42% | | |
| With 3 years of college: | 2% | *Average* | |
| With 4 years of college: | 98% | DAT academic: 19.8 |
| | | | DAT-PAT: | 20 |

### Tuition and Fees

| | |
|---|---|
| **Resident** | 31,950 |
| Average | 24,250 |
| **Nonresident** | 57,253 |
| Average | 37,850 |

(in thousands of dollars)
0    10    20    30    40

Percentage receiving financial aid:  96%

## Introduction

Creation of the University of Colorado/Denver School of Dental Medicine (UCSDODM) was authorized in 1922. The school enrolled its first class of 25 in 1973. Presently, the school enrolls 50 students annually. The small class size is an asset to the teaching and learning process.

## Admission

The majority of students accepted to the School of D.M. have completed at least 4 years of undergraduate work and have received an undergraduate degree. The basic requirement for admission is the completion of at least 90 semester hours (135 quarter hours) with at least 30 hours of upper-division courses for a letter grade. Limitations on Community College work are not more than 60 semester hours (90 quarter hours) will count toward the 90-semester hour minimum. Preference is given to state residents and applicants from Western states under the WICHE agreement. Nonresidents are considered. Students must also complete the basic predental science courses, plus 2 humanities courses and 1 English composition course, and have received letter grades in all required courses. Possible useful electives are courses in business management/finance, studio art, psychology, communications, cell biology, anatomy, biochemistry, physiology, immunology, and histology.

## Curriculum

4-years. *First and second years:* Basic science introduction takes place during this period. Knowledge in these areas is reinforced by critically oriented courses such as oral and organ pathology. Critical experience begins in the sophomore year and continues as increasing levels of competence are acquired. *Third and fourth years:* Behavioral sciences, business administration, history, and ethics are incorporated into the curriculum. An Advanced Clinical Training and Service program enables students to spend much of last 8 months of their schooling gaining exposure in a variety of different clinical settings, such as hospitals and geriatric centers. Certain electives in the clinical sciences and research are offered in the final 2 years.

## Facilities

The overriding vision for the academic health center is interprofessional collaboration in education, research, and patient care/service. This is an exciting time for UCSDODM and the entire University of Colorado/Denver Anschi Medical Group. The School of Dentistry moved into its new comprehensive oral health center equipped with the highest technology, critical care, and educational facilities in August.

## CONNECTICUT

# University of Connecticut School of Dental Medicine

263 Farmington Avenue
Farmington, Connecticut    06030

*Phone:* 860-679-2175          *Fax:* 860-679-1899
*E-mail:* thibodeau@nso.uchc.edu
*WWW:* som.uchc.edu

| Application Filing | | Accreditation | |
|---|---|---|---|
| Earliest: | June 1 | ADA | |
| Latest: | January 10 | | |
| Fee: | $75 | **Degrees Granted** | |
| AADSAS: | yes | DMD, DMD-PhD | |

### Enrollment: 2008–2009 First-Year Class

| | | | | |
|---|---|---|---|---|
| Men: | 21 | 48% | *Mean* | |
| Women: | 23 | 52% | total GPA: | 3.6 |
| Minorities: | 8 | 8% | science: | 3.5 |
| Out of State: | 20 | 48% | | |
| With 2 years of college: | 0% | | *Average* | |
| With 3 years of college: | 0% | | DAT academic: | 20 |
| | | | DAT-PAT: | 20 |

**Tuition and Fees**

| | |
|---|---|
| **Resident** | 25,100 |
| Average | 24,250 |
| **Nonresident** | 50,151 |
| Average | 37,850 |

0    10    20    30    40
(in thousands of dollars)

Percentage receiving financial aid: 90%

## Introduction

The University of Connecticut is a public institution that was originally founded in 1881. The Health Center at the University of Connecticut, established in the 1960s, encompasses the School of Dental Medicine, the School of Medicine, and the John Dempsey Hospital. This dental school is the only public one in New England. The university's main campus is located in Storrs, while the Health Center is situated in a wooded suburban campus in Farmington.

## Admissions (AADSAS)

The basic predental courses are required. Students should have a strong facility in English and should be able to handle quantitative concepts. Credits in behavioral sciences and upper division biology courses are desirable. Thus, courses in biochemistry, cell biology, and molecular biology are recommended. *Transfer and advanced standing:* Not available at this time.

## Curriculum

4-year diagonal. During the first 2 years, students take an integrated course of study in the basic sciences that takes place in multidisciplinary laboratories. The predoctoral curriculum focuses on the biological and epidemiological bases of disease and provides strong preparation in the diagnostic and technical skills required for the practice of dentistry in the twenty-first century. First patients are seen during the second year. The third- and fourth-year clinical component includes comprehensive patient care, self-paced clinics, and rotations.

## Facilities

The school is part of the University of Connecticut Health Center. Satellite clinics are located at the Burgdorf Health Center in Hartford and the Children's Medical Center in Newington.

## Special Features

A combined DMD-PhD program is offered, which takes about 3 additional years to complete.

## DISTRICT OF COLUMBIA

# Howard University College of Dentistry

600 "W" Street, N.W.
Washington, DC    20059

*Phone:* 202-806-0400          *Fax:* 202-806-0354
*E-mail:* ghewittclark@howard.edu
*WWW:* howard.edu.dentistry

| Application Filing | | Accreditation |
|---|---|---|
| Earliest: | May 1 | CDA |
| Latest: | January 15 | |
| Fee: | $45 | **Degrees Granted** |
| AADSAS: | yes | DDS |

### Enrollment: 2008–2009 First-Year Class

| | | | | |
|---|---|---|---|---|
| Men: | 41 | 49% | *Mean* | |
| Women: | 44 | 51% | total GPA: | 3.19 |
| Minorities: | 39 | 48% | science: | 2.9 |
| Out of State: | n/a | n/a | | |
| With 2 years of college: | | 0% | *Average* | |
| With 3 years of college: | | 0% | DAT academic: | 16 |
| | | | DAT-PAT: | 15 |

**Tuition and Fees**

| | |
|---|---|
| **Resident** | 21,065 |
| Average | 24,250 |
| **Nonresident** | 21,065 |
| Average | 37,850 |

0    10    20    30    40
(in thousands of dollars)

Percentage receiving financial aid: 84%

Above data applicable to 2007–2008 academic year.

## Introduction

In 1867 Howard University was established as the largest private, primarily African-American school. Fourteen years later, the College of Dentistry was established. It is the fifth oldest dental school in the United States. The Center for Health Sciences of the University includes colleges of Medicine, Nursing, Pharmacy, and Allied Health Sciences. The 89-acre campus is 5 minutes from downtown Washington, D.C.

## Admissions (AADSAS)

The basic predental courses and 1 year of English are required. A bachelor's degree from an accredited college or university is also required. Recommended courses include biochemistry, human anatomy, physiology, and microbiology. The GPA should be 3.0 and DAT score of 17 in each category. Out-of-state applicants may apply. *Transfer and advance standing* applicants are infrequent.

## Information for Special Applicants

Howard University has devoted many of its activities to the education of minorities, the educationally disadvantaged, women, etc. The college strongly supports this policy and has made many efforts to identify and retain such students with potential to successfully negotiate the dental curriculum and make a meaningful contribution to society.

The College of Dentistry offers the Academic Reinforcement Program, a pre-entrance enrichment program with tutorial assistance for the evaluation of dental applications prior to entrance into the freshman class. These dental applicants are recommended by the admission committee.

## Curriculum

4-year traditional. The goal of the curriculum is that graduates will be competent in the prevention, diagnosis, and treatment of oral diseases and disorders. They also should be knowledgeable about the interrelationship of oral and systemic health. Clinical experience begins in the second year. Basic and clinical sciences are integrated. Special features of the curriculum involve a program for the chronically ill and aged that takes dental care to the home- and institution-bound patient.

## Facilities

The college is housed in a 5-story complex containing classrooms, clinics, laboratories, offices, research facilities, a learning resources area, and convertible clinic-laboratories. Programs are also conducted at the university hospital, as well as other affiliated hospitals.

## Special Features

Many of the school's activities are devoted to the education of minorities, the educationally disadvantaged, and women. This commitment involves a prematriculation and a postmatriculation academic program. Several community-based programs and patient services are offered by the college and other affiliated hospitals.

## FLORIDA

# Nova Southeastern University College of Dental Medicine

3200 South University Drive
Ft. Lauderdale, Florida 33328

*Phone:* 954-262-7311        *Fax:* 954-262-2282
*E-mail:* hippman@nova.edu
*WWW:* dental.nova.edu

| Application Filing | | Accreditation |
|---|---|---|
| Earliest: | June 1 | CDA |
| Latest: | March 1 | |
| Fee: | $50 | **Degrees Granted** |
| AADSAS: | yes | DMD |

### Enrollment: 2008–2009 First-Year Class

| | | | |
|---|---|---|---|
| Men: | 65 | 88% | *Mean* |
| Women: | 9 | 8% | total GPA: 3.5 |
| Minorities: | 6 | 2% | science: 3.6 |
| Out of State: | 45 | 60% | |
| With 2 years of college: | | 0% | *Average* |
| With 3 years of college: | | 6% | DAT academic: 19 |
| | | | DAT-PAT: 18 |

### Tuition and Fees

| | |
|---|---|
| **Resident** | 40,045 |
| Average | 24,250 |
| **Nonresident** | 42,750 |
| Average | 37,850 |

(in thousands of dollars)

Percentage receiving financial aid: n/a

n/a = not available

Above data applicable to 2007–2008 academic year.

## Introduction

Nova Southeastern University is the largest independent institution of higher learning in the state of Florida. It resulted from the merger of Nova University and Southeastern University. The College of Dental Medicine is the newest of the 6 schools in the Health Professions Division and was established in 1996. The other health profession schools are the colleges of Osteopathic Medicine, Pharmacy, Optometry, and Allied Health and Medical Sciences.

## Admissions (AADSAS)

A minimum of 90 semester hours are required and no more than 60 of which will be accepted from a community or junior college in meeting this prerequisite. The basic predental science courses are also necessary. Zoology or microbiology can be substituted for general biology. The required science courses must be completed with a C (2.0) or better grade. Courses in English composition and literature are also required. Additional recommended courses are anatomy, immunology, histology, biochemistry, physiology, principles of management, accounting, communication, art, sculpture, foreign languages, and social sciences. The overall GPA of the applicant should be C+ (2.5) or better. *Transfer and advanced standing:* A limited number will be considered.

## Curriculum

4-year traditional. *First year:* The fall semester includes courses in anatomy, biochemistry, histology, embryology, periodontics, oral medicine, restorative dentistry, and dental materials. The spring semester includes microbiology, immunology, and physiology. Many of the courses will be taught in didactic lectures, laboratory training, seminars, and conferences. *Second year:* The fall semester of 18 weeks will continue studies of restorative dentistry and oral medicine. Pathology, pharmacology, diagnostic radiology, and dental care systems will be introduced into the curriculum. The spring semester will include the following courses: pediatric dentistry, growth and development, endodontics, orthodontics, periodontics, and Introduction to Clinical Practice. *Third year:* The fall semester includes courses in oral surgery, emergency medicine, periodontics, and endodontics. Patient care and patient behavioral techniques will be enhanced along with development of clinical skills through clinical practice. The spring semester consists of clinical practice and oral medicine, periodontics, practice management, and community dentistry. *Fourth year:* The fall and spring semesters will be devoted to expanding clinical expertise in patient care of a variety of individuals. Remaining didactic courses will include optional academic and clinical programs.

## Facilities

The College of Dental Medicine is located in a complex of 8 buildings that house all of the colleges of the Health Professions Division. The major structures include a 5-story Administration Building and Assembly Building containing 2 auditoriums and 8 classrooms. All of the clinic, research, and basic science laboratories for all of the colleges, along with the library, are located in the library/laboratory building. The main dental studies building houses 100 operatories, 4 surgical as well as 4 oral surgery areas, emergency rooms, and radiology operatories. Specialty care units and offices and classrooms are also in the building.

## Special Features

The College of Dental Medicine encourages the application of qualified minority applicants and is committed to a policy of nondiscrimination.

# University of Florida College of Dentistry

P.O. Box 100445
Gainesville, Florida    32610

*Phone:* 352-273-5955          *Fax:* 352-846-0311
*E-mail:* DMDadmissions@dental.ufl.edu
*WWW:* dental.ufl.edu

| Application Filing | | Accreditation | |
|---|---|---|---|
| Earliest: | May 1 | CDA | |
| Latest: | December 1 | | |
| Fee: | $30 | **Degrees Granted** | |
| AADSAS: | yes | DMD | |

### Enrollment: 2008–2009 First-Year Class

| | | | | |
|---|---|---|---|---|
| Men: | 33 | 40% | *Mean* | |
| Women: | 50 | 60% | total GPA: | 3.6 |
| Minorities: | 27 | 33% | science: | 3.5 |
| Out of State: | 12 | 13% | | |
| With 3 years of college: | | 2% | *Average* | |
| With 4 years of college: | | 98% | DAT academic: | 19 |
| | | | DAT-PAT: | 19 |

### Tuition and Fees

| | |
|---|---|
| **Resident** | 24,524 |
| Average | 24,250 |
| **Nonresident** | 51,004 |
| Average | 37,850 |

0      10      20      30      40
(in thousands of dollars)

Percentage receiving financial aid: 88%

## Introduction

The University of Florida was established in 1853. Located on a campus of more than 50,000 students, the University of Florida Health Science Center was founded in 1956. The College of Dentistry admitted its first student in 1972. The Health Science Center, besides a College of Dentistry, includes colleges of Medicine, Nursing, Pharmacy, Veterinary Medicine, and Public Health and Health Professions.

## Admissions (AADSAS)

The basic predental courses are required, and courses in biochemistry, microbiology, molecular biology or genetics, and developmental psychology. Applicants with an overall B+ average as a minimum will receive strongest consideration for admission. A limited number of nonresidents are admitted. *Transfer and advanced standing:* Limited numbers are admitted.

## Curriculum

4-year. Consists of 2 components: (a) core courses that are required of all, and (b) elective courses that are optional. The latter may include a research project. Basic sciences, correlated dental sciences, dental didactic activities, and dental clinical activities are presented in both the core and the electives. *First year:* Devoted to the basic sciences, preclinical technical courses and an introduction to clinical situations. *Second year:* Completion of the basic sciences, preclinical technical courses, and an introduction to comprehensive patient care. *Third year:* Clinical rotations and comprehensive patient care. *Fourth year:* Continues work in comprehensive patient care, extramural rotations, and exposure to private patient practice concepts.

## Facilities

The college, with its 11-story dental clinical-science building, is an integral part of the J. Hillis Miller Health Center located on the university campus. A new computer-based simulation lab, junior-senior laboratory, and state-of-the-art lecture faculty were recently built.

## GEORGIA

# Medical College of Georgia School of Dentistry

1459 Laney Walker Boulevard
Augusta, Georgia    30912

*Phone:* 706-721-3587          *Fax:* 706-721-6276
*E-mail:* osaas@mcg.edu
*WWW:* mcg.edu/careers/dentistry.htm

| Application Filing | | Accreditation | |
|---|---|---|---|
| Earliest: | June 1 | CDA | |
| Latest: | October 15 | | |
| Fee: | $30 | **Degrees Granted** | |
| AADSAS: | no | DMD, DMD-PhD | |

### Enrollment: 2008–2009 First-Year Class

| | | | | | |
|---|---|---|---|---|---|
| Men: | 32 | 48% | *Mean* | | |
| Women: | 34 | 52% | total GPA: | | 3.6 |
| Minorities: | 11 | 26% | science: | | 3.6 |
| Out of State: | 0 | 0% | | | |
| With 3 years of college: | | 0% | *Average* | | |
| With 4 years of college: | | 100% | DAT academic: | | 18 |
| | | | DAT-PAT: | | 19 |

**Tuition and Fees**

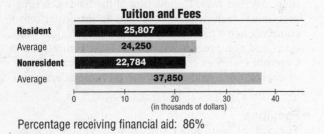

| | |
|---|---|
| Resident | 25,807 |
| Average | 24,250 |
| Nonresident | 22,784 |
| Average | 37,850 |

0    10    20    30    40
(in thousands of dollars)

Percentage receiving financial aid: 86%

## Introduction

In 1828 the Medical College of Georgia was established and in 1965 the School of Dentistry was founded. It offers a DMD program and its modern facilities are located in Augusta. The Medical College of Georgia also has schools of Medicine, Nursing, Allied Health, and Graduate Studies. The School of Dentistry has made significant contributions to research in the field.

## Admissions

Completion of a minimum of 90 semester hours of college level work, the basic predental courses, and 2 semesters in English are required. A course in biochemistry can be substituted for 1 semester of organic chemistry. Comparative anatomy, microbiology, personal management, psychology, and art (drawing and/or sculpturing) are recommended. Only Georgia residents are accepted. *Transfer and advanced standing:* Students are not accepted.

## Curriculum

4-year flexible. Elementary clinical treatment of patients begins at the end of the first year, including restorative dentistry in the fourth semester. Conversely, some basic science courses are not completed until the senior year. Treatment of patients is carried out in a system of comprehensive care, with some in block assignments, so as to simulate private practice of general dentistry. Students participate in off-campus clinical experiences beginning in the summer between the third and fourth years. Students must spend their time in such settings as public health clinics and charitable health programs, as well as at private or government institutions.

## Facilities

The school is on the campus of Medical College of Georgia, which is located on the fringe of the downtown area adjacent to a large complex of health-care facilities.

## Special Features

A combined DMD-PhD program is offered, requiring additional years of study. Students who have been accepted but have recognizable deficiencies can attend a special presession. Students may be provided with tutors, special curricular loads, and self-paced learning packages, if they encounter academic difficulties.

## ILLINOIS

# Southern Illinois University School of Dental Medicine

Building 273
2800 College Avenue, Room 2300
Alton, Illinois   62002

*Phone:* 618-474-7170          *Fax:* 618-474-7249
*WWW:* sive.edu/sdm
*E-mail:* sdmapps@sive.edu

| Application Filing | | Accreditation | |
|---|---|---|---|
| Earliest: | May 15 | CDA | |
| Latest: | February 1 | | |
| Fee: | $20 | **Degrees Granted** | |
| AADSAS: | yes | DMD, BS-DMD | |

### Enrollment: 2008–2009 First-Year Class

| | | | |
|---|---|---|---|
| Men: | 30 | 60% | *Mean* |
| Women: | 20 | 40% | total GPA: 3.6 |
| Minorities: | 5 | 10% | science: 3.4 |
| Out of State: | 0 | | |
| With 3 years of college: | 14% | | *Average* |
| With 4 years of college: | 86% | | DAT academic: 18.4 |
| | | | DAT-PAT: 18 |

**Tuition and Fees**

| | |
|---|---|
| Resident | 26,090 |
| Average | 24,250 |
| Nonresident | 26,090 |
| Average | 37,850 |

0      10      20      30      40
(in thousands of dollars)

Percentage receiving financial aid: 86%

## Introduction

The Southern Illinois University system is one of 2 university systems in Illinois. There are 2 campuses in the system, 1 in Carbondale, and 1 in Edwardsville. The School of Dental Medicine, which was established in 1969, is located in Alton, Illinois, near both Edwardsville and St. Louis. The unique location of the school places it within the urban environment of metropolitan St. Louis and rural southern Illinois.

## Admissions (AADSAS)

The basic predental school courses plus 1 year of English are required. Recommended additional courses can be selected from biochemistry, upper-division biology, quantitative analysis, calculus, literature, art, and sculpturing. Priority is given to state residents. *Transfer and advanced standing:* An applicant accepted for admission to the first-year class who has advanced training in any discipline listed in the curriculum may request advanced placement.

## Curriculum

4-year. *First and second years* are used to present to the student biomedical information on the human organism and information necessary to recognize the disease states in humans. In addition, these 2 years are preparation time for clinical dentistry. The students are first involved in direct patient treatment during the second semester of the second year. *Third year:* Consists of clinical sciences instruction, application-type courses in biomedical sciences, and increasing emphasis on patient care. *Fourth year:* The major portion of the fourth year is spent in comprehensive patient care; in addition, during this time, the student receives instruction in advanced clinical sciences and practice management. The curriculum is designed to incorporate biochemical, clinical, behavioral, and social sciences. This serves to provide the knowledge and experience necessary for comprehensive oral health care. Emphasis is placed on the interrelationship of dentistry and medicine in total patient health management.

## Facilities

The Alton, Illinois, campus is situated in a small-town environment just minutes from downtown St. Louis, Missouri. The campus includes 22 buildings and a modern, state-of-the art dental clinic. Training is also available in hospital programs, private practices, and community health centers.

## Special Features

The school actively encourages applications from persons in those segments of society currently underrepresented in the dental profession.

# University of Illinois at Chicago College of Dentistry

801 South Paulina Street
Chicago, Illinois 60612

*Phone:* 312-996-1020          *Fax:* 312-413-9050
*E-mail:* besprn19@vic.edu
*WWW:* dentistryuic.edu

| Application Filing | | Accreditation | |
|---|---|---|---|
| Earliest: | June 1 | ADA | |
| Latest: | December 1 | | |
| Fee: | $65 | **Degrees Granted** | |
| AADSAS: | yes | DDS, DDS-MS, DDS-PhD | |

### Enrollment: 2008–2009 First-Year Class

| | | | | |
|---|---|---|---|---|
| Men: | 43 | 71% | *Mean* | |
| Women: | 26 | 39% | total GPA: | 3.3 |
| Minorities: | 14 | 20% | science: | 3.4 |
| Out of State: | 5 | 7% | | |
| With 2 years of college: | 0% | | *Average* | |
| With 4 years of college: | 100% | | DAT academic: | 19 |
| | | | DAT-PAT: | 19 |

**Tuition and Fees**

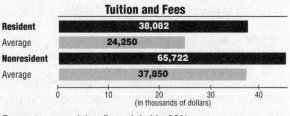

| | |
|---|---|
| Resident | 38,082 |
| Average | 24,250 |
| Nonresident | 65,722 |
| Average | 37,850 |

0   10   20   30   40
(in thousands of dollars)

Percentage receiving financial aid: 80%

## Introduction

The University of Illinois, a public system that was founded in 1867, is an undergraduate and graduate educational institution. The 2 main campuses are located in Chicago and Urbana-Champaign. The College of Dentistry was originally established in 1898 as the Columbian Dental College and later joined the University of Illinois in 1913. It is located on the University of Illinois Chicago campus. In addition to a DDS degree, it offers postgraduate programs in a variety of specialties as well as MS-PhD degrees through the Graduate College. Other health care institutions associated with the university are colleges of Medicine, Nursing, Pharmacy, Associated Health Professions, and a School of Public Health.

## Admissions (AADSAS)

The basic predental science courses plus 1 year of English are required. In addition to the minimal science requirements, highest consideration is given to applicants who complete 3 of the following upper-level science courses: anatomy, physiology, biochemistry, microbiology, cell biology and/or histology. Students interested in practicing in a rural community are encouraged to apply. A minimum GPA of 2.50 is necessary. Most students accepted have much higher GPAs. Very high priority is given to residents. *Transfer and advanced standing:* Under exceptional circumstances students are accepted as transfers.

## Information for Special Applicants

The Urban Health Program aims to assist minority persons (African-Americans, Hispanic Americans, and Native Americans) aspiring to become dentists and to increase the number of minority enrollees at the College of Dentistry. Program services include: academic counseling (advice for predental course planning and selection and interpretation of dental school eligibility requirements), academic retention (prematriculation summer sessions, tutorial services, and nonclinical dental practice workshops), application assistance (advice on application management and procedures), and financial aid. These services are available to all applicants.

## Curriculum

4-year traditional. The basic sciences are the major part of the first two years. Students are introduced to clinical experience in the first year. From then on, clinical emphasis increases, the fourth year comprising clinical practice almost exclusively. Mandatory summer sessions for students take place during the last three years of the program.

## Grading Policy

A letter grading system is used. Examinations include objective essays, completion, and short-answer types. Practical exams for clinical competence are also required.

## Facilities

The college is located in the Health Sciences Center of the University of Illinois at Chicago.

## Special Features

A combined DDS-MS program, which can usually be completed within the basic 4-year period, is offered. A DDS-PhD program is offered, but requires an additional 2 or 3 years.

# INDIANA

## Indiana University School of Dentistry

1121 West Michigan Street
Indianapolis, Indiana   46202

*Phone:* 317-274-8173        *Fax:* 317-278-9066
*E-mail:* rkasberg@iupui.edu
*WWW:* iusd.iupui.edu

| Application Filing | | Accreditation |
|---|---|---|
| Earliest: | May 15 | CDA |
| Latest: | December 1 | |
| Fee: | $50 | **Degrees Granted** |
| AADSAS: | yes | DDS |

### Enrollment: 2008–2009 First-Year Class

| | | | | |
|---|---|---|---|---|
| Men: | 67 | 66% | *Mean* | |
| Women: | 34 | 34% | total GPA: | 3.45 |
| Minorities: | 2 | 2% | science: | 3.3 |
| Out of State: | 31 | 31% | | |
| With 3 years of college: | | 0% | *Average* | |
| With 4 years of college: | | 99% | DAT academic: | 18 |
| | | | DAT-PAT: | 19 |

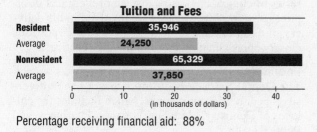

**Tuition and Fees**

| | |
|---|---|
| **Resident** | 35,946 |
| Average | 24,250 |
| **Nonresident** | 65,329 |
| Average | 37,850 |

(in thousands of dollars)

Percentage receiving financial aid:  88%

## Introduction
The Indianapolis campus of Indiana University, established in 1946, is governed by Indiana-Purdue University. The Indiana University School of Dentistry was originally established as the Indiana Dental College in 1879. In 1925 the Dental College joined the university's Medical Center, which includes a medical school, School of Nursing, and a complex of hospitals. Aside from the DDS, the School of Dentistry offers a PhD degree in most departments and has programs in dental hygiene, dental assisting, and dental laboratory technology.

## Admissions (AADSAS)
The basic predental science courses as well as courses in English composition, interpersonal communications/speech, and psychology are required. One-semester courses in anatomy (with lab), physiology (with lab), and biochemistry lectures are also required. Minimum GPA for residents is 2.5 and for nonresidents is 2.7. Recommended additional courses may be selected from cell biology, molecular biology, genetics, business management, and art. Minimum GPA for residents is 2.5, and for nonresidents 2.7. *Transfer and advanced standing:* Information not available.

## Curriculum
4-year traditional. Special clinical correlation lectures are scheduled to achieve an integration of basic and clinical sciences. Clinical experiences begin the first semester of the first year and gradually increase through the second semester of the third year. A multitrack curriculum allows the fourth-year student flexibility to develop a personalized program by electing both intramural and extramural courses of individual interest. *First year:* Students take courses in the biological and preclinical sciences and initiate their hand skills development. *Second year:* The advanced biomedical sciences are presented along with dental sciences and students initiate delivery of comprehensive patient care. *Third and fourth years:* The emphasis is primarily on all aspects of patient care in a variety of clinical settings. These include the school's comprehensive care clinics and community-based clinics. The fourth year also offers opportunities to take elective courses for research.

## Facilities
The school is an integral part of Indiana University's Medical Center. Dental students rotate through hospital-based programs in oral and maxillofacial surgery and pediatric dentistry. They have an opportunity to treat patients who are mentally and physically disabled or medically compromised. Extensive clinical preparation in all disciplines of dentistry is offered throughout the 4-year program.

## Special Features
Following admission, an effort is made to assist any student needing financial, academic, or other types of counseling to ensure satisfactory progress toward graduation.

# IOWA

# University of Iowa College of Dentistry

311 Dental Science Building North
Iowa City, Iowa 52242

*Phone:* 319-335-7157     *Fax:* 319-335-7155
*E-mail:* elaine-brown@uiowa.edu
*WWW:* dentistry.uiowa.edu

| Application Filing | | Accreditation |
|---|---|---|
| Earliest: | June 1 | ADA |
| Latest: | November 1 | |
| Fee: | $60 | **Degrees Granted** |
| AADSAS: | yes | DDS |

### Enrollment: 2008–2009 First-Year Class

| | | | |
|---|---|---|---|
| Men: | 49 | 61% | *Mean* |
| Women: | 31 | 39% | total GPA: 3.7 |
| Minorities: | 11 | 14% | science: 3.6 |
| Out of State: | 23 | 29% | |
| With 3 years of college: | | 2% | *Average* |
| With 4 years of college: | | 95% | DAT academic: 19 |
| | | | DAT-PAT: 19 |

**Tuition and Fees**

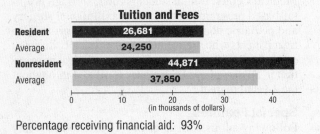

| Resident | 26,681 |
|---|---|
| Average | 24,250 |
| Nonresident | 44,871 |
| Average | 37,850 |

(in thousands of dollars)

Percentage receiving financial aid: 93%

## Introduction

The University of Iowa was established in 1847 and offers both undergraduate and graduate degrees. The University of Iowa College of Dentistry, established in 1900, is located on the 900-acre campus, through which the Iowa River passes. The school offers postgraduate programs in all dental specialties and master's and PhD degrees.

## Admissions (AADSAS)

The applicant's background should include at least 3 years of college work incorporating the basic predental science courses and the English composition, rhetoric, and speech requirements for a bachelor's degree. Recommended additional courses may be selected from biochemistry, upper-division biology, quantitative analysis, calculus, literature, arts, and social sciences. *Transfer and advanced standing:* All applicants must apply through AADSAS for first year admission.

## Curriculum

4-year. *First year:* To achieve a close correlation of the basic sciences with clinical disciplines, students are introduced to clinical situations during this year. *Second year:* Program continues the basic sciences and technical courses, plus definitive clinical patient treatment. *Third year:* Students rotate through a series of clinical clerkships in each of 8 clinical disciplines. *Fourth year:* Seniors are involved in the delivery of comprehensive dental care under conditions closely approximating those in private practice.

## Facilities

The Dental Science Building is part of the university's health sciences campus, which includes the colleges of Dentistry, Medicine, Nursing, Pharmacy, and Public Health.

## Special Features

The Educational Opportunity Program is available to persons of all races and ethnic backgrounds. It provides both financial and academic assistance to a limited number of students who have experienced environmental, economic, or academic hardships that cause them to compete for admission at a disadvantage because their grade point average and DAT scores do not reflect true ability. Program eligibility must be formally requested by the applicant.

# University of Kentucky College of Dentistry

800 Rose Street
Medical Center
Lexington, Kentucky   40536

*Phone:* 859-323-6072            *Fax:* 859-257-5550
*E-mail:* trbriaz@uky.edu
*WWW:* mc.uky.edu/

| Application Filing | | Accreditation | |
|---|---|---|---|
| Earliest: | June 1 | CDA | |
| Latest: | December 1 | | |
| Fee: | $65 | **Degrees Granted** | |
| AADSAS: | yes | DMD | |

### Enrollment: 2008–2009 First-Year Class

| | | | | |
|---|---|---|---|---|
| Men: | 32 | 57% | *Mean* | |
| Women: | 24 | 43% | total GPA: | 3.6 |
| Minorities: | 6 | 10% | science: | 3.5 |
| Out of State: | 16 | 29% | | |
| With 2 years of college: | | 0% | *Average* | |
| With 3 years of college: | | 0% | DAT academic: | 19 |
| | | | DAT-PAT: | 19 |

### Tuition and Fees

| | |
|---|---|
| **Resident** | 22,780 |
| Average | 24,250 |
| **Nonresident** | 46,474 |
| Average | 37,850 |

0    10    20    30    40
(in thousands of dollars)

Percentage receiving financial aid: 95%

## Introduction

The University of Kentucky was established in 1865, and has 13 undergraduate and 1 graduate school. The University of Kentucky College of Dentistry was founded in 1962. Postdoctoral programs are offered in 4 specialties (oral surgery, orthodontics, periodontics and pediatric dentistry) and the school also has strong research and continuing education programs. The College of Dentistry is located in an attractive suburban setting in Lexington.

## Admissions (AADSAS)

The UK College of Dentistry seeks to enroll students whose backgrounds, personalities, and motivations indicate that they will make the best possible future dental practioners. As a state institution, the college gives preference to qualified applicants who are residents of Kentucky; however, a limited number of highly qualified out-of-state applicants are considered each year and such candidates are encouraged to apply. The basic predental courses are required and a bachelor's degree is desirable. *Transfer and advanced standing:* No program is available.

## Curriculum

4-year. The curriculum is based on a diagonal plan. Basic science courses are taught along with clinical applications throughout the program, with clinical work intensifying in the third and fourth years. Clinical experiences begin during the fall of the first year and continue as students gain further competence in delivering dental care to patients. The educational program focuses on learning, competency building, and the development of critical thinking and problem-solving skills in a student-centered environment.

## Grading Policy

The grading policy is based on an A, B, C, F system. This policy emphasizes learning and the development of professional competencies.

## Facilities

The College of Dentistry is an integral part of the University of Kentucky, the Commonwealth's flagship university. The 6-story dentistry building is linked to the University of Kentucky Albert B. Chandler Medical Center, which includes the 5 colleges of Public Health: Dentistry, Medicine, Nursing, Pharmacy, and Health Sciences, and the university's teaching hospital. The main UK campus is across the street, and downtown Lexington is a 10-minute bus ride away.

## Special Features

Financial assistance is available, and the college has a full-time director of this program. Personal and career counseling are also an integral part of the curriculum. Entering students are assigned an advisor who works with them throughout their dental education. Tutorial support services are readily obtained for students needing assistance in developing study skills or mastering content/skill areas.

# University of Louisville School of Dentistry

Health Sciences Center
Louisville, Kentucky   40292

*Phone:* 502-852-5081          *Fax:* 502-852-1210
*E-mail:* dmdadmissions@louisville.edu
*WWW:* louisville.edu/dental

| Application Filing | | Accreditation |
|---|---|---|
| Earliest: | June 1 | CDA |
| Latest: | January 1 | |
| Fee: | $50 | **Degrees Granted** |
| AADSAS: | yes | DMD |

### Enrollment: 2008–2009 First-Year Class

| | | | |
|---|---|---|---|
| Men: | 36 | 42% | *Mean* |
| Women: | 49 | 48% | total GPA: 3.45 |
| Minorities: | 17 | 20% | science: 3.3 |
| Out of State: | 41 | 48% | |
| With 4 years of college: | 100% | | *Average* |
| | | | DAT academic: 17 |
| | | | DAT-PAT: 18 |

### Tuition and Fees

| | |
|---|---|
| **Resident** | 26,540 |
| Average | 24,250 |
| **Nonresident** | 54,072 |
| Average | 37,850 |

0   10   20   30   40
(in thousands of dollars)

Percentage receiving financial aid: 97%

## Introduction

The philosophy of the school is to consider students partners in learning and to provide them with the knowledge and skills to meet the challenges of today's dental profession. Many ULSD graduates choose to practice general dentistry, while others continue their education in a specialty, engage in dental research, or prepare for a career in education. The school focuses on providing its students with a strong clinical education, using pioneering simulation educational techniques.

## Admissions (AADSAS)

Applicants must have earned a minimum of 90 semester hours, including 32 credits of science or health-related coursework. The basic predental science courses best meet this requirement. Recommended courses that may be selected include biochemistry, physiology, histology, anatomy, English composition, and speech. Each class is composed of approximately 55% Kentucky residents and 45% out-of-state students. *Transfer and advanced standing:* rare, but considered on an individual basis.

## Curriculum

4-year traditional. The basic and clinical sciences are integrated. Patient contact is initiated in the first year. The majority of electives are usually taken in the fourth year. *First year:* The basic science and preclinical technique courses, clinical experience in diagnosis and clinical observation/assisting, as well as periodontics. *Second year:* A continuation of the basic science and clinical technique courses. Involvement in patient treatment begins. *Third and fourth years:* Completion of the advanced basic and clinical courses, extensive clinical patient contact, rotations in pediatric dentistry and oral surgery, and exposure to hospital dentistry.

## Grading Policy

Most grading is by letter grades, but several courses are offered, especially in the clinical program, on a Pass/Fail basis.

## Facilities

The school is a state-supported institution located within the University Health Sciences Center (HSC) in downtown Louisville (metropolitan area population of more than 1 million). Founded in 1887, the school is housed in a building that opened in 1970 as part of the HSC. Bonds have been sold to provide funding to complete the total renewal of the clinics and classrooms. Completion of the project is expected by 2010.

## Special Features

An extensive support system of faculty advising, clinical monitoring, and student tutoring serves the needs of all dental students. Counseling services and assistance in developing study skills are also available.

## LOUISIANA

# Louisiana State University*
# School of Dentistry

1100 Florida Avenue, Box 101
New Orleans, Louisiana    70119

*Phone:* 504-941-8124          *Fax:* 504-941-8123
*E-mail:* jweir@lsuhsc.edu
*WWW:* lsusd.lsuhsc.edu

| Application Filing | | Accreditation |
|---|---|---|
| Earliest: | September 1 | CDA |
| Latest: | February 28 | |
| Fee: | $50 | **Degrees Granted** |
| AADSAS: | yes | DDS |

### Enrollment: 2008–2009 First-Year Class

| Men: | 37 | 61% | *Mean* | |
|---|---|---|---|---|
| Women: | 23 | 39% | total GPA: | 3.57 |
| Minorities: | 13 | 21% | science: | 3.5 |
| Out of State: | 7 | 12% | | |
| With 2 years of college: | 0% | | *Average* | |
| With 4 years of college: | 100% | | DAT academic: | 19.7 |
| | | | DAT-PAT: | 19.7 |

**Tuition and Fees**

| Resident | 5,865 |
| Average | 24,250 |
| Nonresident | 13,014 |
| Average | 37,850 |

0    10    20    30    40
(in thousands of dollars)

Percentage receiving financial aid: 89%

*School affected by 2005 hurricane.

## Introduction

The Louisiana State University System was created in 1860. The Louisiana State University School of Dentistry was founded in 1968 and is part of the Louisiana State University Health Sciences Center. The teaching facilities in the basic and clinical sciences were dedicated in 1972. In addition to its DDS program, the School of Dentistry provides educational opportunities on the postgraduate level and programs in dental hygiene and dental laboratory technology.

## Admissions

The basic predental science courses plus 9 semester hours of English are required. Additional courses selected from comparative anatomy, histology, biochemistry, cell and molecular biology, embryology, psychology, sociology, history, philosophy, art, sculpture, and ceramics are recommended. Priority is given to state residents. A few out-of-state residents may be accepted. *Transfer and advanced standing:* Available to selected students in good standing at accredited U.S. schools.

## Curriculum

4-year diagonal. The basic, clinical, and social science courses are presented individually and then interrelated by the free use of correlation courses. As the emphasis on basis and preclinical sciences decreases from year one to year four, the students' exposure to the clinical sciences increases. *First year:* Basic science and preclinical technique courses and behavioral science treatment with limited clinical exposure. *Second year:* A continuation of the basic science and preclinical technique courses with patient treatment in operative dentistry, oral diagnosis, and removable prosthetics. *Third year:* In addition to oral diagnosis, students learn clinical patient treatment in operative dentistry, fixed and removable prosthodontics, pediatric dentistry, oral and maxillofacial surgery, and orthodontics. *Fourth year:* This year focuses on total patient dental care in general surgery. Elective opportunities are available in all departments.

## Facilities

The school is an integral part of the LSU Health Sciences Center. It is located in dental school buildings that contain excellent preclinical and clinical facilities.

## Special Features

Students entering without a degree may earn a bachelor's degree if arrangements are made with their undergraduate school.

## MARYLAND

# University of Maryland Baltimore College of Dental Surgery

650 West Baltimore Street, Room 6410
Baltimore, Maryland   21201-1586

*Phone:* 410-706-7472          *Fax:* 410-706-0945
*E-mail:* dds.admissions@dental.umaryland.edu
*WWW:* dental.umaryland.edu

| Application Filing | | Accreditation |
|---|---|---|
| Earliest: | May 1 | CDA |
| Latest: | January 1 | |
| Fee: | $75 | **Degrees Granted** |
| AADSAS: | yes | DDS, DDS-PhD |

### Enrollment: 2008–2009 First-Year Class

| | | | |
|---|---|---|---|
| Men: | 64 | 49% | *Mean* |
| Women: | 66 | 51% | total GPA: 3.5 |
| Minorities: | 18 | 14% | science: 3.4 |
| Out of State: | 57 | 44% | |
| With 2 years of college: | 0% | | *Average* |
| With 3 years of college: | 99% | | DAT academic: 19.2 |
| With 4 years of college: | 1% | | DAT-PAT: 19.3 |

### Tuition and Fees

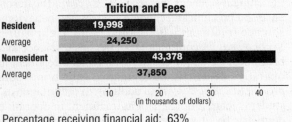

| Resident | 19,998 |
| Average | 24,250 |
| Nonresident | 43,378 |
| Average | 37,850 |

0   10   20   30   40
(in thousands of dollars)

Percentage receiving financial aid: 63%

## Introduction

The University of Maryland system is a public system that was created in 1807. The Baltimore County campus became part of the state university system in 1963. Established in 1840, the dental school at the University of Maryland was the first dental college to exist in the world. The Baltimore College of Dental Surgery is located in the same 32-acre urban campus in downtown Baltimore, as are the schools of Medicine, Pharmacy, Nursing, and Allied Health Professions, as well as Law and Social Work. In 1983 a Center for the Study of Human Performance in Dentistry was established at the school.

## Admissions (AADSAS)

Minimum requirements are 8 credits of inorganic chemistry, general biology, organic chemistry, physics, 6 credits of English composition and 3 credis of biochemistry. Recommended courses include biochemistry, cell and molecular biology, and physiology. Applicants presenting the minimum science requirements should show better than average performance in these courses. Both science and nonscience majors are encouraged to apply. Nonresidents should have a minimum science GPA of 3.2 and DAT of 18. *Transfer and advanced standing:* Students from other U.S. or Canadian schools may be admitted with advanced standing.

## Curriculum

4-year. Integration of biological and clinical sciences takes place using a horizontally and vertically integrated curricula. Preclinical technical courses employ simulators for realism. Elective basic science courses or clinical clerkship programs may be taken in the senior year. Students provide comprehensive patient care for their assigned patients.

## Facilities

A new dental school facility was completed and became operational in the fall of 2006.

## Special Features

Research experience is available at the student's option. A combined DDS-PhD program is also available for qualified applicants. Tutors and a special program are available for those in need of academic assistance while in attendance.

# MASSACHUSETTS

## Boston University, Goldman School of Dental Medicine

100 East Newton Street
Boston, Massachusetts 02118

*Phone:* 617-638-4787     *Fax:* 617-638-4798
*E-mail:* sdmadmis@bu.edu
*WWW:* http://dentalschool.bu.edu

| Application Filing | | Accreditation |
|---|---|---|
| Earliest: | June 1 | CDA |
| Latest: | February 1 | |
| Fee: | $70 | **Degrees Granted** |
| AADSAS: | yes | DMD |

### Enrollment: 2008–2009 First-Year Class

| | | | | |
|---|---|---|---|---|
| Men: | 63 | 55% | *Mean* | |
| Women: | 52 | 45% | total GPA: | 3.3 |
| Minorities: | 31 | 27% | science: | 3.2 |
| Out of State: | 109 | 95% | | |
| With 2 years of college: | | 0% | *Average* | |
| With 3 years of college: | | 0% | DAT academic: | 19 |
| | | | DAT-PAT: | 19 |

**Tuition and Fees**

| | |
|---|---|
| Resident | 44,751 |
| Average | 19,750 |
| Nonresident | 44,751 |
| Average | 29,900 |

0    10    20    30    40
(in thousands of dollars)

Percentage receiving financial aid: 68%

## Introduction

Boston University has been a private school since 1839. As part of Boston University's Medical Center, the Goldman School of Dental Medicine was established in 1963. Also included in Boston University's Medical Center are the School of Medicine, the School of Public Health, and Boston Medical Center Hospital.

## Admissions (AADSAS)

The basic predental sciences plus 1 year of English and 1 year of mathematics (with calculus) are required. Two courses each in psychology, sociology or anthropology, and economics are strongly recommended. There are no geographical restrictions on attendance. *Transfer and advanced standing:* Not available.

## Curriculum

The DMD program requires 4 years of didactic and clinical study. Students integrate a comprehensive understanding of the science of dentistry with an ability to apply clinical judgment and technique. Courses build a foundation of knowledge and teach the analytical skills needed to apply the knowledge. *First year:* Consists of the biomedical sciences, oral radiology, dental assisting techniques, preventive dentistry, preclinical laboratory courses, and a supervised rotation as a dental intern in a private office. *Second year:* Involves continuation of the biomedical sciences and intern rotations alternating with didactic and laboratory courses. *Third and fourth years:* Allow maximum opportunity for team-oriented patient care under faculty supervision. Working in a private practice and management guidance are also provided. A 10-week experience externship is also required, which takes place in a wide choice of sites.

## Grading Policy

A letter grade system is used.

## Facilities

The school is a component of the BU Medical Center and its teaching and clinical facilities are located in Boston's South End. Facilities of affiliated institutions and community-based clinics are also utilized.

## Special Features

The APEX Program offers students the opportunity to function as dental interns in affiliated dental practices. This exposure helps prepare students for managing a dental practice.

# Harvard School of Dental Medicine

88 Longwood Avenue
Boston, Massachusetts  02115

*Phone:* 617-432-0569          *Fax:* 617-432-3881
*E-mail:* 12abet_berner@hsdm.harvard.edu
*WWW:* hsdm.harvard.edu

| Application Filing | | Accreditation | |
|---|---|---|---|
| Earliest: | June 1 | CDA | |
| Latest: | December 15 | | |
| Fee: | $70 | **Degrees Granted** | |
| AADSAS: | yes | DMD, MMSc | |

### Enrollment: 2008–2009 First-Year Class

| | | | | |
|---|---|---|---|---|
| Men: | 12 | 55% | *Mean* | |
| Women: | 10 | 45% | total GPA: | 3.7 |
| Minorities: | 1 | 4% | science: | 3.8 |
| Out of State: | 11 | 50% | | |
| With 2 years of college: | 0 | | *Average* | |
| With 3 years of college: | 0 | | DAT academic: | 21 |
| | | | DAT-PAT: | 22 |

**Tuition and Fees**

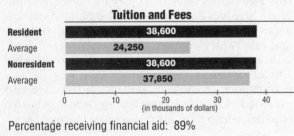

| | |
|---|---|
| **Resident** | 38,600 |
| Average | 24,250 |
| **Nonresident** | 38,600 |
| Average | 37,850 |

0    10    20    30    40
(in thousands of dollars)

Percentage receiving financial aid: 89%

Above data applicable to 2007–2008 academic year.

## Introduction

This school was established in 1867 and was the first university-affiliated dental school in the country. The school sees as its goal the education of its students for leadership in dentistry. The majority of recent graduates have entered postdoctoral programs in clinical specialties or general practice residencies. In addition, students have elected to pursue careers in teaching, research, and public health.

## Admissions (AADSAS)

The basic predental science courses plus 1 year each of calculus and English (preferably composition) are required. Advanced science courses such as biochemistry, physiology, molecular biology, cell biology, or genetics are recommended. Taking the DAT is required and having a score of 19 or higher is recommended. A GPA of 3.0 or higher is desirable. *Transfer and advanced standing:* There is currently no formal advanced standing program.

## Curriculum

4-year. The curriculum is designed with an emphasis on problem-based learning. Students develop skills in critical thinking and problem solving that will enhance their abilities in clinical diagnosis, treatment planning, and delivery of clinical care. In addition, the conceptual and technical aspects of dentistry are taught by utilizing a comprehensive approach to patient care, as opposed to a discipline-based or departmental approach. Each student is required to take a research course and conduct a research project before the end of the fourth year.

## Grading Policy

The Honors/Pass/Fail system is used.

## Facilities

The educational program takes place at the dental school and the Harvard medical school as well as at Harvard-affiliated institutions including Forsyth Institute, Massachusetts General Hospital, Children's Hospital, several VA Medical Centers, other Harvard schools, and the Massachusetts Institute of Technology.

## Special Features

The philosophy of education at HSDM is that dentistry is a specialty of medicine. In keeping with this belief, medical and dental students study together in the New Pathway curriculum at Harvard Medical School during the first 2 years. Dental clinic instruction takes place in treatment teams that use a comprehensive approach to patient care. Both didactic and clinical courses are taught by the problem-based method of study and discussion groups. In this approach, cases based on actual clinical records or investigative problems are used to set the learning objectives. Students are taught critical thinking and problem-solving techniques that will equip them for lifelong learning in the field of dental medicine.

# Tufts University
# School of Dental Medicine

One Kneeland Street
Boston, Massachusetts   02111

*Phone:* 617-636-6639       *Fax:* 617-636-0309
*E-mail:* DenAdmissions@tufts.edu
*WWW:* tufts.edu/dental

| Application Filing | | Accreditation |
|---|---|---|
| Earliest: | May 15 | CDA |
| Latest: | February 1 | |
| Fee: | $70 | **Degrees Granted** |
| AADSAS: | yes | DMD, BS-DMD |

### Enrollment: 2008–2009 First-Year Class

| | | | | |
|---|---|---|---|---|
| Men: | 83 | 50% | *Mean* | |
| Women: | 84 | 50% | total GPA: | 3.4 |
| Minorities: | 69 | 41% | science: | 3.4 |
| Out of State: | 118 | 71% | | |
| With 3 years of college: | 0% | | *Average* | |
| With 4 years of college: | 100% | | DAT academic: | 19 |
| | | | DAT-PAT: | 19 |

**Tuition and Fees**

| | |
|---|---|
| Resident | 62,475 |
| Average | 24,250 |
| Nonresident | 62,475 |
| Average | 37,850 |

0   10   20   30   40
(in thousands of dollars)

Percentage receiving financial aid: 82%

## Introduction

Tufts University has 2 undergraduate and 9 graduate schools. It was originally established in 1852. The School of Dental Medicine was founded in 1868 as the Boston Dental College, which in 1889 joined with Tufts College. The Medical Center includes, in addition to the dental school, the School of Medicine, Sackler School of Graduate Medical Sciences, the Gerald J. and Dorothy R. Friedman School of Nutrition Science and Policy, and other institutions. In addition to the DMD degree, it offers graduate training in many dental specialties.

## Admissions (AADSAS)

The basic predental science courses (but only 1 semester of organic chemistry) plus 1 semester of a writing-intensive humanities course are required. Courses in histology, anatomy, genetics, general psychology, mathematics, economics, statistics, speech, sculpture, and an anthropology course are recommended. A minimum GPA of 3.3 and DAT of 18 are preferred. *Transfer and advanced standing:* Students from foreign dental schools may be considered for advanced standing.

## Curriculum

4-year. The curriculum of the School of Dental Medicine has been designed and modified over the years to reflect the changing needs of the dental profession. The school's primary goal is to develop dental practitioners who are able to utilize their knowledge of the basic principles of human biology and human behavior in conjunction with their technical skills in diagnosing, treating, and preventing oral disease. The DMD program, which extends over a 4-year period, consists of a series of didactic, laboratory, and clinical experiences, all of which are programmed to result in the logical development of concepts and skills. *First year:* The basic science and preclinical technique courses. *Second year:* The courses are concerned with the pathology of the body systems with special emphasis on the oral cavity. Clinical experience is begun under faculty supervision. *Third and fourth years:* These years are primarily clinical and are devoted to the comprehensive care of patients. An integral part of this year is the externship program, which lasts 5 weeks at a facility away from the school.

## Facilities

The school is located in the Tufts Dental Health Science Building, a 10-story structure located in midtown Boston in the Tufts Medical Center.

## Special Features

The school encourages applications from women and minorities.

# MICHIGAN

# University of Detroit—Mercy School of Dentistry

2700 Martin Luther King, Junior Blvd.
Detroit, Michigan    48208

*Phone:* 313-494-6611          *Fax:* 313-494-6659
          313-494-6651
*E-mail:* dental@udmercy.edu
*WWW:* dental.udmercy.edu

| Application Filing | | Accreditation |
|---|---|---|
| Earliest: | May 15 | CDA |
| Latest: | February 1 | |
| Fee: | $75 | **Degrees Granted** |
| AADSAS: | yes | DDS |

### Enrollment: 2008–2009 First-Year Class

| | | | | |
|---|---|---|---|---|
| Men: | 50 | 57% | *Mean* | |
| Women: | 37 | 43% | total GPA: | 3.6 |
| Minorities: | 36 | 41% | science: | 3.6 |
| Out of State: | 27 | 31% | | |
| With 2 years of college: | 1% | *Average* | |
| With 3 years of college: | 2% | DAT academic: | 19 |
| | | | DAT-PAT: | 20 |

**Tuition and Fees**

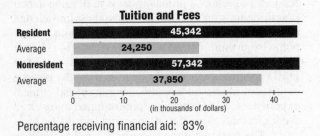

| Resident | 45,342 |
| Average | 24,250 |
| Nonresident | 57,342 |
| Average | 37,850 |

(in thousands of dollars)

Percentage receiving financial aid: 83%

## Introduction

The University of Detroit Mercy School of Dentistry, an independent Catholic institution, is an urban-based school located in metropolitan Detroit. The school serves to deliver oral health care to an extensive patient population as well as community outreach activities. The location provides classrooms, preclinical laboratories, clinics, cafeteria, and a library, an improved environment for learning, research, and patient care. A new clinical simulation laboratory containing patient simulator mannequins and clinical workstations is carefully designed to enhance learning. There is a 42-chair hospital-based satellite clinic. The school is dedicated to educating dentists who are patient-care oriented and skilled in the art of self-evaluation and lifelong learning.

## Admissions (AADSAS)

The basic predental science courses plus a year of English are required. Recommended courses include microbiology, physiology, comparative anatomy, histology, embryology, biochemistry, statistics, and psychology. No priority is given to state residents. *Transfer and advanced standing:* Foreign dental graduates as well as those attending U.S. and Canadian schools are considered.

## Curriculum

The majority of biomedical, behavioral, and preclinical sciences are concentrated in the first 2 years. The freshman curriculum is divided between biomedical and dental sciences, while the sophomore year is devoted primarily to dental sciences taught in a simulation environment. Limited patient care experiences occur in the first and second years. More than half of the curricular time during the third and fourth years is devoted to clinical practice. Patient care experiences are based on an evidence-based, comprehensive care model utilizing the expertise of generalists and specialists. Individual students are assigned a patient family and are responsible for addressing all the patient's dental needs. Outreach clinical rotations occurring during the fourth year expose the student's to alternative practice settings. Patient management and current issues are addressed throughout the curriculum. Research opportunities are available on an elective basis.

## Facilities

The school is located in southwest Detroit and contains well-equipped dental clinics and laboratories. The facilities consist of 187 fully equipped dental units and a simulation laboratory. Senior dental students provide patient care, on an every other week rotation, at the University of Detroit Mercy University Health Center at Detroit Receiving Hospital. This educational experience, a modern 42-operatory clinic, is designed to enable the student to provide comprehensive patient care more similar to the general dental practice setting. Students also rotate on assignments through various satellite clinics and participate in programs in local nursing homes, providing care using portable equipment.

## Special Features

Women and members of minority groups are encouraged to apply. In addition to a DDS degree, the school offers postgraduate studies (Endodontics, Orthodontics, Periodontics, and an AEGD program) as well as a dental hygiene program.

# University of Michigan School of Dentistry

1011 N. University
Ann Arbor, Michigan    48109

*Phone:* 734-763-3316          *Fax:* 734-647-6805
*WWW:* dent.umich.edu

| Application Filing | | | Accreditation | |
|---|---|---|---|---|
| Earliest: | May 15 | | CDA | |
| Latest: | January 15 | | | |
| Fee: | $50 | | **Degrees Granted** | |
| AADSAS: | yes | | DDS | |

### Enrollment: 2008–2009 First-Year Class

| Men: | 56 | 53% | *Mean* | |
|---|---|---|---|---|
| Women: | 49 | 47% | total GPA: | 3.5 |
| Minorities: | 23 | 22% | science: | 3.3 |
| Out of State: | 38 | 36% | | |
| With 2 years of college: | | 0% | *Average* | |
| With 3 years of college: | | 3% | DAT academic: | 19 |
| | | | DAT-PAT: | 18 |

**Tuition and Fees**

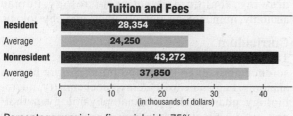

| Resident | 28,354 |
| Average | 24,250 |
| Nonresident | 43,272 |
| Average | 37,850 |

0   10   20   30   40
(in thousands of dollars)

Percentage receiving financial aid: 75%

## Introduction

The University of Michigan System was founded in 1817. The University of Michigan at Ann Arbor is on the main campus, which was founded that same year. Other campuses of the university are located in Dearborn and Flint. Aside from the DDS degree program, the dental school offers programs leading to specialty certification, masters of science degree, PhD in Oral Health Sciences, as well as dental hygiene and continuing education courses.

## Admissions (AADSAS)

The basic predental science courses plus 1 year of English composition are required. Biochemistry, sociology, psychology, and microbiology are also required courses and are highly recommended, and exposure to nonscience courses is encouraged. Each entering class is generally comprised of 60% Michigan residents and 40% nonresidents. *Transfer:* Transfer between dental schools is not available. The School offers an Internationally Trained Dentist Program for foreign-trained dentists.

## Information for Special Applicants

The University of Michigan has a long-standing commitment to the recruitment, retention, and graduation of a culturally diverse student body. It involves a comprehensive approach targeted toward all levels of preparation for professional school admission, beginning with high school. The approach features enhancement of academic skills, interviewing techniques, preadmissions counseling, DAT preparation courses, and financial aid advising to disadvantaged students. Following admission, disadvantaged students are offered a summer prematriculation orientation and a continuing complementary tutorial program to facilitate their retention in dental school. Women, veterans, and members of minority groups are encouraged to apply.

## Curriculum

4-year. Clinical training emphasizing comprehensive patient care begins in the first year and is closely integrated with supporting basic science and preclinical courses. Student research opportunities are available. *First year:* Consists of an Integrated Medical Science (IMS) curriculum along with behavioral sciences and weekly clinical experiences. *Second year:* Continued IMS and preclinical courses with additional clinical experiences. *Third and fourth years:* Involve the clinical sciences and the delivery of comprehensive dental care that approximates private practice. Students also spend several weeks at off-site rotations in community health clinics.

## Facilities

The school's modern quarters were designed to complement the changing concepts in dental education. Preclinical instruction occurs in a simulation laboratory. Pilot programs include audio lectures that can be downloaded to an ipod.

## Special Features

Substantial research facilities, faculty, and activities in basic and applied sciences are features of the school. Women, veterans, and minority group members are encouraged to apply. A summer enrichment program for entering students and students who apply to dental school is offered. Academic counseling and tutorial assistance are available.

# MINNESOTA

# University of Minnesota School of Dentistry

515 Delaware Street S.E.
Minneapolis, Minnesota 55455

*Phone:* 612-625-7477          *Fax:* 612-624-0882
*E-mail:* madde084@umn.edu
*WWW:* dentistry.umn.edu

| Application Filing | | Accreditation | |
|---|---|---|---|
| Earliest: | May 15 | CDA | |
| Latest: | December 1 | | |
| Fee: | $75 | **Degrees Granted** | |
| AADSAS: | yes | DDS | |

### Enrollment: 2008–2009 First-Year Class

| | | | | |
|---|---|---|---|---|
| Men: | 55 | 57% | *Mean* | |
| Women: | 42 | 43% | total GPA: | 3.6 |
| Minorities: | 15 | 15% | science: | 3.6 |
| Out of State: | 31 | 36% | | |
| With 2 years of college: | | 1% | *Average* | |
| With 4 years of college: | | 99% | DAT academic: | 19 |
| | | | DAT-PAT: | 20 |

**Tuition and Fees**

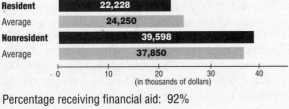

| | |
|---|---|
| **Resident** | 22,228 |
| Average | 24,250 |
| **Nonresident** | 39,598 |
| Average | 37,850 |

0    10    20    30    40
(in thousands of dollars)

Percentage receiving financial aid: 92%

## Introduction

The School of Dentistry, established in 1888, is a state institution and part of the University Health Center. The Center is located on the Minneapolis campus of the university. The school was completed in 1975. A wide range of programs are conducted in the School of Dentistry, including dentistry, dental hygiene, many dental specialties, basic science graduate and other postdoctoral and clinical training programs, and a comprehensive research program. A DDS/PhD program and a Program for Advanced Standing Students (UMN PASS) are also available.

## Admissions (AADSAS)

At least 87 semester credits of 130 quarter credits of liberal arts courses are required from an officially accredited U.S. or Canadian college or university. Required courses must be completed by the end of the regular academic year (i.e., spring) for entry the following fall. They should include: 8 semester credits of English, biology, or zoology with lab, physics, biochemistry with lab, general chemistry with lab, and organic chemistry with lab. In addition 3 semester credits of math, and 3 applied human physiology are required. Other recommended courses include drawing, sculpture, genetics, histology, human anatomy, immunology, microbiology, and physiology.

## Curriculum

The year-round DDS curriculum includes: (a) basic science courses in gross and microscopic human anatomy, human neuroanatomy, biochemistry, microbiology, pharmacology, human physiology, pathology, oral histology, embryology, and genetics; and (b) dentistry courses in operative dentistry, oral anatomy, oral diagnosis, pediatric dentistry, oral surgery, anesthesia, period ontology, roentgenology, biomaterials, fixed and removable prosthodontics, management, jurisprudence, and ethics. A variety of elective experiences is also available.

## Facilities

The School of Dentistry, located in the extensive health sciences complexes on the east bank of the Minneapolis campus, offers Minnesota's only professional program in dentistry. The school's teaching and research facilities are in a health sciences building, which holds shared basic science laboratories and lecture rooms for the health sciences. Its main offices, classrooms, clinics, laboratories, reading and learning resource rooms are in the Malcolm Moos Health Sciences Tower, which provides an innovative setting for education, dental practice, and research.

## Special Features

The University Health Center is located in the Minneapolis Campus of the university, thus students have available to them a variety of academic, cultural, and recreational opportunities.

## MISSISSIPPI

# University of Mississippi School of Dentistry

2500 North State Street
Jackson, Mississippi 39216

*Phone:* 601-984-1080 *Fax:* 601-984-1039
*E-mail:* jduncan@sod.umsmed.edu
*WWW:* http://dentistryumc.edu/

| Application Filing | | Accreditation |
|---|---|---|
| Earliest: | July 1 | CDA |
| Latest: | November 1 | |
| Fee: | $50 | **Degrees Granted** |
| AADSAS: | no | DMD |

### Enrollment: 2008–2009 First-Year Class

| | | | |
|---|---|---|---|
| Men: | 21 | 57% | *Mean* |
| Women: | 16 | 33% | total GPA: 3.7 |
| Minorities: | 6 | 16% | science: 3.6 |
| Out of State: | 0 | 0% | |
| With 3 years of college: | 0% | | *Average* |
| With 4 years of college: | 100% | | DAT academic: 17.7 |
| | | | DAT-PAT: 18.6 |

**Tuition and Fees**

| | |
|---|---|
| **Resident** | 11,530 |
| Average | 24,250 |
| **Nonresident** | 11,530 |
| Average | 37,850 |

0    10    20    30    40
(in thousands of dollars)

Percentage receiving financial aid: 85%

## Introduction
The University of Mississippi is a public school that was established in 1844. The University of Mississippi School of Dentistry, located in the Medical Center, enrolled its first class in 1975. In addition to the School of Dentistry, the University of Mississippi Medical Center contains the schools of Medicine, Nursing, and Health-Related Professions, Graduate Studies in the Medical Sciences, and the University Hospital. The goal of the school is to train general dentists to practice in Mississippi.

## Admissions
The basic predental science courses plus 2 years of English, 1 year each of mathematics (college algebra and/or trigonometry) and psychology is required. Recommended courses include biochemistry, comparative anatomy, histology, cell biology, embryology, microbiology, physical chemistry, quantitative analysis, humanities, communication, and a foreign language. Currently, only legal Mississippi residents are admitted. *Transfer and advanced standing:* Only a few students are admitted with advanced standing.

## Curriculum
4-year modern. A systems approach to a problem-oriented curriculum is used. Clinical experience begins in the second year and is designed to follow the team approach to patient care through all 4 years. Selective courses in the specialty areas of clinical dentistry are available in the last year. Clinical experiences start in the first year with a 1-week continuity project somewhere in the state. These continue throughout the 4 years of the program.

## Facilities
The school is part of the University of Mississippi Medical Center campus. The clinical facilities are self-contained in the dental school building.

## Special Features
By making proper arrangements, students entering without a degree may earn their bachelor's degree while completing the dental program.

## MISSOURI

# University of Missouri—Kansas City School of Dentistry

650 East 25th Street
Kansas City, Missouri   64108

*Phone:* 816-235-2080          *Fax:* 816-235-2157
*E-mail:* 6ighamr@umkc.edu
*WWW:* umkc.edu/dentistry

| Application Filing | | Accreditation |
|---|---|---|
| Earliest: | September 1 | CDA |
| Latest: | October 1 | |
| Fee: | $45 | **Degrees Granted** |
| AADSAS: | yes | DDS |

### Enrollment: 2008–2009 First-Year Class

| | | | |
|---|---|---|---|
| Men: | 63 | 61% | *Mean* |
| Women: | 39 | 39% | total GPA: 3.6 |
| Minorities: | 6 | 6% | science: 3.6 |
| Out of State: | 28 | 25% | |
| With 2 years of college: | 0% | | *Average* |
| With 3 years of college: | 100% | | DAT academic: 18 |
| | | | DAT-PAT: 18 |

### Tuition and Fees

| | |
|---|---|
| **Resident** | 27,813 |
| Average | 24,250 |
| **Nonresident** | 27,813 |
| Average | 37,850 |

(in thousands of dollars)

Percentage receiving financial aid: 89%

## Introduction

The University of Missouri system is public with 4 campuses. Besides Kansas City, campuses are located in Columbia, Rolla, and St. Louis. In 1919 the Kansas City Dental College joined the Western Dental College to become the Kansas City Western Dental College. In 1941 the name changed to the School of Dentistry of the University of Kansas City. The school did not become part of the state university system till 1963. In addition to the DDS degree, the School of Dentistry offers a postdoctoral program leading to a Dental Specialty Certificate and a BS in dental hygiene.

## Admissions (AADSAS)

A minimum of 3 years of predental education is required as well as attainment of other academic and nonacademic criteria. Preference will be given to those who have bachelor's degrees at the time of registration. This includes completing the basic predental science courses as well as 1 year of English composition. Recommended courses may be selected from genetics, logic, mathematics, business, social sciences, psychology, speech, computer science, and humanities. *Transfer and advanced standing:* Students wishing to transfer from another dental school are considered, assuming availability of positions in the appropriate class.

## Curriculum

4-year; 8 semesters plus 2 summer terms (13 weeks each). Emphasis is on preventive and comprehensive dentistry. The student is introduced to clinical procedures during the first year and progresses to the comprehensive treatment of patients during the third and fourth years in a team clinical setting. *First year:* Devoted primarily to the biomedical sciences. Courses are also offered in behavioral dental science, introduction to oral diagnosis, and restorative techniques with associated predental labs. *Second year:* Biomedical sciences continue and preclinical coursework. Fundamentals of operative surgery, prostodontics, and basic endodontics are covered. Clinical care accelerates. *Third year:* Devoted primarily to the clinical practice of dentistry. Patients are assigned to students for comprehensive dental care. Students also attend advanced classes in a wide number of areas. *Fourth year:* This period involves extensive clinical practice and a few courses and seminars.

## Facilities

The school is located in midtown Kansas City. It maintains affiliations with 6 hospitals in the area. It has 2 dental production laboratories in-house and a full-service library with an extensive instructional materials component.

## Special Features

A wide range of personal and/or academic assistance, such as tutoring and counseling, is available as needed.

## NEBRASKA

# Creighton University School of Dentistry

2500 California Plaza
Omaha, Nebraska   68178

*Phone:* 402-280-5022          *Fax:* 402-280-5094
*E-mail:* fayer@creighton.edu
*WWW:* creighton.edu

| Application Filing | | Accreditation | |
|---|---|---|---|
| Earliest: | July 1 | CDA | |
| Latest: | February 1 | | |
| Fee: | $45 | **Degrees Granted** | |
| AADSAS: | yes | DDS | |

### Enrollment: 2008–2009 First-Year Class

| | | | | |
|---|---|---|---|---|
| Men: | 47 | 55% | *Mean* | |
| Women: | 38 | 45% | total GPA: | 3.6 |
| Minorities: | 7 | 8% | science: | 3.5 |
| Out of State: | 79 | 93% | | |
| With 3 years of college: | 0% | | *Average* | |
| With 4 years of college: | 95% | | DAT academic: | 18.5 |
| | | | DAT-PAT: | 18.7 |

### Tuition and Fees

| | |
|---|---|
| Resident | 46,962 |
| Average | 24,250 |
| Nonresident | 46,962 |
| Average | 37,850 |

0    10    20    30    40
(in thousands of dollars)

Percentage receiving financial aid: 92%

## Introduction

Creighton University, a private Catholic school, was established in 1878 but its health science programs did not begin until much later. The Creighton University School of Dentistry was created in 1905. The present dental facility was completed in 1973. In addition to its DDS program, the School of Dentistry, in cooperation with several local junior colleges, is involved in the training of dental auxiliaries. Creighton also has schools of Medicine, Pharmacy, Nursing, and Allied Health Professions.

## Admissions (AADSAS)

The basic predental science courses plus 1 year of English are required. Recommended courses include psychology, modern languages, history, speech, economics, and comparative anatomy. The school has admission agreements with Idaho, New Mexico, Utah, North Dakota, and Wyoming. *Transfer and advanced standing:* Students from other U.S. and Canadian dental schools are considered for advanced standing.

## Curriculum

4-year traditional. Basic and clinical sciences are coordinated by the Department of Oral Biology. Clinical experience begins in the second year. A variety of electives are available in the fourth year. Off-campus clinical opportunities include private practice preceptorships and assignments to hospitals, schools, and clinics. *First year:* The basic and preclinical sciences and an introduction to clinical situations. *Second year:* A continuation of the basic and preclinical sciences with a greater emphasis on preclinical technique courses and an introduction to definitive patient care. *Third year:* A continuation of clinical courses, introduction to practice management, and clinical patient care in a departmental system. *Fourth year:* A continuation of clinical and practical management coursework and delivery of comprehensive dental care.

## Facilities

The dental facility is a modern, 3-level structure containing classrooms, teaching and research laboratories, television studios, and various clinics with over 175 patient treatment stations. The teaching hospital offers additional clinical facilities.

## Special Features

Approximately 92% of the students attending Creighton University School of Dentistry receive some form of financial aid. Most students borrow from federal sources of assistance. There are a small number of scholarships and university-based loans that also are available. These are based on financial need and academic performance and are awarded by both the Committee on Admissions and the Financial Aid Committee of the School of Dentistry.

# University of Nebraska College of Dentistry

40th and Holdrege Streets
Lincoln, Nebraska  68583

*Phone:* 402-472-1363          *Fax:* 402-472-5290
*E-mail:* ckuster@unmc.edu
*WWW:* unmc.edu/dentistry

| Application Filing | | Accreditation | |
|---|---|---|---|
| Earliest: | May 15 | CDA | |
| Latest: | February 1 | | |
| Fee: | $50 | **Degrees Granted** | |
| AADSAS: | yes | DDS | |

### Enrollment: 2008–2009 First-Year Class

| | | | | |
|---|---|---|---|---|
| Men: | 15 | 39% | *Mean* | |
| Women: | 23 | 61% | total GPA: | 3.8 |
| Minorities: | 0 | | science: | 3.7 |
| Out of State: | 11 | 29% | | |
| With 2 years of college: | | 0% | *Average* | |
| With 3 years of college: | | 15% | DAT academic: | 18.5 |
| | | | DAT-PAT: | 17.2 |

### Tuition and Fees

| | |
|---|---|
| **Resident** | 19,207 |
| Average | 24,250 |
| **Nonresident** | 52,135 |
| Average | 37,850 |

0    10    20    30    40
(in thousands of dollars)

Percentage receiving financial aid: 98%

Above data applicable to 2007–2008 academic year.

## Introduction

The University of Nebraska system was founded in 1869, and has campuses in Kearney, Lincoln, and Omaha. The Lincoln Dental College was established in 1899. Less than 20 years later it became a part of the University of Nebraska system and is known as the University of Nebraska College of Dentistry. The school is located on the Lincoln campus. Postgraduate programs are offered in many specialties and a graduate program that leads to the MS degree is available.

## Admissions (AADSAS)

The basic predental science courses plus 1 year of English are required. The college has no specific requirements regarding the absolute minimal scholastic average or DAT scores. Priority is given to applicants from Nebraska, South Dakota, and Wyoming. *Transfer and advanced standing:* Transfer is possible and is determined on an individual basis.

## Curriculum

4-year traditional. The basic sciences are taught by the team method. Students are introduced to clinical observation and personal participation during the first year. Patients are assigned and clinical activity is amplified in the sophomore year. Integration of the basic and clinical sciences is emphasized. Electives may be taken during the senior year. Off-campus clinical experience is provided by means of institutional assignments and a rural rotation program. Research projects are possible and several courses are self-pacing.

## Facilities

Modern preclinical and clinical facilities exist in Lincoln. Hospital affiliations provide opportunities for additional clinical experience. A learning center is available in association with the school library, where the computer facilities and developmental programs are provided.

## Special Features

Counseling is accessible to underrepresented minority applicants.

# NEVADA

# University of Nevada, Las Vegas School of Dentistry
1001 Shadow Lane, MS 7410
Las Vegas, Nevada   89106

*Phone:* 702-774-2520          *Fax:* 702-774-2521
*E-mail:* dentalschool@unlv.edu
*WWW:* dentalschool.unlv.edu

| Application Filing | | Accreditation |
|---|---|---|
| Earliest: | May 15 | Pending |
| Latest: | January 30 | |
| Fee: | $50 | Degrees Granted |
| AADSAS: | yes | DDS |

### Enrollment: 2008–2009 First-Year Class

| | | | Mean | |
|---|---|---|---|---|
| Men: | 48 | 59% | *Mean* | |
| Women: | 34 | 41% | total GPA: | 5 |
| Minorities: | 21 | 26% | science: | 3 |
| Out of State: | 24 | 29% | | |
| With 2 years of college: | | 24% | *Average* | |
| With 3 years of college: | | 76% | DAT academic: | 19 |
| | | | DAT-PAT: | 19 |

### Tuition and Fees

| Resident | 30,837 |
|---|---|
| Average | 24,250 |
| Nonresident | 53,337 |
| Average | 37,850 |

0    10    20    30    40
(in thousands of dollars)

Financial aid: n/a

## Introduction
The University of Nevada was founded in 1957 and is located on a 335-acre campus. The university consists of 12 colleges, which offer undergraduate degree programs. Las Vegas is located in a valley and offers attractive recreational facilities. The first entering class began in September 2002.

## Admissions (AADSAS)
A minimum of 3 years (90 credit) of undergraduate studies is required, but a bachelor's degree is preferred. Also required are the basic predental sciences, plus 2 semesters of English and 1 in biochemistry. Recommended courses are: human or comparative anatomy, physiology, microbiology, histology and genetics, speech, art, sculpture, and business courses. Computer proficiency is desirable. Preference will be given to Nevada residents and students from states without dental schools. *Transfer and advanced standing:* Not available.

## Curriculum
Information not available.

## Facilities
The school is located on the Shadow Lane campus. It occupies more than 110,000 square feet of space and is equipped with more than 165 patient treatment areas.

# NEW JERSEY

# University of Medicine and Dentistry of New Jersey

110 Bergen Street
Newark, New Jersey    07101

*Phone:* 973-972-5362          *Fax:* 973-972-5362
*E-mail:* linfante@umdnj.edu
*WWW:* dentalschool.umdnj.edu

| **Application Filing** | | **Accreditation** |
|---|---|---|
| Earliest: | June 1 | CDA |
| Latest: | December 1 | |
| Fee: | $75 | **Degrees Granted** |
| AADSAS: | yes | DMD, DMD-PhD |

### Enrollment: 2008–2009 First-Year Class

| | | | | |
|---|---|---|---|---|
| Men: | 27 | 52% | *Mean* | |
| Women: | 25 | 48% | total GPA: | 3.6 |
| Minorities: | 4 | 8% | science: | 3.3 |
| Out of State: | 2 | 4% | | |
| With 2 years of college: | | 3% | *Average* | |
| With 3 years of college: | | 8% | DAT academic: | 19 |
| | | | DAT-PAT: | 18 |

**Tuition and Fees**

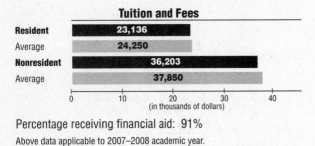

| | |
|---|---|
| Resident | 23,136 |
| Average | 24,250 |
| Nonresident | 36,203 |
| Average | 37,850 |

(in thousands of dollars)

Percentage receiving financial aid: 91%

Above data applicable to 2007–2008 academic year.

## Introduction

The University of Medicine and Dentistry of New Jersey (UMDNJ) is an institution of higher education in the health sciences. As New Jersey's public university of the health sciences, it is the largest such institution in the nation. UMDNJ was created to consolidate and unify all of the state's public programs in medical and dental education. UMDNJ-New Jersey Dental School awards the Doctor of Dental Medicine (DMD) degree upon completion of a comprehensive 4-year program. Graduate dental education is available in Endodontics, Orthodontics, Pediatric Dentistry, Periodontics, Prosthodontics, and Advanced Education in General Dentistry. Hospital residences and fellowships are offered in General Practice Dentistry, Oral Medicine, and in Oral and Maxillofacial Surgery (a 4-year certificate program and a 6-year combined Doctor of Medicine/certificate program).

## Admissions (AADSAS)

The basic predental science courses and 1 year of English are required. A minimum of 3 years of undergraduate credit is required. All applicants must take the DAT. Preference is given to state residents. *Transfer and advanced standing:* Considered only on a space-available basis.

## Curriculum

4-year flexible. Some basic science instruction continues beyond the second year. Clinical activity begins with an Introduction to Clinical Dentistry in the first year. In the next year, students are rotated through clinical departments in a structured manner. During the last year, a student may select a portion of his or her program from clinical courses or research.

## Facilities

Housed in its modern, spacious building on UMDNJ's Newark campus, the New Jersey Dental School provides a setting uniquely suited to an excellent educational experience. Clinic space, research laboratories, and seminar and lecture rooms are designed for optimum efficiency in both teaching and health-care delivery. The dental school building is adjacent to the New Jersey Medical School, the University Hospital, and the George F. Smith Library of the Health Sciences. Also located on the Newark campus are the School of Health-Related Professions, the School of Nursing, the Graduate School of Biomedical Sciences, the School of Public Health, and the Doctors' Office Center, where dental school faculty may engage in faculty practice.

## Special Features

New Jersey Dental School is committed to offering an academic environment where students can learn in a culturally diverse setting so that they may develop skills necessary to provide dental services in a culturally diverse world. Financial, personal, and professional counseling are available from on-campus authorities, and tutorial assistance is provided to students in academic jeopardy. Students are encouraged to participate in summer externships and research opportunities to enhance their dental school curriculum. Many students volunteer their time to serve the community at various elementary and secondary school career days and health fairs and in geriatric outreach programs. Fourth-year students may be selected to participate in the Community-Oriented Dental Education (CODE) program. These students are placed in community-based sites where they provide oral health care to patients in simulated private practice settings with trained staff and under the supervision of faculty. They utilize computer-based scheduling, analyze expense/income, time/productivity, and expense/productivity ratios, manage staff, control the appointment book and inventory, and become involved in infection control and hazard communication standards.

# Columbia University School of Dental and Oral Surgery

630 West 168 Street
New York, New York    10032

*Phone:* 212-305-3478          *Fax:* 212-305-1034
*E-mail:* jmm10@columbia.edu
*WWW:* dental.columbia.edu

**Application Filing**
Earliest:    July 1
Latest:      February 15
Fee:         $70
AADSAS:   yes

**Accreditation**
CDA

**Degrees Granted**
DDS, DDS-MPH
DDS, PAD, DDS, MA

### Enrollment: 2008–2009 First-Year Class
Men:                    17        51%
Women:                16        49%
Minorities:            5         15%
Out of State:    n/a
With 2 years of college:      0%
With 3 years of college:      0%

*Mean*
total GPA:       3.6
science:          3.4

*Average*
DAT academic:   22
DAT-PAT:          19

### Tuition and Fees
Resident       45,760
Average        24,250
Nonresident    45,760
Average        37,850

0    10    20    30    40
(in thousands of dollars)

Percentage receiving financial aid:  96%
Above data applicable to 2007–2008 academic year.

## Introduction
Founded in 1754, Columbia University is a private higher educational system. In 1852 the School of Dental and Oral Surgery was established, and in 1923 it merged with the dental school at Columbia University, the New York Postgraduate School of Dentistry, and the New York School of Dental Hygiene, to become the Columbia University School of Dental and Oral Surgery that exists today. The school has, in addition to its DDS program, postdoctoral and continuing education programs.

## Admissions (AADSAS)
The basic predental science courses plus 1 additional year of English composition and literature are required. Courses in chemistry, biochemistry, mathematics, foreign languages, sociology, history, and the fine industrial arts are recommended. There is no residency requirement. *Transfer and advanced standing:* Qualified graduates of foreign dental schools are considered in July for January admission. They must have taken National Board, Part I, prior to applying and submit scores. Transfers are accepted into the second year only, pending availability.

## Curriculum
4-year traditional. Emphasis is placed on an understanding of broad biomedical principles integrated with clinical dentistry. Initially, students are exposed to the full spectrum of dental problems as observers; subsequently, they are introduced to surgical and manipulative procedures and to methods of diagnosis and prevention. Clinical training is broad in scope. All basic science courses are taken jointly with the medical students of the College of Physicians and Surgeons, during years 1 and 2. *First year:* Focuses on normal human biology and provides for premedical laboratory experience. *Second year:* Focuses on abnormal human biology, and preclinical lab and clinical dentistry courses. *Third year:* Primarily clinical in nature, this year marks the beginning of emphasis on areas of concentration. *Fourth year:* An essential, exclusive clinical year characterized by independent intramural group practices.

## Facilities
The school is an integral part of the Columbia Presbyterian Medical Center within which it occupies 3 floors. These house clinics, research facilities, faculty offices, and student facilities.

## Special Features
A combined DDS-MPH and DDS-MBA is available to selected students, as well as the possibility of completing an MA in research and educational administration.

# New York University College of Dentistry

David B. Kriser Dental Center
345 East 24 Street
New York, New York   10010

*Phone:* 212-998-9818          *Fax:* 212-995-4240
*E-mail:* dentaladmissions@nyu.edu
*WWW:* nyu.edu/dental

| Application Filing | | Accreditation | |
|---|---|---|---|
| Earliest: | June 1 | CDA | |
| Latest: | February 1 | | |
| Fee: | $75 | **Degrees Granted** | |
| AADSAS: | yes | DDS, MS | |

### Enrollment: 2008–2009 First-Year Class

| | | | | | |
|---|---|---|---|---|---|
| Men: | 65 | 63% | *Mean* | | |
| Women: | 38 | 37% | total GPA: | | 3.4 |
| Minorities: | 3 | 3% | science: | | 3.3 |
| Out of State: | 15 | 15% | | | |
| With 2 years of college: | | 0% | *Average* | | |
| With 3 years of college: | | 4% | DAT academic: | | 19 |
| | | | DAT-PAT: | | 18 |

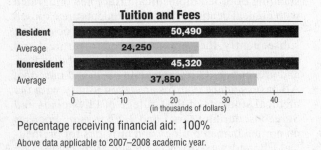

**Tuition and Fees**

| | |
|---|---|
| **Resident** | 50,490 |
| Average | 24,250 |
| **Nonresident** | 45,320 |
| Average | 37,850 |

(in thousands of dollars)

Percentage receiving financial aid: 100%

Above data applicable to 2007–2008 academic year.

## Introduction

New York University opened in 1831. It is a private school with 7 undergraduate and 7 graduate schools. In 1865 the New York University College of Dentistry was established. In addition to the DDS degree, it offers bachelor's and associate degrees in dental hygiene and offers postgraduate and specialty training. There is also a continuing dental education program, an advanced placement program for foreign trained dentists, a program for advanced study in dentistry, dental specialties for international graduates, and an MS degree program in oral biology.

## Admissions (AADSAS)

Students with a GPA of 3.5 or higher may be admitted with 90 credits, including all prerequisite courses, such as the basic predental sciences plus 1 year of English. Recommended courses may be selected from comparative anatomy, embryology, histology, genetics, physiology, mathematics, psychology, sociology, and business management. A BA or BS degree is required from an approved college or university. Out-of-state residents are admitted. *Transfer and advanced standing:* To be eligible for consideration as a transfer student from another dental school, the candidate must be in good standing, without failures or conditions, and eligible for honorable withdrawal from a recognized dental school. Graduate dentists from foreign dental schools may qualify for our Advanced Placement Program for Foreign-Trained Dentists. This is a 3-year program that culminates in a DDS degree from NYU College of Dentistry.

## Curriculum

4-year. *First year:* A balanced program between the study of basic sciences to the practice of dentistry simulation is an integrated sequence of courses that build foundation skills in dentistry and therapy. *Second year:* The biological sciences are directed toward pathology and pathogenesis. *Third year:* The students devote the majority of time to the treatment of patients working alongside fourth-year students in group practices with faculty. *Fourth year:* Encompasses patient care in a general setting.

## Facilities

The Kriser Dental Center comprises 2 contiguous 11-story buildings. The Weissman Clinical Science Building and the Schwartz Hall of Dental Sciences house all the basic science and research departments as well as 576 clinical operatories (distributed among the departments) devoted to the various disciplines of dentistry. Classes are divided into small learning groups of 8 or fewer for closely supervised proactive instruction.

## Special Features

Full scholarships and a large number of partial scholarships are awarded based upon merit. Financial aid (loans and NYU grant scholarships) is available for those who demonstrate need. Early applications are recommended for those who seek financial aid and all types of scholarships.

# State University of New York at Buffalo
# School of Dental Medicine

327 Square Hall, South Campus
3435 Main Street
Buffalo, New York    14214

*Phone:* 716-829-2839          *Fax:* 716-833-3517
*E-mail:* ub-sdm-admissions@buffalo.edu
*WWW:* sdm.buffalo.edu

| Application Filing | | Accreditation |
|---|---|---|
| Earliest: | May 15 | CDA |
| Latest: | January 1 | |
| Fee: | $50 | **Degrees Granted** |
| AADSAS: | yes | DDS, DDS-PhD |

### Enrollment: 2008–2009 First-Year Class

| | | | |
|---|---|---|---|
| Men: | 37 | 61% | *Mean* |
| Women: | 13 | 39% | total GPA: 3.6 |
| Minorities: | 0 | | science: 3.6 |
| Out of State: | 26 | 43% | |
| With 2 years of college: | | 1% | *Average* |
| With 3 years of college: | | 2% | DAT academic: 19 |
| | | | DAT-PAT: 18 |

**Tuition and Fees**

| | |
|---|---|
| **Resident** | 16,200 |
| Average | 24,500 |
| **Nonresident** | 32,000 |
| Average | 37,850 |

0    10    20    30    40
(in thousands of dollars)

Percentage receiving financial aid: 100%

Above data applicable to 2007–2008 academic year.

## Introduction

As 1 of 2 public university systems in the state, the State University of New York was founded in 1948. The State University of New York at Buffalo was created in 1846. In 1962 the Buffalo campus joined the state university system. The School of Dental Medicine was created in 1892 and is now part of the Health Science Center, which includes schools of Medicine, Nursing, Biomedical Sciences, and Health-Related Professions.

## Admissions (AADSAS)

The basic predental courses plus 1 year of English are required. Courses in embryology, biochemistry, genetics, computer science, quantitative chemistry, physical chemistry, calculus, and statistics are recommended. DATs should be taken no later than October of the year before the applicant wishes to matriculate. Preference is given to New York State residents. Applicants are strongly encouraged to seek a clinical experience in dentistry prior to applying. *Transfer and advanced standing:* Students from other dental schools may be considered for transfer with advanced standing into the second-year program.

## Curriculum

4-year. Clinical science studies begin in the first year; students start to provide patient care in the second semester of the freshman year. Integration of the basic and clinical sciences is accomplished in all the clinical courses but is particularly emphasized in such courses as oral biology, oral diagnosis, and oral pathology. In the senior year, students take elective courses in area(s) of their choice. *First year:* Focuses on the basic sciences and preclinical courses. *Second year:* Continuation of the basic sciences with primary focus on preclinical courses. The second semester is devoted to patient care in restorative dentistry and periodontics. *Third year:* Primarily devoted to comprehensive patient care with rotations to area hospitals and medical centers to obtain additional experience in pediatric dentistry, oral surgery, and oncology. *Fourth year:* Intensive clinical experience in various settings and through rotations.

## Facilities

The School of Dental Medicine is one of 5 schools that comprise the Health Science Center. In the summer of 1986 the school was moved to new facilities in the renovated Squire Hall. They include 325 dental units for instructional purposes, new preclinical laboratories, and new basic science and clinical science research facilities. It is one of the most modern facilities of its kind in the country.

## Special Features

Modest class size (86 students) and modern patient care facility. Easy patient access to school clinics. Extensive student summer research program in both basic sciences and clinical sciences.

# Stony Brook University School of Dental Medicine

Rockland Hall
Stony Brook, New York    11794

*Phone:* 631-632-3745          *Fax:* 631-632-7130
*E-mail:* sdmadmissions@notes.cc.sunys6.edu
*WWW:* hsc.stonybrook.edu

| Application Filing | | Accreditation |
|---|---|---|
| Earliest: | July 1 | CDA |
| Latest: | January 15 | |
| Fee: | $75 | **Degrees Granted** |
| AADSAS: | yes | DDS, MPH-PhD |

### Enrollment: 2008–2009 First-Year Class

| | | | |
|---|---|---|---|
| Men: | 25 | 64% | *Mean* |
| Women: | 14 | 36% | total GPA: 3.7 |
| Minorities: | 14 | 36% | science: 3.7 |
| Out of State: | 1 | 3% | |
| With 2 years of college: | | 0% | *Average* |
| With 3 years of college: | | 0% | DAT academic: 21 |
| | | | DAT-PAT: 19 |

**Tuition and Fees**

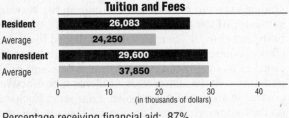

| | |
|---|---|
| **Resident** | 26,083 |
| Average | 24,250 |
| **Nonresident** | 29,600 |
| Average | 37,850 |

(in thousands of dollars)

Percentage receiving financial aid: 87%

## Introduction

Stony Brook, established in 1957, is 1 of the 4 universities in the New York State education system. The School of Dental Medicine was founded in 1973 and is located 60 miles east of New York City on the North Shore of Long Island in a suburban community. The school offers, in addition to a DDS program, postgraduate dental programs in orthodontics, periodontics, endodontics, a PhD program in Oral Biology and Pathology, and a program in Dental Care for the Developmentally Disabled, general practice residency program in conjunction with University Hospital at Stony Brook. The school is a component of the Health Sciences Center, which also includes schools of Medicine, Nursing, Health Technology and Management, and Social Welfare.

## Admissions (AADSAS)

Applicants should demonstrate academic achievement, competence in the sciences, and a general interest in the profession of dentistry. The undergraduate program of study must include the basic predental science courses as well as 1 year of mathematics (with at least 1 semester of calculus or statistics). The DAT is required. All applicants are encouraged to apply early. *Transfer and advanced standing:* not available.

## Curriculum

4-year. The traditional basic sciences are taught predominantly in year 1, with the remainder taught in year 2. The faculty of the school is committed to integrating biomedical, behavioral, and clinical science instruction, in order to achieve a curriculum that instills an appreciation for all disciplines. Courses in oral biology are woven throughout the curriculum and serve as a bridge between the biomedical sciences and clinical dentistry. Students are introduced to the clinic in year 1, and are permitted to start treating patients in year 2. Clinic instruction in years 2 and 3 is a combination of discipline-based and comprehensive care formats. The year 4 General Practice Program is a comprehensive care clinic supported by a faculty of general dentists, with students being supervised by specialists where needed due to the complexity of the case at hand. The importance of research and scholarly activity is emphasized throughout the program.

## Facilities

Physical facilities are equipped to support the diverse educational, research, and patient care programs offered at the school. Dental operators similar to those used in the general practice of dentistry, and provide an attractive and convenient setting for patients. Special suites are available for the teaching and practice of oral surgery and radiology. The clinical facility has been newly renovated, utilizing an electronic record system with computerization at each patient operatory.

## Special Features

Due to the small class size of 39, students attending the school are educated in a highly supportive environment. Academic tutoring, faculty counseling, and individually developed remedial programs are avilable to students under special circumstances, as determined by faculty. Opportunities in patient care, research, outreach, and extracurricular leadership roles are abundant. Consistent with the school policy of selecting students with varied backgrounds, the school encourages applications from qualified individuals from those groups which have in the past been previously underrepresented in the dental profession.

## NORTH CAROLINA

# University of North Carolina School of Dentistry

CB-7450 105 Brauer Hall, CB-7450
Chapel Hill, North Carolina   27589

*Phone:* 919-966-4451          *Fax:* 919-966-5795
*E-mail:* A.D-Guckes@dentistry.unc.edu
*WWW:* www.dent.unc.edu

| Application Filing | | Accreditation | |
|---|---|---|---|
| Earliest: | June 30 | CDA | |
| Latest: | December 1 | | |
| Fee: | $78 | **Degrees Granted** | |
| AADSAS: | yes | DDS, DDS-PhD, DDS-MPH | |

### Enrollment: 2008–2009 First-Year Class

| | | | | |
|---|---|---|---|---|
| Men: | 49 | 49% | *Mean* | |
| Women: | 51 | 51% | total GPA: | 3.4 |
| Minorities: | 25 | 21% | science: | 3.5 |
| Out of State: | 10 | 10% | | |
| With 2 years of college: | | 2% | *Average* | |
| With 3 years of college: | | 93% | DAT academic: | 19 |
| | | | DAT-PAT: | 19 |

### Tuition and Fees

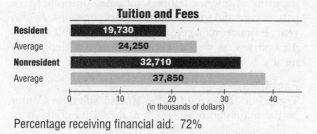

| Resident | 19,730 |
| Average | 24,250 |
| Nonresident | 32,710 |
| Average | 37,850 |

(in thousands of dollars)

Percentage receiving financial aid: 72%

## Introduction

The University of North Carolina system was founded in 1931 and has campuses in Asheville, Chapel Hill, Greensboro, Pembroke, and Wilmington. The University of North Carolina at Chapel Hill was the first state university created in the United States when it was established in 1789. In 1949 the School of Dentistry was created and is considered a part of the Division of Health Affairs. Other schools in the division include the schools of Nursing, Pharmacy, and Public Health. The School of Dentistry offers graduate training in many disciplines and a master's degree in dental hygiene, which prepares graduates for teaching careers.

## Admissions (AADSAS)

The basic predental science courses plus 2 semesters of English are required. Students should complete the regular 4-year curriculum leading to the AB or BS degree. Students not pursuing a degree should complete at least 3 years of accredited college courses (96 semester hours or 144 quarter hours). A maximum of 64 semester hours credit will be accepted from a 2-year community college, and all additional coursework must be completed at a 4-year institution. Foreign trained dentists must enter as first-year students and must submit acceptable scores on the Test of English as a Foreign Language (TOEFL), satisfactory scores on the DAT, and/or acceptable scores on Part I of the National Board Dental Examination. *Transfer and advanced standing:* Transfers are considered on an individual basis. Factors considered will be prior academic record and background, available space in the class, consistency between the curriculum of the 2 schools, and residency status.

## Curriculum

4-year. The goal is to produce dental practitioners qualified to enter general practice, and provide advanced educational programs, research, teaching and/or public service. The first year is highlighted by basic science and dental science courses with participation in preventive patient care activities. During the remaining years, primary emphasis is on the management and delivery of comprehensive care for a family of assigned patients. Patient care activities are supplemented by didactic experiences and numerous enrichment opportunities such as electives, externships, and research. *First year:* Consists of the core basic sciences, introduction to the dental sciences, oral biology, and sequence of preparation courses. *Second year:* Provides a continuation of the basic sciences and advanced dental science and physical diagnosis. Providing comprehensive patient care is initiated. *Third year:* Comprehensive patient care is the major focus, but time is spent on specialty services. *Fourth year:* Intense patient care, extramural rotations, electives, and research.

## Grading Policy

The traditional letter grading system is used, but some courses are graded Pass/Fail.

## Facilities

The school consists of the original dental school building, Braller Hall Office Building, Tarson Hall, and a dental research center. A basic science building and the Division of Health Sciences provide direct support to the programs. A Learning Resources Center is also available.

## Special Features

Both DDS-MPH and DDS-PhD degrees are offered and require additional time.

## OHIO

# Case Western Reserve University School of Dental Medicine

10900 Euclid Avenue
Cleveland, Ohio   44106

*Phone:* 216-368-2460          *Fax:* 216-368-3204
*E-mail:* david.delsky@case.edu
*WWW:* dental.case.edu

| Application Filing | | Accreditation |
|---|---|---|
| Earliest: | May 15 | ADA |
| Latest: | January 1 | |
| Fee: | $45 | **Degrees Granted** |
| AADSAS: | yes | DMD |

### Enrollment: 2008–2009 First-Year Class

| | | | |
|---|---|---|---|
| Men: | 44 | 63% | *Mean* |
| Women: | 26 | 37% | total GPA: 3.61 |
| Minorities: | 19 | 31% | science: 3.57 |
| Out of State: | 6 | 9% | |
| With 3 years of college: | | 4% | *Average* |
| With 4 years of college: | | 90% | DAT academic: 19.4 |
| | | | DAT-PAT: 19.6 |

**Tuition and Fees**

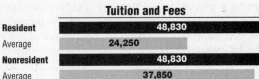

| Resident | 48,830 |
| Average | 24,250 |
| Nonresident | 48,830 |
| Average | 37,850 |

(in thousands of dollars)

Percentage receiving financial aid: 85%

## Introduction

Case Western Reserve University was established in 1826. It is a private school with 4 undergraduate and 7 graduate schools. The Case Western Reserve University School of Dental Medicine was established in 1892 as the dental department of the university. In 1969 the school's facilities were relocated to the Health Sciences Center of the university. Included in the center are the schools of Medicine and Nursing, and University Hospitals of Cleveland.

## Admissions (AADSAS)

The basic predental science courses plus 1 year of English is required. Recommended courses include comparative anatomy, microbiology, physiology, cell biology, and/or biochemistry. A substantial number of out-of-state residents are admitted.

## Curriculum

4-year traditional. Clinical experience is introduced early in the program. Recent curriculum innovations include an integrative experience in preclinical procedures basic to restorative dentistry, and in the comprehensive care concept. A number of multidisciplinary subjects are taught. *First year:* The basic sciences, technical courses, and limited patient care. *Second year:* Continued basic sciences and preclinical courses with increased patient care. *Third year:* At this stage, the clinical science courses include comprehensive patient care and treatment in preceptor groups. *Fourth year:* Practice management and clinical problem-solving courses, as well as comprehensive patient treatment.

## Facilities

The school is located in the Health Sciences Center on the main campus. The dental facility consists of 2 underground and 3 aboveground levels.

# Ohio State University College of Dentistry

305 West 12th Avenue
Columbus, Ohio   43218

*Phone:* 614-292-3361          *Fax:* 614-292-0813
*E-mail:* iannuci.5@dentistry.dent.ohio-state.edu
*WWW:* dent.ohio-state.edu

| Application Filing | | Accreditation | |
|---|---|---|---|
| Earliest: | June 1 | CDA | |
| Latest: | November 15 | | |
| Fee: | $30 | **Degrees Granted** | |
| AADSAS: | yes | DDS, DDS-MS | |

### Enrollment: 2008–2009 First-Year Class

| | | | | |
|---|---|---|---|---|
| Men: | 54 | 66% | *Mean* | |
| Women: | 31 | 34% | total GPA: | 3.6 |
| Minorities: | 3 | 4% | science: | 3.5 |
| Out of State: | 20 | 14% | | |
| With 2 years of college: | 0% | | *Average* | |
| With 3 years of college: | 1% | | DAT academic: | 19 |
| | | | DAT-PAT: | 18 |

### Tuition and Fees

| | |
|---|---|
| Resident | 24,663 |
| Average | 24,250 |
| Nonresident | 53,724 |
| Average | 37,850 |

0    10    20    30    40
(in thousands of dollars)

Above data applicable to 2007–2008 academic year.

## Introduction

The Ohio State University system was established in 1870; the Columbus campus was created in the same year. In 1925 the Ohio State University College of Dentistry moved to Columbus after its beginning as part of Ohio Medical University in 1890. Ohio Medical University joined the Starling Medical College in 1906 and became a component of Ohio State in 1914. The College of Dentistry is located in the Health Sciences Center, which also includes the College of Medicine and Biological Sciences and School of Nursing and Allied Health Sciences.

## Admissions (AADSAS)

The basic predental science courses and 1 year of English composition or literature are required. Recommended courses may be selected from psychology, speech, art, and drawing. A minimum of 20 documented hours of observation in a general dental office is required. *Transfer and advanced standing:* Students from other U.S. schools may be admitted with advanced standing.

## Curriculum

4-year traditional. Clinical experience begins after the first year and a half. The basic and clinical sciences are integrated during both coursework and practice sessions. Ten percent of the senior year must be devoted to electives. Off-campus clinical experience is available at hospitals and clinics. *First year:* The major basic sciences in the form of lectures, laboratory, and self-directed learning. *Second year:* A continuation of the previous year's activities. *Third year:* Clinical experience under faculty supervision is provided in the college, at hospitals, and at other sites. *Fourth year:* Comprehensive dental care under private practice conditions as well as extramural rotations.

## Facilities

The school is located in the Health Sciences Center on the main campus in a 5-story building. Dental clinics are also located in University and Children's Hospitals and in Nisonger Center. City Health Department clinics, VA hospitals, and state institutions also offer facilities for student training.

## Special Features

The College of Dentistry offers DDS-PhD programs in all specialties.

# OKLAHOMA

## University of Oklahoma College of Dentistry

201 N Stonewall Ave.
Oklahoma City, Oklahoma   73117

*Phone:* 405-271-3530          *Fax:* 405-271-3423
*E-mail:* randolph-jones@okhsc.edu
*WWW:* dent.uokhsc.edu

| Application Filing | | Accreditation | |
|---|---|---|---|
| Earliest: | September 1 | CDA | |
| Latest: | December 1 | | |
| Fee: | $65 | **Degrees Granted** | |
| AADSAS: | yes | DDS | |

### Enrollment: 2008–2009 First-Year Class

| | | | | |
|---|---|---|---|---|
| Men: | 26 | 66% | *Mean* | |
| Women: | 13 | 34% | total GPA: | 3.6 |
| Minorities: | 0 | | science: | 3.65 |
| Out of State: | 11 | 3% | | |
| With 2 years of college: | | 1% | *Average* | |
| With 3 years of college: | | 15% | DAT academic: | 19 |
| | | | DAT-PAT: | 17 |

**Tuition and Fees**

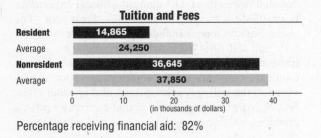

| | |
|---|---|
| Resident | 14,865 |
| Average | 24,250 |
| Nonresident | 36,645 |
| Average | 37,850 |

(in thousands of dollars)

Percentage receiving financial aid: 82%

## Introduction

In 1890 the University of Oklahoma was established. It contains 9 undergraduate and graduate schools. The College of Dentistry is part of the Health Sciences Center, which includes colleges of Medicine, Nursing, Pharmacy, Allied Health, Public Health, and a Graduate College. The dental school offers graduate programs in orthodontics and periodontics.

## Admissions (AADSAS)

The basic predental science courses plus 1 year of English composition or literature are required. Preference is given to Oklahoma residents. Additional courses in biology are recommended. A minimum grade of "C" is required in all prerequisite courses. A minimum of 100 hours of observation and/or work experience is required in a dental clinic or dental laboratory environment. If an applicant has taken the DAT multiple times, the College of Dentistry will consider the DAT report with the highest overall academic average. *Transfer and advanced standings:* Available on an individual basis.

## Curriculum

The four-year curriculum combines foundational studies in biomedical and dental sciences, applied laboratory and simulated clinic experiences, and clinical training and comprehensive patient care. Extensive opportunities for treating patients are a hallmark of the student's training at the College of Dentistry, and it promotes development of strong clinical skills and capable practitioners. The greater part of the biological science instruction is completed in the first two years. Clinical sciences are taught throughout the entire curriculum. The time and emphasis devoted to patient care increases in relation to the student's level of knowledge and skill as he or she progresses through the program. Behavioral sciences instruction, the management of dental practice, and professional responsibility are incorporated throughout the curriculum. Numerous outreach and research activities are also available and strongly encouraged throughout the education experience.

## Facilities

A 5-floor school building houses 5 general practice clinics, 3 specialty clinics, and 180 operatories, as well as the other standard dental school facilities.

## Special Features

Tuition and Fees fee waiver scholarships are available to some minority students qualifying academically and financially for the first academic year. A limited number of Arkansas residents pay in-state tuition and fees. College offers graduate and residency programs in advanced general dentistry, orthodontics, periodontics, and oral and maxillofacial surgery.

## OREGON

# Oregon Health Science University
# School of Dentistry

611 S. W. Campus Drive
Portland, Oregon    97239

*Phone:* 503-494-5274        *Fax:* 503-494-6244
*E-mail:* sodadmit@ohsu.edu
*WWW:* www.ohsu.edu/sod

| Application Filing | | Accreditation |
|---|---|---|
| Earliest: | June 1 | CODA |
| Latest: | November 1 | |
| Fee: | $75 | **Degrees Granted** |
| AADSAS: | yes | DMD, DMD-MS |

### Enrollment: 2008–2009 First-Year Class

| | | | | |
|---|---|---|---|---|
| Men: | 42 | 66% | *Mean* | |
| Women: | 21 | 34% | total GPA: | 3.6 |
| Minorities: | | | science: | 3.6 |
| Out of State: | 30 | 48% | | |
| With 2 years of college: | 0% | | *Average* | |
| With 3 years of college: | 0% | | DAT academic: | 19.5 |
| | | | DAT-PAT: | 18.6 |

### Tuition and Fees

| | |
|---|---|
| **Resident** | 18,582 |
| Average | 24,250 |
| **Nonresident** | 32,562 |
| Average | 37,850 |

0    10    20    30    40
(in thousands of dollars)

Percentage receiving financial aid: 94%

Above data applicable to 2007–2008 academic year.

## Introduction

This dental school was established in 1898. In 1945 the Oregon University School of Dentistry was incorporated into the Oregon state system for higher education and in 1974 it became part of the Oregon Health Science University, which also includes the School of Medicine, School of Nursing, and School of Science and Engineering. The School of Dentistry is located on a 116-acre campus in the wooded hills of southwest Portland.

## Admissions (AADSAS)

The basic predental science courses (physics, physiology, biology, chemistry, and organic chemistry) are required. Recommended additional courses can be selected from cell biology, genetics, histology, molecular biology, microbiology, and neuroscience. Applicants from Oregon, from states certified under the WICHE program, and from the remaining states and Canada are eligible for consideration in the priority order listed.

## Curriculum

4-year traditional. Students see their first patient during their freshman year in the preventive dentistry course. Some subjects are organized into conjoint courses, taught cooperatively by separate departments. Correlation and application of the biological and clinical sciences are emphasized. *First and second years:* The major emphasis is on the biological sciences and preclinical techniques. The summer between the second and third years focuses on clinical experience and oral pathology. *Third and fourth years:* Deal mostly with clinical practice and include courses in practice planning and management. Elective courses enhance the development of clinical skills.

## Facilities

As a part of the Oregon Health Sciences University, the dental school building houses classrooms, a modern clinic containing 200 dental workstations, individual X-ray rooms, and a 72-station clinic simulation lab.

## Special Features

Academic and personal counseling of students is provided through the Office of Admissions and Student Affairs. In addition, students may request an academic advisor at the time of matriculation.

# PENNSYLVANIA

# Temple University Maurice H. Kornberg School of Dentistry

3223 North Broad Street
Philadelphia, Pennsylvania   19140

*Phone:* 215-707-2801          *Fax:* 215-707-5461
*E-mail:* brian.hahn@dental.temple.edu
*WWW:* temple.edu/dentistry/

| Application Filing | | Accreditation | |
|---|---|---|---|
| Earliest: | May 15 | CDA | |
| Latest: | February 1 | | |
| Fee: | $30 | **Degrees Granted** | |
| AADSAS: | yes | DMD, DMD-MBA | |

### Enrollment: 2008–2009 First-Year Class

| | | | | |
|---|---|---|---|---|
| Men: | 68 | 54% | *Mean* | |
| Women: | 57 | 46% | total GPA: | 3.4 |
| Minorities: | 18 | 14% | science: | 3.3 |
| Out of State: | 74 | 59% | | |
| With 3 years of college: | | 4% | *Average* | |
| | | | DAT academic: | 19 |
| | | | DAT-PAT: | 19.1 |

**Tuition and Fees**

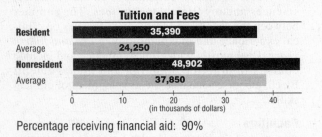

| Resident | 35,390 |
| Average | 24,250 |
| Nonresident | 48,902 |
| Average | 37,850 |

(in thousands of dollars)

Percentage receiving financial aid: 90%

## Introduction

Temple University was established in 1884. It belongs to the Commonwealth System of Higher Education in Pennsylvania. The School of Dentistry was established in 1863 as the Philadelphia Dental College. It joined Temple University in 1907 and is part of the Health Sciences Center, which includes Schools of Medicine, Pharmacy, and Allied Health, and the University Hospital. The School of Dentistry offers programs in continuing education.

## Admissions (AADSAS)

The basic predental science courses and 1 year of English are required. The following science courses are recommended: histology, biochemistry, mammalian anatomy, physiology, and microbiology.

Applications from minority students are encouraged. *Transfer and advanced standing:* Request for transfer will be considered only by current students who are in good academic standing at a dental school in the United States or Canada. Acceptance to transfer is highly selective. Selection factors include academic record, compatibility between the curriculum of the schools, available space and resources, and a personal interview. Kornberg School of Dentistry offers advanced standing for the internationally trained dentist who seeks to practice dentistry in the United States. Admission to advanced standing is highly selective and can occur only if positions are available in the third-year class. Selection factors include academic record, completed credit hours, National Board Parts I and II scores, a comprehensive preclinical skills evaluation conducted by the faculty, and a personal interview.

## Curriculum

4-year. *First year:* Devoted largely to the basic sciences and to the development of skills necessary to complete the procedures used in general practice. *Second year:* Consists of a continuation of the basic science and laboratory courses. This is followed by the Introduction to Clinical Course Dentistry, which includes all phases of dentistry with exposure. *Third year:* Involves clinic rotations during which comprehensive care of assigned patients is provided. Didactic instruction continues. *Fourth year:* This represents a continuation of the responsibilities of the preceding year.

## Facilities

The school is situated in a densely populated, federally designated health provider shortage area in Philadelphia. Dental students perform more than 150,000 clinical procedures per year. The school has a close affiliation with area hospitals and other teaching units of the Health Sciences Center.

## Special Features

The School of Dentistry includes 3 specialty programs, in addition to an advanced education general dentistry program. The School of Dentistry and the School of Business and Management at Temple offer a progam leading to the DMD and MBA dual degrees.

# University of Pennsylvania School of Dental Medicine

240 South 40th Street
Philadelphia, Pennsylvania 19104

*Phone:* 215-898-8943 *Fax:* 215-573-9648
*E-mail:* dental-admissions@pobox.upenn.edu
*WWW:* dental.upenn.edu

| Application Filing | | | Accreditation | |
|---|---|---|---|---|
| Earliest: | June 1 | | CODA | |
| Latest: | January 1 | | | |
| Fee: | $50 | | **Degrees Granted** | |
| AADSAS: | yes | | DMD | |

**Enrollment: 2008–2009 First-Year Class**

| | | | | |
|---|---|---|---|---|
| Men: | 50 | 43% | *Mean* | |
| Women: | 65 | 57% | total GPA: | 3.68 |
| Minorities: | 50 | 43% | science: | 3.64 |
| Out of State: | 97 | 84% | | |
| With 2 years of college: | | 0% | *Average* | |
| With 3 years of college: | | 93% | DAT academic: | 20 |
| | | | DAT-PAT: | 20 |

**Tuition and Fees**

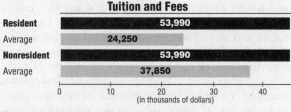

| | |
|---|---|
| Resident | 53,990 |
| Average | 24,250 |
| Nonresident | 53,990 |
| Average | 37,850 |

0   10   20   30   40
(in thousands of dollars)

Percentage receiving financial aid: 80%

## Introduction

The University of Pennsylvania was established in 1740 as a private institution. The University of Pennsylvania School of Dental Medicine was created in 1878. Originally known as the Thomas W. Evans Museum and Dental Institute, it became the School of Dental Medicine in 1964. It is located on the west end of the 250-acre university campus in central Philadelphia, making it accessible to the many educational and cultural facilities in this city.

## Admissions (AADSAS)

The basic predental science courses plus 1 semester of mathematics (calculus preferred) and 2 semesters of English are required. Courses in 1 semester biochemistry, physiology, genetics, and microbiology are recommended. *Transfer and advanced standing:* Students from other U.S. dental schools may be admitted with advanced standing into the second and third years only if space is available.

## Curriculum

The basic science courses are taught in the first and second years through lectures, seminars, and laboratory experiences. Clinical experience begins with dental health education in the first year. The third and fourth years emphasize the general practice of dentistry. Much effort is made to integrate basic and clinical sciences throughout the 4-year program. A highlight of the program is an offering of more than 50 selective courses in a variety of areas. Fourth-year students spend 6 weeks gaining additional clinical skills in a hospital setting.

## Grading Policy

The University of Pennsylvania School of Dental Medicine operates on an A, B, C, F evaluation system. Student performance in lecture and basic science labs is measured by a written objective examination, usually of the multiple-choice and slide identification variety. Achievement in preclinical dental labs is determined by practical exams. Evaluation of clinical performance is based on a composite of daily grades, faculty comments, and competency evaluations. Students who fail a course(s) are reviewed individually by the school's Committee of Student Advancement, which prescribes the course of action to be followed by the student.

## Facilities

The Robert Schattner Center provides facilities for clinical education, patient care, and research. The facility also serves as the school's main entrance, creating a unified Penn Dental campus by linking the Thomas W. Evans Building and the Leon Levy Center for Oral Health Research. The Schattner Center's clinical resources include an emergency/admission clinic, a clinic for medically complex patients, and an oral and maxillofacial surgery facility. The school's varied clinic settings enable student participation in all aspects of oral health education and research. At the center of the school's clinical operations and instruction is the main clinic; located in the Evans Building, it provides facilities for complete oral diagnosis and treatment. Specialty clinics within the Evans Building include a pediatric and special needs clinic, as well as the orthodontic, endodontic, and periodontic clinics.

## Special Features

Opportunities for separate admission to programs in education, biomedical engineering, public health, and business are available.

# University of Pittsburgh School of Dental Medicine

3501 Terrace Street, Suite 2114
Pittsburgh, Pennsylvania   15261

*Phone:* 412-648-8437          *Fax:* 412-648-9571
*E-mail:* dentaladmissions@dental.pitt.edu
*WWW:* dental.pitt.edu

| Application Filing | | Accreditation | |
|---|---|---|---|
| Earliest: | June 1 | CDA | |
| Latest: | November 30 | | |
| Fee: | $35 | **Degrees Granted** | |
| AADSAS: | yes | DMD | |

### Enrollment: 2008–2009 First-Year Class

| | | | | |
|---|---|---|---|---|
| Men: | 39 | 72% | *Mean* | |
| Women: | 14 | 28% | total GPA: | 3.6 |
| Minorities: | 1 | 1% | science: | 3.4 |
| Out of State: | n/a | n/a | | |
| With 2 years of college: | | 0% | *Average* | |
| With 3 years of college: | | 10% | DAT academic: | 19 |
| | | | DAT-PAT: | 18 |

**Tuition and Fees**

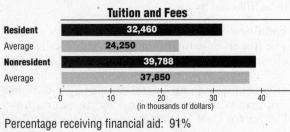

| | |
|---|---|
| Resident | 32,460 |
| Average | 24,250 |
| Nonresident | 39,788 |
| Average | 37,850 |

(in thousands of dollars)

Percentage receiving financial aid: 91%

Above data applicable to 2007–2008 academic year.

## Introduction

The University of Pittsburgh was established in 1787 and has campuses in Pittsburgh, Bradford, Greensburg, and Johnstown. In 1896 the School of Dental Medicine was founded. It is part of the university health complex, the other components being the schools of Medicine, Pharmacy, Nursing, Health-Related Professions, Public Health, and their affiliated hospitals. The School of Dental Medicine offers graduate programs in advanced education in general dentistry and many specialties as well as a dental hygiene program.

## Admissions (AADSAS)

The basic predental science courses plus 1 year of English are required. Recommended courses include biochemistry, upper-division biology courses, art, and sculpture. *Transfer and advanced standing:* Possible if space available.

## Curriculum

4-year. Instruction in the biological and technological principles provides a basis for the clinical prevention of oral disease, the maintenance of oral health, and correction of oral pathology and oral-facial deviations. Clinical contact begins in the second year. Elective programs, or selective research in the third and fourth years, provide in-depth study in areas of student interest. *First year:* Consists of the basic sciences and an introduction to clinical situations in a simulation clinic and clinical assisting. *Second year:* Continuation of the basic sciences and preclinical courses plus definitive clinical patient treatment is initiated. *Third year:* Continuation of dental coursework but major emphasis is on the delivery of comprehensive dental care. *Fourth year:* Training in the delivery of comprehensive health care under conditions similar to those in private practice. Both third- and fourth-year students practice in the comprehensive care area, where faculty rotate through on a semester basis.

## Facilities

The Dental School Building, consisting of a 300-dental chair clinic and modern lecture facilities, is located in the city's Oakland district within the University Health Complex. An audiovisual instructional resource center, consisting of individual stations, is available for study. A new simulation clinic consisting of 80 manequins utilizing air and water provides hands-on experience to first- and second-year students. Live faculty demonstrations are available for student viewing at chairside monitors, as well as faculty monitoring of students' progress.

## Special Features

Postgraduate specialty programs are available in each of the dental areas.

## SOUTH CAROLINA

# Medical University of South Carolina College of Dental Medicine

171 Ashley Avenue
Charleston, South Carolina    29425

*Phone:* 843-792-4892          *Fax:* 843-792-1521
*E-mail:* llinerw@musc.edu
*WWW:* musc.edu/dentistry/dental.html

| Application Filing | | | Accreditation |
|---|---|---|---|
| Earliest: | May 15 | | CDA |
| Latest: | December 1 | | |
| Fee: | $75 | | **Degrees Granted** |
| AADSAS: | yes | | DMD, DMD-PhD |

### Enrollment: 2008–2009 First-Year Class

| | | | |
|---|---|---|---|
| Men: | 40 | 77% | *Mean* |
| Women: | 12 | 23% | total GPA: 3.5 |
| Minorities: | 1 | 2% | science: 3.5 |
| Out of State: | 13 | 25% | |
| With 2 years of college: | 0% | | *Average* |
| With 3 years of college: | 0% | | DAT academic: 19 |
| | | | DAT-PAT: 18 |

### Tuition and Fees

| | |
|---|---|
| **Resident** | 25,430 |
| Average | 24,250 |
| **Nonresident** | 70,944 |
| Average | 37,850 |

0    10    20    30    40
(in thousands of dollars)

Percentage receiving financial aid: 91%

Above data applicable to 2007–2008 academic year.

## Introduction

The College of Dental Medicine, opened in 1967, is part of the Medical University of South Carolina, which was established in 1824. The dental school offers a general practice residency as well as graduate programs in advanced education in general dentistry and in a number of specialties.

## Admissions (AADSAS)

A minimum of 3 years of college work (90 semester hours), including the basic predental science courses plus a science elective, and 1 year each of English, mathematics, and additional science courses are required. *Transfer and advanced standing:* Not possible.

## Curriculum

4-year traditional. The focus of the curriculum is to produce clinicians able to practice dentistry with an understanding of biological principles. The first 2 years include basic science courses and preclinical dental courses, with some clinical observation and experience. It is recommended that the sciences be selected from biochemistry, comparative anatomy, histology, genetics, and microbiology. The final 2 years concentrate on clinical practice. During the fourth year, the student will be assigned rotations at various facilities, thereby experiencing dentistry as it is practiced throughout the state.

## Facilities

The school is located in the Basic Science-Dental Building of the Medical University complex. Dental students also participate in programs at other South Carolina facilities.

## TENNESSEE

# Meharry Medical College School of Dentistry

1005 D. B. Todd Boulevard
Nashville, Tennessee   37208

*Phone:* 615-327-6223           *Fax:* 615-327-6228
*E-mail:* admissions@mmc.edu
*WWW:* mmc.edu/dentschool/

| Application Filing | | Accreditation |
|---|---|---|
| Earliest: | May 15 | CDA |
| Latest: | January 15 | |
| Fee: | $60 | **Degrees Granted** |
| AADSAS: | yes | DDS |

### Enrollment: 2008–2009 First-Year Class

| | | | | |
|---|---|---|---|---|
| Men: | 28 | 55% | *Mean* | |
| Women: | 23 | 45% | total GPA: | 3.2 |
| Minorities: | 49 | 96% | science: | 3.0 |
| Out of State: | 41 | 84% | | |
| With 2 years of college: | 0% | | *Average* | |
| With 3 years of college: | 1% | | DAT academic: | 16 |
| With 4 years of college: | 99% | | DAT-PAT: | 16 |

**Tuition and Fees**

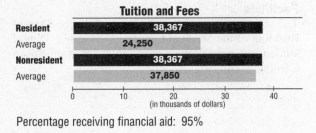

| | |
|---|---|
| Resident | 38,367 |
| Average | 24,250 |
| Nonresident | 38,367 |
| Average | 37,850 |

(in thousands of dollars)

Percentage receiving financial aid: 95%

## Introduction

Meharry Medical College was founded in 1876. In 1886 the School of Dentistry was established. It is located near the center of Nashville. Two other academic divisions are part of the college: the schools of Medicine, and Graduate Studies and Research.

## Admissions (AADSAS)

The basic predental science courses and 1 year of English composition are required. Recommended courses include those in engineering, design, human psychology, speech, and sociology. State residents and students from states with which the school has admission agreements are given priority. *Transfer:* Students from other U.S. and Canadian dental schools.

## Curriculum

4-year flexible. *First year:* Largely devoted to the basic sciences. In addition, there are courses in tooth morphology, behavioral science, analytical reasoning, and critical thinking. *Second year:* Focuses on the preclinical areas, particularly dental pathology and pharmacology. Introductory courses to clinical treatment and diagnosis are given. *Third and fourth years:* These 2 years are devoted to clinical instruction. Students are exposed to learning experiences in the dental specialties. During the senior year, instruction is provided in hospitals in dentistry and public health services.

## Facilities

The school is located on a 24-acre college campus. The basic science, learning resources, hospital, and modern dental facilities have been renovated. Audiovisual, computer assistance, and group and individual study rooms are available.

## Special Features

Research opportunities are available, as well as counseling.

# University of Tennessee College of Dentistry

875 Union Avenue
Memphis, Tennessee 38163

*Phone:* 901-448-6200 *Fax:* 901-448-1265
*E-mail:* wcoleman@utmem.edu
*WWW:* utmem.edu/dentistry/

## Application Filing
Earliest: July 1
Latest: November 30
Fee: $50
AADSAS: no

## Accreditation
CDA

## Degrees Granted
DDS, DDS-MS, DDS-PhD

## Enrollment: 2008–2009 First-Year Class
| | | | |
|---|---|---|---|
| Men: | 58 | 72% | *Mean* |
| Women: | 22 | 28% | total GPA: 3.5 |
| Minorities: | 10 | 13% | science: 3.4 |
| Out of State: | 26 | 33% | |
| With 4 years of college: | 0% | | |

*Average*
DAT academic: 18
DAT-PAT: 19

### Tuition and Fees
Resident 18,368
Average 24,250
Nonresident 18,368
Average 37,850
(in thousands of dollars)

Percentage receiving financial aid: 89%

## Introduction
The University of Tennessee system was established in 1794 with campuses in Chattanooga, Martin, and Knoxville. The University of Tennessee at Memphis was established in 1911 and the Health Sciences Center is located there. The College of Dentistry is a component of this center. It offers a general practice residency program as well as graduate programs in advanced education in general dentistry and a variety of specialties.

## Admissions
The basic predental science courses plus 1 year of English composition and 2 science elective courses are required. These should be selected from comparative anatomy, developmental biology, histology, genetics, microbiology, molecular biology, physiology, and neurobiology. Qualified Tennesseans are given first priority, and a number of Arkansas students are also accepted under a formal agreement. A few additional out-of-state students may be accepted if they possess superior qualifications. *Transfer and advanced standing:* Transfer students with advanced standing from ADA-accredited schools may be accepted where strong similarities exist between the curricula of the institutions. Students requesting transfer must be independently evaluated by a faculty board appointed from the various departments for proper placement in the curriculum.

## Curriculum
4-year traditional. The principal goal is to prepare students for general practice who are professional, people-oriented, knowledgeable, and skillful in delivering comprehensive dental care. To achieve this goal, students are taught to think in terms of problem solving and are given a solid grounding in the basic sciences and appropriate training in the clinical skills. Selected segments of the basic and clinical sciences are presented by an interdisciplinary, team-teaching approach. Students are oriented to clinical activities in the first year. Delivery of patient care begins in the second year. During the senior year, 100 clock hours of electives from special clinical projects, lectures, and research projects are available to students.

## Facilities
The college is located on the Health Sciences Center campus and has a modern clinical facility. Off-campus clinics are also used.

## Special Features
The school encourages applications from minority and disadvantaged students.

## TEXAS

# Baylor College of Dentistry
# Texas A&M University

3302 Gaston Ave.
Dallas, Texas   75246

*Phone:* 214-828-8231          *Fax:* 214-874-4521
*E-mail:* admissions-bcd@bcd.tamhsc.edu
*WWW:* bcd.tambcd.edu

| Application Filing | | Accreditation |
|---|---|---|
| Earliest: | June 1 | CDA |
| Latest: | October 1 | |
| Fee: | $35 | **Degrees Granted** |
| AADSAS: | yes | DDS |

### Enrollment: 2008–2009 First-Year Class

| | | | |
|---|---|---|---|
| Men: | 50 | 50% | *Mean* |
| Women: | 50 | 50% | total GPA: 3.51 |
| Minorities: | 54 | 54% | science: 3.45 |
| Out of State: | 9 | 9% | |
| With 2 years of college: | 0% | | *Average* |
| With 3 years of college: | 0% | | DAT academic: 19 |
| | | | DAT-PAT: 19 |

### Tuition and Fees

| | |
|---|---|
| Resident | 8,732 |
| Average | 19,750 |
| Nonresident | 24,955 |
| Average | 29,900 |

0    10    20    30    40
(in thousands of dollars)

Percentage receiving financial aid: 91%

## Introduction

The Baylor College of Dentistry is located in Dallas' metropolitan area. The school opened in 1905 as the State Dental College and joined the Baylor University system in 1918. Its status changed in 1971 when it became a private, nonprofit, nonsecterian corporation. In 1996 the college joined the Texas A&M University system. It is now a public institution, known as Texas A&M Health Science Center, Baylor College of Dentistry. Graduate programs are offered in a large number of specialties and a continuing education program is also available, as is a BS in dental hygiene.

## Admissions (AADSAS)

The basic predental science courses and 1 year of English are required. Recommended courses include biochemistry, anatomy, physiology, psychology, business management, foreign language, literature, mechanical drawing, and art. Strong preference is given to state residents. *Transfer and advanced standing:* Applicants must meet the school's requirements. There is no advanced standing program for foreign dentists at this time.

## Curriculum

4-year traditional. First- and second-year students devote their time primarily to the basic biological and dental science courses. Starting with the second year, the various subdisciplines of dentistry are emphasized through clinical experiences and didactic instruction. Off-campus clinical experience is provided by means of extramural rotations.

## Facilities

The facilities include a modern 7-story building plus a library, a science research building, and a multilevel parking garage.

# University of Texas Dental Branch at Houston

6516 M.D. Anderson Boulevard
Houston, Texas    77030

*Phone:* 713-500-4151          *Fax:* 713-500-4425
*E-mail:* utdds@uthouston.edu
*WWW:* db.uth.tmc.edu

| Application Filing | | | Accreditation |
|---|---|---|---|
| Earliest: | May 1 | | ADA/SACS |
| Latest: | October 1 | | |
| Fee: | $55 | | **Degrees Granted** |
| AADSAS: | yes | | DDS, MS, DDS/PhD |

### Enrollment: 2008–2009 First-Year Class

| | | | |
|---|---|---|---|
| Men: | 39 | 46% | *Mean* |
| Women: | 45 | 54% | total GPA: 3.6 |
| Minorities: | 12 | 14% | science: 3.5 |
| Out of State: | 1 | 1% | |
| With 3 years of college: | 35% | | *Average* |
| With 4 years of college: | 92% | | DAT academic: 19 |
| | | | DAT-PAT: 19 |

### Tuition and Fees

| | |
|---|---|
| **Resident** | 16,531 |
| Average | 24,250 |
| **Nonresident** | 27,331 |
| Average | 37,850 |

0   10   20   30   40
(in thousands of dollars)

Percentage receiving financial aid: 93%

## Introduction

The Houston Dental Branch was founded in 1905 as the Texas Dental College and later became part of the University of Texas Health Science Center at Houston. This center includes the Dental Branch, the Medical School, the Graduate School of Biomedical Sciences, School of Public Health, School of Nursing, and the School of Health Informatics. The Dental Branch offers graduate and postgraduate dental programs, continuing education, and dental hygiene.

## Admissions (TMDSAS)

A minimum of 90 semester hours, to include prerequisite courses, are required. High priority is given to state residents. *Transfer:* Students from other U.S. and Canadian schools may apply. Transfer students may be admitted to the second- and third-year of classes if space is available and curriculum compatibility is established.

## Curriculum

4-year. The curriculum consists of basic science, preclinical, clinical, behavioral science, and elective instruction. The didactic material is presented in lectures, seminars, problem-based learning sessions, and laboratories. The clinical portion begins with Introduction to the Clinic and continues with patient treatment that is focused on comprehensively managing patient needs in a timely manner based on a well-developed treatment plan. Students are mentored by academic advisers and clinical facilitators. Overall management of the clinical curriculum is through a fully digital electronic patient record. Each class of 84 progresses through the curriculum together. The Dental Branch also has programs in 6 of the dental specialties, advanced general dentist's programs, and dental hygiene.

## Facilities

The school is located in the Texas Medical Center and is housed in a self-contained, 6-floor building. Preclinical training is carried out in multidisciplinary laboratories and a state-of-the-art simulation facility equipped with the latest technology. Clinical activities are performed in individualized clinical cubicles. Extramural rotations are an integral part of clinical training.

# University of Texas Health Science Center at San Antonio Dental School

7703 Floyd Curl Drive
San Antonio, Texas   78229

*Phone:* 210-567-2674          *Fax:* 210-567-2645
*E-mail:* dsprospect@uthscsa.edu
*WWW:* dental.uthscsa.edu

| Application Filing | | Accreditation | |
|---|---|---|---|
| Earliest: | May 1 | CDA | |
| Latest: | October 15 | | |
| Fee: | $55 | **Degrees Granted** | |
| AADSAS: | no | DDS, DDS-PhD | |

### Enrollment: 2008–2009 First-Year Class

| | | | | | |
|---|---|---|---|---|---|
| Men: | 44 | 45% | *Mean* | | |
| Women: | 53 | 55% | total GPA: | 3.8 | |
| Minorities: | 15 | 16% | science: | 3.6 | |
| Out of State: | 4 | 4% | | | |
| With 3 years of college: | 0% | | *Average* | | |
| With 4 years of college: | 100% | | DAT academic: | 19 | |
| | | | DAT-PAT: | 19 | |

### Tuition and Fees

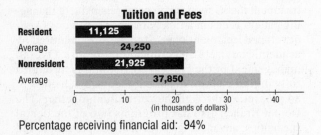

| Resident | 11,125 |
| Average | 24,250 |
| Nonresident | 21,925 |
| Average | 37,850 |

(in thousands of dollars)

Percentage receiving financial aid: 94%

## Introduction
The UTHSCSA Dental School is located in the Health Science Center, whose other components are the Medical School, schools of Nursing and Allied Health Sciences, and the Graduate School of Biomedical Sciences. The Dental School provides graduate education in many specialties as well as general dentistry. The programs in dental hygiene and dental laboratory technology offered by the School of Allied Sciences are housed in the North Campus.

## Admissions
The basic predental science courses and 1 additional year of biology are required. Recommended courses include biochemistry, upper-division biology, advanced literature, conversational Spanish, and those that will assist in the development of manual skills (such as sculpting, ceramics, etc.) Strong preference is given to legal residents of Texas. *Transfer and advanced standing:* Students from other U.S., Canadian, and foreign dental schools may apply for advanced standing on a very limited basis.

## Curriculum
4-year traditional. Some courses are offered in an integrated format. The basic sciences are offered throughout the 4 years. Clinical experience begins in the freshman year and increases thereafter. Juniors are taught the team approach. Seniors are provided with the opportunity to diagnose, plan treatment, and execute clinical procedures on patients under conditions that approximate private practice. Such comprehensive dental care is carried out under supervision at extramural programs off campus.

## Grading Policy
A letter grade system is used.

## Facilities
The school building is designed to facilitate the educational process. It provides an individual cubicle for each lower-level student in multidiscipline laboratories and a fully equipped clinical cubicle for upper-level students. Off-campus facilities are also used.

## Special Features
A combined DDS-PhD program is offered with the Graduate School of Biomedical Sciences.

# VIRGINIA

## Virginia Commonwealth University
## School of Dentistry

P.O. Box 980566
Richmond, Virginia    23005-0566

*Phone:* 804-828-9196            *Fax:* 804-828-5288
*E-mail:* mhealy@vcu.edu
*WWW:* dentistry.vcu.edu

| Application Filing | | Accreditation | |
|---|---|---|---|
| Earliest: | May 15 | CDA | |
| Latest: | November 1 | | |
| Fee: | $70 | **Degrees Granted** | |
| AADSAS: | yes | DDS | |

### Enrollment: 2008–2009 First-Year Class

| | | | | |
|---|---|---|---|---|
| Men: | 65 | 65% | *Mean* | |
| Women: | 35 | 35% | total GPA: | 3.4 |
| Minorities: | 7 | 7% | science: | 3.3 |
| Out of State: | 45 | 45% | | |
| With 3 years of college: | | 2% | *Average* | |
| With 4 years of college: | | 98% | DAT academic: | 19 |
| | | | DAT-PAT: | 20 |

**Tuition and Fees**

| | |
|---|---|
| **Resident** | 19,656 |
| Average | 24,250 |
| **Nonresident** | 38,965 |
| Average | 37,850 |

0    10    20    30    40
(in thousands of dollars)

Percentage receiving financial aid:  85%

## Introduction

Virginia Commonwealth University was established in 1838. The School of Dentistry was founded in 1893 as a division of the University College of Medicine. It is the only dental school in Virginia. The school is located on the Health Sciences campus, which includes schools of Medicine, Nursing, Pharmacy, Allied Health, and basic sciences. In addition to postgraduate programs in many specialties, the school offers an advanced education in dentistry residency (AEGD) program.

## Admissions (AADSAS)

The basic predental science courses plus courses in English are required. Courses in general microbiology, genetics, animal physiology, embryology, immunology, and behavioral sciences as well as courses involving psychomotor skills are recommended. The school accepts both state residents and nonresidents. *Transfer and advanced standing:* Students from other U.S. dental schools may apply for advanced standing into the second and third year only. Foreign dental graduates are also considered. Advanced standing can take place only if positions are available in the appropriate class.

## Curriculum

4-year. The subject matter of the curriculum is divided into the basic, clinical, and social sciences. The basic sciences, including preclinical didactic virtual reality laboratory preparation and comprehensive patient care, begin in the first year. The social sciences cover such topics as dental health needs, health care delivery systems, and practice management. Clinical sciences include preclinical didactic and laboratory preparation and begin in the second year. Didactic work together with laboratory and clinical experiences are offered throughout the 4 years of the curriculum to develop skills vital to the practice of dentistry. Elective courses are offered in the senior year.

## Facilities

The facilities of the school are housed in 3 attached modern buildings, containing clinical facilities, classrooms/laboratories, group and individual study areas, department offices, and a closed-circuit color television studio. Dormitories, athletic facilities, and a student center are located on campus.

## Special Features

Combined DDS-MS and DDS-PhD programs are offered. They require additional time beyond the 4-year DDS program.

## WASHINGTON

# University of Washington School of Dentistry

Health Science Building D323
Box 356365
Seattle, Washington   98195

*Phone:* 206-685-9484          *Fax:* 206-616-2612
*E-mail:* askuwsod@uwashington.edu
*WWW:* dental.washington.edu

| Application Filing | | Accreditation | |
|---|---|---|---|
| Earliest: | June 1 | ADA | |
| Latest: | November 1 | | |
| Fee: | $35 | **Degrees Granted** | |
| AADSAS: | yes | DDS, DDS-PhD | |

### Enrollment: 2008–2009 First-Year Class

| | | | | |
|---|---|---|---|---|
| Men: | 36 | 57% | *Mean* | |
| Women: | 27 | 43% | total GPA: | 3.5 |
| Minorities: | 7 | 8% | science: | 3.5 |
| Out of State: | 5 | 6% | | |
| With 2 years of college: | 0% | | *Average* | |
| With 4 years of college: | 98% | | DAT academic: | 21 |
| | | | DAT-PAT: | 19 |

### Tuition and Fees

| | | |
|---|---|---|
| Resident | 17,425 | |
| Average | 24,250 | |
| Nonresident | 41,429 | |
| Average | 37,850 | |

0    10    20    30    40
(in thousands of dollars)

Percentage receiving financial aid: n/a

## Introduction

The University of Washington was established in 1861. There are 17 undergraduate schools and 1 graduate school. The University of Washington School of Dentistry was founded in 1945 and is now located on the 700-acre main campus. The School of Dentistry is part of the Warren G. Magnuson Health Science Center, whose other components are the schools of Medicine, Nursing, Pharmacy, Public Health, and Community Medicine. In addition to the DDS degree, the school offers a BS in dental hygiene, an MS in dentistry, and graduate training in a variety of specialties leading to a certificate of proficiency.

## Admissions (AADSAS)

One year of biology or zoology, 1 year of general physics, 1 semester/2 quarters of inorganic and organic chemistry, 1 semester/2 quarters of biochem-istry, and 2 semesters/3 quarters general microbiology are required. Entering classes are 75% Washington State residents; the rest are from WICHE states or other states. While a majority of the entering class have completed an undergraduate degree, applicants who have at least 3 years of college coursework are considered. *Transfer and advanced standing:* Transfer students are rarely accepted. There is no advanced standing program.

## Curriculum

4-year. Strong emphasis is placed on integrating study in the basic sciences with study in clinical dental sciences. *First year:* Consists of the basic sciences with an introduction to preclinical techniques. *Second year:* A continuation of preclinical skills, application of basic science principles in a clinical setting, and the beginning of experience in clinical treatment. *Third year:* Devoted to rotations in 9 disciplines plus lectures to enhance diagnostic and technical skills. *Fourth year:* Provides an opportunity for extensive experience in the delivery of comprehensive patient dental care in off-campus sites. A wide choice of electives are available to third- and fourth-year students to meet elective requirements.

## Facilities

As an integral part of the Health Sciences Center, the school has a variety of facility resources available to students.

## Special Features

Students with special backgrounds can utilize the diverse resources of the Health Sciences Center to plan joint MS and/or PhD programs. The University of Washington, School of Dentistry is one of 15 dental schools nationwide selected to participate in this novel 5-year $15 million Robert Wood Johnson Foundation and California Endowment-sponsored program. The program is designed to increase access to dental care for underserved populations and to increase recruitment and retention of disadvantaged and underrepresented minority students.

## WEST VIRGINIA

# West Virginia University School of Dentistry

P.O. Box 9400
Morgantown, West Virginia   26506

*Phone:* 304-293-6646          *Fax:* 304-293-8561
*E-mail:* dentaladmit@hsc.wvu.edu
*WWW:* hsc.wvu.edu/sod/

| Application Filing | | Accreditation |
|---|---|---|
| Earliest: | June 1 | CDA |
| Latest: | November 1 | |
| Fee: | $50 | **Degrees Granted** |
| AADSAS: | yes | DDS, DDS-MS, DDS-PhD |

### Enrollment: 2008–2009 First-Year Class

| | | | | |
|---|---|---|---|---|
| Men: | 23 | 46% | *Mean* | |
| Women: | 27 | 54% | total GPA: | 3.5 |
| Minorities: | 10 | 20% | science: | 3.39 |
| Out of State: | 11 | 22% | | |
| With 3 years of college: | 9% | | *Average* | |
| With 4 years of college: | 98% | | DAT academic: | 17 |
| | | | DAT-PAT: | 18 |

**Tuition and Fees**

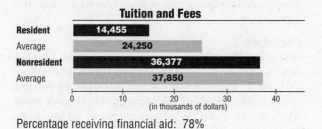

| | |
|---|---|
| Resident | 14,455 |
| Average | 24,250 |
| Nonresident | 36,377 |
| Average | 37,850 |

(in thousands of dollars)

Percentage receiving financial aid: 78%

## Introduction

West Virginia University was established in 1867. The West Virginia University School of Dentistry was opened in 1957 and is part of the Robert C. Byrd Health Sciences Center. The School of Dentistry offers, in addition to the DDS degree, a BS and MS in dental hygiene and graduate training in a number of specialties. Continuing education courses for dentists and auxiliaries are available as is an advanced education in general dentistry program.

## Admissions (AADSAS)

The basic predental science courses and 1 year of English composition and rhetoric are required. Recommended additional courses are biochemistry, comparative anatomy, embryology, microbiology, and psychology. Courses in the humanities and social sciences are also suggested. Applicants must complete at least 90 semester credit hours prior to application. Preference is given to state residents. Nonresidents should have a GPA of at least 3.5 and DAT scores of 17–17. *Transfer and advanced standing:* Limited availability. Contact school for details.

## Curriculum

4-year. Clinical predoctoral observation begins during the first semester of the second year. A transition to hands-on assisting assignments occurs in the second semester of the second year. Clinical experience begins during the summer of the second year. A team leader program has been initiated to ensure that students have the appropriate learning experiences to achieve competency and learn how to manage the needs of a family of patients. A 6-week community rural practice rotation is requried of all senior students.

## Facilities

The school is part of the WVU Health Sciences Center. Modern fully equipped facilities are continually upgraded.

## Special Features

Combined DDS-MS and DDS-PhD in the basic sciences programs are available on an individual basis. They require several years of study in addition to time needed for the dental curriculum.

# WISCONSIN

## Marquette University School of Dentistry

P.O. Box 1881
Milwaukee, Wisconsin   53233

*Phone:* 414-288-3532          *Fax:* 414-288-6505
*E-mail:* dentaladmit@marquette.edu
*WWW:* marquette.edu/dentistry

| Application Filing | | Accreditation | |
|---|---|---|---|
| Earliest: | June 1 | CDA | |
| Latest: | January 1 | | |
| Fee: | $45 | **Degrees Granted** | |
| AADSAS: | yes | DDS | |

### Enrollment: 2008–2009 First-Year Class

| | | | | |
|---|---|---|---|---|
| Men: | 47 | 59% | *Mean* | |
| Women: | 33 | 41% | total GPA: | 3.5 |
| Minorities: | 17 | 21% | science: | 3.5 |
| Out of State: | 40 | 50% | | |
| With 3 years of college: | | 11% | *Average* | |
| With 4 years of college: | | 89% | DAT academic: | 18.3 |
| | | | DAT-PAT: | 19.5 |

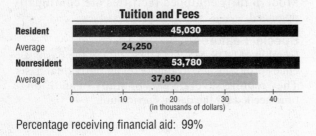

**Tuition and Fees**

| | |
|---|---|
| Resident | 45,030 |
| Average | 24,250 |
| Nonresident | 53,780 |
| Average | 37,850 |

(in thousands of dollars)

Percentage receiving financial aid: 99%

## Introduction

Marquette University was founded in 1881. The Marquette University School of Dentistry was created in 1907 when Milwaukee Medical College merged with Marquette College and formed Marquette University. Graduate programs leading to an MS degree are offered in several specialties. Continuing education courses are available in all phases of dentistry through the year.

## Admissions (AADSAS)

The basic predental science courses and 1 year of English are required, and additional courses in biology and biochemistry are strongly recommended. Other recommended courses are speech, history, philosophy, sociology, political science, economics, accounting, personal finance, and psychology. *Transfer and advanced standing:* Students from other U.S. and Canadian dental schools and foreign dental school graduates can apply for advanced standing only into the second year.

## Curriculum

The curriculum involves students in a model of dental education that mimics a dental practice. Students will be trained to develop and utilize all their skills, as competent clinicians and diagnosticians, to identify and manage the multiple oral health concerns of their patients. Students will take fewer courses. Instead, the curriculum combines courses into itnegrated, multidisciplinary tracks that link traditional dental disciplines and provide learning experiences designed to integrate knowledge, skills, and attitudes. Students will move through curricular tracks as members of small practice groups. They will participate in dental rounds (a concept borrowed from the medical education model) with faculty leading discussions of dental cases and bringing in the pharmacological and medical concerns that should be considered in planning and rendering dental care. Students will dedicate up to 25% of their time working at off-campus dental projects sponsored by Marquette University.

## Grading Policy

The performance of students is evaluated by conventional classroom and clinical testing. Proficiency examinations are carried out in major clinical disciplines to determine the extent of a student's capabilities.

## Facilities

In August 2002, Marquette cut the ribbon on a brand-new, $30 million, 120,000-square-foot dental school and clinic. The new building is designed to house a revamped curriculum, one designed to operate more like a private practice with an emphasis on improved patient care. Effective reciprocal collaborations in dental education exist between the Dental School and the Milwaukee Children's Hospital, Sinai Samaritan Medical Center, and the Zablocki Veterans Administration Hospital. In addition, the School of Dentistry operates several off-campus clinics in underserved areas of the state, which provide additional clinical experience for its students.

## Special Features

A combined BS/DDS program is available on an individual basis, and a DDS+ program encompassing graduate courses in both dental and nondental fields exists.

# Dalhousie University Faculty of Dentistry

5981 University Avenue
Halifax, Nova Scotia   B3H 1W2

*Phone:* 902-494-2274          *Fax:* 902-494-2527
*E-mail:* denadmis@dal.ca
*WWW:* dentistry.dal.ca

| Application Filing | | Accreditation |
|---|---|---|
| Earliest: | September 1 | CDA |
| Latest: | December 1 | |
| Fee: | $75 | **Degrees Granted** |
| AADSAS: | no | DDS |

### Enrollment: 2008–2009 First-Year Class

| | | | |
|---|---|---|---|
| Men: | 23 | 82% | *Mean* |
| Women: | 5 | 18% | total GPA: 3.7 |
| Minorities: | n/a | n/a | science: 3.7 |
| Out of Province: | 7 | 25% | |
| With 2 years of college: | | n/a | *Average* |
| With 3 years of college: | | 100% | DAT academic: 18 |
| | | | DAT-PAT: 16 |

### Tuition and Fees

| | |
|---|---|
| **Resident** | 14,074 |
| Average | 24,250 |
| **Nonresident** | 35,000 |
| Average | 37,850 |

(in thousands of dollars) 0 10 20 30 40

Percentage receiving financial aid: 64%

Above data applies to 2007–2008 academic year.

## Introduction
Dalhousie University, in Nova Scotia, was established in 1818. It is a public, nonsectarian school. The Faculty of Dentistry opened in 1912. Through its Alumni Affair Development, the school provides continuing education courses for dentists and dental hygienists.

## Admissions
A minimum of 10 credits of university study, as well as basic predental science courses including biochemistry, microbiology, and vertebrate physiology, plus 1 writing course and 2 credits from the humanities and/or social sciences, are required. Students are advised to complete their studies toward a bachelor's degree, while completing the required prerequisites for admission. This will enhance their chances for admission. Preference is given to students from the Atlantic Provinces of Canada. The Canadian Dental Association's Dental Aptitude Test must also be completed prior to the December 1 application deadline. Applicants should achieve an average score of 15 or better. *Transfer and advanced standing:* Not possible.

## Curriculum
4-year. Integration of dental, biological, and behavioral sciences is emphasized throughout the 4 years. Didactic and laboratory classes comprise most of the first 2 years, with patient care introduced late in the first year and continued through the second year. The clinically oriented disciplines and total patient care are emphasized during the third and fourth years, respectively. Selective study programs are required during the fourth year. During the last 2 clinical years dental students work together with second-year dental hygiene sttudents during clinical training to provide a team approach to total patient care. Dental assistants are provided, and as a result, experience is attained in 4-handed dentistry and auxiliary utilization.

## Facilities
All subjects are taught in the Dental Building, which has ample and modern facilities. Three adjacent hospitals provide additional clinical facilities.

## Special Features
A limited number of student research fellowships are available on an irregular basis each summer.

# McGill University
# Faculty of Dentistry

3640 University Street
Montréal, Québec   H3A 2B2

*Phone:* 514-398-7203          *Fax:* 514-398-8900
*E-mail:* undergrade@mcgill.ca
*WWW:* mcgill.ca/dentistry

| Application Filing | | Accreditation | |
|---|---|---|---|
| Earliest: | November 15 | CDA | |
| Latest: | January 15 | | |
| Fee: | $80 | **Degrees Granted** | |
| AADSAS: | yes | DMD | |

### Enrollment: 2008–2009 First-Year Class

| | | | | |
|---|---|---|---|---|
| Men: | 10 | 33% | *Mean* | |
| Women: | 20 | 67% | total GPA: | 3.7 |
| Minorities: | n/a | n/a | science: | 3.7 |
| Out of Province: | 16 | 53% | | |
| With 3 years of college: | 33% | | *Average* | |
| With 4 years of college: | 7% | | DAT academic: | 22 |
| | | | DAT-PAT: | 21 |

**Tuition and Fees**

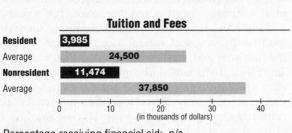

| Resident | 3,985 |
| Average | 24,500 |
| Nonresident | 11,474 |
| Average | 37,850 |

0    10    20    30    40
(in thousands of dollars)

Percentage receiving financial aid: n/a

## Introduction

McGill University was established in 1821 and is a public school. It has 11 undergraduate schools and 17 graduate schools. The dental school offers masters programs in oral biology as well as in oral and maxillofacial surgery.

## Admissions (AADSAS)

Applicants to the 4-year program must have an undergraduate cumulative grade point average (CGPA) of 3.6 or better on a 4.0 scale. Applicants must have received an undergraduate degree, or be in the first year of a course of study at a recognized college or university leading to an undergraduate degree consisting of 120 credits over 8 terms following completion of high school. However, students who have received a diploma of collegial studies (CEGEP) in the Province of Quebec must have completed 90 credits (6 terms) in a Quebec university to obtain the required degree. Similarly, Quebec residents who, having received credit for their diploma of collegial studies, elect to complete their undergraduate degree outside the Province of Quebec (other Canadian provinces, United States, or elsewhere) will be required to complete an undergraduate degree with a minimum of 90 credits (6 terms) at the non-Quebec university to be eligible to apply. Students who fail to complete a DEC before transferring to a non-Quebec university must complete a 4-year degree. Successful candidates must be in receipt of the bachelor's degree by the time of registration for the first year of the dental curriculum. The basic predental courses are required. It is important to note that in all of the above courses Pass/Fail grades are not acceptable. Prerequisite courses completed more than 8 years before must be repeated. Exception may be made for applicants with advanced degrees in the material concerned. University-level courses in biochemistry, cell and molecular biology, and physiology are strongly recommended.

## Curriculum

4-year. The goal of the dental program is for graduates to be competent to begin to work as general practitioners, regardless of their future aspirations. They should have the competence to cope with the dental diseases they will encounter and be qualified to apply the necessary preventive and treatment measures. The basic sciences are taught in conjunction with the Faculty of Medicine during the first 18 months of the program. Introduction to clinical experience begins in the first year, and the integration of basic sciences into clinical dentistry occurs in the second year. The last 2 years are devoted to comprehensive patient dental care.

## Facilities

The faculty is located in downtown Montreal. The preclinical training is provided on the McGill campus in cooperation with the Faculty of Medicine and the clinical training takes place in the McCall Dental Clinic of Montreal General Hospital and other teaching hospitals.

## Special Features

The school trains students in dental science research. This program can lead to a masters of science in Dental Sciences.

# Université de Montréal
# Faculté de Médecine Dentaire

C.P. 6128, Succursale centre-ville
Montréal, Québec   H3C 3J7

*Phone:* 514-343-2223          *Fax:* 514-343-2233
*WWW:* medent.umontreal.ca

| Application Filing | | | Accreditation |
|---|---|---|---|
| Earliest: | January 1 | | CDA |
| Latest: | March 1 | | |
| Fee: | $30 | | **Degrees Granted** |
| AADSAS: | no | | DMD |

### Enrollment: 2008–2009 First-Year Class

| | | | |
|---|---|---|---|
| Men: | 26 | 31% | *Mean* |
| Women: | 59 | 69% | total GPA:    n/a |
| Minorities: | n/a | n/a | science:    n/a |
| Out of Province: | n/a | n/a | |
| With 2 years of college: | 100% | | *Average* |
| With 3 years of college: | n/a | | DAT academic:    n/a |
| | | | DAT-PAT:    n/a |

### Tuition and Fees

| | |
|---|---|
| **Resident** | 2,650 Canadian dollars |
| Average | 24,250 |
| **Nonresident** | 3,000 Canadian dollars |
| Average | 37,850 |

0    10    20    30    40
(in thousands of dollars)

Percentage receiving financial aid: n/a

Average tuition shown is for U.S. schools.

Above data applies to 2007–2008 academic year.

## Introduction

The Université de Montréal was established in 1878. It conducts its classes in French. The Faculté de Médecine Dentaire was established in 1904. Postgraduate programs are offered in a variety of specialties, some of which lead to masters degrees or certificates.

## Admissions

Information is available on the web site at *www.medent.umontreal.* A minimum score of 10 is required on the Canadian DAT on both the carving dexterity and the perception aptitude tests. All candidates must be Canadian citizens or permanent residents. Strong preference is given to provincial residents. Instruction is given in French. *Transfer and advanced standing:* Graduates of nonaccredited foreign dental schools may be admitted with advanced standing if requirements are met and space is available in the second-year class.

## Curriculum

5-year semitraditional. Training in basic sciences and preclinical disciplines are emphasized during the first 2 years of the program. Formal clinical training starts during the second semester of the second year. There is an initiation to the clinic during the predental and the first year of the program. Senior students spend 3 weeks in a hospital off campus to become acquainted with oral surgery and for training in pediatric dentistry. The clinical program of the senior year also offers optional clinical courses. In addition to traditional clinical training, off-campus activities such as exchange programs are available.

## Facilities

The Faculté is located in the main building of the university and occupies the street and second-floor levels of the east end. Students have access to university audiovisual and computer facilities.

## Special Features

All teaching is in the French language. Joint postgraduate programs in the biomedical sciences are offered in association with the medical faculty. Outstanding students are offered summer appointments to enable them to become familiar with clinical and laboratory research.

# Université Laval
# Faculté de Médecine Dentaire

Québec, Québec   G1V 0A6

*Phone:* 418-656-2247          *Fax:* 418-656-2720
*E-mail:* fmd@fmd.ulaval.ca
*WWW:* fmdulaval.ca/md

| Application Filing | | Accreditation |
|---|---|---|
| Earliest: | September 1 | CDA |
| Latest: | March 1 | |
| Fee: | $55 | **Degrees Granted** |
| AADSAS: | no | DMD |

### Enrollment: 2008–2009 First-Year Class

| Men: | 16 | 33% | *Mean* | |
|---|---|---|---|---|
| Women: | 32 | 67% | total GPA: | n/a |
| Minorities: | 0 | 0% | science: | n/a |
| Out of Province: | n/a | n/a | | |
| With 2 years of college: | 50% | | *Average* | |
| With 3 years of college: | 25% | | DAT academic: | n/a |
| | | | DAT-PAT: | 15 |

### Tuition and Fees

| Resident | 3,860 |
|---|---|
| Average | 24,250 |
| Nonresident | n/a |
| Average | n/a |

0    10    20    30    40
(in thousands of dollars)

Percentage receiving financial aid:  n/a

Average tuition shown is for U.S. schools

## Introduction

Laval University was established in 1852 and is the oldest university in North America. It conducts its classes in French. The Université Laval Faculté Médecine Dentaire was founded in 1969. The school also offers a masters program in oral and in maxillo-facial surgery in periodontics, and in geriatric dentistry. The university is primarily a government-funded institution.

## Admissions

The basic predental science courses plus 2 semesters of mathematics are required. Taking the Canadian or American DAT is a mandatory requirement for admission. For the Canadian exam, the written part may be taken in French. A maximum of 47 students per year can be currently accommodated. Ninety percent of the students must be from Quebec province. Only residents of Quebec are accepted. *Transfer and advanced standing:* Not available.

## Curriculum

4-year nontraditional. The first 2 years are devoted to the basic and preclinical sciences. The last 2 years are devoted almost entirely to clinical work. Elective specialization is possible in the senior year. Electives in hospital dentistry, public health, and basic research are available. Self-pacing is possible in a few courses.

## Facilities

The school is equipped with 3 laboratories, 2 dental clinics (97 units), surgery clinic (8 units), and clinic of radiology (9 units). Several services related to dentistry are also available (dental laboratory, store, etc.).

## Special Features

All teaching is in the French language.

# University of Alberta Faculty of Medicine and Dentistry Department of Dentistry

3028 Dentistry-Pharmacy Centre
Edmonton, Alberta   T6G 2N8

*Phone:* 780-492-1319          *Fax:* 780-492-7536
*E-mail:* admissions@dent.ualberta.ca
*WWW:* dent.ualberta.ca

| Application Filing | | Accreditation |
|---|---|---|
| Earliest: | July 1 | CDA |
| Latest: | November 1 | |
| Fee: | $115 | **Degrees Granted** |
| AADSAS: | no | DDS |

### Enrollment: 2008–2009 First-Year Class

| | | | | |
|---|---|---|---|---|
| Men: | 35 | 60% | *Mean* | |
| Women: | 23 | 40% | total GPA: | 3.7 |
| Minorities: | 12 | 21% | science: | 3.8 |
| Out of Province: | n/a | n/a | | |
| With 3 years of college: | 23% | | *Average* | |
| With 4 years of college: | 51% | | DAT academic: | n/a |
| | | | DAT-PAT: | 20.9 |

### Tuition and Fees

| | |
|---|---|
| **Resident** | 18,578 |
| Average | 24,250 |
| **Nonresident** | 18,578 |
| Average | 37,850 |

0      10      20      30      40
(in thousands of dollars)

Percentage receiving financial aid:  n/a

Average tuition shown is for U.S. schools.

## Introduction

The University of Alberta was established in 1906. It is a public institution with both undergraduate and graduate schools. The University of Alberta Department of Dentistry has both Canadian and American Dental Association approval. The school is located on the North Saskatchewan River. Senior students gain experience in treating underprivileged people by service in Northern Alberta.

## Admissions

The basic predental science courses, statistics, and 2 courses in English are required. Recommended electives include psychology, genetics, and biochemistry. The Canadian DAT is mandatory with a minimum score of 15 for Reading Comprehension, perceptual ability, and manual dexterity. A minimum GPA of 3.0 is required. High priority is given to provincial residents, but candidates from other provinces and other countries are admitted. Although it is not necessary to complete requirements for a degree prior to applying, it is to the student's advantage to register in a degree program for preprofessional study. *Transfer and advanced standing:* Not possible.

## Curriculum

The first and second year of the dental program is combined with the MD program. The curriculum is taught in blocks and covers such areas as infection, immunity and inflammation, endocrine system, cardiovascular pulmonary and renal system, gastroenterology and nutrition, reproductive medicine and urology, musculoskeletal system, neurosciences and oncology. These subjects are augmented by dental courses offered by the respective divisions. The lectures, laboratories, seminars, and clinics offered by the Department of Dentistry relate and integrate these fundamental disciplines with the knowledge skills, judgment, and performance required of dental practitioners. In addition to bedside and operating instruction in medicine and surgery, senior students are assigned to the Dental Clinic and the Department of Dentistry, University of Alberta Hospital. An experience in the Satellite Dental Clinic and the external hospitals is required in the final year of the program. Thus, students are able to relate their field of heatlh service to the science of preventing, curing, or alleviating disease in general.

## Facilities

The dental facilities are housed in the Dental Pharmacy Center. The students also rotate through the University External Hospitals, and Northern Alberta Clinics.

## Special Features

Limited research opportunities are available through employment as summer research assistants. The first 2 years of the dental program is combined with the MD program. The school offers a 2-year Master of Science degree in Orthodontics.

# University of British Columbia Faculty of Dentistry

Room 278, 2199 Westbrook Mall
Vancouver, British Columbia   V6T 1Z3

*Phone:* 604-822-8063          *Fax:* 604-822-8279
*E-mail:* fodadms@interchange.ubc.ca
*WWW:* dentistry.ubc.ca

| Application Filing | | Accreditation | |
|---|---|---|---|
| Earliest: | June 1 | CDA | |
| Latest: | November 1 | | |
| Fee: | $200 | **Degrees Granted** | |
| AADSAS: | no | DMD, DMD-MS, MSc, DMD-PhD | |

### Enrollment: 2008–2009 First-Year Class

| | | | | |
|---|---|---|---|---|
| Men: | 22 | 56% | *Mean* | |
| Women: | 17 | 44% | total GPA: | n/a |
| Minorities: | n/a | n/a | science: | n/a |
| Out of Province: | | n/a | | |
| With 3 years of college: | | 10% | *Average* | |
| With 4 years of college: | | 82% | DAT academic: | 21 |
| | | | DAT-PAT: | 22 |

### Tuition and Fees

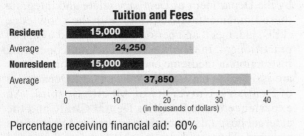

| | |
|---|---|
| **Resident** | 15,000 |
| Average | 24,250 |
| **Nonresident** | 15,000 |
| Average | 37,850 |

(in thousands of dollars)

Percentage receiving financial aid: 60%

Average tuition shown is for U.S. schools.

## Introduction

The University of British Columbia was founded in 1908. It is supported by the province and offers both undergraduate and graduate programs. The University of British Columbia Faculty of Dentistry first opened in 1964. It is a part of the Health Science Center, which includes the faculties of Medicine and Pharmaceutical Sciences, and schools of Nursing, Rehabilitation Medicine, and others. The school is located on a 1,000-acre site on the Point-Grey Peninsula at the west end of Vancouver.

## Admissions

The basic predental science courses plus 1 year each of English, biochemistry, and mathematics are required, and electives in the social sciences and humanities are recommended. Preparatory study for entry must comprise at least 3 years at the college or university level. A minimum GPA of 2.8 (70%) is also required. Taking the Canadian DAT is mandatory. Very strong preference is given to provincial residents.

## Curriculum

The 4-year DMD curriculum utilizes an integrated approach to learning that emphasizes self-directed study, lifelong learning skills, professionalism, and patient-centered care. Years 1 and 2 of the program, taken in partnership with the Faculty of Medicine, focus on the study of the human body, with an emphasis on the whole patient, communications skills, the social contract inherent in the health care professions, and a medical model of care. Years 3 and 4 focus on the orofacial complex, including integrated dental basic and clinical sciences, surgical/psychomotor skills, and patient care, and continuing the emphasis on the whole patient. Didactic learning occurs in a small-group, student-centered format supplemented by lectures, while clinical skills learning integrates simulation and patient care under formalized guidelines for professional behavior. Students are exposed to a broad range of patient care experiences both on campus and at community outreach clinics.

## Facilities

The faculty is located within the Health Sciences Center on the university campus. The facilities of community health clinics and other health care units are also utilized.

## Special Features

Combined DMD-MSc and DMD-PhD programs are available.

# University of Manitoba Faculty of Dentistry

780 Bannatyne Avenue, Room D-113
Winnipeg, Manitoba    R3T 0W2

*Phone:* 204-789-5611          *Fax:* 204-789-3912
*E-mail:* dean_dent@umanitoba.ca
*WWW:* umanitoba.ca/dentistry

| Application Filing | | Accreditation |
|---|---|---|
| Earliest: | November 15 | CDA |
| Latest: | January 22 | |
| Fee: | $75 | **Degrees Granted** |
| AADSAS: | no | DMD |

### Enrollment: 2008–2009 First-Year Class

| | | | | |
|---|---|---|---|---|
| Men: | 16 | 68% | *Mean* | |
| Women: | 14 | 34% | total GPA: | 3.8 |
| Minorities: | n/a | n/a | science: | 3.6 |
| Out of Province: | 5 | 30% | | |
| With 2 years of college: | 17% | | *Average* | |
| With 3 years of college: | 23% | | DAT academic: | 20 |
| | | | DAT-PAT: | 19 |

**Tuition and Fees**

| | |
|---|---|
| **Resident** | 13,595 |
| Average | 24,250 |
| **Nonresident** | 13,595 |
| Average | 37,850 |

0    10    20    30    40
(in thousands of dollars)

Percentage receiving financial aid: 48%

Average tuition shown is for U.S. schools.

Above data applies to 2007–2008 academic year.

## Introduction

In 1957 the University of Manitoba Faculty of Dentistry was established. The school offers specialty training programs in clinical areas and a 2-year dental hygiene program as well as continuing education programs. An opportunity exists for securing masters and PhD degrees in oral biology.

## Admissions

The basic predental science courses and 1 year each of mathematics, biochemistry, and social science, plus 5 electives are required. Very high priority is given to provincial residents. Taking the Canadian DAT is mandatory.

## Curriculum

The basic sciences are taught primarily in the first 2 years. Clinical exposure begins in the first term of the first year. There are no electives; however, all senior students are required to spend 5 weeks in a rural community clinic and one week in a teaching hospital. *First year:* The basic sciences and clinical courses take up the major portion of the program. Also offered is an introduction to clinical patient treatment. *Second year:* The basic sciences and technical courses, plus definitive clinical patient treatment. *Third year:* Focuses primarily on developing skills in comprehensive total patient care. *Fourth year:* Patient-centered clinical treatment in a variety of settings such as hospitals and community extramural programs.

## Grading Policy

Letter grades are used in the didactic and clinical portions of the curriculum and Pass/Fail in selected clinical segments.

## Facilities

The faculty is located on the health science campus in downtown Winnipeg. Additional space is devoted to dental teaching and service in the Health Sciences Center, a consortium of 4 hospitals.

## Special Features

A limited number of undergraduate students are employed in research laboratories during the summer months.

# University of Saskatchewan College of Dentistry

Room B526, Health Sciences Building
107 Wiggins Road
Saskatoon, Saskatchewan S7N 5E4

*Phone:* 306-966-5119 *Fax:* 306-966-5126
*E-mail:* dentistry.admissions@usask.ca
*WWW:* usask.ca/dentistry

| Application Filing | | Accreditation | |
|---|---|---|---|
| Earliest: | August 1 | CDA | |
| Latest: | January 15 | | |
| Fee: | $125 | **Degrees Granted** | |
| AADSAS: | no | DMD | |

### Enrollment: 2008–2009 First-Year Class

| | | | | | |
|---|---|---|---|---|---|
| Men: | 20 | 71% | *Mean* | | |
| Women: | 8 | 29% | total GPA: | | 89.1 |
| Minorities: | n/a | n/a | science: | | n/a |
| Out of Province: | 2 | 7% | | | |
| With 3 years of college: | 8 | 32% | *Average* | | |
| With 4 years of college: | 4 | 25% | DAT academic: | 19.0 | |
| | | | DAT-PAT: | 22.0 | |

**Tuition and Fees**

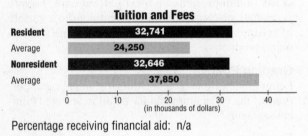

| | |
|---|---|
| Resident | 32,741 |
| Average | 24,250 |
| Nonresident | 32,646 |
| Average | 37,850 |

(in thousands of dollars)

Percentage receiving financial aid: n/a

Average tuition shown is for U.S. schools.

## Introduction

The College of Dentistry offers a fully accredited 4-year Doctor of Dental Medicine (DMD) degree. The college was established in 1965 and graduates approximately 28 qualified dentists each year. Upon successful completion of all courses, graduates of the college are eligible to sit for board examination in Canada and the United States leading to licensure in any province or state.

## Admissions

Applicants must have a minimum overall average of no less than 70% in the required predentistry courses as well as biochemistry, and the equivalent of a full course in the humanities and/or social sciences. In addition to satisfying the predentistry requirements, applicants must have completed at least 60 credit units (2 years) of university-level work and obtain a minimum overall weighted average of 75%. All applicants must take the Dental Aptitude Test (DAT) administered by the Canadian Dental Association. The U.S. Dental Aptitude Test may be used to determine eligibility for admission consideration. However, if accepted, the candidate must write the Canadian DAT in the first term of attendance. DAT results older than 5 years are not accepted for admission purposes.

## Curriculum

4-year. Clinical exposure begins in the first year. Strong efforts are made to closely integrate the basic and dental sciences. *First year:* Consists of basic science courses and a number of dental courses, including Operative Dentistry, Occlusion, and Infection Control. *Second year:* Consists of some basic science courses, as well as advanced dental courses, including participation in patient treatment clinics. *Third year:* The focus is on gaining experience in patient care and treatment, with some preclinical and didactic courses included, as well as a research project course. *Fourth year:* Further experience in patient care and treatment is emphasized, including a Comprehensive Care clinic course.

## Facilities

Preclinical teaching resources include a state-of-the-art clinic simulation facility that allows freshman and sophomore students to learn basic dental procedures, as well as current techniques in infection control, fiber optic technology, and intra-oral imaging. Students learn the practical aspects of dentistry in a variety of clinical settings such as emergency, diagnosis, radiology, oral surgery, and multidisciplinary clinics, which include 80 dental chairs with enhanced ambient lighting and patient privacy screens. An ultra modern 6-chair clinic area with the latest technology allows flexibility to provide additional practice management experience to senior students.

## Special Features

Fourth-year students who meet all their requirements may participate in an option program during the last 2 weeks of their senior year. Approved activities could be undertaken in the College of Dentistry, the adjoining Royal University Hospital, other dental colleges, acceptable alternate institutions, or private dental offices.

# University of Toronto Faculty of Dentistry

124 Edward Street
Toronto, Ontario   M5G 1G6

*Phone:* 416-979-4901      *Fax:* 416-979-4944
*E-mail:* admissions.dental@u.toronto.ca
*WWW:* utoronto.ca/dentistry

| **Application Filing** | | **Accreditation** |
|---|---|---|
| Earliest: | July 1 | CDA |
| Latest: | December 1 | |
| Fee: | $230 | **Degrees Granted** |
| AADSAS: | yes | DDS, DDS-PhD |

### Enrollment: 2008–2009 First-Year Class

| Men: | 24 | 37% | *Mean* | |
|---|---|---|---|---|
| Women: | 41 | 63% | total GPA: | 3.84 |
| Minorities: | n/a | n/a | science: | n/a |
| Out of Province: | 4 | 6% | | |
| With 2 years of college: | | 0% | *Average* | |
| With 3 years of college: | | 21.5% | DAT academic: | 20 |
| | | | DAT-PAT: | 20 |

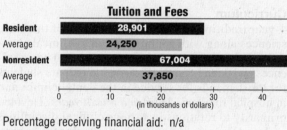

**Tuition and Fees**

| Resident | 28,901 |
| Average | 24,250 |
| Nonresident | 67,004 |
| Average | 37,850 |

(in thousands of dollars)

Percentage receiving financial aid: n/a
Average tuition shown is for U.S. schools.

## Introduction

The School of Dentistry was founded by the Royal College of Dental Surgeons of Ontario in 1875. Seven years earlier, in 1868, the college was given the dual responsibilities of licensing and dental education when the Province of Ontario, in one of its first legislative acts, passed the "Act Respecting Dentistry." In 1888 the school began its affiliation with the University of Toronto when it established the degree of Doctor of Dental Surgery.

## Admissions (AADSAS)

In order to be eligible for admission consideration, applicants must have completed 3 years of university education (at least 15 full courses or equivalent) in a program that demonstrates focus and coherence in education. This education must have included 1 full course in general biochemistry; 1 full course in mammalian physiology; and at least 2 courses in humanities or social sciences. A minimum cumulative GPA of 2.7 at the time of application is required. However, it should be noted that at least 80% of all applicants have a GPA above 3.7. It is recommended that applicants follow a program of study that will provide them with an educational background in keeping with their own interests and possible career opportunities should they not be accepted into Dentistry. *Residency:* Applicants must be Canadian citizens or permanent residents. A maximum of 10% of the first-year places may be offered to out-of-province applicants. NOTE: A limited number of positions are also available for international students (students who can enter or are already in Canada on student authorization). *Transfers within Canada and from the United States:* Canadian citizens or permanent residents currently enrolled in an accredited Canadian or U.S. dental school will be considered for admission, space permitting, into second year only. Applicants must meet all academic and English facility requirements for admission into first year. In addition, dental program equivalency with the DDS program at the University of Toronto must be established. Applicants enrolled in dental schools where the curriculum is not sufficiently equivalent to allow for direct entry into second year at the University of Toronto are not eligible for transfer consideration. Domestic applicants should be aware that the number of second-year places, if any, may vary annually, and in most years no spaces are available.

## Curriculum

The dental program is designed to unify the basic and clinical sciences, as it is believed that scientific and professional development cannot be sharply differentiated, but should proceed concurrently throughout the program. Instruction shifts gradually from an emphasis on the sciences basic to dentistry (first year) to a clinically oriented program (fourth year).

## Facilities

The Faculty of Dentistry has been completely renovated and expanded making it one of the most modern facilities in North America. New modern research laboratories, clinics, offices, and ancillary services, including a computerized clinic management system, enable the faculty to provide the best possible climate for teaching and research.

## Special Features

The staff/student ratio in the DDS program is traditionally set at 1:9. This allows students to receive highly individualized instruction in both the preclinical and clinical components of their dental education.

# University of Western Ontario Schulich School of Dentistry

1151 Richmond Street
London, Ontario    N6A 5C1

*Phone:* 519-661-3744    *Fax:* 519-852-2958
*E-mail:* admissions.dentistry@schulich.uwo.ca
*WWW:* schulich.uwo.ca/dentistry

| Application Filing | | Accreditation | |
|---|---|---|---|
| Earliest: | September 15 | CDA | |
| Latest: | December 1 | | |
| Fee: | $250 | **Degrees Granted** | |
| AADSAS: | no | DDS | |

### Enrollment: 2008–2009 First-Year Class

| | | | | | |
|---|---|---|---|---|---|
| Men: | 27 | 48% | *Mean* | | |
| Women: | 26 | 52% | total GPA: | 3.83 |
| Minorities: | 5 | 10% | science: | n/a |
| Out of Province: | 8 | 15% | | |
| With 2 years of college: | 75% | *Average* | | |
| With 3 years of college: | 20% | DAT academic: | n/a |
| | | | DAT-PAT: | 19 |

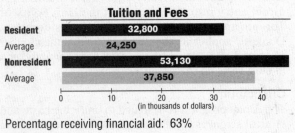

**Tuition and Fees**

| Resident | 32,800 |
| Average | 24,250 |
| Nonresident | 53,130 |
| Average | 37,850 |

(in thousands of dollars)

Percentage receiving financial aid: 63%

Average tuition shown is for U.S. schools.

## Introduction

The University of Western Ontario was chartered in 1878. It is a public school with 14 undergraduate and 4 graduate schools. The school offers, besides its DDS degree, a 3-year masters program in orthodontics and oral biology.

## Admissions

Requirements include successful completion of a second-year program at an Ontario university, or an equivalent second year at another university, provided that the program has included a minimum of 4 honors courses or equivalent within the first 10 courses completed. All applicants must have successfully completed the approved courses in physiology (human or mammalian), biochemistry, and organic chemistry. Canadian candidates must also have taken approved biology, chemistry, and physics courses if an undergraduate degree has not been completed by entry. International candidates must have completed an undergraduate degree or at least 2 years of a dental program, including the mandatory basic science courses for all candidates. Taking the Canadian DAT is mandatory. (The American DAT can be considered for international candidates.) *Transfer and advanced standing:* Transfer is possible into the second year, if a position is available.

## Curriculum

4-year traditional. *First year:* Consists of the basic sciences along with an introduction to clinical situations. *Second year:* Involves the advanced basic sciences and dental courses designed to prepare students for the demands for service in the dental clinics and in hospital rotations. *Third and fourth years:* Devoted primarily to rotations in various clinical disciplines and in delivery of comprehensive dental care to patients in a clinical setting. A Qualifying Program is also offered for graduates of nonaccredited dental programs, which prepares them for Canadian licensing exams. Competitive candidates will be invited to interview.

## Facilities

Teaching takes place at the Dental Science Building.

## Special Features

Good clinical experience throughout program starting with preclinical exposure in a well-equipped simulation clinic.

# APPENDIX A

## A SELF-ASSESSMENT ADMISSION PROFILE

As discussed in Chapter 6, admission to medical or dental school is dependent upon a multiplicity of factors. Some of the specific data associated with admissions criteria are known to you (such as the quality of your GPA, science cumulative average, etc.), while others are either unknown or unpredictable at this time (such as recommendations or aptitude test scores). Nevertheless, of the ten major admission requirements, most can be quantified with adequate accuracy so as to allow you to formulate a reasonably accurate assessment of your admission chances. More importantly, completing an assessment profile will serve to identify your strengths and weaknesses and thus provide you with information as to which of the areas need improvement. (It will, in addition, identify what assets you should, if possible, emphasize about yourself at an interview and in your AMCAS application essay.)

Success with the use of this profile requires accuracy and as much completeness as possible. In dealing with criteria where data are uncertain, you should make a realistic estimate based on the information currently at your disposal. You may, after completion of the assessment profile, wish to review its content, conclusions, and recommendations with your school's Prehealth Professions Advisor in order to validate your facts, assumptions, and interpretation.

Each of the admission criteria listed in the profile will be discussed briefly. (A fuller treatment is given in Chapter 6.)

1. *College attended.* The established admission "track" record to medical and dental schools by students from your own college is the major consideration for this category. A *superior* rating would be used if most applicants from your school succeed in gaining admission, whereas *weak* would reflect the opposite position, and *adequate*, about a 50% acceptance rate. Taking the exact acceptance rate for the most recent year available into consideration will help you identify where in each box to place your mark (such as at the left, right, or middle of the appropriate box).

2. *Grade point average (GPA).* Your current GPA should be plotted on the profile by using the following rating scheme:

|         | Superior | Adequate | Weak    |
|---------|----------|----------|---------|
| Medical | 4.0–3.5  | 3.4–3.2  | 3.1–2.5 |
| Dental  | 4.0–3.3  | 3.2–2.8  | 2.7–2.0 |

You should determine where to place your rating in each box by noting the consistency of your level of academic performance. Thus, a 3.5 GPA representing a 3.5 for each of approximately three years would merit the rating sign being placed at the right end of the *superior* box. However, a 3.5 GPA resulting from the sum of 4.0, 3.5, and 3.0 for each year respectively over a three-year period would mandate that the marker be placed near the left end of the *adequate* box. Placing the marker at the beginning of the superior box, as in the first case, would be misleading, since a downward trend in a GPA suggests an inability to sustain academic work at a superior level over a long course, assuming no mitigating circumstances exist. If such circumstances exist, they should be noted under "Comments."

3. *Science cumulative average.* This should be determined by the sum of your biology, chemistry, physics, and mathematics (B, C, P, M) grades over the length of your college stay (bearing in mind the credit value for each course). The same

considerations applicable to your GPA are relevant to your science cum as noted in item 2 above. Thus, the consistency of your science courses performance should be considered in determining your rating in this category.

4. *MCAT or DAT scores*. Where these are known, your rating can be determined by using the following scheme (given as total exam score range):

|  | Superior | Adequate | Weak |
|---|---|---|---|
| *Medical | 30–45 | 25–29 | 1–24 |
| Dental | 20–30 | 15–19 | 1–14 |

*These figures represent total scores for the Verbal Reasoning, Physical Sciences, and Biological Sciences subtests of the MCAT (see Chapter 7).

This determination is usually available to college juniors, most of whom take the appropriate aptitude exam in April. For lowerclassmen or juniors who plan to take the fall exam, a rough estimate of one's possible aptitude test performance can be attempted by using your SAT I or ACT scores as a reference source. Thus, an average performance on either of these tests can be reflected as an average potential performance on the MCAT or DAT. This should be taken as a working hypothesis subject to revision when the results are in. But for those with average or below average SAT I or ACT scores, this would suggest that a meaningful effort be directed to obtain a more impressive result on the Medical or Dental Aptitude Test.

5. *Recommendations*. Most schools request that students waive their legal right to see letters of recommendation sent out in their behalf. Thus, rating this factor with certainty is impossible. However, you may be able to make a realistic approximation for this category through *discreet* inquiry of a member of your Prehealth Advisory Committee with whom you may have an especially friendly relationship. You should not seek to find out your specific ranking or rating, but rather merely to ascertain whether you can expect your candidacy for admission to professional school to secure either strong, modest, or weak support from the committee.

6. *Extracurricular activities*. Your rating in this category should be obtained after first itemizing your activities and then comparing them with some of your fellow students who are also applying to medical or dental school. On this basis, you can judge if your participation is well above average and thus superior, or well below average or weak, or simply average and therefore adequate.

7. *Professional exposure*. The nature and extent of your professional exposure to medicine or dentistry will determine your rating in this category. Thus, a physician's assistant or former army medical corpsman will gain an especially strong rating. On the other hand, one whose exposure is limited to a discussion with his family physician or dentist should gain only a very modest rating.

8. *Achievements*. By identifying special accomplishments that are of an academic or a nonacademic nature, you will be able to assess if your credentials will stand out from among the multitude of applications received by the professional schools. You can then rate yourself accordingly.

9. *Personal attributes*. This criterion refers to qualities such as appearance, personality, capacity for critical judgment under stress and for perseverance under pressure, level of maturity, innate flexibility of character, etc. These factors will be relevant to your performance at an interview. The conclusions about your own characteristics should be based on evidence that can be exemplified. Your prior history as to your performance at interviews is very relevant in assessing

your rating on this important issue. Thus, individuals who are endowed with innate personal charm and an attractive physical appearance and who are good conversationalists have an enhanced potential for interview success and should rate themselves accordingly.

When you have completed the rating segment of the profile, you are in a position to arrive at an overall assessment of your admission potential, draw conclusions, and draft recommendations on areas where you need to improve.

Your overall assessment should be established by noting where the majority of criteria ratings have been placed. A distribution weighted to the left, where placement of ratings predominates in the superior and adequate categories, should be considered as indicating a good likelihood to achieve success in gaining admission. If the distribution is, however, weighted to the right, the reverse may be true, and an intense remediation effort in appropriate areas is called for.

In drawing your conclusions, you should bear in mind that the criteria are *not* of equal importance — the first five carry greater weight than the last four and your conclusions should be formulated appropriately.

## Self-assessment Admission Profile

Name: _____     Date: _____

College: _____     Class: _____

| Admission Criteria | Superior | Adequate | Weak | Comments |
|---|---|---|---|---|
| 1. College attended | | | | |
| 2. GPA | | | | |
| 3. Science cumulative average | | | | |
| 4. MCAT or DAT scores | | | | |
| 5. Recommendations | | | | |
| 6. Extracurricular activities | | | | |
| 7. Professional exposure | | | | |
| 8. Achievements | | | | |
| 9. Personal attributes | | | | |

n.a. — adequate information is not available on this issue.

*Comments:*

_____

_____

_____

_____

*Overall rating and conclusions:*

_____

_____

*Recommendations:*

1. _____

2. _____

3. _____

# APPENDIX B

## MEDICAL SCHOOL APPLICATION FORM

For many students, a major obstacle to admission can be that of successfully completing the application forms. Many of the forms are lengthy and all should be completed when you are relaxed, not rushed. Read all instructions carefully and answer all questions completely. Don't jeopardize your chances for admission by submitting an incomplete application form. Type all your answers neatly and be sure to review your application before sending it off. If the appearance of your application is in question, obtain a new one and fill it out more carefully. For additional information on applications, read Chapter 6.

Note: You must obtain the current application forms from the schools directly or through one of the application services (AMCAS, AACOMAS, AADSAS). Do not use these sample forms as your final application. They will not be accepted by the schools.

The very few medical schools that do not subscribe to AMCAS have their own application forms. All osteopathic medical schools belong to AACOMAS, which has its own standard application form (see the next page). Note: this application form is included for your reference, even though the form must now be filled out and submitted exclusively online. This application is very similar to the one used by AMCAS. Almost all dental schools belong to AADSAS. Nonsubscribing dental schools have their own application forms.

## AACOMAS Application

See AACOMAS Application instructions before completing this form.

1.  SSN |__|__|__|__|__|__|__|__|__|    2. Name_____
                                                Last                          first                    middle        suffix

3.  Do you have educational materials under another name?    Yes [   ]  No [   ]    If yes, indicate name_____

4.  Preferred Mailing Address_____
                                                Street                                        city
    _____ Telephone ___(___)_____
            state              zip code                          area code        number

5.  Permanent and/or Legal Residence_____
                                                Street                                        city
    _____ Telephone ___(___)_____
        county          state          zip code                  area code        number

6.  Are you a U.S. Citizen?   Yes [   ]    No [   ] If No, what is your residency status?   Temporary [   ]    Permanent [   ]

7.  Gender*  Male [   ]   Female [   ]    8. Birth Date* |__|__|__|__|__|__|

9.  How do you describe yourself?*  (see instructions - choose only one)   Number |__|   Letter (if applicable) |__| _____

10. Parent/Guardian    Name          Living          Occupation       State of          Education/College
                                    Yes   No                          Residence         or highest level

Father_____  [   ] [   ] _____

Mother_____  [   ] [   ] _____

Guardian_____  [   ] [   ] _____

11. Secondary School_____
                        name                    city                  state              year of graduation

12. A. All Undergraduate Colleges Attended/Planning to Attend (list in chronological order)     Check if

| For office use only | Institution Name | Campus/Location/State | Dates of Attendance | Summer Only | Major | Degree Granted or expected (with date) |
|---|---|---|---|---|---|---|
| _____ | _____ | _____ | ____ to ____ | [   ] | _____ | _____ |
| _____ | _____ | _____ | ____ to ____ | [   ] | _____ | _____ |
| _____ | _____ | _____ | ____ to ____ | [   ] | _____ | _____ |
| _____ | _____ | _____ | _____ | [   ] | _____ | _____ |
| _____ | _____ | _____ | _____ | [   ] | _____ | _____ |
| _____ | _____ | _____ | _____ | [   ] | _____ | _____ |

    B. All Graduate or Professional Schools Attended/Planning to Attend (list in chronological order)

| _____ | _____ | _____ | ____ to ____ | [   ] | _____ |
|---|---|---|---|---|---|
| _____ | _____ | _____ | ____ to ____ | [   ] | _____ |
| _____ | _____ | _____ | ____ to ____ | [   ] | _____ |

13. Have you had any U.S. military experience?  Yes [   ]  No [   ]    Was your discharge dishonorable? Yes [   ] No [   ]

14. List employment in chronological order, beginning with your current position:

    Title or Description          Dates                    Level of Responsibility

    _____

    _____

    _____

                                                                            (continue on back)

*See instructions                        DO NOT TYPE OUTSIDE THE BORDER

                                        FOR OFFICE USE ONLY |__|__|__|__|__|

-2-

**ACADEMIC RECORD**

SSN |⎵⎵⎵⎵⎵⎵⎵⎵⎵|     2. Name _____

_last_                          _first_                          _middle_     _suffix_

| | College | Location | Year | Term | Number | Course Name | Type | Academic Status | Subject | Semester Hours | AACOMAS Grade | Actual Grade | AACOMAS Use | | |
|---|---|---|---|---|---|---|---|---|---|---|---|---|---|---|---|
| 1. | | | | | | | | | | | | | | | |
| 2. | | | | | | | | | | | | | | | |
| 3. | | | | | | | | | | | | | | | |
| 4. | | | | | | | | | | | | | | | |
| 5. | | | | | | | | | | | | | | | |
| 6. | | | | | | | | | | | | | | | |
| 7. | | | | | | | | | | | | | | | |
| 8. | | | | | | | | | | | | | | | |
| 9. | | | | | | | | | | | | | | | |
| 10. | | | | | | | | | | | | | | | |
| 11. | | | | | | | | | | | | | | | |
| 12. | | | | | | | | | | | | | | | |
| 13. | | | | | | | | | | | | | | | |
| 14. | | | | | | | | | | | | | | | |
| 15. | | | | | | | | | | | | | | | |
| 16. | | | | | | | | | | | | | | | |
| 17. | | | | | | | | | | | | | | | |
| 18. | | | | | | | | | | | | | | | |
| 19. | | | | | | | | | | | | | | | |
| 20. | | | | | | | | | | | | | | | |
| 21. | | | | | | | | | | | | | | | |
| 22. | | | | | | | | | | | | | | | |
| 23. | | | | | | | | | | | | | | | |
| 24. | | | | | | | | | | | | | | | |
| 25. | | | | | | | | | | | | | | | |
| 26. | | | | | | | | | | | | | | | |
| 27. | | | | | | | | | | | | | | | |
| 28. | | | | | | | | | | | | | | | |
| 29. | | | | | | | | | | | | | | | |
| 30. | | | | | | | | | | | | | | | |
| 31. | | | | | | | | | | | | | | | |
| 32. | | | | | | | | | | | | | | | |
| 33. | | | | | | | | | | | | | | | |
| 34. | | | | | | | | | | | | | | | |
| 35. | | | | | | | | | | | | | | | |
| 36. | | | | | | | | | | | | | | | |
| 37. | | | | | | | | | | | | | | | |
| 38. | | | | | | | | | | | | | | | |
| 39. | | | | | | | | | | | | | | | |
| 40. | | | | | | | | | | | | | | | |
| 41. | | | | | | | | | | | | | | | |
| 42. | | | | | | | | | | | | | | | |
| 43. | | | | | | | | | | | | | | | |
| 44. | | | | | | | | | | | | | | | |
| 45. | | | | | | | | | | | | | | | |
| 46. | | | | | | | | | | | | | | | |
| 47. | | | | | | | | | | | | | | | |
| 48. | | | | | | | | | | | | | | | |

*Subject code of "C" is not a valid code

DO NOT TYPE BELOW BORDER         FOR OFFICIAL USE ONLY _____

-3-

SSN |_|_|_|_|_|_|_|_|_|    2. Name _____

        last                    first                    middle    suffix

| | College | Location | Year | Term | Number | Course Name | Type | Academic Status | Subject | Semester Hours | AACOMAS Grade | Actual Grade | AACOMAS Use | |
|---|---|---|---|---|---|---|---|---|---|---|---|---|---|---|
| 49. | | | | | | | | | | | | | | |
| 50. | | | | | | | | | | | | | | |
| 51. | | | | | | | | | | | | | | |
| 52. | | | | | | | | | | | | | | |
| 53. | | | | | | | | | | | | | | |
| 54. | | | | | | | | | | | | | | |
| 55. | | | | | | | | | | | | | | |
| 56. | | | | | | | | | | | | | | |
| 57. | | | | | | | | | | | | | | |
| 58. | | | | | | | | | | | | | | |
| 59. | | | | | | | | | | | | | | |
| 60. | | | | | | | | | | | | | | |
| 61. | | | | | | | | | | | | | | |
| 62. | | | | | | | | | | | | | | |
| 63. | | | | | | | | | | | | | | |
| 64. | | | | | | | | | | | | | | |
| 65. | | | | | | | | | | | | | | |
| 66. | | | | | | | | | | | | | | |
| 67. | | | | | | | | | | | | | | |
| 68. | | | | | | | | | | | | | | |
| 69. | | | | | | | | | | | | | | |
| 70. | | | | | | | | | | | | | | |
| 71. | | | | | | | | | | | | | | |
| 72. | | | | | | | | | | | | | | |
| 73. | | | | | | | | | | | | | | |
| 74. | | | | | | | | | | | | | | |
| 75. | | | | | | | | | | | | | | |
| 76. | | | | | | | | | | | | | | |
| 77. | | | | | | | | | | | | | | |
| 78. | | | | | | | | | | | | | | |
| 79. | | | | | | | | | | | | | | |
| 80. | | | | | | | | | | | | | | |
| 81. | | | | | | | | | | | | | | |
| 82. | | | | | | | | | | | | | | |
| 83. | | | | | | | | | | | | | | |
| 84. | | | | | | | | | | | | | | |

*Subject code of "C" is not a valid code

List volunteer positions, internships, etc. (include dates): _____
_____
_____
_____
_____

List honors and/or awards if applicable: _____
_____
_____
_____
_____

| Test Scores | | | | |
|---|---|---|---|---|
| Date | Verbal | Phys Sci | Writing | Biology |
| | | | | |
| | | | | |
| | | | | |
| | | | | |
| | | | | |

How many times have you taken the MCAT test? ☐    If you plan to take or retake the MCAT — enter date. ☐ Mo. ☐ yr.

ACADEMIC RECORD

SSN |␣|␣|␣|␣|␣|␣|␣|␣|␣| Name_____
last                          first                          middle        suffix

| | College | Location | Year | Term | Number | Course Name | Type | Academic Status | Subject | Semester Hours | AACOMAS Grade | Actual Grade | AACOMAS Use | |
|---|---|---|---|---|---|---|---|---|---|---|---|---|---|---|
| 85. | | | | | | | | | | | | | | |
| 86. | | | | | | | | | | | | | | |
| 87. | | | | | | | | | | | | | | |
| 88. | | | | | | | | | | | | | | |
| 89. | | | | | | | | | | | | | | |
| 90. | | | | | | | | | | | | | | |
| 91. | | | | | | | | | | | | | | |
| 92. | | | | | | | | | | | | | | |
| 93. | | | | | | | | | | | | | | |
| 94. | | | | | | | | | | | | | | |
| 95. | | | | | | | | | | | | | | |
| 96. | | | | | | | | | | | | | | |
| 97. | | | | | | | | | | | | | | |
| 98. | | | | | | | | | | | | | | |
| 99. | | | | | | | | | | | | | | |
| 100. | | | | | | | | | | | | | | |
| 101. | | | | | | | | | | | | | | |
| 102. | | | | | | | | | | | | | | |
| 103. | | | | | | | | | | | | | | |
| 104. | | | | | | | | | | | | | | |
| 105. | | | | | | | | | | | | | | |
| 106. | | | | | | | | | | | | | | |
| 107. | | | | | | | | | | | | | | |
| 108. | | | | | | | | | | | | | | |
| 109. | | | | | | | | | | | | | | |
| 110. | | | | | | | | | | | | | | |
| 111. | | | | | | | | | | | | | | |
| 112. | | | | | | | | | | | | | | |
| 113. | | | | | | | | | | | | | | |
| 114. | | | | | | | | | | | | | | |
| 115. | | | | | | | | | | | | | | |
| 116. | | | | | | | | | | | | | | |
| 117. | | | | | | | | | | | | | | |
| 118. | | | | | | | | | | | | | | |
| 119. | | | | | | | | | | | | | | |
| 120. | | | | | | | | | | | | | | |
| 121. | | | | | | | | | | | | | | |
| 122. | | | | | | | | | | | | | | |
| 123. | | | | | | | | | | | | | | |
| 124. | | | | | | | | | | | | | | |
| 125. | | | | | | | | | | | | | | |
| 126. | | | | | | | | | | | | | | |
| 127. | | | | | | | | | | | | | | |
| 128. | | | | | | | | | | | | | | |
| 129. | | | | | | | | | | | | | | |
| 130. | | | | | | | | | | | | | | |
| 131. | | | | | | | | | | | | | | |
| 132. | | | | | | | | | | | | | | |
| 133. | | | | | | | | | | | | | | |

DO NOT TYPE BELOW BORDER

PROFESSIONAL SCHOOL ACADEMIC RECORD

SSN |_|_|_|_|_|_|_|_|_|    2. Name_____
                                        *last*                    *first*                    *middle*        *suffix*

Indicate the grading or evaluation system used by your school:

_____

| COLLEGE | LOCATION | YEAR | TERM | COURSE NAME | NUMBER | GRADE | AACOMAS Use |
|---|---|---|---|---|---|---|---|
| | | | | | | | |
| | | | | | | | |
| | | | | | | | |
| | | | | | | | |
| | | | | | | | |
| | | | | | | | |
| | | | | | | | |
| | | | | | | | |
| | | | | | | | |
| | | | | | | | |
| | | | | | | | |
| | | | | | | | |
| | | | | | | | |
| | | | | | | | |
| | | | | | | | |
| | | | | | | | |
| | | | | | | | |
| | | | | | | | |
| | | | | | | | |
| | | | | | | | |
| | | | | | | | |
| | | | | | | | |
| | | | | | | | |
| | | | | | | | |
| | | | | | | | |
| | | | | | | | |
| | | | | | | | |
| | | | | | | | |
| | | | | | | | |
| | | | | | | | |
| | | | | | | | |
| | | | | | | | |
| | | | | | | | |
| | | | | | | | |
| | | | | | | | |
| | | | | | | | |
| | | | | | | | |
| | | | | | | | |

DO NOT TYPE BELOW BORDER

**ACADEMIC RECORD**

SSN |__|__|__|__|__|__|__|__|__|  2. Name_____
                         *last*               *first*             *middle*   *suffix*

| College | Location | Year | Term | Number | Course Name | Type | Academic Status | Subject | Semester Hours | AACOMAS Grade | Actual Grade | AACOMAS Use | | |
|---------|----------|------|------|--------|-------------|------|-----------------|---------|----------------|--------------|--------------|---|---|---|
| | | | | | | | | | | | | | | |
| | | | | | | | | | | | | | | |
| | | | | | | | | | | | | | | |
| | | | | | | | | | | | | | | |
| | | | | | | | | | | | | | | |
| | | | | | | | | | | | | | | |
| | | | | | | | | | | | | | | |
| | | | | | | | | | | | | | | |
| | | | | | | | | | | | | | | |
| | | | | | | | | | | | | | | |
| | | | | | | | | | | | | | | |
| | | | | | | | | | | | | | | |

DO NOT TYPE BELOW BORDER

14.  Employment (continued)
     Title or Description                    Dates                           Level of Responsibility

_____

_____

_____

| It is imperative you answer # 15-19. If # 16-18 are "yes," # 19 is "F," or # 21 is "31-33" explain in Personal Comments |
| --- |

15.  Have you ever matriculated in or attended any medical school as a candidate for the M.D. or D.O. degree?      Yes [  ]   No [  ]

16.  Were you ever the recipient of <u>any</u> action for unacceptable academic performance (e.g. academic probation, dismissal, suspension, disqualification, etc.) <u>or</u> were you ever the recipient of any action for conduct violations (e.g. probation, suspension, dismissal, etc.) by any college or school? See instructions. . . . . . . . . . . . . . . . . . . . . . . . . . . . . . . . Yes [  ]   No [  ]

     If yes, were you ever denied readmission?          Yes [  ]       No [  ]

17.  Have you ever been convicted of a misdemeanor or felony (exclude parking violation)? . . . . . . . . . . . . . . . . . . . Yes [  ]   No [  ]
     If you have a pending misdemeanor or felony, which results in a conviction, it is your responsibility to immediately inform a college of osteopathic medicine if you matriculate to that college

18.  Is a family member a D.O. or M.D.? (If yes, list up to three codes from the instructions) . . . . . . . . . . . . . Yes [  ] [  ] [  ]   No [  ]

19.  How did you first learn about osteopathic medicine? (choose only one, see instructions) . . . . . . . . . . . . . . . . . . . . . . .   [  ]

20.  Have you ever met with an osteopathic college or AACOM representative? (choose only one, see instructions) . . . . . . . .   [  ]

21.  Do you consider yourself disadvantaged? (see instructions for definition and codes). . . . . . . . . . . . . . . . . . . . . . . . . . . .   [  ]

22.  Which choice best describes your prior career/experience? (see instructions for definition and codes). . . . . . . . . . . . . .   [  ]

_PERSONAL COMMENTS/PERSONAL STATEMENT (see AACOMAS Application instructions before completing)_

\
\
\
\
\
\
\
\
\
\
\
\
\
\
\
\
\
\
\
\
\
\

_____

I authorize AACOMAS to release the following information to pre-professional health advisors to assist those advisors in counseling students: my name, the osteopathic medical school at which I matriculate; my state or country of legal residence, as stated in my application materials; my undergraduate institution; and degree date from that institution . . . . . . . . . . . . . . . . . . . . . . . . . . . . . . . . . . Yes [  ]   No [  ]

I have read and understand the instructions and other information in the AACOMAS Instruction Booklet, and consent to release of information provided or otherwise obtained in the course of the application process to the Colleges of Osteopathic Medicine (in the case of AACOMAS Reports, also with the AAMC). I certify that the information submitted in these application materials is complete and correct to the best of my knowledge. I agree that this information may be used by AACOM, its member institutions, and related health organizations for research and development purposes aimed at improving osteopathic medical education and admissions programs.

Date _____   Signature _____

# APPENDIX C

## SAMPLE ESSAYS FOR AMCAS APPLICATION

Most U.S. medical and osteopathic schools make use of the application services, AMCAS and AACOMAS, respectively. The major component of the application used by these services, as well as the dental service (AADSAS), is the blank page allotted for a personal statement or essay (see Chapter 6). This is a valuable opportunity that can impact very significantly on one's admission potential. Appendix C contains 25 sample conventional essays. These, like the two presented in Chapter 6, were written by applicants seeking admission to professional schools. (To avoid any possibility of identifying the writers of these essays, specific names are not used.) These essays are included to give a prospective applicant an insight into the different approaches that can be used. Some are general essays covering personal characteristics, education, relevant experience, and motivation. Other essays are more focused on aspects of the applicant's background. These essays should provide helpful ideas on how to approach the important part of the application process—the essay.

At this point it is useful to summarize the essential elements to be considered when drafting your essay. (Relevant comments on essay writing can also be found in Chapters 2 and 6.)

1. Your essay is very important, as it may determine whether you will be invited for an interview.

2. Your essay can influence interviewers in provided them with a view of you to compare with their idealized image of a prospective compassionate and committed physician.

3. Your efforts in preparing the essay should focus on being self-descriptive and creative, so as to generate an appealing view of your prospects as a medical student, resident, and physician.

4. In drafting your essay be concerned with both the message and writing style. These two elements are linked in producing an impact on the reader.

5. Admissions personnel assume you will have your essay proofread by others, so don't hesitate to do so.

6. Aim to snare the reader's attention with an opening that will engender strong interest in what lies ahead.

7. Remember that a memorable essay will remain in the reader's mind and will influence the discussion of your candidacy as the admissions committee reviews your application.

8. A strong effort should be made to have a central theme that ties up the various elements you present. Avoid simply presenting disconnected statements regarding your past activities. Note that a very common central theme is what motivates you to become a physician.

9. Try to make your essay stand out by highlighting *unique* achievements, experiences, and/or meaningful views on relevant topics.

10. The essay should serve as a device for personal expression rather than a catalog of facts about yourself, which can be indicated elsewhere in the application.

11. When you review your essay, and when you ask others to do so, seek to avoid remarks or statements that suggest that you are egotistical or apologetic. Rather, be sure you have expressed yourself in a confident manner.

12. Feel free to utilize the allotted space to the extent you think is necessary to get your message across.

*Essay 1*

I have elected to apply to medical school because I believe that this unique profession will provide me with a lifetime of personal satisfaction. Moreover, I am convinced that I possess the basic attributes that are essential for those who seek to enter this demanding field. I know that I have the intellectual potential, especially in the sciences, as well as the temperament and drive necessary to meet the challenge that the lifelong study of medicine requires.

I enrolled at _____ University after successfully completing a demanding high school (graduating eighth of 85). I chose _____ because of its reputation for providing both a well-rounded education and a strong science background. I elected to major in general science to obtain the broad base of knowledge that would serve as a solid foundation for my future professional school studies. Aside from the required premedical curriculum, I have taken courses ranging from astronomy to computers, with a concentration in the biological sciences. My educational goal was not grade-oriented, but directed to securing the best grasp of the material. I feel that my academic average, while satisfactory, does not accurately reflect my academic potential, which I feel is significantly higher. I also sought an education that would incorporate non-science courses to the extent possible and I participated in a wide variety of extracurricular activities.

I am patient, self-disciplined, and caring. I like to accept a challenge and I then apply my talents to successfully achieve the realistic goals I set. In the field of experimental medicine, I spent two summers at _____ Hospital. I was engaged in research projects concerned with drug blood levels using various analytical tools, and also did a time-action study to determine the feasibility of laboratory computerization. In my free time, I organized my own band and succeeded in winning several talent contests, as well as being hired to play at a variety of social affairs. Both of these efforts involved assuming responsibilities, demonstrating initiative and leadership capacity, and having good interpersonal ability.

My hospital experience served to convince me of the genuineness of my feeling of empathy for those in need of healing or relief from pain. It also convinced me of the need to keep the patient in proper focus, since technological advances, although most valuable, can tend to impede the establishment of good physician-patient relationships.

While I am not certain at this time in what area of medicine I will find my place, I believe my talents will enable me to contribute to the welfare of those I will serve. I sincerely hope I will be granted the opportunity to pursue my professional goals.

*Essay 2*

My career goal to become a physician is long-standing and deep-rooted. Two of the major drives to attain my professional goal include a broad educational involvement and interest in the sciences and a unique set of life experiences over the past five years that have crystallized my aspirations.

Supplementing this application are transcripts reflecting my scientific exposure. However, what is most significant regarding my career decision is my personal experience. Always athletic, I sustained a sports-related accident at the age of seventeen, and became a patient in a hospital, where surgery and several months of rehabilitation were required. My complete recovery was due to the medical expertise and compassion of my physician, and the patience and support of my physical therapist. I learned a great deal, not only about my medical condition in particular, but also about being a patient and how important an understanding physician is to the healing process. Since then, I have developed a firm conviction that those practicing the healing arts not only restore the body, but give people hope to overcome many of the hardships related to illness.

Due to my experience as a patient, I was removed from familiar surroundings and forced to contend with difficult situations. At nineteen, I again found myself in an unfamiliar setting. This time, it was for a year and a half of college studies overseas. Relocating to a foreign country for an extended period had a strong impact on my individual growth and helped develop my sense of identity and responsibility. I improved my capacity to cope with change, the unknown, and multicultural environments. The ability to adapt, to overcome adversity, and to welcome new and formidable tasks, are skills I will bring with me to the medical profession.

During my college studies abroad, I was fortunate to have a premedical placement in a local hospital. There, I was exposed to the unpredictable and challenging activities of an emergency room. In addition, my school provided me with a type of "settlement house" placement, working with underprivileged, immigrant children. These placements allowed me to learn more about the interrelationship between poverty and the poor utilization of health service.

A constant source of inspiration has come from living in a cohesive, civic-minded community with numerous practicing physicians. I have been impressed with the communal and charitable roles played by the physicians my family knows. Several of these physicians have been especially supportive in my pursuits and have become role models whom I would hope to emulate in the future.

The attainment of a black belt from a prestigious karate school is among the many skills that I have mastered. To achieve this required many years of study, practice, and commitment to a discipline. Training others to master the art of self-defense, while teaching them diligence and perseverance, has solidified these qualities within myself.

My cumulative college index for my studies both in the United States and abroad was 3.9, demonstrating my ability to be scholastically consistent and outstanding in varied academic settings. Throughout my college years, I have been involved in numerous communication arts and educational seminars, such as: Dramatic Society, Speech Club, and preparing instructional/cultural workshops for high school and college students. Upon graduation from college this past June, I accepted a position furnishing outreach services to the homebound elderly. I also plan to take graduate courses in medical ethics.

To me, medicine is unique for its restorative potentials made possible through a combination of advanced technologies and human compassion. I am deeply committed to seeking a career in medicine, and believe that I have the capabilities to succeed.

*Essay 3*

"Please doctor help me!" an elderly woman called out anxiously, while lying on a stretcher in the emergency room at _____ Hospital. "I am not yet a doctor; just try to relax and I will get help right away," I responded.

Before my hospital exposure as a volunteer in the emergency room, I was attracted to a medical career because of the intellectual life that it offers. This appeal was stimulated by my long-standing insatiable scientific curiosity. I m strongly motivated to learn about science in general and medicine in particular. My academic record demonstrates that I have an ability to meet the demanding chal lenges that medical school presents. My GPA rose rapidly from 2.98, which I received in my first semester of freshman year, to the 3.48 that I have now (which includes the 3.93 that I received in the first semester of junior year). I anticipate that I will apply to medical school with a GPA that will exceed 3.50.

A physician needs a great deal more than academic competence. With the enor-mous advances in recent years in diagnostic technology, the patient is no longer the spokesman for his or her body. Although diseases can be detected earlier and there-fore treated more effectively as a result of advances in modern medicine, there has been a tendency for the physician to become more impersonal. I believe the greatest challenge facing a medical practitioner today is to develop an approach that will prevent technology from coming between himself or herself and the patient. Lewis Thomas, in his book, *The Youngest Science,* writes, "Doctors the critics say, are applied scientists, concerned only with the disease at hand but never with the patient as an individual, whole person." If this is true it is quite disturbing because I feel that a good doctor-patient rapport can have a positive impact on a patient's treatment and recovery. A physician must be a confidant, gaining the trust of those he or she is treating. I would seek to utilize the tools of modern medicine to supple-ment, but not replace, an empathizing approach to human suffering and anxiety.

The issue that I am concerned about in the future is how I will react to the ethi-cal challenges that face a medical practitioner today. I am especially interested in the discipline of medical ethics, and I am pleased to see that the subject has been included in the medical school curriculum. I am confident that further training in this area will prepare me to meet these challenges.

One reason why I want a career in medicine is that, as a physician, I will be able to provide care for those who need it. When the elderly woman in the emergency room at _____ Hospital cried for help, I had a strong desire to alleviate her suffering. Considering my innate love of science and my academic achievements in college, I am confident that I will succeed and become a credit to the medical profession.

*Essay 4*

Contemplating what the future holds for a prospective physician in the twenty-first century would suggest the probability of changes in the practice of medicine. While medicine will continue to make significant advances, increased government regulation will impose bureaucratic hardships and technological breakthroughs will increase the pressures toward depersonalization of medical practice. Prospective physicians (as myself) will, therefore, be required to possess the innate personal characteristics that will enable us to accept a sense of gratification for services rendered as a significant measure of compensation for the difficulties that we will have to accept.

In the limited free time available to me, I involved myself in various communal and charitable endeavors, which brought me into contact with the youth and elderly, infirm, indigent, and handicapped. I not only served personally but was motivated to stimulate others to do so and thereby helped improve the life of those less fortunate than myself. By being a service-oriented individual, I hope that my years as a physician will allow me to alleviate the pain of my fellow man and offer the ailing comfort and support during their trying times.

Medicine also offers its professionals a chance to unravel the mysteries of the human being. Its focus on man as a primary subject of study has long intrigued me and it will undoubtedly continue to grant me intellectual stimulation in future years. A summer of research experience in an honors program, an intense emergency medical training course, and acting as a volunteer in the Emergency Room of a local hospital have sparked my interests, and I look forward to contributing my own insights and skills to this ever progressing science.

As a health-care professional entrusted with life and death decisions, a physician must possess the highest intellectual capabilities. My academic career has been characterized by superlatives, and I am confident that this pattern will continue. My selection as salutatorian of my elementary school class and valedictorian of my high school class (with the simultaneous reception of a Governor's Scholarship Award) confirmed that I had the capabilities for superior academic achievement. Excelling in my scholastic studies during my college career in both the science and nonscience courses has reinforced this conviction.

Medicine is both the art and science of healing. As my extracurricular activities and scholastic achievements indicate, I realize the vital importance of both aspects. My background and education have instilled in me the ethical concepts and sense of dedication that the medical professional demands. By becoming a physician qualified to practice in the twenty-first century, I will be afforded the privilege of sharing in the effort to improve the quality of life of my fellow human beings and, simultaneously, the quality of my own life will be more meaningful.

*Essay 5*

While at Yale I have become interested in a career in medicine through my studies and extracurricular activities. Before coming to college I was interested in science and was considering a career in scientific research. In the last three years my attention has become focused on medicine, as I feel this profession offers the best opportunity to pursue my interests in a way that will be beneficial and useful to others.

For three years I have worked in the astronomy department on a variety of research projects. I helped compile the most recent versions of the Yale Bright Star Catalogue and the Yale Parallax Catalogue. These projects allowed me to get a taste of scientific research. Although I learned much from this experience and enjoyed working with the other astronomers, I believe that my abilities would be more usefully applied in some other way.

Medicine first attracted me because it requires a knowledge of several sciences, whereas most fields require (or encourage) knowledge of only one. In my senior research essay I will publish the results of an epidemiological investigation into correlations between high population density and certain pathologies among bacteria, laboratory rats, and humans. The data has been collected from experiments at Yale's Osborn Biology facility and from the Social Science Archives at Yale Computer Center. I hope to have this paper published in both biology and sociology journals.

My major involves sixteen courses, eight from sociology and eight from biology. Of course, in addition to these I have taken the required chemistry, physics, mathematics, and English. I have become especially interested in molecular biology, and now have a small library of books on this subject.

One of the most interesting experiences of the past three years was working in the emergency room of _____ Hospital in _____. I was part of the College Aide Program, which provided Yale students with an opportunity to observe hospital practices in return for volunteer work. I spent about half of my time in the emergency room in the medical and surgical trauma areas helping with suturing procedures, EKGs, IVs, and blood gases. The rest of my time was spent in the labs, helping with routine blood analysis. The shifts were four hours at a time, which was one-third of what many of the physicians worked, yet were still plenty tiring! However, I was so interested in what was happening that the time seemed to pass quickly. I gained a lot of respect and admiration for the doctors who had to deal with the great responsibility and pressure inherent to their profession, and decided that someday I would like to become one of them.

I have always been interested in issues of medical significance and was one of three student speakers (along with a number of academic figures) to make a presentation at the 1990 Bioethics Conference at _____. My talk was on the ethics of genetic engineering, a topic that is still a matter of controversy. At the time I was a freshman at Yale, and our biology department had just announced the results of some startling experiments with mouse embryos that had been genetically engineered.

All of these experiences have convinced me that medicine is an exciting field in which I believe I could make a worthwhile contribution while simultaneously gaining the personal satisfaction that accompanies such an important profession.

### Essay 6

My decision to apply to medical school is a result of considerable preparation and thought, an evaluation of my own abilities, and some experience in the health field.

Among the attributes I believe a physician should possess are dedication, sincerity, and integrity. I believe that my peers consider me to have such qualities and I trust that these qualities should contribute to my professional success.

I've progressed through high school and college, both of which had demanding programs of study, and achieved superior grades. I always found science courses to be of special interest.

My decision to pursue a medical career stems from several motivating factors. Foremost, I have come to appreciate the inherent intellectual and emotional challenges involved in medicine during my research at _____ Hospital. While there I was involved in a research project dealing with the role of Ketoconazole in the treatment of fungal infections. This experience enabled me to directly view the clinical application of research. I have also been exposed to the emotional side of practicing medicine by participating in daily rounds and observing the patients' progress with physicians and other members of the research team. This activity was instrumental in allowing me to appreciate the vital role played by the physician in helping the patient emotionally as well as physically. As a member of this team, I used this opportunity to establish relationships by offering daily encouragement and explanations whenever possible. This unique medical exposure afforded me the opportunity of obtaining both intellectual and emotional satisfaction in a medical context.

The satisfactions derived from challenging intellectual and emotional pursuits have always motivated me to excel. This is underscored by my success as a youth leader in my church and as a coordinator of a blood drive for my school. My duties in the church involve weekly preparation of a portion of the Bible for presentation to the congregation. This entails approximately ten hours per week of preparation and requires a thorough understanding as well as memorization of the lengthy passages. Although extremely demanding of my time and concentration, the rewards of leadership and performing a job well make this task worth undertaking. I anticipate that this congregational leadership role will help me assume responsibilities as an active layman in my community later in my life.

As a coordinator of my school's blood drive, my major responsibility was donor recruitment. This entailed my allaying the fears of prospective donors and arranging all logistical aspects of the drive. My determination and hard work were rewarded by the outstanding achievement of the drive, as noted by the Red Cross for being the most successful drive in New York City.

I am well aware of the physical and emotional difficulties as well as the dedication required in a medical career. This realization has become evident to me through my close relationship with my brother-in-law who is currently a physician in postgraduate training. The demands and responsibilities of his work have often been communicated to me. The challenges and rewards however, are the factors that stand out as providing adequate compensation. I am confident that my personal attributes, coupled with my motivation refined through my various exposure to medicine, will lead me to a satisfying and fruitful career. I feel that I have already proved to myself that, when motivated, I can succeed at a challenging task. It is with this positive attitude that I seek to embark upon a medical career.

*Essay 7*

To the members of the Admission Committee:

I am applying for admission to your school with the aim of securing my M.D. degree as a basis for an eventual career in academic medicine. It is my goal to devote my professional activities to clinical practice, teaching, and research. This career goal evolved naturally during my adolescence, as well as during my college and graduate school studies.

I received my elementary school education at a small private school, where my initial interest in science developed. This interest was enhanced due to my close relationship with a cousin who was a medical technologist. By the time I was in my early teens, I had spent part of each summer in her hospital's laboratory observing the routine and being briefed in terms that were understandable. I became increasingly enthusiastic with my medical science exposure. Gradually, my horizons were expanded when I was fortunate to have the opportunity to observe the activities of the chief pathologist. I not only viewed specimen preparation procedures, but was given explanations of the clinical findings on both gross and microscopic levels. By the end of my freshman year of college, I had observed my first autopsy. Once I had this meaningful exposure, the stimulus to seek a medical career took on a self-propelling dimension. I realized how interesting and challenging the profession was and that it offered the satisfying opportunity to improve the quality of life of those I would have the opportunity to treat.

To attain my goal, I enrolled in a program of science and non-science studies at _____ College, and later, _____ University, where I elected to major in biology. As an upperclassman, I enrolled in some graduate level courses, took part in research, and wrote an honors thesis. I was the second person in the history of the Biology Department to graduate with departmental honors as well as summa cum laude.

My successful research activities, although exciting by themselves, stimulated my interest in a career in academic medicine. Because of the intimate student-graduate student-faculty relationships existing at my school, teaching came into the picture as part of my potential career activities. To further my ambition, I enrolled in our Masters Program and was offered a teaching assistantship. My graduate research so far has resulted in one paper (to be published shortly), another paper in preparation, and hopefully one commercial product. My successful teaching activities have covered a wide variety of undergraduate laboratory courses.

My academic achievements both as an undergraduate and graduate student have been consistently superior except for my sophomore year in college. At that time I was extremely preoccupied with my father's health, which was deteriorating because of emphysema. However, I gained a great deal of career inspiration from the dedicated team of medical personnel who pulled him through. Omitting this unrepresentative year, therefore, my cumulative average would be 3.76 (instead of 3.61), which is consistent with my 3.85 graduate school record.

In conclusion, I am convinced that I have the maturity, interest, and ability to undertake medical studies with a sense of enthusiasm and dedication. I hope you will afford me the opportunity to do so.

## *Essay 8*

One might assume that since my father and grandfather are both physicians, the decision that I too must be a doctor would have been unquestioned. This may be true in many cases but the situation was quite the opposite for me. My decision to enter the medical profession is solely my own, made after a very prolonged period of introspection and soul-searching. My family did not seek to pressure me, but rather helped me to have a well-balanced view of this challenging profession. What I saw was the selfless dedication of my father to his family practice in a low-income area in central New Jersey. His major reward is, for the most part, the satisfaction of providing quality health care to the community he serves, which has always involved a great deal of physical and emotional commitment and self-sacrifice. Therefore, my decision is based not on an idealistic view but a very realistic one of the rewards that a medical career has to offer.

I have always had a great interest in farming. The idea of producing something with my own hands, managing my own affairs, and being my own boss has always meant a great deal to me. As a result, for the past six years I have been operating my own vegetable farm and produce stand. All the vegetables I sell I have grown myself. I have been careful to avoid treating my crops with pesticides and harmful chemicals. I found it especially enjoyable to deal directly with people and I related well to them to the point of building a sizable, steady clientele. In my work I have grown very found of the countryside and I enjoy working in a rural setting.

My love for plants and the soil contributed to my decision to major in biology at my college. After three years of undergraduate work I have found that the more I study biology, the more enthusiastic I become about the subject. This is reflected in my consistent A average in all my biology courses. My less than impressive overall performance during the first two years of college stems from my delay in firmly fixing my career goal until the end of sophomore year. As a result, I did not mobilize all of my intellectual resources toward achieving a strong academic record; however, once I made up my mind about my future, I began to demonstrate that I possess the necessary potential to meet the demands of medical school. I trust that my willingness to undertake the uphill journey to a medical career—although belatedly—will reflect favorably upon the genuineness of my commitment and the sincerity of my motivation. I am convinced that I can succeed in making a significant contribution to the well-being of the people I hope to serve.

After much though, I find that my fundamental reason for wanting to become a physician is simple: I want to establish a family practice in a rural area where dedicated physicians are sorely needed. I realize that the goal I have set may not, in the light of my initial college record, be easily attained. Nevertheless, I firmly believe that when my full record of achievement is reviewed, and the special circumstances discussed above are taken into consideration, I will merit the confidence of being offered a place in your freshman class.

## *Essay 9*

"Mad Scientist" is the name my mother has affectionately called me since childhood. Even as a youngster, my favorite place was my father's laboratory in his medical office. On Sunday afternoons my father would take my four younger brothers and me to his office where we would spend hours viewing slides and "experimenting." It was in this lab that I developed my sense of curiosity, my love of science, and a spirit of adventure.

When I was 17 I left home and spent two years studying and traveling abroad. The experience of living 6,000 miles away from home in a milieu so different from my own provided me with a much broader view of the wide variety of existing culture. The most intriguing aspect of those years was the diversity of personalities I encountered. Among my classmates were natives of Yemen, Iran, England, and France. Every meal we shared resembled a model United Nations with students from many countries expressing varying opinions. I learned to relate to and understand people with whom I seemingly had little in common, and developed close and lasting friendships with them. This unique exposure will undoubtedly prove valuable to me in the years ahead in dealing with people as their physician.

I returned from overseas to pursue my educational and premedical career goals. I selected _____ University because of its academic excellence.

I worked with youth programs organized by the university and was recently appointed to head an educational program for high school students. I was also elected Senior Editor of the student newspaper. This position required an ability to express myself creatively in writing. It also required learning to work with a team while assuming a leadership role.

My summer experiences were an outgrowth of my scientific interests. I worked for a radiologist where I learned about human anatomy, about the fascinating methods now available through modern technology, and how to secure invaluable clinical information. I worked during the same summer with Dr. H., Director of the Rheumatic Diseases laboratory at _____ College of Medicine, studying the immunopathological process involved in cartilage erosion. The following summer I worked with Dr. S. of the Cardiology Department of the Medical School studying the microcirculation of the rat's coronary artery system. This laboratory work introduced me to such divergent procedures as gel electrophoresis and animal surgery and gave me a great respect for scientific inquiry. I am continuing my work with Dr. S. this summer, studying the effects of calcium channel blockers on the inotropy of the rat's myocardium.

All of my experiences mentioned above affected my career choice, and medicine offers a vast array of intellectual challenges. The coming decades will witness a continuation of the exciting technological revolution. I hope to be a part of this creative adventure. At the same time, medicine offers the ultimate in one's service to humanity. There is no greater pleasure than the ability to use one's intellect and abilities to alleviate human pain and suffering.

If accepted, I believe I will be an asset to your freshman class.

## Essay 10

The gratification that I receive from working with and caring for others has been the major motivation behind my desire to become a doctor. My experience growing up as an only child has had much to do with my reaching out toward others, as I often felt isolated as a result of my parents' difficulty understanding English. When I show concern for another person it is because I know how important it can be to have someone show sincere interest and caring.

I have always been interested in serving the needs of others. At my school I was vice-president of a community service organization. I enjoyed working with those who shared the same interest. Some of my best experiences were working with concerned students on blood drives and fund-raisings. A particularly memorable experience was acting as co-chairman of the school's annual Muscular Dystrophy Marathon.

It is difficult to adequately describe the feelings I experience when my caring is rewarded with something as simple as being depended on and being considered a source of comfort. At the local hospital I formed a special relationship with a young patient suffering from multiple sclerosis. I spent many hours in her company, helping to feed her, and talking to her. More recently, I worked with a dedicated staff at another hospital, gift-wrapping hundreds of holiday presents for patients.

My earlier experiences influenced my decision to work this past year as an assistant in oral surgery, where I found great satisfaction comforting and relaxing patients before an operative procedure.

My interest in science has made becoming a doctor an ideal choice. I can remember very vividly the experience of seeing my mother admitted to a hospital because of a problem with her lungs. Before a diagnosis was reached, I wanted to know what was at stake and read all that I could about tuberculosis and cancer. (It turned out to be emphysema and she was successfully treated.) Several years later, this desire to learn about medicine was strongly reinforced as I sat totally absorbed watching open heart surgery. Another situation that has left a very strong impression occurred while I was a volunteer at the hospital's emergency room. I watched doctors and nurses working together under intense time pressure as they attempted to save an elderly man who had been hit by a truck. As I observed them, I could visualize myself being a part of their efforts to sustain life.

My firm commitment to my career goal has strengthened my determination during difficult periods. There were times when my ability to study effectively was disrupted by financial problems, illness, and a less than ideal living situation. In order to avoid a long commute, I often resorted to sleeping nights on dormitory floors and library couches.

Becoming a doctor is an extension of my interest in science and of my desire to lead a life that I consider all-absorbing. I strongly desire a career that involves a total commitment to learning and a responsibility for the welfare of others. The more lives I touch as a doctor, the more meaningful I feel my life becomes. Therefore, I would value the opportunity to pursue my studies at your institution.

## *Essay 11*

My mother was born in what was then the Soviet Union and my father in Poland into an upper middle-class family. They both received advanced education for their time, my father graduating from a university as an engineer and my mother attending a junior college (gimnasium). World War II drastically interrupted their lives and they fled from Poland to the Soviet Union. My father was deported to Siberia, where he managed to survive because of his skills as an engineer. Because he was of service to the government in helping manage a factory in support of the war effort, he was eventually allowed to leave Siberia. He remained in the Soviet Union with my mother where he established himself and they looked forward to a productive life for themselves and their children. As I will relate, things did not work out as planned.

I was born in Moscow, the capital of what is now known as Russia. I received my elementary and high school eduction there and did very well. I always wanted to become a physician. At the age of 17, I was faced with a critical problem that was to drastically alter the course of my life. Then I was eligible to apply for admission to medical school. Naturally, I was very excited. Unfortunately, in spite of my attractive credentials, I was rejected. Subsequently, I learned that the reason for being denied admission was my religion. I thought that this was the end of my dream, since no other option existed for me in Russia to become a physician.

Seeing the extent of my determination, my parents and I realized that the only way to achieve my goal was to emigrate to the United States. We applied for an emigration visa to come to this country. Consequently, this created a multitude of personal hardships for us. After a considerable waiting period, we arrived in America and settled in Seattle. We had very little funds, no knowledge of the English language, and hardly any friends. My father, despite being an engineer by profession, was forced to work as a plumber, while I began each day working before dawn unloading vegetable and fruit trucks. Life was a very hard struggle, but what sustained us was my dream of becoming a physician, since we knew that America was a land of opportunity.

Within a year of my arrival, after attending night school to learn English, I enrolled as a premedical student in college and worked as a volunteer at a local hospital. My academic studies progressed well and I was able to demonstrate my talents in the sciences, especially biology. My hospital work helped me gain extensive contact with patients, doctors, nurses, and administrators. I found that I was able to relate well with each group.

My volunteer work also exposed me to the integral elements of a hospital environment, namely, healing, recovery, suffering, and death. In addition, I was fortunate in having an opportunity to see a variety of surgical procedures and observe the positive impact of good doctor-patient relations. Similarly, I observed the importance of positive interaction between the physician and house staff with ancillary professionals. My broad experience at the hospital, coupled with my academic success as a premedical student, have reinforced my determination to become a physician. Having faced many challenges and overcome numerous obstacles, I believe I am well prepared for the next decisive step in may career, that is, entering medical school. After becoming a well-trained medical doctor, I hope to use my skills to repay my debt of gratitude to this unique country for the opportunities it has granted me.

*Essay 12*

During the freshman and sophomore years at my university, I worked at the city medical center as a physical therapy assistant on a voluntary, part-time basis. In the course of this experience, the most important conversation, relevant to my career goal, was with a nurse. She was exceptionally friendly and a competent professional. During a conversation, I took the liberty of asking her why she had elected to become a nurse rather than a doctor. She replied, "A physician makes a lifetime commitment to medicine; his or her profession must be his or her first priority. However, I wasn't willing to have my profession dominate my life." Her response did not surprise me; rather, it served to reinforce my lifelong commitment to a profession in which I already had become actively associated.

For the next summer, I chose a position that would provide me with a new perspective on medicine. Upon returning home, I began working in the Department of Radiology at the local medical center. My activities were concentrated in the Special Procedures Division, where one of my duties involved assisting the nurses in preparing the patient and the room for scheduled tests. I observed procedures that usually consisted of angiograms, venograms, or percutaneous nephrostomies. I was provided with a detailed explanation in the course of the procedure that was both informative and educational. At the conclusion of each procedure, I paid careful attention as the radiologist read the X-rays, and learned about patient problems and their required treatments. The staff, after getting to know me, encouraged me to spend time with apprehensive patients to try to alleviate some of their anxieties and to be generally supportive. In addition, for one hour each day, I attended class with the interns. There I was introduced to radiological anatomy, interpreting some nuances of complicated X-rays, and listening to discussions of interesting cases.

My experiences at the medical center were so stimulating that I applied for placement for the following summer, and I had the good fortune to be accepted.

The next June I began to work as a research assistant for a prominent surgeon. The investigation concerned the reliability of the criteria for the diagnosis of appendicitis. The justification for this project is the problematic nature of diagnoses as evidenced by the significant negative laparotomy rate. The aim of this study was to assess the feasibility of increasing diagnostic accuracy. A large part of my activities involved using the hospital computer to retrieve, study, and evaluate appropriate patient charts in order to enlarge the statistical sample. My work has made me more appreciative of the importance of medical research. It also showed me how some physicians combine their practice with clinical research.

Reading an article entitled "The Ordeal: Life as a Medical Resident" in the *New York Times Magazine* enhanced my awareness of the strong commitment a physician must make to his or her profession. Unlike the aforementioned nurse, I have been impressed by many doctors with whom I came in contact who were leading rich and rewarding personal lives as well as being totally dedicated to medicine.

Besides a sense of dedication, I am aware that appropriate academic ability is needed to meet the intense demands of medical school and postgraduate training. I elected to attend my university because it is an excellent institution of higher education. I also wanted to be on my own in order to develop the self-confidence necessary to manage my life independently. My academic performance as well as science cumulative average and MCAT scores confirm my ability to handle the rigorous requirements of the basic medical sciences. In the light of both my clinical exposure and educational preparation, I feel confident that I will be prepared for the many challenges of medical education, training, and practice. I look forward to undertaking this unique and exciting adventure.

*Essay 13*

I have elected to apply to medical school because I believe that this unique profession will provide me with a lifetime of personal satisfaction. I am convinced that I possess the basic attributes that are essential for anyone seeking to enter this demanding field. I know that I have the intellectual potential, especially in the sciences, as well as the temperament and drive necessary to meet the many unusual challenges that medicine presents.

I enrolled for my premedical studies at my university after successfully completing four years at a very competitive high school (graduating eighth of 85). I chose this university because of its reputation for providing both a well-rounded education and a strong science background. I elected to major in general science to obtain the broad base of knowledge that would serve as a solid foundation for my future professional studies. Therefore, aside from the required premedical curriculum, I have taken courses ranging from astronomy to computers, with a concentration in the biological sciences. My educational goal was not grade-oriented; rather, it was directed toward securing the best grasp of the material. Therefore, I feel that my academic average, while satisfactory, does not fully reflect my academic potential, which I strongly believe to be significantly higher. I also sought to gain an education incorporating nonscience courses and I participated in a wide variety of extracurricular activities.

I am a patient, self-disciplined, and caring person. I am ready to accept challenges and then apply my talents to achieve realistic goals. In the realm of experimental medicine, I spent two summers at the Graduate Hospital in Philadelphia where I was engaged in research projects concerned with drug blood levels using various analytical tools. I also did a "time-action" study to determine the feasibility of laboratory computerization. In a totally different context, I organized my own band of musicians and succeeded in winning several contests. In addition, I worked at a variety of social affairs. These efforts involved my assuming responsibilities, showing initiative and leadership capacity, and demonstrating good interpersonal skills.

I recognized the importance of several medical-relevant issues. As a result of my hospital experience, I became convinced of the genuineness of my sense of empathy for those in need of healing or amelioration from pain. Also, I recognized the need to keep the patient in focus during the course of treatment, since technological advances, although most valuable, may impede good physician-patient relationships.

While I am uncertain at this time in what area of medicine I will find my place, I believe my talents will enable me to contribute to the welfare of those I will serve in the future. I sincerely hope that I will be granted the opportunity to pursue my professional goals as a medical student.

*Essay 14*

During the third year at my college, I was fortunate to participate in a unique medical program. Hospice (Latin for "way station") is a program designed to comfort terminally ill patients as well as diminish the stress of their families. The idea of tending to the needs of incurable people is very important. It affords an outlet for the feelings and emotional concerns of both the hopelessly ill patient and their relatives. This hospice program is a college course in Sociology of Medicine. It involves regular supportive visits with the families of dying patients at a most sensitive time. I am presently helping to care for an elderly woman suffering from lung cancer. She is in temporary remission and is living at home with her son and daughter-in-law. I am able to appreciate the sad situation, and assist her in coming to terms with the incurable nature of the illness. I believe that the empathy I demonstrate to others enables me to help them. Seeing the patient at home adjust to her circumstances, interacting with her own family, provides a more natural and realistic experience than otherwise would exist in a hospital environment. Based on my experience, I strongly relate to the goals of the Hospice program. My attitude results from my own family's experience with my grandfather's death. While we were unaware of hospice placement at the time, this would have provided an opportunity to help ease the suffering cause by his terminal cancer. My hospice exposure has made me recognize that the physician's contribution can have a powerful impact on people's lives, which extends beyond curative aspects.

While volunteering at two medical institutions, I had a chance to observe physicians and hospitals on a practical level of operation as well as to actively participate in patient care. Although being a minor member of the treatment team, this experience gave me a sense of pride and satisfaction. After spending time in the emergency and operating rooms, unexpectedly, something stirred inside of me. When I gathered my thoughts about my newfound feelings, I realized the message I was receiving was that I too can and should make a meaningful contribution to medicine. In just observing the procedures, I became familiar with useful techniques in dealing with some illnesses. I also became more confident in responding to high-stress situations, where decisions have to be made quickly and calmly. I witnessed a range of problems, from dog bites to heart attacks. I was impressed with the skill, speed, and professionalism of the various physicians, and I felt strongly that I wanted to be part of that dedicated team.

Medicine appeals to me because of its potential to ease people's physical and emotional suffering. My past experiences have stimulated a strong concern and compassion for people. I also have a desire to pursue a career in which I can make maximum use of my attributes and abilities. I believe I have demonstrated through the science and other courses I have completed my intellectual capacity to pursue a medical career. Throughout my undergraduate years, I enjoyed studying a myriad of subjects. Courses in psychology, politics, and English literature all proved to be intellectually stimulating. My major in East Asian studies led to an internship and extensive research in acupuncture. This allowed me to link my studies in this field with my interest in medicine. For my work, I was awarded distinction.

My extracurricular work, as well as my volunteer work for Hospice and the two hospitals, prove to me not only that I can handle responsibility well, but also that I have talent in relating empathetically to others. From my experiences and observations, I have concluded that medicine is a rigorous, demanding, and satisfying profession that I hope to enter next year.

*Essay 15*

My father has been a practicing physician for many years. This naturally influenced my initial interest in medicine; nevertheless, profound personal experiences have convinced me that my goal to become a physician is the most appropriate professional career to select.

Undoubtedly, my father has served as a role model for me. I recognized his ability to combine a concern for the patient's physical well-being with a strong interest in the patient's overall life situation. He views his patients not only from a clinical perspective but as individuals deserving highly personalized attention. This approach had endeared him to his patients and helped build a thriving practice.

I have also admired the fact that my father, while intensely involved in a clinical practice, has been able to set aside time for research. This work has proven to be quite successful. It also has provided him with both a change of pace and a great deal of satisfaction. On the other hand, my mother, a Medicaid administrator, made me aware of the complex issues associated with providing access to medical care for all those in need. Her dedication to enhancing a program that seeks to facilitate such a goal and efforts on behalf of needy individuals has also had a strong positive impact upon me. Through her work, I recognize that there is a moral obligation to provide quality health care to all segments of our society.

It has been my life experiences, however, that have made me fully aware of the realities and complexities of a physician's life. My research laboratory volunteer work at a local medical center enabled me to appreciate the nature of medical investigation to achieve breakthroughs that over the course of time will have practical applicability in patient care. I was able to foresee, after a number of in-depth discussions with my supervisor, how my involvement in the analysis of the data could ultimately have an impact on a number of serious musculoskeletal conditions.

My volunteer hospital exposure to another center has explicitly demonstrated the level of expertise needed to be a competent physician. I recognized that competent service requires in-depth basic science and clinical knowledge combined with manual dexterity skills for diagnostic and treatment purposes. I also came to realize the tragedies that physicians often need to face and unfortunately must accept. While I had the opportunity to observe creative medical and surgical care, I noted that many patients have serious emotional problems that need special attention.

The goal of twenty-first-century medicine is focusing not only on treatment but also on prevention, which will impact significantly on the manner in which future health care providers will practice. This is already reflected in urging women over 50 to have mammograms, seniors to obtain flu shots, and people over 50 to have colonoscopies.

My clinical exposure has by necessity been limited. Consequently, I have sought to avoid developing a prospective residency preference for any specific field. At a later time, I hope to gain a greater and broader exposure to key specialties and perhaps to some subspecialties, which will allow me to make an appropriate selection. Nevertheless, I have ascertained from my hospital experience that both my heart and mind are in full agreement that for me medicine is the career that will provide a lifetime of satisfaction.

*Essay 16*

My desire to become a physician evolved slowly as I progressed through childhood and adolescence. I will relate some important steps in this process.

My curiosity as a child motivated me to examine the structure of insects using magnifying lenses of various strengths. I then moved on to tinkering with a chemistry set that my parents, at my request, purchased for me. Upon entering high school, I had the good fortune to take a biology class with a dedicated teacher. Although this was only an elementary course, the teacher sought to provide us with opportunities to gain relatively sophisticated exposure to more advanced laboratory assignments. His enthusiasm for the subject was infectious and stimulated me to gain a deeper insight into the subject matter. This positive experience served to direct my interest in pursuing a science-oriented career.

A subsequent high school experience made an even stronger impact on me. This involved volunteer work at a state-operated facility for the mentally disabled. I was assigned consistently to a certain patient, a twenty-year-old severely mentally and physically handicapped man. His condition necessitated basic training to perform simple tasks, which for him were quite a challenge. Initially I felt overwhelmed by the situation, but within a short period of time I adjusted and I gradually developed a sense of satisfaction that I could be of some assistance to this unfortunate individual. The overall experience made me cognizant of the importance of providing facilities for those who are mentally and/or physically handicapped. Moreover, I came to recognize the virtue of patience and determination when engaged in helping people. This opportunity for service for someone less fortunate helped motivate me to focus on medicine as a potential career.

Preparing myself in college for my career, I sought to seek an educational background that emphasized both the sciences and humanities. Studying courses in philosophy and English literature was quite stimulating. A course that I took in electron microscopy was a major experience, which gave me an opportunity to gain a direct insight into the ultra structure of cells and tissues. Suddenly, like an explorer, I came in contact with a hidden world. I also gained an appreciation for the effort involved in preparing material that was suitable to be viewed by such an instrument.

I had another insight into the clinical relevance of scientific work when I spent a summer month at a local medical school where I engaged in a research project involving genetics and biochemistry. In addition, I attended some medical school classes and occasionally also conferences. I not only had a glimpse into scientific clinical research but enjoyed working in a medical school environment. I gained a meaningful appreciation for medicine by observing the activities taking place in a variety of departments at an affiliated hospital and came to understand the important role of the physician in this setting. It introduced me to the sophisticated technological elements involved in medical treatment. I also recognized the importance of dedication and compassion in the art of healing the sick.

In summary, a variety of influences have brought me to the stage I am at presently. They have prepared me well for the substantial challenges that lie ahead.

## *Essay 17*

In my quest to gain a realistic perspective about the nature of a medical career, I was able to have a series of intimate conversations with a number of active practitioners. These conversations gave me an insight into their thoughts and feelings about their professional activities and their views on the future of medicine. They have provided me with an image of the essential needs of a physician, as well as what it takes to enter and succeed in the medical profession.

I ascertained two key elements from my conversations with these physicians: One, to serve in this profession it is necessary to have an intense desire for knowledge on an ongoing basis; two, a strong motivation is needed to dedicate oneself to help others in a most meaningful way. These assets presuppose being endowed with good innate intelligence as well as competency in communication skills, which are prerequisites of the healing profession.

Clear evidence of my natural desire to acquire knowledge and my commitment to service are reflected in my activities over the past few years. At college I pursued a broad spectrum of courses. My record also reflects a strong interest in science. These studies were a part of a wide range of academic and extracurricular activities. These endeavors have facilitated my functioning as an informed member of our society. They provided me with a knowledge base in literature, philosophy, history, and psychology. The result of my highly successful studies have given me a sense of accomplishment and a feeling that I have learned the important art of problem solving as well as processing information.

Gaining a broad knowledge base was one of the several goals and achievements of my college experience. I spent much time and effort interacting with others in a helpful and constructive manner. I am an active officer of a college fraternity. I have volunteered to be a host for visiting prospective students, to inform them candidly of the assets and challenges of college campus life in a meaningful personalized manner. I have also served as a teaching assistant in both advanced biology and computer courses. These, as well as a number of other jobs I held, gave me much satisfaction.

I have had an opportunity to be engaged in research at the Department of Medicine of a local medical school. This provided me with a unique opportunity to gain exposure to a variety of important aspects of medicine.

In conclusion, I believe the past few years have been very meaningful for me, as I have accomplished my aim of obtaining a broad education and achieved a greater level of maturity. This will better enable me to interact with a wide variety of individuals as a physician. I hope you will help enable me to do so, by granting me a place in your next freshman class.

## *Essay 18*

My life has been characterized by a strong sense of inquisitiveness about the world around me. This characteristic has remained the hallmark of my life.

As a child I was interested in biological life. I watched ants as they moved about in their habitat. When I found baby chicks that had fallen out of a nest, I attempted to give them food and shelter. As I reached my teens, I implored my parents to get me a small microscope as a part of a science kit. With it I spent considerable time examining a wide variety of specimens and was fascinated by the details of what I saw. In time I began reading books about nature and naturalists.

As a high school student I realized that my academic strengths were in the sciences, but my interests were also in other areas, such as English literature and foreign languages. I also became involved with the varsity basketball team and other extracurricular activities including the school newspaper. All of these were time consuming. Through high school I made a strong effort to keep up with current events and took a particularly strong interest in social and health care problems in our society. I found that reading the "Science Times" section of *The New York Times* was especially interesting and informative. It kept me up to date with recent advances on a variety of scientific fronts. I came to realize that remarkable technical achievements have been made in medicine but some of these generated difficult ethical problems, for example, establishing priorities for organ transplants among critically ill patients. Similarly, placing individuals on respirators whose chances for recovery are quite questionable or discontinuing such devices are challenging moral issues.

Upon entering college my outlook was to follow my intellectual curiosity. I enrolled in science courses and was very stimulated by them. What really moved me toward health care was my volunteer work in a local clinic for handicapped youngsters. I was assigned to supervise two mentally and physically challenged boys once a week during their play activity. It took time and a great deal of patience to establish a good functional relationship with them, but once this preliminary step was achieved I found myself deriving personal satisfaction from my volunteer work.

I was also fortunate to gain exposure to investigative medicine during the course of a two-month summer position at a major hospital's blood center where I was trained in the execution of histocompatibility tests. These are required when matching donors with recipients for bone marrow and kidney transplants. I received considerable gratification by participating in a project that directly helps to extend the lives of seriously ill people.

My college experience in an entirely new and challenging social and educational environment put me to the test. I had to learn self-reliance and how to adapt to new circumstances. I was admitted to the school's Scholars Program after completing my freshman year. This attests to the recognition given for the quality of my work and potential. I was also selected for the varsity baseball team. I feel that my dynamic college program of liberal parts provided me with a rich intellectual experience that is essential for being a well-rounded individual.

In seeking a career in medicine, I know that my inquisitive nature will be continually challenged and that I will need to be ready to adapt and adjust to readily changing knowledge and situations. I believe that I am ready for the demanding adventure that pursuing a career in medicine necessitates.

*Essay 19*

By the time I reached high school, I seriously started to consider my future career goals. After carefully evaluating my various interests, talents, and experiences, I came to the conclusion that for me medicine is the most appropriate one.

One of the strong influences on my life, career-wise, has been our exceptional family physician. In his office, patients felt relaxed and reassured by his presence. His high spirits, humor, and sympathetic manner made everyone feel comfortable. Beneath his graceful personal style was a high degree of professionalism. This kind and gentle man, became over time my role model. He demonstrated how one can be both personally subjective and professionally objective at the same time.

Another person whose impact upon me has been significant was my high school English teacher. She made me realize the importance of communication skills, both oral and written. She instilled in me a strong positive feeling for the work ethic. In medicine, which is a demanding profession, this concept is very important. She also served as an advisor and provided me with considerable encouragement. She even helped me with the process of applying to college.

As a high school graduation present, my father, who is in the export-import business, took me on a trip through several European countries. This was an eye-opening experience that broadened my cultural horizon. I gained a firsthand insight into the life outside of our country. I realized that while outward differences do exist, nevertheless, as people we have common human qualities, feelings, and needs.

My college education focused on securing a strong liberal arts background. My courses ranged from advanced English literature and international politics to astronomy and molecular biology. I spent a summer working in a pharmacology laboratory at a local medical school. This experience afforded me an opportunity to spend time in a medical school environment. I simultaneously became acquainted with the nature and demands of research involving sophisticated experimental equipment.

Medical studies and training are demanding financially, physically, and emotionally. As to the latter, a prolonged serious illness of my much younger sister placed intense stress on our entire household. I realized how wide ranging the effects of a major illness on a family can be and the need for psychological support through such a crisis. This will be an important and enduring lesson for me when I encounter such situations in the course of my future activities.

The road I have chosen to attain my career goal is neither easy nor short. It involves a great deal of effort and sacrifice. Having gotten a glimpse of what can be achieved by a knowledgeable and dedicated physician, I am convinced that I am prepared to accept the challenge.

### Essay 20

A great deal of thought and consideration has gone into my choice of medicine as a career. It involved discussions with my parents, close friends, our respected family physician, and my competent college advisor. But the underlying motive has been my varied and relevant experiences.

While in high school, I felt a persistent desire to be of help to others, so I organized a group of friends having this common interest. We decided to provide assistance to unfortunate people living in a neighborhood homeless shelter. We visited the shelter on a regular basis on weekends. We befriended many residents and became aware of the specific nature of their problems. These involved poverty, loneliness, and depression. We offered them encouragement and urged them to view their lives from a brighter perspective. We also sought to find sources offering professional and financial help to them. To our satisfaction, a good number of the residents responded positively to our efforts. It should be noted that these activities were strongly encouraged by our parents, which helped maintain their momentum. Most probably, this meaningful experience directed me toward a service-oriented career.

Being strongly interested in science, a subject in which I always excelled, the thought of medicine was not far off. To explore my feelings, I decided to spend a summer working in a local hospital. I was able to have the opportunity to gain exposure to the activities of various departments. Being located in a small community, the hospital had an outreach health maintenance program. It involved sending teams of health care professionals to many nearby underserved communities. I joined one of these teams and I was very impressed with the devotion of these professionals, as well as the warm and appreciative reception they got from the families they served. This enlightening experience helped reinforce my aspirations to become a physician.

At college I concentrated on securing a broad liberal arts background. Therefore, I majored in French literature and also took a wide range of courses in humanities. Recognizing that such intellectual activities would not be available to me once I entered a professional school, I chose this path.

My fundamental educational goal has been to be able to become a creative thinker and to master the skills of perceptive observation and analytical problem solving. My achieving these goals will set the foundation for successful medical school experience and postgraduate training.

In addition to a strong sense of dedication and a sound base of medical knowledge, there are other important skills that a physician must have, such as good interpersonal communication abilities. I became aware of this from my own experience with our family physician and from my hospital observation service. To further this skill, I involved myself in a wide range of community activities that required having personal contact with people of varying ages, backgrounds, and walks of life. I found that I could meet this challenge and successfully establish a sound rapport with diverse individuals.

I am confident that my intellectual abilities, determination, and compassion will provide me with the personal assets that will enable me to succeed as a physician in the twenty-first century.

*Essay 21*

It is quite natural that I am anxious to become a physician because I come from a home where the head of the household, my dad, is a successful medical practitioner. It is common at our family dinners to hear my father relating the challenges facing him in dealing with his patients and their problems. He often speaks with gratification about his many triumphs and with distress of occasional defeats. His attitude has left me with a strong impression that medicine is a demanding profession intellectually and emotionally.

The dynamic nature of medicine is especially appealing to me. The impact of revolutionary technical advances coupled with the promise of the effect of molecular biology on medical practice is fascinating. Clearly the twenty-first century will be a time of considerable change in medicine, medical therapy, and in its emphasis on preventive health care. It is an ideal time to join the medical profession.

The fact that medical practice necessitates interaction with a wide range of individuals from all walks of life is particularly appealing to me. My interest in interacting with people is probably due to the fact that I grew up in a large family. In our household, cooperation for the common good is the norm and is accepted social ethic. These feelings were evident to me in high school and college during my active participation in team sports. I felt greatly rewarded by joining my peers in the rough sport of football, whether we won or lost; what counted was a team effort devoted to a common goal.

Having established the path of my career, I defined my college goals to obtain a broad humanistic education supported by a solid grounding in the basic premedical courses. Now that graduation is only a year away, I believe that I am achieving my educational aims.

I chose to major in sociology and minor in psychology. Both my coursework and projects on the whole were stimulating. They opened new vistas in my life experiences. I was fortunate to have knowledgeable and dedicated instructors who have made the intense demands of the coursework worthwhile. My premedical courses were challenging, requiring much effort with a strong emphasis on detail. My superior academic performance reflects my native intellectual abilities as well as the extensive effort I put into my studies.

Supplementing my formal education, like many other students, I arranged to have direct in-patient exposure at a local hospital. This provided me with an opportunity to see the inner workings of a modern teaching institution. I realized the importance of the learning opportunity that a hospital can provide for medical students, interns, and residents. I also came to appreciate the importance of each member of the health care team. The timely coordinated activities of all involved provide the essential services needed to help those who are ill. Working in such an environment and contributing to the extent of my knowledge and abilities was a most satisfying experience. I look forward with great anticipation to joining the medical profession and gaining clinical exposure in a formal manner.

*Essay 22*

What an exciting time to consider becoming a medical student! I make this statement in the light of my relevant extensive reading, my in-depth discussions with physicians, and my volunteer hospital and research experience. As a consequence of this exposure, I came to realize, more fully than before, that in many specialties, advances are taking place in quantum leaps.

Examples of major advances are readily identified in such fields as orthopedic surgery and ophthalmology. In the former, the area of joint replacement has made remarkable progress. This approach has become firmly established for hips and knees. It is now even becoming applicable to the shoulder joint. Yet for the established techniques, refinements are taking place. The same is true for ophthalmology regarding cataract surgery, where lens replacement is now a routine procedure, but valuable technical improvements are still being made. The area of mechanical heart replacement appears on the verge of major advances. On the other hand, the impact of molecular biology is in its early infancy, yet prospects for dramatic therapeutic advances in the foreseeable future are high.

Obviously, dramatic advances in medical sciences have been made. Nevertheless, I recognized that basic clinical progress in patient management is dependent on the following: making an accurate diagnosis; formulating an appropriate treatment protocol; and ensuring that the plan is executed properly by skilled personnel. To formulate a tenable diagnosis requires a solid knowledge base, meaningful experience, and mature clinical judgment. As a future medical student, I consider that my primary obligation is to obtain a fund of knowledge in the basic and clinical sciences. This will provide me with the proper foundation for postgraduate training.

My educational philosophy has over time proven to be sound. Namely, as a high school and college student I sought a good grounding in biology, chemistry, and other related disciplines, as well as superior oral and written communication skills. I have placed considerable emphasis on the art of time management, improving my reading skills, and obtaining a broad humanistic education. I have supplemented my formal education, in which I excelled, with a wide range of extracurricular activities, including varsity sports, drama, and classical cello performances. Maintaining a successful balance to meet the demands of both my formal educational and other nonacademic activities proved quite a challenge. I believe it has adequately been met, and this makes me confident that I will be able to handle the rigorous demands of the medical school curriculum. My achievements have come about by prioritizing my activities, being flexible, making adjustments, and staying focused.

Fortunately, during my college years, I devoted one summer to volunteering for hospital work and another one to laboratory research. In both, I was in an environment among professionals that I found congenial and stimulating. My communication skills served me well when dealing with patients, where I tried to be supportive and helpful, and do what I could to make them comfortable and relaxed. With research investigators, I sought to understand the nature of their scientific problem, so that I could be useful, even if to a limited extent.

I believe my efforts and activities in the past have prepared me well for the important mission that lies ahead. I look forward to meeting the challenges that I will face as a medical student.

## *Essay 23*

Early in my education I looked to find a satisfying answer both rationally and emotionally to the natural question, "Why study medicine?" Certainly, medicine offers a wonderful opportunity for fulfilling one's intellectual desires, while at the same time providing sick patients curative or at least palliative outcomes. I recognized that for physicians prestige does not come automatically, but results from faithfully meeting their awesome responsibilities. This field offers economic security, while allowing, to a considerable extent, professional independence and integrity. Within medicine there is a broad spectrum of specialty opportunities that range from administration to vascular surgery. Thus, upon completing postgraduate training, one can, depending on the specialty, be involved in bringing babies into the world, providing care for children and adolescents, young adults, and the middle-aged, or helping ameliorate chronic illnesses among seniors. Moreover, there is the possibility of a career combining practice, teaching, and research.

In addition, medicine has the special feature that allows physicians to option focusing on patient care, specimen diagnosis, or treatment modalities. Few other professions can offer so many choices that can meet the needs, interests, and talents of a wide variety of gifted individuals. Becoming a physician means joining a unique fraternity of people who have had a profound influence on advancing the quality of human life, especially in the last century.

Having elected to become a physician, I nevertheless faced a number of challenging questions. How will my choice affect my future lifestyle in the short and long term? Will there be attractive professional opportunities available when I am ready to enter the work force? Am I intellectually, physically, and emotionally capable of undertaking such a challenging career? I found it necessary to ask such questions as well as answer them to my satisfaction prior to seeking admission to medical school. Obviously, I have done so in the affirmative.

After having set my goal, I focused my attention on preparing for future success in my medical studies, so, aware of the basic foundations of medicine, I wanted a firm grounding in biology. This would contribute to my preparation for the basic medical sciences that I will face during my first two years as a medical student. The advanced courses that I took in my major, especially molecular biology and genetics, were particularly intellectually stimulating. They have valuable implications for future advances in medicine.

I had the good fortune to work on an honor project under the supervision of a senior biology professor. This provided me with a unique opportunity to enter the world of biological research. Searching the literature, learning, and applying techniques, patiently waiting for results, and finally, interpreting data, proved to be a fascinating experience. This served to prepare me for the summer research assistantship I held in the Department of Physiology at a local medical school. There I was faced with a more complex research problem that required me to make use of sophisticated equipment.

Supplementing my exposure to a medical school environment, I was engaged during my third college summer in volunteer work at the Community General Hospital of my town. The opportunity to observe effective patient care being managed under stressful conditions was very impressive. Seeing the grateful responses of many patients was a moving experience.

I believe medicine will provide me with much professional satisfaction. It is a field in which I am confident I can make a significant contribution.

*Essay 24*

I have been looking forward to the time when I would be eligible to apply for admission to medical school. Finally, after thoroughly evaluating my abilities and motivation, I am convinced that I am ready to undertake this definite step of my life.

I have been enjoying my college studies and extracurricular activities and my academic performance and personal attributes reflect my capabilities. I have been a consistent achiever, having mastered the art of meeting educational challenges. This includes managing time, taking notes and tests, writing term papers and using educational resources such as college and local libraries, the Internet, and so on.

Although I was quite careful not to overextend myself, I did not shy away from enrolling in demanding courses and undertaking honors projects. Proper planning, working at a steady pace, seeking assistance from faculty, and collaborating with classmates proved to be *the* valuable tools in achieving an attractive record. My impressive MCAT scores support my confidence in my native intelligence as well as my abilities in the sciences. Therefore, I am sure I can face the challenges of the medical school curriculum.

Aside from having intellectual talents and scientific interest, my social skills have demonstrated that I am able to communicate well with people on all levels. As a physician, I anticipate having to associate with individuals from many walks of life, differing ages, and various backgrounds. I am confident that I will be able to respond to future patients in an empathetic and respectful manner that will facilitate obtaining their cooperation. I trust that these attributes will serve me well in the future.

As a result of my college studies, especially in honors courses, I have developed a strong appreciation for self-education. Now I realize more fully that continuing education in medicine serves to enhance clinical knowledge, thereby facilitating more accurate diagnoses. Medicine is a scientific field that requires that the doctor act decisively for the patient's benefit, even when data are inconclusive. Additionally, being aware of the most recent advances can increase a physician's self-confidence, because the degree of ambiguity may be diminished. Therefore, keeping up-to-date is a major requirement of medicine, particularly in one's own specialty.

Anticipating my ultimate entry into the field of medicine, I have sought to be cognizant of health-care policy issues. This includes delivery modalities, preventive health care approaches, and the recognition of the impact of different sociocultural backgrounds on patients' medical conditions.

In conclusion, I believe that the personal assets I possess have served me well and brought me to this important stage in my career. During the future course of my medical education and training, I hope to demonstrate my capabilities for varying creative activities. My achievements should prove to be highly beneficial to those who will seek my help in the years ahead.

**Essay 25**

Achieving a meaningful career requires utmost determination and commitment. This was the philosophy of my grandfather, who was a general practitioner and my role model.

While in high school, I decided to become a physician. Since that time, I have expended maximum effort toward my career goal. Reflecting on the source of my commitment, I realized to my surprise that it largely also stems from my long-standing affection for basketball. Let me clarify how I arrived at this rather strange conclusion.

Since my early childhood, I have been an avid player of basketball. I was encouraged in this activity by my parents. They felt that team sports would prove beneficial to my maturation into adulthood, and indeed they have. I also found that I could maintain a superior academic record while at the same time be intensely involved in an extracurricular activity that demanded considerable effort and time. I also learned that teamwork and making the proper decision at the right time are very important. I recognize that practice significantly improves performance and enhances physical coordination to carry out complex tasks. The need to prioritize one's interests so as to focus on certain activities was another valuable lesson.

My intention, while playing basketball, was not to be the best player, but rather to contribute to the team's effort to the best of my abilities. Consequently, I derived personal satisfaction even when my team did not win. As time progressed my self-confidence improved considerably. My readiness to apply myself intensely toward my extracurricular activity became easier, since I recognized the varied benefits I was getting from it.

There are obvious, important similarities between my sports activity and my career plans. Both require hard work and team effort in order to be successful. In addition, manual dexterity comes with practice. This skill is a very valuable asset for patient care. The organizational abilities I learned allowed me to successfully meet my commitments. All of these will certainly prove useful when working under intense pressure in medical school and during postgraduate training.

I am well aware of the enormous demands placed on medical students and residents. Nevertheless, I recognized that it is essential to lead a balanced lifestyle. This means avoiding becoming overextended as well as maintaining a regime of proper nourishment, exercise, relaxation, and sleep. Thus, I feel assured that I am adequately prepared to meet my future responsibilities on the road to becoming a competent physician.

My self-confidence stems from many sources. Among these are my previously noted academic performance and extracurricular activities, as well as experience gained while engaged in volunteer hospital work and research.

My volunteer hospital work two summers ago proved very meaningful. It provided me with a good view of the dynamics of medical care. I had ample opportunity not only to observe the activities in various departments but also to converse with medical students, residents, and attending physicians. I observed firsthand that they were conscientious, diligent, and dedicated to their patients' well-being, even when working under great stress.

My research activities were carried out during the past summer. The position I held was with the biochemistry department at the state medical school. Working in collaboration with others was very stimulating. My supervisor and colleagues were most cooperative and helpful in providing me with guidance and advice that facilitated the progress of the project. I secured a good insight into the demanding character of scientific research and its meticulous concern with detail.

I readily visualize myself joining the field of medicine, since I believe that I have what it takes. I sincerely hope that you will come to share this view.

# APPENDIX D

## MAJOR PROFESSIONAL ALLOPATHIC ORGANIZATIONS _____

**Accreditation Council for Graduate Medical Education**
515 North State Street
Chicago, IL 60610
*www.acgmc.org*

**Aerospace Medical Association**
320 South Henry Street
Alexandria, VA 22314
*www.asma.org*

**AMCAS**
2501 M Street NW
Washington, DC 20037
*www.aamc.org*

**American Academy of Allergy, Asthma and Immunology**
611 East Wells Street
Milwaukee, WI 53202
*www.aaaai.org*

**American Academy of Child and Adolescent Psychiatry**
3615 Wisconsin, NW
Washington, DC 20016
*www.aacpa.org*

**American Academy of Dermatology**
P. O. Box 4014
Schaumburg, IL 60173
*www.aad.org*

**American Academy of Family Physicians**
11400 Tomahawk Creek Parkway
Leewood, KS 66211
*www.aafp.org*

**American Academy of Neurology**
1080 Montreal Avenue
St. Paul, MN 55116
*www.aan.com/professionals*

**American Academy of Ophthalmology**
655 Beach Street
San Francisco, CA 94109
*www.aao.org*

**American Academy of Otolaryngology**
1 Prince Street
Alexandria, VA 22314
*www.entnet.org*

**American Academy of Orthopedic Surgeons**
6300 North River Road
Rosemont, IL 60018
*www.aaos.org*

**American Academy of Pediatrics**
141 Northwest Point Boulevard
Elk Grove, IL 60007
*www.aap.org*

**American Association of Colleges of Osteopathic Medicine**
5550 Friendship Boulevard, Suite 310
Chevy Chase, MD 20815
*www.aacom.org*

**American Association of Dental Schools**
1625 Massachusetts Avenue, NW
Washington, DC 20036
*www.ada.org*

**American Association of Medical Colleges**
2460 North Street NW
Washington, DC 20037
*www.aamc.org*

**American Association of Neurological Surgeons**
22 South Washington Street
Park Ridge, IL 60068
*www.neurosurgery.org*

**American Association of Orthodontists**
401 North Lindbergh Boulevard
St. Louis, MO 63141
*www.aaortho.org*

**American Association of Public Health Physicians**
c/o Armand Start, M.D.
1300 W Belmont Avenue
Chicago, IL 60657
*www.aaphp.org*

**American Board of Medical Specialties**
1007 Church Street, Suite 404
Evanston, IL 60201
*www.abms.org*

**American College of Cardiology**
9111 Old Georgetown Road
Bethesda, MD 20814
*www.acc.org*

**American College of Chest Physicians**
3300 Dundee Road
Northbrook, IL 60062
*www.chestnet.org*

**American College of Emergency Physicians**
P.O. Box 61911
Dallas, TX 75261
*www.accp.org*

**American College of Gastroenterology**
4900B South 31st Street
Arlington, VA 22206
*www.acg.gi.org*

**American College of Medical Genetics**
9650 Rockville Pike
Bethesda, MD 20814
*www.acmg.net*

**American College of Nuclear Medicine**
P.O. Box 175
Landsville, PA 17538
*www.rsha.org*

**American College of Obstetricians and Gynecologists**
409 12th Street SW
Washington, DC 20024
*www.acog.org*

**American College of Physicians—
American Society of Internal Medicine**
190 N. Independence Mall West
Philadelphia, PA 19106
*www.acponline.org*

**American College of Preventive Medicine**
1307 New York Avenue NW
Washington, DC 20005
*www.acpm.org*

**American College of Radiology**
1891 Preston White Drive
Reston, VA 22091
*www.acr.org*

**American College of Rheumatology**
1800 Century Place NE
Atlanta, GA 30345
*www.rheumatology.org*

**American College of Surgeons**
635 North St. Clair Street
Chicago, IL 60611
*www.facs.org*

**American Dental Association**
211 East Chicago Avenue
Chicago, IL 60611
*www.ada.org*

**American Federation for Clinical Research**
6900 Grove Road
Thorofare, NJ 08086
*www.afmr.org*

**American Geriatric Society**
770 Lexington Avenue
New York, NY 10021
*www.americangeriatrics.org*

**American Hospital Association**
1 North Franklin
Chicago, IL 60606
*www.aha.org*

**American Medical Association**
515 North Street
Chicago, IL 60610
*www.ama.org*

**American Medical Student Association**
1902 Association Drive
Reston, VA 22091
*www.amsa.org*

**American Medical Women's Association**
801 North Fairfax Street
Alexandria, VA 22314
*www.amwa.org*

**American Ophthalmologic Society**
c/o W. Banks Anderson, M.D.
Duke University Eye Center
Durham, NC 27710
*www.aosonline.org*

**American Osteopathic Association**
142 East Ontario Street
Chicago, IL 60611
*www.aoa-net.org*

**American Osteopathic College of Rehabilitation Medicine**
2214 Elmira Avenue
Des Plaines, IL 60018
*www.aoa-net.org*

**American Osteopathic Healthcare Association**
5550 Friendship Boulevard, Suite 300
Chevy Chase, MD 20815
*www.aoha.org*

**American Psychiatric Association**
1400 K Street NW
Washington, DC 20005
*www.psych.org*

**American Society of Anesthesiologists**
520 N. Northwest Highway
Park Ridge, IL 60068
*www.asahq.org*

**American Society of Clinical Oncology**
1900 Duke Street, Suite 200
Alexandria, VA 22314
*www.asco.org*

**American Society for Colon and Rectal Surgeons**
85 West Algonquin Road
Arlington Heights, IL 60005
*www.fascrs.org*

**American Society of Hematology**
1900 M Street NW
Washington, DC 20036
*www.hematology.org*

**American Society of Internal Medicine**
2011 Pennsylvania Avenue NW
Washington, DC 20036
*www.asim.org*

**American Society of Nephrology**
1200 19th Street NW
Washington, DC 20036
*www.asn.org*

**American Society of Plastic and Reconstructive Surgeons**
444 East Algonquin Road
Arlington Heights, IL 60005
*www.plasticsurgery.org*

**American Thoracic Society**
1740 Broadway, 14th Floor
New York, NY 10019
*www.thoracic.org*

**American Urological Association**
2425 West Loop South
Suite 300
Houston, TX 77027
*www.auanet.org*

**Association of American Medical Colleges**
2450 N Street NW
Washington, DC 20037
*www.aamc.org*
*www.aamc.org/students/eras/start.htm*

**Canadian Resident Matching Service**
151 Slater Street
802 Ottawa, Ontario, K1P-5H3
Canada
*www.carms.org*

**College of American Pathologists**
325 Waukegan Road
Northfield, IL 60093
*www.cap.org*

**Educational Commission for Foreign Medical Graduates**
3624 Market Street
Philadelphia, PA 19104
*www.edfmg.org*

**Federation of State Medical Boards of the U. S., Inc.**
P. O. Box 19850
Dallas, TX 75261
*www.fsmb.org*

**National Association of Advisors for the Health Professions**
P. O. Box 1518
Champaign, IL 61824
*www.naahp.org*

**National Board of Medical Examiners**
3750 Market Street
Philadelphia, PA 19104
*www.nbme.org*

**National Board of Osteopathic Medical Examiners**
8765 West Higgins Road
Chicago, Il 60631
*www.abome.org*

**National Dental Association**
5506 Connecticut Avenue NW
Washington, DC 20015
*www.nadonline.org*

**National Medical Association**
1012 10th Street NW
Washington, DC 20001
*www.nmanet.org*

**National Resident Matching Program**
2501 M Street NW
Washington, DC 20037
*www.nrmp.org*

**Rehabilitation Physicians Association**
1101 Vermont Avenue NW
Washington, DC 20005
*www.aapmr.org*

**Society of Critical Care Medicine**
8101 East Kaiser Boulevard
Anaheim, CA 92808
*www.sccm.org*

**Society of Thoracic Surgeons**
401 North Michigan Avenue
Chicago, Il 60611
*www.sts.org*

**The College of American Pathologists**
325 Waukegan Road
Northfield, IL 60093
*www.cap.org*

**The Endocrine Society**
4350 East West Highway
Bethesda, MD 20814
*www.endo-society.org*

**The Infectious Disease Society of America**
99 Canal Center Plaza
Suite 600
Alexandria, VA 22314
*www.idsociety.org*

**The American Society for Therapeutic Radiology and Oncology**
12055 Fair Lakes Circle
Fairfax, VA 22033
*www.astro.org*

**The American College of Occupational
and Environmental Medicine**
1114 North Arlington Heights Road
Arlington Heights, IL 60005
*www.acoem.org*

**The American Academy of Physical Medicine
and Rehabilitation**
One IBM Plaza, Suite 2500
Chicago, IL 60611
*www.aapmr.org*

**The American Society of Addiction Medicine**
4601 North Par Avenue
Upper Arcade
Chevy Chase, MD 20815
*www.asam.org*

**The Society of Nuclear Medicine**
1850 Samuel Morse Drive
Reston, VA 20190
*www.snm.org*

# APPENDIX E

## MAJOR PROFESSIONAL OSTEOPATHIC ORGANIZATIONS _____

**American Osteopathic College of Allergy and Immunology**
1625 McDowell Road
Scottsdale, AZ 85257
480-585-1580
*www.aocai.org*

**American Osteopathic College of Anesthesiologists**
17201 East Highway 40
Independence, MO 64055
*www.aoca.org*

**American Osteopathic College of Dermatology**
P.O. Box 7525
Kirksville, MO 63501
800-449-2623
*www.aocd.org*

**American College of Osteopathic Emergency Physicians**
142 East Ontario Street
Chicago, IL 60611
800-521-3709
*www.acoep.org*

**American College of Osteopathic Family Physicians**
330 East Algonquin Road
Arlington Heights, IL 60005
800-323-0794
*www.acofp.org*

**American College of Osteopathic Internists**
3 Bethesda, Metro Center
Bethesda, MD 20814
301-656-8877
*www.acoi.org*

**American Osteopathic Board of Nuclear Medicine**
1000 East 53rd Street
Chicago, IL 60615
*www.acbnm.org*

**American College of Osteopathic Neurologists and Psychiatrists**
28595 Orchard Lake Road
Farmington Hills, MI 48334
748-553-0010
*www.aconp.org*

**American Osteopathic Board of Neuromusculoskeletal Medicine**
3500 De Paw Boulevard
Indianapolis, IN 46268
317-879-1881
*www.academyofosteopathy.org*

**American Osteopathic College of Occupational and Preventive Medicine**
P.O. Box 2606
Leesburg, VA 26177
*www.aocopm.org*

**American College of Osteopathic Obstetricians and Gynecologists**
900 Auburn Road
Pontiac, MI 48342
800-875-6360
*www.acoog.org*

**American Osteopathic College of Ophthalmology, Otolaryngology—
Head and Neck Surgery**
405 W Grand Avenue
Dayton, OH 45405
800-455-9404
*www.acoohns.org*

**American Osteopathic Academy of Orthopedics**
P. O. Box 291690
Davie, FL 83329
800-236-3307
*www.handsurgery.org*

**American Osteopathic College of Pathology**
12368 NW 13th Court
Penbroke Pines, FL 33026
954-432-9640
*www.acop-net.org*

**American Academy of Osteopathic Pediatrics**
142 East Ontario Street
Chicago, IL 60611
312-202-8188
*www.acopeds.org*

**American College of Physical Medicine and Rehabilitation**
One IBM Plaza
Chicago, IL 60611
312-454-9701
*www.acpmr.org*

**American Osteopathic College of Proctology**
9948 Route 682
Athens, OH 45701
740-594-7979
*www.aocp.org*

**American College of Radiology of Osteopathy**
119 East Second Street
Milan, MO 63556
*www.aocr.org*

**American College of Osteopathic Surgeons**
123 North Henry Street
Alexandria, VA 22314
800-888-1312
*www.acos.org*

# APPENDIX F

## ALTERNATIVE MEDICAL TERMINOLOGY _____

### Allopathy
term coined by Dr. Samuel Hahnemann (1755–1843), the German founder of homeopathy. The name represents a combination of the Greek words *allos* (other) and *pathos* (suffering). It is a type of therapy aimed at healing a disease by producing a second condition that is different from the effects of that disease. The name now applies to all but osteopathic medical schools.

### Acupuncture
Chinese technique for treating pain or disease in which needles are inserted in points along meridians that correspond to organs.

### Alexander Technique
technique developed by an Australian actor as a method for improving posture so as to improve health.

### Byur Veda
Indian healing approach that uses diet, herbs, exercise, massage, and scent, prescribed according to body type.

### Bachs Flour Remedy
medicine made from flour and alcohol, based on the formulas of an English physician Edward Bachs (1886–1933).

### Biofeedback
a careful monitoring of body changes by which patients can learn to lower their blood pressure and alter other internal physiological functions.

### Chelation Therapy
infusion of intravenous doses of an aminoxide. It is used to treat AIDS and other diseases and illnesses.

### Shi
Chinese name for the invisible life force.

### Chi Gong
a form of meditation or, as used by some, a type of hand healing.

### Chiropractic
approach developed by D.D. Palmer (1845–1913), combining the Greek names *kheir* (hand) and *practios* (effective). He believed that 95% of illnesses could be cured by manipulating the spine. Most modern chiropractors primarily treat back problems.

### Homeopathy
approach developed by Dr. Samuel Hahnemann. Combining the Greek word *homoest* (similar) and *pathos* (suffering), he treated symptoms on the principle that "like cures like." He prescribed substances that, in healthy patients, caused symptoms similar to those of the diseases he was treating.

### Hydrotherapy
ancient remedy of bathing to promote health. Various combinations of minerals and temperatures are used.

### Imagery
behavior therapy technique in which the patient is conditioned to replace feelings of anxiety with pleasant fantasies.

### Iridology

examining the iris of the eye to diagnose illness.

### Moxibustion

Asian treatment of burning herbs near the skin. The body should benefit from their penetration.

### Naturapathy

system of therapy in which practitioners use natural means, such as herbal remedies, hydrotherapy, homeopathy, nutrition, manipulative modalities, acupuncture, and counseling for treatment.

### Osteopathy

developed by Andrew Taylor Still (1828–1917), an American physician, who believed in applying musculoskeletal manipulation as a therapeutic approach. The profession has changed considerably since it was founded and has moved closer to allopathy.

### Rolfing

deep massage technique developed by an American chemist, Dr. Ida Rolf.

### Shiatsu

Japanese massage technique based on acupuncture concepts.

### Traditional Chinese Medicine

system of healing using acupuncture, herbal medicine, moxibustion, massage, cupping, nutrition, and meditation. Its goal is to balance opposite and complementary aspects of being to enhance the flow of the life force (chi).

# APPENDIX G

## TRACKING TABLES

Applying to medical school requires the processing of all application material in a systematic manner. You must be conscious of deadlines and be aware that all required material must be submitted, or processing of your application will be delayed. Any prolonged delay can negatively impact on your chances for admission.

While medical schools have to handle hundreds of thousands of documents generated by more than 40,000 applicants, your contribution is to see that all material related to your own applications is submitted in a timely fashion. To facilitate that process, this appendix was developed and consists of a series of tracking tables that apply to the application process as a whole, MCAT registration, AMCAS and non-AMCAS school applications, and interviews. Using these tables will facilitate the orderly management of a challenging and critical part of your plan to secure a place in medical school. These tables will also serve to provide you with a record of what you have done and indicate the tasks ahead. It is also important to make copies of all important documents you send out.

The Appendix consists of

Tracking Table 1:  Application Process Sequence

Tracking Table 2:  Medical College Admission Test (MCAT) Record

Tracking Table 3:  Preliminary List of Medical Schools

Tracking Table 4:  Final List of Medical Schools

Tracking Table 5:  Application Schedule—AMCAS Schools

Tracking Table 6:  Interview Record Form for AMCAS Schools

Tracking Table 7:  Application Schedule—Non-AMCAS Schools

**Tracking Table 1:** *Application Process Sequence*
(*Check when complete*)

## FRESHMAN YEAR

_____ Joined your school's premedical society and attended its meetings.

_____ Became personally acquainted with your premedical adviser.

_____ Discussed your career plans with your family physician.

## SOPHOMORE YEAR

_____ Became familiar with the admission process.

_____ Got some hospital and/or research experience.

## JUNIOR YEAR

_____ November–January: Preliminary MCAT Preparation

_____ February. Registered to take the MCAT.

_____ February–April. Intensive MCAT Preparation

_____ April. Took the MCAT.

_____ Solicited faculty recommendation from your advisory committee.

_____ May. Secured AMCAS and non-AMCAS Applications.

_____ Prepared first and revised drafts of your application essay.

_____ June. Completed AMCAS and non-AMCAS applications, including essays.

_____ Completed preliminary MCAT preparation for August examination.

_____ Advised premedical committee where to send recommendations.

_____ July–August. Completed intensive preparation if taking the fall MCAT.

## SENIOR YEAR

_____ September. Checked with premedical advisory office to see if all supporting material is complete.

_____ Took or (retook) fall MCAT.

_____ October. Contacted medical schools to confirm that they received applications.

_____ Completed and submitted supplementary applications.

_____ November. Prepared for interviews.

_____ December–January. Attended interviews.

_____ February. Sent lower senior year transcript (if it helps you).

_____ March. Advised waiting-list schools of interest.

_____ Contacted schools you haven't heard from (by phone and/or letter) expressing interest.

_____ Asked advisor to contact schools on your behalf.

_____ April–August. You can still get an affirmative reply.

_____ Made sure that medical schools know your summer address.

_____ August. If you have still not been accepted, consider the options discussed earlier in the chapter for rejected applicants. Don't give up hope; it may be worth trying again.

**Tracking Table 2:** *Medical College Admission Test (MCAT) Record*
(*Check when complete*)

1. _____ Secured MCAT Registration Packet (This can be obtained from your Pre-medical Advisory Office or MCAT Program, PO Box 4056, Iowa City, IA 52243. (319) 337–1357.

2. _____ Mailed MCAT Registration Form on \_\_\_/\_\_\_/\_\_\_.

3. _____ Received MCAT Registration Permit on \_\_\_/\_\_\_/\_\_\_.

4. _____ Score reporting (if applicable). AMCAS, when forwarding a copy of your record (transmittal notification) to the medical schools you designate, includes your MCAT exam scores. Thus, you need only designate the non-AMCAS schools to which you want your scores sent. (The first six reports are included in the enrollment fee for the exam.) Sent to:

   _____    _____    _____

   _____    _____    _____

5. Sample test scores.
   Verbal reasoning      _____
   Physical sciences     _____
   Biological sciences   _____
   Writing sample        _____

6. MCAT Exam taken \_\_\_/\_\_\_/\_\_\_ (spring/fall).
   MCAT Scores
   Verbal reasoning      _____
   Physical sciences     _____
   Biological sciences   _____
   Writing sample        _____

7. Discussed MCAT scores with advisor \_\_\_/\_\_\_/\_\_\_.
   Recommendation:  Don't retake _____    Retake \_\_\_\_
   Comments: _____

8. Repeat MCAT scores (spring/fall exam), Date taken \_\_\_/\_\_\_/\_\_\_
   Verbal reasoning      _____
   Physical sciences     _____
   Biological sciences   _____
   Writing sample        _____

9. Comparison of MCAT scores (if taken a second time).

        Verbal reasoning + \_\_\_\_ or – \_\_\_\_

        Physical sciences + \_\_\_\_ or – \_\_\_\_

        Biological sciences + \_\_\_\_ or – \_\_\_\_

        Writing sample + \_\_\_\_ or – \_\_\_\_

10. Comparison of performance: Achieved versus desirable scores for the medical schools to which I am applying (see Table 8.1)

| SCHOOL | DESIRABLE SCORES VERBAL / PHYSICAL / BIOLOGICAL | MY SCORES VERBAL / PHYSICAL / BIOLOGICAL |
| --- | --- | --- |
| _____ | \_\_\_ / \_\_\_ / \_\_\_ | \_\_\_ / \_\_\_ / \_\_\_ |
| _____ | \_\_\_ / \_\_\_ / \_\_\_ | \_\_\_ / \_\_\_ / \_\_\_ |
| _____ | \_\_\_ / \_\_\_ / \_\_\_ | \_\_\_ / \_\_\_ / \_\_\_ |
| _____ | \_\_\_ / \_\_\_ / \_\_\_ | \_\_\_ / \_\_\_ / \_\_\_ |
| _____ | \_\_\_ / \_\_\_ / \_\_\_ | \_\_\_ / \_\_\_ / \_\_\_ |
| _____ | \_\_\_ / \_\_\_ / \_\_\_ | \_\_\_ / \_\_\_ / \_\_\_ |
| _____ | \_\_\_ / \_\_\_ / \_\_\_ | \_\_\_ / \_\_\_ / \_\_\_ |
| _____ | \_\_\_ / \_\_\_ / \_\_\_ | \_\_\_ / \_\_\_ / \_\_\_ |
| _____ | \_\_\_ / \_\_\_ / \_\_\_ | \_\_\_ / \_\_\_ / \_\_\_ |
| _____ | \_\_\_ / \_\_\_ / \_\_\_ | \_\_\_ / \_\_\_ / \_\_\_ |
| _____ | \_\_\_ / \_\_\_ / \_\_\_ | \_\_\_ / \_\_\_ / \_\_\_ |
| _____ | \_\_\_ / \_\_\_ / \_\_\_ | \_\_\_ / \_\_\_ / \_\_\_ |
| _____ | \_\_\_ / \_\_\_ / \_\_\_ | \_\_\_ / \_\_\_ / \_\_\_ |
| _____ | \_\_\_ / \_\_\_ / \_\_\_ | \_\_\_ / \_\_\_ / \_\_\_ |
| _____ | \_\_\_ / \_\_\_ / \_\_\_ | \_\_\_ / \_\_\_ / \_\_\_ |
| _____ | \_\_\_ / \_\_\_ / \_\_\_ | \_\_\_ / \_\_\_ / \_\_\_ |
| _____ | \_\_\_ / \_\_\_ / \_\_\_ | \_\_\_ / \_\_\_ / \_\_\_ |
| _____ | \_\_\_ / \_\_\_ / \_\_\_ | \_\_\_ / \_\_\_ / \_\_\_ |
| _____ | \_\_\_ / \_\_\_ / \_\_\_ | \_\_\_ / \_\_\_ / \_\_\_ |
| _____ | \_\_\_ / \_\_\_ / \_\_\_ | \_\_\_ / \_\_\_ / \_\_\_ |

**Tracking Table 3:** *Preliminary List of Medical Schools*

Based on your state of residency, school location, and tuition, as well as your academic credentials and MCAT scores, formulate a preliminary list of where you would conceivably apply. Use data taken from Table 8.1 (Chapter 8) and the profiles (Chapter 9) as well as Table 10.1, which gives the percentage of women (from which the percentage of men can be extrapolated) to see if your choices are realistic.

| SCHOOL | AMCAS YES—NO | TUITION | PERCENTAGE MEN—WOMEN | | CATALOG DATE REQD.—RECVD. | |
|---|---|---|---|---|---|---|
| 1. | | | | | | |
| 2. | | | | | | |
| 3. | | | | | | |
| 4. | | | | | | |
| 5. | | | | | | |
| 6. | | | | | | |
| 7. | | | | | | |
| 8. | | | | | | |
| 9. | | | | | | |
| 10. | | | | | | |
| 11. | | | | | | |
| 12. | | | | | | |
| 13. | | | | | | |
| 14. | | | | | | |
| 15. | | | | | | |
| 16. | | | | | | |
| 17. | | | | | | |
| 18. | | | | | | |
| 19. | | | | | | |
| 20. | | | | | | |

**Tracking Table 4:** *Final List of Medical Schools*

After receiving your MCAT scores, you are in a more favorable position to prepare the definitive list of medical schools to which to apply. Doing so can be viewed as a four-step process.

1. Formulate, with the aid of Table 6.1, the approximate number of schools you think you should apply to in order to secure a place in the incoming freshman medical school class.

2. Determine if this number exceeds the number of schools recommended in Table 3.1. If it does, then using the criteria of affordability of tuition and the percentages of women and minorities accepted (if the last two are relevant), eliminate some schools from list. If further reduction is needed, note your academic credentials and the *mean* data for accepted students for schools you are considering (from Table 8.1), on the table below. You can eliminate schools where there is a wide divergence between the two sets of data.

   Another criterion that can be used for lowering the number of schools, aside from tuition, is the cost associated with an interview. This should be estimated and noted below. If your budget cannot tolerate such an expense and if there are no other mitigating circumstances in favor of the school (see below), it can be dropped from list.

3. If you have some uncertainty about eliminating a specific school, find out how many students from your school have been admitted to it over the last few years. If significant and you can afford it, keep the school on your list. (This information is also useful if you want or need to add schools to your list.)

4. Now check your list with your premedical adviser before acting on it, and make any needed adjustments.

**Tracking Table 4:** *Final List of Medical Schools*

| SCHOOL | GPA | SCIENCE CUM | MCAT SCORES V | P | B | TOTAL TRAVEL COSTS | APPLYING YES | NO | DATE APPLIED |
|--------|-----|-------------|---------------|---|---|--------------------|--------------|----|--------------|
| 1. | | | | | | | | | |
| 2. | | | | | | | | | |
| 3. | | | | | | | | | |
| 4. | | | | | | | | | |
| 5. | | | | | | | | | |
| 6. | | | | | | | | | |
| 7. | | | | | | | | | |
| 8. | | | | | | | | | |
| 9. | | | | | | | | | |
| 10. | | | | | | | | | |
| 11. | | | | | | | | | |
| 12. | | | | | | | | | |
| 13. | | | | | | | | | |
| 14. | | | | | | | | | |
| 15. | | | | | | | | | |
| 16. | | | | | | | | | |
| 17. | | | | | | | | | |
| 18. | | | | | | | | | |
| 19. | | | | | | | | | |
| 20. | | | | | | | | | |

**Tracking Table 5:** *Application Schedule—AMCAS Schools*
(*check when complete*)

1. _____ Secured AMCAS Registration Packet. (This can be secured from your Premedical Advisory Office or from AMCAS, Association of American Medical Colleges, Section for Student Services, 2450 N Street NW, Suite 201, Washington, DC 20037, (202) 828-0600. Allow two weeks for delivery.)

2. _____ Received AMCAS Packet ___/___/___.

3. _____ Requested student copies of my college and/or university records (to accurately prepare application) from:
   Name _____ Date requested ___/___/___
   Name _____ Date requested ___/___/___
   Name _____ Date requested ___/___/___

4. _____ Completed and mailed application (certified, return receipt request recommended) on ___/___/___. (Made a copy for files before sending.)
   Note: earliest date for mailing is June 1.

5. _____ Arranged that my official transcripts be sent by the following colleges and/or universities:
   Name _____ Date requested ___/___/___ Rec'd by AMCAS _____
   Name _____ Date requested ___/___/___ Rec'd by AMCAS _____
   Name _____ Date requested ___/___/___ Rec'd by AMCAS _____

6. ___ Received Transmittal Notification on ___/___/___ Cycle form # _____

7. Phone log:

   Name _____ Phone # _____ Date _____
   Subject _____
   Name _____ Phone # _____ Date _____
   Subject _____
   Name _____ Phone # _____ Date _____
   Subject _____
   Name _____ Phone # _____ Date _____
   Subject _____
   Name _____ Phone # _____ Date _____
   Subject _____
   Name _____ Phone # _____ Date _____
   Subject _____
   Name _____ Phone # _____ Date _____
   Subject _____
   Name _____ Phone # _____ Date _____
   Subject _____
   Name _____ Phone # _____ Date _____
   Subject _____
   Name _____ Phone # _____ Date _____
   Subject _____
   Name _____ Phone # _____ Date _____
   Subject _____

**Tracking Table 6:** *Interview Record Form for AMCAS Schools*
(*Duplicate for each school.*)

Medical School _____

Address _____
       (Street)           (City)         (State)   (Zip)

Phone # _____     FAX # _____

(*Check when completed*)

1. _____     Received interview invitation ___/___/___
2. _____     Interview accepted and scheduled for ___/___/___ at _____ AM _____ PM
3. _____     Travel instructions _____
                     _____
4. _____     Information sources on school:
                 Catalogue _____ available _____ requested ___/___/___
                 Classmates (if already interviewed)
                 Name _____     Phone _____
                 Name _____     Phone _____
                 Name _____     Phone _____
                 Alumnus _____     Phone _____
                 Alumnus _____     Phone _____
5. _____     Interviewers
                 Name _____     Department _____
                 Name _____     Department _____
                 Name _____     Department _____
6. _____     Thank you note(s) sent ___/___/___
                 Phone log:
                 Name _____ Phone # _____ Date ___/___/___
                 Subject _____
                 Name _____ Phone # _____ Date ___/___/___
                 Subject _____
                 Name _____ Phone # _____ Date ___/___/___
                 Subject _____
                 Name _____ Phone # _____ Date ___/___/___
                 Subject _____
                 Name _____ Phone # _____ Date ___/___/___
                 Subject _____
7. Comments _____
_____
_____
_____
_____
_____
_____
_____
_____
_____
_____
_____
_____
_____

**Tracking Table 7:** *Application Schedule—Non-AMCAS Schools*

Medical School _____

Address _____

            (Street)               (City)              (State)     (Zip)

Phone # _____    FAX # _____

*(Check when completed)*

1. _____ Application and catalogue: Date requested ___/___/___
Date received ___/___/___

2. _____ Application deadline ___/___/___

3. _____ MCAT score   Request sending: ___/___/___, *(see also* Tracking Table 2)

4. _____ Completed (and duplicated) application ___/___/___

5. _____ Mailed application (certified, return receipt requested recommended), ___/___/___

6. Requested (for fee) the official college or university transcripts be sent from:
Name _____    Date _____
Name _____    Date _____
Name _____    Date _____

7. _____ Requested letters of recommendation
Premedical Committee    Date ___/___/___  Date sent ___/___/___
Dr. _____    Date ___/___/___  Date sent ___/___/___
Dr. _____    Date ___/___/___  Date sent ___/___/___
Dr. _____    Date ___/___/___  Date sent ___/___/___

8. _____ Received secondary application

9. _____ Returned secondary application ___/___/___

10. _____ Received confirmation that application is complete ___/___/___

11. _____ Interview Offered _____    Not Offered _____
If yes, interview scheduled _____ at _____ (AM/PM)

12. _____ Interviewers:
Name _____    Department _____
Name _____    Department _____
Name _____    Department _____

13. _____ Sent thank you note(s) to interviewers ___/___/___

14. _____ Comments concerning interview: _____

_____

_____

_____

_____

_____

_____

_____

_____

_____

_____

_____

_____

_____

_____

15. _____ Final action taken
    Accepted     _____    ___/___/___
    Rejected     _____    ___/___/___
    Waiting list  _____    ___/___/___

16. _____ Ultimate decision on application (if wait-listed)
    Acceptance   _____
    Rejection     _____

17. _____ Phone log:

Name _____ Phone # _____ Date _____
Subject _____

Name _____ Phone # _____ Date _____
Subject _____

Name _____ Phone # _____ Date _____
Subject _____

Name _____ Phone # _____ Date _____
Subject _____

Name _____ Phone # _____ Date _____
Subject _____

Name _____ Phone # _____ Date _____
Subject _____

Name _____ Phone # _____ Date _____
Subject _____

Name _____ Phone # _____ Date _____
Subject _____

Name _____ Phone # _____ Date _____
Subject _____

Name _____ Phone # _____ Date _____
Subject _____

Name _____ Phone # _____ Date _____
Subject _____

Name _____ Phone # _____ Date _____
Subject _____

Name _____ Phone # _____ Date _____
Subject _____

Name _____ Phone # _____ Date _____
Subject _____

Name _____ Phone # _____ Date _____
Subject _____

Name _____ Phone # _____ Date _____
Subject _____

Name _____ Phone # _____ Date _____
Subject _____

# APPENDIX H

## REGIONAL MAPS
## EAST COAST STATES

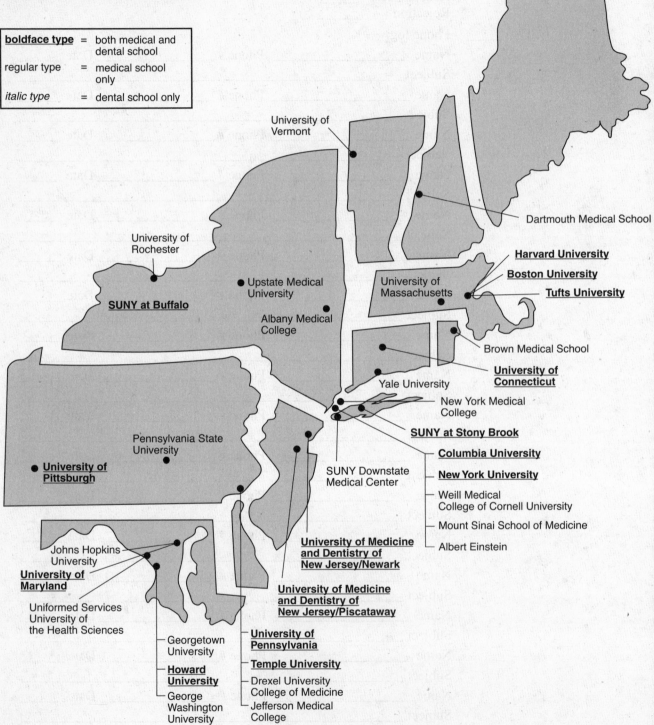

| boldface type | = | both medical and dental school |
| *regular type* | = | medical school only |
| *italic type* | = | dental school only |

University of Vermont

Dartmouth Medical School

University of Rochester

Upstate Medical University

**SUNY at Buffalo**

Albany Medical College

University of Massachusetts

**Harvard University**

**Boston University**

**Tufts University**

Brown Medical School

**University of Connecticut**

Yale University

New York Medical College

**SUNY at Stony Brook**

**Columbia University**

**New York University**

Weill Medical College of Cornell University

Mount Sinai School of Medicine

Albert Einstein

Pennsylvania State University

**University of Pittsburgh**

SUNY Downstate Medical Center

**University of Medicine and Dentistry of New Jersey/Newark**

**University of Medicine and Dentistry of New Jersey/Piscataway**

Johns Hopkins University

**University of Maryland**

Uniformed Services University of the Health Sciences

Georgetown University

**Howard University**

George Washington University

**University of Pennsylvania**

**Temple University**

Drexel University College of Medicine

Jefferson Medical College

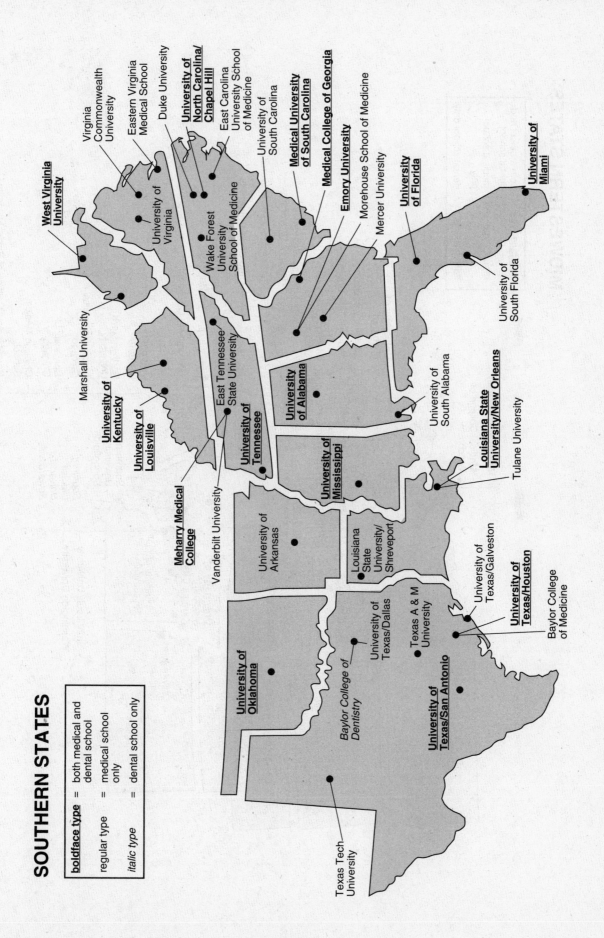

## SOUTHERN STATES

| | | |
|---|---|---|
| **boldface type** | = | both medical and dental school |
| regular type | = | medical school only |
| *italic type* | = | dental school only |

**West Virginia University**

Virginia Commonwealth University

Eastern Virginia Medical School

Duke University

**University of North Carolina/ Chapel Hill**

East Carolina University School of Medicine

University of South Carolina

**Medical University of South Carolina**

**Medical College of Georgia**

Morehouse School of Medicine

**University of Florida**

**University of Miami**

University of Virginia

Wake Forest University School of Medicine

**Emory University**

Mercer University

University of South Florida

Marshall University

**University of Kentucky**

**University of Louisville**

East Tennessee State University

**University of Tennessee**

**University of Alabama**

University of South Alabama

**Louisiana State University/New Orleans**

Tulane University

**Meharry Medical College**

Vanderbilt University

**University of Mississippi**

University of Arkansas

Louisiana State University/ Shreveport

University of Texas/Galveston

**University of Texas/Houston**

Baylor College of Medicine

**University of Oklahoma**

*Baylor College of Dentistry*

University of Texas/Dallas

Texas A & M University

**University of Texas/San Antonio**

Texas Tech University

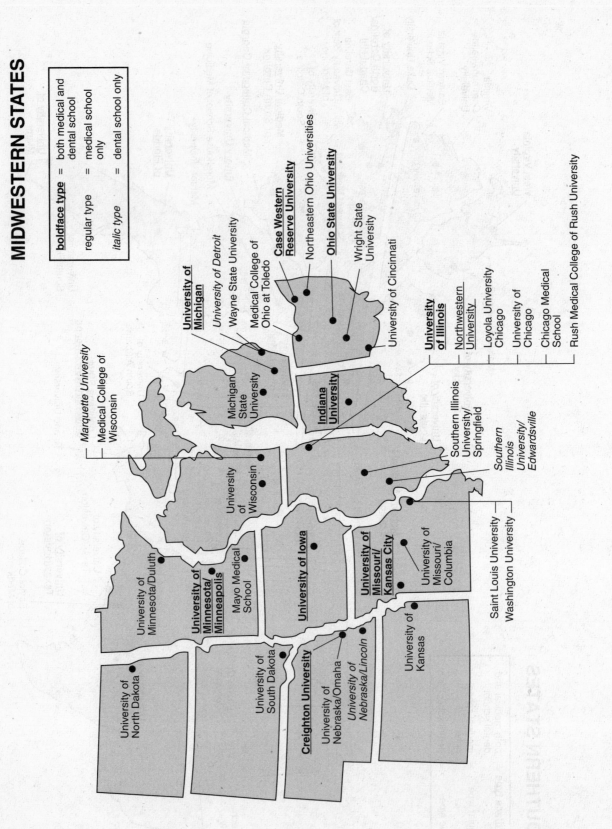

## MIDWESTERN STATES

| | | |
|---|---|---|
| **boldface type** | = | both medical and dental school |
| regular type | = | medical school only |
| *italic type* | = | dental school only |

*Marquette University*
Medical College of Wisconsin

University of Detroit
Wayne State University
Medical College of Ohio at Toledo

**Case Western Reserve University**
Northeastern Ohio Universities

**Ohio State University**

Wright State University

University of Cincinnati

**University of Michigan**

**University of Illinois**

Northwestern University

Loyola University Chicago

University of Chicago

Chicago Medical School

Rush Medical College of Rush University

Michigan State University

**Indiana University**

University of Wisconsin

Southern Illinois University/Springfield

*Southern Illinois University/Edwardsville*

University of Minnesota/Duluth

**University of Minnesota/Minneapolis**

Mayo Medical School

**University of Iowa**

**University of Missouri/Kansas City**

University of Missouri/Columbia

Saint Louis University
Washington University

University of South Dakota

**Creighton University**

University of Nebraska/Omaha

*University of Nebraska/Lincoln*

University of Kansas

University of North Dakota

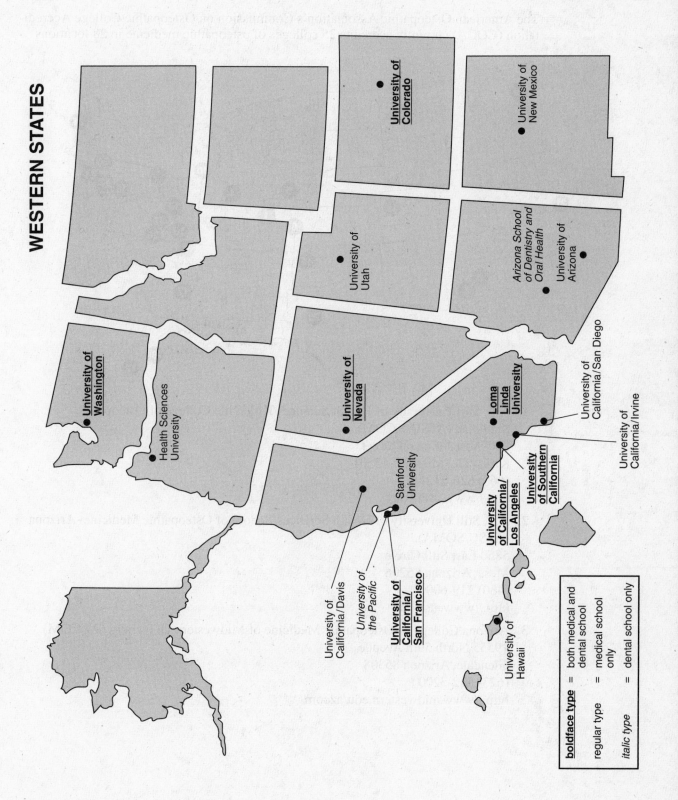

## WESTERN STATES

**University of Colorado**

University of
New Mexico

University of Utah

Arizona School
of Dentistry and
Oral Health

University
of Arizona

**University of
Washington**

Health Sciences
University

**University
of Nevada**

**Loma
Linda
University**

University of California/San Diego

University of
California/Irvine

Stanford
University

**University of California/
Los Angeles**

**University
of Southern
California**

University of
California/Davis

University of
the Pacific

**University of
California/
San Francisco**

University of
Hawaii

| | | |
|---|---|---|
| **boldface type** | = | both medical and dental school |
| regular type | = | medical school only |
| *italic type* | = | dental school only |

# APPENDIX I

## NATIONWIDE DISTRIBUTION OF OSTEOPATHIC MEDICAL SCHOOLS____

The American Osteopathic Association's Commission on Osteopathic College Accreditation (COCA) currently accredits 25 colleges of osteopathic medicine in 28 locations.

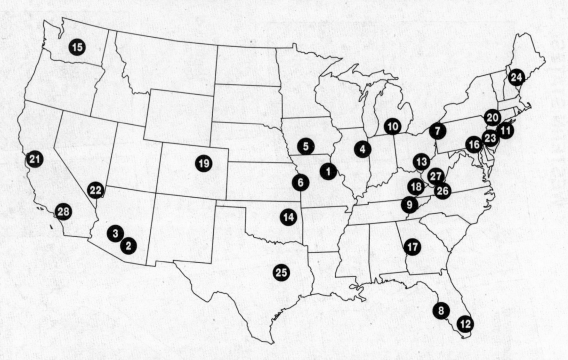

1. A.T. Still University of Health Sciences/Kirksville College of Osteopathic Medicine (ATSU/KCOM)
   800 West Jefferson Street
   Kirksville, Missouri 63501
   (660) 626-2121
   http://www.atsu.edu

2. A.T. Still University of Health Sciences/School of Osteopathic Medicine–Arizona (ATSU/SOMA)
   5850 East Still Circle
   Mesa, Arizona 85206
   (480) 219-6000
   http://www.atsu.edu

3. Arizona College of Osteopathic Medicine of Midwestern University (AZCOM)
   19555 North 59th Avenue
   Glendale, Arizona 85308
   (623) 572-3200
   http://www.midwestern.edu/azcom/

4. Chicago College of Osteopathic Medicine of Midwestern University (CCOM)
   555 31st Street
   Downers Grove, Illinois 60515-1235
   (630) 969-4400
   http://www.midwestern.edu/ccom/

5. Des Moines University–College of Osteopathic Medicine (DMU-COM)
   3200 Grand Avenue
   Des Moines, Iowa 50312
   (515) 271-1400
   http://www.dmu.edu/com/

6. Kansas City University of Medicine and Biosciences
   College of Osteopathic Medicine (KCUMB-COM)
   1750 Independence Boulevard
   Kansas City, Missouri 64106-1453
   (816) 283-2000
   http://www.kcumb.edu

7. Lake Erie College of Osteopathic Medicine (LECOM)
   1858 West Grandview Boulevard
   Erie, Pennsylvania 16509
   (814) 866-6641
   http://www.lecom.edu

8. LECOM–Bradenton Campus (LECOM-Bradenton)
   5000 Lakewood Ranch Boulevard
   Bradenton, Florida 34211-4909
   http://www.lecom.edu/bradenton/

9. Lincoln Memorial University–DeBusk College of Osteopathic Medicine
   (LMU-DCOM)
   6965 Cumberland Gap Parkway
   Harrogate, Tennessee 37752
   (423) 869-3611
   http://www.lmunet.edu/dcom

10. Michigan State University College of Osteopathic Medicine (MSUCOM)
    East Fee Hall
    East Lansing, Michigan 48824
    (517) 355-9616
    http://www.com.msu.edu/

11. New York College of Osteopathic Medicine of New York Institute of Technology
    (NYCOM/NYIT)
    Northern Boulevard
    Old Westbury, New York 11568-8000
    (516) 686-3747
    http://iris.nyit.edu/nycom/

12. Nova Southeastern University–College of Osteopathic Medicine (NSU-COM)
    3200 South University Drive
    Fort Lauderdale, Florida 33328
    (954) 262-1100 or 1-800-356-0026
    http://medicine.nova.edu

13. Ohio University College of Osteopathic Medicine (OUCOM)
Grosvenor, Irvine and Parks Halls
Athens, Ohio 45701
(740) 593-2500
http://www.oucom.ohiou.edu

14. Oklahoma State University Center for Health Sciences–College of Osteopathic Medicine (OSU-COM)
1111 West 17th Street
Tulsa, Oklahoma 74107
(918) 582-1972
http://www.healthsciences.okstate.edu/college/

15. Pacific Northwest University of Health Sciences
College of Osteopathic Medicine (PNWU-COM)
111 South 33rd Street, Suite 104
Yakima, WA 98901
(509) 452-5100
http://www.pnwu.org

16. Philadelphia College of Osteopathic Medicine (PCOM)
4170 City Avenue
Philadelphia, Pennsylvania 19131-1694
(215) 871-6100
http://www.pcom.edu

17. Georgia Campus–Philadelphia College of Osteopathic Medicine (GA-PCOM)
625 Old Peach Tree Road
Gwinett County, Georgia 30024
(678) 225-7531
http://www.pcom.edu/General_Information/georgia/georgia.html

18. Pikeville College School of Osteopathic Medicine (PCSOM)
147 Sycamore Street
Pikeville, Kentucky 41501-1194
(606) 432-9617
http://pcsom.pc.edu

19. Rocky Vista University College of Osteopathic Medicine (RVUCOM)
8401 S. Chambers Rd.
Parker, CO 80134
(303) 373-2008
http://www.rockyvistauniversity.org

20. Touro College of Osteopathic Medicine–New York (TOUROCOM)
230 West 125th Street
New York City, New York 10027
(212) 851-1199
http://www.touro.edu/med/

21. Touro University College of Osteopathic Medicine (TUCOM-CA)
1310 Johnson Lane
Vallejo, California 94592
(707) 638-5200 or 1-888-652-7580
http://www.tu.edu

22. Touro University of Nevada College of Osteopathic Medicine–Nevada Campus (TUNCOM-NV)
    874 American Pacific Drive
    Henderson, Nevada 89014
    http://www.tu.edu/departments.php?id=44

23. University of Medicine and Dentistry of New Jersey–School of Osteopathic Medicine (UMDNJ-SOM)
    One Medical Center Drive, Suite 312
    Stratford, New Jersey 08084
    (856) 566-6000
    http://som.umdnj.edu/

24. University of New England College of Osteopathic Medicine (UNECOM)
    11 Hills Beach Road
    Biddeford, Maine 04005
    (207) 283-0171
    http://www.une.edu/com/

25. University of North Texas Health Science Center at Fort Worth/Texas College of Osteopathic Medicine at Forth Worth (UNTHSC/TCOM)
    3500 Camp Bowie Boulevard
    Fort Worth, Texas 76107
    (817) 735-2000
    http://www.hsc.unt.edu/education/tcom/

26. Edward Via Virginia College of Osteopathic Medicine (VCOM)
    2265 Kraft Drive
    Blacksburg, Virginia 24060
    (540) 443-9106
    http://www.vcom.vt.edu

27. West Virginia School of Osteopathic Medicine (WVSOM)
    400 North Lee Street
    Lewisburg, West Virginia 24901-1961
    (304) 645-6270
    http://www.wvsom.edu

28. Western University of Health Sciences/College of Osteopathic Medicine of the Pacific (Western U/COMP)
    309 East Second Street/College Plaza
    Pomona, California 91766-1889
    (909) 623-6116
    http://www.westernu.edu/comp.html

# APPENDIX J

## MEDICAL AND DENTAL ADMISSIONS AND THE WORLD WIDE WEB

The initial impact on medicine of the development of the information superhighway is outlined in the section on Cybermedicine (see Chapter 18). The communication revolution has also had an influence on medical education in general and medical school admissions in particular. One can file an application to AMCAS by E-mail and plans are being made to be able to apply for residencies in a similar manner. A variety of information sites are currently available and the major ones are listed below.

### Medical and Dental Schools

Most medical and dental schools have a home page on the Web that provides information in excess of what you can secure from the school catalogs. To obtain this information you only need to utilize your Web browser and use the words *medical school*, *dental school*, or the name of the school as search words to locate appropriate Web sites. These addresses change frequently. They are listed in the capsules of individual school profiles in Chapter 9. There are also phone and fax numbers listed there for each school.

### AAMC

*www.aamc.org*
This organization provides information that deals with medical education, personnel, and admissions and is an excellent source to follow current trends in these areas.

### AMSA Home Page

*med.amsa.bu.edu/medical.html*
A good source for lists of medical resources, government sites, and other useful information.

### U.S. Medical Schools

*vumclib.mv.vanderbilt.edu/-aubrey/medstu/medicalschools.html*
This site also provides a list of schools on the Internet, complete with links.

### Medical Education Page

*www.primenet.com/-gwa/med.ed./*
This site provides links to medical news along with an interview feedback source.

### Medical Matrix

*www.medmatrix.org*
This site provides a list of schools as well as medical libraries and hospital information services.

### Duke University's Health Professions Undergraduate Information

*www.duke.edu/SOPH.html*
This site provides information about undergraduate preparation for health career programs, including medicine.

## National Prehealth Student Association (NPSA)

*www.netplace.net/naahp/*
Provides information about a variety of resources that the organization offers its students.

## American Association of Medical Colleges (AAMC)

*www.aamc.org*
This wide-ranging site covers many topics of interest to premedical students. Some headings include Considering a Medical Career and Applying to Medical School as well as information about AMCAS.

## American Association of Colleges of Osteopathic Medicine (AACOM)

*www.aacom.org*
Provides useful and current information about osteopathic schools.

## American Association of Dental Schools

*www.aads.jhu.edu*
Offers a variety of relevant information about dental schools to all of the members of this organization.

## American Medical Association (AMA)

*www.ama-assn.org*
The nation's leading physicians organization provides access to the many services they offer their members.
Other secondary Web sites may be found to be useful.

## Aspiring Docs

*www.aspiringdocs.org*
This Web site seeks to help premedical students navigate the admission process, handle the MCAT, and pay for medical school.
Questions are welcome!

## The Interactive Medical Student Lounge

*falcon.ca.ukans.edu/hsween/*
This site offers the option of asking questions.

## Medweb Educational Resources

*gen.emory.edu/medweb/medweb.ed.html*
Provides links to the National Library of Medicine and the AAMC.

## Erick's Guide to Medical School Admissions

*homepage.seas.upenn.edu/-santos/medGuide.html*
Provides useful links to other premedical sites and personal accounts of getting into medical school.

## Premed

*premedguide.com*
This site offers a wide variety of basic information for premedical students.

# APPENDIX K

## GLOSSARY

*Aerospace Medicine* medical specialty that involves care of those involved in air and space travel and evaluating the impact of such travel on the body.

*American Association of Colleges of Osteopathic Medicine (AACOMAS)* agency that processes applications to all of the osteopathic colleges of medicine.

*American Association of Dental Schools (AADS)* organization that represents American and Canadian dental schools. It provides suggestions for admission standard studies dealing with predental and dental service.

*American Medical Association (AMA)* most prominent professional organization representing U.S. physicians.

*American Medical College Application Service (AMCAS)* agency that processes the distribution of a standard application to the affiliated allopathic medical schools designated by the applicant.

*American Osteopathic Association* professional organization representing osteopathic physicians.

*Anatomy* Known also as gross anatomy, a component of the first-year curriculum that focuses on a study of the structure of the human body, commonly aided by dissection of cadavers.

*Anesthesiology* medical specialty that utilizes drugs or gases to partially or completely alter a patient's state of consciousness so that the patient is impervious to pain. An elective clerkship in this field is usually available in the fourth year.

*Assocation of American Medical Colleges (AAMC)* organization that represents American and Canadian allopathic medical schools. It provides suggestions for admission standards and publishes studies dealing with premedical and medical education.

*Biochemistry* first-year basic science course concerned with the nature and function of the chemical substances involved in normal and abnormal processes such as growth, respiration, or duplication of pathological cells.

*Cardiology* medical specialty concerned with the diagnosis and treatment of diseases of the heart and circulatory system.

*Colon and Rectal Surgery* surgical specialty that treats diseases of and injuries to the lower portion of the digestive tract.

*Dermatology* medical specialty that involves diagnosis and treatment of skin diseases. An elective clerkship is usually available in the fourth year.

*Educational Commission on Foreign Medical Graduates (ECFMG)* agency that processes applications from foreign medical graduates to help facilitate their securing residency appointments in the United States.

*Elective* chosen program of academic work or research in an area of personal interest.

*Embryology* first-year, basic science component of the anatomy that deals with the development of the human body prior to birth and with abnormalities that may occur during fetal development.

*Emergency Medicine* newer medical specialty that deals with the diagnosis and treatment of acute illnesses or injuries. Basic knowledge in this field is provided early on in some schools and a rotation may be required as part of clinical training by others.

***Endocrinology*** medical specialty that is concerned with the diagnosis and treatment of diseases of the hormone-secreting glands.

***Epidemiology*** course that provides an understanding of the factors that influence the spread of disease.

***Family Practice*** medical specialty that provides initial care for all family members. Clinical rotations in this field are commonly required.

***Fifth Pathway*** program of clinical training at an American medical school designed for supplementing the clinical experience of U.S. citizens who are graduates of foreign medical schools. If sastisfactorily completed, it enables them to apply for postgraduate training at an American institution.

***Foreign Medical Graduate (FMG)*** U.S. or foreign citizen who is a graduate of a foreign (non-LCME-accredited) school.

***Gastroenterology*** medical specialty dealing with the diagnosis and treatment of diseases of the digestive tract, liver, and pancreas.

***Genetics*** component of the first-year curriculum that deals with medical problems associated with heredity.

***Gynecology*** medical specialty associated with obstetrics and treatment of diseases of the female reproductive tract. A clerkship that involves this subject is part of the standard third-year curriculum of medical school studies.

***Hematology*** subspecialty of pathology that deals with the diagnosis and treatment of blood disorders.

***Histology*** first-year basic science component of anatomy; involves a study of the microscopic and submicroscopic structure of tissues. This course is commonly linked to the study of cell biology.

***Immunology*** medical specialty that is involved with the diagnosis and treatment of diseases of the immune system such as AIDS.

***Infectious Diseases*** medical specialty concerned with diagnosing and treating illnesses caused by infectious agents ranging from viruses and bacteria to large parasites.

***Intern*** physician in the first year of postgraduate training (PGY1) or *internship*.

***Internal Medicine*** major medical specialty that provides for the diagnosis and treatment of diseases of the body's internal organs. This is a major required clerkship during the third year.

***Medical College Admission Test (MCAT)*** a full-day exam covering the premedical sciences (biology, chemistry, and physics) as well as verbal reasoning and writing skills.

***Medical Ethics*** newer element introduced into medical education that focuses on the moral issues involved in patient care and biomedical research.

***Medical Scientist Training Program (MSTP)*** national Institutes of Health supported program designed to prepare physicians who will be qualified to enter academic medicine and research. Full financial support, which usually extends over seven or eight years, enables candidates to secure combined MD-PhD degrees.

***Microbiology*** basic science commonly taught during the second year. It involves the study of the role of microorganisms such as bacteria and viruses as agents of disease.

*National Intern and Resident Matching Program (NRMP)* procedure that allows eligible U.S., Canadian, and foreign medical school graduates to secure internship appointments on a competitive basis by matching the ranked choices of both hospitals and medical school graduates.

*Neurology* medical specialty that involves diagnosing and treating diseases of the nervous system. A clerkship in this area is usually mandated during the third or fourth year.

*Neurosurgery* surgical subspecialty that deals with the treatment of neurological diseases by operative procedures.

*Nuclear Medicine* subspecialty of radiology that involves the use of radioactive isotopes for diagnostic and especially therapeutic purposes.

*Obstetrics* medical-surgical specialty, which is usually linked with gynecology, that is concerned with the care of pregnant women and the delivery of babies. This is a standard required component of a third-year clerkship.

*Oncology* medical specialty that deals with the diagnosis and treatment of (malignant) tumors.

*Ophthalmology* medical specialty that involves diagnosis and treatment of diseases of the eyes. An elective clerkship in this field is usually available in the fourth year.

*Orthopedic Surgery* surgical specialty that provides for the treatment of bone and joint injuries and diseases.

*Pathology* medical specialty that involves determining postmortem diagnoses of causes of death and analyzing tissue specimens for evidence of disease. This subject is a major component of the second-year curriculum. This field has many subspecialties.

*Pathophysiology* major second-year course (linked to the pathology course) that discusses the impact of disease in altering the physiology of the structure of the body as reflected in the alteration of body tissues.

*Pediatrics* medical specialty that involves the diagnosis and treatment of illnesses in children and adolescents and also provides for preventive care. Clerkship in this field is a standard required component of the third-year curriculum.

*Pharmacology* second-year basic science course that deals with the use of medications and drugs in the treatment of illnesses and diseases and the body's reaction to them.

*Plastic Surgery* surgical subspecialty that involves using surgery for medical, psychological, or cosmetic purposes.

*Postgraduate Year (PGY)* stage in residency training that, depending on the specialty, may extend from three to seven years.

*Psychiatry* specialty that deals with the diagnosis and treatment of mental illnesses. It is a standard required course in the medical curriculum.

*Public Health* program that educates students in medical issues involving the community as a whole.

*Resident* physician in postgraduate training to become a generalist or specialist. This training period is referred to as a *residency.*

*Rotation* set period of time devoted to obtaining undergraduate medical training usually during the third and fourth years of undergraduate medical education.

*Surgery*  application of operative techniques to treat injuries and illnesses. General Surgery is a standard third-year required clerkship. This field has many subspecialties.

*United States Medical Licensing Examination (USMLE)*  three-part examination, given at the end of the second and fourth years of medical school and at the end of the first year of postgraduate training. It is used for promotion, graduation, and licensing purposes.

*Urology*  medical-surgical specialty that treats diseases of the male reproductive tract as well as the urinary tracts in both sexes.

# BIBLIOGRAPHY

Abernethy, V. *Frontiers in Medical Ethics: Applications in a Medical Setting*. Cambridge, Massachusetts: Ballinger, 1982.

Baiev, K. *The Oath: A Surgeon Under Fire*. New York: Walker & Co., 2004.

Belkin, L. *First Do No Harm*. New York: Simon and Schuster, 1993.

Bordley, J. and McGehee, H. *Two Centuries of American Medicine: 1776–1976*. Philadelphia: Saunders, 1976.

Brown, J. *Elizabeth Blackwell*. New York: Chelsea, 1989.

Brown, P. E. (ed.), *Biotechnology and Culture: Bodies, Anxieties and Ethics*. Bloomington, IN: Indiana University Press, 2005.

Castleman, M. *Natures Cures*. Des Moines, Iowa, Rodale Press, 1996.

Chin, E. *This Side of Doctoring: Reflections from Women in Medicine*. Beverly Hills, CA: Sage Publications, 2003.

Coles, R. *The Call of Service*. New York: Houghton Mifflin, 1995.

Drake, M. W. *Working in Health: What You Need to Know to Succeed*. Philadelphia: Davis, 1994.

Duffy, J. *The Healers: The Rise of the Medical Establishment*. New York: McGraw-Hill, 1976.

Engel, J. *Doctors and Reformers: Discussions and Debate over Health Policy, 1925–1950*. Durham: University of South Carolina Press, 2004.

Flexner, J. T. *Doctors on Horseback: Pioneers of American Medicine*. New York: Dover, 1979.

Gawan, E. *Complications: A Surgeon's Notes on an Imperfect Science*. New York: Metropolitan Books, 2004.

Groopman, J. *The Measure of Our Days, a New Beginning at Life's End*. New York: Viking, 1997.

Hendrie, H. *Educating Competent and Human Physicians*. Indianapolis: Indiana University Press, 1990.

Heymann, J. *Equal Partners: A Physician's Call for a New Spirit of Medicine*. Boston: Little Brown, 1995.

Hilfiker, D. *Not All of Us Are Saints*. New York: Hill and Wang, 1995.

Hoffmeir, P. and Bonner, J. *From Residency to Reality*. New York: McGraw-Hill, 1990.

Huyler, F. *The Blood of Strangers*. New York: Owl Books, 2000.

Jamieson, K. *Beyond the Double Bind: Women and Leadership*. New York: Oxford University Press, 1995.

Jonas, S. *Medical Mystery: The Training of Doctors in the United States*. New York: Norton, 1978.

Jeruchim, J. and Shapiro, P. *Women, Mentors, and Success*. New York: Ballantine Books, 1992.

Kaufman, M. *American Medical Education: The Formative Years, 1765–1910*. Westport, Conn.: Greenwood Press, 1976.

Kean, B. H. *One Doctor's Adventures Among the Famous and Infamous from the Jungles of Panama to a Park Avenue Practice*. New York: Ballantine Books, 1990.

Klein, K. *Getting Better: A Medical Student's Story*. Boston: Little, Brown, and Co., 1980.

Knight, J. A. *Medical Student: Doctor in the Making*. New York: Appleton-Century-Crofts, 1973.

Knowles, J. H., ed. *Hospitals, Doctors, and the Public Interest*. Cambridge, Mass.: Harvard University Press, 1965.

Konner, M. *Becoming a Doctor*. New York: Viking, 1987.

Kronhaus, H. *Choosing a Practice*. New York: Springer, 1991.

Lander, L. *Defective Medicine: Risk, Anger, and the Malpractice Crisis*. New York: Farrar, Straus and Giroux, 1978.

Lasser, M. H. *The Art of Learning Medicine*. New York: Appleton-Century-Crofts, 1974.

Laster, Leonard. *Choices After Medical School*. New York: Norton, 1995.

Loomis, F. A. *As Long as Life: The Memoirs of a Frontier Woman Doctor, Mary Canaga Rowland, 1873–1966*. Seattle, Wash.: Storm Peak Press, 1994.

Luchetti, C. *Medicine Women: The Story of Early-American Women Doctors*. New York: Crown, 1999.

Marion, Robert. *Learning to Play God*. New York: Fawcett, 1993.

_____ *The Intern Blues: The Private Ordeals of Three Young Doctors*. New York: Fawcett, 1990.

Noland, S. B. *Doctors: The Biography of Medicine*. New York: Knopf, 1988.

Nolen, W. A. *The Making of a Surgeon*. New York: Pocket Books, 1976.

Pekkamen, J., M.D. *Doctors Talk About Themselves*. New York: Dell, 1988.

Peterkin, A. D. *Staying Human During Residency Training*. 2nd ed. Toronto: University of Toronto Press, 1998.

Porter, K. *The Greatest Benefit to Mankind. A Medical History of Humanity*. New York: Norton, 1998.

Raiber, J. K. *First Do No Harm*. New York: Villard, 1987.

Ramshell, M. (Ed.) *First Year as a Doctor: Real World Stories from America's M.D.s*. New York: Walker and Co., 1995.

Rabinowitz, P. M. *Talking Medicine: America's Doctors Tell Their Stories*. New York: Norton, 1981.

Rafferty, G. W. and McKinley (Eds.) *The Changing Medical Profession*. New York: Oxford, 1993.

Reilly, P. *To Do No Harm: A Journey Through Medical School*. New York: Auburn House, 1987.

Rothman, D. J. Marcus, and U.K. Kicel, S. A. Eds., *Medicine and Western Civilization*. New Brunswick, New Jersey: Rutgers University Press, 1995.

Rothman, E. L. *White Coat: Becoming a Doctor at Harvard Medical School*. New York: Morrow, 1999.

Saks, N. S. *How to Excel in Medical School*, Alexandria, VA: J & S, 1998.

Seager, S. *Psych Ward*. New York: Putnam, 1991.

Seibel, H. R. and Guyer, K. E. *Barron's How to Prepare for the Medical College Admission Test, 10th edition*. Hauppauge, N.Y.: Barron's Educational Series, Inc., 2006.

Seltzer, R. *Down from Troy: A Doctor Comes of Age*. New York: Morrow, 1993.

Shapiro, E. C. and Lowenstein, L. M. (Eds.) *Becoming a Physician: Development of Values and Attitudes in Medicine*. Cambridge, Mass.: Ballinger, 1979.

Smith, R. T. and Edward, M. J. A. *The Internet for Physicians*. New York: Springer, 1997.

Starzl, T. *The Puzzle People: Memoirs, a Transplant Surgeon*. Pittsburgh, Pa.: University of Pittsburgh Press, 1993.

Stone, J. *The Country of Hearts: Journeys, in the Art of Medicine*. New York: Delacorte Press, 1991.

Takakuwa, K. M., Rubashkin, N., and Herzig, K. Z. (Eds.) *What I Learned in Medical School: Personal Stories of Young Doctors*. Berkeley, Los Angeles: University of California Press, 2004.

Tysinger, J. W., *Resumes and Personal Statements for Health Professionals*, 2nd ed., Tucson, Arizona: Galen Press, 1999.

Verghese, A. *My Own Country*. New York: Simon and Schuster, 1995.

Waldenstein, J. G. *Reflections and Recollections from a Long Life with Medicine*. Rome: Ferrata Storti Foundation Publication, 1994.

Walters, B. et al. *Annotated Bibliography of Women in Medicine*. Toronto: Ontario Medical Association, 1993.

Weatherall, D. *Science and the Quiet Art: The Role of Medical Research in Health Care*. New York: Norton, 1995.

Wischnitzer, S. *Survival Guide for Medical Students*. Philadelphia, PA: Hanley & Belfus, and Elsevier, 2001.

Wischnitzer, S. and Wischnitzer, E. *Residency: Selecting, Securing, Surviving and Succeeding*. New York: Cambridge University Press, 2006.

_____ *Top 100 Health-Care Careers*, 2nd ed. Indianapolis, IN: Jist, 2005.

Young, A. *What Patients Taught Me: A Medical Student's Journey*. Susquatch Books, 2004.

# INDEXES

## Index of Osteopathic School Profiles

## Index of Dental School Profiles

# SUBJECT INDEX

# NOTES

# NOTES

# NOTES

**NOTES**

**NOTES**

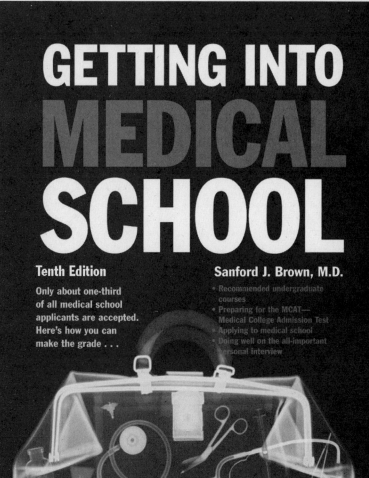

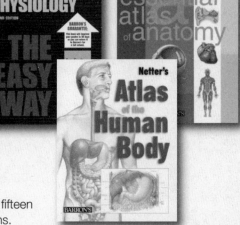